Writers' & Artists' Yearbook 2001

Writers' & Artists' Yearbook 2001

Ninety-fourth Year of Issue

A directory for writers, artists, playwrights, writers for film, radio and television, designers, illustrators and photographers

A & C Black · London

35 Bedford Row, London WC1R 4JH

A CIP catalogue record for this book is available from the British Library.

ISBN 0-7136-5159-8

Printed and bound in France by Aubin
e-mail sales@aubin-imprimeur.fr

Foreword

Rosie Thomas's Celebration was the first in a successful series of novels, of which the most recent is White. She has also recently published Border Crossing, an account of her entry in the 1997 Peking to Paris Motor Challenge.

I don't come from a bookish family, and I had no youthful ambitions to be a writer. We had very few books in the house where I grew up, and the main source of reading matter for me was the Flintshire County Council mobile library van which parked in the village square every other Thursday and from which I borrowed, more or less indiscriminately, as many novels as I was allowed. I sank and then swam in them, but it was more as an escape from the agonising boredom of a rural childhood than a great love for literature itself.

There may have been a reference section somewhere in the van, I can't remember now. *Writers' & Artists' Yearbook* would probably have been there, but at that time I had never heard of it and I would have had no reason to search for it.

My introduction to this volume came years later when I was employed as an editor for its publisher, A & C Black. I worked in the general books division and had no direct contact with the reference section, but I very quickly learned that this particular book was *important*. Prolonged, energetic and close attention was paid to the preparation of each edition. Existing entries were constantly checked and rechecked for accuracy, revised and updated. New material was regularly planned and incorporated. Many copies were printed and sold. All this was plainly a good thing, but it had no personal relevance for me. I was neither an artist or a writer.

Nor did I possess much talent as a publisher and I didn't last long in the job. By this time I had a new baby and I was glad to take a year's voluntary redundancy. I had a lucky 12 months' grace, but I couldn't afford not to have a job in the long term. The question now became – how to earn money by legal and decent means out of the back bedroom, with a baby on my lap? I know, I thought. I'll write a novel. And so I sat down and began.

The advice most regularly given to new authors with a crisp manuscript is, 'find yourself an agent'. In this at least I had an advantage, because I was married to one. Sportingly he agreed to represent me. In due course the novel found a publisher, who offered me an advance against royalties of £3000. We spent most of this on installing central heating in our building site of a house.

Once the book appeared [in 1982] I embarked on the shortest ever promotion tour – one phone-in interview on a local radio station. And the very first caller asked the big question: "How can I become a published author, like you?"

I knew less than nothing about it, and I was barely an author myself, but I took a deep breath and – from somewhere – the right answer came. The first part was what had worked for me, and the second I knew to be correct because I had seen the book in preparation: "Sit down and write what you really want. Then get a copy of *Writers' & Artists' Yearbook*. It will tell you everything you need to know."

Twenty years and 15 books later I am still writing, and I am still giving the same advice. Write not necessarily what you know, but what you care about. And use the *Yearbook*. It won't write yours for you, but it will tell you about everything else.

Rosie Thomas, June 2000

Contents

**Classified index to listings for quick reference*

Literary agents

Art and illustration

Photography and picture research

Societies, prizes and festivals

The Internet

Resources for writers

Publishing practice

Copyright and libel

Finance for writers and artists

Newspapers and magazines

Submitting material

Over a thousand titles are included in the newspapers and magazines section of the Yearbook, almost all of them offering opportunities to the writer. Many publications do not appear in our lists because the market they offer for the freelance writer is either too small or too specialised, or both. We give here some guidelines to bear in mind when submitting material to a newspaper or magazine.

Before submitting material to any newspaper or magazine it is advisable first to contact the relevant editor. The listings beginning on page 3 give the names of editors for each section of the national newspapers and a quick telephone call to a magazine will establish the name of the relevant commissioning editor together with an e-mail address.

Magazine editors frequently complain to us about the unsuitability of many submissions. When submitting by post writers are advised, in their own interests, to enclose postage for the return of unsuitable material.

Study the market

Before submitting articles or features, always study carefully the editorial requirements of a magazine, not only for the subjects dealt with but for the approach, treatment, style and length. These comments will be obvious to the practised writer but the beginner can be spared much disappointment by buying copies of magazines and studying the market in depth.

The importance of studying the market cannot be overemphasised. It is an editor's job to know what readers want, and to see that they get it. Thus, freelance contributions must be tailored to fit a specific market; subject, theme, treatment, length, etc, must meet the editor's requirements. This is looked at further in *Writing for newspapers* on page 132 and *Writing magazine articles* on page 138. For additional information on markets, see the UK volume of *Willings Press Guide*, which is usually available at local reference libraries.

Most newspapers and many magazines these days expect copy to be sent by e-mail (see page 549). Editors who accept postal submissions expect them to be well presented: neatly typed, double spaced, with good margins, on A4 paper is the standard to aim at. If submitting articles on disk always verify with the editor that your system and theirs are compatible before submission. Most editors also require a hard copy (printout) in addition to the disk. See *Preparing and submitting a typescript* on page 248 and *PCs for writers* on page 570.

Illustrations

It is not advisable to send illustrations 'on spec'; check with the editor first. See page 141 for further information; listings of *Picture agencies and libraries* start on page 412.

For a list of magazines and newspapers willing to pay for cartoons, see *Newspapers and magazines which accept cartoons* on page 405, and *A serious look at marketing cartoons* (page 402) offers guidance for success.

Payment

It has always been our aim to obtain and publish the rates of payment offered for contributions by newspapers and magazines. Many publications, however, are reluctant to state a standard rate, since the value of a contribution may be dependent not upon length but upon the standing of the writer or of the information given. Many other periodicals, in spite of efforts to extract more precise information from them, prefer to state 'by negotiation' or 'by arrangement'.

A number of magazines will accept and pay for letters to the editor, brief fillers and gossip paragraphs, as well as puzzles and quizzes. *Magazines by subject area* on page 121 provides a rough guide to these markets.

Overseas contributions

The lists of overseas newspapers and magazines in the *Yearbook* contain only a selection of those journals which offer a market for the freelance writer. For fuller listings, refer to *Willings Press Guide Volume 2 Overseas*. The overseas market for stories and articles is small and editors often prefer their fiction to have a local setting. Some editors require their contributors to be residents of that country.

Some overseas magazine titles have little space for freelance contributions but many of them will consider outstanding work. Potential contributors sending material overseas should always enclose return postage in the form of International Reply Coupons (IRCs) when submitting query proposals or finished articles. IRCs can be exchanged in any foreign country for stamps representing the minimum postage payable on a letter sent from one country to another. It is of course worth checking whether it is acceptable to send material by e-mail.

Using an agent to syndicate material written from overseas is worth considering. Most agents operate on an international basis and are more aware of current market requirements. Again, return postage should always be included.

Newspapers and syndicates

The larger newspapers and magazines buy many of their stories, and the smaller papers buy general articles, through one or other of the well-known syndicates. Another avenue for writers is to send printed copies of their stories published at home to an agent for syndication overseas. Listings for *Syndicates, news and press agencies* start on page 143. Listings of *National newspapers UK and Ireland* start on page 3, and the names of editors are included in each.

Most of the larger UK and overseas newspapers depend for news on their own staffs and press agencies. The most important overseas newspapers have permanent representatives in Britain who keep them supplied, not only with news of especial interest to the country concerned, but also with regular summaries of British news and with articles on events of particular importance. While many overseas newspapers and magazines have a London office, it is usual for manuscripts from freelance contributors to be submitted to the headquarters' editorial office overseas.

See also ...

- *Regional newspapers UK and Ireland*, page 11
- Newspapers are listed together with magazines for *Australia* (page 107), *Canada* (page 113), *New Zealand* (page 116) and *South Africa* (page 118)
- *USA*, page 120
- *Recent changes to newspapers and magazines*, page 131

National newspapers UK and Ireland

Daily Express

Ludgate House, 245 Blackfriars Road,
London SE1 9UX
tel 020-7928 8000 *fax* 020-7620 1654
Albert House, 17 Bloom Street,
Manchester M1 3HZ
tel 0161-236 2112
Editor Rosie Boycott
Daily Mon-Fri 35p Sat 50p
Supplements **Saturday**, **The Sport**

Exclusive news; striking photos. Leader page articles (600 words); facts preferred to opinions. Payment: according to value.

City Editor Patrick Hosking
Diary Editor John McEntee
Environment Editor John Ingham
Features Editor John Price
Foreign Editor Jacqui Goddard
Health Editor Rachel Ellis
Literary Editor Maggie Pringle
Media Editor tba
News Editor Nicola Briggs
Political Editor Tony Bevins
Sports Editor Mike Allen
Women's Editor Fiona Macdonald-Smith

Saturday

fax 020-7922 2753
Editor Sally Ferrari
Free with paper

Daily Mail

Northcliffe House, 2 Derry Street,
London W8 5TT
tel 020-7938 6000 *fax* 020-7937 3251
Editor Paul Dacre
Daily Mon-Fri 35p Sat 50p
Supplement **Weekend**

Highest payment for good, exclusive news. Ideas welcomed for leader page articles (500-800 words). Exclusive news photos always wanted. Founded 1896.

City Editor Andrew Alexander
Diary Editor Nigel Dempster
Education Editor Tony Halpin
Features Editor Veronica Wadley
Deputy Foreign Editor Gerry Hunt
Health Editor Grant Feller
Industrial Editor David Norris
Literary Editor Jane Mays
Media Editor Sean Poulter
Money Editor Tony Hazell
News Editor Tony Gallagher
Picture Editor Paul Silva
Political Editor David Hughes
Showbiz Editor Alison Boshoff
Sports Editor Bryan Cooney
Travel Editor Cathy Wood
Weekend Editor Heather McGlone

Daily Record

Anderston Quay, Glasgow G3 8DA
tel 0141-248 7000 *fax* 0141-242 3340
web site http://www.record-mail.co.uk/rm
London office 1 Canada Square, Canary Wharf,
London E14 5AP
tel 020-7293 3000
Editor-in-Chief Martin Clarke
Daily Mon-Sat 32p
Supplement **Saturday**

Topical articles, from 300-700 words; exclusive stories of Scottish interest and exclusive colour photos.

Features Editor Aileen Easton
Health and Science Correspondent Jim McLean
News Editor Gordon Hay
Picture Editor Stuart Nicol
Political Editor Ron McKenna
Sports Editor Gordon Waddell
Women's Page Editor Ros Paterson

Saturday

Editor Jan Patience
Free with paper

Lifestyle magazine and entertainment guide. Reviews, travel features, shopping, personalities. Payment: by arrangement. Illustrations: colour.

Daily Sport

19 Great Ancoats Street,
Manchester M60 4BT
tel 0161-236 4466 *fax* 0161-236 4535
Editor-in-chief Tony Livesey
Editor Jeff McGowan
Daily Mon-Fri 35p

Factual stories and series. Length: up to 1000 words. Illustrations: b&w and colour photos, cartoons. Payment: £30-£5000. Founded 1988.

Features and News Editor Tony Hore
Sports Editor Mark Smith

Daily Star

Ludgate House, 245 Blackfriars Road,
London SE1 9UX
tel 020-7928 8000 *fax* 020-7922 7960
Editor Peter Hill
Daily Mon-Sat 30p

Hard news exclusives, commanding substantial payment. Major interviews with big-star personalities; short features; series based on people rather than things; picture features. Payment: short features £75-£100; full page £250-£300; double page £400-£600, otherwise by negotiation. Illustrations: line, half-tone. Founded 1978.

Deputy Editor Hugh Whittow
Entertainment Editor Gareth Morgan
Features Editor Dawn Neesom
News Editor Kieron Saunders
Political Editor tba
Sports Editor Jim Mansell

The Daily Telegraph

1 Canada Square, Canary Wharf,
London E14 5DT
tel 020-7538 5000 *fax* 020-7538 6242
Editor Charles Moore
Daily Mon-Fri 45p Sat 75p
Supplements **Appointments**, **Arts & Books**, **dotcom.telegraph**, **Money-Go-Round**, **Motoring**, **Property**, **Telegraph Magazine**, **Television & Radio**, **T2**, **Weekend**

Articles on a wide range of subjects of topical interest considered. Preliminary letter and synopsis required. Length: 700-1000 words. Payment: by arrangement. Founded 1855.

Arts Editor Sarah Crompton
City Editor Neil Collins
Education Editor John Clare
Environment Editor Charles Clover
Fashion Editor Hilary Alexander
Features Editor Corinna Honan
Foreign Editor Stephen Robinson
Health Features Editor Christine Doyle
Health News Editor Celia Hall
Literary Editor John Coldstream
Media Editor Tom Leonard
News Editor Neil Darbyshire
Picture Editor Bob Bodman
Political Editor George Jones
Sports Editor David Welch

Telegraph Magazine

Editor Emma Soames
Free with Sat paper

Short profiles (about 1600 words); articles of topical interest. Preliminary study of the magazine essential. Illustrations: all types. Payment: by arrangement. Founded 1964.

Electronic Telegraph

e-mail et@telegraph.co.uk
web site http://www.telegraph.co.uk/
Editor Derek Bishton
Daily Free to Internet subscribers

Based on *The Daily Telegraph*, contains news, sport, City, features, Internet News, Hyperlinks to Archive. Founded 1994.

Juiced

web site http://www.juiced.com
Weekly Free to Internet subscribers

Student magazine.

Planet

web site http://www.the-planet.co.uk
Free to Internet subscribers

Travel writing from the *Daily Telegraph* and the *Sunday Telegraph*.

Financial Times

1 Southwark Bridge, London SE1 9HL
tel 020-7873 3000 *fax* 020-7873 3076
web site http://www.ft.com
Editor Richard Lambert
Daily Mon-Sat 85p
Supplements **Business Books**, **Companies & Markets**, **FT-IT**, **How To Spend It**, **Surveys**, **Weekend FT**, **Weekend Money**

Articles of financial, commercial, industrial and economic interest. Length: 800-1000 words. Payment: by arrangement. Founded 1888.

Arts Editor Peter Aspden
Banking Editor George Graham
Deputy Editor Peter Martin
Head of Consumer Industries John Willman
Features Editor John Gapper
Financial Editor Martin Dickson
Foreign Editor Will Dawkins
International Affairs Editor Quentin Peel
Markets Editor Philip Coggan
News Editor Lionel Barber
Head of Observer Michael Cassell
Political Editor Robert Peston
Small Businesses Editor Katherine Campbell
Surverys Editor Rhys David
Travel Editor Jill James
Weekend FT Editor Julia Cuthbertson

The Guardian

119 Farringdon Road, London EC1R 3ER
tel 020-7278 2332 *fax* 020-7837 2114
164 Deansgate, Manchester M60 2RR
tel 0161-832 7200 *fax* 0161-832 5351
Editor Alan Rusbridger
Daily Mon-Fri 45p Sat 75p
Supplements **The Editor**, **Education**, **Friday Review**, **G2**, **Online**, **Society**, **Space**, **The Week**, **Weekend**

Few articles are taken from outside contributors except on its specialist pages. Length: not exceeding 1200 words. Illustrations: news and features photos. Payment: from £170.83 per 1000 words; from £50.94 for illustrations. Founded 1821.

Arts Editor Don Glaister
Books Editor Claire Armitstead
Deputy Editor Georgina Henry
Economics Editor Larry Elliot
Education Editor Will Woodward
Fashion Editor Jess Cartner-Morley
Features Editor Ian Katz
Financial Editor Paul Murphy
Foreign Editor Ed Pilkington
Home Editor Harriet Sherwood
Media Editor Janine Gibson
News Editor Clare Margetson
Political Editor Michael White
Religious Editor Stephen Bates
Science Editor Tim Radford
Sports Editor Ben Clissitt
Travel Editor Charlie Burgess
Women's Editor Libby Brooks

Weekend

Editor Katherine Viner
Free with Sat paper

Features on world affairs, major profiles, food and drink, home life, the arts, travel, leisure, etc. Also good reportage on social and political subjects. Illustrations: b&w photos and line, cartoons. Payment: apply for rates.

Guardian Online

web site http://www.guardian.co.uk

The Herald

Scottish Media Newspapers Ltd, 195 Albion Street, Glasgow G1 1QP
tel 0141-552 6255 *fax* 0141-552 2288
web site http://www.cims.co.uk/herald
London office 3 Waterhouse Square, 138-142 Holborn, London EC1N 2NY
tel 020-7882 1100
Editor Harry Reid
Daily Mon-Sat 48p

Articles up to 1000 words. Founded 1783.

Arts Editor Keith Bruce
Associate Editor John Ryan
Business Editor Robert Powell
Chief Financial Editor Ronnie Dundas
Deputy Editor Alf Young
Diary Editor Tom Shields
European Correspondent Rory Watson
Executive Editor Colin McDiarmid
Associate Features Editor Drew Allan
Managing Editor Bob Jeffrey
News Editor Bill McDowall
Sports Editor Iain Scott

The Independent

1 Canada Square, Canary Wharf, London E14 5DL
tel 020-7293 2000 *fax* 020-7293 2435
Editor-in-Chief Simon Kelner
Daily Mon-Fri 45p Sat 80p
Supplements **Business Review, Education, The Information, Review, Traveller, Weekend Review, Your Money**

Occasional freelance contributions; preliminary letter advisable. Payment: by arrangement. Founded 1986.

Arts Editor Ian Irvine
Business & City Editor Jeremy Warner
Education Editor Judith Judd
Environment Editor Mike McCarthy
Features Editor Laurence Earle
Foreign Editor Leonard Doyle
Health Editor Jeremy Laurance
Literary Editor Boyd Tonkin
Media Editor Jojo Moyes
News Editor Jason Burt
Picture Editor Lynn Cullen
Political Editor Andrew Grice
Sports Editor Paul Newman

The Independent Magazine

Editor Andrew Tuck
Free with Sat paper

Profiles and illustrated articles of topical interest; all material commissioned. Preliminary study of the magazine essential. Length: 500-3000 words. Illustrations: cartoons; commissioned colour and b&w photos. Payment: by arrangement. Founded 1988.

Independent on Sunday

1 Canada Square, Canary Wharf, London E14 5DL
tel 020-7293 2000 *fax* 020-7293 2043
Editor Janet Street-Porter
Deputy Editor Michael Williams
Sun £1.10
Supplements **Business, Culture, Reality, The Sunday Review, Smart Moves, Sport, Travel**

News, features and articles. Illustrated, including cartoons. Payment: by negotiation. Founded 1990.

Business Editor Jason Nissé
Comment Editor Charlie Courtauld
Culture Editor Marcus Field
Environment Editor Geoffrey Lean
Foreign Editor James Roberts
News & Arts Editor Barry Hugill
Picture Editor Andy Blackmore
Political Editor Jonathan Carr-Brown
Reality Editor Louise France
Sports Editor Neil Morton

The Sunday Review

tel 020-7293 2000 *fax* 020-7293 2027
Editor Richard Askwith

Free with paper

Original features of general interest with potential for photographic illustration. Material mostly commissioned. Length: 1000-5000 words. Illustrations: transparencies. Payment: £150 per 1000 words.

Irish Independent

Independent House, 90 Middle Abbey Street, Dublin 1, Republic of Ireland
tel (01) 7055333 *fax* (01) 8720304/8731787
Editor Vincent Doyle
Daily Mon-Sat IR90p

Special articles on topical or general subjects. Length: 700-1000 words. Payment: editor's estimate of value.

Business Editor Frank Mulrennan
Deputy Editor Michael Wolsey
Diary Editor Angela Phelan
Features Editor Peter Carvosso
News Editor Philip Molloy
Picture Editor Danny Thornton
Political Editor Chris Glennon
Sports Editor Patrick J. Cunningham

Irish Times

11-15 D'Olier Street, Dublin 2, Republic of Ireland
tel (01) 6792022 *fax* (01) 6719407
Editor Conor Brady
Daily Mon-Sat 95p

Mainly staff-written. Specialist contributions (800-2000 words) by commission on basis of ideas submitted. Payment: at editor's valuation. Illustrations: photos and line drawings.

Arts Editor Victoria White
Business Editor Bill Murdoch
Features Editor Sheila Wayman
Finance Editor Paul O'Neill
Foreign Editor Paul Gillespie
Literary Editor Caroline Walsh
News Editor Willy Clingan
Picture Editor Dermot O'Shea
Political Editor Geraldine Kennedy
Special Reports Editor Ray Comiskey
Sports Editor Malachy Logan

The Irish Times on the Web

web site http://www.irish-times.co.

Mail on Sunday

Northcliffe House, 2 Derry Street, London W8 5TS
tel 020-7938 6000 *fax* 020-7937 3829
Editor Peter Wright
Sun 90p
Supplements **Financial Mail on Sunday**, **Night & Day**, **Review**, **You**

Articles. Payment: by arrangement. Illustrations: line, half-tone; cartoons. Founded 1982.

City Editor Alex Brummer
Diary Editor Nigel Dempster
Features Editor Sian James
Literary Editor Susanna Gross
News Editor Paul Field
Picture Editor Andy Kyle
Political Editor Simon Walters
Sports Editor Dan Evans

Financial Mail on Sunday

tel 020-7938 6984
e-mail fmos@mailonsunday.co.uk
web site http://www.financialmail.co.uk
Free with paper

Acting Editor Allan Piper
City Editor William Kay
Personal Finance Editor Jeff Prestridge

City, industry, business, and personal finance. News stories up to 1500 words. Payment by arrangement. Full colour illustrations and photography commissioned.

Night & Day

tel 020-7938 7051 *fax* 020-7937 7488
Editor Christena Appleyard
Free with paper

Interviews, entertainment-related features and TV listings. Length: 1000-3000 words. Illustrations: colour photos. Founded 1993.

Review

Editor Richard Addis

Investigative journalism, reportage, features, and film, TV, book and theatre reviews.

You

Editor Dee Nolan
Features Editor Jane Phillimore
Free with paper

Women's interest features. Length: 500-2500 words. Payment: by arrangement. Illustrations: full colour and b&w drawings commissioned; also colour photos.

The Mirror

1 Canada Square, Canary Wharf, London E14 5AP
tel 020-7293 3000 *fax* 020-7293 3409
Editor Piers Morgan
Daily Mon-Sat 32p
Supplements **Mirror Football Mania**, **Mirror TVplus**

Top payment for exclusive news and news pictures. Freelance articles used, and ideas bought: send synopsis only. 'Unusual' pictures and those giving a new angle on the news are welcomed; also cartoons. Founded 1903.

Business Editor Clinton Manning
Environment Editor Jeremy Armstrong
Features Editor Mark Thomas

Health Editor Jill Palmer
Letters Editor Jo Dipple
News Editor David Leigh
Picture Editor Ian Down
Political Editor Peter MacMahon
Sports Editor Des Kelly

Morning Star

(formerly Daily Worker)
People's Press Printing Society Ltd,
Cape House, 787 Commercial Road,
London E14 7HG
tel 020-7538 5181 *fax* 020-7538 5125
e-mail morsta@geo2.poptel.org.uk
Editor John Haylett
Daily Mon-Sat 50p

Newspaper for the labour movement. Articles of general interest. Illustrations: photos, cartoons, drawings. Founded 1930.

Arts, Media & Features Editor Mike Parker
Diary Editor Mike Ambrose
Financial Editor Richard Maybin
Foreign Editor Brian Denny
Health Editor Leigh Arnold
Industrial Editor Ian Morrison
News Editor Ian Morrison
Political Editor Mike Ambrose
Sports Editor Alex Reid

News of the World

1 Virginia Street, London E1 9XR
tel 020-7782 1000 *fax* 020-7583 9504
Editor Rebekah Wade
Deputy Editor Andy Coulson
Sun 60p

Uses freelance material. Payment: by negotiation. Founded 1843.

Assistant Editor (Features) Gary Thompson
Money Editor Peter Prendergast
News Editor Phil Taylor
Political Editor Ian Kirby
Royal Editor Clive Goodman
Sports Editor Mike Dunn
Travel Editor Tony Harris

Sunday Magazine

Phase 2, 5th Floor, 1 Virginia Street,
London E1 9BD
tel 020-7782 7900 *fax* 020-7782 7474
Editor Judy McGuire
Free with paper

The Observer

119 Farringdon Road, London EC1R 3ER
tel 020-7278 2332 *fax* 020-7713 4250
Editor Roger Alton
Sun £1
Supplements **Business**, **Cash**, **Escape**, **Life**, **The Observer Review**, **Screen**, **Sport**

Some articles and illustrations commissioned. Payment: by arrangement. Founded 1791.

Arts Editor Jane Ferguson
Business Editor Emily Bell
City Editor Paul Farrelly
Economics Editor William Keegan
Education Editor Martin Bright
Fashion Editor Jo Adams
Features Editor Gaby Wood
Foreign Editor Peter Beaumont
Literary Editor Robert McCrum
Media Correspondent John Arlidge
News Editor Andy Malone
Picture Editor Greg Whitmore
Political Editor Kamal Ahmed
Review Editor Lisa O'Kelly
Sports Editor Brian Oliver
Travel Editor Desmond Balmer

Life

tel 020-7713 4175 *fax* 020-7239 9837
Editor Sheryl Garratt
Free with paper

Commissioned features. Length: 2000-3000 words. Illustrations: first-class colour and b&w photos. Payment: NUJ rates; £150 per illustration.

The Observer Online

web site http://www.observer.co.uk

Scotland on Sunday

108 Holyrood Road, Edinburgh EH8 8AS
tel 0131-620 8620 *fax* 0131-620 8491
Glasgow office tel 0141-332 6163
Editor John C. McGurk
Sun 70p

Features on all subjects, not necessarily Scottish. Payment: £88 per 1000 words. Founded 1988.

News Editor Ian Stewart
Political Editor Iain Martin

Scotland on Sunday Magazine

Editor Margot Wilson
Free with paper

The Scotsman

Barclay House, 108 Holyrood Road,
Edinburgh EH8 8AS
tel 0131-620 8620 *fax* 0131-620 8615
Editor Rebecca Hardy
Daily Mon-Fri 42p Sat 50p
Supplements **S2**, **Saturday Magazine**

Considers articles on political, economic and general themes which add substantially to current information. Prepared to commission topical and controversial series from proved authorities. Length: 800-1000 words. Illustrations: outstanding news pictures, cartoons. Payment: by arrangement. Founded 1817.

Arts Editor Rona Johnson
Business Editor Ken Symon

Education Editor Seonag MacKinnon
Features Editor tba
Foreign Editor Andrew McLeod
Literary Editor Catherine Lockerbie
News Editor tba
Political Editor (Westminster) John Hibbs
Assistant Editor (Politics) Iain Martin
Saturday Magazine Editor Sandra Colamartino
Sports Editor Donald Walker
S2 Editor Charlotte Ross

The Star

Independent Star Ltd, Star House, 62A Terenure Road North, Dublin 6w, Republic of Ireland
tel (01) 4901228 *fax* (01) 4902193/4902188
Editor Gerard Colleran
Daily Mon-Sat 60p

General articles relating to news and sport, and features. Length: 1000 words. Illustrations: colour photos. Payment: by negotiation. Founded 1989.

Deputy Editor Danny Smyth
News Editor Dave O'Connell
Picture Editor Bernard Phelan
Political Editor Stephen O'Brien
Acting Sports Editor Kieran Cunningham

The Sun

News Group Newspapers Ltd, Virginia Street, London E1 9XP
tel 020-7782 4000 *fax* 020-7488 3253
Editor David Yelland
Daily Mon-Fri 28p, Sat 30p
Supplement **Super Goals, Sportsweek**

Takes freelance material, including cartoons. Payment: by negotiation. Founded 1969.

Business Editor Ian King
Features Editor Sam Carlisle
Health Editor Jacqui Thornton
Letters Editor Sue Cook
News Editor Sue Thompson
Picture Editor Geoff Webster
Political Editor Trevor Kavanagh
Showbiz Editor Dominic Mohan
Sports Editor Paul Ridley
Travel Editor Lisa Bielfeld
Women's Editor Vicki Grimshaw

Sunday Business

3 Waterhouse Square, Holborn Bars, 142 Holborn, London EC1N 2NP
tel 020-7961 0000 *fax* 020-7961 0102
Editor Jeff Randall
Sun £1

Standalone Sunday newspaper for the business and financial community. All aspects of business news with in-depth features ranging from captains of industry to the entrepreneurial and small business sector. Wide economic coverage, IT news, and personal finance features. Length: from 200-word news stories to 2500-word features. Payment: by arrangement.

City Editor Richard Wachman
Deputy Editor Richard Northedge
Diary Editor Damien McCrystal
Economics Editor Martin Essex
Features Editor Vivien Goldsmith
News Editor Frank Kane
Stock Markets Editor Matthew Guarente

The Sunday Business Post

80 Harcourt Street, Dublin 2, Republic of Ireland
tel (01) 6026000 *fax* (01) 6796496/6796498
Editor Damien Kiberd
Sun £1.10

Features on financial, economic and political topics; also lifestyle, media and science articles. Illustrations: colour and b&w photos, graphics, cartoons. Payment: by negotiation. Founded 1989.

Arts Editor Marion McKeon
Business Editor Ted Harding
Features Editor Jennifer O'Connell
Financial Editor Ruth Marchand
IT Editor Tom Golden
Media Editor Christine Doherty
News Editor Aileen O'Toole
Political Editor Mark O'Connell

Sunday Express

Ludgate House, 245 Blackfriars Road, London SE1 9UX
tel 020-7928 8000 *fax* 020-7620 1653
Editor Rosie Boycott
Sun 90p
Supplement **Sunday Express Magazine**

Exclusive news stories, photos, personality profiles and features of controversial or lively interest. Length: 800-1000 words. Payment: top rates. Founded 1918.

City Editor Patrick Tooher
Features Editor Sue Mathias
Literary Editor Maggie Pringle
News Editor Simon Young
Political Editor Jon Craig
Sports Editor Mike Allen

Sunday Express Magazine

fax 020-7928 7262
Editor Lesley Thomas
Free with paper

Sunday Herald

Scottish Media Publishing Ltd, 200 Renfield Street, Glasgow G2 3PR
tel 0141-302 7800 *fax* 0141-302 7809
web site http://www.sundayherald.com
Editor Andrew Jaspan
Sun
Supplements **Directory, Seven Days, Sport, Sunday Herald Magazine**

News and stories about Scotland, its characteristics and people. Opportunities for freelances with quality contacts. Founded 1999.

Business Editor Kenny Kemp
Deputy Editor Richard Walker
Features Editor Barry Didcock
Magazine Editor Kathleen Morgan
News Editor David Milne
Political Editor Torquil Crichton
Sports Editor David Dick

Sunday Independent

Independent House, 90 Middle Abbey Street, Dublin 1, Republic of Ireland
tel (01) 7055333 *fax* (01) 7055779
Editor Aengus Fanning
Sun £1

Special articles. Length: according to subject. Illustrations: topical or general interest, cartoons. Payment: at editor's valuation.

Arts Editor Ronan Farren
Business Editor Shane Ross
Deputy Editors Anne Harris, Willie Kealy
Political Editor Jody Corcoran
Sports Editor Adhamhnan O'Sullivan

Sunday Life

124 Royal Avenue, Belfast BT1 1EB
tel 028-9026 4300 *fax* 028-9055 4507
e-mail betty.arnold@belfasttelegraph.co.uk
Editor Martin Lindsay
Sun 65p

Items of interest to Northern Ireland Sunday tabloid readers. Payment: by arrangement. Illustrations: colour and b&w pictures and graphics. Founded 1988.

Features Editor Sue Corbett
News Editor Martin Hill
Photographic Editor Fred Hoare
Sports Editor Jim Gracey
Women's Page Editor Sue Corbett

Sunday Mail

Anderston Quay, Glasgow G3 8DA
tel 0141-248 7000 *fax* 0141-242 3587
web site http://www.record-mail.co.uk/rm
London office 1 Canada Square, Canary Wharf, London E14 5AP
Editor Peter Cox
Sun 60p
Supplement **XS**

Exclusive stories and pictures (in colour if possible) of national and Scottish interest; also cartoons. Payment: above average.

Assistant Editor Andrew Sannholm
Deputy Editor Allan Rennie
Features Editor Susie Cormack
Financial Editor Magnus Gardham
Health Editor Dr Gareth Smith
News Editor Iain Ferguson
Picture Editor David Robertson
Showbiz Editor Billy Sloan
Sports Editor George Cheyne
Women's Page Editor Melanie Reid
XS Editor Liz Steele

Sunday Mirror

1 Canada Square, Canary Wharf, London E14 5AP
tel 020-7293 3000 *fax* 020-7293 3939
Editor Colin Myler
Sun 60p
Supplement **Personal**

Concentrates on human interest news features, social documentaries, dramatic news and feature photos. Ideas, as well as articles, bought. Payment: high, especially for exclusives. Founded 1963.

Associate Editor John McShane
Deputy Editor Fiona Wyton
Executive Editor (Pictures) Paul Bennett
Editor (Sport) Steve McKenlay
Executive Editor (Features) Jane Johnson
News Editor tba

Personal

tel 020-7293 3826 *fax* 020-7293 3835
Contact Katy Bravery, Paul Bennett
Free with paper

Human interest, celebrity articles, and original amusing ideas. Length: 1000 words. Illustrations: colour photos. Payment: articles and photographs high, especially for exclusives. Founded 1988.

The Sunday People

1 Canada Square, Canary Wharf, London E14 5AP
tel 020-7293 3000 *fax* 020-7293 3810
Editor Neil Wallis
Sun 60p
Supplements **Sunday People Magazine**

Investigative features, single articles and series considered; pictures should be supplied with contributions if possible. Features should be of deep human interest, whether the subject is serious or lighthearted. Very strong sports following. Exclusive news and news-feature stories also considered. Payment: rates high, even for tips that lead to published news stories.

Features Editor Alison Phillips
News Editor David Wooding
Picture Editor tba
Political Editor Nigel Nelson
Sports Editor Lee Clayton

Sunday People Magazine

Editor Amanda Cable
Free with paper

/ Post

ɔmson & Co. Ltd, 144 Port Dundas Road,
w G4 0HZ
tel 0141-332 9933 *fax* 0141-331 1595
Albert Square, Dundee DD1 9QJ
tel (01382) 223131 *fax* (01382) 201064
185 Fleet Street, London EC4A 2HS
tel 020-7400 1030 *fax* 020-7400 1089
Editor Russell Reid
Sun 60p

Human interest, topical, domestic and humorous articles, and exclusive news. Payment: on acceptance.

The Sunday Post Magazine

tel (01382) 223131 *ext* 5820 *fax* (01382) 201064
Editor Maggie Dun
Monthly Free with paper

General interest articles. Length: 1000-2000 words. Illustrations: colour transparencies. Payment: varies. Founded 1988.

Sunday Sport

19 Great Ancoats Street, Manchester M60 4BT
tel 0161-236 4466 *fax* 0161-236 4535
Executive Editor Tony Livesey
Editor Mark Harris
Sun 60p

Founded 1986.

Assistant Editor Simon Dean
Deputy Editor Jon Wise
Features Editor Sarah Stephens
News Editor Paul Carter
Picture Editor Paul Currie
Sports Editor Marc Smith

Sunday Telegraph

1 Canada Square, Canary Wharf,
London E14 5DT
tel 020-7538 5000 *fax* 020-7513 2504
Editor Dominic Lawson
Sun £1
Supplements **Appointments**, **City**, **Review**, **Sport**, **Sunday Telegraph Magazine**

Occasional freelance material accepted.

Arts Editor Anna Murphy
City Editor Neil Bennett
Comment Editor Mark Law
Deputy Editor Matthew d'Ancona
Diary Editor Adam Helliker
Executive Editor Con Coughlin
Features Editor Sandy Mitchell
Foreign Editor Robin Gedye
Literary Editor Miriam Gross
News Editor Chris Boffey
Picture Editor Nigel Skelsey
Sports Editor John Ryan

Sunday Telegraph Magazine

tel 020-7538 7590 *fax* 020-7538 7074
e-mail sunmag@telegraph.co.uk
Editor Lucy Tuck
Executive Editor Rebecca Tyrrel
Free with paper

All material is commissioned. Founded 1995.

The Sunday Times

1 Pennington Street, London E98 1ST
tel 020-7782 5000 *fax* 020-7782 5658
web site http://www.sunday-times.co.uk
Editor John Witherow
Sun £1.10
Supplements **Appointments**, **Doors**, **Business**, **Culture**, **Funday Times**, **Money**, **News Review**, **Rich List**, **Sport**, **Style**, **The Sunday Times Magazine**, **Travel**

Special articles by authoritative writers on politics, literature, art, drama, music, finance and science, and topical matters. Payment: top rate for exclusive features. Illustrations: first class photos of topical interest and pictorial merit welcome; also topical drawings and cartoons. Founded 1822.

Culture Editor Helen Hawkins
Economics Editor David Smith
Education Correspondent Judith O'Reilly
Literary Editor Caroline Gascoigne
News Editor Charles Hymas
News Review Sarah Baxter
Chief Political Correspondent Eben Black
Sports Editor Alex Butler
Travel Editor Christine Walker

The Sunday Times Magazine

tel 020-7782 7000
Editor Robin Morgan
Free with paper

Articles and pictures. Illustrations: colour and b&w photos. Payment: by negotiation.

The Sunday Times Scotland

Times Newspapers Ltd, 124 Portman Street, Kinning Park, Glasgow G41 1EJ
tel 0141-420 5100 *fax* 0141-420 5262
Editor Mark Douglas-Home
Free with *The Sunday Times*

News, features and sport. Illustrations: colour photos, cartoons and graphics. Payment: £100 per feature; £50 for illustrations. Founded 1988.

The Sunday Tribune

Tribune Publications plc, 15 Lower Baggot Street, Dublin 2, Republic of Ireland
tel (01) 661 5555 *fax* (01) 661 5302
e-mail editorial@tribune.ie
Editor Matt Cooper
Sun £1
Supplements **People**, **Review**

Newspaper containing news (inc. foreign), articles, features and photo features. Length: 600-2800 words. Illustrations: colour and b&w photos and cartoons. Payment: £100 per 1000 words; £100 for illustrations. Founded 1980.

Arts Editor Lise Hand
Business Editor Brian Carey
Deputy Editor Paddy Murray
News Editor Martin Wall
Photo Desk Bea McMunn
Sports Editor Mark Jones
Supplements Editor Ros Dee

The Times

1 Pennington Street, London E1 9XN
tel 020-7782 5000 *fax* 020-7488 3242
web site http://www.the-times.co.uk
Editor Peter Stothard
Daily Mon-Fri 35p Sat 60p
Supplements **Interface, Meg@, Metro, The Times 2, The Times 3, Times Law, The Times Magazine, Times Sport, Vision, Weekend**

Outside contributions considered from: experts in subjects of current interest and writers who can make first-hand experience or reflection come readably alive. Phone appropriate section editor. Length: up to 1200 words. Founded 1785.

Arts Editor Sarah Vine
Business/City Editor Patience Wheatcroft
Deputy Editor Ben Preston
Education Editor John O'Leary
Environment Correspondent Nick Nuttall
Features Editor Sandra Parsons
Foreign Editor Bronwen Maddox
Industrial Correspondent Christine Buckley
Literary Editor Erica Wagner
Media Editor Ray Snoddy
Medical Correspondent Helen Rumbelow
News Editor Michael Gove
Political Editor Philip Webster
Science Editor Nigel Hawkes
Sports Editor David Chappell
Weekend Times Acting Editor Angus Clarke

The Times Magazine
Editor Gill Morgan
Free with Sat paper

Features. Illustrated.

Wales on Sunday

Thomson House, Havelock Street, Cardiff CF10 1XR
tel 029-2058 3583 *fax* 029-2058 3725
Editor Alan Edmunds
Sun 65p

National Sunday newspaper of Wales offering comprehensive news, features and entertainments coverage at the weekend, with a particular focus on events in Wales. Accepts general interest articles, preferably with a Welsh connection. Founded 1989.

News Editor Ceri Gould
Senior Assistant Editor Mike Smith
Sports Editor Paul Abbandonato

Regional newspapers UK and Ireland

Regional newspapers are listed in alphabetical order under region. Some will accept and pay for letters to the editor, brief fillers, and gossip paragraphs, as well as puzzles and quizzes. See also Writing for newspapers on page 132.

Belfast

Belfast Telegraph

124-144 Royal Avenue, Belfast BT1 1EB
tel 028-90321242 *fax* 028-90554506 (also photographic), 9055 4540 (news only), 9055 4517 (features), 90554508 (sport)
web site http://www.belfasttelegraph.co.uk
Editor Edmund Curran
Daily Mon-Sat 26p

Features Editor John Caruth
News Editor Paul Connolly
Picture Editor Gerry Fitzgerald
Sports Editor John Laverty

Any material relating to Northern Ireland. Payment: by negotiation. Founded 1870.

Irish News

113-117 Donegall Street, Belfast BT1 2GE
tel 028-9032 2226 *fax* 028-9033 7505
Editor tba
Daily Mon-Sat 35p

Business Editor Jim Fitzpatrick
Features Editor Ann-Marie McFarl
News Editor tba
Picture Editor Brendan Murphy
Sports Editor John Haughey

Articles of historical and topical interest. Payment: by arrangement. Founded 1855.

News Letter

46-56 Boucher Crescent, Boucher Road, Belfast BT12 6QY
tel 028-9068 0000 *fax* 028-9066 4412
Editor Geoff Martin
Daily Mon-Sat 35p
Features Editor Geoff Hill
Picture Editor John Rush
Sports Editor Brian Millar

Pro-Union. Founded 1737.

Channel Islands

Guernsey Press and Star

Braye Road, Vale, Guernsey GY1 3BW
tel (01481) 240240 *fax* (01481) 240235
Editor Nick Machon
Daily Mon-Sat 34p
Features Editor Jackie Chappell
News Editor James Falla
Sports Editor Rob Batiste

News and feature articles. Length: 500-700 words. Illustrations: colour and b&w photos. Payment: by negotiation. Founded 1897.

Jersey Evening Post

PO Box 582, Five Oaks, St Saviour, Jersey JE4 8XQ
tel (01534) 611611 *fax* (01534) 611622
e-mail editorial@jerseyeveningpost.com
Editor Chris Bright
Daily Mon-Sat 38p
Features Editor Richard Pedley
News Editor Sue le Ruez
Picture Editor Peter Mourant
Sports Editor Ron Felton

News and features with a Channel Islands angle. Length: 1000 words (articles/features), 300 words (news). Illustrations: colour and b&w. Payment: £85 (articles/features), £25 (news); £30. Founded 1890.

Cork

Evening Echo (Cork)

Cork Examiner Publications Ltd,
1-6 Academy Street, Cork, Republic of Ireland
tel (021) 272722 *fax* (021) 802135
Editor Brian Feeney
Daily Mon-Sat IR50p
Deputy Editor Maurice Gubbins
News Editor Ailin Quinlan
Picture Editor Brian Lougheed
Sports Editor Simon Lewis

Articles, features and news for the area. Illustrations: colour prints.

The Examiner

1-6 Academy Street, Cork, Republic of Ireland
tel (021) 272722, 802153 (newsroom)
fax (021) 275477
e-mail (department)@examiner.ie
web site http://www.examiner.ie
Editor Brian Looney
Daily Mon-Sat IR90p
Features Editor Dan Buckley
News Editor Brian Carroll
Picture Editor Norma Cuddihy
Sports Editor Tony Leen

Features. Material mostly commissioned. Length: 1000 words. Payment: by arrangement. Founded 1841.

Dublin

Evening Herald

90 Middle Abbey Street, Dublin 1, Republic of Ireland
tel (01) 8731333
e-mail eveningherald@unison.independent.ie
Editor Gerard O'Regan
Daily Mon-Sat IR65p
Assistant Editor Philip Nolan
Deputy Editor Noirin Hegarty
Design Editor Eamonn Gibson
Features Editor David Robbins
News Editor Martin Brennan
Pictures Editor Declan Cahill
Sports Editor David Courtney

Articles. Payment: by arrangement. Illustrations: line, half-tone, cartoons.

East Anglia

Cambridge Evening News

Winship Road, Milton, Cambs. CB4 6PP
tel (01223) 434434 *fax* (01223) 434415
e-mail ColinGrant@cambridge-news.co.uk
Editor Colin Grant
Daily Mon-Sat 33p
Features Editor Angela Singer
News Editor Helen Montgomery
Picture Editor Keith Heppell
Sports Editor Cyrus Pundole

The voice of Mid-Anglia – news, views and sport. Illustrations: colour prints, b&w and colour graphics. Payment: by negotiation. Founded 1888.

East Anglian Daily Times

30 Lower Brook Street, Ipswich, Suffolk IP4 1AN
tel (01473) 230023 *fax* (01473) 233228
Editor Terry Hunt
Daily Mon-Fri 42p Sat 47p
Features Editor Julian Ford

News Editor Mark Hindle
Picture Editor Paul Nixon
Sports Editor Nick Garnham

Features of East Anglian interest, preferably with pictures. Length: 500 words. Illustrations: colour, b&w. Payment: negotiable; illustrations NUJ rates. Founded 1874.

Eastern Daily Press

Prospect House, Rouen Road,
Norwich NR1 1RE
tel (01603) 628311 *fax* (01603) 612930
web site http://www.ecn.co.uk
Editor Peter Franzen
London office House of Commons Press Gallery, House of Commons, London SW1A 0AA
tel 020-7219 3384 *fax* 020-7222 3830
Daily Mon-Wed 40p, Thur, Fri 45p, Sat 50p

Limited market for articles of East Anglian interest not exceeding 900 words. Founded 1870.

Evening News

Prospect House, Rouen Road,
Norwich NR1 1RE
tel (01603) 628311 *fax* (01603) 219060
Editor Bob Crawley
Daily Mon-Sat 32p
Features Editor Derek James
News Editor Adrian Galvin
Picture Editor Nolan Lincoln
Sports Editor David Cuffley

Interested in local news-based features. Length: up to 500 words. Payment: NUJ or agreed rates. Founded 1882.

East Midlands

Burton Mail

Burton Daily Mail Ltd, 65-68 High Street,
Burton on Trent DE14 1LE
tel (01283) 512345 *fax* (01283) 515351
Editor Brian J. Vertigen
Daily Mon-Sat 30p
Features Editor Bill Pritchard
News and Picture Editor Andy Parker
Sports Editor Rex Page

Features, news and articles of interest to Burton and south Derbyshire readers. Length: 400-500 words. Illustrations: colour and b&w. Payment: by negotiation. Founded 1898.

Chronicle & Echo, Northampton

Northamptonshire Newspapers Ltd,
Upper Mounts, Northampton NN1 3HR
tel (01604) 467000 *fax* (01604) 467190
Editor Mark Edwards
Daily Mon-Sat 30p

Articles, features and news – mostly commissioned – of interest to the Northampton area. Length/illustrations: varies. Payment: by negotiation. Founded 1931.

Derby Evening Telegraph

Northcliffe House, Meadow Road, Derby DE1 2DW
tel (01332) 291111 *fax* (01322) 253027
web site http://www.thisisderbyshire.co.uk
Editor Keith Perch
Daily Mon-Sat 29p
Features Editor Nigel Powlson
News Editor Andy Wright
Picture Editor Stuart Wilde
Sports Editor tba

Articles and news of local interest. Payment: by negotiation.

The Leicester Mercury

St George Street, Leicester LE1 9FQ
tel 0116-251 2512 *fax* 0116-253 0645
Editor Nick Carter
Daily Mon-Sat 27p

Occasional articles, features and news; submit ideas to editor first. Length/payment: by negotiation. Founded 1874.

Nottingham Evening Post

Castle Wharf House, Nottingham NG1 7EU
tel 0115-948 2000 *fax* 0115-964 4032
e-mail nep.editorial@dial.pipex.com
web site http://www.thisisnottingham.co.uk
Daily Mon-Sat 29p

Material on local issues considered. Founded 1878.

London

Evening Standard

Northcliffe House, 2 Derry Street, London W8 5EE
tel 020-7938 6000
web site http://www.thisislondon.com
Editor Max Hastings
Daily Mon-Fri 35p
Features Editor Bernice Davison
News Editor Stephen Clackson
Picture Editor David Ofield
Sports Editor Simon Greenberg

Articles of general interest considered, 1500 words or shorter; also news, pictures and ideas. Founded 1827.

ES Magazine
Editor Mimi Spencer
Weekly Free with paper

Feature ideas, exclusively about London. Payment: by negotiation. Illustrations: all types.

North

Evening Chronicle

Newcastle Chronicle and Journal Ltd,
Thomson House, Groat Market,
Newcastle upon Tyne NE1 1ED
tel 0191-232 7500 *fax* 0191-232 2256
Editor Alison Hastings
Daily Mon-Sat 28p
Features Editor Emma Walker
News Editor Mick Smith
Picture Editor Rod Wilson
Sports Editor Paul New

News, photos and features covering almost every subject of interest to readers in Tyne and Wear, Northumberland and Durham. Payment: by arrangement.

Evening Gazette

North Eastern Evening Gazette Ltd,
Borough Road, Middlesbrough TS1 3AZ
tel (01642) 245401 *fax* (01642) 232014
e-mail editor@eveninggazette.co.uk
Editor Paul Robertson
Daily Mon-Sat 27p

News, and topical and lifestyle features. Length: 600-800 words. Illustrations: line, half-tone, colour, graphics, cartoons. Payment: £75 per 1000 words; scale rate or by agreement for illustrations. Founded 1869.

Hartlepool Mail

Northeast Press Ltd, New Clarence House,
Wesley Square, Hartlepool TS24 8BX
tel (01429) 274441 *fax* (01429) 869024
e-mail mail.news@northeast-press.co.uk
Editor John Knighton
Daily Mon-Sat 30p
Assistant Editor (Content) Neil Hunter
Features Editor Bernice Saltzer
Picture Editor Dirk van der Werff
Sports Editor Roy Kelly

Features of local interest. Length: 500 words. Illustrations: colour, b&w photos, line, cartoons. Payment: by negotiation. Founded 1877.

The Journal

Thomson House, Groat Market,
Newcastle upon Tyne NE1 1ED
tel 0191-232 7500 *fax* 0191-261 8869
e-mail journal@ncjlib.demon.co.uk
Editor Gerard Henderson
Daily Mon-Sat 34p
Features Editor Rosie Walker
News Editor Richard Kirkman
Picture Editor Simon Greener (acting)
Sports Editor Kevin Dinsdale

News, sport items and features of topical interest considered. Payment: by arrangement.

The Northern Echo

Priestgate, Darlington, Co. Durham DL1 1NF
tel (01325) 381313 *fax* (01325) 380539
Editor Peter Barron
Daily Mon-Sat 30p
Features Editor Chris Lloyd
News Editor Nigel Burton
Picture Editor Mike Gibb
Sports Editor Nick Loughlin

Articles of interest to North-East and North Yorkshire; all material commissioned. Preliminary study of newspaper advisable. Length: 800-1000 words. Illustrations: line, half-tone, colour – mostly commissioned. Payment: by negotiation. Founded 1870.

North-West Evening Mail

Newspaper House, Abbey Road,
Barrow-in-Furness, Cumbria LA14 5QS
tel (01229) 821835 *fax* (01229) 840164/832141
Editor Sara Hadwin
Daily Mon-Sat 30p
News Editor Peter Leydon
Sports Editor Leo Clarke

'The Voice of Furness and West Cumbria.' Articles, features and news. Length: 500 words. Illustrations: b&w photos and occasional artwork. Payment: £30 (minimum); £10 for illustrations. Founded 1898.

The Sunday Sun

Thomson House, Groat Market,
Newcastle upon Tyne NE1 1ED
tel 0191-201 6330 *fax* 0191-230 0238
e-mail scoop@sundaysun.co.uk
web site http://www.sundaysun.co.uk
Editor Peter Montellier
Sun 60p

Key requirements: immediate topicality and human sidelights on current problems. Particularly welcomed are special features of family appeal and news stories of special interest to the North of England. Length: 200-700 words. Payment: normal lineage rates, or by arrangement. Illustrations: photos. Founded 1919.

Sunderland Echo

Echo House, Pennywell, Sunderland,
Tyne & Wear SR4 9ER
tel 0191-534 3011 *fax* 0191-534 5975
web site http://www.sunderland.com/echo
Editor Andrew Smith
Daily Mon-Sat 30p

Local news, features and articles. Length: 500 words. Illustrations: colour and b&w photos, line, cartoons. Payment: negotiable. Founded 1875.

North West

Bolton Evening News

Newspaper House, Churchgate, Bolton, Lancs. BL1 1DE
tel (01204) 522345 *fax* (01204) 365068
e-mail ben_editorial@newsquest.co.uk
Daily Mon-Sat 28p

Articles, particularly those with South Lancashire appeal. Length: up to 500 words. Illustrations: photos. Founded 1867.

Daily Post

PO Box 48, Old Hall Street,
Liverpool L69 3EB
tel 0151-227 2000 *fax* 0151-236 4682
Editor Alastair Machray
Daily Mon-Sat 32p
Features Editor Andrew Forgrave
News Editor Andrew Edwards
Picture Editor Steve Shakeshaft
Sports Editor Richard Williamson

Articles of general interest and topical features of special interest to North West England and North Wales. No verse or fiction. Payment: according to value. News and feature illustrations. Founded 1855.

The Gazette, Blackpool

Blackpool Gazette & Herald Ltd,
Avroe House, Avroe Crescent,
Blackpool Business Park,
Squires Gate, Blackpool FY4 2DP
tel (01253) 400888 *fax* (01253) 361870
e-mail bpl_editorial@upn.co.uk
web site http://www.blackpoolonline.co.uk
Editor tba, *Managing Director* Philip Welsh
Daily Mon-Sat 28p

Local news and articles of general interest, with photos if appropriate. Length: varies. Payment: on merit. Founded 1929.

Lancashire Evening Post

Oliver's Place, Fulwood, Preston PR2 9ZA
tel (01772) 254841 *fax* (01772) 880173
Editor Roger Borrell
Daily Mon-Sat 28p

Topical articles on all subjects. Area of interest Wigan to Lake District, Lancs, and coast. Length: 600-900 words. Illustrations: colour and b&w photos, cartoons. Payment: by arrangement.

Lancashire Evening Telegraph

Newspaper House, High Street, Blackburn, Lancs. BB1 1HT
tel (01254) 678678
web site http://www.thisislancashire.co.uk
Editor Kevin Young
Daily Mon-Sat 26p
News Editor Nick Nunn
Picture Editor John Napier
Sports Editor Neil Bramwell

Will consider general interest articles, such as property, motoring, finance, etc. Payment: by arrangement. Founded 1886.

Liverpool Echo

PO Box 48, Old Hall Street, Liverpool L69 3EB
tel 0151-227 2000 *fax* 0151-236 4682
web site http://www.liverpool.com
Editor Mark Dickinson
Daily Mon-Sat 30p
News Editor Andrew Edwards
Picture Editor Stephen Shakeshaft
Sports Editor Ken Rogers

Articles of up to 600-800 words of local or topical interest; also cartoons. Payment: according to merit; special rates for exceptional material. This newspaper is connected with, but independent of, the *Liverpool Daily Post.* Articles not interchangeable.

Manchester Evening News

164 Deansgate, Manchester M60 2RD
tel 0161-832 7200 editorial *fax* 0161-834 3814
features fax 0161-839 0968
Editor Paul Horrocks
Daily Mon-Sat 30p
Features Editor Maggie Henfield
News Editor Lisa Roland
Picture Editor Robert Ridley
Sports Editor Peter Spencer

Feature articles of up to 1000 words, topical or general interest and illustrated where appropriate, should be addressed to the Features Editor. Payment: on acceptance.

Oldham Chronicle

PO Box 47, Union Street, Oldham, Lancs. OL1 1EQ
tel 0161-633 2121 *fax* 0161-627 0905
Editor Jim Williams
Daily Mon-Fri 30p

News and features on current topics and local history. Length: 1000 words. Illustrations: colour and b&w photos and line. Payment: £20-£25 per 1000 words; £16.32-£21.90 for illustrations. Founded 1854.

Northern Ireland – see Belfast

Scotland

Aberdeen Evening Express

Aberdeen Journals Ltd, PO Box 43, Lang Stracht, Mastrick, Aberdeen AB15 6DF
tel (01224) 690222 *fax* (01224) 699575
Editor Donald Martin
Daily Mon-Sat 28p
Features Editor Scott Begbie
News Editor Sally McDonald
Sports Editor Jim Strachan

Lively evening paper reading. Illustrations: colour and b&w, cartoons. Payment: by arrangement.

The Courier and Advertiser

D.C. Thomson & Co. Ltd, 80 Kingsway East, Dundee DD4 8SL
tel (01382) 223131 *fax* (01382) 454590
e-mail courier@dcthomson.co.uk
web site http://www.thecourier.co.uk
London office 185 Fleet Street, London EC4A 2HS
tel 020-7400 1030 *fax* 020-7400 1089
Daily Mon-Sat 32p

Founded 1816 and 1801.

Dundee Evening Telegraph and Post

D.C. Thomson & Co. Ltd, 80 Kingsway East, Dundee DD4 8SL
tel (01382) 223131 *fax* (01382) 454590
London office 185 Fleet Street, London EC4A 2HS
tel 020-7400 1030 *fax* 020-7400 1089
Daily Mon-Sat 25p

Edinburgh Evening News

108 Holyrood Road, Edinburgh EH8 8AS
tel 0131-620 8620 *fax* 0131-620 8696
Editor John McLellan
Daily Mon-Sat 30p
Features Editor Sandra Dick
News Editor David Lee
Picture Editor Tony Marsh
Sports Editor Martin Dempster

Features on current affairs, preferably in relation to our circulation area. Women's talking points, local historical articles; subjects of general interest.

Glasgow Evening Times

195 Albion Street, Glasgow G1 1QP
tel 0141-552 6255 *fax* 0141-553 1355
web site http://www.eveningtimes.co.uk
Editor Charles McGhee
Daily Mon-Sat 30p

Founded 1876.

Inverness Courier

PO Box 13, 9-11 Bank Lane, Inverness IV1 1QW
tel (01463) 233059 *fax* (01463) 243439
e-mail courier@zetnet.co.uk
Editor John Macdonald
2 p.w. Tue 39p Fri 42p
News Editor Hector Mackenzie
Sports Editor David Beck

Articles of Highland interest only. Unsolicited material accepted. Illustrations: colour and b&w photos. Payment: by arrangement. Founded 1817.

The Press and Journal

Lang Stracht, Aberdeen AB15 6DF
tel (01224) 690222
e-mail pj.editor@ajl.co.uk
web site http://www.thisisnorthscotland.co.uk
Editor Derek Tucker
Daily Mon-Sat 35p
Deputy Editor Kay Drummond
News Editor David Knight
Picture Desk Steve Bain
Sports Editor Jim Dolan

Contributions of Scottish interest. Payment: by arrangement. Illustrations: half-tone. Founded 1748.

The Sun

News International Newspapers, Scotland, 124 Portman Street, Kinning Park, Glasgow G41 1EJ
tel 0141-420 5200 *fax* 0141-420 5248
Editor Bruce Waddell
Daily Mon-Sat 28p
News Editor Alan Muir
Picture Editor Mark Sweeney
Sports Editor Steve Wolstencroft

Scottish edition of *The Sun*. Illustrations: transparencies, colour and b&w prints, colour cartoons. Payment: by arrangement. Founded 1985.

South East

Evening Echo

Newspaper House, Chester Hall Lane, Basildon, Essex SS9 1RE
tel (01268) 522792 *fax* (01268) 282884
Editor Martin McNeill
Daily Mon-Fri 32p
Features Editor Pamela Horne
News Editor Claire Ogley
Picture Editor Nick Ansell
Sports Editor Paul Alton

Mostly staff-written. Only interested in local material. Payment: by arrangement. Founded 1969.

Kent Today

395 High Street, Chatham,
Kent ME4 4PQ
tel (01634) 830600 *fax* (01634) 829484
Daily Mon-Fri 25p
News Editor Sarah Clarke
Picture Editor Barry Hollis
Sports Editor Mike Rees

Paper with emphasis on local news and sport, plus regular feature pages. National news; with editions covering the Medway Towns, Gravesend and Dartford, Swale. Illustrations: line, half-tone.

The News, Portsmouth

The News Centre, Hilsea,
Portsmouth PO2 9SX
tel 023-9266 4488 *fax* 023-92673363
e-mail feedback@thenews.co.uk
web site http://www.thenews.co.uk
Editor Mike Gilson
Daily Mon-Sat 30p
Features Editor John Millard
News Editor Ruth Butler
Picture Editor Pete Langdown
Sports Editor Dave King

Articles of relevance to southeast Hampshire and West Sussex. Payment by arrangement. Founded 1877.

Reading Evening Post

8 Tessa Road, Reading, Berks. RG1 8NS
tel 0118-918 3000 *fax* 0118-959 9363
Editor Andy Murrill
Daily Mon-Fri 25p
Features Editor Kate Magee
News Editor Ian Francis
Picture Editor Steve Templeman
Sports Editor Dave Wright

Topical articles based on current local news. Length: 800-1200 words. Payment: based on lineage rates. Illustrations: half-tone. Founded 1965.

The Southern Daily Echo

Newspaper House, Test Lane, Redbridge,
Southampton SO16 9JX
tel 023-8042 4777 *fax* 023-8042 4770
Editor Ian Murray
Daily Mon-Sat 30p
Features Editor Andy Bissell
News Editor Gordon Sutter
Picture Editor Paul Collins
Sports Editor David Briers
Supplements Editor Jane Sullivan

News, articles, features, sport. Length: varies. Illustrations: line, half-tone, colour. Payment: NUJ rates. Founded 1888.

South West

The Bath Chronicle

Bath Newspapers, Windsor House,
Windsor Bridge, Bath BA2 3AU
tel (01225) 322322 *fax* (01225) 322291
Editor David Gledhill
Daily Mon-Sat 32p
Features Editor Matt Mills
News Editor Paul Wiltshire
Picture Editor Kevin Bates
Sports Editor Neville Smith

Welcomes local news and features. Length: 200-500 words. Illustrations: colour photos. Payment: 8p-15.7p per printed line; £5 per photo where commissioned. Founded 1760.

Bristol Evening Post

Temple Way, Bristol BS99 7HD
tel 0117-934 3000
Editor Mike Lowe
Daily Mon-Sat 28p
Features Editor Matthew Shelley
News Editor Kevan Blackadder
Picture Editor Peter Watson
Sports Editor Chris Bartlett

Takes freelance news and articles. Payment: by arrangement. Founded 1932.

The Citizen

Gloucestershire Newspapers Ltd, St John's Lane,
Gloucester GL1 2AY
tel (01452) 424442 *fax* (01452) 420664
Editor Spencer Feeney
Daily Mon-Sat 30p

Local news and features for Gloucester and its districts. Length: 1000 words (articles/features), 300 words (news). Illustrations: colour. Payment: negotiable.

Dorset Echo

Southern Newspapers plc, Fleet House,
Hampshire Road, Weymouth, Dorset DT4 9XD
tel (01305) 830930 *fax* (01305) 830956
e-mail newsdesk@dorsetecho.co.uk
Editor David Murdock
Daily Mon-Sat 28p
Features Editor Mike Clarke
News Editor Paul Thomas
Picture Editor Jim Tampin
Sports Editor Paul Baker

News and occasional features (1000-2000 words). Illustrations: b&w photos. Payment: by negotiation. Founded 1921.

Express & Echo

Express & Echo Publications Ltd, Heron Road,
Sowton, Exeter, Devon EX2 7NF
tel (01392) 442211 *fax* (01392) 442294/442287

Editor Steve Hall
Daily Mon-Sat 27p
Features Editor Sue Kemp
Head of Content Chris Styles
Picture Editor John Ffoulkes
Sports Editor Simon Mills

Features and news of local interest. Length: 500-800 words (features), up to 400 words (news). Illustrations: colour. Payment: lineage rates; illustrations negotiable. Founded 1904.

Gloucestershire Echo

Cheltenham Newspaper Co. Ltd, 1 Clarence Parade, Cheltenham, Glos. GL50 3NY
tel (01242) 271900 *fax* (01242) 271803
Editor Anita Syvret
Daily Mon-Sat 30p

Specialist articles with Gloucestershire connections; no fiction. Material mostly commissioned. Length: 350 words. Payment: £30 per article, negotiable. Founded 1873.

Sunday Independent (West of England)

Southern Newspapers plc, Burrington Way, Plymouth PL5 3LN
tel (01752) 206600 *fax* (01752) 206164
Editor Nikki Rowlands
Sun 60p

News features on West Country topics; features/articles with a nostalgic theme; short quirky news briefs (must be original). Length: 600 words (features/articles), 300 words (news). Illustrations: colour, b&w. Payment: by arrangement. Founded 1808.

Western Daily Press

Bristol Evening Post and Press Ltd, Temple Way, Bristol BS99 7HD
tel 0117-934 3000 *fax* 0117-934 3574
web site http://www.westpress.co.uk
Editor Ian Beales
Daily Mon-Sat 34p

National, international or West Country topics for features or news items, from established journalists, with or without illustrations. Payment: by negotiation. Founded 1858.

The Western Morning News

Brest Road, Derriford, Plymouth PL6 5AA
tel (01752) 765500 *fax* (01752) 765535
Editor Barrie Williams
Daily Mon-Sat 34p
News Editor Jason Clark
Picture Editor Michael Cranmer
Sports Editor Rick Cowdery

Articles plus illustrations considered on West Country subjects. Founded 1860.

Wales

South Wales Argus

South Wales Argus Ltd, Cardiff Road, Maesglas, Newport, Gwent NP9 1QW
tel (01633) 777219 *fax* (01633) 777202
Editor Gerry Keighley
Daily Mon-Sat 32p

News and features of relevance to Gwent. Length: 500-600 words (features); 350 words (news). Illustrations: colour prints and transparencies. Payment: £30 (features), £20 (news) per item; £20-£25 (photos). Founded 1892.

South Wales Echo

Thomson House, Havelock Street, Cardiff CF1 1XR
tel 029-2058 3583/20223333 *fax* 029-2058 3624
Editor Robin Fletcher
Daily Mon-Sat 30p

Evening paper: features, showbiz, news features, personality interviews. Length: up to 700 words. Illustrations: photos, cartoons. Payment: by negotiation. Founded 1884.

The Western Mail

Thomson House, Havelock Street, Cardiff CF10 1XR
tel 029-2058 3583 *fax* 029-2058 3652
Editor Neil Fowler
Daily Mon-Fri 35p Sat 40p

Articles of political, industrial, literary or general and Welsh interest are considered. Illustrations: topical general news and feature pictures, cartoons. Payment: according to value; special fees for exclusive news. Founded 1869.

West Midlands

Birmingham Evening Mail

28 Colmore Circus, Queensway, Birmingham B4 6AX
tel 0121-236 3366 *fax* 0121-625 1105
London office 1 Canada Square, Canary Wharf, London E14 5AP
tel 020-7293 3000 *fax* 020-7293 3793
Editor I. Dowell
Daily Mon-Sat 30p

Features of topical Midland interest considered. Length: 400-800 words. Payment: by arrangement. Founded 1870.

The Birmingham Post

PO Box 18, 28 Colmore Circus,
Birmingham B4 6AX
tel 0121-236 3366 *fax* 0121-625 1105
London office 22nd Floor, 1 Canada Square,
Canary Wharf, London E14 5AP
tel 020-7293 3455 *fax* 020-7293 3400
Editor N. Hastilow
Daily Mon-Sat 37p
Features Editor Peter Bacon
News Editor Chris Russon
Picture Editor Paul Vokes
Sports Editor Mark Woodward

Authoritative and well-written articles of industrial, political or general interest are considered, especially if they have relevance to the Midlands. Length: up to 1000 words. Payment: by arrangement.

Coventry Evening Telegraph

Corporation Street, Coventry CV1 1FP
tel 024-7663 3633 *fax* 024-7655 0869
Editor Alan Kirby
Daily Mon-Sat 32p

Topical, illustrated articles with a Coventry or Warwickshire interest. Length: up to 600 words. Payment: by arrangement.

Express and Star

Queen Street, Wolverhampton WV1 1ES
tel (01902) 313131 *fax* (01902) 319721
e-mail general@expressandstar.co.uk
web site http://www.westmidlands.com
Editor Warren Wilson
London office Room 110, Temple Chambers,
Temple Avenue, London EC4Y 0DT
Daily Mon-Sat 30p
Features Editor Jim Walsh
News Editor John Bray
Picture Editor Geoff Wright
Sports Editor Steve Gordos

Founded 1874.

The Sentinel

Staffordshire Sentinel Newspapers Ltd,
Sentinel House, Etruria,
Stoke-on-Trent ST1 5SS
tel (01782) 602525 *fax* (01782) 602616
e-mail editor@thesentinel.co.uk
web site http://www.thisisstaffordshire.co.uk
Editor Sean Dooley
Daily Mon-Sat 27p
Arts and Features Editor Roy Coates
Business Correspondent Andrew Stanistreet
News Editor Michael Wood
Picture Editor Trevor Slater
Sports Editor Alex Martin

Articles and features of topical interest to the north Staffordshire/south Cheshire area. Illustrations: colour and b&w. Payment: by arrangement. Founded 1873.

Shropshire Star

Ketley, Telford TF1 4HU
tel (01952) 242424 *fax* (01952) 254605
Editor Adrian Faber
Daily Mon-Sat 28p
News Editor Sarah Jane Smith
Picture Editor Ken Done
Sports Editor Keith Harrison
Supplements Dept Sharon Walters

Evening paper: news and features. No unsolicited material; write to features editor with outline of ideas. Payment: by arrangement. Founded 1964.

Sunday Mercury

Colmore Circus, Birmingham B4 6AZ
tel 0121-236 3366 *fax* 0121-233 0271
Editor Fiona Alexander
Sun 55p
Features Editor Bernard Cole
News Editor Bernard Cole
Picture Editor Adam Fradgley
Sports Editor Lee Gibson

News specials or features of Midland interest. Illustrations: colour, b&w, cartoons. Special rates for special matter.

Yorkshire/Humberside

Evening Courier

PO Box 19, King Cross Street,
Halifax HX1 2SF
tel (01422) 260200 *fax* (01422) 260341
web site http://www.halifaxcourier.co.uk
Editor Edward Riley
2 per day Mon-Sat 30p
Features Editor William Marshall
News Editor John Kenealy
Sports Editor Ian Rushworth

Articles of local interest and background to news events. Length: up to 500 words. Illustrations: colour photos. Payment: £25-£40 per article; photos per quality/size used. Founded 1832.

Evening Press

York and County Press, PO Box 29,
76-86 Walmgate, York YO1 9YN
tel (01904) 653051 *fax* (01904) 612853
Editor Elizabeth Page
Daily Mon-Sat 30p
Assistant Editor Chris Buxton
News Editor Francine Clee
Picture Editor Martin Oates
Sports Editor Martin Jarred

Articles of North and East Yorkshire interest, humour, personal experience of current affairs. Length: 500-1000 words. Payment: by arrangement. Illustrations: line, half-tone, cartoons. Founded 1882.

Grimsby Evening Telegraph

80 Cleethorpe Road, Grimsby,
North East Lincolnshire DN31 3EH
tel (01472) 360360 *fax* (01472) 372257
e-mail grimsbytelegraph@dial.pipex.com
web site http://www.grimsbytelegraph.co.uk
Editor Peter Moore
Daily Mon-Sat 27p
Features Editor Barrie Farnsworth
News Editor Stephen Richards
Picture Editor David Moss
Sports Editor Geoff Ford

Considers general interest articles. Illustrations: line, half-tone, colour, cartoons. Payment: by arrangement. Founded 1897.

The Huddersfield Daily Examiner

Examiner News & Information Services Ltd,
PO Box A26, Queen Street South,
Huddersfield HD1 2TD
tel (01484) 430000 *fax* (01484) 437789
e-mail editor@examiner.co.uk
web site http://www.examiner.co.uk
Editor John Williams
Daily Mon-Fri 32p
Features editor Andrew Flynn
Picture editor Neil Atkinson

No contributions required at present. Payment: £10-£15 (short features). Founded 1871.

The Star

York Street, Sheffield S1 1PU
tel 0114-276 7676 *fax* 0114-272 5978
web site http://www.sheffweb.co.uk
Editor Peter Charlton
Daily Mon-Sat 27p
Features Editor Paul License
News Editor Bob Westerdale
Picture Editor Dennis Lound
Sports Editor Martin Smith

Well-written articles of local character. Length: about 500 words. Payment: by negotiation. Illustrations: topical photos, line drawings, graphics, cartoons. Founded 1887.

Telegraph & Argus

Hall Ings, Bradford, West Yorkshire BD1 1JR
tel (01274) 729511 *fax* (01274) 723634
e-mail bradford.editorial@telegraph-and-argus.co.uk
web site http://www.thisisbradford.co.uk
Editor Perry Austin-Clarke
Daily Mon-Sat 28p
Chief Photographer Simon Waites
Features Editor Jan Brierley
News Editor Damian Bates
Sports Editor Alan Birkinshaw

Evening paper: news, articles and features relevant to or about the people of West Yorkshire. Length: up to 1000 words. Illustrations: line, half-tone, colour. Payment: features from £15; line from £5, b&w and colour photos by negotiation. Founded 1868.

Yorkshire Evening Post

PO Box 168, Wellington Street, Leeds LS1 1RF
tel 0113-2432701 *fax* 0113-2388535
Editor N.R. Hodgkinson
Daily Mon-Sat 30p
Features Editor Anne Pickles
News Editor David Helliwell
Picture Editor Andy Manning
Sports Editor Martin Rose

News stories and feature articles. Illustrations: colour and b&w, cartoons. Payment: by negotiation. Founded 1890.

Yorkshire Post

Wellington Street, Leeds LS1 1RF
tel 0113-243 2701 *fax* 0113-238 8537
web site http://www.ypn.co.uk
Editor Tony Watson
London office 27 Albemarle Street,
London W1X 3FA
tel 020-7408 9622
Daily Mon-Sat 38p
Features Editor Michael Hickling
Head of Content John Furbisher
Picture Editor Nigel Roddis
Sports Editor Bill Bridge

Authoritative and well-written articles on topical subjects of general, literary or industrial interests. Length: max. 1200 words. Illustrations: photos and frequent pocket cartoons (single column width), topical wherever possible. Payment: by arrangement. Founded 1754.

Magazines UK and Ireland

Listings for regional newspapers start on page 11 and listings for national newspapers start on page 3. For quick reference, magazines are listed by subject area on page 121. See page 131 for recent changes to newspapers and magazines.

Accountancy

40 Bernard Street, London WC1N 1LD
tel 020-7833 3291 *fax* 020-7833 2085
e-mail postmaster@theabg.demon.co.uk
web site http://www.abgweb.com
Editor Brian Singleton-Green
Monthly £52.50 p.a.

Articles on accounting, taxation, financial, legal and other subjects likely to be of professional interest to accountants in practice or industry, and to top management generally; cartoons. Payment: £130 per page. Founded 1889.

Accountancy Age

VNU Business Publications, VNU House, 32-34 Broadwick Street, London W1A 2HG
tel 020-7316 9236 *fax* 020-7316 9250
e-mail accountancy_age@vnu.co.uk
web site http://www.accountancyage.com
Editor Damian Wild
Weekly £2 (£100 p.a.)

Articles of accounting, financial and business interest. Illustrations: colour photos; freelance assignments commissioned. Payment: by arrangement. Founded 1969.

Accounting & Business

Association of Chartered Certified Accountants, 10-11 Lincolns Inn Fields, London WC2A 3BP
tel 020-7396 5966 *fax* 020-7396 5958
e-mail accounting&business@acca.org.uk
web site http://www.acca.org.uk
Editor John Rogers Prosser
10 p.a. £85 p.a.

Journal of the Association of Chartered Certified Accountants. Accountancy, finance and business topics of relevance to accountants and finance directors. Length: 1300 words. Payment: £150 per 1000 words. Illustrated. Founded 1998.

ace

Tennis GB, 9-11 North End Road, London W14 8ST
tel 020-7605 8000 *fax* 020-7602 2323
Editor Dominic Bliss
11 p.a. £2.60

International high profile tennis, including interviews with top players, coaching articles, big tournament reports, health and fitness. Submit synopsis in first instance. Payment: 15p per word. Founded 1996.

Active Life

Lexicon Editorial Group Services, 1st floor, 1-5 Clerkenwell Road, London EC1M 5PA
tel 020-7253 5775 *fax* 020-7253 5676
e-mail activelife@lexicon-uk.com
Editor Helene Hodge
Bi-monthly £2.30

Lifestyle advice for the over 50s, including holidays and health, fashion and food, finance and fiction, hobbies and home, personality profiles. Submit ideas in writing. Length: 600-1200 words. Illustrations: colour. Payment: £100 per 1000 words; photos by negotiation. Founded 1989.

Acumen

6 The Mount, Higher Furzeham, Brixham, South Devon TQ5 8QY
tel (01803) 851098
Editor Patricia Oxley
Tri-annual (Jan/May/Sept) £12.50 p.a.

Poetry, literary and critical articles, reviews, literary memoirs, etc, 130pp or more. Send sae with submissions. Payment: small. Founded 1985.

Aeromodeller

Nexus Special Interests Ltd, Nexus House, Azalea Drive, Swanley, Kent BR8 8HU
tel (01322) 660070 *fax* (01322) 667633
Editor Pete Norrington
13 p.a. £2.50

Articles and news concerning model aircraft. Suitable articles and first-class photos by outside contributors are always considered. Length: 750-2000 words, or by arrangement. Illustrations: photos and line drawings to scale. Payment: by negotiation. Founded 1935.

Aeroplane Monthly

IPC Magazines Ltd, King's Reach Tower, Stamford Street, London SE1 9LS
tel 020-7261 5849 *fax* 020-7261 5269
Editor Michael Oakey
Monthly £3.20

Articles and photos relating to historical aviation. Length: up to 3000 words. Illustrations: line, half-tone, colour, cartoons. Payment: £50 per 1000 words, payable on publication; photos £10-£40; colour £80 per page. Founded 1973.

Africa Confidential

Blackwell Publishing Ltd, 73 Farringdon Road, London EC1M 3JQ
tel 020-7831 3511 *fax* 020-7831 6778
web site http://www.africa-confidential.com
Editor Patrick Smith
Fortnightly £278 p.a.

News and analysis of political and economic developments in Africa. Unsolicited contributions welcomed, but must be exclusive and not published elsewhere. Length: 1200-word features, 200-word pointers. Payment: £200 per 1000 words. No illustrations. Founded 1960.

Africa: St Patrick's Missions

St Patrick's, Kiltegan, Co. Wicklow, Republic of Ireland
tel (0508) 73600 *fax* (0508) 73622
e-mail spsoff@iol.ie
web site http://www.spms.org
Editor Rev. Gary Howley
9 p.a. £5 p.a. (IR£6)

Articles of missionary and topical religious interest. Length: up to 1000 words. Illustrations: line, half-tone, colour.

African Business

IC Publications Ltd, 7 Coldbath Square, London EC1R 4LQ
tel 020-7713 7711 *fax* 020-7713 7970
e-mail icpubs@dial.pipex.com
Editor Anver Versi
Monthly £2.50

Articles on business, economic and financial topics of interest to businessmen, ministers, officials concerned with African affairs. Length: 400-750 words; shorter coverage 100-400 words. Illustrations: line, half-tone. Payment: £80 per 1000 words; £1 per column cm for illustrations. Founded 1978.

Agenda

5 Cranbourne Court, Albert Bridge Road, London SW11 4PE
tel/fax 020-7228 0700
e-mail agendapoetry@btinternet.com
Editor William Cookson, *Assistant Editor* Anita Money
Quarterly £26 p.a. (libraries, institutions and overseas: rates on application); £20 OAPs/students

Poetry and criticism. Study the journal before submitting MSS with an sae. Illustrations: half-tone. Payment: variable.

Air International

Key Publishing Ltd, PO Box 100, Stamford, Lincs. PE9 1XQ
tel (01780) 755131 *fax* (01780) 757261
e-mail English@keymags.demon.co.uk
Editor Malcolm English
Monthly £2.80

Technical articles on aircraft; features on topical aviation subjects – civil and military; historical aviation subjects. Length: up to 5000 words. Illustrations: colour transparencies/prints, b&w prints/line drawings, cartoons. Payment: £50 per 1000 words or by negotiation; £20 colour, £10 b&w. Founded 1971.

Air Pictorial International

HPC Publishing, Drury Lane, St Leonards-on-Sea, East Sussex TN38 9BJ
tel (01424) 720477 *fax* (01424) 443693/434086
Editor Barry C. Wheeler
Monthly £2.85

Covers all aspects of aviation. Many articles commissioned; will consider competent articles exploring fresh ground or presenting an individual point of view on technical matters. Illustrated, mainly with photos. Payment: by arrangement.

Amateur Gardening

IPC Magazines Ltd, Westover House, West Quay Road, Poole, Dorset BH15 1JG
tel (01202) 440840 *fax* (01202) 440860
e-mail amateurgardening@ipc.co.uk
Editor Adrian Bishop
Weekly £1.10

Topical, practical or newsy articles up to 1200 words of interest to keen gardeners. Payment: by arrangement. Illustrations: colour. Founded 1884.

Amateur Photographer

(incorporating Photo Technique)
IPC Magazines Ltd, King's Reach Tower, Stamford Street, London SE1 9LS
tel 020-7261 5100 *fax* 020-7261 5404
e-mail amateurphotographer@ipc.co.uk

Editor Garry Coward-Williams
Weekly £1.75

Original articles of pictorial or technical interest, preferably illustrated with either photos or diagrams. Good instructional features especially sought. Length preferred: (unillustrated) 400-800 words; articles up to 1500 words; (illustrated) 2-4 pages. Payment: weekly, rates according to usage. Illustrations unaccompanied by text considered – indicate if material can be held on file. Founded 1884.

Amateur Stage

Platform Publications Ltd, Hampden House, 2 Weymouth Street, London W1N 3FD
tel 020-7636 4343 *fax* 020-7636 2323
e-mail cvtheatre@aol.com
web site http://www.amdram.org.uk/amstagel.htm
Editor Charles Vance
Monthly £2.40

Articles on all aspects of the amateur theatre, preferably practical and factual. Length: 600-2000 words. Illustrations: photos, line drawings. Payment: none. Founded 1946.

Ambit

17 Priory Gardens, London N6 5QY
tel 020-8340 3566
web site http://www.ambit.co.uk
Poetry Editors Martin Bax, Henry Graham, Carol-Ann Duffy, *Prose Editors* J.G. Ballard, Geoff Nicholson, *Art Editor* Mike Foreman
Quarterly £6 inc. p&p (£24 p.a. UK, £26/$52 p.a. overseas; £35 p.a., £37/$74 p.a. institutions)

Poetry, short fiction, art, poetry reviews. New and established writers and artists. Payment: by arrangement. Illustrations: line, half-tone, colour. Founded 1959.

American Markets Newsletter

175 Westland Drive, Glasgow G14 9JQ
e-mail sheila.oconnor@juno.com
Editor Sheila O'Connor
10 p.a. £34 p.a. (£63 for 2 years)

Editorial guidelines for US, Canadian and other overseas markets, plus information on press trips, non-fiction/fiction markets and writers' tips. Sample issue £3.95 (payable to S. O'Connor).

Amiga Format

Future Publishing Ltd, 30 Monmouth Street, Bath BA1 6PS
tel (01225) 442244 *fax* (01225) 732341
e-mail amformat@futurenet.co.uk
web site http://www.futurenet.co.uk
Editor Ben Vost
13 p.a. £5.99 (disk) £5.99 (CD)

Features, news, interviews, reviews covering the whole of the Amiga market. Length: 100-150 words (news). Payment: £85 per 750 words. Colour transparencies and digital images. Founded 1989.

AN Magazine

(formerly Artists Newsletter)
AN Publications, 1st Floor, Turner Building, 7-15 Pink Lane, Newcastle upon Tyne NE1 5DW
tel 0191-241 8000 *fax* 0191-241 8001
e-mail edit@anpubs.demon.co.uk
Contact Julie Crawshaw
Monthly £3 (£25 p.a.)

Articles, news and features for practising artists and makers. Illustrations: transparencies, colour and b&w photos. Payment: £100 per 1000 words. Founded 1980.

Angler's Mail

IPC Magazines Ltd, King's Reach Tower, Stamford Street, London SE1 9LS
tel 020-7261 5778 *fax* 020-7261 6016
Editor Roy Westwood
Weekly £1

News items about coarse and sea fishing. Payment: by agreement.

Angling Times

EMAP Active Ltd, Bushfield House, Orton Centre, Peterborough PE2 54W
tel (01733) 266222/264666 *fax* (01733) 465844
e-mail john.kelly@ecm.emap.com
Editor John Kelly
Weekly 85p

Articles, pictures, news stories, on all forms of angling. Illustrations: line, half-tone, colour. Payment: by arrangement. Founded 1953.

Animals and You

D.C. Thomson & Co Ltd, Albert Square, Dundee DD1 9QJ
tel (01382) 223131 *fax* (01382) 225511
185 Fleet Street, London EC4A 2HS
tel 020-7400 1030 *fax* 020-7400 1089
Fortnightly (Fri) £1.20

Features, stories and pin-ups for girls who love animals. Founded 1998.

Antiques and Collectables

Western Publishing Ltd, PO Box 2552, Bath BA1 3YP
tel (01225) 311077 *fax* (01225) 334619
e-mail antiques.collectables@btinternet.com
web site http://www.antiques-collectables.co.uk
Editor George Perrott
Monthly £2.20

Features on ceramics, furniture, glass, memorabilia, ephemera etc aimed at the antiques trade and general collectors. Includes price guide and news. Write with idea in first instance. Length: 1500-2000 (features). Illustrations: transparencies and colour prints. Payment £100-£150; none. Founded 1998.

The Antique Dealer & Collectors Guide

PO Box 805, London SE10 8TD
tel 020-8691 4820
Editor Philip Bartlam
Monthly £2.75

Articles on antique collecting and art. Length: 1500-2000 words. Payment: £76 per 1000 words. Illustrations: half-tone, colour.

Antiques & Art Independent

PO Box 1945, Comely Bank, Edinburgh EH4 1AB
tel (07000) 765 263 *fax* 0131-332 4481
Publisher/Editor Tony Keniston
Quarterly £2

Newspaper for the British antiques and art trade. News, gossip and controversial personal views on all aspects of the antiques world welcome. People stories only. Approach in writing with ideas. Length: 600 words (articles), 200 words (news). Illustrations: b&w prints. Payment: by negotiation. Founded 1997.

Apollo

1-2 Castle Lane, London SW1E 6DR
tel 020-7233 6640 *fax* 020-7630 7791
Editor David Ekserdjian
Monthly £7.80

Scholarly articles of about 2500 words on art, architecture, ceramics, furniture, armour, glass, sculpture, and any subject connected with art and collecting. Payment: by arrangement. Illustrations: half-tone, colour. Founded 1925.

The Aquarist and Pondkeeper

Inline Magazines Ltd, Suite 4, Invicta Business Centre, Orbital Park, Ashford, Kent TN24 0HB
tel (01233) 500021 *fax* (01233) 500070
Editor Derek Lambert
Monthly £2.25

Illustrated authoritative articles by professional and amateur biologists, naturalists and aquarium hobbyists on all matters concerning life in and near water, conservation and herpetology. Length: about 1500 words. Illustrations: line, half-tone, colour, cartoons. Payment: by arrangement. Founded 1924.

Aquila

New Leaf Publishing Ltd, PO Box 2518, Eastbourne, East Sussex BN21 2BB
tel (01323) 431313 *fax* (01323) 731136
e-mail aquila@pavilion.co.uk
web site http://www.aquila.co.uk/aquila
Editor Jackie Berry
Monthly £31.50 p.a. (£19.95 6 months)

Dedicated to encouraging children aged 8-13 to reason and create, and to develop a caring nature. Short stories and serials of up to 4 parts. Occasional features commissioned from writers with specialist knowledge. Approach in writing with ideas and sample of writing style, with sae. Length: 700-800 words (features), 1000-1100 words (stories or per episode of a serial). Illustrations: colour and b&w, cartoons. Payment: £75 (features); £90 (stories), £80 (per episode). Founded 1993.

The Architects' Journal

EMAP Business Communications, 151 Rosebery Avenue, London EC1R 4GB
tel 020-7505 6700 *fax* 020-7505 6701
Editor Isobel Allen
Weekly £1.80 (£75 p.a.)

Articles (mainly technical) on architecture, planning and building accepted only with prior agreement of synopsis. Illustrations: photos and drawings. Payment: by arrangement. Founded 1895.

Architectural Design

John Wiley & Sons Ltd, 4th Floor, International House, Ealing Broadway Centre, London W5 5DB
tel 020-8326 3800 *fax* 020-8326 3801
Editor Maggie Toy
6 double issues p.a. £90 p.a. (£60 p.a. students)

International magazine comprising an extensively illustrated thematic profile presenting architecture and critical interpretations of architectural history, theory and practice. Uncommissioned articles not accepted. Illustrations: drawings and photos, line (colour preferred). Payment: by arrangement. Founded 1930.

The Architectural Review

EMAP Construct, 151 Rosebery Avenue, London EC1R 4GB
tel 020-7505 6725 *fax* 020-7505 6701
e-mail peterd@construct.emap.co.uk
web site http://www.arplus.com/
Editor Peter Davey
Monthly £5.95

Articles on architecture and the allied arts. Writers must be thoroughly qualified. Length: up to 3000 words. Payment: by arrangement. Illustrations: photos, drawings, etc. Founded 1896.

Architecture Today

161 Rosebery Avenue, London EC1R 4QX
tel 020-7837 0143 *fax* 020-7837 0155
Editors Ian Latham, Mark Swenarton
10 p.a. £3 Free to architects

Mostly commissioned articles and features on today's European architecture. Length: 200-800 words. Illustrations: colour. Payment: by negotiation. Founded 1989.

Arena

EMAP Metro Ltd, 5th Floor, Mappin House, 4 Winsley Street, London W1N 7AR
tel 020-7689 9999 *fax* 020-7689 0901
Editor Greg Williams
Monthly £3

Profiles, articles on a wide range of subjects intelligently treated; art, architecture, politics, sport, business, music, film, design, media, fashion. Length: up to 3000 words. Illustrations: b&w and colour photos. Payment: £200 per 1000 words; varies for illustrations. Founded 1986.

Army Quarterly & Defence Journal

1 West Street, Tavistock, Devon PL19 8DS
tel (01822) 613577/612785 *fax* (01822) 612785
Editor T.D. Bridge
Quarterly £52 p.a. (£138 3-yr saver contract)

Articles on a wide range of British, UN, Commonwealth and worldwide defence issues, historical and current; also Quarterly Diary, Defence Contracts, International Defence Reports, reviews. Preliminary letter with synopsis preferred. Length: 1000-4800 words. Illustrations: b&w photos, line drawings, maps. Payment: by arrangement. Founded 1829.

Art & Craft

Scholastic Ltd, Villiers House, Clarendon Avenue, Leamington Spa, Warks. CV32 5PR
tel (01926) 887799 *fax* (01926) 883331
e-mail art&craft@scholastic.co.uk
Editor Siân Morgan
Monthly £2.35

Articles offering fresh, creative ideas of a practical nature, based on teaching art, design and technology in the National Curriculum, for teachers. Articles by teachers and other experts. Illustrations: colour. Payment: by arrangement. Founded 1936.

The Art Book

Laughton Cottage, Laughton, Nr Lewes, East Sussex BN8 6DD
tel (01323) 811759 *fax* (01323) 811756
e-mail sward@mistral.co.uk
web site http://www.blackwellpublishers.co.uk/journals/artbook
Editor Sue Ward
4 p.a. (personal £23/$37 p.a.)

Magazine of the Association of Art Historians. Critical reviews of newly published books in the field of decorative, fine and applied art, art history, photography, architecture and design. Payment: none. Founded 1993.

Art Business Today

The Fine Art Trade Guild, 16-18 Empress Place, London SW6 1TT
tel 020-7381 6616 *fax* 020-7381 2596
e-mail abt@fineart.co.uk
web site http://www.fineart.co.uk/sumabt.htm
Editor Annabelle Ruston
5 p.a. £19 p.a.

Distributed to the fine art and framing industry. Covers essential information on new products and technology, market trends and business analysis. Length: 800-1600 words. Illustrations: colour photos, cartoons. Payment: by arrangement. Founded 1991.

Art Monthly

Britannia Art Publications Ltd, Suite 17, 26 Charing Cross Road, London WC2H 0DG
tel 020-7240 0389 *fax* 020-7497 0726
e-mail info@artmonthly.co.uk
web site http://www.artmonthly.co.uk
Editor Patricia Bickers
10 p.a. £3.25

Features on modern and contemporary visual artists and art history, art theory and art-related issues; exhibition and book reviews. All material commissioned. Length: 750-1500 words. Illustrations: b&w photos. Payment: features £100-£150; none for photos. Founded 1976.

The Art Newspaper

70 South Lambeth Road, London SW8 1RL
tel 020-7735 3331 *fax* 020-7735 3332
Editor Anna Somers Cocks
11 p.a. £4.50 (£45 p.a.)

International coverage of the art market, news, commentary. Length: 200-1000 words. Illustrations: b&w photos. Payment: £120 per 1000 words. Founded 1990.

Art Review

Art Review Ltd, Hereford House,
23-24 Smithfield Street, London EC1A 9LB
tel 020-7236 4880 *fax* 020-7236 4881
e-mail info@art-review.co.uk
Editor Charlotte Mullins
Monthly £3.95

Art news, features and reviews. Commissioned work only. Payment: from £200 per 1000 words. Illustrations: line, colour. Founded 1949.

The Artist

The Artists' Publishing Co. Ltd, Caxton House,
63-65 High Street, Tenterden, Kent TN30 6BD
tel (01580) 763673
Editor Sally Bulgin
Monthly £2.35

Practical, instructional articles on painting for all amateur and professional artists. Payment: by arrangement. Illustrations: line, half-tone, colour. Founded 1931.

Artists and Illustrators

The Fitzpatrick Building, 188-194 York Way,
London N7 9QR
tel 020-7700 8500 *fax* 020-7700 4985
Editor Jim Manson
Monthly £2.60

Practical and business articles for amateur and professional artists. Length: 1000-1500 words. Illustrations: colour transparencies. Payment: variable. Founded 1986.

Asian Times

Ethnic Media Group, 1st Floor, 148 Cambridge
Heath Road, London E1 5QJ
tel 020-7702 8012 *fax* 020-7702 7937
Editor Sanjay Gohil
Weekly 50p

News stories, articles and features of interest to Britain's Asian community. Founded 1983.

Astronomy Now

Pole Star Publications, PO Box 175, Tonbridge,
Kent TN10 4ZY
tel (01732) 367542 *fax* (01732) 356230
e-mail editorial@astronow.cix.co.uk
Managing Editor Steven Young
Monthly £2.50

Aimed at amateur and professional astronomers. Interested in news items and longer features on astronomy and some space-related activities. Writers' guidelines available (send sae). Length: 1500-3000 words. Illustrations: line, half-tone, colour. Payment: 5p per word; from £10 per photo. Founded 1987.

Athletics Weekly

Descartes Publishing Ltd, 13 Cavell Court,
Lincoln Road, Peterborough PE1 2RJ
tel (01733) 898440 *fax* (01733) 898441
e-mail nigel.walsh@ecm.emap.com
Editor Nigel Walsh
Weekly £1.95

News and features on track and field athletics, road running, cross country, fell and race walking. Material mostly commissioned. Length: 1000-3000 words. Illustrations: colour and b&w action and head/shoulder photos, line. Payment: varies. Founded 1946.

Attitude

Northern & Shell plc, Northern & Shell Tower,
City Harbour, London E14 9GL
tel 020-7308 5090 *fax* 020-7308 5075
e-mail amattera@norshell.co.uk
Editor Adam Mattera
Monthly £2.50

Men's style magazine aimed primarily but not exclusively at gay men. Covers style/fashion, interviews, reviews. Illustrations: colour transparencies, b&w prints. Payment: £150 per 1000 words; £100 per full page illustration. Founded 1994.

The Author

84 Drayton Gardens, London SW10 9SB
tel 020-7373 6642
Editor Derek Parker
Quarterly £7

Organ of The Society of Authors. Commissioned articles from 1000-2000 words on any subject connected with the legal, commercial or technical side of authorship. Little scope for the freelance writer: preliminary letter advisable. Illustrations: line, occasional cartoons. Payment: by arrangement. Founded 1890.

Auto Express

Dennis Publishing Ltd, 19 Bolsover Street,
London W1P 7HJ
tel 020-7631 1433 *fax* 020-7917 5556
Editor David Johns
Weekly £1.30

News stories, and general interest features about drivers as well as cars. Illustrations: colour photos. Payment: features £250 per 1000 words; photos, varies. Founded 1988.

Autocar

Haymarket Publishing Ltd, 60 Waldegrave Road,
Teddington, Middlesex TW11 8LG
tel 020-8267 5630 *fax* 020-8267 5759
e-mail autocar@compuserve.com

Editor Patrick Fuller
Weekly £2

Articles on all aspects of cars, motoring and the motor industry: general, practical, competition and technical. Illustrations: line (litho), colour and electronic (Illustrator). Press day news: Thursday. Payment: varies; mid-month following publication. Founded 1895.

Babycare and Pregnancy

(formerly First Steps)
D.C. Thomson & Co. Ltd, 80 Kingsway East, Dundee DD4 8SL
tel (01382) 223131 *fax* (01382) 452491
Editor Irene K. Duncan
Monthly £1.90

Cares about the mother and her needs as well as the baby. Interested in articles on pregnancy, birth and childcare, and fillers. Illustrations: colour transparencies and colour artwork. Length/payment: negotiable. Founded 1994.

Back Street Heroes

9 White Lion Street, London N1 9XJ
tel 020-7837 8727 *fax* 020-7837 7064
Editor Stu Garland
Monthly £2.70

Custom motorcycle features plus informed lifestyle pieces. Illustrations: colour, cartoons. Payment: by arrangement. Founded 1983.

Balance

British Diabetic Association, 10 Queen Anne Street, London W1M 0BD
tel 020-7323 1531 *fax* 020-7637 3644
e-mail balance@diabetes.org.uk
web site http://www.diabetes.org.uk
Editor John Isitt
Bi-monthly £2

Articles on diabetes and related health and lifestyle issues. Length: 1000-2000 words. Payment: by arrangement. Illustrations: colour. Founded 1935.

Ballroom Dancing Times

The Dancing Times Ltd, Clerkenwell House, 45-47 Clerkenwell Green, London EC1R 0EB
tel 020-7250 3006 *fax* 020-7253 6679
e-mail ballroom@dancing-times.co.uk
web site http://www.dt-ltd@dircon.co.uk
Editor Mary Clarke, *Executive Editor* Bronya Seifert
Monthly £1.15

Ballroom and social dancing from every aspect, but chiefly from the serious competitive, teaching and medal test angles. Well-informed freelance articles are occasionally used, but only after preliminary arrangements. Payment: by arrangement. Illustrations: action photos preferred, b&w or colour. Founded 1956.

The Banker

Maple House, Tottenham Court Road, London W1P 9LL
tel 020-7896 2507 *fax* 020-7896 2507
e-mail stephen.timewell@ft.com
Editor Stephen Timewell
Monthly £189 p.a.

Articles on investment banking and finance, retail banking, banking technology, banking services and systems; bank analysis and top 1000 listings. Illustrations: half-tones and full colour of people, charts, tables, maps etc. Founded 1926.

Baptist Times

PO Box 54, 129 Broadway, Didcot, Oxon OX11 8XB
tel (01235) 517670 *fax* (01235) 517678
Editor John Capon
Weekly 50p

Religious or social affairs material, up to 1000 words. Payment: by arrangement. Illustrations: half-tone. Founded 1855.

BBC magazines – see page 301

The Beano

D.C. Thomson & Co. Ltd, Albert Square, Dundee DD1 9QJ
tel (01382) 223131 *fax* (01382) 322214
185 Fleet Street, London EC4A 2HS
tel 020-7400 1030 *fax* 020-7400 1089
Weekly 52p

Comic strips for children. Series, 11-22 pictures. Payment: on acceptance.

Fun Size Beano
2 p.m. 70p

Founded 1997.

Bella

H. Bauer Publishing, Shirley House, 25-27 Camden Road, London NW1 9LL
tel 020-7241 8000 *fax* 020-7241 8056
Editor Jackie Highe
Weekly 62p

General interest magazine for women: practical articles on fashion and beauty, health, cooking, home, travel; real life stories, plus fiction up to 2000 words. Payment: by arrangement. Illustrations: line including cartoons, half-tone, colour. Founded 1987.

Best

Grunar + Jahr (UK), 197 Marsh Wall, London E14 9SG

tel 020-7519 5500 *fax* 020-7519 5516
Editor Louise Court
Weekly 62p

Short stories. No other uncommissioned work accepted, but always willing to look at ideas/outlines. Length: 1000 words for short stories, variable for other work. Illustrations: line, half-tone, colour, cartoons. Payment: by agreement. Founded 1987.

Best of British

Ian Beacham Publishing, Bank Chambers, 27A Market Place, Market Deeping, Lincs. PE6 8EA
tel/fax (01778) 342814
e-mail beacham@british.fsbusiness.co.uk
Editor Peter Kelly
Monthly £2.50

Nostalgic features about life in the 1930s, 1940s and 1950s and personal memories. Length: max. 1000 words. Illustrations: colour and b&w. Payment: from £20 (words); £10 (pictures). Founded 1994.

The Big Issue

236-240 Pentonville Road, London N1 9JY
tel 020-7526 3200
Editor Matthew Collin
Weekly £1

Features, news, reviews, interviews – of general interest and on social issues. Length: features 500-2000 words. No short stories or poetry. Illustrations: colour and b&w photos and line. Payment: £150 per 1000 words. Founded 1991.

The Big Issue in the North

The Big Issue in the North Ltd, 135-141 Oldham Street, Manchester M4 1LL
tel 0161-834 6300 *fax* 0161-819 5000
Editor Kate Markey
Weekly £1

Articles of general interest and on social issues; arts features and news covering the north of England. No fiction or poetry, except by the homeless. Contact the news, arts or deputy editor to discuss ideas. Length: 1500 words (features/articles), 300-500 (news), 700 (arts features), 350 words (comment). Payment: £90 per 1000 words. Colour transparencies, puzzles and quizzes. Founded 1992.

The Big Issue in Scotland

The Big Issue in Scotland Ltd, 29 College Street, Glasgow G1 1QH
tel 0141-559 5555 *fax* 0141-552 3200
e-mail edit.scot@bigissue.com
Editor Ken Laird
Weekly £1

Features on human rights, animal issues, green issues, injustices, Scotland, medical, scientific, the paranormal, health and crime, plus news and reviews. Length: 1000-2000 words (articles); 500-800 words (news). Illustrations: colour and b&w. Payment: £95 per 1000 words; £30 per photo/illustration. Founded 1993.

The Big Issues

110 Amien Street, Dublin 1, Republic of Ireland
tel (01) 8553969
Editor Rosemarie Meleady
Fortnightly IR£2

News and entertainment: politics, current affairs, social issues (especially), celebrity interviews. No fiction or poetry. Articles welcome. Approach in writing with a brief outline and angle first. Length: 700-1200 words. Payment: minimum 10p per word. Founded 1994.

Bike

EMAP Active Ltd, Bushfield House, Orton Centre, Peterborough PE2 5UW
tel (01733) 237111 *fax* (01733) 465858
e-mail hugo.wilson@ecm.emap.com
Editor Hugo Wilson
Monthly £3.20

Motorcycle magazine: interested in articles, features, news. Length: articles/features 1000-3000 words. Illustrations: colour and b&w photos, line, cartoons. Payment: £150 per 1000 words; illustrations per size/position. Founded 1971.

Bird Keeper

IPC Magazines Ltd, King's Reach Tower, Stamford Street, London SE1 9LS
tel 020-7261 6116 *fax* 020-7261 6095
Editor Colin Mitchell
Monthly £2.50

Articles on the care, health and breeding of pet birds, beginner bird keepers and how-to. Send synopsis of ideas. Payment: by negotiation. Founded 1988.

Bird Watching

EMAP Active Ltd, Apex House, Oundle Road, Peterborough PE2 9NP
tel (01733) 898100 *fax* (01773) 315984
e-mail dave.cromack@ecm.emap.com
Editor David Cromack
Monthly £2.65

Broad range of bird-related features and photography, particularly looking at bird behaviour, bird news, reviews and birdwatching sites. Emphasis on providing accurate information in entertaining ways. Send synopsis first. Length: 1200 words. Illustrations: colour photos, cartoons. Payment: by negotiation. Founded 1986.

Birding World

Sea Lawn, Coast Road, Cley next the Sea, Holt, Norfolk NR25 7RZ
tel (01263) 740913 *fax* (01263) 741014
e-mail steve@birdingworld.co.uk
web site http://www.birdingworld.co.uk
Editor Steve Gantlett
Monthly £38 p.a. (£45 p.a. Europe; £50 p.a. rest of the world, airmail)

Magazine for keen birdwatchers. Articles and news stories about mainly European ornithology, with the emphasis on ground-breaking new material. Length: up to 3000 words (articles); up to 1500 words (news). Illustrations: good quality colour photos of birds. Payment: up to £25 per 500 words; £10-£40 (illustrations). Founded 1987.

Birdwatch

Solo Publishing Ltd, 3rd Floor, Leroy House, 436 Essex Road, London N1 3QP
tel 020-7704 9495 *fax* 020-7704 2767
Editor Dominic Mitchell
Monthly £2.65

Topical articles on all aspects of birds and birding, including conservation, identification, sites and habitats, equipment, overseas expeditions. Length: 700-1500 words. Illustrations: colour slides, b&w photos, colour and b&w line. Payment: from £40 per 1000 words; colour: photos £15-£40, cover £70, line by negotiation; b&w: photos £10, line £10-£40. Founded 1991.

Bizarre

John Brown Publishing Ltd, The New Boathouse, 136-142 Bramley Road, London W10 6SR
tel 020-7565 3000 *fax* 020-7565 3053
e-mail bizarre@johnbrown.co.uk
web site http://www.bizarremag.com
Editor Joe Gardiner
Monthly £2.70

Features on strange events, adventure, cults, weird people, celebrities, etc. Study the magazine for style before submitting ideas by post or fax. No fiction. Length: 1200-2000 words. Payment: £100 per 1000 words. Colour transparencies and prints: £200 per dps, £125 per page. Founded 1997.

Black Beauty & Hair

Hawker Publications, 13 Park House, 140 Battersea Park Road, London SW11 4NB
tel 020-7720 2108 *fax* 020-7498 3023
e-mail info@blackbeauty.co.uk
web site http://www.blackbeauty.co.uk
Editor Irene Shelley
Bi-monthly £2.20

Beauty and style articles relating specifically to the black woman; celebrity features. True-life stories and salon features. Length: approx. 1000 words. Illustrations: colour and b&w photos. Payment: £95 per 1000 words; photos £25-£75. Founded 1982.

Bliss!

EMAP Élan Ltd, Endeavour House, 189 Shaftesbury Avenue, London WC2H 8JG
tel 020-7437 9011 *fax* 020-7208 3591
Editor Liz Nice
Monthly £1.70

Glamorous young women's glossy magazine. Bright intimate American-style format, with real life stories and reports, beauty, fashion, shopping, advice, quizzes. Payment: by arrangement. Founded 1995.

Blueprint

ETP Ltd, Rosebery House, 41 Springfield Road, Chelmsford CM2 6JJ
tel (01245) 491717 *fax* (01245) 499110
e-mail eiggibson@wilmington.co.uk
Editor Grant Gibson, *Managing Editor* Aidan Walker
11 p.a. £3.75

The magazine of modern architecture and design and contemporary culture. Interested in articles, features and reviews. Length: up to 2500 words. Illustrations: colour and b&w photos and line. Payment: negotiable. Founded 1983.

BMA News Review

British Medical Association, BMA House, Tavistock Square, London WC1H 9JP
tel 020-7383 6122 *fax* 020-7383 6566
Editor Julie Coulson

GP edition

20 p.a. £58 p.a.

News and features.

Hospital doctors edition

12 p.a. £58 p.a.

News and features. Length: 700-1200 words (features), 100-400 words (news). Illustrations: transparencies, colour and b&w artwork and cartoons. Payment: by negotiation. Founded 1966.

BMW Magazine

River Publishing, Victory House, Leicester Square, London WC2H 7QH
tel 020-7306 0304 *fax* 020-7306 0303

e-mail jevans@riverltd.co.uk
Editor Justin Evans
Quarterly £3.50

Lifestyle magazine for BMW car and bike owners. Discuss ideas for features and articles with the editor before submitting material. Length: 800-2500 (articles/features); 50-400 (news). Illustrations: colour. Payment £250 per 1000 words; £100 per quarter-page illustration. Founded 1996.

Boards

Yachting Press Ltd, 196 Eastern Esplanade, Southend-on-Sea, Essex SS1 3AB
tel (01702) 582245 *fax* (01702) 588434
e-mail 106003.3405@compuserve.com
web site http://www.boards.co.uk
Editor Bill Dawes
Monthly during summer, Bi-monthly during winter £2.80 (9 p.a.)

Articles, photos and reports on all aspects of windsurfing and boardsailing. Payment: by arrangement. Illustrations: line, halftone, colour, cartoons. Founded 1982.

The Book Collector

(incorporating Bibliographical Notes and Queries)
The Collector Ltd, PO Box 12426,
London W11 3GW
tel/fax 020-7792 3492
e-mail info@thebookcollector.co.uk
Editorial Board Nicolas Barker (Editor), A. Bell, J. Fergusson, T. Hofmann, D. McKitterick, Joan Winterkorn
Quarterly £38 p.a. (£40/$64 overseas)

Articles, biographical and bibliographical, on the collection and study of printed books and MSS. Payment: for reviews only. Founded 1952.

Book and Magazine Collector

Diamond Publishing Group Ltd,
43-45 St Mary's Road, London W5 5RQ
tel 020-8579 1082 *fax* 020-8566 2024
Editor Crispin Jackson
Monthly £2.90

Articles about collectable authors/publications/subjects. Articles must be bibliographical and include a full bibliography and price guide (no purely biographical features). Approach in writing with ideas. Length: 2000-4000 words. Illustrations: colour and b&w artwork. Payment: £30 per 1000 words. Founded 1984.

Books Ireland

11 Newgrove Avenue, Dublin 4,Republic of Ireland
tel (01) 2692185 *fax* (01) 260 4927
e-mail booksi@eircom.net
Editor Jeremy Addis, *Features Editor* Shirley Kelly
Monthly (exc. Jan, Jul, Aug) IR£2.40 (IR£22 p.a.)

Reviews of Irish-interest and Irish-author books, articles of interest to librarians, booksellers and readers. Length: 800-1400 words. Payment: £35 per 1000 words. *New Writing* section (showcase for unpublished poetry and prose). Length: 2500 words. Payment: token only (£5-£20). Founded 1976.

Books Magazine

39 Store Street, London WC1E 7DB
tel 020-7629 2900 *fax* 020-7419 2111
Editor Liz Thomson
Quarterly £1.50

Reviews, features, interviews with authors. No unsolicited MSS. Payment: negotiable but little bought in. Founded 1987.

The Bookseller

J. Whitaker and Sons Ltd, 12 Dyott Street, London WC1A 1DF
tel 020-7420 6000 *fax* 020-7420 6103
e-mail letters.to.editor@bookseller.co.uk
web site http://www.the-bookseller.com
Editor Nicholas Clee
Weekly £149 p.a.

Journal of the publishing and bookselling trades. While outside contributions are welcomed, most of the journal's contents are commissioned. Length: about 1000-1500 words. Payment: by arrangement. Founded 1858.

Bowls International

Key Publishing Ltd, PO Box 100, Stamford, Lincs. PE9 1XQ
tel (01780) 755131 *fax* (01780) 757261
Editor Melvyn Beck
Monthly £2.20

Sport and news items and features; occasional, bowls-oriented short stories. Illustrations: colour transparencies, b&w photos, occasional line, cartoons. Payment: sport/news approx. 25p per line, features approx. £50 per page; colour £25, b&w £10. Founded 1981.

Brewing & Distilling International

52 Glenhouse Road, London SE9 1JQ
tel 020-8859 4300 *fax* 020-8859 5813
e-mail bdilondon@dial.pipex.com
web site http://www.bdinews.com
Editor Bruce Stevens
Monthly £48 p.a. (£82/$115 p.a. airmail)

Journal for brewers, maltsters, hop merchants, distillers, soft drinks manufacturers, bottlers and allied traders, circulating in over 80 countries. Technical and marketing articles (average 1000 words) accepted, by prior arrangement, from authors with specialist knowledge. Illustrations: line drawings, photos. Payment: by agreement. Founded 1865.

British Birds

Fountains, Park Lane, Blunham, Bedford MK44 3NJ
tel/fax (01767) 640025
Managing Editor Dr J.T.R. Sharrock
Monthly £63.50 p.a.

Original observations relating to birds of Britain, Europe and North Africa. Illustrations: line, half-tone, colour. Payment: none for articles, nominal for illustrations. Founded 1907.

British Deaf News

7 Empire Court, Albert Street, Redditch, Worcs. B97 4DA
tel (01527) 592034, 592044 (text)
fax (01527) 592083 *videophone* (01527) 595318
web site http://www.britishdeafnews.com
Editor Catya Neilson
Monthly £1.25, £15 p.a. non-members (£1/£12 p.a. members)

Journal of the British Deaf Association. Articles, news items, letters dealing with deafness. Payment: by arrangement. Illustrations: line, half-tone. Founded 1955.

British Journal of General Practice

14 Princes Gate, Hyde Park, London SW7 1PU
tel 020-7581 3232 *fax* 020-7584 6716
e-mail journal@rcgp.org.uk
web site http://www.rcgp.org.uk
Editor Dr David Jewell BA, MB, BChir, MRCGP
Monthly £130 p.a. (£147 overseas, £166.50 airmail)

Articles relevant to general medical practice. Illustrations: half-tone, colour. Payment: none.

The British Journal of Photography

Timothy Benn Publishing, 39 Earlham Street, London WC2H 9LD
tel 020-7306 7000 *fax* 020-7306 7112
e-mail jt@benn.co.uk
web site http://www.bjphoto.co.uk
Editor Jon Tarrant
Weekly £1.50

Articles on professional, commercial and press photography, and on the more advanced aspects of amateur, technical, industrial, medical, scientific and colour photography. Illustrations: line, half-tone, colour. Payment: by arrangement. Founded 1854.

British Journalism Review

BJR Publishing Ltd, c/o University of Luton Press, Faculty of Humanities, University of Luton, 75 Castle Street, Luton, Beds. LU1 3AJ
tel (01582) 743297 *fax* (01582) 743298
e-mail ulp@luton.ac.uk
Editor Geoffrey Goodman
Quarterly £25 p.a. (overseas rates on application)

Comment/criticism/review of matters published by, or of interest to, the media. Length: 1000-3000 words. Illustrations: b&w photos. Payment: by arrangement. Founded 1989.

British Medical Journal

BMA House, Tavistock Square, London WC1H 9JR
tel 020-7387 4499 *fax* 020-7383 6418
e-mail editor@bmj.com
web site http://www.bmj.com
Editor Richard Smith BSc, MB, ChBEd, MFPHM, FRCPE
Weekly £7.90

Medical and related articles. Payment: by arrangement. Founded 1840.

British Philatelic Bulletin

Royal Mail, 2-14 Bunhill Row, London EC1Y 8HQ
fax 020-7847 3359
Editor J.R. Holman
Monthly 85p

Articles on any aspect of British philately – stamps, postmarks, postal history; also stamp collecting in general. Length: up to 1500 words (articles); 250 words (news). Payment: £45 per 1000 words. Illustrations: colour. Founded 1963.

British Postmark Bulletin

Fortnightly £10 p.a. (£21.75 p.a. overseas)

Articles on British postmarks – past and present. Founded 1971.

British Printer

Miller Freeman UK Ltd, Sovereign Way, Tonbridge, Kent TN9 1RW
tel (01732) 377207 *fax* (01732) 377316
e-mail rhayes@unmf.com
web site http://www.dotprint.com
Editor Rod Hayes
Monthly £75 p.a.

Articles on technical and aesthetic aspects of printing processes and graphic reproduction. Payment: by arrangement. Illustrations: photos, line drawings and diagrams, cartoons. Founded 1888.

Broadcast

EMAP Media, 33-39 Bowling Green Lane, London EC1R 0DA
tel 020-7505 8014 *fax* 020-7505 8050

Editor Lucy Rouse
Weekly £2.40

News and authoritative articles designed for all concerned with the UK and international TV and radio industry, and with programmes and advertising on TV, radio, video, cable, satellite, digital. Illustrations: colour, b&w, line, cartoons. Payment: by arrangement.

Brownie

The Guide Association, 17-19 Buckingham Palace Road, London SW1W 0PT
tel 020-7834 6242
e-mail MarionT@guides.org.uk, chq@guides.org.uk
web site http://www.guides.org.uk
Editor Marion Thompson
Monthly £1.30

Official Magazine of The Guide Association. Short articles for Brownies (girls 7-10 years); fiction with Brownie background (700-800 words); puzzles; 'things to make', etc. Illustrations: colour. Payment: £50 per 1000 words; varies for illustrations.

Budgerigar World

The County Press, Bala, Gwynedd LL23 7PG
tel (01678) 520262 *fax* (01678) 521262
Editor Terry A. Tuxford, 145 Western Way, Basingstoke, Hants RG22 6EX
tel (01256) 328898 *fax* (01256) 329462
e-mail 101610.1547@compuserve.com
Monthly £30 p.a.

Articles about exhibition budgerigars. Payment: by arrangement. Illustrations: half-tone, colour. Founded 1982.

Building

The Builder Group, Exchange Tower, 2 Harbour Exchange Square, London E14 9GE
tel 020-7560 4000 *fax* 020-7560 4004
e-mail 106173.632@compuserve.com
Editor Adrian Barrick
Weekly £2.20

Covers the entire professional, industrial and manufacturing aspects of the building industry. Articles on architecture and techniques at home and abroad considered, also news and photos. Payment: by arrangement. Founded 1842.

Building Design

Miller Freeman UK Ltd, City Reach, 5 Greenwich View Place, Millharbour, London E14 9NN
tel 020-7861 6467 *fax* 020-7861 6261
Editor Louise Rogers
Weekly Controlled circulation (£65 p.a.)

News and features on all aspects of building design. All material commissioned. Length: up to 1500 words. Illustrations: colour and b&w photos, line, cartoons. Payment: £120 per 1000 words; illustrations by negotiation. Founded 1970.

Built Environment

Alexandrine Press, PO Box 15, 51 Cornmarket Street, Oxford OX1 3EB
tel (01865) 724627 *fax* (01865) 792309
e-mail representative@ara.i-way.co.uk
Editors Prof Sir Peter Hall, Prof David Banister
Quarterly £75 p.a.

Articles about architecture, planning and the environment. Preliminary letter advisable. Length: 1000-5000 words. Payment: by arrangement. Illustrations: photos and line.

Bunty

D.C. Thomson & Co. Ltd, Albert Square, Dundee DD1 9QJ
tel (01382) 223131 *fax* (01382) 322214
185 Fleet Street, London EC4A 2HS
tel 020-7400 1030 *fax* 020-7400 1089
Weekly 75p

Vividly told picture-story serials for young girls of school age.

Burlington Magazine

14-16 Duke's Road, London WC1H 9AD
tel 020-7388 1228 *fax* 020-7388 1230
e-mail editorial@burlington.org.uk
Editor Caroline Elam
Monthly £11

Deals with the history and criticism of art; book and exhibition reviews; illustrated monthly Calendar section. Potential contributors must have special knowledge of the subjects treated; MSS compiled from works of reference are unacceptable. Length: 500-5000 words. Payment: up to £100. Illustrations: b&w and colour photos. Founded 1903.

Buses

Ian Allan Publishing Ltd, Riverdene Business Park, Molesey Road, Hersham, Surrey KT12 4RG
tel (01932) 266600 *fax* (01932) 266601
Editor Alan Millar, PO Box 3759, Glasgow G41 5YN
tel 0141-427 6294 *fax* 0141-427 9594
Monthly £2.95

Articles of interest to both road passenger transport operators and bus enthusiasts. Preliminary enquiry essential. Illustrations: colour transparencies, half-tone, line maps. Payment: on application. Founded 1949.

Business Life

Premier Media Partners, Haymarket House, 1 Oxenden Street, London SW1Y 4EE
tel 020-7925 2544 *fax* 020-7839 4508
Editor Sandra Harris
Monthly Free

Inflight magazine for British Airways. Articles and features of interest to the European business traveller. All material commissioned; approach in writing with ideas. Length: 850-1500 words. Illustrations: colour photos and line. Payment: £300 per 1000 words; £100-£400 for illustrations. Founded 1985.

Business Scotland

Peebles Media Group, Bergius House, Clifton Street, Glasgow G3 7LA
tel 0141-567 6000 *fax* 0141-331 1395
Editor Graham Lironi
Monthly Controlled circulation

Features, profiles and news items of interest to business and finance in Scotland. Payment: by arrangement. Founded 1947.

Business Traveller

Perry Publications Ltd, Russell Square House, 10-12 Russell Square, London WC1B 5ED
tel 020-7580 9898 *fax* 020-7580 6676
e-mail editorial@businesstraveller.com
web site http://www.btonline.co.uk
Editor Julia Brookes
Monthly £2.90

Articles, features and news on consumer travel aimed at individual frequent international business travellers. Submit ideas with recent clippings and a CV. Length: varies. Illustrations: colour for destinations features; send lists to Deborah Miller, Picture Editor. Payment: on application. Founded 1976.

BusinessMatters

GMC Publications, Castle Place, 166 High Street, Lewes, East Sussex BN7 1XU
tel (01273) 477374 *fax* (01273) 487692
Editor Peter Roper
Bi-monthly £3.95

How to run and market small- to medium-sized businesses. Articles based on case studies; relevant news. Length: 400-800 words. Illustrations: colour, cartoons. Payment: £60 per 500 words; £50 per illustration. Founded 1992.

Cable Guide

Cable Guide Ltd, 172 Tottenham Court Road, London W1P 0JJ
tel 020-7419 7300 *fax* 020-7419 7299
web site http://www.cableguide.co.uk
Editor Robin Jarossi
Monthly £3.25

Features and interviews about programmes featured on cable TV, together with programme listings for cable channels. All material commissioned. Length: up to 1000 words. Illustrations: colour transparencies. Payment: £550 per 1000 words, photo fees negotiable. Founded 1986.

Cage & Aviary Birds

IPC Magazines Ltd, King's Reach Tower, Stamford Street, London SE1 9LS
tel 020-7261 6116 *fax* 020-7261 6095
Editor tba
Weekly £1

News on all aspects of birds and bird-keeping. Practical articles on bird-keeping. First-hand knowledge only. Quality pictures always welcome. Illustrations: line, half-tone, colour. Payment: by arrangement. Founded 1902.

Camcorder User

(incorporating Video Editing and Desktop Video)
WV Publications, 57-59 Rochester Place, London NW1 9JU
tel 020-7331 1000 *fax* 020-7331 1242
e-mail wvmags@compuserve.com
Editor Adrian Justins
Monthly £2.75

Features on film/video-making techniques, specifically tailored to the amateur enthusiast. Material mostly commissioned. Length: 1000-2500 words. Illustrations: colour and b&w; contact editor for details. Payment: by arrangement. Founded 1988.

Campaign

Haymarket Business Publications Ltd, 174 Hammersmith Road, London W6 7JP
tel 020-7413 4036 *fax* 020-7413 4507
e-mail 100560.1626@compurserve.com
Editor Stefano Hatfield
Weekly £2.10

News and articles covering the whole of the mass communications field, particularly advertising in all its forms, marketing and the media. Features should not exceed 2000 words. News items also welcome. Press day, Wednesday. Payment: by arrangement.

Camping Magazine

Warner Group Publications, The Maltings, West Street, Bourne, Lincs. PE10 9PH
tel/fax (01778) 391116

Editor David Ogle
Monthly £2.30

Covers the spectrum of camping and related activities in all shapes and forms – camping is more than a tent on a site! Lively, anecdotal articles written to guidelines and photos are welcome. Talk to editor first. Length: 500-1500 words on average. Illustrations: colour. Payment: by arrangement. Founded 1961.

Car

EMAP Active Ltd, Angel House,
338-346 Goswell Road, London EC1V 7QP
tel 020-7477 7399 *fax* 020-7477 7282
e-mail car@ecm.emap.com
Editor Greg Fountain
Monthly £3.20

Top-grade journalistic features on car driving, car people and cars. Length: 1000-2500 words. Payment: minimum £250 per 1000 words. Illustrations: b&w and colour photos to professional standards. Founded 1962.

Car Mechanics

Cudham Tithe Barn, Berrys Hill, Cudham,
Kent TW16 3AG
tel (01959) 541444 or (01733) 203749
fax (01959) 541400
e-mail info@kelsey.co.uk
Editor Phil Weeden
Monthly £2.80

Practical articles on maintaining, repairing and uprating modern cars for DIY plus the motor trade. Always interested in finding new talent for our rather specialised market but please study a recent copy before submitting ideas or features. Preliminary letter or phone call outlining feature recommended. Payment: by arrangement. Illustrations: line drawings, colour prints or transparencies. Rarely use words only; please supply text and pictures.

Caravan Magazine

IPC Country & Leisure Media Ltd, Link House,
Dingwall Avenue, Croydon CR9 2TA
tel 020-8686 2599 *fax* 020-8781 6044/8760 0973
web site http://www.linkhouse.co.uk/
Editor Rob McCabe
Monthly £2.60

Lively articles based on real experience of touring caravanning, especially if well illustrated by photos. General countryside or motoring material not wanted. Payment: by arrangement. Founded 1933.

Caribbean Times

(incorporating African Times)
Ethnic Media Group, 1st Floor,
148 Cambridge Heath Road, London E1 5QJ
tel 020-7702 8012 *fax* 020-7702 7937
e-mail ct@eeye.demon.co.uk
Editor Emmanuel Dunseath
Weekly 50p

News stories, articles and features of interest to Britain's African-Caribbean community. Founded 1981.

Carousel – The Guide to Children's Books

7 Carrs Lane, Birmingham B4 7TG
tel 0121-643 6411 *fax* 0121-643 3152
Editor Jenny Blanch
3 p.a. £9.75 p.a. (£13 p.a. Europe; £16 p.a. rest of world)

Reviews of fiction, non-fiction and poetry books for children, plus in-depth articles; profiles of authors and illustrators. Length: 1200 words (articles); 150 words (reviews). Illustrations: colour and b&w. Payment: by arrangement. Founded 1995.

Cat World

Ashdown Publishing Ltd, Avalon Court,
Star Road, Partridge Green,
West Sussex RH13 8RY
tel (01403) 711511 *fax* (01403) 711521
e-mail lisa@catworld.co.uk
web site http://www.catworld.co.uk
Editor Lisa Lidderdale
Monthly £2.25

Bright, lively articles on any aspect of cat ownership. Articles on breeds of cats and veterinary articles by acknowledged experts only. No unsolicited fiction. All submissions by e-mail or on disk. Illustrations: colour prints or transparencies. Payment: by arrangement; £7.50 per illustration. Founded 1981.

Caterer & Hotelkeeper

Reed Business Information Ltd, Quadrant House,
The Quadrant, Sutton, Surrey SM2 5AS
tel 020-8652 8680 *fax* 020-8652 8973/8947
Editor Forbes Mutch
Weekly £1.80

Articles on all aspects of the hotel and catering industries. Length: up to 1500 words. Illustrations: line, half-tone, colour. Payment: by arrangement. Founded 1893.

Catholic Gazette

The Chase Centre, 114 West Heath Road,
London NW3 7TX
tel 020-8458 3316 *fax* 020-8905 5780

e-mail gazette@cms.org.uk
web site http://www.cms.org.uk/gazette
Editor Fr. Peter Stanton
Monthly £1.20

Articles on evangelisation and the Christian life. Length: up to 2000 words. Illustrations: b&w photos, line, cartoons. Payment: by arrangement. Founded 1910.

The Catholic Herald

Herald House, Lambs Passage, Bunhill Row, London EC1Y 8TQ
tel 020-7588 3101 *fax* 020-7256 9728
e-mail catholic@atlas.co.uk
web site http://www.catholicherald.co.uk
Editor Dr William Oddie
Weekly 60p

Independent newspaper covering national and international affairs from a Catholic/Christian viewpoint as well as church news. Length: articles 600-1100 words. Illustrations: photos of Catholic and Christian interest. Payment: by arrangement.

Catholic Pictorial

Media House, Mann Island, Pier Head, Liverpool L3 1DQ
tel 0151-236 2191 *fax* 0151-236 2216
Editor David Mahon
Weekly 50p

News and photo features (maximum 800 words plus illustration) of Merseyside, regional and national Catholic interest only; also cartoons. Has a strongly social editorial and is a trenchant tabloid. Payment: by arrangement. Founded 1961.

Catholic Times

1st Floor, St James's Buildings, Oxford Street, Manchester M1 6FP
tel 0161-236 8856 *fax* 0161-237 5590
Editor Kevin Flaherty
Weekly 60p

News (400 words) and news features (800 words) of Catholic interest. Illustrations: colour and b&w photos. Payment: £30-£80; photos £50. Relaunched 1993.

Cencrastus: Scottish & International Literature, Arts and Affairs

Unit One, Abbeymount Techbase, 2 Easter Road, Edinburgh EH8 8EJ
tel/fax 0131-661 5687
e-mail cencrastus@hotmail.com
Editor Raymond Ross, *Managing Editor* Kate Kelman
Quarterly £2.95 (back copies £2.50); £12 p.a.

Articles, short stories, poetry, reviews. Payment: by arrangement. Illustrations: line, half-tone. Founded 1979.

Chapman

4 Broughton Place, Edinburgh EH1 3RX
tel 0131-557 2207 *fax* 0131-556 9565
e-mail editor@chapman-pub.co.uk
web site http://www.chapman-pub.co.uk
Editor Joy Hendry
Quarterly £4 (£16 p.a.)

'Scotland's Quality Literary Magazine.' Poetry, short stories, reviews, criticism, articles on Scottish culture. Illustrations: line, half-tone, cartoons. Payment: £8.00 per page; illustrations by negotiation. Founded 1969.

Chartered Secretary

(formerly Administrator)
16 Park Crescent, London W1N 4AH
tel 020-7580 4741 *fax* 020-7323 1132
e-mail chartsec@dial.pipex.com
web site http://www.icsa.org.uk/icsa/
Monthly £4 (£50 p.a. post free UK)

Official Journal of The Institute of Chartered Secretaries and Administrators. Practical and topical articles (750-1600 words) on law, finance and management affecting company secretaries and other senior administrators in business, nationalised industries, local and central government and other institutions in Britain and overseas. Payment: by arrangement.

Chat

IPC Magazines Ltd, King's Reach Tower, Stamford Street, London SE1 9LS
tel 020-7261 6565 *fax* 020-7261 6534
Editor Keith Kendrick
Weekly 64p

Tabloid weekly for women; fiction. Length: up to 800 words. Payment: by arrangement. Founded 1986.

Chemist & Druggist

Miller Freeman UK Ltd, Miller Freeman House, Sovereign Way, Tonbridge, Kent TN9 1RW
tel (01732) 377487 *fax* (01732) 367065
e-mail chemdrug@unmf.com
web site http://www.dotpharmacy.com
Editor Patrick Grice
Weekly £137 p.a.

'The newsweekly for pharmacy.' News stories and feature items relating to any aspect of community pharmacy or small independent retailing. Length: 1000 or 1500 words (features), up to 300 words (news). Illustrations: colour. Payment: £125 per 1000 words. Founded 1859.

Child Education

Scholastic Publications Ltd, Villiers House, Clarendon Avenue, Leamington Spa, Warks. CV32 5PR
tel (01926) 887799 *fax* (01926) 883331
Editor Gill Moore
Monthly £2.85

For teachers and nursery staff concerned with children aged 3-8. Articles by specialists on practical teaching ideas and methods. Length: 600-1200 words. Payment: by arrangement. Profusely illustrated with photos, line drawings and cartoons; also large full colour pictures. Founded 1924.

The China Quarterly

School of Oriental and African Studies, Thornhaugh Street, Russell Square, London WC1H 0XG
tel 020-7898 4063 *fax* 020-7898 4849
e-mail chinaq@soas.ac.uk
Editor Dr Richard Louis Edmonds
Quarterly £39/$68 p.a. (£76/$135 institutions, £20/$35 students)

Articles on contemporary China. Length: 8000 words approx.

Choice

1st Floor, Kings Chambers, 39-41 Priestgate, Peterborough PE1 1FR
tel (01733) 555123 *fax* (01733) 427500
Editor-in-Chief Sue Dobson
Monthly £2.30

Pre- and retirement magazine for 50+ readership. Positive attitude to life – experiences, hobbies, holidays, finance, relationships. Most of the magazine commissioned. If suggesting feature material, include selection of cuttings of previously published work. Payment: by agreement, on publication. Founded 1974.

Christian Herald

Christian Media, 96 Dominion Road, Worthing, West Sussex BN14 8JP
tel (01903) 821082 *fax* (01903) 821081
e-mails news@christianherald.org.uk
features@christianherald.org.uk
web site http://www.christianherald.org.uk
Weekly 60p

Evangelical Christian paper with strong emphasis on news and current affairs. Features up to 800 words – profiles, the changing church, Christians, and contemporary culture (e.g. media, TV, music); cartoons. No short stories. Payment: £20-£60, depending on length/pictures used.

Church of England Newspaper

10 Little College Street, London SW1P 3SH
tel 020-7878 1545 *fax* 020-7976 0783
Weekly 50p

Anglican news and articles relating the Christian faith to everyday life. Evangelical basis; almost exclusively commissioned articles. Study of paper desirable. Length: up to 1000 words. Illustrations: photos, line drawings, cartoons. Payment: c. £40 per 1000 words; photos £22, line by arrangement. Founded 1828.

Church of Ireland Gazette

36 Bachelor's Walk, Lisburn, Co. Antrim BT28 1XN
tel (01846) 675743 *fax* (01846) 675743
Editor Rev. Canon C.W.M. Cooper
Weekly 30p

Church news, articles of religious and general interest. Length: 600-1000 words. Payment: according to length and interest. New Series 1963. Founded 1885.

Church Times

33 Upper Street, London N1 0PN
tel 020-7359 4570 *fax* 020-7226 3073
e-mail editor@churchtimes.co.uk
web site http://www.churchtimes.co.uk
Editor Paul Handley
Weekly 50p

Articles on religious topics are considered. No verse or fiction. Length: up to 1000 words. Illustrations: news photos, sent promptly. Payment: £100 per 1000 words; Periodical Publishers' Association negotiated rates for illustrations. Founded 1863.

Classic & Sports Car

Haymarket Specialist Motoring Publications Ltd, Somerset House, Somerset Road, Teddington, Middlesex TW11 8RU
tel 020-8943 5995 *fax* 020-8943 5844
Editor James Elliott
Monthly £3.25

Features on classic cars and sportscars; shows, news and reviews, features and stories. Illustrations: half-tone, colour. Payment: £150 per 1000 words; varies for illustrations. Founded 1982.

Classic Boat & The Boatman

Link House, Dingwall Avenue, Croydon CR9 2TA
tel 020-8686 2599 *fax* 020-8781 6535
e-mail cb@ipc.co.uk
web site http://www.classicboat.co.uk
Editor Dan Houston
Monthly £3.50

Cruising and technical features, restorations, events, new boat reviews, practical, maritime history; news. Study of magazine essential: read 3-4 back issues and send for contributors' guidelines. Length: 500-2000 words. Illustrations: colour and b&w photos; line drawings of hulls. Payment: £75-£100 per published page. Founded 1987.

Classic Cars

EMAP Active Ltd, Bushfield House, Orton Centre, Peterborough PE2 5UW
tel (01733) 465798 *fax* (01733) 465857
e-mail classic.cars@ecm.emap.com
web site http://www.classiccarsworld.co.uk
Editor John Westlake
Monthly £3.25

Specialist articles on older cars. Length: from 500-4000 words (subject to prior contract). Illustrations: half-tone, colour, cartoons. Payment: by negotiation.

Classic CD

Future Publishing, 30 Monmouth Street, Beauford Court, Bath BA1 2BW
tel (01225) 442244 *fax* (01225) 462986
e-mail nevans@futurenet.co.uk
Editor Neil Evans
Monthly £3.95

Covers classical music on CD. Aims to inform, educate and entertain, with features on composers and performers, reviews and news. Commissioned material only. Length: up to 2000 words. Illustrations: colour and b&w photos, b&w line, including collage and cartoons. Payment: £125 per 1000 words; colour up to £300, b&w £35 1/8 page. Founded 1990.

Classic Stitches

D.C. Thomson & Co. Ltd, 80 Kingsway East, Dundee DD4 8SL
tel (01382) 462276 *fax* (01382) 452491
e-mail editorial@classicstitches.com
web site http://www.classicstitches.com
Editor Mrs Bea Neilson
Bi-monthly £3.50

Creative needlework ideas and projects; needlework-based features on designers, collections, work-in-progress and exhibitions. Submissions also welcome for e-mag on web site. Length: 1000-2000 words. Illustrations: colour photos, preferably not 35 mm. Payment: negotiable. Founded 1994.

Classical Music

Rhinegold Publishing Ltd, 241 Shaftesbury Avenue, London WC2H 8EH
tel 020-7333 1742 *fax* 020-7333 1769
e-mail classical.music@rhinegold.co.uk
web site http://www.rhinegold.co.uk
Editor Keith Clarke
Fortnightly £2.95

News, opinion, features on the classical music business. All material commissioned. Illustrations: b&w photos and line; colour covers. Payment: minimum £100 per 1000 words; from £50 for illustrations. Founded 1976.

Classics

SPL, Berwick House, 8-10 Knoll Rise, Orpington, Kent BR6 0PS
tel (01689) 887200 *fax* (01689) 838844
e-mail classics@splpublishing.co.uk
Editor Andrew Noakes
Monthly £3.20

News photos and stories of classic car interest and illustrated features on classic car history, repairs, maintenance and restoration. Study magazine before submitting material. Features must have high level of subject knowledge and technical accuracy. Length: up to 2000 words (features); 200 words (news). Illustrations: colour and b&w. Payment: £120 per 1000 words plus £100 per set of supporting photos (features); £120 per 1000 words plus photos based on £100 per page (news). Founded 1997.

Climber

Warners Group Publications plc, West Street, Bourne, Lincs. PE10 9PH
tel (01778) 391117
Editor Bernard Newman
Monthly £2.60

Articles on all aspects of mountaineering in Great Britain and abroad, and on related subjects. Study of magazine essential. Length: 1500-2000 words, illustrated (colour transparencies). Payment: according to merit. Founded 1962.

Coin News

Token Publishing Ltd, 1 Orchard House, Duchy Road, Heathpark, Honiton, Devon EX14 1YP
tel (01404) 46972 *fax* (01404) 44788
Editor John W. Mussell
Monthly £2.65

Articles of high standard on coins, tokens, paper money. Length: up to 2000 words. Payment: by arrangement. Founded 1964.

Commando

D.C. Thomson & Co. Ltd, Albert Square, Dundee DD1 9QJ
tel (01382) 223131 *fax* (01382) 322214

185 Fleet Street, London EC4A 2HS
tel 020-7400 1030 *fax* 020-7400 1089
8 p.m. 70p

Fictional war stories told in pictures. Scripts: about 135 pictures. Synopsis required as an opener. New writers encouraged; send for details. Payment: on acceptance.

Commercial Motor

Reed Business Information Ltd, Quadrant House, The Quadrant, Sutton, Surrey SM2 5AS
tel 020-8652 3302/3303 *fax* 020-8652 8969
Editor-in-Chief Brian Weatherley
Weekly £1.40

Technical and road transport articles only. Length: up to 1500 words. Payment: varies. Illustrations: drawings and photos. Founded 1905.

Communicate

DMG Business Media Ltd, Queensway House, 2 Queensway, Redhill, Surrey RH1 1QS
tel (01737) 768611 *fax* (01737) 855470
Editor Simon Dux
Monthly Controlled circulation

Covers all aspects of telecommunications management: analysis pieces (200-700 words), features (1000-2000 words), case studies (300 words). Some material commissioned. Illustrations: colour photos, line, diagrams. Payment: £200 per 1000 words; illustrations by negotiation. Founded 1980.

Community Care

Reed Business Information Ltd, Quadrant House,The Quadrant, Sutton, Surrey SM2 5AS
tel 020-8652 4861 *fax* 020-8652 4739
Editor Polly Neate
Weekly £1.50

Articles of professional interest to local authority and voluntary body social workers, managers, teachers and students. Preliminary letter advisable. Length: 900-1500 words. Payment: at current rates. Founded 1974.

Company

National Magazine House, 72 Broadwick Street, London W1V 2BP
tel 020-7439 5000
e-mail company.mail@natmags.co.uk
Editor Sam Baker
Monthly £2.30

Articles on a wide variety of subjects, relevant to young, independent women. Most articles are commissioned. Payment: usual magazine rate. Illustrated. Founded 1978.

Computer Weekly

Reed Business Information Ltd, Quadrant House, The Quadrant, Sutton, Surrey SM2 5AS
tel 020-8652 3122 *fax* 020-8652 8979
web site http://www.computerweekly.co.uk
Editor Karl Schneider, *News Editor* Lindsay Clark
Weekly £1.90

Feature articles on IT-related topics for business/industry users. Length: 1200 words. Illustrations: b&w photos, line, cartoons. Payment: £250 per 1000 words; negotiable for illustrations. Founded 1966.

Computing

VNU Business Publications, VNU House, 32-34 Broadwick Street, London W1A 2HG
tel 020-7316 9601 *fax* 020-7316 9160
web site http://www.computingnet.co.uk
Editor Peter Kirwan
Weekly £100 p.a.

Features and news items on corporate procurement and deployment of IT infrastructure, and on applications and implications of computers and telecommunications. Particular sections address the IT professional career development, and the desktop computing environment. Length: 1600-2200 words. Payment: by negotiation. Illustrations: colour photos, line drawings, cartoons. Founded 1973.

Condé Nast Traveller

Vogue House, Hanover Square, London W1R 0AD
tel 020-7499 9080 *fax* 020-7493 3758
e-mail traveller@msmail.condenast.co.uk
web site http://www.cntraveller.co.uk
Editor Sarah Miller
Monthly £3

Highly illustrated features on travel, style, food and wine, beauty and health. Illustrations: colour. Payment: by arrangement. Founded 1997.

Contemporary Review

(incorporating the Fortnightly)
Contemporary Review Co. Ltd, PO Box 1242, Oxford OX1 4FJ
tel/fax (01865) 201529
Editor Dr Richard Mullen
Monthly £3.25

Independent review dealing with questions of the day, chiefly politics, international affairs, religion, literature, the arts. Mostly commissioned, but with limited scope for freelance authors with authoritative knowledge. TS returned only if sae enclosed. Intending contributors should study journal first. Length: 2000-3000 words. No illustrations. Payment: £5 per page (500 words), 2 complimentary copies. Founded 1866.

contemporary visual arts

Suite K101, Tower Bridge Business Complex, 100 Clements Road, London SE16 4DG
tel 020-7740 1204 *fax* 020-7252 0203
e-mail cva@gbhap.com
web site http://www.gbhap.com/cont.visarts
Editor Keith Patrick
Bi-monthly £4.95

Articles and reviews on all aspects of contemporary art; book reviews. Length: articles 1000-2000 words, reviews 500 words. Illustrations: colour photos. Payment: £100 per 1000 words; none for photos. Founded 1992.

Control & Instrumentation

Centaur Publishing Ltd, St Giles House, 50 Poland Street, London W1V 4AX
tel 020-7970 4119 *fax* 020-7970 4191
e-mail pgay@centaur.co.uk
web site http://www.e4engineering.com
Editor Paul Gay
Monthly £93 p.a.

Authoritative main feature articles on measurement, automation, control systems, instrumentation and data processing; also export, business and engineering news. Regular supplement entitled *Sys.Build* details all aspects of system building and system integration – news, projects, feedback, comment and features. Length of articles: 750 words for highly technical pieces, 1000-2500 words main features. Payment: according to value. Illustrations: photos and drawings of equipment using automatic techniques, control engineering personalities, cartoons. Founded 1958.

Cosmetic World News

21 Piccadilly, London W1V 9PF
tel 020-7589 0589 *fax* 020-7838 0908
e-mail murray-pearce@cosmeticworldnews.com
web site http://www.cosmeticworldnews.com
Editor M.A. Murray-Pearce, *Features Editor* Norman Clare
Bi-monthly £96 p.a.

International news magazine of perfumery, cosmetics and toiletries industry. Worldwide reports, photo-news stories, articles (500-1000 words) on essential oils and new cosmetic raw materials, and exclusive information on industry's companies and personalities welcomed. Payment: by arrangement, minimum 10p per word. Illustrations: b&w and colour photos or colour separations. Founded 1949.

Cosmopolitan

National Magazine House, 72 Broadwick Street, London W1V 2BP
tel 020-7439 5000 *fax* 020-7439 5016
Editor-in-Chief Lorraine Butler
Monthly £2.60

Articles. Commissioned material only. Payment: by arrangement. Illustrated. Founded 1972.

Country

Summerhouse Publishing Ltd, St James Yarn Mill, Whitefriars, Norwich NR3 1XU
tel (01603) 664242 *fax* (01603) 664410
Editor Gill Crawley
Monthly £2.95

Magazine of the CGA. News and features covering rural events, countryside, leisure, heritage, homes and gardens. Some outside contributors used; approach in writing in first instance. Payment: by arrangement. Founded 1893.

Country Homes and Interiors

IPC Magazines Ltd, King's Reach Tower, Stamford Street, London SE1 9LS
tel 020-7261 6451 *fax* 020-7261 6895
Editor Katherine Hadley
Monthly £2.75

Articles on property, country homes, interior designs. Illustrations: colour. Payment: from £250 per 1000 words. Founded 1986.

Country Life

IPC Magazines Ltd, King's Reach Tower, Stamford Street, London SE1 9LS
tel 020-7261 7058 *fax* 020-7261 5139
Editor Clive Aslet
Weekly £2.40

Illustrated journal chiefly concerned with British country life, social history, architecture and the fine arts, natural history, agriculture, gardening and sport. Length: about 1000 or 1300 words (articles). Illustrations: mainly colour photos. Payment: according to merit. Founded 1897.

Country Living

National Magazine House, 72 Broadwick Street, London W1V 2BP
tel 020-7439 5000 *fax* 020-7439 5093
Editor Susy Smith
Monthly £3

Up-market magazine for country dwellers and townies who have the country at heart. No unsolicited material and do not send valuable transparencies. Illustrations: line, half-tone, colour. Payment: by arrangement. Founded 1985.

Country Quest

7 Aberystwyth Science Park, Aberystwyth, Ceredigion SY23 3AH
tel (01970) 611611 *fax* (01970) 624699
Editor Beverly Davies
Monthly £2

Illustrated articles on matters relating to countryside, history and personalities of Wales and border counties. No fiction. Illustrated work preferred. Length: 700-1500 words. Payment: by arrangement.

Country Smallholding

Broad Leys Publishing Company, Buriton House, Station Road, Newport, Saffron Walden, Essex CB11 3PL
tel (01799) 540922 *fax* (01799) 541367
e-mail helen@countrysmallholding.com
web site http://www.countrysmallholding.com
Editor Helen Sears
Monthly £2.25

The magazine for smallholders. Practical, how-to articles, and seasonal features, on organic gardening, small-scale poultry and livestock keeping, country crafts, cookery and smallholdings. Approach editor in writing with ideas. Length: up to 2000 words. Illustrations: colour and b&w photos, line for instructive articles. Payment: £30 per 1000 words; photos £10, £40 cover. Founded 1975 as *Home Farm*.

Country Walking

EMAP Active Ltd, Apex House, Oundle Road, Peterborough PE2 9NP
tel (01733) 898100 *fax* (01733) 890657
Editor Lynne Maxwell
Monthly £2.60

Features and readers' stories. Length: 1200 words on average (features), 800 words (stories), more if commissioned. Illustrations: colour transparencies. Payment: £100 per 1000 words, £35 fee for readers' stories; £15 (1/4 page), £50 (full page). Founded 1987.

The Countryman

IPC Magazines, King's Reach Tower, Stamford Street, London SE1 9LS
tel 020-7261 7262
Editor Tom Quinn
Every 6 weeks £2.40

Every department of rural life except field sports. Copy must be trustworthy, well-written, brisk, cogent and light in hand. Articles up to 1200 words. Skilful sketches of life and character from personal knowledge and experience. Dependable natural history based on writer's own observation. Really good matter from old unpublished letters and MSS. Study magazine before submitting material. Illustrations: b&w and colour photos and drawings, but all must be exclusive and out of the ordinary. Payment: £70 per 1000 words minimum, usually more, according to merit. Founded 1927.

Creative Camera

CC Publishing, 5 Hoxton Square, London N1 6NU
tel 020-7729 6993
e-mail info@ccamera.demon.co.uk
web site http://www.ccamera.demon.co.uk
Editor David Brittain
Bi-monthly £3.95

Illustrated articles and pictures dealing with serious photography, sociology of, history of and criticism of photos; book and exhibition reviews. Arts Council supported. Payment: by arrangement. Illustrations: b&w, colour. Founded 1968.

The Cricketer International

Third Street, Langton Green, Tunbridge Wells, Kent TN3 0EN
tel (01892) 862551 *fax* (01892) 863755
e-mail editorial@cricketer.co.uk
Editor Peter Perchard
Monthly £2.75

Articles on cricket at any level. Illustrations: line, half-tone, colour, cartoons. Payment: £50 per 1000 words; illustrations minimum £17.50. Founded 1921.

Critical Quarterly

Blackwell Publishers, 108 Cowley Road, Oxford OX4 1JF
web site http://www.blackwellpublishers.co.uk
Quarterly £31 p.a. (£62 p.a. institutions)

Fiction, poems, literary criticism. Length: 2000-5000 words. Study magazine before submitting MSS. Payment: by arrangement. Founded 1959.

Cumbria and Lake District Magazine

(formerly Cumbria)
Dalesman Publishing Company Ltd, Stable Courtyard, Broughton Hall, Skipton, North Yorkshire BD23 3AE
tel (01756) 701381 *fax* (01756) 701326
e-mail editorial@dalesman.co.uk

Editor Terry Fletcher
Monthly £1.10

Articles of genuine rural interest concerning Lakeland and Cumbria. Short length preferred. Illustrations: line drawings and first-class photos. Payment: according to merit. Founded 1951.

Custom Car

Kelsey Publishing Ltd, Cudham Tithe Barn, Berry's Hill, Cudham, Kent TN16 3AG
tel (01959) 541444 *fax* (01959) 541400
e-mail customcar@kelsey.co.uk
web site http://www.kelsey.co.uk/custom
Editor Kev Elliott
Monthly £2.80

Customising, drag racing and hot rods. Length: by arrangement. Payment: by arrangement. Founded 1970.

CWU Voice

150 The Broadway, London SW19 1RX
tel 020-8971 7200 *fax* 020-8971 7437
web site http://www.cwu.org
Head of Communications Chris Proctor
Monthly Free to members

Main journal of CWU members. Articles on postal and telecommunications workers in the UK and abroad and on other questions of interest to a trade union readership. Payment: NUJ rates. Illustrations: line and colour. Founded 1920.

Cycling Today

Yachting Press Ltd, 196 Eastern Esplanade, Southend-on-Sea, Essex SS1 3AS
tel (01702) 582245 *fax* (01702) 588434
Editor Guy Andrews
Monthly £2.60

Material mostly commissioned. Accepts unsolicited travel/expedition features (UK and abroad), written to style (emphasis on anecdotes and on characters met, rather than bland travelogue) with professional-quality colour transparencies, including cycle action shots; and general cycling news. Length: features 1500-2000 words, news 150-200 words. Payment: £150 per feature inc. pix; news £20 per item. Founded 1993 as *New Cyclist*.

Cycling Weekly

IPC Music and Sport Ltd, Link House, Dingwall Avenue, Croydon CR9 2TA
tel 020-8774 0811 *fax* 020-8686 0947
Editor Robert Garbutt
Weekly £1.60

Racing and technical articles; topical photos with a cycling interest considered; cartoons. Length: not exceeding 1500 words. Payment: by arrangement. Founded 1891.

Cyphers

3 Selskar Terrace, Dublin 6, Republic of Ireland
fax (01) 4978866
IR£6 for 3 issues
Editors Leland Bardwell, Pearse Hutchinson, Eiléan Ní Chuilleanáin, Macdara Woods

Poems, fiction, articles on literary subjects, translations. Payment: £10 per page. Founded 1975.

Dairy Farmer

Miller Freeman UK Ltd, 4 Friars Courtyard, Princes Street, Ipswich IP1 1RJ
tel (01473) 401379 *fax* (01473) 232822
e-mail dairyfarmer@dotfarming.com
Editor Rachael Porter
Monthly Controlled circulation

In-depth, technical articles on all aspects of dairy farm management and milk marketing. Length: normally 800-1400 words with colour photos. Payment: by arrangement.

Dalesman

Dalesman Publishing Company Ltd, Stable Courtyard, Broughton Hall, Skipton, North Yorkshire BD23 3AE
tel (01756) 701381 *fax* (01756) 701326
e-mail editorial@dalesman.co.uk
Editor Terry Fletcher
Monthly £1.35

Articles and stories of genuine rural interest concerning Yorkshire (1000-1500 words). Payment: according to merit. Illustrations: line drawings and first-class photos preferably featuring people. Founded 1939.

Dance & Dancers

214 Panther House, 38 Mount Pleasant, London WC1X 0AP
tel/fax 020-7837 2711
Editor John Percival
Monthly £1.75

Specialist features, reviews on modern/classical dance, dancers. Length: by prior arrangement. Payment: by arrangement. Illustrations: line, half-tone; colour covers. Founded 1950.

Dancing Times

The Dancing Times Ltd, Clerkenwell House, 45-47 Clerkenwell Green, London EC1R 0EB
tel 020-7250 3006 *fax* 020-7253 6679
e-mail dt@dancing-times.co.uk
web site http://www.dt-ltd.dircon.co.uk
Editor Mary Clarke

Editorial Adviser Ivor Guest
Executive Editor Frances Palmer
Monthly £2.20

Ballet, contemporary dance and all forms of stage dancing from general, historical, critical and technical angles. Well-informed freelance articles used occasionally, but only after preliminary arrangements. Payment: by arrangement. Illustrations: occasional line, action photos preferred; colour invited. Founded 1910.

The Dandy

D.C. Thomson & Co. Ltd, Albert Square, Dundee DD1 9QJ
tel (01382) 223131 *fax* (01382) 322214
185 Fleet Street, London EC4A 2HS
tel 020-7400 1030 *fax* 020-7400 1089
Weekly 52p

Comic strips for children. 10-12 pictures per single page story, 18-20 pictures per 2-page story. Promising artists are encouraged. Payment: on acceptance.

Fun Size Dandy

2 p.m. 70p

Founded 1997.

Darts World

World Magazines Ltd, 28 Arrol Road, Beckenham, Kent BR3 4PA
tel 020-8650 6580 *fax* 020-8654 4343
Editor Tony Wood
Monthly £1.95

Articles and stories with darts theme. Illustrations: half-tone, cartoons. Payment: £40-£50 per 1000 words; illustrations by arrangement. Founded 1972.

Day by Day

Woolacombe House, 141 Woolacombe Road, London SE3 8QP
tel 020-8856 6249
Editor Patrick Richards
Monthly 90p

Articles and news on non-violence and social justice. Reviews of art, books, films, plays, musicals and opera. Cricket reports. Short poems and very occasional short stories in keeping with editorial viewpoint. Payment: £2 per 1000 words. No illustrations required. Founded 1963.

Dental Update

George Warman Publications (UK) Ltd, Unit 2, Riverview Business Park, Walnut Tree Close, Guildford, Surrey GU1 4UX
tel (01483) 304944 *fax* (01483) 303191
e-mail geowarman@aol.com
web site http://www.gwarman.co.uk/dupdate/
Editor Angela Stroud
10 p.a. £65 p.a. (£29 p.a. students; £45 p.a. vocational trainees)

Clinical articles pertinent to general dental practice. Submit synopsis in first instance. All articles are subject to review by specialist referees. Illustrations: line, colour. Payment: £100-£150 per 1000 words, £25 letters to editor; £75 cover photos only. Founded 1973.

Derbyshire Life and Countryside

Heritage House, Lodge Lane, Derby DE1 3HE
tel (01332) 347087/8/9 *fax* (01332) 290688
Monthly £1.30

Articles, preferably illustrated, about Derbyshire life, people and history. Length: up to 800 words. Some short stories set in Derbyshire accepted; no verse. Payment: according to nature and quality of contribution. Illustrations: photos of Derbyshire subjects. Founded 1931.

Descent

Wild Places Publishing, 51 Timbers Square, Cardiff CF24 3SH
tel/fax 029-2048 6557
e-mail descent@wildplaces.co.uk
web site http://www.caving.uk.com
Editor Chris Howes
Bi-monthly £2.65

Articles, features and news on all aspects of cave and mine sport exploration. Submissions must match magazine style. Length: up to 2000 words (articles and features), up to 1000 words (news). Illustrations: colour and b&w. Payment: on consideration of material. Founded 1969.

The Dickensian

The Dickens Fellowship, Dickens House, 48 Doughty Street, London WC1N 2LF
Editor Dr Malcolm Andrews, School of English, Rutherford College, University of Kent, Canterbury, Kent CT2 7NX
fax (01227) 827001
e-mail M.Y.Andrews@ukc.ac.uk
3 p.a. £9.50 p.a. (£12 p.a. institutions; overseas rates on application)

Welcomes articles on all aspects of Dickens' life, works and character. Payment: none. Send contributions (enclose sae if return required) and editorial correspondence to the editor.

Director

116 Pall Mall, London SW1Y 5ED
tel 020-7766 8950 *fax* 020-7766 8840
Editor Joanna Higgins

Monthly £3

Authoritative business-related articles. Send synopsis of proposed article and examples of printed work. Length: 500-3000 words. Payment: by arrangement. Illustrations: colour. Founded 1947.

Dirt Bike Rider

Lancaster & Morecambe Newspapers Ltd,
Victoria Street, Morecambe, Lancs. LA4 4AG
tel (01524) 833111 *fax* (01524) 425469
e-mail dbr@keymags.demon.co.uk
Editor Gary Pinchin
Monthly £2.65

Features, track tests, coverage on all aspects of off-road motor-cycling. Length: up to 1000 words. Illustrations: half-tone, colour, cartoons. Founded 1981.

Disability Now

(published by Scope)
6 Market Road, London N7 9PW
tel 020-7619 7323 *fax* 020-7619 7331
Minicom 020-7619 7332
e-mail editor@disabilitynow.org.uk
web site http://www.@disabilitynow.org.uk
Editor Mary Wilkinson
Monthly £18 p.a., free to people on income support; tape version free to people with visual impairment or severe disability

Newspaper for people with different types of disability, carers and professionals, and anyone interested in disability. News and comment on anything of interest in the disability field: benefits, services, equipment, jobs, politics, motoring, holidays, sport, relationships, the arts. All regular contributors have a disability (unless they are a parent of someone with a disability). Preliminary letter desirable. Founded 1957.

Diva

Millivres Ltd, Worldwide House,
116-134 Bayham Street, London NW1 0BA
tel 020-7482 2576 *fax* 020-7284 0329
e-mail diva@gaytimes.co.uk
web site http://www.gaytimes.co.uk
Editor Gillian Rodgerson
Monthly £2

Lesbian life and culture: articles, features, news, short fiction. Length: 1000-2000 words (articles/features); 300-500 words (news); 1000-2000 words (short stories). Illustrations: colour and b&w. Payment: £10 per 100 words; £30-£50 per photo; £25-£80 per drawing. Founded 1994.

Diver

55 High Street, Teddington, Middlesex TW11 8HA
tel 020-8943 4288 *fax* 020-8943 4312
e-mail 100737.2226@compuserve.com
web site divernet@www.divernet.com
Editor Nigel Eaton
Monthly £2.95

Articles on sub aqua diving and related developments. Length: 1500-4000 words. Illustrations: line, half-tone and colour. Payment: by arrangement. Founded 1953.

Dogs Today

Pet Subjects Ltd, Pankhurst Farm, Bagshot Road, West End, Woking, Surrey GU24 9QR
tel (01276) 858880 *fax* (01276) 858860
e-mail dogstoday@dial.pipex.com
Editor Beverley Cuddy
Monthly £2.95

Study of magazine essential before submitting ideas. Interested in human interest dog stories, celebrity interviews, holiday features and anything unusual – all must be entertaining and informative and accompanied by illustrations. Length: 800-1200 words. Illustrations: colour, preferably transparencies, colour cartoons. Payment: negotiable. Founded 1990.

Dorset Life – The Dorset Magazine

95 North Street, Wareham, Dorset BH20 4AE
tel (01929) 551264 *fax* (01929) 552099
e-mail office@dorsetlife.co.uk
Editor John Newth
Monthly £1.85

Articles (500-1200 words), photos (colour) and line drawings with a specifically Dorset theme. Payment: by arrangement. Founded 1967.

The Downside Review

Downside Abbey, Stratton-on-the-Fosse,
Nr Bath, Somerset BA3 4RH
tel (01761) 235136
Editor Dom Dunstan O'Keeffe
Quarterly £6 (£22 p.a.)

Articles and book reviews on theology, metaphysics, mysticism and modernism, and monastic and church history. Payment: not usual.

Drapers Record

EMAP Business Communications, Angel House,
338-346 Goswell Road, London EC1V 7QP
tel 020-7520 1500 *fax* 020-7837 4699
Editor-in-Chief Eric Musgrave
Weekly £2.40

Business editorial aimed at fashion

retailers, large and small. Payment: by negotiation. Illustrations: colour and b&w: photos, drawings and cartoons. Founded 1887.

Early Music

Oxford University Press, 70 Baker Street, London W1M 1DJ
tel 020-7616 5902 *fax* 020-7616 5901
e-mail jnl.early-music@oup.co.uk
web site http://www.oup.co.uk/earlyj
Editor Tess Knighton
Quarterly £10.50 (£43 p.a., institutions £72 p.a.)

Lively, informative and scholarly articles on aspects of medieval, renaissance, baroque and classical music. Payment: £20 per 1000 words. Illustrations: line, half-tone, colour. Founded 1973.

East Lothian Life

1 Beveridge Row, Belhaven, Dunbar, East Lothian EH42 1TP
tel/fax (01368) 863593
Editor Pauline Jaffray
Quarterly £2

Articles and features with an East Lothian slant. Length: up to 1000 words. Illustrations: b&w photos, line, cartoons. Payment: negotiable. Founded 1989.

Eastern Art Report

Eastern Art Publishing Group, PO Box 13666, 27 Wallorton Gardens, London SW14 8WF
tel 020-8392 1122 *fax* 020-8392 1422
e-mail ear@eapgroup.com
Managing Sajid Rizvi, *Executive Editor* Shirley Rizvi
Bi-monthly £10.95 (individual £25 p.a., institutions £40 p.a.)

Original, well-researched articles on all aspects of the visual arts – Islamic, Indian, Chinese and Japanese; reviews. Length of articles: min. 1500 words. Illustrations: colour transparencies, b&w photos; no responsibility accepted for unsolicited material. Payment: by arrangement. Founded 1989.

Eastern Eye

Ethnic Media Group, 1st Floor, 148 Cambridge Heath Road, London E1 5QJ
tel 020-7702 8012 *fax* 020-7702 7937
Editor Sanjay Gohil
Weekly 70p

Articles, features and news of interest to British Asians. Magazine covers music, fashion, film gossip. Freelance material considered. Illustrations: colour. Founded 1989.

The Ecologist

Unit 18, Chelsea Wharf, 15 Lots Road, London SW10 0QJ
tel 020-7351 3578 *fax* 020-7351 3617
e-mail ecologist@gn.apc.org
Editors Edward Goldsmith, Zac Goldsmith
6 p.a. £3.50

Fully-referenced articles on economic, social and environmental affairs from an ecological standpoint. Study magazine first for level and approach. Length: 1000-5000 words. Illustrations: line, half-tone. Payment: by arrangement.

Economica

STICERD, London School of Economics, Houghton Street, London WC2A 2AE
tel 020-7955 7855 *fax* 020-7242 2357
Editors Prof F.A. Cowell, Prof Alan Manning
Quarterly £24 (apply for subscription rates)

Learned journal covering the fields of economics, economic history and statistics. Payment: none. Founded 1921; New Series 1934.

The Economist

25 St James's Street, London SW1A 1HG
tel 020-7830 7000
web site http://www.economist.com
Editor Bill Emmott
Weekly £2.60

Articles staff-written. Founded 1843.

The Edge

65 Guinness Buildings, Fulham Palace Road, London W6 8BD
tel 020-7460 9444
e-mail grahamevans@cwcom.net
web site http://www.users.globalnet.co.uk/~houghtong/edge.htm
Editor Graham Evans
Quarterly £2.95

Interviews and features: books, films, music, modern popular culture; imaginative stories for today and tomorrow. Return postage essential. Payment: £20-£300 negotiable. Founded 1996.

Edinburgh Review

22A Buccleugh Place, Edinburgh EH8 9LN
tel/fax 0131-651 1415
e-mail Edinburgh.Review@ed.ac.uk
Editor Alex Thomson
Tri-annual £17 p.a. (individual)

Fiction, poetry, clearly written articles on Scottish and international cultural and philosophical ideas. Payment: by arrangement. Founded 1969.

Education Journal

17 Park Road, Hampton Hill, Middlesex TW12 1HE
tel/fax 020-8979 9473
Editor George Low
Monthly £38 p.a.

Features on policy, management and professional development issues. Major documents and reports gutted down to a brief digest; documents and research listings. Research section combining original reports and updates on research projects. Coverage of parliamentary debates and answers to parliamentary questions, giving statistical data by LEA. Reference section that includes coverage of all circulars, conference reports and opinion column. Length: 1000 words. Illustrations: photos, cartoons. Payment: by arrangement. Founded 1903; relaunched 1996.

Electrical Review

Reed Business Information Ltd, Quadrant House, The Quadrant, Sutton, Surrey SM2 5AS
tel 020-8652 3113 *fax* 020-8652 8951
Editor Paul Doughty
Fortnightly £3.50

Technical and business articles on electrical and control engineering; outside contributions considered. Electrical news welcomed. Illustrations: photos and drawings, cartoons. Payment: according to merit. Founded 1872.

Electrical Times

Reed Business Information Ltd, Quadrant House, The Quadrant, Sutton, Surrey SM2 5AS
tel 020-8652 8736 *fax* 020-8652 8972
Editor Paul Doughty
Monthly £2.75

Business and technical articles of interest to contractors and installers in the electrical industries, with illustrations as necessary. Length: 750-1000 words. Payment: negotiable. Illustrations: line, half-tone, colour, cartoons. Founded 1891.

Electronics Times

Miller Freeman UK Ltd, City Reach, 5 Greenwich View Place, Millharbour, London E14 9NN
tel 020-8876 6417 *fax* 020-8861 6253
e-mail luke.collins@unmf.com
Editor Luke Collins
Weekly £3.25 (£85 p.a.)

News, reviews and features on the electronics industry. Length: 2000 words (features), 200 words (news). Illustrations: colour transparencies, colour and b&w artwork and cartoons. Payment: variable. Founded 1978.

Elle (UK)

EMAP Élan, Endeavour House, 189 Shaftesbury Avenue, London WC2H 8JG
tel 020-7437 9011 *fax* 020-7208 3599
Editor Fiona McIntosh
Monthly £2.50

Commissioned material only. Payment: by arrangement. Illustrations: colour. Founded 1985.

Empire

Mappin House, 4 Winsley Street, London W1N 7AR
tel 020-7436 1515/1601 *fax* 020-7312 8249
web site http://www.empireonline.com
Editor Emma Cochrane
Monthly £2.70

Guide to film and video: articles, features, news. Length: various. Illustrations: colour and b&w photos. Payment: approx. £300 per 1000 words; varies for illustrations. Founded 1989.

The Engineer

Centaur Communications Ltd, St Giles House, 50 Poland Street, London W1V 4AX
tel 020-7970 4106 *fax* 020-7970 4189
e-mail pcarslake@centaur.co.uk
web site http://www.e4engineering.com
Editor Paul Carslake
50 p.a. Controlled circulation (£118 p.a.)

Articles, features and news on the business, innovation and technology, including profiles, analysis. Length: news up to 400 words, features average 1000 words. Illustrations: colour transparencies or prints; line diagrams, graphs. Payment: by negotiation. Founded 1856.

Engineering

Gillard Welch Ltd, Chester Court, High Street, Knowle, Solihull, West Midlands B93 0LL
tel (01564) 771772 *fax* (01564) 774776
Editor Jonathan Ward
11 p.a. £5.95

'For innovators in technology, manufacturing and management': features and news. Contributions considered on all aspects of engineering, particularly design. Illustrations: colour. Founded 1866.

The English Garden

Romsey Publishing Ltd, Glen House, Stag Place, London SW1E 5AQ
tel 020-7233 9191 *fax* 020-7630 8084
e-mail editorial@theenglishgarden.co.uk
Editor Vanessa Berridge

Monthly £2.95

Features and photography on English gardens, plant genera and garden design. Send written synopsis. Length: 1000 words. Illustrations: colour photos and artwork. Payment: variable. Founded 1997.

English Historical Review

Oxford University Press, Great Clarendon Street, Oxford OX2 6DP
tel (01865) 556767
web site http://www.oup.co.uk/enghis/
Editors Dr J.R. Maddicott, Dr Jean Dunbabin
5 p.a. £104/$204 p.a. institutions, £44/$86 p.a. students

High-class scholarly articles, documents, and reviews or short notices of books. Contributions are not accepted unless they supply original information and should be sent direct to Dr J.R. Maddicott, Editor, EHR, Exeter College, Oxford OX1 3DP. Books for review should be sent to Dr J. Dunbabin, Editor, EHR, St Anne's College, Oxford OX2 6HS. Payment: none. Founded 1886.

Enterprise

Martin Leach Publishing, 3rd Floor,
2-6 Northburgh Street, London EC1V 0AY
tel 0171-608 8000 *fax* 0171-608 8001
e-mail ml.edit@btinternet.com
Editor Bronagh Miskelly
Bi-monthly £2.25

'The magazine for today's growing businesses': news, features and profiles of companies and people. Length: 1500 words (features). Illustrations: colour transparencies and artwork. Payment: £225 per 1000 words; £300 per illustration. Founded 1991.

Envoi

44 Rudyard Road, Biddulph Moor,
Stoke-on-Trent, Staffs. ST8 7JN
tel (01782) 517892
Editor Roger Elkin
3 p.a. £12 p.a.

New poetry, including sequences, collaborative works and translations, reviews, articles on modern poets and poetic style; poetry competitions; editorial criticism of subscribers' poems (with sae) at no charge. Sample copy: £3.00. Payment: 2 complimentary copies. Founded 1957.

The Erotic Review

EPS-MacHo, 4th Floor, Maddox House,
1 Maddox Street, London W1V 9WA
tel 020-7437 8887 *fax* 020-7437 3528
e-mail eroticreview@eps.org.uk
web site http://www.eps.org.uk
Editor Rowan Pelling
Monthly £2.95

Up-market literary magazine for sensualists and libertines. Length: 1000 words (articles and features), 1000-2000 (short stories). Illustrations: colour and b&w prints, artwork and cartoons. Payment: £50-£75 (articles and features), £75-£150 (short stories); £50 (prints and artwork), £40 (cartoons). Founded 1997.

ES Magazine – see Evening Standard in Regional newspapers UK and Ireland, page 11

Esquire

National Magazine House, 72 Broadwick Street, London W1V 2BP
tel 020-7439 5000 *fax* 020-7312 3920
Editor Peter Howarth
Monthly £3.20

Quality men's general interest magazine – articles, features. No unsolicited material or short stories. Length: various. Illustrations: colour and b&w photos, line. Payment: by arrangement. Founded 1991.

Essentials

IPC Magazines Ltd, King's Reach Tower,
Stamford Street, London SE1 9LS
tel 020-7261 6970
Editor Karen Livermore
Monthly £2

Features, plus fashion, health and beauty, cookery. Illustrations: colour. Payment: by negotiation. Founded 1988.

Essex Countryside

Dugard House, Peartree Road, Stanway,
Colchester CO3 5JX
tel (01206) 571348 *fax* (01206) 366982
Editor Andy Tilbrook
Monthly £1.70

Features, profiles and occasional short stories, all with Essex emphasis. Length: up to 1200 words. Illustrations: colour and b&w photos. Payment: negotiable. Founded 1953.

Estates Gazette

151 Wardour Street, London W1V 4BN
tel 020-7437 0141 *fax* 020-7437 0294
Editor Peter Bill
Weekly £2.20

Property, legislation, planning, architecture – articles, features and business news. Length: 1500 words. Illustrations: colour, line, cartoons. Payment: none. Founded 1858.

European Chemical News

Reed Business Information, Quadrant House, The Quadrant, Sutton, Surrey SM2 5AS
tel 020-8652 3187 *fax* 020-8652 3375
e-mail ecne@rbi.co.uk
Editor John Baker
Weekly £314 p.a. Europe (£353 p.a. overseas)

Articles and features concerning business, markets and investments in the chemical industry. Length: 1000-2000 words; news items up to 400 words. Payment: £120-£150 per 1000 words.

Eventing

IPC Magazines Ltd, Room 2105, King's Reach Tower, Stamford Street, London SE1 9LS
tel 020-7261 5388 *fax* 020-7261 5429
Editor Kate Green
Monthly £3.10

News, articles, features, event reports and opinion pieces – all with bias towards the sport of horse trials. Mostly commissioned, but all ideas welcome. Length: up to 1500 words. Illustrations: colour and b&w, mostly commissioned. Payment: by arrangement; illustrations £30-£45. Founded 1984.

Evergreen

PO Box 52, Cheltenham, Glos. GL50 1YQ
tel (01242) 537900 *fax* (01242) 537901
Roy Faiers
Quarterly £2.95

Articles about Britain's famous people and infamous characters, its natural beauty, towns and villages, history, traditions, odd customs, legends, folklore, etc; regular articles on old films, songs, radio programmes and variety acts. Length 250-2000 words. Also 'meaningful rather than clever' poetry. Illustrations: colour transparencies. Payment: £15 per 1000 words, £4 poems. Founded 1985.

Everyday Practical Electronics

Wimborne Publishing Ltd, Allen House, East Borough, Wimborne, Dorset BH21 1PF
tel (01202) 881749 *fax* (01202) 841692
e-mail editorial@epemag.wimborne.co.uk
web site http://www.epemag.wimborne.co.uk
Editor Mike Kenward
Monthly £2.65

Constructional and theoretical articles aimed at the student and hobbyist. Length: 1000-5500 words. Payment: £55-£90 per 1000 words. Illustrations: line, half-tone, cartoons. Founded 1971.

Executive PA

Hobsons, Bateman Street, Cambridge CB2 1LZ
tel (01223) 354551 *fax* (01223) 273436
e-mail executive.pa@hobsons.co.uk
Editor Penny Cottee
Quarterly Complimentary

Business to business for working senior secretaries. Length: 700-1400 words. Illustrations: colour. Payment: £140 per 1000 words. Founded 1991.

Executive Woman

Saleworld Ltd, 2 Chantry Place, Harrow, Middlesex HA3 6NY
tel 020-8420 1210 *fax* 020-8420 1691/3
e-mail info@execwoman.com
web site http://www.execwoman.com
Editor Angela Giveon
Bi-monthly £2.50

News and features with a holistic approach to the world of successful working women. Strong business features; articles on management, personnel, networking and mentoring. Length: 500-1000 words. Illustrations: colour and b&w. Payment: £150 per 1000 words; £50-£100. Founded 1987.

Expecting Our Baby

IPC Magazines Ltd, King's Reach Tower, Stamford Street, London SE1 9LS
tel 020-7261 7986 *fax* 020-7261 6542
web site http://www.ipc.co.uk
Editor Rhoda Parry, *Editor-in-Chief* Jayne Marsden
Monthly £2.20

Aimed at first-time mums and dads, including product information as well as health news and features on pregnancy and baby care; also readers' birth stories (£25 for 500 words). Material mostly commissioned. Length: varies. Illustrations: brilliant, colour photos of mums- and dads-to-be and newborn babies. Payment: negotiable. Founded 1994.

The Face

EMAP Metro Ltd, Exmouth House, Pine Street, London EC1R 0JL
tel 020-7689 9999 *fax* 020-7689 0300
Editor Johnny Davis
Monthly £2.70

Articles on music, fashion, films, popular youth culture. Contributors must be familiar with the magazine, its audience and culture. Illustrations: half-tone, colour. Payment: £250 per 1000 words; illustrations approx. £150 per page. Founded 1980.

Family Law

21 St Thomas Street, Bristol BS1 6JS
tel 0117-923 0600 *fax* 0117-925 0486
e-mail familylaw@jordanpublishing.co.uk
web site http://www.familylaw.co.uk
Editors Elizabeth Walsh, Miles McColl
Monthly £107 p.a.

Articles dealing with all aspects of the law as it affects the family, written from a legal or socio-legal point of view. Length: from 1000 words. Payment: by arrangement. No illustrations. Founded 1971.

Family Tree Magazine

61 Great Whyte, Ramsey, Huntingdon, Cambs. PE26 1HJ
tel (01487) 814050
Editor Sue Fearn
Monthly £2.30 (£25.30 p.a.)

Articles on any genealogically related topics. Payment: £35 per 1000 words. Founded 1984.

Farmers Weekly

Reed Business Information, Quadrant House, The Quadrant, Sutton, Surrey SM2 5AS
tel 020-8652 4911 *fax* 020-8652 4005
e-mail farmers.weekly@rbi.co.uk
web site http://www.fwi.co.uk
Editor Stephen Howe
Weekly £1.40

Articles on agriculture from freelance contributors will be accepted subject to negotiation. Founded 1934.

Farming News

Miller Freeman UK Ltd, Miller Freeman House, Sovereign Way, Tonbridge, Kent TN9 1RW
tel (01732) 377209 *fax* (01732) 377675
e-mail farming.news@unmf.com
web site http://www.farming.news.com
Editor Jim van den Bos
Weekly £1.40 (£66 p.a.)

News, business, technical features and articles. Payment: by arrangement. Founded 1983.

Fashion Forecast International

23 Bloomsbury Square, London WC1A 2PJ
tel 020-7637 2211 *fax* 020-7637 2248
e-mail itbd@itbdhquk.demon.co.uk
Managing Editor Stephen Higginson
2 p.a. (Feb, Aug) £30 p.a. UK/Europe, £40 p.a. outside Europe

Refocused as a trend publication, featuring future styling for men's, women's and children's wear. Half the styling and illustration (colour and b&w) is done in house; the balance is contracted out. Payment: by arrangement. Founded 1946.

Fasttrack

Angela Mortimer plc, 1-3 Frederick's Place, London EC2R 8AB
tel 020-7494 1448 *fax* 020-7606 2010
e-mail editors@fasttrack.u-net.com
web site http://www.goldensquare.com
Editor Laura Pank
Quarterly £3.50

'The magazine for professional and executive personnel.' Work-related features and articles for people in business, including technology and training. Length: 750-1500 (features/articles); 300-750 words (news). Illustrations: colour and b&w. Payment: £300 for 1500 words (features), £200 for 750 words (news). Founded 1995.

Feng Shui for Modern Living

Centennial Publishing plc, 1st Floor, 1-5 Clerkenwell Road, London EC1M 5PA
tel 020-7251 5489 *fax* 020-7251 5490
e-mail info@fengshui-magazine.com
web site http://www.fengshui-magazine.com
Editor Miss Nimita Parmar
Monthly £2.95

Features based on the influence of Feng Shui on interior design, decorating, gardens and lifestyle in the West. Length: 1000-2000 words (features), up to 200 words (news). Illustrations: colour transparencies. Payment: £125 per 1000 words; £40 per photo. Founded 1998.

FHM (For Him Magazine)

EMAP Metro, Mappin House, 4 Winsley Street, London W1N 7AR
tel 020-7436 1515 *fax* 020-7312 8191
e-mail fhm@ecm.emap.com
web site http://www.erack.com/fhm
Editor Anthony Noguera
Monthly £2.70

Features, fashion, grooming, travel (adventure) and men's interests. Length: 1200-2000 words. Illustrations: colour and b&w photos, line and colour artwork. Payment: by negotiation. Founded 1987.

The Field

IPC Magazines Ltd, King's Reach Tower, Stamford Street, London SE1 9LS
tel 020-7261 5198 *fax* 020-7261 5358
web site http://www.thefield.co.uk
Monthly £3.10

Specific, topical and informed features on the British countryside and country pursuits, including natural history, field sports, gardening and rural conservation. Overseas subjects considered but opportunities for such articles are limited. No fiction or children's material. Articles, length 800-2000 words, by outside contributors considered; also topical 'shorts' of 200-300 words on all countryside matters. Illustrations: colour photos of a high standard. Payment: on merit. Founded 1853.

Film Review

Visual Imagination Ltd, 9 Blades Court, Deodar Road, London SW15 2NU
tel 020-8875 1520 *fax* 020-8875 1588
e-mail filmreview@visimag.com
Editor Neil Corry
Monthly £2.80

Features and interviews on mainstream cinema; film and video reviews. No fiction. Length: 1000-3000 words (features), 350 words (reviews). Illustrations: colour and b&w. Payment: £80 per 1000 words; £20 for first image, £10 per additional image. Founded 1950.

Financial Adviser

FT Finance Ltd, Maple House, 149 Tottenham Court Road, London W1P 9LL
tel 020-7896 2525 *fax* 020-7896 2699/2588
Editor Kevin O'Donnell
Weekly (£90 p.a.) Free to financial intermediaries working in financial services

Topical personal finance news and features. Length: variable. Payment: by arrangement. Founded 1987.

Financial Mail on Sunday – see Mail on Sunday in National newspapers UK and Ireland, page 3

Fire

Queensway House, 2 Queensway, Redhill, Surrey RH1 1QS
tel (01737) 855433 *fax* (01737) 855470
Managing Editor Simon Hoffman
Monthly £6.95 (£56.07 p.a.)

Articles on firefighting and fire prevention from acknowledged experts only. Length: 850 words. Illustrations: dramatic firefighting or fire brigade rescue colour photos sometimes bought. Also *Fire Europe* and *Fire International*. Payment: by arrangement. Founded 1908.

Fishing News

Emap Business International, Meed House, 21 John Street, London WC1N 2BP
tel 020-7470 6209 *fax* 020-7831 9362
e-mail timo@meed.emap.co.uk
Editor Tim Oliver
Weekly 90p

News and features on all aspects of the commercial fishing industry. Length: up to 1000 words (features), up to 500 words (news). Illustrations: colour and b&w photos. Payment: negotiable. Founded 1913

Flicks

Flicks Publications Ltd, First floor, 25 The Coda Centre, 189 Munster Road, London SW6 6AW
tel 020-7381 8811 *fax* 020-7381 1811
e-mail nick@flicks.co.uk
Editor Nick Thomas
Monthly £1.95 (£23.50 p.a.)

Articles, features and reviews on new mainstream film releases; reviews of videos, DVDs, soundtrack CDs and film tie-ins. Length: 100-1200 words. Illustrations: colour. Payment: by negotiation. Founded 1985.

Flight International

Reed Business Information Ltd, Quadrant House, The Quadrant, Sutton, Surrey SM2 5AS
tel 020-8652 3842 *fax* 020-8652 3840
e-mail flight.international@rbi.co.uk
web site http://www.flightinternational.com
Editor C. Reed
Weekly £2.20

Deals with all branches of aerospace: operational and technical articles, illustrated by photos, engineering cutaway drawings; also news, paragraphs, reports of lectures, etc. News press days: Thu, Fri. Illustrations: tone, line, colour. Payment: by agreement. Founded 1909.

Fly-Fishing & Fly-Tying

Rolling River Publications, Aberfeldy Road, Kenmore, Perthshire PH15 2HF
tel/fax (01887) 830526
e-mail MarkB.ffft@btinternet.com
web site http://www.flyfishing-and-flytying.co.uk
Editor Mark Bowler
8 p.a. £2.50

Fly-fishing and fly-tying articles, fishery features, limited short stories, some fishing travel. Length: 800-1500 words. Illustrations: colour photos. Payment: by arrangement. Founded 1990.

Focus

Gruner + Jahr of the UK, 197 Marsh Wall, London E14 9SG
tel 020-7519 5500 *fax* 020-7519 5515
e-mail focusmag@focusmag.demon.co.uk
Editor Nick Smith
Monthly £2.60

'Tomorrow's science today.' Articles, features and news with a science-based or technical slant. All material is commissioned. Length: 500-3000 words (features), 50-200 words (news). Illustrations: colour prints, transparencies and artwork. Payment: £300 per 1000 words; £250 per full-page photo (negotiable). Founded 1993.

Folio

64-65 North Road, St Andrews, Bristol BS6 5AQ
tel 0117-942 8491 *fax* 0117-942 0369
e-mail editor@venue.co.uk
web site http://www.venue.co.uk
Editor Dave Higgitt
Monthly Free

Magazine for the Bristol, Bath and Cheltenham area. Articles, features, interviews and news on people, places and events with a local connection. No short stories or poems. Unsolicited material considered. Length: 600-2000 words (features), variable (news). Illustrations: colour and b&w. Payment: by negotiation. Founded 1994.

Football Picture Story Library

D.C. Thomson & Co. Ltd, Albert Square, Dundee DD1 9QJ
tel (01382) 223131 *fax* (01382) 322214
185 Fleet Street, London EC4A 2HS
tel 020-7400 1030 *fax* 020-7400 1089
2 p.m. 70p

Football stories for boys told in pictures.

For Women

Fantasy Publications, 4 Selsdon Way, London E14 9GL
tel 020-7308 5363 *fax* 020-7308 5075
Fiction Editor Elizabeth Coldwell
6-weekly £3.50

Women's magazine with erotic emphasis. Features on sex and health; erotic fiction and photos. Submit written synopsis for features; erotic fiction welcomed on spec. Fiction guidelines on receipt of sae. Length: 1500-2000 words. Illustrations: colour and b&w photos. Payment: £150 per story (fiction), features by arrangement; £150 per illustration. Founded 1991.

Fortean Times

Box 2409, London NW5 4NP
tel/fax 020-7485 5002
e-mail rickard@forteantimes.com
web site http://www.forteantimes.com/
Editors Bob Rickard, Paul Sieveking
Monthly £2.70

The journal of strange phenomena, experiences, related subjects and philosophies. Articles, features, news, reviews. Length: 500-3000 words; longer by arrangement. Illustrations: colour photos, line and tone art, cartoons. Payment: by negotiation. Founded 1973.

Fortnight – An Independent Review of Politics and the Arts

7 Lower Crescent, Belfast BT7 1NR
tel 028-9023 2353/9031 1337/9032 4141
fax 028-9023 2650
e-mail mairtin@fortnite.dnet.co.uk
Editors John O'Farrell, Mairtin Crawford
Monthly £2.20

Current affairs analysis, reportage, opinion pieces, cultural criticism, book reviews, poems. Illustrations: line, half-tone, cartoons. Payment: by arrangement. Founded 1970.

FourFourTwo

(incorporating Goal)
Haymarket Specialist Publications Ltd, Somerset House, Somerset Road, Teddington TW11 8RT
tel 020-8267 5337 *fax* 020-8267 5354
Editor Michael Hann
Monthly £2.90

Football magazine with 'adult' approach: interviews, in-depth features, issues pieces, odd and witty material. Length: 2000-3000 (features), 100-500 words (news/latest score). Illustrations: colour transparencies and artwork, b&w prints. Payment: £150 per 1000 words. Founded 1994.

FRANCE Magazine

Normandy House, 311 High Street, Cheltenham, Glos. GL50 3FB
tel (01242) 259850 *fax* (01242) 259869
e-mail editorial@francemag.com
Editor Philip Faiers
Quarterly £4.25

An armchair journey to the real France – features and articles ranging from cuisine to customs to architecture to exploring the hidden France. Informed speculative submissions welcome. Length: 800-2500 words. Illustrations: colour transparencies (mounted and captioned). Payment:

£100 per 1000 words; £50 per page/pro rata for illustrations. Founded 1989.

Frank

EMAP Élan Ltd, Endeavour House,
189 Shaftesbury Avenue, London WC2H 8JG
tel 020-7437 9011 *fax* 020-7208 3373
e-mail quitefrankly@frankmag.co.uk
web site http://www.virgin.net/frank/
Editor Harriet Quick
Monthly (quarterly from autumn 1999) £2.70

Young women's lifestyle magazine with the focus on fashion and a strong features base. Unsolicited material considered. Length: up to 2000 words. Illustrations: transparencies, colour and b&w prints. Payment: £250 per 1000 words. Founded 1997.

Freelance Market News

Sevendale House, 7 Dale Street,
Manchester M1 1JB
tel 0161-237 1827 *fax* 0161-228 3533
e-mail fmn@writersbureau.com
Editor Angela Cox
11 p.a. £29 p.a.; £17 6 issues

Information on UK and overseas publications with editorial content, submission requirements and contact details. News of editorial requirements for writers. Features on the craft of writing, competitions, letters page. Founded 1968.

Freelance Photographer

(formerly Photon)
Icon Publications Ltd, Maxwell Place,
Maxwell Lane, Kelso, Roxburghshire TD5 7BB
tel (01573) 226032 *fax* (01573) 226000
e-mail david@maxwellplace.demon.co.uk
web site http://www.freelancephotographer.co.uk/photon/
Editor David Kilpatrick
6 p.a. £2.95

Illustrated features on professional and craft photography. All material commissioned. Length: 750-2500 words. Illustrations: b&w and colour photos. Payment: £50-£300 per feature, including photos. Founded 1989.

Fresh Produce Journal

Lockwood Press Ltd, 430-438 Market Towers,
1 Nine Elms Lane, London SW8 5NN
tel 020-7622 6677 *fax* 020-7720 2047
e-mail editorial@fpj.co.uk
Editor Dominic Weaver
Weekly £1.80

Articles dealing with fruit, vegetable and flower trades on the marketing aspects of production but particularly importing, distribution and post-harvest handling; articles should average 500-700 words. Payment: by arrangement. Illustrations: half-tone. Founded 1895.

The Friend

New Premier House, 150 Southampton Row,
London WC1B 5BQ
tel 020-7387 7549
e-mail editorial@thefriend.org
web site http://www.thefriend.org
Editor Harry Albright
Weekly 82p

Material of interest to the Religious Society of Friends and like-minded people; political, social, economic or devotional, considered from outside contributors. Length: up to 1200 words. Illustrations: b&w or colour prints, b&w line drawings. Payment: not usually but will negotiate a small fee with professional writers. Founded 1843.

Fun Size Beano – see The Beano

Fun Size Dandy – see The Dandy

The Furrow

St Patrick's College, Maynooth, Co. Kildare,
Republic of Ireland
tel (01) 6286215 *fax* (01) 7083908
e-mail furrow.office@may.ie
Editor Rev. Ronan Drury
Monthly IR£1.60

Religious, pastoral, theological, social articles. Length: 3000 words. Payment: average £15 per page (450 words). Illustrations: line, half-tone. Founded 1950.

The Garden

Apex House, Oundle Road,
Peterborough PE2 9NP
tel (01733) 898100 *fax* (01733) 466885
e-mail thegarden@rhs.org.uk
Editor Ian Hodgson
Monthly £3

Journal of The Royal Horticultural Society. Features of horticultural or botanical interest on a wide range of subjects. Commissioned material only. Length: 1200-2500 words. Illustrations: 35mm or medium format colour transparencies, occasional b&w prints, botanical line drawings. Payment: varies. Founded 1866.

Garden Answers

(incorporating Practical Gardening)
EMAP Active Ltd, Apex House, Oundle Road,
Peterborough PE2 9NP

tel (01733) 898100 *fax* (01733) 466857
Editor Jim Ward
Monthly £2.40

Commissioned features and articles on all aspects of gardening. Study of magazine essential. Approach by letter with examples of published work. Length: 750 words. Illustrations: colour transparencies and artwork. Payment: by negotiation. Founded 1982.

Garden News

EMAP Active Ltd, Apex House, Oundle Road, Peterborough PE2 9NP
tel (01733) 898100 *fax* (01733) 466857
e-mail sarah.page@ecm.emap.com
Editor Sarah Page
Weekly £1

Up-to-date information on everything to do with plants, growing and gardening. Illustrations: line, colour, cartoons. Payment: by negotiation. Founded 1958.

Gardens Illustrated

John Brown Publishing, 136-142 Bramley Road, London W10 6SR
tel 020-7565 3000 *fax* 020-7565 3056
e-mail gardens@johnbrown.co.uk
web site http://www.gardensillustrated.com
Editor Rosie Atkins
10 p.a. £3.50

Upmarket, inspirational glossy for those interested in garden history, plants and gardening merchandise. Material mostly commissioned; send synopsis, samples of past work and sae to the editor. Length: 1000 words. Illustrations: colour. Payment: by negotiation. Founded 1993.

Gay Times

Ground Floor, Worldwide House, 116-134 Bayham Street, London NW1 0BA
tel 020-7482 2576 *fax* 020-7284 0329
Editor Colin Richardson
Monthly £2.50

Feature articles, full news and review coverage of all aspects of gay and lesbian life. Length: up to 2000 words. Illustrations: colour, line and half-tone, cartoons. Payment: by arrangement. Founded 1982.

Geographical Journal

Royal Geographical Society (with the Institute of British Geographers), Kensington Gore, London SW7 2AR
tel 020-7591 3025 *fax* 020-7591 3001
e-mail g.lowman@rgs.org
Editor Prof A. Millinglon
4 p.a. £30 (post free), (£75 p.a.)

Papers on all aspects of geography and development of current interest and concern. Large reviews section. Illustrations: photos, maps, diagrams. Founded 1893.

Geographical Magazine

(under licence from the Royal Geographical Society)
Campion Interactive Publishing Ltd, 47c Kensington Court, London W8 5DA
tel 020-7938 4011 *fax* 020-7938 4022
e-mail magazine@geographical.co.uk
Editor-in-Chief Miranda Haines
Monthly £2.75

Topical geography in a broad sense and travel . Illustrations: colour slides or vintage material; maps and graphs always needed. Payment: by negotiation. Founded 1935.

Geological Magazine

Cambridge University Press, The Edinburgh Building, Shaftesbury Road, Cambridge CB2 2RU
tel (01223) 312393
Editors Prof I.N. McCave, Dr N.H. Woodcock, Dr M.J. Bickle, Dr T.J. Palmer
Bi-monthly (£198 p.a. institutions, £42 p.a. students, US$324 USA/Canada/Mexico)

Original articles on all earth science topics containing the results of independent research by experts. Also reviews and notices of current geological literature, correspondence on geological subjects – illustrated. Length: variable. Payment: none. Founded 1864.

Gibbons Stamp Monthly

Stanley Gibbons Ltd, 5 Parkside, Ringwood, Hants BH24 3SH
tel (01425) 472363 *fax* (01425) 470247
e-mail gsm@stanleygibbons.co.uk
Editor Hugh Jefferies
Monthly £2.10 (£25.20 p.a.)

Articles on philatelic topics. Contact the editor first. Length: 500-2500 words. Payment: by arrangement, £30 or more per 1000 words. Illustrations: photos, line, stamps or covers.

Gifts International

Nexus Media Ltd, Nexus House, Azalea Drive, Swanley, Kent BR8 8HU
tel (01322) 660070 *fax* (01322) 667633
Editor Mary Brittain
Bi-monthly £21 p.a. (£31 p.a. Europe airmail, £37 p.a. rest of the world)

News of gift industry – products, trends, shops; articles on retailing, exporting, importing, manufacturing, crafts (UK and abroad). Illustrations: products, news.

Girl About Town Magazine

7-9 Rathbone Street, London W1P 1AF
tel 020-7636 6651 *fax* 020-7255 2352
Editor Bill Williamson
Weekly Free

Articles of general interest to women. Length: about 1100-1500 words. Payment: negotiable. Founded 1973.

Girl Talk – see page 301

Glaucus

Glaucus House, 14 Corbyn Crescent, Shoreham-by-Sea, West Sussex BN43 6PQ
tel (01273) 465433 *fax* (01273) 465433
e-mail bmlss@compuserve.com
web site http://cbr.nc.us.mensa.org/homepages/bmlss
Editor Andy Horton
Bi-annual £22 p.a.; bi-monthly Newsletter

Journal of the British Marine Life Study Society, aimed at the popular market. Observations and scientific research on the natural history, and related subjects, of the marine environment surrounding the British Isles. Send sae for Guide to submissions. Length: up to 2500 words. Illustrations: b&w line, occasional b&w photos. Payment: expenses only. Founded 1990.

Golf Monthly

IPC Magazines Ltd, King's Reach Tower, Stamford Street, London SE1 9LS
tel 020-7261 7237 *fax* 020-7261 7240
e-mail golfmonthly@ipc.co.uk
Editor Jane Carter
Monthly £2.80

Original articles on golf considered (not reports), golf clinics, handy hints. Illustrations: half-tone, colour, cartoons. Payment: by arrangement. Founded 1911.

Golf Weekly

EMAP Active Ltd, Bretton Court, Bretton, Peterborough PE3 8DZ
tel (01733) 465209 *fax* (01733) 465248
Editor Bob Warters
Weekly £1.70

News, tournament reports and articles on golf of interest to golfers. Payment: 15p per word published. Illustrations: photos of golf news and new courses.

Golf World

Emap Active Ltd, Bretton Court, Bretton, Peterborough PE3 8DZ
tel (01733) 264666 *fax* (01733) 465221
Editor David Clarke
Monthly £2.90

Expert golf instructional articles, 500-3000 words; general interest articles, personality features 500-3000 words. Little fiction. Payment: by negotiation. Illustrations: line, half-tone, colour, cartoons. Founded 1962.

Good Health

Attic Futura (UK) Ltd, 16-18 Berners Street, London W1P 3DD
tel 020-7664 6400 *fax* 020-7637 4645
Editor tba
Monthly £2.30

Covers all aspects of family health and wellbeing with emphasis given to feeling good about yourself. No unsolicited articles; submit synopsis of feature idea. Illustrations: colour transparencies. Payment: by negotiation. Founded 1997.

Good Housekeeping

National Magazine House, 72 Broadwick Street, London W1V 2BP
tel 020-7439 5000 *fax* 020-7439 5591
Editor-in-Chief Lindsay Nicholson
Monthly £2.50

Articles on topics of interest to intelligent women. No unsolicited features or stories accepted; approach by letter only. Domestic subjects covered by staff writers. Personal experiences and humorous articles occasionally used. Length: 700-2400 words. Payment: magazine standards. Illustrations: mainly commissioned. Founded 1922.

GQ

Vogue House, Hanover Square, London W1R 0AD
tel 020-7499 9080 *fax* 020-7495 1679
web site http://www.gq/magazine.co.uk
Editor Dylan Jones
Monthly £2.90

Style, fashion and general interest magazine for men. Illustrations: b&w and colour photos, line drawings, cartoons. Payment: by arrangement. Founded 1988.

Granta

2-3 Hanover Yard, Noel Road, London N1 8BE
tel 020-7704 9776 *fax* 020-7704 0474
web site http://www.granta.com
Editor Ian Jack
Quarterly £8.99 (£24.95 p.a.)

Original literary fiction, non-fiction and journalism. Study magazine before submitting work. No poems, essays or reviews. Length: determined by content. Illustrations: photos. Payment: by arrangement. Founded 1889; new series 1979.

Greetings Today

(formerly Greetings Magazine)
Lema Publishing, Unit No. 1, Queen Mary's Avenue, Watford, Herts. WD1 7JR
tel (01923) 250909 *fax* (01923) 250995
Publisher Malcolm Naish, *Editor* Vicky Hancocks
Monthly £35 p.a. (other rates on application)

Articles, features and news related to the greetings card industry; includes Artists Directory for aspiring artists wishing to attract the eye of publishers. Mainly written in-house; some material taken from outside. Length: varies. Illustrations: line, colour and b&w photos. Payment: by arrangement. Founded 1999; first published 1972.

The Grocer

(incorporating CTN – Confectioner, Tobacconist, Newsagent)
William Reed Publishing Ltd, Broadfield Park, Crawley, West Sussex RH11 9RT
tel (01293) 613400 *fax* (01293) 610333
e-mail editorial@the-grocer.co.uk
Editor Clive Beddall
Weekly £1.20

Trade journal: articles or news or illustrations of general interest to the grocery and provision trades. Payment: by arrangement. Founded 1861.

The Grower

Nexus Media Ltd, Nexus House, Azalea Drive, Swanley, Kent BR8 8HU
tel (01322) 660070 *fax* (01322) 666408
e-mail nxhort@compuserve.com
Editor Peter Rogers
Weekly £1.30

News and practical articles on commercial horticulture, covering all sectors including fruit, vegetable, salad crop and ornamentals. Founded 1923.

Guiding

17-19 Buckingham Palace Road, London SW1W 0PT
tel 020-7834 6242 *fax* 020-7828 8317
Editor Jan Clampett
Monthly £1.40

Official magazine of The Guide Association. Articles of interest to women of all ages, with special emphasis on youth work and the Guide Movement. Articles on simple crafts, games and the outdoors especially welcome. Length: 300-400 words. Illustrations: line, halftone, colour, cartoons. Payment: £70 per 1000 words; £100 full colour page.

H & P

(formerly Horse & Pony)
EMAP Active Ltd, Apex House, Oundle Road, Peterborough PE2 9NP
tel (01733) 898100 *fax* (01733) 466843
Editor Amanda Stevenson
4-weekly £2.15

All material relevant to young people with equestrian interests. Payment: on value to publication rather than length. Illustrations: colour, with a strong story line, cartoons. Founded 1970.

Hairflair

James Kimber Publishing Ltd, Freebournes House, Freebournes Road, Witham, Essex CM8 3US
tel (01376) 534547 *fax* (01376) 534565
Editor Ruth Page
Bi-monthly £2.20

Hair, beauty, fashion – and related features – for the 16-35 age group. Preliminary letter essential. Length: 800-1000 words. Illustrations: colour and b&w photos. Payment: negotiable. Founded 1985.

Hampshire – The County Magazine

74 Bedford Place, Southampton SO15 2DF
tel 023-8022 3591/8033 3457
Monthly £1.90

Factual articles concerning all aspects of Hampshire and Hampshire life, past and present. Length: 400-1000 words. Payment: by arrangement. Illustrations: mainly colour photos and line drawings. Founded 1960.

Harpers & Queen

National Magazine House, 72 Broadwick Street, London W1V 2BP
tel 020-7439 5000 *fax* 020-7439 5506
Editor Fiona Macpherson
Monthly £3

Features, fashion, beauty, art, theatre, films, travel, interior decoration – all commissioned. Illustrations: line, wash, full colour and 2- and 3-colour, and photos. Founded 1929.

Having a Baby

National Magazine Co Ltd, 72 Broadwick Street, London W1V 2BP
tel 020-7439 5000 *fax* 020-7439 5337
e-mail hab@natmags.co.uk
Editor Sarah Wilson
Monthly £2.60

Magazine for women covering all aspects of pregnancy and childbirth and life with children aged up to 3 years; plus health, beauty, fashion. Length: up to 1500 words.

Illustrations: colour transparencies. Payment: by arrangement. Founded 1994.

Health Club Management

Leisure Media Company Ltd,
Portmill House, Portmill Lane, Hitchin, Herts. SG5 1DJ
tel (01462) 431385 *fax* (01462) 433909
e-mail catherine@leisuremedia.com
web site http://www.leisuremedia.co.uk
Editor Catherine Larner
Monthly £48 p.a. with *Leisure Management* magazine

Official publication of the Fitness Industry Association. Articles on the operation of health clubs, day spas, fitness and sports centres, items on consumer issues and lifestyle trends as they affect club management are all welcomed. Length: up to 1500 words. Illustrations: colour and b&w photos. Payment: by arrangement. Founded 1995.

Health and Efficiency – H&E Magazine

New Freedom Publications Ltd, Burlington Court, Carlisle Street, Goole, East Yorkshire DN14 5EG
tel (01405) 769712 *fax* (01405) 763815
e-mail newfreedom@btinternet.com
web site http://www.h-and-e.co.uk
Editor Mark Nisbet
Monthly £2.95

Articles on naturist travel, clubs, beaches and naturist lifestyle experiences from the UK, Europe and the world. Length: 700-1500 words. Illustrations: line, colour transparencies and prints featuring naturists in natural settings; also cartoons, humorous fillers and features with naturist themes. Payment: by negotiation but guidelines for contributors and basic payment rates available on request.

Health & Fitness

Nexus Media Ltd, Nexus House, Azalea Drive, Swanley, Kent BR8 8HU
tel (01322) 660070 *fax* (01322) 616319
e-mail editorial@hfonline.co.uk
web site http://www.hfonline.co.uk
Editor Mary Comber
Monthly £2.30

Articles on all aspects of health and fitness. Illustrations: line, half-tone, colour. Payment: by arrangement. Founded 1984.

Healthy Eating

Market Link Publishing plc, The Mill, Bearwalden Business Park, Wendens Ambo, Saffron Walden, Essex CB11 4JX
tel (01799) 544239 *fax* (01799) 544205
Editor Kathryn Custance
Monthly £2.50

Articles on health and nutrition, how food affects the body, celebrity food and health stories. Length: 1000-1200 words. Illustrations: colour food photography and illustrations. Payment: £150-£250 per article; £30-£50 for illustrations; £25-£80 for transparencies. Founded 1990.

Hello!

Wellington House, 69-71 Upper Ground, London SE1 9PQ
tel 020-7667 8700 *fax* 020-7667 8716
Editor Maggie Koumi
Weekly £1.45

News-based features – showbusiness, celebrity, royalty; exclusive interviews. Payment: by arrangement. Illustrated. Founded 1988.

Here's Health

EMAP Esprit, Greater London House, Hampstead Road, London NW1 7EJ
tel 020-7874 0200
Editor Elaine Griffiths
Monthly £2.40

Articles on alternative medicine, complementary health, holistic living, environment, nutrition and natural treatment success stories. Preliminary letter and clippings essential. Length: 750-1800 words. Payment: on publication.

Hertfordshire Countryside

Beaumonde Publications Ltd, 4 Mill Bridge, Hertford, Herts. SG14 1PY
tel (01992) 553571, (01462) 431237
fax (01992) 587713
Editor Sandra Small
Monthly £1.25

Articles of county interest. No poetry. Length: 1000 words. Payment: £30 per 1000 words. Illustrations: line, half-tone. Founded 1946.

Hi-Fi News & Record Review

Link House, Dingwall Avenue, Croydon CR9 2TA
tel 020-8686 2599 *fax* 020-8781 6046
e-mail 101574.223@compuserve.com
Editor Steve Harris
Monthly £2.75

Articles on all aspects of high quality sound recording and reproduction; also extensive record review section and supporting musical feature articles. Audio matter is essentially technical, but should be presented in a manner suitable for music lovers interested in the nature of sound. Length: 2000-3000 words. Illustrations: line, half-tone. Payment: by arrangement. Founded 1956.

History

Editorial office History Department, University of Exeter, Exeter EX4 4RJ
tel (01392) 264297
Published by Blackwell (Oxford) for the Historical Association, 59a Kennington Park Road, London SE11 4JH *tel* 020-7735 3901
Editor Joseph Smith
Quarterly £38 p.a. (£16 p.a. members)

Historical articles and reviews by experts. Length: usually up to 8000 words. Illustrations: only exceptionally. Payment: none. Founded 1916.

History Today

20 Old Compton Street, London W1V 5PE
tel 020-7534 8000
e-mail admin@historytoday.com
web site http://admin@historytoday.com
Editor Peter Furtado
Monthly £3.40

History in the widest sense – political, economic, social, biography, relating past to present; world history as well as British. Length: articles 3500 words; shorter news/views pieces 600-1200 words. Illustrations: from prints and original photos. Please do not send original material until publication is agreed. Payment: by arrangement. Founded 1951.

Home and Country

104 New King's Road, London SW6 4LY
tel 020-7731 5777 *fax* 020-7736 4061
Editor Susan Seager
Monthly £1.50

Journal of the National Federation of Women's Institutes for England and Wales. Publishes material related to the Federation's and members' activities; also considers articles of general interest to women, particularly country women, e.g. craft, environment, humour, health, rural life stories, of 800-1200 words. Illustrations: colour and b&w photos and drawings, cartoons. Payment: by arrangement. Founded 1919.

Home and Family

The Mothers' Union, Mary Sumner House, 24 Tufton Street, London SW1P 3RB
tel 020-7222 5533 *fax* 020-7222 1591
Editor Jill Worth
Quarterly £1.25

Short articles related to Christian family life. Payment: approx. £70 per 1000 words. Illustrations: colour photos. Founded 1954.

Home Words

G.J. Palmer & Sons Ltd, St Mary's Works, St Mary's Plain, Norwich, Norfolk NR3 3BH
tel (01603) 612914 *fax* (01603) 624483
Publisher G.A. Knights
Monthly

Illustrated C of E magazine insert. Articles of popular Christian interest with an Anglican slant (400-800 words) with relevant photos; also cartoons. Payment: by arrangement. Founded 1870.

HomeFlair Magazine

Hamerville Magazines Ltd, Regal House, Regal Way, Watford, Herts. WD2 4YJ
tel (01923) 237799 *fax* (01923) 246927
e-mail homeflair@hamerville.co.uk
Editor Nicola Shannon
Monthly £1.90

Homes' conversions, inspirational looks, what's new in products and design. Approach in writing, with samples of previously published work. Payment: by arrangement. Illustrated. Founded 1990.

Homes and Gardens

IPC Magazines Ltd, King's Reach Tower, Stamford Street, London SE1 9LS
tel 020-7261 5000 *fax* 020-7261 6247
Editor Matthew Line
Monthly £2.80

Articles on home interest or design, particularly well-designed British interiors (snapshots should be submitted). Length: articles, 900-1000 words. Illustrations: all types. Payment: generous, but exceptional work required; varies. Founded 1919.

Homes & Ideas

IPC Magazines Ltd, King's Reach Tower, Stamford Street, London SE1 9LS
tel 020-7261 7494 *fax* 020-7261 7495
Editor tba
Monthly £2

Features on any aspect of style for the home. Send cuttings to the features dept. Length: by arrangement. Illustrations: colour photos and drawings. Payment: NUJ rates plus; illustrations by arrangement. Founded 1993.

Homestyle

Essential Publishing, 1-4 Eaglegate, East Hill, Colchester, Essex CO1 2PR

tel (01206) 796911 *fax* (01206) 796922
Editor Hayley Chilver
Monthly £1.80

Ideas and practical features on home and garden improvements. Merchandise reviews. Length: 2 or 4-page spreads. Illustrations: colour transparencies. Payment: by negotiation. Founded 1992.

Horse & Hound

IPC Magazines Ltd, King's Reach Tower, Stamford Street, London SE1 9LS
tel 020-7261 6315 *fax* 020-7261 5429
e-mail jenny_sims@ipc.co.uk
web site http://www.ipc.co.uk
Editor Arnold Garvey
Weekly £1.65

Special articles, news items, photos, on all matters appertaining to equestrian sports. Payment: by negotiation.

Horse and Rider

Haslemere House, Lower Street, Haslemere, Surrey GU27 2PE
tel (01428) 651551 *fax* (01428) 653888
e-mail djm@djmurphy.co.uk
web site http://www.horseandridermagazine.co.uk
Editor Alison Bridge, *Assistant Editor* Danielle Pascoe
Monthly £2.40

Sophisticated magazine covering all forms of equestrian activity at home and abroad. Good writing and technical accuracy essential. Length: 1500-2000 words. Illustrations: photos and drawings, the latter usually commissioned. Payment: by arrangement. Founded 1959.

Horticulture Week

Haymarket Magazines Ltd, 174 Hammersmith Road, London W6 7JP
tel 020-8267 4977
Editor Pete Weston
Weekly £1.75 (£75 p.a.)

News, technical and business journal for the nursery and garden centre trade, landscape industry and public parks and sports ground staff. Outside contributions considered. No fiction. Length: 500-1500 words. Illustrations: line, half-tone, colour. Payment: by arrangement.

Hortus

Bryan's Ground, Stapleton, Nr Presteigne, Herefordshire LD8 2LP
tel (01544) 260001 *fax* (01544) 260015
e-mail all@hortus.co.uk
web site http://www.hortus.co.uk
Editor David Wheeler
Quarterly £30 p.a. (UK)

Articles on decorative horticulture: plants, gardens, history, design, literature, people; book reviews. Length: 1500-5000 words, longer by arrangement. Illustrations: line, half-tone and wood-engravings. Payment: by arrangement. Founded 1987.

Hospital Doctor

Reed Healthcare Publishing, Quadrant House, The Quadrant, Sutton, Surrey SM2 5AS
tel 020-8652 8745 *fax* 020-8652 8701
Editor Tim Burrowes
Weekly Free to 45,000 doctors. (£70 p.a.)

Commissioned features of interest to all grades and specialities of hospital doctors; demand for news tip-offs. Length: features 800-1500 words. Illustrations: colour photos, transparencies, cartoons and commissioned artwork. Payment: £130 per 1000 words features, £12 per 100 words news. Founded c.1980.

Hot Air

John Brown Contract Publishing Ltd, The New Boathouse, 136-142 Bramley Road, London W10 6SR
tel 020-7565 3000 *fax* 020-7565 3202
Editor Alex Finer
Quarterly Free

Inflight magazine for Virgin Atlantic Airways. Sport, trends/lifestyle, celebrities. Length: 1500-3000 words. Illustrations: high quality colour transparencies. Payment: by negotiation. Founded 1984.

Hot Press

13 Trinity Street, Dublin 2, Republic of Ireland
tel (01) 6795077/6795091 *fax* (01) 6795097
e-mail hotpress@iol.ie
web site http://www.hot-press.com
Editor Niall Stokes
Fortnightly IR£1.95

High-quality, investigative stories, or punchily written offbeat pieces, of interest to 16-39-year-olds, including politics, music, sport, sex, religion – whatever's happening on the street. Length: varies. Illustrations: b&w photos, colour sometimes used. Payment: by negotiation. Founded 1977.

Hotel and Catering Review

Jemma Publications Ltd, Marino House, 52 Glasthule Road, Sandycove, Co. Dublin, Republic of Ireland
tel (01) 2800000 *fax* (01) 2801818
e-mail fcorr@homenet.ie
Editor Frank Corr
Monthly IR£22 p.a.

Short news and trade news pieces.

Length: approx. 200 words. Features. Payment: £100 per 1000 words. Illustrations: half-tone, cartoons.

House & Garden

Vogue House, Hanover Square, London W1R 0AD
tel 020-7499 9080 *fax* 020-7629 2907
Editor Susan Crewe
Monthly £2.90

Articles (always commissioned), on subjects relating to domestic architecture, interior decorating, furnishing, gardening, household equipment, food and wine.

House Beautiful

National Magazine House, 72 Broadwick Street, London W1V 2BP
tel 020-7439 5500 *fax* 020-7439 5595
Editor Libby Norman
Monthly £2

Specialist 'home' features for the homes of today. Preliminary study of magazine advisable. Payment: according to merit. Illustrated. Founded 1989.

HouseBuilder

56-64 Leonard Street, London EC2A 4JX
tel 020-7608 5130
Editor Ben Roskrow
11 p.a. £66 p.a.

Official Journal of the HouseBuilders Federation published in association with the National House-Building Council. Technical articles on design, construction and equipment of dwellings, estate planning and development, and technical aspects of house-building, aimed at those engaged in house and flat construction and the development of housing estates. Preliminary letter advisable. Length: articles from 500 words, preferably with illustrations. Payment: by arrangement. Illustrations: photos, plans, construction details, cartoons.

HQ Poetry Magazine

(The Haiku Quarterly)
39 Exmouth Street, Swindon SN1 3PU
tel (01793) 523927
Editor Kevin Bailey
3-4 p.a. £2.60 (4 issues £9 p.a. UK, £12 p.a. non-UK)

A range of experimental and traditional poetry from all over the world. About one third of the content is devoted to haikuesque and imagistic poetry. Plus review section and articles. Payment: small. Founded 1990.

HU (The Honest Ulsterman)

HU Publications, PO Box 15, Holywood, Co. Down BT18 9UP
Editor Tom Clyde
3 p.a. £2.50

Poetry, short stories, reviews, critical articles, poetry pamphlets. Payment: notional. Founded 1968.

i-D Magazine

Universal House, 251-255 Tottenham Court Road, London W1P 0AE
tel 020-7813 6170 *fax* 020-7813 6179
e-mail editor@i-Dmagazine.co.uk
Editor Avril Mair
Monthly £2.80

International fashion orientated magazine. Includes music, art, design and technology. Will consider unsolicited ideas. Illustrations: colour and b&w photos. Payment: £100 per 1000 words; photos £50 per page. Founded 1980.

Ideal Home

IPC Magazines Ltd, King's Reach Tower, Stamford Street, London SE1 9LS
tel 020-7261 5000 *fax* 020-7261 6697
Editor Isobel McKenzie-Price
Monthly £2

Lifestyle magazine, articles usually commissioned. Contributors advised to study editorial content before submitting material. Payment: according to material. Illustrations: usually commissioned. Founded 1920.

The Illustrated London News

20 Upper Ground, London SE1 9PF
tel 020-7805 5555 *fax* 020-7805 5911
Editor Alison Booth
2-3 p.a. £2.50

Two special issues published annually: Summer and Christmas, plus occasional additional issues to tie in with major events. Focuses on London and the UK: culture, the arts, people, dining, fashion, entertainment. All material commissioned but ideas welcome. Founded 1842.

In Balance

(formerly Herts. Holistic Health Magazine)
The Pintail Group Ltd, 50 Parkway, Welwyn Garden City, Herts. AL8 6HH
tel (01707) 339007 *fax* (01707) 395550
e-mail vbrown@pintail.u-net.com
Editor Val Reynolds Brown
Quarterly £1.50

Holistic health and lifestyle magazine and therapy directory covering London and the southeast. Features on alternative therapies and related environmental issues. Ideas welcome. Length: 1000-3000 words. Payment: negotiable. Founded 1990.

In Britain

Premier Media Partners, Haymarket House, 1 Oxendon Street, London SW1Y 4EE
tel 020-7925 2544 *fax* 020-7976 1088
e-mail in_britain@premiermp.com
Editor Andrea Spain
Monthly £2.75 (£23.95 p.a. UK/Europe; $39.95 p.a. US)

Upmarket features magazine about places and people in Britain. Very limited freelance material is accepted. Illustrated. Payment: by arrangement. Founded 1930.

In Dublin

6-7 Camden Place, Dublin 2, Republic of Ireland
tel (01) 4784322 *fax* (01) 4781055
Editor Declan Lawn
Fortnightly IR£1.95

Dublin-related news features, oddball items, humour and interviews. Length: 500-1000 words. Payment: £80 per 1000 words. Illustrated. Founded 1976.

The Independent Magazine – see The Independent in National newspapers UK and Ireland, page 3

Index on Censorship

Lancaster House, 33 Islington High Street, London N1 9LH
tel 020-7278 2313 *fax* 020-7278 1878
e-mail judith@indexoncensorship.org
web site http://www.indexoncensorship.org
Editor-in-Chief Ursula Owen
Bi-monthly £8.99 (£39 p.a.)

Articles up to 3000 words dealing with all aspects of free speech and political censorship. Illustrations: b&w, cartoons. Payment: £75 per 1000 words. Founded 1972.

The Indexer

Society of Indexers, Globe Centre, Penistone Road, Sheffield S6 3AE
tel 0114-281 3060
e-mail cshuttle@dircon.co.uk
web site http://www.socind.demon.co.uk/publics.htm
Executive Editor Christine Shuttleworth
2 p.a. (£40 p.a.) Free to members

The International Journal of Indexing. Articles of interest to professional indexers and providers and users of information in any form. Payment: none. Founded 1958.

Infant Projects

Scholastic Ltd, Villiers House, Clarendon Avenue, Leamington Spa, Warks. CV32 5PR
tel (01926) 887799 *fax* (01926) 333325
e-mail EarlyYears@Scholastic.co.uk
Editor Jane Bishop
Bi-monthly £2.85

Practical articles suggesting project activities for teachers of children aged 4-7; material mostly commissioned. Length: 500-1000 words. Illustrations: colour photos and line illustrations, colour posters. Payment: by arrangement. Founded 1978.

The Inquirer

1-6 Essex Street, London WC2R 2HY
tel 020-7240 2384
Editor Keith Gilley
Fortnightly 45p

Journal of news and comment for Unitarians and religious liberals. Articles, liberal and progressive in tone, of general religious, social, cultural and international interest. Length: up to 750 words. Payment: none. Founded 1842.

Inspirations For Your Home

GE Publishing Ltd, 133 Long Acre, London WC2E 9AD
tel 020-7836 0519 *fax* 020-7836 0280
Editor Deborah Barker
Monthly £2.50

Practical features on all aspects of home interest – home design, cookery, crafts, gadgets. Length: 800-2000 words. Payment: by arrangement. Illustrated. Founded 1993.

Insurance Age

EMAP Business Communications, 33-39 Bowling Green Lane, London EC1R 0DA
tel 020-7505 8161 *fax* 020-7505 8186
e-mail rachelg@finance.emap.co.uk
web site http://www.insuranceage.com
Editor Rachel Gordon
Monthly

News and features on general insurance and the broker market, personal, commercial, health and Lloyd's of London. Illustrations: transparencies. Payment: by negotiation. Founded 1979.

Insurance Brokers' Monthly

7 Stourbridge Road, Lye, Stourbridge, West Midlands DY9 7DG
tel (01384) 895228 *fax* (01384) 893666
e-mail info@brokersmonthly.co.uk
web site http://www.brokersmonthly.co.uk
Editor Brian Susman

Monthly £4

Articles of technical and non-technical interest to insurance brokers and others engaged in the insurance industry. Occasional articles of general interest to the City, on finance, etc. Length: 1000-1500 words. Payment: from £40 per 1000 words on last day of month following publication. Authoritative material written under true name and qualification receives highest payment. Illustrations: line and half-tone, 100-120 screen. Founded 1950.

InterMedia

International Institute of Communications, Tavistock House South, Tavistock Square, London WC1H 9LF
tel 020-7388 0671 *fax* 020-7380 0623
Editor Daniella Goldman
Bi-monthly £70 p.a.

International journal concerned with policies, events, trends and research in the field of communications, broadcasting, telecommunications and associated issues, particularly cultural and social. Preliminary letter essential. Illustrations: b&w line. Payment: by arrangement. Founded 1970.

International Affairs

Royal Institute of International Affairs, Chatham House, 10 St James's Square, London SW1Y 4LE
tel 020-7957 5700 *fax* 020-7957 5710
e-mail IA-CH@riia.org
web site http://www.riia.org
Quarterly £14 (£40 p.a.individuals, £94 p.a. institutions)

Serious long-term articles on international affairs; more than 100 books reviewed each quarter. Preliminary letter advisable. Article length: average 7000 words. Illustrations: none. Payment: by arrangement. Founded 1922.

Internet

EMAP Active Ltd, Angel House, 338-346 Goswell Road, London EC1V 7QP
tel 020-7880 7438
web site http://www.internet-magazine.com
Editor Tanya Kreisky
Monthly £3.25

Magazine for consumer users, people who use the net at work and business users. Articles, news and features and guide to web sites on the Internet. Length: 1500-2500 words. Illustrations: colour photos, artwork. Payment: £170 per 1000 words. Founded 1994.

Interzone

217 Preston Drove, Brighton, East Sussex BN1 6FL
tel (01273) 504710
Editor David Pringle
Monthly £3 (£32 p.a.)

Science fiction and fantasy short stories, articles, interviews and reviews. Please read magazine before submitting. Length: 2000-6000 words. Illustrations: line, half-tone, colour. Payment: by arrangement. Founded 1982.

Investors Chronicle

4B Floor, Maple House, 149 Tottenham Court Road, London W1P 9LL
tel 020-7896 2525 *fax* 020-7896 2078
Editor Ceri Jones
Weekly £2.95

Journal covering investment and personal finance. Occasional outside contributions for surveys are accepted. Payment: by negotiation.

Ireland of the Welcomes

Irish Tourist Board, Baggot Street Bridge, Dublin 2, Republic of Ireland
tel (01) 6024000 *fax* (01) 6024335
e-mail iow@irishtouristboard.ie
web site http://www.irelandofthewelcomes.com
Editor Letitia Pollard
Bi-monthly IR£2.50

Irish items with cultural, sporting or topographical background designed to arouse interest in Irish holidays. Mostly commissioned – preliminary letter advised. No unsolicited MSS. Length: 1200-1800 words. Payment: by arrangement. Illustrations: scenic and topical transparencies, line drawings, some cartoons.

Ireland's Own

Channing House, Upper Rowe Street, Wexford
tel (053) 40140 *fax* (053) 340191
Editors Gerry Breen, Margaret Galvin
Weekly 50p

Short stories: non-experimental, traditional with an Irish orientation (2000-2500 words); articles of interest to Irish readers at home and abroad (750-1000 words); general and literary articles (750-1000 words). Monthly special bumper editions, each devoted to a particular seasonal topic. Suggestions for new features considered. Payment: varies according to quality and length. Illustrations: photos, cartoons. Founded 1902.

Irish Farmers Journal
Irish Farm Centre, Bluebell, Dublin 12, Republic of Ireland
tel (01) 4199500 *fax* (01) 4520876
e-mail editdept@ifj.ie
web site http://www.farmersjournal.ie
Editor Matthew Dempsey
Weekly IR£1.20 (£1)

Readable, technical articles on any aspect of farming. Length: 700-1000 words. Payment: £100-£150 per article. Illustrated. Founded 1948.

Irish Journal of Medical Science
Royal Academy of Medicine, 6 Kildare Street, Dublin 2, Republic of Ireland
tel (01) 6767650 *fax* (01) 6611684
e-mail journal@rami.ie
web site http://www.rami.ie
Quarterly IR£20 (IR£70 EU, IR£110 outside EU)

Official Organ of the Royal Academy of Medicine in Ireland. Original contributions in medicine, surgery, midwifery, public health, etc; reviews of professional books, reports of medical societies, etc. Illustrations: line, half-tone, colour.

Irish Medical Times
15 Harcourt Street, Dublin 2, Republic of Ireland
tel (01) 4757461 *fax* (01) 4757467
e-mail editor@imt.ie
web site http://www.imt.ie
Editor Aindreas McEntee
Weekly IR£3 (IR£145 p.a.)

Medical articles, also humorous articles with medical slant. Length: 850-1000 words. Payment: £60 per 1000 words. Illustrations: line, half-tone, colour, cartoons.

Irish Printer
Jemma Publications Ltd, 52 Glasthule Road, Sandycove, Co. Dublin, Republic of Ireland
tel (01) 2800000 *fax* (01) 2801818
e-mail fcorr@homenet.ie
Editor Frank Corr
Monthly IR£22 p.a.

Technical articles and news of interest to the printing industry. Length: 800-1000 words. Illustrations: colour and b&w photos. Payment: £100 per 1000 words; photos £30. Founded 1974.

IT (Irish Tatler)
Smurfit Publications Ltd, 2 Clanwilliam Court, Lower Mount Street, Dublin 2, Republic of Ireland
tel (01) 6623158 *fax* (01) 6619757
Editor Leanne de Cerbo
Monthly IR£2.10

General interest women's magazine: beauty, interiors, fashion, cookery, current affairs, reportage and celebrity interviews. Length: 2000-4000 words. Payment: by arrangement.

J17
EMAP Élan, Endeavour House, 189 Shaftesbury Avenue, London WC2H 8JG
tel 020-7208 3408 *fax* 020-7208 3590
Editor Sophie Wilson
Monthly £1.70

Articles of interest to girls aged 14-16: fashion, beauty, pop, and various features; investigative pieces; quizzes. Payment: by arrangement. Illustrations: colour. Founded 1983.

Jane's Defence Weekly
Sentinel House, 163 Brighton Road, Coulsdon, Surrey CR5 2YH
tel 020-8700 3700 *fax* 020-8763 1007
web site http://www.jdw.janes.com
Editor Clifford Beal
Weekly £180 p.a. (5-year archive on CD-Rom)

International defence news; military equipment; budget analysis, industry, military technology, business, political, defence market intelligence. Payment: minimum £198 per 1000 words used. Illustrations: line, half-tone, colour. Founded 1984.

Jazz Journal International
Jazz Journal Ltd, 3 and 3A Forest Road, Loughton, Essex IG10 1DR
tel 020-8532 0456/0678 *fax* 020-8532 0440
Publisher and Editor-in-Chief Eddie Cook
Monthly £3.20

Articles on jazz, record reviews. Telephone or write before submitting material. Payment: by arrangement. Illustrations: photos. Founded 1948.

Jewish Chronicle
25 Furnival Street, London EC4A 1JT
tel 020-7415 1500
Editor Edward J. Temko
Weekly 55p

Authentic and exclusive news stories and articles of Jewish interest from 500-1500 words are considered. There is a lively arts and leisure section, as well as regular travel pages. Payment: by arrangement. Illustrations: of Jewish interest, either topical or feature. Founded 1841.

The Jewish Quarterly
PO Box 2078, London W1A 1JR

tel/fax 020-8830 5367 (editorial)
Editor Matthew Reisz
Quarterly £3.95 (£15 p.a., £17.50 p.a. Europe, £25 p.a. overseas)

Articles of Jewish interest, literature, history, music, politics, poetry, book reviews, fiction. Illustrations: half-tone. Founded 1953.

Jewish Telegraph

Telegraph House, 11 Park Hill, Bury Old Road, Prestwich, Manchester M25 0HH
tel 0161-740 9321 *fax* 0161-740 9325
1 Shaftesbury Avenue, Leeds LS8 1DR
tel 0113-295 6000 *fax* 0113-295 6006
Harold House, Dunbabin Road, Liverpool L15 6XL
tel 0151-475 6666 *fax* 0151-475 2222
4 May Terrace, Giffnock, Glasgow G46 6LD
tel 0141-621 4422 *fax* 0141-621 4333
Editor Paul Harris
Weekly Man. 35p, Leeds 25p, Liverpool 25p, Glasgow 40p

Non-fiction articles of Jewish interest, especially humour. Exclusive Jewish news stories and pictures, international, national and local. Length: 1000-1500 words. Payment: by arrangement. Illustrations: line, half-tone, cartoons. Founded 1950.

Journal of Alternative and Complementary Medicine

9 Rickett Street, London SW6 1RU
tel 020-7385 0012 *fax* 020-7385 4566
Editor Graeme Miller
Monthly £2.95 (£33.50 p.a.)

Feature articles (up to 2000 words) and news stories (up to 250 words). Unsolicited material welcome but not eligible for payment unless commissioned. Illustrations: line, half-tone, colour. Payment: by negotiation. Founded 1983.

Journalist

NUJ, Acorn House, 314 Gray's Inn Road, London WC1X 8DP
tel 020-7278 7916 *fax* 020-7837 8143
e-mail the.journalist @mcr1.poptel.org.uk
Editor Tim Gopsill
Bi-monthly £2.50 (£12 p.a., £20 p.a. overseas)

Magazine of the National Union of Journalists (mailed to all members). Accepts material relating to journalism, trade unionism and general conditions in the media – newspapers, magazines, books, broadcasting and electronic. Mainly contributed by members, and outside written contributions not paid.

Junior Education

Scholastic Ltd, Villiers House, Clarendon Avenue, Leamington Spa, Warks. CV32 5PR
tel (01926) 887799 *fax* (01926) 883331
Editor Mrs Terry Saunders
Monthly £2.85

For teachers, educationalists and students concerned with children aged 7-12. Articles by specialists on practical teaching ideas and methods, plus in-depth coverage and debate on news issues in education. Length: 800-1000 words. Payment: by arrangement. Illustrated with photos and drawings; includes colour poster. Founded 1977.

Junior Focus

Scholastic Ltd, Villiers House, Clarendon Avenue, Leamington Spa, Warks. CV32 5PR
tel (01926) 887799 *fax* (01926) 883331
Editor Libby Russell
Monthly £2.70

Aimed at teachers of 7-12 year olds, each issue is based on a theme, closely linked with the National Curriculum. Includes A1 and A3 full-colour posters, 16 pages of photocopiable material and 12 pages of articles. All material commissioned. Length: 800 words. Illustrations: commissioned colour; welcomes samples of work from new illustrators. Payment: £100 per double-page spread; varies for illustrations. Founded 1982.

Justice of the Peace

Butterworth-Tolley, 2 Addiscombe Road, Croydon CR9 5AF
tel 020-8686 9141 *fax* 020-8686 3155
e-mail jpn@tolleys.co.uk
Editor Adrian Turner
Weekly £183.50 p.a.

Professional journal. Articles on magisterial and local government law and associated subjects including family law, criminology, medico-legal matters, penology, police, probation. Information on articles and contributions sent on request. Length: 3000 words. Payment: £200 per feature article. Founded 1837.

Kerrang!

EMAP Metro Ltd, Mappin House, 4 Winsley Street, London W1N 7AR
tel 020-7436 1515 *fax* 020-7312 8910
Editor Phil Alexander
Weekly £1.50

News, views and reviews; the noise of the new generation. All material commissioned. Illustrations: colour. Payment: by arrangement. Founded 1981.

Kids Alive! (The Young Soldier)

The Salvation Army, 101 Newington Causeway, London SE1 6BN
tel 020-7367 4910 *fax* 020-7367 4710
e-mail kidsalive@salvationarmy.org.uk
Editor Ken Nesbitt
Weekly 20p (£26 p.a.)

Children's magazine: stories, pictures, cartoon strips, puzzles etc, Christian-based with emphasis on education re addictive substances. Payment: by arrangement. Illustrations: half-tone, line and 4-colour line, cartoons. Founded 1881.

Kids Out

Time Out Guides Ltd, Universal House, 251 Tottenham Court Road, London W1P 0AB
tel 020-7813 6018 *fax* 020-7813 6153
e-mail guides@timeout.co.uk
Editor Melanie Dakin
Monthly £2

Contains a comprehensive calendar of London events in London for families, plus travel, education and parenting articles of interest to parents of under 16 year-olds in the London area. Also game, book, software and film reviews. For picture requirements call Kerri Miles 020-7813 6089. Length: 200-8000 words. Payment: £100 per 1000 words. Founded 1995.

The Lady

39-40 Bedford Street, Strand, London WC2E 9ER
tel 020-7379 4717 *fax* 020-7836 4620
Editor Arline Usden
Weekly 75p

British and foreign travel, countryside, human-interest, celebrity interviews, animals, cookery, art and antiques, historic-interest and commemorative articles (preliminary letter advisable for articles dealing with anniversaries). Send proposals for articles by post or fax; do not phone. Length: 900-1200 words; Viewpoint: 600 words. Annual Short Story Competition with prize of £1000 plus. Winning entries printed in magazine. Illustrations: colour transparencies, b&w photos and drawings. Payment: by arrangement. Founded 1885.

Lancashire Magazine

33 Beverley Road, Driffield, Yorkshire YO25 6SD
tel/fax (01377) 253232
Editor Winston Halstead
Bi-monthly £1.40

Articles about people, life and character of all parts of Lancashire. Length: 1000 words. Payment: £35-£40 approx. per published page. Illustrations: line, half-tone, colour. Founded 1977.

Lancet

84 Theobalds Road, London WC1X 8RR
tel 020-7611 4100 *fax* 020-7611 4466
web site http://www.thelancet.com
Editor Dr Richard Horton
Weekly £5

Research papers, review articles, editorials, correspondence and commentaries on the international medicosocial scene. Consult the editor before submitting material. Founded 1823.

Land & Liberty

Suite 427, The London Fruit Exchange, Brushfield Street, London E1 6EL
tel 020-7377 8885 *fax* 020-7377 8886
e-mail HGF_IGU@compuserve.com
Editor Fred Harrison
Quarterly £3 (£12 p.a.)

Articles on land economics, land taxation, land prices, land speculation as they relate to housing, the economy, production, politics. Study of journal essential. Length: up to 3000 words. Payment: by arrangement. Illustrations: half-tone. Founded 1894.

The Latest

Gloucester House, 45 Gloucester Street, Brighton BN1 4EW
tel (01273) 818150 *fax* (01273) 818152
e-mail canon@pavilion.co.uk
web site http://www.thelatest.co.uk
Editor Bill Smith
Monthly 30p

Lively local newspaper (covering Sussex, Surrey, South London, Hampshire and Dorset) for young professionals. Contains news and arts features, listings. Payment: £100 per 1000 words. Founded 1996.

The Lawyer

Centaur Communications Group, 50 Poland Street, London W1V 4AX
tel 020-7970 4614 *fax* 020-7970 4640
e-mail lawyer.edit@chiron.co.uk
web site http://www.the-lawyer.co.uk
Editor Catrin Griffiths, *Editor-in-Chief* Sean Brierley
Weekly £1.75 (£60 p.a.)

News, articles, features and views relevant to the legal profession. Length: 600-900 words. Illustrations: as agreed. Payment: £125-£150 per 1000 words. Founded 1987.

Legal Week

Global Professional Media Ltd,
99 Charterhouse Street, London EC1M 6HR
tel 020-7566 5600 *fax* 020-7253 8505
e-mail jmalpas@gpmuk.com
web site http://www.legalweek.net
Editor John Malpas
Weekly £2.45

News and features aimed at business lawyers. Length: 750-1000 words (features), 300 words (news). Payment: £150 upwards (features), £75-£100 (news). Considers unsolicited material and welcomes ideas for articles and features. Founded 1999.

Legal Week Benchmarker
Bi-monthly

Features for in-house lawyers.

Legal IT
Bi-monthly

News and features for IT decision-makers in the legal industry.

The Leisure Manager

The Institute of Leisure and Amenity Management, ILAM House, Lower Basildon, Reading, Berks. RG8 9NE
tel (01491) 874800 *fax* (01491) 874801
Editor Jonathan Ives
Monthly £40 p.a. (£50 p.a. overseas)

Official Journal of The Institute of Leisure and Amenity Management. Articles on amenity, children's play, tourism, leisure, parks, entertainment, recreation and sports management, cultural services. Payment: by arrangement. Illustrations: line, half-tone. Founded 1985.

Leisure Painter

63-65 High Street, Tenterden, Kent TN30 6BD
tel (01580) 763315 *fax* (01580) 765411
Editor Jane Stroud
Monthly £2.35

Instructional articles on painting and fine art. Payment: £75 per 1000 words. Illustrations: line, half-tone, colour, original artwork. Founded 1966.

Leisureweek

Centaur Publishing Ltd, St Giles House, 50 Poland Street, London W1V 4AX
tel 020-7970 4000 *fax* 020-7970 4891
e-mail leisure-week@centaur.co.uk
Editor Michael Nutley
Weekly £2

News and features relating to the leisure industry. All material commissioned. Length: features from 800 words, news from 200 words. Illustrations: line, half-tone. Payment: by agreement. Founded 1989.

The Library

(published by Oxford University Press for the Bibliographical Society)
The Brotherton Library, University of Leeds, Leeds LS2 9JT
Editor Dr O.S. Pickering
Quarterly £88 p.a. (£33 p.a. to members)

Articles up to 15,000 words as well as shorter Notes, embodying original research on subjects connected with bibliography; reviews. Illustrations: line, half-tone. Payment: none. Founded 1889.

Life – see The Observer in National newspapers UK and Ireland, page 3

Life & Work: Magazine of the Church of Scotland

121 George Street, Edinburgh EH2 4YN
tel 0131-225 5722 *fax* 0131-240 2207
e-mail lifework@dial.pipex.com
Editor Rosemary Goring
Monthly 90p

Articles not exceeding 1200 words and news; poems and occasional stories. Study the magazine and contact editor first. Payment: up to £75 per 1000 words, or by arrangement. Illustrations: photos and line, cartoons.

Lincolnshire Life

PO Box 81, Lincoln LN1 1HD
tel (01522) 527127 *fax* (01522) 560035
e-mail editorial@lincolnshirelife.co.uk
web site http://www.lincolnshirelife.co.uk
Editor Judy Theobald
Monthly £1.60

Articles and news of county interest. Length: up to 1200 words. Illustrations: colour photos and line drawings. Payment: varies. Founded 1961.

The Linguist

The Institute of Linguists, Saxon House, 48 Southwark Street, London SE1 1UN
tel 020-7690 9665 *fax* 020-7607 6824
e-mail patricia.treasure@dial.pipex.com
web site http://www.frankdesign.co.uk/linguist
Editor Pat Treasure
Bi-monthly £5 (£25 p.a.)

Articles of interest to professional linguists in translating, interpreting and teaching fields. Articles usually contributed, but payment by arrangement. All contributors have special knowledge of the subjects with which they deal. Length: 1500-2000 words. Illustrations: line, half-tone.

The List

The List Ltd, 14 High Street, Edinburgh EH1 1TE
tel 0131-558 1191 *fax* 0131-557 8500
e-mail editor@list.co.uk
Editor Mark Fisher
Fortnightly £1.95

Events guide for Glasgow and Edinburgh covering film, theatre, music, clubs, books, city life, art, and TV and video. Considers unsolicited material and welcomes ideas. Length: 200 words (articles), 800 words and above (features). Illustrations: transparencies and colour prints. Payment: £20 (articles), from £60 (features); £25-£50. Founded 1985.

The Literary Review

44 Lexington Street, London W1R 3LH
tel 020-7437 9392 *fax* 020-7734 1844
Editor-in-Chief Auberon Waugh
Monthly £3 (£30 p.a.)

Reviews, articles of cultural interest, interviews, profiles, monthly poetry competitions. Material mostly commissioned. Length: articles and reviews 800-1500 words. Illustrations: line and b&w photos. Payment: £25 per article; none for illustrations. Founded 1979.

Live & Kicking Magazine – see page 301

Loaded

IPC Media, King's Reach Tower,
Stamford Street, London SE1 9LS
tel 020-7261 5000 *fax* 020-7261 5640
e-mail (features) tammy_butt@ipc.co.uk
(handbook) johnny_cigarette@ipc.co.uk
web site http://www.uploaded.com
Acting Editor John Perry
Monthly £2.80

Magazine for men aged 18-30. Music, sport, sex, humour, travel, fashion, hard news and popular culture. Address longer features (2000 words) to Features Editor, and shorter items to Handbook Editor. Payment: by arrangement. Founded 1994.

Local Government Chronicle

EMAP Business Publishing, 33-39 Bowling Green Lane, London EC1R 0DA
tel 020-7833 7311 *fax* 020-7837 2725
Editor Jake Arnold-Forster
Weekly £3.25

Articles relating to financial, political, legal and administrative work of the local government manager. Payment: by arrangement. Illustrations: half-tone, cartoons. Founded 1855.

The Local Historian

(formerly The Amateur Historian)
British Association for Local History,
25 Lower Street, Harnham, Salisbury,
Wilts. SP2 8EY
tel (01722) 332158 *fax* (01722) 413242
Editor Dr Margaret Bonney, 7 Carisbrooke Park, Knighton, Leicester LE2 3PQ
Reviews Editor Peter Christie, 30 Lime Grove, Bideford, North Devon EX39 3JL
web site http://www.balh.co.uk
Quarterly £6

Articles, popular in style but based on original historical research, covering methods of research, sources and background material helpful to regional, local and family historians – histories of particular places, people or incidents not wanted. Reviews of recently published books on local history (send to Reviews Editor). Length: maximum 7000 words. Illustrations: line and photos. Payment: none. Founded 1952.

The Log

The British Air Line Pilots Association, 81 New Road, Harlington, Hayes, Middlesex UB3 5BG
tel 020-8476 4000 *fax* 020-8476 4077
e-mail ginaalexander@balpa.org.uk
web site http://www.balpa.org.uk/
Chief Editor Capt. I.G. Frow
6 p.a. £14 p.a. (UK non-members), £22 (overseas non-members)

Journal of the British Air Line Pilots Association. Articles relating to aviation, travel, medical, news, etc. Length: 2000 words (articles), 1000 words (short stories). Illustrations: b&w photos, cartoons and sketches. Payment: £15 per article; £5-£25 (illustrations). Founded 1937.

LOGOS

5 Beechwood Drive, Marlow, Bucks. SL7 2DH
tel/fax (01628) 477577
Editor Gordon Graham
Quarterly £40 p.a. (£80 p.a. institutions)

In-depth articles on publishing, librarianship and bookselling with international or interdisciplinary appeal. Length: 3500-7000 words. Payment: 25 offprints/copy of issue. Founded 1990.

London Magazine: A Review of the Arts

30 Thurloe Place, London SW7 2HQ
tel 020-7589 0618
Editor Alan Ross, Deputy *Editor* Jane Rye
Bi-monthly £5.99 (£28.50 p.a.)

Poems, stories (2000-5000 words), literary memoirs, critical articles, features on art, photography, sport, theatre, cinema, music, architecture, events, reports from abroad, drawings. Sae necessary. Payment: by arrangement. Founded 1954.

London Review of Books

28 Little Russell Street,
London WC1A 2HN
tel 020-7209 1101 *fax* 020-7209 1102
e-mail edit@lrb.co.uk
Editor Mary-Kay Wilmers
Fortnightly £2.75

Features, essays, poems. Payment: by arrangement. Founded 1979.

Looks

EMAP Élan, Endeavour House,
189 Shaftesbury Avenue, London WC2H 8JG
tel 020-7437 9011 *fax* 020-7208 3586
Editor Margi Conklin
Monthly £1.80

Fashion, beauty and hair for 15-24 age range; features, especially with a celebrity bias. No unsolicited material, but ideas welcome. Length: up to 2000 words. Illustrations: colour, b&w. Payment: by arrangement.

MacUser

Dennis Publishing Ltd, 19 Bolsover Street,
London W1P 7HJ
tel 020-7917 7629 *fax* 020-7636 5668
e-mail edit@macuser.co.uk
web site http://www.macuser.co.uk
Editor Karen Harvey
Fortnightly £2.99

News, reviews, tutorials and features on Apple Macintosh computer products and topics of interest to their users. Commissioned reviews of products compatible with Mac computers required. Occasional requirement for features relating to Mac-based design and publishing and general computing and Internet issues. Ideas welcome. Length: 2500-5000 words (features), approx. 500 words (news), 300-2500 words (reviews). Illustrations: commissioned from Mac-based designers. Payment: £170 per 1000 words; competitive (artwork). Founded 1985.

Magpie

Odeon House, Eyre Square, Galway,
Republic of Ireland
tel 091-567600 *fax* 091-567635
e-mail info@magpie.ie
web site http://www.magpie.ie
Editor Declan Varley
Monthly IR£1.50

News, features and humour relating to the West of Ireland. Welcomes ideas for articles and features and regularly uses freelance material. Length: 800 words (articles and features). Payment: £80. Illustrations: colour. Founded 1998.

make: the magazine of women's art

(formerly Women's Art Magazine)
Women's Art Library, Fulham Palace,
Bishops Avenue, London SW6 6EA
tel/fax 020-7384 1110
e-mail womensart.lib@ukonline.co.uk
Editor Rebecca Gordon Nesbitt
Quarterly £3

International contemporary art, exhibitions and events, reviews, interviews. Profiles and critically considers the context of women's art practice. Contact editor for commissioning details.

Making Music

Nexus Media Ltd, Nexus House, Azalea Drive,
Swanley, Kent BR8 8HU
tel (01322) 660070 *fax* (01322) 616319
e-mail makingmusic@cerbernet.co.uk
web site http://cerbernet.co.uk/makingmusic/
Editor Paul Quinn
Monthly £18 p.a.

Technical, musicianly and instrumental features on rock, pop, blues, dance, world, jazz, soul; little classical. Length: 500-2500 words. Payment: £95 per 1000 words. Illustrations: colour, including cartoons and photos. Founded 1986.

Management Today

174 Hammersmith Road, London W6 7JP
tel 020-8267 4600 *fax* 020-7267 4966
Editor Rufus Olins
Monthly £40 p.a.

Company profiles and analysis – columns from 1000 words, features up to 3000 words. Payment: £300 per 1000 words. Illustrations: colour transparencies, always commissioned. Founded 1966.

Marie Claire

European Magazines Ltd, 2 Hatfields,
London SE1 9PG
tel 020-7261 5240 *fax* 020-7261 5277

e-mail marieclaire@ipc.co.uk
Editor Liz Jones
Monthly £2.60

Feature articles of interest to today's woman; plus fashion, beauty, health, food, drink and travel. Commissioned material only. Payment: by negotiation. Illustrated in colour. Founded 1988.

Market Newsletter

Bureau of Freelance Photographers,
Focus House, 497 Green Lanes,
London N13 4BP
tel 020-8882 3315/6 *fax* 020-8886 5174
Editor John Tracy
Monthly Private circulation

Current information on markets and editorial requirements of interest to writers and photographers. Founded 1965.

Marketing Week

St Giles House, 50 Poland Street, London W1V 4AX
tel 020-7970 4000 *fax* 020-7970 6721
web site http://www.marketing-week.co.uk/mw001
Editor Stuart Smith
Weekly £2.30

Aimed at marketing management. Accepts occasional features and analysis. Length: 1000-2000 words. Payment: £200 per 1000 words. Founded 1978.

Maxim

Dennis Publishing Ltd, 19 Bolsover Street,
London W1P 7HJ
tel 020-7631 1433 *fax* 020-7917 7663
e-mail editorial.maxim@dennis.co.uk
web site http://www.maxim-magazine.co.uk
Editor Tom Loxley
Monthly £2.80

Glossy men's lifestyle magazine with news, features and articles. All material is commissioned. Length: 1500-2500 words (features), 150-500 words (news). Illustrations: transparencies, colour and b&w cartoons. Payment: by negotiation. Founded 1995.

Mayfair

2 Archer Street, London W1V 8JJ
tel 020-7292 8000 *fax* 020-7734 5030
e-mail mayfair@pr-org.co.uk
Editor Steve Shields
Monthly £2.60

Glamour magazine. Unusual features: 'crazy, dangerous, sexy or just plain mad.' Only features accompanied by relevant illustrative material will be considered. Founded 1966.

Medal News

Token Publishing Ltd, 1 Orchard House, Duchy Road, Heathpark, Honiton, Devon EX14 1YT
tel (01404) 46972 *fax* (01404) 44788
e-mail info@medal-news.com
web site http://www.medal-news.com
Editor John Mussell
10 p.a. £2.85

Well-researched articles on military history with a bias towards medals. Length: up to 2000 words. Illustrations: b&w preferred. Payment: £20 per 1000 words; none for illustrations. Founded 1989.

Media Week

Quantum Publishing Ltd, Quantum House,
19 Scarbrook Road, Croydon CR9 1LX
tel 020-8565 4317 *fax* 020-8565 4394
e-mail mweeked@media.emap.co.uk
Editor Patrick Barrett
Weekly £1.85

News and analysis of UK advertising media industry. Illustrations: full colour and b&w. Founded 1985.

Melody Maker

IPC Magazines Ltd, King's Reach Tower,
Stamford Street, London SE1 9LS
tel 020-7261 6229 *fax* 020-7261 6706
Editor Mark Sutherland
Weekly £1.20

Technical, entertaining and informative articles on rock and pop music. Payment: by arrangement. Illustrations: line, halftone, colour.

Men Only

2 Archer Street, London W1V 8JJ
tel 020-7292 8000 *fax* 020-7734 5030
Publisher Paul Raymond, *Editor* Nevile Player
Monthly £2.60

High quality glamour photography; explicit sex stories (no erotic fiction); male interest features – sport, humour, entertainment, hedonism! Proposals welcome. Payment: by arrangement. Founded 1971.

Men's Health

Rodale Press Ltd, 7-10 Chandos Street,
London W1M 0AD
tel 020-7291 6000 *fax* 020-7291 6060
Editor Phil Hilton
10 p.a. £2.90

Active pursuits, grooming, fitness, fashion, sex, career and general men's interest issues. Length 1000-4000 words. Ideas on any subject welcome. No unsolicited MSS. Payment: by arrangement. Founded 1994.

Methodist Recorder

122 Golden Lane, London EC1Y 0TL
tel 020-7251 8414
e-mail editorial@methodistrecorder.co.uk
web site http://www.methodistrecorder.co.uk
Editor Moira Sleight
Weekly 52p

Methodist newspaper; ecumenically involved. Limited opportunities for freelance contributors. Preliminary letter advised. Founded 1861.

Military Modelling

Nexus Special Interests Ltd, Nexus House, Azalea Drive, Swanley, Kent BR8 8HU
tel (01322) 660070 *fax* (01322) 667633
Editor Ken Jones
Monthly £2.75

Articles on military modelling. Length: up to 2000 words. Payment: by arrangement. Illustrations: line, half-tone, colour.

Mind

Oxford University Press, Great Clarendon Street, Oxford OX2 6DP
tel (01865) 56767 *fax* (01865) 267773
web site http://www.oup.co.uk/jnls/list/mind
Editor Dr Michael Martin
Quarterly £9 (£30 p.a. UK/Europe, $56 p.a. rest of world; institution/student rates on application)

Review of philosophy intended for those who have studied and thought on this subject. Articles from about 5000 words; shorter discussion notes; critical notices and reviews. Payment: none. Founded 1876.

Minx

Emap Élan, Endeavour House, 189 Shaftesbury Avenue, London WC2H 8JG
tel 020-7208 3428 *fax* 020-7208 3323
e-mail [name]@ecm.emap.com
Editor Vanessa Thompson
Monthly £2.30

Magazine for stylish twenty-somethings with fashion and thought-provoking features. Outlines for readers' diaries and relevant first-person stories only can be sent on spec. Founded 1996.

Mizz

IPC Magazines Ltd, King's Reach Tower, Stamford Street, London SE1 9LS
tel 020-7261 6319 *fax* 020-7261 6032
e-mail mizz@ipc.co.uk
web site http://www.ipc.co.uk
Editor Lucie Tobin
Fortnightly £1.25

Articles on any subject of interest to teenage girls. Approach in writing. Payment: by arrangement. Illustrated. Founded 1985.

Mobile and Cellular Magazine

Nexus Media, Nexus House, Azalea Drive, Swanley, Kent BR8 8HU
tel (01322) 660070 *fax* (01322) 661257
Editor Peter Sayer
Monthly £38 p.a.

Aimed at radio communications professionals – technical features, company profiles and news analysis; cartoons. Length: features up to 1500 words, analysis up to 800 words. Payment: £150 per 1000 words. Ceased publication May 2000.

Model Boats

Nexus Special Interests Ltd, Nexus House, Azalea Drive, Swanley, Kent BR8 8HU
tel (01322) 660070 *fax* (01322) 667633
Editor John L. Cundell *tel* (01525) 382847
13 p.a. £2.30

Articles, drawings, plans, sketches of model boats. Payment: £25 per page; plans £100. Illustrations: line, half-tone. Founded 1964.

Model Engineer

Nexus Special Interests Ltd, Nexus House, Azalea Drive, Swanley, Kent BR8 8HU
tel (01322) 660070 *fax* (01322) 667633
Editor Mike Chrisp
2 p.m. £2

Detailed description of the construction of models, small workshop equipment, machine tools and small electrical and mechanical devices; articles on small power engineering, mechanics, electricity, workshop methods, clocks and experiments. Payment: up to £35 per page. Illustrations: line, half-tone, colour. Founded 1898.

Modern Believing

(formerly Modern Churchman)
The Lincoln Theological Institute for the Study of Religion in Society, University of Sheffield, 36 Wilkinson Street, Sheffield S10 2GB
Editor The Revd Canon Dr Martyn Percy
Quarterly £4

Covers 'liberal theology in the contemporary world'. Length: up to 3500 words. Intending contributors advised to write to the editor for a copy of instructions to authors. Founded 1911.

Modern Language Review

Modern Humanities Research Association, King's College, Strand, London WC2R 2LS
Quarterly £88 p.a. (£105.50 overseas, $211 USA)

Articles and reviews of a scholarly or specialist character on English, Romance,

Germanic and Slavonic languages and literatures. Payment: none, but offprints are given. Founded 1905.

Modern Painters

Fine Art Journals Ltd, Universal House,
251-255 Tottenham Court Road,
London W1P 9AD
tel 020-7580 5618 *fax* 020-7580 5615
Editor Karen Wright
Quarterly £4.95

Journal of modern fine arts and architecture – commissioned articles and features; also interviews. Length: 1000-2500 words. Payment: £120 per 1000 words. Illustrated. Founded 1986.

Modern Woman Nationwide

Meath Chronicle Ltd, Market Square, Navan,
Co. Meath, Republic of Ireland
tel (046) 21442 *fax* (046) 23565
Editor Margot Davis
Monthly IR50p

Articles and features on a wide range of subjects of interest to women over the age of 18 (e.g. politics, religion, health and sex). Length: 200-1000 words. Illustrations: colour and b&w photos, line drawings and cartoons. Payment: NUJ rates. Founded 1984.

Mojo

EMAP Metro, Mappin House, 4 Winsley Street,
London W1N 7AR
tel 020-7436 1515 *fax* 020-7312 8296
e-mail mojo@ecm.emap.com
web site http://www.mojomagazine.co.uk
Editor Paul Trynka
Monthly £3.10

Serious rock music magazine: interviews, news and reviews of books, live shows and albums. Length: up to 10,000 words. Illustrations: colour and b&w photos, colour caricatures. Payment: £180 per 1000 words; £150-£350 illustrations. Founded 1993.

MoneyMarketing

Centaur Communications Ltd, St Giles House,
50 Poland Street, London W1V 4AX
tel 020-7970 4000 *fax* 020-7970 4397
Editor Grant Ringshaw
Weekly £1.50

News, features, surveys and viewpoints; cartoons. Length: features from 900 words. Illustrations: b&w photos, colour and b&w line. Payment: £150 per 1000 words; colour line £200, b&w line £150. Founded 1985.

Moneywise

RD Publications Ltd, 11 Westferry Circus,
Canary Wharf, London E14 4HE
tel 020-7715 8465 *fax* 020-7715 8725
web site http://www.moneywise.co.uk
Editor Matthew Vincent
Monthly £2.95

Financial and consumer interest features, articles and news stories. Length: 1500-2000 words. Illustrations: willing to see designers, illustrators and photographers for fresh new ideas. Payment: by arrangement. Founded 1990.

The Month

114 Mount Street, London W1Y 6AH
tel 020-7491 7596 *fax* 020-7629 6936
e-mail themonth@dial.pipex.com
Editor Tim Noble SJ
Monthly £1.50

Review of Christian thought, and world affairs, with arts and literary sections, edited by the Jesuit Fathers. Preliminary letter desirable. Length: up to 2500 words. Payment: by arrangement. Illustrations: b&w photos. Founded 1864.

More!

EMAP Élan, Endeavour House, 189 Shaftesbury
Avenue, London WC2H 8JG
tel 020-7208 3165 *fax* 020-7208 3595
Editor Marina Gask
Fortnightly £1.35

Celebrities, fun and sexy features, 'how to' articles aimed at young women. Short erotic fiction. Study of magazine essential. Length: 900-1100 words. Payment: £150 per 1000 words. Illustrated. Founded 1988.

Mother & Baby

EMAP Esprit, Greater London House,
Hampstead Road, London NW1 7EJ
tel 020-7874 0200
web site http://www.motherandbaby.co.uk
Editor tba
Monthly £1.90

Features and practical information including pregnancy and birth and babycare advice. Expert attribution plus real-life stories. Length: 1000-1500 words. Payment: by negotiation. Illustrated. Founded 1956.

Motor Boat and Yachting

IPC Magazines Ltd, King's Reach Tower,
Stamford Street, London SE1 9LS
tel 020-7261 5333 *fax* 020-7261 5419
e-mail mby@ipc.co.uk
web site http://www.mby.com

Editor Alan Harper
Monthly £2.95
General interest as well as specialist motor boating material welcomed. Features up to 2000 words considered on all sea-going aspects. Payment: varies. Illustrations: photos (mostly colour and transparencies preferred). Founded 1904.

Motor Boats Monthly

IPC Magazines Ltd, King's Reach Tower, Stamford Street, London SE1 9LS
tel 020-7261 7256 *fax* 020-7261 7900
e-mail mbm@ipc.co.uk
web site http://www.motorboatsmonthly.co.uk
Editor Kim Hollamby
Monthly £2.90
News on motorboating in the UK and Europe, cruising features and anecdotal stories. Mostly commissioned – send synopsis to editor. Length: news up to 200 words, features up to 4000 words. Illustrations: colour transparencies. Payment: by arrangement. Founded 1987.

Motor Caravan Magazine

Link House Magazines Ltd, Link House, Dingwall Avenue, Croydon CR9 2TA
tel 020-8686 2599 *fax* 020-8781 6044
e-mail motorcaravan@lhm.co.uk
web site http://www.linkhouse.co.uk/motorcaravan
Editor Gary Martin
Monthly £2.50
Practical features, touring features (home and abroad). Length: up to 1500 words. Payment: £50 per page. Illustrations: line, half-tone, colour, cartoons. Founded 1985.

Motor Cycle News

EMAP Active Ltd, 20-22 Station Road, Kettering NN15 7HH
tel (01536) 411111 *fax* (01536) 411750
e-mail mcn@mcnl.demon.co.uk
web site http://www.erack.com/mcw
Editor Rob McDonnell
Weekly £1.15
Features (up to 1000 words), photos and news stories of interest to motorcyclists. Founded 1955.

Motorcaravan Motorhome Monthly (MMM)

PO Box 44, Totnes TQ9 5XB
Editor Mike Jago
Monthly £2.80
Articles including motorcaravan travel, owner reports and DIY. Length: up to 2500 words. Payment: by arrangement. Illustrations: line, half-tone, colour prints and transparencies. Founded 1966 as Motor Caravan and Camping.

Ms London

Independent Magazines, 7-9 Rathbone Street, London W1P 1AF
tel 020-7636 6651
Editor Cathy Howes
Weekly Free
Features and lifestyle pieces of interest to young professional working women with a contemporary London bias. All material commissioned. Length: 800-1400 words. Illustrations: no unsolicited illustrations; enquire first. Payment: by negotiation. Founded 1968.

Music and Letters

Editorial Dr Nigel Fortune, Dr Jeanice Brooks, Dr Katharine Ellis, Music Department, Royal Holloway, University of London, Egham, Surrey TW20 0EX
tel (01784) 443532
Other matters OUP (Journals Production), Great Clarendon Street, Oxford OX2 6DP
Quarterly £41 p.a. (personal rate)
Scholarly articles, up to 10,000 words, on musical subjects, neither merely topical nor purely descriptive. Technical, historical and research matter preferred. Illustrations: music quotations and plates. Payment: none. Founded 1920.

Music Teacher

Rhinegold Publishing Ltd, 241 Shaftesbury Avenue, London WC2H 8EH
tel 020-7333 1747 *fax* 020-7333 1769
e-mail music.teacher@rhinegold.co.uk
Editor Lucien Jenkins
Monthly £3.45
Information and articles for both school and private music teachers, including reviews of books, music, CD-Roms, videos and other music-education resources. Articles and illustrations must both have a teacher, as well as a musical, interest. Length: articles 1000-3000 words. Payment: by arrangement. Founded 1908.

Music Week

Miller Freeman Entertainment Ltd, 8 Montague Close, London SE1 9UR
tel 020-7620 3636 *fax* 020-7401 8035
Editor Selina Webb
Weekly £3.35 (£130 p.a.)
News and features on all aspects of producing, manufacturing, marketing and retailing music. Payment: by negotiation. Founded 1959.

Musical Opinion

2 Princes Road, St Leonards-on-Sea,
East Sussex TN37 6EL
tel (01424) 715167 *fax* (01424) 712214
Editor Denby Richards
Quarterly (plus supplements) £3.50 (£26 p.a.)

Suggestions for contributions of musical interest, scholastic, educational, anniversaries, ethnic, and also relating to the organ world. Record, video, CD-Rom, opera, festival, book, music reviews. All editorial matter must be commissioned. Payment: on publication. Illustrations: b&w photos, cartoons. Founded 1877.

Musical Times

63A Jamestown Road,
London NW1 7DB
Editor Nicholas Williams
4 p.a. For subscription rates *tel* (01442) 879097

Musical articles, reviews, 500-6000 words. All material commissioned; no unsolicited material. Illustrations: music. Founded 1844.

My Weekly

D.C. Thomson & Co. Ltd, 80 Kingsway East,
Dundee DD4 8SL
tel (01382) 223131 *fax* (01382) 452491
185 Fleet Street, London EC4A 2HS
tel 020-7400 1030 *fax* 020-7400 1089
Weekly 54p

Serials, from 30,000-80,000 words, suitable for family reading. Short complete stories of 1000-3500 words with humorous, romantic or strong emotional themes. Articles on TV stars and on all subjects of women's interest. Contributions should appeal to women everywhere. Payment: on acceptance. Illustrations: colour and b&w. Founded 1910.

My Weekly Puzzle Time

D.C. Thomson & Co. Ltd, Albert Square,
Dundee DD1 9QJ
tel (01382) 223131 *fax* (01382) 322214
Monthly £1.50

Broad range of puzzles appealing mainly to women. Entertainment value more important than intellectual. Payment: by arrangement. No illustrations. Founded 1993.

My Weekly Story Collection

D.C. Thomson & Co. Ltd, Albert Square,
Dundee DD1 9QJ
tel (01382) 223131 *fax* (01382) 322214
185 Fleet Street, London EC4A 2HS
tel 020-7400 1030 *fax* 020-7400 1089
4 p.m. 70p

35,000-37,500-word romantic stories aimed at the post-teenage market. Payment: by arrangement; competitive for the market. No illustrations.

The National Trust Magazine

The National Trust, 36 Queen Anne's Gate,
London SW1H 9AS
tel 020-7222 9251 *fax* 020-7222 5097
web site http://www.nationaltrust.org.uk
Editor Gaynor Aaltonene
3 p.a. Free to members

News and features on the conservation of historic houses, coasts and countryside in the UK. Length: 1000 words (features), 200 words (news). Illustrations: colour transparencies and artwork. Payment: by arrangement; picture library rates. Founded 1969.

Nationwide Magazine

BLA Group Ltd, Vinery Court, 50 Banner Street,
London EC1Y 8QE
tel 020-7577 9300 *fax* 020-7577 9344
Group Editor Alison Thomas
2 p.a. Free to customers

Home interest and financial articles for Nationwide customers. Founded 1994.

Natural World

River Publishing, Victory House,
14 Leicester Place, London WC2H 7QH
tel 020-7306 0304 *fax* 020-7306 0303
Editor Sarah-Jane Forder
3 p.a. Free to members

National magazine of The Wildlife Trusts. Short articles on UK nature conservation, particularly the work of Trusts; contributors normally have special knowledge of subjects on which they write. Length: up to 1200 words. Payment: by arrangement. Illustrations: line, colour. Founded 1981.

Naturalist

The University, Bradford BD7 1DP
tel (01274) 234212 *fax* (01274) 234231
e-mail m.r.d.seaward@bradford.ac.uk
Editor Prof M.R.D. Seaward MSc, PhD, DSc
Quarterly £20 p.a.

Original papers on all kinds of British natural history subjects, including various aspects of geology, archaeology and environmental science. Length: immaterial. Illustrations: photos and line drawings. Payment: none. Founded 1875.

Nature

Macmillan Magazines Ltd, Porters South,
4-6 Crinan Street, London N1 9XW

tel 020-7833 4000 *fax* 020-7843 4596
e-mail nature@nature.com
web site http://www.nature.com
Editor Philip Campbell
Weekly £5.45

Devoted to scientific matters and to their bearing upon public affairs. All contributors of articles have specialised knowledge of the subjects with which they deal. Illustrations: line, half-tone. Founded 1869.

Nautical Magazine

Brown, Son & Ferguson, Ltd, 4-10 Darnley Street, Glasgow G41 2SD
tel 0141-429 1234 *fax* 0141-420 1694
e-mail info@skipper.co.uk
web site http://www.skipper.co.uk
Editor L. Ingram-Brown MIMgt, MBIM, MRIN
Monthly £29.40 p.a. (£33 p.a. overseas)

Articles relating to nautical and shipping profession, from 1500-2000 words; also translations. Payment: by arrangement. No illustrations. Founded 1832.

Needlecraft

Future Publishing Ltd, 30 Monmouth Street, Bath BA1 2BW
tel (01225) 442244 *fax* (01225) 732398
e-mail debora.bradley@futurenet.co.uk
Editor Debora Bradley
4-weekly £2.99

Mainly project-based stitching designs with step-by-step instructions. Features with tight stitching focus (e.g. technique, personality). Length: 1000 words. Illustrated. Payment: £150-£200. Founded 1991.

.net The Internet Magazine

Future Publishing Ltd, Beaufort Court, 30 Monmouth Street, Bath BA1 2BW
tel (01225) 442244 *fax* (01225) 732291
e-mail netmag@futurenet.co.uk
web site http://www.netmag.co.uk
Editor Paul Douglas
Monthly CD edition £3.99 (non-CD edition £2.99)

Articles, features and news on the Internet. Length: 1000-3000 words. Payment: negotiable. Illustrations: colour. Founded 1994.

New Beacon

RNIB, 224 Great Portland Street, London W1N 6AA
tel 020-7388 1266
Editor Ann Lee
Monthly £2

Articles on all aspects of living with a visual impairment (blindness or partial sight). Published in clear print, braille, disk and tape editions. Length: from 500 words. Payment: by arrangement. Illustrations: half-tone. Founded 1930; as *Beacon* 1917.

New Buckinghamshire Countryside

Beaumonde Publications Ltd, 4 Mill Bridge, Hertford SG14 1PY
tel (01992) 553571 *fax* (01992) 587713
Editor Sandra Small (01462) 431237
Bi-monthly £1.25

Articles relating to Buckinghamshire. No poetry. Length: 1000 words. Illustrations: colour transparencies and b&w prints, artwork. Payment: £30 per article. Founded 1995.

New Electronics

Findlay Publications Ltd, Franks Hall, Franks Lane, Horton Kirby, Dartford, Kent DA4 9LL
tel (01322) 222222 *fax* (01322) 289577
e-mail ne@findlay.co.uk
web site http://www.neon.co.uk
Editor Graham Pitcher
Fortnightly (£88 p.a. UK, £165 p.a. airmail)

Technical/technology news articles, case studies, and career and skills development articles. Length: 1500 words (features), 800 words (news). Illustrations: colour photos, artwork and cartoons. Payment: £120 per 1000 words. Founded 1968.

New Humanist

Rationalist Press Association, Bradlaugh House, 47 Theobald's Road, London WC1X 8SP
tel 020-7430 1371 *fax* 020-7430 1271
e-mail jim.herrick@rationalist.org.uk
Editor Jim Herrick
Quarterly £2.50

Articles on current affairs, philosophy, science, literature and humanism. Length: 1000-3000 words. Illustrations: b&w photos. Payment: nominal; none for photos. Founded 1885.

New Impact

Anser House of Marlow, Courtyard Offices, 3 High Street, Marlow, Bucks. SL7 1AX
tel (01628) 481581 *fax* (01628) 475570
Managing Editor Elaine Sihera
Bi-monthly £42 p.a. (business), £32 p.a. (individual), £20 p.a. (faculties)

'Promoting enterprise, training and diversity.' Articles, features and news on any aspect of training, business and women's issues to suit a multicultural audience; also profiles of personalities, short stories. Length: 900-1000 words.

Illustrations: b&w photos if related to profiles. Payment: £40 (depending on merit); none for photos. Founded 1993.

New Internationalist

55 Rectory Road, Oxford OX4 1BW
tel (01865) 728181 *fax* (01865) 793152
e-mail ni@newint.org
web site http://www.newint.org
Editors Vanessa Baird, Chris Brazier, David Ransom, Nikki van der Gaag
Monthly £2.50 (£24.85 p.a.)

World issues, ranging from food to feminism to peace – examines one subject each month. Length: up to 2000 words. Illustrations: line, half-tone, colour, cartoons. Payment: £75 per 1000 words. Founded 1973.

New Law Journal

Butterworth & Co. (Publishers) Ltd, Halsbury House, 35 Chancery Lane, London WC2A 1EL
tel 020-7400 2579 *fax* 020-7400 2583
Editor-in-Chief James Morton, *Editor* Silvia Rice
48 p.a. £4.50

Articles and news on all aspects of the legal profession. Length: up to 1800 words. Payment: by arrangement. Founded 1965.

New Library World

MCB University Press, 60-62 Toller Lane, Bradford, West Yorkshire BD8 9BY
tel (01274) 777700 *fax* (01274) 785200
web site http://www.mcb.co.uk/nlw.htm
7 p.a. £1999 p.a.

Professional and bibliographical articles. Includes Librarians' World (6 p.a.), 16pp newsletter 'for librarians by librarians'. Payment: none. Founded 1898.

New Media Age

Centaur Newsletters, St Giles House, 50 Poland Street, London W1V 4AX
tel 020-7970 4000 *fax* 020-7970 4899
e-mail mikeb@centaur.co.uk
Editor Mike Butcher
Weekly £164 p.a.

News and articles on on-line advertising, marketing, publishing and e-commerce. Phone first with ideas; no uncommissioned material. Length: 1000-3000 (articles), 250 words (news). Payment: £180 per 1000 words. Founded 1995.

New Musical Express

IPC Magazines Ltd, 25th Floor, King's Reach Tower, Stamford Street, London SE1 9LS
tel 020-7261 5000 *fax* 020-7261 5185
Editor Ben Knowles
Weekly £1.15

Authoritative articles and news stories on the world's rock and movie personalities. Length: by arrangement. Preliminary letter or phone call desirable. Payment: by arrangement. Illustrations: action photos with strong news angle of recording personalities, cartoons.

New Scientist

RBI Ltd, 151 Wardour Street, London W1V 4BN
tel 020-8652 3500 *fax* 020-7331 2772
e-mail news@newscientist.com
web site http://www.newscientist.com
Editor Jeremy Webb
Weekly £2

Authoritative articles of topical importance on all aspects of science and technology (length: 1000-3000 words); preliminary letter or telephone call desirable. Short items from specialists also considered for Science, This Week, Forum and Technology. Intending contributors should study recent copies of the magazine. Payment: varies but average £300 per 1000 words. Illustrations: line, half-tone, colour, cartoons.

New Statesman

(formerly New Statesman & Society)
Victoria Station House, 191 Victoria Street, London SW1E 5NE
tel 020-7828 1232 *fax* 020-7828 1881
e-mail info@newstatesman.co.uk
Editor Peter Wilby
Weekly £2

Interested in news, reportage and analysis of current political and social issues at home and overseas, plus book reviews, general articles and coverage of the arts, environment and science seen from the perspective of the British Left but written in a stylish, witty and unpredictable way. Length: strictly according to the value of the piece. Illustrations: commissioned for specific articles, though artists' samples considered for future reference; occasional cartoons. Payment: by agreement. Founded 1913.

New Theatre Quarterly

Oldstairs, Kingsdown, Deal, Kent CT14 8ES
Editors Clive Barker, Simon Trussler
e-mail simon@country-setting.co.uk
Quarterly £15 (£32 p.a.)

Articles, interviews, documentation, reference material covering all aspects of live theatre. An informed, factual and serious approach essential. Preliminary discussion and synopsis desirable. Payment: by arrangement. Illustrations: line, half-tone. Founded 1985; as *Theatre Quarterly* 1971.

New Welsh Review

Chapter Arts Centre, Market Road, Cardiff CF5 1QE
tel/fax 029-2066 5529/2051 5014
e-mail robin@nwrc.demon.co.uk
Editor Robin Reeves
Quarterly £5.95 (£18 p.a., £34 2 yrs)

Literary – critical articles, short stories, poems, book reviews, interviews and profiles. Especially, but not exclusively, concerned with Welsh writing in English. Theatre in Wales section. Length: (articles) up to 4000 words. Illustrations: line, half-tone, cartoons; colour cover. Payment: £15-£35 per 1000 words (articles); £10-£25 per poem, £40-£70 per short story, £15-£35 per review, £10-£20 per illustration. Founded 1988.

New Woman

EMAP Élan, Endeavour House, 189 Shaftesbury Avenue, London WC2H 8JG
tel 020-7437 9011 *fax* 020-7208 3585
Editor Jo Elvin
Monthly £2.50

Features up to 2000 words. Occasionally accepts unsolicited articles; enclose sae for return. No fiction. Payment: at or above NUJ rates. Illustrated. Founded 1988.

New World

United Nations Association, 3 Whitehall Court, London SW1A 2EL
tel 020-7930 2931 *fax* 020-7930 5893
e-mail UNA_UK@compuserve.com
web site http://www.una-uk.org
4 p.a. £1

Review of UN activities, of UNA campaigns and of different viewpoints on major international issues confronting the United Nations. Occasionally takes cartoons. No payment.

The New Writer

(incorporating Acclaim and Quartos)
PO Box 60, Cranbrook, Kent TN17 2ZR
tel (01580) 212626 *fax* (01580) 212041
e-mail thenewwriter@hotmail.com
web site http://www.tnwriter.free-online.co.uk
Editor Suzanne Ruthven
Publisher Merric Davidson
10 p.a. £3.25

Features, short stories from guest writers and from subscribers, poems, news and reviews. Seeks forward-looking articles on all aspects of the written word that demonstrate the writer's grasp of contemporary writing and current editorial/publishing policies. Length: approx. 1000 words (articles), longer pieces considered; 1000-2000 words (features). Payment: £20 per 1000 words (articles), £10 (stories), £3 (poems). Founded 1996.

Night & Day – see Mail on Sunday in National newspapers UK and Ireland, page 3

19

IPC Magazines Ltd, King's Reach Tower, Stamford Street, London SE1 9LS
tel 020-7261 6410
Editor Samantha Warwick
Monthly £2.10

Glossy fashion and general interest magazine for young women aged 17-22, including beauty, celebrities and social features of strong contemporary interest. All illustrations commissioned. Payment: by arrangement. Founded 1968.

Numismatic Chronicle

Department of Coins and Medals, British Museum, London WC1B 3DG
Editor Richard Ashton
£24 per annual volume

Journal of the Royal Numismatic Society. Articles on coins and medals. Articles relating to coins and medals are unpaid, and contributions should reach a high academic standard. Founded 1839.

Nursery Projects

Scholastic Ltd, Villiers House, Clarendon Avenue, Leamington Spa, Warks. CV32 5PR
tel (01926) 887799 *fax* (01926) 883331
e-mail earlyyears@scholastic.co.uk
web site http://www.scholastic.co.uk
Editor Jane Morgan
Monthly £2.85

Practical theme-based activities for educators working with 3-5 year-olds. All ideas based on the Early Learning Goals. Material mostly commissioned. Length: 500-1000 words. Illustrations: colour and b&w; colour posters. Payment: by arrangement. Founded 1997.

Nursery World

Admiral House, 66-68 East Smithfield, London E1W 1BX
tel 020-7782 3120

e-mail pcreview@futurenet.co.uk
web site http://www.futurenet.co.uk
Editor Garrick Webster
Monthly £4.99

Features, previews, reviews of PC entertainment – commissioned only, by arrangement. Illustrations: colour transparencies; ideas for line art, diagrams, charts, etc. Payment: by negotiation.

PCS, The Magazine

Public and Commercial Services Union,
160 Falcon Road, London SW11 2LN
tel 020-7924 2727 *fax* 020-7924 1847
Editor Val Stansfield
10 p.a. Free to members

Well-written articles on civil service, trade union and general subjects considered. Length: 750-1400 words. Also photos and humorous drawings of interest to civil servants. Illustrations: line, half-tone. Payment: NUJ rates.

Peace News

5 Caledonian Road, London N1 9DX
tel 020-7278 3344 *fax* 020-7278 0444
e-mail peacenews@gn.apc.org
web site http://www.gn.apc.org/peacenews
Quarterly £2.50

Political articles based on nonviolence in every aspect of human life. Illustrations: line, half-tone. No payment. Founded 1936.

Peakland Walker

Magmaker Ltd, 33 Park Road, Bakewell,
Derbyshire DE45 1AX
tel/fax (01629) 812034
e-mail rolysmith@compuserve.com
web site http://www.owg.uk/rolysmith
Editor Roly Smith
Quarterly £2.50

Features with a walking bias and/or relating to countryside/rural issues connected with the Peak District. Length: 1200-2000 words. Illustrations: colour. Payment: £60 per 1000 words. Founded 1997.

Peninsular Magazine

Cherrybite Publications, Linden Cottage,
45 Burton Road, Little Neston,
Cheshire CH64 4AE
tel 0151-353 0967
e-mail helicon@globalnet.co.uk
Editor Shelagh Nugent
Quarterly £3.50

Literary magazine: essential to read a current issue before sending MSS. Regular competitions with prizes. Length: up to 4000 words. Payment: £5 per 1000 words. Founded 1996.

Pensions World

Butterworths Tolley, Tolley House,
2 Addiscombe Road, Croydon CR9 5AF
tel 020-8686 9141 *fax* 020-8760 0588
e-mail stephanie_hawthorne@tolley.co.uk
web site http://www.pensionsworld.co.uk
Editor Stephanie Hawthorne
Monthly £70 p.a.

Specialist articles on pensions, investment and law. No unsolicited articles; all material is commissioned. Length: 1500 words. Payment: by negotiation. Founded 1972.

People Management

Personnel Publications Ltd, 17 Britton Street,
London EC1M 5NQ
tel 020-7880 6200 *fax* 020-7336 7635
Editor Steve Crabb
Fortnightly £5 (£80 p.a.)

Journal of the Institute of Personnel and Development. News items and feature articles on recruitment and selection, training and development; pay and performance management; industrial psychology; employee relations; employment law; working practices and new practical ideas in personnel management in industry and commerce. Length: up to 2500 words. Payment: by arrangement. Illustrations: contact art editor.

People's Friend

D.C. Thomson & Co. Ltd, 80 Kingsway East,
Dundee DD4 8SL
tel (01382) 223131 *fax* (01382) 452491
185 Fleet Street, London EC4A 2HS
tel 020-7400 1030 *fax* 020-7400 1089
Weekly 54p

Illustrated weekly appealing to women of all ages and devoted to their personal and home interests, especially knitting, fashion and cookery. Serials (60,000-70,000 words) and complete stories (1500-3000 words) of strong romantic and emotional appeal. Stories for children are considered. No preliminary letter required. Illustrations: colour and b&w. Payment: on acceptance. Founded 1869.

People's Friend Story Collection

D.C. Thomson & Co. Ltd, 2 Albert Square,
Dundee DD1 9QJ
tel (01382) 223131*fax* (01382) 322214
185 Fleet Street, London EC4A 2HS
tel 020-7400 1030 *fax* 020-7400 1089
2 p.m. £1

50,000-55,000-word family and romantic stories aimed at 30+ age group. Payment: by arrangement. No illustrations.

Perfect Home

DMG Home Interest Magazines Ltd,
Equitable House, Lyon Road, Harrow,
Middlesex HA1 2EW
tel 020-8515 2000 *fax* 020-8515 2080
e-mail perfecthome@dmgexhib.co.uk
Editor Julia Smith
Monthly £1.80

Home-related features: readers' homes, craft, finance, DIY, show houses, product testing/reviews, gardening. Length: 800-1000 words. Payment: by merit. Illustrated. Founded 1992.

Period Living & Traditional Homes

EMAP Élan, Endeavour House,
189 Shaftesbury Avenue, London WC2H 8JG
tel 020-7437 9011 *fax* 020-7434 0656
Editor Gary Mason
Monthly £2.70

Articles and features on decoration, furnishings, renovation of period homes; gardens, crafts, decorating in a period style. Illustrated. Payment: varies, according to work required. Founded 1990.

Personal – see Sunday Mirror in National newspapers UK and Ireland, page 3

Personal Computer World

VNU House, 32-34 Broadwick Street,
London W1A 2HG
tel 020-7316 9000 *fax* 020-7316 9313
e-mail pcw@vnu.co.uk
web site http://www.pcw.co.uk
Editor Riyad Emeran
Monthly £2.99

Articles about computers; reviews. Length: 800-5000 words. Payment: from £150 per 1000 words. Illustrations: line, half-tone, colour. Founded 1978.

Personal Finance

Charterhouse Communications, Arnold House,
36-41 Holywell Lane, London EC2A 3SF
tel 020-7827 5454 *fax* 020-7827 0567
e-mail nik.rome@charterhouse-communications.co.uk
Editor Juliet Oxborrow
Monthly £2.60

Articles and features on savings and investment, general family finance, of interest both to new investors and financially aware readers. All material commissioned: submit ideas in writing to the editor in first instance. Illustrations: colour and b&w photos, colour line drawings. Payment: £190 per 1000 words; £90-£250 illustrations. Founded 1994.

Picture Postcard Monthly

15 Debdale Lane, Keyworth, Nottingham NG12 5HT
tel 0115-937 4079 *fax* 0115-937 6197
e-mail reflections@argonet.co.uk
web site http://www.postcard.co.uk.ppm
Editor Brian Lund
Monthly £1.95 (£22 p.a.)

Articles, news and features for collectors of old or modern picture postcards. Length: 500-2000 words. Illustrations: colour and b&w. Payment: £25 per 1000 words; 50p per print. Founded 1978.

Pig Farming

Wharfedale Road, Ipswich IP1 4LG
tel (01473) 241122 *fax* (01473) 240501
Editor Roger Abbott
Monthly £28 p.a.

Practical, well-illustrated articles on all aspects of pigmeat production required, particularly those dealing with new ideas in pig management, feeding, housing, health and hygiene, product innovation and marketing. Length: 800-1200 words. Payment: by arrangement. Illustrations: line, half-tone, colour.

Pilot

The Clock House, 28 Old Town, London SW4 0LB
tel 020-7498 2506 *fax* 020-7498 6920
e-mail pilotmagazine@compuserve.com
web site http://www.pilotweb.co.uk
Editor James Gilbert
Monthly £2.95

Feature articles on general aviation, private and business flying. Illustrations: line, half-tone, colour, cartoons. Payment: £100-£1000 per article on acceptance; £26 for each photo used. Founded 1968.

The Pink Paper

72 Holloway Road, London N7 8NZ
tel 020-7296 6000 *fax* 020-7957 0046
e-mail editorial @pinkpaper.co.uk
Editor Justin Webb
Weekly Free

National news magazine for lesbians and gay men. Features (500-1000 words) and news (100-500 words) plus lifestyle section (features 350-1000 words) on any gay-related subject. Illustrations: b&w photos and line plus colour 'scene' photos. Payment: £40-£90 for words; £30-£60 for illustrations. Founded 1987.

Planet

PO Box 44, Aberystwyth, Ceredigion SY23 3ZZ
tel (01970) 611255 *fax* (01970) 611197
Editor John Barnie
6 p.a. £2.75 (£13 p.a.)

Short stories, poems, topical articles on Welsh current affairs, politics, the environment and society. New literature in English. Length of articles: 1000-3500 words. Payment: £40 per 1000 words for prose; £25 minimum per poem. Illustrations: line, half-tone, cartoons. Founded 1970-9; relaunched 1985.

Playdays – see page 301

Plays & Players Applause

Northway House, 1379 High Road, London N20 9LP
tel 020-8343 9977 *fax* 020-8492 0439
Editor Sandra Rennie
Monthly £2.95

Articles, reviews and photos on world theatre. Payment: by arrangement. Illustrations: line, photos.

PN Review

(formerly Poetry Nation)
Carcanet Press Ltd, 4th Floor, Conavon Court, 12 Blackfriars Street, Manchester M3 5BQ
tel 0161-834 8730 *fax* 0161-832 0084
e-mail pnr@carcanet.u-net.com
web site http://www.carcanet.co.uk
Editor Michael Schmidt
6 p.a. £4.99 (£29.50 p.a.)

Poems, essays, reviews, translations. Submissions by post only. Payment: by arrangement. Founded 1973.

Poetry Ireland Review/Éigse Éireann

Bermingham Tower, Upper Yard, Dublin Castle, Dublin 2, Republic of Ireland
tel (01) 671 4632 *fax* (01) 671 4634
e-mail poetry@iol.ie
Managing Editor Theo Dorgan, *Editor* Biddy Jenkinson
Quarterly IR£5.99 (IR£24/$52 p.a.)

Poetry. Features and articles by arrangement. Payment: £10 per contribution or one year's subscription. Founded 1981.

Poetry London

1A Jewel Road, London E17 4QU
tel/fax 020-8521 0776
e-mail pdaniels@easynet.co.uk
Editors Pascale Petit, Peter Daniels, Scott Verner, Anna Robinson
3 p.a. £9.50 p.a.

Poems of the highest standard, articles/reviews on any aspect of modern poetry. Comprehensive listings of poetry events and resources. Contributors must be knowledgeable about contemporary poetry. Payment: £20 minimum. Founded 1988.

Poetry Nottingham International

71 Saxton Avenue, Heanor, Derbyshire DE75 7PZ
Editor Cathy Grindrod
Quarterly £2.75 (£10 p.a. UK, 17 p.a. overseas)

Poems; letters; articles up to 500 words on current issues in the poetry world. Payment: complimentary copy. Founded 1946.

Poetry Review

22 Betterton Street, London WC2H 9BU
tel 020-7420 9880 *fax* 020-7240 4818
e-mail poetrysoc@dial.pipex.com
web site http://www.poetrysoc.com/
Editor Peter Forbes
Quarterly £27 p.a. (£35 p.a. institutions, schools and libraries)

Poems, features and reviews; also cartoons. Send no more than 6 poems with sae. Preliminary study of magazine essential. Payment: £40 per poem.

Poetry Wales

1st Floor, 2 Wyndham Street, Bridgend CF31 1EF
Books for review Amy Wack, 20 Denton Road, Canton, Cardiff CF5 1PE
e-mail poetrywales@seren.force9.co.uk
Editor Robert Minhinnick
Quarterly £3 (£12 p.a. inc. postage)

Poems mainly in English and mainly by Welsh people or resident: other contributors (and Welsh language poetry) also published. Articles on Welsh literature in English and in Welsh, as well as on poetry from other countries. Special features; reviews on poetry and wider matters. Payment: by arrangement. Founded 1965.

Police Journal

Vathek Publishing, 5 Millennium Court, Derby Road, Douglas, Isle of Man IM2 3EW
tel (01624) 661857 *fax* (01624) 679915
e-mail mlw@vathek.com
Publisher Mairwen Lloyd-Williams
Quarterly £72 p.a.

Articles of technical or professional interest to the Police Service throughout the world. Payment: by negotiation. Illustrations: half-tone. Founded 1928.

Police Review

The Quadrangle, 1st Floor, 180 Wardour Street, London W1A 4YG

tel 020-7851 9701 *fax* 020-7287 4765
Editor Gary Mason
Weekly £1.50

News and features of interest to the police and legal professions. Length: 200-2000 words. Illustrations: colour and b&w photos, line, cartoons. Payment: NUJ rates. Founded 1893.

The Political Quarterly

Basil Blackwell Ltd, 108 Cowley Road, Oxford OX4 1JF
tel (01865) 791100
Editors Tony Wright MP, House of Commons, Westminster, London SW1A 0AA; *and* Andrew Gamble, Professor of Politics, University of Sheffield S10 2TU
Literary Editor Prof Donald Sassoon, History Dept, Queen Mary and Westfield College, Mile End Road, London E1 4NS
Assistant Editor Gillian Bromley, 1 Kings Head Court, New Street, Chipping Norton, Oxon OX7 5LP
5 p.a. (£93 p.a. institutions, £20 p.a. individuals)

Topical aspects of national and international politics and public administration; takes a progressive, but not a party, point of view. Send articles to Assistant Editor. Length: average 5000 words. Payment: about £100 per article. Founded 1930.

Pony Magazine

Haslemere House, Lower Street, Haslemere, Surrey GU27 2PE
tel (01428) 651551 *fax* (01428) 653888
Editor Janet Rising, *Assistant Editor* Sarah Lee
Monthly £1.65

Lively articles and short stories with a horsy theme aimed at young readers, 8 to 14 years old. Technical accuracy and young, fresh writing essential. Length: up to 800 words. Payment: by arrangement. Illustrations: drawings (commissioned), photos, cartoons. Founded 1949.

Popular Crafts

Nexus Special Interests Ltd, Nexus House, Azalea Drive, Swanley, Kent BR8 8HU
tel (01322) 660070 *fax* (01322) 616319
e-mail debbie.moss@nexusmedia.com
web site http://www.popularcrafts.com
Editor Debbie Moss
Monthly £2.50

Covers all kinds of crafts. Projects with full instructions, profiles and successes of craftspeople, news on craft group activities, readers' homes, celebrity interviews, general craft-related articles. Welcomes written outlines of ideas. Payment: by arrangement. Illustrated.

Post Magazine & Insurance Week

Timothy Benn Publishing Ltd, 39 Earlham Street, London WC2H 9LD
tel 020-7306 7000 *fax* 020-7306 7101
e-mail postmag@benn.co.uk
Editor-in-Chief David Worsfold
Weekly £2 (£99 p.a.)

Commissioned specialist articles on topics of interest to insurance professionals; news, especially from overseas stringers. Length: 1200-1500 words. Illustrations: colour photos and illustrations, colour and b&w cartoons and line drawings. Payment: £150-£200 per 1000 words; photos £30-£120, cartoons/line by negotiation. Founded 1840.

Poultry World

Quadrant House, The Quadrant, Sutton, Surrey SM2 5AS
tel 020-8652 4020 *fax* 020-8652 4042
e-mail poultry.world@rbi.co.uk
Editor John Farrant
Monthly £2.20

Articles on poultry breeding, production, marketing and packaging. News of international poultry interest. Payment: by arrangement. Illustrations: photos, line.

PR Week

Haymarket Marketing Publications, 174 Hammersmith Road, London W6 7JP
tel 020-8267 4520 *fax* 020-8267 4509
Editor Kate Nicholas
Weekly Controlled circulation; £1.85 (£72 p.a.)

News and features on public relations. Length: approx. 800-3000 words. Payment: £185 per 1000 words. Illustrations: colour and b&w. Founded 1984.

Practical Boat Owner

Westover House, West Quay Road, Poole, Dorset BH15 1JG
tel (01202) 440820
e-mail pbo@ipc.co.uk
web site http://www.ybw.com
Editor Rodger Witt
Monthly £2.90

Hints, tips and practical articles for cruising skippers – power and sail. Send synopsis first. Payment: by negotiation. Illustrations: photos or drawings. Founded 1967.

Practical Caravan

Haymarket Magazines Ltd, 60 Waldegrave Road, Teddington, Middlesex TW11 8LG
tel 020-8943 5629 *fax* 020-8943 5777
e-mail practicalcaravan@dial.pipex.com
Editor John Evans

Monthly £2.70

Caravan-related travelogues, human interest features, technical and DIY matters. Length: 1500-2500. Illustrations: Colour. Payment: £120 per 1000 words; negotiable. Founded 1967.

Practical Fishkeeping

(incorporating Fishkeeping Answers)
EMAP Apex, Apex House, Oundle Road, Peterborough PE2 9NP
tel (01733) 898100
Editor Steve Windsor
Monthly £2.50

Practical fishkeeping in tropical and coldwater aquaria and ponds. Heavy emphasis on inspiration and involvement. Good colour photography always needed, and used. No verse or humour, no personal biographical accounts of fishkeeping unless practical. Payment: by worth. Founded 1966.

Practical Householder

Nexus Media Ltd, Nexus House, Azalea Drive, Swanley, Kent BR8 8HU
tel (01322) 660070 *fax* (01322) 667633
Editor John McGowan
Monthly £2.15

Articles about 1500 words in length, about practical matters concerning home improvement. Payment: according to subject. Illustrations: line, half-tone. Founded 1955.

Practical Parenting

IPC Media, King's Reach Tower, Stamford Street, London SE1 9LS
tel 020-7261 5058 *fax* 020-7261 6542
Editor-in-Chief Jayne Marsden
Monthly £2.10

Articles on parenting, baby and childcare, health, psychology, education, children's activities, personal birth/parenting experiences. Send synopsis, with sae. Illustrations: commissioned only; colour: photos, line. Payment: by agreement. Founded 1987.

Practical Photography

EMAP Active Ltd, Apex House, Oundle Road, Peterborough PE2 9NP
tel (01733) 898100 *fax* (01733) 315984
e-mail practical.photography@ecm.emap.com
Editor William Cheung
Monthly £2.80

Features on any aspect of photography with practical bias. Mostly written by staff journalists, but freelance ideas welcome. Send brief synopsis only in first instance. Illustrations: line, half-tone, colour, cartoons. Payment: from £50 per 1000 words; from £10 b&w or colour. Founded 1959.

Practical Wireless

PW Publishing Ltd, Arrowsmith Court, Station Approach, Broadstone, Dorset BH18 8PW
tel (01202) 659910 *fax* (01202) 659950
e-mail rob@pwpublishing.ltd.uk
Editor Rob Mannion G3XFD
Monthly £2.50

Articles on the practical and theoretical aspects of amateur radio and communications. Constructional projects. Illustrations: in b&w and colour; photos, line drawings and wash half-tone for offset litho. Payment: by arrangement. Founded 1932.

Practical Woodworking

Nexus Special Interests Ltd, Nexus House, Azalea Drive, Swanley, Kent BR8 8HU
tel (01322) 660070 *fax* (01322) 667633
Editor Mark Chisholm
Monthly £2.60

Articles of a practical nature covering any aspect of woodworking, including woodworking projects, tools, joints or timber technology. Payment: £70 per published page. Illustrated.

The Practising Midwife

(formerly Modern Midwife)
Hochland & Hochland Ltd, The Precinct Centre, Oxford Road, Manchester M13 9QA
tel 0161-273 6811 *fax* 0161-273 4340
e-mail practimid@hochland.demon.co.uk
Editor Julia Magill-Cuerden
Monthly £35 p.a.

Disseminates research-based material to a wide professional audience. Research and review papers, viewpoints and news items pertaining to midwifery, maternity care, women's health and neonatal health with both a national and an international perspective. All articles submitted are anonymously reviewed by at least 2 external acknowledged experts. Length: 1000-2000 words (articles); 150-400 words (news); up to 1000 words (viewpoints). Illustrations: colour transparencies and artwork. Payment: by arrangement. Founded 1991.

The Practitioner

Miller Freeman UK Ltd, City Reach, 5 Greenwich View Place, Millharbour, London E14 9NN

tel 020-7861 6472 *fax* 020-7861 6259
e-mail gmatkin@unmf.com
Editor Harvey Jones
Monthly £11 (£71 p.a. UK, $168 p.a. overseas)

Articles of interest to GPs and vocational registrars, and others in the medical profession. Payment: approx. £200 per 1500 words. Founded 1868.

Prediction

Link House, Dingwall Avenue,
Croydon CR9 2TA
tel 020-8686 2599 *fax* 020-8781 6044
Editor Jo Logan
Monthly £2.10

Articles on astrology and all occult subjects. Length: up to 2000 words. Payment: by arrangement. Illustrations: for cover use only: large colour transparencies (i.e. not 35mm). Founded 1936.

Press Gazette

Quantum Publishing Ltd, Quantum House,
19 Scarbrook Road, Croydon CR9 1LX
tel 020-8565 4200 *fax* 020-8565 4295
Editor Philippa Kennedy
Weekly £1.90

News and features of interest to journalists and others working in the media. Length: 1200 words (features), 300 words (news). Payment: approx. £200 (features), news stories negotiable. Founded 1965.

Pride

Hamilton House, 55 Battersea Bridge Road,
London SW11 3AX
tel 020-7228 3110 *fax* 020-7228 3130
Managing Editor Dionne St Hill
Monthly £2.20

Lifestyle magazine incorporating fashion and beauty, travel, food and entertaining articles for the young woman of colour. Length: 1000-3000 words. Illustrations: colour photos and drawings. Payment: £100 per 1000 words. Founded 1993; relaunched 1997, 1998.

Priests & People

Blackfriars, 64 St Giles, Oxford OX1 3LY
tel (01865) 514845
Editor Rev. D.C. Sanders OP
Monthly £2.30

Journal of pastoral theology especially for parish ministers and for Christians of English-speaking countries. Illustrations: occasional b&w photos. Length and payment by arrangement.

Prima

Gruner + Jahr (UK), 197 Marsh Wall,
London E14 9SG
tel 020-7519 5500 *fax* 020-7519 5514
Editor Maire Fahey
Monthly £1.90

Articles on fashion, crafts, health and beauty, cookery; features. Illustrations: half-tone, colour. Founded 1986.

Print it! magazine

Paper Publications Ltd, Church House,
Church Lane, Kings Langley, Herts. WD4 8JP
tel (01923) 261555 *fax* (01923) 261118
e-mail printit-mag@paper-pub.co.uk
web site http://www.printit-mag.co.uk
Editor Margaret Curle
Bi-monthly £2.75

Practical features on the equipment, software and services needed by everyday computer users to produce better printed communications. Payment: £150 per 1000 words. Founded 1999.

Printing World

Miller Freeman UK Ltd, Miller Freeman House,
Sovereign Way, Tonbridge, Kent TN9 1RW
tel (01732) 364422 *fax* (01732) 377552
Editor Terry Ulrick
Weekly £2.75 (£90 p.a., overseas US$206 p.a.)

Commercial, technical, financial and labour news covering all aspects of the printing industry in the UK and abroad. Outside contributions. Payment: by arrangement. Illustrations: line, half-tone, colour, cartoons. Founded 1878.

Private Eye

6 Carlisle Street, London W1V 5RG
tel 020-7437 4017 *fax* 020-7437 0705
e-mail strobes @cix.compulink.co.uk
web site http://www.compulink.co.uk/~private-eye/
Editor Ian Hislop
Fortnightly £1.20

Satire. Payment: by arrangement. Illustrations: b&w, line, cartoons. Founded 1961.

Professional Nurse

EMAP Healthcare Ltd, Greater London House,
Hampstead Road, London NW1 7EJ
tel 020-7874 0384 *fax* 020-7874 0386
e-mail pn@healthcare.emap.co.uk
Editor Carolyn Scott
Monthly £36 p.a.

Clinical articles of interest to the professional nurse. Length: articles: 2000-3000 words; letters: 250-500 words. Payment: by arrangement. Illustrations: commissioned. Founded 1985.

Professional Photographer

Market Link Publishing Ltd, The Mill, Bearwalden Business Park, Wendens Ambo, Saffron Walden, Essex CB11 4GB
tel (01799) 544246 *fax* (01799) 544205
Editor Eileen Martin
Monthly £2.95

Articles on professional photography, including technical articles, photographer profiles and coverage of issues affecting the industry. Length: 1000-2000 words. Illustrations: colour and b&w prints and transparencies, diagrams if appropriate. Payment: from £90 per page for articles; pro rata for illustrations. Founded 1961.

Prospect

Prospect Publishing Ltd, 4 Bedford Square, London WC1B 3RA
tel 020-7255 1281 *fax* 020-7255 1279
e-mail editorial@prospect-magazine.co.uk
web site http://www.prospect-magazine.co.uk
Editor David Goodhart
Monthly £3.50

Politics and current affairs. Essays, features, special reports, reviews, short stories, opinions/analysis. Length: 3000-6000 words (essays, special reports, short stories), 1000 words (opinions). Illustrations: colour and b&w. Payment: by negotiation. Founded 1995.

Publishing News

39 Store Street, London WC1E 7DB
tel 020-7692 2900
web site http://www.publishingnews.co.uk
Editor Rodney Burbeck
Weekly £1.90

Articles and news items on the book publishing and bookselling industry. Payment: £120 per 1000 words. Founded 1979.

Pulse

Miller Freeman UK Ltd, City Reach, 5 Greenwich View Place, Millharbour, London E14 9NN
tel 020-7861 6483 *fax* 020-7861 6257
e-mail pulse@unmf.com
Editor Howard Griffiths
Weekly £122 p.a.

Articles and photos of direct interest to GPs. Purely clinical material can only be accepted from medically qualified authors. Length: up to 750 words. Payment: £150 average. Illustrations: b&w and colour photos. Founded 1959.

Punch

Liberty Publishing, 100 Brompton Road, London SW3 1ER
tel 020-7225 6716 *fax* 020-7225 6766
e-mail edit@punch.co.uk
Editor James Steen
Fortnightly £1.50

A satirical and investigative magazine with cartoons. Illustrations: colour and b&w. Payment: by arrangement. Founded 1841; relaunched 1996.

Q Magazine

EMAP Metro, Mappin House, 4 Winsley Street, London W1N 7AR
tel 020-7436 1515 *fax* 020-7312 8247
e-mail q@ecm.emap.com
web site http://www.qonline.co.uk
Editor Andy Pemberton
Monthly £2.80

Glossy modern guide to more than just rock music. All material commissioned. Length: 1200-2500 words. Illustrations: colour and b&w photos. Payment: £180 per 1000 words; illustrations by arrangement. Founded 1986.

Quaker Monthly

Quaker Home Service, Friends House, Euston Road, London NW1 2BJ
tel 020-7663 1018 *fax* 020-7663 1001
Editor Elizabeth Cave
Monthly 85p (£13.25 p.a.)

Articles, poems, reviews, expanding the Quaker approach to the spiritual life. Writers should be members or attenders of a Quaker meeting. Illustrations: line, half-tone. Payment: none. Founded 1921.

QWF

PO Box 1768, Rugby CV21 4ZA
tel (01788) 334302
e-mail qwfmagazine@hotmail.com
Editor Jo Good
Bi-monthly £3.95 (£23 p.a.)

Thought-provoking short stories by female writers (no traditional romances, domestic crises or mainstream fiction) and articles of general interest. Study magazine first. Length: up to 4000 words. Payment: £5 (articles), £10 (short stories). Annual short story competition (up to 5000 words) in any style or genre, on any theme; first prize: £200. Founded 1994.

RA Magazine

Royal Academy of Arts, Burlington House, Piccadilly, London W1V 0DS
tel 020-7300 5820 *fax* 020-7300 5881
Editor Nick Tite
Quarterly £4

Topical articles relating to the Royal

Academy, its history and its exhibitions. Length: 500-1500 words. Illustrations: consult editor. Payment: £100 per 1000 words; illustrations by negotiation. Founded 1983.

Racing Post

Trinity Mirror, Floor 23, One Canada Square, Canary Wharf, London E14 5AP
tel 020-7293 3291 *fax* 020-7293 3758
e-mail editor@racingpost.co.uk
web site http://www.racingpost.co.uk
Editor Alan Byrne
Mon-Fri £1 Sat £1.10

News on horseracing, greyhound racing and sports betting. Founded 1986.

Radio Control Models and Electronics

Nexus Special Interests Ltd, Nexus House, Azalea Drive, Swanley, Kent BR8 8HU
tel (01322) 660070 *fax* (01322) 667633
Editor Graham Ashby
Monthly £2.65

Well-illustrated articles on topics related to radio control. Payment: £35 per published page. Illustrations: line, half-tone. Founded 1960.

Radio Times

BBC Worldwide Ltd, 80 Wood Lane, London W12 0TT
tel (0870) 608 4455 *fax* 020-8433 3923
e-mail radio.times@bbc.co.uk
web site http://www.radiotimes.com
Editor Sue Robinson
Weekly 79p

Articles that preview the week's programmes on British TV and radio. All articles are specially commissioned – ideas and synopses are welcomed but not unsolicited MSS. Length: 600-2500 words. Payment: by arrangement. Illustrations: mostly in colour; photos, graphic designs or drawings.

Rail

EMAP Active Publications, Apex House, Oundle Road, Peterborough PE2 9NP
tel (01733) 898100 *fax* (01733) 466859
e-mail rail@ecm.emap.com
Managing Editor Nigel Harris
Fortnightly £2

News and in-depth features on current UK railway operations. Length: 2000-3000 words (features), 250-400 words (news). Illustrations: colour and b&w photos and artwork. Payment: £75 per 1000 words; £20 per photo except cover (£70) and Comment (£50). Founded 1981.

Railway Gazette International

Reed Business Information, Quadrant House, The Quadrant, Sutton, Surrey SM2 5AS
tel 020-8652 8608 *fax* 020-8652 3738
web site http://www.railwaygazette.com
Editor Murray Hughes
Monthly £64 p.a.

Deals with management, engineering, operation and finance of railways worldwide. Articles of practical interest on these subjects are considered and paid for if accepted. Illustrated articles, of 1000-3000 words, are preferred. A preliminary letter is required.

Railway Magazine

IPC Magazines Ltd, King's Reach Tower, Stamford Street, London SE1 9LS
tel 020-7261 5821 *fax* 020-7261 5269
Editor Nick Pigott
Monthly £2.80

Illustrated magazine dealing with all railway subjects; no fiction or verse. Articles from 1500-2000 words accompanied by photos. Preliminary letter desirable. Payment: by arrangement. Illustrations: colour transparencies, half-tone and line. Founded 1897.

The Rambler

The Ramblers' Association, 2nd Floor, Camelford House, 87-90 Albert Embankment, London SE1 7TW
tel 020-7339 8500 *fax* 020-7339 8501
e-mail ramblers@london.ramblers.org.uk
web site http://www.ramblers.org.uk
Editor Paul Rees
Quarterly Free to members

Magazine of The Ramblers' Association. Articles on walking, access to countryside and related issues. Material mostly commissioned. Length: about 1000 words. Illustrations: colour slides. Payment: by agreement. Founded 1935.

Reader's Digest

The Reader's Digest Association Ltd, 11 Westferry Circus, Canary Wharf, London E14 4HE
tel 020-7715 8000
e-mail excerpts@readersdigest.co.uk/r_feedback.htm
web site http://www.readersdigest.co.uk
Editor Russell Twisk
Monthly £2.25

Original anecdotes – £200 for up to 150 words – are required for humorous features. Booklet 'Writing for Reader's Digest' available £4.50 post free.

Real Money

Perspective Publishing, 408 The Fruit and Wool Exchange, Brushfield Street, London E1 6EP
tel 020-7426 0424 *fax* 020-7426 0042
e-mail real-money@newsdesk.globalnet.co.uk
web site http://www.real-money.co.uk
Editor Mark Frary
Monthly £2.50

Finance issues from a lifestyle angle aimed at 25-45 year-olds. Considers unsolicited material and welcomes ideas for features. Length: 500-2000 (articles and features). Illustrations: transparencies, colour prints and artwork, colour and b&w cartoons. Payment: by negotiation. Founded 1999.

Reality

Redemptorist Publications, Orwell Road, Rathgar, Dublin 6, Republic of Ireland
tel (01) 4922488 *fax* (01) 4922654
Editor Rev. Gerry Moloney CSSR
Monthly 85p

Illustrated magazine for Christian living. Articles on all aspects of modern life, including family, youth, religion, leisure. Illustrated articles, b&w photos only. Short stories. Length: 1000-1500 words. Payment: by arrangement; average £50 per 1000 words. Founded 1936.

Red

EMAP Élan, Endeavour House,
189 Shaftesbury Avenue, London WC2H 8JG
tel 020-7437 9011 *fax* 020-7208 3218
Editor Sally Brampton
Monthly £2.70

High-quality articles on topics of interest to women aged 35-45: humour, memoirs, interviews and well-researched investigative features. Approach with ideas in writing in first instance. Length: 2000-3000 words. Illustrations: transparencies. Payment: NUJ rates. Founded 1998.

Red Pepper

Socialist Newspaper (Publications) Ltd,
1A Waterlow Road, London N19 5NJ
e-mail redpepper@online.rednet.co.uk
web site http://www.redpepper.org.uk
Editor Hilary Wainwright
Monthly £1.95

Independent radical magazine: news and features on politics, culture and everyday life of interest to the left and greens. Material mostly commissioned. Length: news/news features 200-800 words, other features 800-2000 words. Illustrations: b&w photos, cartoons, graphics. Payment: for investigations, otherwise only exceptionally. Founded 1994.

Reform

(published by United Reformed Church)
86 Tavistock Place,
London WC1H 9RT
tel 020-7916 8630 *fax* 020-7916 2021 (fao 'Reform')
e-mail reform@urc.org.uk
Editor David Lawrence
Monthly £1.25 (£10 p.a.)

Articles of religious or social comment. Length: 600-1000 words. Illustrations: line, half-tone, colour, cartoons. Payment: by arrangement. Founded 1972.

Report

ATL, 7 Northumberland Street,
London WC2N 5DA
tel 020-7782 1517 *fax* 020-7925 0529
e-mail newsdesk@atl.org.uk
web site http://www.atl.org.uk
Editor Heather Pinnell
8 p.a. £2.50 (£10 p.a. UK; £12 p.a. overseas)

The magazine from the Association of Teachers and Lecturers (ATL). Features, articles, comment, news about nursery, primary, secondary and further education. Payment: minimum £120 per 1000 words.

Retail Week

EMAP Maclaren, Leon House, 233 High Street, Croydon, Surrey CR0 9XT
tel 020-8277 5331 *fax* 020-8277 5344
Acting Editor Neill Denny
Weekly Controlled circulation (£105 p.a.)

Features and news stories on all aspects of retail management. Length: up to 1000 words. Illustrations: colour photos. Payment: by arrangement. Founded 1988.

The Rialto

PO Box 309, Aylsham, Norwich NR11 6LN
Editor Michael Mackmin
3 p.a. £4.25 (£12 p.a., £8 p.a. low income)

Poetry and criticism. Sae essential. Payment: by arrangement. Founded 1984.

Ride

EMAP Active Ltd, Bushfield House,
Orton Centre, Peterborough PE2 5UW
tel (01733) 237111 *fax* (01733) 465804
Editor Tim Thompson
Monthly £2.80

Review features on tests of used motorbikes, services and related products. Length: 2000 words (features), 200 words (news). Illustrations: colour. Payment: £120 per 1000 words (features), £200 per 1000 words (news); £220 per day (photos). Founded 1995.

Right Start
Needmarsh Publishing Ltd, 71 Newcomen Street, London SE1 1YT
tel 020-7403 0840 *fax* 020-7378 6883
Editor Lynette Lowthian
Bi-monthly £1.95

Features on all aspects of pre-school and infant education, child health and behaviour. No unsolicited MSS. Length: 1200-1500 words. Illustrations: colour photos, line. Payment: varies. Founded 1989.

Rugby World
IPC Magazines Ltd, Kings Reach Tower, Stamford Street, London SE1 9LS
tel 020-7261 6830 *fax* 020-7261 5419
e-mail Paul_Morgan@ipc.co.uk
Editor Paul Morgan
Monthly £2.95

Features and exclusive news stories on rugby. Length: approx. 1200 words. Illustrations: colour photos, cartoons. Payment: £120. Founded 1960.

Runner's World
Rodale Press Ltd, 7-10 Chandos Street, London W1M 0AD
tel 020-7291 6000 *fax* 020-7291 6080
e-mail rwedit@rodale.co.uk
web site http://www.runnersworld.co.uk
Editor Steven Seaton
Monthly £2.90

Articles on jogging, running and fitness. Payment: by arrangement. Illustrations: line, half-tone, colour, cartoons. Founded 1979.

Running Fitness
EMAP Active Ltd, Bretton Court, Bretton, Peterborough PE3 8DZ
tel (01733) 264666 *fax* (01733) 267198
Editor Paul Larkins
Monthly £2.60

Practical articles on all aspects of running lifestyle, especially road running training and events, and advice on health, fitness and injury. Illustrations: colour photos, cartoons. Payment: by negotiation. Founded 1985.

RUSI Journal
Whitehall, London SW1A 2ET
tel 020-7930 5854 *fax* 020-7321 0943
e-mail journal@rusi.org
web site http://www.rusi.org
Contact Editorial Manager
Bi-monthly £7.50

Journal of the Royal United Services Institute for Defence Studies. Articles on international security, the military sciences, defence technology and procurement, and military history; also book reviews and correspondence. Length: 3000-3500 words. Illustrations: b&w photos, colour transparencies, maps and diagrams. Payment: £12.50 per printed page upon publication.

Safety Education
Royal Society for the Prevention of Accidents, Edgbaston Park, 353 Bristol Road, Birmingham B5 7ST
tel 0121-248 2000 *fax* 0121-248 2001
web site http://www.rospa.org.uk
Editor Carole Wale
3 p.a. £8.75 p.a. for members of Safety Education Department (£10.29 p.a. non-members)

Articles on every aspect of good practice in safety education including safety of teachers and pupils in school, and the teaching of road, home, water, leisure and personal safety by means of established subjects on the school curriculum. All ages. Commissioned material only. Illustrations: line, half-tone, colour. Payment: by negotiation. Founded as *Child Safety* 1937; became *Safety Training* 1940; 1966.

Saga Magazine
The Saga Building, Middelburg Square, Folkestone, Kent CT20 1AZ
tel (01303) 771523 *fax* (01303) 776699
Editor Paul Bach
Monthly £13.95 p.a.

Articles relevant to interests of 50-plus age group, and profiles of celebrities in same age group. Mostly commissioned or written in-house, but genuine exclusives always welcome. Length: 1200-1600 words. Illustrations: colour transparencies, commissioned colour artwork. Payment: competitive rate. Founded 1984.

Sainsbury's: The Magazine
New Crane Publishing, 20 Upper Ground, London SE1 9PD
tel 020-7633 0266 *fax* 020-7401 9423
Editor Michael Wynn Jones
Monthly £1

Features: general, food and drink, health and humour; all material commissioned. Length: from 1500 words. Illustrations: colour and b&w photos and line illustrations. Payment: varies; £300 per full page for illustrations. Founded 1993.

Satellite Times

Everpage Ltd, The Stables, West Hill Grange, North Road, Horsforth, Leeds LS18 5HG
tel 0113-258 5008 *fax* 0113-258 9745
Editor-in-Chief Juliet Cross
Monthly £2.20

TV and film personality articles and interviews, sports articles, music, competitions. Payment: from £120 per 1000 words. Founded 1988.

Scale Models International

Nexus Special Interests Ltd, PO Box 6018, Linslade, Leighton Buzzard LU7 7RS
tel/fax (01525) 850938
e-mail scalemodels@compuserve.com
Editor Kelvin Barber
Bi-monthly £2.50

Articles on scale models. Length: up to 2500 words. Payment: £25-£30 per page. Illustrations: line, half-tone, colour.

School Librarian

The School Library Association, Liden Library, Barrington Close, Liden, Swindon, Wilts. SN3 6HF
tel (01793) 617838 *fax* (01793) 537374
e-mail info@SLA.org.uk
web site http://www.rmplc.co.uk/eduweb/sites/mleech
Editor Raymond Astbury *tel* (01745) 730203
e-mail 101704.2701@compuserve.com
Acting Review Editor Chris Brown
SL2001 Editor Elspeth Scott
Quarterly Free to members (£45 p.a.)

The official journal of the School Library Association. Reviews of books, CD-Roms, web pages and other library resources from pre-school to young adult. Articles on school library organisation, use and skills, and on authors and illustrators. Length: 1800-3000 words. Payment: by arrangement. Founded 1937.

Science Progress

Science Reviews, 41-43 Green Lane, Northwood, Middlesex HA6 3AE
tel (01923) 823586 *fax* (01923) 825066
e-mail scilet@scilet.com
Editors Prof David Phillips, Prof Robin Rowbury
Quarterly £120 p.a. (£134 p.a. overseas)

Articles of 6000 words on new scientific developments, written so as to be intelligible to workers in other disciplines. Imperative to submit synopsis before full-length article. Payment: by arrangement. Illustrations: line, half-tone.

Scientific Computing World

Cambridge Publishers Ltd, 53-54 Sydney Street, Cambridge CB2 3HX
tel (01223) 477411 *fax* (01223) 327356
web site http://www.scientific-computing.com
Editor Dr Tom Wilkie
6 p.a. Free to qualifying subscribers

Features on hardware and software developments for the scientific community, plus news articles and reviews. Length: 800-2000 words. Illustrations: colour transparencies, photos, electronic graphics. Payment: by negotiation. Founded 1994.

Scotland on Sunday Magazine – see Scotland on Sunday in National newspapers UK and Ireland, page 3

The Scots Magazine

D.C. Thomson & Co. Ltd, 2 Albert Square, Dundee DD1 9QJ
tel (01382) 223131 *fax* (01382) 322214
e-mail scotsmagazine@dcthomson.co.uk
web site http://www.scotsmagazine.com
Monthly £1.25

Articles on all subjects of Scottish interest. Short stories, poetry, but must be Scottish. Illustrations: colour and b&w photos. Payment: £22 per 1000 words; from £12. Founded 1739.

Scottish Book Collector

c/o 36 Lauriston Place, Edinburgh EH3 9EZ
tel 0131-228 4837 *fax* 0131-228 3904
e-mail jennie@scotbooksmag.demon.co.uk
web site http://www.scotbooksmag.demon.co.uk
Editor Jennie Renton
Quarterly £2.50

Articles on collecting Scottish books; literary/bibliographical articles on books published in Scotland or by Scottish writers. Length: 1500-2500 words. Payment: £25 per article. Founded 1987.

Scottish Educational Journal

Educational Institute of Scotland, 46 Moray Place, Edinburgh EH3 6BH
tel 0131-225 6244 *fax* 0131-220 3151
web site http://www.eis.org.uk
Editor Simon Macaulay
6 p.a. plus Specials £15 p.a.

The Scottish Farmer

Caledonian Publishing Ltd, 6th Floor, 195 Albion Street, Glasgow G1 1QP
tel 0141-302 7700 *fax* 0141-302 7799
Editor Alasdair Fletcher

Weekly £1.35

Articles on agricultural subjects. Length: 1000-1500 words. Payment: £80 per 1000 words. Illustrations: line, half-tone, colour. Founded 1893.

Scottish Field

Special Publications, Royston House, Caroline Park, Edinburgh EH5 1QJ
tel 0131-551 2942 *fax* 0131-551 2938
e-mail editor@scottishfield.co.uk
Editor Archie Mackenzie
Monthly £2.90

Will consider all material with a Scottish link and good photos. Payment: by negotiation. Founded 1903.

Scottish Home and Country

42A Heriot Row, Edinburgh EH3 6ES
tel 0131-225 1724 *fax* 0131-225 8129
e-mail magazine@swri.demon.co.uk
Editor Airlie Fleming
Monthly 80p

Articles on crafts, cookery, travel, personal experience, DIY; humorous rural stories; fashion, health, books. Length: up to 1000 words, preferably illustrated. Illustrations: colour prints/transparencies, b&w, cartoons. Payment: by arrangement. Founded 1924.

Scottish Memories

Lang Syne Publishers Ltd, The Clydeway Centre, 45 Finnieston Street, Glasgow G3 8JU
tel 0141-204 3104 *fax* 0141-204 3101
e-mail http://www.argyll
web site internet.co.uk/scotmem
Editor George Forbes
Monthly £2.25

Features on any aspect of Scottish nostalgia or history, from primeval times to the 1990s. Contact editor with an outline in first instance. Length: 1000 words. Illustrations: colour and b&w. Payment: £70 per 1000 words; £20 per photo. Founded 1993.

Scouting

The Scout Association, Baden-Powell House, Queens Gate, London SW7 5JS
tel 020-7584 7030 *fax* 020-7590 5124
Editor Ron Crabb
Monthly £1.70

Magazine of the Scout Association. Ideas, news, views, features and programme resources for Leaders and Supporters. Training material, accounts of Scouting events and articles of general interest with Scouting connections. Illustrations: photos – action shots preferred rather than static posed shots for use with articles or as fillers or cover potential, cartoons. Payment: on publication by arrangement.

Screen International

EMAP Business Publishing, 33-39 Bowling Green Lane, London EC1R 0DA
tel 020-7505 8080 *fax* 020-7505 8117
e-mail ScreenInternational@compuserve.com
Managing Editor Denis Seguin
Weekly £2

International news and features on the international film business. No unsolicited material. Length: variable. Payment: by arrangement.

Scuba World

Freestyle Publications Ltd, Alexander House, Ling Road, Tower Park, Poole, Dorset BH12 4NZ
tel (01202) 735090 *fax* (01202) 733969
web site http://www.freepubs.co.uk
Editor Donna Vincent
Monthly £2.75

The official magazine of the Sub-Aqua Association. Articles, features, news and short stories related to diving. Unsolicited material welcome. Length: 1500-2000 words (articles/features); 200-1000 words (news); 800 words (short stories); 2000 words (interviews). Payment: negotiable. Founded 1990.

Sea Angler

EMAP Active Ltd, Bushfield House, Orton Centre, Peterborough PE2 5UW
tel (01733) 465791 *fax* (01733) 465658
Editor Mel Russ
Monthly £2.50

Topical articles on all aspects of sea-fishing around the British Isles. Payment: by arrangement. Illustrations: colour. Founded 1973.

Sea Breezes

Units 28-30, Spring Valley Industrial Estate, Braddan, Isle of Man IM2 2QS
tel (01624) 626018 *fax* (01624) 661655
Editor A.C. Douglas
Monthly £2.50

Factual articles on ships and the sea past and present, preferably illustrated. Length: up to 4000 words. Illustrations: line, half-tone, colour. Payment: by arrangement. Founded 1919.

Select Magazine

EMAP Metro, Mappin House, 4 Winsley Street, London W1N 5AR

tel 020-7436 1515 *fax* 020-7637 0456
Editor Andrew Harrison
Monthly £2.40

Off-the-wall youth/music feature ideas for hip 18-25-year-olds. Length: decided on commissioning. Illustrations: colour and b&w rock/pop photography with an arty/provocative bent. Payment: £120 per 1000 words; illustrations £110 per page. Founded 1990.

Sewing World

Traplet Publications Ltd, Traplet House, Severn Drive, Upton Upon Seven, Worcs. WR8 0JL
tel (01684) 594505 *fax* (01684) 594586
e-mail sw@traplet.co.uk
Editor Wendy Gardiner
Monthly £2.75

'Sewing magazine for sewing machine enthusiasts.' Articles and step-by-step projects. Length: 1000-1500 words (articles). Illustrations: colour. Payment: £100 per article including illustrations. Founded 1995.

She

National Magazine House, 72 Broadwick Street, London W1V 2BP
tel 020-7439 5000 *fax* 020-7312 3981
Editor Alison Pylkkanen
Monthly £2.50

No unsolicited MSS. Ideas with synopses welcome on subjects ranging from health and relationships to child care. Payment: NUJ freelance rates. Illustrations: photos, cartoons. Founded 1955.

Sherlock Holmes – The Detective Magazine

(formerly The Sherlock Holmes Gazette)
Overdale, 69 Greenhead Road, Huddersfield HD1 4ER
tel/fax (01484) 426957
e-mail overdale@btinternet.com
web site http://www.pmh.uk.com/sherlock.htm
Editor David Stuart Davies
6 p.a. £3.50

Articles relating to Sherlock Holmes and Conan Doyle, and crime fiction and writers. Also short stories. Length: 1600 words (articles), 7000-12,000 words (short stories). Illustrations: colour and b&w prints. Payment: £20-£25 (articles), short stories by negotiation. Founded 1991.

Shine

Attic Futura Ltd, 17-18 Berners Street, London W1P 3DD
tel 020-7664 6564 *fax* 020-7637 4645
Editor Lucy Bulmer
Monthly £2.50

Glossy health, beauty and lifestyle subjects aimed at women aged 25-34. Welcomes ideas for features. Length: 800-2000 words (features). Illustrations: transparencies, colour and b&w prints. Payment: £150-£450 (words). Founded 1999.

Ship & Boat International

Royal Institution of Naval Architects, 10 Upper Belgrave Street, London SW1X 8BQ
tel 020-7235 4622 *fax* 020-7245 6959
Editor Andy Smith
Monthly £55 p.a.

Technical articles on the design, construction and operation of all types of specialised small ships and workboats. Length: 500-1500 words. Payment: by arrangement. Illustrations: line and half-tone, photos and diagrams.

Ships Monthly

IPC Country & Leisure Media Ltd, 222 Branston Road, Burton-on-Trent, Staffs. DE14 3BT
tel (01283) 542721 *fax* (01283) 546436
Editor Iain Wakefield
Monthly £2.25

Illustrated articles of shipping interest – both mercantile and naval, preferably of 20th century ships. Well-researched, factual material only. No short stories or poetry. 'Notes for Contributors' available. Mainly commissioned material; preliminary letter essential, with sae. Payment: by arrangement. Illustrations: half-tone and line, colour transparencies and prints. Founded 1966.

Shoot

IPC Magazines Ltd, King's Reach Tower, Stamford Street, London SE1 9LS
tel 020-7261 6287 *fax* 020-7261 6019
Editor Colin Mitchell
Weekly 95p

Football magazine for young males. News, features, profiles of big names in football, posters. Length: 300-400 words (features), 100 words (news). Illustrations: colour transparencies, artwork and cartoons. Payment: negotiable. Founded 1969.

Shooting Times and Country Magazine

IPC Magazines Ltd, King's Reach Tower, Stamford Street, London SE1 9LS
tel 020-7261 6180 *fax* 020-7261 7179

Editor tba
Weekly £1.50
Articles on fieldsports, especially shooting, and on related natural history and countryside topics. Unsolicited MSS not encouraged. Length: up to 2000 words. Payment: by arrangement. Illustrations: photos, drawings, colour transparencies. Founded 1882.

The Short Wave Magazine

Arrowsmith Court, Station Approach, Broadstone, Dorset BH18 8PW
tel (01202) 659910 *fax* (01202) 659950
e-mail kevin@pwpublishing.ltd.uk
web site http://www.pwpublishing.ltd.uk
Editor Kevin Nice
Monthly £2.75 (£30 p.a.)
Technical and semi-technical articles, 500-5000 words, on design, construction and operation of radio receiving equipment. Radio-related photo features welcome. Payment: £55 per page. Illustrations: line, half-tone, colour. Founded 1937.

Shout

D.C. Thomson & Co. Ltd, Albert Square, Dundee DD1 9QJ
tel (01382) 223131 *fax* (01382) 200880
185 Fleet Street, London EC4A 2HS
tel 020-7400 1030 *fax* 020-7400 1089
Fortnightly £1.20
Colour gravure magazine for 12-16 year-old girls. Pop, film and 'soap' features and pin-ups; general features of teen interest; emotional features, fashion and beauty advice. Illustrations: colour transparencies. Payment: on acceptance. Founded 1993.

The Shropshire Magazine

77 Wyle Cop, Shrewsbury, Shropshire SY1 1UT
tel (01743) 361979 *fax* (01743) 362128
Editor Keith Parker
Monthly £1.50
Articles on topics related to Shropshire, including countryside, history, characters, legends, education, food; also home and garden features. Length: up to 1500 words. Illustrations: colour. Founded 1950.

Sight and Sound

British Film Institute, 21 Stephen Street, London W1P 2LN
tel 020-7255 1444 *fax* 020-7436 2327
Editor Nick James
Monthly £2.90
Topical and critical articles on the cinema of any country; book reviews; reviews of every film theatrically released in London; reviews of every video released; regular columns from the USA and Europe. Length: 1000-5000 words. Payment: by arrangement. Illustrations: relevant photos, cartoons. Founded 1932.

The Sign

G.J. Palmer & Sons Ltd, St Mary's Works, St Mary's Plain, Norwich, Norfolk NR3 3BH
tel (01603) 615995 *fax* (01603) 624483
Publisher G.A. Knights
Monthly 5p
Leading national insert for C of E parish magazines. Articles of interest to parishes. No poems. Items should bear the author's name and address; return postage essential. Length: up to 450 words, accompanied by photos/illustrations. Payment: by arrangement. Founded 1905.

Signal, Approaches to Children's Books

Lockwood, Station Road, South Woodchester, Stroud, Glos. GL5 5EQ
tel (01453 75) 5566/2208 *fax* (01453 87) 8599
Editor Nancy Chambers
3 p.a. £4.75 (£13.25 p.a.)
Articles on any aspect of children's books or the children's book world. Length: no limit but average 2500-3000 words. Payment: £3 per printed page. Illustrations: line occasionally. Founded 1970.

Ski and Board

The Ski Club of Great Britain, The White House, 57-63 Church Road, London SW19 5SB
tel 020-8410 2000 *fax* 020-8410 2001
e-mail s&b@skiclub.co.uk
web site http://www.skiclub.co.uk
Editor Gillian Williams
Monthly (Oct-Jan) £2.75
Articles, features, news, true life stories, ski tips, equipment reviews, resort reports – all in connection with skiing. Welcomes ideas for articles and features. Length: 600-2000 words. Illustrations: colour transparencies, colour and b&w artwork and cartoons. Payment: £200 per 1000 words; £100-£200 per photo/illustration. Founded 1903.

The Skier and The Snowboarder Magazine

Mountain Marketing Ltd, 1st Floor, Squires House, 205 High Street, West Wickham, Kent BR4 0PH
tel 020-8777 4426 *fax* 020-8777 8789

e-mail skierandsnowboarder@hotmail.com
Editor Frank Baldwin
5 p.a. (July-May) £2.75

Ski features, based around a good story. Length: 800-1000 words. Illustrations: colour action ski photos. Payment: by negotiation. Founded 1984.

Sky Magazine

EMAP Men's Media, Mappin House, 4 Winsley Street, London W1N 7AR
tel 020-7436 1515 *fax* 020-7312 8248
e-mail sky@ecm.emap.com
web site http://www.skymag.co.uk
Editor Michael Hogan
Monthly £2.70

People, movies, music and style. Length: varies. Illustrations: colour and b&w photos. Payment: by arrangement.

Slimmer Magazine

Aceville Publications Ltd, Castle House, 97 High Street, Colchester CO1 1TH
tel (01206) 564782 *fax* (01206) 564214
e-mail aceville@globalnet.co.uk
Editor Helen Tudor
Bi-monthly £1.95

Features on health, nutrition, slimming. Personal weight loss stories. Sae essential. Length: 600 or 1200 words. Payment: by arrangement. Founded 1972.

Slimming Magazine

EMAP Esprit, Greater London House, Hampstead Road, London NW1 7EJ
tel 020-7347 1854 *fax* 020-7347 1863
Editor Juliette Kellow
11 p.a. £1.85

Articles on psychology, lifestyle and health related to diet and nutrition. Approach editor in writing with ideas. Length: 1000-1500 words. Payment: by negotiation. Founded 1969.

Smallholder

Hook House, Hook Road, Wimblington, March, Cambs. PE15 0QL
tel/fax (01354) 741182
e-mail edit@smallholder.co.uk
web site http://www.smallholder.co.uk
Editor Liz Wright
Monthly £2

Articles of relevance to small farmers about livestock and crops, organics, conservation, poultry, equipment. Items relating to the countryside considered. Send for copy. Payment: £20 per 1000 words or by arrangement. Illustrations: line, half-tone, cartoons. Founded 1985.

Smash Hits

EMAP Metro, Mappin House, 4 Winsley Street, London W1N 7AR
tel 020-7436 1515 *fax* 020-7636 5792
Editor John McKie
Fortnightly £1.45

News interviews and posters of pop, TV and film stars. Illustrations: colour photos. Payment: £100 per page and per photo.

Snooker Scene

Cavalier House, 202 Hagley Road, Edgbaston, Birmingham B16 9PQ
tel 0121-454 2931 *fax* 0121-452 1822
Editor Clive Everton
Monthly £2 (£18 p.a.)

News and articles about snooker and billiards. Payment: by arrangement. Illustrations: photos. Founded 1971.

Snoop

Snoop Publications Ltd, 5A High Street, Southall, Middlesex UB1 3HA
tel 020-8571 7700 *fax* 020-8571 6006
e-mail editor@snoop.co.uk
web site http://www.snooplife.com
Editor Raj Kaushal
Monthly £1.50

Entertainment and lifestyle magazine for second and third generation UK Asians (16-35 year-olds): interviews, music, films, fashion, gossip and gigs. Features and articles by arrangement. Founded 1997.

Solicitors Journal

Sweet & Maxwell, 100 Avenue Road, London NW3 3PF
tel 020-7393 7000 *fax* 020-7393 7880
e-mail solicitorsjournal@sweetandmaxwell.co.uk
Weekly £149 for 48 issues

Articles, by practising lawyers or specialist journalists, on subjects of practical interest to solicitors. Articles on spec should be sent on disk or by e-mail. Length: up to 1800 words. Payment: by negotiation. Founded 1856.

Somerset Magazine

Smart Print Publications Ltd, 23 Market Street, Crewkerne, Somerset TA18 7JU
tel (01460) 270011 *fax* (01460) 270022
Editor Roy Smart
Monthly £2.25

Articles, features with particular reference to Somerset locations, facilities and other interests. Length: 1000-1500 words. Illustrations: half-tone, colour. Payment: by arrangement. Founded 1977 as Somerset & West.

The Songwriter

International Songwriters Association,
PO Box 46, Limerick City, Republic of Ireland
tel (061) 228837
Editor James D. Liddane
Monthly Available to members only

Articles on songwriting and interviews with music publishers and recording company executives. Length: 400-5000 words. Payment: from £100 per page and by arrangement. Illustrations: photos. Founded 1967.

Songwriting and Composing

Sovereign House, 12 Trewartha Road,
Praa Sands, Penzance, Cornwall TR20 9ST
tel (01736) 762826 *fax* (01736) 763328
e-mail songmag@aol.com
web site http://www.songwriters-guild.co.uk
General Secretary Carole Jones
Quarterly Free to members

Magazine of the Guild of International Songwriters and Composers. Short stories, articles, letters relating to songwriting, publishing, recording and the music industry. Payment: negotiable upon content £25-£60. Illustrations: line, half-tone. Founded 1986.

Speaking English

English Speaking Board (International),
26A Princes Street, Southport, Merseyside PR8 1EQ
tel (01704) 501730 *fax* (01704) 539637
e-mail admin@esbuk.demon.co.uk
web site http://www.esbuk.demon.co.uk
Editor Susan Karaska
£20 p.a. (ESB membership inc. 2 issues)

Serious articles (1000-plus words) on spoken English, communication ventures and training, poetry, drama, and English-teaching from primary to university levels, in Britain and overseas. Payment: by arrangement. Founded 1968.

The Spectator

56 Doughty Street, London WC1N 2LL
tel 020-7405 1706 *fax* 020-7242-0603
Editor Boris Johnson
Weekly £2.20

Articles on current affairs, politics, the arts; book reviews. Illustrations: colour and b&w, cartoons. Payment: on merit. Founded 1828.

Speech and Drama

4 Fane Road, Old Marston, Oxford OX3 0SA
tel (01865) 728304
web site http://www.stsd.org.uk
Editor Dr Paul Ranger
2 p.a. £7 p.a. (£12.50 overseas)

Journal of the Society of Teachers of Speech and Drama. Covers theatre, drama and all levels of education relating to speech and drama; specialist articles only; preliminary abstract of 300 words; photos welcome. Length: 1500-2000 words. Payment: none. Founded 1951.

Sport First

20-26 Brunswick Place, London N1 6DZ
tel 020-7490 7575 *fax* 020-7490 7666
e-mail editorial@sportfirst.com
web site http://www.sportfirst.com
Editor Chris Mann
Weekly 60p

Tabloid Sunday newspaper covering all sports. Length: 800 words (articles), 300-800 words (news). No unsolicited contributions. Payment: £150 per 1000 words. Founded 1998.

Springboard

30 Orange Hill Road, Prestwich,
Manchester M25 1LS
tel 0161-7735911
e-mail leobrooks@rammy.com
Editor Leo Brooks
Quarterly £8 p.a.

Articles on writing, competition news, markets. Winning articles, stories and poems from internal competitions – £45 prize money each quarter. Includes copy of *The Curate's Egg*, poetry submissions for which contributors receive free copy. Founded 1990.

The Squash Player

460 Bath Road, Longford, Middlesex UB7 0EB
tel (01753) 775511 *fax* (01753) 775512
e-mail editor@squashplayer.co.uk
Editor Ian McKenzie
10 p.a. £39.95 p.a.

Covers all aspects of playing squash. All features are commissioned – discuss ideas with editor. Length: 1000-1500 words. Illustrations: unusual photos (e.g. celebrities), cartoons. Payment: £75 per 1000 words; £25-£40 for illustrations. Founded 1971.

Staffordshire Life Magazine

Staffordshire Newsletter Ltd, The Publishing Centre, Derby Street, Stafford ST16 2DT
tel (01785) 257700 *fax* (01785) 253287
e-mail editor@staffordshirelife.co.uk
Editor Philip Thurlow-Craig
10 p.a. £1.50

County magazine for Staffordshire. Historical articles; features on county personalities. No short stories. Contact the editor in first instance. Length: 500-800 words. Illustrations: colour transparencies and prints. Founded 1948; relaunched 1980.

The Stage

(incorporating Television Today)
Stage House, 47 Bermondsey Street, London SE1 3XT
tel 020-7403 1818 *fax* 020-7357 9287
Editor Brian Attwood
Weekly 90p

Original and interesting articles on professional stage and broadcasting topics may be sent for the editor's consideration. Length: 500-800 words. Payment: £100 per 1000 words. Founded 1880.

Stamp Lover

National Philatelic Society, British Philatelic Centre, 107 Charterhouse Street, London EC1M 6PT
tel 020-7336 0882
Editor Michael Furnell
6 p.a. £2

Original articles on stamps and postal history. Illustrations: line, half-tone. Payment: by arrangement. Founded 1908.

Stamp Magazine

IPC Focus Network, 9 Dingwall Avenue, Croydon CR9 2TA
tel 020-8686 2599 *fax* 020-8781 6044
Editor Steve Fairclough
Monthly £2.40

Informative articles and exclusive news items on stamp collecting and postal history. No preliminary letter. Payment: by arrangement. Illustrations: line, half-tone, colour. Founded 1934.

Stand Magazine

School of English, University of Leeds, Leeds LS2 9JT
tel 0113-233 4794 *fax* 0113-233 4791
Editors Michael Hulse, John Kinsella
Quarterly £6.50 plus p&p (£25 p.a.)

Poetry, short stories, translations, literary criticism. Send sae/IRCs for return. Annual Short Story Competition for unpublished original short story in English (see page 536) and annual Poetry Competition. Payment: £75 per 1000 words of prose; £40 per poem. Founded 1952.

Staple New Writing

Padley Rise, Nether Padley, Grindleford, Hope Valley, Derbyshire S32 2HE
tel (01433) 631949
Editors Ann Atkinson, Elizabeth Barrett
3 p.a. £10 p.a.

Poetry and short stories. Payment: under review. Founded 1982.

Starburst

Visual Imagination Ltd, 9 Blades Court, Deodar Road, London SW15 2NU
tel 020-8875 1520 *fax* 020-8875 1588
e-mail starburst@vismag.com
web site http://www.wisimag.com
Editor Andrew Cartmel
Monthly plus 4 specials p.a. £3.25

Features and interviews on all aspects of science fiction. Length: 2000 words. Illustrations: colour and b&w photos. Payment: £80 per 1000 words; £10-20 per image. Founded 1977.

Studies, An Irish quarterly review

35 Lower Leeson Street, Dublin 2, Republic of Ireland
tel (01) 6766785 *fax* (01) 6762984
e-mail studies@s-j.ie
web site http://www.studiesirishreview.com
Editor Rev. Noel Barber SJ
Quarterly IR£4

General review of social comment, literature, history, the arts. Articles written by specialists for the general reader. Critical book reviews. Preliminary letter. Length: 3500 words. Founded 1912.

Studio Sound

Miller Freeman Entertainment Ltd, 8 Montague Close, London SE1 9UR
tel 020-7940 8500 *fax* 020-7407 7102
Editor Tim Goodyer
Monthly £5

Articles on all aspects of professional sound recording. Technical and operational features on the functional aspects of sound recording, AV postproduction and broadcast; general features on studio affairs. Length: widely variable. Payment: by arrangement. Illustrations: line, half-tone, colour. Founded 1959.

Success Now

(formerly Personal Success)
Sphinx Inc. Ltd, Compass House, 30-36 East Street, Bromley, Kent BR1 1QU
tel 020-8402 5252 *fax* 020-8402 5353
e-mail colin@successnow.co.uk
web site http://www.successnow.co.uk
Editor Colin C. Edwards

Quarterly £2.95

Positive and inspirational articles on business and human development; features on success stories of entrepreneurs, famous people, business trailblazers and motivated individuals. Length: 2500 words (features), 450 words (news). Illustrations: colour photos, artwork. Payment: rates on application. Founded 1993.

Suffolk Norfolk Life

Today Magazines Ltd, Barn Acre House, Saxtead Green, Woodbridge, Suffolk IP13 9QJ
tel (01728) 685 832 *fax* (01728) 685 842
e-mail todaymagazines@lineone.net
web site http://www.today-magazines.com
Editor William Locks
Monthly £1.25

Articles relevant to Suffolk and Norfolk – current topics plus historical items, art, leisure, etc. Considers unsolicited material and welcomes ideas for articles and features. Length: 900-1000 words. Illustrations: transparencies, colour and b&w prints, b&w artwork and cartoons. Payment: £25-£30 per article. Founded 1989.

Sugar

Attic Futura (UK) Ltd, 17-18 Berners Street, London W1P 3DD
tel 020-7664 6400 *fax* 020-7636 5055
Editor Jennifer Stringer
Monthly £1.90

Magazine for young women aged 13-17. Fashion, beauty, entertainment, features. Interested in real-life stories (1200 words), quizzes. Payment: by arrangement. Opportunities for freelance writers, illustrators and designers. Founded 1994.

Sunday Express Magazine – **see Sunday Express in National newspapers UK and Ireland, page 3**

Sunday Magazine – **see News of the World in National newspapers UK and Ireland, page 3**

Sunday People Magazine – **see Sunday People in National newspapers UK and Ireland, page 3**

The Sunday Post Magazine – **see Sunday Post in National newspapers UK and Ireland, page 3**

The Sunday Review – **see Independent on Sunday in National newspapers UK and Ireland, page 3**

Sunday Telegraph Magazine – **see Sunday Telegraph in National newspapers UK and Ireland, page 3**

The Sunday Times Magazine – **see The Sunday Times in National newspapers UK and Ireland, page 3**

Swimming Times

Swimming Times Ltd, 41 Granby Street, Loughborough LE11 3DU
tel (01509) 632207 *fax* (01509) 632213
Editor Peter Hassall
Monthly £1.70

Official journal of the Amateur Swimming Association and the Institute of Swimming Teachers and Coaches. Reports of major events and championships; news and features on all aspects of swimming including synchronised swimming, diving and water polo, etc; accompanying photos where appropriate; short fiction with a swimming theme. Unsolicited material welcome. Length: 800-1500 words. Payment: by arrangement. Founded 1923.

The Tablet

1 King Street Cloisters, Clifton Walk, London W6 0QZ
tel 020-8748 8484 *fax* 020-8748 1550
e-mail thetablet@thetablet.co.uk
web site http://www.thetablet.co.uk/
Editor John Wilkins
Weekly £1.45

The senior Catholic weekly. Religion, philosophy, politics, society, books and arts. International coverage. Freelance work welcomed. Length: 1500 words. Illustrations: cartoons. Payment: by arrangement. Founded 1840.

Take a Break

H. Bauer Publishing Ltd, 25-27 Camden Road, London NW1 9LL
tel 020-7241 8000 *fax* 020-7241 8052
Editor John Dale
Weekly 64p

Lively, tabloid women's weekly. True life features, celebrities, health and beauty, family, travel; short stories (up to 1500 words); lots of puzzles. Payment: by arrangement. Illustrated. Founded 1990.

Take a Break's Take a Puzzle

H. Bauer Publishing, 1st Floor, 1-5 Maple Place, London W1P 5FX
tel 020-7462 4745 *fax* 020-7462 4762
e-mail take.puzzle@bauer.co.uk
Editor Douglas Carter
Monthly £1.50

Puzzles. Fresh ideas always welcome. Illustrations: colour transparencies and b&w prints and artwork. Work supplied on Mac-compatible disk preferred. Payment: from £25 per puzzle, £30-£90 for picture puzzles and for illustrations not an integral part of a puzzle. Founded 1991.

tate: the art magazine

Spafax Publishing, Avon House, Kensington Village, Avonmore Road, London W14 8TS
tel 020-7906 2002 *fax* 020-7906 2004
e-mail tmarlow@aspenplc.co.uk
Editor Tim Marlow
3 p.a. £3.50

Independent visual arts magazine: features, news, interviews, reviews, previews and opinion pieces. Length: up to 5000 words but usually commissioned. Illustrations: colour and b&w photos. Payment: negotiable. Founded 1993.

Tatler

Vogue House, Hanover Square, London W1R 0AD
tel 020-7499 9080 *fax* 020-7409 0451
web site http://www.tatler.co.uk
Editor Geordie Grieg
Monthly £2.80

Smart society magazine favouring sharp articles, profiles, fashion and the arts. Illustrations: colour, b&w, but all commissioned. Founded 1709.

The Teacher

National Union of Teachers, Hamilton House, Mabledon Place, London WC1H 9BD
tel 020-7380 4708 *fax* 020-7387 8458
Editor Mitch Howard
8 p.a. Free to NUT members

Articles, features and news of interest to all those involved in the teaching profession. Length: 750 words. Payment: NUJ rates to NUJ members. Founded 1872.

Technology Ireland

Enterprise Ireland, Strand Road, Dublin 4, Republic of Ireland
tel (01) 206 6337 *fax* (01) 206 6342
Editor Tom Kennedy
Monthly IR£33 p.a. (IR£38 p.a. overseas)

Articles, features, reviews, news on current science and technology. Length: 1500-2000 words. Illustrations: line, half-tone, colour. Payment: varies. Founded 1969.

Telegraph Magazine – see The Daily Telegraph in National newspapers UK and Ireland, page 3

Television

Reed Business Information Ltd, Quadrant House, The Quadrant, Sutton, Surrey SM2 5AS
tel 020-8652 8120 *fax* 020-8652 8956
Monthly £2.80

Articles on the technical aspects of domestic TV and video equipment, especially servicing, long-distance TV, constructional projects, satellite TV, video recording, teletext and viewdata, test equipment, monitors. Payment: by arrangement. Illustrations: photos and line drawings for litho. Founded 1950.

Tempo

Boosey & Hawkes, Music Publishers, Ltd, 295 Regent Street, London W1R 8JH
tel 020-7580 2060 *fax* 020-7436 5675
e-mail tempo2@boosey.com
web site http://www.temporeview.com
Editor Calum MacDonald
Quarterly £3.50 (£17.50 p.a.)

Authoritative articles on contemporary music. Length: 2000-4000 words. Payment: by arrangement. Illustrations: music type, occasional photographic or musical supplements.

Tennis World

Market Link Publishing plc, The Mill, Bearwalden Business Park, Wendens Ambo, Saffron Walden, Essex CB11 4JX
tel (01799) 544200 *fax* (01799) 544201
Editor Alastair McIver
Monthly £2.50

Tournament reports, topical features, personality profiles, instructional articles. Length: 600-1500 words. Payment: by arrangement. Illustrations: line, half-tone, colour.

TGO (The Great Outdoors) Magazine

Caledonian Magazines Ltd, 6th Floor, 195 Albion Street, Glasgow G1 1QQ
tel 0141-302 7700 *fax* 0141-302 7799
e-mail tgo@calmags.co.uk (editorial)
Editor Cameron McNeish
Monthly £2.60

Articles on walking or lightweight camping in specific areas, preferably illustrated. Length: 1200-1800 words. Payment: by arrangement. Illustrations: colour. Founded 1978.

that's life!

H. Bauer Publishing Ltd, 25-27 Camden Road, London NW1 9LL
tel 020-7241 8000 *fax* 020-7462 4741
Editor Janice Turner
Weekly 49p

Dramatic true life stories about women. Length: average 1000 words. Illustrations: colour photos and cartoons. Payment: £650. Founded 1995.

Theology

SPCK, Holy Trinity Church, Marylebone Road, London NW1 4DU
tel 020-7387 5282 *fax* 020-7388 2352
e-mail theology@spck.org.uk
Editor William Jacob
Bi-monthly £3.75

Articles and reviews on theology, ethics, Church and Society. Length: up to 3500 words. Payment: none. Founded 1920.

Therapy Weekly

EMAP Healthcare Ltd, Greater London House, Hampstead Road, London NW1 7EJ
tel 020-7874 0360 *fax* 020-7874 0368
Editor Melissa Oliveck
Weekly Free to NHS and local authority therapists (£47.50 p.a.)

Articles of interest to chartered physiotherapists, occupational therapists and speech and language therapists. Guidelines to contributors available. Send proposals only initially. Length: up to 1000 words. Illustrations: colour and b&w photos, line, cartoons. Payment: by arrangement. Founded 1974 as *Therapy*.

The Third Alternative

TTA Press, 5 Martins Lane, Witcham, Ely, Cambs. CB6 2LB
tel (01353) 777931
e-mail ttapress@aol.com
web site http://www.tta-press.freewire.co.uk
Editor Andy Cox
Quarterly £3.25 (£18 for 6 issues)

Extraordinary new fiction: science fiction, fantasy, horror, slipstream. Also interviews with, and profiles of, authors and film-makers. Send sae with all submissions. Considers unsolicited material and welcomes ideas for articles and features. Length: 3000 words (articles and features), short stories unrestricted. Illustrations: send samples and portfolios. Payment: £20 per 1000 words. Founded 1994.

Third Way

St Peter's, Sumner Road, Harrow, Middlesex HA1 4BX
tel 020-8423 8494 *fax* 020-8423 5367
e-mail editor@thirdway.org.uk
10 p.a. £2.90

Aims to present biblical perspectives on the political, social and cultural issues of the day. Payment: by arrangement on publication. Founded 1977.

This Caring Business

1 St Thomas' Road, Hastings, East Sussex TN34 3LG
tel (01424) 718406 *fax* (01424) 718460
e-mail vivshep@aol.com
Editor Michael J. Monk
Monthly £50 p.a.

Specialist contributions relating to the commercial aspects of nursing and residential care, including hospitals. Payment: £100 per 1000 words. Illustrations: line, half-tone. Founded 1985.

This England

PO Box 52, Cheltenham, Glos. GL50 1YQ
tel (01242) 577775
Editor Roy Faiers
Quarterly £3.75

Articles on towns, villages, traditions, customs, legends, crafts of England; stories of people. Length: 250-2000 words. Payment: £25 per page and pro rata. Illustrations: line, half-tone, colour. Founded 1968.

Time Out

Time Out Group Ltd, Universal House, 251 Tottenham Court Road, London W1P 0AB
tel 020-7813 3000 *fax* 020-7813 6001
web site http://www.timeout.com
Editor Laura Lee Davies
Weekly £1.95

Listings magazine for London covering all areas of the arts, plus articles of consumer and news interest. Illustrations: colour and b&w. Payment by negotiation. Founded 1968.

The Times Magazine – **see The Times in National newspapers UK and Ireland, page 3**

The Times Educational Supplement

Admiral House, 66-68 East Smithfield, London E1W 1BX

tel 020-7782 3000 *fax* 020-7782 3202 (news), 020-7782 3919 (features), 020-7782 3205 (opinion articles)
e-mail copy@tes.co.uk, friday@tes.co.uk (outlines)
web site http://www.tes.co.uk
Editor Caroline St John-Brooks
Weekly £1.10

Articles on education written with special knowledge or experience; news items; books, arts and equipment reviews. Advisable to check with news or picture editor before submitting. Outlines of feature ideas should be faxed or e-mailed. Illustrations: suitable photos and drawings of educational interest, cartoons. Payment: standard rates, or by arrangement.

Times Educational Supplement Scotland

Scott House, 10 South St Andrew Street, Edinburgh EH2 2AZ
tel 0131-557 1133 *fax* 0131-558 1155
Editor Willis Pickard
Weekly £1.10

Articles on education, preferably 800-1000 words, written with special knowledge or experience. News items about Scottish educational affairs. Illustrations: line, half-tone. Payment: by arrangement. Founded 1965.

Times Higher Education Supplement

Admiral House, 66-68 East Smithfield, London E1W 1BX
tel 020-7782 3000 *fax* 020-7782 3300
Editor Auriol Stevens
Weekly £1.20

Articles on higher education written with special knowledge or experience, or articles dealing with academic topics. Also news items. Illustrations: suitable photos and drawings of educational interest. Payment: by arrangement. Founded 1971.

The Times Literary Supplement

Admiral House, 66-68 East Smithfield, London E1W 1BX
tel 020-7782 3000 *fax* 020-7782 3100
Editor Ferdinand Mount
Weekly £2.20

Will consider poems for publication, literary discoveries and articles, particularly of an opinionated kind, on literary and cultural affairs. Payment: by arrangement.

Today's Golfer

EMAP Active Ltd, Bretton Court, Bretton, Peterborough PE3 8DZ
tel (01733) 264666 *fax* (01733) 465248
Editor Neil Pope
Monthly £2.99

Specialist features and articles on golf instruction and equipment. Founded 1988.

Top of the Pops – see page 301

Top Santé Health & Beauty

Emap Elán, Endeavour House, 189 Shaftesbury Avenue, London WC2H 8JG
tel 020-7938 3033 *fax* 020-7938 5464
Editor Annabel Goldstaub
Monthly £1.95

Articles, features and news on all aspects of health and beauty. Ideas welcome. Length: 1-2 pages. Illustrations: colour photos and drawings. Payment: £200 per 1000 words; illustrations by arrangement. Founded 1993.

Total Film

99 Baker Street, London W1N 1FB
tel 020-7317 2600 *fax* 020-7317 2644
e-mail totalfilm@futurenet.co.uk
Editor Matt Mueller
Monthly £2.80

Movie magazine covering all aspects of film. Phone to discuss ideas before submitting material. Length: 400 words (news items); 1000 words (funny features); 400/800/1500 words (interviews). Payment: £150 per 1000 words; free-£1500 per picture. Founded 1996.

Total Football

Future Publishing Ltd, 30 Monmouth Street, Bath BA1 2BW
tel (01225) 442244 *fax* (01225) 732248
e-mail richard.jones@futurenet.co.uk
Editor Richard Jones
Monthly £2.80

News, features and reviews of domestic and international football events and related stories. Illustrations: colour and b&w. Payment: 12-15p a word/variable page rate. Founded 1995.

Toy Trader

Peebles Publishing Group, Brookmead House, Thorney Leys Business Park, Witney, Oxon OX8 7GE
tel (01993) 775545 *fax* (01993) 778884
e-mail toytrader@peebl.com
web site http://www.toy.co.uk/toytrader
Editor Sarah Sheppard
Monthly £60 p.a.

Trade magazine specialising in anything to do with toys, games, children's products, licensing, TV and cinema for children and electronic gaming, circulated to manufacturers and retailers. Length: by negotiation. Illustrations: colour photos and diagrams. Payment: by negotiation. Founded 1908.

Traveller

Wexas Ltd, 45 Brompton Road, London SW3 1DE
tel 020-7589 0500 *fax* 020-7581 1357
e-mail traveller@wexas.com
Editor Jonathan Lorie
Quarterly Free to UK travel club members; back numbers £2.50 (£3 overseas), payable to Wexas

Serious travel writing. Narrative features describe personal journeys to remarkable places (mainly non-Western). Unsolicited material considered if prose and pictures are excellent. Length: 1200-1600 words. Illustrations: transparencies. Payment: £150 per 1000 words; colour £35 (£75 cover). Founded 1970.

Tribune

308 Gray's Inn Road, London WC1X 8DY
tel 020-7278 0911
Editor Mark Seddon, *Reviews Editor* Caroline Rees
Weekly £1

Political, literary, with Socialist outlook. Informative articles (about 700 words), news stories (250-300 words). No unsolicited reviews or fiction. Payment: by arrangement. Illustrations: cartoons, photos.

Trout and Salmon

EMAP Active Ltd, Bushfield House, Orton Centre, Peterborough PE2 5UW
tel (01733) 237111 *fax* (01733) 465820
e-mail sandy.leventon@ecm.emap.com
Editor Sandy Leventon
Monthly £2.60

Articles of good quality with strong trout or salmon angling interest. Length: 400-2000 words, accompanied if possible by colour transparencies or good-quality colour prints. Payment: by arrangement. Illustrations: line, colour transparencies and prints, cartoons. Founded 1955.

Truck & Driver

Reed Business Information, Quadrant House, The Quadrant, Sutton, Surrey SM2 5AS
tel 020-7652 3682 *fax* 020-7652 8988
Editor Dave Young
Monthly £1.90

News, articles on trucks, personalities and features of interest to truck drivers. Words (on disk or electronically) and picture packages preferred. Length: approx. 2000 words. Illustrations: colour transparencies and artwork, cartoons. Payment: negotiable. Founded 1984.

Trucking International

A & S Publishing, Messenger House, 35 St Michael's Square, Gloucester GL1 1HX
tel (01452) 307181 *fax* (01452) 415817
Editor Richard Simpson
Monthly £2

For truck drivers, owner-drivers and small fleet operators: news, articles, features and technical advice. Length: 750-2500 words. Illustrations: mostly 35 mm colour transparencies. Payment: by negotiation. Founded 1983.

TV Quick

H. Bauer Publishing Ltd, 25-27 Camden Road, London NW1 9LL
tel 020-7241 8000 *fax* 020-7241 8066
Editor Lori Miles
Weekly 62p

Real life features, readers' tips and letters. No fiction. Payment: £250 (real life stories). Founded 1991.

TVTimes Magazine

IPC Magazines Ltd, 10th Floor, King's Reach Tower, Stamford Street, London SE1 9LS
tel 020-7261 7000 *fax* 020-7261 7777
Editor Peter Genower
Weekly 69p

Features with an affinity to ITV, BBC1, BBC2, Channels 4 and 5, satellite and radio personalities and TV generally. Length: by arrangement. Photographs: commissioned only. Payment: by arrangement.

U magazine

Smurfit Communications, 2 Clanwilliam Court, Lower Mount Street, Dublin 2, Republic of Ireland
tel (01) 240 5300 *fax* (01) 661 9757
e-mail letters@umagazine.ie
Editor Ray Walsh
Monthly IR£2.30

Fashion and beauty magazine for 18-25 year-old Irish women, with celebrity interviews, talent profiles, real-life stories, sex and relationship features, plus regular pages on the arts, the club scene, music and film. Also travel, interiors, health, food, horoscopes. Material mostly commissioned. Payment: varies. Founded 1978.

Ulster Grocer

Greer Publications, 5B Edgewater Business Park, Belfast Harbour Estate, Belfast BT3 9JQ
tel 028-9078 3200 *fax* 028-9078 3210

e-mail mail@ulsterbusiness.com
Editor Brian McCalden
Monthly Controlled circulation

Topical features (500-1000 words) on agribusiness – retail and manufacturing – and exhibitions; news (200 words) with a Northern Ireland bias. All features commissioned; no speculative articles accepted. Illustrations: colour and b&w photos. Payment: features £75, news £30; photos £40. Founded 1972.

Under Five Contact

Pre-school Learning Alliance,
69 Kings Cross Road, London WC1X 9LL
tel 020-7833 0991 *fax* 020-7837 4942
e-mail pla@pre-school.org.uk
Editor Ann Henderson
10 p.a. £25 p.a.

Articles on the role of adults – especially parents/preschool workers – in young children's learning and development, including children from all cultures and those with special needs. Length: 1000 words. Payment: £50 per article. Founded 1962.

The Universe

1st Floor, St James's Buildings, Oxford Street, Manchester M1 6FP
tel 0161-236 8856 *fax* 0161-236 8530
Editor Joe Kelly
Weekly 50p

Catholic Sunday newspaper. News stories, features and photos on all aspects of Catholic life required; also cartoons. MSS should not be submitted without sae. Payment: by arrangement. Founded 1860.

Vanity Fair

The Condé Nast Publications Ltd, Vogue House, Hanover Square, London W1R 0AD
tel 020-7499 9080 *fax* 020-7493 1962
web site http://www.vanityfair.co.uk
London Editor Henry Porter
tel 020-7221 6228 *fax* 020-7221 6269
Monthly £2.80

Media, glamour and politics for grown-up readers. No unsolicited material. Payment: by arrangement. Illustrated.

The Vegan

The Vegan Society, Donald Watson House, 7 Battle Road, St Leonards-on-Sea, East Sussex TN37 7AA
tel (01424) 427393 *fax* (01424) 717064
e-mail terrybevis@vegansociety.com
Editor Terry Bevis
Quarterly £1.95

Articles on animal rights, nutrition, cookery, agriculture, Third World, health. Length: approx. 1500 words. Payment: by arrangement. Illustrations: photos, cartoons, line drawings – foods, animals, livestock systems, crops, people, events; colour for cover. Founded 1944.

Venue

Ventrogreen Ltd, 64-65 North Road, Bristol BS6 5AQ
tel 0117-942 8491 *fax* 0117-942 0369
e-mail editor@venue.co.uk
web site http://www.venue.co.uk
Editor Nigel Tassell
Fortnightly £1.90

Listings magazine for Bristol and Bath combining comprehensive entertainment information with local features, profiles and interviews. Length: by agreement. Illustrations: colour and b&w. Payment: £8 per 100 words. Founded 1982.

The Veterinary Review

John C. Alborough Ltd, Lion Lane, Needham Market, Suffolk IP6 8NT
tel (01449) 723800 *fax* (01449) 723801
e-mail enquiries@jca.uk.com
Editor Anna Cooper
Bi-monthly £40 p.a.

News, articles – both topical and general – and product listings for veterinarians. Payment: negotiable.

Farm & Country Retailer

News, articles and product listings for the agricultural supply trade.

Viz

House of Viz, PO Box 1PT, Newcastle upon Tyne NE99 1PT
fax 0191-241 4244
e-mail web@johnbrown.co.uk
web site http://www.viz.co.uk
Editor Chris Donald
6 p.a. £1.75

Cartoons, spoof tabloid articles, spoof advertisements. Illustrations: half-tone, line, cartoons. Payment: £300 per page (cartoons). Founded 1979.

Vogue

Vogue House, Hanover Square, London W1R 0AD
tel 020-7499 9080 *fax* 020-7408 0559
web site http://www.vogue.co.uk
Editor Alexandra Shulman
Monthly £3.10

Fashion, beauty, health, decorating, art, theatre, films, literature, music, travel, food and wine. Length: articles from 1000 words. Illustrated.

The Voice

370 Coldharbour Lane, London SW9 8PL
tel 020-7737 7377 *fax* 020-7274 8994
e-mail veeteeay@gn.apc.org
Acting Editor Mike Best
Weekly 65p

News, general and arts features of interest to black readers. Illustrations: colour and b&w photos. Founded 1982.

woman2woman

Last Mon of each month

Supplement addressing the needs and aspirations of young Black Britons with a focus on a female readership.

Wanderlust

PO Box 1832, Windsor SL4 1YT
tel (01753) 620426
web site http://www.wanderlust.co.uk
Editor Lyn Hughes
Bi-monthly £2.95

Features on independent adventure and special-interest travel. Send sae for 'Guidelines for contributors'. Length: up to 2500 words. Illustrations: high quality colour slides (send stocklist first). Payment: by arrangement. Founded 1993.

War Cry

The Salvation Army, 101 Newington Causeway, London SE1 6BN
tel 020-7367 4900 *fax* 020-7367 4710
e-mail warcry@salvationarmy.org.uk
web site http://www.salvationarmy.org/warcry
Editor Major Nigel Bovey
Weekly 20p (£26 p.a.)

Voluntary contributions: Christian comment on contemporary issues, human interest stories of personal Christian faith; puzzles. Illustrations: line and photos, cartoons. Founded 1879.

Wasafiri

Queen Mary & Westfield College,
Dept of English & Drama, Mile End Road,
London E1 4NS
tel 020-7882 3120 *fax* 020-8980 6200
e-mail wasafiri@qmw.ac.uk
web site http://www.qmw.ac.uk/~english/publications/wasafiri.html
Editor Susheila Nasta
Managing Editor Richard Dyer
Bi-annual £14 p.a. (£24 p.a. institutions)

Published at University of London. Short stories, poetry, reviews, essays on literature and film, interviews. Covers literatures in English from Africa, Asia, the Caribbean, Black Britain and the Diaspora. Submit MSS in duplicate, with an sae. Illustrations: b&w photos. Payment: negotiable. Founded 1984.

Waterways World

Waterways World Ltd, The Well House,
High Street, Burton-on-Trent, Staffs. DE14 1JQ
tel (01283) 742951 *fax* (01283) 742957
e-mail ww@wellhouse.easynet.co.uk
Editor Hugh Potter
Monthly £2.40

Feature articles on all aspects of inland waterways in Britain and abroad, including historical material; factual and technical articles preferred. No short stories or poetry. Send sae for 'Notes for WW Contributors'. Payment: £37 per 1000 words. Illustrations: colour transparencies or prints, line. Founded 1972.

Wedding and Home

IPC Magazines Ltd, King's Reach Tower,
Stamford Street, London SE1 9LS
tel 020-7261 7471 *fax* 020-7261 7459
e-mail weddingandhome@ipc.co.uk
Editor Christine Hayes
Deputy Editor Helen Salmon
Bi-monthly £3.80

Ideas and inspiration for modern brides. Fashion and beauty, information for grooms, real life weddings, planning advice, gift list ideas and honeymoon features. Approach Deputy Editor in writing or by e-mail. Most features are commissioned to regular freelances but ideas will receive consideration if presented clearly and briefly. Payment: by negotiation. Founded 1985.

Weekend – see The Guardian in National newspapers UK and Ireland, page 3

The Weekly News

D.C. Thomson & Co. Ltd, Albert Square,
Dundee DD1 9QJ
tel (01382) 223131
137 Chapel Street, Manchester M3 6AA
tel 0161-834 5122
144 Port Dundas Road, Glasgow G4 0HZ
tel 0141-332 9933
185 Fleet Street, London EC4A 2HS
tel 020-7400 1030
Weekly 45p

Real-life dramas of around 2000 words told in the first person. Non-fiction series with lively themes or about interesting people. Keynote throughout is strong human interest. Joke sketches. Illustrations: cartoons. Payment: on acceptance.

Weight Watchers Magazine

Bloomsbury House Ltd, 1 Cecil Court,
49-55 London Road, Enfield, Middlesex EN2 6DN
tel 020-8342 2222 *fax* 020-8342 2223
8 p.a. £1.70

Features: health, beauty, news, astrology; food-orientated articles; success stories. All material commissioned. Length: 1/2-3 pages. Illustrations: colour photos and cartoons. Payment: by arrangement.

West Lothian Life

Ballencrieff Cottage, Ballencrieff Toll, Bathgate, West Lothian EH48 4LD
tel (01506) 632728 *fax* (01506) 635444
e-mail wll@pages.clara.net
web site http://home.clara.net/pages
Editor Susan Coon
Quarterly £2

Articles, profiles etc with a West Lothian angle. Length: 800-3000 words. Illustrations: colour and b&w photos, b&w artwork and cartoons. Payment: £20 per 1000 words. Founded 1995.

What Camcorder

(formerly Video Camera)
WV Publications & Exhibitions,
57-59 Rochester Place, London NW1 9JU
tel 020-7331 1000 *fax* 020-7331 1242
e-mail whatcamcorder@yahoo.co.uk
Editor Tracey Smith
Monthly £2.95

Technique articles on how to use camcorders and equipment tests of camcorders and accessories. Material mostly commissioned. Length: 1000-1500 words. Illustrations: colour photos, diagrams. Payment: £95 per 1000 words; £70 per page for illustrations. Founded 2000.

What Car?

Haymarket Motoring Magazines Ltd,
60 Waldegrave Road, Teddington,
Middlesex TW11 8LG
tel 020-8267 5688 *fax* 020-8267 5750
Editor Steve Fowler
Monthly £3.30

Road tests, buying guide, consumer stories and used car features. No unsolicited material. Illustrations: colour and b&w photos, line drawings. Payment: by negotiation. Founded 1973.

What Laptop & Handheld PC

Crimson Publishing, 14 Northfields,
London SW18 1UU
tel 020-8875 5600 *fax* 020-8875 5601
e-mail letters@whatlaptop.co.uk
web site http://www.whatlaptop.co.uk
Editor Ian Delaney
Monthly £2.99

Non-technical news, reviews and help for anyone who wants to buy or has bought a portable computer. Discuss ideas for features with Editor in first instance; welcomes ideas for features. Length: up to 1600 words. Payment: by arrangement. Founded 1999.

What's on TV

IPC Magazines Ltd, 10th Floor, King's Reach Tower, Stamford Street, London SE1 9LS
tel 020-7261 7769 *fax* 020-7261 7739
Editor Mike Hollingsworth
Weekly 40p

Features on TV programmes and personalities. All material commissioned. Length: up to 500 words. Illustrations: colour and b&w photos, cartoons. Payment: by agreement. Founded 1991.

When Saturday Comes

When Saturday Comes Ltd, 17A Perseverance Works, 38 Kingsland Road, London E2 8DD
tel 020-7729 1110 *fax* 020-7729 9417
e-mail editorial@wsc.co.uk
web site http://www.wsc.co.uk
Editor Andy Lyons
Monthly £1.95

Features on football from the fans' perspective. Read the magazine for style first. Length: 500-2000 words. Illustrations: colour and b&w photos, occasional illustrations. Payment: £50-£100 for words; £50-£75 for illustrations. Founded 1986.

Wine

Quest Magazines Ltd, Wilmington Publishing,
6-8 Underwood Street, London N1 7JQ
tel 020-7549 2572 *fax* 020-7549 8622
e-mail wine@wilmington.co.uk
Acting Editor Richard Davies
11 p.a. £3.10

Articles, features and news on new developments in wine; travelogues, tastings and profiles. Illustrations: colour. Payment: £125 per 1000 words. Founded 1983.

Wisden Cricket Monthly

The New Boathouse, 136-142 Bramley Road,
London W10 6SR
tel 020-7565 3000 *fax* 020-7565 3077
e-mail wisden@johnbrown.co.uk
web site http://www.wisden.com
Editor Tim de Lisle
Monthly £2.60

Cricket articles of exceptional interest (unsolicited pieces seldom used). Length: up to 3000 words. Payment: by arrangement. Illustrations: half-tone, colour. Founded 1979.

Woman

IPC Magazines Ltd, King's Reach Tower, Stamford Street, London SE1 9LS
tel 020-7261 5000 *fax* 020-7261 5997
Editor Carole Russell
Weekly 64p

Human interest stories and practical articles of varying length on all subjects of interest to women. Payment: by arrangement. Illustrations: colour transparencies and photos. Founded 1937.

Woman Alive

(formerly Christian Woman)
Christian Media Centre, 96 Dominion Road, Worthing, West Sussex BN14 8JP
tel (01903) 821082 *fax* (01903) 821081
e-mail womanalive@christianmedia.org.uk
Editor Elizabeth Trundle
Monthly £1.90

Aimed at women aged 25 upwards. Celebrity interviews, topical features, Christian issues, 'Day in the life of' profiles of women in interesting occupations, Christian testimonies, fashion, beauty, health, crafts. Unsolicited material should include colour slides or b&w photos. Length: 'Day in the life of'/testimonies 750 words, interviews/features 1300 words. Payment: £50 per 1000 words published. Founded 1982.

Woman and Home

(incorporating Living)
IPC Magazines Ltd, King's Reach Tower, Stamford Street, London SE1 9LS
tel 020-7261 5000 *fax* 020-7261 7346
Acting Editor Sarah Kilby
Monthly £1.90

Centres on the personal and home interests of the lively-minded mature, modern woman. Articles dealing with fashion, beauty, leisure pursuits, gardening, home style; features on topical issues, people and places. Fiction: complete stories from 3000-4500 words in length. Illustrations: commissioned colour photos and sketches. Please note: non-commissioned work is rarely accepted and regrettably cannot be returned. Founded 1926.

The Woman Writer

118 Forest Edge, Buckhurst Hill, Essex 1G9 5AB
e-mail oneder@btinternet.com
web site http://www.author.uk/swwj.html
Editor Doreen Friend
4 p.a. Free to members

Periodical of the Society of Women Writers and Journalists. See under Societies section for further information. Founded 1894.

Woman's Journal

IPC Magazines Ltd, King's Reach Tower, Stamford Street, London SE1 9LS
tel 020-7261 6622 *fax* 020-7261 7061
Editor Elsa McAlonan
Monthly £2.30

Magazine devoted to the looks and lives of intelligent women aged 30 plus: interviews and articles (1000-2000 words) dealing with topical subjects and personalities; fashion, beauty and health, food and interiors. No fiction accepted. Illustrations: full colour, line and wash, first-rate photos. Payment: by arrangement. Founded 1927.

Woman's Own

IPC Connect Ltd, King's Reach Tower, Stamford Street, London SE1 9LS
tel 020-7261 5000
Editor Terry Tavner
Weekly 64p

Modern women's magazine aimed at the 20-35 age group. No unsolicited features or fiction. Illustrations: colour and b&w: interior decorating and furnishing, fashion. Address work to relevant department editor. Payment: by arrangement.

Woman's Realm

IPC Magazines Ltd, King's Reach Tower, Stamford Street, London SE1 9LS
tel 020-7261 5000
Editor Mary Frances
Weekly 64p

Lively general interest weekly magazine. Articles on topical issues, celebrities, health, cookery, fashion, beauty, home; fiction. Human interest features; dramatic emotional stories. No unsolicited features or fiction accepted. Payment: by arrangement. Illustrated. Founded 1958.

Woman's Way

Smurfit Communications, 2 Clanwilliam Court, Lower Mount Street, Dublin 2, Republic of Ireland

tel (01) 240 5300 *fax* (01) 661 9757
e-mail ltayler@smurfit-comms.ie
Editor Lucy Tayler
Weekly 85p

Human interest, personality interviews, features on fashion, beauty, celebrities and investigations, short stories. Length: 1000-1500 words. Payment: approx. £50-£100. Founded 1963.

Woman's Weekly

IPC Connect Ltd, King's Reach Tower, Stamford Street, London SE1 9LS
tel 020-7261 5000 *fax* 020-7261 6322
Editor Gilly Sinclair
Weekly 60p

Lively, family-interest magazine. One serial, averaging 4000 words each instalment, of strong romantic interest, and several short stories of 1000-2500 words of general emotional interest. Celebrity and strong human interest features; also inspirational and entertaining personal stories. Payment: by arrangement. Illustrations: full colour fiction illustrations, small sketches and photos. Founded 1911.

Women's Health

WV Publications & Exhibitions, 57-59 Rochester Place, London NW1 9JU
tel 020-7331 1000 *fax* 020-7331 1242
e-mail wvmags@compuserve.com
Editor Christine Morgan
Monthly £2.20

Lifestyle magazine for women covering a wide range of issues from fashion and fitness to health and beauty – but from an unconventional angle. Length: 1800-2000 words. Payment: by negotiation. Founded 1998.

The Woodworker

Nexus Special Interests Ltd, Nexus House, Azalea Drive, Swanley, Kent BR8 8HU
tel (01322) 660070
Editor Mark Ramuz
Monthly £2.65

For the craft and professional woodworker. Practical illustrated articles on cabinet work, carpentry, wood polishing, wood turning, wood carving, rural crafts, craft history, antique and period furniture; also wooden toys and models, musical instruments; timber procurement, conditioning, seasoning; tool, machinery and equipment reviews. Payment: by arrangement. Illustrations: line drawings and photos.

The Word

Divine Word Missionaries, Donamon, Roscommon, Republic of Ireland
tel/fax (0903) 62608
e-mail wordeditor@eircom.net
Editor Fr Tom Cahill SVD
Monthly 75p

General interest magazine with religious emphasis. Illustrated articles up to 2000 words and good picture features. Payment: by arrangement. Illustrations: photos and large colour transparencies, cartoons. Founded 1936.

Workbox Magazine

Ebony Media Ltd, Heathlands Business Park, Heathlands Road, Liskeard, Cornwall PL14 4DH
tel (01579) 340100 *fax* (01579) 340200
e-mail workbox@ebony.co.uk
web site http://www.ebony.co.uk/workbox
Editor Victor Briggs
Bi-monthly £1.95

Features, of any length, on all aspects of needlecrafts. No 'how-to' articles. Send sae with enquiries and submissions. Illustrations: good colour transparencies. Payment: by agreement. Founded 1984.

The World of Embroidery

The Embroiderers' Guild, PO Box 42B, East Molesey, Surrey KT8 9BB
e-mail magsmag@compuserve.com
web site http://www.hiraeth.com/world-emb
tel 020-8943 1229
6 p.a. £4.15 (£24.90 p.a.)

Articles on historical and contemporary embroidery by curators, artists and craftsmen; exhibition and book reviews; saleroom report; diary of events. Illustrations: line, half-tone, colour. Payment: by arrangement.

World Fishing

Nexus Media Ltd, Nexus House, Azalea Drive, Swanley, Kent BR8 8HU
tel (01322) 660070 *fax* (01322) 616324
Editor Mark Say
Monthly £49 p.a.

International journal of commercial fishing. Technical and management emphasis on catching, processing and marketing of fish and related products; fishery operations and vessels covered worldwide. Length: 500-1500 words. Payment: by arrangement. Illustrations: photos and diagrams for litho reproduction. Founded 1952.

The World of Interiors

The Condé Nast Publications Ltd,
Vogue House, Hanover Square,
London W1R 0AD
tel 020-7499 9080 *fax* 020-7493 4013
e-mail interiors@msmail.condenast.co.uk
web site http://www.worldofinteriors.co.uk
Editor Min Hogg
Monthly £3.50

All material commissioned: send synopsis/visual reference for article ideas. Length: 1000-1500 words. Illustrations: colour photos. Payment: £500 per 1000 words; photos from £100. Founded 1981.

World Soccer

IPC Magazines Ltd, King's Reach Tower,
Stamford Street, London SE1 9LS
tel 020-7261 5737 *fax* 020-7261 7474
Editor Gavin Hamilton
Monthly £2.40

Articles, features, news concerning football, its personalities and worldwide development. Length: 600-2000 words. Illustrations: colour and b&w photos, cartoons. Payment: by arrangement. Founded 1960.

The World Today

The Royal Institute of International Affairs,
Chatham House, 10 St James's Square,
London SW1Y 4LE
tel 020-7957 5700 *fax* 020-7957 5710
e-mail wt-ch@riia.org
web site http://www.riia.org
Editor Graham Walker
Monthly £2.50

Analysis of international issues and current events by journalists, diplomats, politicians and academics. Length: 1700-3000 words. Payment: nominal. Founded 1945.

World Wide Writers

Writers International Ltd, 1st Floor, Briggs House,
26 Commercial Road, Ashley Cross, Poole,
Dorset BH14 0JR
tel (01202) 716043 *fax* (01202) 740995
e-mail writintl@globalnet.co.uk
web site http://www.worldwidewriters.com
Editor Frederick E. Smith
Bi-monthly £5.99 (£30 p.a.)

Original, unpublished short stories. Winners of the magazine's competition each quarter are published alongside the work of established authors. All types of story are considered, which should be literate rather than literary. Length: 2500-5000 words. Payment: £625 (1st prize), £315 (2nd prize), £200 (3rd prize), £125 (runners up). Founded 1997.

World's Children

Save the Children, 17 Grove Lane, London SE5 8RD
tel 020-7703 5400 *fax* 020-7708 2508
e-mail publications@scfuk.org.uk
web site http://www.savethechildren.org.uk
Editor Kate O'Malley
Quarterly Sent free to regular donors

Magazine of Save the Children. Articles on child welfare and rights, related to Save the Children's work overseas and in the UK. No unsolicited features. Illustrations: colour and b&w photos. Founded 1920.

Writers' Forum

Writers' International Ltd, 1st Floor,
Briggs House, 26 Commercial Road,
Ashley Cross, Poole BH14 0JR
tel (01202) 716043 *fax* (01202) 740995
e-mail writintl@globalnet.co.uk
web site http://www.users.globalnet.co.uk/~writintl
Publisher John Jenkins
6 p.a. £3 (£18 p.a.)

Welcomes articles on any aspect of the craft and business of writing. Length: 800-2000 words. Payment: by arrangement. Administrators of 2 annual prizes: the Petra Kenney Memorial Poetry Prize (total £1750) and a Short Story Competition (total £300), plus poetry and short story competitions for subscribers in each issue. Founded 1993.

World Wide Writers

£5.99 6 p.a. (£30 p.a.)

Original, previously unpublished short stories considered. Length: 2500-5000. Prizes for best stories published.

Writers' News

PO Box 168, Wellington Street, Leeds LS1 1RF
tel 0113-238 8333 *fax* 0113-238 8330
Editor Derek Hudson
Monthly £44.90 p.a. (£39.90 p.a. CC/DD)

News, competitions and articles on all aspects of writing. Length: 800-1500 words. Illustrations: line, half-tone. Payment: by arrangement. Founded 1989.

Writing Magazine

PO Box 168, Wellington Street, Leeds LS1 1RF
tel 0113-238 8333 *fax* 0113-238 8330
Editor Derek Hudson
Bi-monthly £2.75 (free to *Writers News* subscribers)

Articles on all aspects of writing. Length: 800-1500 words. Illustrations: line, half-tone. Payment: by arrangement. Founded 1992.

Yachting Monthly

IPC Magazines Ltd, King's Reach Tower, Stamford Street, London SE1 9LS
tel 020-7261 6040 *fax* 020-7261 7555
Editor Sarah Norbury
Monthly £2.75

Articles on all aspects of seamanship, navigation, the handling of sailing craft, and their design, construction and equipment. Well-written narrative accounts of cruises in yachts. Length: up to 2250 words (articles), up to 2500 words (narratives). Illustrations: colour transparencies and prints, cartoons. Payment: quoted on acceptance. Founded 1906.

Yachting World

IPC Magazines Ltd, King's Reach Tower, Stamford Street, London SE1 9LS
tel 020-7261 6800 *fax* 020-7261 6818
e-mail yachting_world@ipc.co.uk
Editor Andrew Bray
Monthly £3.15

Practical articles of an original nature, dealing with sailing and boats. Length: 1500-2000 words. Payment: varies. Illustrations: colour transparencies, drawings, cartoons. Founded 1894.

Yachts and Yachting

196 Eastern Esplanade, Southend-on-Sea, Essex SS1 3AB
tel (01702) 582245 *fax* (01702) 588434
Editor Frazer Clark
Fortnightly £2.35

Short articles which should be technically correct. Payment: by arrangement. Illustrations: line, half-tone, colour. Founded 1947.

Yorkshire Ridings Magazine

33 Beverley Road, Driffield, Yorkshire YO25 6SD
tel/fax (01377) 253232
Editor Winston Halstead
Bi-monthly £1.25

Articles exclusively about people, life and character of the 3 Ridings of Yorkshire. Length: up to 1000 words. Payment: approx. £35-£40 per published page. Illustrations: colour, b&w photos; prints preferred. Founded 1964.

You – see Mail on Sunday in National newspapers UK and Ireland, page 3

You & Your Wedding

You & Your Wedding Publications Ltd, Silver House, 31-35 Beak Street, London W1R 3LD
tel 020-7440 3838 *fax* 020-7287 8655
Editor Carole Hamilton
Bi-monthly £3.80

Articles, features and news covering all aspects of planning a wedding. Submit ideas in writing only. Illustrations: colour. Payment: £300 per 1000 words.

Young People Now

National Youth Agency, 17-23 Albion Street, Leicester LE1 6GD
tel 0116-285 3700 *fax* 0116-285 3775
e-mail ypn@nya.org.uk
web site http://www.nya.org.uk
Editor Tim Burke
Monthly £2 (£22.80 p.a.)

Informative articles, highlighting issues of concern to all those who work with young people, including youth workers, probation and social services, Connexions Service, teachers and volunteers. Guidelines for contributors available on request. Founded 1989.

Young Writer

Glebe House, Weobley, Herefordshire HR4 8SD
tel (01544) 318901 *fax* (01544) 318901
e-mail youngwriter@enterprise.net
web site http://www.mystworld.com/youngwriter
Editor Kate Jones
3 p.a. £2.75 (£7.50 for 3 issues)

Specialist magazine for young writers under 18 years: ideas for them and writing by them. Includes interviews of famous writers by children, fiction and non-fiction pieces, poetry; also explores words and grammar, issues related to writing (e.g. dyslexia), plus competitions with prizes. Length: 750 or 1500 words (features), up to 400 words (news), 750 words (short stories – unless specified otherwise in a competition), poetry of any length. Illustrations: colour – drawings by children, snapshots to accompany features. Payment: most children's material is published without payment; £25-£100 (features); £25 (cover cartoon). Founded 1995.

Your Cat Magazine

BPG (Bourne) Ltd, Roebuck House, 33 Broad Street, Stamford, Lincs. PE9 1RB
tel (01780) 766199 *fax* (01780) 766416
e-mail suebpgroup@talk21.com
Editor Sue Parslow
Monthly £2.30

Practical advice on the care of cats and kittens, general interest items and news on cats, and true life tales and fiction. Length: 800-1500 (articles), 200-300 (news), up to 1000 (short stories). Illustrations: colour transparencies and prints. Payment: £80 per 1000 words. Founded 1994.

Your Dog Magazine

BPG (Stamford) Ltd, Roebuck House,
33 Broad Street, Stamford, Lincs. PE9 1RB
tel (01780) 766199 *fax* (01780) 766416
e-mail sarahbpgroup@talk21.com
Editor Sarah Wright
Monthly £2.65

Articles and information of interest to dog lovers; features on all aspects of pet dogs. Length: approx. 1500 words. Illustrations: colour transparencies, prints and line drawings. Payment: £80 per 1000 words. Founded 1994.

Your Garden

IPC Magazines Ltd, Westover House,
West Quay Road, Poole, Dorset BH15 1JG
tel (01202) 440870 *fax* (01202) 440860
Editor Adrienne Wild
Monthly £2.40

Anything on gardening for the enthusiastic beginner. Commissioned material only; send brief synopsis of ideas. Length: 800-2000 words. Illustrations: colour photos and line. Payment: £100 per published 1000 words. Founded 1993.

Yours

Apex House, Oundle Road,
Peterborough PE2 9NP
tel (01733) 898100 *fax* (01733) 466863
Editor Neil Patrick
Monthly £1

Features and news about and /or of interest to the over-60s age group, including nostalgia and short stories. Study of magazine essential; approach in writing in first instance. Length: articles up to 1000 words, short stories up to 1800 words. Illustrations: preferably colour transparencies/prints but will consider good b&w prints/line drawings, cartoons. Payment: at editor's discretion or by agreement. Founded 1973.

Zene

TTA Press, 5 Martins Lane, Witcham, Ely,
Cambs. CB6 2LB
tel (01353) 777931
e-mail ttapress@aol.com
web site http://www.tta-press.freewire.co.uk
Editor 'Team Zene'
Bi-monthly 12 p.a. (subscription only)

A guide to the world's independent (or small) press, featuring contributors' guidelines to magazines and books from several countries, plus reviews and news for writers seeking markets for their work. Length: 1000 words (features). Payment: negotiable. Founded 1995.

Zest

National Magazine House, 72 Broadwick Street,
London W1V 2BP
tel 020-7439 5000 *fax* 020-7312 3750
e-mail zest.mail@natmags.co.uk
Editor Eve Cameron
Monthly £2.50

Health and beauty magazine. Commissioned material only: health, fitness and beauty, features, news and shorts. Length: 50-2000 words. Illustrations: colour and b&w photos and line. Payment: £250 per 1000 words. Founded 1994.

Newspapers and magazines overseas

Listings are given for newspapers and magazines in Australia (below), Canada (page 113), New Zealand (page 116) and South Africa (page 118). For information on submitting material to the USA, see page 120. Newspapers are listed under the towns in which they are published.

Australia

(Adelaide) Advertiser

121 King William Street, Adelaide, SA 5000
tel (08) 8206 2000 *fax* (08) 8206 3669
London office PO Box 481, 1 Virginia Street, London E1 9BD
tel 020-7702 1355 *fax* 020-7702 1384
Editor Mel Mansell
Daily Mon-Fri 80c Sat $1.20

Descriptive and news background material, 400-800 words, preferably with pictures; also cartoons. Founded 1858.

(Adelaide) Sunday Mail

121 King William Street, Adelaide, SA 5000
postal address GPO Box 339, Adelaide, SA 5001
tel (08) 8206 2000 *fax* (08) 8206 3646
web site http://www.news.com.au
Editor K. Sullivan
Weekly $1.40

Founded 1912.

AQ – Journal of Contemporary Analysis

Australian Institute of Political Science, PO Box 145, Balmain, NSW 2041
tel (02) 9810 5642 *fax* (02) 9810 2406
web site http://www.aips.net.au
Editor Paul Best
Quarterly $55 p.a. individuals, $95 p.a. institutions ($105 overseas)

Peer-reviewed articles for the informed non-specialist on politics, law, economics, social issues, etc. Length: 3500 words preferred. Payment: none. Founded 1929.

Aussie Post

(formerly Australasian Post)
Pacific Publications Pty Ltd, 35-51 Mitchell Street, McMahons Point, NSW 2060
Private Bag 9100, North Sydney, NSW 2059
tel (02) 9464 3129 *fax* (02) 9464 3169
e-mail aussiepost@pacpubs.com.au/
Editor Gill Chalmers
Weekly $3.50

Feature stories about Australia and Australians, both urban and rural; characters and achievers, known and unknown; short stories and poems. Material mostly commissioned. Length: 750-1000 words. Illustrations: colour transparencies. Payment: $300-500 per feature/illustration. Founded 1864.

Australian Bookseller & Publisher

D.W. Thorpe, 18 Salmon Street, Port Melbourne, Victoria 3207
tel (03) 9245 7370 *fax* (03) 9245 7395
e-mail bookseller.publisher@thorpe.com.au
web site http://www.thorpe.com.au
Editor Lorien Kaye
Monthly $70 p.a. ($105 p.a. NZ/Asia; $115 p.a. USA/Canada; $125 p.a. UK/Europe)

Founded 1921.

The Australian Financial Review

GPO Box 506, Sydney, NSW 2001
tel (02) 9282 2512 *fax* (02) 9282 3137
London office 95 Fetter Lane, London EC4A 1HE
tel 020-7242 0044 *fax* 020-7242 0066
New York office Suite 1720, 317 Madison Avenue, New York, NY 10017
tel 212-398-9494
Editor Colleen Ryan
Daily Mon-Fri $1.60

Investment business and economic news and reviews; government and politics, production, banking, commercial, and Stock Exchange statistics; company analysis. General features in Friday *Weekend Review* supplement.

Australian Flying

Yaffa Publishing Group, 17-21 Bellevue Street, Surry Hills, NSW 2010

tel (02) 9281 2333 *fax* (02) 9281 2750
e-mail yaffa@flex.com.au
Editor Doug Nancarrow
London office 64 The Mall, London W5 5LS
tel 020-8579 4836
Editor Robert Logan
6 p.a. $5.50

Covers the Australian aviation industry, from light aircraft to airliners. Payment: by arrangement.

Australian Geographic

PO Box 321, Terrey Hills, NSW 2084
tel (02) 9450 2344 *fax* (02) 9450 2990
web site http://www.australiangeographic.com.au
Editor Terri Cowley
Quarterly $45 p.a.

Articles and features about Australia, particularly life, technology and wildlife in remote parts of the country. Material mostly commissioned. Length: articles, 300-800 words, features, 2000-3000 words. Illustrations: all commissioned. Payment: from $500 per 1000 words; illustrations by negotiation. Founded 1986.

Australian Home Beautiful

35-51 Mitchell Street, McMahons Point, NSW 2060
tel (02) 9464 3000 *fax* (02) 9464 3263
e-mail homebeaut@pacpubs.com.au
Editor W. Buttner
Monthly $4.90

Deals with home building, interior decoration, furnishing, gardening, cookery, etc. Short articles with accompanying photos with Australian slant accepted. Preliminary letter advisable. Payment: Australian average. Founded 1913.

Australian House and Garden

54 Park Sgtreet, Sydney, NSW 1028
postal address GPO Box 4088, Sydney, NSW 1028
tel (02) 9282 8456 *fax* (02) 9267 4912
e-mail h&g@acp.com.au
Editor Anny Friis
Monthly $5.20

Factual articles dealing with interior decorating, home design, gardening, wine, food. Preliminary letter essential. Payment: by arrangement. Illustrations: line, half-tone, colour. Founded 1948.

Australian Journal of International Affairs

Department of International Relations, RSPAS, Australian National University, Canberra, ACT 0200
tel (06) 249 2169 *fax* (06) 279 8010
Editor Dr Ramesh Thakur, Vice-Rector (Peace & Governance), United Nations University, 53-70 Jingumae 5-chome, Shibuya-ku, Tokyo 150-8925, Japan
3 p.a. Personal rate A$64 p.a., institutions A$132 p.a. (Australia); other rates on application

Scholarly articles on international affairs. Length: 3000-7000 words. Payment: none.

Australian Journal of Politics and History

Department of Government, University of Queensland, St Lucia, Queensland 4067
tel (07) 3365 3163 *fax* (07) 3365 1388
e-mail g.stokes@mailbox.uq.edu.au
Editors Geoffrey Stokes and Ross Johnston
4 p.a. $50 (US $50, UK £30) individuals; $100 (US$125, UK £75) institutions

Australian, European, Asian, Pacific and international articles. Special feature: regular surveys of Australian Foreign Policy and State and Commonwealth politics. Length: 8000 words max. Illustrations: line, only when necessary. Payment: none.

Australian Photography

Yaffa Publishing Group, 17-21 Bellevue Street, Surry Hills, NSW 2010
tel (02) 9281 2333 *fax* (02) 9281 2750
e-mail yaffa@flex.com.au
Editor Robert Keeley
Monthly $4.95

Illustrated articles: picture-taking techniques, technical. Length: 1200-2500 words with colour and/or b&w prints or slides. Payment: $80 per page. Founded 1950.

Australian Powerboat

Yaffa Publishing Group, GPO Box 606, Sydney, NSW 1041
tel (02) 9213 8257 *fax* (02) 9281 2750
Editor Ian Macrae
Bi-monthly $5.20

Articles and news on boats and boating, racing, water skiing and products. Length: 1500 words (articles), 200 words (news). Illustrations: colour (transparencies preferred). Payment: $100 per 1000 words; from $30. Founded 1976.

Australian Short Stories

Howard Firkin, 73 Mooltan Street, Flemington, Victoria 3031
tel (03) 9370 4858
Quarterly $9.95

Contemporary short stories from around the world. Length: 500-5000 words. Illustrations: b&w artwork. Payment $90 per 1000 words; $70 illustrations. Founded 1983.

The Australian Way

BRW Media, Level 2, 469 Latrobe Street, Melbourne, Victoria 3000
postal address GPO Box 55A, Melbourne, Victoria 3001
tel (03) 9603 3888 *fax* (03) 9642 0852
Editor Tom Brentnall
Monthly Free

Inflight magazine for Qantas Airways. Articles of international interest; profiles, business, design, science, sport, travel, third-person stories that use locations as a backdrop, and pictorial essays. Length: 50-2000 words. Illustrations: colour transparencies. Payment: by negotiation. Founded 1986.

The Australian Women's Weekly

Australian Consolidated Press Ltd, 54 Park Street, Sydney, NSW 1028
postal address GPO Box 4178, Sydney, NSW 1028
tel (02) 9282 8000 *fax* (02) 9267 4459
e-mail dthomas@acp.com.au
Editor Deborah Thomas
Monthly $4

Fiction and features. Length: fiction 1000-5000 words; features 750-1500 words plus colour or b&w photos. Payment: according to length and merit. Fiction illustrations: sketches by own artists and freelances.

The Big Issue Australia

GPO Box 4911VV, Melbourne, Victoria 3001
tel (03) 9663 4522 *fax* (03) 9663 4252
e-mail bigissue@infoxchange.net.au
Editor Simon Castles
Fortnightly $3

Profiles and features of general interest and on social issues, plus international and local news, arts reviews. No fiction. Length: 1000-2500 words (features), up to 900 words (news), 250 words (reviews). Payment: 15c per word (features and news), $30 (reviews). Colour and b&w cartoons (approx. $100). Founded 1996.

(Brisbane) The Courier-Mail

Queensland Newspapers Pty Ltd, Campbell Street, Bowen Hills, Brisbane, Queensland 4006
tel (07) 3666 8000 *fax* (07) 3666 6696
e-mail cmletters@qnp.newsltd.com.au
web site http://www.news.com.au
Editor-in-Chief C. Mitchell
Daily 80c

(Brisbane) The Sunday Mail

Queensland Newspapers Pty Ltd, PO Box 130, Campbell Street, Bowen Hills, Brisbane, Queensland 4006
tel (07) 3666 6276 *fax* (07) 3666 6692
e-mail smletters@qnp.newsltd.com.au
Editor Michael Prain
Weekly $1.30

Anything of general interest. Length: up to 1500 words. Illustrations: line, photos, b&w and colour, cartoons. Rejected MSS returned if postage enclosed.

The Bulletin with Newsweek

54 Park Street, Sydney, NSW 2000
tel (02) 282 8200 *fax* (02) 267 4359
Editor Lyndall Crisp
Weekly $3.30

General interest articles, features; humour. Length: 750 words per page, max. 2100 words. Illustrations: colour photos and cartoons. Payment: $450 per 1000 words published; $100 colour cartoons and photos, according to size used.

Cleo

Level 4, 54 Park Street, Sydney, NSW 1028
tel (02) 9282 8617 *fax* (02) 9267 4368
Editor Deborah Thomas
Monthly $4.90

Articles (relationship, emotional, self-help) up to 3000 words, short quizzes. Payment: by negotiation. Founded 1972.

Countryman

50 Hasler Road, Osborne Park, Western Australia 6017
tel (08) 9482 3322 *fax* (08) 9482 3324
e-mail countryman@wanews.com.au
Editor Gary McGay
Weekly $1

Agriculture, farming or country interest features and service columns. Payment: standard rates. Illustrations: line, half-tone, colour, cartoons.

Dance Australia

Yaffa Publishing Group, Box 606, GPO Sydney, NSW 2001
tel (02) 281 2333 *fax* (02) 281 2750
e-mail yaffa@yaffa.com.au
Editor Karen van Ulzen
Bi-monthly $5.50

Articles and features on all aspects of dance in Australia. Material mostly commissioned, but will consider unsolicited contributions. Illustrations: b&w photos, line drawings, cartoons. Payment: $200 per 1000 words; illustrations by negotiation. Founded 1980.

Dolly

54 Park Street, Sydney, NSW 1028
tel (02) 9282 8437 *fax* (02) 9267 4911
web site http://dolly.ninemsn.com.au
Editor Eliza O'Hare
Monthly $4

Features on teen fashion, health and beauty, personalities, music, social issues and how to cope with growing up, etc. Length: not less than 1000 words. Illustrations: colour, b&w, line, cartoons. Payment: by arrangement. Founded 1970.

Electronics Australia with ETI

PO Box 199, Alexandria, NSW 1435
tel (02) 9353 0620 *fax* (02) 9353 0613
e-mail electaus@fpc.com.au
web site http://www.electronicsaustralia.com.au
Editor Graham Cattley
Monthly $5.95

Articles on technical television and radio, hi-fi, popular electronics, microcomputers and avionics. Length: up to 2000 words. Payment: by arrangement. Illustrations: line, half-tone, cartoons.

Elle (Australia)

Level 4, 80 Clarence Street, Sydney, NSW 2000
tel (02) 9249 3553 *fax* (02) 9249 3555
Editor Marina Go
Monthly $5.20

Profiles, news reports, cultural essays, fashion stories. Length: 300-3000 words. Payment: varies. Founded 1990.

Fishing World Magazine

Yaffa Publishing Group, 17-21 Bellevue Street, Surry Hills, NSW 2010
tel (02) 9281 2333 *fax* (02) 9281 2750
web site http://www.yaffa.com.au/fw
Editor Jim Harnwell
Monthly $4.95

Rock, surf, stream, deep sea and game fishing, with comprehensive sections on gear, equipment and boats. Payment: by arrangement.

Geo Australasia

Hallmark Editions, PO Box 84, Hampton, Victoria 3188
tel (03) 9555 7377 *fax* (03) 9555 7599
e-mail hallmark@halledit.com.au
Editor Peter Stirling
Bi-monthly $7.95 ($55 p.a. surface mail, $85 p.a. airmail)

Non-fiction articles on wildlife, adventure, culture and lifestyles, natural history and the environment in Australia, New Zealand, the Pacific and SE Asia. Length: 1500-3000 words. Payment: $600-$1500 by arrangement. Illustrations: photos, colour transparencies. Founded 1978.

Harper's Bazaar

ACP Publishing Pty Ltd, 54 Park Street, Sydney, NSW 2000
tel (02) 9282 8703 *fax* (02) 9267 4456
e-mail bazaar@acp.com.au
Editor Karin Upton Baker
10 p.a. $6.50

Fashion, health and beauty, celebrity news, plus features. Length: 3000 words. Illustrations: colour and b&w photos. Payment: $500 per 1000 words; $150. Founded 1998.

Herald of the South

173 Mona Vale Road, Ingleside, NSW 2101
tel (02) 9913 2771 *fax* (02) 9970 7275
e-mail herald@bahai.org.au
Quarterly $28 p.a.

The Baha'i magazine for world citizens focusing on new and challenging perpsectives to global issues. Features, fiction and non-fiction. Length: up to 3500 words. Illustrations: colour and b&w photos. Payment: by negotiation. Founded 1925.

Hobo

PO Box 166, Hazelbrook, NSW 2779
web site http://www.inkstream.com.au/hobo
Editor Dane Thwaites
Quarterly $20 p.a. (A$25p.a. New Zealand, A$30 p.a. elsewhere)

Poetry, Haiku, book reviews, articles about poetry and Haiku. Payment: approx. $12 per page. No illustrations. Founded 1993.

HQ Magazine

Level 5, 74-84 Foveaux Street, Surry Hills, NSW 2010
tel (02) 9281 3111 *fax* (02) 9281 3122
e-mail hq@terraplanet.com.au
web site http://www.terraplanet.com.au
Editor Lisa Anthony
Bi-monthly $6.50

General interest features and profiles for a literate readership. Length: 1500-5000 words. Illustrations: colour and b&w photos. Payment: by negotiation. Founded 1989.

Imago: new writing

School of Media & Journalism, QUT, GPO Box 2434, Brisbane, Queensland 4001
tel (07) 3864 2976 *fax* (07) 3864 1810
Editor Philip Neilsen
3 p.a. $40 p.a. airmail

New writing: short stories, poems, essays and articles on writers and writing or on some aspect of Australian culture. Length: 2000-3000 words (articles), 1500-3000 words (stories), 14-40 lines (poems). Payment: by arrangement on publication. No illustrations. Founded 1989.

(Launceston) Examiner

Box 99A, PO Launceston, Tasmania 7250
tel (03) 633 15111 *fax* (03) 633 47328
Editor Rod Scott
Daily 80c

Accepts freelance material. Payment: by arrangement.

(Melbourne) Age

The Age Company Ltd, 250 Spencer Street, Melbourne, Victoria 3000
tel (03) 9600 4211 *fax* (03) 9601 2412
Associate Publisher and Editor Michael Gawenda, *Managing Editor* Malcolm Schmidtke
London office 95 Fetter Lane, London EC4A 1HE
tel 020-7242 0044 *fax* 020-7242 0066
Daily Mon-Fri $1 Sat $1.70 Sun $1.50

Independent liberal morning daily; room occasionally for outside matter. *Good Weekend* (illustrated weekend magazine); *News Extra*; *Saturday Extra* (includes literary reviews). Accepts occasional freelance material.

(Melbourne) Herald Sun

HWT Tower, 40 City Road, Southbank, Victoria 3006
tel (03) 9292 1816 *fax* (03) 9292 1776
Editor Peter Blunden
Daily Mon-Fri 70c Sat 90c Sun $1.20

Accepts freelance articles, preferably with illustrations. Length: up to 750 words. Illustrations: half-tone, line, cartoons. Payment: on merit.

(Melbourne) Sunday Herald Sun

HWT Tower, 40 City Road, Southbank, Victoria 3006
tel (03) 9292 2000 *fax* (03) 9292 2080
Editor Alan Howe
Weekly $1.30

Accepts freelance articles, preferably with illustrations. Length: up to 2000 words. Illustrations: colour. Payment: on merit.

New Woman

Level 4, 45 Jones Street, Ultimo, NSW 2007
tel (02) 9692 2000 *fax* (02) 9692 2488
Editor Saska Graville
Monthly $5

Self-development for the 30-something woman: articles, features, fashion, beauty, health, reviews and book excerpts. Material mostly commissioned. Length: average 1200 words. Payment: 55c a word. Illustrated. Founded 1989.

NW Magazine

54 Park Street, Sydney, NSW 2000
tel (02) 9282 8285 *fax* (02) 9264 6005
Editor Philip Barker
Weekly $3

News and features on celebrities, food, new products, fashion and astrology. Illustrated. Payment: by negotiation. Founded 1993.

Overland

PO Box 14146 MCMC, Melbourne, Victoria 8001
tel (03) 9688 4163 *fax* (03) 9688 4883
e-mail overland@vu-edu.au
Editor Ian Syson
Quarterly $36 p.a.

Literary and cultural. Australian material preferred. Payment: by arrangement. Illustrations: line, half-tone, cartoons.

People Magazine

54 Park Street, Sydney, NSW 2000
tel (02) 282 8743 *fax* (02) 267 4365
Editor Simon Butler-White
Weekly $2.90

National weekly news-pictorial. Mainly people stories. Photos depicting exciting happenings, glamour, show business, unusual occupations, rites, customs. Payment: $300 per page, text and photos.

(Perth) The Sunday Times

34-40 Stirling Street, Perth, Western Australia 6000
tel (08) 9326 8476 *fax* (08) 9226 8316
Editor Brian Crisp
Weekly $1.30

Topical articles to 800 words. Payment: on acceptance. Founded 1897.

(Perth) The West Australian

55 Hasler Road, Osborne Park, Western Australia 6017
tel (09) 9482 3111 *fax* (09) 9482 3452
Editor Paul Murray
Daily Mon-Fri 70c Sat $1.20

Articles and sketches about people and events in Australia and abroad. Length: 300-700 words. Payment: Award rates or better. Illustrations: line, half-tone. Founded 1833.

Quadrant

46 George Street, Fitzroy, Victoria 3065
postal address PO Box 1495, Collingwood, Victoria 3066

tel (03) 9417 6855 *fax* (03) 9416 2980
e-mail quadrnt@ozemail.com.au
Editor P.P. McGuinness
Monthly $6

Articles, short stories, verse, etc. Prose length: 2000-5000 words. Payment: min. $90 articles/stories, $60 reviews, $40 poems; illustrations by arrangement.

Reader's Digest (Australia)

PO Box 4353, Sydney, NSW 2001
tel (02) 690 6111 *fax* (02) 9690 6211
Editor-in-Chief Bruce Heilbuth
Monthly $4.95

Articles on Australian subjects by commission only. No unsolicited MSS accepted. Length: 2500-5000 words. Payment: up to $6000 per article; brief filler paragraphs, $50-$250. Illustrations: half-tone, colour.

Rock

Wild Publications Pty Ltd, PO Box 415, Prahran, Victoria 3181
tel (03) 9826 8482 *fax* (03) 9826 3787
e-mail rock@wild.com.au
web site http://www.rock.com.au
Editor Naomi Peters
Quarterly $8.99

Australian rockclimbing and mountaineering articles, features and news. Length: 2000 words (articles/features), 200 words (news). Illustrations: colour transparencies. Payment: $85 per page (words and pictures). Founded 1978.

Scuba Diver

Yaffa Publishing Group, 17-21 Bellevue Street, Surry Hills, NSW 2010
tel (02) 9281 2333 *fax* (02) 9281 2750
e-mail yaffa@flex.com.au
Editor Sue Crowe
Bi-monthly $5.95

News, features, articles and short stories on scuba diving. Length: 1500 words (articles/features), 300-800 words (news), 800-1000 (short stories). Illustrations: colour. Payment: $70 per page, negotiable (words and pictures).

She

ACP Publishing Pty Ltd, 54 Park Street, Sydney, NSW 2000
tel (02) 9282 8585 *fax* (02) 9267 4457
Editor Kate Mahon
Monthly $5.20

Lifestyle magazine for women aged 25-39. Length: 2000 words, variable (articles/ features). Illustrations: colour and b&w. Founded 1993.

The Sun-Herald

GPO Box 506, Sydney, NSW 2001
tel (02) 9282 2822 *fax* (02) 9282 2151
Publisher and Editor Alan Revell
London office John Fairfax (UK) Ltd, 93 Fetter Lane, London EC4A 1HE
tel 020-7242 0044
Weekly $1.20

Topical articles to 1000 words; news plus sections on current affairs, social issues, entertainment, finance, sport and travel. Payment: by arrangement.

(Sydney) The Daily Telegraph

News Ltd, 2 Holt Street, Surry Hills, NSW 2010
tel (02) 9288 3000 *fax* (02) 9288 2300
Editor-in-Chief Col Allan
Daily Mon-Fri 80c Sat $1.20

Modern feature articles and series of Australian or world interest. Length: 1000-2000 words. Payment: according to merit/length.

The Sydney Morning Herald

PO Box 506, Sydney, NSW 2001
tel (02) 9282 2858
Publisher and Editor-in-Chief Gregory Hywood
London office 95 Fetter Lane, London EC4A 1HE
tel 020-7242 0044 *fax* 020-7242 0066
Daily $1

Saturday edition has pages of literary criticism and also magazine articles, plus glossy colour magazine. Topical articles 600-4000 words. Payment: varies, but minimum $100 per 1000 words. Illustrations: all types. Founded 1831.

(Sydney) The Sunday Telegraph

News Ltd, 2 Holt Street, Surry Hills, Sydney, NSW 2010
tel (02) 9288 3305 *fax* (02) 9288 2300
Editor Roy Miller
Weekly $1

News and features. Illustrations: transparencies. Payment: varies. Founded 1935.

Vogue Australia

170 Pacific Highway, Greenwich, NSW 2065
postal address Locked Bag 2550, Crows Nest, NSW 1585
tel (02) 9964 3817 *fax* (02) 9964 3763
Editor Kirstie Clements
Monthly $5.90

Articles and features on fashion, beauty, health, business, people and the arts of interest to the modern woman of style and high spending power. Ideas welcome. Length: from 1000 words. Illustrations: colour and b&w. Founded 1959.

Wild

Wild Publications Pty Ltd, PO Box 415, Prahran, Victoria 3181
tel (03) 9826 8482 *fax* (03) 9826 3787
e-mail wild@wild.com.au
web site http://www.wild.com.au
Editor Naomi Peters
4 p.a. $7.99

'Australia's wilderness adventure magazine.' Illustrated articles of first-hand experiences of the Australian wilderness, plus book and track reviews, product tests. Send sae for guidelines for contributors. Length: 2500 words (articles), 200 words (news). Colour transparencies. Payment: $125 per published page. Founded 1981.

Woman's Day

54-58 Park Street, Sydney, NSW 2000
tel (02) 9282 8000 *fax* (02) 9267 4360
Editor-in-Chief Bob Cameron
Weekly $3

National women's magazine; news, show business, fiction, fashion, general articles, cookery, home economy.

Canada

The Beaver: Exploring Canada's History

Canada's National History Society, Suite 478, 167 Lombard Avenue, Winnipeg, Manitoba R3B 0T6
tel 204-988-9300 *fax* 204-988-9309
Editor Annalee Greenberg
Bi-monthly $27.50 p.a. ($31.50 USA, $33.50 p.a. elsewhere)

Articles, historical and modern, on Canadian history. Length: 1500-4000 words, with illustrations. Payment: on acceptance, approx. 20c per word. Illustrations: b&w and colour photos or drawings.

Books in Canada

50 St Clair Avenue East, 3rd Floor, Toronto, Ontario M4T 1M9
tel 416-924-2777 *fax* 416-924-8682
e-mail bic@inscroll.com
Editor Diana Kuprel
9 p.a. $4.50

Commissioned reviews, informed criticism and articles on Canadian literary, intellectual and political books. Query first – do not send unsolicited material. Payment: 10c per word. Founded 1971.

C international contemporary art

PO Box 5, Station B, Toronto, Ontario M5T 2T2
tel 416-539-9495 *fax* 416-539-9903
e-mail cmag@istar.ca
Editor Joyce Mason
Quarterly US$8.25

Arts and artists' projects, features, reviews. Accepts submissions. Length: features (varies), reviews (500 words). Illustrations: transparencies, photos. Payment: $250-$500 features, $100 reviews. Founded 1972.

The Canadian Forum

35 Britain Street, 3rd Floor, Toronto, Ontario M5A 1R7
tel 416-362-0726 *fax* 416-362-3939
e-mail canadian.forum@sympatico.ca
Editor Robert Chodos
10 p.a. $4 ($28 p.a.)

Articles on public affairs and the arts; book reviews. Length: up to 2500 words. Payment: varies. Illustrations: line and photos.

Canadian Interiors

Crailer Communications, 360 Dupont Street, Toronto, Ontario M5R 1V9
tel 416-966-9944 *fax* 416-966-9946
Editor Sheri Craig
8 p.a. $34.24 p.a. (US$75 p.a. elsewhere)

Articles on all aspects of the interior design industry. Illustrations: half-tone, colour.

Canadian Literature

167-1855 West Mall, University of British Columbia, Vancouver, BC V6T 1Z2
tel 604-882-2780 *fax* 604-822-5504
Editor E.M. Kröller
4 p.a. $40 p.a. individual; $55 p.a. institutions (outside Canada add $15 postage)

Articles on Canadian writers and writing in English and French. No fiction. Length: up to 5000 words. Payment: none. Founded 1959.

Canadian Theatre Review (CTR)

Dept of Drama, University of Guelph, Guelph, Ontario N1G 2W1
Contact Editorial Committee
Quarterly $10.50 ($35 p.a.)

Feature and review articles on Canadian theatre aimed at theatre professionals, academics and general audience; book and play reviews. Send MSS accompanied by PC compatible disk. Length: 2000-3000 words. Illustrations: b&w. Payment: $200-275 (features/articles), $75 (book/play reviews). Founded 1974.

Canadian Yachting

Kerrwil Publications Ltd, 395 Matheson Boulevard East, Mississauga, Ontario L4Z 2H2
tel 905-890-1846 *fax* 905-890-5769
e-mail canyacht@kerrwil.com
web site http://www.canyacht.com
Editor Heather Ormerod
6 p.a. $3.95

Features, news and views. Query letters preferred. Length: regulars, 1000-2000 words; features, 1800-2700 words. Illustrations: line, half-tone, colour, cartoons. Payment: up to $350 regulars, up to $350 features; $50-$250 line, $30-$100 photos, $200 cover shots. Founded 1974.

Chatelaine

777 Bay Street, Toronto, Ontario M5W 1A7
tel 416-596-5425
Editor Rona Maynard
Monthly $2.99

Women's interest articles; Canadian angle preferred. Payment: on acceptance; from $1000.

Chickadee

The Owl Group, Bayard Press Canada, 179 John Street, Suite 500, Toronto, Ontario M5T 3G5
tel (416) 340 2700 *fax* (416) 340 9769
e-mail hilary@owl.on.ca
web site http://www.owlkids.com
Editor Hilary Bain
9 p.a. $2.95 ($24 p.a. Canada, US$14.95 USA, $34 rest of world)

Highly illustrated mix of stories and activities on the theme of the world around kids; aimed at children aged 6-9. Length: 10-100 words (articles), 800-900 words (fiction). Illustrations: colour. Payment: $250 (fiction). Founded 1979.

The Dalhousie Review

Dalhousie University, Halifax, Nova Scotia B3H 3J5
tel 902-494-2541 *fax* 902-494-3561
e-mail Dalhousie.Review@dal.ca
Editor Ronald Huebert, *Associate Editor* Robert M. Martin
3 p.a. ($32.10 p.a., $85.60 for 3 years; ($40/$100 outside Canada)

Articles on history, literature, political science, philosophy, sociology, popular culture, fine arts; short fiction; verse; book reviews. Usually not more than 3 stories and 10-12 poems in any one issue. Length: prose, up to 5000 words; verse, less than 40 words. Contributors receive 2 copies of issue and 10 offprints of their work.

Equinox

11450 Albert-Hudon Blvd, Montreal, Montreal, QC H1G 3J9
tel 514-327-4464 *fax* 514-327-0514
e-mail eqxmag@globetrotter.net
Editor Martin Silverstone
Bi-monthly ($22.95 p.a. Canada; Can.$29 p.a. USA; Can.$35 elsewhere)

Magazine of discovery in science, human cultures, technology and geography. Accepts articles on hard science topics (length: 250-350 words); welcomes queries (2-3-page outline) for specific assignments. No phone queries please. Illustrations: colour transparencies. Payment: by arrangement. Founded 1982.

The Fiddlehead

Campus House, University of New Brunswick, PO Box 4400, Fredericton, NB E3B 5A3
tel 506-453-3501
Editor Ross Leckie
Quarterly $9 ($26 p.a.)

Reviews, poetry, short stories. Payment: approx. $10-$12 per printed page. Founded 1945.

(Hamilton) The Spectator

44 Frid Street, Hamilton, Ontario L8N 3G3
tel 905-526-3333
web site http://www.hamiltonspectator.com
Publisher Patrick J. Collins
Daily Mon-Fri 75c Sat $1.75

Articles of general interest, political analysis and background; interviews, stories of Canadians abroad. Length: 800 words maximum. Payment: rate varies. Founded 1846.

Inuit Art Quarterly

2081 Merivale Road, Nepean, Ontario K2G 1G9
tel 613-224-8189 *fax* 613-224-2907
e-mail iaq@inuitart.org
web site http://www.inuitart.org
Editor Marybelle Mitchell
Quarterly $6.25

Features, original research, artists' perspectives, news. Freelance contributors are expected to have a thorough knowledge of the arts. Length: varies. Illustrations: colour and b&w photos and line. Payment: by arrangement. Founded 1985.

Journal of Canadian Studies

Trent University, Peterborough, Ontario K9J 7B8
tel 705-748-1279 *fax* 705-748-1564
e-mail jcs_rec@trentu.ca
Editors Robert M. Campbell, Kerry Cannon
Quarterly US$35 p.a. (US$55 p.a. institutions)

Major academic review of Canadian studies. Articles of general as well as scholarly interest on history, politics, literature, society, arts. Length: 7000-10,000 words.

The Malahat Review

University of Victoria, PO Box 1700 STN CSC, Victoria, BC V8W 2Y2
tel 250-721-8524
e-mail malahat@uvic.ca
web site http://web.uvic.ca/malahat
Editor Marlene Cookshaw
Quarterly $30 p.a. ($40 p.a. overseas)

Short stories, poetry, short plays, reviews, some graphics. Payment: $30 per magazine page. Illustrations: half-tone. Founded 1967.

Performing Arts & Entertainment in Canada (PA&E)

104 Glenrose Avenue, Toronto, Ontario M4T 1K8
tel 416-484-4534 *fax* 416-484-6214
Editor Karen Bell
Quarterly $8 p.a. ($14 p.a. elsewhere)

Feature articles on Canadian theatre, music, dance and film artists and organisations; technical articles on scenery, lighting, make-up, costumes, etc. Length: 600-1200 words. Payment: $150-$175, one month after publication. Illustrations: b&w photos, colour slides. Founded 1961.

Photo Life

1 Dundas Street West, Suite 2500, PO Box 84, Toronto, Ontario M5G 1Z3
tel 800-905-7468 *fax* 800-664-2739
e-mail apex@photolife.com
web site http://www.photolife.com
Editor Suzie Ketene
8 p.a. $3.95

Covers all aspects of photography of interest to amateur and professional photographers. Length: 1500-2500 words. Illustrations: colour and b&w photos. Payment: by arrangement. Founded 1976.

Queen's Quarterly

Queen's University, Kingston, Ontario K7L 3N6
tel 613-533-2667 *fax* 613-533-6822
e-mail qquarter@post.queensu.ca
web site http://info.queensu.ca/quarterly
Editor Dr Boris Castel
Quarterly $6.50 ($20 p.a.; $40 p.a. institutions)

A multidisciplinary scholarly journal aimed at the general educated reader – articles, short stories and poems. Length: 2500-3500 words (articles), 2000 (stories). Payment: by negotiation. Founded 1893.

Quill & Quire

70 The Esplanade, Suite 210, Toronto, Ontario M5E 1R2
tel 416-360-0044 *fax* 416-955-0794
e-mail quill@idirect.com
Editor Scott Anderson
12 p.a. $59.95 p.a. (outside Canada $85p.a.)

Articles of interest about the Canadian book trade. Payment: from $100. Illustrations: line, half-tone. Subscription includes Canadian Publishers Directory (2 p.a.). Founded 1935.

Reader's Digest (Canada)

1100 René Levesque Blvd. W, Montreal, Quebec H3B 5H5
tel 514-940-0751
Editor Murray Lewis
Monthly $3.25

Original articles on all subjects of broad general appeal, thoroughly researched and professionally written. Outline or query only. Length: 3000 words approx. Payment: from $2700. Also previously published material. Illustrations: line, half-tone, colour.

Saturday Night

300-1450 Don Mills Road, Toronto, Ontario M3B 2X7
tel 416-386-2789 *fax* 416-386-2779
Editor Dianna Symonds

Magazine of Canada's people, politics, business, entertainment and life. For non-fiction send a query letter, including details of preliminary research and writing experience. For fiction, send MSS with sae or IRCs for its return. No poetry. Length: 1500-4000 words. Payment: $1 per word. Founded 1887.

(Toronto) The Globe and Mail

444 Front Street West, Toronto, Ontario M5V 2S9
Publisher Phillip Crawley, *Editor* Richard Addis
Daily 60c

Unsolicited material considered. Payment: by arrangement. Founded 1844.

Toronto Life

59 Front Street East, Toronto, Ontario M5E 1B3
tel 416-364-3333 *fax* 416-861-1169
Editor John Macfarlane
Monthly $3.95

Articles, profiles on Toronto and Torontonians. Illustrations: line, half-tone, colour. Founded 1966.

Toronto Star

One Yonge Street, Toronto, Ontario M5E 1E6
tel 416-367-2000
London office Level 4A, PO Box 495, Virginia Street, London E1 9XY *tel* 020-7833 0791
Daily Mon-Fri 30c Sat$1 Sun 75c

Features, life, world/national politics. Payment: by arrangement. Founded 1892.

(Vancouver) Province

200 Granville Street, Suite 1, Vancouver, BC V6C 3N3
tel 604-605-2063 *fax* 604-606-2720
Editor-in-Chief Vivienne Sosnowski
Daily Mon-Fri 60c Sun $1

Founded 1898.

Vancouver Sun

200 Granville Street, Vancouver, BC V6C 3N3
tel 604-605-2180 *fax* 604-605-2323
e-mail jcruickshank@pacpress.southam.ca
web site http://www.vancouversun.com
Editor-in-Chief John Cruickshank
London office Southam News of Canada, 8 Heath Mansions, Hampstead Grove, London NW3 6SL
tel 020-7435 5103
Daily Mon-Thu 75c Fri, Sat $1.25

Mix arts magazine. Travel, Op-Ed pieces considered. Payment: by arrangement.

Wascana Review of Contemporary Poetry & Short Fiction

c/o English Department, University of Regina, Regina, Sask. S4S 0A2
tel 306-585-4302 *fax* 306-585-4827
web site http://www.uregina.ca./wrhome.htm
Editor Kathleen Wall
Bi-annual $10 p.a. ($12 p.a. outside Canada)

Criticism, short stories, poetry, reviews. Manuscripts from freelance writers welcome. Length: prose, not more than 6000 words; verse, up to 100 lines. Payment: $3 per page for prose; $10 per printed page for verse; $3 per page for reviews. Contributors also receive 2 free copies and a year's subscription. Founded 1966.

Windspeaker

15001-112 Ave NW, Edmonton, Alberta T5M 2V6
tel 780-455-2700 *fax* 780-455-7639
Editor Debora Lockyer
Monthly ($36 p.a.)

National newspaper by and about Aboriginal people: articles, features, news, guest editorials. Send for 'Freelancer's guidelines'. Length: 300-800 words. Illustrations: prefer colour prints. Payment: $3.00 per published column inch; $15-$50 per photo. Founded 1983.

Winnipeg Free Press

1355 Mountain Avenue, Winnipeg, MB R2X 3B6
tel 204-697-7000 *fax* 204-697-7412
Editor Nicholas Hirst
Daily Mon-Fri 25c Sat $1.25 Sun 35c

Some freelance articles. Payment: $100. Founded 1872.

New Zealand

(Auckland) New Zealand Herald

PO Box 32, Auckland
tel (09) 379-5050 *fax* (09) 373-6421
e-mail editor@herald.co.nz
web site http://www.nzherald.co.nz
Editor Steve Davis
Editor-in-Chief Gavin Ellis
Daily Mon-Fri 90c Weekend $1.20

Topical and informative articles 800-1100 words. Payment: minimum $150-$300. Illustrations: colour negatives or prints. Founded 1863.

(Auckland) Sunday News

PO Box 1327, Auckland
tel (09) 302-1300 *fax* (09) 358-3003
e-mail editor@sunday-news.co.nz
Editor Clive Nelson
Weekly Sun $1.10

News, sport and showbiz, especially with New Zealand interest. Illustrations: colour and b&w photos. Founded 1963.

(Auckland) Sunday Star-Times

News Media Auckland Ltd, PO Box 1327, Auckland 1
tel (09) 302-1300 *fax* (09) 309-0258
e-mail feedback@star-times.co.nz
Editor Suzanne Chetwin
Sun $1.30

(Christchurch) The Press

Private Bag 4722, Christchurch
tel (03) 379-0940 *fax* (03) 364-8238
Editor Tim Pankhurst
Daily 70c

Articles of general interest not more than 800 words. Illustrations: photos and line drawings, cartoons. Payment: by arrangement.

Christchurch Star

PO Box 1467, Christchurch
tel (03) 379-7100 *fax* (03) 366-0180
Editor Mike Fletcher
Bi-weekly Free

Will consider freelance material, excluding travel; also cartoons. Founded 1868.

(Dunedin) Otago Daily Times

PO Box 181, Dunedin
tel (03) 477-4760 *fax* (03) 474-7422
e-mail odt.editor@alliedpress.co.nz
web site http://www.odt.co.nz
Editor R.L. Charteris
Daily 80c

Any articles of general interest up to 1000 words, but preference is given to NZ writers. Topical illustrations and personalities. Payment: current NZ rates. Founded 1861.

Hawke's Bay Today

PO Box 180, Karamu Road North, Hastings
tel (06) 878-5155 *fax* (06) 876-0655
Editor J. Eagle
Daily 70c

Limited requirements. Payment: $40 upwards for articles, $10 upwards for photos. Illustrations: web offset.

(Invercargill) The Southland Times

PO Box 805, Invercargill
tel (03) 218-1909 *fax* (03) 214-9905
e-mail editor@stl.co.nz
web site http://www.press.co.nz
Editor F.L. Tulett
Mon-Fri 70c Sat 80c

Articles of up to 800 words on topics of Southland interest. Payment: by arrangement. Illustrations: line, half-tone, colour, cartoons. Founded 1862.

Management

Profile Publishing, PO Box 5544, Auckland
tel (09) 630-8940 *fax* (09) 630-1046
e-mail sprofile@iconz.co.nz
Editor Sherrill Tapsell
Monthly $5.95

Articles on the practice of management skills and techniques, individual and company profiles, coverage of business trends and topics. A NZ/Australian angle or application preferred. Length: 2000 words. Payment: by arrangement; minimum 23c per word. Illustrations: photos, line drawings.

(Napier) The Daily Telegraph

PO Box 343, Napier
tel (06) 835-4488 *fax* (06) 835-1129
e-mail editor@telegraph.co.nz
Editor L.H. Pierard
Daily 70c

Limited market for features. Illustrations: line, half-tone, colour. Payment: $50 upwards per 1000 words; $20 a picture. Founded 1871.

The Nelson Mail

PO Box 244, 15 Bridge Street, Nelson
tel (03) 548-7079 *fax* (03) 546-2802
e-mail nml@nelsonmail.co.nz
Editor David Mitchell
Daily 70c

Features, articles on NZ subjects. Length: 500-1000 words. Payment: up to $100 per 1000 words. Illustrations: half-tone, colour.

(New Plymouth) The Daily News

PO Box 444, Currie Street, New Plymouth
tel (06) 758-0559 *fax* (06) 758-6849
e-mail editor@tnl.co.nz
Editor Murray Goston
Daily 70c

Articles preferably with a Taranaki connection. Payment: by negotiation. Illustrations: half-tone, cartoons. Founded 1857.

The New Zealand Farmer

NZ Rural Press Ltd, PO Box 4233, 300 Great South Road, Greenlane, Auckland 5
tel (09) 520-9451 *fax* (09) 520-9459
e-mail ruralprs@iconz.co.nz
Editor Sean Stephens
Weekly $2.30

Authoritative, simply written articles on new developments in livestock husbandry, grassland farming, cropping, farm machinery, marketing.

New Zealand Woman's Day

Private Bag 92512, Wellesley Street, Auckland
tel (09) 308-2718 *fax* (09) 357-0978
Editor Michele Crawshaw
Weekly $3.10

Celebrity interviews, exclusive news stories, short stories, gossip. Length: 1000 words. Illustrations: colour transparencies; payment according to use. Payment: £400. Founded 1989.

She

Private Bag 92512, Wellesley Street, Auckland 1036
tel (09) 308-2735 *fax* (09) 302-0667
e-mail she@acpnz.co.nz
Editor Debra Millar
Monthly $5.95

Lifestyle magazine for young women. Length: 1000-2000 words (features), 300 words (profiles). Illustrations: colour. Payment: negotiable. Founded 1996.

Straight Furrow

Rural Press, PO Box 4233, Auckland
tel (09) 520 9451 *fax* (09) 520 9459
Editor Sean Stephens
Fortnightly

News and features of interest to the farming/rural sector with emphasis on agri-political issues. Length: 500 words news, 1000 words features. Illustrations: colour and b&w photos. Payment: 25c per published word; $20 per published photo. Founded 1933.

Takahe

Takahe Collective Trust, PO Box 13335, Christchurch 8001
tel (03) 359-8133
3-4 p.a. $24 p.a. ($32 p.a. international)

Quality short fiction and poetry by both new and established writers. Payment: approx. $30 per issue. Founded 1989.

The Timaru Herald

PO Box 46, Bank Street, Timaru
tel (03) 684-4129 *fax* (03) 688-1042
e-mail editor@hcl.co.nz
Editor D.H. Wood
Daily 60c

Topical articles. Payment: by arrangement. Illustrations: colour or b&w prints.

(Wellington) The Evening Post

PO Box 3740, 40 Boulcott Street, Wellington
tel (04) 474-0444 *fax* (04) 474-0237
e-mail editor@evpost.co.nz
Editor's fax (04) 474-0536
Editor Suzanne Carty
Daily Mon-Fri 80c Sat 90c

General topical articles, 600 words. Payment: NZ current rates or by arrangement. News illustrations, cartoons. Founded 1865.

Your Home and Garden

Australian Consolidated Press (New Zealand) Ltd, Private Bag 92512, Wellesley Street, Auckland
tel (09) 308-2700 *fax* (09) 377 6725
Editor Claire McCall
Monthly $5.95

Advice, ideas and projects for homeowners – interiors and gardens. Length: 1000 words. Illustrations: good quality colour transparencies. Payment: 30c per word/ $75 per transparency. Founded 1991.

South Africa

(Cape Town) Cape Times

Newspaper House, 5th Floor, 122 St George's Mall, Cape Town 8001
tel (021) 488-4911 *fax* (021) 488 4744
postal address PO Box 11, Cape Town 8000
Editor John Scott
London office Mediaforce Ltd, 1 Gunpowder Square, Fleet Street, London EC4A 3EP
tel 020-7583 2100 *fax* 020-7353 2111
Daily R1.70

Contributions must be suitable for a daily newspaper and must not exceed 800 words. Illustrations: photos of outstanding South African interest. Founded 1876.

Car

PO Box 180, Howard Place 7450
tel (021) 531-1391 *fax* (021) 532-2698
e-mail car@rsp.co.za
web site http://www.cartoday.com
Editor John Wright
Monthly R9.95

New car announcements with pictures and full colour features of motoring interest. Payment: by arrangement. Illustrations: colour, cartoons. Founded 1957.

Caxton Magazines

PO Box 32083, Mobeni 4060, Natal
tel (031) 422-041

Bona

Monthly R5.50

Articles on fashion, cookery, sport, music of interest to black people. Length: up to 3000 words. Payment: by arrangement. Illustrations: line, half-tone, colour, cartoons.

Farmer's Weekly

Editor C. Venter
Weekly R6.95

Articles, generally illustrated, up to 1000 words, on all aspects of practical farming and research with particular reference to conditions in Southern Africa. Includes women's section which accepts suitable, illustrated articles. Illustrations: line, half-tone, colour, cartoons. Payment: according to merit. Founded 1911.

Garden and Home

Editor Margaret Wasserfall
Monthly R12.95

Well-illustrated articles on gardening, suitable for southern hemisphere. Articles for home section on furnishings, flower arranging, food. Payment: by arrangement. Illustrations: half-tone, colour, cartoons.

Living and Loving

Editor Fiona Wayman
Monthly R8.50

Romantic fiction, 1500-4000 words. Articles dealing with first-person experiences; baby, family and marriage, medical articles up to 3000 words. Payment: by merit. Illustrations: line, half-tone, colour, cartoons. Founded 1970.

Your Family
Editor Debbie-Lee Kelly
Monthly R8.50
Cookery, knitting, crochet and homecrafts. Family drama, happy ending. Payment: by arrangement. Illustrations: continuous tone, colour and line, cartoons.

Daily Dispatch
Dispatch Media (Pty) Ltd, 33 Caxton Street, East London 5201
tel (043) 702-2000 *fax* (043) 743 5155
e-mail eledit@iafrica.com
web site http://www.dispatch.co.za
Editor Gavin Stewart
Daily Mon-Sat R1.40
Newspaper for the Eastern Cape region. Features of general interest, especially successful development projects in developing countries. Colour and b&w photographs, artwork, cartoons. Contributions welcome. Length: approx. 1000 words (features). Payment: R250; R50 photographs. Founded 1872.

(Durban) The Mercury
Independent Newspapers KwaZulu-Natal Ltd, PO Box 950, Durban 4000
tel (031) 308-2332 *fax* (031) 308-2357
Editor D. Pather
Daily Mon-Fri R2.80
Serious background news and inside details of world events. Length: 700-900 words. Illustrations: photos of general interest. Founded 1852.

Femina Magazine
Associated Magazines, Box 3647, Cape Town 8000
tel (021) 464-6200 *fax* (021) 461 4290
e-mail femina@assocmags.co.za
Editor Jane Raphaely
Monthly R11.25
For busy young professionals, often with families. Humour, personalities, real-life drama, medical breakthroughs, popular science, news-breaking stories and human interest. Payment: by arrangement. Illustrated.

Independent Newspapers Holdings Ltd
Contributions PO Box 1014, Johannesburg 2000
Cape Town **Argus** Daily R1.70
Weekend Argus Sat R3.90
Cape Times R2.70
Durban **Daily News** R1.60
The Saturday Paper R2.20
Ilanga R1.40
Post (Natal) R3
Natal Mercury R2.40
Sunday Tribune R4
Johannesburg **The Star** R2.30
Saturday Star R2.70
Sunday Star R2.50
Sunday Independent R6
Sowetan R1.30
Pretoria **Pretoria News** R1.90
web site http://www.star.co.za
Accepts articles of general and South African interest; also cartoons. Payment: in accordance with an editor's assessment.

The Star & SA Times online
web site http://www.satimes.press.net/

(Johannesburg) Sunday Times
PO Box 1742, Saxonwold 2132
tel (011) 280-5102 *fax* (011) 280-5111
e-mail suntimes@tml.co.za
Editor M.W. Robertson
Sun R4.95
Illustrated articles of political or human interest, from a South African angle if possible. Maximum 1000 words long and 2 or 3 photos. Shorter essays, stories and articles of a light nature from 500-750 words. Payment: average rate £100 a column. Illustrations: colour and b&w photos, line drawings.

Natal Witness
244 Longmarket Street, Pietermaritzburg, KwaZulu-Natal 3201
tel (033) 355-1111 *fax* (033) 355-1122
e-mail features@witness.co.za
Editor J.H. Conyngham
Daily R2
Accepts topical articles. All material should be submitted direct to the editor in Pietermaritzburg. Length: 500-1000 words. Payment: average of R350 per 1000 words. Founded 1846.

Southern Cross
PO Box 2372, Cape Town 8000
tel (021) 465-5007 *fax* (021) 465-3850
e-mail scross@global.co.za
Editor Michael Shackleton
Weekly R2
National English-language Catholic weekly. Catholic news reports, world and South African. Length: 700-word articles.

Illustrations: cartoons of Catholic interest from freelance contributors. Payment: 10c per word; illustrations R23.10.

Woman's Value

Nasionale Media, PO Box 1802, Cape Town 8000
tel (021) 406-2205 *fax* (021) 406-2929
e-mail adonald@naspers.com
web site http://www.womansvalue.com
Editor Ann Donald
Monthly R9.55

Features on beauty, food, finance, knitting, needlecraft, crafts, home and garden, health and parenting; short stories. 1000-word accounts of experiences published on the 'My own story' page. Length: up to 1200 words (features/stories). Payment: by negotiation. Colour transparencies. Founded 1980.

World Airnews

PO Box 35082, Northway, Durban 4065
tel (031) 564-1319 *fax* (031) 563-7115
Editor Tom Chalmers
Monthly £36 p.a.

Aviation news and features with an African angle. Payment: by negotiation.

USA

The Yearbook does not contain a detailed list of US magazines and journals. The Overseas volume of Willings Press Guide is the most useful general reference guide to US publications, available in most reference libraries. For readers with a particular interest in the US market, the publications listed here will be helpful (please make payments to the US in US funds).

American Markets Newsletter

175 Westland Drive, Glasgow G14 9JQ
e-mail sheila.oconnor@juno.com
Editor Sheila O'Connor
10 p.a. £34 p.a. (£63 for 2 years)

Editorial guidelines for US, Canadian and other overseas markets, plus information on press trips, non-fiction/fiction markets and writers' tips. Sample issue £3.95 (payable to S. O'Connor).

Willings Press Guide

Hollis Directories Ltd, 7 High Street, Teddington, Middlesex TW11 8EL
tel 020-8977 7711 *fax* 020-8977 1133
e-mail willings@hollis-pr.co.uk
web site http://www.hollis-pr.co.uk
£225 2-volume set; or £170 UK volume, £170 international volume

Two volumes contain details on 50,000 newspapers, broadcasters, periodicals and special interest titles in the UK and internationally. Usually available at local reference libraries or direct from the publisher. Also available on CD-Rom and the Internet.

The Writer

The Writer Inc., 120 Boylston Street, Boston, MA 02116
Monthly $29 p.a. ($39 p.a. Canada, $59 p.a. foreign)

Contains articles of instruction on all writing fields, lists of markets for MSS and special features of interest to freelance writers everywhere.

The Writer Inc. also publishes books on writing fiction, non-fiction, poetry, articles, plays, etc.

Writer's Digest

Writer's Digest Books (address below)
($27 plus $10 surface post, $56 airmail p.a.)

Monthly magazine for writers who want to write better and sell more; aims to inform, instruct and inspire the freelance.

Writer's Digest Books

Writer's Digest Books, 1507 Dana Avenue, Cincinnati, OH 45207

Also publishes annually *Novel and Short Story Writer's Market, Children's Writer's and Illustrator's Market, Poet's Market, Photographer's Market, Artist's & Graphic Designer's Market, Guide to Literary Agents* and many other books on creating and selling writing and illustrations.

The Writer's Handbook

The Writer Inc. (address above)
$32.95 plus $3.25 shipping & handling; $4.25 s&h Canada; $4.75 s&h foreign ($33.20 p.a. book rate)

A substantial volume containing 110 chapters, each written by an authority, giving practical instruction on a wide variety of aspects of freelance writing and includes details of 3300 markets, payment rates and addresses.

Writer's Market

Writer's Digest Books (address above)
($27.99 plus $4 p&p)

An annual guidebook giving editorial requirements and other details of over 4000 US markets for freelance writing. Also available on CD-Rom.

Submitting manuscripts

When submitting material to US journals, include a covering letter, together with return postage in the form of International Reply Coupons (IRC). IRCs can be exchanged in any foreign country for stamps representing the minimum postage payable on a letter sent from one country to another. Make it clear what rights are being offered for sale as some editors like to purchase MSS outright, thus securing world copyright, i.e. the traditional British market as well as the US market. Send the MSS direct to the US office of the journal and not to any London office.

In many cases it is best to send a preliminary letter giving a rough outline of your article or story (enclose IRCs for a reply). Most magazines will send a leaflet giving guidance to authors.

Magazines by subject area

These lists can be only a broad classification. They should be regarded as a pointer to possible markets and should be used with discrimination. Addresses for magazines start on page 21.

Fiction (see also Literary)

The following take short stories, unless otherwise stated. 'Long' refers to long complete stories, from 35,000 words upwards.

Active Life
Acumen
Ambit
Aquila
Australian Short Stories (Aus.)
The Australian Women's Weekly
Bella
Best
Brownie
Cencrastus
Chat
Chickadee (Can.)
The Dalhousie Review (Can.)
The Edge
Femina Magazine (SA)
The Fiddlehead (Can.)
Fly-Fishing & Fly-Tying
HU (The Honest Ulsterman) (Ire.)
Imago (Aus.)
Infant Projects
Interzone
Ireland's Own
The Lady
Living and Loving (SA)
London Magazine
The Malahat Review (Can.)
More!
My Weekly (also serials)
My Weekly Story Collection (long only)
New Impact
New Zealand Woman's Day (NZ)
Overland (Aus.)
Peninsular Magazine
People's Friend (also serials)
People's Friend Story Collection (long only)
Planet
Pride
Prospect
Quadrant (Aus.)
QWF
Reality (Ire.)
Saturday Night (Can.)
The Scots Magazine
Scuba Diver* (Aus.)
Songwriting and Composing
Springboard
Stand Magazine
Staple New Writing
Starburst
Takahe (NZ)
Take a Break
Wascana Review (Can.)
Woman and Home (also serials)
Woman's Day (Aus.)
Woman's Own
Woman's Way (Ire.)
Woman's Weekly (also serials)
Young Writer
Yours

Letters to the Editor

The Australian Women's Weekly
Bella
Best
The Big Issue
The Big Issue in Scotland
Bizarre
Caravan Magazine
Chat
Child Education
Control & Instrumentation
Dental Update
Dolly (Aus.)
Electrical Times
Expecting Our Baby
Femina Magazine (SA)
Freelance Market News
The Furrow (Ire.)
Ideal Home
Junior Education
Modern Painters
Moneywise
Mother & Baby
Motor Caravan Magazine
My Weekly
New Scientist
NW Magazine (Aus.)
New Zealand Woman's Day (NZ)
Park Home & Holiday Caravan
Police Journal
Practical Householder
Practical Parenting
Practical Photography
Practical Woodworking

Prima
Right Start
Saga Magazine
She
Shout
Slimmer Magazine
Slimming Magazine
Take a Break
Television
that's life!
TV Quick
The Weekly News
What's on TV
Woman
Woman's Day (Aus.)
Woman's Own
Woman's Realm
Woman's Way (Ire.)
Woman's Weekly
Yours

Gossip paragraphs

Art Business Today
Australian Bookseller & Publisher
The Big Issue
Bliss!
Broadcast
Campaign
Car
Church of England Newspaper
Classical Music
Country Life
Cycling Weekly
Dirt Bike Rider
Drapers Record
Electrical Times
Eventing
Farming News
Film Review
Flicks
FourFourTwo
Fresh Produce Journal
Garden News
Geographical Magazine
Gibbons Stamp Monthly
Golf Weekly
Golf World
Hampshire – The County Magazine
Health and Efficiency – H&E Magazine
Horse & Hound
Irish Farmers Journal
Irish Medical Times
Irish Printer
Journalist
The Lawyer
Making Music
Marketing Week
Men Only
Mojo
Music Week
New Statesman
The New Welsh Review
Nursing Times
Opera Now
PC Review
PCS, The Magazine
Pilot
The Pink Paper
Police Review
Pride
Private Eye
Punch
Radio Times
Red Pepper
Retail Week
Rugby World
Runner's World
Running Fitness
Satellite Times
The Scottish Farmer
Shoot
Shout
The Stage
Success Now
The Tablet
tate: the art magazine
Therapy Weekly
Total Football
Venue
Woman
Woman's Realm
World Soccer
Writers' Forum

Brief filler paragraphs

Active Life
Africa Confidential
American Markets Newsletter
The Architects' Journal
Athletics Weekly
Australian Bookseller & Publisher
Babycare and Pregnancy
Ballroom Dancing Times
Bella
Best of British
The Big Issue
Black Beauty & Hair
Bliss!
Blueprint
Boards
British Journal of General Practice
Broadcast
Cage and Aviary Birds
Car
Cat World
Cencrastus
Christian Herald
Classic Cars
Climber
Communicate
Country Life
Country Smallholding
The Countryman
Cycling Weekly
Dorset Life – The Dorset Magazine
Drapers Record
Electrical Times
Eventing
Executive PA
Farming News
The Field
Film Review
Flight International
Fly-Fishing & Fly-Tying
Fortean Times
FourFourTwo
FRANCE Magazine
Freelance Market News
Fresh Produce Journal
Garden News
Geographical Magazine
Gibbons Stamp Monthly
Gifts International
Golf Weekly
Golf World
Greetings Today
Hampshire – The County Magazine
Health and Efficiency – H&E Magazine
Health & Fitness
Hi-Fi News & Record Review
Horse & Hound
Horticulture Week
Hortus
Hotel and Catering Review (Ire.)
The Illustrated London News
Insurance Age
Inuit Art Quarterly (Can.)
Ireland of the Welcomes
Ireland's Own
Irish Farmers Journal
Irish Medical Times
Irish Printer
Jane's Defence Weekly
Journalist
Justice of the Peace
Kids Out
The Lawyer
Making Music
Marketing Week
Men Only
Model Engineer
Motor Boat and Yachting
Motor Boats Monthly
My Weekly
Nautical Magazine
New Scientist

The New Welsh Review
The New Writer
The New Zealand Farmer
Nursing Times
The Oldie
Opera Now
Organic Gardening
Overland (Aus.)
Peninsular Magazine
Picture Postcard Monthly
Pig Farming
Pilot
The Pink Paper
Police Review
Pony Magazine
Post Magazine & Insurance Week
Practical Caravan
Practical Fishkeeping
Practical Woodworking
Pride
Priests & People
Printing World
Private Eye
QWF
Radio Times
Railway Gazette International
Railway Magazine
Reader's Digest
Reader's Digest (Aus.)
Red Pepper
Runner's World
Running Fitness
Satellite Times
School Librarian
The Scottish Farmer
Sea Breezes
Shoot
Slimmer Magazine
Snooker Scene
Somerset Magazine
The Songwriter (Ire.)
Songwriting and Composing
Southern Cross (SA)
The Squash Player
The Stage
Stamp Lover
Staple New Writing
Studio Sound
Success Now
The Tablet
tate: the art magazine
Technology Ireland
TGO
Therapy Weekly
This England
Total Football
Toy Trader
Trucking International
TV Quick
Venue
Waterways World
Weight Watchers Magazine
Woman
Woman's Realm
Woman's Weekly
The Woodworker
World Airnews (SA)
World Fishing
World Soccer
Yachts and Yachting
Young People Now
Young Writer
Your Dog

Puzzles and quizzes

The following take puzzles and/or quizzes on an occasional or, in some cases, regular basis. Ideas must be tailored to suit each publication; approach in writing in the first instance.

Army Quarterly & Defence Journal
Art Business Today
Baptist Times
Best of British
The Big Issue in the North
Bird Watching
Bliss!
Brownie
Cage and Aviary Birds
Catholic Gazette
Chickadee (Can.)
Choice
Cleo (Aus.)
Country Life
The Cricketer International
The Dandy
Darts World
Dirt Bike Rider
Disability Now
Dolly (Aus.)
East Lothian Life
Electrical Times
Essentials
Everyday Practical Electronics
Farmers Weekly (SA)
Film Review
Financial Adviser
Fire
Fishing World Magazine (Aus.)
Football Picture Story Library
Garden and Home (SA)
Golf Monthly
Golf World
Guiding
H & P
Health and Efficiency – H&E Magazine
Here's Health
Hertfordshire Countryside
Horse & Hound
Hospital Doctor
Hotel and Catering Review (Ire.)
HouseBuilder
The Illustrated London News
Ireland's Own
Irish Medical Times
J17
Journalist
Kids Alive!
Kids Out
Living and Loving (SA)
The Log
Making Music
Men Only
Methodist Recorder
My Weekly Puzzle Time
(Napier) The Daily Telegraph (NZ)
New Impact
New Scientist
New World
19
Nursing Times
Opera
Opera Now
Park Home & Holiday Caravan
PCS, The Magazine
Peakland Walker
Performing Arts & Entertainment in Canada (Can.)
Picture Postcard Monthly
Pilot
Practical Photography
The Practitioner
Prospect
Publishing News
Reality (Ire.)
Red Pepper
Runner's World
Running Fitness
Satellite Times
The Scottish Farmer
Scottish Home and Country
She
Shoot
The Short Wave Magazine
Shout
Snooker Scene
Southern Cross (SA)
The Spectator
The Stage
Sugar
The Tablet
Take a Break
Take a Break's Take a Puzzle
TGO
Therapy Weekly
The Times Educational Supplement
Toy Trader
Trout and Salmon
TV Quick

The Universe
War Cry
Waterways World
West Lothian Life
Woman
Woman's Weekly
The Woodworker
The Word (Ire.)
World Soccer
Writers' Forum
Young People Now
Young Writer
Your Family (SA)

UK ethnic weekly newspapers

Asian Times
Caribbean Times
Eastern Eye
The Voice

Women's interest magazines (see also Health and home)

The Australian Women's Weekly
Bella
Best
Black Beauty & Hair
Bliss!
Bona (SA)
Chat
Chatelaine (Can.)
Company
Cosmopolitan
Country Living
Diva
Elle (Aus.)
Elle (UK)
Essentials
Executive PA
Executive Woman
Femina Magazine (SA)
For Women
Frank
Girl About Town Magazine
Good Housekeeping
Hairflair
Harper's Bazaar (Aus.)
Harpers & Queen
Having a Baby
Hello!
Home and Country
Home Words
HQ Magazine (Aus.)
IT (Ire.)
The Lady
Living and Loving (SA)
Looks
Marie Claire
Modern Woman Nationwide (Ire.)
More!
Mother & Baby
Ms London
My Weekly
My Weekly Puzzle Time
New Woman
New Woman (Aus.)
New Zealand Woman's Day (NZ)
19
Nursery World
Office Secretary
OK! Magazine
ONtheBALL
People's Friend
The Pink Paper
Pride
Prima
Red
Right Start
She
She (Aus.)
She (NZ)
Sugar
Take a Break
Tatler
that's life!
U magazine (Ire.)
Vanity Fair
Vogue
Vogue Australia
Wedding and Home
Woman
Woman Alive
Woman and Home
Woman's Day (Aus.)
Woman's Journal
Woman's Own
Woman's Realm
Woman's Value (SA)
Woman's Way (Ire.)
Woman's Weekly
Women's Health
World's Children
Your Family (SA)
You & Your Wedding

Men's interest magazines

Arena
Attitude
Country
Esquire
FHM (For Him Magazine)
Gay Times
GQ
Loaded
Maxim
Mayfair
Men Only
Men's Health
The Pink Paper

Children's and young adult magazines

Animals and You
Aquila
The Beano
Brownie
Bunty
Chickadee (Can.)
Commando
The Dandy
Dolly (Aus.)
Football Picture Story Library
H & P
Hot Press (Ire.)
i-D Magazine
J17
Looks
Mizz
Pony Magazine
Scouting
Shoot
Shout
Sky Magazine
Smash Hits
Young Writer

Subject articles

Advertising, design, printing and publishing (see also Literary)

Arena
Australian Bookseller & Publisher
The Author
Blueprint
Books Ireland
The Bookseller
British Journalism Review
British Printer
Campaign
Canadian Interiors
The Face
Freelance Market News
Greetings Today
The Indexer
Irish Printer
Journalist
Market Newsletter
Media Week
New Media Age
PR Week
Press Gazette
Printing World
Publishing News
The World of Interiors
Young Writer

Agriculture, farming and horticulture

Country Life
Country Smallholding
The Countryman
Countryman (Aus.)
Dairy Farmer
Farmer's Weekly
Farmer's Weekly (SA)
Farming News
The Field
Fresh Produce Journal
The Grower
Horticulture Week
Irish Farmers Journal
The New Zealand Farmer
Pig Farming
Poultry World
Scottish Farmer
Smallholder
Straight Furrow (NZ)

Architecture and building

The Architects' Journal
Architectural Design
The Architectural Review
Architecture Today
Blueprint
Building
Building Design
Built Environment
Country Homes and Interiors
Country Life
Education Journal
Estates Gazette
Homes and Gardens
House & Garden
HouseBuilder
Ideal Home
The Local Historian

Art and collecting

AN Magazine
The Antique Dealer & Collectors Guide
Antiques & Art Independent
Antiques and Collectables
Apollo
Art Business Today
Art Monthly
The Art Newspaper
Art Review
The Artist
Artists and Illustrators
Book and Magazine Collector
Burlington Magazine
C international contemporary art (Can.)
Coin News
contemporary visual arts
Country Life
Creative Camera
Eastern Art Report
Gibbons Stamp Monthly
The Illustrated London News
Inuit Art Quarterly (Can.)
Leisure Painter
Medal News
Modern Painters
Numismatic Chronicle
RA Magazine
Stamp Lover
Stamp Magazine
tate: the art magazine
make: the magazine of women's art
The World of Embroidery
The World of Interiors

Aviation

Aeromodeller
Aeroplane Monthly
Air International
Air Pictorial International
Australian Flying
Flight International
The Log
Pilot
World Airnews (SA)

Blind and partially sighted

Published by the Royal National Institute for the Blind in braille unless otherwise stated (see under Book publishers UK and Ireland)
3-FM
Absolutely Boys (also disk)
Absolutely Girls (also disk)
Access IT (also disk)
After Hours
Aphra (women's magazine; also disk)
BBC on Air (also disk)
Blast Off! (also disk)
Braille Chess Magazine
Braille Journal of Physiotherapy
Braille at Bedtime
Braille Music Magazine (also disk)
Braille Radio Times
Braille TV Times (5 regions)
Broadcast Times (disk only)
Busy Solicitor's Digest (also disk)
Channels of Blessing (also abridged in Moon; also disk)
Come Gardening
Compute IT (also disk)
Contention (also disk)
Conundrum (also disk)
Daily Bread (also disk)
Diane (Moon)
Eye Contact (also print)
Good Vibrations (also disk)
High Browse (also print, tape and disk)
Light of the Moon (Moon)
The Moon Magazine (Moon)
Money Matters (also disk)
Music Magazine (also disk)
New Beacon (also print, tape and disk)
News to You? (also print, tape and disk)
Physiotherapists' Quarterly
Piano Tuners' Quarterly (also print, tape and disk)
Progress (also disk)
Rhetoric (also disk)

Scientific Enquiry (also disk)
Shaping Up (also disk)
Shop Window (also disk)
Slugs and Snails (also disk)
SP (Starting Price: men's magazine; also disk)
Spotlight (also print, tape and disk)
Sugar and Spice (also disk)
Theological Times (also tape and disk)
Upbeat (also disk)
The Weekender (also Moon and disk)
You & Your Child (also disk)
VisAbility (also print and tape)
Welcome to a World of ... (also disk)

Business, industry and management

Brewing & Distilling International
Business Life
Business Scotland
BusinessMatters
Chartered Secretary
Communicate
Cosmetic World News
CWU Voice
Director
European Chemical News
Executive PA
Executive Woman
Fashion Forecast International
Fasttrack
Fire
Fishing News
Land & Liberty
Leisureweek
Management (NZ)
Management Today
Mobile and Cellular Magazine
Nationwide Magazine
New Impact
Office Secretary
People Management
The Political Quarterly
Success Now
The Woodworker

Cinema and films

Campaign
The Edge
Empire
Film Review
Flicks
New Statesman
Screen International
Sight and Sound
Studio Sound
Total Film

Computers

Amiga Format
Computer Weekly
Computing
Internet
MacUser
.net The Internet Magazine
New Media Age
PC Answers
PC Direct
PC Review
Personal Computer World
Scientific Computing World

Economics, accountancy and finance

Accountancy
Accountancy Age
Accountancy & Business
Active Life
Africa Confidential
African Business
The Australian Financial Review
The Banker
Business Scotland
Choice
Contemporary Review
Economica
The Economist
Financial Adviser
The Grower
Insurance Age
Insurance Brokers' Monthly
Investors Chronicle
Land & Liberty
Local Government Chronicle
MoneyMarketing
Moneywise
New Statesman
Pensions World
Personal Finance
Post Magazine & Insurance Week
Studies (Ire.)
Tribune

Education

Amateur Stage
Aquila
Art & Craft
Carousel – The Guide to Children's Books
Child Education
Education Journal
Guiding
Infant Projects
Junior Education
Junior Focus
Linguist
Local Historian
Modern Language Review
Music Teacher
New Impact
New Statesman
Nursery Projects
Nursery World
Practical Parenting
Reality (Ire.)
Report
Right Start
Safety Education
School Librarian
Scottish Educational Journal
Speaking English
The Teacher
Theology
The Times Educational Supplement
Times Educational Supplement Scotland
Times Higher Education Supplement
Tribune
Under Five Contact
World's Children
Young People Now

Engineering and mechanics (see also Architecture, Aviation, Business, Motor transport, Nautical, Radio, Sciences)

Car Mechanics
Control & Instrumentation
Electrical Review
Electrical Times
Electronics Australia with ETI
Electronics Times
The Engineer
Engineering
European Chemical News
Everyday Practical Electronics
Fire
Mobile and Cellular Magazine
Model Engineer
New Electronics
Practical Woodworking
Rail
Railway Gazette International
Railway Magazine

Gardening

Amateur Gardening
Country
Country Smallholding
Country Life
The English Garden
The Field
The Garden
Garden and Home (SA)
Garden Answers
Garden News
Gardens Illustrated
Homestyle
Hortus
House & Garden
Organic Gardening
Your Garden

Health and home (see also Women's interest magazines)

Active Life
Australian Home Beautiful
Australian House and Garden
Babycare and Pregnancy
Canadian Interiors
Choice
Classic Stitches
Country Homes & Interiors
Cycling Today
Expecting Our Baby
Feng Shui for Modern Living
Garden and Home (SA)
Good Health
Having a Baby
Health and Efficiency – H&E Magazine
Health & Fitness
Healthy Eating
Here's Health
Home and Family
Homes and Gardens
Homes and Ideas
HomeFlair Magazine
Homestyle
House & Garden
House Beautiful
Ideal Home
In Balance
Inspirations For Your Home
Jewish Telegraph
Kids Out
Perfect Home
Period Living & Traditional Homes
Practical Householder
Practical Parenting
Running Fitness
Safety Education
Saga Magazine
Sainsbury's: The Magazine
Scottish Home and Country
Slimmer Magazine
Slimming Magazine
The Vegan
Weight Watchers Magazine
Wine
Woman's Value (SA)
Women's Health
The World of Embroidery
The World of Interiors
Your Family (SA)
Your Home and Garden (NZ)
Yours
Zest

History and archaeology

Best of British
Coin News
Country Quest
English Historical Review
Evergreen
Geographical Magazine
History
History Today
Illustrated London News
In Britain
The Local Historian
The National Trust Magazine
Picture Postcard Monthly
Scottish Memories
Studies (Ire.)

Hotel, catering and leisure

Caterer & Hotelkeeper
Health Club Management
Hotel and Catering Review (Ire.)
The Leisure Manager
Leisureweek

Humour and satire

Private Eye
Punch
Viz

Inflight magazines

The Australian Way
Business Life
Hot Air

Legal and police

Family Law
Justice of the Peace
The Lawyer
Legal Week
New Law Journal
Police Journal
Police Review
Solicitors Journal

Leisure interests, pets (see also Nautical, Sports)

ace
Aeromodeller
Astronomy Now
Bird Keeper
Bird Watching
Birding World
Birdwatch
Boards
British Birds
British Philatelic Bulletin
Camping Magazine
Caravan Magazine
Classic Stitches
Classics
Climber
Country Walking
Dogs Today
Family Tree Magazine
The Field
Gibbons Stamp Monthly
Guiding
In Britain
Military Modelling
Model Boats
Model Engineer
Motor Caravan Magazine
Motorcaravan & Motorhome Monthly
Needlecraft
Our Dogs
Park Home & Holiday Caravan
Popular Crafts
Practical Caravan
Practical Fishkeeping
Radio Control Models and Electronics
The Rambler
Scale Models International
Scottish Field
Scouting
Scuba Diver (Aus.)
Scuba World
Sewing World
Stamp Lover
Stamp Magazine
Swimming Times
Time Out
Wine

The Woodworker
Workbox Magazine
Your Cat Magazine
Your Dog Magazine

Literary (see also Poetry)

American Markets Newsletter
Australian Bookseller & Publisher
Australian Short Stories
The Author
The Book Collector
Books in Canada
Books Ireland
Books Magazine
The Bookseller
British Journalism Review
The Canadian Forum
Canadian Literature
Carousel – The Guide to Children's Books
Cencrastus
Chapman
Contemporary Review
Critical Quarterly
The Dalhousie Review (Can.)
The Dickensian
The Edge
Edinburgh Review
The Fiddlehead (Can.)
Granta
Hobo (Aus.)
Imago (Aus.)
Index on Censorship
The Indexer
Journal of Canadian Studies
Journalist
The Library
The Literary Review
LOGOS
London Magazine
London Review of Books
The Malahat Review (Can.)
Market Newsletter
Modern Language Review
New Library World
New Statesman
The New Welsh Review
The New Writer
The Oldie
Orbis
Outposts Poetry Quarterly
Overland (Aus.)
Peninsular Magazine
Planet
Prospect
Publishing News
Quadrant (Aus.)
Queen's Quarterly (Can.)
Quill & Quire (Can.)
QWF
Reality (Ire.)
Scottish Book Collector
Signal
The Spectator
Springboard
Stand Magazine
Starburst
Studies (Ire.)
Takahe (NZ)
The Times Literary Supplement
Tribune
Wasafiri
Wascana Review (Can.)
The Woman Writer
Writers' Forum
Writers' News
Writing Magazine
Young Writer

Local government and civil service

Justice of the Peace
Local Government Chronicle
PCS, The Magazine

Marketing and retailing

Drapers Record
Gifts International
Greetings Today
The Grocer
Marketing Week
Retail Week
Toy Trader
Ulster Grocer

Medicine and nursing

Balance
BMA News Review
British Deaf News
British Journal of General Practice
British Medical Journal
Chemist & Druggist
Community Care
Dental Update
Disability Now
Hospital Doctor
Irish Journal of Medical Science
Irish Medical Times
Journal of Alternative and Complementary Medicine
Lancet
Nursery World
Nursing Times
The Practising Midwife
The Practitioner
Professional Nurse
Pulse
Therapy Weekly
This Caring Business
The Veterinary Review
Young People Now

Military

Army Quarterly & Defence Journal
Jane's Defence Weekly
RUSI Journal

Motor transport and cycling

Auto Express
Autocar
Back Street Heroes
Bike
BMW Magazine
Buses
Car
Car (SA)
Car Mechanics
Classic & Sports Car
Classic Cars
Classics
Commercial Motor
Custom Car
Cycling Today
Cycling Weekly
Dirt Bike Rider
Motor Cycle News
Ride
Truck & Driver
Trucking International
What Car?

Music and recording

Arena
Classic CD
Classical Music
Early Music
The Face
Hi-Fi News & Record Review
i-D Magazine
Jazz Journal International
Kerrang!
Making Music
Melody Maker
Mojo
Music and Letters
Music Teacher
Music Week
Musical Opinion
Musical Times
New Musical Express
Opera
Opera Now
The Organ

Q Magazine
Select Magazine
Sky Magazine
Smash Hits
The Songwriter (Ire.)
Songwriting and Composing
Studio Sound
Tempo

Natural history (see also Agriculture, Rural life)

The Aquarist and Pondkeeper
Bird Keeper
Bird Watching
Birding World
Birdwatch
British Birds
Budgerigar World
Cage & Aviary Birds
Cat World
Chickadee (Can.)
Dogs Today
The Ecologist
Equinox (Can.)
Geo Australasia
Geographical Magazine
Glaucus
Guiding
The National Trust Magazine
Natural World
Naturalist
Nature
Our Dogs

Nautical and marine

Australian Powerboat
Canadian Yachting (Can.)
Classic Boat & The Boatman
Diver
Motor Boat and Yachting
Motor Boats Monthly
Nautical Magazine
Practical Boat Owner
Sea Breezes
Ship & Boat International
Ships Monthly
Yachting Monthly
Yachting World
Yachts and Yachting

Photography

Amateur Photographer
Australian Photography
The British Journal of Photography
Camcorder User
Creative Camera
Freelance Photographer Market Newsletter
Photo Life (Can.)
Practical Photography
Professional Photographer
What Camcorder

Poetry

**Magazines that only take the occasional poem; check with the editor before submitting*

Acumen
Agenda
Ambit
Best of British
British Journal of General Practice*
Brownie*
Catholic Pictorial*
Cencrastus
Chapman
Chickadee (Can.)
Contemporary Review*
The Cricketer International*
Critical Quarterly
Cumbria and Lake District Magazine
Cyphers (Ire.)
Dalesman*
The Dalhousie Review (Can.)
Day by Day*
East Lothian Life
Edinburgh Review
Envoi
The Fiddlehead (Can.)
Fishing World Magazine (Aus.)*
Fortnight (Ire.)
Herald of the South (Aus.)
Hobo (Aus.)
Home and Country*
HQ Poetry Magazine
HU (The Honest Ulsterman) (Ire.)
Imago (Aus.)
Infant Projects
Jewish Chronicle*
Jewish Quarterly*
Lancet*
Life & Work*
The Literary Review
London Magazine
London Review of Books
The Malahat Review (Can.)
Modern Believing
The Month
The New Welsh Review
Orbis
Organic Gardening*
Outposts Poetry Quarterly
Overland (Aus.)
Oxford Poetry
Peninsular Magazine
Planet
PN Review
Poetry Ireland Review/Éigse Éireann
Poetry London
Poetry Nottingham International
Poetry Review
Poetry Wales
Pride
Quadrant (Aus.)
Quaker Monthly*
Reform*
The Rialto
The Scots Magazine*
Scuba Diver* (Aus.)
Songwriting and Composing*
Springboard
Stand Magazine
Staple New Writing
Takahe (NZ)
Third Way*
The Times Literary Supplement*
Traveller*
Tribune*
Wasafiri
Wascana Review (Can.)
West Lothian Life*
Young People Now*
Young Writer
Yours

Politics

Africa Confidential
Australian Journal of International Affairs
Australian Journal of Politics and History
The Big Issues (Ire.)
The China Quarterly
Christian Herald
Contemporary Review
Fortnight (Ire.)
The Illustrated London News
International Affairs
Justice of the Peace
Local Government Chronicle
New Internationalist
New Statesman
Peace News
The Political Quarterly

Prospect
Red Pepper
Studies (Ire.)
Tribune
The World Today

Radio, TV and video

Broadcast
Cable Guide
Campaign
Electronics Australia with ETI
Empire
Film Review
Flicks
Hi-Fi News & Record Review
InterMedia
New Statesman
Opera Now
Practical Wireless
Radio Times
Satellite Times
The Short Wave Magazine
The Stage
Studio Sound
Television
Tribune
TV Quick
TVTimes Magazine
What's on TV

Religion, philosophy and New Age

Baptist Times
Catholic Gazette
The Catholic Herald
Catholic Pictorial
Catholic Times
Christian Herald
Church of England Newspaper
Church of Ireland Gazette
Church Times
Contemporary Review
Day by Day
The Downside Review
Feng Shui for Modern Living
Fortean Times
The Friend
The Furrow (Ire.)
Herald of the South (Aus.)
Home and Family
Home Words
Inquirer
Jewish Chronicle
The Jewish Quarterly
Jewish Telegraph
Kids Alive!
Life & Work
Methodist Recorder
Mind
Modern Believing
The Month
New Humanist
Priests & People
Quaker Monthly
Reality (Ire.)
Reform
The Sign
Southern Cross (SA)
Studies (Ire.)
The Tablet
Theology
Third Way
The Universe
War Cry
Woman Alive
The Word (Ire.)

Rural life and country (see also Natural history)

Aussie Post (Aus.)
Country
Country Life
Country Quest
The Countryman
Cumbria and Lake District Magazine
Dalesman
Derbyshire Life and Countryside
Dorset Life – The Dorset Magazine
East Lothian Life
Essex Countryside
Evergreen
The Field
Hampshire – The County Magazine
Hertfordshire Countryside
In Britain
Lancashire Magazine
Lincolnshire Life
The Local Historian
The National Trust Magazine
New Buckinghamshire Countryside
Peakland Walker
The Rambler
The Scots Magazine
Scottish Field
Scottish Home and Country
Shooting Times and Country Magazine
The Shropshire Magazine
Somerset Magazine
Staffordshire Life Magazine
This England
Waterways World
West Lothian Life
Yorkshire Ridings Magazine

Sciences

Equinox (Can.)
Focus
Geological Magazine
Mind
Nature
New Scientist
Science Progress
Scientific Computing World
Technology Ireland

Sports and games (see also Leisure interests, Motor transport, Nautical)

ace
Ang;er's Mail
Angling Times
Athletics Weekly
Australian Powerboat
Bowls International
The Cricketer International
Darts World
Eventing
The Field
Fishing World Magazine (Aus.)
Fly-Fishing & Fly-Tying
FourFourTwo
Golf Monthly
Golf Weekly
Golf World
Horse & Hound
Horse and Rider
ONtheBALL
Our Dogs
Rock (Aus.)
Rugby World
Runner's World
Running Fitness
Scottish Field
Scuba Diver (Aus.)
Scuba World
Sea Angler
Shoot
Shooting Times and Country Magazine
Ski and Board
The Skier and The Snowboarder
Snooker Scene
Sport First
The Squash Player
Swimming Times
Tennis World
Today's Golfer
Total Football
Trout and Salmon
When Saturday Comes
Wisden Cricket Monthly
The Word (Ire.)
World Fishing
World Soccer

Theatre, drama and dancing (see also Cinema, Music)

Amateur Stage
Ballroom Dancing Times
The Canadian Forum
Canadian Theatre Review
Dance & Dancers
Dance Australia
Dancing Times
The Illustrated London News
In Britain
New Statesman
New Theatre Quarterly
Performing Arts & Entertainment in Canada
Plays & Players Applause
Radio Times
Reality (Ire.)
Speech and Drama
The Stage
Tribune
TV Quick
TVTimes Magazine

Travel and geography

Australian Geographic
Caravan Magazine
Condé Nast Traveller
Equinox (Can.)
FRANCE Magazine
Geo Australasia
Geographical Journal
Geographical Magazine
The Illustrated London News
In Britain
In Dublin (Ire.)
Ireland of the Welcomes
The Local Historian
Natal Witness (SA)
Traveller
Wanderlust
Wild (Aus.)

Recent changes to newspapers and magazines

The following changes have taken place since the last edition of the Yearbook.

Changes of name and mergers

The Australian Quarterly *now* AQ – Journal of Contemporary Analysis
Dairy Farmer and Dairy Beef Producer *now* Dairy Farmer
Greetings Magazine *now* Greetings Today
Guiding Magazine *now* Guiding
Health & Efficiency International *now* Health and Efficiency – H&E Magazine
Horse & Pony *now* H & P
InformationWeek
Inspirations *now* Inspirations For Your Home
The Journal incorporated into The Voice
Modern Woman *now* Modern Woman Nationwide
My Weekly Story Library *now* My Weekly Story Collection
New Weekly *now* NW Magazine
Our Baby *now* Expecting Our Baby
Peak & Pennine *now* Peakland Walker
People's Friend Library *now* People's Friend Story Collection
Photo Technique merged with Amateur Photographer
Poetry London Newsletter *now* Poetry London
Professional Photographer & Digital Pro *now* Professional Photographer
Rambling Today *now* The Rambler
Today's Runner *now* Running Fitness
Video Camera *now* What Camcorder
The Woman Journalist *now* The Woman Writer

Titles ceased publication

Beano Comic Library
Big!
Bunty Library
Dandy Comic Library
Fore!
Helicon Poetry Magazine
M
Parents
Total Sport

Writing for newspapers

A newspaper may be only ink on paper but it's alive, feeding on topicality, originality and the quality of writing on its pages. The contributors an editor longs to hear from identify with the readers and understand what they want. Such contributors are never short of work and enjoy great personal satisfaction. ***Jill Dick*** *looks at newspapers from the freelance's point of view.*

Freelance writers are essential in newspaper production. The sense of excitement, of being reborn every week, every day or even several times a day, and of living on a fast-moving platform of people and events makes papers grow and thrive – and the work of freelances, each with a fresh view of the outside world, is invaluable.

Newspapers offer writers an enormous variety of markets. In the UK and Ireland there are 17 national daily papers and 20 national Sunday papers, plus dozens of supplements and booklets, representing thousands of separate opportunities a year for freelance contributions. The nationals fall into three groups – quality, middle-range and popular – each with its own characteristics, ranging from *The Times* and the *Daily Telegraph*, to the *Daily Mail* and the *Star*; from the *Observer* to the *Sunday People* and from the *Sunday Express* to the *Sunday Mirror*. Add to these hundreds of evening and weekly regional newspapers and an increasing number of free papers – and the total is staggering.

The size and quality of the readership are vital elements in market study. Advertisers want to know this too, and freelance writers can benefit greatly from the information advertisers use for their own purposes. It is not unusual for a serious Sunday newspaper to reserve 60% of the whole paper for advertisements and to carry as many as 150 display and over 4000 classified ads in a single edition.

Advertisers (with big money at stake) take pains to target the readers most likely to buy their wares or use their services: editors have the same idea in mind when considering whether to accept or reject work from freelances. Will this particular copy encourage readers to buy the paper or make them pleased they did so to the extent that they will buy the next edition too? That's how close you need to get to the readers for consistent success.

There is no better way of finding out who they are and how they think and live than making a close, regular and up-to-date study of the papers you'd like to write for. Analyse their content, their page layout and format and discover why they print what they do. Even such attention to detail isn't infallible, for at best it can only reveal what they printed and were interested in yesterday or last week. As for what they'll want tomorrow and next week …

Ideas

If ideas jostle for priority in your head almost without thinking you may have a natural bent for newspaper writing. Even if they don't, remember journalism is a craft which almost anyone can learn, and gathering ideas is just part of it. No matter where you live or work, whom you meet, how you spend your time or what your hobbies and interests may be, you'll find a story. Feature, filler, news item, article, review, regular series, specialist column, interview, diary item, letter, anecdote, profile, preview; in buying a paper readers instinctively ask themselves, 'What's in it for me?' You are providing the answer. To help you there are several well-established market guides, the best being the *Writers' & Artists' Yearbook*, *Willings Press Guide* and *Benn's Media Guide*.

To provide a list of topics to write about would be counter-productive. Dry lists of ideas can encourage stultified thinking; countless writers have stared at such lists and tried to wrench inspiration from them; countless editors have seen (and rejected) the results. In any case, more is needed than an idea. A unique slant on one may be the pointer to a worthwhile venture but a newspaper 'story' is most likely to be successful when it arrives in your head eager, if not desperate, to be told.

Whatever your chosen topic, remember that fishermen bait their hooks not with what they like, but with what fish like. There are many hard lessons to learn about freelancing and one of the toughest is that you have to write not just the stories that appeal to you, but the stories that will sell.

It pays to look ahead, particularly in ways other writers may not. This is not always easy to do and you will have to work hard on your copy before ever writing a word. Research can never be skimped. A thinly researched piece quickly lands on the reject pile if another author has taken more time and trouble to delve into the subject than you have. The real value of research lies not only in the facts and figures you have unearthed but also in the greater understanding you can give your readers from what you have yourself understood. In these modern times the Internet offers easy and rapid results to any researcher – but beware. The Internet has no overall controlling body and I (or anyone else) could put up a web site of wholly invented 'facts'; a wise writer will always confirm research material elsewhere. Reference libraries offer extensive facilities for researching anything and everything, but the most comprehensive single volume to help you is *Research for Writers* by Ann Hoffmann. As your pile of researched material grows so will your interest and enthusiasm. To write well you have to be interested in what you're writing, or at least make yourself interested. If you're not, why should anyone else be?

Style

Style is of equal importance. Beginners sometimes think the lifespan of a newspaper, particularly a daily, is so short that it's not worth bothering about style; this is a big mistake.

Written work submitted to editors or features editors needs to stop them in their tracks or at least intrigue them sufficiently to contact you about development of a point here or getting a picture there. So important is this 'must have' attribute that such features are called 'page-stoppers' in newspaper offices.

Remember the importance of character in newspaper articles:, papers are alive because people are alive. Show rather than tell and use the active rather than the passive voice. Write using all five senses, in short sentences when you want to quicken the pace. Never be afraid to evoke emotion to give your copy a human face, mindful that writing for newspapers is not literary work: it is practical. Too often journalists fail to give characters life – even though the people featured in their copy are alive, not fictional creations. Features may be based entirely on facts but it is their relevance to people that makes them viable. Make yourself the bringer of comfort, an inspiration, an instructor or a wallower in nostalgia. Give readers information about education, medical services, local transport, job opportunities; all are important to people. Above all, let your originality show through – in what you say and how you say it.

But a couple of warnings: be careful not to fill your piece with little more than your own opinion and personal experiences; unless you are famous or well known in the locality, such views are unlikely to be required. And remember that if your story is tagged to a news event (as some of the best often are), whatever its theme, be sure it is not out of date, having been overtaken by more recent events.

Original freelance copy on an editor's desk is more welcome than a tea-break. A good feature writer can write about virtually anything. When you do so make it strong; plunge right into your story, make them laugh, cry, want to know more, swear, feel encouraged, understand something or someone better, agree, disagree – or whatever you choose – but make sure they do or feel *something*.

Specialist spots

Writing a regular page/halfpage/column/corner is not a commission won without effort, often over a number of years. Editors will want to know you will be able to sustain an unlimited time at the job, that your copy will constantly be fresh and innovative and, most importantly, that it will always arrive on time. But when satisfied about these criteria, most are only too glad to hand over responsibility for a portion of the paper and know it is being handled efficiently. Making editors aware of your worth by previously selling them other copy is a good basis for seeking a regular column for yourself.

The golden rule that applies for all copy is that (short of real and rare emergencies) it must never be late. To be calm about accepting deadlines you need to plan ahead carefully, to accept your own limits in terms of the research needed for a particular job of work and the time it is likely to take you to write it and (the best and only true safety net) to have plenty of copy ready in your private store.

What types of regular columns are popular with readers? Their themes are boundless: nature, profiles of famous people, chess, horoscopes, self-help, crosswords, competitions, children's and women's pages, young mothers, pop music, pets, food – anything that interests people will make a good column. As writing a column will get you known and your work constantly read you should be prepared for the feedback from readers. This can be one of the most rewarding aspects of column-running if you don't let it take up too much of your writing time. And at the end of every month you are guaranteed a pre-negotiated fee without having to invoice anyone.

A few topics generally fall into a separate category: travel, sport, motoring, business and finance among them. These are nearly always covered by staff writers and freelance contributions to these sections have to be exceptional, if not unique.

Reviews

The distinctive task of reviewing books, drama, films, videos, radio and television programmes is seldom work for beginners. Sometimes a person who is not even thought of as a writer but who is famous in another sphere might be invited to contribute – a politician or a top sportsman, perhaps – to attract readers with the name of the reviewer rather than the quality of the review but the established papers have their own trained and experienced staff reviewers.

How, then, do you gain experience? For all categories of reviewing it is at the discretion of editors (or features editors) that you may be given a chance. And the only way to build up a solid reputation is to keep writing the copy they want when (or preferably just before) they want it.

Reporting

National dailies and Sunday papers rely on staff reporters and news agencies to maintain a flow of news and reports from prearranged locations, as do leading regional papers. With competition fierce between them, none can afford to miss the capturing and reporting of events as they happen; there can be little or no room for the *ad hoc* freelance in these circumstances.

The local and regional scene is very different. With a sound reputation for filing local news stories a freelance reporter may find work as a regular contributor or on the staff of a local paper, and will soon discover that local reporters are hardworking folk at the very root of a paper's activities. They are likely to be out and about collecting information from tip-offs supplied by the office, waiting to file the latest news on a 'running' story or they might be engaged on any one of a dozen duties in the circulation area. It's the place where many a leading journalist began learning the craft.

Reporters carry considerable responsibility in a challenging job that should not be undertaken without careful consideration. Being committed to maintaining a flow of news from a small town or village or district can be a chore when you want to go on holiday, or if you are ill, or if you just don't feel like doing it. But the first rule of the job is not to let your community down. Doing the 'calls' will be a regular task. This means you will call on the people or organisations likely to tell you what's going on: the police and fire stations, local hospitals, the town hall, the Citizens Advice Bureau, the morgue, the courts, schools, health clinics, community centres – anywhere and everywhere in the locality where a spokesperson is able and willing to give you news or the basis of a news story to pass on to readers of the paper.

Being a reporter will almost certainly bring you more rewards than cash. Your writing skills will benefit by making quick decisions about your copy, learning how to present it clearly in print and over the phone; you will develop an increasing awareness of what is and what is not newsworthy and your confidence will increase.

Letters, fillers, anecdotes and humour

Writers may complain that computerised page layout leaves fewer spaces for small items but (as in all marketing) it is a matter of finding your own openings. It is sometimes worthwhile amassing a good collection of fillers and filing them to an editor as a single package. Fillers, be they Letters to the Editor, snippets to make readers laugh or small pieces of general interest, are covered by the same copyright protection as their weightier brothers: the original copy belongs to the writer and only an exact copy of it by an unauthorised person infringes that copyright. Other people taking up the ideas in themes or fillers are quite free to develop them as they wish – in fact Letters to the Editor are generally chosen with just this in mind: that the original may generate sufficient interest for other readers to write more letters with their views.

To a freelance writer nothing observed or overheard is ever wasted. Humour is nearly always welcome and the newspaper world is full of surprises: a writer friend persuaded the editor of her evening paper that a 'funny' corner would give readers at least one thing to laugh at every day. That's her column now and readers love it. It's easy to laugh at humour, not easy to write it and virtually impossible to teach someone how to do it. If you can, you're lucky.

Business

Never be deterred by the thought that a freelance writer must also be a seller – or be afraid to discuss what you will be paid for work accepted. Bona fide freelances have to deal with tax self-assessment but with this status you can claim many benefits, setting some of your expenses against tax and even working at a tax loss. To satisfy the Inland Revenue you must demonstrate that you are a professional writer, that you are trying to make a profit and that you are eligible to be taxed in such a capacity. This means your taxable income from writing will be the amount you receive in fees less expenses wholly and exclusively incurred in the pursuit of your writing. If you hold another full-time job it may not be easy to substantiate your writing credentials, but being able to produce genuine records and receipts and to demonstrate a proper businesslike approach to your writing work will be to your advantage.

Perhaps the most important rule to observe is this: never give your copy away or sell it for less than its real value. Above all, write what editors want – that's the simple recipe. A newspaper may be only ink on paper but it's alive, feeding on topicality, originality and the quality of the writing on its pages. The contributor an editor longs to hear from identifies with readers and understands what they want. Such a contributor has plenty to write about, works hard to achieve success and enjoys great personal satisfaction.

Jill Dick has spent many years working for national, regional and local newspapers as a feature writer, columnist, reviewer and departmental editor. Her published books include *Freelance Writing for Newspapers* and *Writing for Magazines*, both now in second editions and published by A & C Black.

Errors and pitfalls

In his role as Readers' Editor of the Guardian, ***Ian Mayes*** *compiles corrections, clarifications and apologies for the newspaper. In this article he highlights the importance of accuracy of language.*

My brief as the Readers' Editor or internal ombudsman of the *Guardian* – the first newspaper in Britain to make such a full-time appointment – is to act impartially to resolve differences between readers or other complainants and the paper. It is true that since 1995 I have been an assistant editor of the *Guardian* so how, you may wonder, can I really act fairly in mediating between the paper and its critics? Under the terms of my contract as Readers' Editor I have been set apart from the editorial authority of the paper. That means that the editor cannot sack me – to do that he would have to gain a majority vote of the Scott Trust, which owns the paper and exists, among other reasons, to guard the *Guardian*. Neither he nor any member of his staff can veto anything I care to run in the daily Corrections and Clarifications column, or that I write about the paper in my own column which appears on Saturdays. In fact, since I started at the end of 1997, I have been left completely free to get on with the job to the best of my ability, which is exactly what I expected.

I think I can say that there has never been a dull moment. In the first two years we had more than 12,000 calls from readers and published nearly 3000 corrections, clarifications and apologies. They appear daily in a prominent position, on the leader page of the paper, where readers' letters also appear. A few readers have been appalled by the revelation of mistakes in such profusion, prompting the question, Don't you ever get anything right? Well, yes, we get most things right. The overwhelming majority of readers understand that in gathering in such a short time the vast amount of material we publish daily, perfect accuracy and precision of expression are not always possible. We publish in an average week more than enough words to make a fat book, the length of *Crime and Punishment* or *Moby-Dick*, or – the example I prefer – *Don Quixote*. Weighed against this, the corrections, even on a bad day, may seem less damning.

Most of the *Guardian's* staff journalists, of whom there are more than 350, would not want to return to the old way of automatically resisting almost every complaint. Indeed, since the *Guardian* introduced its corrections column other papers seem to have found it easier to own up and apologise when they get things wrong. One commentator has even suggested that corrections are becoming fashionable. The *Guardian* journalists, if I may risk speaking for them, see the regular publication of corrections as the only honest way of proceeding. It now seems astonishing that it took us so long to start. The insupportable position, we can now see much more clearly, was for the paper to chastise others for lack of accountability while remaining unaccountable itself.

The importance of accuracy

The majority of the crimes we commit are minor ones which neither harm anyone nor significantly detract from the integrity or veracity of the reports in which the mistakes occur. However, half a dozen journalists have been severely reprimanded by the editor and one has left the paper. These cases usually involved breaches of the rules, the code of practice, ratified by the Press Complaints Commission (PCC), which all newspapers in Britain agree to abide by. If you are thinking of writing for newspapers or magazines then you need to be familiar with the PCC code since it requires editors and publishers to see that it is observed rigorously "not only by their staff but by anyone who contributes to their publications." (You can get a copy free by writing to: The Society of Editors, The University Centre, Granta Place, Mill Lane, Cambridge CB2 1RU.) By the way, the code begins by reminding us all that accuracy is the first requirement. The best piece of advice I can give to anyone beginning to write for newspapers is, remember you are writing about real people and not fictional characters of your own invention to do with as you wish.

As a matter of fact, I first contributed to the *Guardian*, long before I joined the staff of the paper, as a freelance in 1963. I submitted a piece about the return of Laurie Lee to Slad, the Gloucestershire village in which *Cider With Rosie* is set. The piece was published, but the byline read Ian Hayes. It was, I have to say, a bit of a disappointment, although a useful reminder that daily journalism is a rough and tumble.

Some of my colleagues have suggested that I seized my present job as the perfect, if somewhat belated, opportunity to get my own back. That is not true, of course, but I do think names are important. Getting them wrong is at the very least a discourtesy and at worst a lapse of professional standards. If someone says his name is Smith, ask him how he spells it. If someone says her name is Catherine, is it Cathryn, Kathryn, Katharine … You need to be particularly careful when part of the name you want to use is also that of some other well-known person. One of the many *Guardian* corrections involving names read: "In one of our editions yesterday the poem *Cost of Life* was attributed to Andrew Morton, 'the poet laureate', a title held by the real author of the piece, Andrew Motion. Andrew Morton is the biographer of Princess Diana and Monica Lewinsky."

One piece of advice, which may seem startlingly obvious, is to read carefully what you have written before you submit it to anyone. You are responsible for the accuracy of what you write and you are also responsible for the cleanliness of the copy you submit. Misspellings, jumbled word orders and misplaced apostrophes are all things that conspire to give an editor the idea that you have not really bothered – and if you can't be bothered why should a busy editor take the trouble? The poor sub-editor, the person who prepares copy for print, is blamed for everything. Interestingly, when I analysed the cause of a sequence of 100 errors corrected in the *Guardian*, the largest group comprised mistakes by writers – mistakes that the most vigilant sub-editor could not have been expected to catch. Mistakes attributable primarily to the sub-editor formed the smallest group.

The choice of words

It may be all right to believe that what you say is more important than the way that you say it. But it is heresy to continue the thought and add that therefore the way in which you say something does not really matter. Certainly it is true that clarity is more important than style, but that is not the same thing. More people write to me at the *Guardian* about our use and abuse of English than about any other single subject. They want to know why we do not know when to use its and it's, or who and whom: "It's a mystery to me. The paper prides itself on its use of English. Those to whom these words are addressed will know who they are."

Why do we use words that do not mean what we think they mean, and indeed sometimes mean the direct opposite? We said quite recently, intending to be complimentary, that a team of architects was best known outside Britain for "the eye-boggling regional government building that enervates the centre of Marseilles." Passing over the fact that we no longer put an s on the end of Marseille, any more than we spell Lyon 'Lyons' or Siena 'Sienna', that description expressed the exact opposite of the writer's intended remark, that the building 'energised' the centre of the city. The list of words in this category is quite long: fulsome, mitigate, inchoate, celibate, refute, disinterest ... When you add a word to your vocabulary make sure you really get to know it. The spelling check on your computer will not help you to do that. The dictionary will.

Journalists, and anyone partaking of journalism, should extend their curiosity for the world around them to the language they use in describing it. Whether this would save us from one of the more common kinds of linguistic error, the homophone, or near homophone, words which sound like the one which should have been used but differ in meaning, I do not know. These errors, which I often add to the corrections column as 'Homophone corner', are a source of great entertainment to readers of the *Guardian*, so perhaps it would be a pity if they disappeared altogether (not very likely to happen). For example, we described somewhere as "the original farming, fishing and fouling [instead of fowling] hamlet"; we spoke about Prince Andrew's way of walking as "a rolling gate" [instead of gait]; and we lamented the presence of "loudmouthed and chauvinistic boars" [instead of boors, or perhaps even bores] ...

Perhaps the only important piece of advice I have to offer is this: If you are just beginning, don't be intimidated or put off by anything I have said. I agree with the historian J.H. Plumb who said, "Nothing blights the creative spirit so much as fear of a solecism." If you want to write you should read. But if you are really going to write, I hope that nothing will stop you.

Ian Mayes is the Readers' Editor at the *Guardian*.

Writing magazine articles

For the would-be writer there can be little doubt that magazine articles offer the easiest way to get into print. ***John Hines*** *offers guidance to potential contributors.*

The article market is vast and is growing steadily. New magazines appear almost daily and, although some founder, many of them survive. The subject material covered by these magazines is so varied that few writers would find their special interests not included.

The magazines range from the modest budget publications to the expensive glossies. Beginners can cut their teeth on the lower end of the market, knowing that, although the fees are modest, the competition is small. These publications provide an excellent start for building skills, self-confidence and credibility. The opportunity for steadily moving up-market is there for the taking, until the writer reaches the level which fulfils his or her ambitions.

The idea

Established article writers usually have files bulging with ideas. They will include newspaper and magazine clippings, jottings from television and radio programmes and personal observations. Almost anything which intrigues the writer or fires the imagination is worth a place in the ideas file. There is an adage in the writing world that it pays to write about what you know. Certainly this is a good idea, for you write more comfortably and competently on a familiar subject, but the wise diversify as well.

In selecting subjects, it is most rewarding to pick those which interest you or, better still, fascinate you. They provide absorbing research and can result in articles rich in original thought with your enthusiasm showing through. As a freelance, you have the luxury of being able to pick and choose, so why not select those articles which are a pleasure to write?

Market study

Successful writers know that effective market study is vital. Any editor will tell you that the vast majority of unsolicited material which lands on their desk is quite unsuitable. The material may be wrong in length, style or choice of subject. Yet studying a copy of the magazine could have helped to avoid these mistakes.

Try to read at least two recent copies of the magazine for which you are aiming to write. Analyse it carefully. Check the number of articles which are staff written (the staff are usually listed in the front of the magazine). By studying several issues you may also discover that there are contributors with regular slots and so deduce the opportunities which exist for the freelance.

If the magazine looks promising, study the type of subject which the editor favours. Check the approximate length of the average article. Ask yourself if the magazine's style is one with which you would be comfortable or to which you could adapt.

Few writers seem to study the advertisements and this is a big mistake. Advertising agencies spend a great deal of money on painstaking expert research, aimed at identifying the typical reader. By studying the advertisements you can benefit from this valuable information which can be most helpful when slanting your article to the readers' interests.

Willings Press Guide, Vol. 1 is an excellent comprehensive source of information on the UK print media. In particular, its classified index can be invaluable for finding a market for those difficult-to-place articles. If you are interested in selling to foreign markets, *Vol. 2* gives international coverage, apart from the UK. There is now a CD-Rom that covers even more titles than the printed volumes.

Studying the *Writers' & Artists' Yearbook* can give you a good insight into the requirements of many magazines, even including the fees they pay.

Freelance Market News is the best market newsletter for the freelance writer (see further reading, page 143). However, the finest market information is that which freelances compile for themselves from personal experience. A card filing system is useful here but, like all market information, its value depends on its being kept up to date.

Research and accuracy

Although some articles can be written from personal experience or knowledge, most articles require some sound current research. Public libraries can be very helpful, particularly if you enlist the help of a qualified librarian rather than a library assistant. The copyright libraries, of which the British Library is the best known, are superb. Would-be researchers must establish their bona fides before being issued with a ticket. (See also *Books, research and reference* on page 565.)

All facts should be checked for accuracy, going back to the source wherever possible. The books of others are not infallible, even reference books. Errors can be embarrassing and inevitably attract unwelcome letters from readers. File your researched material away for future use; an effective filing system is essential. The best book on the subject is *Research for Writers* by Ann Hoffmann (see further reading, page 143).

The Internet can offer a vast amount of research material, particularly in the form of published articles. As some Internet sources may include information of dubious quality, your routine check for accuracy should be made conscientiously.

Research may entail interviewing people and this is a skill which the freelance should consider developing. For effective interviews, sound preparation is important. Research in advance as much as possible about the interviewee and their field of interest. Make a list of important questions in logical sequence. But be prepared to divert from your questions and follow any unexpected revelations. If you use a tape recorder, test it beforehand and always carry spare batteries and tapes. It is essential to have a notebook as a back-up and to carry spare pens.

Sensitivity and courtesy should be the criteria for all interviewing for normal articles. Start with easy general questions. Guide the interview gently, but firmly. Wind up the interview as you began, on an easy note. The interviewee should be left with the feeling that it has been an enjoyable experience. Some interviewees ask if they can vet the finished article. You should always politely refuse, but do offer to allow them to withdraw anything they may regret saying.

For more information on interviewing technique, see *Freelance Writing for Newspapers* and *The Way to Write Magazine Articles* in the further reading list on page 143.

Non-linear thinking

A stumbling block for many inexperienced writers is beginning their article, particularly when faced with a daunting mass of notes, clippings and research references. Related research material must be associated and the various aspects considered in order of importance. However, when marshalling material, we often tend to arrange it in a linear fashion, rather like a shopping list. This tends to restrict our thinking on each point.

It has been found that non-linear thinking stimulates ideas and their logical development. I use this method as a framework for my articles, particularly those which are complex. Non-linear flow-of-thought patterns are easy to compile and to use. The subject is written in the centre of a large sheet of paper with the major aspects to be covered radiating from it. From these, further spurs are drawn, filling in other important material. Less significant points are added on minor spurs until all aspects are covered. Never discard these patterns; file them away for future use as a valuable concise reference to your research material.

A detailed explanation of this method, together with illustrations of typical non-linear patterns, is given in *The Way to Write Magazine Articles*; and more general coverage can be found in *Use Your Head* (see further reading, page 143).

The article structure

We all develop our own style, but it is important to learn to modify it to suit the requirements of our market. The majority of articles are relatively short and must put over their story crisply without wasting words. Often this can best be done with fairly short sentences and relatively short paragraphs. Never write long convoluted sentences which require reading more than once to understand.

The opening

The first paragraph of an article has special importance. It must grip the editor's attention immediately, its purpose being to force the editor to read on. You can often make your opening irresistible by selecting a point from your article which is intriguing, startling or even audacious.

The body

You will not sell an article on the strength of its opening. The body of the article must fulfil the promise of that good first paragraph. It is here that the main text or message of your article will be unfolded. Your thought patterns will help you to move logically from one aspect to the next in a smooth progression and ensure that nothing important is left out.

The end

The poor article appears to finish when the writer runs out of ideas. A good ending must aim to tie up any loose ends positively. The way it does this depends a great deal on the subject. It can be speculative – a look into the future, perhaps. It might go back to answer a question posed in the beginning. Avoid a mere recap of the main text for this gives a weak ending. Try to set aside some 'meat' to include in the ending; this could leave the reader with a strong point to ponder over.

Dialogue

Dialogue can breathe life into an article and give it sparkle. It must be used judiciously, for over-use may unbalance the article. It is often effective when used appropriately as the first sentence of an article.

The typescript

The conventional layout of a typescript is described in *Preparing and submitting a typescript* on page 248. However, an article for the British magazine market needs the addition of a typed cover sheet with the writer's name and address in the top right-hand corner, the article's title centred halfway down the page followed by the writer's name. If you are using a pseudonym it goes here, not at the top.

About two-thirds down the page on the left should be the number of words in the article and two or three lines' space below, the rights which you are offering the editor. For normal practical purposes this would be First British Serial Rights, usually abbreviated to 'FBSR offered' – see below. The cover sheet is not used for USA markets.

An increasing number of editors are asking writers to submit their articles on disk or even electronically. It pays you to provide this facility if you can. You should always verify with the editor that your system and theirs are compatible before submission. You will find that most editors also require a hard copy (printout) in addition to the disk or electronic copy. For more information, see *Writers and the Internet* on page 549).

Illustrations

Good illustrations enhance an article, making it more saleable. The writer/illustrator also receives an extra fee. It is self-evident that all article writers should try to produce that editors' delight – the words and pictures package. If you are a reasonable photographer, you are halfway there. If you are not, there is little excuse for not trying with one of the fully automatic cameras which are available today.

Study magazines to see, not only whether they use black and white or colour, but also the way they use illustrations. Do they tend to be small and plentiful to assist in the understanding of the text? Does the editor favour large dramatic pictures, sometimes covering as much as a whole page or even two? Finally, can your pictures match those in the magazine?

Your pictures must be pin-sharp and properly exposed. They must avoid all the basic mistakes of composition which are outlined in any photographic primer. For black and white you should submit glossy, borderless prints, 254 x 203mm (10 x 8in). Transparencies are demanded by most quality magazines for their colour illustrations, although a small but growing number of periodicals will consider colour prints. You must always confirm that a magazine uses colour prints before submitting them. For covers, most magazines use 35mm transparencies, but many prefer a larger format. Illustrations are covered in depth in *The Way to Write Magazine Articles* (see further reading, page 143.)

Writers who turn to supplementing their writing with photography rarely look back. They report better sales and increased earnings.

Rights

By offering First British Serial Rights you are inviting the magazine to publish your article once and for the first time in Britain. You are retaining the right to sell it elsewhere in the world. Some editors will try to wring all rights from you. Do not give way as it leaves the magazine free to sell your article worldwide and pocket the proceeds.

Second British Serial Rights are rarely sold, but a magazine may ask to buy them if they see your article in print and wish to reproduce it themselves. You would normally accept, but as Second Rights earn lower fees than First Rights, it is not worth making a particular effort to sell them. It pays to rewrite the original article, reslanting it to suit the new market and possibly introducing some new material. This effectively makes it a new article for which the First Rights may be legitimately offered.

The sales strategy

Probably the most common reason for good articles failing to get published is lack of a sound sales strategy. A surprisingly large number of writers complete a good article and then peddle it hopefully around the markets. This is quite the wrong way. Your article must always be written specifically for the market you have in mind. Your sales strategy should begin the moment you look at your material and can say: 'Yes, there is enough here for a good article.' You then use your market study to find a number of likely magazines which might publish such an article.

Query letters

The sound query letter is essential for sustained success in the article-writing field. Examine your list of possible magazines and arrange them in order of your preference. Select the top one and write your query letter to its editor. Keep it brief and state your idea for the article, mentioning any special slant you have in mind. If you are qualified in any way to write such an article or if you have a 'track-record' of writing in that field, you should say so. Also mention if you have suitable illustrations.

Ask the editor how many words he or she would like to see. It is particularly important to ask for the magazine's rates for contributors. Always enclose an sae. The query letter is your initial shop-window and its quality should be the best of which you are capable. If the editor turns down the idea, write immediately to the next magazine on your list and so on.

If the editor likes your idea, you may get a commission, but if you are unknown it is more likely that you will be asked to submit the article on spec.

An acceptance is the usual outcome from an editor's expression of interest. As you become better at matching subject to magazine, writing shrewd query letters and producing sound articles, your rejections should drop to virtually nil.

On acceptance, the professional freelance looks around for another outlet. Writing is easy, it is the research which takes the time. Make sure you get the maximum from your research (see above).

The pathway to successful article writing

- have a good idea for a subject;
- find a suitable market;
- produce an interesting and well-written article for that market;
- submit a professional-looking typescript;
- have a sound sales strategy throughout.

Payment

Some magazines pay on acceptance, but the majority pay on publication. Avoid those magazines which hold your material on spec with no guarantee of ultimate publication. Never be afraid to question offers of low rates, for many editors will negotiate. If low rates are not improved upon, be professional and withdraw the offer of your article.

If a magazine defaults on payment, you should always consider pursuing the matter, even as far as the Small Claims Court. The Society of Authors has an excellent pamphlet on Small Claims procedure (free to members; £5, post free, to non-members).

Fresh fields

When you have written articles extensively on a subject, it may be worth considering whether the subject is suitable for a non-fiction book (see *The Way to Write Non-fiction*, below). If so, your articles could be valuable as evidence of your writing skills, your knowledge of the subject and the wide interest the subject can generate. Many writers have used their published articles as a means of gaining an advance contract for a non-fiction book.

John Hines is a freelance writer and lecturer covering a wide range of interests, but specialises in health and the environment. He lectures extensively on writing, both in the UK and abroad.

Further reading

Buzan, Tony, *Use Your Head*, BBC, revised edn, 1995

Dick, Jill, *Freelance Writing for Newspapers*, A & C Black, 2nd edn, 1998

Dick, Jill, *Writing for Magazines*, A & C Black, 2nd edn, 1996

Freelance Market News, Sevendale House, 7 Dale Street, Manchester M1 1JB (on subscription)

Hines, John, *The Way to Write Magazine Articles*, Hamish Hamilton, repr. 1995

Hines, John, *The Way to Write Non-fiction*, Hamish Hamilton, 1990, o.p.

Hoffmann, Ann, *Research for Writers*, A & C Black, 6th edn, 1999

Howard, Godfrey, *The English Guide*, Pan Macmillan, 1994, o.p.

Legat, Michael, *The Nuts and Bolts of Writing*, Robert Hale, repr. 1999

Peak, Steve and Fisher, Paul (eds), *The Media Guide*, Fourth Estate, annual

The Oxford Writers' Dictionary, Oxford Reference, 1990

Willings Press Guide, Hollis Directories Ltd, annual

Syndicates, news and press agencies

Before submitting material, you are strongly advised to make preliminary enquiries and to ascertain terms of work. Strictly speaking, syndication is the selling and reselling of previously published work although some news and press agencies handle original material.

Academic File Information Services

Eastern Art Publishing Group, PO Box 13666,
27 Wallorton Gardens, London SW14 8WF
tel 020-8392 1122 *fax* 020-8392 1422
e-mail afis@eapgroup.com
web site http://www.eapgroup.com
Managing Editor Sajid Rizvi, *Executive Editor* Shirley Rizvi

Feature and photo syndication with special reference to the developing world and immigrant communities in the West. Founded 1985.

Advance Features

Stubbs Wood Cottage, Hammerwood,
East Grinstead, West Sussex RH19 3QE
tel/fax (01342) 850480
web site http://www.advancefeatures.uk.com
Managing Editor Peter Norman

Supplies text and visual services to the national and regional press in Britain and newspapers overseas. Instructional graphic panels on a variety of subjects. Text services (weekly); stars, nature, business. Crosswords: daily, weekly and theme; general puzzles. Daily and weekly cartoons for the regional and national press (not single cartoons).

Alpha incorporating London News Service

63 Gee Street, London EC1V 3RS
tel 020-7336 0632 *fax* 020-7253 8419
Managing Director Ray Blumire

Worldwide syndication of features and photos.

The Associated Press Ltd

(News Department), The Associated Press House,
12 Norwich Street, London EC4A 1BP
tel 020-7353 1515 *fax* 020-7353 8118

Atlantic Syndication Partners

17-18 Haywards Place,
London EC1R 0EQ
tel 020-7566 0360 *fax* 020-7566 0388
Contact Trevor York

Worldwide syndication of newspaper features, photos, cartoons, strips and book serialisations. Agency represents the international syndication of Associated Newspapers (*Daily Mail*, *Mail on Sunday*, *Evening Standard*).

Australian Associated Press

12 Norwich Street, London EC4A 1QJ
tel 020-7353 0153 *fax* 020-7583 3563

News service to the Australian, New Zealand and Pacific Island press, radio and TV. Founded 1935.

Neil Bradley Puzzles

Linden House, 34 Hardy Barn, Shipley, Derbyshire DE75 7JA
tel/fax (01773) 768960
e-mail bradcart@aol.com
Director Neil Bradley

Supplies visual puzzles to national and regional press; emphasis placed on variety and topicality with work based on current media listings. Work supplied on disk or prints to Mac or PC. Daily single frame and strip cartoons. Contact for free booklet and disk demo. Founded 1981.

Bulls Presstjänst AB

Tulegatan 39, Box 6519, S-11383 Stockholm, Sweden
tel (08) 55520600 *fax* (08) 55520665
e-mail kontakt@bulls.se
web site http://www.bulls.se

Bulls Pressedienst GmbH

Eysseneckstrasse 50, D-60322 Frankfurt am Main, Germany
tel (069) 959 270 *fax* (069) 959 27111
e-mail sales@bullspress.de

Bulls Pressetjeneste A/S

Ebbells Gate 3, N-0183 Oslo, Norway
tel 22 98 26 60 *fax* 22 20 49 78
e-mail bullsosl@online.no

Bulls Pressetjeneste

Östbanegade 9, 1th, DK-2100 Copenhagen, Denmark
tel 35 38 90 99 *fax* 35 38 25 16
e-mail kjartan@bulls.dk

Bulls Finskaförsäljnings AB

Keskuskatu 1B, FIN-00100, Helsinki, Finland
tel (09) 612 96 50 *fax* (09) 757 06 34
e-mail ilkka@bullsress.fi

Bulls Press

ul. Chocimska 28, Pokoj 509, 00-791 Warsawa, Poland
tel (22) 845 90 10 *fax* (22) 845 90 11
e-mail krzysztof@bulls.com.pl

Bulls Press

Mere Pst 8, EE 0001 Tallinn, Estonia
tel (2) 61 30 663 *fax* (2) 64 64 133
e-mail meelik@division.ee

Market newspapers, magazines, weeklies and advertising agencies in Sweden, Denmark, Norway, Finland, Iceland, Poland, The Baltic States, Germany, Austria and German-speaking Switzerland.

Syndicates human interest picture stories; topical and well-illustrated background articles and series; photographic features dealing with science, people, personalities, glamour; genre pictures for advertising; condensations and serialisations of best-selling fiction and non-fiction; cartoons, comic strips, film and TV rights, merchandising and newspaper graphics on-line via modem or ISDN.

The Canadian Press

Associated Press House, 12 Norwich Street, London EC4A 1QE
tel 020-7353 6355 *fax* 020-7583 4238
Chief Correspondent Helen Branswell

London Bureau of the national news agency of Canada. Founded 1919.

Central Press Features

Temple Way, Bristol BS99 7HD
tel 0117-934 3600 *fax* 0117-934 3639
e-mail mail@central-press.co.uk
Editor Ken Elkes

Supplies features, cartoons, crosswords, horoscopes and graphics strips to newspapers, magazines and other publications (including Internet sites) in 50 countries. Included in over 100 daily and weekly services are columns of international interest on health and beauty, medicine, employment, sports, house and home, motoring, computers, film and video, children's features, gardening, celebrity profiles, food and drink, finance and law. Also runs a parliamentary service and TV listings service, as well as supplying editorial material for advertising features.

Children's Express UK

Exmouth House, 3-11 Pine Street, London EC1R 0JH
tel 020-7833 2577 *fax* 020-7278 7722
e-mail enquiries@childrensexpress.btinternet.com
web site http://www.childrens-express.org
Chief Executive Huw Meredith, *Chairman* Stephanie Williams

Offers young people aged 8-18 the opportunity to write on issues of importance to them, for newspapers, radio and TV. It operates after school and at weekends. Founded 1995.

J.W. Crabtree and Son

Cheapside Chambers, 43 Cheapside, Bradford BD1 4HP
tel (01274) 732937 (office), (01535) 655288 (home)
fax (01274) 732937

News, general, trade and sport; information and research for features undertaken. Founded 1919.

Daily & Sunday Telegraph Syndication

The Telegraph Group Ltd, 1 Canada Square, Canary Wharf, London E14 5DT
tel 020-7538 7505 *fax* 020-7538 7319
e-mail syndicat@telegraph.co.uk

News, features, photography; worldwide distribution and representation.

Environmental & Occupational Health Research Foundation

Penrose House, Birtles Road, Whirley, Cheshire SK10 3JQ
tel/fax (01625) 615323
e-mail eorhfl@aol.com
Managing Editor Peggy Bentham

Undertakes individual commissions and syndicates articles to diverse science and technology journals and general consumer media. Peer reviewed and accredited contributors from academia and professional institutions.

Euro-Digest Features

34A Compton Avenue, Brighton BN1 3PS
tel (01273) 233615 *fax* (01273) 203622
Directors Edward Whitehead, Andrew C.F. Whitehead, Diane Askew

Represents European press. Human interest and travel features. Occasional news items. Particularly interested in material from Scotland, Northern Ireland and Wales. Commission: by arrangement, according to subject etc.

Europa-Press

Saltmätargatan 8, 1st Floor, Box 6410, S-113 82, Stockholm, Sweden
tel 8-34 94 35 *fax* 8-34 80 79
e-mail red.led@europapress.se
Managing Director Tord Steinsvik

Market: newspapers, magazines and weeklies in Sweden, Denmark, Norway, Finland, and the Baltic states. Syndicates high quality features of international appeal such as topical articles, photo-features – b&w and colour, women's features, short stories, serial novels, non-fiction stories and serials with strong human interest, crime articles, popular science, cartoons, comic strips.

Europress Features (UK)

18 St Chads Road, Didsbury, Nr Manchester M20 9WH
tel 0161-445 2945

Representation of newspapers and magazines in Europe, Australia, United States. Syndication of top-flight features with exclusive illustrations – human interest stories – showbusiness personalities. 30-35% commission on sales of material successfully accepted; 40% on exclusive illustrations.

Express Enterprises

(division of Express Newspapers plc)
Ludgate House, 245 Blackfriars Road, London SE1 9UX
tel 020-7922 7903 *fax* 020-7922 7871

Text and pictures from all Express titles. Archive from 1900. Numerous strips and political cartoons. Material handled worldwide for freelance journalists.

Frontline Photo Press Agency

18 Wall Street, Norwood, South Australia 5067
postal address PO Box 162, Kent Town, SA 5071
tel (08) 8333 2691 *fax* (08) 8364 0604
e-mail info@frontline.net.au
web site http://www.frontline.net.au
Director Carlo Irlitti

Photographic press agency specialising in sports coverage. Services provided: news, interviews, features, articles and photos for newspapers, magazines and other media. Digital photo wire services.

Syndicates sports, celebrity, travel, men's, women's, human and general interest features and articles with photos. Welcomes approaches from individuals and organisations abroad. Assignments undertaken. Rates negotiable. Founded 1988.

Gemini News Service

9 White Lion Street, London N1 9PD
tel 020-7278 1111 *fax* 020-7278 0345
e-mail gemini@panoslondon.org.uk
Editor Dipankar De Sarkar

Network of freelance contributors and specialist writers all over the world. Specialists in news-features of international, topical and development interest. Preferred length 800-1200 words.

Graphic Syndication

4 Reyntiens View, Odiham, Hants RG29 1AF
tel (01256) 703004
e-mail mike@business-cartoons.co.uk
web site http://www.members.tripod.co.uk/mike_flanagan
Manager M. Flanagan

Cartoon strips and single frames supplied to newspapers and magazines in Britain and overseas. Terms: 50%. Founded 1981.

India-International News Service

Head office Jute House, 12 India Exchange Place, Calcutta 700001, India
tel 2209563, 4791009
Proprietor Euro Ing H. Kothari BSc, DWP(Lond), FIMechE, FIE, FVI. FInstD, FRAS, FRSA

'Calcutta Letters' and Air Mail news service from Calcutta. Specialists in industrial and technical news.

INS (International News Service)/ Irish News Service

7 King's Avenue, Minnis Bay, Birchington-on-Sea, East Kent CT7 9QL
tel (01843) 845022
Editor and Managing Director Barry J. Hardy PC, *Photo Editor* Jan Vanek, *Secretary* K.T. Byrne

News, sport, book and magazine reviews (please forward copies), TV, radio, photographic department; also equipment for TV films, etc.

International Fashion Press Agency

Penrose House, Birtles Road, Whirley, Cheshire SK10 3JQ
tel/fax (01625) 615323
e-mail IFPressAgy@aol.com
Directors P. Bentham (managing), P. Dyson, S. Fagette, L.C. Mottershead, L.B. Fell, T.R. Fox

Monitors and photographs international fashion collections and developments in textile and fashion industry. Specialist writers on health, fitness, beauty and personalities. Undertakes individual commissioned features. Supplies syndicated columns/pages to press, radio and TV (NUJ staff writers and photographers).

International Press Agency (Pty) Ltd

PO Box 67, Howard Place 7450, South Africa
tel (021) 531 1926 *fax* (021) 531 8789
e-mail inpra@iafrica.com
Manager Mrs T. Temple
UK office 17 Fairmount Road, London SW2 2BJ
tel/fax 020-8674 9283
Managing Editor Mrs U.A. Barnett PhD

South African agents for many leading British, American and continental press firms for the syndication of comic strips, cartoons, jokes, feature articles, short stories, serials, press photos for the South African market. Founded 1934.

Joker Feature Service (JFS)

PO Box 253, 6040 AG, Roermond, The Netherlands
tel (0475) 337338 *fax* (0475) 315663
e-mail j.f.s@tip.nl
Managing Director Ruud Kerstens

Feature articles, serial rights, tests, cartoons, comic strips and illustrations, puzzles. Handles TV features, books, Internet sites; also production for merchandising.

Knight Features

20 Crescent Grove, London SW4 7AH
tel (0207) 622 1467 *fax* (0207) 622 1522
e-mail pknight@easynet.co.uk
Director Peter Knight, *Associates* Ann King-Hall, Gaby Martin, Andrew Knight

Worldwide selling of strip cartoons and major features and serialisations. Exclusive agent in UK and Republic of Ireland for United Feature Syndicate and Newspaper Enterprise Association of New York. Founded 1985.

London News Service – see Alpha incorporating London News Service

London Sports Reporting Agency

Ground Floor, 13-16 Faro Close, Coates Hill Road, Bromley, Kent BR1 2RR
tel 020-8467 1951
e-mail 100654.463@compuserve.com
Editor Christopher Harte, *Managers* Michael Latham (Northern Region), David Fox (South West Region), Diana Harding (South East Region), Dave Hammond (Scotland)

News and reporting service for sporting events. Research facilities for radio and TV, particularly sports documentaries. Commission: NUJ rates. Name change to National Sports Reporting Agency late 2000/early 2001. Founded 1994.

Maharaja Features Pvt. Ltd

5-226 Sion Road East, Bombay 400022, India
tel 22-4097951 *fax* 22-4097801
e-mail mahafeat@bom2.vsnl.net.in
web site http://www.welcomeindia.com/maharaja
Editor K.R.N. Swamy, *Managing Editor* K.R. Padmanabhan

Syndicates feature and pictorial material, of interest to Asian readers, to newspapers and magazines in India, UK and abroad. Specialists in well-researched articles on India by eminent authorities for publication in prestige journals throughout the world. Also topical features 1000-1500 words. Illustrations: b&w prints and colour transparencies.

Mirror Syndication International

22nd Floor, 1 Canada Square, Canary Wharf, London E14 5AP
tel 020-7293 3700 *fax* 020-7293 2712
e-mail desk@mirpix.com
web site http://www.mirpix.com

Supplies publishing material and international rights for news text and pictures from Mirror Group Newspapers and other large publishing houses. Extensive picture library of all subjects.

National Association of Press Agencies (NAPA)

41 Lansdowne Crescent, Leamington Spa, Warks. CV32 4PR
tel (01926) 424181 *fax* (01926) 424760
Directors Denis Cassidy, Chris Johnson, Barrie Tracey, Peter Steele, John Quinn

NAPA is a network of independent, established and experienced press agencies serving newspapers, magazines, TV and radio networks. Founded 1980.

New Blitz Literary & TV Agency

Via di Panico 67, 00186 Rome, Italy
tel/fax (06) 686 4859
e-mail bono@uniroma3.it
Manager Giovanni A.S. Congiu

Syndicates worldwide: cartoons, comic strips, humorous books with drawings, feature and pictorial material, topical, environment, travel. Average rates of commission 60/40%, monthly report of sales, payment 60 days after the date of monthly report.

New Zealand Press Association

12 Norwich Street, London EC4A 1EJ
tel 020-7353 5430 *fax* 020-7583 3563
Chief Correspondent Kip Brook

Chandra S. Perera

Cinetra, 437 Pethiyagoda, Kelaniya-11600, Sri Lanka
tel 94-1-911885 *fax* 94-1-541414/332867/323910
ATTN CHANDRA PERERA
Cinetra Worldwide Createch (Pvt) Ltd, 126/3rd floor, 10B YMBA Building, Fort, Colombo 1, Sri Lanka
tel/fax 94-1-323910

Press and TV news, news films on Sri Lanka and Maldives, colour and b&w photo news and features, photographic and film coverages, screenplays and scripts for TV and films, press clippings. Broadcasting, TV and newspapers; journalistic features, news, broadcasting and TV interviews.

Pixfeatures

5 Latimer Road, Barnet, Herts. EN5 5NU
tel 020-8449 9946 *fax* 020-8441 2725
Contact Peter Wickman
Spanish office tel 00349 6647 6379
Contact Roy Wickman

News agency and picture library. Specialises in selling Spanish pictures and features to British and European press.

The Press Association

292 Vauxhall Bridge Road, London SW1V 1AE
tel 020-7963 7000 *fax* 020-7963 7192
web site http://www.pressassociation.press.net
Chief Executive/Editor-in-Chief Paul Potts, *Commercial Director* Clive Marshall

PA News Fast and accurate news, photography and information to print, broadcast and electronic media in the UK and Ireland.

PA Sport In-depth coverage of national and regional sports, transmitting a huge range of stories, results, pictures and updates every day.

PA Listings Page- and screen-ready information from daily guides to 7-day supplements on sports results, TV and radio listings, arts and entertainment, financial and weather listings tailored to suit requirements.

PA Enterprises Top quality content including news and sport for a wide range of multimedia customers.

PA WeatherCentre Continuously updated information on present and future weather conditions; consultancy services for media and industry. Founded 1868.

Press Features Syndicate

9 Paradise Close, Eastbourne, East Sussex BN20 8BT
tel (01323) 728760
Editor Harry Gresty

Specialises in photo-features, both b&w and colour. Seek human interest, oddity, glamour, pin-ups, scientific, medical, etc., material suitable for marketing through own branches in London, San Francisco, Paris, Hamburg, Milan, Stockholm, Amsterdam (for Benelux), Helsinki.

Rann Communication

6th Floor, 117 King William Street, Adelaide, SA 5000, Australia
postal address GPO Box 958, Adelaide, SA 5001
tel (08) 8211 7771 *fax* (08) 8212 2272
e-mail chrisran@rann.com.au
Proprietor C.F. Rann

Full range of professional PR, press releases, special newsletters, commercial intelligence, media monitoring. Welcomes approaches from organisations requiring PR representation or press release distribution. Founded 1977.

Reuters Limited

85 Fleet Street, London EC4P 4AJ
tel 020-7250 1122

Singer Media Corporation

Seaview Business Park, 1030 Calle Cordillera, Unit 106, San Clemente, CA 92673, USA
tel 949-498-7227
e-mail singer@deltanet.com
Vice-President Helen J. Lee

Features (celebrity interviews and profiles, business, health, fitness, beauty, diet, self-help, how-to, etc), cartoons, puzzles and quizzes of international appeal for international and domestic syndication. Represented in most countries abroad. No local or national material; no comic strips. Query first.

UK Features

38 The Woodlands, Esher, Surrey KT10 8DB
tel 020-8398 5676 *fax* 020-8398 9051
Proprietor Robin Corry

Human interest and general features. Payment: £100-200 for an early tip-off. Founded 1979.

United Press International

80 Silverthorne Road, London SW8 3XA
tel 020-7675 9960 (news), 020-7675 9967 (admin), 020-7675 9991 (business development)
e-mail www.upi.com

Universal Pictorial Press & Agency Ltd

29-31 Saffron Hill, London EC1N 8SW
tel 020-7421 6000 *fax* 020-7421 6006
e-mail postmaster@uppa.demon.co.uk
Managing Director T.R. Smith

Photographic news agency and picture library: the UK's leading archive for British and international personalities from 1944 to present. Digital archive from 1994 with full ISDN facilities. Founded 1929.

Visual Humour

5 Greymouth Close, Stockton-on-Tees TS18 5LF
tel (01642) 581847/0121-705 4087
fax (01642) 581847
Contact Peter Dodsworth

Daily and weekly humorous cartoon strips; also single panel cartoon features (not single cartoons) for possible syndication in the UK and abroad. Picture puzzles also considered. Submit photocopy samples only initially, with sae. Founded 1984.

Yaffa Syndicate Pty Ltd

17-21 Bellevue Street, Surry Hills, NSW 2010, Australia
tel (02) 9213-8209 *fax* (02) 9281-2750

Books

Submitting material

Each year, thousands of typescripts are submitted to publishers by hopeful authors but only a small proportion are accepted for publication. Some are needlessly rejected either because they were sent to the wrong publisher, or because the publisher's submission procedure was not followed. We give here some guidelines to consider before submitting material.

First, and most importantly, choose the right publisher. It is a waste of time and money to send the typescript of a novel to a publisher who publishes no fiction, or poetry to one who publishes no verse. By studying the entries in the *Yearbook*, examining publishers' lists of publications, or by looking for the names of suitable publishers in the relevant sections in libraries and bookshops, you will find the names of several publishers which might be interested in seeing your material.

Secondly, approach the publisher in the way they prefer. Many publishers will not accept unsolicited material – you must enquire first if they would be willing to read the whole work. A few publishers are prepared to speak on the telephone, allowing you to describe, briefly, the work on offer. Most prefer a preliminary letter; and many publishers, particularly of fiction, will only see material submitted through a literary agent. It has to be said that some publishing houses, the larger ones in particular, may well employ all three methods!

Enclose a synopsis of the work, and two or three sample chapters, with your preliminary letter, plus return postage (International Reply Coupons if you are writing from outside the country or if you are submitting material from the UK to the Irish Republic). Writers have been known to send out such letters in duplicated form, an approach unlikely to stimulate a publisher's interest. Remember, also, that whilst every reasonable care will be taken of material in the publishers' possession, responsibility cannot be accepted if material is lost or damaged. Never send your only copy of the typescript. For more information, see *Preparing and submitting a typescript* on page 248. An alphabetical listing of publishers' names and addresses follows on page 151. For classified lists, see below.

Fiction

See page 220 for a list of *Publishers of fiction*, by fiction genre. A full list of *Literary agents* starts on page 348.

Poetry

Publishers which consider poetry for adults are listed in *Publishers of poetry* on page 286. See also the article *Poetry into print* on page 275 and *Poetry organisations* on page 280.

Children's books

The market for children's books is considered in *Writing and the children's book market* on page 252 and the list of *Children's book publishers and packagers* on page 259, which includes publishers of poetry for children. A list of *Literary agents for children's books* is on page 368.

Small presses

It is beyond the scope of the *Yearbook* to list all the many smaller publishers which have either a limited output, or that specialise in poetry, avant-garde or other fringe publishing. We include details of some of the better-known small poetry houses but for a comprehensive listing refer to *Small Presses & Little Magazines in the UK and Ireland* (available from the Stationery Office Oriel Bookshop, 18-19 High Street, Cardiff CF10 1PT *tel* (029) 2039 5548.

Self-publishing

Authors are strongly advised not to pay for the publication of their work. A reputable firm of publishers will undertake publication at its own expense, except possibly for works of an academic nature. See *Doing it on your own* on page 262 for an introduction to self-publishing, *Vanity publishing* on page 266, and *Publishing agreements* on page 619.

See also ...

- *Book publishers* in *Australia*, page 223; in *Canada*, page 226; in *New Zealand*, page 229; in *South Africa*, page 231; and in the *USA*, page 233
- *Literary agents*, page 347
- *Top hundred chart of 1999 paperback fastsellers*, page 267
- *Book packagers*, page 214
- *Publishers of plays*, page 346

Book publishers UK and Ireland

**Member of the Publishers Association or Scottish Publishers Association*
†Member of the Irish Book Publishers' Association

AA Publishing*

Automobile Association, Fanum House, Basingstoke, Hants RG21 4EA
tel (0990) 448866 *fax* (01256) 322575
web site http://www.theaa.co.uk
Managing Director John Howard, *Marketing and International Sales Director* S.J. Mesquita, *Editorial Manager* Michael Buttler

Travel, atlases, maps, leisure interests, including Baedeker, Essential, Thomas Cook and Explorer Travel Guides. Founded 1979.

Abacus – see Little, Brown and Company (UK)*

ABC-Clio Ltd

(formerly Clio Press Ltd)
Old Clarendon Ironworks, 35A Great Clarendon Street, Oxford OX2 6AT
tel (01865) 311350 *fax* (01865) 311358
e-mail tsloggett@abc-clio.ltd.uk
web site http://www.abc-clio.com
Directors Tony Sloggett (managing), Bob Neville (UK editorial and production)

General and academic reference: history, art, photography, mythology, literature, ethnic studies; bibliography. Publishes *World Bibliographical Series* (comprehensive guides to individual countries), *The Clio Montessori Series*, *Electronic Library* (CD-Roms and web versions of abstracting services in modern art, American studies and history). Subsidiary of ABC-CLIO Inc. Founded 1971.

Absolute Press

Scarborough House, 29 James Street West, Bath BA1 2BT
tel (01225) 316013 *fax* (01225) 445836
e-mail sales@absolutepress.demon.co.uk
web site http://www.absolutepress.demon.co.uk
Publisher Jon Croft, *Directors* Amanda Bennett (sales), Bronwen Douglas (marketing)

General list: cookery, food-related topics, wine, lifestyle, popular culture, travel. Streetwise maps, accordian fold, and laminated city maps. No fiction. *Outlines* series of monographs on gay and lesbian artists. No unsolicited MSS. Founded 1979.

Academic Press – see Harcourt Publishers Ltd

Academy Editions – acquired by Wiley Europe Ltd*

Access Press – see HarperCollins Publishers*

Ace Books – see Age Concern Books

Acorn Editions – see James Clarke & Co. Ltd*

act-two ltd*

(formerly Two-Can Design)
346 Old Street, London EC1V 9RB
tel 020-7684 4000 *fax* 020-7613 3371
e-mail info@act-two.co.uk
Directors Andrew Jarvis (chairman), Sara Lynn (creative)

Children's: reference and non-fiction books, magazines, video and multimedia products. Founded 1987.

Actinic Press – see Cressrelles Publishing Co. Ltd

Addison-Wesley – imprint of Pearson Education

Adlard Coles Nautical – see A & C Black (Publishers) Ltd*

Age Concern Books

(formerly Ace Books)
Age Concern England, 1268 London Road, London SW16 4ER
tel 020-8679 8000 *fax* 020-8679 6069
e-mail books@ace.org.uk

Publisher Richard Holloway, *Marketing Manager* Michael Addison
Health and care, advice, finance, gerontology. Founded 1973.

Airlife Publishing Ltd
101 Longden Road, Shrewsbury, Shrops. SY3 9EB
tel (01743) 235651 *fax* (01743) 232944
e-mail airlife@airlifebooks.com
web site http://www.airlifebooks.com
Directors Andrew Johnston (sales), Peter Holmes (finance), Anne Cooper (rights)
Aviation, technical and general, military. Founded 1976.
Swan Hill Press (imprint)
web site http://www.swanhillbooks.com
Managing Editor P. Coles
Natural history, wildlife, arts, travel, equestrian, fishing, country sports and pursuits.

Aladdin/Watts – see The Watts Publishing Group Ltd*

Ian Allan Publishing Ltd
Riverdene Business Park, Molesey Road, Hersham, Surrey KT12 4RG
tel (01932) 266600 *fax* (01932) 266601
e-mail info@ianallanpub.co.uk
web site http://www.ianallanpub.co.uk
Publishing Manager Peter Waller
Transport: railways, aircraft, shipping, road; naval and military history; reference books and magazines; sport and cycling guides; no fiction.
Dial House (imprint)
General: sport, cycling.
Midland Publishing Ltd (imprint)
Transport: railways, aviation; naval and military history.
Oxford Publishing Company (imprint)
Transport: railways, road.

George Allen & Unwin Publishers Ltd – acquired by HarperCollins Publishers*

J.A. Allen
Clerkenwell House, 45-7 Clerkenwell Green, London EC1R 0HT
tel 020-7251 2661 *fax* 020-7490 4958
Publisher Caroline Burt
Specialist publishers of books on the horse and equestrianism including bloodstock breeding, racing, polo, dressage, horse care, carriage driving, breeds, veterinary and farriery. Technical books usually commissioned but willing to consider any serious, specialist MSS on the horse and related subjects. No fiction or autobiography. Imprint of **Robert Hale Ltd**. Founded 1926.

W.H. Allen – acquired by Virgin Publishing Ltd

Allen Lane – see Penguin UK*

Allison & Busby Ltd
114 New Cavendish Street, London W1M 7FD
tel 020-7636 2942 *fax* 020-7323 2023
e-mail all@allisonbusby.co.uk
web site http://www.allisonandbusby.ltd.uk
Directors David Shelley (publishing), Fiona Hague (marketing), Deborah Hatfield (editorial)
Literary fiction, crime fiction. Biography and history with a literary theme. Writers' Guides. New proposals accepted (send synopsis and sample pages initially) but sae essential.

The Alpha Press – see Sussex Academic Press

AN Publications
First Floor, Turner Building, 7-15 Pink Lane, Newcastle upon Tyne NE1 5DW
tel 0191-241 8000 *fax* 0191-241 8001
e-mail edit@anpubs.demon.co.uk
web site http://www.anweb.co.uk
Programme Co-ordinator Louise Coysh
AN's programme incorporates *AN Magazine*, AN Advice, AN Live, AN web site. Publishes model contracts covering commissions, residencies, selling, galleries, dealers and agents, and a reproduction licence. Founded 1980.

Anchor – see Transworld Publishers*

Andersen Press Ltd
20 Vauxhall Bridge Road, London SW1V 2SA
tel 020-7840 8700 (editorial) *fax* 020-7233 6263
e-mail 101370.533@compuserve.com
Managing Director/Publisher Klaus Flugge, *Directors* Philip Durrance, Joëlle Flugge (company secretary)
Children's books: picture books, novelties and fiction (send synopsis and full MS with sae); no short stories. International co-productions. Founded 1976.

The Angels' Share – see Neil Wilson Publishing Ltd

Anness Publishing
88-89 Blackfriars Road, London SE1 8HA
tel 020-7401 2077 *fax* 020-7633 9499

Managing Director Paul Anness, *Publisher* Joanna Lorenz

Practical illustrated books on crafts, cookery and gardening, and children's non-fiction. Founded 1989.

Hermes House (imprint)

Illustrated promotional and bargain books on practical subjects.

Lorenz Books (imprint)

Lifestyle, cookery, crafts, gardening, and all practical illustrated subjects.

Antique Collectors' Club

5 Church Street, Woodbridge, Suffolk IP12 1DS
tel (01394) 385501 *fax* (01394) 384434
Managing Director Diana Steel

Fine art, antiques, gardening and garden history, architecture. Founded 1966.

Anvil Books/The Children's Press†

45 Palmerston Road, Dublin 6, Republic of Ireland
tel (01) 4973628 *fax* (01) 4968263
Directors Rena Dardis (managing), Margaret Dardis (editorial)

Anvil: Irish history and biography. Children's Press: Irish adventure, fiction, ages 9-14. No unsolicited MSS. Founded 1964.

Anvil Press Poetry

Neptune House, 70 Royal Hill, London SE10 8RF
tel 020-8469 3033 *fax* 020-8469 3363
e-mail anvil@anvilpresspoetry.com
web site http://www.anvilpresspoetry.com
Director Peter Jay

Poetry. Submissions only with sae. Founded 1968.

Appletree Press Ltd†

14 Howard Street South, Belfast BT7 1BA
tel 028-9024 3074 *fax* 028-9024 6756
e-mail reception@appletree.ie
web site http://www.appletree.ie
Director John Murphy

Gift books, biography, cookery, guidebooks, history, Irish interest, literary criticism, music, photographic, social studies, sport, travel. Founded 1974.

Arc Publications

Nanholme Mill, Shaw Wood Road, Todmorden, Lancs. OL14 6DA
tel (01706) 812338 *fax* (01706) 818948
Partners Rosemary Jones, Tony Ward (general editor), Angela Jarman, *Associate Editors* David Morley (UK), John Kinsella (international), Jean Boase-Beier

Poetry. MSS with sae only.

Arcadia Books Ltd

15-16 Nassau Street, London W1N 7RE
tel 020-7436 9898 *fax* 020-7637 7357
e-mail info@arcadiabooks.co.uk
web site http://www.arcadiabooks.co.uk
Managing Director Gary Pulsifer, *Publishing Manager* Daniela de Groote

Original paperback fiction, fiction in translation, autobiography, biography, travel, gender studies, gay books. No unsolicited MSS. Enquiry letters must include sae. Founded 1996.

Architectural Press – see Reed Educational and Professional Publishing Ltd*

Arkana – former imprint of The Penguin Press

Arms & Armour Press – see Cassell & Co

E.J. Arnold – see Nelson Thornes Ltd

Edward Arnold – now Arnold, see Hodder Headline Ltd*

Arrow Books Ltd – see Random House Group Ltd*

Art Trade Press Ltd

9 Brockhampton Road, Havant, Hants PO9 1NU
tel 023-9248 4943
Editorial Director J.M. Curley

Publishers of *Who's Who in Art*.

Ashgate Publishing Ltd

Gower House, Croft Road, Aldershot, Hants GU11 3HR
tel (01252) 331551 *fax* (01252) 344405
e-mail info@ashgatepub.co.uk
Editors Sarah Markham (social sciences), Katherine Hodkinson (social work and public service), John Hindley (aviation management), Thomas Gray (history), Pamela Edwardes (art history), Rachel Lynch (music and literary studies), Sarah Lloyd (philosophy and theology), Val Rose (regional science), Kirsten Howgate (politics and international relations)

Publishes a wide range of academic research in the social sciences and humanities, professional practice publications in the management of business and public services, and illustrated books on art, architecture and design. Founded 1967.

Dartmouth (imprint)
Editor John Irwin

Law and legal studies.

Gower (imprint)
Editor Jo Gorderham
Business and management.

Lund Humphries (imprint)
Editor Lucy Myers
Art and design.

Variorum (imprint)
Editor John Smedley
History.

Ashmolean Museum Publications

Beaumont Street, Oxford OX1 2PH
tel (01865) 278009/27801 *fax* (01865) 278018
web site http://www.ashmol.ox.ac.uk/
Publications Officer Ian Charlton

Fine and applied art of Europe and Asia, archaeology, history, numismatics. Photographic archive. Founded 1683.

Aslib

(The Association for Information Management)
Staple Hall, Stone House Court, London EC3A 7PB
tel 020-7903 0000 *fax* 020-7903 0011
e-mail pubs@aslib.com
web site http://www.aslib.com
Head of Publications Sarah Blair

Information management, librarianship, information science, general reference, translation, copyright, the Internet, knowledge management, records management, computing. Founded 1924.

Associated University Presses – see Golden Cockerel Press

The Athlone Press Ltd

1 Park Drive, London NW11 7SG
tel 020-8458 0888 *fax* 020-8201 8115
e-mail athlonepress@btinternet.com
Directors Brian Southam (chairman), Doris Southam (managing), Tristan Palmer (editorial), Philip Kogan

Anthropology, architecture, art, Asian studies, economics, film studies, history, language, law, literature, medical, music, oriental, philosophy, politics, psychology, religion, science, sociology, cultural studies. Founded 1949.

Atlantic Europe Publishing Co. Ltd

Greys Court Farm, Greys Court,
Henley-on-Thames, Oxon RG9 4PG
tel (01491) 628188 *fax* (01491) 628189
e-mail info@atlanticeurope.com
web site http://www.AtlanticEurope.com
Directors Dr B.J. Knapp, D.L.R. McCrae

Children's colour illustrated information books, co-editions and primary class books: science, geography, technology, mathematics, history. Associate company: **Earthscape Editions** (see Book packagers). Founded 1990.

Attic Press[†]

Crawford Business Park, Crosses Green, Cork, Republic of Ireland
tel (021) 4321725 *fax* (021) 4315329
e-mail s.wilbourne@ucc.ie
web site http://www.iol.ie/~atticirl/
Publisher Sara Wilbourne

Books by and about women in the areas of social and political comment, women's studies, reference guides and handbooks. Imprint of **Cork University Press**. Founded 1984.

Aureus Publishing Ltd

24 Mafeking Road, Cardiff CF23 5DQ
tel/fax 029-2045 5200
e-mail meuryn.hughes@aureus.co.uk
web site http://www.aureus.co.uk
Director Meuryn Hughes

Rock and pop titles, autobiography, sport, religion; also music. Founded 1993.

Aurum Press Ltd

25 Bedford Avenue, London WC1B 3AT
tel 020-7637 3225 *fax* 020-7580 2469
e-mail aurum@attglobal.net
Directors André Deutsch (chairman), Bill McCreadie (managing), Piers Burnett (editorial)

General, illustrated and non-illustrated adult non-fiction: biography and memoirs, visual arts, film, home interest, travel. Founded 1977.

Award Publications Ltd

1st Floor, 27 Longford Street, London NW1 3DZ
tel 020-7388 7800 *fax* 020-7388 7887
Managing Director Ron Wilkinson

Children's books: full colour picture story books; early learning, information and activity books. No unsolicited material. Preliminary letter of enquiry essential. Founded 1954.

Azure Books – see Society for Promoting Christian Knowledge*

Bernard Babani (Publishing) Ltd

The Grampians, Shepherds Bush Road, London W6 7NF
tel 020-7603 2581/7296 *fax* 020-7603 8203
Directors S. Babani, M.H. Babani BSc (Eng)

Practical handbooks on radio, electronics and computing.

Baillière Tindall Ltd – see Harcourt Publishers Ltd

Duncan Baird Publishers

Sixth Floor, Castle House, 75-76 Wells Street, London W1P 3RE
tel 020-7323 2229 *fax* 020-7580 5692
Directors Duncan Baird (managing), Bob Saxton (editorial), Roger Walton (art), Alex Mitchell (international sales), Nick Foster (financial)

Non-fiction, illustrated reference. Founded 1994.

Bantam – see Transworld Publishers*

Bantam Children's Books – see Transworld Publishers*

Bantam Press – see Transworld Publishers*

Barefoot Books Ltd

PO Box 95, Kingswood, Bristol BS30 5BH
tel 0117-932 8885 *fax* 0117-932 8881
e-mail sales@barefoot-books.com
web site http://www.barefoot-books.com
Publisher Tessa Strickland

Children's picture books: myth, legend, fairytale. No unsolicited MSS. Founded 1993.

Barrie & Jenkins – see Random House Group Ltd*

Bartholomew – see HarperCollins Publishers*

Basement Press – see Attic Press†

B.T. Batsford Ltd

9 Blenheim Court, Brewery Road, London N7 9NT
tel 020-7700 7611 *fax* 020-7700 4552
e-mail batsford@chrysalisbooks.co.uk
web site http://www.batsford.com
Director Roger Huggins

Chess and bridge, art techniques, film, fashion and costume, practical craft, gardening, embroidery, lace, woodwork. A member of the Chrysalis Group plc. Founded 1843.

BBC Worldwide Ltd – see page 301*

Belitha Press

London House, Great Eastern Wharf, Parkgate Road, London SW11 4NQ
tel 020-7978 6330 *fax* 020-7223 4936
e-mail info@belithapress.co.uk
web site http://www.belithapress.co.uk
Contact Chester Fisher

Illustrated children's non-fiction for international co-editions: art, atlases, geography, history, natural history, reference, science. Imprints include Big Fish and Learning World. Subsidiary of CBMG plc. Founded 1980.

Bell & Hyman Ltd – acquired by HarperCollins Publishers*

Bellew Publishing Co. Ltd

The Nightingale Centre, 8 Balham Hill, London SW12 9EA
tel 020-8673 5611 *fax* 020-8675 2142
e-mail info@bellewpublishing.demon.co.uk
Chairman Ian McCorquodale, *Managing Director* Ib Bellew

Sociology, politics, art and art criticism, some fiction, poetry. Founded 1983.

David Bennett Books Ltd

Kiln House, 210 New Kings Road, London SW6 4NZ
tel 020-7731 6444 *fax* 020-7731 6554
Managing Director Peter Osborn

Highly illustrated children's fiction and non-fiction; baby books, interactive play books and gift books for the young. Subsidiary of CBMG plc. Founded 1989.

Berg Publishers

150 Cowley Road, Oxford OX4 1JJ
tel (01865) 245104 *fax* (01865) 791165
e-mail enquiry@berg.demon.co.uk
Managing Director Kathryn Earle

Social anthropology, cultural studies, dress and fashion studies, European studies, politics, history. Founded 1983.

Berkswell Publishing Co. Ltd

PO Box 420, Warminster, Wilts. BA12 9XB
tel/fax (01985) 840189
Directors J.N.G. Stidolph, S.A. Abbott

Books of local interest, field sports, royalty; *The Churchwarden's Yearbook*. Ideas and MSS welcome.

Berlitz Publishing Co. Ltd

4th Floor, 9-13 Grosvenor Street, London W1X 9FB
tel 020-7518 8300 *fax* 020-7518 8310
Managing Director Roger Kirkpatrick

Travel, language and related multimedia. Founded 1970.

BFI Publishing

British Film Institute, 21 Stephen Street, London W1P 2LN
tel 020-7255 1444 *fax* 020-7580 8434
web site http://www.bfi.org.uk
Head of Publishing Andrew Lockett

Film and media studies; general audience film books. Founded 1982.

Clive Bingley Ltd – see Library Association Publishing*

Birnbaum – see HarperCollins Publishers*

A & C Black (Publishers) Ltd*

35 Bedford Row, London WC1R 4JH
tel 020-7242 0946 *fax* 020-7831 8478
e-mail enquiries@acblack.co.uk
Chairman and Joint Managing Director Charles Black, *Joint Managing Director* Jill Coleman, *Directors* Colin Adams, Oscar Heini (production), Robert Kirk (Christopher Helm, ornithology), Susan Kodicek (sales), Paul Langridge (rights), Janet Murphy (Adlard Coles Nautical), Nigel Newton, Kathy Rooney, Terry Rouelett (distribution)

Children's and educational books (including music) for 3-15 years (preliminary enquiry appreciated – fiction guidelines available on request); ceramics, art & craft, drama, ornithology, reference (*Who's Who*), sport, theatre, travel, books for writers. Subsidiary of Bloomsbury Publishing plc. Founded 1807.

Adlard Coles Nautical (imprint)
web site http://www.adlardcoles.co.uk
Editorial Director Janet Murphy

Nautical.

Christopher Helm (imprint)
Editorial Director Robert Kirk

Ornithology.

The Herbert Press (imprint)

Visual arts.

Black Ace Books

PO Box 6557, Forfar DD8 2YS
tel (01307) 465096 *fax* (01307) 465494
web site http://www.blackacebooks.com
Publisher Hunter Steele, *Art, Publicity and Sales* Boo Wood

New fiction, Scottish and general; new editions of outstanding recent fiction. Non-fiction: biography, history, psychology and philosophy. No unsolicited MSS or submissions from outside the UK. Send only: one-page covering letter, one-page synopsis, one full page of text and large sae. Imprints: Black Ace Books, Black Ace Paperbacks. Founded 1991.

Black Butterfly – see Writers & Readers Ltd

Black Lace – see Virgin Publishing Ltd

Black Swan – see Transworld Publishers*

Blackstaff Press Ltd†

Blackstaff House, Wildflower Way, Apollo Road, Belfast BT12 6TA
tel 028-9066 8074 *fax* 028-9066 8207
e-mail info@blackstaffpress.com
web site http://www.blackstaffpress.com
Managing Director Anne Tannahill

Fiction, poetry, biography, history, politics, natural history, humour, education. Founded 1971.

Blackstone Press Ltd

Aldine Place, London W12 8AA
tel 020-8740 2277 *fax* 020-8743 2292
Directors Alistair MacQueen (managing), Heather Saward (editorial), Jeremy Stein (sales & marketing)

Law books for practitioners and students. Contact Alistair MacQueen with ideas, or send MSS. Founded 1988.

The Blackwater Press – see Folens Publishing Company

Blackwell Publishers*

(Basil Blackwell Ltd)
108 Cowley Road, Oxford OX4 1JF
tel (01865) 791100 *fax* (01865) 791347
Directors Nigel Blackwell (chairman), René Olivieri (managing), Philip Carpenter, Sue Corbett, Mark Houlton, John Davey, Stephan Chambers, Carolyn Dougherty

Economics, education (academic), geography, history, industrial relations, linguistics, literature and criticism, politics, psychology, social anthropology, social policy and administration, sociology, theology, business studies, professional, law, reference, feminism, information technology, philosophy. Founded 1922.

InfoSource International (division)
InfoSource House, 54 Marston Street, Oxford OX4 1JU
tel (01865) 244068 *fax* (01865) 791347
Directors René Olivieri, Mark Houlton

Computer-based training, skills assessment and instructor manuals. Specialist areas include: PC applications (e.g. Microsoft Excel, WordPerfect, Lotus 1-2-3), networks and Internet.

Shakespeare Head Press (imprint)

Finely printed books; scholarly works.

Blackwell Science Ltd*

Osney Mead, Oxford OX2 0EL
tel (01865) 206206 *fax* (01865) 721205
web site http://www.blackwell-science.com
Chairman Nigel Blackwell, *Managing Director* Robert Campbell, *Directors* Jonathan Conibear,

Peter Saugman (editorial), Martin Wilkinson (finance), John Strange (production)

Medicine, nursing, dentistry, veterinary medicine, life sciences, earth sciences, chemistry, professional including construction, allied health. Founded 1939.

Fishing News Books (imprint)
tel (01865) 206081
Publisher Nigel Balmforth

Commercial fisheries, aquaculture, fish biology.

Blake Publishing

(incorporating Smith Gryphon Ltd)
3 Bramber Court, 2 Bramber Road, London W14 9PB
tel 020-7381 0666 *fax* 020-7381 6868
e-mail words@blake.co.uk
Managing Director John Blake, *Deputy Managing Director* Rosie Ries, *Executive Editor* Adam Parfitt, *Production Editor* Michelle Signore

Popular non-fiction, including biographies and true crime. No unsolicited fiction. Founded 1991.

Blandford Press – former imprint of Cassell & Co

Bloodaxe Books Ltd

PO Box 1SN, Newcastle upon Tyne NE99 1SN
tel (01434) 240500 *fax* (01434) 240505
e-mail editor@bloodaxebooks.demon.co.uk
Directors Neil Astley, Simon Thirsk

Poetry, literary criticism. No e-mail or fax submissions. Founded 1978.

Bloodlines – see The Do-Not Press

Bloomsbury Publishing plc*

38 Soho Square, London W1V 5DF
tel 020-7494 2111 *fax* 020-7434 0151
web site http://www.bloomsbury.com
Chairman and Chief Executive Nigel Newton, *Directors* Liz Calder (publishing), Alexandra Pringle (publishing), Alan Wherry (international), Kathy Rooney (reference), David Ward (sales), Minna Fry (marketing), Katie Collins (publicity), Ruth Logan (rights), Penny Edwards (production), Matthew Hamilton (paperbacks), Sarah Odedina (children's), Colin Adams (finance), Will Webb (design), Jill Coleman

Fiction, biography, illustrated, reference, travel, children's, trade paperback and mass market paperback. Founded 1986.

Boatswain Press Ltd

Dudley House, 12 North Street, Emsworth, Hants PO10 7DQ
tel (01243) 377977 *fax* (01243) 379136
Directors Piers Mason, Anthea Mason

Yachting titles, nautical almanacs.

Bodley Head – see Random House Group Ltd*

Bodley Head Children's – see Random House Group Ltd*

Booth-Clibborn Editions

12 Percy Street, London W1P 9FB
tel 020-7637 4255 *fax* 020-7637 4251
e-mail info@booth-clibborn.com
web site http://www.booth-clibborn-editions.co.uk

Illustrated books on art, popular culture, graphic design, photography. Founded 1974.

Bounty – see Octopus Publishing Group

Bowker-Saur

Windsor Court, East Grinstead House, East Grinstead, West Sussex RH19 1XA
tel (01342) 326972 *fax* (01342) 335612
e-mail customer.services@bowker-saur.co.uk
web site http://www.bowker-saur.co.uk
Group Publishing Director Gerard Dummett

Bibliographies, trade and reference directories, library and information science journals, electronic publishing, abstracts and indexes. Division of **Reed Business Information**.

Headland Business Information (imprint)

Business information newsletters and journals.

Boxtree – see Macmillan Publishers Ltd*

Marion Boyars Publishers Ltd*

24 Lacy Road, London SW15 1NL
tel 020-8788 9522 *fax* 020-8789 8122
Directors Arthur Boyars, Catheryn Kilgarriff

Literary fiction, psychology, feminism, music, drama, cinema, dance, biography.

Boydell & Brewer Ltd

PO Box 9, Woodbridge, Suffolk IP12 3DF

Medieval studies, history, literature, archaeology, art history. No unsolicited MSS. Founded 1969.

Bradt Travel Guides

19 High Street, Chalfont St Peter, Bucks. SL9 9QE
tel (01753) 893444 *fax* (01753) 892333
e-mail info@bradt-travelguides.com
web site http://www.bradt-travelguides.com
Managing Director Hilary Bradt

Guides for the adventurous traveller who seeks off-beat places and 'the dreamer who would like to travel there but never will'. Bradt series: *Country Guides*,

Hiking Guides, Rail Guides, Road Guides, Wildlife Guides. Founded 1973.

Brandon Book Publishers Ltd – see Mount Eagle Publications Ltd[†]

Brassey's (UK) Ltd

9 Blenheim Court, Brewery Road, London N7 9NT
tel 020-7700 7611 *fax* 020-7700 4552
web site http://www.brasseys.com
Editorial Caroline Bolton

Military technology, military history and illustrated military reference works. Sports reference books. Founded 1886. A member of the Chrysalis Group plc.

Conway Maritime Press (imprint)
Editorial John Lee

Highly illustrated reference books on naval history and maritime culture, ship design and ship modelling.

Putnam Aeronautical Books (imprint)
Editorial John Lee

Highly illustrated reference books on specialist aviation histories and studies of aerospace manufacturers.

Nicholas Brealey Publishing

36 John Street, London WC1N 2AT
tel 020-7430 0224 *fax* 020-7404 8311
web site http://www.nbrealey-books.com
Managing Director Nicholas Brealey

Critical issues facing business in the new century – from E-business to consumer behaviour, from science applied to business success to an understanding of global change. Founded 1992.

Breedon Books Publishing Co. Ltd

Breedon House, 3 The Parker Centre, Derby DE21 4SZ
tel (01332) 384235 *fax* (01332) 292755
e-mail anton@breedonbooks.co.uk
Directors Anton Rippon (chairman and editorial), Patricia Rippon, Graham Hales (production)

Heritage, local history, archive photography, local guidebooks, sports history – especially soccer. Preliminary letter essential. Founded 1981.

Breese Books Ltd

164 Kensington Park Road, London W11 2ER
tel 020-7727 9426 *fax* 020-7229 3395
e-mail martin@sherlockholmes.co.uk
web site http://www.sherlockholmes.co.uk
Publisher Martin Breese

Conjuring books, Sherlock Holmes pastiches and *Breese's Guide to Modern First Editions*. Submit a one-page synopsis together with sae for return of unsuitable material. Founded 1980.

Brewin Books Ltd

Doric House, 56 Alcester Road, Studley, Warks. B80 7LG
tel (01527) 854228/85362 *fax* (01527) 852746
e-mail admin@brewinbooks.com
web site http://www.brewinbooks.com
Publishing Director Alan Brewin

Non-fiction: Midland regional history (Birmingham, Warwickshire, Worcs., etc), transport history, biography (with Midlands connection). Founded 1976.

Brilliant Publications*

The Old School Yard, Leighton Road, Northall, Dunstable, Beds. LU6 2HA
tel (01525) 222844 *fax* (01525) 221250
e-mail editorial@brilliantpublications.co.uk
web site http://www.brilliantpublications.co.uk
Managing Director Priscilla Hannaford

Books for teachers and others concerned with the education of 0-13 year-olds. Subjects covered include English, mathematics, science, geography and history. Study catalogue or visit web site before sending proposal. Founded 1993.

Brimax Books – see Octopus Publishing Group

Bristol Classical Press – see Gerald Duckworth & Co. Ltd

Britannica.co.uk.ltd

3rd Floor, Golden Square, London W1R 3AF
tel 020-7862 4000 *fax* 020-7862 4040
Managing Director Jason Plent

British Academic Press – see I.B.Tauris & Co. Ltd

The British Library (Publications)*

Publishing Office, The British Library, 96 Euston Road, London NW1 2DB
tel 020-7412 7704 *fax* 020-7412 7768
e-mail blpublications@bl.uk
web site http://www.bl.uk
Managers David Way (publishing), Lara Speicher (managing editor), Catherine Britton (sales and marketing)

Bibliography, book arts, music, maps, oriental, manuscript studies, history, literature, facsimiles, audio-visual, and multimedia CD-Rom. Founded 1973.

British Museum Press*

46 Bloomsbury Street, London WC1B 3QQ
tel 020-7323 1234 *fax* 020-7436 7315

web site http://www.britishmuseum.co.uk
Managing Director Patrick Wright, *Head of Publishing* Emma Way

Art history, archaeology, numismatics, history, oriental art and archaeology, horology. Division of The British Museum Company Ltd. Founded 1973.

Brockhampton Press – see Caxton Publishing Group

Brown, Son & Ferguson, Ltd*

4-10 Darnley Street, Glasgow G41 2SD
tel 0141-429 1234 (24 hours) *fax* 0141-420 1694
e-mail info@skipper.co.uk
web site http://www.skipper.co.uk
Editorial Director L. Ingram-Brown

Nautical books; plays; Scout, Cub Scout, Brownie Guide and Guide story books. Founded 1860.

Brown Wells & Jacobs Ltd

Foresters Hall, 25-27 Westow Street, London SE19 3RY
tel 020-8771 5115 *fax* 020-8771 9994
e-mail postmaster@popking.demon.co.uk
web site http://www.bwj.org
Managing Director Graham Brown

Children's non-fiction novelty and pop-ups. Founded 1979.

Brunner/Routledge – see Psychology Press Ltd

Bryntirion Press

(formerly Evangelical Press of Wales)
Bryntirion, Bridgend, Mid Glamorgan CF31 4DX
tel (01656) 655886 *fax* (01656) 656095
e-mail press@draco.uk.com
Chief Executive Gerallt Wyn Davies, *Press Manager* Huw Kinsey

Theology and religion (in English and Welsh). Founded 1955.

Buildings of England – see Penguin UK*

Burns & Oates

(Publishers to the Holy See)
Wellwood, North Farm Road, Tunbridge Wells, Kent TN2 3DR
tel (01892) 510850 *fax* (01892) 515903
e-mail searchpress@searchpress.com
Director Martin de la Bedoyere

Theology, philosophy, spirituality, church history, Catholic interest, craft books with religious themes. Founded 1847.

Butterworth Heinemann UK – see Reed Educational and Professional Publishing Ltd*

Butterworths Tolley

Halsbury House, 35 Chancery Lane, London WC2A 1EL
tel 020-7400 2500 *fax* 020-7400 2842
e-mail stephen.stout@butterworths.co.uk
Managing Director Stephen J. Stout

Division of Reed Elsevier (UK) Ltd.

Butterworths (imprint)
Legal books, journals, looseleaf and electronic services; tax and accountancy books, journals and looseleaf and electronic services.

Fourmat (imprint)
Books and legal forms for lawyers, business and the professions.

Charles Knight (imprint)
Looseleaf legal works and periodicals on local government law, construction law and technical subjects.

Tolley (imprint)
Law, taxation, accountancy, business.

Cadogan Guides

West End House, 11 Hills Place, London W1R 1AG
tel 020-7287 6555 *fax* 020-7734 1733
e-mail guides@morrispub.co.uk
Editorial Director Vicki Ingle

Travel guides. Founded 1982.

Calder Publications Ltd

126 Cornwall Road, London SE1 8TQ
tel 020-7633 0599
Director John Calder

European, international and British fiction and plays, art, literary, music and social criticism, biography and autobiography, essays, humanities and social sciences, European classics. No unsolicited MSS. Inquiry letters must include an sae. Series include: *English National Opera Guides, New Paris Editions, Scottish Library, New Writing and Writers, Platform Books, Opera Library, Historical Perspectives.*

Calmann and King Ltd – see Laurence King Publishing

Cambridge University Press*

The Edinburgh Building, Shaftesbury Road, Cambridge CB2 2RU
tel (01223) 312393 *fax* (01223) 315052
e-mail information@cup.cam.ac.uk
web site http://www.cup.cam.ac.uk
Chief Executive of the Press and University Printer Jeremy Mynott MA, PhD

Anthropology and archaeology, art and architecture, astronomy, biological sciences, classical studies, computer science, dictionaries, earth sciences, economics, educational (primary, secondary, tertiary), educational software, engineering, film, English language teaching, history, language and literature, law, mathematics, medical sciences, music, oriental, philosophy, physical sciences, politics, psychology, reference, technology, social sciences, theology, religion. Journals (humanities, social sciences, science and professional). The Bible and Prayer Book. Founded 1534.

Campbell Books – see Macmillan Publishers Ltd*

Canongate Books Ltd*

14 High Street, Edinburgh EH1 1TE
tel 0131-557 5111 *fax* 0131-557 5211
e-mail info@canongate.co.uk
web site http://www.canongate.net
Publisher Jamie Byng, *Directors* David Graham (managing), Ronnie Shanks (finance), Jim Hutcheson (art), Neville Moir (non-executive), *Senior Editor* Judy Moir

Adult general non-fiction and fiction: Scottish Interest, Pocket Canons, literary fiction, art, travel, mountaineering, translations, poetry, philosophy, religion, history and biography. Founded 1973.

Canongate Classics (imprint)
Senior Editor Rory Watson

Reprint series of key works of Scottish literature ranging from fiction to poetry, to biography, philosophy and travel.

Canongate Crime (imprint)
Senior Editor Carlos McVeigh

Crime fiction and non-fiction – hard-boiled, literary and noir, including Canongate Crime Classics.

Mojo Books (imprint)
Senior Editor Jim Irvin

Music reference, biography and history.

Payback Press (imprint)
Senior Editor Colin McLear

Afro-American and Jamaican culture: non-fiction, fiction, music, poetry, biography.

Rebel Inc. (imprint)
Senior Editor Kevin Williamson

Counter cultural fiction and non-fiction: Rebel Inc. Classics.

Canterbury Press Norwich

St Mary's Works, St Mary's Plain, Norwich, Norfolk NR3 3BH
tel (01603) 612914 *fax* (01603) 624483
e-mail admin@scm-canterburypress.co.uk
Publisher Christine Smith

C of E doctrine, theology, liturgy, general interest, reference and resource, histories and associated topics, hymn books. Division of SCM-Canterbury Press Ltd, a subsidiary of Hymns Ancient & Modern Ltd.

Jonathan Cape – see Random House Group Ltd*

Jonathan Cape Children's Books – see Random House Group Ltd*

Carcanet Press Ltd

4th Floor, Conavon Court, 12-16 Blackfriars Street, Manchester M3 5BQ
tel 0161-834 8730 *fax* 0161-832 0084
e-mail pnr@carcanet.u-net.com
web site http://www.carcanet.co.uk
Director Michael Schmidt

Poetry, *Fyfield* series, Oxford Poets, translations. Founded 1969.

Carlton Books

20 Mortimer Street, London W1N 7RD
tel 020-7612 0400 *fax* 020-7612 0401
e-mail enquiries@carltonbooks.co.uk
web site http://www.carlton.com
Directors Jonathan Goodman (managing), John Maynard (operations), Piers Murray Hill (publishing), Russell Porter (design), Adrian Whitton (finance), Keith Allen-Jones (international sales)

Popular music, lifestyle, sport, games, quizzes and puzzles, film, popular science, New Age, TV tie-ins, criminology, illustrated reference. Founded 1992.

Carroll & Brown – see Metro Publishing Ltd

Frank Cass & Co. Ltd

Newbury House, 890-900 Eastern Avenue, Newbury Park, Ilford, Essex IG2 7HH
tel 020-8599 8866 *fax* 020-8599 0984
Directors Frank Cass (chairman), Stewart Cass (managing), A.E. Cass, H.J. Osen, M.P. Zaidner

History, economic and social history, military and strategic studies, politics, international affairs, development studies, African studies, Middle East studies, law, business management and academic journals in all of these fields.

Woburn Press (imprint)
Educational.

Cassell (academic, professional and contemporary studies lists) – see The

Continuum International Publishing Group Ltd

Cassell & Co

Wellington House, 125 Strand, London WC2R 0BB
tel 020-7420 5555 *fax* 020-7240 7261
Managing Director John Mitchinson, *Deputy Managing Director* Annabel Merullo

Part of The Orion Publishing Group Ltd. Founded 1848.

Cassell Illustrated
Publishing Director, Weidenfeld & Nicolson Michael Dover, *Publishing Director, Ward Lock* Margaret Little

Quality illustrated non-fiction: gardening, cookery, wine, art and design, health and lifestyle, history, popular culture, archaeology, British heritage, literature, Discovery books, fashion, architecture, natural history, sport and adventure.

Cassell Military (including Arms & Armour) (imprint)
Publishing Director Angus MacKinnon

Military history and militaria.

Cassell Reference (imprint)
Publishing Director Richard Milbank

Language and general interest reference.

Hachette UK (imprint)
Publishing Director Jackie Strachan

Travel, computing, French wine guides and gift books.

Seven Dials (imprint)
Managing Editor Nic Cheetham

Quality illustrated paperbacks: food and drink, gardening, heritage, history, lifestyle, art.

Castle House Publications Ltd

3 Linden Close, Tunbridge Wells, Kent TN4 8HH
tel (01892) 539606 *fax* (01892) 517773
e-mail enquiries@castlehouse.co.uk
Director D. Reinders

Medical. Founded 1973.

Cat's Whiskers – see The Watts Publishing Group Ltd*

Kyle Cathie Ltd

122 Arlington Road, London NW1 7HP
tel 020-7692 7215 *fax* 020-7692 7260
e-mail general.enquiries@kyle-cathie.com
Publisher and Managing Director Kyle Cathie

Health, beauty, food and drink, gardening, reference, style, design. Founded 1990.

Catholic Truth Society

40-46 Harleyford Road, London SE11 5AY
tel 020-7640 0042 *fax* 020-7640 0046
Chairman Rt Rev. Peter Smith DCL, LLB, *General Secretary* Fergal Martin LLB, LLM

General books of Roman Catholic and Christian interest, bibles, prayer books and pamphlets of doctrinal, historical, devotional or social interest. MSS of 11,000-15,000 words with up to 6 illustrations considered for publication as pamphlets. Founded 1868.

Cavendish Publishing Ltd*

The Glass House, Wharton Street, London WC1X 9PX
tel 020-7278 8000 *fax* 020-7278 8080
e-mail info@cavendishpublishing.com
web site http://www.cavendishpublishing.com
Publishing Director Sonny Leong, *Managing Editor* Jo Reddy

A wide range of legal and medico-legal books and journals. Founded 1990.

Caxton Publishing Group

20 Bloomsbury Street, London WC1B 3QA
tel 020-7636 7171 *fax* 020-7636 1922
Directors John Maxwell (managing), Jack Cooper (deputy managing)

Reprints, promotional books, remainders. Imprints: Caxton Editions, Brockhampton Press, Knight Paperbacks.

CBD Research Ltd

15 Wickham Road, Beckenham, Kent BR3 5JS
tel 020-8650 7745 *fax* 020-8650 0768
e-mail cbdresearch@compuserve.com
Directors G.P. Henderson, S.P.A. Henderson, C.A.P. Henderson, A.J.W. Henderson

Directories, reference books, bibliographies, guides to business and statistical information. Founded 1961.

Chancery House Press (imprint)

Unusual non-fiction/reference works. Preliminary letter and synopsis with return postage essential.

Centaur Press – acquired by Open Gate Press*

Century – see Random House Group Ltd*

Chadwyck-Healey Ltd*

The Quorum, Barnwell Road, Cambridge CB5 8SW
tel (01223) 215512 *fax* (01223) 215513
e-mail marketing @chadwyck.co.uk
web site http://www.chadwyck.co.uk
Vice-President/General Manager Steven Hall, *Vice-President, Sales and Marketing* Steve Sidaway, *Vice-President, Publishing* Julie Carroll-Davis

CD-Roms: News and business information, bibliographies and reference works, literature, history, arts, statistics, cartography and climate. Founded 1973.

Chambers Harrap Publishers Ltd*
7 Hopetoun Crescent, Edinburgh EH7 4AY
tel 0131-556 5929 *fax* 0131-556 5313
e-mail admin@chambersharrap.co.uk
Managing Director Maurice Shepherd, *Chambers Publishing Manager* Elaine Higgleton, *Harrap Publishing Manager* Patrick White
English language and bilingual dictionaries, reference. No unsolicited MSS. Write enclosing CV and synopsis.

Chameleon – former imprint of André Deutsch Ltd*

Chancery House Press – see CBD Research Ltd

Geoffrey Chapman – see The Continuum International Publishing Group Ltd

Chapman Publishing*
4 Broughton Place, Edinburgh EH1 3RX
tel 0131-557 2207 *fax* 0131-556 9565
e-mail editor@chapman-pub.co.uk
web site http://www.chapman-pub.co.uk
Editor Joy Hendry
Poetry and drama: *Chapman New Writing Series*. Founded 1970.

Paul Chapman Publishing Ltd
6 Bonhill Street, London EC2A 4PU
tel 020-7374 0645 *fax* 020-7374 8741
web site http://www.paulchapmanpublishing.co.uk
Consultant P.R. Chapman, *Commissioning Editor* Marianne Langrange
Education. Subsidiary of **SAGE Publications Ltd**.

Chatham Publishing – see Gerald Duckworth & Co. Ltd

Chatto & Windus – see Random House Group Ltd*

Chester House Publications – see Methodist Publishing House

The Chicken House – see Egmont Children's Books

Child's Play (International) Ltd
Ashworth Road, Bridgemead, Swindon, Wilts. SN5 7YD
tel (01793) 616286 *fax* (01793) 512795
e-mail allday@childs-play.com
web site http://www.childs-play.com
Chairman Adriana Twinn, *Publisher* Neil Burden
Children's educational books: board picture, activity and play books; fiction and non-fiction. Founded 1972.

Chivers Press Ltd
Windsor Bridge Road, Bath BA2 3AX
tel (01225) 335336 *fax* (01225) 310771
web site http://www.chivers.co.uk
Directors Julian Batson (managing), Nicole Kirkman (publishing), Michael Bowen (finance)
Large print books and complete and unabridged audiobooks: general fiction, crime, romance, mystery/thrillers, westerns, non-fiction. Does not publish original books. Imprints: Chivers Large Print, Chivers Audio Books, Black Dagger Crime, Windsor Large Print, Galaxy Children's Large Print, Cavalcade. Founded 1979.

Churchill Livingstone – see Harcourt Publishers Ltd

Cicerone Press
2 Police Square, Milnthorpe, Cumbria LA7 7PY
tel (015395) 62069 *fax* (015395) 63417
e-mail info@cicerone.demon.co.uk
web site http://www.cicerone.co.uk
Managing Director Jonathan Williams
Guidebooks to the great outdoors – walking, mountaineering, climbing, cycling, etc in Britain, Europe, and worldwide. Founded 1969.

Cima Books†
32 Great Sutton Street, London EC1V 0NB
tel 020-7253 7960 *fax* 020-7253 7967
e-mail mail@cimabooks.co.uk
web site http://www.cimabooks.co.uk
Directors Mark Collins (managing), Lucinda Richards (publishing)
Lifestyle and interiors and mind, body and spirit. Founded 1999.

Clarendon Press – former imprint of Oxford University Press*

T. & T. Clark
59 George Street, Edinburgh EH2 2LQ
tel 0131-225 4703 *fax* 0131-220 4260
e-mail mailbox@tandtclark.co.uk
web site http://www.tandtclark.co.uk
Managing Director Geoffrey F. Green MA, PhD
Theology, philosophy, law. Founded 1821.

James Clarke & Co. Ltd*
PO Box 60, Cambridge CB1 2NT
tel (01223) 350865 *fax* (01223) 366951
e-mail publishing@lutterworth.com
web site http://www.lutterworth.com

Managing Director Adrian Brink

Theology, academic, reference books. Founded 1859.

Acorn Editions (imprint)

Sponsored books.

Lutterworth Press (subsidiary)

The arts, biography, children's books (fiction, non-fiction, picture, rewards), educational, environmental, general, history, leisure, philosophy, science, sociology, theology and religion.

Patrick Hardy Books (imprint)

Children's fiction.

Cló Iar-Chonnachta Teo.†

Indreabhán, Conamara, Co. Galway, Republic of Ireland
tel (091) 593307 *fax* (091) 593362
e-mail cic@iol.ie
web site http://www.cic.ie
Director Micheál Ó Conghaile, *General Manager* Deirdre O'Toole

Mostly Irish-language – novels, short stories, plays, poetry, songs, history; cassettes (writers reading from their works in Irish and English). Promotes the translation of contemporary Irish fiction and poetry into other languages. Founded 1985.

Richard Cohen Books – see Metro Publishing Ltd

Peter Collin Publishing Ltd

1 Cambridge Road, Teddington TW11 8DT
tel 020-8943 3386 *fax* 020-8943 1673
e-mail info@petercollin.com
web site http://www.petercollin.com
Directors P.H. Collin (managing), S.M.H. Collin, F. Collin

Specialised dictionaries covering many subjects – from business to computing, medicine to tourism, law to banking. Bilingual language dictionaries in various subjects and languages. Founded 1985.

Collins – see HarperCollins Publishers*

Collins & Brown

London House, Great Eastern Wharf, Parkgate Road, London SW11 4NQ
tel 0171-924 2575 *fax* 0171-924 7725
Directors Kate MacPhee (managing), Colin Ziegler (publishing), Jane Allison (international rights, sales), Terry Shaughnessy (sales and marketing)

Lifestyle and interiors, gardening, photography, practical arts, health and beauty, hobbies and crafts, natural history, history, ancient civilisation and astrology, fantasy art and general interest. Subsidiary of CBMG plc. Founded1989.

Belitha Press

See page 155.

David Bennett Books

See page 155.

Paper Tiger (imprint)

Contact Colin Ziegler

Fantasy art.

Parkgate Books

Publisher Lisa Simpson

Promotional books.

Pavilion Books

See page 193.

Colourpoint Books*†

Unit D5, Ards Business Centre, Jubilee Road, Newtownards, Co. Down BT23 4YH
tel (028) 9182 0505 *fax* (028) 9182 1900
e-mail info@colourpoint.co.uk
web site http://www.colourpoint.co.uk
Directors Sheila Johnston (commissioning editor), Norman Johnston (transport editor), *Administrator* Michelle Chambers, *Marketing and Publicity* Sharon Patterson

Educational textbooks: transport – shipping, aviation, buses, road and railways; religion; Irish interest. Initial approach in writing please, with full details of proposal and sample chapters. Include return postage. Founded 1993.

The Columba Press†

55A Spruce Avenue, Stillorgan Industrial Park, Blackrock, Co. Dublin, Republic of Ireland
tel (1) 2942556 *fax* (1) 2942564
e-mail info@columba.ie
web site http://www.columba.ie
Publisher and Managing Director Seán O'Boyle

Religion (Roman Catholic and Anglican) including pastoral handbooks, spirituality, theology, liturgy and prayer; counselling and self-help. Founded 1985.

Condé Nast Books – see Random House Group Ltd*

Conran Octopus – see Octopus Publishing Group

Conservative Policy Forum

(formerly the Conservative Political Centre)
32 Smith Square, London SW1P 3HH
tel 020-7984 8086 *fax* 020-7984 8272
e-mail cpf@conservative-party.org.uk
Director James Walsh

Politics, current affairs. Founded 1945 as the Conservative Political Centre.

Constable & Robinson Ltd*

3 The Lanchesters, 162 Fulham Palace Road, London W6 9ER
tel 020-8741 3663 *fax* 020-8748 7562
e-mail enquiries@constablerobinson.com
web site http://www.constablerobinson.com
Non-Executive Chairman Benjamin Glazebrook, *Managing Director* Nick Robinson, *Directors* Jan Chamier, Nova Jayne Heath, Adrian Andrews

Unsolicited sample chapters, synopses and ideas welcome with return postage. Do not send MSS; no e-mail submissions. Founded 1890 (Constable); 1983 (Robinson).

Constable (hardbacks)
Editorial Director Carol O'Brien

Biography, autobiography, crime fiction, general and military history, psychology, travel, climbing, landscape photography, outdoor-pursuits guidebooks.

Robinson (paperbacks)
Senior Commissioning Editor Krystyna Green

Crime, science fiction, *Daily Telegraph* health books, the Mammoth series, psychology, true crime, military history, *Smarties* children's books.

Consumers' Association – see Which? Ltd*

The Continuum International Publishing Group Ltd

Wellington House, 125 Strand, London WC2R 0BB
tel 020-7420 5555 *fax* 020-7240 7261
e-mail info@continuumbooks.com
web site http://www.continuumbooks.com
Chairman and Chief Executive Philip Sturrock, *Directors* Frank Roney (finance), Robin Baird-Smith (publishing), Janet Joyce (editorial), John Parsons (sales and marketing)

Cassell (academic, professional and contemporary studies lists)
Director/Publisher Janet Joyce

Humanities, social sciences, tourism and business, education.

Geoffrey Chapman (imprint)
Director/Publisher Robin Baird-Smith

Religion and theology, particularly Roman Catholic.

Leicester University Press (imprint)
Director/Publisher Janet Joyce

Academic books, especially medieval history, museum studies, political theory.

Mansell Publishing (imprint)
Director/Publisher Janet Joyce

Bibliographies in all academic subject areas and monographs in urban and regional planning, Islamic studies, librarianship, history.

Mowbray (imprint)
Director/Publisher Robin Baird-Smith

Religion and theology, both Anglican and non-denominational.

Pinter (imprint)
Director/Publisher Janet Joyce

Academic and professional specialising in social sciences, including international relations, politics, economics, new technology, linguistics, communications, religious studies.

Conway Maritime Press – see Brassey's (UK) Ltd

Leo Cooper – see Pen & Sword Books Ltd

Corgi – see Transworld Publishers*

Cork University Press[†]

Crawford Business Park, Crosses Green, Cork, Republic of Ireland
tel (021) 4902980 *fax* (021) 4315329
e-mail corkunip@ucc.ie
Publisher Sara Wilbourne

Irish literature, history, cultural studies, medieval studies, English literature, musicology, poetry, translations. Founded 1925.

Cornwall Books – see Golden Cockerel Press

Coronet – see Hodder Headline Ltd*

Council for British Archaeology

Bowes Morrell House, 111 Walmgate, York YO1 9WA
tel (01904) 671417 *fax* (01904) 671384
e-mail archaeology@compuserve.com
web site http://www.britarch.ac.uk
Director George Lambrick, *Publications Officer* Kate Sleight

British archaeology – academic; practical handbooks; general interest archaeology. Founded 1944.

Countryside Books

2 Highfield Avenue, Newbury, Berks. RG14 5DS
tel (01635) 43816 *fax* (01635) 551004
web site http://www.countrysidebooks.co.uk
Partners Nicholas Battle, Suzanne Battle

Books of local or regional interest, usually on a county basis: walking, outdoor activities, local history; also genealogy, aviation. Founded 1976.

Countrywise Press – see Barry Rose Law Publishers Ltd

Crescent Moon Publishing

PO Box 393, Maidstone, Kent ME14 5XU
tel (01622) 729593
e-mail jrobinson@crescentmoon.org.uk
web site http://www.crescentmoon.org.uk
Director Jeremy Robinson, *Editors* Cassidy Hughes, B.D. Barnacle

Literature, poetry, fine art, cultural studies, media, cinema, feminism. Founded 1988.

Cressrelles Publishing Co. Ltd

10 Station Road Industrial Estate, Colwall, Malvern, Herefordshire WR13 6RN
tel/fax (01684) 540154
Directors Leslie Smith, Simon Smith

General publishing. Founded 1973.

Actinic Press (imprint)

Chiropody.

Garnet Miller (imprint)

Plays and theatre textbooks.

Kenyon-Deane (imprint)

Plays and drama textbooks for amateur dramatic societies. Plays for women.

Crown House Publishing Ltd*

Crown Buildings, Bancyfelin, Carmarthen SA33 5ND
tel (01267) 211345 *fax* (01267) 211882
e-mail books@crownhouse.co.uk
web site http://www.crownhouse.co.uk
Directors Martin Roberts (chairman), Glenys Roberts, David Bowan (editorial), Karen Bowman (secretary), Bridget Shine (publishing)

Psychology, personal growth, stress management, business, education, health. Founded 1998.

The Crowood Press

The Stable Block, Ramsbury, Marlborough, Wilts. SN8 2HR
tel (01672) 520320 *fax* (01672) 520280
e-mail enquiries@crowood.demon.co.uk
Directors John Dennis (chairman), Ken Hathaway (managing)

Sport, motoring, aviation, military, climbing and walking, fishing, country sports, farming, natural history, gardening, DIY, crafts, dogs, equestrian, games. Founded 1982.

Helmsman (imprint)

Nautical.

Current Science Group

34-42 Cleveland Street, London W1P 6LB
tel 020-7323 0323 *fax* 020-7580 1938
e-mail csg@cursci.co.uk
web site http://www.current-science-group.com
Chairman Vitek Tracz

Biological sciences, medicine, pharmaceutical science, Internet communities, electronic publishing.

James Currey Ltd

73 Botley Road, Oxford OX2 0BS
tel (01865) 244111 *fax* (01865) 246454
Directors James Currey, Prof Wendy James FBA, Dr Douglas H. Johnson, Keith Sambrook

Academic studies of Africa, Caribbean, Third World: history, anthropology, archaeology, economics, agriculture, politics, literary criticism, sociology. Founded 1985.

Curzon Press Ltd

15 The Quadrant, Richmond, Surrey TW9 1BP
tel 020-8948 4660 *fax* 020-8332 6735
e-mail publish@curzonpress.co.uk
web site http://www.curzonpress.co.uk
Managing Director/Publisher Malcolm Campbell

Academic/scholarly books and journals in the humanities, social sciences, language and linguistics, business, economics, politics in the context of Asia. Imprints: Japan Library, Caucasus World. Founded 1970.

Cygnus Arts – see Golden Cockerel Press

Dalesman Publishing Co. Ltd

Stable Courtyard, Broughton Hall, Skipton, North Yorkshire BD23 3AE
tel (01756) 701381 *fax* (01756) 701326
e-mail editorial@dalesman.co.uk
Chairman T.J. Benn, *Managing Director* C.G. Benn, *General Manager* R. Flanagan

Countryside books and magazines covering the North of England. Founded 1939.

Terence Dalton Ltd

Water Street, Lavenham, Sudbury, Suffolk CO10 9RN
tel (01787) 249289 *fax* (01787) 248267
Directors T.A.J. Dalton, E.H. Whitehair

Inland waterways construction, use and abuse. Contract publisher for the Chartered Institution of Water and Environmental Management. Founded 1966.

The C.W. Daniel Company Ltd

1 Church Path, Saffron Walden, Essex CB10 1JP
tel (01799) 521909 *fax* (01799) 513462
e-mail daniel_publishing@dial.pipex.com
Directors Ian Miller, Jane Miller

Natural healing, Bach Flower Remedies, homoeopathy, aromatherapy, mysticism. Founded 1902.

L.N. Fowler & Co Ltd (imprint)
Directors Ian Miller, Jane Miller
Mysticism, astrology.

Health Science Press (imprint)
Directors Ian Miller, Jane Miller
Homoeopathy.

Neville Spearman Publishers (imprint)
Editorial Director Sebastian Hobnut
Mysticism, metaphysical.

Dartmouth Publishing Co. Ltd – subsidiary of Ashgate Publishing Ltd

Darton, Longman & Todd Ltd*

1 Spencer Court, 140-142 Wandsworth High Street, London SW18 4JJ
tel 020-8875 0155 *fax* 020-8875 0133
e-mail editorial@darton-longman-todd.co.uk
Editorial Director Brendan Walsh

Religious books and bibles, including the following themes: bible study, spirituality, prayer and meditation, anthologies, daily readings, healing, counselling and pastoral care, bereavement, personal growth, mission, political, environmental and social issues, biography/autobiography, theological and historical studies. Founded 1959.

Darwen Finlayson Ltd – see Phillimore & Co. Ltd

David & Charles Children's Books

Winchester House, 259-269 Old Marylebone Road, London NW1 5XJ
tel 020-7616 7200 *fax* 020-7616 7201
Directors Neil A. Page (managing), Pippa Rubinstein (publishing), Mandy Suhr (editorial), Paula Burgess (art)

Picture books, novelty books, board books, story collections and 'entertainment' for under-7 age group. Division of **David & Charles Ltd**. Founded 1994.

David & Charles Ltd

Brunel House, Newton Abbot, Devon TQ12 4PU
tel (01626) 323200 *fax* (01626) 323317
Directors Neil A. Page (managing), Pippa Rubinstein (publishing)

High quality illustrated non-fiction specialising in crafts, hobbies, art techniques, cookery, gardening, natural history, equestrian, DIY. Founded 1960.

Christopher Davies Publishers Ltd

PO Box 403, Swansea SA1 4YF
tel/fax (01792) 648825
Directors Christopher Talfan Davies (editorial), K.E.T. Colayera, D.M. Davies

History, leisure books, sport and general of Welsh interest, Welsh dictionaries, *Triskele Books*. Founded 1949.

Dean – see Egmont Children's Books

Dedalus Ltd

24 St Judith's Lane, Sawtry, Cambs. PE17 5XE
tel/fax (01487) 832382
e-mail DedalusLimited@compuserve.com
Chairman Juri Gabriel, *Directors* Eric Lane (managing), Robert Irwin (editorial), Lindsay Thomas (marketing), Mike Mitchell (translations)

Original fiction in English and in translation; Empire of the Senses; Dedalus European Classics. Founded 1983.

Giles de la Mare Publishers Ltd

PO Box 25351, London NW5 1ZT
tel 020-7485 2533 *fax* 020-7485 2534
e-mail gilesdelamare@dial.pipex.com
Chairman Giles de la Mare

Non-fiction: art, architecture, biography, history, music, travel. Telephone before submitting MSS. Founded 1995.

J.M. Dent – now incorporated into The Orion Publishing Group Ltd

André Deutsch Ltd*

76 Dean Street, London W1V 5HA
tel 020-7316 4450 *fax* 020-7316 4499
web site http://www.vci.co.uk
Managing Director Alasdair Ogilvie, *Editorial Director* Louise Dixon

Subsidiary of VCI plc. Founded 1950.

André Deutsch (imprint)
Film/TV, popular entertainment, music, comedy, sport, biography, history and current affairs, popular culture, cookery/craft.

André Deutsch Classics (imprint)
Children's hardback classic books.

Granada Media Group (imprint)
Official TV tie-in books, publishing interests of Liverpool Football Club.

Madcap (imprint)
Innovative, fun and accessible children's titles.

Manchester United Books (imprint)
Publishing interests of Manchester United Football Club.

Rangers Books (imprint)
Publishing interests of Glasgow Rangers Football Club.

Dial House – see Ian Allan Publishing Ltd

diehard

91-93 Main Street, Callander FK17 8BQ
tel (01877) 339449
3 Spittal Street, Edinburgh EH3 9DY
tel 0131-229 7252
Directors Ian William King (managing), Sally Evans King (marketing)

Contemporary drama, Scottish poetry.

Discovery Walking Guides Ltd

10 Tennyson Close, Dallington, Northampton NN5 7HJ
tel/fax (01604) 752576
web site http://www.walking.demon.co.uk/
Chairman Rosamund C. Brawn

'Warm island' walking guides and plant and flower guides to European holiday destinations; 'Tour & Trail' digital cartographic large-scale maps. Founded 1994.

The Do-Not Press

PO Box 4215, London SE23 2QD
tel 020-8698 7833 *fax* 020-8698 7834
e-mail thedonotpress@zoo.co.uk
web site http://www.thedonotpress.co.uk
Publisher Jim Driver

No unsolicited MSS. Preliminary letter and sae essential. Very small list so opportunities limited. Founded 1995.

Bloodlines (imprint)
Crime fiction.

John Donald

Unit 8, Canongate Venture, 5 New Street, Edinburgh EH8 8BH
tel 0131-556 6660 *fax* 0131-557 6250
Director Hugh Andrew

British history, archaeology, ethnology, local history, vernacular architecture, general non-fiction. Imprint of Birlinn Ltd. Founded 1973.

Dorling Kindersley Ltd

9 Henrietta Street, London WC2E 8PS
tel 020-7836 5411 *fax* 020-7836 7570
web site http://www.dk.com
Ceo Antony Forbes Watson, *Publisher* Christopher Davis, *Group Directors* Andrew Welham (managing UK), Charlie Power (finance), Anita Fulton (legal), Danny Gurr (USA)

High quality illustrated books on non-fiction subjects, including health, atlases, travel, cookery, gardening, crafts and reference; also children's non-fiction, picture books and fiction. Bought by Pearson plc in 2000. Founded 1974.

Doubleday (UK) – see Transworld Publishers*

Dref Wen

28 Church Road, Whitchurch, Cardiff CF14 2EA
tel 029-2061 7860 *fax* 029-2061 0507
Directors Roger Boore, Anne Boore, Gwilym Boore, Alun Boore

Original Welsh language novels for children and adult learners. Original, adaptations and translations of foreign and English language full-colour picture story books for children. Educational material for primary/secondary schoolchildren in Wales and England. Founded 1970.

Dryden Press – see Harcourt Publishers Ltd

Dublar Scripts

204 Mercer Way, Romsey, Hants SO51 7QJ
tel (01794) 501377 *fax* (01794) 502538
e-mail scripts@dublar.freeserve.co.uk
web site http://www.dublar.co.uk
Managing Director Robert Heather

Pantomimes, one-act and full-length plays. Drama and comedy. Founded 1994.

Sleepy Hollow Pantomimes (imprint)
Pantomime scripts.

Duck Editions – see Gerald Duckworth & Co. Ltd

Gerald Duckworth & Co. Ltd

61 Frith Street, London W1V 5TA
tel 020-7434 4242 *fax* 020-7434 4420
e-mail info@duckworth-publishers.co.uk
web site http://www.ducknet.co.uk
Directors Stephen Hill (chairman), Thomas J. Hedley (Ceo and publisher), Gillian Hawkins (sales and marketing), Sarah Such (editorial), Deborah Blake (editorial), John Betts (academic)

General trade publishers with a strong academic division. Imprints: Bristol Classical Press and Chatham Publishing; naval and maritime history. Founded 1898.

Duck Editions (imprint)
Publisher Thomas J. Hedley, *Editorial Director* Sarah Such

Contemporary fiction and non-fiction. Founded 1998.

Martin Dunitz Ltd

The Livery House, 7-9 Pratt Street, London NW1 0AE
tel 020-7482 2202 *fax* 020-7267 0159
e-mail info@dunitz.co.uk
web site http://www.dunitz.co.uk
Managing Director Martin Dunitz

Books, journals and slide atlases in: cardiology, dentistry, dermatology, gastroenterology, gynaecology, haematology, metabolic bone disease, neurology, obesity, oncology, ophthalmology, orthopaedics, otorhinolaryngology, pathology, plastic surgery, psychiatry, radiology, respiratory medicine, rheumatology, sports medicine, surgery, ultrasound, urology. A member of the **Taylor & Francis Group plc**. Founded 1978.

Earthlight – **see Simon & Schuster***

Earthscan Publications Ltd – **see Kogan Page Ltd***

East-West Publications (UK) Ltd

134 Clock Tower Road, Isleworth, Middlesex TW7 6DT
tel 020-8758 0999 *fax* 020-8758 9777
Chairman L.W. Carp

General non-fiction, Eastern studies, sufism. No unsolicited MSS; please write first. Founded 1977.

Gallery Children's Books (imprint)
Quality children's books.

Ebury Press – **see Random House Group Ltd***

Edinburgh University Press*

22 George Square, Edinburgh EH8 9LF
tel 0131-650 4218 *fax* 0131-662 0053
Chairman David Martin, *Managing Director* Timothy Wright, *Editorial Director* Ms Jackie Jones

Academic and general publishers. Archaeology, cultural studies, Islamic studies, geography, history, linguistics, literature (criticism), philosophy, politics, Scottish studies, American studies, religious studies.

Polygon (imprint)
tel 0131-650 8436
New international fiction and poetry, oral history, general, Scottish, social and political (*Determinations* series). Preliminary enquiry preferred.

Éditions Aubrey Walter

BCM 6159, London WC1 3XX
tel (01366) 328101 *fax* (01366) 328102
e-mail aubrey@gmppubs.co.uk
Publisher Aubrey Walter

Visual work by gay artists and photographers, usually in the form of a monograph showcasing one artist's work. Work may be submitted on disk, e-mail, transparency, photocopy or photograph.

The Educational Company of Ireland

Ballymount Road, Walkinstown, Dublin 12, Republic of Ireland
tel (01) 4500611 *fax* (01) 4500993
e-mail info@edco.ie
web site http://www.edco.ie
Executive Directors F.J. Maguire (chief executive), R. McLoughlin, *Financial Controller*
M. Proudfoot, *Sales and Marketing Manager*
M. Harford-Hughes

Trading unit of Smurfit Ireland Ltd. Educational MSS on all subjects in English or Irish language.

Educational Explorers

11 Crown Street, Reading, Berks. RG1 2TQ
tel (01734) 873101 *fax* (01734) 873103
e-mail explorers@cuisenaire.co.uk
web site http://www.cuisenaire.co.uk
Directors M.J. Hollyfield, D.M. Gattegno

Educational, mathematics: *Numbers in colour with Cuisenaire Rods*, languages: *The Silent Way*, literacy, reading: *Words in Colour*; educational films. No unsolicited material. Founded 1962.

Eel Pie – **see Plexus Publishing Ltd**

Egmont Children's Books

239 Kensington High Street, London W8 6SA
tel 020-7761 3500 *fax* 020-7761 3510
e-mail firstname.surname@ecb.egmont.com
Chairman Julie Goldsmith, *Managing Director* Susannah McFarlane

Children's books: picture books, fiction (ages 4-16), illustrated non-fiction, licensed character list. Publishes under Mammoth, Heinemann Young Books, Methuen Children's Books, Egmont World, Dean.

World International
See page 212.

The Chicken House (an Egmont joint venture company)
2 Palmer Street, Frome, Somerset BA11 1DS
tel (01373) 454488 *fax* (01373) 454499
Managing Director Barrie Cunningham
Fiction and non-fiction for 7+, picture books.

Element Books

The Old School House, The Courtyard, Bell Street, Shaftesbury, Dorset SP7 8BP
tel (01747) 851448 *fax* (01747) 855721
web site http://www.elementbooks.com, www.elementkids.com
Directors Michael Mann (chairman and publisher), David Alexander (chief executive), Clive Turner (Coo), Julia McCutchen (managing/editorial), Roger Lane (production),

Elinor Bagenal (children's books, editorial), Clare Armstrong (group production)

Complementary health, personal development, self-help, psychology, philosophy, religion, colour illustrated books. Children's non-fiction, fiction, picture books and board books. Founded 1978.

11:9 – see Neil Wilson Publishing Ltd

Edward Elgar Publishing Ltd

Glensanda House, Montpellier Parade, Cheltenham, Glos. GL50 1UA
tel (01242) 226934 *fax* (01242) 262111
e-mail info@e-elgar.co.uk
web site http://www.e-elgar.co.uk
Managing Director Edward Elgar

Economics and other social sciences. Founded 1986.

Elliot Right Way Books

Kingswood Buildings, Brighton Road, Lower Kingswood, Tadworth, Surrey KT20 6TD
tel (01737) 832202 *fax* (01737) 830311
e-mail info@right-way.co.uk
Managing Directors Clive Elliot, Malcolm Elliot

Independent publishers of practical non-fiction 'how to' paperbacks. The low-price *Right Way* series includes games, pastimes, horses, pets, motoring, sport, health, business, public speaking and jokes, financial and legal, cookery and etiquette. Similar subjects are covered in the *Clarion* series of large-format paperbacks, sold in supermarkets and bargain bookshops. No freelance proofreaders or editors required. Founded 1946.

Aidan Ellis Publishing

Whinfield, Herbert Road, Salcombe, Devon TQ8 8HN
tel (01548) 842755 *fax* (01548) 844356
e-mail aidan@aepub.demon.co.uk
web site http://www.demon.co.uk/aepub
Publisher Aidan Ellis

Non-fiction: gardening, maritime, art, general. Founded 1971.

ELM Publications

Seaton House, Kings Ripton, Huntingdon, Cambs. PE17 2NJ
tel (01487) 773238 *fax* (01487) 773359
web site http://www.elm-training.co.uk
Managing Director Sheila Ritchie

Educational books and resources; books and training aids (tutor's packs and software) for business and management; software simulations; library and information studies. Actively seeking good, tested management skills training materials. Telephone in the first instance, rather than send MSS. NB: Publishes mainly to curricula and course syllabi. Founded 1977.

Elm Tree Books – former imprint of Hamish Hamilton/Penguin

Elsevier Science Ltd

The Boulevard, Langford Lane, Kidlington, Oxford OX5 1GB
tel (01865) 843000 *fax* (01865) 843010
Managing Director/Coo Gavin Howe, *Editorial Director (Social Sciences)* B. Barret, *Editorial Director (Materials Science and Engineering)* Peter Desmond

Journal, magazine and book publishers in science, technology and medicine. Imprints: Pergamon, Elsevier Applied Science, Elsevier Trends Journals, Butterworth Heinemann Journals.

Enitharmon Press

36 St George's Avenue, London N7 0HD
tel 020-7607 7194 *fax* 020-7607 8694
e-mail books@enitharmon.demon.co.uk
Director Stephen Stuart-Smith

Poetry, literary criticism, fiction, translations, artists' books. No unsolicited MSS. No freelance editors or proofreaders required. Founded 1967.

Epworth Press

c/o Methodist Publishing House, 20 Ivatt Way, Peterborough PE3 7PG
tel (01733) 332202 *fax* (01733) 331201
Editorial Committee Rev. Gerald Burt (editorial secretary), Dr Valerie Edden, Dr E. Dorothy Graham, Rev. Dr Emmanuel M. Jacob, Rev. Dr Ivor H. Jones, Rev. Dr John A. Newton (chairman), Rev. Dr Cyril S. Rodd, Rev. Michael J. Townsend

Religion, theology, church history, worship, Bible commentaries.

Eurobook Ltd – see Peter Lowe (Eurobook Ltd)

Euromonitor plc

60-61 Britton Street, London EC1M 5NA
tel 020-7251 8024 *fax* 020-7608 3149
e-mail info@euromonitor.com
web site http://www.euromonitor.com
Directors T.J. Fenwick (managing), R.N. Senior (chairman)

Business and commercial reference, marketing information, European and International Surveys, directories. Founded 1972.

Europa Publications Ltd

11 New Fetter Lane, London EC4P 4EE
tel 020-7583 9855 *fax* 020-7842 2249
e-mail sales@europapublications.co.uk
Directors R. Horton (managing), J.P. Desmond, P. Kelly

Directories, international relations, reference, yearbooks. A member of **Taylor & Francis Group plc**.

Evangelical Press of Wales – see Bryntirion Press

Evans Brothers Ltd*

2A Portman Mansions, Chiltern Street, London W1M 1LE
tel 020-7487 0920 *fax* 020-7487 0921
Directors S.T. Pawley (managing), Brian D. Jones (international publishing), A.O. Ojora (Nigeria), *UK Publisher* Su Swallow

Educational books, particularly preschool, school library and teachers' books for the UK, including the Rainbows series of graded information books for 5-8-year-olds; primary and secondary for Africa, the Caribbean and Brazil. Founded 1908.

Everyman – see The Orion Publishing Group Ltd

Everyman's Library

Gloucester Mansions, 140A Shaftesbury Avenue, London WC2H 8HD
tel 020-7539 7600 *fax* 020-7379 4060
Publisher David Campbell, *Finance Director* Mark Bicknell

Everyman's Library (clothbound reprints of the classics); *Everyman's Library Children's Classics*; *Everyman's Library Pocket Poets*; *Everyman Guides*; *Everyman City Guides*; *Everyman-EMI MusicCompanions*; *Cadogan Chess*.

Exley Publications Ltd

16 Chalk Hill, Watford, Herts. WD1 4BN
tel (01923) 250505 *fax* (01923) 818733/800440
Directors Dalton Exley, Helen Exley (editorial), Lincoln Exley, Richard Exley

Popular colour gift books for an international market. Forty new titles a year. No unsolicited MSS. Founded 1976.

Faber & Faber Ltd*

3 Queen Square, London WC1N 3AU
tel 020-7465 0045 *fax* 020-7465 0034
web site http://www.faber.co.uk
Chairman Matthew Evans, *Directors* John Bodley, Walter Donohue, Valerie Eliot, Toby Faber (managing), Laurence Long, Julian Loose, Chris McLaren, Joanna Mackle, Jon Riley, Peter Simpson

High quality general fiction and non-fiction; all forms of creative writing, including plays. Write to Sales Dept for current catalogues. Unsolicited submissions for the children's list not accepted. For information on submission procedure ring 020-7465 0189. For practical and security reasons submissions by fax or on disk cannot be accepted, except by special arrangement. Allow 6-8 weeks for a response. Freelance editors and proofreaders without in-house experience need not apply.

Fabian Society

11 Dartmouth Street, London SW1H 9BN
tel 020-7227 4900 *fax* 020-7976 7153
e-mail info@fabian-society.org.uk
web site http://www.fabian-society.org.uk
General Secretary Michael Jacobs

Current affairs, political thought, economics, education, environment, foreign affairs, social policy. Also controls NCLC Publishing Society Ltd. Founded 1884.

CJ Fallon

Lucan Road, Palmerstown, Dublin 20, Republic of Ireland
tel (01) 6166400 *fax* (01) 6166499
e-mail editorial@cjfallon.ie
Executive Directors H.J. McNicholas (managing), P. Tolan (financial), N. White (editorial)

Educational text books. Founded 1927.

Falmer Press – now RoutledgeFalmer

Farming Press

Miller Freeman UK Ltd, Miller Freeman House, Sovereign Way, Tonbridge, Kent TN9 1RW
tel (01732) 377539 *fax* (01732) 377465
e-mail farmingpress@unmf.com
web site http://www.farmingpress.com
Publishing Manager Alison Stevens

Technical agriculture, farm machinery, veterinary; books, videos, audio, CD-Roms. Founded 1951.

Fernhurst Books

Duke's Path, High Street, Arundel, West Sussex BN18 9AJ
tel (01903) 882277 *fax* (01903) 882715
e-mail sales@fernhurstbooks.co.uk
web site http://www.fernhurstbooks.co.uk
Publisher Tim Davison

Sailing, watersports. Founded 1979.

David Fickling Books – see Scholastic Children's Books*

Financial Times Prentice Hall – imprint of Pearson Education

First and Best in Education Ltd*
(incorporating Hamilton House Publishing)
Earlstrees Court, Earlstrees Road, Corby, Northants. NN17 4HH
tel (01536) 399004 *fax* (01536) 399012
e-mail FirstBest9@aol.com
Contact Anne Cockburn (editor)
Education-related books. Currently actively recruiting new writers for schools; ideas welcome. Sae must accompany submissions. Founded 1992.

Fishing News Books – see Blackwell Science Ltd*

Fitzroy Dearborn Publishers
310 Regent Street, London W1R 5AJ
tel 020-7636 6627 *fax* 020-7636 6982
e-mail post@fitzroydearborn.com
web site http://www.fitzroydearborn.com
Managing Director Daniel Kirkpatrick, *Senior Commissioning Editor* Lesley Henderson, *Publisher* Roda Morrison, *Marketing Executive* Warren Prentice
Reference books: history, media studies, design, art, literature, philosophy and religion, music, business, science, international affairs, social sciences. Founded 1994.

Flambard Press
Stable Cottage, East Fourstones, Hexham, Northumberland NE47 5DX
tel (01434) 674360 *fax* (01434) 674178
Managing Editor Peter Lewis, *Deputy Editor* Margaret Lewis
Poetry and fiction (literary and crime). Only book-length submissions with sae. Preliminary letter preferred. Founded 1990.

Flame – see Hodder Headline Ltd*

Flamingo – see HarperCollins Publishers*

Flicks Books
29 Bradford Road, Trowbridge, Wilts. BA14 9AN
tel (01225) 767728 *fax* (01225) 760418
e-mail flicks.books@dial.pipex.com
Partners Matthew Stevens (publisher), Aletta Stevens
Cinema, TV, related media. Founded 1986.

Floris Books*
15 Harrison Gardens, Edinburgh EH11 1SH
tel 0131-337 2372 *fax* 0131-346 7516
e-mail floris@floris.demon.co.uk
Editors Christopher Moore, Gale Winskill
Religion, science, Celtic studies, craft; children's books: picture and board books, activity books. Founded 1978.
Flyways (imprint)
Children's fiction paperbacks for the more able reader.

Focal Press – see Reed Educational and Professional Publishing Ltd*

Fodor Guides – see Random House Group Ltd*

Folens Ltd*
Albert House, Apex Business Centre, Boscombe Road, Dunstable LU5 4RL
tel (01582) 472788 *fax* (01582) 472575
e-mail folens@folens.com
web site http://www.folens.com
Managing Director Malcolm Watson
Primary and secondary educational books, learn at home books. Founded 1987.

Folens Publishing Company
Unit 8, Broomhill Business Park, Broomhill Road, Tallaght, Dublin 24, Republic of Ireland
tel (01) 4515311 *fax* (01) 4515306
Chairman Dirk Folens, *Directors* John O'Connor (managing), Anna O'Donovan (secondary), Deirdre Whelan (primary)
Educational (primary, secondary, comprehensive, technical, in English and Irish), educational children's magazines.
The Blackwater Press† (imprint)
General non-fiction, Irish interest.

Fontana Press – former imprint of HarperCollins Publishers*

G.T. Foulis & Co. – see Haynes Publishing, Special Interest Publishing Division

W. Foulsham & Co. Ltd
The Publishing House, Bennetts Close, Slough, Berks. SL1 5AP
tel (01753) 526769 *fax* (01753) 535003
Managing Director B.A.R. Belasco, *Editorial Director* W. Hobson
General know-how, cookery, health and alternative therapies, hobbies and games, gardening, sport, travel guides, DIY, collectibles, popular new age. Founded 1819.
Foulsham (imprint)
Editor Wendy Hobson
Quantum (imprint)
Editor Wendy Hobson

Mind, body and spirit, popular philosophy and practical psychology.

The Foundational Book Company

(for The John W. Doorly Trust)
PO Box 659, London SW3 6SJ
tel 020-7584 1053
Trustee for Publications Mrs Peggy M. Brook

Spiritual Science.

Foundery Press – see Methodist Publishing House

Fount – see HarperCollins Publishers*

Four Courts Press†

Fumbally Court, Fumbally Lane, Dublin 8, Republic of Ireland
tel (01) 4534668 *fax* (01) 4534672
e-mail info@four-courts-press.ie
web site http://www.four-courts-press.ie
Managing Director Michael Adams

Academic books in the humanities, especially history, Celtic and medieval studies, art, theology. Founded 1969.

Fourmat – see Butterworths Tolley

Fourth Estate Ltd*

6 Salem Road, London W2 4BU
tel 020-7727 8993 *fax* 020-7792 3176
Directors Victoria Barnsley (managing), Patric Duffy (financial), Christopher Potter (publishing), Nicky Eaton (publicity), Stephen Page (sales and deputy managing), James Kellow (marketing)

Current affairs, literature, popular culture, fiction, humour, politics, science, popular reference, TV tie-ins. No unsolicited MSS. Founded 1984.

Fourth Estate Paperbacks (imprint)
Publishes paperback editions of Fourth Estate hardback titles.

Guardian Books (imprint)
Books stemming from the *Guardian* newspaper.

L.N. Fowler & Co. Ltd – see The C.W. Daniel Company Ltd

Framework Press Educational Publishers Ltd*

GHPD, Halley Court, Jordan Hill, Oxford OX2 8EJ
tel (01865) 314194 *fax* (01865) 314116
e-mail liz.cartmell@repp.co.uk
Commissioning Editor Liz Cartmell

School management, professional development, vocational, English, PSHE and Citizenship. Founded 1983.

Franklin Watts – see The Watts Publishing Group Ltd*

Free Association Books

57 Warren Street, London W1P 5PA
tel 020-7388 3182 *fax* 020-7388 3187
e-mail fab@fa-b.com
web site http://www.fa-b.com
Publisher and Managing Director T.E. Brown

Social sciences, psychoanalysis, psychotherapy, counselling, cultural studies, social welfare, addiction studies, child and adolescent studies. Also contemporary fiction, including works in translation. No poetry, science fiction or fantasy. Founded 1984.

W.H. Freeman

Macmillan Press Ltd, Houndmills, Basingstoke, Hants RG21 6XS
tel (01256) 332807 *fax* (01256) 330688
Sales Director E. Warner

Science, medicine, economics, psychology, archaeology.

Samuel French Ltd*

52 Fitzroy Street, London W1P 6JR
tel 020-7387 9373 *fax* 020-7387 2161
e-mail theatre@samuelfrench-london.co.uk
web site http://www.samuelfrench-london.co.uk
Directors Charles R. Van Nostrand (chairman, USA), Vivien Goodwin (managing), Amanda Smith, Paul Taylor, *Consultant* John Bedding

Publishers of plays and agents for the collection of royalties. Founded 1830.

FT Law & Tax – incorporated into Sweet & Maxwell*

David Fulton Publishers Ltd*

Ormond House, 26-27 Boswell Street, London WC1N 3JD
tel 020-7405 5606 *fax* 020-7831 4840
e-mail mail@fultonbooks.co.uk
web site http://www.fultonbooks.co.uk
Chairman David Fulton, *Managing Director* David Hill, *Editorial Director* John Owens, *Marketing Director* Pamela Fulton

Initial and continuing teacher education (special needs, primary and secondary), educational management and psychology. Unsolicited MSS not returned. Founded 1987.

Funfax Ltd

9 Henrietta Street, London WC2E 8PS
tel 020-7836 5411 *fax* 020-7836 7570
Managing Director Roger Priddy

Children's books for the international

mass markets: non-fiction information, fun activity and novelty, preschool and stickers. Bought by Pearson plc in 2000. Founded 1990.

Gaia Books Ltd

66 Charlotte Street, London W1P 1LR
tel (01453) 752985 *fax* (01453) 752987
Directors Joss Pearson (managing), David Pearson, Lars Kjeldsen

Illustrated reference books on ecology, natural living, health, mind. Submissions (outline and sample chapter) to MD.

Gairm Publications

(incorporating Alex MacLaren & Sons)
29 Waterloo Street, Glasgow G2 6BZ
tel/fax 0141-221 1971
Editorial Director Derick Thomson

(Gaelic and Gaelic-related only) dictionaries, language books, novels, poetry, music, children's books, quarterly magazine, *Gairm*. Founded 1952.

Gallery Children's Books – see East-West Publications (UK) Ltd

The Gallery Press

Loughcrew, Oldcastle, Co. Meath, Republic of Ireland
tel/fax (049) 8541779
e-mail gallery@indigo.ie
Editor/Publisher Peter Fallon

Poetry, drama, occasionally fiction, by Irish authors. Allied company: Deerfield Publications Inc., USA. Founded 1970.

Garland Publishing – see Taylor & Francis Group plc*

Garnet Miller – see Cressrelles Publishing Co. Ltd

Garnet Publishing Ltd

8 Southern Court, South Street, Reading RG1 4QS
tel (01189) 597847 *fax* (01189) 597356
e-mail enquiries@garnet-ithaca.demon.co.uk
Editorial Manager Emma G. Hawker

Art, architecture, photography, fiction religious studies, travel and general, mainly on Middle and Far East, and Islam. Founded 1991.

Ithaca Press (imprint)
Post-graduate academic works, especially on the Middle East.

South Street Press (imprint)
Non-fiction, including *Behind the Headlines* series.

Gateway Books – see Gill & Macmillan Ltd

The Gay Men's Press

(Millivres Prowler Ltd)
PO Box 3220, Brighton BN2 5AU
tel (01273) 672823 *fax* 01273) 672159
e-mail peterburton@easicom.com
Commissioning Editor Peter Burton

Gay-related issues: primarily fiction from literary to popular; limited non-fiction.

Geddes & Grosset*

David Dale House, New Lanark ML11 9DJ
tel (01555) 665000 *fax* (01555) 665694
e-mail info@gandg.sol.co.uk
Publishers Ron Grosset, Mike Miller

Popular reference, children's picture books, non-fiction and activity books. Founded 1988.

Gee & Son (Denbigh) Ltd

Chapel Street, Denbigh, Denbighshire LL16 3SW
tel (01745) 812020 *fax* (01745) 812825
Directors E. Evans, E.M. Evans

Oldest Welsh publishers. Books of interest to Wales, in Welsh and English. Founded 1808.

Geographia – now Bartholomew – see HarperCollins Publishers*

Stanley Gibbons Publications*

Parkside, Christchurch Road, Ringwood, Hants BH24 3SH
tel (01425) 472363 *fax* (01425) 470247
e-mail sales@stangib.demon.co.uk
Chief Executive T. McQuillan

Philatelic handbooks, stamp catalogues and albums, *Gibbons Stamp Monthly*. Founded 1856.

Robert Gibson & Sons Glasgow Ltd

17 Fitzroy Place, Glasgow G3 7SF
tel 0141-248 5674 *fax* 0141-221 8219
web site http://robert.gibsonsons@btinternet.com
Directors R.G.C. Gibson, M. Pinkerton, H.C. Crawford, N.J. Crawford (editorial)

Educational and textbooks. Founded 1885.

Gill & Macmillan Ltd†

Hume Avenue, Park West, Dublin 12, Republic of Ireland
tel (01) 500 9500 *fax* (01) 500 9599
web site http://www.gillmacmillan.ie

Biography or memoirs, educational (secondary, university), history, literature, cookery, current affairs, guidebooks. Founded 1968.

Gateway Books (imprint)
Spirituality, ecology, metaphysics and alternative science.
Newleaf (imprint)
Mind, body and spirit, popular psychology, self-help, health and healing, lifestyle.

Ginn & Co. – see Reed Educational and Professional Publishing Ltd*

Mary Glasgow – see Nelson Thornes Ltd

Godsfield Press Ltd
259 Old Marylebone Road, London NW1 5XJ
tel 020-7616 7200 *fax* 020-7616 7201
e-mail firstname.surname@davidandcharles.co.uk
Publisher Debbie Thorpe
Highly illustrated books for adults in the area of mind, body and spirit with an emphasis on practical application and personal spiritual awareness. Division of **David & Charles Ltd**. Founded 1994.

Golden Cockerel Press
16 Barter Street, London WC1A 2AH
tel 020-7405 7979 *fax* 020-7404 3598
e-mail lindesay@btinternet.com
Contact Tamar Lindesay
Academic.
Associated University Presses (imprint)
Literary criticism, art, music, history, film, theology, philosophy, Jewish studies, politics, sociology.
Cornwall Books (imprint)
Antiques, history, film.
Cygnus Arts (imprint)
The arts.

The Goldsmith Press
Newbridge, Co. Kildare, Republic of Ireland
tel (045) 433613 *fax* (045) 434648
e-mail de@iol.ie
Directors V. Abbott, D. Egan, *Secretary* E. Hendy
Literature, art, Irish interest, poetry. Unsolicited MSS not returned. Founded 1972.

Victor Gollancz Ltd – see The Orion Publishing Group Ltd

Gomer Press
Llandysul, Ceredigion SA44 4QL
tel (01559) 362371 *fax* (01559) 363758
Directors Jonathan Lewis, John H. Lewis, *Editors* Mairwen Prys Jones, Gordon Jones, Bethan Matthews
Literature and non-fiction with a Welsh background or relevance: biography, history, aspects of Welsh culture, children's books. No unsolicited MSS; preliminary letter essential. Founded 1892.

Government Supplies Agency
Publications Division, 4-5 Harcourt Road, Dublin 2, Republic of Ireland
tel (01) 6613111 *fax* (01) 4752760
Government and international publications including EU, OECD, UN, World Trade Organisation, Nordic Council, ILO and Council of Europe.

Gower Publishing Ltd – subsidiary of Ashgate Publishing Ltd

Grafton – now HarperCollins Paperbacks*

Graham & Whiteside Ltd
Tuition House, 5-6 Francis Grove, London SW19 4DT
tel 020-8947 1011 *fax* 020-8947 1163
e-mail sales@major-co-data.com
Directors A.M.W. Graham, R.M. Whiteside, P.L. Murphy
Directories for international business and professional markets. Founded 1995.

Granada Media Group – see André Deutsch Ltd*

Granta Publications
2-3 Hanover Yard, Noel Road, London N1 8BE
tel 020-7704 9776 *fax* 020-7704 0474
web site http://www.granta.com
Book Publisher Gail Lynch, *Publishing Director* Neil Belton, *Magazine Editor* Ian Jack
Literary fiction, autobiography, political non-fiction. Founded 1982.

Green Books
Foxhole, Dartington, Totnes, Devon TQ9 6EB
tel/fax (01803) 863843
e-mail greenbooks@gn.apc.org
web site http://www.greenbooks.co.uk
Publisher John Elford
Environment (practical and philosophical). No fiction or children's books. No MSS; synopsis and covering letter please. Founded 1987.

Green Print – see Merlin Press Ltd

Greenhill Books/Lionel Leventhal Ltd
Park House, 1 Russell Gardens, London NW11 9NN
tel 020-8458 6314 *fax* 020-8905 5245
e-mail LionelLeventhal@compuserve.com
web site http://www.greenhillbooks.com
Managing Director Lionel Leventhal
Military history. Founded 1984.

Gresham Books Ltd
The Gresham Press, 46 Victoria Road,
Oxford OX2 7QD
tel (01865) 513582 *fax* (01865) 512718
e-mail greshambks@btinternet.com
web site http://www.gresham-books.co.uk
Chief Executive Paul Lewis

Hymn books, Prayer books, Service books, school histories.

Grub Street
The Basement, 10 Chivalry Road,
London SW11 1HT
tel 020-7924 3966/738 1008 *fax* 020-7738 1009
e-mail post@grubstreet.co.uk
web site http://www.grubstreet.co.uk
Principals John B. Davies, Anne Dolamore

Adult non-fiction: military, aviation history, cookery, wine. Founded 1989.

Guardian Books – see Fourth Estate Ltd*

Guild of Master Craftsman Publications Ltd
Castle Place, 166 High Street, Lewes,
East Sussex BN7 1XU
tel (01273) 477374/47844 *fax* (01273) 487692
Managing Director Alan Phillips

Practical, illustrated crafts, including needlecrafts, dolls' houses, woodworking and other leisure and hobby subjects. Founded 1979.

Guinness World Records*
338 Euston Road, London NW1 3BD
tel 020-7891 4567 *fax* 020-7891 4501
Director of Print Media Tim Footman, *Director of Television* Michaeal Feldman

The Guinness Book of Records, general reference, music and sports reference. Founded 1954.

Gwasg Bryntirion Press – see Bryntirion Press

Gwasg Gee – see Gee & Son (Denbigh) Ltd

Gwasg y Dref Wen – see Dref Wen

Hachette UK – see Cassell & Co

Peter Halban Publishers Ltd
22 Golden Square, London W1R 3PA
tel 020-7437 9300 *fax* 020-7437 9512
e-mail books@halban.com
Directors Martine Halban, Peter Halban

General non-fiction; history and biography; Jewish subjects and Middle East. No unsolicited MSS considered; preliminary letter essential. Founded 1986.

Robert Hale Ltd
Clerkenwell House, 45-47 Clerkenwell Green,
London EC1R 0HT
tel 020-7251 2661 *fax* 020-7490 4958
Directors John Hale (managing and editorial), Robert Kynaston (financial), Martin Kendall (marketing), Betty Weston (rights)

Adult general non-fiction and fiction. Founded 1936.

Hamilton House Publishing – see First and Best in Education Ltd*

Hamish Hamilton – see Penguin UK*

Hamish Hamilton Children's – see Penguin UK*

Hamlyn/Octopus – see Octopus Publishing Group

Harcourt Publishers Ltd
24-28 Oval Road, London NW1 7DX
tel 020-7424 4200 *fax* 020-7482 2293/485 4752
Managing Director Peter H. Lengemann

Scientific and medical.

Academic Press (division)
Managing Director Jan Velterop

Academic and reference.

Baillière Tindall Ltd (division)
Managing Director Andrew Stevenson

Medical, veterinary, nursing, pharmaceutical books and journals.

Churchill Livingstone (division)
Managing Director Andrew Stevenson

Medical, nursing, pharmaceutical books and journals.

Dryden Press (division)
Managing Director Peter H. Lengemann

Educational books (college, university), economics, business.

Holt Rhinehart & Winston (division)
Managing Director Peter H. Lengemann

Educational books.

Mosby International (division)
6th Floor, Lynton House, 7-12 Tavistock Square,
London WC1H 9LB
tel 0171-388 7676 *fax* 0171-391 6555
Managing Director Derrick Holman

W.B. Saunders Co. Ltd (division)
Managing Director Andrew Stevenson

Medical and scientific.

Patrick Hardy Books – see James Clarke & Co. Ltd*

Harlem River Press – see Writers & Readers Ltd*

Harlequin Mills & Boon Ltd*

Eton House, 18-24 Paradise Road, Richmond, Surrey TW9 1SR
tel 020-8288 2800 *fax* 020-8288 2899
Directors Fredrik Gejrot (managing), Alan Boon (Editor Emeritus), Stuart Barber (financial), Angela Meredith (production), Alan Dawson (retail sales/ marketing), Karin Stoecker (editorial), Liz Bylow (direct marketing), Mike Creffield (information technology), Janet Oldham (human resources)

Founded 1908.

Medical Historical
Senior Editors S. Hodgson, L. Fildew
Romance fiction.

Mills & Boon (imprint)
Senior Editors T. Shapcott, S. Bell
Contemporary romance fiction in paperback and hardback.

Mira Books (imprint)
Senior Editor L. Fildew
Women's fiction.

Silhouette (imprint)
Senior Editor L. Stonehouse
Popular romantic women's fiction.

HarperCollins Publishers*

77-85 Fulham Palace Road, London W6 8JB
tel 020-8741 7070 *fax* 020-8307 4440
web site http://www.fireandwater.com
Executive Chairman and Publisher tba, *Group Managing Director* tba, *Divisional Managing Directors* Adrian Bourne (trade), Stephen Bray (cartographic/general reference), Kate Harris (education/children's/dictionaries)

All fiction and trade non-fiction must be submitted through an agent. Unsolicited submissions should be made in the form of a typewritten synopsis. Founded 1819.

Access Press (imprint)
Travel guides.

Bartholomew (imprint)
Maps, atlases, electronic products.

Birnbaum (imprint)
Travel guides.

Collins (imprints)
Collins Crime, Collins Classics, Collins Educational, Collins bibles, Collins Liturgical Books, Collins Dictionaries, Collins Cobuild, Collins Gems, Collins New Naturalist Library, Collins Willow, Collins Longman.

Collins (children's imprint)
Publishing Directors Gail Penston, Gillie Russell
Includes Jets, Yellow Storybooks, Red Storybooks, fiction for older children and toddler books.

Collins Children's Audio (imprint)

Collins Children's Books (imprint)

Collins Picture Lions (imprint)
Children's picture paperbacks.

Collins Tracks (imprint)
Young adult books.

Flamingo (imprint)
Publishing Director Philip Gwyn Jones
Literary fiction and non-fiction in hardback and paperback.

Fount (imprint)
Managing Director Adrian Bourne
Religious.

HarperCollins (imprints)
Publishing Directors Michael Fishwick (non-fiction), Nick Sayers (fiction)
Audiobooks, business, hardbacks (fiction and non-fiction), paperbacks (fiction and non-fiction), religious.

HarperCollins Electronic Products
Managing Director Kate Harris
CD-Rom, floppy disk and on-line. Specialises in special interest, children's, reference and interactive fiction.

Lions (imprint)
Publishing Director Gail Penston
Children's books.

Marshall Pickering (imprint)
Managing Director Adrian Bourne
Theology, music, popular religion, illustrated children's, Christian books.

Nicholson (imprint)
Managing Director Stephen Bray
London maps, atlases and guidebooks. Waterways maps and guidebooks.

Thorsons (imprint)
Complementary medicine, health and nutrition, business and management, self-help and positive thinking, popular psychology, parenting and childcare, astrology, tarot and divination, mythology and psychic awareness.

Times Books (imprint)
Managing Director Stephen Bray
World atlases and maps, thematic atlases, reference, guides and crosswords.

Tolkien (imprint)
Projects Director David Brawn

Voyager (imprint)
Publishing Director Jane Johnson

Science fiction, fantasy, media tie-ins.

Willow (imprint)
Publishing Director Michael Doggart

Sport.

Harrap – see Chambers Harrap Publishers Ltd

The Harvill Press

2 Aztec Row, Berners Road, London N1 0PW
tel 020-7704 8766 *fax* 020-7704 8805
web site http://www.harvill-press.com
Publisher and Chairman Christopher MacLehose, *Directors* David Tebbutt (managing), Guido Waldman (editorial), Katharina Bielenberg (sales), Margaret Stead (publishing/rights), Paul Baggaley (marketing), *Production Manager* Simon Rhodes

English-language and world literature in translation (literary fiction, non-fiction and some first-class narrative thrillers); monographs in the fields of ethnography, art, horticulture and natural history. Unsolicited MSS only accepted with sae. Founded 1946.

Hawk Books

Suite 309, Canalot Studios, 222 Kensal Road, London W10 5BN
tel 020-8969 8091 *fax* 020-8968 9012
Director Patrick Hawkey

Comics, nostalgia, juveniles, art. Founded 1986.

Haynes Publishing

Sparkford, Yeovil, Somerset BA22 7JJ
tel (01963) 440635 *fax* (01963) 440023
Directors J.H. Haynes (chairman), A.C. Haynes, I.P. Mauger, D.J. Reach, A.J. Sperring, K.C. Fullman (managing), C. Davies, D.J. Hermelin, C.G. Magnus, M. Minter

Car and motorcycle service and repair manuals, car handbooks/servicing guides; DIY books for the home; car, motorcycle, motorsport and leisure activities.

Haynes Motor Trade Division (imprint)
Director Matthew Minter

Car and motorcycle service and repair manuals and technical data books.

Haynes Special Interest Publishing Division (imprint)
Editorial Director Darryl Reach

Cars, motorcycles, motorsport, related biographies, practical maintenance and renovation.

Hazar Publishing Ltd

147 Chiswick High Road, London W4 2DT
tel 020-8742 8578 *fax* 020-8994 1407
e-mail hazar@compuserve.com
Managing Director Greg Hill, *Editor* Marie Clayton

Children's picture and novelty books; adult non-fiction: architecture and design. Founded 1992.

Headland Business Information – see Bowker-Saur

Headland Publications

Editorial office Ty Coch, Galltegfa, Llanfwrog, Ruthin, Denbighshire LL15 2AR
and 38 York Avenue, West Kirby, Wirral CH48 3JF
Director and Editor Gladys Mary Coles

Poetry, anthologies of poetry and prose. No unsolicited MSS. Founded 1970.

Headline – see Hodder Headline Ltd*

Headline Book Publishing Ltd – see Hodder Headline Ltd*

Headline Feature – see Hodder Headline Ltd*

Headway – see Hodder Headline Ltd*

Health Science Press – see The C.W. Daniel Company Ltd

Heinemann Educational – see Reed Educational and Professional Publishing Ltd*

Heinemann English Language Teaching – now Macmillan Heinemann English Language Teaching

Heinemann Young Books – see Egmont Children's Books

William Heinemann – see Random House Group Ltd*

Helicon Publishing Ltd

42 Hythe Bridge Street, Oxford OX1 2EP
tel (01865) 204204 *fax* (01865) 204205
e-mail admin@helicon.co.uk
web site http://www.helicon.co.uk
Directors David Attwooll (managing), Maria Quantrill (finance), Hilary McGlynn (editorial), John Normansell (production), Sheila Lambie (sales and marketing), Clare Painter (rights)

General and subject encyclopedias and dictionaries in book, CD-Rom and on-line form. Text and illustrations on the Hutchinson Database are continuously updated offering flexible licensing, co-edition and packaging opportunities. Founded 1992.

Christopher Helm – see A & C Black (Publishers) Ltd*

Helmsman – see The Crowood Press

Henderson Publishing Ltd – now Funfax Ltd

The Herbert Press – see A & C Black (Publishers) Ltd*

Hermes House – see Anness Publishing

Nick Hern Books Ltd

The Glasshouse, 49A Goldhawk Road, London W12 8QP
tel 020-8749 4953 *fax* 020-8746 2006
e-mail info@nickhernbooks.demon.co.uk
Publisher Nick Hern

Theatre, professionally produced plays, screenplays. Initial letter required. Founded 1988.

Hilmarton Manor Press

Calne, Wilts. SN11 8SB
tel (01249) 760208 *fax* (01249) 760379
e-mail mailorder@hilmartonpress.co.uk
web site http://www.hilmartonpress.co.uk
Editorial Director Charles Baile de Laperriere

Fine art, photography, antiques, visual arts, wine. Founded 1964.

Hippo – see Scholastic Children's Books*

Hippopotamus Press

22 Whitewell Road, Frome, Somerset BA11 4EL
tel/fax (01373) 466653
Editors Roland John, Anna Martin

Poetry, essays, criticism. Publishes *Outposts Poetry Quarterly*. Poetry submissions from new writers welcome. Founded 1974.

HMSO Books – see The Stationery Office/National Publishing*

Hobsons Publishing plc

Bateman Street, Cambridge CB2 1LZ
tel (01223) 460366 *fax* (01223) 323154
Non-executive Director Charles Sinclair, *Chairman* Martin Morgan, *Directors* Chris Letcher (managing), Frances Halliwell, David Harrington, Nicola Anson

Database publisher of educational and careers information under licence to CRAC (Careers Research and Advisory Centre). Also publishes accommodation guides under Johansens brand. Founded 1974.

Hodder Headline Ltd*

338 Euston Road, London NW1 3BH
tel 020-7873 6000 *fax* 020-7873 6024
Chairman Richard Handover, *Group Chief Executive* Tim Hely Hutchinson, *Directors* Martin Neild (managing, Hodder & Stoughton General), Sue Fletcher (deputy managing, Hodder & Stoughton General), Mary Tapissier (managing, Children's; chairman, Religious), Amanda Ridout (managing, Headline), Malcolm Edwards (managing, Australia and New Zealand), Philip Walters (managing, Educational), Richard Stileman (managing, Arnold), Jon Mortimore (finance), Charles Nettleton (managing, religious), Tony Bryars (managing, Bookpoint)

Founded 1986.

Arnold (division)
Managing Director Richard Stileman, *Humanities* Chris Wheeler, *Medical* Nick Dunton

Academic and professional books and journals.

Headline Book Publishing Ltd (division)
Managing Director Amanda Ridout, *Publishing Directors* Jane Morpeth (fiction), Heather Holden-Brown (non-fiction), *Publishers* Bill Massey (Headline Feature), Geraldine Cooke (Review), Ian Marshall (Sports), *Associate Publishers* Marion Donaldson (Headline), Clare Foss (Headline)

Publishes under Headline, Headline Feature and Review. Commercial and literary fiction; popular non-fiction including sport and sports yearbooks, cookery, autobiography and biography, history, science, popular culture, TV tie-ins, gardening, humour, reference.

Hodder Children's Books (division)
Managing Director Mary Tapissier, *Publishing Director* Margaret Conroy

Publishes under Hodder Children's Books (picture books, fiction and non-fiction) and Hodder Wayland (illustrated non-fiction and reference).

Hodder & Stoughton Educational (division)
Managing Director Philip Walters, *Humanities, Science, Scotland and Vocational* Elisabeth Tribe, *Languages, Business and Psychology* Tim Gregson-Williams, *English, Mathematics, Teach Yourself and Trade Education* Katie Roden

Publishes under Hodder & Stoughton Educational, Teach Yourself, Headway. Textbooks for the primary, secondary, tertiary and further education sectors and for self-improvement.

Hodder & Stoughton General (division)
Managing Director Martin Neild, *Deputy Managing Director* Sue Fletcher, *Non-fiction* Roland

Philipps, *Sceptre* Carole Welch, Nicholas Blincoe, *Fiction* Carolyn Mays, *Audio* Rupert Lancaster

Publishes under Hodder & Stoughton, Coronet, Flame, New English Library, Sceptre, Lir. Commercial and literary fiction; biography, autobiography, history, self-help, humour, travel and other general interest non-fiction; audio.

Lir (imprint))

Fiction and non-fiction Irish writing.

Hodder & Stoughton Religious (division)
Managing Director Charles Nettleton, *Editorial Directors* Emma Sealey (bibles and liturgical), Judith Longman (religious trade)

Publishes under New International Version of the Bible, Hodder Christian Paperbacks. Help Yourself, Bibles, commentaries, liturgical works (both printed and software), Christian paperbacks.

Hogarth Press – imprint of Random House Group Ltd*

Hollis Directories Ltd

Harlequin House, 7 High Street, Teddington, Middlesex TW11 8EL
tel 020-8977 7711 *fax* 020-8977 1133
e-mail gary@hollis-pr.co.uk
web site http://www.hollis-pr.co.uk
Managing Director Gary Zabel

Publications include *Willings Press Guide*, *Hollis Press & PR Annual*, *Hollis Sponsorship Yearbook* and *Advertisers Annual*.

Holt, Rhinehart & Winston – see Harcourt Publishers Ltd

Holtzbrinck Online Publishing – see Macmillan Publishers Ltd*

Honno Ltd (Welsh Women's Press)

Y Seler, Coleg Diwinyddol, Aberystwyth, Ceredigion SY23 2LT
tel/fax (01970) 623150
e-mail gol.honno@virgin.net
web site http://freespace.virgin.net/gol.honno
Editor Gwenllïan Dafydd, *Secretary* Rosanne Reeves *tel* (029) 20515014

Literature written by women in Wales or with a Welsh connection. All subjects considered – fiction, non-fiction, poetry, autobiographies. Honno is a collective. Founded 1986.

How To Books Ltd

3 Newtec Place, Magdalen Road, Oxford OX4 1RE
tel (01865) 793806 *fax* (01865) 248780
e-mail info@howtobooks.co.uk
web site http://www.howtobooks.co.uk
Publisher and Managing Director Giles Lewis, *Commissioning Editor* Nikki Read

Reference. *How To* series of accessible books to help people improve their lives and develop their skills. *Pathways* series of personal, business and career development books. *Essentials* series teaches specific skills to busy people. Subjects covered: business and management, computers and the net, general reference, career choices, career development, living and working abroad, personal finance, personal development, self-employment and small business, study skills and student guides, creative writing, home and family. Book proposals welcome. Authors are given assistance and guidance in the development of their books. Founded 1991.

Hugo's Language Books Ltd

9 Henrietta Street, London WC2E 8PS
tel 020-7836 5411 *fax* 020-7836 7570
Editorial Director Robin Wood

Hugo's language books and courses. Bought by Pearson plc in 2000. Founded 1864.

Hunt & Thorpe – see John Hunt Publishing Ltd

John Hunt Publishing Ltd

(incorporating Hunt & Thorpe, Arthur James Ltd)
46A West Street, New Alresford, Hants SO24 9AU
tel (01962) 736880 *fax* (01962) 736881
e-mail john@johnhuntpub.demon.co.uk
Director John Hunt

Children's and adult religious, full colour books for the international market. MSS welcome; send sae. Founded 1989.

C. Hurst & Co. (Publishers) Ltd*

38 King Street, London WC2E 8JZ
tel 020-7240 2666, (night) 020-7624 8713
fax 020-7240 2667
e-mail hurst@atlas.co.uk
web site http://www.hurstpub.co.uk
Directors Christopher Hurst, Michael Dwyer

Scholarly 'area studies' covering contemporary history, politics, sociology and religion of Europe, former USSR, Middle East, Asia and Africa. Founded 1967.

Hutchinson – see Random House Group Ltd*

ICSA Publishing Ltd*

16 Park Crescent, London W1N 4AH
tel 020-7612 7020/7038 *fax* 020-7323 1132
e-mail icsa.pub@icsa.co.uk
web site http://www.icsapublishing.co.uk
Joint Managing Directors Clare Grist Taylor, Susan Richards

Official publishing company of the Institute of Chartered Secretaries and Administrators. Professional business information for the corporate, public and not-for-profit sectors in a range of formats. Founded 1981.

Idol – see Virgin Publishing Ltd

In Pinn – see Neil Wilson Publishing Ltd

In Print Publishing Ltd

38 Ship Street, Brighton BN1 1AB
tel (01273) 205599 *fax* (01273) 739737
Directors Michael Forster, Sarie Forster

Special interest travel (including literary guides), Japan, Southeast Asia, guides to teaching English. Founded 1990.

Indigo – see The Orion Publishing Group Ltd

InfoSource International – see Blackwell Publishers*

Institute of Personnel and Development

IPD House, 35 Camp Road, London SW19 4UX
tel 020-8971 9000 *fax* 020-8263 3333
e-mail publish@ipd.co.uk
web site http://www.ipd.co.uk/newbooks
Head of Publishing Judith Dennett

Personnel management, training and development.

Institute of Physics Publishing*

Dirac House, Temple Back, Bristol BS1 6BE
tel 0117-929 7481 *fax* 0117-930 1186
e-mail nicki.dennis@ioppublishing.co.uk
web site http://www.bookmark.iop.org
Head of Book Publishing Nicki Dennis, *Sales and Marketing Manager* Colin Fenton

Monographs, graduate texts, conference proceedings and reference works in physics and physics-related science and technology; also popular science titles.

Institute of Public Administration†

Vergemount Hall, Clonskeagh, Dublin 6, Republic of Ireland
tel (01) 2697011 *fax* (01) 2698644
e-mail tmcnamara@ipa.ie
web site http://www.ipa.ie
Head of Publishing Tony McNamara

Government, economics, politics, law, public management, social policy and administrative history. Founded 1957.

Inter-Varsity Press*

38 De Montfort Street, Leicester LE1 7GP
tel 0116-255 1754 *fax* 0116-254 2044
e-mail ivp@uccf.org.uk
Managing Editor Mrs S. Carter

Theology and religion.

Irish Academic Press Ltd†

44 Northumberland Road, Ballsbridge, Dublin 4, Republic of Ireland
tel (01) 6688244 *fax* (01) 6601610
e-mail info@iap.ie
web site http://www.iap.ie
Directors Stewart Cass, Frank Cass, Michael Philip Zaidner

Publishes under the imprints **Irish University Press** and **Irish Academic Press**. Scholarly books especially in 19th and 20th century history and literature. Founded 1974.

Ithaca Press – see Garnet Publishing Ltd

Arthur James Ltd – incorporated into John Hunt Publishing Ltd

Jane's Information Group

163 Brighton Road, Coulsdon, Surrey CR5 2YH
tel 020-8700 3700 *fax* 020-8700 3704
web site http://www.janes.com/janes.html
Managing Director Alfred Rolington

Professional publishers in hardcopy and electronic multimedia of military, aviation, naval, defence, non-fiction, reference, police, geo-political; CD-Rom games in association with Electronic Arts; consumer books in association with **HarperCollinsPublishers**.

Jarrold Publishing

Whitefriars, Norwich NR3 1TR
tel (01603) 763300 *fax* (01603) 662748
Directors Caroline Jarrold (managing), Margot Russell-King (sales and marketing), David Loombe (finance)

UK travel guidebooks, pictorial books and calendars. About 30 titles a year. Unsolicited MSS, synopses and ideas welcome but approach in writing before submitting to Sarah Letts, Editor. Division of Jarrold & Sons Ltd. Founded 1770.

John Jones Publishing Ltd

Unit 12, Clwydfro Business Centre, Ruthin, Denbighshire LL15 1NJ

tel (01824) 704856/705272 *fax* (01824) 705272
e-mail mail@johnjonespublishing.ltd.uk
web site http://www.johnjonespublishing.ltd.uk
Directors John Idris Jones (managing), Denise Idris Jones, David Owen

Paperbacks in English with a Welsh background: biography, history, children's, tourism. Founded 1979.

Jordan Publishing Ltd

21 St Thomas Street, Bristol BS1 6JS
tel 0117-918 1232 *fax* 0117-918 1406
web site http://www.jordanpublishing.co.uk
Managing Director Richard Hudson

Law and business administration. Also specialist Family Law imprint (including the *Family Law Journal*). Books, looseleaf services, serials, CD-Roms and on-line.

Michael Joseph – see Penguin UK*

The Journeyman Press – see Pluto Press

Karnak House

300 Westbourne Park Road, London W11 1EH
tel/fax 020-7243 3620
Directors Amon Saba Saakana (managing), Seheri Sujai (art)

Specialists in African/Caribbean studies worldwide: anthropology, education, Egyptology, fiction, history, language, linguistics, literary criticism, music, parapsychology, philosophy, prehistory. Founded 1979.

The Kenilworth Press Ltd

Addington, Buckingham MK18 2JR
tel (0129 671) 5101 *fax* (0129 671) 5148
e-mail mail@kenilworthpress.co.uk
Directors David Blunt, Deirdre Blunt

Equestrian, including official publications for the British Horse Society. Founded 1989. Incorporates Threshold Books; founded 1970.

Kenyon-Deane – see Cressrelles Publishing Co. Ltd

Laurence King Publishing

71 Great Russell Street, London WC1B 3BN
tel 020-7831 6351 *fax* 020-7831 8356
e-mail enquiries@calmann-king.co.uk
web site http://www.laurence-king.com
Directors Robin Hyman (chairman), Laurence King (managing), Lesley Ripley Greenfield (editorial: college and fine arts), Judith Rasmussen (production), John Stoddart (financial)

Illustrated books on design, art, architecture, carpets and textiles. Imprint of **Calmann & King Ltd**, book packagers. Founded 1991.

Kingfisher Publications plc*

(formerly Larousse plc)
New Penderel House, 283-288 High Holborn, London WC1V 7HZ
tel 020-7903 9999 *fax* 020-7242 4979
e-mail sales@kingfisherpub.co.uk
Chairman Bertil Hessel, *Directors* Marc Zagar (finance), John Richards (production)

Kingfisher (imprint)
Publishing Directors Gill Denton (non-fiction), Ann-Janine Murtagh (fiction)

Children's books. No unsolicited MSS or synopses considered.

Jessica Kingsley Publishers*

116 Pentonville Road, London N1 9JB
tel 020-7833 2307 *fax* 020-7837 2917
e-mail post@jkp.com
web site http://www.jkp.com
Director Jessica Kingsley

Psychology, psychotherapy, psychiatry, arts therapies, social work, special needs (especially autism and Asperger's Syndrome), education, law, anthropology. Founded 1987.

Kluwer Publishing

145 London Road, Kingston-upon-Thames, Surrey KT2 6SR
tel 020-8247 1262 *fax* 020-8547 2637
e-mail info@.croner.cch.co.uk
web site http://www.croner.cch.co.uk
Managing Director Hans Staal

Law, taxation, finance, insurance, looseleaf information services. Subsidiary of Croner.CCH Group. Founded 1972.

Knight Paperbacks – see Caxton Publishing Group

Charles Knight – see Butterworths Tolley

Knockabout Comics

10 Acklam Road, London W10 5QZ
tel 020-8969 2945 *fax* 020-8968 7614
e-mail knockcomic@aol.com
web site http://www.knockabout.com
Editors Tony Bennett, Carol Bennett

Humorous and satirical graphic novels for an adult readership. Founded 1975.

Kogan Page Ltd*

120 Pentonville Road, London N1 9JN
tel 020-7278 0433 *fax* 020-7837 6348
Managing Director Philip Kogan, *Directors* Pauline Goodwin (editorial), Peter Chadwick (production and editorial), Gordon Watts (financial), Philip

Mudd (editorial), Julie McNair (sales)
Education, training, educational and training technology, journals, business and management, human resource management, transport and distribution, marketing, sales, advertising and PR, finance and accounting, directories, small business, careers and vocational, personal finance, environment. Founded 1967.

Earthscan Publications Ltd (subsidiary)
Directors Philip Kogan, Jonathan Sinclair-Wilson (editorial)
Third World and environmental issues including politics, sociology, environment, economics, current events, geography, health.

Ladybird – see Penguin UK*

Larousse – former imprint of Kingfisher Publications plc*

Lawrence & Wishart Ltd

99A Wallis Road, London E9 5LN
tel 020-8533 2506 *fax* 020-8533 7369
e-mail lw@l-w-bks.demon.co.uk
web site http://www.l-w-bks.co.uk
Directors S. Davison (editorial), J. Rodrigues, B. Kirsch, M. Seaton, J. Rutherford, A. Greenaway, G. Andrews
Cultural studies, current affairs, history, socialism and Marxism, political philosophy, politics, popular culture.

Leicester University Press – see The Continuum International Publishing Group Ltd

Lennard Publishing

Windmill Cottage, Mackerye End, Harpenden, Herts. AL5 5DR
tel (01582) 715866 *fax* (01582) 715121
e-mail lennard@lenqap.demon.co.uk
Directors K.A.A. Stephenson, R.H. Stephenson
Media tie-ins, sponsored books, special commissions. No unsolicited MSS. Division of Lennard Associates Ltd.

Letts Educational

Aldine House, Aldine Place, London W12 8AW
tel 020-8740 2266 *fax* 020-8743 8451
e-mail mail@lettsed.co.uk
web site http://www.lettsed.co.uk/
Directors Stephen Baker (managing), Wayne Davies (publishing), Lee Warren (financial)
Accountancy and taxation; children's; computer science; economics; educational and textbooks; industry, business and management; mathematics and statistics; vocational training and careers; homework and revision books. Associate and subsidiary companies: Granada Learning, NFER Nelson, Black Cat, Granada Media, Semerc. Founded 1979.

Lewis Masonic

Riverdene Business Park, Molesey Road, Hersham, Surrey KT12 4RG
tel (01932) 266600 *fax* (01932) 266601
Masonic books; *Masonic Square Magazine*. Founded 1870.

John Libbey & Co. Ltd

PO Box 276, Eastleigh SO50 5YS
tel (023) 8065 0208 *fax* (023) 8065 0259
e-mail johnlibbey@aol.com
Director John Libbey
Medical: nutrition, obesity, epilepsy, neurology, nuclear medicine, oncology. Film/cinema, animation. Founded 1979.

Library Association Publishing*

7 Ridgmount Street, London WC1E 7AE
tel 020-7255 0590 *fax* 020-7255 0591
e-mail lapublishing@la-hq.org.uk
web site http://www.la-hq.org.uk/lapublishing
Managing Director Janet Liebster
Library and information science, information technology, reference works, directories, bibliographies.

Clive Bingley Ltd (imprint)
Library and information science, reference works.

Libris Ltd

10 Burghley Road, London NW5 1UE
tel 020-7482 2390 *fax* 020-7485 4220
Directors Nicholas Jacobs, S.A. Kitzinger
Literature, literary biography, German studies, bilingual poetry. Founded 1986.

The Lilliput Press Ltd†

62-63 Sitric Road, Dublin 7, Republic of Ireland
tel (01) 6711647 *fax* (01) 6711233
e-mail lilliput@indigo.ie
web site http://indigo.ie/~lilliput
Managing Director Antony T. Farrell
General and Irish literature: essays, biography/autobiography, fiction, criticism; Irish history; philosophy; contemporary culture; nature and environment. Founded 1984.

Frances Lincoln Ltd

4 Torriano Mews, Torriano Avenue, London NW5 2RZ
tel 020-7284 4009 *fax* 020-7485 0490
e-mail reception@frances-lincoln.com
Directors Frances Lincoln (managing), Janetta Otter-Barry (editorial, children's books)

Illustrated, international co-editions: gardening, interiors, health, spirituality, art, gift, children's books. Founded 1977.

Lion Publishing plc*
Peter's Way, Sandy Lane West, Oxford OX4 5HG
tel (01865) 747550 *fax* (01865) 747568
web site http://lion-publishing.co.uk
Directors Denis Cole, Tony Wales, Rebecca Winter (editorial), Paul Clifford (managing), John O'Nions, Roy McCloughry
Reference, paperbacks, illustrated children's books, educational, gift books, religion and theology; all reflecting a Christian position. No adult fiction. Send preliminary letter before submitting MSS. Founded 1971.

Lions – see HarperCollins Publishers*

Lir – see Hodder Headline Ltd*

Little Hippo – see Scholastic Children's Books*

Little Tiger Press – see Magi Publications

Little, Brown and Company (UK)*
Brettenham House, Lancaster Place, London WC2E 7EN
tel 020-7911 8000 *fax* 020-7911 8100
Chief Executive David Young, *Directors* Ursula Mackenzie (publisher), Barbara Boote (editorial), Alan Samson (editorial), David Kent (home sales), Nigel Batt (financial), Charles Viney (export sales), Terry Jackson (marketing)
Hardback and paperback fiction, general non-fiction and illustrated books. No unsolicited MSS. Founded 1988.

Abacus (division)
Editorial Director Richard Beswick
Trade paperbacks.

Illustrated (division)
Editor Julia Charles
Hardback photographic and art books.

Orbit (imprint)
Editorial Director Tim Holman
Science fiction and fantasy paperbacks.

Virago (division)
Publisher Lennie Goodings, *Senior Editor* Sally Abbey
Fiction, including Modern Classics Series, biography, autobiography and general non-fiction which highlight all aspects of women's lives.

Warner (division)
Editorial Directors Barbara Boote, Alan Samson, Hilary Hale, Imogen Taylor
Paperbacks: original fiction and non-fiction; reprints.

X Libris (imprint)
Editor Sarah Shrubb
Erotic fiction for women.

Liverpool University Press
4 Cambridge Street, Liverpool L69 7ZU
tel 0151-794 2233/7 *fax* 0151-794 2235
e-mail sandrob@liverpool.ac.uk
web site http://www.liverpool-unipress.co.uk
Publisher Robin Bloxsidge
Academic and scholarly books in a range of disciplines. Special interests: art history, education, European and American literature, science fiction criticism, social, political, economic and ancient history, archaeology, veterinary science, urban and regional planning. New series established include *Modern French Writers* and *Public Sculpture of Britain*. Founded 1899.

Livewire – see The Women's Press

Lonely Planet Publications
10A Spring Place, London NW5 3BH
tel 020-7428 4800 *fax* 020-7428 4828
e-mail go@lonelyplanet.co.uk
web site http://www.lonelyplanet.com/
Directors Tony Wheeler, Maureen Wheeler, *General Manager UK* Charlotte Hindle
Country and regional guidebooks, city guides, phrasebooks, walking guides, travel atlases, city maps, diving and snorkelling guides, pictorial books, condensed guides, restaurant guides, health guides, food guides, cycling guides, wildlife guides. Branch office established 1991.

Longman – imprint of Pearson Education*

Lorenz Books – see Anness Publishing

Peter Lowe (Eurobook Ltd)
PO Box 52, Wallingford, Oxon OX10 0XU
tel (01865) 858333 *fax* (01865) 858263
e-mail eurobook@compuserve.com
Director P.S. Lowe
Publishers of popular science and related subjects (including natural history) as illustrated non-fiction. Age 12+ but no general or teen fiction. Founded 1968.

Lund Humphries – see Ashgate Publishing Ltd

Lutterworth Press – see James Clarke & Co. Ltd*

Macdonald Young Books – now Hodder Children's Books – see Hodder Headline Ltd*

McGraw-Hill Publishing Company Europe*

McGraw-Hill House, Shoppenhangers Road, Maidenhead, Berks. SL6 2QL
tel (01628) 502500 *fax* (01628) 770224
e-mail (contact)@mcgraw-hill.com
web site http://www.mcgraw-hill.co.uk
Directors Alan Martin (operations), John Black (higher education Northern Europe), Rupert Mitchell (trade and professional Northern Europe), *Vice-President Central Europe/MEA* Italo Raimondi

Technical, scientific, professional reference.

Macmillan Publishers Ltd*

25 Eccleston Place, London SW1W 9NF
tel 020-7881 8000 *fax* 020-7881 8001
Chief Executive Richard Charkin, *Directors* R. Barker, M. Barnard, C.J. Paterson, A. Soar, G.R.U. Todd

Macmillan Children's Books Ltd (division)
Managing Director Kate Wilson, *Publishing Director (Picture Books and Gift Books)* Alison Green, *Editorial Director (Campbell Books)* Dereen Taylor, *Publishing Director (Fiction and Poetry)* Sarah Davies, *Associate Publisher (Fiction)* Marion Lloyd, *Editorial Director (Poetry and Non-fiction)* Gaby Morgan

Publishes under **Macmillan**, **Pan**, **Campbell Books**. Picture books, fiction, poetry, non-fiction, early learning, pop-up, novelty, board books. No unsolicited material.

Pan Macmillan Ltd (division)
Chairman Adrian Soar

Publishes under **Boxtree**, **Macmillan**, **Pan**, **Papermac**, **Picador**, **Sidgwick & Jackson**.

Boxtree (imprint)
fax 0171-881 8280
Publisher Gordon Wise, *Channel 4 projects* Charlie Carman

TV and film tie-ins (adult and children's non-fiction); illustrated and general non-fiction; mass market paperbacks linked to TV, film, rock and sporting events; humour.

Macmillan General Books (imprint)
Publisher Jeremy Trevathan, *Editorial Directors* Imogen Taylor (fiction), Beverley Cousins (crime), Peter Lavery (thrillers), Georgina Morley (non-fiction), *Publishing Manager (Macmillan Audio)* Alison Muirden

Novels, crime, science fiction, fantasy and horror. Autobiography, biography, business, gift books, health and beauty, history, humour, natural history, travel, philosophy, politics and world affairs, psychology, theatre and film, gardening and cookery, encyclopedias. Founded 1843.

Pan (imprint)
Publisher Clare Harington

Fiction: novels, crime, science fiction, fantasy and horror. Non-fiction: sports, theatre and film, travel, gardening and cookery, encyclopedias, general. Founded 1947.

Papermac (imprint)
Senior Editor Clare Harington

Serious non-fiction: history, biography, science, political economy, cultural criticism and art history. Founded 1965.

Picador (imprint)
Publisher Peter Straus, *Editorial Directors* Ursula Doyle, Maria Rejt

Literary international fiction and non-fiction, poetry. Founded 1972.

Sidgwick & Jackson (imprint)
Publisher Gordon Wise

Military and war, music, pop and rock. MSS, synopses and ideas welcome. Send to submissions editor, with return postage. Founded 1908.

Holtzbrinck Online Publishing (division)
Managing Director Ian Jacobs, *Production Director* John Peacock, *Executive Web Producer* Sara Lloyd, *Editorial and Publishing Director* Jane Turner, *International Sales and Marketing Director* Alex Lankester

Reference works in academic, professional and vocational subjects, online resources. Founded 2000.

Macmillan Education Ltd (division)
Macmillan Oxford, Between Towns Road, Oxford OX4 3PP
tel (01865) 405700 *fax* (01865) 405701
Chairman Christopher Paterson, *Joint Managing Directors* Mike Esplen, Christopher Harrison, *Publishing Directors* Sue Bale, Alison Hubert, *Finance Director* Paul Emmett

English language teaching materials. School and college textbooks and materials in all subjects for international markets.

Macmillan Heinemann English Language Teaching
Macmillan Oxford, Between Towns Road, Oxford OX4 3PP
tel (01865) 405700 *fax* (01865) 405701
Chairman Christopher Paterson, *Managing Directors* Mike Esplen, Chris Harrison, *Director,*

ELT Publishing Sue Bale
English language teaching materials.
Macmillan Press Ltd (division)
Managing Director D. Knight, *Publishing Directors* J. Dixon (academic), S. Kennedy (politics), S. Rutt (professional business/management), F. Arnold (humanities/social sciences), Christopher Glennie (business/computer science/engineering)
Textbooks and monographs in academic, professional and vocational subjects. Rebranded Palgrave from September 2000.

Julia MacRae Books – see Random House Group Ltd*

Madcap – see André Deutsch Ltd*

Magi Publications
1 The Coda Centre, 189 Munster Road, London SW6 6AW
tel 020-7385 6333 *fax* 020-7385 7333
Publisher Monty Bhatia, *Editor* Linda Jennings
Little Tiger Press (imprint)
e-mail info@littletiger.co.uk
Quality children's picture books and novelty books. New material will be considered from authors and illustrators, but enquire first. Founded 1987.

Mainstream Publishing Co. (Edinburgh) Ltd*
7 Albany Street, Edinburgh EH1 3UG
tel 0131-557 2959 *fax* 0131-556 8720
e-mail mainstream.pub@btinternet.com
web site http://www.mainstreampublishing.com
Directors Bill Campbell, Peter MacKenzie, Fiona Brownlee (marketing), Sharon Atherton (publicity), Ray Cowie (sales), Neil Graham (production)
Biography, autobiography, art, photography, sport, health, guidebooks, humour, literature, current affairs, history, politics. Founded 1978.
Mainstream Sport (imprint)
Sport.

Mammoth – see Egmont Children's Books

Management Books 2000 Ltd
(incorporating Mercury Books)
Cowcombe House, Cowcombe Hill, Chalford, Glos. GL6 8HP
tel (01285) 760722 *fax* (01285) 760708
e-mail m.b.2000@virgin.net
web site http://www.mb2000.com
Directors N. Dale-Harris (publisher), R. Hartman
Business and lifeskills books.

Manchester United Books – see André Deutsch Ltd*

Manchester University Press*
Oxford Road, Manchester M13 9NR
tel 0161-273 5539 *fax* 0161-274 3346
e-mail mup@man.ac.uk
web site http://www.man.ac.uk/mup
Chief Executive David Rodgers
Works of academic scholarship: literary criticism, cultural studies, media studies, art history, design, architecture, history, politics, economics, international law, modern language texts. Textbooks and monographs. Founded 1912.

Mandarin – acquired by Random House Group Ltd*

Mandrake of Oxford
PO Box 250, Oxford OX1 1AP
tel (01865) 243671 *fax* (01865) 432929
e-mail krm@mandrake.cix.co.uk
web site http://www.compulink.co.uk/~mandrake/
Directors Kris Morgan, Shantidevi Nath
Occult and bizarre. Founded 1986.

Mansell Publishing – see The Continuum International Publishing Group Ltd

Manson Publishing Ltd*
73 Corringham Road, London NW11 7DL
tel 020-8905 5150 *fax* 020-8201 9233
e-mail manson@man-pub.demon.co.uk
Managing Director Michael Manson
Medical, scientific, veterinary. Founded 1992.

Mantra Publishing
5 Alexandra Grove, London N12 8NU
tel 020-8445 5123 *fax* 020-8446 7745
e-mail sales@mantrapublishing.com
web site http://www.mantrapublishing.com
Managing Director M. Chatterji
Children's multicultural picture books; multilingual friezes/posters; dual language books/cassettes; South Asian literature/teenage fiction; CD-Roms and videos. Founded 1984.

Marino Books – see The Mercier Press†

Marshall Pickering – see HarperCollins Publishers*

Marshall Publishing*
The Orangery, 161 New Bond Street, London W1Y 8PA
tel 020-7291 8222 *fax* 020-7291 8233
e-mail info@marshallpublishing.com
web site http://www.marshallmedia.com
Directors Richard Harman (chairman), Nick

Croydon (Ceo), Barbara Anderson Marshall, Barry Baker (operations), John Christmas, Katharine Toseland, Andrew Lee

Highly illustrated non-fiction: health, gardening, home and DIY, physical fitness, travel, natural history, children's information reference. Founded 1997.

Martin Books

Grafton House, 64 Maids Causeway, Cambridge CB5 8DD
tel (01223) 366733 *fax* (01223) 461428
Editorial Director Janet Copleston

Cookery, gardening, illustrated non-fiction and sponsored publishing. Imprint of Simon & Schuster UK Ltd.

Kenneth Mason Publications Ltd

Dudley House, 12 North Street, Emsworth, Hants PO10 7DQ
tel (01243) 377977 *fax* (01243) 379136
Directors Kenneth Mason (chairman), Piers Mason (managing), Michael Mason, Anthea Mason

Nautical, slimming, health, fitness; technical journals. Founded 1958.

Kevin Mayhew Ltd

Buxhall, Suffolk IP14 3BW
tel (01449) 737978 *fax* (01449) 737834
e-mail kevinmayhewltd@msn.com
Directors Kevin Mayhew (chairman), Gordon Carter (managing) Ray Gilbert (production), Jonathan Bugden (sales)

Christianity: prayer and spirituality, pastoral care, preaching, liturgy worship, children's, youth work, drama, instant art. Music: hymns, organ and choral, contemporary worship, piano and instrumental. Contact Editorial Dept before sending MSS/synopses. Founded 1976.

Medical Historical – see Harlequin Mills & Boon Ltd*

Medici Society Ltd

Grafton House, Hyde Estate Road, London NW9 6JZ
tel 020-8205 2500 *fax* 020-8205 2552

Publishers of Medici Prints, greetings cards and other colour reproductions. Art, nature and illustrated children's books. Send preliminary letter with brief details of the work marked for the attention of the Art Director.

Melrose Press Ltd

St Thomas Place, Ely, Cambs. CB7 4GG
tel (01353) 646600 *fax* (01353) 646601
e-mail tradesales@melrosepress.co.uk
Directors R.A. Kay, J.M. Kay, B.J. Wilson, N.S. Law (editorial), C. Emmett FCA, V.A. Kay, J.E. Pearson

International biographical reference works, including *International Authors & Writers Who's Who*, *International Who's Who in Poetry* and *Poets' Encyclopedia*. Founded 1969.

Mentor Books†

43 Furze Road, Sandyford Industrial Estate, Dublin 18, Republic of Ireland
tel (01) 2952112 *fax* (01) 2952114
e-mail all@mentorbooks.ie
web site http://www.mentorbooks.ie
Managing Director Daniel McCarthy, *Managing Editor* Claire Haugh

General: adult fiction and non-fiction, children's, guide books, biographies, history. Educational: languages, history, geography, business, maths. Founded 1979.

The Mercat Press*

James Thin Ltd, 53-59 South Bridge, Edinburgh EH1 1YS
tel 0131-622 8222 *fax* 0131-557 8149
e-mail enquiries@jthin.co.uk
web site http://www.mercatpress.com
Chairman D. Ainslie Thin, *Editorial managers* Tom Johnstone, Sean Costello, Camilla James

Scottish books of general and academic interest. No fiction or new poetry. Founded 1970.

The Mercier Press†

5 French Church Street, Cork, Republic of Ireland
tel (021) 4275040 *fax* (021) 4274969
e-mail books@mercier.ie
web site http://www.mercier.ie/mercier
Directors G. Eaton (chairman), J.F. Spillane (managing), M.P. Feehan, J. O'Donoghue

Irish literature, folklore, history, politics, humour, ballads, education, theology, law. Founded 1944.

Marino Books (imprint)

16 Hume Street, Dublin 2, Republic of Ireland
tel (01) 6615299 *fax* (01) 6618583
e-mail books@marino.ie
Publisher Jo O'Donoghue

Fiction, children's fiction, current affairs, health, mind and spirit, general non-fiction.

Merehurst Ltd

Ferry House, 51-57 Lacy Road, London SW15 1PR
tel 020-8355 1480 *fax* 020-8355 1499
Publisher/Ceo Anne Wilson, *Group General Manager* Mark Smith, *International Sales Director* Mark Newman, *Coo* Sharon Miller, *Key Accounts Manager* Debbie Kent

Crafts and hobbies, cake art, cookery,

homes and interiors, children's non-fiction, gardening, DIY.

Merlin Press Ltd

PO Box 30705, London WC2E 8QD
tel 020-7836 3020 *fax* 020-7497 0309
e-mail info@merlinpress.co.uk
Managing Director Anthony Zurbrugg

Radical history and social studies. Letters/ synopses only please.

Green Print (imprint)

Green politics and the environment.

Merrell Publishers Ltd

42 Southwark Street, London SE1 1UN
tel 020-7403 2047 *fax* 020-7407 1333
e-mail mail@merrellpublishers.com
web site http://www.merrellpublishers.com
Publisher Hugh Merrell, *Editorial Director* Julian Honer, *Art Director* Matt Hervey

Art, architecture, photography, textiles and design.

Merrow Publishing Co. Ltd

2 Abbey Road, Darlington, Co. Durham DL3 8LR
tel/fax (01325) 351661
Directors Dr J.G. Cook (editorial), J.A. Verdon, A.M. Creasey

Textiles, plastics, popular science, scientific. Founded 1951.

Methodist Publishing House

20 Ivatt Way, Peterborough PE3 7PG
tel (01733) 332202 *fax* (01733) 331201
e-mail sales@mph.org.uk
Chief Executive Brian Thornton

Hymn and service books, general religious titles, church supplies. Founded 1773.

Chester House Publications (imprint)

Children and youth titles.

Foundery Press (imprint)

Ecumenical titles.

Methuen Academic – now incorporated into Routledge*

Methuen Children's Books – see Egmont Children's Books

Methuen Publishing Ltd

(former imprint of Random House)
215 Vauxhall Bridge Road, London SW1V 1EJ
tel 020-7798 1600 *fax* 020-7828 2098
Managing Director Peter Tummons, *Publishing Director* Max Eilenberg, *Sales Manager* Danny Parnes, *Publicity Manager* Margot Weale

Literary fiction and non-fiction: biography, autobiography, travel, history, drama, humour, film, performing arts, plays. No unsolicited MSS. Synopses considered.

Metro Publishing Ltd

19 Gerrard Street, London W1V 7LA
tel 020-7734 1411 *fax* 020-7734 1811
Managing Director Susanne McDadd, *Publisher* Alan Brooke, *Editorial Manager* Mary Remnant, *Sales Director* John Wright, *Publicity Manager* Becke Parker

Carroll & Brown (imprint)
Publishers Amy Carroll, Denise Brown

Illustrated full-colour non-fiction: health, cookery, New Age, self-help.

Richard Cohen Books (imprint)

Biography, current affairs, history, politics, sport, fiction.

Metro Books (imprint)

Non-fiction: biography, autobiography, military, health, popular psychology, cookery, childcare. Founded 1995.

Michelin Travel Publications

The Edward Hyde Building, 38 Clarendon Road, Watford, Herts. WD1 1SX
tel (01923) 415000 *fax* (01923) 415052
web site http://www.michelin-travel.com
Head of Travel Publications J. Lewis

Tourist guides, maps and atlases, hotel and restaurant guides; children's activity books.

Midland Publishing Ltd – see Ian Allan Publishing Ltd

Milestone Publications

62 Murray Road, Horndean, Waterlooville PO8 9JL
tel (023) 9259 7440 *fax* (023) 9259 1975
e-mail info@gosscrestedchina.co.uk
web site http://www.gosscrestedchina.co.uk
Managing Director Nicholas J. Pine

Heraldic china, antique porcelain, business, economics. Publishing and bookselling division of Goss & Crested China Ltd. Founded 1967.

Millennium – see The Orion Publishing Group Ltd

Harvey Miller Publishers*

2 Byron Mews, Fleet Road, London NW3 2NQ
tel 020-7284 4359 *fax* 020-7267 8764
e-mail sarah.kane@brepols.com
web site http://www.brepols.com
Publisher Johan Van der Beke, *Editor-in-Chief* Elly Miller

Art history. Imprint of Brepols Publishers.

Miller's – see Octopus Publishing Group

J. Garnet Miller
10 Station Road Industrial Estate, Colwall, Malvern, Herefordshire WR13 6RN
tel/fax (01684) 540154
Directors Leslie Smith, Simon Smith

Plays and theatre textbooks, especially for amateur dramatic societies. Division of **Cressrelles Publishing Ltd**. Founded 1951.

Miller Freeman Information Services
Riverbank House, Angel Lane, Tonbridge, Kent TN9 1SE
tel (01732) 362666 *fax* (01732) 367301

Over 20 directories for business and industry, including *Benn's Media* and *The Knowledge*, guides for the media and film and TV markets respectively. Subsidiary of Miller Freeman UK Ltd.

Mills & Boon – see Harlequin Mills & Boon Ltd*

Mira Books – see Harlequin Mills & Boon Ltd*

The MIT Press – see under USA in Overseas book publishers, page 239

Mitchell Beazley – see Octopus Publishing Group

Mojo Books – see Canongate Books Ltd*

Monarch Books
Concorde House, Grenville Place, London NW7 3SA
tel 020-8959 3668 *fax* 020-8959 3678
e-mail tonyc@angushudson.com
Editor Tony Collins

Christian books: (Monarch) issues of faith and society; (MARC) leadership, mission, evangelism. Submit synopsis/2 sample chapters only with return postage.

Moonstone – see Michael O'Mara Books Ltd

Morrigan Book Company
Killala, Co. Mayo, Republic of Ireland
tel/fax (096) 32555
e-mail gerry.kennedy@online.ie
Publisher Gerry Kennedy, *Administrator* Hilary Kennedy

Non-fiction: general Irish interest, biography, history, local history, folklore and mythology. Founded 1979.

Mosby International – see Harcourt Publishers Ltd

Mount Eagle Publications Ltd†
(incorporating Brandon Book Publishers Ltd, 1982)
PO Box 32, Dingle, Co. Kerry, Republic of Ireland
tel (353) 66 9151463 *fax* (353) 66 9151234
Publisher Steve MacDonogh

Fiction, biography and current affairs. No unsolicited MSS.

Mowbray – see The Continuum International Publishing Group Ltd

MQ Publications Ltd
254-258 Goswell Road, London EC1V 7EB
tel 020-7490 7732 *fax* 020-7253 7358
e-mail mqp@btinternet.com
Ceo Zaro Weil

Craft, style, photography, fine art, gift books. Founded 1993.

John Murray (Publishers) Ltd*
50 Albemarle Street, London W1X 4BD
tel 020-7493 4361 *fax* 020-7499 1792
Chairman John R. Murray (general books marketing), *Managing Director* Nicholas Perren, *Directors* Grant McIntyre (general editorial), Judith Reinhold (educational marketing), *Company Secretary* David Weakley

General: art and architecture, biography and autobiography, letters and diaries, travel, exploration and guidebooks, Middle East, Asia, India and sub-continent, general history, health education, aviation, craft and practical. No unsolicited MSS please. Also self teaching in all subjects in *Success Studybook* series. Founded 1768.

National Christian Education Council*
(incorporating International Bible Reading Association)
1020 Bristol Road, Selly Oak, Birmingham B26 6LB
tel 0121-472 4242 *fax* 0121-472 7575
e-mail ncec@ncec.org.uk
web site http://www.ncec.org.uk

Training material for children and youth workers in the Church. Worship resources for use in primary schools. Christian drama and musicals, Activity Club material and Bible reading resources.

The National Trust
36 Queen Anne's Gate, London SW1H 9AS
tel 020-7222 9251 *fax* 020-7447 6641
Publisher Margaret Willes

History, cookery, architecture, gardening, guidebooks, children's non-fiction. No unsolicited MSS. Founded 1895.

The Natural History Museum Publishing Division

Cromwell Road, London SW7 5BD
tel 020-7938 5336 *fax* 020-7938 5010
e-mail j.hogg@nhm.ac.uk
web site http://www.nhm.ac.uk/info/publishing
Head of Publishing Jane Hogg

Natural sciences; entomology, botany, geology, mineralogy, palaeontology, zoology, history of natural history. Founded 1881.

Nautical Books – now Adlard Coles Nautical – see A & C Black (Publishers) Ltd*

NCVO Publications

(incorporating Bedford Square Press)
Regent's Wharf, 8 All Saints Street, London N1 9RL
tel 020-7713 6161 *fax* 020-7713 6300
e-mail ncvo@ncvo-vol.org.uk
web site http://www.ncvo-vol.org.uk
Head of Publications Maria Kane

Imprint of the National Council for Voluntary Organisations. Practical guides, reference books, directories and policy studies on voluntary sector concerns including management and trustee development, legal, finance and fundraising, self-help and Europe. No unsolicited MSS accepted.

Nelson Thornes Ltd*

(formed from the merger of Thomas Nelson & Sons Ltd and Stanley Thornes (Publishers) Ltd)
Delta Place, 27 Bath Road, Cheltenham, Glos. GL53 7TH
tel (01242) 267100 *fax* (01242) 221914
e-mail name@nelsonthornes.com
web site http://www.nelsonthornes.com
Directors Oliver Gadsby (managing), Adrian Ford, Brian Carvell, Paul Vinson, Adrian Wheaton, Peter Oates, Sonia Raphael

Print and electronic publishers for the educational market: primary, secondary, further education, higher education, professional. Imprints: E.J. Arnold, Mary Glasgow. Part of the Wolters Kluwer Group of Companies.

New Beacon Books

76 Stroud Green Road, London N4 3EN
tel 020-7272 4889 *fax* 020-7281 4662
Directors John La Rose, Sarah White, Michael La Rose, Janice Durham

Small specialist publishers: general non-fiction, fiction, poetry, critical writings, concerning the Caribbean, Africa, African-America and Black Britain. No unsolicited MSS. Founded 1966.

New Cavendish Books

3 Denbigh Road, London W11 2SJ
tel 020-7229 6765/792 9984 *fax* 020-7792 01027
e-mail narisa@new-cav.demon.co.uk

Specialist books for the collector; art reference, Thai guidebooks. Founded 1973.

River Books (associate imprint)
The art and architecture of Southeast Asia.

New English Library – see Hodder Headline Ltd*

New Holland Publishers (UK) Ltd*

Chapel House, 24 Nutford Place, London W1H 6DQ
tel 020-7724 7773 *fax* 020-7724 6184
e-mail postmaster@nhpub.co.uk
Managing Director John Beaufoy, *Publishing Director* Yvonne McFarlane

Illustrated books on natural history, travel, cookery, needlecrafts and handicrafts, interior design, DIY, gardening.

New Island Books*

2 Brookside, Dundrum Road, Dundrum, Dublin 14, Republic of Ireland
tel (01) 2986867/2989937 *fax* (01) 2982783
e-mail nibedit@brookside.iol.ie
Directors Edwin Higel (managing), Fergal Stanley

Fiction, poetry, drama, humour, biography, current affairs. Founded 1992.

New Orchard Editions – former imprint of Cassell & Co

New Playwrights' Network

10 Station Road Industrial Estate, Colwall, Nr Malvern, Herefordshire WR13 6RN
tel/fax (01684) 540154
Publishing Director Leslie Smith

General plays for the amateur, one-act and full length.

New Theatre Publications

254 Tithepit Shaw Lane, Warlingham, Surrey CR6 9AQ
tel/fax 020-8651 4119
e-mail paul.beard@new-playwrights.demon.co.uk
web site http://www.plays4theatre.com
Directors Paul Beard, Ian Hornby

Plays for the professional and amateur stage. Founded 1987.

Newleaf – see Gill & Macmillan Ltd

Newnes – see Reed Educational and Professional Publishing Ltd*

Nexus – see Virgin Publishing Ltd

Nexus Special Interests Ltd

Nexus House, Azalea Drive, Swanley, Kent BR8 8HU
tel (01322) 660070 *fax* (01322) 668421
Manager B. Burkinshaw

Modelling, model engineering, woodworking, aviation, railways, military, crafts, electronics, home brewing and winemaking.

NFER-NELSON Publishing Co. Ltd*

Darville House, 2 Oxford Road East, Windsor, Berks. SL4 1DF
tel (01753) 858961 *fax* (01753) 856830
e-mail edu&hsc@nfer-nelson.co.uk
web site http://www.nfer.nelson.co.uk

Testing, assessment and management publications and services for education, business and health care. Founded 1981.

Nia – see the X Press

Nicholson – see HarperCollins Publishers*

James Nisbet & Co. Ltd

78 Tilehouse Street, Hitchin, Herts. SG5 2DY
tel (01462) 438331 *fax* (01462) 431528
Directors Miss E.M. Mackenzie-Wood, Mrs A.A.C. Bierrum

Dictionaries, educational (infants, primary, secondary), business management. Founded 1810.

Northcote House Publishers Ltd

Horndon House, Horndon, Tavistock, Devon PL19 9NQ
tel (01822) 810066 *fax* (01822) 810034
Directors B.R.W. Hulme, A.V. Hulme (secretary)

Careers, education and education management, educational dance and drama, English literature (*Writers and their Work*). Founded 1985.

W.W. Norton & Company

10 Coptic Street, London WC1A 1PU
tel 020-7323 1579 *fax* 020-7436 4553
Managing Director Alan Cameron

History, biography, current affairs, English and American literature, economics, music, psychology, science. Founded 1980.

NWP – see Neil Wilson Publishing Ltd

Oak Tree Press†

Merrion Building, Lower Merrion Street, Dublin 2, Republic of Ireland
tel (01) 6761600 *fax* (01) 6761644
e-mail oaktreep@iol.ie
web site http://www.oaktreepress.com
Directors Brian O'Kane, Rita O'Kane, *General Manager* David Givens

Business management, accountancy, law. Founded 1991.

O'Brien Educational

20 Victoria Road, Rathgar, Dublin 6, Republic of Ireland
tel (01) 4923333 *fax* (01) 4922777
e-mail books@obrien.ie
web site http://www.obrien.ie
Directors Michael O'Brien, Bride Rosney

Humanities, science, environmental studies, history, geography, English, Irish, art, commerce, music, careers, media studies. Founded 1976.

The O'Brien Press Ltd†

20 Victoria Road, Rathgar, Dublin 6, Republic of Ireland
tel (01) 4923333 *fax* (01) 4922777
e-mail books@obrien.ie
web site http://www.obrien.ie
Directors Michael O'Brien, Ide Ni Laoghaire, Ivan O'Brien

History, biography, general fiction and non-fiction, politics, architecture, topography, humour, music, true crime, travel, walking guides, Irish interest, children's (fiction and non-fiction), tapes/CDs. Series include *Pocket Books*, *Another Ireland*, *Other World* (science fiction, fantasy, horror), *Pandas* (age 5-6), *Flyers* (age 6+). Founded 1974.

The Octagon Press Ltd

PO Box 227, London N6 4EW
tel 020-8348 9392 *fax* 020-8341 5971
e-mail octagon@schredds.demon.co.uk
web site http://www.octagonpress.com
Managing Director George R. Schrager

Psychology, philosophy, Eastern religion. Unsolicited MSS not accepted. Founded 1972.

Octopus Publishing Group

2-4 Heron Quays, London E14 4JP
tel 020-7531 8400 *fax* 020-7531 8650
e-mail firstname.lastname@octopus-publishing.co.uk
web site http://www.octopus-publishing.co.uk
Chief Executive Derek Freeman, *Executive Directors* Laura Bamford, Helen Barlow

Bounty (imprint)
tel 020-7531 8601 *fax* 020-7531 8607
e-mail bountybooksinfo-bp@bountybooks.co.uk
Publisher/Managing Director Laura Bamford

Promotional publishing, adult books.

Brimax Books (imprint)
tel 020-7531 8598 *fax* 020-7531 8607
e-mail brimax@brimax.octopus.co.uk
Publisher/Managing Director Laura Bamford
Mass market picture books for children.

Conran Octopus (imprint)
tel 020-7531 8628 *fax* 020-7531 8627
e-mail info-co@conran-octopus.co.uk
web site http://www.conran-octopus.co.uk
Managing Director Caroline Proud
Quality illustrated books, particularly lifestyle, cookery, gardening.

Hamlyn/Octopus (imprint)
tel 020-7531 8573 *fax* 020-7537 0514
e-mail info-ho@hamlyn.co.uk
web site http://www.hamlyn.co.uk
Publisher/Managing Director Alison Goff
Popular illustrated non-fiction, particularly cookery, gardening, craft, sport, film tie-ins, rock'n'roll.

Miller's (imprint)
The Cellars, High Street, Tenterden, Kent TN30 6BN
tel (01580) 766411 *fax* (01580) 766100
e-mail firstname.lastname@millers.uk.com
Publisher/Managing Director Jane Aspden
Quality illustrated books on antiques and collectibles.

Mitchell Beazley (imprint)
tel 020-7531 8400 *fax* 020-7531 8650
e-mail info-mb@mitchell-beazley.co.uk
Publisher/Managing Director Jane Aspden
Quality illustrated books, particularly antiques, gardening, craft and interiors, wine.

Philip's (imprint)
tel 020-7531 8459 *fax* 020-7531 8460
e-mail george.philip@philips-maps.co.uk
web site http://www.philips-maps.co.uk
Publisher/Managing Director John Gaisford
Atlases, maps, astronomy, encyclopedias, globes.

Oldcastle Books Ltd

18 Coleswood Road, Harpenden, Herts AL5 1EP
tel/fax (01582) 761264
e-mail ion@noexit.co.uk
web sites http://www.noexit.co.uk
www.pocketessentials.com
Director Ion Mills
Imprints: No Exit Press (crime fiction), Oldcastle (gambling), Pocket Essentials (inexpensive reference guides). Founded 1985.

The Oleander Press

17 Stansgate Avenue, Cambridge CB2 2QZ
tel (01223) 244688
Managing Director P. Ward
Travel, language, literature, Libya, Arabia and Middle East, Cambridgeshire, humour, reference. Preliminary letter required before submitting MSS; please send sae for reply. Founded 1960.

Michael O'Mara Books Ltd

9 Lion Yard, Tremadoc Road, London SW4 7NQ
tel 020-7720 8643 *fax* 020-7627 8953
Chairman Michael O'Mara, *Managing Director* Lesley O'Mara
General non-fiction: Children's books, history, ancient history, humour, anthologies; biography and royal books. Founded 1985.

Moonstone (imprint)
Mind, body and spirit.

Omnibus Press/Music Sales Ltd*

8-9 Frith Street, London W1V 5TZ
tel 020-7434 0066 *fax* 020-7434 3310
e-mail music@musicsales.co.uk
Head of Sales Hilary Power
Rock music biographies, books about music. Founded 1976.

On Stream Publications Ltd

Currabaha, Cloghroe, Blarney, Co. Cork, Republic of Ireland
tel/fax (353) 21-4385798
e-mail info@onstream.ie
web site http://www.onstream.ie
Owner Rosalind Crowley
Cookery, wine, travel, human interest non-fiction, local history, academic and practical books. Founded 1986.

Oneworld Publications

185 Banbury Road, Oxford, Oxon OX2 7AR
tel (01865) 310597 *fax* (01865) 310598
e-mail info@oneworld-publications.com
web site http://www.oneworld-publications.com
Directors Juliet Mabey (editorial), Novin Doostdar (finance), Helen Coward (sales)
Social issues, psychology, self-help, religion, world religion, inter-religious dialogue, Islamic studies, philosophy, history, teenage non-fiction. Founded 1984.

Onlywomen Press Ltd

40 St Lawrence Terrace, London W10 5ST
tel 020-8354 0796 *fax* 020-8960 2817
e-mail 100756.1242@compuserve.com
Managing Director Lilian Mohin
Lesbian feminist: theory, fiction, poetry, crime fiction and cultural criticism. Founded 1974.

Open Books Publishing Ltd

Willow Cottage, Cudworth, Nr Ilminster, Somerset TA19 0PS
tel/fax (01460) 52565
e-mail patrickta@aol.com
Directors P. Taylor (managing), C. Taylor

Gardening. Founded 1974.

Open Gate Press*

(incorporating Centaur Press, founded 1954)
51 Achilles Road, London NW6 1DZ
tel 020-7431 4391 *fax* 020-7431 5129
e-mail books@opengatepress.co.uk
web site http://www.opengatepress.co.uk
Directors Jeannie Cohen, Elisabeth Petersdorff, George Frankl, Sandra Lovell

Psychoanalysis, philosophy, social sciences, religion, animal rights, the environment. Founded 1988.

Open University Press*

Celtic Court, 22 Ballmoor, Buckingham MK18 1XW
tel (01280) 823388 *fax* (01280) 823233
e-mail enquiries@openup.co.uk
web site http://www.openup.co.uk
Directors John Skelton (managing), Jacinta Evans (editorial), Sue Hadden (production), Barry Clarke (financial)

Education, management, psychology, sociology, criminology, counselling, cultural and media studies, health and social welfare, gender studies. Founded 1977.

Orbit – see Little, Brown and Company (UK)*

Orchard Books – see The Watts Publishing Group Ltd*

The Orion Publishing Group Ltd

Orion House, 5 Upper St Martin's Lane, London WC2H 9EA
tel 020-7240 3444 *fax* 020-7379 6158
Directors Jean-Louis Lisimachio (chairman), Anthony Cheetham (chief executive), Peter Roche (managing)

No unsolicited MSS; approach in writing in first instance. Founded 1992.

Illustrated (division)
Contact Michael Dover

Illustrated non-fiction: design, cookery, wine, gardening, art and architecture, natural history and personality based books.

Mass Market (division)
Managing Director Susan Lamb

Mass market fiction and non-fiction under **Everyman**, **Orion** and **Phoenix** imprints.

Orion (division)
Directors Malcolm Edwards (managing), Rosemary Cheetham (publisher), Jane Wood

Hardcover fiction and non-fiction.

Victor Gollancz Ltd (imprint)
Director Mike Petty

Biography and autobiography, current affairs, history, travel; fiction, literary fiction, crime, science fiction, fantasy. In association with Peter Crawley: *Master Bridge Series*.

Indigo (imprint)
Editorial Director Mike Petty

Literary fiction and general non-fiction.

Millennium (imprint)
Contact Simon Spanton

Science fiction and fantasy.

Orion Children's Books (division)
Managing Director and Publisher Judith Elliott

Children's fiction and non-fiction.

Osprey Publishing Ltd

Elms Court, Chapel Way, Botley, Oxford OX2 9LP
tel (01865) 727022 *fax* (01865) 727017/727019
e-mail osprey@osprey-publishing.co.uk
web site http://www.ospreypublishing.com
Managing Director Jonathan Parker, *Finance Director* Sarah Lough, *Vice-President, American Operations* Bill Corsa

Illustrated military history from around the world. Founded 1969.

Peter Owen Ltd

73 Kenway Road, London SW5 0RE
tel 020-7373 5628/370 6093 *fax* 020-7373 6760
e-mail admin@peterowen.com
Directors Peter L. Owen (managing), Antonia Owen (editorial)

Art, belles lettres, biography, literary fiction, general non-fiction, sociology, theatre. Do not send fiction without telephoning first unless it is by an established novelist.

Oxford Illustrated Press – see Haynes Publishing, Special Interest Publishing Division

Oxford Publishing Company – see Ian Allan Publishing Ltd

Oxford University Press*

Great Clarendon Street, Oxford OX2 6DP
tel (01865) 556767 *fax* (01865) 556646
e-mail enquiry@oup.co.uk
web site http://www.oup.co.uk
Chief Executive and Secretary to the Delegates Henry Reece, *Group Finance Director* Roger

Boning, *Academic Division Managing Director* Ivon Asquith, *UK Educational Division Managing Director* Fiona Clarke, *ELT Division Managing Director* Peter Mothersole, *Group Personnel Director* Martin Havelock

Anthropology, archaeology, architecture, art, belles-lettres, bibles, bibliography, children's books (fiction, non-fiction, picture), commerce, current affairs, dictionaries, drama, economics, educational (infants, primary, secondary, technical, university), English language teaching, electronic publishing, essays, foreign language learning, general history, hymn and service books, journals, law, maps and atlases, medical, music, oriental, philosophy, poetry, political economy, prayer books, reference, science, sociology, theology and religion, educational software. Trade paperbacks published under the imprint of Oxford Paperbacks. Founded 1478.

Paladin – now Flamingo – see HarperCollins Publishers*

Pan – see Macmillan Publishers Ltd*

Pan Macmillan Ltd – see Macmillan Publishers Ltd*

Pandora Press – see Rivers Oram Press

Paper Tiger – see Collins & Brown

Papermac – see Macmillan Publishers Ltd*

Paragon Press

1A Tower Square, Leeds LS1 4HZ
tel 0113-209 5771 *fax* 0113-209 5600
e-mail editorial@paragonpress.org.uk
web site http://www.paragonpress.org.uk
Director Dorothy James, *Managing Editor* Reggie Sharp

Fiction (adult and teenage), children's, biography, education (*Paragon Summaries* series). Founded 1998.

Parkgate Books – see Collins & Brown

Paternoster Publishing

PO Box 300, Carlisle, Cumbria CA3 0QS
tel (01228) 512512 *fax* (01228) 593388
e-mail info@paternoster-publishing.com
Publisher Mark Finnie

Biblical studies, Christian theology, ethics, history, mission. Imprints: Paternoster Press, Partnership, Regnum, Rutherford House, OM Publishing, Solway, Challenge, Paternoster Periodicals, SP Media, Alpha Books.

Stanley Paul – see Random House Group Ltd*

Pavilion Books Ltd

London House, Great Eastern Wharf, Parkgate Road, London SW11 4NQ
tel 020-7350 1230 *fax* 020-7350 1260
Publisher Colin Webb, *Editorial Directors* Vivien James (adult), Pamela Webb (children's)

Cookery, gardening, travel, humour, sport, art, children's. Subsidiary of CBMG plc. Founded 1980.

Pavilion Publishing (Brighton) Ltd

8 St George's Place, Brighton BN1 4GB
tel (01273) 623222 *fax* (01273) 625526
e-mail pavpub@pavilion.co.uk
web site http://www.pavpub.com
Directors Jan Alcoe, Chris Parker

Health and social care training: learning disability, mental health, community care management, older people, young people. Founded 1987.

Payback Press – see Canongate Books Ltd*

Pearson Education*

Edinburgh Gate, Harlow, Essex CM20 2JE
tel (01279) 623623 *fax* (01279) 431059
e-mail pearsoned-ema.com
web site http://www.pearsoned.com
Ceo Peter Jovanovich, *President of Pearson Europe, Middle East & Africa* Nigel Portwood

The new enterprise created following the acquisition by Pearson plc of Simon & Schuster's educational business. Imprints include Longman, Financial Times Prentice Hall, Addison-Wesley, Prentice Hall. It publishes materials for school pupils, students and practitioners globally.

Pelham Books – former imprint of Michael Joseph/Penguin

Pen & Sword Books Ltd

47 Church Street, Barnsley, South Yorkshire S70 2AS
tel (01226) 734222 *fax* (01226) 734438
e-mail charles@pen-and-sword.demon.co.uk
web site http://www.pen-and-sword.co.uk
Chief Executive Charles Hewitt, *Publishing Manager* Henry Wilson

Military history; *Battleground* series. Imprints: Leo Cooper, Pen & Sword Paperbacks.

Wharncliffe* (imprint)
Local history.

Penguin UK*

27 Wrights Lane, London W8 5TZ
tel 020-7416 3000 *fax* 020-7416 3099
web site http://www.penguin.co.uk
Ceo Anthony Forbes Watson

Adult and children's lists include fiction, non-fiction, poetry, drama, classics, reference and special interest areas. Reprints and new work. Owned by Pearson plc.

Penguin General Books (division)
Managing Director Helen Fraser, *Publishing Directors* Tony Lacey (Viking/Hamish Hamilton/Penguin), Tom Weldon (Michael Joseph/Penguin), Juliet Annan (Viking/Hamish Hamilton/Penguin), *Publishers* Simon Prosser (Hamish Hamilton/Penguin), Louise Moore (Michael Joseph/Penguin fiction)

No unsolicited MSS or synopses.

Hamish Hamilton (imprint)
Fiction, belles-lettres, biography and memoirs, current affairs, history, literature, politics, travel. No unsolicited MSS or synopses.

Michael Joseph (imprint)
Biography and memoirs, current affairs, fiction, history, humour, travel, health, spirituality and relationships, sports, general leisure, illustrated books. No unsolicited MSS or synopses.

Penguin (imprint)
Adult paperback books – wide range of fiction, non-fiction, TV and film tie-ins. No unsolicited MSS or synopses.

Viking (imprint)
Fiction, general non-fiction; literature, biography, autobiography, current affairs, history, travel, popular culture, reference. No unsolicited MSS or synopses.

The Penguin Press (division)
Managing Director Andrew Rosenheim, *Publishing Directors* Stuart Proffitt, Nigel Wilcockson

Serious adult non-fiction, reference, specialist and classics. Imprints: Allen Lane, Buildings of England, Penguin Classics, Penguin 20th Century Classics.
Approach in writing only.

Frederick Warne (division)
web site http://www.peterrabbit.com
Managing Director Sally Floyer

Classic children's publishing and merchandising including *Beatrix Potter*™, *Flower Fairies*, *Orlando*. No unsolicited MSS or synopses.

Ventura (division)
Managing Director Sally Floyer

Producer and packager of *Spot* titles by Eric Hill. No unsolicited MSS or synopses.

Puffin (division)
web site http://www.puffin.co.uk
Managing Director Philippa Milnes-Smith

Children's paperback list, publishing in virtually all fields including fiction, non-fiction, poetry, picture books, media-related titles. Imprints: Hamish Hamilton Children's, Viking Children's (hardback). No unsolicited MSS or synopses.

Penguin Audiobooks (division)
Contact Anna Hopkins

Ladybird (division)
Managing Director Michael Herridgo

Children's books for 0-10 year-olds – babies, toddlers, preschoolers, general and home educational (infants, primary, junior and secondary).

Pergamon – see Elsevier Science Ltd

Peterloo Poets

The Old School Chapel, Sand Lane, Calstock, Cornwall PL18 9QX
tel (01822) 833473
Publishing Director Harry Chambers, *Trustees* Brian Perman, David Selzer, Rose Taw, *Honorary President* Charles Causley CBE

Poetry. Founded 1976.

Phaidon Press Ltd

Regent's Wharf, All Saints Street, London N1 9PA
tel 020-7843 1000 *fax* 020-7843 1010
Publisher Richard Schlagman, *Managing Director* Andrew Price, *Directors* Amanda Renshaw, Frances Johnson

Fine art and art history, architecture, design, decorative arts, photography, music, fashion, film.

Philip's – see Octopus Publishing Group

Phillimore & Co. Ltd

(incorporating Darwen Finlayson Ltd)
Shopwyke Manor Barn, Chichester, West Sussex PO20 6BG
tel (01243) 787636 *fax* (01243) 787639
e-mail bookshop@phillimore.co.uk
web site http://www.phillimore.co.uk
Directors Philip Harris JP (chairman), Noel Osborne MA, FSA (managing), Hilary Clifford Brown (marketing)

Local and family history; architectural history, archaeology, genealogy and heraldry; also Darwen County History series and History from the Sources series. Founded 1897.

Phoenix House – see The Orion Publishing Group Ltd

Piatkus Books

5 Windmill Street, London W1P 1HF
tel 020-7631 0710 *fax* 020-7436 7137
e-mail info@piatkus.co.uk
web site http://www.piatkus.co.uk
Managing Director Judy Piatkus, *Directors* Philip Cotterell (marketing), Gill Cormode (editorial)

Fiction, biography, self-help, health, mind, body and spirit, business, careers, women's interest, how-to and practical, popular psychology, cookery, parenting and childcare, paranormal. Founded 1979.

Picador – see Macmillan Publishers Ltd*

Piccadilly Press

5 Castle Road, London NW1 8PR
tel 020-7267 4492 *fax* 020-7267 4493
Directors Brenda Gardner (publisher and managing), Philip Durrance (secretary)

Early picture books and parental advice trade paperbacks; trade paperback teenage information and humorous teenage fiction. Founded 1983.

Pimlico – see Random House Group Ltd*

Pinter – see The Continuum International Publishing Group Ltd

Pipers' Ash Ltd

Pipers' Ash, Church Road, Christian Malford, Chippenham, Wilts. SN15 4BW
tel (01249) 720563 *fax* (0870) 0568916
e-mail pipersash@supamasu.demon.co.uk
web site http://www.supamasu.demon.co.uk
Editorial Director Alfred Tyson

Poetry, contemporary short stories, science fiction stories; short novels, biographies, plays, philosophy, translations, children's, general non-fiction. Founded 1976.

Pitkin Unichrome Ltd

Healey House, Dene Road, Andover, Hants SP10 2AA
tel (01264) 409200 *fax* (01264) 334110
e-mail guides@pitkin.u-net.com
web site http://www.britguides.com
Managing Director Heather Hook, *Managing Editor* Shelley Grimwood

Illustrated souvenir guides.

Pitman Publishing – now Financial Times Prentice Hall; see Pearson Education*

The Playwrights Publishing Company

70 Nottingham Road, Burton Joyce, Notts. NG14 5AL
tel 0115-931 3356
e-mail tonybreeze@yahoo.co.uk
Proprietor Liz Breeze, *Consultant* Tony Breeze

One-act and full-length drama: serious work and comedies, for mixed cast, all women or schools. Reading fee and sae required. Founded 1990.

Plexus Publishing Ltd

55A Clapham Common Southside, London SW4 9BX
tel 020-7622 2440 *fax* 020-7622 2441
e-mail plexus@plexusuk.demon.co.uk
web site http://www.plexusbooks.com
Directors Terence Porter (managing), Sandra Wake (editorial)

Film, music, biography, popular culture, fashion. Founded 1973.

Eel Pie (imprint)

Film, music, biography, popular culture, fashion.

Pluto Press

345 Archway Road, London N6 5AA
tel 020-8348 2724 *fax* 020-8348 9133
e-mail pluto@plutobks.demon.co.uk
web site http://www.plutobooks.com
Directors Roger van Zwanenberg (managing), Anne Beech (editorial), *Head of Sales and Marketing* John Sadler

Sociology, economics, history, politics, cultural, international, women's studies, legal studies, Irish studies, Black studies, Third World and development, anthropology, media studies. Imprint: Journeyman Press. Founded 1968.

Pocket Books – see Simon & Schuster*

Point – see Scholastic Children's Books*

The Policy Press

University of Bristol, 34 Tyndall's Park Road, Bristol BS8 1PY
tel 0117-9546800 *fax* 0117-9737308
e-mail tpp@bris.ac.uk
web site http://www.policypress.org.uk
Publishing Manager Alison Shaw, *Editorial Manager* Dawn Louise Rushen, *Marketing and Sales Manager* Julia Mortimer

Social science publisher, specialising in

social and public policy, social work and social welfare. Founded 1996.

Polity Press

65 Bridge Street, Cambridge CB2 1UR
tel (01223) 324315 *fax* (01223) 461385
Directors Anthony Giddens, David Held, John Thompson

Social and political theory, politics, sociology, history, economics, psychology, media and cultural studies, philosophy, theology, literary theory, feminism, human geography, anthropology. Founded 1983.

Polygon – see Edinburgh University Press*

Poolbeg Group Services Ltd†

123 Baldoyle Industrial Estate, Baldoyle, Dublin 13, Republic of Ireland
tel (01) 8321477 *fax* (01) 8321430
e-mail poolbeg@iol.ie
Directors Kieran Devlin (managing), Philip MacDermott (chairman)

Fiction, public interest, women's interest, history, politics, current affairs. Imprints: Poolbeg, Poolbeg for Children. Founded 1976.

Portland Press Ltd

59 Portland Place, London W1N 3AJ
tel 020-7580 5530 *fax* 020-7323 1136
e-mail editorial@portlandpress.com
web site http://www.portlandpress.com
Directors Glyn D. Jones (managing), Chris J. Finch (finance), Rhonda C. Oliver (publishing), John Day (IT)

Biochemistry and molecular life science books for graduate, post-graduate and research students. Illustrated science books for children: Making Sense of Science series. Founded 1990.

Prentice Hall – imprint of Pearson Education

Prion Books

Imperial Works, Perren Street, London NW5 3ED
tel 020-7482 4248 *fax* 020-7482 4203
e-mail books@prion.co.uk
Managing Director Barry Winkleman

Popular culture, humour, drink, literary and historical reprints, health and beauty. Founded 1982.

Prism Press Book Publishers Ltd

The Thatched Cottage, Partway Lane, Hazelbury Bryan, Sturminster Newton, Dorset DT10 2DP
tel (01258) 817164 *fax* (01258) 817635
Directors Julian King, Diana King

Non-fiction, including health, food, psychology, politics, ecology. Synopses and ideas welcome, but no complete MSS. Founded 1974.

Profile Books Ltd

58A Hatton Garden, London EC1N 8LX
tel 020-7404 3001 *fax* 020-7404 3003
e-mail info@profilebooks.com
web site http://www.profilebooks.com
Publisher and Managing Director Andrew Franklin, *Editorial Director* Stephen Brough

General non-fiction: current affairs, politics, social sciences, history, psychology, business, management. Also publishes in association with the *Economist* and the *London Review of Books*. No unsolicited MSS; phone or send preliminary letter. Founded 1996.

PSI

(Policy Studies Institute)
100 Park Village East, London NW1 3SR
tel 020-7468 0468 *fax* 020-7388 0914
e-mail pubs@psi.org.uk

Economic, cultural and social policy, political institutions, social sciences.

Psychology Press Ltd

27 Church Road, Hove, East Sussex BN3 2FA
tel (01273) 207411 *fax* (01273) 205612
e-mail info@psypress.co.uk
web site http://www.psypress.co.uk

Psychology textbooks and monographs. A member of the **Taylor and Francis Group plc**.

Brunner/Routledge (imprint)
Clinical psychology and psychiatry.

Puffin – see Penguin UK*

Pulp Books

PO Box 12171, London N19 3HB
tel 020-7700 3409
e-mail editorial@pulpfact.demon.co.uk
Publisher Elaine Palmer

Novels by new British and Irish writers. Send synopsis/sample chapters. Founded 1997.

Pulp Faction (imprint)
Short fiction (occasional series supported by the London Arts Board).

Purple House Ltd

75 Banbury Road, Oxford OX2 6PE
tel (01865) 511999 *fax* (01865) 553916
e-mail info@purplehouse.com
web site http://www.purplehouse.com
Managing Director William Gompertz

Non-fiction: Art (*Media Careers* series) and media-related (*Zoo* series) books for the professional and consumer markets. Founded 1998.

Putnam Aeronautical Books – see Brassey's (UK) Ltd

Quadrille Publishing

5th Floor, Alhambra House, 27-31 Charing Cross Road, London WC2H 0LS
tel 020-7839 7117 *fax* 020-7839 7118
Directors Alison Cathie (managing), Anne Furniss (publishing), Jane O'Shea (editorial), Mary Evans (art), Marlis Ironmonger (commercial), Vincent Smith (production)

Illustrated non-fiction: cookery, craft, health and medical, gardening, interiors, magic. Founded 1994.

Quantum – see W. Foulsham & Co. Ltd

Quartet Books Ltd

27 Goodge Street, London W1P 2LD
tel 020-7636 3992 *fax* 020-7637 1866
e-mail quartetbooks@easynet.co.uk
Chairman N.I. Attallah, *Managing Director* Jeremy Beale, *Publishing Director* Stella Kane

General fiction and non-fiction, foreign literature in translation, classical music, jazz, contemporary music, biography. Member of the Namara Group. Founded 1972.

Queen Anne Press

Windmill Cottage, Mackerye End, Harpenden, Herts. AL5 5DR
tel (01582) 715866 *fax* (01582) 715121
e-mail queenanne@lenqap.demon.co.uk
Directors K.A.A. Stephenson, R.H. Stephenson

Sport and leisure activities. No unsolicited MSS. Division of Lennard Associates Ltd.

Quiller Press Ltd

46 Lillie Road, London SW6 1TN
tel 020-7499 6529 *fax* 020-7381 8941
e-mail greenwood@quiller.conx.uk
Directors J.J. Greenwood, A.E. Carlile

Publishers of sponsored books: guidebooks, history, industry, humour, architecture, cookery, collectables, country sports.

Radcliffe Medical Press Ltd

18 Marcham Road, Abingdon, Oxon OX14 1AA
tel (01235) 528820 *fax* (01235) 528830
e-mail contact.us@radcliffemed.com
Directors Andrew Bax (managing), Gill Nineham (editorial), Margaret McKeown (financial), *Head of Marketing* Gregory Moxon

Healthcare development and management, child health, palliative care, nursing, pharmacy, dentistry. Founded 1987.

Ragged Bears Publishing Ltd

Milborne Wick, Sherborne, Dorset DT9 4PW
tel (01963) 251600 *fax* (01963) 250889
e-mail info@raggedbears.co.uk
web site http://www.raggedbears.co.uk
Managing Director Henrietta Stickland, *Submissions Editor* Barbara Lamb

Pre-school and primary age picture and novelty books. Takes very few unsolicited ideas as the list is small. Send sae for return of MSS; do not send original artwork. Imprints: Ragged Bears, Spindlewood. Founded 1984.

Random House Group Ltd*

20 Vauxhall Bridge Road, London SW1V 2SA
tel 020-7840 8400 *fax* 020-7233 8791
e-mail randomhouse.co.uk
Chairman/Ceo Gail Rebuck, *Directors* Simon Master (chairman), Ian Hudson (managing) Amelia Thorpe (managing, Ebury Press), Mike Broderick (UK sales), Anthony McConnell (finance), Susan Sandon (publicity and marketing), Stephen Esson (production), Arthur Tanner (human resources)

Subsidiary of Bertelsmann AG.

Arrow Books Ltd (imprint)
tel 020-7840 8516 *fax* 020-7233 6127
Director Andy McKillop (publishing)

Fiction, non-fiction, fantasy, crime, humour, film tie-ins.

Barrie & Jenkins (imprint of **Ebury Press**)
tel 020-7840 8400 *fax* 020-7233 6057
Associate Publisher, Ebury Press Julian Shuckburgh

Art, antiques and collecting, architecture, decorative and applied arts.

Jonathan Cape (imprint)
tel 020-7840 8576 *fax* 020-7233 6117
Directors Dan Franklin, Robin Robertson, Tom Maschler, Kate Harbinson (publicity)

Biography and memoirs, current affairs, drama, fiction, history, poetry, travel. Imprints: **Bodley Head**, **Yellow Jersey Press** (sport).

Century (imprint)
tel 020-7840 8555 *fax* 020-7233 6127
Directors Kate Parkin (publisher), Mark Booth, Oliver Johnson

Fiction, classics, romance, biography, autobiography, general non-fiction, film tie-ins; *Century Business Books*.

Chatto & Windus (imprint)
tel 020-7840 8522 *fax* 020-7233 6123

Directors Alison Samuel (publishing), Penny Hoare, Hannah Corbett (publicity)

Art, belles-lettres, biography and memoirs, current affairs, drama, essays, fiction, history, poetry, politics, philosophy, translations, travel, hardbacks and paperbacks. No unsolicited MSS.

Condé Nast Books (imprint of **Ebury Press**)

Ebury Press Special Books (division)
tel 020-7840 8400 *fax* 020-7840 8406
Directors Amelia Thorpe (managing) Fiona MacIntyre (publisher), Julian Shuckburgh (associate), Isabel Duffy (publicity)

Art and antiques, biography, buddhism, cookery, gardening, health and beauty, homes and interiors, personal development, spirituality, sport, entertainment, travel guides, TV tie-ins. Unsolicited MSS welcome.

Fodor Guides (imprint of **Ebury Press**)
Worldwide annual travel guides.

William Heinemann (imprint)
tel 020-7840 8400 *fax* 020-7233 8791
Publishing Directors Lynne Drew (fiction), Ravi Mirchandani (non-fiction), Katie Gunning (publicity)

Fiction and general non-fiction: crime, thrillers, women's fiction, history, biography, science. No unsolicited MSS and synopses considered.

Hutchinson (imprint)
tel 020-7840 8564 *fax* 020-7233 7870
Directors Sue Freestone (publishing), Anthony Whittome, Paul Sidey (editorial), Sarah Whale (publicity)

Belles-lettres, biography, memoirs, thrillers, crime, current affairs, general history, politics, translations, travel, film tie-ins.

Stanley Paul (imprint of **Ebury Press**)
tel 020-7840 8400 *fax* 020-7233 6057

Pimlico (imprint)
tel 020-7840 8630 *fax* 020-7233 6117
Publishing Director Will Sulkin

History, biography, literature.

Random House Audio Books
tel 020-7840 8400
Manager Kate Elton

Random House Children's Books (division)
tel 020-7840 8400 *fax* 020-7233 6058
Head of Publishing Gill Evans, *Executive Publisher (Cape)* Ian Craig, *Publishing Directors* Caroline Roberts, Anne McNeil, *Publisher (Cape)* Tom Maschler

Publishes under Bodley Head Children's, Jonathan Cape Children's Books, Hutchinson Children's, Julia MacRae Books, Red Fox, Tellastory. Picture books, fiction, poetry, music, non-fiction, audio cassettes.

Rider (imprint of **Ebury Press**)
Publishing Director Fiona MacIntyre, *Editorial Consultant* Judith Kendra

Buddhism, religion and philosophy, psychology, ecology, health and healing, mysticism, meditation and yoga.

Secker and Warburg (imprint)
tel 020-7840 8649 *fax* 020-7233 6117
Directors Geoff Mulligan (editorial), Hannah Corbett (publicity)

Literary fiction, general non-fiction. No unsolicited MSS/synopses.

Transworld Publishers (division)
See page 208.

Vermilion (imprint of **Ebury Press**)

Vintage (imprint)
tel 020-7840 8400
Publisher Caroline Michel, *Associate Publishing Director* Will Sulkin

Quality fiction and non-fiction.

Rangers Books – see André Deutsch Ltd*

Ransom Publishing Ltd*

Ransom House, Unit 1, Brook Street, Watlington, Oxon OX9 5PP
tel (01491) 613711 *fax* (01491) 613733
e-mail ransom@ransompublishing.co.uk
web site http://www.ransom.co.uk
Directors Jenny Ertle (managing), Robert Ertle (sales), Steve Rickard (creative)

Primary education: literacy, numeracy, science, multimedia. Founded 1995.

The Reader's Digest Association Ltd*

11 Westferry Circus, Canary Wharf, London E14 4HE
tel 020-7715 8000 *fax* 020-7715 8181
Managing Director A.T. Lynam-Smith, *Editorial Directors* R.G. Twisk (magazine), Cortina Butler (general books), Nigel Begbie (condensed books and reading series)

Monthly magazine, condensed and series books; also DIY, car maintenance, gardening, medical, handicrafts, law, touring guides, encyclopedias, dictionaries, nature, folklore, atlases, cookery; music; videos.

Reader's Digest Children's Publishing Ltd

King's Court, Parsonage Lane, Bath BA1 1EF

tel (01225) 473204 *fax* (01225) 443324
e-mail cathy_jones@readersdigest.co.uk
Managing Director Brian Cearnes

Reader's Digest Children's Publishing (imprint)
Mass market children's and novelty information books. Fully owned subsidiary of Reader's Digest Association Inc. Founded 1980.

Reaktion Books

77-79 Farringdon Road, London EC1M 3JU
tel 020-7404 9930 *fax* 020-7404 9931
e-mail info@reaktionbooks.co.uk
web site http://www.reaktionbooks.co.uk
Editorial Director Michael R. Leaman

Art history, design, architecture, history, cultural studies, Asian studies, travel and photography. Founded 1985.

Rebel Inc. – see Canongate Books Ltd*

Red Fox – see Random House Group Ltd*

Reed Books – now Octopus Publishing Group

Reed Business Information

Windsor Court, East Grinstead House, Wood Street, East Grinstead, West Sussex RH19 1XA
tel (01342) 326972 *fax* (01342) 335612
e-mail information@reedinfo.co.uk
web site http://www.reedbusiness.com
Managing Director John Minch

Directories and reference books covering professional and industrial sectors, including *Kompass*, *Kelly's*, *Dial* and *The Bankers' Almanac*. Part of Reed Elsevier plc. Founded 1983.

William Reed Directories

Broadfield Park, Crawley, West Sussex RH11 9RT
tel (01293) 613400 *fax* (01293) 610322
e-mail directories@william-read.co.uk
web site http://www.foodanddrink.co.uk
Managing Director Maria Farmery, *Editorial Manager* Ian Tandy, *Group Sales Manager* Colin Martin

Publishers of leading business-to-business directories and reports, including *The Grocer Marketing Directory* and *The Grocer Food & Drink Directory*.

Reed Educational and Professional Publishing Ltd*

Halley Court, Jordan Hill, Oxford OX2 8EJ
tel (01865) 310533 *fax* (01865) 314641
e-mail reed.educational@repp.co.uk
web site http://www.repp.co.uk
Chief Executive John Philbin

Architectural Press (imprint)
web site http://www.architecturalpress.com
Publisher Neil Warnock-Smith
Architecture, the environment, planning, townscape, building technology; general.

Butterworth Heinemann UK (imprint)
Linacre House, Jordan Hill,
Oxford OX2 8EJ
tel (01865) 310366 *fax* (01865) 310898
web site http://www.bh.com
Managing Director Philip Shaw
Books and electronic products across business, technical, medical fields for students and professionals.

Focal Press (imprint)
web site http://www.focalpress.com
Publisher Jenny Welham
Professional, technical and academic books on photography, broadcasting, film, television, radio, audiovisual and communication media.

Ginn & Co. (imprint)
fax (01865) 314189
Managing Director Paul Shuter
Textbook/other educational resources for primary schools.

Heinemann Educational (imprint)
Managing Director Bob Osborne
Textbooks, literature and other educational resources for all levels.

Newnes (imprint)
fax (01865) 314641
web site http://www.newnespress.com
Publisher Matthew Deans
Technical books in electronics and engineering.

Rigby Heinemann (imprint)
fax (01865) 314189
Managing Director Paul Shuter
Textbook/other educational resources for primary schools.

Religious and Moral Education Press

St Mary's Works, St Mary's Plain, Norwich, Norfolk NR3 3BH
tel (01603) 612914 *fax* (01603) 624483
e-mail admin@scm-canterburypress.co.uk
Publisher Mary Mears

Books for primary and secondary school pupils, college students, and teachers on religious, moral, personal and social education. Division of SCM-Canterbury Press Ltd, a subsidiary of Hymns Ancient & Modern Ltd.

Review – see Hodder Headline Ltd*

Reynolds & Hearn Ltd

61A Priory Road, Kew, Richmond,
Surrey TW9 3DH
tel 020-8940 5198 *fax* 020-8940 7679
e-mail richard.reynolds@rhbooks.com
web site http://www.rhbooks.com
Directors Richard Reynolds (managing), Marcus Hearn (editorial), David O'Leary, Geoffrey Wolfson

Film, TV, entertainment, media. Founded 1999.

Rider – see Random House Group Ltd*

Rigby Heinemann – see Reed Educational and Professional Publishing Ltd*

Rivelin Grapheme Press

Merlin House, Church Street, Hungerford, Berks. RG17 0JG
tel (01488) 684645 *fax* (01488) 683018
Director Snowdon Barnett

Poetry. Send introductory letter enclosing one short poem. Founded 1984.

River Books – see New Cavendish Books

Rivers Oram Press

144 Hemingford Road, London N1 1DE
tel 020-7607 0823 *fax* 020-7609 2776
e-mail ro@riversoram.demon.co.uk
Directors Elizabeth Rivers Fidlon (managing), Anthony Harris

Non-ficton: social and political science, current affairs, social history, gender studies, sexual politics, cultural studies and photography. Founded 1991.

Pandora Press (imprint)
Managing Editor Caroline Lazar

Feminist press publishing. General non-fiction: biography, arts, media, health, current affairs, reference and sexual politics.

Robinson Publishing Ltd – see Constable & Robinson Ltd

Robson Books

10 Blenheim Court, Brewery Road, London N7 9NT
tel 020-7700 7444 *fax* 020-7700 4552
Publisher Jeremy Robson

General non-fiction, biography, music, humour, sport. Unsolicited MSS discouraged; ideas with synopses welcome with sae. A member of the Chrysalis Group plc. Founded 1973.

George Ronald

46 High Street, Kidlington, Oxon OX5 2DN
tel/fax (01235) 529137
e-mail sales@grpubl.demon.co.uk
Managers W. Momen, E. Leith

Religion, specialising in the Baha'i Faith. Founded 1939.

Barry Rose Law Publishers Ltd

Little London, Chichester, West Sussex PO19 1PG
tel (01243) 775552/779174 *fax* (01243) 779278
e-mail books@barry-rose-law.co.uk

Law, local government, police, legal history. Founded 1972.

Countrywise Press

Reprints in paperback of hardcover books from Barry Rose; some non-law titles.

Rosendale Press Ltd

8 Ponsonby Place, London SW1P 4PT
tel 020-7834 1123 *fax* 020-7834 1240
Chairman Timothy S. Green, *Editorial Director* Maureen P. Green

Food and drink, gourmet guides/travel, business and investment, health and lifestyle. No unsolicited MSS. Founded 1987.

Rough Guides Ltd

62-70 Shorts Gardens, London WC2H 9AB
tel 020-7556 5000 *fax* 020-7556 5050
e-mail mail@roughguides.co.uk
web site http://www.roughguides.com
Directors Mark Ellingham, Martin Dunford, John Fisher, Jonathan Buckley, Susanne Hillen, Richard Trillo

Travel guides, music reference guides, reference guides. Founded 1982.

Round Hall Ltd

Sweet & Maxwell Group, 43 Fitzwilliam Place, Dublin 2, Republic of Ireland
tel (01) 6625301 *fax* (01) 6625302
e-mail info@roundhall.ie
Director and General Manager Elanor McGarry

Law.

Roundhouse Publishing Ltd

Millstone, Limers Lane, Northam, North Devon EX39 2RG
tel (01237) 474474 *fax* (01237) 474774
e-mail roundhouse.pub@virgin.net
web site http://www.roundhouse.net
Publisher Alan T. Goodworth

Film, cinema, and performing arts; reference books. No unsolicited MSS. Founded 1991.

Route

School Lane, Glasshoughton, Castleford, West Yorkshire WF10 4QH
tel (01977) 603028 *fax* (01977) 512819
e-mail books@route-online.com

web site http://www.route-online.com
www.openingline.co.uk
Contact Ian Daley
Fiction imprint of Yorkshire Art Circus. Specialises in contemporary fiction and has a commitment to new writing. Looking for novels/novellas and publishes an annual collection of short fiction (check for current theme). Unsolicited MSS discouraged; send for fact sheet or visit web site for submission guidelines. Also manages the writers programme, The Opening Line.

Routledge – see Taylor & Francis Group plc*

RoutledgeFalmer – see Taylor & Francis Group plc*

Royal National Institute for the Blind
PO Box 173, Peterborough, Cambs. PE2 6WS
tel (0845) 7023153 *fax* (01733) 371555
e-mail cservices@rnib.org.uk
web site http://www.rnib.org.uk
textphone (0845) 7585691
Magazines, catalogues and books for blind and partially sighted people, to support daily living, leisure, learning and employment reading needs. Produced in braille, audio, large/legible print, disk and Moon. For complete list of magazines see page 125. Founded 1868.

Ryland Peters & Small
Cavendish House, 51-55 Mortimer Street, London W1N 7TD
tel 020-7436 9090 *fax* 020-7436 9790
e-mail louise.sherwin-stark@rps.co.uk
Directors David Peters (managing), Gabriella Le Grazie (art), Alison Starling (publishing), Joanna Everard (rights), Gerald Wratten (UK sales and marketing), Meryl Silbert (production)
Highly illustrated books on cookery, craft, interiors and gardening. Founded 1995.

SAGE Publications Ltd*
6 Bonhill Street, London EC2A 4PU
tel 020-7374 0645 *fax* 020-7374 8741
e-mail info@sagepub.co.uk
web site http://www.sagepub.co.uk
Directors Stephen Barr (managing), Peter Heilbrunn, Ian Eastment, Mike Birch, Matt Jackson, Ziyad Marar, Richard Fidczuk, Michael Melody (USA), Sara Miller McCune (USA), Paul R. Chapman (USA)
Social sciences, behavioural sciences, humanities, software. Founded 1971.

The Saint Andrew Press*
121 George Street, Edinburgh EH2 4YN
tel 0131-225 5722 *fax* 0131-220 3113
e-mail cofs.standrew@dial.pipex.com
Acting Publishing Manager Derek Auld
Theology and religion, church and local history. Section of Church of Scotland Board of Communication.

St Paul's
St Paul's Publishing, 187 Battersea Bridge Road, London SW11 3AS
tel 020-7978 4300 *fax* 020-7978 4370
e-mail editions@stpauls.org.uk
Theology, ethics, spirituality, biography, education, general books of Roman Catholic and Christian interest. Founded 1948.

Salamander Books Ltd
8 Blenheim Court, Brewery Road, London N7 9NT
tel 020-7700 7799 *fax* 020-7700 3918
Directors David Spence (managing), Colin Gower (sales)
Cookery, crafts, military, natural history, music, gardening, hobbies, transport, sports. Imprint: Vega. A member of the Chrysalis Group plc. Founded 1973.

Sapphire – see Virgin Publishing Ltd

W.B. Saunders Co. Ltd – see Harcourt Publishers Ltd

S.B. Publications
c/o 19 Grove Road, Seaford, East Sussex BN25 1TP
tel (01323) 893498 *fax* (01323) 893860
e-mail sales@sbpublications.swinternet.co.uk
web site http://www.sbpublications.swinternet.co.uk
Proprietor Stephen Benz
Local history (illustrated by postcards/ old photographs), local themes (e.g. walking books, guides), maritime history, transport, specific themes. Founded 1987.

Sceptre – see Hodder Headline Ltd*

Schofield & Sims Ltd
Dogley Mill, Fenay Bridge, Huddersfield HD8 0NQ
tel (01484) 607080 *fax* (01484) 606815
e-mail schofield_and_sims@compuserve.com
Managing Director J. Stephen Platts
Educational: nursery, infants, primary, children's books; posters. Founded 1901.

Scholastic Ltd*
Villiers House, Clarendon Avenue, Leamington Spa, Warks. CV32 5PR
tel 020-7421 9000 *fax* 020-7421 9001
web site http://www.scholastic.co.uk
Directors D.M.R. Kewley (managing), M.R.

Robinson (USA), R.M. Spaulding (USA), D.J. Walsh (USA)

Children's Division
Publishing Director Richard Scrivener

See **Scholastic Children's Books***

Direct Marketing
Managing Director, Book Fair Division Will Oldham, *Managing Director, School Book Clubs and Continuities* Victoria Birkett, *Managing Director* Mike Crossley, *Sales and Marketing Director* Gavin Lang

Children's book clubs and school book fairs.

Educational Division
Publishing Director Anne Peel

Publishers of books for teachers (*Bright Ideas* and other series), primary classroom resources and magazines for teachers (*Child Education, Junior Education* and others). Founded 1964.

Scholastic Children's Books*

Commonwealth House,
1-19 New Oxford Street,
London WC1A 1NU
tel 020-7421 9000 *fax* 020-7421 9001
e-mail publicity@scholastic.co.uk
web site http://www.scholastic.co.uk/zone
Publishing Director Richard Scrivener

Imprint of **Scholastic Ltd**.

David Fickling Books (imprint)
Quality fiction and picture books.

Hippo (imprint)
Children's paperbacks – fiction and non-fiction. No unsolicited MSS.

Little Hippo (imprint)
Picture books.

Point (imprint)
Fiction for 11+.

Scholastic Press (imprint)
Quality fiction.

Science Museum Publications

Science Museum, Exhibition Road,
London SW7 2DD
tel 020-7942 4361 *fax* 020-7942 4362
e-mail publicat@nmsi.ac.uk
web site http://www.nmsi.ac.uk
Publications Manager Ela Ginalska

History of science and technology, public understanding of science, history of photography, railway history, museum guides.

SCM Press*

9-17 St Albans Place, London N1 0NX
tel 020-7359 8033 *fax* 020-7359 0049
e-mail scmpress@btinternet.com
Editor Alex Wright

Theological books with special emphasis on biblical, philosophical and modern theology; books on sociology of religion and religious aspects of current issues. Division of SCM-Canterbury Press Ltd. Founded 1929.

Scottish Academic Press*

22 Hanover Street, Edinburgh EH2 2EP
tel 0131-220 6061 *fax* 0131-225 3991
Editor Dr Douglas Grant

All types of academic books and books of Scottish interest. Founded 1969.

SCP Publishers Ltd*

(trading as Scottish Cultural Press)
Unit 13D, Newbattle Abbey Business Annexe,
Newbattle Road, Dalkeith EH22 3LJ
tel 0131-660 6366 *fax* 0131-660 6414
e-mail scp@sol.co.uk
web site http://www.scottishbooks.com
Director Brian Pugh

Literature, poetry, history, archaeology, biography and environmental history. Founded 1992.

SCP Children's Ltd
(trading as Scottish Children's Press)
tel 0131-660 4757 *fax* 0131-660 6414
Director Avril Gray

Scottish fiction, Scottish non-fiction and Scots language, children's writing.

Scribner – see Simon & Schuster*

Scripture Union*

207-209 Queensway, Bletchley, Milton Keynes, Bucks. MK2 2EB
tel (01908) 856000 *fax* (01908) 856111
e-mail postmaster@scriptureunion.org.uk

Christian books and Bible reading materials for people of all ages; educational and worship resources for churches; children's fiction and non-fiction; adult non-fiction. Founded 1867.

Seafarer Books

102 Redwald Road, Rendlesham, Woodbridge, Suffolk IP12 2TE
tel (01394) 420789
Commissioning Editor Patricia Eve

Books on traditional sailing, mainly narrative.

Search Press Ltd

Wellwood, North Farm Road, Tunbridge Wells, Kent TN2 3DR
tel (01892) 510850 *fax* (01892) 515903
e-mail searchpress@searchpress.com

Directors Martin de la Bédoyère (managing), Rosalind Dace (editorial)

Arts, crafts, leisure, gardening. Founded 1962.

Secker and Warburg – see Random House Group Ltd*

Seren

First Floor, 38-40 Nolton Street, Bridgend CF31 3BN
tel (01656) 663018 *fax* (01656) 649226
e-mail mickfelton@seren.force9.co.uk
Director Mick Felton

Poetry, fiction, drama, history, film, literary criticism, biography, art – mostly with relevance to Wales. Founded 1981.

Serpent's Tail

4 Blackstock Mews, London N4 2BT
tel 020-7354 1949 *fax* 020-7704 6467
e-mail info@serpentstail.com
web site http://www.serpentstail.com
Director Peter Ayrton

Fiction and non-fiction in paperback; literary and non-mainstream work, and work in translation. Approach with query letter please; do not send complete MSS. Sae essential as is familiarity with list. Founded 1986.

Seven Dials – see Cassell & Co

Severn House Publishers

9-15 High Street, Sutton, Surrey SM1 1DF
tel 020-8770 3930 *fax* 020-8770 3850
e-mail editorial@severnhouse.com
web site http://www.severnhouse.com
Chairman Edwin Buckhalter, *Editorial Director* Marisa McGreevy

Hardcover adult fiction for the library market: romances, thrillers, detective, adventure, war, science fiction. No unsolicited MSS.

Shakespeare Head Press – see Blackwell Publishers*

Sheed & Ward Ltd

4 Rickett Street, London SW6 1RU
tel 020-7610 2722 *fax* 020-7610 3373
Directors M.T. Redfern, K.G. Darke, A.M. Redfern

History, philosophy, theology, catechetics, scripture and religion titles, mostly by Catholic authors. Founded 1926.

Sheldon Press – see Society for Promoting Christian Knowledge*

Sheldrake Press

188 Cavendish Road, London SW12 0DA
tel 020-8675 1767 *fax* 020-8675 7736
e-mail mail@sheldrakepress.demon.co.uk
web site http://www.sheldrakepress.demon.co.uk
Publisher J.S. Rigge

History, travel, architecture, cookery, music; stationery. Founded 1979.

Shepheard-Walwyn (Publishers) Ltd

Suite 34, 26 Charing Cross Road, London WC2H 0DH
tel 020-7240 5992 *fax* 020-7379 5770
e-mail books@shepheard-walwyn.co.uk
Directors A.R.A. Werner, M.M. Werner

History, political economy, philosophy; illustrated gift books, some originated in calligraphy; Scottish interest. Founded 1971.

John Sherratt & Son Ltd

Hotspur House, 2 Gloucester Street, Manchester M1 5QR
tel 0161-236 9963 *fax* 0161-236 2026
Managing Director P.A. Westaway

Educational (primary, secondary, technical, university), medical, practical handbooks, collectors' books.

Shire Publications Ltd

Cromwell House, Church Street, Princes Risborough, Bucks. HP27 9AA
tel (01844) 344301 *fax* (01844) 347080
e-mail shire@shirebooks.co.uk
web site http://www.shirebooks.co.uk
Director J.W. Rotheroe

Discovering paperbacks, Shire Albums, Shire Archaeology, Shire Natural History, Shire Ethnography, Shire Egyptology, Shire Garden History. Founded 1966.

Sidgwick & Jackson – see Macmillan Publishers Ltd*

Sigma Press

1 South Oak Lane, Wilmslow, Cheshire SK9 6AR
tel (01625) 531035 *fax* (01625) 536800
e-mail info@sigmapress.co.uk
web site http://www.sigmapress.co.uk
Partners Graham Beech, Diana Beech

Leisure: country walking, cycling, regional heritage, sport, cookery, health, fitness, folklore. Founded 1979.

Signet Books – former imprint of Michael Joseph/Penguin

Silhouette – see Harlequin Mills & Boon Ltd*

Simon & Schuster*

Africa House, 64-78 Kingsway,
London WC2B 6AH
tel 020-7316 1900 *fax* 020-7316 0333
Directors Ian Chapman (managing), Suzanne Baboneau (fiction publisher), Martin Fletcher (editorial, mass-market fiction and Scribner), Diane Spivey (rights), Helen Gummer (editorial, non-fiction)

Fiction; non-fiction: reference, music, travel, mass-market paperbacks. Founded 1986.

Earthlight (imprint)
Science fiction and fantasy.

Pocket Books (imprint)
Mass-market fiction and non-fiction paperbacks.

Scribner (imprint)
Literary fiction.

Simon & Schuster Audioworks
Fiction, non-fiction and business.

Touchstone (imprint)
Quality upmarket non-fiction paperbacks.

Skoob Books Ltd

76A Oldfield Road, London N16 0RS
tel/fax 020-7275 9811
e-mail books@skoob.com
web site http://www.skoob.com
Director I.K. Ong, *Editorial* M. Lovell

Literary guides, cultural studies, oriental literature. Unsolicited summaries with samples and sae welcome. Founded 1979.

Sleepy Hollow Pantomimes – see Dublar Scripts

Smith Gryphon Ltd – see Blake Publishing

Colin Smythe Ltd*

PO Box 6, Gerrards Cross,
Bucks. SL9 8XA
tel (01753) 886000 *fax* (01753) 886469
web site http://www.colinsmythe.co.uk
Directors Colin Smythe (managing and editorial), Peter Bander van Duren, A. Norman Jeffares, Ann Saddlemyer, Leslie Hayward

Biography, phaleristics, heraldry, Irish literature and literary criticism, folklore, crafts and history. Founded 1966.

Society for Promoting Christian Knowledge*

Holy Trinity Church, Marylebone Road,
London NW1 4DU
tel 020-7387 5282 *fax* 020-7388 2352
e-mail publishing@spck.co.uk
Director of Publishing Simon Kingston

Founded 1698.

Azure Books (imprint)
Editor Alison Barr
Biography and letters, personal growth and relationships, history, humour, spirituality, travel.

Sheldon Press (imprint)
Editorial Director Joanna Moriarty
Popular medicine, health, self-help, psychology, business.

SPCK (imprint)
Editorial Director Joanna Moriarty
Theology and academic, liturgy, prayer, spirituality, biblical studies, educational resources, mission, gospel and culture.

Triangle (imprint)
Editor Alison Barr
Popular Christian paperbacks.

Society of Genealogists Enterprises Ltd

14 Charterhouse Buildings, Goswell Road,
London EC1M 7BA
tel 020-7251 8799 *fax* 020-7250 1800
e-mail sales@sog.org.uk
web site http://www.sog.org.uk/
Managing Director Robert I.N. Gordon, *General Manager* Andrew Rylah

Genealogy and family history books, and guides to records.

South Street Press – see Garnet Publishing Ltd

Souvenir Press Ltd

43 Great Russell Street, London WC1B 3PA
tel 020-7580 9307-8 and 7637 5711/2/3
Managing Director Ernest Hecht BSc (Econ), BCom

Archaeology, biography and memoirs, educational (secondary, technical), fiction, general, humour, practical handbooks, psychiatry, psychology, sociology, sports, games and hobbies, travel, supernatural, parapsychology, illustrated books.

SPCK – see Society for Promoting Christian Knowledge*

Neville Spearman Publishers – see The C.W. Daniel Company Ltd

Specialist Crafts Ltd

(formerly Dryad)
PO Box 247, Leicester LE1 9QS
tel 0116-251 0405 *fax* 0116-251 5015
e-mail post@speccrafts.co.uk

web site http://www.speccrafts.co.uk
Joint Managing Director P.A. Crick
'How to' booklets on various art and craft skills. *Specialist Crafts 500* series full colour craft booklets and patterns. Suppliers of over 9000 art and craft items.

Spellmount Ltd
The Old Rectory, Staplehurst, Kent TN12 0AZ
tel (01580) 893730 *fax* (01580) 893731
e-mail enquiries@spellmount.com
web site http://www.spellmount.com
Proprietor Jamie A.G. Wilson
Ancient, 15th through to 20th century history/military history. Send sae with submissions please. Founded 1984.

Spindlewood – see Ragged Bears Publishing Ltd

Spon Press – see Taylor & Francis Group plc*

Springer-Verlag London Ltd
Sweetapple House, Catteshall Road, Godalming, Surrey GU7 3DJ
tel (01483) 418800 *fax* (01483) 415151
e-mail postmaster@svl.co.uk
web site http://www.springer.co.uk
Managing Director John Watson, *Executive Directors* D. Goetz, R. Gebauer
Medicine, computing, engineering, astronomy, mathematics, food science. Founded 1972.

Stacey International
128 Kensington Church Street, London W8 4BH
tel 020-7221 7166 *fax* 020-7792 9288
e-mail stacey_international@compuserve.com
Directors Max Scott (managing), Kitty Carruthers (publishing executive), Tom Stacey (consultant)
Illustrated non-fiction, encyclopedic books on regions and countries, Islamic and Arab subjects, world affairs, art, travel, belles-lettres. Founded 1974.

Stainer & Bell Ltd
PO Box 110, Victoria House, 23 Gruneisen Road, London N3 1DZ
tel 020-8343 3303 *fax* 020-843 3024
e-mail post@stainer.co.uk
web site http://www.stainer.co.uk
Directors Keith Wakefield (joint managing), Carol Wakefield (joint managing and secretary), John Hosier CBE, Antony Kearns, Andrew Pratt, Nicholas Williams
Books on music, religious communication. Founded 1907.

Harold Starke Publishers Ltd*
Pixey Green, Stadbroke, Eye, Suffolk IP21 5NG
tel (01379) 388334 *fax* (01379) 388335
203 Bunyan Court, Barbican, London EC2Y 8DH
tel 0171-588 5195
Directors Harold K. Starke, Naomi Galinski (editorial)
Specialist, scientific, medical, reference.

Stainer & Bell Ltd – see (Ireland) Government Supplies Agency

The Stationery Office/National Publishing*
Head office St Crispins, Duke Street, Norwich NR3 1PD
tel (0870) 6005522 *fax* (0870) 6005533
e-mail orders@bheso.co.uk
web site http://www.tso-online.co.uk
Chief Executive, National Publishing Fred Perkins, *Business Development Director* Kevan Lawton
Archaeology, architecture, art, business, current affairs, directories and guidebooks, educational (primary, secondary, technical, university), general, heritage, history, naval and military, medical, pharmaceutical, professional, practical handbooks, reference, science, sociology, yearbooks (including *Whitaker's Almanack*).

Patrick Stephens Ltd – see Haynes Publishing, Special Interest Publishing Division

Sterling Publishing Group plc
PO Box 839, 86-88 Edgware Road, London W2 2YW
tel 020-7258 0066 *fax* 020-7723 5766
Chairman Christopher Haines, *Chief Executive* Simone Kesseler, *Directors* R. Harrison, D. Watson, L.S. Garman, C. Gillings, R. Panton Corbett
International business-to-business publishing. Reference, management and technology directories, leisure, commemorative publishing, exhibition organising. Founded 1978.

Stride Publications
11 Sylvan Road, Exeter, Devon EX4 6EW
e-mail rml@madbear.demon.co.uk
web site http://www.madbear.demon.co.uk/stride
Managing Editor Rupert M. Loydell
Poetry, literary experimental novels and short fiction collections, contemporary music and visual arts, interviews. Submissions in writing only (not by e-mail). Founded 1980.

Summersdale Publishers Ltd

46 West Street, Chichester, West Sussex PO19 1RP
tel (01243) 771107 *fax* (01243) 786300
e-mail enquiries@summersdale.com
web site http://www.summersdale.com
Editor Liz Kershaw

Travel, humour, gift books, TV/film tie-ins, and Internet publishing. Seeking strong, commercial non-fiction. Founded 1990.

Sunflower Books

12 Kendrick Mews, London SW7 3HG
tel/fax 020-7589 1862
e-mail mail@sunflowerbooks.co.uk
web site http://www.sunflowerbooks.co.uk/
Directors P.A. Underwood (editorial), J.G. Underwood, S.J. Seccombe

Travel guidebooks.

Sussex Academic Press

PO Box 2950, Brighton BN2 5SP
tel (01273) 699533 *fax* (01273) 621262
e-mail edit@sussex-academic.co.uk
web site http://www.sussex-academic.co.uk
Editorial Director Anthony Grahame

Theology and religion, British history and Middle East studies. Founded 1994.

The Alpha Press (imprint)
Religion, history, sport.

Sutton Publishing Ltd

Phoenix Mill, Thrupp, Stroud, Glos. GL5 2BU
tel (01453) 731114 *fax* (01453) 731117
Directors David Hogg (managing), Peter Clifford (publishing), Nick Carter (sales and marketing)

General and academic publishers of high quality illustrated books: history, military, biography, transport, archaeology. Founded 1978.

Swan Hill Press – see Airlife Publishing Ltd

Swedenborg Society

20-21 Bloomsbury Way, London WC1A 2TH
tel 020-7405 7986 *fax* 020-7831 5848
e-mail swed.soc@netmatters.co.uk
web site http://www.swedenborg.co.uk

The Writings of Swedenborg.

Sweet & Maxwell*

100 Avenue Road, London NW3 3PF
tel 020-7393 7000 *fax* 020-7393 7010
Directors Mike Dixon (managing), Jackie Rhodes, Barbara Grandage, Alina Lourie, Derek Sturdy, Antonia Rodgers, Anthony Kinahan, Kevin Waterman, Anne Hayes, Christine Miskin, Janson Woodhall, Alan Wells, Paul Riddle

Law. Part of Thomson Professional Information UK. Founded 1799; incorporated 1889.

Take That Ltd

PO Box 200, Harrogate, North Yorkshire HG1 2YR
tel (01423) 507545 *fax* (01423) 526035
e-mail sales@takethat.co.uk
web site http://www.takethat.co.uk
Managing Director Chris Brown

Internet/computing, business, finance, gambling. Send sae with synopsis/samples. Founded 1986.

Tamarind Ltd

PO Box 52, Northwood, Middlesex HA6 1UN
tel 020-8866 8808 *fax* 020-8866 5627
e-mail tamrindltd@aol.com
Managing Director Verna Wilkins

Multicultural children's picture books and educational material. Publications give a high positive profile to black children. Unsolicited material welcome with return postage. Founded 1987.

Tango Books – imprint of Sadie Fields Productions Ltd, book packagers

Tarquin Publications

Stradbroke, Diss, Norfolk IP21 5JP
tel (01379) 384218 *fax* (01379) 384289
e-mail tarquin-books.demon.co.uk
web site http://www.tarquin-books.demon.co.uk
Partners Gerald Jenkins, Margaret Jenkins

Mathematics and mathematical models; paper cutting, paper engineering and pop-up books for intelligent children. No unsolicited MSS; send suggestion or synopsis in first instance. Founded 1970.

Tate Gallery Publishing Ltd

Millbank, London SW1P 4RG
tel 020-7887 8869/70 *fax* 020-7887 8878
Managing Director Celia Clear, *Senior Manager* Brian McGahon, *Sales and Marketing Manager* Daniel Scott, *Production Manager* Tim Holton, *Head of Licensing* Emma Williams

Publishers for Tate in London, Liverpool and St Ives. Exhibition catalogues, art books, diaries, calendars, posters and stationery in the field of British and modern art. Founded 1996.

I.B.Tauris & Co. Ltd

Victoria House, Bloomsbury Square, London WC1B 4DZ
tel 020-7831 9060 *fax* 020-7831 9061
e-mail mail@ibtauris.com
web site http://www.ibtauris.com
Directors I. Bagherzade (chairman and publisher), Jonathan McDonnell (managing)

History, biography, politics, international relations, current affairs, Middle East, cultural and media studies, film, art, archaeology, travel guides. Founded 1983.

British Academic Press (imprint)
Academic monographs on history, political science and social sciences.

Tauris Parke Books (imprint)
Illustrated books on architecture, design, photography, cultural history and travel.

Tauris Parke Paperbacks (imprint)
Non-fiction trade paperbacks: biography, history, travel, cinema, art, cultural history.

Taylor & Francis Group plc*

11 New Fetter Lane, London EC4P 4EE
tel 020-7583 9855 *fax* 020-7842 2298
e-mail info@tandf.co.uk
web site http://www.tandf.co.uk
Chief Executive Anthony R. Selvey, *Managing Director, Taylor & Francis Books Ltd* Roger Horton

Europa Publications (imprint)
See page 170.

Garland Publishing (imprint)
Science textbooks and scholarly works.

Psychology Press Ltd
See page 196.

Routledge (imprint)
web site http://www.routledge.com
Addiction, anthropology, archaeology, Asian studies, business, classical studies, counselling, criminology, development and environment, dictionaries, economics, education, geography, health, history, Japanese studies, library science, language, linguistics, literary criticism, media and culture, nursing, performance studies, philosophy, politics, psychiatry, psychology, reference, social administration, social studies/sociology, women's studies.

RoutledgeFalmer (imprint)
Education books.

Spon Press (imprint)
Architecture, civil engineering, construction, leisure and recreation management, sports science.

Taylor & Francis (imprint)
Educational (university), science: physics, mathematics, chemistry, electronics, natural history, pharmacology and drug metabolism, toxicology, technology, history of science, ergonomics, production engineering, remote sensing, geographic information systems.

UCL Press (imprint)
History, philosophy, politics, cultural studies, planning and geography, social research methods, sociology.

Teach Yourself – see Hodder Headline Ltd*

Telegraph Books

The Daily Telegraph, 1 Canada Square, Canary Wharf, London E14 5DT
tel 020-7538 6826 *fax* 020-7538 6064
Publisher Susannah Charlton

Business, personal finance, crosswords, sport, travel and guides, cookery and wine, general, gardening, history – all by *Telegraph* journalists and contributors, and co-published with major publishing houses. Founded 1920.

Tellastory – see Random House Group Ltd*

Tempus Publishing Group Ltd

The Mill, Brimscombe Port, Stroud, Glos. GL5 2QG
tel (01453) 883300 *fax* (01453) 883233
Directors Alan Sutton (chief executive), Paul Raffle (finance), Michael Walton (operations), Kirsty Sutton (operations, USA), Peter Kemmis Betty (publishing)

Local history: England, Scotland, Ireland, Wales; sport; industrial and transport history, archaeology. Founded 1993.

Thames & Hudson Ltd*

181A High Holborn, London WC1V 7QX
tel 020-7845 5000 *fax* 020-7845 5050
e-mail mail@thameshudson.co.uk
web site http://www.thamesandhudson.com
Directors T.M. Neurath (managing), S. Baron (editorial), J.R. Camplin (editorial), N. Stangos (editorial), T.L. Evans (sales and marketing), C.M. Kaine (design)

Illustrated non-fiction for an international audience, especially art, architecture, graphic design, garden and landscape design, archaeology, cultural history, historical reference, fashion, photography, ethnic arts, mythology and religion.

Thames Publishing

14 Barlby Road, London W10 6AR
tel/fax 020-8969 3579
Publishing Manager John Bishop

Books about music (not pop), particularly British composers and musicians. Preliminary letter essential. Founded 1970.

D.C. Thomson & Co. Ltd – Publications

2 Albert Square, Dundee DD1 9QJ
London office 185 Fleet Street, London EC4A 2HS

Publishers of newspapers and periodicals. Children's books (annuals), based on weekly magazine characters; fiction. For fiction guidelines, send a large sae to Central Fiction Dept.

Stanley Thornes (Publishers) Ltd – see Nelson Thornes Ltd*

Thorsons – see HarperCollins Publishers*

Times Books – see HarperCollins Publishers*

Titan Books

144 Southwark Street, London SE1 0UP
tel 020-7620 0200 *fax* 020-7620 0032
e-mail readerfeedback@titanemail.com
Publisher and Managing Director Nick Landau, *Editorial Director* Katy Wild

Graphic novels, including *Simpsons* and *Batman*, featuring comic strip material; film and TV tie-ins and cinema reference books, including *Star Wars* and *Star Trek*. No fiction or children's proposals and no unsolicited material without preliminary letter please; send large sae for current author guidelines. Division of Titan Publishing Group Ltd. Founded 1981.

Tolkien – see HarperCollins Publishers*

Tolley – see Butterworths Tolley

Touchstone – see Simon & Schuster*

Town House and Country House†

Trinity House, Charleston Road, Ranelagh, Dublin 6, Republic of Ireland
tel (01) 4972399 *fax* (01) 4970927
e-mail books@townhouse.ie
Directors Treasa Coady, Jim Coady

General illustrated non-fiction, popular fiction, art, archaeology and biography. Founded 1981.

Transworld Publishers*

61-63 Uxbridge Road, London W5 5SA
tel 020-8579 2652 *fax* 020-8579 5479
e-mail info@transworld-publishers.co.uk
Managing Director Mark Barty-King, *Deputy Managing Directors* Barry Hempstead (operations), Patrick Janson-Smith (publishing), *Deputy Publisher, Adult Trade Books* Larry Finlay, *Associate Publisher* Honor Wilson-Fletcher, *Publisher, Children's and Young Adult Books* Philippa Dickinson

Division of **Random House Group Ltd**; subsidiary of Bertelsmann AG.

Anchor (imprint)
Publisher John Saddler
Literary fiction and non-fiction.

Bantam (imprint)
Publishing Director Francesca Liversidge
Paperback general fiction and non-fiction.

Bantam Press (imprint)
Publishing Director Sally Gaminara
Fiction, general, cookery, business, crime, health and diet, history, humour, military, music, paranormal, self-help, science, travel and adventure, biography and autobiography.

Bantam Children's Books (division)
Publisher Philippa Dickinson
Paperback young adult books and series.

Black Swan (imprint)
Editorial Director Bill Scott-Kerr
Paperback quality fiction.

Corgi (imprint)
Editorial Director Bill Scott-Kerr
Paperback general fiction and non-fiction.

Corgi Children's Books (division)
Publisher Philippa Dickinson
Children's paperback picture books, fiction and poetry.

Doubleday (UK) (imprint)
Publisher Marianne Velmans
General fiction and non-fiction.

Doubleday Children's Books (imprint)
Publisher Philippa Dickinson
Hardback picture books, fiction and poetry for children.

Also: Expert Gardening Books, IDG Computer Books *Frommer's* Travel Guides, *Cliffs Notes*.

Treehouse Children's Books Ltd

Page Farm, Newtown, West Pennard, Glastonbury, Somerset BA6 8NN
tel (01458) 835757 *fax* (01458) 835758
e-mail richard.powell4@virgin.net
Editorial Director Richard Powell

Preschool children's books and novelty books. Founded 1989.

Trentham Books Ltd*

Westview House, 734 London Road, Oakhill, Stoke-on-Trent, Staffs. ST4 5NP
tel (01782) 745567 *fax* (01782) 745553
e-mail tb@trentham.books.co.uk
web site http://www.trentham-books.co.uk

Editorial office 28 Hillside Gardens,
London N6 5ST
tel 020-8348 2174
Directors Prof John Eggleston (managing), Dr Gillian Klein (editorial), Barbara Wiggins (executive)

Education (including specialist fields – multi-ethnic issues, equal opportunities, bullying, design and technology, early years), social policy, sociology of education, European education, women's studies. Does not publish books for use by parents or children, or fiction, biography, reminiscences and poetry. Founded 1978.

Triangle – see Society for Promoting Christian Knowledge*

Trotman & Company Ltd

2 The Green, Richmond, Surrey TW9 1PL
tel 020-8486 1150 *fax* 020-8486 1161
web site http://www.trotmanpublishing.co.uk
Chairman A.F. Trotman, *Publishing Director* Morfydd Jones

Higher education guidance, careers, classroom resources. Founded 1970.

Two-Can Design – see act-two ltd*

UCL Press Ltd – see Taylor & Francis Group plc*

Unicorn Books

16 Laxton Gardens, Paddock Wood,
Kent TN12 6BB
tel (01892) 833648 *fax* (01892) 833577
Director R. Green

Militaria, music, transport.

University of Exeter Press*

Reed Hall, Streatham Drive, Exeter,
Devon EX4 4QR
tel (01392) 263066 *fax* (01392) 263064
e-mail uep @exeter.ac.uk
web site http://www.ex.ac.uk/uep/
Publisher Simon Baker

Academic and scholarly books on history, local history (Exeter and the South West), archaeology, classical studies, English literature, film history, performance studies, medieval studies, linguistics, modern languages, European studies, maritime studies, mining history. Founded 1958.

University of Wales Press

6 Gwennyth Street, Cathays,
Cardiff CF24 4YD
tel 029-2023 1919 *fax* 029-2023 0908
e-mail press@press.wales.ac.uk
web site http://www.wales.ac.uk/press
Director Susan Jenkins

Academic and educational (Welsh and English). Publishers of *Welsh History Review, Studia Celtica, Llên Cymru, Y Gwyddonydd, Efrydiau Athronyddol, Contemporary Wales, Welsh Journal of Education, Journal of Celtic Linguistics,* ALT-J (Association for Learning Technology Journal), *Borderlines, Kantian Review. Founded 1922.*

Merlin Unwin Books

Palmers House, 7 Corve Street, Ludlow,
Shropshire SY8 1DB
tel (01584) 877456 *fax* (01584) 877457
e-mail books@merlinunwin.co.uk
web site http://www.merlinunwin.co.uk
Proprietor Merlin Unwin

Fishing and country books. Founded 1990.

Unwin Hyman Academic – incorporated into Routledge; see Taylor and Francis Group plc*

Unwin Hyman Ltd – acquired by HarperCollins Publishers*

Usborne Publishing*

Usborne House, 83-85 Saffron Hill,
London EC1N 8RT
tel 020-7430 2800 *fax* 020-7430 1562
e-mail mail@usborne.co.uk
Directors Peter Usborne, Jenny Tyler (editorial), Robert Jones, David Lowe, Keith Ball, David Harte, Lorna Hunt, Richard Curry

Children's books: reference, practical, craft, natural history, science, languages, history, geography, fiction. Founded 1973.

V&A Publications

160 Brompton Road, London SW3 1HW
tel 020-7938 9663 *fax* 020-7938 9973
web site http://www.vam.ac.uk
Head of Publications Mary Butler

Popular and scholarly books on fine and decorative arts, architecture, contemporary design, fashion and photography. Founded 1980.

Van Nostrand Reinhold – acquired by John Wiley & Sons Inc.; see overseas book publishers, page 247

Variorum – see Ashgate Publishing Ltd

Ventura – see Penguin UK*

Veritas Publications†

Veritas House, 7-8 Lower Abbey Street, Dublin 1, Republic of Ireland
tel (01) 8788177 *fax* (01) 8786507

Religion, including social and educational works, and material relating to the media of communication. An agency of the Irish Catholic Bishops' Commission on Communications.

Vermilion – see Random House Group Ltd*

Verso Ltd

6 Meard Street, London W1V 3HR
tel 020-7437 3546 *fax* 020-7734 0059
e-mail verso@verso.co.uk
Directors George Galfalvi (executive chairman), Colin Robinson (managing), Robin Blackburn, Tariq Ali, Perry Anderson

Politics, sociology, economics, history, philosophy, cultural studies. Founded 1970.

Viking – see Penguin UK*

Viking Children's – see Penguin UK*

Vintage – see Random House Group Ltd*

Virago – see Little, Brown and Company (UK)*

Virgin Publishing Ltd

Thames Wharf Studios, Rainville Road, London W6 9HA
tel 020-7386 3300 *fax* 020-7386 3360
Chairman Robert Devereux, *Directors* Robert Shreeve (managing), Kenneth Ibbett, *Management* Humphrey Price (editorial director, general), Carolyn Thorne (editorial director, illustrated), Louise Cavanagh (publishing director, travel), K.T. Forster (international sales), Amy Nelson-Bennett (marketing), Susan Atkinson (publicity), Ray Mudie (sales), Nigel Williams (financial), Rod Green (senior editor, general)

Virgin (imprint)
Editorial Humphrey Price (general non-fiction), Carolyn Thorne (illustrated), Rod Green (general, film and TV tie-ins, humour), Louise Cavanagh (travel), Jonathan Taylor (sport), David Gould (reference), Ian Gittins (music)

Popular culture: entertainment, showbiz, arts, film and TV, music, humour, biography and autobiography, popular reference, true crime, sport, travel.

Black Lace (imprint)
Senior Editor Kerri Sharp

Erotic fiction by women for women.

Idol (imprint)
Editor Kathleen Bryson

Homoerotic fiction for men.

Nexus (imprint)
Editor James Marriott

Erotic fiction.

Sapphire (imprint)
Editor Kathleen Bryson

Lesbian erotic fiction.

Virtue Books Ltd

Edward House, Tenter Street, Rotherham S60 1LB
tel (01709) 365005 *fax* (01709) 829982
Directors Peter E. Russum, Margaret H. Russum, Michael G. Virtue (editorial)

Books for the professional chef, catering and drink.

The Vital Spark – see Neil Wilson Publishing Ltd

VNR – see Wiley Europe Ltd*

Voyager – see HarperCollins Publishers*

Walker Books Ltd*

87 Vauxhall Walk, London SE11 5HJ
tel 020-7793 0909 *fax* 020-7587 1123
e-mail mail@walkerbooks.co.uk
Directors David Heatherwick, David Lloyd, Roger Alexander, Michael Blake, Judy Burdsall, Amelia Edwards, Sarah Foster, Harold G. Gould OBE, Mike McGrath, Henryk Wesolowski, Jane Winterbotham, *Company Secretary* Richard Wilkinson

Children's – mainly picture books; junior and teenage fiction. Founded 1979.

Warburg Institute

University of London, Woburn Square, London WC1H 0AB
tel 020-7862 8949 *fax* 020-7862 8955
e-mail warburg@sas.ac.uk
web site http://www.sas.ac.uk/warburg/

Cultural and intellectual history, with special reference to the history of the classical tradition.

Ward Lock – see Cassell & Co

Ward Lock Educational Co. Ltd

BIC Ling Kee House, 1 Christopher Road, East Grinstead, West Sussex RH19 3BT
tel (01342) 318980 *fax* (01342) 410980
Directors Au Bak Ling (chairman, Hong Kong), Au King Kwok (Hong Kong), Au Wai Kwok (Hong Kong), Albert Kw Au (Hong Kong), *General Manager* Penny Kitchenham

Primary and secondary pupil materials, Kent Mathematics Project: KMP BASIC and KMP Main series covering Reception to GCSE, Reading Workshops, Take Part

Series and Take Part Starters, teachers' books, music books, Target Series for the National Curriculum: Target Science and Target Geography, religious education. Founded 1952.

Frederick Warne – see Penguin UK*

Warner – see Little, Brown and Company (UK)*

Warner/Chappell Plays Ltd – see Josef Weinberger Plays Ltd

The Watts Publishing Group Ltd*
96 Leonard Street, London EC2A 4XD
tel 020-7739 2929 *fax* 020-7739 2318
Directors Marlene Johnson (managing), Francesca Dow (publishing, Orchard), Philippa Stewart (publishing, Franklin Watts), George Spicer (sales), Elaine Ward (production), Claire Hurst (rights)

Cat's Whiskers (imprint)
Publishing Director Philippa Stewart
Children's picture books.

Franklin Watts (division)
Publishing Director Philippa Stewart
Children's illustrated non-fiction, reference, education. Imprint: Aladdin/Watts.

Orchard Books (division)
Publishing Director Francesca Dow
Children's picture books, fiction, poetry, novelty books, board books.

Wayland – now Hodder Wayland – see Hodder Headline Ltd*

Websters International Publishers Ltd
2nd Floor, Axe & Bottle Court, 70 Newcomen Street, London SE1 1YT
tel 020-7940 4700 *fax* 020-7940 4701
Chairman and Publisher Adrian Webster, *Managing Director* Jean-Luc Barbanneau, *Publishing Director* Susannah Webster
Wine, food, travel, health. Founded 1983.

Weidenfeld & Nicolson – see Cassell & Co

Josef Weinberger Plays Ltd
12-14 Mortimer Street, London W1N 7RD
tel 020-7580 2827 *fax* 020-7436 9016
e-mail general.info@jwmail.co.uk
web site http://www.josef-weinberger.com
Stage plays only, in both acting and trade editions. Preliminary letter essential.

Wharncliffe – see Pen & Sword Books Ltd

Which? Ltd*
2 Marylebone Road, London NW1 4DF
tel 020-7770 7000 *fax* 020-7770 7660
e-mail books@which.net
Chief Executive Sheila McKechnie, *Head of Publishing* Gill Rowley
Part of Consumers' Association. Founded 1957.

Which? Books (imprint)
Travel, restaurant, hotel and wine guides, medicine, law and personal finance for the layman, gardening, careers, DIY – all branded *Which? Books*.

J. Whitaker & Sons Ltd*
12 Dyott Street, London WC1A 1DF
tel 020-7420 6000 *fax* 020-7836 2909
Directors Jonathan Nowell, Chris Ostrom, Paul Pounsford, Richard Knight, Martin Whitaker (managing)
Reference including *The Bookseller* (1858), *Whitaker's Books in Print* (1874), and other book trade directories.

Whittet Books Ltd
Hill Farm, Stonham Road, Cotton, Stowmarket, Suffolk IP14 4RQ
tel (01449) 781877 *fax* (01449) 781898
e-mail annabel@whittet.dircon.co.uk
Directors Annabel Whittet, John Whittet
Natural history, countryside, poultry, pets, horses. Founded 1976.

Whurr Publishers Ltd*
19B Compton Terrace, London N1 2UN
tel 020-7359 5979 *fax* 020-7226 5290
e-mail info@whurr.co.uk
Managing Director Colin Whurr
Disorders of human communication, medicine, psychology, psychiatry, psychotherapy, occupational therapy, physiotherapy, nursing. Founded 1987.

Wiley Europe Ltd*
(incorporating Interscience Publishers)
Baffins Lane, Chichester, West Sussex PO19 1UD
tel (01243) 779777 *fax* (01243) 775878
e-mail europe@wiley.co.uk
web site http://www.wiley.co.uk
Managing Director J.H. Jarvis, *Publishing Director, P&T Division* S. Mair, *Director, STM Journal Publishing* M. Davis, *Director, STM Book Publishing* E. Kirkwood
Physics, chemistry, mathematics, statistics, engineering, architecture, computer science, biology, medicine, earth science, psychology, business, economics, finance. Imprints: Chancery Law, Halsted Press, Interscience, Jossey-Bass, Wiley-

Heyden, Wiley-Interscience, Wiley-Liss, Wiley ValuSource, WILEY-VCH, VNR.

Willow – see HarperCollins Publishers*

Neil Wilson Publishing Ltd*

303A The Pentagon Centre, 36 Washington Street, Glasgow G3 8AZ
tel 0141-221 1117 *fax* 0141-221 5363
e-mail info@nwp.sol.co.uk
web site http://www.nwp.co.uk
Managing Director Neil Wilson

The Angels' Share (imprint)
web site http://www.angelshare.co.uk
Whisky-related matters (leisure, reference, history, memoir); other food and drink categories.

11:9 (imprint)
tel 0141-221 1109
web site http://www.11-9.co.uk
Scottish Arts Council/National Lottery-funded project to bring new Scottish fiction writing to the marketplace.

In Pinn (imprint)
web site http://www.theinpinn.co.uk
The outdoors: travel, hillwalking, climbing, fishing.

NWP (imprint)
Scottish interest subjects including history, biography, culture and reference.

The Vital Spark (imprint)
web site http://www.vitalspark.co.uk
Scottish humour.

Philip Wilson Publishers Ltd

143-149 Great Portland Street, London W1N 5FB
tel 020-7436 4490 *fax* 020-7436 4403
e-mail pwp@monoclick.co.uk
Chairman P. Wilson
Fine and applied art, collecting, museums. Founded 1975.

The Windrush Press

Little Window, High Street, Moreton-in-Marsh, Glos. GL56 0LL
tel (01608) 652012/652025 *fax* (01608) 652125
e-mail windrush@windrushpress.com
web site http://www.windrushpress.com
Managing Director Geoffrey Smith, *Publishing Director* Victoria Huxley
History, military history, *The Traveller's History* series, ancient mysteries, humour. Founded 1987.

Wisley Handbooks – former imprint of Cassell & Co

Woburn Press – see Frank Cass & Co. Ltd

Wolfhound Press[†]

68 Mountjoy Square, Dublin 1, Republic of Ireland
tel (01) 8740354 *fax* (01) 8720207
Publisher Seamus Cashman, *Editor* Emer Ryan
Literary studies and criticism, fiction, art, biography, history, young readers, children's and teenage fiction, law, gift titles, cookery, general non-fiction. Submissions with IRCs. Founded 1974.

The Women's Press

34 Great Sutton Street, London EC1V 0DX
tel 020-7251 3007 *fax* 020-7608 1938
web site http://www.the-womens-press.com
Managing Director Elsbeth Lindner
Books by women in the areas of literary and crime fiction, biography and autobiography, health, politics, handbooks, literary criticism, psychology and self-help, the arts. Founded 1978.

Livewire (imprint)
Books for young women.

Woodhead Publishing Ltd

Abington Hall, Abington, Cambridge CB1 6AH
tel (01223) 891358 *fax* (01223) 893694
e-mail wp@woodhead-publishing.com
web site http://www.woodhead-publishing.com
Managing Director Martin Woodhead
Materials engineering, welding, textiles, finance, investment, banking, business, food science and technology. Founded 1989.

Wordsworth Editions Ltd*

6 London Street, London W2 1HL
tel 020-7706 8822 *fax* 020-7706 8833
e-mail editorial@wordsworth-editions.com
Directors Michael Trayler (managing), Helen Trayler (operations), Laelia Hartnoll (editorial)
Reprints of classic books: literary, children's, American, women's, military; myth, legend and folklore; poetry; reference. Founded 1987.

World International Ltd

Deanway Technology Centre, Wilmslow Road, Handforth, Cheshire SK9 3FB
tel (01625) 650011 *fax* (01625) 650040
e-mail sales@egmont.uk.com
Directors Ian Findlay (managing), David Smith (finance), David Riley (publishing)
Books for children of all ages; early learning, activity, annuals; character publishing including *Mr Men*.

Writers & Readers Ltd

2A Britannia Row, London N1 8PA
tel 020-7226 2522 *fax* 020-7359 1406

e-mail begin@writersandreaders.com
web site http://www.writersandreaders.com
Publisher Glenn Thompson

African/Black studies, architecture, performing arts, media, history, music, philosophy, photography, poetry, political studies, psychology, religion, science, social issues, spirit and body, US studies, women/ gender studies, *For Beginners* documentary comic book series. No unsolicited MSS. Founded 1974.

Black Butterfly (imprint)
Multicultural children's books.

Harlem River Press (imprint)
Poetry anthologies and spiritual writing by Black women writers, Black political studies.

X Libris – see Little, Brown and Company (UK)*

The X Press

6 Hoxton Square, London N1 6NU
tel 020-7729 1199 *fax* 020-7729 1771
e-mail vibes@xpress.co.uk
Editorial Director Dotun Adebayo, *Marketing Director* Steve Pope

Black interest popular novels, particularly reflecting contemporary ethnic experiences. *Black Classics* series: reprints of classic novels by black writers. Founded 1992.

Nia (imprint)
Literary black fiction.

Y Lolfa Cyf.

Talybont, Ceredigion SY24 5AP
tel (01970) 832304 *fax* (01970) 832782
e-mail ylolfa@ylolfa.com
web site http://www.ylolfa.com
Directors Robat Gruffudd, Enid Gruffudd, Garmon Gruffudd, *Editor* Lefi Gruffudd

Welsh-language popular fiction and non-fiction, music, children's books; Welsh-language tutors; English-language political books and a range of Welsh-interest books for the tourist market. Founded 1967.

Yale University Press London*

23 Pond Street, London NW3 2PN
tel 020-7431 4422 *fax* 020-7431 3755
e-mail firstname.lastname@yaleup.co.uk
Managing Director John Nicoll

Art, architecture, history, economics, political science, literary criticism, Asian and African studies, religion, philosophy, psychology, history of science. Founded 1961.

Yellow Jersey Press – see Random House Group Ltd*

Zed Books Ltd*

7 Cynthia Street, London N1 9JF
tel 020-7837 4014 (general) *fax* 020-7833 3960
e-mail zed @ zedbooks.demon.co.uk
web site http://www.zedbooks.demon.co.uk
Editors Robert Molteno, Louise Murray

Social sciences on international issues; women's studies, cultural studies, development and environmental studies; area studies (Africa, Asia, Caribbean, Latin America, Middle East and the Pacific). Founded 1976.

Zoë Books Ltd

15 Worthy Lane, Winchester, Hants SO23 7AB
tel (01962) 851318 *fax* (01962) 843015
e-mail enquiries@zoebooks.co.uk
web site http://www.zoebooks.co.uk
Directors I.Z. Dawson (managing publishing), A.R. Davidson

Publishers of children's information books for the school and library markets in the UK; specialists in co-editions for world markets. No unsolicited MSS. No opportunities for freelances. Founded 1990.

Book packagers

Many modern illustrated books are created by book packagers, whose special skills are in the areas of book design and graphic content. In-house desk editors and art editors match up the expertise of specialist writers, artists and photographers who usually work on a freelance basis.

Aetos Ltd

69 Warminster Road, Bathampton,
Bath & NE Somerset BA2 6RU
tel (01225) 425745 *fax* (01225) 444966
e-mail ron@aetos.demon.co.uk
General Manager Athina Adams-Florou, *Publishing Manager* Ron Adams

Full packaging/production service, from original concept to delivery of film or finished copies. Specialises in illustrated educational and general interest books. Publishers' commissions undertaken. Opportunities for freelances.

Aladdin Books Ltd

28 Percy Street, London W1P 0LD
tel 020-7323 3319 *fax* 020-7323 4829
e-mail aladdin@dircon.co.uk
Directors Charles Nicholas, Bibby Whittaker

Full design and book packaging facility specialising in children's non-fiction and reference. Founded 1980.

Albion Press Ltd

Spring Hill, Idbury, Oxon OX7 6RU
tel (01993) 831094 *fax* (01993) 831982
Directors Emma Bradford, Neil Philip

Quality integrated illustrated titles. Specialises in children's books. Supply finished books. Publishers' commissions undertaken. No unsolicited MSS. Founded 1984.

Alphabet & Image Ltd

Marston House, Marston Magna, Yeovil, Somerset BA22 8DH
tel (01935) 851331 *fax* (01935) 851372
Directors Anthony Birks-Hay, Leslie Birks-Hay

Complete editorial, picture research, photographic, design and production service for illustrated books on ceramics, fine art, horticulture, architecture, history, etc. Imprint: Marston House. Founded 1972.

Amber Books Ltd

Bradley's Close, 74-77 White Lion Street, London N1 9PF
tel 020-7520 7600 *fax* 020-7520 7606/7607
e-mail info@amberbooks.co.uk
Managing Director Stasz Gnych, *Rights and Operations Director* Sara Ballard, *Managing Editor* Sally Harper, *Head of Production* James Bann, *Military Editor* Charles Catton, *Design Manager* Mark Batley, *Picture Manager* Lisa Wren, *Naval Editor* Naomi Waters

Illustrated non-fiction. Subject areas include military, aviation, transport, crime, general reference and maritime. Opportunities for freelances. Imprints: Brown Books Ltd. Founded 1989.

Andromeda Oxford Ltd

11-13 The Vineyard, Abingdon, Oxon OX14 3PX
tel (01235) 550296 *fax* (01235) 550330
e-mail mail@andromeda.co.uk
web site http://www.andromeda.co.uk
Directors David Holyoak (managing), Graham Bateman (publishing), Clive Sparling (production), Andrew Flatt (finance)

Produces for the international market adult and junior reference books: history, natural history, geography, science, art; children's information and activity books. Founded 1986.

BCS Publishing Ltd

2nd Floor, Temple Court, 109 Oxford Road, Cowley, Oxford OX4 2ER
tel (01865) 770099 *fax* (01865) 770050
e-mail bcs-publishing@dial.pipex.com
Managing and Art Director Steve McCurdy, *Managing Editor* Penelope Isaac

Specialises in the preparation of illustrated non-fiction; provides a full creative, design, editorial and production service. Opportunities for freelances. Commissioned work undertaken.

Bellew Publishing Co. Ltd

8 Balham Hill, London SW12 9EA
tel/fax 020-8675 2142
Chairman Ian McCorquodale, *Managing Director* Ib Bellew

Adult and children's illustrated titles from origination of idea through concept and design to production. Founded 1983.

Bender Richardson White

PO Box 266, Uxbridge, Middlesex UB9 5NX
tel (01895) 832444 *fax* (01895) 835213
e-mail brw@brw.co.uk
Partners Lionel Bender, Kim Richardson, Ben White

Book and multimedia packaging, specialising in children's natural history, science and family information. Opportunities for freelances. See also **Lionheart Books**. Founded 1990.

BLA Publishing Ltd

BIC Ling Kee House, 1 Christopher Road, East Grinstead, West Sussex RH19 3BT
tel (01342) 318980 *fax* (01342) 410980
Directors Au Bak Ling (chairman, Hong Kong), Albert Kw Au (Hong Kong), *Contact* Penny Kitchenham

High quality illustrated reference books, particularly science dictionaries and encyclopedias, for the international market. Founded 1981.

Book Packaging and Marketing

3 Murswell Lane, Silverstone, Towcester, Northants. NN12 8UT
tel/fax (01327) 858380
Proprietor Martin F. Marix Evans

Illustrated general and informational non-fiction and reference for adults, especially military history, travel, countryside. Product development and project management; editorial and marketing consultancy. Very limited opportunities for freelances. Founded 1990.

Breslich & Foss Ltd

20 Wells Mews, London W1P 3FJ
tel 020-7580 8774 *fax* 020-7580 8784
Directors Paula G. Breslich, K.B. Dunning

Books produced from MS to bound copy stage from in-house ideas. Specialising in the arts, crafts, gardening, health, gift and novelty, children's. Founded 1978.

Brown Packaging Books Ltd

Bradley's Close, 74-77 White Lion Street, London N1 9PF
tel 020-7520 7600 *fax* 020-7520 7606/7607
e-mail info@amberbooks.co.uk
Managing Director Stasz Gnych, *Rights and Operations Director* Sara Ballard, *Managing Editor* Sally Harper, *Head of Production* James Bann, *Military Editor* Charles Catton, *Design Manager* Mark Batley, *Picture Manager* Lisa Wren, *Naval Editor* Naomi Waters

Highly illustrated non-fiction. Subject areas include military, aviation, transport, crime, general reference and maritime. Opportunities for freelances. Imprint: Brown Books Ltd. Founded 1989.

Brown Partworks Ltd

8 Chapel Place, Rivington Street, London EC2A 3DQ
tel 020-7920 7500 *fax* 020-7920 7501
e-mail info@brownpartworks.co.uk
web site http://www.brownpartworks.co.uk
Marketing Director Sharon Hutton

Book, partwork and continuity set packaging services for trade, promotional and international publishers. Opportunities for freelances. Founded 1989.

Brown Wells & Jacobs Ltd

Foresters Hall, 25-27 Westow Street, London SE19 3RY
tel 020-8771 5115 *fax* 020-8771 9994
e-mail postmaster@popking.demon.co.uk
web site http://www.bwj.org
Director Graham Brown

Design, editorial, illustration and production of high quality non-fiction illustrated children's books. Specialities include pop-ups and novelties. Opportunities for freelances. Founded 1979.

C&B Packaging

London House, Great Eastern Wharf, Parkgate Road, London SW11 4NQ
tel 0171-924 2575 *fax* 0171-924 7725
e-mail roger.bristow@cb-packaging.co.uk
Managing Director Roger Bristow, *Publishing Director* Denis Kennedy

Quality illustrated non-fiction book production from conception: editorial/ design, reproduction, print. Opportunities for freelances. Division of **Collins & Brown Ltd**. Founded 1998.

Calmann & King Ltd

71 Great Russell Street, London WC1B 3BN
tel 020-7831 6351 *fax* 020-7831 8356
e-mail enquiries@calmann-k.co.uk
Directors Robin Hyman, Laurence King, Judy Rasmussen, Lesley Ripley Greenfield, John Stoddart

Illustrated books on art history, architecture, design and graphic design. Imprint: **Laurence King**. Founded 1976.

Cambridge Language Services Ltd

Greystones, Allendale, Northumberland NE47 9PX
tel/fax (01434) 683200
e-mail paul@oakleaf.demon.co.uk
Managing Director Paul Procter

Suppliers to publishers, societies and other organisations of customised database management systems, with advanced retrieval mechanisms, and electronic publishing systems for the preparation of dictionaries, reference books, encyclopedias, catalogues, journals, archives. PC (windows) based. Founded 1982.

Cameron Books

PO Box 1, Moffat, Dumfriesshire DG10 9SU
tel (01683) 220808 *fax* (01683) 220012
e-mail editorial@cameronbooks.co.uk
web site http://www.cameronbooks.co.uk
Directors Ian A. Cameron, Jill Hollis

Illustrated non-fiction: fine arts (including environmental and land art), film, the decorative arts, crafts, architecture, design, antiques, collecting, natural history, environmental studies, social history, food. Founded 1976. **Edition** Design, editing, typesetting, production work from concept to finished book for galleries, museums, institutions and other publishers. Founded 1975.

Carroll & Brown Ltd

20 Lonsdale Road, London NW6 6RD
tel 020-7372 0900 *fax* 020-7372 0460
e-mail carbro.gen@virgin.net
Directors Amy Carroll (managing), Denise Brown (creative)

Editorial and design through to final film and printing of cookery, health, craft, mind, body and spirit, and lifestyle titles. Opportunities for freelances. Founded 1989.

Roger Coote Publishing

Gissing's Farm, Fressingfield, Eye, Suffolk IP21 5SH
tel (01379) 588044 *fax* (01379) 588055
e-mail rgc@ndirect.co.uk
Director Roger Goddard-Coote

High quality illustrated children's non-fiction titles for trade, institutional and international markets. Commissions undertaken. Freelance opportunities for editors and designers. Founded 1989.

Cowley Hunter Ltd

8 Belmont, Bath BA1 5DZ
tel (01225) 339999 *fax* (01225) 339995
Directors Clyde Hunter (managing), Stewart Cowley (publishing), Rob Kendrew (production)

Children's international co-editions. Novelty format creation. Licence and character publishing developments. Information and early learning. Founded 1998.

D & N Publishing

Membury Business Park, Lambourn Woodlands, Hungerford, Berks. RG17 7TJ
tel (01488) 71210 *fax* (01488) 71220
e-mail DandNpub@aol.com
Partners David and Namrita Price-Goodfellow

Production from MS to printed book. Specialises in taking raw MS and doing all necessary liaison, editorial, design and production work up to when book is ready to print, but can also organise printing. Specialises in natural history, travel, craft, transport. Founded 1991.

Design Eye Ltd

4-6 Dunmow Road, Bishop's Stortford, Herts. CM23 5HL
tel (01279) 655115 *fax* (01279) 655151
Managing Director Lee Robinson

Packager and publisher of interactive kit books for adults and children: arts and crafts, science, history and fiction. Opportunities for freelances. Member of the Quarto Group. Founded 1988.

Diagram Visual Information Ltd

195 Kentish Town Road, London NW5 2JU
tel 020-7482 3633 *fax* 020-7482 4932
Director Bruce Robertson

Research, writing, design and illustration of reference books, supplied as film or disk. Opportunities for freelances. Founded 1967.

Earthscape Editions

Greys Court Farm, Greys Court, Henley on Thames, Oxon RG9 4PG
tel (01491) 628188 *fax* (01491) 628189
Partners B.J. Knapp, D.L.R. McCrae

High quality, full colour, illustrated children's text and information books, including co-editions, for education and library market. Send MSS to Atlantic Europe Publishing Co. Ltd (associate company); sae essential for return of MSS. Founded 1987.

Eddison Sadd Editions Ltd

St Chad's House, 148 King's Cross Road, London WC1X 9DH
tel 020-7837 1968 *fax* 020-7837 2025
e-mail reception@eddisonsadd.co.uk

Directors Nick Eddison, Ian Jackson, David Owen, Elaine Partington, Charles James, Susan Cole

Illustrated non-fiction books and kits for the international co-edition market. Broad, popular list with emphasis on New Age and complementary health. Founded 1982.

First Rank Publishing

5 Rochester Gardens, Hove, East Sussex BN3 3NW
tel (01273) 326376
Proprietor Byron Jacobs

Packager and publisher of sports, games and leisure books. No unsolicited MSS but ideas and synopses welcome. Payment usually fees. Also provides editorial, production and typesetting services. Founded 1996.

Focus Publishing

The Courtyard, 26 London Road, Sevenoaks, Kent TN13 1AP
tel (01732) 742456 *fax* (01732) 743381
e-mail focus-publishing@netway.co.uk
web site http://www.focus-publishing.netway.co.uk
Partners Guy Croton, Caroline Watson

Illustrated non-fiction: gardening, wine and food, sex and health, sport, aviation, DIY and crafts, computers. Opportunities for freelances. Founded 1997.

Graham-Cameron Publishing & Illustration

The Studio, 23 Holt Road, Sheringham, Norfolk NR26 8NB
tel (01263) 821333 *fax* (01263) 821334
Directors Mike Graham-Cameron, Helen Graham-Cameron

Educational and children's books; information publications; sponsored publications. Illustration agency with 37 artists. Editorial and production services. No unsolicited MSS. Founded 1984.

Haldane Mason Ltd

59 Chepstow Road, London W2 5BP
tel 020-7792 2123 *fax* 020-7221 3965
e-mail haldane.mason@dial.pipex.com
Directors Ron Samuel, Sydney Francis

High-quality packager of illustrated general non-fiction for the international market. Areas include: arts and crafts, children's, cookery, health, New Age, lifestyle, popular reference, travel, sport. Opportunities for freelances. Founded 1992.

Hardlines

Park Street, Charlbury, Oxon OX7 3PS
tel (01608) 811255 *fax* (01608) 811442
e-mail info@hardlines.co.uk
web site http://www.hardlines.co.uk
Partners P. Wilkinson, G. Walker

Primary, secondary, academic ducation (geography, science, modern languages) and co-editions (travel guides, gardening cookery). Opportunities for freelances. Founded 1985.

Hart McLeod

14 Greenside, Waterbeach, Cambridge CB5 9HP
tel (01223) 861495 *fax* (01223) 862902
e-mail hmcl@dial.pipex.com
Partners Graham Hart, Chris McLeod

Primarily educational and general non-fiction with particular experience of revision books, school texts. Opportunities for freelances. Founded 1985.

Angus Hudson Ltd

Concorde House, Grenville Place, London NW7 3SA
tel 020-8959 3668 *fax* 020-8959 3678
Directors Angus Hudson (chairman), Nicholas Jones (managing), Stephen Price (production), Geoffrey Benge, William Brooks

Children's and religious international co-editions, from concept to finished copies. Publishing imprints: Candle Books and Concorde House Books. Founded 1971.

The Ivy Press Ltd

The Old Candlemakers, West Street, Lewes, East Sussex BN7 2NZ
tel (01273) 487440 *fax* (01273) 487441
e-mail surname@ivypress.co.uk
Directors Peter Bridgewater, Jenny Manstead, Terry Jeavons

Illustrated books on the arts, lifestyle and design. Opportunities for freelances. Founded 1995.

Lennard Books

Windmill Cottage, Mackerye End, Harpenden, Herts. AL5 5DR
tel (01582) 715866 *fax* (01582) 715121
e-mail lennard@lenqap.demon.co.uk
Directors K.A.A. Stephenson, R.H. Stephenson

Sport, personalities, TV tie-ins, humour. Division of Lennard Associates Ltd.

Lexus Ltd

13 Newton Terrace, Glasgow G3 7PJ
tel 0141-221 5266 *fax* 0141-226 3139
e-mail pt@lexus.win-uk.net
Director P.M. Terrell

Reference book publishing (especially bilingual dictionaries) as contractor, packager, consultant; translation. Founded 1980.

Lionheart Books

10 Chelmsford Square, London NW10 3AR
tel 020-8459 0453 *fax* 020-8451 3681
e-mail lionheart.brw@btinternet.com
Partners Lionel Bender (editorial), Madeleine Bender (editorial), Ben White (design)

Handles all aspects of editorial and design packaging of, mostly, children's illustrated science, natural history and history projects. See also **Bender Richardson White**. Founded 1985.

Market House Books Ltd

2 Market House, Market Square, Aylesbury, Bucks. HP20 1TN
tel (01296) 484911 *fax* (01296) 437073
e-mail mhb_aylesbury@compuserve.com
Directors Dr Alan Isaacs, Dr John Daintith, P.C. Sapsed

Compilation of dictionaries, encyclopedias, and reference books. Founded 1970.

Marshall Cavendish Books

119 Wardour Street, London W1V 3TD
tel 020-7734 6710 *fax* 020-7439 1423
Head of Books Liz Dennis

Cookery, crafts, gardening, do-it-yourself, general illustrated non-fiction. Founded 1969.

Marshall Editions Ltd

The Orangery, 161 New Bond Street, London W1Y 9PA
tel 020-7291 8222 *fax* 020-7291 8233
e-mail info@mediakey.u-net.com
web site http://www.marshallmedia.com
Directors Richard Harman (chairman), Barbara Anderson (publisher), Nick Croydon (Ceo), Barry Baker (operations), Ellen Dupont (editorial, adult), Cindy O'Brien (editorial, children's), Andy Lee (finance), Belinda Ioni Rasmussen (international rights)

Highly illustrated non-fiction for adults and children, including health, gardening, lifestyle, self-improvement, leisure, popular science and visual information for children. Founded 1977.

Monkey Puzzle Media Ltd

Gissing's Farm, Fressingfield, Eye, Suffolk IP21 5SH
tel (01379) 588044 *fax* (01379) 588055
e-mail rgc@ndirect.co.uk
Directors Roger Goddard-Coote (managing), Alex Edmonds (publishing)

High-quality illustrated children's and adult non-fiction for trade, institutional and mass markets worldwide. Publishers' commissions undertaken.

Orpheus Books Ltd

2 Church Green, Witney, Oxon OX8 6AW
tel (01993) 774949 *fax* (01993) 700330
e-mail post@orpheusbooks.demon.co.uk
Executive Directors Nicholas Harris (editorial, design and marketing), Joanna Turner (production and administration)

Children's illustrated non-fiction/reference. Opportunities for freelance artists. Founded 1992.

Oyster Books

Unit 4, Kirklea Farm, Badgworth, Axbridge, Somerset BS26 2QH
tel (01934) 732251 *fax* (01934) 732514
e-mail pearls@oysterbooks.co.uk
Directors Tim Wood, Ali Brooks, Donna Webber

Specialises in high-quality children's books and book/toy gift items. Founded 1985.

Pinwheel Ltd

Station House, 8-13 Swiss Terrace, London NW6 4RR
tel 020-7586 5100 *fax* 020-7483 1999
e-mail admin@pinwheel.co.uk
Managing Director Sarah Fabiny

Novelty books for children under 5. Opportunities for freelances. Founded 1995.

Playne Books Ltd

Chapel House, Trefin, Haverfordwest, Pembrokeshire SA62 5AU
tel (01348) 837073 *fax* (01348) 837063
e-mail playne.books@virgin.net
Design and Production David Playne, *Editor* Gill Davies

Specialises in highly illustrated adult non-fiction and books for very young children. All stages of production undertaken from initial concept (editorial, design and manufacture) to delivery of completed books. Founded 1987.

Mathew Price Ltd

The Old Glove Factory, Bristol Road, Sherborne, Dorset DT9 4HP
tel (01935) 816010 *fax* (01935) 816310
e-mail mathewp@mathew-price.com
Chairman Mathew Price

Illustrated fiction and non-fiction children's books for all ages for the international market. Specialist in flap, pop-up, paper-engineered titles. Founded 1983.

Quarto Children's Books Ltd

3rd Floor, The Fitzpatrick Building, 188-194 York Way, London N7 9QP
tel 020-7607 3322 *fax* 020-7700 2951

Publisher Bob Morley

Highly illustrated non-fiction children's books. **Apple Press** (imprint) Leisure, domestic and craft pursuits; cookery, gardening, sport, transport, children's.

Quarto Publishing plc/Quintet Publishing Ltd

The Old Brewery, 6 Blundell Street, London N7 9BH
tel 020-7700 6700 *fax* 020-7700 4191
Directors L.F. Orbach, R.J. Morley, M.J. Mousley

International co-editions. Founded 1976/84.

Sadie Fields Productions Ltd

Penthouse Studio, 4C/D West Point, 36-37 Warple Way, London W3 0RG
tel 020-8746 1171 *fax* 020-8746 1170
e-mail sales@tangobooks.co.uk
Directors Sheri Safran, David Fielder

Creates and produces international co-editions of pop-up, hologram, touch-and-feel, and other novelty books for children. Imprint: Tango Books. Founded 1983.

Salariya Book Company

25 Marlborough Place, Brighton BN1 1UB
tel (01273) 603306 *fax* (01273) 621619
e-mail salariya@fastnet.co.uk
Director David Salariya

Children's non-fiction. Founded 1989.

Savitri Books Ltd

115J Cleveland Street, London W1P 5PN
tel 020-7436 9932 *fax* 020-7580 6330
Director Mrinalini S. Srivastava

Packaging, publishing, design, production. Founded 1983.

The Templar Company plc

Pippbrook Mill, London Road, Dorking, Surrey RH4 1JE
tel (01306) 876361 *fax* (01306) 889097
Directors Richard Carlisle, Amanda Wood, Ruth Huddleston, Graeme East

Children's gift, novelty, picture and illustrated information books; most titles aimed at international co-edition market. Established links with major co-publishers in USA, Australia and throughout Europe.

Toucan Books Ltd

4th Floor, 32-38 Saffron Hill, London EC1N 8FH
tel 020-7404 8181 *fax* 020-7404 8282
Directors Robert Sackville West, Adam Nicolson, Jane MacAndrew

International co-editions; editorial, design and production services. Founded 1985.

Tucker Slingsby

5th Floor, Berkeley House, 73 Upper Richmond Road, London SW15 2SZ
tel 020-8874 3400 *fax* 020-8874 3004
Directors Janet Slingsby, Del Tucker

Creation, editorial and design to disk, film or finished copy of children's books, magazines and general interest adult books. Commissioned work undertaken. Opportunities for freelances and picture book artists. Founded 1993.

Ventura Publishing Ltd

27 Wrights Lane, London W8 5TZ
tel 020-7416 3000 *fax* 020-7416 3070
Managing Director Sally Floyer

Specialises in production of the *Spot* books by Eric Hill.

Webb & Bower (Publishers) Ltd

9 Duke Street, Dartmouth, Devon TQ6 9PY
tel (01803) 835525 *fax* (01803) 835552
Director Richard Webb

Specialises in licensing illustrated non-fiction books. Founded 1975.

Wordwright Books

25 Oakford Road, London NW5 1AJ
tel 020-7284 0056 *fax* 020-7284 0041
e-mail wordwright@clara.co.uk
Director Charles Perkins

Full packaging/production service – from concept to delivery of film or finished copies. Produces illustrated non-fiction. Also assesses and prepares MSS for the US market. Publishes a small general fiction list. Founded 1987.

Publishers of fiction

Addresses for Book publishers UK and Ireland start on page 151.

Adventure/thrillers

Allison & Busby
Bantam
Bantam Press
Black Ace Books
Black Swan
Blackstaff Press (Ire.)
Blake Publishing
Bloomsbury Publishing
Marion Boyars Publishers
Brandon Book Publishers
Chatto & Windus
Richard Cohen Books
Corgi
Coronet
Doubleday (UK)
Fourth Estate
Gairm Publications
Robert Hale
HarperCollins Publishers
Headline Book Publishing
William Heinemann
Hodder & Stoughton
Hutchinson Books
Michael Joseph
Little, Brown
Macmillan Publishers
New English Library
Onlywomen Press
Orion
Pan
Penguin Books
Piatkus Books
Random House Group
Sceptre
Severn House Publishers
Simon & Schuster
Souvenir Press
Vintage
Virago Press
Warner

Crime/mystery/suspense

Allison & Busby
Arrow Books
Bantam
Bantam Press
Black Swan
Blake Publishing
Bloomsbury Publishing
Marion Boyars Publishers
Canongate Books
Richard Cohen Books
Collins Crime
Constable & Co.
Corgi
Coronet
The Do-Not Press
Faber & Faber
Flambard Press
Fourth Estate
Gairm Publications
Robert Hale
Hamish Hamilton
HarperCollins Publishers
Headline Book Publishing
William Heinemann
Hodder & Stoughton
Hutchinson Books
Michael Joseph
Little, Brown
Macmillan Publishers
New English Library
The O'Brien Press (Ire.)
Michale O'Mara Books
Onlywomen Press
Orion
Pan
Penguin Books
Piatkus Books
Polygon
Random House Group
Sceptre
Serpent's Tail
Severn House Publishers
Souvenir Press
Town House and Country House (Ire.)
Viking
Vintage
Virago Press
Warner – Futura
Wolfhound Press (Ire.)
The Women's Press
The X Press

Gay/lesbian

Arcadia Books
Bantam
Black Swan
Marion Boyars Publishers
Richard Cohen Books
Corgi
Faber & Faber
Fourth Estate
GMP Publishers
Hamish Hamilton
HarperCollins Publishers
Little, Brown
Macmillan Publishers
The O'Brien Press (Ire.)
Michael O'Mara Books
Onlywomen Press
Penguin Books
Polygon
Serpent's Tail
Vintage
Virago Press
The Women's Press

General

Abacus
Allison & Busby
Arcadia Books
Aureus Publishing
Bantam
Bantam Press
Basement Press (Ire.)
Black Ace Books
Black Swan
Blackstaff Press (Ire.)
Blake Publishing
Bloomsbury Publishing
Marion Boyars Publishers
Brandon Book Publishers (Ire.)
Jonathan Cape
Century
Chatto & Windus
Cló Iar-Chonnachta Teo. (Ire.)
Richard Cohen Books
The Collins Press (Ire.)
Corgi
Doubleday (UK)

Gerald Duckworth & Co.
Faber & Faber
Fourth Estate
Gairm Publications
The Gallery Press (Ire.)
Garnet Publishing
Gee & Son (Denbigh)
Victor Gollancz
Robert Hale
Hamish Hamilton
HarperCollins Publishers
Headline Book Publishing
William Heinemann
Hodder & Stoughton
Honno
Hutchinson Books
Michael Joseph
Karnak House
Little, Brown
Macmillan Publishers
Marino Books (Ire.)
Mentor Press (Ire.)
The Mercier Press
New English Library
The O'Brien Press (Ire.)
Michael O'Mara Books
Orion
Pan Books
Paternoster Publishing
Penguin Books
Piatkus Books
Pimlico
Pipers' Ash
Pocket Books
Poolbeg Press (Ire.)
Pulp Books
Quartet Books
Random House Group
Route
Sceptre
Secker and Warburg
Seren
Serpent's Tail
Severn House Publishers
Simon & Schuster
Souvenir Press
Touchstone
Town House and Country House (Ire.)
Viking
Vintage
Virago
Warner
Wolfhound Press (Ire.)
Worldwide Books
Y Lolfa Cyf. (Welsh language)

Historical

Allison & Busby
Bantam
Bantam Press
Black Ace Books
Blackstaff Press (Ire.)
Canongate Books
Jonathan Cape
Richard Cohen Books
Doubleday (UK)
Everyman's Library
Fourth Estate
Gee & Son (Denbigh)
Victor Gollancz
Robert Hale
HarperCollins Publishers
Headline Book Publishing
William Heinemann
Hodder & Stoughton
C. Hurst & Co. (Publishers)
Hutchinson Books
Michael Joseph
Karnak House
Little, Brown
Macmillan Publishers
The O'Brien Press (Ire.)
Michael O'Mara Books
Onlywomen Press
Orion
Pan
Penguin Books
Piatkus Books
Pimlico
Random House Group
Sceptre
Severn House Publishers
Simon & Schuster
Souvenir Press
Vintage
Virago Press
Warner
Wolfhound Press (Ire.)

Literary

Abacus
Allison & Busby
Arcadia Books
Bantam
Bantam Press
Bellew Publishing Co.
Black Ace Books
Black Swan
Blackstaff Press (Ire.)
Bloomsbury Publishing
Marion Boyars Publishers
Calder Publications
Canongate Books
Jonathan Cape
Chatto & Windus
Richard Cohen Books
Corgi
Dedalus
Doubleday (UK)
Gerald Duckworth & Co.
Enitharmon Press
Everyman's Library
Faber & Faber
Flamingo
Fourth Estate
Gee & Son (Denbigh)
Victor Gollancz
Granta Publications
Robert Hale
Hamish Hamilton
HarperCollins Publishers
Harvill
Headland Publications
William Heinemann
Hodder & Stoughton
Honno
Hutchinson Books
Indigo
Karnak House
Libris
Little, Brown
Macmillan Publishers
Methuen
The O'Brien Press (Ire.)
Onlywomen Press
Orion
Peter Owen
Pan
Paternoster Publishing
Penguin Books
Phoenix
Piatkus Books
Picador
Pimlico
Polygon
Poolbeg Press (Ire.)
Random House Group
Sceptre
Scottish Cultural Press
Secker and Warburg
Seren
Serpent's Tail
Skoob Books
Souvenir Press
Stride Publications
Viking
Vintage
Virago Press
Wolfhound Press (Ire.)
The Women's Press
The X Press

Romantic

Bantam
Bantam Press
Black Swan
Blake Publishing
Corgi
Coronet
Doubleday (UK)
Robert Hale
Harlequin Mills & Boon

Headline Book Publishing
William Heinemann
Hodder & Stoughton
Little, Brown
Macmillan Publishers
Monarch Publications
Onlywomen Press
Orion
Pan
Piatkus Books
Random House Group
Scarlet
Severn House Publishers
Silhouette
Town House and Country House (Ire.)
Warner

Science fiction/fantasy

Arrow Books
Bantam
Bantam Press
Black Swan
Blake Publishing
Marion Boyars Publishers
Corgi
Coronet
Victor Gollancz
HarperCollins Publishers
Headline Book Publishing
Hodder & Stoughton
Little, Brown
Macmillan Publishers
Millennium
New English Library
The O'Brien Press (Ire.)
Onlywomen Press
Orbit
Orion
Pan
Penguin Books
Pipers' Ash
Random House Group
Severn House Publishers
Souvenir Press
Voyager
Wolfhound Press (Ire.)
The Women's Press

Short stories

Allison & Busby
Arcadia Books
Blackstaff Press (Ire.)
Marion Boyars Publishers
Jonathan Cape
Chatto & Windus
Canongate Books
Everyman's Library
Flambard Press
Fourth Estate
Gairm Publications
Gee & Son (Denbigh)
Granta Publications
Hamish Hamilton
William Heinemann
Hodder & Stoughton
Honno
Karnak House
Macmillan Publishers
Onlywomen Press
Pan
Penguin Books
Pipers' Ash
Polygon
Random House Group
Scottish Cultural Press
Secker and Warburg
Seren
Severn House Publishers
Y Lolfa Cyf.

Other

Ethnic

Allison & Busby
Marion Boyars Publishers
Canongate Books
C. Hurst & Co. (Publishers)
Souvenir Press
The Women's Press
The X Press

Erotic

Black Lace
Marion Boyars Publishers
Idol
Nexus
Michael O'Mara Books
Souvenir Press
X Libris
The X Press

Graphic

Knockabout Comics
Titan Books

Horror

Black Ace Books
Chapman
Robert Hale
Severn House Publishers
Warner

Humour

Black Swan
Canongate Books
Corgi
Victor Gollancz
Robert Hale
Michael O'Mara Books
Paternoster Publishing
Piccadilly Press
Souvenir Press
Warner

New/experimental

Arcadia Books
Black Ace Books
Marion Boyars Publishers
Canongate Books
Polygon
Serpent's Tail
Stride Publications
The X Press

Translations

Allison & Busby
Arcadia Books
Marion Boyars Publishers
Canongate Books
Dedalus
Enitharmon Press
Everyman's Library
Granta Publications
The Harvill Press
Peter Owen
Quartet Books
Serpent's Tail
Souvenir Press

War

Canongate Books
Robert Hale
Severn House Publishers
Souvenir Press

Westerns

Robert Hale

Book publishers overseas

Listings are given for book publishers in Australia (below), Canada (page 226), New Zealand (page 229), South Africa (page 231) and the USA (page 233).

Australia

**Member of the Australian Publishers Association*

Access Press

54 Railway Parade, Bassendean, Western Australia 6054
postal address PO Box 446, Bassendean, Western Australia 6054
tel (08) 9379 3188 *fax* (08) 9379 3199
Managing Editor Helen Weller

Australiana, poetry, children's, history, general. Privately financed books published and distributed. Founded 1979.

Allen & Unwin Pty Ltd*

9 Atchison Street, PO Box 8500, St Leonards, NSW 2065
tel (02) 8425 0100 *fax* (02) 9906 2218
e-mail frontdesk@allen.unwin.com.au
web site http://www.allen-unwin.com.au

General trade, including fiction and children's books, academic, especially social science and history.

The Australian Council for Educational Research Ltd*

19 Prospect Hill Road, Private Bag 55, Camberwell, Victoria 3124
tel (03) 9277 5555 *fax* (03) 9277 5500
e-mail info@acer.edu.au

Range of books and kits: for teachers, trainee teachers, parents, psychologists, counsellors, students of education, researchers.

Blackwell Science Asia Pty Ltd

54 University Street, South Carlton, Victoria 3053
tel (03) 9347 0300 *fax* (03) 9347 5001
e-mail Dimi.Katsieris@blacksci-asia.com.au
web site http://www.blackwell-science.com/
Group President Mark Robertson

Medical, healthcare, life, earth sciences, professional.

Butterworths*

Tower 2, 475-495 Victoria Avenue, Chatswood, NSW 2067
tel (02) 9422 2222 *fax* (02) 9422 2444
web site http://www.butterworths.com.au
Managing Director Murray Hamilton, *Editorial/ Deputy Managing Director* J. Broadfoot

Legal, tax and commercial. Division of Reed International Books Australia Pty Ltd.

Cambridge University Press Australian Branch*

10 Stamford Road, Oakleigh, Melbourne, Victoria 3166
tel (03) 9568 0322 *fax* (03) 9563 1517
web site http://www.cup.edu.au
Director Sandra McComb

Academic, educational, reference, English as a second language.

Craftsman House

Level 1, Tower A, 112 Talavera Road, North Ryde, NSW 2113
tel (02) 9878 8222 *fax* (02) 9878 8122
Directors Nevill Drury (publishing), Martin Gordon (chairman), Anna Mayo (marketing manager)

Australian and European fine arts. Division of Fine Arts Press Pty Ltd. Founded 1981.

Dominie Pty Ltd

Drama Department, 8 Cross Street, Brookvale, NSW 2100
tel (02) 9905 0201 *fax* (02) 9905 5209
e-mail dominie@dominie.com.au
web site http://www.dominie.com.au

Australian representatives of publishers of plays and agents for the collection of royalties for Samuel French Ltd, incorporating Hanbury Plays and Samuel French Inc., The Society of Authors, ACTAC, Bakers Plays of Boston, Pioneer Drama and Dramatic Publishing.

Harcourt Australia Pty Ltd

30-52 Smidmore Street, Marrickville, NSW 2204
tel (02) 9517 8999 *fax* (02) 9550 6007
Managing Director Brian M. Brennan

Novels, children's, academic, medical and scientific books. Imprints: Harcourt Brace; Holt, Rinehart and Winston; W.B. Saunders/Ballière Tindall; Dryden Press; Saunders College; The Psychological Corporation; Academic Press, Churchill Livingstone; Morgan Kaufmann; Industrial Press; Technomic Publishing, Mosby. Established 1972.

HarperCollins Publishers (Australia) Pty Limited Group*

25-31 Ryde Road, Pymble, NSW 2073
postal address PO Box 321, Pymble, NSW 2073
tel (02) 9952 5000 *fax* (02) 9952 5555
Managing Director Barrie Hitchon

Literary fiction and non-fiction, popular fiction, reference, biography, autobiography, current affairs, sport, lifestyle, health/self-help, humour, true crime, travel, Australiana, history, business, gift/stationery, religion.

Hill of Content Publishing Co. Pty Ltd*

86 Bourke Street, Melbourne, Victoria 3000
tel (03) 9662 2282 *fax* (03) 9662 2527
e-mail hocpub@collinsbooks.com.au
Directors M. Slamen, M.G. Zifcak, M. Anderson

Health, philosophy, and mind, body and spirit. Founded 1965.

Hodder Headline Australia Pty Ltd*

Level 22, 201 Kent Street, Sydney, NSW 2000
tel (02) 8248 0800 *fax* (02) 8248 0810
e-mail auspub@hha.com.au
web site http://www.hha.com.au
Directors Malcolm Edwards (managing), Tim Hely Hutchinson, Lisa Highton, Mary Drum, David Cocking, Keith Hammill, Mary Tapissier

General, children's. No unsolicited MSS.

Kangaroo Press – see Simon & Schuster (Australia) Pty Ltd

LBC Information Services*

PO Box 3502, Rozelle, NSW 2039
tel (02) 8587 7000 *fax* (02) 8587 7100
e-mail lbccustomer@lbc.com.au
web site http://www.lbc.com.au

Accountancy and taxation, law.

Lonely Planet Publications*

Corner Maribyrnong and Parker Streets, Footscray 3011, Victoria
tel (03) 9819 1877 *fax* (03) 9819 6459
e-mail talk2us@lonelyplanet.com.au
web site http://www.lonelyplanet.com

Travel guidebooks, phrasebooks, travel literature, pictorial books, city maps, atlases; diving and snorkelling, walking, health, restaurant and pre-departure guidebooks. New series include world food, condensed pocket guides, cycling guides and wildlife guidebooks. Offices in London, Paris and Oakland, USA. Founded 1973.

Lothian Books*

11 Munro Street, Port Melbourne, Victoria 3207
tel (03) 9645 1544 *fax* (03) 9646 4882
e-mail books@lothian.com.au
Chairman/Managing Director P. Lothian, *Directors* E. McDonald, B. Hilliard

Juveniles, health, gardening, reference, Australian history, business, sport, biography, New Age, humour.

Macmillan Education Australia Pty Ltd*

Melbourne office 627 Chapel Street, South Yarra, Victoria 3205
tel (03) 9825 1025 *fax* (03) 9825 1010
e-mail meapl@macmillan.com.au
Sydney office Suite 310, Henry Lawson Business Centre, Birkenhead Point, Carey Street, Drummoyne, NSW 2047
tel (02) 9719 8944 *fax* (02) 9719 8613
e-mail measyd@macmillan.com.au
Directors Richard Charkin (chief executive – UK), Ross Gibb (executive chairman), Shane Armstrong (managing), Peter Huntley (sales), Sandra Iversen (primary publishing), Rex Parry (secondary publishing), George Smith (production), *Company Secretary/Financial Controller* Terry White

Educational books.

Melbourne University Press*

268 Drummond Street, Carlton, Victoria 3053
postal address PO Box 278, Carlton South, Victoria 3053
tel (03) 9347 3455 *fax* (03) 9349 2527
Chairman Prof Barry Sheeham, *Director* John Meckan

Academic, scholastic and cultural; educational textbooks and books of reference. Imprint: Miegunyah Press. Founded 1922.

Mimosa Publications Pty Ltd – see Weldon International Pty Ltd*

Nelson Thomson Learning*

102 Dodds Street, South Melbourne, Victoria 3205
tel (03) 9685 4111 *fax* (03) 9685 4199
e-mail customerservices@nelson.com.au
web site http://www.nelson.com.au

Educational books.

Pan Macmillan Australia Pty Ltd*
Level 18, 31 Market Street, Sydney, NSW 2000
tel (02) 9261 5611 *fax* (02) 9261 5047
e-mail pansyd@macmillan.com.au
Directors Ross Gibb (chairman), James Fraser (publishing), Roxarne Burns (publishing), Siv Toigo (finance), Peter Phillips (sales), Jeannine Fowler (publicity and marketing)

Commercial and literary fiction; children's fiction, non-fiction and character products; non-fiction; sport.

Penguin Books Australia Ltd*
487 Maroondah Highway, Ringwood, Victoria 3134
postal address PO Box 257, Ringwood, Victoria 3134
tel (03) 9871 2400 *fax* (03) 9870 9618
Managing Director P.J. Field, *Publishing Director* R.P. Sessions

Fiction, general non-fiction, current affairs, sociology, economics, environmental, travel guides, anthropology, politics, children's, health, cookery, gardening, pictorial and general books relating to Australia under Penguin Books and Viking imprints. Founded 1946.

Random House Australia Pty Ltd*
20 Alfred Street, Milson's Point, NSW 2061
tel (02) 9954 9966 *fax* (02) 9954 4562
e-mail random@randomhouse.com.au
Managing Director Juliet Rogers, *Chairman* Geoff Rumpf, *Deputy Managing Director* Margaret Seale, *Head of Publishing, Random House* Jane Palfreyman, *Publisher, Bantam Doubleday* Fiona Henderson, *Children's Publisher* Linsay Knight, *Managing Editor, Illustrated* Penny Martin, *Head of Sales and Marketing* Lou Johnson and Amanda Roberts, *Head of Publicity* Maggie Hamilton, *Rights and Permissions* Nerrilee Weir

General fiction and non-fiction; children's, illustrated. MSS submissions – for Random House phone before submitting; for Transworld Publishers send non-fiction by mail, fiction via an agent unless with positive reports from MSS assessment agents. Imprints: Anchor, Anderson, Arrow, Avon, Ballantine, Bantam Books, BBC Worldwide, Black Swan, Broadway Books, Century, Chatto & Windus, Corgi, Crown Publishing Group, Dell Publishing, Doubleday, Ebury, Egmont, Fodor, Hamlyn Children's, Heinemann, Hutchinson, Jonathan Cape, Knopf Publishing, Living Books, Mammoth UK, Minerva, Pantheon, Pavilion, Pimlico, Random House, Ravette, Red Fox, Rider, Robinson, Running Press, Secker & Warburg, Sesame Street, Vermilion, Vintage, Virgin. Subsidiary of Bertelsmann AG.

Reed Educational & Professional Publishing Australia*
22 Salmon Street, Port Melbourne, Victoria 3207
tel (03) 9245 7111 *fax* (03) 9245 7333
Managing Director David O'Brien

Art, chemistry, chemical engineering, environmental studies, geography, geology, health, nutrition, history, mathematics, physics, languages. Primary, Secondary; electronic publishing. Division of Reed Elsevier Australia. Founded 1982.

Reeve Books
54 Railway Parade, Bassendean, Western Australia 6054
postal address PO Box 446, Bassendean, Western Australia 6054
tel (08) 9379 3188 *fax* (08) 9379 3199
Managing Director/Editor Helen Weller

Biography, local history, general non-fiction. Commissioned works only. Founded 1987.

Rigby Heinemann – now Reed Educational & Professional Publishing Australia*

Samuel French Ltd – see Dominie Pty Ltd

Scholastic Australia Pty Ltd*
PO Box 579, Gosford, NSW 2250
tel (02) 4328 3555 *fax* (02) 4323 3827
Managing Director Ken Jolly

Children's fiction/non-fiction; educational materials for elementary schools, teacher reference. Founded 1968.

Simon & Schuster (Australia) Pty Ltd
20 Barcoo Street, East Roseville, NSW 2069
postal address PO Box 507, East Roseville, NSW 2069
tel (02) 9415 9900 *fax* (02) 9417 4292
Managing Director Jon Attenborough, *Publishing Director* Angelo Loukakis

General non-fiction including anthropology, child care, hobbies, house and home, how-to, craft, biography, motivation, management, outdoor recreation, sport, travel. Imprints: Simon & Schuster Australia, Kangaroo Press.

Transworld Publishers (Aust) Pty Ltd – merged with Random House Australia Pty Ltd*

University of Queensland Press

PO Box 6042, St Lucia, Queensland 4067
tel (07) 3365 2127 *fax* (07) 3365 7579
e-mail craig@uqp.uq.edu.au
web site http://www.uqp.uq.edu.au
General Manager L.C. Muller

Scholarly works, tertiary texts, Australian fiction, young adult fiction, poetry, history, general interest. Founded 1948.

University of Western Australia Press*

UWA, Nedlands 6907, Western Australia
tel (08) 9380 3670 *fax* (08) 9380 1027
e-mail uwap@cyllene.uwa.edu.au
web site http://www.uwapress.uwa.edu.au

History, natural history, literary criticism, Asian studies, Aboriginal studies, biography, children's picture books. Imprints: Cygnet Books, Staples, Tuart House, UWA Press. Founded 1954.

Viking – see Penguin Books Australia Ltd*

Weldon International Pty Ltd*

43-45 Victoria Street, North Sydney, NSW 2060
tel (02) 9955 0091 *fax* (02) 9955 9390
Chairman Kevin Weldon

Mimosa Publications Pty Ltd (division)
Primary school education.

Weldon Owen (division)
Cookery, natural science, aerial photography, encyclopedic reference works, young readers' non-fiction.

Weldon Russell (division)
Illustrated non-fiction including natural history, cookery, gardening, ancient history, general reference books and gift books.

Wild & Woolley Pty Ltd*

PO Box 41, Glebe, NSW 2037
tel (02) 9692 0166 *fax* (02) 9552 4320
web site http://www.fastbooks.com.au
Director Pat Woolley

Offers short-run paperback printing for self-publishing writers. Founded 1974.

John Wiley & Sons Australia, Ltd*

33 Park Road, Milton, Queensland 4064
tel (07) 3859 9755 *fax* (07) 3859 9715
e-mail name@johnwiley.com.au
Managing Director P. Donoughue

Educational, technical, atlases, professional, reference, trade. Imprints: John Wiley & Sons, Jacaranda Press. Founded 1954.

Wrightbooks Pty Ltd*

5 Horne Street, Elsternwick, Victoria 3185
postal address PO Box 270, Elsternwick, Victoria 3185
tel (03) 9532 7082 *fax* (03) 9532 7084
e-mail wbooks@ozemail.com.au
web site http://www.wrightbooks.com.au
Managing Director/Publisher Geoff Wright, *Editorial Director* Lesley Beaumont

Finance, investment, money management, personal development, business management. Unsolicited MSS welcome. Founded 1988.

Canada

**Member of the Canadian Publishers' Council*
†Member of the Association of Canadian Publishers

Addison-Wesley Canada – merged with Prentice Hall Canada to form Pearson Education Canada*

Annick Press Ltd†

15 Patricia Avenue, Toronto, Ontario M2M 1H9
tel 416-221-4802 *fax* 416-221-8400
e-mail annick@annickpress.com
web site http://www.annickpress.com
Co-editors Rick Wilks, Colleen MacMillan

Preschool to juvenile fiction and non-fiction. Founded 1975.

Butterworths Canada Ltd

75 Clegg Road, Markham, Ontario L6G 1A1
tel 905-479-2665 *fax* 905-479-2826
e-mail info@butterworths.ca

Law and accountancy. Division of Reed Elsevier plc.

Canada Publishing Corporation†

164 Commander Boulevard, Scarborough, Ontario M1S 3C7
tel 416-293-8141 *fax* 416-293-9009

Publishers of elementary and secondary school textbooks; general trade/consumer publications including cookbooks, business, sport and fiction; professional and reference materials; annual publications, including *Canadian Global Almanac* and *Who's Who in Canada*. Founded 1844.

Canadian Stage and Arts Publications Ltd

104 Glenrose Avenue, Toronto, Ontario M4T 1K8
tel 416-484-4534 *fax* 416-484-6214
President/Publisher George Hencz

Primarily children's books of an educational nature, art books. Also publishes quarterly *Performing Arts & Entertainment in Canada* (Editor: Karen Bell).

CDG Books Canada Inc.†
99 Yorkville Avenue, Suite 400, Toronto, Ontario M5R 3K5
tel 416-963-8830 *fax* 416-923-4821
Trade book publishers. Founded 1905.

The Charlton Press
2040 Yonge Street, Suite 208, Toronto, Ontario M4S 1Z9
tel 416-488-1418 *fax* 416-488-4656
e-mail chpress@charltonpress.com
web site http://www.charltonpress.com
President W.K. Cross
Collectibles, numismatics, Sportscard price catalogues. Founded 1952.

Doubleday Canada Ltd*
105 Bond Street, Toronto, Ontario M5B 1Y3
tel 416-340-0777 *fax* 416-340-1069
Chairman Abraham Simkin, *President/Publisher* John Neale
General trade non-fiction: current affairs, politics; fiction; children's fiction and illustrated. Division of **Random House of Canada Ltd**. Founded 1942.

Douglas & McIntyre Ltd†
2323 Quebec Street, Suite 201, Vancouver, BC V5T 4S7
tel 604-254-7191 *fax* 604-254-9099
e-mail dm@douglas-mcintyre.com
General list, including Greystone Books imprint: Canadian biography, art and architecture, natural history, history, native studies, Canadian fiction. Children's division (Groundwood Books) specialises in fiction and illustrated flats. No unsolicited MSS. Founded 1964.

ECW Press†
2120 Queen Street E, Toronto, Ontario M4E 1E2
tel 416-694-3348 *fax* 416-698-9906
e-mail ecw@sympatico.ca
web site http://www.ecw.ca/press
President Jack David, *Secretary-Treasurer* Robert Lecker
Popular culture, sports, humour, general trade books, biographies, guidebooks. Founded 1979.

Fitzhenry & Whiteside Ltd*†
195 Allstate Parkway, Markham, Ontario L3R 4T8
tel 905-477-9700 *fax* 905-477-9179
e-mail godwit@fitzhenry.ca
tel 1-800-387-9776 (toll free) *fax* 1-800-260-9777 (toll free)
Director Sharon Fitzhenry
Trade, educational, college books. Founded 1966.

Gage Educational Publishing Company – see Canada Publishing Corporation†

Gold Eagle Books – see Harlequin Enterprises Ltd*

Harcourt Canada Ltd*
55 Horner Avenue, Toronto, Ontario M8Z 4X6
tel 416-255-4491 *fax* 416-255-4046
e-mail firstname_lastname@harcourt.com
web site http://www.harcourtcanada.com
Educational materials from K-College, medical texts, psychological testing products.

Harlequin Enterprises Ltd*
225 Duncan Mill Road, Don Mills, Ontario M3B 3K9
tel 416-445-5860 *fax* 416-445-8655
Chairman/Ceo Brian E. Hickey, *President* Stuart Campbell
Romance, action adventure, mystery. Founded 1949.

Gold Eagle Books (imprint)
Senior Editor/Editorial Co-ordinator Feroze Mohammed
Series action adventure fiction.

Harlequin Books (imprint)
Editorial Director Randall Toye
Contemporary and historical romance fiction in series.

Mira Books (imprint)
Editorial Director Dianne Moggy
Women's fiction: contemporary and historical dramas, family sagas, romantic suspense and relationship novels.

Silhouette Books (imprint)
Editorial Director Tara Gavin
Contemporary romance fiction in series.

Worldwide Library (imprint)
Senior Editor/Editorial Co-ordinator Feroze Mohammed
Contemporary mystery fiction. Reprints only.

HarperCollins Publishers Ltd*
Suite 2900, Hazelton Lanes, 55 Avenue Road, Toronto, Ontario M5R 3L2
tel 416-975-9334 *fax* 416-975-9884
web site http://www.harpercanada.com
President Claude Primeau

Publishers of literary fiction and non-fiction, business books, history, politics, biography, spiritual and children's books. Founded 1989.

Irwin Publishing Ltd†
325 Humber College Blvd, Toronto, Ontario M9W 7C3
tel 416-798-0424 *fax* 416-798-1384
e-mail irwin@irwin-pub.com
President Brian O'Donnell, *Chairman* Jack Stoddart
Educational books at the elementary, high school and college levels.

Key Porter Books Ltd†
70 The Esplanade, 3rd Floor, Toronto, Ontario M5E 1R2
tel 416-862-7777 *fax* 416-862-2304
e-mail aporter@keyporter.com
web site http://www.keyporter.com
Publisher/Ceo Anna Porter, *President/Editor-in-Chief* Susan Renouf, *Vice-President/Director of Publishing* Clare McKeon
Fiction, nature, history, Canadian politics, conservation, humour, biography, autobiography, health, children's books. Founded 1981.

Kids Can Press Ltd†
29 Birch Avenue, Toronto, Ontario M4V 1E2
tel 416-925-5437 *fax* 416-960-5437
e-mail info@kidscan.com
Publisher Valerie Hussey
Juvenile/young adult books.

Knopf Canada*
33 Yonge Street, Suite 210, Toronto, Ontario M5E 1G4
tel 416-777-9477 *fax* 416-777-9470
web site http://www.randomhouse.com
Publisher, Vice-President Louise Dennys
Literary fiction and non-fiction. Division of **Random House of Canada Ltd**. Founded 1991.

Lone Pine Publishing
10145-81 Avenue, Edmonton, Alberta T6E 1W9
tel 780-433-9333 *fax* 780-433-9646
Chairman and Founder Grant Kennedy, *President* Shane Kennedy
Natural history, recreation and wildlife guidebooks, gardening, popular history. Founded 1980.

McClelland & Stewart Inc.†
481 University Avenue, Suite 900, Toronto, Ontario M5G 2E9
tel 416-598-1114 *fax* 416-598-7764
Chairman/President/Ceo Avie Bennett
General. Founded 1906.

McGill-Queen's University Press†
3430 McTavish Street, Montreal, Quebec H3A 1X9
tel 514-398-3750 *fax* 514-398-4333
e-mail mqup@mqup.mcgill.ca
web site http://www.mcgill.ca/mqup
Queen's University, Kingston, Ontario K7L 3N6
tel 613-533-2155 *fax* 613-533-6822
e-mail mqup@qucdn.queensu.ca
web site http://www.mcgill.ca/mqupress
Academic, non-fiction, poetry. Founded 1969.

McGraw-Hill Ryerson Ltd*
300 Water Street, Whitby, Ontario L1N 9B6
tel 905-430-5000 *fax* 905-430-5020
web site http://www.mcgrawhill.ca
Educational and trade books.

Mira Books – see Harlequin Enterprises Ltd*

Nelson Thomson Learning*
(formerly ITP Nelson)
1120 Birchmount Road, Scarborough, Ontario M1K 5G4
tel 416-752-9100 *fax* 416-752-9646
President/Ceo George W. Bergquist, *Vice President of Finance/Cfo* Lesley Gouldie, *Vice President of Human Resources* Marlene Fedorkow, *Vice President, Media Services* Susan Cline, *Vice President, Operations* Ed Bierman, *VP, College* Ron Kelly, *Vice President, School* Greg Pilon, *Editorial Director, Higher Education* Evelyn Veitch
School (K-12), college and university, career education, measurement and guidance, professional and reference, ESL titles. Founded 1914.

Oberon Press
400-350 Sparks Street, Ottawa, Ontario K1R 7S8
tel/fax 613-238-3275
General.

Oxford University Press, Canada
70 Wynford Drive, Don Mills, Ontario M3C 1J9
tel 416-441-2941 *fax* 416-444-0427
web site http://www.oupcan.com
President Joanna Gertler
General, educational and academic.

Pearson Education Canada*
(formerly Prentice Hall Canada and Addison-Wesley Canada)
26 Prince Andrew Place, Toronto, Ontario M3C 2T8
tel 416-447-5101 *fax* 416-443-0948
web site http://www.pearsoned.ca
President Tony Vander Woude
Academic, technical, educational, children's and adult, trade.

Penguin Books Canada Ltd*
10 Alcorn Avenue, Suite 300, Toronto,
Ontario M4V 3B2
tel 416-925-2249 *fax* 416-925-0068
web site http://www.penguin.ca
Joint President, Publisher and Editor-in-Chief Cynthia Good
Joint President and Ceo Don Howard
Cfo Tim Man
Literary fiction, memoir, non-fiction (history, business, current events). Founded 1974.

Pippin Publishing Corporation
Suite 232, 85 Ellesmere Road, Toronto,
Ontario M1R 4B9
tel 416-510-2918 *fax* 416-510-3359
e-mail jld@pippinpub.com
web site http://www.pippinpub.com
President/Editorial Director Jonathan Lovat Dickson
ESL/EFL, teacher reference, adult basic education, school texts (all subjects).

Prentice Hall Canada – merged with Addison-Wesley Canada to form Pearson Education Canada*

Random House of Canada Ltd*
33 Yonge Street, Suite 210, Toronto,
Ontario M5E 1G4
tel 416-777-9477 *fax* 416-777-9470
web site http://www.randomhouse.com
105 Bond Street, Toronto,
Ontario M5B 1Y3
tel 416-340-0777 *fax* 416-977-8488
Chairman John Neale, *President and Publisher* David Kent
Imprints: Ballantine Canada, Doubleday Canada, Knopf Canada, Random House Canada, Seal Books, Vintage Canada. Subsidiary of Bertelsmann AG. Founded 1944.

Silhouette Books – see Harlequin Enterprises Ltd*

Stoddart Publishing Co. Ltd†
34 Lesmill Road, Don Mills,
Ontario M3B 2T6
tel 416-445-3333 *fax* 416-445-5967
e-mail stoddart@genpub.com
web site http://www.genpub.com/stoddart
Fiction and non-fiction.

Tundra Books Inc.†
481 University Avenue, Suite 802, Toronto,
Ontario M5G 2E9
tel 416-598-4786 *fax* 416-598-0247
High quality children's picture books.

University of Toronto Press Inc.†
10 St Mary Street, Suite 700, Toronto,
Ontario M4Y 2W8
tel 416-978-2239 *fax* 416-978-4738
e-mail publishing@utpress.utoronto.ca
web site http://www.utpress.utoronto.ca
President/Publisher George L. Meadows

Worldwide Library – see Harlequin Enterprises Ltd*

New Zealand

**Member of the New Zealand Book Publishers' Association*

Ashton Scholastic Ltd – see Scholastic New Zealand Ltd*

Auckland University Press*
University of Auckland, Private Bag 92019,
Auckland
tel (09) 373-7528 *fax* (09) 373-7465
e-mail aup@auckland.ac.nz
web site http://www.auckland.ac.nz/aup
Director Elizabeth Caffin
NZ history, NZ poetry, Maori and Pacific studies, politics, sociology, literary criticism, art history, biography, media studies, women's studies. Founded 1966.

David Bateman Ltd*
30 Tarndale Grove, Bush Road, Albany,
Auckland
postal address PO Box 100242,
North Shore Mail Centre,
Auckland 10
tel (09) 415-7664 *fax* (09) 415-8892
e-mail bateman@bateman.co.nz
Chairman/Publisher David L. Bateman, *Directors* Janet Bateman, Paul Bateman (joint managing), Paul Parkinson (joint managing)
Natural history, gardening, encyclopedias, sport, art, cookery, historical, juvenile, travel, motoring, maritime history, business. Founded 1979.

Bush Press Communications Ltd
4 Bayview Road, Hauraki Corner, Takapuna,
Auckland 1309
postal address PO Box 33-029, Takapuna,
Auckland 1309
tel/fax (09) 486-2667
e-mail bush.press@clear.net.nz
Governing Director/Publisher Gordon Ell
NZ non-fiction, particularly outdoor, nature, travel, architecture, crafts, Maori, popular history; children's non-fiction. Founded 1979.

Butterworths of New Zealand Ltd*
205-207 Victoria Street, Wellington 1
postal address PO Box 472, Wellington 1
tel (04) 385-1479 *fax* (04) 385-1598
e-mail Hellen.Papadopoulos@butterworths.co.nz
Publishing Director Hellen Papadopoulos
Law, accountancy.

The Caxton Press
113 Victoria Street, Christchurch, PO Box 25-088
tel (03) 366-8516 *fax* (03) 365-7840
Director E.B. Bascand
Fine printers and publishers since 1935 of NZ books of many kinds, including biography, history, natural history, travel, gardening.

Dunmore Press Ltd*
PO Box 5115, Palmerston North
tel (06) 358-7169 *fax* (06) 357-9242
e-mail dunmore@xtra.co.nz
web site http://www.dunmore.co.nz
Directors Murray Gatenby, Sharmian Firth
Education, history, sociology, business studies, general non-fiction. Founded 1970.

Godwit Publishing Ltd – acquired by Random House New Zealand Ltd*

HarperCollins Publishers (New Zealand) Ltd*
PO Box 1, Auckland
tel (09) 443-9400 *fax* (09) 443-9403
web site http://www.harpercollins.co.nz
Publishers of general literature, teen fiction, non-fiction, reference books, trade paperbacks.

Hodder Moa Beckett Publishers Ltd*
PO Box 100-749, North Shore Mail Centre, Auckland 1330
tel (09) 478-1000 *fax* (09) 478-1010
e-mail admin@hoddermoa.co.nz
Managing Director Kevin Chapman, *Managing Editor* Linda Cassells, *Commissioning Editor* Warren Adler
Sport, gardening, cooking, travel, atlases, general.

Mallinson Rendel Publishers Ltd*
Level 5, 15 Courteney Place, PO Box 9409, Wellington
tel (04) 802-5012 *fax* (04) 802-5013
e-mail publisher@mallinsonrendel.co.nz
Directors Ann Mallinson, David Rendel
Children's books. Founded 1980.

Nelson Price Milburn Ltd*
1 Te Puni Street, Petone
postal address PO Box 38-945, Wellington Mail Centre, Wellington
tel (04) 568-7179 *fax* (04) 568-2115
e-mail npm@xtra.co.nz
postal address PO Box 38-945, Wellington Mail Centre, Wellington
Children's fiction, primary school texts, especially school readers and maths, secondary educational.

New Zealand Council for Educational Research*
Box 3237, Education House, 178-182 Willis Street, Wellington 1
tel (04) 384-7939 *fax* (04) 384-7933
e-mail info@nzcer.org.nz
web site http://www.nzcer.org.nz
Director Richard Watkins, *Publisher* Bev Webber
Education, including educational policy and institutions, early childhood education, educational achievement tests, Maori education, curriculum and assessment, etc. Founded 1934.

Oxford University Press*
PO Box 11-149, Ellerslie, Auckland 5
tel (09) 525-8020 *fax* (09) 525-1072
e-mail henryj@oup.com.au
web site http://www.oup.com.au
NZ Academic/College Publisher Jill Henry

Pearson Education New Zealand Ltd*
Private Bag 102908, North Shore Mail Centre, Glenfield, Auckland 10
tel (09) 444-4968 *fax* (09) 444-4957
e-mail rosemary.stagg@awl.co.nz
NZ educational books.

Random House New Zealand Ltd*
Private Bag 102950, North Shore Mail Centre, Auckland 10
tel (09) 444-7197 *fax* (09) 444-7524
Managing Director M. Moynahan
Fiction, general non-fiction, gardening, cooking, art, business, health. Subsidiary of Bertelsmann AG. Founded 1977.

Reed Publishing (New Zealand) Ltd*
(incorporating Reed Consumer Books and Heinemann Education)
39 Rawene Road, Private Bag 34901, Birkenhead, Auckland 10
tel (09) 480-4950 *fax* (09) 480-4999
Chairman John Holloran, *Managing Director* Alan Smith
NZ literature, specialist and general titles, primary, secondary and tertiary textbooks. Imprints: George Philip, Conran Octopus, Mitchell Beazley, Reed Publishing Group Australia Pty Ltd,

Heinemann Young Books, Secker & Warburg, Hamlyn, Bounty, Dean, Buzz, Minerva, Mandarin, Cedar, Methuen Drama, Brimax, Budget Books, Octopus Publishing Group, Ginn & Company, Heinemann Education Books, Rigby Heinemann (Australia), Rigby (USA), Heinemann Education Books Inc. (USA).

Scholastic New Zealand Ltd*

21 Lady Ruby Drive, East Tamaki, Auckland
postal address Private Bag 94407, Greenmount, Auckland
tel (09) 274-8112 *fax* (09) 274-8114
General Manager David Peagram, *Publishing Manager* Christine Dale

Children's books. Founded 1962.

Shortland Publications*

2B Cawley Street, Ellerslie, Auckland 5
tel (09) 526-6200 *fax* (09) 526-4499
Submissions Heather Peach, Shortland Publications, Private Bag 11904, Ellerslie, Auckland 5
e-mail hpeach@shortland.co.nz

International primary reading market: potential authors should familiarise themselves with Shortland products. Currently seeking submissions for: *Junior novels* (ages 9-13) – Fictional MSS 8000-20,000 words long; non-fiction MSS significantly shorter. Looking for fresh ideas. *Emergent/early and fluency reading material*, 8-24pp – stories need to be predictable and to feature supports for the child learning to read, e.g. repetition of vocabulary and sentence structure. *Cocky's Circle* – 24pp read-to books for 2-6 year-olds. Stories must lend themselves to a different illustration on each page. Fantasy and humour are always good sellers. All submissions should cater for an international market; include sae. Founded 1984.

University of Otago Press*

University of Otago, PO Box 56, Dunedin
tel/fax (03) 479-8807 (03) 479-8385
e-mail university.press@otago.ac.nz
Managing Editor Wendy Harrex

Student texts and scholarly works in all disciplines and general books, including Maori and women's studies, natural history and environmental studies, health and fiction. Also publishes journals including *Landfall* and the *Women's Studies Journal*. Founded 1958.

Victoria University Press*

Victoria University of Wellington, PO Box 600, Wellington
tel (04) 463-6580 *fax* (04) 463-6581
e-mail victoria-press@vuw.ac.nz
web site http://www.vup.vuw.ac.nz
Publisher Fergus Barrowman

Academic, scholarly books on NZ history, sociology, environment, law, biology; Maori language; fiction, plays, poetry. Founded 1974.

Viking Sevenseas Ltd

23B Ihakara Street, Paraparaumu
tel/fax (04) 902-9990
e-mail viking@the.net.nz
Managing Director M.B. Riley

Natural history books on New Zealand.

South Africa

**Member of the Publishers' Association of South Africa*

Jonathan Ball Publishers (Pty) Ltd

10-14 Watkins Street, Denver Ext. 4, Johannesburg
postal address Box 33977, Jeppestown 2043
tel (011) 622-2900 *fax* (011) 622-3553

Ad Donker (division)
Africana, literature, history, academic.

Jonathan Ball/HarperCollins (division)
General publications, reference books, business, history, politics.

Delta Books (division)
General non-fiction.

Cambridge University Press

(African Branch)
Dock House, Portswood Ridge, Victoria & Alfred Waterfront, Cape Town 8001
tel (021) 419-8414
e-mail information@cup.co.za
web site http://www.cup.cam.ac.uk
Director Hanri Pieterse

Educational, ELT and academic publishers serving primary and secondary schools, further education, distance education, technikons and universities. Also publishes primary reading materials in 21 mother tongue languages.

Delta Books – see Jonathan Ball Publishers (Pty) Ltd*

HarperCollins Publishers (SA) (Pty) Ltd – see Jonathan Ball Publishers (Pty) Ltd*

Jacklin Enterprises (Pty) Ltd

PO Box 521, Parklands 2121
tel (011) 652-1800 *fax* (011) 314-2984
e-mail mjacklin@jacklin.co.nz
Managing Director M.A.C. Jacklin

Children's fiction and non-fiction; Afrikaans large print books. Subjects include aviation, natural history, romance, general science, technology and transportation. Imprints: Mike Jacklin, Kennis Onbeperk, Daan Retief.

Juta & Company Ltd*

PO Box 14373, Kenwyn 7790, Cape Town
tel (021) 797-5101 *fax* (021) 762-7424
e-mail books@juta.co.za
web site http://www.juta.co.za
Ceo Rory Wilson

School, academic, professional, law and electronic. Founded 1853.

Maskew Miller Longman (Pty) Ltd*

Howard Drive, Pinelands 7405
postal address PO Box 396, Cape Town 8000
tel (021) 531-7750 *fax* (021) 531-4049
web site http://www.mml.co.za

Educational and general publishers.

Oxford University Press Southern Africa*

Vasco Boulevard, NI City, Cape Town 7460
postal address PO Box 12119, NI City, Cape Town 7463
tel (021) 595-4400 *fax* (021) 595-4430
e-mail oxford@oup.co.za
Managing Director Kate McCallum

David Philip Publishers (Pty) Ltd*

PO Box 23408, Claremont 7735, Western Cape
tel (21) 6744-136 *fax* (21) 6743-358
e-mail dpp@iafrica.com
web site http://www.twisted.co.za/dpp
Managing & Marketing Director Bridget Impey, *Publishing Director* Russell Martin, *Non-executive Directors* David Philip, Marie Philip, Wilmot James, G.J. Gerwell, Njabulo Ndebele

Academic, history, social sciences, politics, theology, biography, belles-lettres, reference books, fiction, cartoons, educational, children's books. Founded 1971.

Ravan Press (Pty) Ltd

4th Floor, Randhill, 104 Bordeaux Drive, Randburg
postal address PO Box 145, Randburg 2125
tel (011) 789-7636 *fax* (011) 789-7653
Executive Chairman G.E. de Villiers

South African studies: history, politics, social studies; fiction, literature, children's, educational. Founded 1972.

Shuter and Shooter (Pty) Ltd*

230 Church Street, Pietermaritzburg 3201, KwaZulu-Natal
postal address PO Box 109, Pietermaritzburg 3200, KwaZulu-Natal
tel (0331) 946-830/948-881 *fax* (0331) 427-419
e-mail dryder@shuter.co.za
Publishing Director D.F. Ryder

Primary and secondary educational, science, biology, history, maths, geography, English, Afrikaans, biblical studies, music, teacher training, agriculture, accounting, early childhood, dictionaries, African languages. Founded 1925.

Struik Publishers (Pty) Ltd*

Cornelius Struik House, 80 McKenzie Street, Cape Town 8001
tel (021) 462-4360 *fax* (021) 462-4379
Managing Director Steve Connolly

General illustrated non-fiction. Division of Struik New Holland Publishing (Pty) Ltd.

Unisa Press*

PO Box 392, Pretoria 0003
tel (012) 429-3051 *fax* (012) 429-3221
e-mail unisa-press@unisa.ac.za
web site http://www.unisa.ac.za/dept/press/index.html
Head Phoebe Van Der Walt

Theology and all academic disciplines. Publishers of University of South Africa. Imprint: UNISA. Founded 1957.

Van Schaik Publishers*

PO Box 12681, Hatfield, Pretoria 0028
tel (012) 342-2765 *fax* (012) 433-563
e-mail jlvschai@jlvanschaik.com
web site http://www.jlvanschaik.com

Publishers of books in English, Afrikaans and African languages. Specialists in textbooks and fiction (school books) in 11 official languages. Founded 1914.

Witwatersrand University Press*

PO Wits, Johannesburg 2050
tel (011) 484-5910 *fax* (011) 484-5971
e-mail wup@iafrica.com
web site http://www.wits.ac.za/wup.html

Zebra Press

PO Box 5563, Rivonia 2128
tel (011) 807-2292 *fax* (011) 803-1783

Publishers of non-fiction books, especially business, motivational and lifestyle, as well as contemporary South African interest. Imprint of Struik New Holland Publishing (Pty) Ltd.

USA

**Member of the Association of American Publishers Inc.*

Abbeville Press

22 Cortlandt Street, 32nd Floor, New York, NY 10007
tel 212-577-5555 *fax* 212-577-5579
Publisher/President Robert Abrams

Art and illustrated books. Founded 1977.

Abingdon Press

PO Box 801, Nashville, TN 37202-0801
tel 615-749-6404 *fax* 615-749-6512
web site http://www.abingdon.org
Senior Vice President, Publishing Harriett Jane Olson

General interest, professional, academic and reference – primarily directed to the religious market.

Harry N. Abrams Inc.

100 Fifth Avenue, New York, NY 10011
tel 212-206-7715 *fax* 212-645-8437
Ceo/President/Editor-in-Chief Paul Gottlieb

Art and architecture, photography, natural sciences, performing arts, children's books. No fiction. Founded 1949.

Andrews McMeel Publishing*

4520 Main Street, Kansas City, MO 64111
tel 816-932-6700 *fax* 816-932-6706
Vice-President/Editorial Director Christine Schillig

General trade publishing; emphasis on humour, how-to, self-help, women's issues.

Applause Theatre Book Publishers

1841 Broadway, New York, NY 10023
tel 212-765-7880 *fax* 212-765-7875
President/Publisher Glenn Young

Plays, theatre, cinema, entertainment. Founded 1980.

Arcade Publishing

141 Fifth Avenue, New York, NY 10010
tel 212-475-2633 *fax* 212-353-8148
e-mail arcadeinfo@arcadepub.com
web site http://www.arcadepub.com
President/Publisher Richard Seaver, *Associate Publisher/Marketing Director* Jeannette Seaver, *General Manager* Cal Barksdale

General trade, including adult hard cover and paperbacks.

Atlantic Monthly Press – see Grove/Atlantic Inc.

Avery – see The Putnam Publishing Group

Avon Books

The Hearst Corporation, 1350 Avenue of the Americas, New York, NY 10019
tel 212-261-6800 *fax* 212-261-6895
web site http://www.avonbooks.com/
Senior Vice-President/Publisher Lou Aronica

All subjects, fiction and non-fiction. Founded 1941.

Walter H. Baker Company

PO Box 699222, Quincy, MA 02269
tel 617-745-0805 *fax* 617-745-9891
web site http://www.bakersplays.com
President Charles Van Nostrand, *Editor* John B. Welch, *UK Agent* Samuel French Ltd

Plays and books on the theatre. Also agents for plays. Founded 1845.

The Ballantine Publishing Group*

1540 Broadway, New York, NY 10036
tel 212-782-9000 *fax* 212-302-7985
web site http://www.randomhouse.com
President/Publisher Gina Centrello

Trade and mass-market general fiction, science fiction and non-fiction. Imprints: Ballantine Books, Ballantine Wellspring, Del Rey, Fawcett, Ivy, Library of Contemporary Thought, One World. Division of **Random House Inc.**

Bantam Dell Publishing Group*

1540 Broadway, New York, NY 10036
tel 212-782-9000 *fax* 212-302-7985
web site http://www.randomhouse.com
President/Publisher Irwyn Applebaum

General fiction and non-fiction. Imprints: Bantam Hardcover, Bantam Mass Market, Bantam Trade Paperback, Crimeline, Delacorte Press, Dell, Delta, Dial Press, Domain, DTP, Fanfare, Island, Spectra. Division of **Random House Inc.**

Barron's Educational Series Inc.

250 Wireless Boulevard, Hauppage, NY 11788
tel 516-434-3311 *fax* 516-434-3723
web site http://www.barronseduc.com
President Manuel H. Barron, *Executive Vice President* Ellen Sibley

Test preparation, juvenile, cookbooks, crafts, business, pets, gardening, family and health, art, study guides, school guides. Founded 1941.

Beacon Press

25 Beacon Street, Boston, MA 02108
tel 617-742-2110 *fax* 617-723-3097
Director Helene Atwan

General non-fiction in fields of religion, ethics, philosophy, current affairs, gender studies, environmental concerns, African-American studies, anthropology and women's studies, nature.

Berkley Publishing Group
375 Hudson Street, New York, NY 10014
tel 212-366-2000 *fax* 212-366-2666
e-mail online@penguinputnam.com
web site http://www.penguinputnam.com
President David Shanks, *President and Publisher, Berkley Books* Leslie Gelbman, *Executive Director, Trade Paperbacks* Louise Burke

Fiction and general non-fiction. Imprints: Ace Books, Berkley Books, Boulevard, Diamond Books, HP Books, Jam, Jove, Perigee, Prime Crime, Riverhead Books (paperback). Division of **Penguin Putnam Inc.** Founded 1954.

Berkley Books (imprint)
President and Publisher Leslie Gelbman

Fiction and general non-fiction for adults. Imprints: Ace Books, Berkley Books, Boulevard Books, Diamond Books, Jam, Jove, Prime Crime. Founded 1954.

HP Books (imprint)
Editorial Director, Automotive Michael Lutfy

Non-fiction trade paperbacks. Founded 1964.

Perigee Books (imprint)
Vice President/Publisher John Duff

Non-fiction paperbacks: psychology, spirituality, reference, etc. Founded 1980.

Riverhead Books (Trade Paperback)
Editor Christopher Knutsen

Fiction and general non-fiction for adults. Founded 1995.

Betterway Books – see Writer's Digest Books

BlueHen – see The Putnam Publishing Group

R.R. Bowker*
121 Chanlon Road, New Providence, NJ 07974
tel 908-464-6800 *fax* 908-464-3553
President Ira T. Siegel

Bibliographies and reference tools for the book trade and literary and library worlds, available in hardcopy, on microfiche, online and CD-Rom. Reference books for music, art, business, computer industry, cable industry and information industry. A Reed Reference Publishing company.

Boyds Mills Press
815 Church Street, Honesdale, PA 18431
tel 570-253-1164 *fax* 570-253-0179
web site http://www.boydsmillpress.com
Publisher Kent Brown Jr, *President* Clay Winters, *Editorial Director* Larry Rosler, *Art Director* Tim Gillner

Fiction, non-fiction, and poetry trade books for children. Founded 1990.

Burford Books
PO Box 388, Short Hills, NJ 07078
tel 973-258-0960 *fax* 973-258-0113
e-mail pburford@aol.com
President Peter Burford

Outdoor activities: golf, sports, fitness, nature, travel. Founded 1997.

Cambridge University Press*
(North American Branch)
40 West 20th Street, New York, NY 10011
tel 212-924-3900 *fax* 212-691-3239
web site http://www.cup.org
Director Richard L. Ziemacki

Candlewick Press
2067 Massachusetts Avenue, Cambridge, MA 02140
tel 617-661-3330 *fax* 617-661-0565
Editor-in-Chief Liz Bicknell, *Senior Editor* Mary Lee Donovan, *Editor* Gale Pryor, *Editor-at-Large* Amy Ehrlich

Children's books – 6 months to 14 years: board books, picture books, novels, non-fiction, novelty books. Submit material through a literary agent. Subsidiary of **Walker Books Ltd**, UK. Founded 1991.

Carroll & Graf Publishers Inc.
19 West 21st Street, Suite 601, New York, NY 10010
tel 212-889-8772
Publisher/Editor Kent Carroll, *Subrights* Martine Ballen, *Foreign Rights* Lena Dixon

Mystery and crime, popular fiction, history, biography, literature, literary fiction. Founded 1983.

Chronicle Books
85 Second Street, 6th Floor, San Francisco, CA 94105
tel 415-537-3730 *fax* 415-537-4460
web site http://www.chroniclebooks.com
Publisher Jack Jensen, *Associate Publishers* Christine Carswell, Craig Hetzer, Nion McEvoy, Victoria Rock

Cooking, art, fiction, general, children's, gift, new media, gardening, regional, nature. Founded 1967.

Coffee House Press
27 N 4th Street, Suite 400, Minneapolis, MN 55401
tel 612-338-0125 *fax* 612-338-4004
UK Representation Patricia Moosbrugger

tel 212-569-3618 *fax* 212-569-3633
Literary fiction and poetry; collectors' editions. Founded 1984.

Columbia University Press*

562 West 113th Street, New York, NY 10025
tel (0243) 842165 *fax* (0243) 842167
UK 1 Oldlands Way, Bognor Regis, West Sussex PO22 9SA
tel (0243) 842165 *fax* (0243) 842167
Editor-in-Chief Kate Wittenberg
General reference works in print and electronic formats, translations and serious non-fiction of more general interest.

Concordia Publishing House

3558 S Jefferson Avenue, St Louis, MO 63118
tel 314-268-1000 *fax* 314-268-1329
Executive Vice-President, Editorial Barry Bobb
Religious books, Lutheran perspective. Few freelance MSS accepted; query first. Founded 1869.

The Continuum Publishing Company Inc.

370 Lexington Avenue, New York, NY 10017-6503
tel 212-953-5858 *fax* 212-953-5944
e-mail contin@tiac.net
web site http://www.continuum-books.com
Chairman/Publisher Werner Mark Linz
General non-fiction, education, literature, psychology, politics, sociology, literary criticism, religious studies. Founded 1980.

Cornell University Press*

(including ILR Press and Comstock Publishing Associates)
Sage House, 512 East State Street, Ithaca, NY 14850
tel 607-277-2338 *fax* 607-277-2374
e-mail cupressinfo@cornell.edu
web site http://www.cornellpress.cornell.edu
Director John G. Ackerman
Scholarly books. Founded 1869.

Council Oak Books

1290 Chestnut Street, Suite 2, San Francisco, CA 94109
tel 415-931-6868 *fax* 415-931-5353
e-mail calla@sky4.com
Publishing Director Melissa Lilly, *Editor-in-Chief* Kevin Bentley
Non-fiction: native American, multicultural, life skills, life accounts, Earth awareness, meditation. Founded 1984.

The Countryman Press

PO Box 748, Rte 12N, Mount Tom Building, Woodstock, VT 05091
tel 802-457-4826 *fax* 802-457-1678
e-mail countrymanpress@wwnorton.com
web site http://www.countrymanpress.com
Editor-in-Chief Helen Whybrow
Outdoor recreation guides for anglers, hikers, cyclists, canoeists and skiers, US travel guides, New England non-fiction, how-to books, country living books, books on nature and the environment, classic reprints and general non-fiction. No unsolicited MSS. Division of **W.W. Norton & Co. Inc.** Founded 1973.

Crown Publishing Group*

299 Park Avenue, New York, NY 10170
tel 212-572-2408 *fax* 212-940-7408
President/Publisher Chip Gibson
General fiction, non-fiction, illustrated books. Imprints: Bell Tower, Clarkson Potter, Crown Publishers Inc., Harmony Books, Three Rivers Press. Division of **Random House Inc.**

DAW Books Inc.

375 Hudson Street, 3rd Floor, New York, NY 10014
tel 212-366-2096 *fax* 212-366-2090
e-mail daw@penguinputnam.com
web site http://www.dawbooks.com
Publishers Elizabeth R. Wollheim, Sheila E. Gilbert
Science fiction, fantasy, horror, mainstream thrillers: originals and reprints. Imprints: DAW/Fantasy, DAW/Fiction, DAW/Science Fiction. Affiliate of **Penguin Putnam Inc.** Founded 1971.

Dell Publishing – now Bantam Dell Publishing Group*

Dial Books for Young Readers – see Penguin Putnam Books for Young Readers

Doubleday Broadway Publishing Group*

1540 Broadway, New York, NY 10036
tel 212-782-9000 *fax* 212-302-7985
web site http://www.randomhouse.com
President/Publisher Stephen Rubin
General fiction and non-fiction. Imprints: Anchor Bible Dictionary, Anchor Bible Reference Library, Currency, Doubleday, Doubleday Bible Commentary, Doubleday/Galilee, Doubleday/Image, Nan A. Talese, The New Jerusalem Bible. Division of **Random House Inc.**

Dover Publications Inc.

31 E 2nd Street, Mineola, NY 11501
tel 516-294-7000 *fax* 516-742-5049

Vice-President, Editorial Paul Negri
Art, architecture, antiques, crafts, juvenile, food, history, folklore, literary classics, mystery, language, music, math and science, nature, design and ready-to-use art. Founded 1941.

Dutton
(formerly Dutton/Signet)
375 Hudson Street, New York, NY 10014
tel 212-366-2000 *fax* 212-366-2666
e-mail online@penguinputnam.com
web site http://www.penguinputnam.com
President Carole Baron, *Vice President/Publisher/Editorial Director* Lori Lipsky, *Editor-in-Chief* Brian Tart
Fiction and general non-fiction for adults. Imprint: Dutton. Division of **Penguin Putman Inc.**

Dutton Children's Books – see Penguin Putnam Books for Young Readers

Facts On File Inc.
11 Penn Plaza, 15th Floor, New York, NY 10001-2006
tel 212-967 8800 *fax* 212-967 9196
President Mark McDonnell
General reference books and services for colleges, libraries, schools and general public. Founded 1940.

Farrar, Straus & Giroux Inc.
19 Union Square West, New York, NY 10003
tel 212-741-6900 *fax* 212-633-9385
Publisher/Editor-in-Chief Jonathan Galassi
General publishers.

Firebrand Books
141 The Commons, Ithaca, NY 14850
tel 607-272-0000
web site http://www.firebrandbooks.com
Editor/Publisher Nancy K. Bereano
Feminist and lesbian fiction and non-fiction. Founded 1986.

Fodor's Travel Publications Inc. – see Random House Inc.*

Four Walls Eight Windows
39 West 14th Street, Room 503, New York, NY 10011
tel 212-206-8965 *fax* 212-206-8799
e-mail edit@fourwallseightwindows.com
web site http://www.fourwallseightwindows.com
Publisher John Oakes
Fiction, history, current affairs, biography, environment, health. No unsolicited submissions accepted. Founded 1987.

Samuel French Inc.
45 West 25th Street, New York, NY 10010
tel 212-206-8990 *fax* 212-206-1429
Play publishers and authors' representatives (dramatic).

David R. Godine, Publisher Inc.
9 Hamilton Place, Boston, MA 02108
tel 617-451-9600 *fax* 617-350-0250
e-mail info@godine.com
web site http://www.godine.com
President David R. Godine
Fiction, photography, poetry, art, biography, children's, essays, history, typography, architecture, nature and gardening, music, cooking, words and writing, and mysteries. Founded 1970.

Golden Books Family Entertainment
888 Seventh Avenue, New York, NY 10106
tel 212-547-6700 *fax* 212-547-6788
Chairman/Ceo Richard E. Snyder, *Coo* Richard Collins
Children's books, educational workbooks and products, electronic books and software, children's videos. Founded 1907.

Greenwillow Books
1350 Avenue of the Americas, New York, NY 10019
tel 212-261-6500 *fax* 212-261-6619
Senior Vice-President/Editor-in-Chief Susan Hirschman
Children's books. Division of **William Morrow & Co. Inc.**

Grosset & Dunlap – see Penguin Putnam Books for Young Readers

Grove/Atlantic Inc.
841 Broadway, New York, NY 10003-4793
tel 212-614-7850 *fax* 212-614-7886
Publisher Morgan Entrekin
MSS of permanent interest, fiction, biography, autobiography, history, current affairs, social science, belles-lettres, natural history. Imprints: Atlantic Monthly Press, Grove Press.

Harcourt Trade Division*
525 B Street, Suite 1900, San Diego, CA 92101
tel 619-231-6616 *fax* 619-699-6320
web site http://www.harcourtbrace.com
President/Publisher, Adult Books Dan Farley, *Vice President/Publisher, Children's Books* Louise Pelan
General publishers. Fiction, history, biography, etc. Division of Harcourt Inc.

HarperCollins Publishers*

10 East 53rd Street, New York, NY 10022
tel 212-207-7000 *fax* 212-207-7145
web site http://www.harpercollins.com
HarperCollins SanFrancisco 1160 Battery Street, San Francisco, CA 94111
tel 415-477-4400 *fax* 415-477-4444
President/Ceo Jane Friedman

Fiction, history, biography, poetry, science, travel, cookbooks, juvenile, educational, business, technical and religious. No unsolicited material; all submissions must come through a literary agent. Founded 1817.

HarperInformation (division)
Imprints: HarperBusiness, HarperResource, Access Travel, William Morrow Cookbooks.

HarperSanFrancisco (division)
Imprint: HarperSanFrancisco.

HarperTrade (division)
Imprints: HarperCollins, Perennial, Cliff Street Books, The Ecco Press, Quill, Amistad, HarperAudio, Large Print Editions, and Regan Books (*President and Publisher* Judith Regan).

Morrow/Avon (division)
Imprints: William Morrow, Avon, HarperTorch, Eos, HarperEntertainment.

HarperCollins Children's Books Group
1350 6th Avenue, New York, NY 10019
tel 212-261-6500
President/Publisher Susan Katz
Imprints: Greenwillow Books, Joanna Cotler Books, Laura Geringer Books, HarperCollins, HarperFestival, HarperTrophy, Avon, Tempest.

Harvard University Press*

79 Garden Street, Cambridge, MA 02138-1499
tel 617-495 2600 *fax* 617-495-5898
web site http://www.hup.harvard.edu
Director William P. Sisler, *Editor-in-Chief/ Assistant Director* Aida D. Donald

History, philosophy, literary criticism, politics, economics, sociology, music, science, classics, social sciences, behavioural sciences, law.

Hastings House Book Publishers

9 Mott Avenue, Suite 203, Norwalk, CT 06850
tel 203-838-4083 *fax* 203-838 4084
e-mail PLeers@aol.com
web site http://www.upub.com
Publisher Peter Leers, *Associate Editor* Rachel Borst, *Editor* Vallerie Huyghue

Travel, general non-fiction, controversy, how-to.

D.C. Heath and Co. – acquired by Houghton Mifflin Company*

Hill & Wang

19 Union Square West, New York, NY 10003
tel 212-741-6900 *fax* 212-633-9385
Publisher Elisabeth Sifton, *Editor* Lauren M. Osborne, *Consulting Editor* Arthur W. Wang

General non-fiction, history, drama. Division of **Farrar, Straus & Giroux Inc**. Founded 1956.

Hippocrene Books Inc.

171 Madison Avenue, New York, NY 10016
tel 212-685-4371 *fax* 212-779-9338
e-mail orders@hippocrenebooks.com
web site http://www.hippocrenebooks.com
President/Editorial Director George Blagowidow, *Publisher* Jacek Galazka

Foreign language books, international cookbooks, foreign language dictionaries, love poetry, travel, military history, Polonia, general trade. Founded 1971.

Holiday House

425 Madison Avenue, New York, NY 10017
tel 212-688-0085
President John Briggs, *Vice-President/Editor-in-Chief* Regina Griffin

General children's books. Send query letter before submitting MSS. Always include sae. No multiple submissions, please. Founded 1935.

Henry Holt and Company LLC*

115 West 18th Street, New York, NY 10011
tel 212-886-9200 *fax* 212-633-0748
President/Publisher John Sterling

History, biography, nature, science, self-help, novels, mysteries; books for young readers; trade paperback line, computer books. Founded 1866.

Houghton Mifflin Company*

222 Berkeley Street, Boston, MA 02116
tel 617-351-5000
Executive Vice-President/Publisher, Trade and Reference Division Wendy J. Strothman

Fiction and non-fiction – history, political science, biography, nature (Peterson Guides), and gardening guides; both adult and juvenile. Imprints: Mariner (original and reprint paperbacks); Chapters (cookbooks). Length: 60,000-180,000 words; juveniles, any reasonable length. Founded 1832.

HP Books – see Berkley Publishing Group

Hyperion*

114 Fifth Avenue, New York, NY 10011
tel 212-633-4400 *fax* 212-633-4811
Vice-President/Publisher Robert Miller, *Vice-President/Publisher (Hyperion Books for Children)* Lisa Holton

General fiction and non-fiction, children's books. Division of Buena Vista Publishing, formerly Disney Book Publishing Inc. Founded 1990.

Indiana University Press

601 North Morton Street, Bloomington, IN 47404-3797
tel 812-855-4203 *fax* 812-855-8507
e-mail iupress@indiana.edu
web site http://www.indiana.edu/~iupress
Director Peter-John Leone

African studies, Russian and East European studies, semiotics, literary criticism, music, history, women's studies, Jewish studies, African-American studies, film, folklore, philosophy, medical ethics, archaeology, anthropology, paleontology. Reference and high level trade books. Founded 1950.

International Marine Publishing

PO Box 220, Camden, Maine 04843
tel 207-236-4837 *fax* 207-236-6314
e-mail nancy_dowling@mcgraw-hill.com
web site http://www.internationalmarine.com
Editorial Director Jonathan F. Eaton

Imprints: International Marine (boats, boating and sailing); Ragged Mountain Press (sport, adventure/travel, natural history). Division of the McGraw-Hill Companies. Founded 1992.

The Johns Hopkins University Press*

2715 North Charles Street, Baltimore, MD 21218-4319
tel 410-516-6971 *fax* 410-516-6968
Director James D. Jordan

History, literary criticism, classics, politics, economic development, environmental studies, biology, medical genetics, consumer health, history, religion. Founded 1878.

Keats Publishing

2020 Avenue of the Stars, Suite 300, Los Angeles, CA 90067

Natural health, alternative medicine, nutrition and medical books. Division of **NTC/Contemporary Publishing Group**. Founded 1971.

Knopf Publishing Group*

299 Park Avenue, New York, NY 10170
tel 212-572-2600 *fax* 212-572-8700
web site http://www.randomhouse.com
President Sonny Mehta

General literature, fiction, belles-lettres, sociology, politics, history, nature, science, etc. Imprints: Alfred A. Knopf Inc., Anchor, Everyman's Library, Pantheon Books, Schocken Books, Vintage Books. Division of **Random House Inc.**

Krause Publications

700 East State Street, Iola, WI 54990-0001
tel 715-445-2214 *fax* 715-445-4087
e-mail info@Krause.com
web site http://www.Krause.com
Acquisitions Editor Paul Kennedy

Antiques and collectibles, sewing and crafts, ceramics, outdoors, hunting, Internet, lifestyle.

Little, Brown & Company

3 Center Plaza, Boston, MA 02108
tel 617-227-0730
Chief Executive Larry Kirshbaum

General literature, especially fiction, non-fiction, biography, history, trade paperbacks, books for boys and girls. Imprint: Bulfinch Press (art and photography).

Lothrop, Lee & Shepard Books

1350 Avenue of the Americas, New York, NY 10019
tel 212-261-6641 *fax* 212-261-6648
Vice-President/Editor-in-Chief Susan Pearson

Children's books only. Division of **William Morrow & Co. Inc.** Founded 1904.

The Lyons Press

123 West 18th Street, 6th Floor, New York, NY 10011
tel 212-620-9580 *fax* 212-929-1836
President/Publisher Tony Lyons

Outdoor sport, natural history, sports, art, general fiction and non-fiction. Founded 1978.

Macmillan General Reference USA

1633 Broadway, New York, NY 10019
tel 212-654-8500
Senior Vice-President/Publisher Lloyd Short

General trade reference: travel, horticulture, cookery. Imprints: Alpha, ARCO, Audel, Baedeker's, Betty Crocker, Burpee, Cassell's Spectrum, Frommer's, Horticulture, Howell Book House, J.K. Lasser, Macmillan Cooking and Gardening, Macmillan Travel, Monarch,

The Unofficial Guides, Webster's New World, Weight Watchers.

Macmillan Publishing USA
1633 Broadway, New York, NY 10019
web site http://www.mcp.com
Computer science, general and mass-market non-fiction, high school and college reference and text books. Divisions: Macmillan Computer Publishing, Macmillan Digital Publishing, Macmillan Reference USA.

McGraw-Hill*
11 West 19th Street, New York, NY 10011
tel 212-337 4098
web site http://www.mcgraw-hill.com
Group Vice-President Theodore Nardin
Professional and reference: engineering, scientific, business, architecture, encyclopedias; college textbooks; high school and vocational textbooks: business, secretarial, career; trade books; training materials for industry. Division of The McGraw-Hill Companies.

McPherson & Company
PO Box 1126, Kingston, NY 12402
tel/fax 914-331-5807
e-mail bmcpher@ulster.net
web site http://www.mcphersonco.com
Publisher Bruce R. McPherson
Literary fiction; non-fiction: art criticism, writings by artists, film-making, etc; occasional general titles (e.g. anthropology). No poetry. No unsolicited MSS; query first. Founded 1974.

Microsoft Press
One Microsoft Way, Redmond, WA 98052-6399
tel 425-882-8080 *fax* 425-936-7329
Publisher James Brown, *Editorial Director* Kim Fields
Computer books. Division of Microsoft Corp. Founded 1983.

Milkweed Editions
430 First Avenue North, Suite 400, Minneapolis, MN 55401
tel 612-332-3192 *fax* 612-332-6248
Publisher/Editor Emilie Buchwald
Fiction, poetry, essays, the natural world, children's novels (ages 8-14). Founded 1979.

The MIT Press*
5 Cambridge Center, Cambridge, MA 02142-1493
tel 617-253-5646 *fax* 617-258-6779
web site http://mitpress.mit.edu
Director Frank Urbanowski, *Editor-in-Chief* Laurence Cohen
Architecture, art and design, cognitive sciences, neuroscience, linguistics, computer science and artificial intelligence, economics and finance, philosophy, environment and ecology, natural history. Founded 1961.

Morehouse Publishing Co.
PO Box 1321, Harrisburg, PA 17105
tel 717-541-8130 *fax* 717-541-8128
President Kenneth Quigley, *Publisher* Mark J.H. Fretz
Religious books, religious education, texts, seminary texts, children's books.

William Morrow & Co. Inc.
1350 Avenue of the Americas, New York, NY 10019
tel 212-261-6500 *fax* 212-261-6595
Publisher Michael Murphy
General literature, fiction and juveniles. Imprints: Greenwillow Books, Lothrop, Lee & Shepard, Morrow Jr Books, Tambourine Books, Mulberry/Beech Tree/Tupelo.

Morrow Jr. Books
1350 Avenue of the Americas, New York, NY 10019
tel 212-261-6500 *fax* 212-261-6689
Senior Vice-President, Publisher Barbara Lalicki
Children's books only. No unsolicited material accepted. Division of **William Morrow & Co. Inc**.

The Naiad Press Inc.
PO Box 10543, Tallahassee, FL 32302
tel 850-539-5965 *fax* 850-539-9731
web site http://www.naiadpress.com
Ceo Barbara Grier
Lesbian fiction; non-fiction: bibliographies, biographies, essays. Founded 1973.

NAL
375 Hudson Street, New York, NY 10014
tel 212-366-2000 *fax* 212-366-2666
e-mail online@penguinputnam.com
web site http://www.penguinputnam.com
President/Publisher Louise Burke, *Vice President/Executive Director/Editorial* Carolyn Nichols
Fiction and general non-fiction. Imprints: Mentor, Meridian, New American Library, Onyx, Roc, Signet, Signet Classics, Topaz. Division of **Penguin Putnam Inc.** Founded 1948

Thomas Nelson Publisher

501 Nelson Place, Nashville, TN 37214-1000
tel 615-889-9000 *fax* 615-391-5225
Senior Vice President of Publishing Charles Moore

Bibles, religious, non-fiction and fiction general trade books. Founded 1798.

North Light Books – see Writer's Digest Books

W.W. Norton & Company Inc.

500 Fifth Avenue, New York, NY 10110
tel 212-354-5500 *fax* 212-869-0856
e-mail ftp@wwnorton.com
web site http://www.wwnorton.com

General fiction and non-fiction, music, boating, psychiatry, economics, family therapy, social work, reprints, college texts, science.

NTC/Contemporary Publishing Group, Inc.

4255 West Touhy Avenue, Lincolnwood, IL 60712-1975
tel 847-679-5500 *fax* 847-679-2494
Vice President and Publisher John Nolan

Non-fiction. Imprints: Peter Bedrick, Contemporary Books, Country Roads Press, Jamestown Publishers, Lowell House, Masters Press, National Textbook Co., NTC Business Books, Passport Books, Quilt Digest Press, VGM Career Horizons.

Orchard Books

95 Madison Avenue, New York, NY 10016
tel 212-951-2600 *fax* 212-213-6435
e-mail jwilson@grolier.com
web site http://Grolier.com
President/Publisher Judy V. Wilson

Books for children and young adults; picture books, fiction. Founded 1987.

Ottenheimer Publishers Inc.

5 Park Center Court, Suite 300, Onwings Mill, MD 21117
tel 410-902-9100 *fax* 410-902-7210
Directors Allan T. Hirsh, Jr, Allan T. Hirsh, III

Juvenile and adult non-fiction, reference. Founded 1890.

The Overlook Press*

386 West Broadway, 4th Floor, New York, NY 10012
tel 212-965-8400 *fax* 212-965-9834
President and Publisher Peter Mayer, *Publishing Director* Tracy Carns

Non-fiction, fiction, children's books.

Oxford University Press Inc.*

198 Madison Avenue, New York, NY 10016
tel 212-726-6000 *fax* 212-726-6455
web site http://www.oup-usa.org

Scholarly, professional, reference, bibles, college textbooks, religion, medicals, music.

Pantheon Books – imprint of Knopf Publishing Group*

Peachtree Publishers Ltd

494 Armour Circle NE, Atlanta, GA 30324-4088
tel 404-876-8761 *fax* 404-875-2578
President and Publisher Margaret Quinlin, *Editorial Director* Kathy Landwehr

Children's picture books and novels. Non-fiction subjects include self-help, parenting, education, health, the American South, cookbooks and gardening; also gift books and fiction. Founded 1977.

Pelican Publishing Company*

PO Box 3110, Gretna, LA 70054
tel 504-368-1175 *fax* 504-368-1195
e-mail office@pelicanpub.com
Publisher/President Milburn Calhoun

Art and architecture, cookbooks, travel, music, business, children's. Founded 1926.

Penguin AudioBooks – see Viking Penguin

Penguin Books – see Viking Penguin

Penguin Putnam Books for Young Readers

345 Hudson Street, New York, NY 10014
tel 212-366-2000 *fax* 212-366-2666
e-mail online@penguinputnam.com
web site http://www.penguinputnam.com
President/Publisher Douglas Whiteman

Children's: picture books, board and novelty books, young adult novels, mass merchandise products. Imprints: Dial Books for Young Readers, Dutton Children's Books, Dutton Interactive, Phyllis Fogelman Books, Grosset & Dunlap, PaperStar, Philomel, Planet Dexter, Platt & Munk, Playskool, Price Stern Sloan, PSS, Puffin Books, G.P. Putnam's Sons, Viking Children's Books, Frederick Warne. Division of **Penguin Putnam Inc.** Founded 1997.

Dial Books for Young Readers (imprint)
fax 212-414-3394
President/Publisher Nancy Paulsen, *Editorial Director* Laura Hornik, *Vice President/Publisher, Phyllis Fogelman Books* Phyllis Fogelman

Children's fiction and non-fiction, picture books, board books, interactive books, novels.

Dutton Children's Books (imprint)
President/Publisher Stephanie Lurie, *Editor-in-Chief/Associate Publisher* Lucia Monfried, *Editorial Director, Dutton Children's Trade* Donna Brooks
Picture books, young adult novels, non-fiction photographic books. Founded 1852.

Grosset & Dunlap (imprint)
President, Penguin Putnam Young Readers Merchandise Group Jane O'Connor
Children's: picture books, activity books, fiction and non-fiction. Imprints: Grosset & Dunlap, Platt & Munk, Somerville House USA, Planet Dexter. Founded 1898.

Price Stern Sloan (imprint)
Vice President/Publisher Jon Anderson
Children's books: novelty/lift-flaps, activity books, middle-grade fiction, middle-grade and YA non-fiction, cutting-edge graphic readers, picture books, books plus. Imprints: Crazy Games, Doodle Art, Planet Dexter, Serendipity, Troubador Press, Wee Sing. Founded 1963.

Puffin Books (imprint)
President/Publisher Tracy Tang, *Associate Publisher/Managing Editor* Gerard Mancini
Children's paperback books. Founded 1935.

G.P. Putnam's Sons (imprint)
President/Publisher Nancy Paulsen
Children's hardcover and paperback books. Imprints: G.P. Putnam's Sons, Philomel Books, PaperStar. Founded 1838.

Viking Children's Books (imprint)
President Regina Hayes, *Executive Editor* Deborah Brodie
Fiction, non-fiction, picture books. Founded 1925.

Frederick Warne (imprint)
Original publisher of Beatrix Potter's *Tales of Peter Rabbit*. Founded 1865.

Penguin Putnam Inc.

(formerly Penguin USA and Putnam Berkley)
375 Hudson Street, New York, NY10014
tel 212-366-2000 *fax* 212-366-2666
e-mail online@penguinputnam.com
web site http://www.penguinputnam.com
President, The Penguin Group David Wan, *President/Ceo* Phyllis Grann, *Coo* David Shanks
Publisher of consumer books in both hardcover and paperback for adults and children; also produces maps, calendars, audiobooks and mass merchandise products. Adult imprints: Ace, Ace/Putnam, Allen Lane The Penguin Press, Avery, Berkley Books, BlueHen, Boulevard, DAW, Dutton, Grosset/Putnam, HP Books, Jove, Mentor, Meridian, Onyx, Penguin, Penguin Classics, Penguin Compass, Perigee, Plume, Prime Crime, Price Stern Sloan Inc., Putnam, G.P. Putnam's Sons, Riverhead Books, Roc, Signet, Signet Classics, Jeremy P. Tarcher, Topaz, Viking, Viking Compass, Viking Studio, Marian Wood Books. Children's imprints: Dial Books for Young Readers, Dutton Children's Books, Grosset & Dunlap, PaperStar, Philomel Books, Planet Dexter, Price Stern Sloan Inc., Puffin, G.P. Putnam's Sons, Viking Children's Books, Wee Sing, Frederick Warne. Divisions: **Berkley Publishing Group**, **Dutton**, **Plume**, **NAL**, **Penguin Putnam Books for Young Readers**, **The Putnam Publishing Group**, **Viking Penguin**.

Penn State University Press*

820 North University Drive, USB1, Suite C, University Park, PA 16802
tel 814-865-1327 *fax* 814-863-1408
web site http://www.psu.edu/psupress
Editor-in-Chief Peter Potter
Art history, literary criticism, religious studies, philosophy, political science, sociology, history, Russian and East European studies, Latin American studies and medieval studies. Founded 1956.

Perigee Books – see Berkley Publishing Group

The Permanent Press and Second Chance Press

4170 Noyac Road, Sag Harbor, NY 11963
tel 631-725-1101 *fax* 631-725-8215
web site http://www.thepermanentpress.com
Directors Martin Shepard, Judith Shepard
Quality fiction. Founded 1978.

Plume

375 Hudson Street, New York, NY 10014
tel 212-366-2000 *fax* 212-366-2666
e-mail online@penguinputnam.com
web site http://www.penguinputnam.com
Chairman Susan Petersen Kennedy, *President* Clare Ferraro, *Editor-in-Chief* Rosemary Ahern
Fiction and general non-fiction for adults. Division of **Penguin Putnam Inc.**

Pocket Books*

1230 Avenue of the Americas, New York, NY 10020
tel 212-698-7000 *fax* 212-698-7007
web site http://www.SimonSays.com

President/Publisher Judith M. Curr, *Vice President/Editorial Director* Emily Bestler
General fiction and non-fiction, trade hardcovers and paperbacks, mass market paperbacks. Imprints: Archway Paperbacks, Minstrel Books, Washington Square Press, MTV Books. Division of Simon & Schuster Consumer Group. Founded 1939.

Price Stern Sloan – see Penguin Putnam Books for Young Readers

Princeton University Press*

41 William Street, Princeton, NJ 08540
tel 609-258-4900 *fax* 609-258-6305
web site http://www.pup.princeton.edu
Director Walter Lippincott, *Editor-in-Chief* Ann Wald
Scholarly and scientific books on all subjects. Founded 1905.

Puffin Books – see Penguin Putnam Books for Young Readers

The Putnam Publishing Group

375 Hudson Street, New York, NY 10014
tel 212-366-2000 *fax* 212-366-2666
e-mail online@penguinputnam.com
web site http://www.penguinputnam.com
General trade books for adults; books on cassette. Imprints: Avery, BlueHen, G.P. Putnam's Sons, Riverhead Books, Jeremy P. Tarcher, Tarcher/Penguin, Putnam Berkley Audio, Marian Wood Books. Division of **Penguin Putnam Inc.**

Avery (imprint)
Executive Editor Laura Shepherd
Health and nutrition. Founded 1976.

BlueHen (imprint)
Editors Frederick Ramey, Greg Michaelson
Hardcover and paperback literary fiction and non-fiction.

Putnam Berkley Audio (imprint)
Senior Editor David Highfill
Founded 1996.

G.P. Putnam's Sons (imprint)
Senior Vice President and Publisher Neil Nyren
Fiction and general non-fiction for adults; books on cassette. Founded 1838.

Riverhead Books (Hardcover) (imprint)
Publisher Susan Petersen Kennedy
Fiction and general non-fiction for adults. Founded 1995.

Jeremy P. Tarcher (imprint)
President Jeremy P. Tarcher, *Publisher* Joel Fotinos
Non-fiction, general trade books in hardcover and paperback for adults. Founded 1965.

Marian Wood Books (imprint)
Vice President/Editor Marian Woods

G.P. Putnam's Sons (adult) – see The Putnam Publishing Group

G.P. Putnam's Sons (children's) – see Penguin Putnam Books for Young Readers

Rand McNally

PO Box 7600, Chicago, IL 60680
tel 847-329-2178
Chairman John Macomber, *President/Ceo* Richard Davis
Maps, guides, atlases, educational publications, globes and children's geographical titles and atlases in print and electronic formats.

Random House Inc.*

1540 Broadway, New York, NY 10036
tel 212-782-9000 *fax* 212-302-7985
299 Park Avenue, New York, NY 10170
280 Park Avenue, New York, NY 10017
tel 212-572-2600 *fax* 212-572-8700
Chairman/Ceo Peter Olson, *President/Coo* Erik Engstrom
General fiction and non-fiction, children's books. Subsidiary of Bertelsmann AG.

Random House Audio Publishing Group (division)
President Jenny Frost
BDD Audio Publishing, Random House Audio Publishing.

Random House Children's Media Group (division)
President Kristina Peterson
Imprints: Children's Publishing – Crown Books for Young Readers, CTW Publishing, Delacorte Press, Disney Books, Doubleday Books for Young Readers, Dragonfly Books, First Choice Chapter Books, Knopf Books for Young Readers, Knopf Paperbacks, Laurel-Leaf, Picture Yearling, Random House Children's Publishing, Skylark, Starfire, Yearling Books; Children's Media.

Random House Diversified Publishing Group (division)
President Jenny Frost
Random House Large Print Publishing; Random House Value Publishing (Children's Classics, Crescent Books, Derrydale, Gramercy Books, Testament Books, Wings Books).

The Random House Information Group (division)
President Bonnie Ammer
Imprints: Fodor's Travel Publications, Living Language, Princeton Review, Random House Reference, Random House Puzzles and Games.

Random House Trade Publishing Group (division)
President/Editor-in-Chief Ann Godoff
Imprints: Random House Adult Trade Books, The Modern Library, Villard Books.

Riverhead Books (Hardcover) – see The Putnam Publishing Group

Riverhead Books (Trade Paperback) – see Berkley Publishing Group

Rizzoli International Publications Inc.
300 Park Avenue South, New York, NY 10010
tel 212-387-3400 *fax* 212-387-3535
Publisher Marta Hallett
Art, architecture, photography, fashion, gardening, design, gift books, cookbooks. Founded 1976.

Rodale Books
33 East Minor Street, Emmaus, PA 18098
tel 610-967-5171 *fax* 610-967-8961
President, Book Division Pat Corpora
General health, women's health, men's health, senior health, alternative health, fitness, healthy cooking, gardening, pets, spirituality/inspiration, trade health. Founded 1930.

Rough Guides – see Viking Penguin

Routledge Inc.
29 West 35th Street, New York, NY 10001
tel 212-244-3336 *fax* 212-563-2269
President and Publisher Colin Jones, *Vice President and Associate Publisher* Kenneth Wright
Literary criticism, history, philosophy, psychology and psychiatry, politics, women's studies, education, anthropology, religion, lesbian and gay studies, classical studies, reference.

Running Press Book Publishers
125 S 22 St, Philadelphia, Pennsylvania 19103
tel 215-567-5080 *fax* 215-568 2919
President Stuart Teacher, *Publisher* Carlo DeVito, *Design Director* Bill Jones, *Production Director* Bill Luckey, *Editorial Director* Jennifer Worick
Art, craft/how-to, general non-fiction, children's books. Imprints: Courage Books, Running Press Miniature Editions. Founded 1972.

Rutgers University Press*
100 Joyce Kilmer Avenue, Piscataway, NJ 08854-8099
tel 732-445-7762 *fax* 732-445-7039
web site http://www.rutgerspress.rutgers.edu
Directors Marlie Wasserman, *Editor-in-Chief* Leslie Mitchner
Women's studies, anthropology, film and media studies, sociology, public health, popular science, cultural studies, literature, religion, history of medicine, Asian-American studies, African-American studies, American history, American studies, art history. Founded 1936.

St Martin's Press Inc.*
175 Fifth Avenue, New York, NY 10010
tel 212-674-5151 *fax* 212-420-9314
Trade, reference, college.

Schocken Books – imprint of Knopf Publishing Group*

Scholastic Inc.*
555 Broadway, New York, NY 10012
tel 212-343-6100 *fax* 212-343-6930
web site http://www.scholastic.com
Chairman/President/Ceo Richard Robinson, *Executive Vice President, Book Group* Barbara Marcus, *Executive Vice President, Scholastic Entertainment* Deborah Forte, *Executive Vice President, Learning Ventures* Margery Mayer
Innovative textbooks, magazines, technology and teacher materials for use in both school and the home. Founded 1920.

Scribner – imprint of Simon & Schuster Trade Division*

Sheridan House Inc.*
145 Palisade Street, Dobbs Ferry, NY 10522
tel 914-693-2410 *fax* 914-693-0776
e-mail sheribks@aol.com
web site http://www.sheridanhouse.com
President Lothar Simon
Sailing, nautical, travel. Founded 1940.

Simon & Schuster Children's Publishing Division*
1230 Avenue of the Americas, New York, NY 10020
tel 212-698-7200 *fax* 212-605 3068
President/Publisher Rick Richter
Preschool to young adult, fiction and non-fiction, trade, library and mass market. Imprints: Aladdin Paperbacks, Atheneum Books for Young Readers, Little Simon,

Margaret K. McElderry Books, Simon & Schuster Books for Young Readers, Simon Spotlight. Division of Simon & Schuster. Founded 1924.

Simon & Schuster Trade Division*

1230 Avenue of the Americas, New York, NY 10020
tel 212-698-7000 *fax* 212-698-7007
President/Publisher Carolyn K. Reidy

General fiction and non-fiction. Imprints: H&R Block, Lisa Drew Books, Fireside, The Free Press, Free Press Paperbacks, Hudson River Editions, Kaplan, Rawson Associates, Scribner, Scribner Classics, Scribner Paperback Fiction, Scribner Poetry, S&S Libros en Espanol, S&S Editions, Simon & Schuster, Touchstone. Division of Simon & Schuster. Founded 1924.

Soho Press Inc.*

853 Broadway, New York, NY 10003
tel 212-260-1900 *fax* 212-260-1902
e-mail sohopress.com
web site http://www.sohopress.com
Publisher Juris Jurjevics, *Associate Publisher* Laura Hruska

Literary fiction, commercial fiction, mystery, thrillers, travel, memoir, general non-fiction. Founded 1986.

Stackpole Books

5067 Ritter Road, Mechanicsburg, Pennsylvania 17055-6921
tel 717-796-0411 *fax* 717-796-0412
e-mail sales@stackpolebooks.com
web site http://www.stackpolebooks.com
Directors David Detweiler (chairman), David Ritter (president), Judith Schnell (editorial)

Nature, outdoor sports, Pennsylvania, crafts and hobbies, history, military history. Founded 1930.

Stanford University Press*

Stanford, CA 94305-2235
tel 650-723-9434 *fax* 650-725-3457
Director Norris Pope

Scholarly non-fiction.

Strawberry Hill Press

3848 SE Division Street, Portland, OR 97202
tel 503-235-5989
President Jean-Louis Brindamour PhD, *Executive Vice-President/Art Director* Ku Fu-Sheng, *Treasurer* Edward E. Serres

Health, self-help, cookbooks, philosophy, religion, history, drama, science and technology, biography, mystery, Third World. No unsolicited MSS; preliminary letter and return postage essential. Founded 1973.

Jeremy P. Tarcher – see The Putnam Publishing Group

Theatre Arts Books

29 West 35th Street, New York, NY 10001
tel 212-216-7877
Publishing Director William Germano

Theatre, performance, dance and allied books – acting techniques, voice, movement, costume, etc; a few plays. Division of **Routledge Inc**.

Time Life Inc.*

2000 Duke Street, Alexandria, VA 22314
tel 703-838-7000 *fax* 703-838-7225
President/Ceo Steven L. Janas

Non-fiction: art, cooking, crafts, food, gardening, health, history, home maintenance, nature, photography, science. Subsidiary of Time Warner Inc. Founded 1961.

Tor Books

175 Fifth Avenue, 14th Floor, New York, NY 10010
tel 212-388-0100 *fax* 212-388-0191

Fiction: general, historical, western, suspense, mystery, horror, science fiction, fantasy, humour, juvenile, classics (English language); non-fiction: adult and juvenile. Affiliate of **St Martin's Press Inc**. Founded 1980.

Tuttle Publishing/Periplus Editions

153 Milk Street, Boston, MA 02109
tel 617-951-4080 *fax* 617-951-4045
Periplus Editions, 5 Little Road 08-01, Singapore 536983
tel 65-280-3320 *fax* 65-280-6290
Publisher Eric Oey, *President* Michael Kerber, *Editorial Director* Jan Johnson

Asian art, culture, cooking, gardening, Eastern philosophy, martial arts, health. Founded 1948.

United Publishers Group – see Hastings House Book Publishers

The University of Alabama Press

Box 870380, Tuscaloosa, AL 35487
tel 205-348-5180 *fax* 205-348-9201
Director Nicole Mitchell, *Managing Editor* Elizabeth May

American and Southern history, African-American studies, religion, rhetoric and communication, Judaic studies, literary criticism, anthropology and archaeology. Founded 1945.

The University of Arkansas Press

The University of Arkansas, 201 Ozark Avenue, Fayetteville, AR 72701
tel 501-575-3246 *fax* 501-575-6044
e-mail uaprinfo@cavern.uark.edu
Director Lawrence J. Malley
Biography, history, humanities, literary criticism, Middle East studies, poetry. Founded 1980.

University of California Press*

2120 Berkeley Way, Berkeley, CA 94720
tel 510-642-4247 *fax* 510-643-7127
Director James H. Clark
Publishes scholarly books, books of general interest, series of scholarly monographs and scholarly journals.

University of Chicago Press*

5801 South Ellis Avenue, Chicago, IL 60637
tel 773-702-7700 *fax* 773-702-9756
Director Paula Barker Duffy
Scholarly books and monographs, religious and scientific books, general trade books, and 54 scholarly journals.

University of Illinois Press

1325 South Oak Street, Champaign, IL 61820
tel 217-333-0950 *fax* 217-244-8082
Director Willis G. Regier
American studies (history, music, literature), poetry, working-class and ethnic studies, communications, regional studies, architecture, philosophy and women's studies. Founded 1918.

The University of Massachussetts Press

PO Box 429, Amherst, MA 01004-0429
tel 413-545-2217 *fax* 413-545-1226
web site http://www.umass.edu/umpress
Director Bruce G. Wilcox
Scholarly books and works of general interest: American studies and history, black and ethnic studies, women's studies, cultural criticism, architecture and environmental design, literary criticism, poetry, fiction, philosophy, political science, sociology, books of regional interest. Founded 1964.

The University of Michigan Press

839 Greene Street, PO Box 1104, Ann Arbor, MI 48106
tel 734-764-4388 *fax* 734-615-1540
e-mail um.press@umich.edu
web site http://www.press.umich.edu/
Director Colin Day, *Assistant Director* Mary Erwin, *Executive Editor* LeAnn Fields, *Managing Editor* Christina Milton
Scholarly works in literature, classics, history, theatre, women's studies, political science, law, anthropology, economics; textbooks in English as a second language; regional trade titles, health policy and management. Founded1930.

University of Missouri Press

2910 LeMone Boulevard, Columbia, MO 65201
tel 573-882-7641 *fax* 573-884-4498
web site http://www.system.missouri.edu/upress
Director/Editor-in-Chief Beverly Jarrett, *Acquisitions Editor* Clair Willcox
American and European history, American, British and Latin American literary criticism, journalism, political philosophy, art history, regional studies; short fiction. Founded 1958.

University of New Mexico Press

1720 Lomas Boulevard NE, Albuquerque, NM 87131-1591
tel 505-277-2346 *fax* 505-277-9270
e-mail unmpress@unm.edu
Director Elizabeth C. Hadas
Western history, anthropology, archaeology, Latin American studies, photography, multicultural literature. Founded 1929.

The University of North Carolina Press*

PO Box 2288, 116 South Boundary Street, Chapel Hill, NC 27514
tel 919-966-3561 *fax* 919-966-3829
Director Kate Douglas Torrey
American history, American studies, Southern studies, European history, women's studies, Latin American studies, political science, anthropology and folklore, classics, regional trade. Founded 1922.

University of Oklahoma Press*

1005 Asp Avenue, Norman, OK 73019-0445
tel 405-325-5111 *fax* 405-325-4000
Director John N. Drayton
History of American West, American Indian studies, Mesoamerican studies, classical studies, women's studies, natural history, political science. Founded 1928.

University of Pennsylvania Press

4200 Pine Street, Philadelphia, PA 19104-4011
tel 215-898-6261 *fax* 215-898-0404
web site http://www.upenn.edu/pennpress
Director Eric Halpern
American and British history, anthropology, art, architecture, business, cultural studies, economics, folklore, ancient

studies, human rights, literature, medicine, Pennsylvania regional studies, gender studies. Founded 1890.

University of Tennessee Press*

293 Communications Building, Knoxville, TN 37996-0325
tel 865-974-3321 *fax* 865-974-3724
e-mail gadair@utk.edu
web site http://www.sunsite.utk.edu/utpress
Director Jennifer Siler

American studies: women's studies, African-American studies, ethnomusicology, folklore, history, religion, anthropology, political science, vernacular architecture, material culture, literature. Native American studies; cultural and ethnic studies; studies in most disciplines on Appalachia and the Southeast; regional fiction. Founded 1940.

University of Texas Press*

PO Box 7819, Austin, TX 78713-7819
tel 512-471-7233 *fax* 512-320-0668
e-mail utpress@uts.cc.utexas.edu
web site http://www.utexas.edu/utpress/
Director Joanna Hitchcock, *Assistant Director and Editor-in-Chief* Theresa May, *Assistant Director and Financial Officer* Joyce Lewandowski

Scholarly non-fiction: anthropology, classics and the Ancient World, conservation and the environment, film and media studies, geography, Latin American and Latino studies, Middle Eastern studies, natural history, ornithology, Texas and Western studies. Founded 1950.

University of Washington Press

PO Box 50096, Seattle, WA 98145-5096
tel 206-543-4050 *fax* 206-543-3932
Director Patrick Soden, *Associate Director/Editor-in-Chief* Naomi B. Pascal

Anthropology, Asian-American studies, Asian studies, art and art history, aviation history, environmental studies, forest history, Jewish studies, literary criticism, marine sciences, Middle East studies, music, regional studies, including history and culture of the Pacific Northwest and Alaska, Native American studies, resource management and public policy, Russian and East European studies, Scandinavian studies. Founded 1909.

University Press of Kansas

2501 West 15th Street, Lawrence, KS 66049-3905
tel 785-864-4155 *fax* 785-864-4586
e-mail mail@newpress.upress.ukans.edu
web site http://www.kansaspress.ku.edu
Director Fred Woodward, *Editor-in-Chief* Michael Briggs, *Senior Production Editor* Melinda Wirkus, *Assistant Director/Marketing Manager* Susan K. Schott

American history, military history, American political thought, American presidency studies, law and constitutional history, political science and philosophy. Founded 1946.

Van Nostrand Reinhold – acquired by John Wiley & Sons

Viking – see Viking Penguin

Viking Children's Books – see Penguin Putnam Books for Young Readers

Viking Penguin

375 Hudson Street, New York, NY 10014
tel 212-366-2000 *fax* 212-366-2666
e-mail online@penguinputnam.com
web site http://www.penguinputnam.com
Chairman Susan Petersen Kennedy, *President* Clare Ferraro

Fiction and general non-fiction for adults. Imprints: Stephen Greene Press, Pelham, Penguin Books, Penguin Classics, Penguin Compass, Rough Guides, Viking, Viking Compass, Viking Studio, Penguin AudioBooks, Allen Lane The Penguin Press. Division of **Penguin Putnam Inc.** Founded 1975.

Penguin AudioBooks (imprint)
Senior Editor David Highfill

Imprints: Penguin AudioBooks, Penguin HighBridge Audio. Founded 1990.

Penguin Books (imprint)
Senior Vice President/Publisher/Editor-in-Chief Kathryn Court

Fiction and general non-fiction for adults. Imprints: Penguin, Penguin Classics, Penguin Compass, Penguin 20th Century Classics. Founded 1935.

Rough Guides (imprint)
345 Hudson Street, New York, NY 10014
tel 212-414-3635 *fax* 212-414-3352
e-mail rough@panix.com
web site http://www.roughguides.com
Publisher (UK) Mark Ellingham, *Associate Publisher (US)* Jean Marie Kelly

Trade paperbacks, travel guides, phrasebooks, music reference, music CDs and Internet reference. Founded 1982.

Viking (imprint)
Associate Publishers Ivan Held, Paul Slovak

Fiction and general non-fiction for adults. Founded 1925.

Viking Studio (imprint)
Editor-in-Chief Christopher Sweet
High production, non-fiction art and illustrated books and giftbooks. Founded 1988.

Viking Studio – see Viking Penguin

Walker & Co.

435 Hudson Street, New York, NY 10014
tel 212-727-8300 *fax* 212-727-0984
Publisher George Gibson, *Mystery* Michael Seidman, *Juvenile* Emily Easton
General publishers, biography, popular science, health, business, mystery, history, juveniles. Founded 1960.

Frederick Warne – see Penguin Putnam Books for Young Readers

Warner Books Inc.*

1271 Avenue of the Americas, New York, NY 10020
tel 212-522-7200 *fax* 212-522-7991
Ceo Laurence K. Kirshbaum, *President/Coo/Publisher* Maureen Mahon Egen
Paperback originals and reprints, fiction and non-fiction, trade paperbacks and hardcover books, audio books, gift books. Subsidiary of Time Warner Inc. Founded 1961.

WaterBrook Press*

5446 North Academy, Suite 200, Colorado Springs, CO 80918
tel 719-590-4999 *fax* 719-590-8977
web site http://www.randomhouse.com
President/Publisher Dan Rich
Broad range of Christian fiction and non-fiction. Imprint: Harold Shaw Publishing. Division of **Random House Inc.**

Watson-Guptill Publications

1515 Broadway, New York, NY 10036
tel 212-764-7300 *fax* 212-536-5359
President/Publisher Glenn Heffernan, *Vice-President, Marketing and Sales* Harriet Pierce, *Senior Acquisitions Editors* Candy Raney, Bob Nirkand
Art, architecture, crafts, entertainment, drama, film, interior design, photography, popular culture, music, theatre. Imprints: Amphoto, Back Stage Books, Billboard Books, Radio Amateur Callbook, Watson-Guptill, The Whitney Library of Design. Founded 1937.

Franklin Watts

Sherman Turnpike, Danbury, CT 06813
tel 203-797-3500 *fax* 203-797-6986
School and library books for grades K-12.

Westminster John Knox Press

100 Witherspoon Street, Louisville, KY 40202-1396
tel 502-569-5043 *fax* 502-569-5113
e-mail wjk@ctr.pcusa.org
web site http://www.wjk.org
Executive Editor Stephanie Egnotovich
Religious, academic, reference, general.

John Wiley & Sons Inc.*

605 Third Avenue, New York, NY 10158-0180
tel 212-850-6000 *fax* 212-850-6088
e-mail info@wiley.com
web site http://www.wiley.com
President/Ceo William Pesce
Specialises in scientific and technical books and journals, textbooks and educational materials for colleges and universities, as well as professional and consumer books and subscription services. Subjects include business, computer science, electronics, engineering, environmental studies, reference books, science, social sciences, multimedia, and trade paperbacks. Founded 1807.

Marian Wood Books – see The Putnam Publishing Group

Writer's Digest Books

1507 Dana Avenue, Cincinnati, OH 45207
tel 513-531-2690 *fax* 513-531-7107
Market Directories, books for writers, photographers and songwriters.

Betterway Books (imprint)
How-to in home building, remodelling, woodworking, sports, home organisation, theatre, genealogy.

North Light Books (imprint)
Fine art, decorative art, graphic arts instruction books.

Yale University Press*

302 Temple Street, New Haven, CT 06511
postal address PO Box 209040, New Haven, CT 06520
tel 203-432-0960 *fax* 203-432-0948/2394
e-mail firstname.lastname@yale.edu
Director John G. Ryden
Scholarly books and art books.

Preparing and submitting a typescript

A well-presented typescript will make a good impression on the publisher's reader. ***Michael Legat*** *gives below guidelines on how best to present your typescript.*

A well-presented typescript (sometimes still called a manuscript) or printout is not only easier for the publisher's reader to read, but indicates a professional attitude on the part of the author. Most material for potential publication is nowadays produced on a word processor (see *PCs for writers* on page 570), but work produced on a typewriter is entirely acceptable. On the other hand, most publishers refuse even to consider handwritten typescripts and no publisher will accept them as final copy.

Presentation

A neat typescript is essential not only to make a good impression but also for the publisher's copy editor to work on. Keep your corrections to the typescript to a minimum, and retype any pages which look messy.

Margins of at least 3cm on all sides (left, right, top and bottom) are essential to accommodate editorial amendments and instructions from the copy editor or designer to the typesetter. Use the same margins throughout, so that the type on each page is of the same width and so that, except at the beginning and end of chapters, there will be the same number of lines on each page. Chapters should always begin on a new page. If you use a word processor, do not use its facility for justifying the type on the right hand side – justify on the left side only.

Lay out the text in double spacing, i.e. a full line of space between two lines of copy. This will allow room for any last minute changes you may want to make and for the copy editor's amendments. Indent the first line of each paragraph a few spaces and do not leave a blank line between paragraphs unless you want to indicate a change of subject, scene, time or viewpoint. Be as consistent as possible in your choice of variant spellings, capitalisation, use of sub-headings, etc. For example, use either -ise or -ize suffixes consistently throughout.

Number the pages (or 'folios', as publishers prefer to call them) straight through from beginning to end – don't start each chapter at folio 1. If you need to include an extra folio after, say, folio 27, call it folio 27a and write at the foot of folio 27: 'Folio 27a follows'. Then write at the foot of 27a: 'Folio 28 follows'. Don't do this too often or you will confuse and irritate your readers.

Create a front page (unnumbered) for your typescript. Type the title of the book about halfway down the page, with your name (or pen name) immediately beneath. Type your name and address in the bottom left hand corner. It is worth including your name and address on the last folio too, in case the first folio becomes detached.

Produce your finished material on standard A4 paper whether you use a type-

Manuscript checklist

- Allow generous margins
- Use double spacing
- Number each folio
- Include a front page
- Keep a duplicate of the manuscript

writer or a word processor and linked printer (in the latter case do not use continuous listing paper), and use one side of the paper only.

Fastening the typescript together

Publishers prefer to handle each folio separately, so do not use a binder which will make this impossible; ring binders are just about acceptable, but it is best to place the typescript in a cardboard envelope folder which will obviate the need for pins (which scratch), paperclips (which pick up other papers from a busy editor's desk) or staples (which make it awkward to read the typescript). Do not use plastic folders, which tend to slip if placed in a pile, as frequently happens.

Word count

The length of a book is referred to by publishers as 'the extent'. You will need to know the approximate number of words in your book when you send out letters asking if you may submit it for a publisher's consideration. Use the word count facility on your word processor, or simply count the number of words on a few full pages to get an average and then multiply that figure by the number of pages in the typescript.

Submitting your typescript

Choosing the right publisher

You will save time and postage if you check first that you are sending your typescript to a publisher who will consider it. Publishers specialise – it is no use sending your romantic novel to a firm which publishes fiction but only of the most highbrow, 'literary' genre, and even less use to send it to a firm which publishes no fiction at all. (For an index of *Publishers of fiction* see page 220.) By studying entries in the *Yearbook*, examining publishers' lists of publications, or by looking in the relevant sections of libraries and bookshops, you will find the names of publishers who might be interested in seeing your work, including the paperback houses; remember, though, that paperback publishers are often linked to a hardcover firm (the *Yearbook* gives details of these relationships), and you should submit your material to one or other of them, but not both, because they work closely together.

It is important to make the right approach to a publisher. Many publishers will not accept unsolicited material, and others are willing to consider submissions only from an agent (listings of literary agents start on page 348), and these conditions are usually indicated in their entries in the *Yearbook*. It is wise in all cases to enquire first, by letter, whether the publisher would be willing to read your material. There is no point whatsoever in asking for an interview – the publisher will not want to talk to you about the book before reading it.

The preliminary letter

This will save you time, money and possible frustration. Most publishers prefer to see a brief, businesslike preliminary letter together with a synopsis of the book and the first couple of chapters. From this the publisher can judge whether the book will fit the list, in which case you will be asked to send the complete typescript, either immediately or when it is completed. This procedure is especially advisable for non-fiction – most non-fiction books are commissioned as the result of an initial submission in the form of a synopsis and specimen chapters.

It is permissible to send your material simultaneously to more than one publisher, provided that you inform each pub-

Treatment for plays

For plays, use capitals for character names and underline stage directions in red by hand. If a traditional typewriter is employed, use red for names of characters, stage directions, etc, and black for dialogue. See also *Presenting scripts for television and film* on page 311.

lisher that the book is being considered elsewhere at the same time.

Always enclose return postage, whether for a letter or the typescript itself. Remember too that whilst publishers take every reasonable care of material, they will not accept responsibility for loss or damage while it is in their possession, so it is essential always to keep a copy of your typescript, with all changes to the text incorporated in it.

Disks and e-mails

Few publishers are currently willing to consider work submitted on disk or by e-mail, but these methods of submission will undoubtedly become commonplace before many years have passed. At the present time, however, after a book in typescript has been accepted for publication, the publisher will almost certainly ask the author to supply a disk containing the final text.

Waiting for a decision

There is usually a considerable interval between submission and the publisher's decision. Most publishers acknowledge receipt of typescripts; if you do not receive one it is advisable to check that the material has arrived. Apart from that, it is not worth chasing the publisher for a quick decision, which is unlikely to speed the process, unless your book is of a topical nature.

You should hear from the publisher within about two months. During this time the typescript will have been read 'in house' or sent to one or more advisers whose opinions the publisher respects. Favourable readers' reports may mean that the publisher will immediately accept the typescript (although probably not before consulting the production, sales, subsidiary rights and other departments), especially if it fits easily into the current publishing programme and if it is clearly saleable. On the other hand, a publisher may hesitate, despite glowing reports, and seek further opinions and explore various options before reaching a final decision. Publishers want to be sure that they will be able to sell their wares profitably, and if they are doubtful of recouping the money they will have to invest in the book – probably at least £5000 – and making a profit, it will be rejected despite the readers' enthusiasm.

If you have not had a decision after two months, write either a tactful letter saying 'I don't want to rush you but ...' or, alternatively, request an immediate decision, and be prepared to start again with another publisher.

If your book is rejected, although some publishers may give you their reasons for turning it down, most will not, nor in either case should you expect to be able to discuss the matter further, unless specifically invited to do so. Publishers do not have the time to spend on books and authors which they are not going to publish. If, in the course of rejection, the publisher should be complimentary about your work, you can take the remarks at face value – publishers do not encourage rejected authors unless they mean it.

Illustrations

If illustrations form a large part of your proposed book and you expect to provide them yourself, then they should be included with the typescript. If sending specimen chapters, then you should also include sample illustrations (this applies largely to children's picture books and to travel and technical books). Do not send originals – duplicate photographs, photocopies of line drawings and so on will ensure that little harm is done if illustrations go astray.

In the case of a children's book which you intend to illustrate yourself, obviously one finished piece of artwork is essential, plus photocopies of roughs for the rest (it is not wise to finish all the artwork before acceptance of the book – the publisher will decide on the number of illustrations to be used, and their sizes, which may not be in accordance with your original plan). If you have written a children's story, or the text for a picture book, do not ask a friend to supply the illustrations; the publisher who likes your story may not admire your friend's artwork, and will prefer to find and commission a different artist. Of course, this does not apply when an artist and author work closely together to develop an idea; in that case it is best to start by finding a publisher who likes the artist's work before submitting the story. See *Writing and the children's book market* on page 252, *Illustrating for children's books* on page 256, and *Children's book publishers and packagers* on page 259.

Travel typescripts should be accompanied by a sketch map to show the area you are writing about, with sufficient detail with which to follow the account.

If the illustrations are not your own artwork or photographs, it is best to establish early on who is responsible for the illustration costs; a seemingly generous advance against royalties might be less attractive if you have to gather the pictures, obtain permission for their use, and foot the bills.

Quotations

It is normally the author's responsibility to obtain and pay for permission to quote written material which is in copyright. Permission should always be sought from the publisher of the quoted work, not from the author. There are no standard fees for quotation: for fashionable modern writers and for the lyrics of popular songs permission may be very costly, but in other cases only a nominal fee is charged. It is permissible to quote a short extract (up to 400 words, or up to 40 lines of a poem, but not more than one quarter of the poem) under a convention known as 'fair dealing', but only for purposes of criticism or review. Fair dealing does not apply to use in anthologies. The source of any quotation must always be fully acknowledged.

Although this is your area of responsibility, you should ask your publisher for advice before embarking on the clearance of permissions for any copyright material, including illustrations.

Proofs

When the publisher accepts your typescript, if you have used a word processor you will probably be asked to supply a copy on disk. The files containing the work should be unformatted plain text – doing a fancy layout will be a waste of time, as it will be unformatted by the publisher or typesetter. Having the book on disk will save time in production, as well as cutting down the margin for errors creeping into the text.

As the author you should see the finalised copy of the typescript before it goes to the typesetter. This is really your last chance to pick up any typing errors which have previously been missed, to make any other changes, and to approve of or challenge any amendments made by the publisher's copy editor. This applies also to highly illustrated books, such as children's or 'coffee table' books, on which the designer and editor will have worked in tandem to marry the text and the pictures on each page, sometimes modifying the text to produce a satisfactory end result.

After seeing the finalised copy, you may be sent either a computer printout which has had all the last minute amendments incorporated, or galley proofs or page proofs. The printout will bear no resemblance to the finished book, but will contain everything that will appear in that book; galley proofs, produced by the typesetter, are columns of continuous text; page proofs have been made up into pages, including page numbers, headlines, illustrations, and so on.

Corrections can be made at any of these stages (see *Correcting proofs* on page 597 for the conventional proof-correcting marks), but it is a costly business, especially where page proofs are concerned. You will probably have signed a contract undertaking to pay the cost of corrections (other than printer's errors) over, say, 10-15% of the cost of composition. This does not mean that you can change 10 or 15 lines in every hundred – even small changes are very expensive – but you are entitled of course to correct any errors made by the printer or typesetter.

Michael Legat became a full-time writer after a long and successful publishing career. He is the author of a number of highly regarded books on publishing and writing.

Writing and the children's book market

Over 9000 new children's titles are published in the UK each year. ***Chris Kloet*** *suggests how a potential author can best ensure that their work is published.*

Children's book publishing can be difficult for the first-time writer to break into. It is a diverse, overcrowded market, with more than 30,000 titles currently in print. Children's publishers tend to fill their lists with commissioned books by writers they publish regularly, so they may lack space or be reluctant to take a risk with an untried author. This is a selective, highly competitive, market-led business. Since every new book is expected to meet its projected sales target, your writing must demonstrate solid sales potential, as well as strength and originality, if it is to stand a chance of being published.

Is your work right for today's market? Literary tastes and fashions change. Publishers cater to children whose reading is now almost certainly different from that of your own childhood. In the present electronic media-driven age, few want cosy tales about fairies and bunnies, jolly talking cars or magic teapots. Nor anything remotely imitative. Editors choose original, lively material – something witty, innovative and pacey. They look for polished writing with a fresh, contemporary voice that speaks directly and engages today's critical, media-savvy young readers, who are often easily bored.

Develop a sense of the market so that you can judge the potential for your work. Read widely and critically across the children's book spectrum for an overview, especially noting recent titles. As you read, pay attention to the different categories, series, genres and publishers' imprints. This will help you to pinpoint likely publishers. Before submitting your typescript, ensure that your targeted publisher currently publishes in your particular form or genre. Request catalogues from their marketing department; check out their web site. Consult the publisher's entry under *Book publishers UK and Ireland* (see page 151). Many publishing houses now stipulate 'No unsolicited MSS or synopses'. Don't spend your time and postage sending work to them; choose instead a publisher who accepts unsolicited work.

You might consider approaching a literary agent who knows market trends, publishers' lists and the faces behind them (see *Literary agents for children's books* on page 368). Some editors regard agents as filters and may prefer submissions from them, knowing that a preliminary critical eye has been cast over them.

Picture books

Books for babies and toddlers are often board books and novelties. Unless you are also a professional illustrator (see *Illustrating for children's books* on page 256) they present few opportunities for a writer. Picture books are aimed at children aged between two and five or six, and are usually 32 pages long giving 12-14 double-page spreads, and illustrated in colour.

Although a story written for this format should be simple, it must be structured, with a compelling beginning, middle and end. The theme should interest and be appropriate for the age and experience of its audience. As the text is likely to be reread, it should possess a satisfying rhythm (but beware of rhymes). Ideally, it should be fewer than 1000 words (and could be much shorter), must offer scope for illustration and, finally, it needs strong international appeal. Reproducing full-colour artwork is costly and the originating publisher must be confident of achieving co-productions with publishers overseas, to keep unit costs down. It has to be said: it is a tough field.

Submit a picture book text typed either on single-sided A4 sheets, showing page breaks, or as a series of numbered pages, each with its own text. Do not go into details about illustrations, but simply note anything that is not obvious from the text that needs to be included in the pictures.

Younger fiction

This area of publishing, which has expanded in recent years, presents opportunities for the new writer. It covers stories written for the post-picture book stage, when children are reading their first whole novels. Texts vary in length and complexity, depending on the age and fluency of the reader, but tend to be between 1000 and 8000 words long.

Publishers bring out titles under the umbrella of various series, each targeted at a particular level of reading experience and competency. Categories are: beginning or first readers, developing or newly confident, confident, and fluent readers. Note that these are not the same as reading schemes published for the schools market and do not require a restricted vocabulary. Stories for the bottom end of the age range are usually short, straight-through narratives illustrated throughout in colour, whereas those for older children are broken down into chapters and may be illustrated in black and white. The table (overleaf) lists publishers' requirements for some currently published series. Check that your material is correct in terms of length and interest level when approaching a publisher with a submission for a series.

Genre fiction

Another growth area in children's publishing is that of genre fiction. Usually published in paperback series, titles are sometimes the work of a single author, but might also be novels from different authors writing in a similar vein. Recent successes include Lucy Daniels' *Animal Ark* series of animal stories, and the spooky *Goosebumps* series by R.L. Stine. Much fiction aimed at teenagers is published in genre series.

General fiction

Many novels for children aged 9-12 are published, not in series, but as 'stand alone' titles, each judged on its own merits. The scope for different types of stories is wide – adventure stories, fantasies, historical novels, science fiction, ghost and horror stories, humour, and stories of everyday life. Generally, their length is 20,000-40,000 words. Anything longer may present the publisher with an unpalatably high price point for the book. This is a rough guide and is by no means fixed. For example, J.K. Rowling's highly successful first novel, *Harry Potter and the Philosopher's Stone*, weighs in at more than 220 closely printed pages.

Perhaps more than in other areas of juvenile fiction, the individual editor's tastes will play a significant part in the publishing decision, i.e they want authors' work which *they* like. They also need to feel confident of a new writer's ability to go on to write further books for their lists – nobody is keen to invest in an author who is just a one-book wonder.

When submitting your work it is probably best to send the entire typescript (see *Preparing and submitting a typescript* on page 248). Although some people advise sending in a synopsis with the first three chapters, a prospective publisher will need to see whether you can sustain a reader's interest to the end of the book.

Teenage fiction

As noted earlier, much of the published output for teenaged readers is published in series, sometimes under different series gen- res. While some publishers regard this age group as a difficult market to target, others make this type of writing a large part of their lists. Many of the most successful in this area publish 'stand alone' teenage novels, a notoriously hard field, only rarely. However, there are notable exceptions, as the recent success

Publisher	Series name	Length	Age group	Comments
Andersen Press	Tigers	3000-5000 words 64 pages	6-9	B&w illustrations throughout
A & C Black	Comix	2500 words 64 pages	7-9	Action stories illustrated in a comic-strip style
	Graffix	4000 words 80 pages	9-12	B&w graphic novels
	Rockets	1200 words x 4 48 pages each	5-7	4 stories linked by central character/ scenario; b&w illustrations throughout
Bloomsbury	Young Fiction	2500 words 64 pages	5-7	B&w illustrations throughout
	Middle Fiction	6000 words 64 pages	7-9	B&w illustrations throughout
Collins Children's Books	Young Fiction	2000 words 64 pages	5-7	B&w illustrations throughout
	Middle Fiction	6000-8000 words	7-9	B&w illustrations throughout
Egmont Children's Books	Blue Bananas	1200-1500 words 48 pages	5-7	Colour illustrations
	Yellow Bananas	3000 words 48 pages	7-9	Chapter stories. Colour illustrations
	Story Books	6000 words 64 pages	5-7	4 linked stories: family, school, friendship
	Reads	8000 words 96 pages	9-11	B&w illustrations throughout
	Epix	1500-2000 words 48 pages	9-11	B&w graphic novels
	Telling Times	9000-11,000 words 96 pages	10-12	Historical fiction factual background
	Telling Tales	7000-9000 words 64 pages	10-12	Author biographies
Franklin Watts	Leapfrog	500-700 words 32 pages	4-6	Colour illustrations throughout
Hodder Children's Books	My First Read Alone	1500 words 48/64 pages	5	B&w illustrations throughout
	Read Alone	2000-4000 words 48/64 pages	6-7	B&w illustrations throughout
	Story Book	8000-12,000 words 96/128 pages	7-9	B&w illustrations throughout
	Signature	20,000-45,000 words	10+	
Hodder Wayland	Bright Stars	700 words 32 pages	5-7	Colour illustrations throughout
	Shooting Stars	1500-1750 words 48 pages	6-8	Colour and b&w illustrations
	Super Stars	2250-2500 words 48 pages	7-9	Colour and b&w illustrations
	Mega Stars	4000 words 64 pages	8-10	B&w illustrations
	Tremors	2500 words 48 pages	7-10	B&w illustrations
	Scientists	2500 words 48 pages	7-10	Colour and b&w illustrations

Publisher	Series name	Length	Age group	Comments
Hodder Wayland (cont.)	Historical Story Books	2500 words 48 pages	7-10	Colour and b&w illustrations
Kingfisher	I Am Reading	1500-2000 words 48 pages	5+	Colour illustrations throughout
Orchard	Crunchies	1000-1500 words	5-7	B&w line illustrations
	Super Crunchies	5000 words	7-9	B&w line illustrations
	Red Apples	25,000 words	9-11	
	Black Apples	30,000-40,000 words	12+	
Penguin Group	First Young Puffin	1000 words 32 pages	5-7	Colour illustrations
	Colour Young Puffin	3000 words 64 pages	6-8	Colour illustrations
	Young Puffin	8000-10,000 words 96 pages	7-9	B&w line illustrations
	Surfers	13,000 words	9-12	B&w chapter heads
Random House Children's Books	Red Fox Read Alones	3000-4000 words 64 pages	6-9	B&w illustrations throughout
Scholastic Children's Books	Young Hippo	3500-10,000 words 64-128 pages	5-9	B&w illustrations throughout
	Hippo	15,000-25,000	8-11	
	Point	30,000	12+	
Transworld Children's Books	Corgi Pups	2000-2500 words 64 pages	5-8	B&w illustrations throughout
	Young Corgi	4000-10,000 words 64/80 pages	6-9	B&w illustrations throughout
Walker Books	Story Books	6000-10,000 words	4-7	Stories around central character
	Sprinters	2000 words	6-8	B&w illustrations throughout
	Racers	7,500-15,000 words	7-10	B&w illustrations throughout

of a controversial novel such as *Junk*, by Melvin Burgess, and Philip Pullman's *His Dark Materials* trilogy goes to prove.

Non-fiction

The last few years have seen fundamental and striking changes in the type of information books published for the young. Hitherto the province, by and large, of specialist publishers catering for the educational market, the field has now broadened to encompass an astonishing range of presentations and formats which are attractive to the young reader. Although the illustrated text book approach still has its place in schools, increasingly, children are wooed into learning about many topics via entertaining and accessible paperback series such as the *Horrible Histories* published by Scholastic, and a host of similar series from other publishers. In writing for this market, it goes without saying that you must research your subject thoroughly and be able to put it across clearly, with an engaging style. Check out the various series and ask the publishers for any guidelines. You will be well advised to check that there is a market for your book before you actually write it, as researching a subject can be both time consuming and costly. Submit a proposal to your targeted publisher, outlining the subject matter and the level of treatment, and your ideas about the audience for your book.

Chris Kloet worked as Children's Publisher (1984-97) at Victor Gollancz Ltd, and now works as a freelance children's editor and book consultant. She has written and reviewed children's books and has lectured widely on the subject.

Illustrating for children's books

The world of children's publishing is big business. The huge range of books published each year all carry artwork – lots of it. ***Maggie Mundy*** *offers guidance for people who are at the start of their career in illustrating for children's books.*

The portfolio

Your portfolio should reflect the best of you and your work, and should speak for itself. Keep its content simple – if too many styles are included, for instance, your work will not leave a lasting impression.

Include some artwork other than those carried out for college projects, e.g. an illustration from a timeless classic to show your abilities, and something modern which reflects your own taste and the area in which you wish to work.

If your strength is for black and white illustration, include pieces with and without tone and with or without a wash. Some publishers want line and tone and some want only line. As cross hatching and stippling can add a lot of extra time to an illustration deadline, it might be advisable to leave out these samples. If you can, include a selection of humour as it can be used effectively in educational books and elsewhere. It is best not to sign and date your work: some artworks can stand the test of time and still look good after a year or two, but if it looks dated ... so is the illustrator!

An A3 portfolio is probably the ideal size. Place your best piece of artwork on the opening page and your next best piece on the last page. See *Freelancing for beginners* on page 385 for further information on portfolio presentation.

Looking at the market

Start by looking thoroughly at what is being published today for children. Take your studies to branches of big retail chains, some independent bookshops, as well as your local library (a helpful librarian should be able to tell you which are the most borrowed books). Absorb the picture books, explore the novelty books, look at the variety of colour covers, and note the range of black line illustrations inside books for children and teenagers. Make a list of the publishers you think may be able to use your particular style.

By making these investigations you will gain an insight into not only the current trends and styles but also the much favoured, oft-published classic children's literature. Most importantly, it will help you identify your market.

In books for a young age range every picture must tell the story – some books have no text and the illustrations say it all. Artwork should be uncluttered, shapes clear, and colour bright. If this does not appeal to you, go up a year or two and note the extra details that are added to the artwork (which still tells the story). Children now need to see more than just clear shapes: they need extra details added to the scene – e.g. a quirky spider hanging around, or a mouse under the bed.

Children are your most critical audience: never think that you can get away with 'any old thing'. Indeed, at the Bologna Book Fair it is a panel of children which judges what they consider to be the best picture book.

Current trends

Innovative publishers are always on the lookout for something new in illustration styles: something completely different from the tried and tested. More and more they are turning to European and overseas illustrators, often sourced from the Bologna Book Fair exhibitions and illustrators catalogue.

Philip Hopman, a Dutch illustrator, has made great strides into British publishing, with his brilliantly observed black line work. Among the many titles he has illustrated is a book for the late Leon Garfield, as well as a poetry book by Spike Milligan. He partnered Roger McGough in the hilarious and successful title *The Magic Fountain* (Bodley Head) and his artwork is used in Jostein Gaarder's *The Frog Castle* (Orion). He can make a dead fish look disgusted to have to lie in a fishmongers.

Today, virtually any medium can be used on any colour paper. Belgian Marjolein Pottie is another young illustrator to watch out for. Her picture books are done on black paper, using the paper itself to make the outlines. A new discovery in the UK, she is also to be published in the USA by Simon & Schuster and HarperCollins.

Always strive to improve on your work. Don't be afraid to try out something different and to work it up into acceptable examples. Above all, don't get left behind.

Making approaches for work

With your portfolio arranged and your target audience in mind, compile a list of publishing houses, packagers and magazines which you think may be suitable for your work.

An agent should know exactly where to place your work, and this may be the easier option (see below). However, you may wish to market yourself by making and going to appointments until you crack your first job.

Alternatively, you could make up a simple broadsheet comprising a black and white and two or three colour illustrations, together with your contact details, and have it colour photocopied or printed. Send a copy to either the Art Director, the Creative Director or the Senior Commissioning Editor (for picture books) of each potential client on your list. Try to find out the name of the person you would like to see your work. Wait at least a week and then follow up your mailing with a phone call to ask if someone would like to see your portfolio.

Know your capabilities

Know your strengths, but be even more aware of your weaknesses. You will gain far more respect if you admit to not being able to draw something particularly well than by going ahead and producing an embarrassing piece of artwork and having it rejected. You will be remembered for your professional honesty and that client may well try to give you a job where you can use your expertise.

Publishers need to know that you can turn out imaginative, creative artwork while closely following a text or brief, and be able to meet their deadline. It may take an illustrator three weeks to prepare roughs for 32 pages, three weeks to finish the artwork, plus a week to make any corrections. In addition, time has to be allowed for the roughs to be returned. On this basis, how many books can an illustrator realistically take on? Scheduling is of paramount importance (see below).

You will need to become familiar with 'publishing speak' – terms such as gutters, full bleed, holding line, overlays, vignettes, tps, etc. If you don't know the meaning of a term, ask – after all, if you have only recently left college you will not be expected to know all the jargon.

In the course of your work you will have to deal with such issues as contracts, copyright, royalties, public lending rights, rejection fees, etc. The Association of Illustrators, which exists to give help to illustrators in all areas, is well worth joining.

Organising your workload

When you have reached the stage when you have jobs coming through on a fairly regular basis, organise a comprehensive schedule for yourself so you do not overburden yourself with work. Include on it when roughs have to be submitted, how much work you can fit in while waiting for their approval, the deadline for the artwork, and so on. A wall chart can be helpful for this but another system may work better for you.

It is totally unacceptable to deliver artwork late. If you think that you might run over time with your work, let your client know in advance as it may be possible to reach a new agreement for delivery.

Payment

There are two ways in which an illustrator may be paid for a commission for a book: a flat fee on receipt and acceptance of the artwork, or by an advance against a royalty of future sales. The advance offered could be less than a flat fee but it may result in higher earnings overall. If the book sells well, the illustrator will receive royalty payments twice a year for as long the book is in print.

You need to know from the outset how you are going to be paid. If it is by a flat fee, you may be given an artwork order with a number to be quoted when you invoice. Always read through orders to make sure you understand the terms and conditions. If you haven't been paid within 30 days, send a statement to remind the client, or make a quick phone call to ask when you can expect to receive payment.

With a royalty offer, a contract will be drawn up and this must be checked carefully. One of the clauses will state the breakdown of how and when you will be paid.

Once you have illustrated your first book you should register with the Public Lending Right office (see page 626) so that you can receive a yearly payment on all UK library borrowings. You will need to cooperate with the author regarding percentages before submitting your own form. The PLR office will give you a reference number, and you then submit details to them of each book you illustrate. It mounts up and is a nice little earner!

Agents

The role of the agent is to represent the illustrator to the best of their ability and to the illustrator's best advantage. A good agent knows the marketplace and will promote illustrators' work where it will count. An agent may ask you to do one or two sample pieces to strengthen your portfolio, giving them a better chance of securing work for you.

Generally speaking, agents will look after you, your work schedules, payments, contracts, royalties, copyright issues, and try to ensure you have a regular flow of work which you not only enjoy but will stretch your talents to taking on bigger and better jobs. Without exposing your weaknesses, check that you have adequate time in which to do a job and that you are paid a fair rate for the work.

Some illustrators manage well without an agent, and having one is not necessarily a pathway to fame and fortune. Choose carefully: you need to both like and trust the agent and vice versa.

Agents' charges range from 25% to 30%. Find out from the outset how much a prospective agent will charge.

Finally

Do not be downhearted if progress is at first slow. Everyone starts by serving an apprenticeship, and it is a great opportunity to learn, absorb and soak up as much of the business as possible. Ask questions, get all the advice you can, and use what you learn to improve your craft and thereby your chances of landing a job. Publishers are always on the lookout for fresh talent and new ideas, and one day your talent will be the one they want.

Maggie Mundy has been representing illustrators for children's books since 1983. Her agency represents 25 European and British illustrators for children's books.

Children's book publishers and packagers

A quick reference guide to children's book publishers and packagers by subject area. Listings for Book publishers UK and Ireland start on page 151 and listings for Book packagers start on page 214.

Picture books

Book publishers
act-two
Andersen Press
Award Publications
Bantam Children's Books
Barefoot Books
David Bennett Books
A & C Black
Black Butterfly
Bloomsbury Publishing
Bodley Head Children's
Brimax Books
Brown Wells & Jacobs
Jonathan Cape Children's Books
Child's Play (International)
David & Charles Children's Books
André Deutsch
Dorling Kindersley
Element Books
Floris Books
Gairm Publications (Gaelic)
Gomer Press
Hamish Hamilton Children's
HarperCollins Publishers
Hawk Books
Hazar Publishing
Heinemann Young Books
Hippo Books
Hodder & Stoughton
Hunt & Thorpe
Hutchinson Children's
Kingfisher
Ladybird Books
Frances Lincoln
Lion Publishing
Little, Brown
Peter Lowe (Eurobook Ltd)
Lutterworth Press
Macmillan Children's Books
Julia MacRae Books
Madcap
Magi Publications
Mammoth
Mantra Publishing
Medici Society
Methuen Children's Books
The O'Brien Press (Ire.)
Michael O'Mara Books
Orchard Books
Orion Children's Books
Oxford University Press
Paternoster Publishing
Pavilion Books
Piccadilly Press
Poolbeg for Children (Ire.)
Puffin
Ragged Bears
Reader's Digest Children's Books
Red Fox
Scholastic Children's Books
Scripture Union
Tamarind
Tango Books
Transworld Publishers
Usborne Publishing
Ventura Publishing
Viking Children's
Walker Books
Frederick Warne
Wolfhound Press (Ire.)
World International

Book packagers
Aladdin Books
Albion Press
Bellew Publishing
Graham-Cameron
Angus Hudson
Marshall Editions
Orpheus Books
Oyster Books
Mathew Price
Sadie Fields Productions
The Templar Company
Tucker Slingsby
Ventura Publishing

Fiction

Book publishers
Andersen Press
Anvil Books/The Children's Press (Ire.)
Award Publications
Bantam Children's Books
A & C Black
Black Butterfly
Bloomsbury Publishing
Bodley Head Children's
Brimax Books
Brown, Son & Ferguson
Canongate Books
Jonathan Cape Children's Books
Child's Play (International)
David & Charles Children's Books
André Deutsch
Dorling Kindersley
Element Books
Evans Brothers
Everyman's Library
Faber & Faber
Flyways
Gairm Publications (Gaelic)
Gomer Press (English/Welsh)
Hamish Hamilton Children's
Patrick Hardy Books
HarperCollins Publishers
Hawk Books
Heinemann Young Books
Hippo
Hodder & Stoughton
Honno
Hutchinson Children's
Kingfisher
Ladybird Books
Lion Publishing
Peter Lowe (Eurobook Ltd)
Lutterworth Press
Macmillan Children's Books
Julia MacRae Books
Mammoth
Mantra Publishing
Marino Books (Ire.)

Kevin Mayhew
Methuen Children's Books
Michael O'Mara Books
The O'Brien Press (Ire.)
Orchard Books
Orion Children's Books
Oxford University Press
Pavilion Books
Piccadilly Press
Point
Poolbeg for Children (Ire.)
Puffin
Ragged Bears
Reader's Digest Children's Books
Red Fox
Robinson
Schofield & Sims
Scholastic Press
Scripture Union
Tamarind
Tango Books
D.C. Thomson
Transworld Publishers
Usborne Publishing
Viking Children's
Walker Books
Wolfhound Press (Ire.)
World International
Y Lolfa Cyf. (Welsh)

Book packagers

Albion Press
Oyster Books
Mathew Price

Non-fiction

Book publishers

act-two
Aladdin/Watts
Anness Publishing
Anvil Books/The Children's Press (Ire.)
Apple Press
Atlantic Europe Publishing Co.
Award Publications
Bantam Children's Books
Belitha Press
David Bennett Books
A & C Black
Black Butterfly
Boxtree (film/TV tie-ins)
Brimax Books
Brown Wells & Jacobs
Child's Play (International)
André Deutsch
Dorling Kindersley
Element Books
Evans Brothers
Exley Publications
First and Best in Education
Folens (Ire.)
Funfax
Geddes & Grosset
Gomer Press (English/Welsh)
HarperCollins Publishers
Heinemann Young Books
Hippo
Hodder & Stoughton
Hodder Wayland
Kingfisher
Ladybird Books
Frances Lincoln
Lion Publishing
Little, Brown
Peter Lowe (Eurobook Ltd)
Lutterworth Press
Macmillan Children's Books
Julia MacRae Books
Madcap
Mantra Publishing
Marshall Publishing
Medici Society
Merehurst
Michelin Travel Publications
The National Trust
New Orchard Editions
The O'Brien Press (Ire.)
Michael O'Mara Books
Oxford University Press
Paternoster Publishing
Pavilion Books
Piccadilly Press
Poolbeg for Children (Ire.)
Puffin
Ragged Bears
Reader's Digest Children's Books
Salamander Books
Science Museum Publications
Schofield & Sims
Scholastic Children's Books
Scripture Union
Tango Books
Transworld Publishers
Usborne Publishing
Walker Books
Frederick Warne
Wolfhound Press (Ire.)
World International
Y Lolfa Cyf. (Welsh)
Zoë Books

Book packagers

Aladdin Books
Alphabet & Image
Andromeda Oxford
Bellew Publishing
Bender Richardson White
Breslich & Foss
Brown Wells & Jacobs
Roger Coote Publishing
Cowley Hunter
Diagram Visual Information
Earthscape Editions
Graham-Cameron
Haldane Mason
Lionheart Books
Marshall Editions
Monkey Puzzle Media
Orpheus Books
Oyster Books
Mathew Price
Quarto Children's Books
The Templar Company
Toucan Books
Tucker Slingsby
Wordwright Books

Other

Activity and novelty

Book publishers

act-two
Andersen Press
Apple Press
Award Publications
David Bennett Books
Bloomsbury Publishing
Brimax Books
Brown Wells & Jacobs
Child's Play (International)
David & Charles Children's Books
André Deutsch
Dorling Kindersley
Exley Publications
First and Best in Education
Floris Books
Funfax
Geddes & Grosset
Hazar Publishing
Heinemann Young Books
Hippo
Kingfisher
Ladybird Books
Frances Lincoln
Lion Publishing
Lutterworth Press
Macmillan Children's Books
Magi Publications
Mammoth
Kevin Mayhew
Methuen Children's Books
Michelin Travel Publications
The O'Brien Press (Ire.)
Madcap
Michael O'Mara Books
Orchard Books
Orion Children's Books
Oxford University Press
Pavilion Books
Puffin
Ragged Bears
Reader's Digest Children's Books

Robinson
Salamander Books
Scholastic Children's Books
Scripture Union
Tango Books
Tarquin Publications
Transworld Publishers
Treehouse Children's Books
Usborne Publishing
Walker Books
Frederick Warne
World International

Book packagers
Aladdin Books
Andromeda Oxford
Bellew Publishing
Breslich & Foss
Brown Wells & Jacobs
Roger Coote Publishing
Cowley Hunter
Graham-Cameron
Angus Hudson
Lionheart Books
Monkey Puzzle Media
Orpheus Books
Oyster Books
Playne Books
Mathew Price
Quarto Children's Books
Sadie Fields Productions
The Templar Company
Tucker Slingsby

Audiobooks

Book publishers
Award Publications
Child's Play (International)
André Deutsch
Funfax
HarperCollins Publishers
Hodder Headline
Ladybird Books
Mantra Publishing
The O'Brien Press (Ire.)
Random House Audio Books
St Pauls
Scholastic Children's Books
Scripture Union
Tellastory
Usborne Publishing

Multimedia

Book publishers
act-two
Dorling Kindersley
Ginn
HarperCollins
Heinemann Educational
Hodder Headline
Hodder Wayland
Macmillan
Mantra Publishing
Nelson Thornes
Oxford University Press
Paternoster Publishing
Puffin
Random House Group
St Pauls
Usborne Publishing
Frederick Warne

Book packagers
Roger Coote Publishing
Monkey Puzzle Media
Oyster Books

Poetry

Book publishers
Andersen Press
Award Publications
Bantam Children's Books
Barefoot Books
A & C Black
Bloomsbury Publishing
Bodley Head Children's
Jonathan Cape Children's Books
André Deutsch
Evans Brothers
Everyman's Library
Faber & Faber
Gairm Publications
Gomer Press (English/Welsh)
HarperCollins Publishers
Heinemann Young Books
Hutchinson Children's
Kingfisher
Frances Lincoln
Lutterworth Press
Macmillan Children's Books
Mammoth
Methuen Children's Books
Orchard Books
Oxford University Press
Paternoster Publishing
Puffin
Ragged Bears
Red Fox
Scholastic Children's Books
Transworld Publishers
Usborne Publishing
Viking Children's
Walker Books
Wolfhound Press (Ire.)

Religion

Book publishers
Award Publications
Child's Play (International)
Dorling Kindersley
Element Books
HarperCollins Publishers
Hunt & Thorpe
Kingsway Publications
Lion Publishing
Frances Lincoln
Lutterworth Press
Mantra Publishing
Kevin Mayhew
Marshall Pickering
Medici Society
National Christian Education Council
Oxford University Press
Paternoster Publishing
Ragged Bears
Reader's Digest Children's Books
George Ronald
St Pauls
Scripture Union
Society for Promoting Christian Knowledge

Book packagers
Graham-Cameron
Angus Hudson
Lionheart Books
Marshall Editions
Oyster Books

Doing it on your own

Reasons for self-publishing are varied. Many highly respected comtemporary and past authors have published their own works. ***Peter Finch*** *introduces the concept and outlines the implications of such an undertaking.*

Why bother?

You've tried all the usual channels and been turned down; your work is uncommercial, specialised, technical, out of fashion; you are concerned with art while everyone else is obsessed with cash; you need a book out quickly; you want to take up small publishing as a hobby; you've heard that publishers make a lot of money out of their authors and you'd like a slice – all reason enough. But be sure you understand what you are doing before you begin.

But isn't this cheating? It can't be real publishing – where is the critical judgement? Publishing is a respectable activity carried out by firms of specialists. Writers of any ability never get involved.

But they do. Start self-publishing and you'll be in good historical company: Horace Walpole, Balzac, Walt Whitman, Virginia Woolf, Gertrude Stein, John Galsworthy, Rudyard Kipling, Beatrix Potter, Lord Byron, Thomas Paine, Mark Twain, Upton Sinclair, W.H. Davies, Zane Grey, Ezra Pound, D.H. Lawrence, William Carlos Williams, Alexander Pope, Robbie Burns, James Joyce, Anaïs Nin and Lawrence Stern. All these at some time in their careers dabbled in doing it themselves. William Blake did nothing else. He even made his own ink, handprinted his pages and got Mrs Blake to sew on the covers.

But today it's different?

Not necessarily. This is not vanity publishing we're talking about although if all you want to do is produce a pamphlet of poems to give away to friends then self-publishing will be the cheapest way. Doing it yourself today can be a valid form of business enterprise. Being twice shortlisted for major literary prizes sharpened Timothy Mo's acumen. Turning his back on mass-market paperbacks, he published *Brownout on Breadfruit Boulevard* on his own. Michael Tod's badger trilogy, *The Silver Tide*, has been paperbacked by Orion, Susan Hill self-produced her short stories, *Listening to the Orchestra*, and as an example to us all Jill Paton Walsh's self-published *Knowledge of Angels* was shortlisted for the Booker Prize.

Can anyone do it?

Certainly. If you are a writer then a fair number of the required qualities will already be in hand. If, in addition, you can put up a shelf then the manufacture of the book to go on it will not be beyond you. The more able and practical you are then the cheaper the process will be. The utterly inept will need to pay others to help them, but it will still be self-publishing in the end.

Where do I start?

With research. Read up on the subject. Make sure you know what the parts of a book are. Terms like *verso*, *recto*, prelims, typeface and point size all have to lose their mystery. You will not need to become an expert but you will need a certain familiarity. Don't rush. Learn.

What about ISBN numbers?

International Standard Book Numbers – a standard bibliographic code, individual to each book published, are used by booksellers and librarians alike. They are issued by the Standard Book Numbering Agency at a cost of £50 plus VAT for ten. Self-publishers may balk at this apparently inordinate expense but the ISBN is the device used by the trade to track titles and if you are serious about your book should be regarded as essential. The Agency issues a free information pack (12 Dyott Street, London WC1A 1DF *tel* 020-7420 6008). See *Frequently asked questions about ISBNs* on page 623.

Next?

Put your book together – be it the typed pages of your novel, your selected poems or your story of how it was in the forces – and see how large a volume it will make. See *Preparing and submitting a typescript* on page 248 for guidelines on how to lay out the text.

No real idea of what your book should look like? Anything will not do. Go to your local bookshop and hunt out a few contemporary examples of volumes produced in a style you would like to emulate. Ask the manager for advice. Take your typescript and your examples round to a number of local printers (find these through *Yellow Pages*) and ask for a quote.

How much?

It depends. How long is a piece of string? You will not get a pamphlet of poems out for less than a few hundred pounds while a hardbacked work of prose will cost several thousand. Unit cost is important. The larger the number of copies you have printed the less each will cost. Print too many and the total bill will be enormous. Books are no longer cheap; perhaps they never were.

Can I make it cost less?

Yes. Do some of the work yourself. If you want to publish poems and you are prepared to use a text set by a home word processor, you will make a considerable saving. Many word processing programs today have desktop publishing (DTP) facilities which will enhance the look of your text. See *PCs for writers* on page 570. Could you accept home production, run the pages off on an office photocopier, then staple the sheets? Editions made this way can be very presentable.

For longer texts keyed in on a word processor, savings can be made by supplying the work on disk directly to a printer. They can import your text into their program without the need for any rekeying.

Home binding, if your abilities lie in that direction, can save a fair bit. What it all comes down to is the standard of production you want and indeed at whom your book is aimed. Books for the commercial marketplace need to look like their fellows; specialist publications can afford to be more eccentric.

Who decides how it looks?

You do. No one should ever ask a printer simply to produce a book. You should plan the design of your publication with as much care as you would a house extension. Spend as much time and money as you can on the cover. It is the part of the book your buyer will see first.

Low print run printers

Start by asking a few local printers for quotes. It is also worth trying:

Axxent Ltd, The Short Run Book Company
St Stephen's House, Arthur Road, Windsor, Berks SL4 1RY
Contact John M. Cox
tel (01733) 856300
e-mail sales@short-run.demon.co.uk

The Better Book Company Ltd
Warblington Lodge, The Gardens, Warblington, Hants PO9 2XH
Contact Jude James Garvey
tel (01428) 682937
e-mail betterbook@argonet.co.uk

Evergreen Graphics
11 The Drive, Craigwell-on-Sea, Aldwick, West Sussex PO21 4DU

Ex-Libris Press Book Production
1 The Shambles, Bradford on Avon, Wilts. BA15 1JS
Contact Roger Jones

Anthony Rowe Ltd
Bumper's Way, Bristol Road, Chippenham SN14 6LM

How many copies should I produce?

Small press poetry pamphlets sell about 300 copies, new novels sometimes manage 1000, literary paperbacks 10,000, mass-market blockbusters over a million. But that is generally where there is a sales team and whole distribution organisation behind the book. You are an individual. You must do everything yourself. Do not, on the one hand, end up with a prohibitively high unit cost by ordering too few copies. One hundred of anything is usually a waste of time. On the other hand can you really sell 3000? Will shops buy in dozens? They will probably only want twos and threes. Take care. Research your market first.

How do I sell it?

With all your might. This is perhaps the hardest part of publishing. It is certainly as time consuming as both the writing of the work and the printing of it put together. To succeed here you need a certain flair and you should definitely not be of a retiring nature. If you intend selling through the trade (and even if you don't you are bound to come into contact with bookshop orders at some stage), your costing must be correct and worked out in advance. Shops will want at least 33% of the selling price as discount. You'll need about the same again to cover your distribution, promotion and other overheads, leaving the final third to cover production costs and any profit you may wish to make. Multiply your unit production cost by at least four. Commerical publishers often multiply by as much as nine.

Do not expect the trade to pay your carriage costs. Your terms should be 33% post free on everything bar single copy orders. Penalise these by reducing your discount to 25%. Some shops will suggest that you sell copies to them on sale or return. This means that they only pay you for what they sell and then only after they've sold it. This is a common practice with certain categories of publications and often the only way to get independent books into certain shops; but from the self-publisher's point of view it should be avoided if at all possible. Cash in hand is best but expect to have your invoices paid by cheque at a later date. Buy a duplicate pad in order to keep track of what's going on. Phone the shops you have decided should take your book or turn up in person and ask to see the buyer. Letters and sample copies sent by post will get ignored. Get a freelance distributor to handle all of this for you if you can. Check the trade section of Cassell's *Directory of Publishing* or advertise for one in *The Bookseller.* If you can contract one they will want another 12% or so commission on top of the shops' discount – but expect to have to go it alone.

What about promotion?

A vital aspect often overlooked by beginners. Send out as many review copies as you can, all accompanied by slips quoting selling price and name and address of the publisher. Never admit to being that per-

Useful organisations

Author-Publisher Network
SKS, St Aldhelm, 20 Paul Street, Frome, Somerset BA11 1DX
web site http://www.author.co.uk
Founded by John Dawes

A non-profit, self-publishers' self-help organisation. Runs courses and lectures; publishes *Write to Publish*, an essential newsletter for self-publishers; compiles a catalogue of members' publications; offers co-operative promotional schemes and has one of the best self-publishers sites on the Internet – provides information and sales opportunities in equal quantity. Membership: £25.

The National Small Press Centre
BM Bozo, London WC1N 3XX
Director John Nicholson
Press Officer Cecilia Boggis

A point of focus for small, self- and independent publishers. Offers advice surgeries, book ordering services, publicity, help with origination and design, mounts exhibitions and workshops, holds a comprehensive reference library. Publishes *News From The Centre* (bi-monthly) and *Small Press Listings* (quarterly); joint annual subscription £15; the Centre's *Handbook* costs £12 (plus £1.50 postage).

son yourself. Invent a name: it will give your operation a professional feel. Ring up newspapers and local radio stations ostensibly to check that your copy has arrived but really to see if they are prepared to give your book space. Buying advertising space rarely pays for itself but good local promotion with 100% effort will generate dividends.

What about depositing copies at the British Library?

Under the Copyright Acts the British Library, the Bodleian Library, Oxford, The University Library, Cambridge, The National Library of Scotland, the Library of Trinity College Dublin and the National Library of Wales are all entitled to a free copy of your book which must be sent to them within one month of publication. One copy should go direct to the Legal Deposit Office at The British Library, Boston Spa, Wetherby, West Yorkshire LS23 7BY. The other libraries use an agent, Mr A.T. Smail, at 100 Euston Street, London NW1 2HQ *tel* 020-7388 5061. Contact him directly to find out how many copies he requires.

What if I can't manage all this myself?

You can employ others to do it for you. If you are a novelist and you opt for a package covering everything, it could set you back more than £10,000. A number of publishers and associations advertise such services in writers' journals and in the Sunday classifieds. 'Authors. Publish with us.' is a typical ploy. They will do a competent job for you, certainly, but you will still end up having to do the bulk of the selling yourself. It is a costly route, fraught with difficulty. Do the job on your own if you possibly can.

And what if it goes wrong?

Put all the unsolds under the bed or give them away. It has happened to lots of us. Even the big companies who are experienced at these things have their regular flops. It was an adventure and you did get your book published. On the other hand you may be so successful that you'll be at the London Book Fair selling the film rights and wondering if you've reprinted enough.

Can the Internet help?

Certainly. The web, with which many authors are now actively engaged, offers unrivalled opportunity for self-promulgation. This rapidly developing and highly flexible medium enables participants to promote themselves and their work internationally for as little as the cost of a few phone calls. Initial investment may be high – you need a decent computer, a modem and a set of software – but the benefits can be enormous. And it's fun. Some authors are happy simply to advertise their books while others produce complete on-line electronic versions for the world to read. The process may at first appear difficult but it is actually no more complex than traditional publishing.

Peter Finch runs Academi, the Welsh National Literature Promotion Agency and Society of Writers. He is a poet, former bookseller and small publisher and author of the best-selling *How to Publish Yourself* (Allison & Busby). His web site contains further advice for self-publishers: dialspace.dial.pipex.com/peter.finch/

Further reading

Baverstock, Alison, *How to Market Books*, Kogan Page, 1999

Coleman, Vernon, *How to Publish Your Own Book*, Blue Books, 1998

Domanski, Peter and Irvine, Philip, *A Practical Guide to Publishing Books Using Your PC*, Domanski-Irvine Books, 1997

Finch, Peter, *How to Publish Yourself*, Allison & Busby, 3rd edn, 1997

Foster, Charles, *Editing, Design and Book Production*, Journeyman, 1993

Godber, Bill, Webb, Robert, and Smith, Keith, *Marketing for Small Publishers*, Journeyman, 1992

Kennedy, Angus J., *The Rough Guide to the Internet 2000*, Rough Guides Ltd, 1999

Nicholson, John (ed.), The National Small Press Centre Handbook, NSPC, 1998

Ross, Tom and Marilyn, *The Complete Guide to Self-Publishing*, Writer's Digest Books, 1994

Spicer, Robert, *Publishing A Book*, How To Books, 3rd edn, 1998

Vanity publishing

Vanity publishers produce copies of a book in return for a fee paid by its author. The job they undertake is very different from that carried out by a publisher, which invests its own money in the whole publishing process. Authors considering vanity publishing should exercise caution.

Publishers very rarely ask authors to pay for the production of their work, to contribute to its cost, or to undertake purchase of copies. Exceptions may be a book of an extremely specialised nature with a very limited market, or perhaps the first book of poems by a talented new writer. In such cases, especially if the book makes a significant contribution to its subject, an established and reliable publisher may be prepared to accept a subvention from the author to make publication possible, and such financial grants often come from scientific or other academic foundations or funds. This is a very different procedure from that of the vanity publisher who claims to perform, for a fee to be paid by the author, all the many functions involved in publishing a book.

Manufacture *v.* publication

Some vanity publishers clearly state the services they provide and are open in all their dealings. However, the promotional material sent out by many vanity publishers makes claims which prove to be lacking in substance and foundation. The Advertising Standards Authority, with the support of the Committee of Advertising Practice, has issued revised guidelines to advertisers in an endeavour to reduce misleading claims made by some vanity publishers in their follow-up material. Several national newspaper and magazine groups are now refusing advertisements from vanity publishers. In their effort to secure business, vanity publishers may give exaggerated praise to an author's work and arouse equally unrealistic hopes of its commercial success. True publishers invest their own money in the whole publishing process: editorial, design, manufacturing, selling and distribution. The vanity publisher usually invests the author's money in but one part of this process: manufacture.

The distressing reports the *Writers' & Artists' Yearbook* office has received from embittered victims of vanity publishers underlines the importance of reading with extreme care the contracts offered by such publishers. The Society of Authors (see page 507) publishes a *Quick Guide to Vanity/Subsidy Publishing and Self-*

Vanity publishing considerations

Authors who want to use their money to publish their own books through a vanity publisher should:

- assume that they are paying to see their work in print and not expect to recoup their money;
- not immediately believe all the claims of a vanity publisher's promotional material;
- treat with caution enthusiastic praise by a vanity publisher of a typescript submitted;
- not sign anything without first consulting the Society of Authors or a solicitor with knowledge of publishing practice;
- ask to see examples of reviews received from the national press;
- ask to see a sample of a book published by them to assess the standard of publication;
- make sure that the vanity publisher is connected with a distributor.

Publishing (£1 to non-members). To those still in doubt the Society offers further help.

Often, these contacts will provide for the printing of, say, 2000 copies of the book, usually at a quite exorbitant cost to the author, but will leave the 'publisher' under no obligation to bind more than a very limited number. Alternatively, the vanity publisher may promise to print any number of copies for an author, but actually print only 100 copies or fewer.

Frequently, too, the author will be expected to pay extra for the cost of any effective advertising, while the 'publisher' makes little or no effort to promote the distribution and sale of the book. The names and imprints of vanity publishers are well known to literary editors and, with some worthy exceptions, their productions are rarely reviewed in any important periodical. Such books are unlikely to be stocked by major booksellers.

Mainstream publishers receive a very large number of unsolicited typescripts, only a small percentage of which are published. Typescripts may be rejected because they are not of an acceptable standard, because they do not fit in with the kind of books the publisher normally produces or because the market for them is too small or too local. In any case, getting a typescript accepted by a mainstream publisher requires careful targeting and perseverance.

If you are unable to persuade a mainstream publisher to take your typescript and decide to publish at your own expense, you could consider the possibility of self-publishing (see page 262). If you decide to approach a vanity publisher do so with caution and do not expect any commercial gain from your investment.

Having checked that the sum asked for is a reasonable one, and the publisher will provide the services you require, take the attitude that you are paying simply for the pleasure of seeing your work in print. You are less likely to be disappointed.

Top hundred chart of 1999 paperback fastsellers

Every year since 1979 ***Alex Hamilton*** *has compiled for the Guardian a survey comprising a table of the 100 topselling paperbacks published for the first time during that year by British publishers. He describes here its terms of reference, and reviews some major figures and trends of the last 20 years.*

Bestsellers and fastsellers

A distinction must be made between 'bestsellers' and the term used here – 'fastsellers'. Bestsellers have the real commercial pedigree. Sometimes, but not always, they make a strong showing in the fastseller lane, but among bestselling authors are hundreds whose books began slowly and only over many years vindicate the faith of the original publisher. D.H. Lawrence and George Orwell are two authors whose sales in their lifetimes were modest, but posthumous interest spectacular.

Poetry

While serious poets never repeat Lord Byron's triumph in becoming a bestseller and 'famous overnight', and the only two works with short lines in two decades of fastsellers were collections of comic verse, a poet such as Eliot, not to mention Shakespeare and Chaucer, will in the long term rack up sales in millions. And an outside event, such as the Nobel Prize for Seamus Heaney in 1995, produces an immediate harvest. In 1998, the year when the Oxford University Press announced the closure of its poetry section to save money, the late Poet Laureate, Ted Hughes, with the last book of his life, *Birthday Letters*, headed the hardcover selling lists with 145,000 copies, and won every award for which the book could qualify. Its paperback version just squeezes into this year's fastseller list.

Fiction and non-fiction

The staple of publishing has long been Bibles, classic authors, cookbooks, dictionaries and other reference books (the trade's bridge into CD-Rom.) Although the bulk of counter sales, and of library borrowings, consists of fiction, the top individual titles for the century, with figures over 20 million copies include most of these categories. *The Guinness Book of Records*, for example, in its many editions, has passed 85 million copies. However, gross figures worldwide for hardcover, paperback and translation editions of prolific authors such as Agatha Christie, Alistair MacLean, Mickey Spillane, Stephen King and Catherine Cookson are claimed to be from 50 million to 300 million copies. In all her long writing life Cookson was never off the lists, and her running Transworld sale when she died in 1998 was 53.5 million, with seven unpublished titles to come.

Popular authors mostly have international appeal, but not always. Dennis Wheatley, for instance, had a big following in Britain, but the 'British' quality he prided himself on did not travel; overseas he was hardly read. At his death he had 50 books in print with a combined sale of 41 million, but the foreign share was slight. Compare the late Barbara Cartland who, with over 500 titles, was so prolific as to compete with herself: her individual books never show on the list, but together they do loom large. She is said to have been discovered recently by the Chinese millions.

The fastseller list on pages 000-0 is limited to paperbacks that appeared for the first time in that year from British publishers (regardless of hardcover provenance). It is tempting to enter old titles revived to synchronise with films and television serials, because tie-ins have strong effects (e.g. Keneally's *Schindler's Ark* and Harris's *Silence of the Lambs* both tripled their sales to 800,000 and 1,580,000 respectively) when reissued to coincide with film versions, but except when the figure is very large, I exclude them.

Looking at the figures

From 1979 until the recession of the 1990s there were always between 102 and 125 titles that passed the 100,000 mark – a convenient round figure for those who make comparisons – but now the figure is rising: this year there were 139. While publishers naturally highlight the performances of their own authors, it was never my aim to make the list look like a competition. Nor can it be used as an index to publishing efficiency, or solvency. It is best seen as a reflection of popular taste accentuated by aggressive marketing.

A distortion for titles published at the end of the period may be suspected, but actually it rarely makes much difference. Booksellers now use electronic stock control that better enables them to match ordering to demand. The significant sale of new paperbacks, particularly by established authors, takes place within a few weeks of their appearance, although a few do enter the magic circle of bestsellers: *Captain Corelli's Mandolin* by Louis de Bernières has gone on to sell 1.6 million copies after achieving only 60,000 in its first year.

Electronic point-of-sale monitors have much improved the accuracy of weekly 'top 10' newspaper charts, thereby probably increasing their influence on sales, and extending the shelf-life of certain already popular titles, but perhaps shading out less familiar titles. Beneficiaries include such titles as *The Little Book of Calm*, Helen Fielding's rueful picture of a 'thirty-something' single woman, *Bridget Jones's Diary*, and Frank McCourt's memoir *Angela's Ashes*, all rolling towards two million, chasing Jung Chang's Chinese saga *Wild Swans*.

The authors

Over a 20-year period, the fastseller lists indicate conservative attitudes among buyers. For instance, fewer than 10% of authors come from outside the Anglo-American axis (which itself divides about 60-30). Few authors appear in the top 25 (which earn between them much the same as the rest put together) who have not appeared somewhere on the list in previous years. (1998 provided three exceptions, 1999 only one.) Once established on it, an author has only to turn in a regular supply of similar works to stay there. Being comfortable with a formula is therefore a psychological asset for writers with commercial ambitions. However, like actors when typecast, they may find too late that the market does not let them escape. One author trapped in his own formula was thriller writer Peter Cheyney, who gave his publisher a book unlike his others and was told to bury it, lest it confuse his loyal following.

The leading figures of the 1980s were Wilbur Smith (now with more than 25 novels past the million and 30 million sales), Stephen King (25 million), Dick Francis (19 million), Barbara Taylor Bradford, Len Deighton, Catherine Cookson, Jeffrey Archer, Danielle Steel and Victoria Holt, with Jilly Cooper coming through at the end (and adding up, now, to 12 million). To these (minus Victoria Holt, who died) the 1990s added regular front-runners in John Grisham and Maeve Binchy, with Patricia Cornwell as a top 10 reliable. Cookson, King, Francis and Steel are the only four in every list since 1979 (Deighton dropped out in 1998, to enjoy some travel).

The author's name is like a brand. While only seven of 2000 titles were volumes of short stories, two had sales over 750,000, because they were by Frederick Forsyth and Jeffrey Archer, and two reached 500,000 (Archer and Rosamund Pilcher).

More than half the buyers of books have always been women but for most of the 1980s hardly more than a quarter of the authors were. However, in the 1990s their presence steadily increased, from 25% rising to a new plateau between 35% and 40%, and up again this year to 45%.

Genres

Some 80% of the top hundred paperback fastsellers is usually fiction – often the proportion is even higher. Regular elements of the non-fiction remainder are diet books, the horoscope division of astrology, joke books, showbiz lives and exploitations based on big movies (e.g. anything by Spielberg). Cookery books, being basically tools in daily use, are essentially hardcover bestsellers (with Delia Smith selling close on a million copies of one new book in 1999). Of fiction, genres take up most slots, particularly adventure and naval yarns, thrillers and crime, horror stories, family sagas and a mixed bag of romances, from historical to 'Gothic' to the now faded bodice-rippers and 'sex'n'shopping', and career conflict stories under the vague umbrella of 'women's fiction'. The current fashion is for humorous accounts of the 'city girl's' experience, sharing flats, finding a job, troubled about finding a man. Lately a similar genre, a mirror image, has been devised for the 'town boy'.

There is otherwise no obvious category of 'men's fiction' that might once have included authors like Mickey Spillane and Harold Robbins (whose world sales had reached 130 million in his 1970s heyday). Perhaps there was a slight hint in the popularity of heroics by SAS men, war commanders and pilots who have been shot down, but it was never a fully developed genre. In the 1970s and early 1980s, with authors such as Russell Braddon and Sven Hassel, war outsold sex. Unlike old soldiers the interest never wholly faded away, but as the Russian bear became sick it slackened, while the balloon of the spy story, inflated by Ian Fleming and crewed by Frederick Forsyth, Len Deighton, John le Carré, *et al*, fell with the Berlin Wall.

Science fantasy does better than science fiction of a harder, more experimental kind. Westerns never figured, despite the fame of authors such as Zane Grey, Louis L'Amour and J.T. Edson. Contrary to widespread opinion, erotica have never made publishers an opulent living. Specialised imprints dedicated to soft porn have to be content with maximum sales of around 25,000, and their living is made more precarious by material on the Internet. Comic books, on the edge of being non-books, and collections of cartoonists of genius, appear *passim*, and quickly fade. Travellers' tales

No	Title	Genre	Author	Imprint
1	**Tara Road**	Novel	Maeve Binchy (Ire.)	Orion
2	**H. Potter: Chamber of Secrets**	Juvenile	J.K. Rowling (Br.)	Bloomsbury
3	**The Street Lawyer**	Thriller	John Grisham (US)	Arrow
4	**Point of Origin**	Thriller	Patricia Cornwell (US)	Warner
5	**About a Boy**	Novel	Nick Hornby (Br.)	Phoenix
6	**Rainbow Six**	Thriller	Tom Clancy (US)	Penguin
7	**The Long Road Home**	Romance	Danielle Steel (US)	Corgi
8	**Mirror Image**	Romance	Danielle Steel (US)	Corgi
9	**Eleventh Commandment**	Novel	Jeffrey Archer (Br.)	HarperCollins
10	**Who Wants to be a Millionaire?**	Quiz book	Various (Br.)	Boxtree
11	**The Solace of Sin**	Saga	Catherine Cookson (Br.)	Corgi
12	**Archangel**	Thriller	Robert Harris (Br.)	Arrow
13	**Bag of Bones**	Thriller	Stephen King (US)	NEL
14	**The Loop**	Novel	Nicholas Evans (Br.)	Corgi
15	**The Klone and I**	Romance	Danielle Steel (US)	Corgi
16	**Tell Me Your Dreams**	Thriller	Sidney Sheldon (US)	HarperCollins
17	**Charlotte Gray**	Novel	Sebastian Faulks (Br.)	Vintage
18	**When the Wind Blows**	Thriller	James Patterson (US)	Feature
19	**Field of 13**	Crime	Dick Francis (Br.)	Pan
20	**Carpe Jugulum**	Fantasy	Terry Pratchett (Br.)	Corgi
21	**Riley**	Saga	Catherine Cookson (Br.)	Corgi
22	**Notes from a Big Country**	Travel	Bill Bryson (US)	Black Swan
23	**Southern Cross**	Thriller	Patricia Cornwell (US)	Warner
24	**Other People's Children**	Novel	Joanna Trollope (Br.)	Black Swan
25	**The Last Continent**	Fantasy	Terry Pratchett (Br.)	Corgi
26	**The Breaker**	Crime	Minette Walters (Br.)	Pan
27	**The Gilded Cage**	Saga	Josephine Cox (Br.)	Headline
28	**Widow for One Year**	Novel	John Irving (US)	Black Swan
29	**Tomorrow the World**	Saga	Josephine Cox (Br.)	Headline
30	**Sight for Sore Eyes**	Thriller	Ruth Rendell (Br.)	Arrow
31	**A Certain Justice**	Thriller	P.D. James (Br.)	Penguin
32	**Come Together**	Novel	Lloyd & Rees (Br.)	Arrow
33	**Mr Maybe**	City girl	Jane Green (Br.)	Penguin
34	**Blast from the Past**	Humour	Ben Elton (Br.)	Black Swan
35	**Angels Flight**	Thriller	Michael Connelly (US)	Orion
36	**Net Force: Hidden Agendas**	Thriller	Tom Clancy (US)	Feature
37	**Sudden Change of Heart**	Saga	Barbara T. Bradford (Br.)	HarperCollins
38	**Snap Happy**	Romance	Fiona Walker (Br.)	Coronet
39	**Net Force: Night Moves**	Thriller	Tom Clancy (US)	Feature
40	**Stalingrad**	History	Antony Beevor (Br.)	Penguin
41	**Amsterdam**	Novel	Ian McEwan (Br.)	Vintage
42	**Shadow Watch**	Thriller	Tom Clancy (US)	Penguin
43	**Dead Souls**	Crime	Ian Rankin (Br.)	Orion
44	**The Hammer of Eden**	Thriller	Ken Follett (Br.)	Pan
45	**Star Wars: Episode 1**	Juvenile	Patricia C. Wrede (US)	Scholastic
46	**Suddenly Single**	Novel	Sheila O'Flanagan (Ire.)	Headline
47	**Seize the Night**	Thriller	Dean Koontz (US)	Headline
48	**Charlie**	City girl	Lesley Pearse (Br.)	Penguin
49	**Black Notice**	Thriller	Patricia Cornwell (US)	Little, Brown
50	**She's the One**	Novel	Cathy Kelly (Ire.)	Headline

Price	Month	Home	Export	Total	Gross (RRP)	No
£6.99	May	658,321	450,612	1,108,933	£7,751,442	**1**
£4.99	Jan	868,611	156,361	1,024,972	£5,114,610	**2**
£5.99	Feb	636,181	357,220	993,401	£5,950,472	**3**
£5.99	June	491,332	159,930	651,262	£3,901,059	**4**
£6.99	Mar	442,770	105,850	548,620	£3,834,854	**5**
£6.99	Aug	418,619	127,500	546,119	£3,817,372	**6**
£5.99	Mar	417,189	121,990	539,179	£3,229,682	**7**
£5.99	Nov	387,756	113,787	501,543	£3,004,243	**8**
£5.99	April	337,390	163,780	501,170	£3,002,008	**9**
£5.99	Nov	486,157	123	486,280	£2,912,817	**10**
£5.99	Feb	353,991	120,531	474,522	£2,842,387	**11**
£5.99	Oct	342,258	127,901	470,159	£2,816,252	**12**
£6.99	June	347,325	120,529	467,854	£3,270,299	**13**
£5.99	July	321,711	131,823	453,534	£2,716,669	**14**
£5.99	Aug	360,052	90,120	450,172	£2,696,530	**15**
£6.99	Mar	215,424	230,316	445,740	£3,115,723	**16**
£6.99	July	363,520	70,103	433,623	£3,031,025	**17**
£5.99	July	328,769	98,918	427,687	£2,561,845	**18**
£5.99	Sept	271,833	140,846	412,679	£2,471,947	**19**
£5.99	Nov	312,530	83,053	395,583	£2,369,542	**20**
£5.99	Oct	344,795	38,894	383,689	£2,298,297	**21**
£6.99	Sept	303,645	74,530	378,175	£2,643,443	**22**
£5.99	Dec	254,012	107,771	361,783	£2,167,080	**23**
£6.99	Feb	309,896	51,670	361,566	£2,527,346	**24**
£5.99	May	259,193	78,575	337,768	£2,023,230	**25**
£5.99	June	236,357	92,047	328,404	£1,967,140	**26**
£5.99	Sept	296,927	28,426	325,353	£1,948,864	**27**
£7.99	June	177,754	135,533	313,287	£2,503,163	**28**
£5.99	Feb	277,169	34,859	312,028	£1,869,048	**29**
£5.99	Sept	233,277	68,921	302,198	£1,810,166	**30**
£6.99	Jan	250,256	47,200	297,456	£2,079,217	**31**
£5.99	Feb	236,894	59,202	296,096	£1,773,615	**32**
£6.99	June	282,583	10,646	293,229	£2,049,671	**33**
£6.99	July	229,909	54,608	284,517	£1,988,774	**34**
£5.99	Sept	172,616	110,000	282,616	£1,692,870	**35**
£6.99	May	176,240	104,267	280,507	£1,960,744	**36**
£5.99	July	208,389	58,825	267,214	£1,600,612	**37**
£5.99	May	191,261	58,468	249,729	£1,495,877	**38**
£6.99	Nov	167,148	81,020	248,168	£1,734,694	**39**
£12.99	May	231,583	12,287	243,870	£3,167,871	**40**
£6.99	May	191,073	49,731	240,804	£1,683,220	**41**
£5.99	Dec	160,922	72,000	232,922	£1,395,203	**42**
£5.99	Nov	159,022	72,500	231,522	£1,386,817	**43**
£5.99	Oct	101,921	125,150	227,071	£1,360,155	**44**
£4.99	May	223,644	0	223,644	£1,115,984	**45**
£5.99	Nov	205,031	18,414	223,445	£1,338,436	**46**
£5.99	June	140,505	82,514	223,019	£1,335,884	**47**
£5.99	Jan	195,205	22,924	218,129	£1,306,593	**48**
£10.99	July	41,677	175,911	217,588	£2,391,292	**49**
£5.99	April	176,547	39,811	216,358	£1,295,984	**50**

No	Title	Genre	Author	Imprint
51	**The Chimney Sweeper's Boy**	Crime	Barbara Vine (Br.)	Penguin
52	**Last Chance Saloon**	City girl	Marian Keyes (Ire.)	Penguin
53	**A Patchwork Planet**	Novel	Anne Tyler (US)	Vintage
54	**Driving Over Lemons**	Travel	Chris Stewart (Br.)	Sort Of
55	**The Tesseract**	Novel	Alex Garland (Br.)	Penguin
56	**The Waiting Time**	Thriller	Gerald Seymour (Br.)	Corgi
57	**No Safe Place**	Thriller	Richard N. Patterson (US)	Arrow
58	**Moon Island**	Novel	Rosie Thomas (Br.)	Arrow
59	**Ralph's Party**	City girl	Lisa Jewell (Br.)	Penguin
60	**Every Dead Thing**	Thriller	John Connolly (Ire.)	Coronet
61	**OP Centre State of Siege**	Thriller	Tom Clancy (US)	HarperCollins
62	**Monsoon**	Adventure	Wilbur Smith (S. Afr.)	Macmillan
63	**The Hanging Garden**	Crime	Ian Rankin (Br.)	Orion
64	**The Kissing Garden**	Romance	Charlotte Bingham (Br.)	Bantam
65	**Georgiana**	Biography	Amanda Foreman (Br.)	HarperCollins
66	**Polly**	Novel	Freya North (Br.)	Arrow
67	**My Legendary Girlfriend**	Town boy	Mike Gayle (Br.)	Flame
68	**Rosie Meadows Regrets**	Novel	Catherine Alliott (Br.)	Headline
69	**Filth**	Novel	Irvine Welsh (Br.)	Vintage
70	**Flight of Eagles**	Thriller	Jack Higgins (Br.)	Penguin
71	**Hanna's Daughters**	Novel	M. Fredericksson (Swed.)	Phoenix
72	**Day of Confession**	Thriller	Alan Folsom (US)	Warner
73	**The English**	Society	Jeremy Paxman (Br.)	Penguin
74	**LA Connections: The Novel**	Novelettes	Jackie Collins (Br.)	Pan
75	**Snow Falcon**	Novel	Stuart Harrison (NZ)	HarperCollins
76	**The Surgeon of Crowthorne**	History	Simon Winchester (Br.)	Penguin
77	**Armadillo**	Novel	William Boyd (Br.)	Penguin
78	**Head Over Heels**	Novel	Jill Mansell (Br.)	Headline
79	**Aches & Pains**	Humour	Maeve Binchy (Ire.)	Orion
80	**The New Flower Expert**	Gardening	D.G. Hessayon (Br.)	Expert
81	**Pilot's Wife**	Novel	Anita Shreve (US)	Abacus
82	**Message in a Bottle**	Romance	Nicholas Sparks (US)	Bantam
83	**When Morning Comes**	Saga	Audrey Howard (Br.)	Coronet
84	**A Man in Full**	Novel	Tom Wolfe (US)	Picador
85	**Losing My Virginity**	Autobiog.	Richard Branson (Br.)	Virgin
86	**Sharpe's Triumph**	Hist. Novel	Bernard Cornwell (Br.)	HarperCollins
87	**Ashes to Ashes**	Thriller	Tami Hoag (US)	Orion
88	**City Woman**	City girl	Patricia Scanlan (Br.)	Bantam
89	**The Ties that Bind**	Saga	Lyn Andrews (Br.)	Headline
90	**Southern Cross**	Thriller	Patricia Cornwell (US)	Little, Brown
91	**The Corner House**	Saga	Ruth Hamilton (Br.)	Corgi
92	**Beyond the Shining Water**	Saga	Audrey Howard (Br.)	Coronet
93	**The Lazarus Child**	Novel	Robert Mawson (Br.)	Bantam
94	**Kremlin Device**	Thriller	Chris Ryan (Br.)	Arrow
95	**Speaking in Tongues**	Thriller	Jeffery Deaver (US)	Coronet
96	**Making of Minty Malone**	City girl	Isabel Wolff (Br.)	HarperCollins
97	**Buried Alive!**	Juvenile	Jacqueline Wilson (Br.)	Yearling
98	**The Keys to the Garden**	Saga	Susan Sallis (Br.)	Corgi
99	**Star Wars Storybook**	Scriptbook	George Lucas (US)	Scholastic
100	**Birthday Letters**	Poetry	Ted Hughes (Br.)	Faber

Price	Month	Home	Export	Total	Gross (RRP)	No
£5.99	Mar	160,353	54,150	214,503	£1,284,873	**51**
£9.99	Oct	157,850	56,000	213,850	£2,136,362	**52**
£6.99	Mar	178,279	32,380	210,659	£1,472,506	**53**
£6.99	June	170,116	31,416	201,532	£1,408,709	**54**
£6.99	July	173,437	22,000	195,437	£1,366,105	**55**
£5.99	Jan	136,886	53,270	190,156	£1,139,034	**56**
£5.99	June	127,800	62,083	189,883	£1,137,399	**57**
£5.99	July	170,120	17,764	187,884	£1,125,425	**58**
£5.99	May	184,348	3,424	187,772	£1,124,754	**59**
£5.99	Oct	136,075	47,772	183,847	£1,101,244	**60**
£6.99	Sept	115,818	66,518	182,336	£1,274,529	**61**
£10.99	Oct	121,558	58,944	180,502	£1,983,717	**62**
£5.99	Feb	128,109	52,109	180,218	£1,079,506	**63**
£5.99	Aug	147,954	31,732	179,686	£1,076,319	**64**
£8.99	June	172,057	3,845	175,902	£1,581,359	**65**
£5.99	May	156,673	17,892	174,565	£1,045,644	**66**
£6.99	Feb	149,927	24,373	174,300	£1,218,357	**67**
£5.99	May	156,959	16,236	173,195	£1,037,438	**68**
£6.99	Aug	128,373	43,662	172,035	£1,202,525	**69**
£5.99	Feb	144,215	27,000	171,215	£1,025,578	**70**
£6.99	June	43,036	126,764	169,800	£1,186,902	**71**
£5.99	Aug	92,795	76,587	169,382	£1,014,598	**72**
£7.99	Sept	161,299	5,370	166,669	£1,331,685	**73**
£5.99	Sept	129,981	35,491	165,472	£991,177	**74**
£5.99	Nov	79,866	85,327	165,193	£989,506	**75**
£6.99	June	103,746	60,635	164,381	£1,149,023	**76**
£6.99	Jan	154,725	9,499	164,224	£1,147,926	**77**
£5.99	June	152,629	8,897	161,526	£967,541	**78**
£3.99	Sept	84,400	73,000	157,400	£628,026	**79**
£8.99	April	135,324	21,577	156,901	£1,410,540	**80**
£6.99	Mar	29,298	123,487	152,785	£1,067,967	**81**
£5.99	Jan	72,079	79,796	151,875	£909,731	**82**
£5.99	April	115,863	34,896	150,759	£903,046	**83**
£10.00	Nov	65,249	82,252	147,501	£1,475,010	**84**
£9.99	June	128,727	18,408	147,135	£1,469,879	**85**
£5.99	July	138,772	7,476	146,248	£876,026	**86**
£5.99	Nov	84,700	59,800	144,500	£865,555	**87**
£5.99	June	134,783	8,340	143,123	£857,307	**88**
£5.99	Aug	136,970	4,205	141,175	£845,638	**89**
£9.99	Jan	20,767	120,065	140,832	£1,406,912	**90**
£5.99	May	135,357	4,960	140,317	£840,499	**91**
£5.99	Oct	115,363	24,419	139,782	£837,294	**92**
£5.99	April	97,937	41,085	139,022	£832,742	**93**
£5.99	April	102,284	36,128	138,412	£829,088	**94**
£5.99	Aug	87,059	51,164	138,223	£827,956	**95**
£5.99	Aug	122,335	15,681	138,016	£826,716	**96**
£3.99	May	130,567	4,197	134,764	£537,708	**97**
£5.99	Dec	124,984	6,716	131,700	£788,883	**98**
£5.99	May	130,851	0	130,851	£783,797	**99**
£7.99	April	115,086	14,176	129,262	£1,032,803	**100**

had no significant presence until the American Bill Bryson's flattering farewell journey around Britain sold more copies in one year (1996) than any other travelogue has in 20. But the 1999 chart does include a travel newcomer with the oddly named imprint, Sort Of. Mark Ellingham, founder of Rough Guides, created it specially to publish *Driving Over Lemons*.

Heavyweight to juvenile

Hardly more than a dozen titles in any list could count on reviews from serious book pages. However, in recent years, broadly since the television interest, the Booker Prize has taken winners into the fastseller list (witness Arundati Roy in 1998, the highest to date, and Ian McEwan in 1999). When it works, this award seems to establish books rather than authors, and not all winners make a second appearance. Still the potential of non-category fiction is evinced by Picador's results for Humberto Eco's *The Name of the Rose*, Tom Wolfe's *The Bonfire of the Vanities* and Salman Rushdie's *Midnight's Children*, all with sales of well over half a million copies. Unprecedented success for a war history, obtained by Stalingrad in 1999, shows the lift that warm reviews can give to a serious study.

But the phenomenon at the end of the century was a sequence of books by J.K. Rowling about a schoolboy wizard called Harry Potter. The combined 1999 sales for three titles passed 4 million in British markets and 16 million in America. With this small cluster of books she became as popular with children as the late Roald Dahl and Terry Pratchett, who is equally at home on the wilder shores of technology, and whose 37 titles with Transworld sell 1,750,000 copies a year. Mention must also be made of the American horror writer R.L. Stine, with a claim to a worldwide sale of 220 million for his 60 children's books.

The year 1999

The new element for the trade in recent years has been to adapt to price flexibility, since the end of the Net Book Agreement (whereby booksellers observed publishers' cover prices). At present, the discounting focus is on top hardcover titles. For a small number, surprisingly high figures are reported. (Thus, in 1999 alone, Harris's grotesque thriller *Hannibal* sold 656,000 copies, McCourt's *'Tis* sold 437,174, and Sir Alex Ferguson's *Managing My Life* sold 480,715.) Paperback sales are less affected by discounts, but perhaps 10% should be deducted from the aggregate money gross shown. The most common price point is still £5.99 (59 examples).

In a gradually declining market for books, the fastsellers' performance seems still the most stable element. The aggregate went up from 25.38 million to 28.1 million, with the notional turnover improved from £171.1 million to £181.1 million (the first 25 titles account for 13.5 million books and £82.2 million). Export continues to suffer badly from the strength of the pound; its share dropped from 28.5% to 25%, the lowest ever.

Looking back on genres that have raised hopes in recent times, few fulfil their promise. Those that do are new subdivisions of the categories of thriller, horror and romance – the three central strands of bestsellerdom, not only of the past 25 years but the whole century.

The Western has disappeared into the sunset; the modest flutter in travel writing in the late eighties subsided; fantasy now does better than hardcore science fiction. *The X-files*, prominent in the mid-1990s, dwindled into the small screen. 'Green books', after looking as if they would be as uplifting commercially as sermons in the 19th century, have not much expanded their original niche market. The heralded wave of books for the millennium was unimpressive, despite an undertow of New Age challenges to religious orthodoxy. At the turn of the century some publishers wondered if books on self-determination, 'the road less travelled', might take. Not the sort of road mass-market books often take. But it sounds right for that new imprint, Sort Of.

Alex Hamilton is a journalist and award-winning travel writer, and the author of several novels and volumes of short stories.

Poetry

Poetry into print

***John Whitworth** has submitted hundreds of poems and has had dealings with a number of publishers of poetry. He gives advice here 'from the handle end of the long spoon that poets use to sup with those they would persuade or bamboozle into printing, even paying for, their work.'*

Constant readers of these columns may suppose that I do not update my material. Be assured that I do – magazines and publishers wax and wane and I try to keep abreast. But, even in these days of publishing on the Internet (rather like making your poems into paper boats and sending them down the Yangtse it seems to me), the basics seem to stay the same and my general advice likewise. If your poems are good they will find a publisher if you persevere. Do I believe this? Yes I do and so should you.

There are two things to say at the outset. Do not expect to make more than pin money *directly* from publication of your work. You may, in the fullness of time, make quite a tidy sum *indirectly* – I mean you get work because you are a published poet: readings, workshops, reviewing and so forth, if you like any of that sort of thing. But if you get £50 for a poem from a national magazine you may feel very satisfied, and as for your published slim volumes – they will not sell in four figures, nor do the publishers, except in a very few instances, expect them to. In a sense, nearly all poetry publishing is vanity publishing. Nobody is in it for the money.

And, secondly, as one poet put it to me, do not have too much respect for the taste of individual literary editors. She is right. An editor is not God (whatever he or she thinks). Remember that, though it can be hard if you are diffident (and most poets are). But this person is just like you; the fact that he or she (nearly always he) is warming an editorial chair may mean many things. It certainly does not mean papal infallibility. If Snooks of the *Review* sends back your work, despatch it immediately to Snurd of the *Supplement*. And if Snurd concurs with Snooks, they may both be wrong, indeed neither may actually have read through (or at all) what you sent. Grit your teeth and send to Snarl and then to Snivel. Do not be discouraged by rejection. If your poems are as good as you can make them and have been submitted in as professional a way as you can manage, then just keep on sending them out. I started writing poems in 1968, wrote my first good one in 1972, and was paid my first proper money (£40 from the Arts Council) in 1976. The first book was published in 1980. So patience and a thick skin are big advantages.

It does help, of course, to have read the magazine you are making submissions to. This will prevent you sending your bawdy ballad to *The Times Literary Supplement (TLS)* or concrete poetry to the *Literary Review*. And I am assuming that you actually are interested in the craft of poetry and the names of, say, Milton, Tennyson and Eliot mean something to you. You will also be interested to know what Heaney, Harrison and Hannah actually do. You don't have to like it, but you ought to want to know about it. If no one is writing anything remotely like your work, perhaps you should ask yourself why that might be. On the other hand, remember the words of Charlie Coburn, the old music-hall singer: 'I sang my song to them, and they didn't like it. So I sang it again, and they still didn't like it. So I sang it a third time and one of them thought he might just get to like it if I changed the tune and altered the words.

So I sang it again, just exactly the same way, and after a bit they all liked it.'

Submitting your work to magazines

I asked a number of poets about this. Some of them said they never submitted to magazines at all, because they disliked being rejected. I must say I think that a rather craven attitude, but you *can* carve out a poetic reputation through workshops and readings. You must be good at putting yourself about in public and have the time and energy to expend on it. All who did submit work regularly agreed on a number of basics:

• Submit your poem on an A4 sheet, typed or printed out from a word processor. One poet, David Phillips, reckoned his percentage of successful submissions had gone up appreciably since he bought his word processor, and he assumed it was because his work now looked much more professional. It might be, of course, that it has just got better. Do not type it in italic, capitals or mock cursive. Keep it simple.

• Put your name and address at the bottom of each poem. Editors, reasonably, do not keep your letters, only the poems that interest them. You might consider one of those rubber stamps. I know a number of poets who have them, though I don't myself.

• Fold the poem once and put it into the sort of envelope designed to take A4 folded once. I don't know why poets like to scrunch their verses into tiny envelopes, but don't do it. Don't go to the other extreme either and send it decorated with admonitions not to bend, etcetera. Include a stamped, self-addressed envelope of the same size. This really is important. Shakespeare himself would be consigned to the wpb without an appropriate sae.

• Do not send just one poem. Do not send 20 poems. Send enough to give a reasonable flavour of your work – say about four or five. Long poems are less likely to be accepted than short poems. If you write different kinds of things, then make sure your selection covers a fair few of these kinds. Send what you think of as your best work, but do not be surprised if what is finally accepted is the one you put in at the last minute, 'to make the others look better' as Larkin lugubriously puts it. And if an editor says he or she likes your work and would like to see more, then send more as soon as possible. The editor wasn't just being polite. Editors aren't. It was said because it was meant.

• At this point there is generally some po-faced stuff about never sending the same poem to more than one editor simultaneously. As it happens, I don't do this, but some well-known poets do. And indeed, if Snurd of the *Supplement* sits on your poems for six months, what are you supposed to do, since the polite follow-up letter recommended will, almost certainly, have no effect at all, except to waste your time and your stamps? The real reason for not making multiple submissions is the embarrassment when the same poem is accepted by two editors at once. I once, inadvertently, won two microscopic prizes in poetry competitions for the same poem. What did I do? I kept my mouth shut and cashed the cheques, that's what I did.

• You wouldn't have been daft enough to send off your *only* copies of poems to Snurd, would you? *Of course* he lost them and it's all your own silly fault. No you can't sue him but you'll know better next time. Send photocopies and keep your originals. Editors don't mind photocopies. Why should they? They look a lot better than the original all covered in Tippex.

• Keep your covering letter short, but if you have been published in reputable places then it will do no harm to say so.

Submitting poems

- Submit poems on an A4 sheet, simply typed.
- Put your name and addess at the bottom of each sheet.
- Fold the sheet only once and use an A5 envelope.
- Send about four or five poems.
- Consider whether to submit the same poem simultaneously to more than one editor.
- Always keep copies of your poems.
- Include a short covering letter.

This advice comes from Duncan Forbes. Selling poems is very like selling anything else, so blow your own trumpet, but don't blow for too long. Don't ask the editor for help in the advancement of your poetic career. Being rude won't help either. Artists are supposed to be rude and a lot of them are, too, but it hasn't actually helped them to anything except an ulcer or a punch on the nose.

Which magazines?

You could start with the *TLS* but I wouldn't advise it. One editor (not from the *TLS*) said honestly that he tended to reject, more or less unread, poems from anyone he had never heard of. Before you play with the big boys perhaps you ought to have some sort of a record in the little magazines. Some pay and some do not. What matters is not the cash but whether you feel proud or ashamed to be seen in the thing. The Poetry Library at the South Bank Centre (Royal Festival Hall, London SE1 8XX) publishes a list of poetry magazines, and if you can get along there (very convenient for Waterloo Station and open 11am-8pm except Mondays), you can nose around among the back numbers and see what is appealing to you. If you can't do that, then a letter with an sae will get you the list (see also page 282).

Judge where you think you will fit in, and buy yourself a big sheet of second-class stamps. Send off your work and be prepared to be reasonably patient. Most editors reply in the end. Little magazines have a high mortality rate, so be prepared for a particularly crushing form of disappointment – having your work accepted by a magazine which promptly ceases publication. It happens to us all; it goes on happening to me. The Poetry Library also sends out for an sae of 40p a satisfying wodge of bumph about poetry publishing in general. Worth the money.

Some inexperienced poets seem very worried that editors will filch their 'ideas' and pay them nothing, but poems are not made up of ideas; they are made up of words, and if anyone prints your poem without permission they are infringing your copyright and you can threaten them with all sorts of horrible things. But, honestly, this is a buyer's market, and even the editor of that badly photocopied rag has more material than can be used.

There seems to be a new kind of organisation that solicits poems. Often with names like Global or International, they don't ask for money up front, so are not exactly vanity presses. But they encourage you in marketers' prose to buy super-duper anthologies for £40 or so. Harmless, I suppose, but I'd rather appear in something less pretentious along with some poets I had actually heard of.

Subscribe to *Poetry Review,* the magazine of the Poetry Society. It's quarterly, expensive and the best poetry magazine. *Poetry Wales* and the *New Welsh Review* are both beautifully produced. Earlier remarks about 'relentless celticity' may now be unfair. Particularly since Robert Minhinnick has taken over at *Poetry Wales. HU (Honest Ulsterman)* is interesting and intelligent, but currently taking ages to look at submissions (mine anyway), even longer than *Ambit*, which is lively, sexy and full of good artwork.

Stand tell me that, though 'their roots are in the North', their 'interests are wide ranging and certainly not parochial'. On the evidence of the September 1999 issue they sent me this is certainly true, and the world is now their oyster. Alan Ross's *London Magazine* is excellent as ever and has the world's fastest turn-around – you get your rejection almost before you've posted the material, said one disgruntled poet, but Ross does accept work too and scribbles cryptic encouragement from time to time. Definitely something to aspire to.

PN Review, an offshoot of Carcanet (or the other way round) is good critically and prints a wide range of poems. The *Rialto* has excellent poetry. *Acumen* and *Outposts* are good respectable places for new poets. *Tabla* is annual; you can get into it through their competition. Poems are goodish. I don't know why I haven't mentioned the *Frogmore Papers* before. Independent, lively, full of good poetry though Jeremy Hardy ought to beef up the crits. *Poetry London* is well produced (actually most magazines are well produced these days and we have the computer to thank for this); the poets come from all over the place, turn-around is quick thanks to Pascale Petit, and the critical section is sharp and interesting. This is a personal list, magazines I read from time to time. (See the list on page 129 for the poetry magazines listed in this *Yearbook*.)

Of the national newspapers, the *Express* prints a poem every day. You can send to Harry Eyres and you may get £25 – I didn't but Michael Conaghan did. The *Independent* prints a daily poem from published collections; they don't pay. The *Observer* and the *Sunday Times* print poems; the *Sunday Telegraph* and the *Independent on Sunday* don't.

The two literary heavyweights are the *Times Literary Supplement* and the *London Review of Books*, and both publish poetry.

Have you tried submitting abroad, to Australia, New Zealand, Canada or the USA? The Post Office will tell you about International Reply Coupons, and there is a good article on this in *Connections Winter 98/99*, published by South East Arts. I tried and had some luck!

Small press information

The Stationery Office Oriel Bookshop
18-19 High Street, Cardiff CF1 2BZ
Publishes *Small Presses and Little Magazines of the UK and Ireland.*

The National Small Press Centre
BM BOZO, London WC1N 3XX
Publishes *Small Press Listings* quarterly.

Photon Press
The Light House, 37 The Meadows, Berwick-upon-Tweed, Northumberland TD15 1NY
Light's List, now in its 15th year, is a list of over 1450 magazines worldwide. It costs £2 including p&p.

The Poetry Library
Royal Festival Hall, South Bank Centre, London SE1 8XX
tel 020-7921 0943/0664 *fax* 020-7921 0939
Lists of poetry magazines, poetry bookshops, current competitions, etc. See also page 282.

Book publication

Every poet wants to get a book out. How do you do it? One pretty sure way is to win a big prize in a competition, the National or the biennial Arvon or Harry Chambers' Peterloo. Otherwise, you wait until you have reached the stage of having had two or three dozen poems published in reputable places; then you type out enough poems for a collection, traditionally 64pp but collections seem to be getting longer, and send them out, keeping your own copy and including return postage. I suppose you do. I first got published by talking to Anthony Thwaite in a pub; everybody needs a slice of luck. I know some excellent poets who are still trying to place their first book and, contrariwise, there are books ... Poetry, like most things, goes in fashions. But don't be in a hurry. Wait until you have a reputation in the magazines and small presses. Neil Astley at Bloodaxe reckons more than 90% of what comes through his letterbox he sends back, and he has usually had an eye on the successful ones before they got around to submitting.

Who do you send out to? Faber are still out in front (though they did turn down Larkin's *The Less Deceived*, the most influential book of English poems in the last 50 years). It is not that their poets are better, but Faber promote them heavily and care about them. And being a Faber poet puts you in the company of Eliot and Larkin. Penguin have revived their excellent *Modern Poets* series and have 12 titles so far. Most other big publishers do poetry – fortunes wax and wane with the person, often a poet, nearly always a man, in the editorial chair.

But being published by a household name does not mean selling thousands – hundreds are more common. Publishers like to have poetry on their list as a badge of virtue, but often they don't want to know much about it, they don't promote it and they don't persist with it. The book sinks or swims, and usually it sinks. (Publishers that consider poetry for adults are listed in *Publishers of poetry* on page 286; *Children's book publishers and packagers* on page 259 includes publishers of poetry for children.)

Specialist poetry presses (some, though not all of which, publish nothing but poetry) produce books that look every bit as good and, in most cases, sell every bit as well (or badly). Bloodaxe, Peterloo and Carcanet, none of them London-based, are leaders in the field.

Bloodaxe sounds fearsomely dismissive, but the name is from a Viking who conquered Northumbria. They have more titles and possibly better poets than Faber but they still fail the railway bookstall test. 'From traditional formalists to post-modernists', says Neil Astley. Half the poets on his list are women – good if you are a woman. Carcanet publish Elizabeth Jennings, Sophie Hannah and the Wizard of Oz, Les Murray, which indicates Michael Schmidt's catholicity and willingness to go outside this country. He welcomes typescripts but wishes people would read some of the books on his list first. Good advice; every publisher has a style, just as every magazine has.

Harry Chambers at Peterloo has a reputation for publishing late starters. Kirkpatrick Dobie's first book came out in the poet's 84th year – excellent! Dana Gioia, the American 'new formalist', Ann Drysdale and quizzical Ursula Fanthorpe are his biggest guns.

Back in the metropolis, Anvil has Carol Ann Duffy and Michael Hamburger along with lots of poetry in translation. Enitharmon has Anthony Thwaite, Myra Schneider and Gary Geddes from Canada, but little arts money for some unfathomable reason. Seren, the imprint of Poetry Wales, publishes the lively Sheena Pugh and Paul Groves, who isn't obviously Welsh. Headland has Simon Rae of the *Guardian* fame. Of course there are all those OUP poets, cruelly jettisoned and looking for homes. But honestly, there are lots (really *lots*) more small presses and information on them can be obtained through the organisations listed in the box.

Competitions

Some poets are snooty about these (perhaps they don't win?) and of course competitions are supposed to make money for the organisers. But in my experience, they (judge, organiser, entrant, prizewinner) are honest and unknowns (everyone starts as an unknown) sometimes win big prizes, and often pick up smaller ones. Many a poet's published career has started with a competition win. I like it when the judge is a published poet – a badge of respectability, I think. Try the small ones. Prize money of £200 or less deters big names (not me though!).

You might consider subscribing to *Writers News*, now owned by the *Yorkshire Post*. Their literary competitions specifically exclude published poets like me and their stuff on poetry is good, if elementary. It's also a good place to find out about other competitions. If you can do light verse, why not enter the competitions run by the *Spectator* and the *New Statesman*? I've won sometimes, Wendy Cope used to, and so have a couple of members of my local writing groups. Lots of kudos, some money and the occasional bottle of scotch. Go for it! For more information on current competitions, see page 283 and *Prizes and awards* on page 512.

Getting on radio

Michael Conaghan, who has had many poems broadcast, says BBC local radio – more talk than its commercial equivalent – is the place to start. Find out who is responsible for Arts programming and contact them. 'Short punchy, topical work is probably what they want, and events/festivals concentrate their minds wonderfully. Nationally, Radio 1's Mark Radcliffe is a notable friend to poets.'

Poetry on the Internet

The poet Peter Howard writes an Internet column for *Poetry Review* and suggests you can submit to electronic magazines or set up your own site and get people to visit it. You can even set up your own magazine

– there's no extra charge. 'Everything's up for grabs – there are no real reputations yet, though they're forming', he says.

Poetry for children

Not a dustbin for grown-up rejects. There seems to be a market in the USA. Over here, you can self-publish books of poems and flog them locally. Schools pay poets (some with more brass neck than talent) to give readings and workshops. Poet Lindsay Macrae thinks it helps to be young and female (she is), but Roger McGough and Kit Wright are old(ish) and male. There is an inner circle of editors attached to publishers who trawl likely names for inclusion in anthologies; I've never actually had a poem accepted by this route but live in hopes.

Vanity/subsidy publishing

Never give a publisher money. That is what they give to you. If you want your work in print and nobody will do it for you without a cheque, then do it yourself. See *Doing it on your own* on page 262. You could buy yourself a secondhand word processor with the money you save by not answering that advertisement!

Making your poems better

Read more poetry, and I mean modern poetry. You can't write it if you don't read it. There are some good how-to books. *Writing Poetry and Getting Published* by Matthew Sweeney and John Hartley Williams (Hodder) is my favourite in the UK. *The Practice of Poetry* (Harper Perennial) edited by Robin Behn and Chase Twichell ditto in the USA. John Hollander's *Rhyme's Reason* (Yale) is good on poetic forms. *The Princeton Handbook of Poetic Terms* by Alex Preminger (Princeton) is good on most things. Take a course, join a group; your local Regional Arts Board (see page 492) will know who they are. The Muse chooses her favourites, but be a bit welcoming.

John Whitworth has published seven books of poetry, including *From the Sonnet History of Modern Poetry* (with drawings by Gerald Mangan) and, for children, *The Complete Poetical Works of Phoebe Flood* (Hodder). He has been a Faber anthologist, both judge and prize-winner in national poetry competitions, and has been published in national newspapers and on radio and television.

Poetry organisations

Poetry is one of the easiest writing art forms to begin with, though the hardest to excel at or earn any money from. Many organisations offer advice, information and resources to writers and readers at all levels, and as many as possible are included here. ***Christina Patterson****, director of the* ***Poetry Society*** *lists below the organisations which can help poets take their poetry further.*

Where to get involved

The Poetry Society

22 Betterton Street, London WC2H 9BU
tel 020-7420 9880 *fax* 020-7240 4818
fax 020-7384 3264
e-mail info@poetrysoc.com
web site http://www.poetrysoc.com

The Poetry Society was set up to help poetry and poets thrive in Britain. Now a registered charity funded by the Arts Council of England, the Society offers free advice and information to members and non-members on writing poetry and getting published. Membership is open to anyone interested in poetry and includes 4 issues of the magazine *Poetry Review* and 4 issues of the newsletter *Poetry News*.

The Society also publishes education

resources (see later); promotes National Poetry Day; runs a critical service called Poetry Prescription (£50 for 100 lines – 20% discount to members); provides an education advisory and training service, school membership, youth membership and a thriving web site. A range of events and readings take place at the Poetry Café and the BT Poetry Studio at the Society's headquarters in Covent Garden. In 1998, the Society was awarded a lottery grant to run a 2-year project to enable hundreds of poet-in-residence and short-term placements for poets to bring poetry to a range of new locations – from chain stores to gas platforms.

Competitions run by the Society include the National Poetry Competition in association with BT, the largest open poetry competition in Britain each year with a first prize of £5000, the biannual European Poetry Translation Prize and the Simon Elvin Young Poet Awards. Membership: £32 full, £25 concessions. Founded 1909.

Poetry Ireland

Bermingham Tower, Upper Yard, Dublin Castle, Dublin 2, Republic of Ireland
tel (01) 671 4632
e-mail poetry@iol.ie
web site http://www.poetryireland.ie

Poetry Ireland is the national poetry organisation for Ireland. It is grant-aided by both Northern and Southern Arts Councils of Ireland and is a resource centre with the Austin Clarke Library, of over 10,000 titles. It publishes the quarterly magazine *Poetry Ireland Review* and the bi-monthly newsletter *Poetry Ireland News*. Poetry Ireland organises readings in Dublin and nationally, and runs a Writers-in-Schools Scheme.

The Poetry Book Society

Book House, 45 East Hill, London SW18 2RX
tel 020-8870 8403 *fax* 020-8877 1615
e-mail info@poetrybooks.co.uk
web site http://www.poetrybooks.co.uk

This unique book club for readers of poetry was founded in 1953 by T.S. Eliot, and is funded by the Arts Council of England. Every quarter, selectors choose one outstanding publication (the PBS Choice), and recommend 4 other titles. Members can receive some or all of these books free and are also offered substantial discounts on other poetry books. The Poetry Book Society also administers the T.S. Eliot prize (see page 519), produces the quarterly membership magazine, the *Bulletin*, and has an education service providing teaching materials for primary and secondary schools. Write for membership details.

The British Haiku Society

PO Box 1974, Bristol BS88 3BB
General Secretary Alan J. Summers
tel (07979) 656775, *Pager* 04325 215042
e-mail asummers@dircon.co.uk

The British Haiku Society runs 'The Hackett' annual haiku competition; organises tutorials, workshops and critical comment; and provides information to promote the appreciation of haiku, senryu, tanka and renga. It publishes the journal *Blithe Spirit* (4 p.a.), a newsletter for its members called the *Brief* (5 p.a.), as well as books and the *Haiku Kit* – a teachers' guide for schools suitable for all age groups. Write for membership details. Founded 1990.

Survivors Poetry

Diorama Arts Centre, 34 Osnaburgh Street, London NW1 3ND
tel 020-7916 5317 *fax* 020-7916 0830
e-mail survivor@survivorspoetry.org.uk
Director Clare Douglas, *Outreach* Sharon Holder, *Finance Worker/Administrator* Demet Dayanch, *Information and Volunteer Co-ordinator* Lisa Boardman

Survivors Poetry provides poetry workshops, performances, readings, publishing, networking and training for survivors of mental distress in London and the UK. Survivors Poetry is funded by the Arts Council of England and was founded in 1991 by 4 poets who have had first-hand experience of the mental health system. It works in partnership with local and national arts, mental health, community, statutory and disability organisations. Its outreach project has established a network of 28 writers' groups in the UK.

Where to get information

Your local library should have information about the local poetry scene. Many libraries are actively involved in promoting poetry as well as having modern poetry available for loan. Local librarians promote writing activities with, for example, projects like Poetry on Loan and Poetry Places information points in West Midlands Libraries.

The Poetry Library

Level 5, Royal Festival Hall, London SE1 8XX
tel 020-7921 0943/0664 *fax* 020-7921 0939
e-mail poetrylibrary@rfh.org.uk
web site http://www.poetrylibrary.org.uk

The principal roles of the Poetry Library are to collect and preserve all poetry published in the UK since about 1912 and to act as a public lending library. The Library also keeps a wide range of international poetry. It has 2 copies of each title available and a collection of about 40,000 titles in English and English translation. The Library also provides an education service (see later).

Founded in 1953 by the Arts Council, the Library runs an active information service, which includes a unique noticeboard for lost quotations, and tracing authors and publishers from extracts of poems. Current awareness lists are available for magazines, publishers, competitions, bookshops, groups and workshops, evening classes and festivals on receipt of a large sae. The Library also stocks a full range of British poetry magazines as well as a selection from abroad. When visiting the Library, look out for the Voice Box, a performance space for literature; a programme is available from 020-7921 0906.

Open 11am-8pm Tuesday to Sunday. Membership: free with proof of identity and current address.

The Northern Poetry Library

County Library, The Willows, Morpeth, Northumberland NE61 1TA
tel (01670) 534514 (poetry enquiries)
tel (01670) 534524 (poetry dept)

The Northern Poetry Library has over 14,000 titles and magazines covering poetry published since 1945. For information about epic through to classic poetry, a full text database is available of all poetry from 600-1900. A postal lending service is available to members, who pay for return postage.

Membership: free to anyone living in the areas of Tyne and Wear, Durham, Northumberland, Cumbria and Cleveland. Founded 1968.

The Scottish Poetry Library

5 Crichton's Close, Canongate, Edinburgh EH8 8DT
tel 0131-557 2876 *fax* 0131-557 8393
e-mail inquiries@spl.org.uk
web site http://www.spl.org.uk

The Scottish Poetry Library is run along similar lines to the Poetry Library in London. It specialises in 20th century poetry written in Scotland, in Scots, Gaelic and English. It also collects some pre-20th-century poetry and contemporary poetry from all over the world. Information and advice is given, and visits by individuals, groups and schools are welcome. Borrowing is free of charge and there is a membership scheme (£20 p.a.), which includes use of the members' reading room and a regular newsletter. It has branches in libraries and arts centres throughout Scotland and also runs a library touring service. Readings and exhibitions are regularly organised, particularly during the Edinburgh Festival. Founded 1984.

Poeziecentrum

Hoornstraat 11, B-9000 Ghent, Belgium
tel 0032 9 225 2225
fax 0032 9 225 9054

Poeziecentrum (poetry centre) offers general information about translated and non-translated poetry. It has a library of 20,000 titles (including English, Scottish, American, Canadian and South African poetry), 600 magazines and 5000 archives including press cuttings, periodicals and biographical information. It also promotes the study of poetry (particularly in schools), offers advice on writing, publishing and competitions, and publishes many collections, including its own magazine *Poezierant* (bi-monthly). Founded 1980.

Regional Arts Boards (RABs)

5 City Road, Winchester, Hants SO23 8SD
tel (01962) 851063 *fax* (01962) 842033

Local literature officers can provide information on local poetry groups, workshops and societies (see page 492). Many RABs give grant aid to local publishers and magazines and help fund festivals, literature projects and readings, and some run critical services.

The Internet

You can get many links with good Internet poetry magazines by trying the following addresses.

The Poetry Kit
http://www.poetrykit.org
The Poetry Society of America
http://www.poetrysociety.org

Where to get poetry books

See the Poetry Book Society on page 281. The Poetry Library provides a list of bookshops stocking poetry. For second-hand mail order poetry books try:

Peter Riley

27 Sturton Street, Cambridge CB1 2QG
tel (01223) 576422
e-mail priley@dircon.co.uk

The Poetry Bookshop

The Ice House, Brook Street, Hay-on-Wye HR3 5BQ
tel (01497) 821812

Where to celebrate poetry

Festival information should be available from Regional Arts Boards. See also *Literature festivals* on page 543.

The British Council

Information Officer, Literature Dept,
The British Council, 11 Portland Place,
London W1N 4EJ
web site http://www.britishcouncil.org/arts/literature

Send a large sae or visit the web site for a list of forthcoming festivals.

Where to perform

In London, Big Word, Express Excess and Vice Verso are 3 of the liveliest venues and they regularly feature the best performers, while Poetry Unplugged at the Poetry Café (22 Betterton Street) is famous for its weekly open mike nights (Tuesdays 7pm). Other performance venues listed below have readings. For up-to-date information, read *Time Out* and *What's On in London*).

Big Word
Finnegan's Wake, 2 Essex Road, London N1
tel 020-7354 2016
Express Excess
The Enterprise, 2 Haverstock Hill, London NW3
tel 020-7485 2659
Vice Verso
Bread and Roses, 68 Clapham Manor Street, London SW4
tel 020-8341 6085
Terrible Beauty
Troubadour Coffee House,
265 Old Brompton Road, London SW5
tel 020-7370 1434
Voice Box
Level 5, Royal Festival Hall, London SE1
tel 020-7960 4242
Apples and Snakes Performance Poetry
Battersea Arts Centre, Lavender Hill,
London SW11
tel 020-7223 2223

For venues outside London, check local listings, and ask at libraries and Regional Arts Boards.

Competitions

There are now hundreds of competitions to enter and as the prizes increase, the highest being £5000 (1st prize in the National Poetry Competition and the Arvon Foundation International Poetry Competition), so does the prestige associated with winning such competitions.

To decide which competitions are worth entering, make sure you know who the judges are and think twice before paying large sums for an anthology of 'winning' poems which will only be read by entrants wanting to see their own work in print. The Poetry Library publishes a list of competitions each month (available free on receipt of a large sae). See also *Poetry into print* on page 275 and *Prizes and awards* on page 512.

Literary prizes are given annually to published poets and as such are non-competitive. A complete list of awards is given in the *Guide to Literary Prizes* (published by Book Trust, 2000, £6.99); it also produces a free leaflet on grants and awards.

Where to write poetry

The Arvon Foundation

The Arvon Foundation at Lumb Bank
Hebden Bridge, West Yorkshire HX7 6DF
tel (01422) 843714 *fax* (01422) 843714
The Arvon Foundation at Totleigh Barton
Sheepwash, Beaworthy,
Devon EX21 5NS
tel 01409 231338 *fax* 01409 231338

The Arvon Foundation at Moniack Mhor
Teavarren, Kiltarlity, Beauly,
Inverness-shire IV4 7HT
tel (01463) 741675

The Arvon Foundation's 3 centres run 5-day residential courses throughout the year to anyone over the age of 16, providing the opportunity to live and work with professional writers. Writing genres explored include poetry, narrative, drama, writing for children, song writing and the performing arts. Bursaries are available to those receiving benefits. Founded in 1968.

The Poetry School

1A Jewel Road, London E17 4QU
tel/fax 020-8223 0401 *tel* 020-8985 0090
e-mail poetryschl@aol.com

Using London venues, the Poetry School offers a core programme of tuition in reading and writing poetry. It provides a forum to share experience, develop skills and extend appreciation of both traditional and innovative aspects of poetry.

The Poet's House/Teach na hÉigse

Clonbarra, Falcarragh, County Donegal,
Republic of Ireland
tel 00 353 74 65470 *fax* 00 353 74 65471
e-mail phouse@iol.ie

The Poets House runs 3 10-day poetry courses in July and August. An MA degree in creative writing is validated by Lancaster University, and the Irish Language Faculty includes Cathal O'Searcaigh. The poetry faculty comprises 30 writers, including Paul Durcan and John Montagu.

Ty Newydd

Taliesin Trust, Ty Newydd, Llanystumdwy,
Criccieth, Gwynedd LL52 0LW
tel (01766) 522811 *fax* (01766) 523095
e-mail tynewydd@dial.pipex.com

Ty Newydd runs week-long writing courses encompassing a wide variety of genres, including poetry, and caters for all levels, from beginners to published poets. All the courses are tutored by published writers. Writing retreats are also available.

Write Away

East Midlands Arts, Mountfields House,
Epinal Way, Loughborough, Leics. LE11 0QE
tel (01509) 218292 *fax* (01509) 262214
web site http://www.arts.org.uk

The next programme of residential writing courses begins in September 2000. A variety of types of writing is studied.

Internet and local groups

On the Internet. It is worth searching for discussion groups and chat rooms on the Internet. There are plenty of them; John Kinsella's is highly recommended, which is junk mail-resistant and highly informative:

John Kinsella's poetryetc@listbot.com
Peter Howard's poetry@lists.cyberware.co.uk
www.writerswrite.com/

Locally. Local groups vary enormously so it is worth shopping around to find one that suits your poetry. Up-to-date information can be obtained from Regional Arts Boards.

The Poetry Library publishes a list of groups for the Greater London area which will be sent out on receipt of a large sae.

Help for young poets and teachers

The Poetry Library

Children's Section, Royal Festival Hall,
London SE1 8XX
tel 020-7921 0664
web site http://www.poetrylibrary.org.uk

For young poets, the Poetry Library has about 4000 books incorporating the SIGNAL Collection of Children's Poetry. It also has a multimedia children's section, from which cassettes and videos are available to engage children's interest in poetry.

The Poetry Library has an education service for teachers and writing groups. Its information file covers all aspects of poetry in education. There is a separate collection of books and materials for teachers and poets who work with children in schools, and teachers may join a special membership scheme to borrow books for the classroom.

National Association of Writers in Education (NAWE)

PO Box 1, Sheriff Hutton, York YO60 7YU
tel/fax (01653) 618429
e-mail paul@nawe.co.uk
web site http://www.nawe.co.uk

NAWE is a national organisation, which aims to widen the scope of writing in education, and co-ordinate activities between writers, teachers and funding bodies. It publishes the magazine *Writing in Education* and is author of a writers' database which can identify writers who fit the given criteria (e.g. speaks several languages, works well with special needs, etc) for schools, colleges and the community. Publishes *Reading the Applause: Reflections on Performance Poetry by Various Artists*. Write for membership details.

Poetry Society Education

The Poetry Society, 22 Betterton Street, London WC2H 9BU
tel 020-7420 9894 *fax* 020-7240 4818

Poetry Society Education sponsors poets in residence in educational settings from BBC Education to festivals and playgroups. A publication celebrating National Poetry Day is sent free to every school, giving an insight into the best of contemporary verse.

Schools membership (£45 secondary, £25 primary) offers publications, training opportunities for teachers and poets, and a consultancy service matching poets to places, and display materials. Poetryclass, an INSET training project funded by the DfEE, employs poets to train teachers at primary and secondary level. Under 18-year-olds can join the Society for £10 and benefit from regular performance opportunities, a national network of criticism and advice, and copies of the quarterly *Poetry News*.

Poetry Society publications for schools include *The Poetry Book for Primary Schools* and *Jumpstart Poetry in the Secondary School*, a young poets pack and posters for school Key Stage 1 to GCSE requirements. A full catalogue of poetry resources, details of youth membership, the Young National Poetry Competition, school membership and education residencies are available from the Education Department.

Young Book Trust and Bookstart

Book House, 45 East Hill, London SW18 2QZ
tel 020-8516 2977 *fax* 020-8516 2978
e-mail booktrust@dial.pipex.com

Young Book Trust, the children's division of Book Trust offers advice and information on all aspects of children's reading and books to promote reading. It runs a library of all children's books published over the last two years. It organises Children's Book Week, usually held in October, co-ordinating national activities throughout the week. It also offers an information service, including information on authors (Authorbank), and publishes a newsletter. A subscription service is available for schools, libraries, colleges, bookshops and publishers.

Book Trust also runs Bookstart, an innovative 2-year national project which gives free advice and books to parents/ carers attending their baby's health checks.

Young poetry competitions

Children's competitions are included in the competition list provided by the Poetry Library (free on receipt of a large sae).

Young National Poetry Competition

The Poetry Society, 22 Betterton Street, London WC2H 9BU

Free entry for 11 to 18-year-olds with unique prizes.

Further Reading

Baldwin, Michael, *The Way to Write Poetry*, Hamish Hamilton, 1982

Chisholm, Alison, *The Craft of Writing Poetry*, Allison & Busby, 1992, o.s.

Chisholm, Alison, *A Practical Poetry Course*, Allison & Busby, 1994

Clifford, Johnathon, *Vanity Press and The Proper Poetry Publishers*, Johnathon Clifford, 1994

Corti, Doris, *Writing Poetry*, Writers News, 1994

Fairfax, John, and John Moat, *The Way to Write*, Elm Tree Books, 1995

Finch, Peter, *How to Publish Your Poetry*, Allison & Busby, 2nd edn, 1998

Forbes, Peter, *Scanning the Century*, Penguin Books, 1999

Guide to Literary Prizes, Book Trust, 2000

Hamilton, Ian, *The Oxford Companion to Twentieth Century Poetry in English*, OUP, 1994, o.p.

Hyland, Paul, *Getting into Poetry*, Bloodaxe, 2nd edn, 1997

Livingstone, Dinah, *Poetry Handbook for Readers and Writers*, Macmillan, 1992

O'Brien, Sean, *The Firebox*, Picador, 1999, o.p.

Reading the Applause: Reflections on Performance Poetry by Various Artists, NAWE, 1999

Riggs, Thomas, (ed.) *Contemporary Poets*, St James Press, 6th edn, 1996, 7th edn due Oct 2000

Roberts, Philip Davies, *How Poetry Works: the Elements of English Poetry*, Penguin Books, 1996

Sansom, Peter, *Writing Poems*, Bloodaxe, 1994, reprinted 1997

Sweeney Matthew, and John Williams, *Teach Yourself Writing Poetry*, Hodder and Stoughton, 1997

USA

Fulton, Len, *Directory of Poetry Publishers*, Dustbooks, USA, 15th edn, 1999-2000

Fulton, Len, *The International Directory of Little Magazines and Small Presses*, Dustbooks, USA, 35th edn, 1999-2000

Jerome, Judson, *Poet's Market: Where and How to Publish Your Poetry*, Writer's Digest Books, USA, annual

Preminger, Alex, *New Princeton Encyclopedia of Poetry and Poetics*, Princeton University Press, 3rd edn 1993

Publishers of poetry

Anvil Press Poetry
Arc Publications
Bellew Publishing
Blackstaff Press (Ire.)
Bloodaxe Books
Marion Boyars Publishers
Jonathan Cape
Carcanet Press
Chapman Publishing
Chatto & Windus
Cló Iar-Chonnachta Teo. (Ire.) (Irish language only)
diehard
Enitharmon Press
Everyman's Library
Faber & Faber
Flambard Press
Gairm Publications
The Gallery Press (Ire.)
Gee & Son (Denbigh)
The Goldsmith Press (Ire.)
Headland Publications
Hippopotamus Press
Honno
Libris
Liverpool University Press
New Beacon Books
Onlywomen Press
Oxford University Press
Payback Press
Penguin UK
Peterloo Poets
Pipers' Ash
Polygon
Random House Group
Rivelin Grapheme Press
Scottish Cultural Press
Seren
Stride Publications
Writers & Readers

Television, film and radio

Writing for television

Writing for television can be an extremely rewarding career and one that can be started at virtually any age. ***Anji Loman Field*** *says anyone with the right aptitude and attitude can succeed. Here she gives sound advice for the potential screenwriter.*

The markets

There are various openings for new writers in television, but apart from competitions and special projects these are hardly ever advertised. The openings fall into four categories:

Single drama

There are fewer slots nowadays for the single play – a 30- or even 60-minute one-off drama is highly unlikely to find a market. Occasionally broadcasters will gather single 90-minute plays together under a collective banner (e.g. Screens One and Two; Love Bites; Obsession) but it's best to think of individual projects as either standalone 90-minute television films, two-parters or even four-parters. Ask television companies for their current guidelines on single drama and film.

Series and serials

Although it has been known for a new writer to sell an original series or serial, it is a relatively rare occurrence. Writers with a track record of writing for existing strands are far more likely to be taken seriously. Long-running soaps like *EastEnders*, *Emmerdale* and *Family Affairs* are often in the market for new writers, but check first. If the door is open, a good 'calling card script' is usually the way in. Submit an original piece of work in a similar genre that is at least an hour long and shows your ability to create believable characters, write sparkling dialogue and tell a compelling story. You may be invited to try out for one of these long-running shows.

Dramatisations/adaptations

A new writer is extremely unlikely to be commissioned to adapt or dramatise someone else's work for television. However, if there's something you really want to adapt and you can afford to take out an 'option' on the rights (or already own them, if it is your own novel or play) then write the script on spec. If you have a good script and can show that you own the rights, you could succeed.

Situation comedy

This is the one area where production companies and broadcasters are desperate for new talent, and there are several competitions open to new writers. If you are a good comedy writer and market your work well, you will undoubtedly succeed (see 'Writing situation comedy' below).

Aptitude and attitude

The first prerequisite in writing for television is that you enjoy the medium, and actually watch the kinds of shows that you would be interested in writing for. A cynical approach will always show through. And before sitting down to write that first television script, arm yourself with the appropriate skills by examining the medium as a whole.

- **Tape the kind of show you'd like to**

write for and analyse it. How many scenes are there? What length are they? How much of the story happens 'off camera'? Knowing the answers to these questions will help you to understand the grammar of screen, and enable you to write a more professional script.

• **Study the structure of story telling.** There are plenty of books on the subject, and although it is never a good idea to follow structural paradigms to the letter, absorb as much information as possible so that the essential 'rules' on character, motivation and plot filter through into your writing.

• **Read scripts.** Some are published in book form, but a huge variety of scripts are also available from specialist book shops such as Offstage (*tel* 020-7485 4996) and the Screenwriter's Store (*tel* 020-8469 2244).

• **If you want to write sitcom, see as many live recordings of shows as possible.** This enables you to understand the techniques involved in television production, and particularly the physical constraints imposed by the studio. Free tickets for sitcom recordings are always available – phone the broadcasters for information.

• **Be realistic.** Don't make your first project too ambitious in terms of screen time, locations or special effects. If you can 'contain the action' and make your first script affordable to shoot, it is far more likely to be taken seriously.

Learning the craft

Even the most successful and experienced screenwriters say they never stop learning. Some have been lucky enough to learn the skill of writing for the screen in a subliminal way. For example, Lynda La Plante (*Prime Suspect*) was an actress with plenty of opportunity for studying scripts and production techniques before she turned her hand to writing; John Sullivan (*Only Fools and Horses*) worked in the props department at the BBC on countless sitcoms, and used to take the scripts home to study. But there are other ways to learn. Script workshops are particularly useful.

There are many courses and workshops available. These range from small self-help groups, where writers give each other feedback on their work, to full- and part-time Screenwriting MA courses at universities (e.g. in London, Sheffield, Bournemouth, Manchester and Leeds). Evening classes are springing up in local colleges, and there are even script workshops on the Internet. Workshops can help in the following ways:

• **Discipline**. The hardest thing most writers ever have to do is sit down and face that blank screen or page. Joining a script workshop – where you *have* to deliver an outline or a treatment, or the next 20 pages of your script by a certain date – provides the push that so many writers need.

• **Feedback**. Reading and giving feedback on other people's work helps you to focus on getting your own script right. It is also good to get used to the idea of showing your own work to others and getting their feedback. Television writing is generally a collaborative process and writers need to be pleasant to work with, and receptive to ideas. Knowing when to argue a point and when to concede are crucial skills which can be developed in good writing workshops.

• **Rewriting**. Learn to Love the Rewrite. It is such a major achievement to get to the end of a first draft that it is all too easy to rush to the post box and send it off to several production companies at once. *Four Weddings and a Funeral*, a Channel 4-funded project, went through 17 rewrites before finally reaching the screen. So before you post your masterpiece:

• Leave it to 'settle' for a few days and do something completely different – allow your head to clear completely. Then re-read the script from beginning to end – from as objective a viewpoint as possible – and make necessary changes.

• Get feedback so that you're sure your script is ready to send. Be warned: knowing how to read and analyse a script properly is a particular skill. Unless they are equipped in this area, *never* ask your friends or relations to read your script. Their comments could either lull you into a false sense of security or destroy your

Useful information

Euroscript
Suffolk House, 1-8 Whitfield Place,
London W1P 5SF
tel/fax 020-7387 5880
e-mail euroscript@netmatters.co.uk
web site http://www.euroscript.co.uk
A media project of the EU to advance European scriptwriting in the form of distance training that develops scripts; reads, selects and promotes scripts and writers; runs workshops and supports writers' groups; and runs 2 film story competitions twice a year (deadlines: 30 April and 31 October each year).

London Film & Video Development Agency
114 Whitfield Street,
London W1P 5RW
tel 020-7383 7755
(incorporating the London Production Fund
tel 020-7383 7766)
Offers grants that enable writers, producers and directors to make their projects. Send sae for further information.

The Screenwriters' Workshop
(formerly London Screenwriters' Workshop)
Suffolk House, 1-8 Whitfield Place,
London W1P 5SF
tel/fax 020-7387 5511
web site http://www.lsw.org.uk
Educational charity that runs regular courses, workshops and events, and publishes a quarterly newsletter. (See also page 497.)

National Association of Television Program Executives (NATPE)
452 Oakleigh Road North, London N20 0RZ
tel 020-8361 3793 *fax* 020-8368 3824
web site http://www.natpe.org
Contact Pam Smithard
Non-profit TV programming and software association dedicated to the continued growth and success of the global TV marketplace. Year-round activities include the annual conference and exhibition, which reaches tens of thousands of key decisionmakers in virtually every sector of the TV industry.

PACT (Producers' Alliance for Cinema and Television)
45 Mortimer Street, London W1N 7TD
tel 020-7331 6000 *fax* 020-7331 6700
Serves the feature film and independent TV production sector. The *PACT Guide* lists contacts in all areas (£30 to non-members). (See also page 487.)

Regional Arts Boards
Many RABs offer grants that enable writers, producers and directors to make their projects. Contact your local Arts Board for details (see page 492).

The Spotlight
7 Leicester Place, London WC2H 7BP
tel 020-7437 7631
Publishes a book called *Contacts*, which contains useful information and contact addresses. The 2000-2001 edition is available from October.

The Writers' Guild of Great Britain
430 Edgware Road,
London W2 1EH
tel 020-7723 8074
web site http://www.writers.org.uk/guild
Trade organisation for professional writers. Negotiates rates for TV drama with the BBC and the ITV Network Centre. (See also page 509.)

confidence for ever. Feedback from other writers in your workshop group is best. There are some organisations (including the Screenwriters' Workshop) which offer a professional script feedback service for a moderate fee.

Writing situation comedy

Situation comedy writing is the most lucrative area of television, and deservedly so. Have you ever tried making an audience laugh several times a minute for 25 minutes for at least six weeks running, and maybe (in the case of *Last of the Summer Wine*) for 20 long years?

Despite its name, sitcom is less about situation and much more about character. It is better to start with funny and engaging characters in mind and then (if it isn't part and parcel of the character) find the perfect situation in which to place them than it is to begin with the premise 'nobody's ever set a sitcom in a nuclear power station before'. It is not the setting that makes the audience laugh, it is the characters.

A good exercise in seeing if you can write funny material is to write an episode of an existing sitcom. If *Fawlty Towers* is your all-time favourite, study a few episodes and then try your own. It will never get made, but you'll learn a lot in the process – and sample scripts like this are often useful as calling card scripts.

Some of the broadcast companies issue guidelines on writing situation comedy. Phone the comedy departments at the BBC, LWT and Carlton for information, or the Programme Support Unit at Channel 4 (020-7396 4444) for their excellent 'beginner's guide to sitcom writing' pack – available for a small fee.

Competitions

Broadcasters occasionally run writing competitions or 'new writing initiatives'. Check their web sites – and general screenwriters' web sites – for up-to-date information. Also, watch out for annual awards run by organisations such as PAWS (People's Awareness of Science), the BBC (e.g. the Dennis Potter Play of the Year Award, see page 533), and the Orange Prize for Screenwriting (*web site* http://www.orangeprize.com *tel* (07970) 111999). Details can be found in the trade press and via relevant web sites and screeenwriting organisations. See also *Prizes and awards* section on page 512.

Breaking in

Do you need an agent?

Many new writers are keen to get an agent before they attempt to sell anything, but this can be an arduous process and there are few agents prepared to take on a completely untried writer.

The best way to get an agent is to first get an offer of a deal on a project. Most *bona fide* production companies and broadcasters will happily recommend a selection of agents to writers they want to do business with. If you can phone an agent and say 'so-and-so wants to option/commission my project and has recommended you as an agent' s/he is far more likely to be interested. And at that point you can pick and choose the agent who is right for you, rather than going with the first one to say "yes".

Selling yourself

Once you are sure you have a good script, where do you send it? If you've done your homework, you will already know which channel is the most likely to be interested. But often it is better to send to an independent production company rather than directly to a broadcaster, so do a bit more research. Check out the companies that are making the kind of show you've written and approach them first.

A preliminary letter or phone call can save you time and money because some smaller companies simply don't have the resources to read unsolicited material. If you feel that a certain production company is absolutely right for your project, write a letter giving a brief synopsis of the project and asking if they will read the script. If they agree, your script will join the 'solicited' pile. And if it fits the bill, they may even pick it up and develop it. But don't expect overnight results. It can sometimes take many months before scripts are even read by small and/or busy companies.

Sending your script directly to a broadcaster can lead to a commission, but unless you target a particular producer whose work you admire you will probably have less control over who you work with.

Being 'discovered'

If you can get your work 'rehearse-read' by actors in front of an audience it will help your writing, and may even lead to discovery. Many script readings are attended by development executives from television and production companies and there are many stories of individuals being picked up from such projects. TAPS (Television Arts Performance Showcase) (020-8977 3252), Player-Playwrights (020-8883 0371) and the Screenwriters' Workshop, all organise rehearsed readings.

Development hell

This is the place between finding someone who wants to produce your script and waiting for the 'suits' at the television companies to give the final go-ahead for the project. In the meantime you will have been paid, perhaps just an option fee, or maybe a commission fee for a script or two. Either way, *never put all your eggs in one development basket.* Aim eventually to have several projects bubbling under for every one that comes to the boil.

A realistic optimism is required for this game. Don't believe anything wonderful will happen until you actually have that signed contract in front of you. In the meantime keep writing, keep marketing and, if you possibly can, keep making contacts in the industry. If you're good at schmoozing, go to as many industry events as possible and make new contacts. If you can send a script to a producer with a covering letter saying 'I heard your talk the other day ...' you will immediately arouse interest.

Coping with rejection

The standard rejection letter is the worst part of this business. When it is accompanied by your returned script – looking decidedly un-read – it is very easy to become disillusioned. The trick is this: change your mental attitude to the point where if you don't receive at least one rejection letter in the post every day, you feel rejected! So long as you are absolutely sure that your work is good, keep sending it out. Sooner or later you'll get a nicer, more personalised rejection letter, and then eventually perhaps even a cup of tea with the producer ...

Selling ideas

Completely new writers do occasionally sell ideas but are much more likely to sell the idea alone, i.e. the 'format rights', and will probably end up not writing the script. If you have a great calling card script or two, or have had a few episodes of something produced, your ideas will be taken much more seriously. At this stage you might well sell a project on the basis of a short outline or synopsis, and be paid to write the script(s).

All scripts must be typed and properly formatted if they are to be taken seriously. If you dread the practical aspects of getting your script onto the page it might be worth investing in a screenwriting software program for your computer. They take the pain out of screenwriting by auto-formatting and numbering the pages and scenes, thus enabling you to move scenes around and restructure your script with ease. Such facilities allow writers to concentrate wholly on the creative process and can therefore be quite liberating, even for those who type well. Contact the Screenwriters' Store for details and advice.

Summary

Writing for television is not generally something that can be taken up as a hobby. It may look easy but huge amounts of work and commitment are required in order to succeed. If that doesn't put you off, and it is what you really want to do, then go for it. And good luck!

Anji Loman Field worked as a television producer for several years before turning to writing. She has since written drama, comedy drama and animation for film and television, and has taught writing at the Screenwriters' Workshop, the Royal College of Art and the London Institute.

Further reading

Friedmann, Julian, *How to Make Money Scriptwriting*, Boxtree, 1995, o.p.

Kelsey, Gerald, *Writing for Television*, A & C Black, 3rd edn, 1999

Seger, Linda, *Making a Good Script Great*, Samuel French Inc. (pbk), 1994

Vogler, Christopher, *The Writer's Journey*, Pan, 2nd revised edn, 1999

Wolfe, Ronald, *Writing Comedy*, Robert Hale, (pbk), 1997

Writing drama for radio

Writing drama for radio allows a freedom which none of the other performing arts can give. ***Lee Hall*** *guides the radio drama writer to submit a script which will be both well received and merit production.*

With upwards of 300 hours of radio drama commissioned each year, radio is an insatiable medium and, therefore, one which is constantly seeking new blood. It is no surprise to find that many of our most eminent dramatists, such as Pinter and Stoppard, did important radio work early in their careers.

Although the centrality of radio has been eclipsed somewhat by television and fringe theatre, it continues to launch new writers, and its products often find popular recognition in other media (for example, the film version of Anthony Mingella's *Truly Madly Deeply*). Because radio is often cited as the discoverer and springboard of so many talents, this should not obscure the fact that many writers make a living primarily out of their radio writing and the work itself is massively popular, with plays regularly getting audiences of over 500,000 people.

For the dramatist, the medium offers a variety of work which is difficult to find anywhere else: serials, dramatisations, new commissions of various lengths (from a couple of minutes to several hours), musicals, soap operas, adaptations of the classics, as well as a real enthusiasm to examine new forms.

Because it is no more expensive to be in the Hindu Kush than to be in a laundrette in Deptford, the scope of the world is only limited by the imagination of the writer. However, though radio drama in the 'Fifties and 'Sixties was an important conduit for absurdism, there is a perceived notion that radio drama on the BBC is domestic, Home Counties and endlessly trotting out psychological trauma in a rather naturalistic fashion. This is not a fair assessment of the true range of work presented. The BBC itself is anxious to challenge this idea and as the face of broadcasting changes, there is a conscious move to attract new audiences with new kinds of work.

Get to know the form

Listen to as many plays as possible, read plays that are in print, and try to analyse what works, what doesn't and why. This may seem obvious, but it is easy to fall back on your preconceived notions of what radio plays are. The more you hear other people's successes and failures, the more tools you will have to discriminate when it comes to your own work.

Plays on radio tend to fit into specific time slots: 30, 60, 75, 90 minutes, and each slot will have a different feel – an afternoon play will be targeted at a different audience from one at 10.30pm.

A radio play will be chosen on artistic grounds but nevertheless a writer should be familiar with the market. This should not be seen as an invitation merely to copy forms or to try to make your play 'fit', but an opportunity to gain some sense of what the producers are dealing with. Producers are looking for new and fresh voices, ones which are unique, open new areas or challenge certain preconceptions. This is not to suggest you should be wilfully idiosyncratic but to be aware that it is the individuality of your 'voice' that people will notice.

Write what you feel strongly about, in the way that most attracts you. It should be bold, personal, entertaining, challenging and stimulating. Radio has the scope to explore drama that wouldn't get produced in theatres or on television, so treat it as the most radical forum for new writing. How many times have you listened to the radio with the sense that you've heard it all before? Never feel limited by what exists but be aware how your voice can enrich the possibilities of the future.

Who to approach

Opportunities for writing for radio in the UK are dominated by the BBC. Whilst there are increasing opportunities with independent stations, BBC Radio Drama overwhelms the field. Its output is huge. The variety of the work – from soaps to the classics – makes it the true national repertory for drama in its broadest sense. However, the BBC is increasingly commissioning productions from independent producers, so you can:

- send your unsolicited script to the BBC's New Writing Initiative (see page 297) where it will be assessed by a reader. If they find it of interest they will put you in contact with a suitable producer.
- approach a producer directly. This may be a producer at the BBC or at an independent company (see page 329). Both will give a personal response based on their own taste, rather than an institutional one.

Producers have a broad role: they find new writers, develop projects, edit the script, cast the actors, record and edit the play, and even write up the blurb for the *Radio Times*. Because of this intense involvement, the producer needs to have a strong personal interest in the writer or writing when they take on a project.

The system of commissioning programmes at the BBC is such that staff producers or independent production companies offer projects to commissioning editors to decide upon. Thus, a writer must be linked to a producer in the first instance to either get their play produced or get a commission for a new piece of work. Therefore, going direct to a producer can be a convenient short cut, but it requires more preparation.

Approaching a producer

Discovering and developing the work of new writers is only a small part of a producer's responsibilities, so be selective. Do your homework – there is little point in sending your sci-fi series to a producer who exclusively produces one-off period comedies.

To help decide which producer will be the most receptive to your work, become familiar with the work of each producer you are intersted in and the type of writers they work with. Use the *Radio Times* to help with your research and listen to as many of their plays as possible. It is well worth the effort in order to be sure to send your play to the right person. If you can quote the reasons why you've chosen them in particular, it can only help to get a congenial reception. It will also give you confidence in their response, as the comments – good or bad – will be from someone you respect.

Submitting your work

Don't stuff your manuscript into an envelope as soon as you've written 'The End'. You owe it to yourself to get the script into the best possible state before anyone sees it. First impressions matter and time spent refining will pay dividends in attracting attention.

Ask a person you trust to give you some feedback. Try to edit the work yourself, cutting things that don't work and spending time revising and reinventing anything which you think could be better. Make sure that what you send is the best you can possibly do.

Producers have mountains of scripts to read. The more bulky your tome the less enthusiastically it will be received. (It's better to send a sparkling 10-page sample than your whole 300-page masterpiece.) Try to make the first scene excellent. The more you can surprise, engage or delight in the first few pages, the more chance the rest will be carefully read. The adage that a reader can tell whether a play is any good after the first three pages might be wholly inaccurate but it reflects a cynicism versed by the practice of script reading. The reader will probably approach your script with the expectation that it is unsuitable, and part of getting noticed is jolting them out of their complacency.

Have your script presentably typed. Make sure your letter of introduction is well informed and shows that you haven't just picked a name at random. Do not send it to more than one producer at a time, as this is considered bad etiquette. And don't expect an instantaneous response – it may take a couple of months before you receive a reply. Don't be afraid of calling up if they keep you waiting for an unreasonable length of time, but don't badger people as this will inevitably be counterproductive.

Finally

Don't be discouraged by rejection and *don't* assume that because one person has rejected your script that it is no good. It is all a question of taste. Use the criticism positively to help your work, not as a personal attack.

Lee Hall's first radio play, *I Luv U, Jimmy Spud*, won the Alfred Bradley Bursary Award, The Richard Imison Award, and the Society of Authors/Sony Award in 1996. He has written several other plays for BBC Radio, as well as the series *God's Country*, which included the award-winning play *Spoonface Steinberg*, and a serial dramatisation of Mario Vargas Llosa's *Aunt Julia and the Scriptwriter*.

Digital broadcasting

Digital broadcasting is expanding rapidly. ***David Teather*** *introduces this new media and looks at the implications for writers.*

Digital broadcasting offers choice from hundreds of channels and the chance to offer interactive services to viewers. As many as 10 digital services are able to occupy the frequency previously occupied by one analogue service. Picture quality is far sharper using digital transmission.

Interactive services are so far only being used for e-commerce – for instance, Sky's television shopping and banking service Open. Ultimately, though, viewers will be able to link straight from a programme to associated web sites, merchandising or on-line discussion points covering issues raised in a show. Digital transmission costs are also much lower which makes it more commercially viable for niche channels to exist.

The technical explanation

The BBC offers this definition: "Digital Broadcasting is transmission by converting sound and picture into binary digits – a series of ones and noughts. Digital signals are more robust than analogue signals and can occupy parts of the spectrum unavailable to analogue. A process of compression also allows many digital services within the space taken by one analogue service."

The story so far

The first company to launch digital services was Sky and it hopes to have some 5 million digital subscribers by the end of 2000. Its customer numbers for pay-TV stations had plateaued, but are now rising again as a result of digital broadcasting.

Of the cable companies, Telewest began its digital services at the end of 1999 and NTL (which now owns Cable & Wireless) started in mid 2000. ONdigital, a joint venture between Carlton Communications and Granada which enables digital services to be sent via traditional roof-top aerials, is aiming for one million customers by the end of 2000.

The uptake of digital services was given a huge boost when the fierce competition for subscribers led Sky to scrap the £200 charge for the set-top boxes needed to unscramble the digital signal. ONdigital was forced to follow suit.

End of analogue

The government is aiming to switch off analogue and would like to do so before 2010, by which time digital set-top boxes will have been almost entirely replaced by television sets able to receive digital television signals. However, it fears the outcry which will inevitably follow when pensioners are forced to buy new sets.

Free to air

There are a number of free-to-air digital channels. The BBC has, controversially, set up three new channels: BBC Choice shows reruns from the previous week as well as some entertainment-based original programming; BBC Knowledge is an education channel; and BBC News 24 – as the name suggests – screens news 24 hours a day. Rival companies such as Sky have argued that the licence fee should not be used to prop up stations like News 24 in a commercial marketplace.

ITV Network's ITV2 also shows 'catch-up' episodes of programmes such as *Coronation Street*, as well as trumpeting a large number of US imports, including a late night double bill of Jerry Springer and David Letterman.

All of the five existing free-to-air channels are also available in digital format although at the time of going to press, ITV was refusing to offer its channels for broadcast on the Sky's satellite distribution platform.

Video on demand

The next step in the digital revolution is video on demand. A number of companies are trialling systems, including the cable firms and a new breed of young companies, such as Video Networks, Filmgroup, Yes Television and Future TV. Users will be able to download films or television programmes at will, and fast forward, pause and rewind them. Programme-makers like the BBC have already sold packages to some of the video-on-demand firms and writers need to consider the implications for the potential sell-on of copyright.

Video on demand will become widespread with the advent of a technology called ADSL (Asymmetrical Digital Subscriber Line), which upgrades existing copper telephone wires for high bandwidth use such as pay-TV without the need to dig up roads. ADSL should become readily available on BT's networks by mid-2001. A ban on broadcasting being carried over BT's lines is to be lifted from 1 January.

Digital technology in the next few years will enable video-quality film to be sent over mobile phone networks. The mobile phone industry is expecting to have the networks and handsets with larger screens available by 2003.

New channels, new opportunities?

The explosion of new channels may suggest that there will be an equally huge demand for new writing talent to help fill the extra airtime. Through a joint venture with Flextech Television, the BBC has six pay-TV channels, including UK Gold, UK Play and UK Drama. The evidence so far, however, is that money is being spent largely on three things: sports rights, movies and US imports. Most original programming on pay-TV channels is very low budget and is far more likely to be a cookery or pop music show than original drama.

Unfortunately, rather than playing to their own strengths, the BBC and ITV appear to be drawn into competing with the entertainment channels at their level. "Once upon a time the BBC set the standards of quality and everyone else had to try and compete," says one writer. "That doesn't happen any more. Now the BBC competes with the others for crap."

The level of competition among broadcasters now also means that where original drama is being commissioned it is often low budget. In fact, many writers believe that in the short term digital technology has not opened opportunities at all and see the future as pretty bleak. Management gurus, though, maintain that 'content is king' and that those broadcasters who triumph will be the ones who produce the most compelling programming.

Copyrights

The Writers' Guild notes a recent case where a writer saw a 30-year-old show he had penned being repeated again and again on a pay-TV channel and demanded to know why he wasn't being paid. It turned out that he had signed his rights away in 1972.

If the explosion of channels made possible by digital technology isn't leading to a wave of new commissioning then writers could at least hope for healthier repeat fees. The culture of broadcasters forcing writers to sign away their rights for a lump sum so that they can show a programme whenever they like is becoming increasingly prevalent. The usual royalty is 5.6% of the sale price, which gives the owner the right to show the programme a set number of times over a given period.

Broadcasters blame the need to sell to the US market programmes which are unencumbered by copyright issues. When selling work, writers should remember how many more times, potentially, a programme will appear on air because of the growth in distribution platforms, and therefore at least try to protect their rights. The rapid changes in technology has also led writers' unions to recommend that contracts over the shortest space of time possible are agreed.

Original programming

There are at last some encouraging signs, however, led by Channel 4 and followed by Sky. Channel 4 has long supported new writing talent through its backing of British film and has found its own pay-TV distribution outlet with FilmFour.

In 1999, Sky committed some £90 million to new programming with mixed results, including *Dream Team* and the heavily publicised sci-fi comedy *The Strangerers*. However, Sky's original programming has largely been forced upon it as the cost of acquiring top US content has soared due to increased competition – the reason why it lost the rights to show *Friends* and *ER*, two of Sky One's biggest ratings pullers, to Channel 4. Sky's commitment to original programming is also uncertain after the departure of Elisabeth Murdoch who championed British-produced content at Sky.

Sky Pictures is trying to emulate the success of FilmFour, albeit from a mass audience pitch. Its first two films were a biopic of footballer George Best and *Saving Grace* staring Brenda Blethyn. In early 2000, NTL, now Britain's largest cable company, committed its first spend to original programming.

Digital radio

The attributes of digital radio are similar to those of television. It was supposed to be the next revolution, but it has yet to catch on.

The growth of stations is still in its infancy. In London, for instance, there will be three so-called 'multiplexes' of eight stations awarded to various consortia of existing radio groups. Interactive services will be on offer with the most obvious for radio including up-to-date traffic or weather reports displayed on a digital monitor on request. Digital radio could also lead to music or programming on demand similar to that of digital television programming.

A number of stations are now being broadcast in both digital and analogue as well as a growing number in digital alone. So far, though, the industry has been held back by the prohibitive cost of hardware – the radios currently cost around £300.

David Teather is Media Business Correspondent at the *Guardian*.

BBC network television and radio

At the time of going to press, the BBC was in the process of being reorganised. For up-to-date information contact the relevant department.

The new structure

The BBC has undergone a major restructuring, introduced by BBC Director-General Greg Dyke on 3 April 2000, with the creation of four programming divisions: Drama, Entertainment and Children; Factual and Learning; Sport; and News. BBC Broadcast and BBC Production have been abolished.

In the areas of sport, children's and education, commissioning and programme-making are now integrated. A New Media division is now developing the BBC's interactive television on-line activities.

Television genre commissioners in drama, entertainment and features now work with the television channel controllers to strengthen the BBC's output in these areas.

The disbanding of the Independent Commissioning Group has not diminished the value the BBC now places on the contribution of independents. However, in future they will take the same commissioning routes as in-house producers.

The restructuring also gives output guarantees for in-house departments, including Nations and English Regions, and longer term commissions to enable better planning and a greater focus on creativity.

web site http://www.bbc.co.uk/
Director, Television Mark Thompson
Controller, BBC 1 Peter Salmon
Controller, BBC 2 Jane Root
Head of Programming BBC Choice Stuart Murphy
Director, Radio Jenny Abramsky
Controller, Radio 1 Andy Parfitt
Controller, Radio 2 Jim Moir
Controller, Radio 3 Roger Wright
Controller, Radio 4 Helen Boaden
Controller, Radio 5 Live Bob Shennan

Drama, Entertainment and Children

Director Alan Yentob

Drama

BBC Television Centre, Centre House, Wood Lane, London W12 7SB
tel 020-8743 8000

The New Writing Initiative
Room 6058, BBC Broadcasting House, London W1A 1AA
tel 020-7580 4468

Drama Development in the North
BBC New Broadcasting House, Oxford Road, Manchester M60 1SJ
tel 0161-200 2020

BBC Broadcasting Centre
Pebble Mill Road, Birmingham B5 7QQ
tel 0121-432 8888

Drama has departments in London, Birmingham and Manchester and produces a broad range of plays, serials, series and readings for TV, film, BBC Radio 3, BBC Radio 4 and BBC World Service.

Unsolicited scripts for TV and film, single plays and radio drama, are co-ordinated by the New Writing Initiative. Scripts should be submitted one at a time. The Initiative also produces detailed guidelines on script construction, markets and contacts (for address see above). Since competition is fierce, reading the guidelines is advisable before submitting a script. All writers submitting scripts are considered for the Initiative's highly targeted writing schemes and workshops.

The Manchester team also operates radio drama workshops, primarily for writers in the North of England. For further information contact Drama Development in the North.

The Birmingham radio team reads the

unsolicited scripts of writers in the Midlands, East Anglia and South West but does not have a formal new writing department. The TV operation also reads unsolicited scripts on an informal basis. Both offices are based at BBC Broadcasting Centre.
Controller, Drama Production Colin Adams
Head of Series Mal Young
Head of Films and Single Drama David Thompson
Head of Development Television Series Patrick Spence
Head of Development Television Serials Pippa Harris
Senior Executive Producer BBC ONE Films and Serials Jane Tranter
Senior Executive Producer BBC TWO Serials Hilary Salmon
Head of Development Single Dramas and Films Tracey Scoffield
Casting Executive, Drama Series Jane Deitch
Head of Radio Drama and New Services Kate Rowland
Executive Producer TV Drama Series, Birmingham Richard Langridge
Development Co-ordinator TV Drama, Birmingham Terry Barker
Executive Producer Radio Drama and Editor, The Archers, Birmingham Vanessa Whitburn
Executive Producer Radio Drama, Manchester Sue Roberts
Head of Drama, BBC World Service Gordon House
New Writing Initiative Co-ordinator Lucy Hannah

Entertainment

BBC Television Centre, Wood Lane, London W12 7RJ
tel 020-8743 8000
web site http://www.bbc.co.uk/writeon

Entertainment welcomes new half-hour TV situation comedy scripts and material is reviewed by its Comedy Script Unit. Radio is also a good entry point for new comedy writers, performers and ground-breaking innovative series such as sketch shows and panel games.

The department produces *Writers Guidelines*, a detailed information pack which includes advice on how to write radio and TV scripts, current trends, available markets, contacts, free audience opportunities and further reading (available by sending an A4 first class sae to Comedy Script Unit, Room 4088). Writers are strongly advised to read the *Writers Guidelines* before submitting scripts one at a time, as competition is high. It has an informative web site.
Controller of Entertainment Paul Jackson
Head of Light Entertainment David Young
Editor, Radio Entertainment John Pidgeon
Head of Comedy Geoffrey Perkins
Head of Comedy Entertainment Jon Plowman
Editor, Comedy Sophie Clarke-Jervoise
Script Executive Bill Dare
Head of Music Entertainment Trevor Dann

Children's

BBC Television Centre, Wood Lane, London W12 7RJ
tel 020-8743 8000

Opportunities are limited for new writers in this highly competitive area. Unsolicited material is read by the department, preferably in the form of synopses of ideas. The preferred genre is contemporary comedy and drama series for weekdays after school aimed at the 7-12 year-old age range.
Head of Children's Nick Pickard
Executive Producer Drama Elaine Sperber
Head of Entertainment Chris Bellinger
Programme Executive New Media Greg Childs
Development Producer Anne Gilchrist

Factual and Learning

Joint Directors Lorraine Heggessey, Michael Stevenson

Entertainment and Features, Manchester

BBC New Broadcasting House, PO Box 27, Oxford Road, Manchester M60 1SJ
tel 0161-200 2020

A bi-media department which makes programmes for both radio and TV. It is responsible for a wide range of factual, entertainment and music programming, and specialises in spotting new comedy talent and aims to see all new stand-up performers/writers in the North West. Write with details of events to Comedy Entertainment, Room 4033.
Head of Entertainment and Features Wayne Garvie
Executive Producer Entertainment Programmes Kieron Collins
Executive Producer Factual and Popular Culture Alan Brown
Executive Producer Factual Features Claire Powell
Executive Producer Lifestyle and New Channels Emma Westcott
Head of African Caribbean Unit Angela Ferreira
Development Executive Helen Bullough

Education

BBC White City, 201 Wood Lane,
London W12 7TS
tel 020-8752 5252
web site http://www.bbc.co.uk/education

Education commissions a vast range of TV, radio, print and on-line material to support both formal and informal learning across all age groups and levels. The digital TV channel, BBC KNOWLEDGE, extends the learning and information experience still further.

Head of Programmes, BBC Knowledge Liz Cleaver
Head of Commissioning, Education for Children Frank Flynn
Head of Commissioning, Education for Adults Fiona Chesterton
Head of Learning Support Steve Pollock

Features, Bristol

BBC Broadcasting House,
Whiteladies Road,
Bristol BS8 2LR
tel 01179-732211

Produces a range of factual leisure, information and documentary programmes for radio and TV. The department also specialises in animation and new talent initiatives, including *Picture This* and *10X10*.

Head of Features, Bristol Jeremy Gibson
Deputy Head and Managing Editor, TV Andy Battern Foster
Head of Development Tom Ware
Joint Editors, Radio Fiona Couper, Elizabeth Burke
Senior Executive Producer, Leisure Mark Hill
Senior Executive Producer, Observational Documentaries Tessa Finch
Executive Producer, Animation Colin Rose

Arts and Classical Music

BBC Television Centre,
East Tower, Wood Lane,
London W12 9RJ
tel 020-8743 8000

Landmark arts series, magazine programmes and live music are a hallmark of this department.

Head of Arts and Classical Music Kim Evans
Head of Classical Music (Radio and Orchestras) Dr John Evans
Head of Classical Music, Television Peter Maniura
Managing Editor Alex Graham

Documentaries and History

BBC White City, 201 Wood Lane,
London W12 7TS
tel 020-8752 5252

Primarily a TV department, making observational documentaries, it is developing history as a bi-media service (both TV and radio). It is also responsible for the Disability Programme Unit and for the Community Programme Unit, which is the home of *Video Diaries* and *Video Nation* (the 50-minute and 2-minute slots on BBC TWO which feature members of the public and their life stories).

Head of Documentaries and History Paul Hamann
Head of History Laurence Rees
Executive Producer, Community Programmes Bob Long

Features and Events

BBC White City, 201 Wood Lane, London W12 7TS
tel 020-8752 5252

This bi-media department makes popular, factual and leisure programmes including cookery, gardening, consumer, crime busting, mysteries and travel. It also brings its specialist expertise to great national occasions and major royal events.

Head of Features and Events Anne Morrison
Chief Assistant Donna Taberer
Editor, Television Development Vicki Barrass
Executive Editor, Radio Graham Ellis

Natural History Unit

BBC Broadcasting House, Whiteladies Road,
Bristol BS8 2LR
tel 01179-732211

Makes specialist programmes with established experts.

Head of Natural History Unit Keith Scholey
Head of Development Michael Bright
Commercial Director Ailish Heneberry
Editor Radio Sarah Blunt

Religion

BBC New Broadcasting House, PO Box 27,
Oxford Road, Manchester M60 1SJ
tel 0161-200 2020

Produces a wide range of religious, moral and ethical programmes for radio and TV which, while recognising Christianity as

the UK's dominant faith, explore a wide range of faiths and issues.
Head of Religious Broadcasting Rev Ernest Rea
Managing Editor Helen Alexander

Science

BBC White City, 201 Wood Lane, London W12 7TS
tel 020-8752 5252

Produces programmes ranging from popular, fun magazine shows to landmark series and documentaries for both radio and TV.
Head of BBC Science Glenwyn Benson
Deputy Head and Executive Editor John Lynch
Head of Development Emma Swain
Executive Editor, Business and Industry Robert Thirkell
Editor, Radio Science Unit Harry Dean

Network Production, Birmingham

BBC Broadcasting Centre, Pebble Mill Road, Birmingham, B5 7QQ
tel 0121-432 8888

A vast range of radio and TV programming which encompasses Asian, consumer affairs, leisure, lifestyle, motoring, music and rural affairs.
Head of Network Production Kate Marsh
Head of New Media Tony Steyger
Head of Programme Development Jane Booth
Editor, Motoring and Leisure Sports Jon Bentley
Editor, Lifestyle and Entertainment Roger Casstles
Editor, Factual and Music Chris Marshall
Editor, Asian Unit Paresh Solanki

News

BBC Television Centre, Wood Lane, London W12 7RJ
tel 020-8743 8000

BBC News is the biggest news organisation in the world with over 2000 journalists, 50 bureaus worldwide and 13 networks and services across TV, radio and new media.

Its News Trainee Scheme is highly regarded in the industry. Advertised annually in the national press and promoted at appropriate career fairs, it is a bi-media broadcast journalists' training course, covering all aspects of radio and TV production and reporting. After formal training in each area, working attachments are arranged to gain practical experience. In addition, jobs are advertised in the national press and on the web site: http://www.bbc.co.uk/jobs.
Director, News Tony Hall
Deputy Chief Executive Richard Sambrook
Assistant Chief Executive and Head of Political Programmes Mark Damazer
Head of Current Affairs Helen Boaden
Head of Radio News Steve Mitchell
Head of New Media Richard Deverell
Head of TV News Roger Mosey
Head of Newsgathering Adrian Van Klaveren
Executive Editor TV News Malcolm Balen
Executive Editor TV Daily Current Affairs Jon Barton
Executive Editor Radio Daily Current Affairs Anne Koch
Controller, Television News Channels Tim Orchard
Managing News Editor, News 24 Margaret Budy

Sport

BBC Television Centre, Wood Lane, London W12 7RJ
tel 020-8743 8000

Multimedia coverage of a wide range of sports in the UK and worldwide.
Acting Director, Sport Richard Sambrook
Executive Editor, Magazines and Documentaries Philip Bernie
Executive Editor, Radio Gordon Turnbull
Executive Editor, Television Dave Gordon

World Service

Bush House, Strand, London WC2B 4PH
tel 020-7240 3456
web site http://www.bbc.co.uk/worldservice

BBC World Service provides radio services in English and 42 other languages, via short wave and in an increasing number of cities around the world, on MW and FM. The English service is also available 24 hours a day in real audio on the Internet. Classic contemporary drama, novels, short stories, soap operas and poetry are all a feature of its English service, plus a wide range of arts, documentaries, education, features, music, religious affairs, science, sports and youth programmes. In addition, BBC World Service provides on-the-spot coverage of world news, giving a global perspective of international events.
Director, BBC World Service Mark Byford
Deputy Director Caroline Thomson
Director, News and Programme Commissioning Bob Jobbins
Controller, World Service English Network Andrew Taussig

Worldwide

BBC Woodlands, 80 Wood Lane, London W12 0TT
tel 020-8433 2000
web site http://www.bbc.worldwide.com

BBC Worldwide Ltd is the commercial arm of the BBC. It makes money from broadcast-related businesses and returns cash to the BBC to invest in new programming. Publishing forms a significant part of its activities.

Chief Executive Rupert Gavin
Managing Director, UK Regions and Deputy CE Peter Teague
Director, New Media Jeremy Mayhew

Audio cassettes and CDs. Around 130 audio cassettes and CDs of BBC radio and TV programmes are released every year, mainly comedy, readings and dramatised serials. Pitch ideas to:
Editorial Director, Spoken Word Audio Mary Kalemkarian

Books and videos. Ideas for books or videos that would extend audience enjoyment of a BBC radio or TV programme should be pitched, according to subject matter, via a short synopsis to:
Arts and drama Emma Broughton
History, science and travel Sue Kerr
News and natural history Carl White
Music Jessica Gibson
Sport, motoring and comedy Ben Dunn/Joe Mahoney
Gardening, cookery, home interest and health Viv Bowler/Nicky Copeland
Teen/children's interest Mandy Cleeve

Magazines. Freelance contributions are regularly used by BBC Worldwide magazines, but the use of unsolicited material is rare as the editorial links closely to BBC programme content. Ideas for articles that clearly fit the remit of a magazine should be pitched via a short written summary to the Editor.
Radio Times Sue Robinson
BBC Good Food Orlando Murrin
BBC Gardeners' World Adam Pasco
BBC Good Homes Julie Savill
BBC History Magazine Greg Neale
BBC Homes & Antiques Judith Hall
BBC Top Gear Magazine Kevin Blick
BBC Match of the Day Tim Glynne-Jones
BBC Music Magazine Helen Wallace
BBC Wildlife Magazine Rosamund Kidman Cox (BBC Bristol address)

All ideas for BBC children's and teen magazines (*Top of the Pops, Live & Kicking, Girl Talk, FBX, BBC Learning is Fun, Robot Wars, BBC Smart, Noddy, BBC Toybox, Playdays, Teletubbies, Spot, Bob the Builder, Tell Me Why, Star Hill Ponies* and *Tweenies*) should be sent to:
Editorial Director, Family Group Nicky Smith

Nations and Regions

BBC Henry Wood House, Langham Place, London W1A 1AA
tel 020-7580 4468
web site http://www.bbc.co.uk/around the uk

BBC National & Regional Broadcasting is responsible for over 80% of all the BBC's domestic output – about 7000 hours of TV and over 250,000 of radio. BBC Northern Ireland, BBC Scotland and BBC Wales produce a growing number of programmes for the BBC's TV and radio networks, as well as providing comprehensive services for viewers and listeners in their own nations. The BBC's English Regions are responsible for 10 TV regional news and current affairs services across England, and for 40 BBC local radio stations with their emphasis on news and information for their local communities.
Director, National & Regional Broadcasting Pat Loughrey

BBC Northern Ireland

BBC Broadcasting House, Ormeau Avenue, Belfast BT2 8HQ
tel 028-9033 8000
web site http://www.bbc.co.uk/ni

BBC Northern Ireland produces a broad spectrum of radio and TV programmes, both for the network and for its home audience. Output includes news and current affairs, documentaries, education, entertainment, sport, music, Irish language and religious programmes. It also has a thriving drama department which reads unsolicited scripts across all genre, i.e. single, serials, series, feature films and the short film scheme *Northern Lights*, which is aimed at new talent from within Northern Ireland.

In addition to making network radio programmes, broadcasting on BBC Radio 1, 2, 3, 4, and 5 Live and BBC World Service, BBC Northern Ireland also makes programmes for its local radio listeners.

Controller, BBC Northern Ireland tba
Head of Broadcasting Anna Carragher
Head of News and Current Affairs Andrew Colman
Head of Factual and Learning tba
Head of Entertainment and Events tba
Head of Drama Robert Cooper
Editor Foyle Ana Leddy
Head of Marketing and Development Peter Johnston
Head of Resources Stephen Beckett

BBC Radio Ulster
BBC Broadcasting House, Ormeau Avenue, Belfast BT2 8HQ
tel 028-9033 8000

BBC Radio Foyle
8 Northland Road, Londonderry BT48 7JO
tel (028) 7126 2244

BBC Scotland

BBC Broadcasting House, Queen Margaret Drive, Glasgow G12 8DG
tel 0141-339 8844
web site http://www.bbc.co.uk/scotland

BBC Scotland is the BBC's most varied production centre outside London, providing BBC TV and radio networks and BBC World Service with pivotal drama, comedy, entertainment, children's, leisure, documentaries, religion, education, arts, music, special events news, current affairs and political coverage. Internet development is also a key element of production activity.

Its drama department, along with Scottish Screen, is responsible for the highly successful initiative, *Tartan Shorts*, which promotes film-making in the nation and provides a platform for emerging Scottish creative talent, including actors, writers, directors and producers.

In addition to making network output, more than 700 hours of TV programming per year is transmitted on BBC ONE Scotland and BBC TWO Scotland, and a further 500 hours on the new digital service BBC CHOICE Scotland. BBC Radio Scotland is the country's only national radio station, and is on air 18 hours a day, 7 days a week. Local programmes are also broadcast on Radio Scotland's FM frequency in the Northern Isles, and there are daily local bulletins for listeners in the Highlands, Grampian, Borders, and the southwest. BBC Radio Nan Gaidheal provides a Gaelic service on a separate FM frequency for around 40 hours a week.

Controller, BBC Scotland John McCormick
Head of Broadcast Ken MacQuarrie
Head of Production Colin Cameron
Head of News and Current Affairs Blair Jenkins
Head of Drama Barbara McKissack
Head of Resources Andy Davy

BBC Radio Scotland
BBC Broadcasting House, Queen Margaret Drive, Glasgow G12 8DG
tel 0141-338 8844

BBC Radio Nan Gaidheal
Rosebank, Church Street, Stornoway, Isle of Lewis PA87 2LS
tel (0851) 705000

BBC Wales

BBC Broadcasting House, Llandaff, Cardiff CF5 2YQ
tel 029-2032 2000
web site http://www.bbc.co.uk/wales

BBC Wales provides a wide range of services in Welsh and in English, on radio, TV and on-line. This includes 12 hours a week of programmes on BBC ONE Wales and BBC TWO Wales and a further 10 hours a week on the digital channel BBC CHOICE Wales. Regular output includes the flagship news programme *Wales Today*, the current affairs strand *Week In Week Out*, the arts series *The Slate*, and the rugby magazine *Scrum V*. A further 10 hours are shown on the Welsh-language channel S4C including the news programme *Newyddion*, the nightly drama serial *Pobol y Cwm* plus a range of programmes for schools. Its 2 radio stations, BBC Radio Wales, broadcasting in English, and BBC Radio Cymru, broadcasting in Welsh, each provide 18 hours a day of news, entertainment, music and sports output. Political coverage on all services has expanded as a result of the creation of the National Assembly for Wales. BBC Wales also makes popular drama, documentaries, education and music programmes for audiences throughout the UK, including the biennial *Cardiff Singer of the World* competition, accompanied by the BBC National Orchestra of

Wales. It also co-produces animated versions of literary classics including the Oscar-nominated *Canterbury Tales.*
Controller, BBC Wales Menna Richards
Head of Programmes (English) tba
Head of Programmes (Welsh) tba
Head of Production John Geraint
Head of News and Current Affairs Aled Eirug
Editor, Radio Wales tba
Editor, Radio Cymru tba
Commissioning Editor, BBC Choice Wales Nick Evans
Head of Drama Matthew Robinson
Head of Sport Arthur Emyr
Head of Factual tba
Head of Arts tba
Head of Music tba
Music Director, BBC National Orchestra of Wales David Murray

BBC Radio Cymru (Welsh language)
BBC Broadcasting House, Llandaff, Cardiff CF5 2YQ
tel 029-2032 2000

BBC Radio Wales (English language)
BBC Broadcasting House, Llandaff, Cardiff CF5 2YQ
tel 029-2032 2000

BBC regional television and local radio

The BBC's English Regions are responsible for 10 TV regional news and current affairs services across England, and for 40 BBC local radio stations with their emphasis on news and information for their local communities.

BBC English regions (TV and radio)

BBC Broadcasting Centre, Pebble Mill Road, Birmingham B5 7QQ
tel 0121-432 8888
Controller, English Regions Andy Griffee
Head of Editorial Development Roy Roberts
Heads of Regional and Local Programmes see below

BBC East

St Catherine's Close, All Saints Green, Norwich NR1 3ND
tel (01603) 619331
Head of Regional and Local Programmes David Holdsworth

BBC Radio Cambridgeshire
PO Box 96, Hills Road, Cambridge CB2 1LD
tel (01223) 259696

BBC Essex
198 New London Road, Chelmsford CM2 9AB
tel (01245) 616000

BBC Radio Norfolk
Norfolk Tower, Surrey Street, Norwich NR1 3PA
tel (01603) 617411

BBC Radio Northampton
Broadcasting House, Abington Street, Northampton NN1 2BE
tel (01604) 239100

BBC Radio Suffolk
Broadcasting House, St Matthew's Street, Ipswich IP1 3EP
tel (01473) 250000

BBC Three Counties Radio
PO Box 3CR, Luton, Beds. LU1 5XL
tel (01582) 637400

BBC East Midlands

London Road, Nottingham NG2 4UU
tel 0115-955 0500
Head of Regional and Local Programmes Craig Henderson

BBC Radio Derby
PO Box 269, Derby DE1 3HL
tel (01332) 361111

BBC Radio Leicester
Epic House, Charles Street, Leicester LE1 3SH
tel 0116-251 6688

BBC Radio Lincolnshire
Radio Buildings, PO Box 219, Newport, Lincoln LN1 3XY
tel (01522) 511411

BBC Radio Nottingham
York House, Mansfield Road, Nottingham NG1 3JB
tel 0115-955 0500

The BBC Asian Network
Epic House, Charles Street, Leicester LE1 3SH
tel 0116-251 6688

BBC South East

Elstree Centre, Clarendon Road, Borehamwood, Herts. WD6 1JF
tel 020-8953 6100
Head of Regional and Local Programmes Jane Mote

BBC London Live
35C Marylebone High Street, London W1A 4LG
tel 020-7224 2424

BBC Radio Kent
Sun Pier, Chatham, Kent ME4 4EZ
tel (01634) 830505

BBC Southern Counties Radio
Broadcasting Centre, Guildford GU2 5AP
tel (01483) 306306

BBC North

Broadcasting Centre, Woodhouse Lane, Leeds LS2 9PX
tel 0113-244 1188
Head of Regional and Local Programmes Colin Philpott

BBC Radio Humberside
9 Chapel Street, Hull HU1 3NU
tel (01482) 323232

BBC Radio Leeds
Broadcasting Centre, Woodhouse Lane, Leeds LS2 9PN
tel 0113-244 2131

BBC Radio Sheffield
Ashdell Grove, 60 Westbourne Road, Sheffield S10 2QU
tel 0114-268 6185

BBC Radio York
20 Bootham Row, York YO3 7BR
tel (01904) 641351

BBC North East and Cumbria

Broadcasting Centre, Barrack Road, Newcastle upon Tyne NE99 2NE
tel 0191-232 1313
Head of Regional and Local Programmes Olwyn Hocking

BBC Radio Cleveland
PO Box 95FM, Newport Road, Middlesbrough TS1 5DG
tel (01642) 225211

BBC Radio Cumbria
Annetwell Street, Carlisle CA3 8BB
tel (01228) 592444

BBC Radio Newcastle
Broadcasting Centre, Barrack Road, Newcastle upon Tyne NE99 1RN
tel 0101-232 4141

BBC North West

New Broadcasting House, Oxford Road, Manchester M60 1SJ
tel 0161-200 2020
Head of Regional and Local Programmes Martin Brooks

BBC GMR
PO Box 951, Oxford Road, Manchester M60 1SD
tel 0161-200 2000

BBC Radio Lancashire
26 Darwen Street, Blackburn, Lancs. BB2 EA
tel (01254) 262411

BBC Radio Merseyside
55 Paradise Street, Liverpool L1 3BP
tel 0151-708 5500

BBC South

Broadcasting House, Havelock Road, Southampton SO14 7PU
tel 023-80226201
Head of Regional and Local Programmes Eve Turner

BBC Radio Berkshire
PO Box 1044, Reading, Berks. RG4 8PH
tel 0118-946 4200

BBC Radio Oxford
269 Banbury Road, Oxford OX2 7DW
tel (01865) 311444

BBC Radio Solent
Broadcasting House, Havelock Road, Southampton SO14 7PU
tel 023-8063 1311

BBC South West

Broadcasting House, Seymour Road, Mannamead, Plymouth PL3 5BD
tel (01752) 229201
Head of Regional and Local Programmes Leo Devine

BBC Radio Cornwall
Phoenix Wharf, Truro, Cornwall TR1 1UA
tel (01872) 275421

BBC Radio Devon
PO Box 5, Broadcasting House, Seymour Road, Mannamead, Plymouth PL1 1XT
tel (01752) 260323

BBC Radio Guernsey
Commerce House, Les Banques, St Peter Port, Guernsey GY1 2HS
tel (01481) 728977

BBC Radio Jersey
18 Parade Road, St Helier, Jersey JE2 3PL
tel (01534) 870000

BBC West

Broadcasting House, Whiteladies Road, Bristol BS8 2LR
tel 0117-973 2211
Head of Regional and Local Programmes Rhodri Talfan Davies

BBC Radio Bristol
PO Box 194, Bristol BS99 7QT
tel 0117-974 1111

BBC Radio Gloucestershire
London Road, Gloucester GL1 1SW
tel (01452) 308585

BBC Radio Somerset Sound
(part of Radio Bristol)
14-15 Paul Street, Taunton, Somerset TA1 3PF
(01823) 252437

BBC Wiltshire Sound
Broadcasting House, Prospect Place, Swindon SN1 3RW
tel (01793) 513626

BBC West Midlands

Pebble Mill Road, Birmingham B5 7QQ
tel 0121-432 8888
Head of Regional and Local Programmes Roy Roberts

BBC Coventry & Warwickshire
Holt Court, 1 Greyfriars Road, Coventry CV1 2WR
tel (02476) 231231

BBC Hereford & Worcester
Hylton Road, Worcester WR2 5WW
tel (01905) 748485

BBC Radio Shropshire
2-4 Boscobel Drive, Shrewsbury SY1 3TT
tel (01743) 248484

BBC Radio Stoke
Cheapside, Hanley, Stoke on Trent ST1 1JJ
tel (01782) 208080

BBC Radio WM
PO Box 206, Broadcasting Centre, Pebble Mill Road, Birmingham B5 7SD
tel 0121-432 8484

BBC broadcasting rights and terms

Contributors are advised to check latest details of fees with the BBC.

Rights and terms – television

Specially written material

Fees for submitted material are paid on acceptance. For commissioned material, half the fee is paid on commissioning and half on acceptance as being suitable for television. All fees are subject to negotiation above the minima.

• Rates for one performance of a 60-minute original television play are a minimum of £4728 for a play written by a beginner and a 'going rate' of £7450 for an established writer, or *pro rata* for shorter or longer timings.

• Fees for a 50-minute episode in a series during the same period are a minimum of £3900 for a beginner and a 'going rate' of £5634 for an established writer.

• Fees for a 50-minute dramatisation are a minimum of £2721 for a beginner and a 'going rate' of £4010 for an established writer.

• Fees for a 50-minute adaptation of an existing stage play or other dramatic work are a minimum of £1640 for a beginner and a 'going rate' of £2403 for an established writer.

Specially written light entertainment sketch material

• The rates for sketch material range from £32.53 per minute for beginners with a 'going rate' of £65.66 for established writers.

• The fee for a quickie or news item is half the amount of the writer's per minute rate.

• Fees for submitted material are payable on acceptance and for commissioned material half on signature and half on acceptance.

Published material

• Prose works: £19.36 per minute.
• Poems: £22.59 per half minute.

Stage plays and source material for television

• Fees for stage plays and source novels are negotiable.

Rights and terms – radio

Specially written material

Fees are assessed on the basis of the type of material, its length, the author's status and experience in writing for radio. Fees for submitted material are paid on acceptance. For commissioned material, half the fee is paid on commissioning and half on acceptance as being suitable for broadcasting.

• Rates for specially written radio dramas in English (other than educational programmes) are £42.57 a minute for beginners and a 'going rate' of £64.80 a minute for established writers. This rate covers two broadcasts.

Specially written short stories

• Fees range from £131 for 15 minutes.

Published material

Domestic radio

• Dramatic works: £12.85 per minute.
• Prose works: £12.85 per minute.
• Prose works required for dramatisation: £10.02 per minute.
• Poems: £12.85 per half minute.

World Service Radio (English)

• Dramatic works: £6.43 per minute for

broadcasts within a seven-day period.
- Prose works: £6.43 per minute for broadcasts within a seven-day period.
- Prose works required for dramatisation: £5.02 per minute for broadcasts within a seven-day period.
- Poems: £6.43 per half minute for broadcasts within a seven-day period.
- Foreign Language Services are approximately one-fifth of the rate for English Language Services.

Television and radio

Repeats in BBC programmes

- Further proportionate fees are payable for repeats.

Use abroad of recordings of BBC programmes

If the BBC sends abroad recordings of its programmes for use by overseas broadcasting organisations on their own networks or stations, further payments accrue to the author, usually in the form of additional percentages of the basic fee paid for the initial performance or a royalty based on the percentage of the distributors' receipts. This can apply to both sound and television programmes.

Value Added Tax

There is a self-billing system for VAT which covers radio, external services and television for programmes made in London.

Talks for television

Contributors to talks will be offered the standard television talks contract which provides the BBC certain rights to broadcast the material in a complete, abridged and/or translated manner, and which provides for the payment of further fees for additional usage of the material whether by television, domestic radio or external broadcasting. The contract also covers the assignment of material and limited publication rights. Alternatively, a contract taking in all standard rights may be negotiated. Fees are arranged by the contract authorities in London and the Regions.

Talks for radio

Contributors to talks for domestic Radio and World Service broadcasting may be offered either:
- the standard talks contract which takes rights and provides for residual payments, as does the television standard contract; or
- an STC (Short Talks Contract) which takes all rights except print publication rights where the airtime of the contribution does not exceed five minutes and which has set fees or disturbance money payable; or
- an NFC (No Fee Contract) where no payment is made which provides an acknowledgement that a contribution may be used by the BBC.

Independent national television

BSkyB
Grant Way, Isleworth, Middlesex TW7 5QD
tel 020-7705 3000 *fax* 020-7705 3030/3113
web site http://www.sky.com

Channel 5 Broadcasting Ltd
22 Long Acre, London WC2E 9LY
tel 020-7497 5225 *fax* 020-7497 5222
The fifth and last national 'free to air' terrestrial 24-hour TV channel. Commissions a wide range of programmes to suit all tastes.

Channel 4 Television Corporation
124 Horseferry Road, London SW1P 2TX
tel 020-7396 4444 *fax* 020-7306 8347
web site http://www.channel4.com
Commissions and purchases programmes (it does not make them) for broadcast during the whole week throughout the United Kingdom (except Wales). Also broadcasts subscription film channel FilmFour.

GMTV
London Television Centre, Upper Ground, London SE1 9TT
tel 020-7827 7000 *fax* 020-7827 7001
ITV's national breakfast TV service, 6.00-9.25am, 7 days a week.

Independent Television Commission (ITC)
33 Foley Street, London W1P 7LB
tel 020-7255 3000 *fax* 020-7306 7800
e-mail publicaffairs@itc.org.uk
web site http://www.itc.co.uk
Licenses and regulates all commercially funded TV services in the UK, including cable and satellite services as well as terrestrial services.

ITN
200 Gray's Inn Road, London WC1X 8XZ
tel 020-7833 3000
web site http://www.itn.co.uk
Provides the national and international news programmes for ITV, Channel 4 and Channel 5.

ITV Network Ltd
200 Gray's Inn Road, London WC1X 8HF
tel 020-7843 8000 *fax* 020-7843 8158
web site http://www.itv.co.uk

NTL
NTL House, Bartley Wood Business Park, Bartley Way, Hook, Hants RG27 9UP
tel (01256) 752000 *fax* (01256) 752100
web site http://www.ntl.co.uk

ONdigital
346 Queenstown Road, London SW8 4DG
tel 020-7819 8000 *fax* 020-7819 8100
web site http://www.ondigital.co.uk

S4C
Parc Ty Glas, Llanishen, Cardiff CF4 5DU
tel 029-20747444 *fax* 029-20754444
e-mail s4c@s4c.co.uk
web site http://www.s4c.co.uk
The Welsh Fourth Channel. S4C's analogue service broadcasts 32 hours per week in Welsh: 22 hours are commissioned from independent producers and 10 hours are produced by the BBC. Most of Channel 4's output is rescheduled to complete this service. S4C's digital service broadcasts 12 hours per day in Welsh.

Teletext Ltd
101 Farm Lane, London SW6 1QJ
tel 020-7386 5000 *fax* 020-7386 5002
e-mail enquiries@teletext.co.uk
web site http://www.teletext.co.uk

Independent regional television

It is advisable to check before submitting any ideas/material – in all cases, scripts are preferred to synopses. Programmes should be planned with natural breaks for the insertion of advertisements. These companies also provide some programmes for Channel 4.

Anglia Television Ltd
Anglia House, Norwich NR1 3JG
tel (01603) 615151 *fax* (01603) 631032
e-mail angliatv@angliatv.co.uk
web site http://www.angliatv.com
48 Leicester Square, London WC2H 7FB
tel 020-7389 8555 *fax* 020-7930 8499
Provides programmes for the East of England, daytime discussion programmes, drama, documentaries and Survival natural history programmes for the ITV Network. Drama submissions only through an accredited agency or similar source.

Border Television plc
The Television Centre, Carlisle CA1 3NT
tel (01228) 25101
Provides programmes for, Cumbria, the Borders and the Isle of Man, during the whole week. Ideas for programmes, but not drama programmes, are considered from outside sources. Suggestions should be sent to Neil Robinson, Controller of Programmes.

Carlton Broadcasting
101 St Martin's Lane, London WC2N 4AZ
tel 020-7240 4000 *fax* 020-7240 4171
Provides ITV programmes for London and the South East from Monday to Friday.

Carlton Broadcasting, Central Region
Central Court, Gas Street, Birmingham B1 2JT
tel 0121-643 9898 *fax* 0121-643 4897
Carlton Studios, Lenton Lane, Nottingham NG7 2NA
tel 0115-986 3322 *fax* 0115-964 5552
Unit 9, Windrush Court, Abingdon Business Park, Abingdon, Oxon OX1 1SA
tel (01235) 554123 *fax* (01235) 524024
Provides ITV programmes for the East, West and South Midlands 7 days a week.

Carlton Broadcasting, West Country Region
Langage Science Park, Plymouth PL7 5BQ
tel (01752) 333333 *fax* (01752) 333444
e-mail westcountryregion@carltontv.co.uk
Provides programmes for South West England throughout the week. In-house production mainly news, regional current affairs and topical features; other regional features commissioned from independent producers. Conduit to the Network for independent production packages.

Channel Television
The Television Centre, St Helier, Jersey JE1 3ZD
tel (01534) 816816 *fax* (01534) 816817
e-mail broadcast@channeltv.co.uk
Provides programmes for the Channel Islands during the whole week relating mainly to Channel Islands news, events and current affairs.

Grampian Television plc
Queens Cross, Aberdeen AB15 4XJ
tel (01224) 846846 *fax* (01224) 846800
e-mail gtv@grampiantv.co.uk
Harbour Chambers, Dock Street, Dundee DD1 3HW
tel (01382) 591000 *fax* (01382) 591010
23-25 Huntly Street, Inverness IV3 5PR
tel (01463) 242624
Seaforth House, 54 Seaforth Road, Stornoway HS1 2SD
tel (01851) 704433 *fax* (01851) 706406
Provides programmes for North Scotland during the whole week.

Granada Television Ltd
Granada Television Centre, Manchester M60 9EA
tel 0161-832 7211 and
Upper Ground, London SE1 9LT
tel 020-7620 1620
The ITV franchise holder for the North

West of England. Produces programmes across a broad range for both its region and the ITV Network. Writers are advised to make their approach through agents who would have some knowledge of Granada's current requirements.

HTV Ltd

HTV Wales, The Television Centre, Culverhouse Cross, Cardiff CF5 6XJ
tel 029-2059 0590 and
HTV West, The Television Centre, Bristol BS4 3HG
tel 01179-722 722
e-mail htv@htv.co.uk
web site http://www.htv.co.uk

Provides programmes for Wales and West of England during the whole week. Produces programmes for home and international sales.

LWT

The London Television Centre, London SE1 9LT
tel 020-7620 1620

Provides programmes for Greater London and much of the Home Counties area from Friday 5.15pm to Monday 6.00am (excluding 6.00-9.25am on Sat/Sun).

Meridian Broadcasting

Television Centre, Southampton, Hants SO14 0PZ
tel 023-8022 2555 *fax* 023-8033 5050
web site http://www.meridiantv.com

The ITV franchise holder for the South and South East. Meridian produces quality drama, factual, sport and children's programming for the ITV network.

Scottish Television – Network Production

3 Waterhouse Square, 138-142 Holborn, London EC1N 2YN
tel 020-7882 1000 *fax* 020-7882 1005
web site http://www.smg.plc.uk

Wholly owned subsidiary of SMG plc, making drama and other programmes for the ITV network. The SMG plc Television Division also includes Ginger Television.

Material (STV): ideas and formats for long-form series with or without a Scottish flavour. Approach Controller of Drama, Philip Hinchcliffe.

Material (Ginger): produces compelling programmes for groups of all ages. Programming includes *TFI Friday* and *The Priory*.

Tyne Tees Television Ltd

The Television Centre, City Road, Newcastle upon Tyne NE1 2AL
tel 0191-261 0181 *fax* 0191-261 2302
e-mail tyne.tees@granadamedia.com

Serving the North of England 7 days a week, 24 hours a day.

UTV

Havelock House, Ormeau Road, Belfast, Northern Ireland BT7 1EB
tel 028-9032 8122 *fax* 028-9024 6695
e-mail info@utvlive.com
web site http://www.utvlive.com

Provides programmes for Northern Ireland during the whole week.

Yorkshire Television Ltd

The Television Centre, Leeds LS3 1JS
tel 0113-243 8283 *fax* 0113-244 5107

Yorkshire Television is a Network Company which produces many programmes for the ITV Network and the Yorkshire area 7 days a week. Material preferred submitted through agents. Wholly owned subsidiary of Granada Media Group.

Presenting scripts for television and film

There is an old saying that the plot of the best movie can be written on a postcard. However, whether your aim is to write a big feature film or a television play to be made on film (as most are nowadays), you must be prepared to write the full screenplay. ***Jean McConnell*** *describes how to lay out your manuscript and how to submit it for consideration.*

What is a screenplay?

A screenplay should tell a story in terms of visual action and dialogue spoken by the characters. A script for a full-length feature film running about one and a half hours will be about 100-130 pages long. Whether it is a feature film, a short film for children, say, or a documentary, it is better to present a version which is too short rather than too long.

Elaborate camera directions are not necessary as a shooting script will be made at a later stage. Your job is to write the master scenes, clearly broken down into each incident and location.

Layout

Individual companies may vary slightly in their house style but the general layout of a screenplay, either for a feature film or television film, is illustrated on page 313. The following points should be noted.

- Each scene should be numbered on the left and given a title which indicates whether the scene is an interior or an exterior, where it takes place, and the lighting conditions, i.e. day or night. The situation of each scene should be standardised; don't call your 'sitting room' a 'lounge' the next time you come to it, or people will think you mean a different place.
- Note that the dialogue is spaced out, with the qualifying directions such as '(frowning)' on a separate line, slightly inset from the dialogue. Double space each speech from the previous one.
- Always put the names of the characters in CAPITALS, except when they occur in the actual dialogue. Double space the stage directions from the dialogue, but single space the lines of the stage directions themselves.
- Use A4 size paper. Leave at least a 4cm margin on the left and a reasonably wide right-hand margin. It is false economy to cram the page. Use one side of the sheet only.
- Only give the camera directions when you feel it to be essential. For instance, if you want to show something from a particular character's point of view, or if you think you need it to make a point, i.e. 'HARRY approaches the cliff edge and looks down. LONG SHOT – HARRY'S POINT OF VIEW. ALICE fully clad is walking into the sea. CUT TO: CLOSE UP OF HARRY'S HORRIFIED FACE.' Note the camera directions are put in capital letters on a separate line, as in the specimen page.
- Character sketches should appear in the body of the screenplay, e.g. PETE enters. He is a man you wouldn't want to meet in a dark alley.

Preparation of manuscript

The title page should give the name and nature of your piece. Also include your (or your agent's) address. The second page should give a list of the main characters.

Add a front and back cover and bind your screenplay, securing the pages firmly. Make sure you have saved it on disk or retain a master copy. Never part with the only copy you possess. If you do, it will surely get lost.

Submission

Try to get an agent. A good agent will give you a fair opinion of your work and, if your work is worthwhile, he or she will know the particular film company which will want to buy it. Remember that if film companies state that they will only consider material sent through an agent, they definitely mean it.

If you are sending your manuscript to a company direct, it is advisable to first check as far as possible in case it is already working on a similar idea.

Attach a stamped, addressed envelope to your manuscript whether sending it through an agent or direct. Most companies have a story department, to which you should address your material. As story editors are very busy people, you can make their life easier by complying with the submission notes listed in the box.

Accept that this is really a tough market, namely because:

- films cost so much to make today that the decision to go ahead is only taken after a great many important factors have been satisfied and an even greater number of important people are happy about it;
- writing a screenplay calls for knowledge and appreciation of the technicalities of film-making, as well as the ability to combine dialogue, action and pictures, throughout in the language of a visual medium.

Submission notes

If you have based your screenplay on someone else's published work you should make the fact clear in a covering letter, stating that:

- the material is no longer in copyright, or
- you yourself own the copyright, or at least an option on it, or
- you have not obtained the copyright but have reason to believe that there would be no difficulty in doing so.

Apart from a note of any relevant credits you may already possess, do not regale the editor with your personal details, unless they bear a direct relation to the material submitted. For instance, if your story concerns a brain surgeon, then it would be relevant for the editor to know that you actually are one. Otherwise, trust your work to stand on its own merit.

There is no need to mention if your work has been turned down by other companies, however regretfully. The comments of others will not influence a story editor one way or the other.

Do not suggest actors or actresses you would like to play your characters. This decision is entirely out of your hands.

Don't pester the company if you don't get a reply, or even an acknowledgement, for some weeks. Most companies will formally acknowledge receipt and then leave you in limbo for at least six weeks. However, after about three months or so, a brief letter politely asking what has happened is in order. A telephone call is unlikely to be helpful. It is possible the company may have liked your work enough to have sent it to America, or to be getting further readers' opinions on it. This all takes time. If they don't like it, you will certainly get your manuscript back in due course.

The treatment

If a producer likes the idea of your screenplay, he or she may ask to see a treatment. A treatment can range from a basic outline through to a synopsis of the story with a breakdown of the main characters and some of the key scenes written in detail. Its aim is to demonstrate the style and general flavour of the piece and may be wanted before the whole script is read and/or in order to interest his or her colleagues. It may be no more than half a dozen pages but it is likely to be your major selling document. So do your best to thrill the producer to the core in a couple of minutes flat.

13. INT. BARN DAY

ALAN regards ELIZABETH anxiously. ELIZABETH is staring at the large wine vat. She backs away from it and crosses to the door, where she turns.

ELIZABETH
I still think the police ought to know.

She goes out. ALAN listens as her footsteps retreat. Then he crosses quickly to the vat, climbs up and heaves at the lid.

CUT TO:

14. EXT. FARMYARD DAY

DONALD intercepts ELIZABETH as she crosses the yard.

DONALD
What does he say?

ELIZABETH
Nothing.

DONALD
(frowning)
Right. Now it's my turn.

He starts for the barn. ELIZABETH watches him go.

CUT TO:

15. INT. BARN DAY

DONALD'S shadow falls across the threshold. He hesitates, his eyes getting used to the gloom.

DONALD
Alan?

ALAN lets the lid of the vat fall. He jumps down. He stands quite still as DONALD crosses to him. The two men eye each other silently. ALAN turns away.

DONALD
(with sudden realisation)
You knew it was there ... didn't you?

CUT TO:

CLOSE-UP OF ALAN'S FACE: IT IS HAGGARD

ALAN
I hoped to God it wouldn't be.

Television and film producers

***Jean McConnell** advises on submitting a screenplay for consideration.*

The recommended approach for placing material is through a recognised literary agent. Most film companies have a story department to which material can be sent for consideration by its editors. If you choose to submit material direct, first check with the company to make sure it is worth your while.

It is a fact that many of the feature films these days are based on already best-selling books. However, there are some companies, particularly those with a television outlet, which will sometimes accept unsolicited material if it seems to be exceptionally original.

When a writer submits material direct to a company, some of the larger ones – usually those based in the United States – may request that a Release Form be signed before they are prepared to read it. This document is ostensibly designed to absolve the company from any charge of plagiarism if they should be working on a similar idea; and also to limit their liability in the event of any legal action. Writers must make up their own minds whether they wish to sign this but, in principle, it is not highly recommended.

It should be noted that there are a number of independent companies making films specifically for television presentation. These are included in the list below of companies currently in active production.

Jean McConnell is a founder member of the Writers' Guild of Great Britain. She has written screenplays, radio and stage plays, and books. She is a member of the Crime Writers' Association and the Society of Women Writers and Journalists.

Aardman Animations

Gas Ferry Road, Bristol BS1 6UN
tel 0117-984 8485 *fax* 0117-984 8486
web site http://www.aardman.com
Producer, Broadcast/Features Michael Rose

Specialists in model animation. No unsolicited treatments. Founded 1972.

Absolutely Productions

Alhamra House, 27-31 Charing Cross Road, London WC2H 0AU
tel 020-7930 3113 *fax* 020-7930 4114
e-mail info@absolutely-uk.com
web site http://www.absolutely-uk.com
Contact Miles Bullough

Drama and comedy screenplays for cinema and TV, and TV entertainment programmes. Founded 1989.

British Lion

Pinewood Studios, Iver, Bucks. SL0 0NH
tel (01753) 651279 *fax* (01753) 656391
Contact Peter Snell

Screenplays and treatments for cinema; TV drama and sitcoms. No unsolicited material. Founded 1927.

Brook Lapping Productions Ltd

6 Anglers Lane, London NW5 3DG
tel 020-7428 3100 *fax* 020-7284 0626
Development Executives Anne Lapping, Brian Lapping, Phillip Whitehead, Norma Percy

TV documentaries and current affairs.

Carlton Television Productions

35-38 Portman Square, London W1H 0NU
tel 020-7486 6688 *fax* 020-7486 1132
Director of Programmes Steve Hewlett

Makes programmes for Carlton Central Broadcasting, Carlton Broadcasting and Carlton Westcountry Television to supply ITV and other broadcasters.

Catalyst Film and Television International Ltd

Brook Green Studios, 186 Shepherds Bush Road, London W6 7LL
tel 020-7603 7030 *fax* 020-7603 9519
Contact Head of Drama Development

Screenplays/novels for adaptation for TV. Only consider material submitted through an agent or publisher. Founded 1991.

Celador Productions Ltd

39 Long Acre, London WC2E 9JT
tel 020-7240 8101 *fax* 020-7836 1117

All material should be submitted through an agent.

Chatsworth Television Ltd

97-99 Dean Street, London W1V 5RA
tel 020-7734 4302 *fax* 020-7437 3301
e-mail television@chatsworth-tv.co.uk
Managing Director Malcolm Heyworth

Entertainment, factual and drama. Sister companies in TV distribution and licensing. Founded 1980.

Children's Film and Television Foundation Ltd

Elstree Film Studios, Borehamwood, Herts. WD6 1JG
tel 020-8953 0844 *fax* 020-8207 0860
e-mail annahome@cftf.onyxnet.co.uk

Involved in the development and co-production of films for children and the family, both for the theatric market and for TV.

Childsplay Productions Ltd

8 Lonsdale Road, London NW6 6RD
tel 020-7328 1429 *fax* 020-7328 1416
Contact Kim Burke

Children's (not preschool) and family TV programming; chiefly drama. Founded 1984.

The Comic Strip Ltd

1st Floor, 143 Wardour Street, London W1V 3TB
tel 020-7437 8855 *fax* 020-7437 8866
Contact Rebecca Jeffrey, Peter Richardson

Screenplays for cinema and TV; half-hour comedy and drama series. Founded 1980.

The Walt Disney Company Ltd

3 Queen Caroline Street, London W6 9PE
tel 020-8222 1000 *fax* 020-8222 2795

Screenplays not accepted by London office. Must be submitted by an agent to The Walt Disney Studios in Burbank, California.

Fairwater Films Ltd

68 Vista Rise, Llandaff, Cardiff CF5 2SD
tel/fax 029-2057 8488
e-mail tbarnes@netcomuk.co.uk
Managing Director Tony Barnes

Animation for cinema and TV; live action entertainment. All material should be submitted through an agent. Founded 1982.

Feelgood Fiction Ltd

49 Goldhawk Road, London W12 8QP
tel 020-8746 2535 *fax* 020-8740 6177
e-mail feelgood@feelgoodfiction.co.uk
Managing Director Philip Clarke, *Drama Producer* Laurence Bowen

Film and TV drama.

The First Film Company Ltd

38 Great Windmill Street, London W1V 7PA
tel 020-7439 1640 *fax* 020-7437 2062
Producers Roger Randall-Cutler, Rob Cheek

Screenplays for cinema. All material should be submitted through an agent. Founded 1984.

Focus Films Ltd

The Rotunda Studios, rear of 116-118 Finchley Road, London NW3 5HT
tel 020-7435 9004 *fax* 020-7431 3562
e-mail focus@pupix.demon.co.uk
Contact Head of Development

Screenplays for cinema. Will only consider material submitted through an agent. Founded 1982.

Mark Forstater Productions Ltd

27 Lonsdale Road, London NW6 6RA
tel 020-7624 1123 *fax* 020-7624 1124
Contact Rosie Homan

Film and TV production. No unsolicited scripts, please.

Front Page Films

507 Riverbank House, 1 Putney Bridge Approach, London SW6 3JD
Contact Script Editor

Screenplays for cinema. Founded 1985.

Gaia Communictions

Sanctuary House, 35 Harding Avenue, Eastbourne, East Sussex BN22 8PL
tel (01323) 727183 *tel/fax* (01323) 734809
e-mail production@gaiacommunications.co.uk
web site http://www.gaiacommunications.co.uk
Director Robert Armstrong, *Script Editor* Loni von Gruner

Specialises in Southeast regional documentary programmes, particularly historical and tourist. Send synopsis in first instance with sae for return of material. Founded 1987.

Noel Gay Television

1 Albion Court, Galena Road, London W6 0QT
tel 020-8600 5200 *fax* 020-8600 5222
e-mail ngtv@noelgay.co.uk
web site http://www.noelgay.co.uk

Contact Anne Mensah
Treatments for TV; entertainment, comedy and drama. Founded 1987.

Granada Film

The London TV Centre, Upper Ground, London SE1 9LT
tel 020-7737 8681 *fax* 020-7737 8682
Head of Film Pippa Cross
Screenplays for cinema: major commercial feature films and smaller UK-based films. No unsolicited material. Founded 1989.

Hartswood Films

Twickenham Studios, The Barons, St Margaret's, Twickenham, Middlesex TW1 2AW
tel 020-8607 8736 *fax* 020-8607 8744
Producers Beryl Vertue, Sue Vertue, Elaine Cameron
Screenplays for cinema and TV; comedy and drama. No unsolicited material. Founded 1981.

Hat Trick Productions Ltd

10 Livonia Street, London W1V 3PH
tel 020-7434 2451 *fax* 020-7287 9791
Contact Denise O'Donoghue
Situation and drama comedy series and light entertainment shows. Founded 1986.

The Jim Henson Company

30 Oval Road, London NW1 7DE
tel 020-7428 4000 *fax* 020-7428 4001
Contact Angus Fletcher (Senior VP, International Television), Sophie Finston (International Development Manager)
Screenplays for cinema and TV; fantasy, family and children's programmes – usually involving puppetry or animatronics. All material should be submitted through an agent. Founded 1979.

Mike Hopwood Productions Ltd

Winton House, Stoke Road, Stoke-on-Trent ST4 2RW
tel (01782) 848800 *fax* (01782) 749447
Contact Development Executive
Screenplays for cinema; drama and factual TV programmes. Founded 1991.

Ignition Films Ltd

1 Wickham Court, Bristol BS16 1DQ
tel 0117-958 3087 *fax* 0117-965 7674
Contact Terry Flaxton
Screenplays for cinema and TV; arts/drama and documentaries, plays. Material only accepted through agents. Founded 1983.

Illuminations

19-20 Rheidol Mews, Rheidol Terrace, London N1 8NU
tel 020-7288 8400 *fax* 020-7359 1151
e-mail linda@illumin.co.uk
web site http://www.illumin.co.uk
Contact Linda Zuck
Screenplays for TV; cultural documentaries, arts and entertainment for broadcast TV. All material should be submitted through an agent. Founded 1982.

Kensington Films and Television Ltd

60 Charlotte Street, London W1P 2AX
tel 020-7927 8458 *fax* 020-7927 8798
Screenplays for cinema and TV drama. No unsolicited material. Founded 1993.

Brian Lapping Associates – merged with Brook Associates Ltd to form Brook Lapping Productions Ltd

Little Bird Company Ltd

9 Grafton Mews, London W1P 5LG
tel 020-7380 3980 *fax* 020-7380 3981
e-mail firstname@littlebird.co.uk
Contact M. Pope
Screenplays for cinema and TV. Founded 1982.

Little Dancer Ltd

Avonway, 3 Naseby Road, London SE19 3JJ
tel 020-8653 9343
e-mail Littledancer@compuserve.com
Producer Robert Smith
Screenplays for cinema and TV; drama. Founded 1992.

London Film Productions Ltd

35 Davies Street, London W1Y 1FN
tel 020-7499 7800 *fax* 020-7499 7994
Chairman J. Eliasch
No unsolicited material considered.

Malone Gill Productions Ltd

27 Campden Hill Road, London W8 7DX
tel 020-7937 0557 *fax* 020-7376 1727
e-mail ikonic@compuserve.com
Contact Georgina Denison
TV programmes. Founded 1978.

Maya Vision International Ltd

43 New Oxford Street, London WC1A 1BH
tel 020-7836 1113 *fax* 020-7836 5169
e-mail maya@mayavisn.demon.co.uk
Producer/Director Rebecca Dobbs
Features, TV dramas and documentaries. No unsolicited scripts. Founded 1982/3.

Monogram Productions Ltd

27-29 Berwick Street, London W1V 3RF
tel 020-7734 9873 *fax* 020-7734 9874
Managing Director Eileen Quinn

Screenplays for cinema and TV; drama series and serials only. All material should be submitted through an agent. Founded 1997.

MW Entertainments

48 Dean Street, London W1V 5HL
tel 020-7734 7707 *fax* 020-7734 7727
e-mail mw@michaelwhite.co.uk

Screenplays for cinema and TV. Treatments and synopses only. Founded 1963.

Pagoda Film & Television Corporation

Twentieth Century House, 31-32 Soho Square, London W1V 6AP
tel 020-7534 3500 *fax* 020-7534 3501
e-mail pag@pagodafilm.co.uk
Contact Head of Development

Screenplays for cinema and TV. Continues to work with established talent but is changing its focus to nurture new writers. Founded 1997.

Penumbra Productions Ltd

80 Brondesbury Road, London NW6 6RX
tel 020-7328 4550 *fax* 020-7328 3844
e-mail 101621.3135@compuserve.com
Contact H.O. Nazareth

Drama for feature films and TV; documentaries for TV; non-broadcast videos to commissions. Founded 1981.

Picture Palace Films Ltd

13 Egbert Street, London NW1 8LJ
tel 020-7586 8763 *fax* 020-7586 9048
e-mail picpalace@compuserve.com
web site http://www.picturepalace.com
Contact Malcolm Craddock

Screenplays for cinema and TV; low budget films; TV drama series. Material only considered if submitted through an agent. Founded 1971.

Planet 24 Ltd

195 Marsh Wall, London E14 9SG
tel 020-7345 2424 *fax* 020-7345 9400
Managing Director Mary Durkan

Light entertainment, factual entertainment, music, features and computer animation. Bought by Carlton Communications.

Portman Productions Ltd

167 Wardour Street, London W1V 3TA
tel 020-7468 3400 *fax* 020-7468 3499
Chief Executive Officer Timothy Buxton

TV drama and feature films. Founded 1944.

Portobello Pictures Ltd

14-15 D'Arblay Street, London W1V 3FP
tel 020-7379 5566 *fax* 020-7379 5599
Contact Ed Whitmore, Eric Abraham

Screenplays for cinema. Founded 1987.

Praxis Films Ltd

PO Box 290, Market Rasen, Lincs. LN3 6BB
tel (01472) 399976 *fax* (01472) 399976
e-mail info@praxisfilms.com
web site http://www.praxisfilms.com
Contact Lori Wheeler, Head of Development

Documentaries, news, current affairs, all factual genres for TV. Drama and movies, web sites, new media in development. Founded 1985.

Real Creatives Worldwide

14 Dean Street, London W1V 5AH
tel 020-7437 4188 *fax* 020-7437 4221
e-mail realcreate@aol.com
web site http://www.realcreativesworldwide.com
Directors F.L. Rasala, M. Rasala, M. Maco

Writers, producers and directors of motion pictures and TV programmes. Also packages movie ideas and scripts for submission to Hollywood studios and TV companies worldwide. Founded 1984.

Red Rooster Television Ltd

14-15 D'Arblay Street, London W1V 3FP
tel 020-7439 6969 *fax* 020-7439 6767
Managing Director Mervyn Watson, *General Manager* Sam King

TV drama series and serials. All material should be submitted through an agent. Founded 1982.

September Films Ltd

Silver House, 35 Beak Street, London W1R 3LD
tel 020-7494 1884 *fax* 020-7439 1194
Contact Kate Thompson, Head of Development

Expanding in both drama and films for both theatrical and TV. Founded 1989.

SH Production

Robert Symes, Green Dene Cottage, Honeysuckle Bottom, East Horsley, Surrey KT24 5TD
tel/fax (01483) 281792

Broadcast and non-broadcast commercial material, English and German voiceovers for films, video production. Founded 1988.

Specific Films

25 Rathbone Street, London W1P 1AG
tel 020-7580 7476 *fax* 020-7494 2676
e-mail specificfilms@compuserve.com
Contact Michael Hamlyn

Feature-length screenplays.

Spice Factory UK Ltd

81 The Promenade, Peacehaven,
Brighton BN10 8LS
tel (01273) 585275, 587495 *fax* (01273) 585304
e-mail sfactory@fastnet.co.uk
Contact Jason Piette, Michael Cowan

Feature films, TV drama, series and light entertainment. Looking for young talented writers and directors. Founded 1995.

Talisman Films Ltd

5 Addison Place, London W11 4RJ
tel 020-7603 7474 *fax* 020-7602 7422
e-mail email@talismanfilms.com
Contact Anna Kirkwood

Screenplays for cinema and TV. Material only considered if submitted through an agent. Founded 1991.

TalkBack Productions

36 Percy Street, London W1P 0LN
tel 020-7323 9777 *fax* 020-7637 5105

TV situation comedies and comedy dramas. Send unsolicited material to PA to Managing Director; material through an agent to Peter Fincham. Founded 1981.

Tiger Aspect Productions Ltd

5 Soho Square, London W1V 5DE
tel 020-7434 0672 *fax* 020-7287 1448
Contact Katie Waters (drama), Claire Davies (comedy)

TV drama, comedy and sitcoms. All material should be submitted through an agent. Founded 1993.

Twentieth Century Fox Productions Ltd

Twentieth Century House, 31-32 Soho Square, London W1V 6AP
tel 020-7437 7766 *fax* 020-7434 2170

Will not consider unsolicited material.

Twenty Twenty Television

20 Kentish Town Road, London NW1 9NX
tel 020-7284 2020 *fax* 020-7284 1810
e-mail twentytwenty@dial.pipex.com
Executive Producers Claudia Milne, Paul Woolwich

Current affairs, documentaries, travel films, science and educational programmes, drama. Founded 1982.

United Productions

48 Leicester Square, London WC2H 7FB
tel 020-7389 8555 *fax* 020-7930 8499
Chief Executive John Willis

Producers of TV and film. Founded 1996.

Warner Bros. Productions Ltd

Warner House, 98 Theobald's Road,
London WC1X 8WB
tel 020-7984 5000

Screenplays for cinema. Will only consider material submitted through an agent.

Warner Sisters Film & TV Ltd

The Cottage, Pall Mall Deposit, 124 Barlby Road, London W10 6BL
tel 020-8960 3550 *fax* 020-8960 3880

Screenplays for cinema and TV; TV programmes. All material should be submitted through an agent. Founded 1984.

Working Title Films

Films 76 Oxford Street, London W1N 9FD
tel 020-7307 3000 *fax* 020-7307 3001/2/3
e-mail dan.shepherd@unistudios.com
Head of Development Debra Hayward (films), *Development Executive* Chris Clark (films)

Screenplays for films.

TV 77 Shaftesbury Avenue, London W1V 8HQ
tel 020-7494 4001 *fax* 020-7255 8600
Head of Television Simon Wright

Screenplays for TV drama and comedy.

WT2 76 Oxford Street, London W1N 9FD
Head of Development Natascha Wharton, *Development Executive* Rachel Prior

Low budget films. Founded 1984.

World Productions Ltd

Norman House, 105-109 Strand,
London WC2R 0AA
tel 020-7240 1444 *fax* 020-7240 3740
e-mail world-productions.com
web site http://www.world-productions.com
Drama Manager Liza Mellody

Screenplays for TV; TV drama series and serials.

Zenith Entertainment plc

43-45 Dorset Street, London W1H 4AB
tel 020-7224 2440 *fax* 020-7224 3194
e-mail zenith@zenith.tv.co.uk

Screenplays for cinema; TV drama. No unsolicited scripts.

Independent national radio

Commercial Radio Companies Association (CRCA)

(formerly Association of Independent Radio Companies – AIRC)
77 Shaftesbury Avenue, London W1V 7AD
tel 020-7306 2603 *fax* 020-7470 0062
e-mail info@crca.co.uk
web site http://www.crca.co.uk

CRCA is the trade body for UK commerical radio. It represents commercial radio to Government, the Radio Authority, copyright societies and other organisations concerned with radio. CRCA is a source of advice to members and acts as a clearing house for radio information. CRCA runs the Radio Advertising Clearance Centre. It jointly owns Radio Joint Audience Research Ltd (RAJAR) with the BBC, JICRIT Ltd (an electronic means of buying, selling and accounting for radio advertisements) with the IPA, and also owns the Network Chart Show, sponsored by Pepsi.

CRCA is a founder member of the Association of European Radios (AER), which lobbies European institutions on behalf of commercial radio.

Classic FM

7 Swallow Place, London W1R 7AA
tel 020-7343 9000 *fax* 020-7344 2700
e-mail enquiries@classicfm.co.uk
web site www.classicfm.co.uk

Digital One Ltd

7 Swallow Place, London W1R 7AA
tel 020-7518 2620 *fax* 020-7518 2605
e-mail info@digitalone.co.uk
web site http://www.ukdigitalradio.com

Commercial digital radio multiplex operator. Founded 1999.

IRN (Independent Radio News)

6th Floor, 200 Gray's Inn Road, London WC1X 8XZ
tel 020-7430 4090 *fax* 020-7430 4092
e-mail news@irn.co.uk

National news provider to all UK commercial radio stations, including live news bulletins, sport and financial news, and coverage of the House of Commons.

Oneword

Landseer House, 19 Charing Cross Road, London WC2H 0ES
tel 020-7976 3030 *fax* 020-7930 9460
e-mail info@oneword.co.uk
web site http://www.oneword.co.uk
Managing Director Ben Budworth

Book readings, plays, comedy, reviews and commentaries for national transmission. Founded 2000.

The Radio Authority

Holbrook House, 14 Great Queen Street, London WC2B 5DG
tel 020-7430 2724 *fax* 020-7405 7062
e-mail info@radioauthority.org.uk
web site http://www.radioauthority.org.uk

Licenses and regulates Independent Radio. Plans frequencies, awards licences, regulates programming and advertising, and plays an active role in the discussion and formulation of policies which affect the Independent Radio industry and its listeners.

Talk Radio

76 Oxford Street, London W1N 0TR
tel 020-7636 1089 *fax* 020-7636 1053

Virgin 1215

1 Golden Square, London W1R 4DJ
tel 020-7434 1215 *fax* 020-7434 1197
e-mail virgin@vradio.co.uk
web site http://www.virginradio.com

Independent local radio

**Stations offering some/occasional opportunities for creative input from local writers. Check with the station before submitting material.*

England

Alton
Delta FM 102, Prospect Place, Mill Lane, Alton, Hants GU34 2SY
tel (01420) 544444 *fax* (01420) 544044
e-mail studio@delta102.freeserve.co.uk

Aylesbury
MIX 96, Friars Square Studios, 11 Bourbon Street, Aylesbury, Bucks. HP20 2PZ
tel (01296) 399396 *fax* (01296) 398988

Barnstaple
Lantern FM, Unit 2B, Lauder Lane, Barnstaple, Devon EX31 3TA
tel (01271) 340340 *fax* (01271) 340345

Basingstoke
107.6 Kestrel FM, 2nd Floor, Paddington House, The Walks Shopping Centre, Basingstoke RG21 7LJ
tel (01256) 694000 *fax* (01256) 694111

Bassetlaw
Trax FM, PO Box 444, Worksop, Notts. S80 1GP
tel (01909) 500611 *fax* (01909) 500445

Bedford
B97 Chiltern FM, 55 Goldington Road, Bedford MK40 3LT
tel (01234) 272400 *fax* (01234) 218580

Birmingham
96.4 FM BRMB *and* Capital Gold (1152), 9 Brindley Place, 4 Oozells Square, Birmingham B1 2DJ
tel 0121-245 5000 *fax* 0121-245 5245
e-mail info@brmb.co.uk

Birmingham
Galaxy 102.2, 1 The Square, 111 Broad Street, Birmingham B15 1AS
tel 0121-695 0000 *fax* 0121-695 0055
e-mail mail@galaxy1022.co.uk

Blackpool
The Wave 96.5, 965 Mowbray Drive, Blackpool, Lancs. FY3 7JR
tel (01253) 304965 *fax* (01253) 301965
e-mail any@thewavefm.co.uk

Birmingham
Radio XL 1296 AM, KMS House, Bradford Street, Birmingham B12 0JD
tel 0121-753 5353 *fax* 0121-753 3111

Bolton & Bury
Tower FM, The Mill, Brownlow Way, Bolton BL1 2RA
tel (01204) 387000 *fax* (01204) 534065

Bournemouth
Classic Gold 828 *and* 2CR FM, 5 Southcote Road, Bournemouth BH1 3LR
tel (01202) 259259 *fax* (01202) 255244

Bradford
Sunrise FM, Sunrise House, 30 Chapel Street, Little Germany, Bradford BD1 5DN
tel (01274) 735043 *fax* (01274) 728534

Bradford, Huddersfield & Halifax
Classic Gold 1278/1530 *and* The Pulse, Pennine House, Forster Square, Bradford BD1 5NE
tel (01274) 203040 *fax* (01274) 203130
e-mail general@pulse.co.uk

Brighton*
Surf 107, PO Box 107, Brighton BN1 1QG
tel (01273) 386107 *fax* (01273) 273107
e-mail info@Surf107.co.uk

Bristol & Bath
Classic Gold 1260 AM, PO Box 2020, Watershed, Canons Road, Bristol BS99 7SN
tel 0117-984 3200 *fax* 0117-984 3202
e-mail reception@gwrfm@musicradio.com
web site http://www.gwrfm.musicradio.com

Bristol & Bath
GWR FM, PO Box 2000, Watershed, Canons Road, Bristol BS99 7SN
tel 0117-984 3200 *fax* 0117-984 3202
e-mail reception@gwrfm@musicradio.com
web site http://www.gwrfm.musicradio.com

Cambridge
107.9 The Eagle, Sturton Street,
Cambridge CB1 2QF
tel (01223) 722300 *fax* (01223) 577686

Cambridge & Newmarket
Q103 FM, Enterprise House, The Vision Park,
Chivers Way, Histon, Cambs. CB4 9WW
tel (01223) 235255 *fax* (01223) 235161
e-mail reception@q103.musicradio.com

Canterbury
106 CTFM Radio, 16 Lower Bridge Street,
Canterbury, Kent CT1 2HQ
tel (01227) 789106 *fax* (01227) 785106
e-mail e-mail@ctfm.co.uk

Carlisle
CFM, PO Box 964, Carlisle CA1 3NG
tel (01228) 818964 *fax* (01228) 819444

Chelmsford
107.7 Chelmer FM, 6th Floor, Cater House,
High Street, Chelmsford, Essex CM1 1AL
tel (01245) 259400 *fax* (01245) 259558
e-mail mail@chelmerfm.co.uk
web site http://www.chelmerfm.co.uk

Cheltenham
107.5 Cat FM, Regent Arcade, Cheltenham,
Glos. GL50 1JZ
tel (01242) 699555 *fax* (01242) 699666
e-mail catfm@netcomuk.co.uk
web site http://www.catfm.co.uk

Chesterfield & North Derbyshire
Peak 107 FM, Radio House, Foxwood Road,
Chesterfield S41 9RF
tel (01246) 269107 (01246) 269933
e-mail info@peak107.co.uk
web site http://www.peak107.co.uk

Chichester, Bognor Regis & Littlehampton*
Spirit FM, Dukes Court, Bognor Road,
Chichester, West Sussex PO19 2FX
tel (01243) 773600 *fax* (01243) 786464
e-mail info@spiritfm.net

Colchester
SGR Colchester, Abbeygate Two,
9 Whitewell Road, Colchester CO2 7DE
tel (01206) 575859 *fax* (01206) 561199

Cornwall, Plymouth & West Devon
Pirate FM102·2/8, Carn Brea Studios,
Wilson Way, Redruth, Cornwall TR15 3XX
tel (01209) 314400 *fax* (01209) 314345
e-mail enquiries@piratefm102.co.uk

Coventry
Classic Gold 1359 *and* Mercia FM,
Hertford Place, Coventry CV1 3TT
tel (01203) 868200 *fax* (01203) 868202
e-mail mercia@musicradio.com

Coventry
Kix 96, Watch Close, Spon Street,
Coventry CV1 3LN
tel 024-7652 5656 *fax* 024-7655 1744
e-mail kix962@aol.com

Darlington
Alpha 103.2, Radio House, 11 Woodland Road,
Darlington, Co. Durham DL3 7BJ
tel (01325) 255552 *fax* (01325) 255551
e-mail admin@alpharadio.demon.co.uk

Derby
Ram FM, 2nd Floor, Norwich Union House,
35-36 Irongate, Derby DE1 3GA
tel (01332) 292945 *fax* (01332) 292229

Doncaster
Trax FM, PO Box 444, Doncaster DN4 5GW
tel (01302) 341166 *fax* (01302) 326104

Dover & Folkestone
Neptune Radio, PO Box 1068, Dover CT16 1GB
and PO Box 964, Folkestone CT18 8GG
tel (01304) 202505 *fax* (01304) 212717

East of England
Vibe FM, Reflection House, The Anderson Centre,
Olding Road, Bury St Edmunds IP33 3TA
tel (01284) 718800 *fax* (01284) 718839
e-mail studios@vibefm.co.uk

East Lancashire
Asian Sound Radio, Globe House, Southall
Street, Manchester M3 1LG
tel 0161-288 1000 *fax* 0161-288 9000
e-mail asr@aol.com

East Midlands
Century 106, City Link,
Nottingham NG2 4NG
tel 0115-910 6100 *fax* 0115-910 6107
e-mail radio@century106.com
web site http://www.century106.com

Eastbourne*
Sovereign Radio, 14 St Mary's Walk, Hailsham,
East Sussex BN27 1AF
tel (01323) 442700 *fax* (01323) 442866
e-mail sovereignradio.co.uk
web site http://www.1075 sovereignradio.co.uk

Exeter & Torbay
Westward Radio *and* Gemini FM,
Hawthorn House, Exeter Business Park,
Exeter, Devon EX1 3QS
tel (01392) 444444 *fax* (01392) 444433

Fenland*
X-Cel FM, 46 Camel Road, Littleport, Ely,
Cambs. CB6 1EW
tel (01353) 865102 *fax* (01353) 865105
e-mail [name] @xcel.fm.co.uk
web site http://www.xcelfm.co.uk

Along the M20 towards Folkestone and the Kent channel ports
Channel Travel Radio, Main Control Building, Eurotunnel UK Terminal, PO Box 2000, Folkestone, Kent CT18 8XY
tel (01303) 283873 *fax* (01303) 283874

Gloucester & Cheltenham
Classic Gold 774 *and* Severn Sound FM, Bridge Studios, Eastgate Centre, Gloucester GL1 1SS
tel (01452) 313200 *fax* (01452) 313213
e-mail reception@severnfm.musicradio.com

Great Yarmouth & Lowestoft
The Beach, PO Box 103.4, Lowestoft, Suffolk NR32
tel (07000) 001035 *fax* (07000) 001036
e-mail 103.4@thebeach.co.uk

Great Yarmouth & Norwich
Broadland 102·4 FM *and* Classic Gold Amber, St George's Plain, 47-49 Colegate, Norwich NR3 1DB
tel (01603) 630621 *fax* (01603) 666353
e-mail sales@broadland102.co.uk
web site http://www.broadland102.co.uk

Guernsey
Island FM, 12 Westerbrook, St Sampson, Guernsey GY2 4QQ, Channel Islands
tel (01481) 242000 *fax* (01481) 249676
e-mail kevin@islandfm.guernsey.net
web site http://www.islandfm.guernsey.net

Guildford
County Sound Radio 1566 AM *and* 96.4 The Eagle, Dolphin House, North Street, Guildford, Surrey GU1 4AA
tel (01483) 300964 *fax* (01483) 531612
e-mails onair@countysound.co.uk, eagle@countysound.co.uk

Harlow
Ten 17, Latton Bush Centre, Southern Way, Harlow, Essex CM18 7BU
tel (01279) 432415 *fax* (01279) 445289
e-mail studios@ten17.co.uk

Harrogate
97.2 Stray FM, PO Box 972, Station Parade, Harrogate HG1 5YF
tel (01423) 522972 *fax* (01423) 522922
e-mail @972strayfm.co.uk

Haslemere
Delta FM 97.1, 65 Weyhill, Haslemere, Surrey GU27 1HN
tel (01428) 651971 *fax* (01428) 658971
e-mail delta@ukrd.com

Hastings
107.8 Arrow FM, Priory Meadow Centre, Hastings, East Sussex TN34 1PJ
tel (01424) 461177 *fax* (01424) 422662
e-mail info@arrowfm.co.uk

Havering
Active 107.5 FM, Lambourne House, 7 Western Road, Romford, Essex RM1 3LD
tel (01708) 731643 *fax* (01708) 730383

Hereford, Worcester & Kidderminster
Wyvern FM, 5 Barbourne Terrace, Worcester WR1 3JZ
tel (01905) 612212 *fax* (01905) 746637
e-mail wyvernfm@musicradio.com

Hertford, Ware, Hatfield, Welwyn Garden City & Stevenage*
HertBeat FM, PO Box 299, Hertford SG14 3XN
fax (01992) 505362
e-mail info@hertbeat.com
web site http://www.hertbeat.com

High Wycombe
ElevenSeventy, PO Box 1170, High Wycombe, Bucks HP13 6YT
tel (01494) 446611 *fax* (01494) 445400

Hinckley, Nuneaton & surrounding area
Fosseway Radio, PO Box 107, Hinckley, Leics. LE10 1WR
tel (01455) 614151 *fax* (01455) 616888
e-mail enquiries@fossewayradio.co.uk

Huddersfield
Home 107.9, The Old Stableblock, Lockwood Park, Huddersfield HD1 3UR
tel (01484) 321107 *fax* (01484) 311107

Humberside
Magic 1161 AM *and* 96.9 Viking FM, Commercial Road, Hull HU1 2SG
tel (01482) 325141 *fax* (01482) 587067
web sites http://www.magic1161.co.uk *and* www.vikingfm.co.uk

Ipswich & Bury St Edmunds
Classic Gold Amber (Suffolk) *and* SGR-FM, Radio House, Alpha Business Park, White House Road, Ipswich IP1 5LT
tel (01473) 461000 *fax* (01473) 741200
e-mail sgrfm.co.uk

Isle of Man*
Manx Radio, PO Box 1368, Broadcasting House, Douglas, Isle of Man IM99 1SW
tel (01624) 682600 *fax* (01624) 682604
e-mail postbox@manxradio.com
web sites http://www.manxradio.com *and* http://www.radiott.com

Isle of Wight
Isle of Wight Radio, Dodnor Park, Newport PO30 5XE
tel (01983) 822557 *fax* (01983) 822109
e-mail admin@iwradio.co.uk

Jersey
Channel 103 FM, 6 Tunnell Street, St Helier, Jersey JE2 4LU, Channel Islands
tel (01534) 888103 *fax* (01534) 887799
e-mail chan103@itl.net

Kent
Capital Gold (1242 and 603) *and* Invicta FM, Radio House, John Wilson Business Park, Whitstable, Kent CT5 3QX
tel (01227) 772004 *fax* (01227) 771558
e-mail info@invictaradio.co.uk

Kettering
KCBC, PO Box 1074, Centre 2000, Kettering, Northants. NN16 8ZH
tel (07000) 1074 1074 *fax* (01536) 517390
e-mail fm107.4@kcbc.co.uk

Kings Lynn
KL.FM 96·7, 18 Blackfriars Street, Kings Lynn, Norfolk PE30 1NN
tel (01553) 772777 *fax* (01553) 766453
e-mail klfmradio.co.uk

Kingston upon Thames
107.8 FM Thames Radio, Brentham House, 45c High Street, Hampton Wick, Kingston upon Thames KT1 4DG
tel 020-8288 1300 *fax* 020-8288 1312
e-mail events@thamesradio.co.uk
web site http://www.thamesradio.co.uk

Leeds
96.3 Aire FM *and* Magic 828, 51 Burley Road, Leeds LS3 1LR
tel 0113-283 5500 *fax* 0113-283 5501

Leicester
Leicester Sound, Granville House, Granville Road, Leicester LE1 7RW
tel 0116-256 1300 *fax* 0116-256 1303
e-mail leicestersound@musicradio.com

Leicester
Sabras, Radio House, 63 Melton Road, Leicester LE4 6PN
tel 0116-261 0666 *fax* 0116-266 7776

Lincolnshire & Newark*
Lincs FM, Witham Park, Waterside South, Lincoln LN5 7JN
tel (01522) 549900 *fax* (01522) 549911
e-mail enquiries@lincsfm.co.uk

Liverpool
Radio City 96·7 *and* Magic 1548, 8-10 Stanley Street, Liverpool L1 6AF
tel 0151-227 5100 *fax* 0151-471 0330
web site http://www.radiocity967.com

London
Choice FM, 291-299 Borough High Street, London SE1 1JG
tel 020-7378 3969 *fax* 020-7378 3911 (South London); *tel* 020-8348 1033 *fax* 020-8348 1044 (North London)

London
Millennium 106.8 FM, Harrow Manor Way, Thamesmead, London SE2 9XH
tel 020-8311 3112 *fax* 020-8312 1930

London, Greater
95.8 Capital FM *and* Capital Gold (1548), 30 Leicester Square, London WC2H 7LA
tel 020-7766 6000 *fax* 020-7766 6100

London, Greater
Country 1035 AM, 33-35 Wembley Hill Road, Wembley, Middlesex HA9 8RT
tel 020-8733 1300 *fax* 020-8733 1393

London, Greater
Heart 106·2, The Chrysalis Building, Bramley Road, London W10 6SP
tel 020-7468 1062 *fax* 020-7470 1062
e-mail (initial.surname)@heart1062.co.uk

London, Greater
Jazz FM 102.2, 26-27 Castlereagh Street, London W1H 6DJ
tel 020-7706 4100 *fax* 020-7723 9742
e-mail info@jazzfm.com

London, Greater
Kiss 100 FM, Kiss House, 80 Holloway Road, London N7 8JG
tel 020-7700 6100 *fax* 020-7700 3979

London, Greater
LBC 1152 AM *and* News Direct 97·3 FM, 200 Gray's Inn Road, London WC1X 8XZ
tel 020-7973 1152 *fax* 020-7973 8833
e-mail jackiek@lnr.uk.co

London, Greater
963/972 Liberty Radio, 7th Floor, Trevor House, 100 Brompton Road, London SW3 1ER
tel 020-7893 8966 *fax* 020-7893 8965

London, Greater
Magic 105.4 FM, The Network Building, 97 Tottenham Court Road, London W1 9HF
tel 020-7504 7000 *fax* 020-7504 7001

London, Greater*
Premier Christian Radio, Glen House, Stag Place, London SW1E 5AG
tel 020-7316 1300 *fax* 020-7233 6706
e-mail premier@premier.org.uk
web site http://www.premier.org.uk

London, Greater
Spectrum International Radio, International Radio Centre, 204-206 Queenstown Road, London SW8 3NR
tel 020-7627 4433 *fax* 020-7627 3409

e-mail spectrum@spectrum558am.co.uk
web site http://www.spectrum558am.co.uk

London, Greater
Sunrise Radio, Sunrise House, Sunrise Road, Southall, Middlesex UB2 4AU
tel 020-8574 6666 *fax* 020-8813 9800

London, Greater
Virgin 105.8, 1 Golden Square, London W1R 4DJ
tel 020-7434 1215 *fax* 020-7434 1197
e-mail virgin@vradio.co.uk
web site http://www.virginradio.com

London, Greater
Xfm, 30 Leicester Square, London WC2H 7LA
tel 020-7766 6600 *fax* 020-7766 6601

London (Lewisham)
FLR 107.3, PO Box 1073, London SE14 6WA
tel 020-8691 9202 *fax* 020-8691 9193
e-mail enquiries@ukrd.com

London (North)
London Greek Radio, Florentia Village, Vale Road, London N4 1TD
tel 020-8800 8001 *fax* 020-8800 8005
e-mail lgrhgc@globalnet.co.uk

London (North)
London Turkish Radio, 185B High Road, London N22 6BA
tel 020-8881 0606/2020 *fax* 020-8881 5151

Loughborough & neighbouring parts of North West Leicestershire
107 Oak FM, PO Box 107, Loughborough LE11 5XP
tel (01509) 211711 *fax* (01509) 246107

Ludlow
Sunshine 855, Sunshine House, Waterside, Ludlow, Shropshire SY8 1PE
tel (01584) 873795 *fax* (01584) 875900

Luton/Bedford
Chiltern FM *and* Classic Gold 792/828, Chiltern Road, Dunstable, Beds. LU6 1HQ
tel (01582) 676200 *fax* (01582) 676231/201
e-mail chilternfm@musicradio.com

Macclesfield
Silk FM, Radio House, Bridge Street, Macclesfield, Cheshire SK11 6DJ
tel (01625) 268000 *fax* (01625) 269010
e-mail mail@silkfm.com

Manchester
Key 103 *and* Magic 1152, Castle Quay, Castlefield, Manchester M5 4PR
tel 0161-288 5000 *fax* 0161-288 5001

Manchester
1458 Lite AM, Quay West, Trafford Wharf Road, Trafford Park, Manchester M17 1FL
tel 0161-872 1458 *fax* 0161-872 0206

Greater Manchester, Merseyside & South & Central Lancashire
Galaxy 102, 127-129 Portland Street, Manchester M1 6ED
tel 0161-228 0102 *fax* 0161-228 1020
web site http://www.galaxy102.co.uk

Mansfield & Ashfield
Mansfield 103.2 FM, The Media Suite, Brunts Business Centre, Samuel Brunts Way, Mansfield, Notts. NG18 2AH
tel (01623) 646666 *fax* (01623) 660606

Medway towns
Medway FM, Berkeley House, 186 High Street, Rochester ME1 1EY
tel (01634) 841111 *fax* (01634) 841122
e-mail studio@medwayfm.com

Merseyside
107.6 Crash FM, 27 Fleet Street, Liverpool L1 4AR
tel 0151-707 3107 *fax* 0151-707 3109
e-mail crashfm@btinternet.com
web site http://www.107.6crashfm.com

Milton Keynes
FM 103 Horizon, Broadcast Centre, Vincent Avenue, Crownhill Industry, Milton Keynes MK8 0AB
tel (01908) 269111 *fax* (01908) 564063
e-mail fm103horizon@musicradio

Morecambe Bay
The Bay 96.9 FM, PO Box 969, St George's Quay, Lancaster LA1 3LD
tel (01524) 848747 *fax* (01524) 848787
e-mail (staffname)@thebay.co.uk

Newbury
Kick FM, The Studios, 42 Bone Lane, Newbury, Berks. RG14 5SD
tel (01635) 841600 *fax* (01635) 841010

North East England
Century Radio, Century House, PO Box 100, Gateshead NE8 2YX
tel 0191-477 6666 *fax* 0191-477 1771
e-mail name@centurynortheast.com

North West England
Century 105, Century House, Waterfront Quay, Salford Quays, Manchester M5 2XW
tel 0161-400 0105 *fax* 0161-400 1105

North West England
Jazz FM 100.4, The World Trade Centre, Exchange Quay, Manchester M5 3EJ
tel 0161-877 1004 *fax* 0161-877 1005
e-mail jazzinfo@jazzfm.com

Northampton
Classic Gold 1557 *and* Northants 96, 19-21 St Edmunds Road, Northampton NN1 5DY
tel (01604) 795600 *fax* (01604) 795601
e-mail reception@northants96.musicradio.com

Nottingham & Derby
96 Trent FM *and* Classic Gold Gem,
29-31 Castle Gate, Nottingham NG1 7AP
tel 0115-952 7000 *fax* 0115-912 9302
e-mails admin@gemam.musicradio.com *and* admin@trentfm.musicradio.com

Oldham & surrounding area*
Revolution 96.2, PO Box 962, Oldham OL1 1FE
tel 0161-628 8787 (temp) *fax* 0161-628 0905

Oxford
Oxygen 107.9 FM, Suite 41, Westgate Centre, Oxford OX1 1PD
tel (01865) 724442 *fax* (01865) 726161
e-mail mail@oxygen.demon.co.uk

Oxford & Banbury
FOX FM, Brush House, Pony Road, Oxford OX4 2XR
tel (01865) 871000 *fax* (01865) 871036
e-mail fox@foxfm.co.uk

Peterborough
Classic Gold 1332 AM, PO Box 2020, Queensgate Centre, Peterborough PE1 1LL
tel (01733) 460460 *fax* (01733) 281445

Peterborough
102·7 Hereward FM, PO Box 225, Queensgate Centre, Peterborough PE1 1XJ
tel (01733) 460460 *fax* (01733) 281445

Peterborough
Lite FM, 2nd Floor, 5 Church Street, Peterborough PE1 1XB
tel (01733) 898106 *fax* (01733) 898107

Plymouth
Plymouth Sound AM *and* Plymouth Sound FM, Earl's Acre, Plymouth PL3 4HX
tel (01752) 227272 *fax* (01752) 670730
e-mail plymouth.com

Poole, Bournemouth & surrounding area*
The NRG (Bournemouth) Ltd, PO Box 1234, Bournemouth BH1 2AD
tel (01202) 318100 *fax* (01202) 318111
e-mail name@the-nrg.co.uk
web site http://www.the-nrg.co.uk

Portsmouth, Havant, Gosport & Fareham*
Victory 107.4, Media House, Tipner Wharf, Twyford Avenue, Portsmouth PO2 8PE
tel (02392) 639 922 *fax* (02392) 639933

Preston & Blackpool
Magic 999 *and* Rock FM, PO Box 999/PO Box 974, Preston, Lancs. PR1 1XR
tel (01772) 556301 *fax* (01772) 201917

Reading, Basingstoke & Andover
Classic Gold 1431/1485 *and* 2-TEN FM, PO Box 2020, Reading RG31 7FG
tel 0118-945 4400 *fax* 0118-928 8483
e-mail mail2tenfm@musicradio.com

Reigate & Crawley
Breeze 1521 *and* Mercury FM, The Stanley Centre, Kelvin Way, Crawley, West Sussex RH10 2SE
tel (01293) 519161 *fax* (01293) 560927
e-mail studio@mercuryfm.co.uk

Rutland & Stamford
Rutland Radio, 40 Melton Road, Oakham, Rutland LE15 6AY
tel (01572) 757868 *fax* (01572) 757744
e-mail enquiries@rutlandradio.co.uk

St Albans & Watford
96.6 Oasis FM, 9 Christopher Place Shopping Centre, St Albans, Herts. AL3 5DQ
tel (01727) 831966 *fax* (01727) 834456
e-mail studios@oasisfm.co.uk

Salisbury
Spire FM, City Hall Studios, Malthouse Lane, Salisbury, Wilts. SP2 7QQ
tel (01722) 416644 *fax* (01722) 416688
e-mail admin@spirefm.co.uk

Scarborough
Yorkshire Coast Radio, PO Box 962, Scarborough, North Yorkshire YO12 5YX
tel (01723) 500962 *fax* (01723) 501050
e-mail mail@minsterfm.demon.co.uk

Severn Estuary
Galaxy 101, Millennium House, 27 Baldwin Street, Bristol BS1 1SE
tel 0117-901 0101 *fax* 0117-901 4666
e-mail addressee@galaxy101.co.uk

Shaftesbury
97.4 Vale FM, Longmead, Shaftesbury SP7 8QQ
tel (01747) 855711 *fax* (01747) 855722

Slough, Windsor & Maidenhead
106·6 Star FM, The Observatory Shopping Centre, Slough, Berks. SL1 1LH
tel (01753) 551066 *fax* (01753) 512277
e-mail onair@starfm.co.uk

Solent area
Wave 105.2 FM, 5 Manor Court, Barnes Wallis Road, Segensworth East, Fareham PO15 5TH
tel (01489) 481050 *fax* (01489) 481060
e-mail studio@wave105.com

South Hampshire
Capital Gold (1170 and 1557) *and* Ocean FM *and* Power FM, Radio House, Whittle Avenue, Segensworth West, Fareham PO15 5SH
tel (01489) 589911 *fax* (01489) 589453
e-mail info@oceanradio.co.uk

South Yorkshire
Hallam FM *and* Magic AM, Radio House, 900 Herries Road, Sheffield S6 1RH

tel 0114-285 3333/2121 *fax* 0114-285 3159
e-mail programmes@hallamfm.co.uk @magicam.co.uk

Southampton
South City FM, City Studios, Marsh Lane, Southampton SO14 3ST
tel/fax 023-8022 0020

South-East Staffordshire
Centre FM, 5-6 Aldergate, Tamworth, Staffs B79 7DJ
tel (01827) 318000 *fax* (01827) 318002

Southend & Chelmsford
Breeze *and* Essex FM, Radio House, Clifftown Road, Southend-on-Sea, Essex SS1 1SX
tel (01702) 333711 *fax* (01702) 345224
e-mails studios@breeze.co.uk @essexfm.co.uk
web sites http://www.breeze.co.uk www.essexfm.co.uk

Southern Gloucestershire
FM 107 The Falcon, Brunel Mall, London Road, Stroud, Glos. GL5 2BP
tel (01453) 767369 *fax* (01453) 757107
e-mail info@thefalcon.org
web site http://www.thefalcon.org

Southport
107.9 Dune FM, The Power Station, Victoria Way, Southport PR8 1RR
tel (01704) 502500 *fax* (01704) 502540
e-mail dunefm@aol.com

Stockport
Imagine FM, Regent House, Heaton Lane, Stockport SK4 1BX
tel 0161-285 4545 *fax* 0161-285 1010
e-mail recipient@imaginefm.net

Stoke-on-Trent
Signal One *and* BIG AM, Stoke Road, Stoke-on-Trent ST4 2SR
tel (01782) 747047 *fax* (01782) 744110
e-mail recipient@signalradio.com

Stratford upon Avon*
FM 102* – The Bear, The Guard House Studios, Banbury Road, Stratford upon Avon CV37 7HX
tel (01789) 262636 *fax* (01789) 263102
e-mail studio@thebear.co.uk

Sunderland*
Sun FM, PO Box 1034, Sunderland SR5 2TA
tel 0191-548 1034 *fax* 0191-548 7171

East Sussex
Capital Gold (1323 and 945) *and* Southern FM, Radio House, PO Box 2000, Brighton BN41 2SS
tel (01273) 430111 *fax* (01273) 430098

Swindon & West Wiltshire
Classic Gold 936/1161 AM *and* GWR FM, PO Box 2000, Swindon SN4 7EX
tel (01793) 842600 *fax* (01793) 842602
e-mail reception@gwrfm.musicradio.com

Teesside
TFM *and* Magic 1170, Radio House, Yale Crescent, Thornaby, Stockton-on-Tees TS17 6AA
tel (01642) 888222 *fax* (01642) 868288

Telford*
Telford FM, PO Box 1074, Telford TF3 3WG
tel (01952) 280011 *fax* (01952) 280010

Tendring*
Dream 100 FM, Northgate House, St Peters Street, Colchester CO1 1HT
tel (01206) 764466 *fax* (01206) 715102
e-mail info@Dream100.com

Thanet
TLR, Imperial House, 2-14 High Street, Margate, Kent CT9 1DH
tel (01843) 220222 *fax* (01843) 299666
e-mail paul.mccartney@tlrfm.co.uk

Tunbridge Wells & Sevenoaks
KFM, 1 East Street, Tonbridge, Kent TN9 1AR
tel (01732) 369200 *fax* (01732) 369201

Tyne & Wear
Galaxy 105-106, Kingfisher Way, Silverlink Business Park, Tyne & Wear NE28 9ND
tel 0191-206 8000
web site http://www.galaxy1056.co.uk

Tyne & Wear
Magic 1152, Radio House, Swalwell, Newcastle upon Tyne NE99 1BB
tel 0191-420 3040 *fax* 0191-488 9222

Tyne & Wear
Metro FM, Newcastle upon Tyne NE99 1BB
tel 0191-420 0971 *fax* 0191-488 9222

Wakefield
Ridings FM, PO Box 333, Wakefield WF2 7YQ
tel (01924) 367177 *fax* (01924) 367133
e-mail enquiries@ridingsfm.co.uk

Warrington, Widnes & Runcorn
107.2 Wire FM, Warrington Business Park, Long Lane, Warrington WA2 8TX
tel (01925) 445545 *fax* (01925) 657705
e-mail wirefm.com

Wellingborough*
Connect FM, Church Street, Wellingborough, Northants. NN8 4XX
tel (01933) 224972 *fax* (01933) 442333
e-mail info@connectfm.co.uk
web site http://www.connectfm.co.uk

West Cumbria
CFM, PO Box 964, Carlisle CA1 3NG
tel (01228) 818964 *fax* (01228) 819444

West Midlands
100·7 Heart FM, 1 The Square, 111 Broad Street, Birmingham B15 1AS

tel 0121-695 0000 *fax* 0121-696 1007
e-mail (initial.surname)@heartfm.com

West Somerset
Quay West Radio, Harbour Studios,
The Esplanade, Watchet, Somerset TA23 0AJ
tel (01984) 634900 *fax* (01984) 634811
e-mail quaywestradio@csi.com

Weymouth & Dorchester
Wessex FM, Radio House, Trinity Street,
Dorchester, Dorset DT1 1DJ
tel (01305) 250333 *fax* (01305) 250052

Wigan & St Helens
102.4 Wish FM, Orrell Lodge, Orrell Road,
Wigan WN5 8HJ
tel (01942) 761024 *fax* (01942) 777694
e-mail general@wishfm.com

Winchester*
Win 107.2 FM, PO Box 1072, The Brooks,
Winchester SO23 8FT
tel (01962) 841071 *fax* (01962) 841079
e-mail info@win1072.com
web site http://www.win1072.com

Wirral
The Buzz 97.1, Media House, Claughton Road,
Birkenhead L45 6EY
tel 0151-650 1700 *fax* 0151-647 5427

Wolverhampton
107.7 The Wolf, 10th Floor, Mander House,
Wolverhampton WV1 3NB
tel (01902) 571070 *fax* (01902) 571079
e-mail studio@thewolf.co.uk

Wolverhampton, Shrewsbury & Telford
Beacon Radio FM *and* Classic Gold WABC,
267 Tettenhall Road, Wolverhampton WV6 0DQ
tel (01902) 461300 *fax* (01902) 461299

Yeovil & Taunton
Orchard FM, Haygrove House, Taunton TA3 7BT
tel (01823) 338448 *fax* (01823) 320444

York
Minster FM, PO Box 123, Dunnington,
York YO1 5ZX
tel (01904) 488888 *fax* (01904) 488811
e-mail mail@minsterfm.demon.co.uk
web site http://www.minsterfm.demon.co.uk

Yorkshire
Galaxy 105, Josephs Well, Hanover Walk,
Leeds LS3 1AB
tel 0113-213 0105 *fax* 0113-213 1055
e-mail name@galaxy105.co.uk

Yorkshire Dales, with Skipton
Yorkshire Dales Radio, YDR House, Gargrave
Road, Skipton, North Yorkshire BD23 1YD
tel (01756) 799991 *fax* (01756) 799771

Scotland

Aberdeen
Northsound One *and* Northsound Two,
45 Kings Gate, Aberdeen AB15 4EL
tel (01224) 337000 *fax* (01224) 400003
e-mails northsound1@srh.co.uk,
northsound2@srh.co.uk

Arbroath*
RNA FM, Radio North Angus, Arbroath Infirmary,
Rosemount Road, Arbroath, Angus DD11 2AT
tel (01241) 879660 *fax* (01241) 439664
web site http://listen.to/rna

Ayr
West FM *and* West Sound AM, Radio House,
54A Holmston Road, Ayr KA7 3BE
tel (01292) 283662 *fax* (01292) 283665
e-mail westfm@srh.co.uk, westsound@srh.co.uk

The Borders
Radio Borders, Tweedside Park, Galashiels TD1 3TD
tel (01896) 759444 *fax* (01896) 759494

Central Scotland
Beat 106 Ltd, The Fourwinds Pavilion,
Pacific Quay, Glasgow G51 1EB
tel 0141-566 6106 *fax* 0141-566 6110
web site http://www.beat106.com

Central Scotland*
Scot FM, 1 Albert Quay, Leith EH6 7DN
tel 0131-625 8400 *fax* 0131-625 8401
e-mail name@scot.fm.com

Dundee*
Wave 102 FM, 8 South Tay Street,
Dundee DD1 1PA
tel (01382) 901000 *fax* (01382) 900999

Dundee/Perth*
Radio Tay AM* *and* Tay FM, 6 North Isla Street,
Dundee DD3 7JQ
tel (01382) 200800 *fax* (01382) 423252
e-mail tayam@srh.co.uk, tayfm@srh.co.uk

Edinburgh
Forth FM *and* Forth AM, Forth House,
Forth Street, Edinburgh EH1 3LF
tel 0131-556 9255 *fax* 0131-558 3277
e-mail forthfm.co.uk, fortham.co.uk
web site http://www.forthonline.co.uk

Fife
Kingdom FM, Haig House, Haig Business Park,
Balgonie Road, Markinch, Fife KY7 6AQ
tel (01592) 753753 *fax* (01592) 757788
e-mail info@kingdomfm.co.uk

Fort William
Nevis Radio, Inverlochy, Fort William PH33 6LU
tel (01397) 700007 *fax* (01397) 701007
e-mail nevisradio@lochaber.co.uk

Glasgow
Clyde 1 FM *and* Clyde 2, Clydebank Business Park, Clydebank, Glasgow G81 2RX
tel 0141-565 2200 *fax* 0141-565 2265
e-mails clyde1@srh.co.uk, clyde2@srh.co.uk

Inverness
Moray Firth Radio, PO Box 271, Scorguie Place, Inverness IV3 8UJ
tel (01463) 224433 *fax* (01463) 243224
e-mail mfr@mfr.uk.com

Inverurie
NECR, Town House, Kintore, Inverurie AB51 0US
tel (01467) 632909 *fax* (01467) 632969

Lanarkshire
Clan FM, Radio House, Rowantree Avenue, Newhouse Industrial Estate, Newhouse, Lanarkshire ML1 5RX
tel (01698) 733107
e-mail studio@clan-fm.co.uk
web site http://www.clan-fm.co.uk

Oban*
Oban FM, 132 George Street, Oban, Argyll PA34 5NT
tel (01631) 570057 *fax* (01631) 570530

Paisley
96.3 QFM, 26 Lady Lane, Paisley PA1 2LG
tel 0141-887 9630 *fax* 0141-887 0963
e-mail sales@q-fm.demon.co.uk

Peterhead
Waves Radio Peterhead, Unit 2, Blackhouse Industrial Estate, Peterhead AB42 1BW
tel (01779) 491012 *fax* (01779) 490802
e-mail waves@radiophd.freeserve.co.uk
web site http://www.wavesfm.com

Pitlochry & Aberfeldy*
Heartland FM*, Atholl Curling Rink, Lower Oakfield, Pitlochry, Perthshire PH16 5HQ
tel (01796) 474040 *fax* (01796) 474007

Shetland
SIBC, Market Street, Lerwick, Shetland ZE1 0JN
tel (01595) 695299 *fax* (01595) 695696
e-mail info@sibc.co.uk
web site http://www.sibc.co.uk

Stirling
Central FM, 201 High Street, Falkirk FK1 1DU
tel (01324) 611164 *fax* (01324) 611168

Stranraer, Dumfries & Galloway
South West Sound, Campbell House, Bankend Road, Dumfries DG1 4TH
tel (01387) 250999 *fax* (01387) 265629

Ullapool*
Lochbroom FM, Mill Street, Ullapool, Ross-shire IV26 2UN
tel (01854) 613131 *fax* (01854) 613132
web site http://www.lochbroom.co.uk

Western Isles
Isles FM, PO Box 333, Stornoway, Isle of Lewis HS1 2PU
tel (01851) 703333 *fax* (01851) 703322
e-mail admin@islesfm.co.uk
web site http://www.islesfm.co.uk

Northern Ireland

Belfast
City Beat 96.7, Lamont Buildings, Stranmills Embankment, Belfast BT9 5FN
tel (028) 9020 5967 *fax* (028) 9020 0023

Coleraine*
Q97.2FM, 24 Cloyfin Road, Coleraine BT52 2NU
tel (028) 703 59100 *fax* (028) 703 26666

Londonderry
Q102·9 FM, The Riverside Suite, Old Waterside Railway Station, Duke Street, Londonderry, BT47 6DH
tel (028) 7134 4449/311000 *fax* (028) 7131 1177
e-mail q102@iol.ie
web site http://q102-fm.com

Northern Ireland
Cool FM, PO Box 974, Belfast BT1 1RT
tel (01247) 817181 *fax* (01247) 814974
e-mail music@coolfm.co.uk

Northern Ireland
Downtown Radio, Newtownards, Co. Down BT23 4ES
tel (028) 9181 5555 *fax* (028) 9181 8913
e-mail programmes@downtown.co.uk

Wales

Caernarfon
Champion 103 FM, Llys y Dderwen, Parc Menai, Bangor, Gwynedd LL57 4BN
tel (01978) 752202 *fax* (01978) 758565
e-mail eira@championfm.co.uk

Cardiff & Newport
Red Dragon FM, Radio House, West Canal Wharf, Cardiff CF1 5XL
tel (01222) 384041 *fax* (01222) 384014
e-mail mail@rdfm.co.uk

Cardiff & Newport
Touch Radio, West Canal Wharf, Cardiff CF1 5XL
tel (01222) 384041 *fax* (01222) 384014

Ceredigion*
Radio Ceredigion, Yr Hen Ysgol Gymraeg, Ffordd Alexandra, Aberystwyth, Ceredigion SY23 1LF
tel (01970) 627999 *fax* (01970) 627206

Heads of South Wales Valleys
Valleys Radio, Festival Park, Victoria, Ebbw Vale NP3 6XW
tel (01495) 301116 *fax* (01495) 300710
e-mail admin@valleysradio.co.uk

Montgomeryshire
Radio Maldwyn, The Studios, The Park, Newtown, Powys SY16 2NZ
tel (01686) 623555 *fax* (01686) 623666
e-mail radio.maldwyn@ukonline.co.uk

North Wales Coast
Coast FM, Media House, Conway Road, Colwyn Bay LL28 5AB
tel (01492) 534555 *fax* (01492) 535248

Swansea
Swansea Sound, PO Box 1170, Victoria Road, Gowerton, Swansea SA4 3AB
tel (01792) 511170 *fax* (01792) 511171
e-mail admin@swanseasound.co.uk

Swansea
The Wave 96·4 FM, PO Box 964, Victoria Road, Gowerton, Swansea SA4 3AB
tel (01792) 511964*fax* (01792) 511965
e-mail admin@thewave.co.uk

Wrexham & Chester
Marcher Gold *and* MFM 103.4, The Studios, Mold Road, Gwersyllt, Wrexham LL11 4AF
tel (01978) 752202 *fax* (01978) 759701

Independent radio producers

Many writers approach independent production companies direct and, increasingly, BBC Radio is commissioning independent producers to make programmes.

Boom Media Ltd
PO Box 17, Halesworth, Suffolk IP19 0JZ
tel (01986) 781722 *fax* (01986) 781733
e-mail ideas@boom-media.demon.co.uk
Director Nick Patrick
Features and docs with an East Anglian bias, sports' features, popular culture, East Anglian drama. Founded 1993.

Cork Campus Radio
Level 3, Áras na Mac Léinn, University College Cork, Cork City, Republic of Ireland
tel (021) 902170 *fax* (021) 903108
e-mail radio@ucc.ie
Contact Sinéad O'Donnell, Station Manager
Produces dramatic works by new writers; stories of 1800-2000 words from the annual Fallen Leaves Short Story Competition; and the weekly *On the Road* documentary series. Founded 1995.

Fast Forward Productions
22 Fleshmarket Close, Edinburgh EH1 1DY
tel 0131-220 0200 *fax* 0131-220 2297
Producer Adrian Quine
Aviation. Founded 1994.

Festival Radio Productions
PO Box 107, Brighton, East Sussex BN1 1QG
tel (01273) 669595 *fax* (01273) 669596
Managing Director Daniel Nathan
Plays, docs, features and programmes. Founded 1989.

The Fiction Factory
14 Greenwich Church Street, London SE10 9BJ
tel 020-8853 5100 *fax* 020-8293 3001
e-mail radio@fictionfactory.co.uk
Creative Director John Taylor
Plays, dramatisations, documentaries, arts features, readings and family drama mainly for BBC radio (R4, R2, World Service, etc). Original radio drama scripts considered if targeted at existing BBC slots. Script reading fee except for submissions from established writers – some student exemptions. No charge for considering programme ideas and outlines. Founded 1993.

The Flying Dutchman Company
5-7 Hughes Mews, 143 Chatham Road, London SW11 6HJ
tel 020-7223 9067 *fax* 020-7585 0459
e-mail info@flyingdutchman.co.uk
Managing Director Michael Cameron
Plays, docs and other programmes on all topics. No unsolicited scripts. Please send synopsis only. Founded 1988.

Heavy Entertainment Ltd

208-209 Canalot Studios, 222 Kensal Road, London W10 5BN
tel 020-8960 9001/2 *fax* 020-8960 9003
e-mail scripts@heavy-entertainment.co.uk
Company Directors David Roper, Nick St George

Audiobooks, radio documentaries and comedy. Partners in Oneword – the plays, books and comedy radio station. Founded 1992.

Mike Hopwood Productions Ltd

Winton House, Stoke Road, Stoke-on-Trent, Staffs. ST4 2RW
tel (01782) 848800 *fax* (01782) 749447
Editor Mike Hopwood

Plays, docs, comedy, soaps, light entertainment. Founded 1991.

IRDP

PO Box 518, Manningtree, Essex CO11 1XD
tel (01206) 299088
web site www.irdp.co.uk/

New writing schemes for radio and theatre, and professional independent productions.

Mediatracks

93 Columbia Way, Blackburn, Lancs. BB2 7EA
tel (01254) 691197 *fax* (01254) 723505
e-mail info@mediatracks.co.uk
Contact Steve Johnson

Music and general interest docs for BBC local radio network. Founded 1987.

Mr Punch Productions

139 Kensington High Street, London W8 6SU
tel 020-7368 0088 *fax* 020-7368 0051
Director Stewart Richards

Plays and dramatisations for broadcast on BBC Radio 4 and for audiobooks. Founded 1993.

Partners in Sound Ltd

The Tower, Church Studios, North Villas, London NW1 9AY
tel 020-7485 0873 *mobile* (0973) 221 479
fax 020-7428 0541
e-mail partners_insound@compuserve.com
Director Ian Willox

No unsolicited scripts.

Penumbra Productions Ltd

80 Brondesbury Road, London NW6 6RX
tel 020-7328 4550 *fax* 020-7328 3844
e-mail 101621.3135@compuserve.com
Contact R. Elsgood

Drama and documentaries for Radio 3 and 4. Founded 1981.

Planet 24

Norex Court, Thames Quay, 195 Marsh Wall, London E14 9SG
tel 020-7345 2424 *fax* 020-7345 9400
Managing Director Alex Connock

Scripts, synopses and ideas for plays, docs and other programmes. Founded 1991.

Quantum Radio Productions Ltd

22 Fleshmarket Close, Edinburgh EH1 1DY
tel 0131-220 0200 *fax* 0131-220 2297
e-mail quine@quantumradio.demon.co.uk
Producer Adrian Quine

Sponsored syndicated radio programmes.

Rewind Productions Ltd

The Media Centre, 131-151 Great Titchfield Street, London W1P 8AE
tel 020-7665 8202 *fax* 020-7665 8201
Managing Director Simon Hughes, *Programme Development Manager* Olivia Landsberg

Plays, docs, popular and classical music, comedy and game shows. Founded 1989.

SH Radio

Robert Symes, Green Dene Cottage, Honeysuckle Bottom, East Horsley, Surrey KT24 5TD
tel/fax (01483) 281792

Broadcast and non-broadcast commercial material (English and German). Founded 1988.

Smooth Operations

PO Box 286, Cambridge CB1 4TW
tel (01223) 880835 *fax* (01223) 881647
e-mail info@smoothoperations.com
Contact Nick Barraclough
6 Millgate, Delph, Oldham OL3 5JG
tel (01457) 873752 *fax* (01457) 878500
e-mail info@smoothoperations.com
web site http://www.smoothoperations.com
Contact John Leonard

Music-based docs and series. Founded 1992.

Testbed Productions

5th Floor, 14-16 Great Portland Street, London W1N 5AB
tel 020-7436 0555 *fax* 020-7436 2800
Directors Viv Black, Nick Baker

Docs and other programmes; ideas for interviews, feature series, magazine, plays and panel/quiz games. Founded 1992.

Television and radio overseas

Opportunities are outlined here for submitting material to television and radio companies in Australia, Canada, Republic of Ireland, New Zealand and South Africa.

Australia

Australian Broadcasting Corporation (ABC)

Box 9994, Sydney, NSW 2001
tel (02) 9333 1500 *fax* (02) 9333 5305
e-mail comments@your.abc.net.au
web site http://www.abc.net.au
Manager for Europe Australian Broadcasting Corporation, 54 Portland Place, London W1N 4DY

Provides TV and radio programmes in the national broadcasting service; operates Radio Australia; and co-ordinates a network of 6 symphony orchestras and on-line services.

ABC TV restricts its production resources to work closely related to the Australian environment. ABC radio also looks principally to Australian writers for the basis of its drama output. However, ABC radio is interested in reading or auditioning new creative material of a high quality from overseas sources and this may be submitted in script or taped form. No journalistic material is required. Talks on international affairs are commissioned.

Federation of Australian Commercial Television Stations (FACTS)

44 Avenue Road, Mosman, NSW 2088
tel (02) 9960 2622 *fax* (02) 9969 3520
General Manager Tony Branigan

Represents all 48 commercial TV stations.

Federation of Australian Radio Broadcasters Ltd

PO Box 299, St Leonards, NSW 1590
tel (02) 9906 5944 *fax* (02) 9906 5128
Ceo David Bacon

Association of privately owned radio stations.

Canada

Canadian Broadcasting Corporation

250 Lanark Avenue, PO Box 3220, Stn. 'C', Ottawa, Ontario K1Y 1E4
tel 613-724-1200
e-mail commho@ottawa.cbc.ca
web site http://www.cbc.radio-canada.ca

CTV Inc.

9 Channel Nine Court, Toronto, Ontario M1S 4B5
tel 416-332-5000 *fax* 416-332-5054

Republic of Ireland

Radio Telefís Éireann (RTÉ)

Donnybrook, Dublin 4
tel (01) 208 3111 *fax* (01) 208 3080
web site http://www.rte.ie

The Irish national broadcasting service operating radio and TV.

Television Ongoing production of both a rural and an urban drama serial. Currently of interest: one-off drama productions, drama series, serials (preferably contemporary) and situation comedies (preferably set in Ireland or of strong Irish interest), with preferred length of commercial half hour or one hour. Proposals for serials suitable for a young adult network 2 audience, either cutting edge or humorous, which could exploit a low cost DV production model are of particular interest. Full scripts will not be considered – treatments and series/ serial outlines only, except in cases where projects are already part funded. Before submitting material to the Independent Productions Unit, Current Affairs, Drama, Features or Young People's programmes, authors are advised to write to the department in question to establish initial interest, timing of commissioning rounds, etc.

Radio Short stories (length 13-14 minutes) in Irish or English suitable for broadcasting; plays (running 28 or 58 minutes) are welcome. Guidelines on writing for radio drama are available from the RTÉ Radio Drama Department, Radio Centre, Donnybrook, Dublin 4.

Independent Radio and Television Commission (IRTC)

Marine House, Clanwilliam Place, Dublin 2, Republic of Ireland
tel (01) 6760966 *fax* (01) 6760948
e-mail info@irtc.ie
web site http://www.irtc.ie

Statutory body with responsibility for independent broadcasting in Ireland. To date, its activities have included the establishment of:

- an independent TV programme service (TV3);
- a national radio service (100-102 Today FM);
- 22 local commercial radio services;
- a special interest radio service;
- 13 community/community of interest radio services;
- 5 hospital/institutional radio services;
- approximately 15 short-term special event licences per annum.

It is envisaged that further licences will be granted in 2000 for both commercial and non-commercial radio stations.

New Zealand

The Radio Network of New Zealand Ltd

Private Bag 92198, Auckland
tel (09) 373-0000 *fax* (09) 367-4650
Ceo Kevin Malone

A radio company controlling a NZ-wide group of 52 commercial radio stations in metropolitan and provincial markets. The station brand groups are Newstalk ZB, Classic Hits, ZM, Easy Listening i, Hauraki, Radio Sports Network, and Community.

Television New Zealand Ltd

PO Box 3819, Auckland
tel (09) 377-0630 *fax* (09) 375-0934
web site http://www.tvnz.co.nz
Chairman Rosanne Meo, *Ceo* Rick Ellis

A state-owned enterprise, TVNZ is charged with operating a commercially successful TV business, acting with social responsibility in the provision of quality services, in particular the provision of TV programmes which reflect and foster New Zealand's identity and culture, both in New Zealand and internationally, and which are in the overall national interest.

Local and international activities include programme production, outside broadcasting services (through subsidiary company Moving Pictures), multimedia development, merchandising, Teletext, signal distribution and programming supply and transmission consultancy services in Australia, South-East Asia and the Pacific.

South Africa

South African Broadcasting Corporation (SABC)

Private Bag X1, Auckland Park 2006
tel (011) 714-9111 *fax* (011) 714-3106
web site http://www.sabc.co.za

Television Operates 6 TV services (4 free-to-air and 2 pay-TV). Three of the free-to-air channels, SABC1, SABC2 and SABC3, accept scripts in English for drama and comedy, either for one-off programmes or series.

Radio Operates 19 internal radio networks and one external radio service. The service which makes the greatest use of written material in English is SAFM.

Drama One-hour plays of all kinds welcomed. Half-hour plays are occasionally broadcast.

Short stories Short stories of all kinds (1500-1800 words) are welcomed.

Children's programmes Short stories, plays and serials (maximum 15 minutes) may be submitted.

Talks Most are locally commissioned, but outstanding material of particular interest may be submitted (3-10 minutes).

Theatre

Marketing a stage play

Despite the financial problems facing many subsidised theatres and the mounting costs of commercial productions, there are still plenty of companies interested in producing new plays and supporting new writers. Indeed, the sheer number and variety of such companies can be daunting. ***Ben Jancovich*** *examines the options.*

Selecting the theatre

Given the financial costs of submitting a play and the emotional strain in waiting for a response, it is important to take the time to research where a submission is most likely to gain a positive response. Start by recognising the disparate nature of contemporary outlets for new plays. Study the box (right) and decide on which kind of theatre company you should concentrate your efforts.

Clearly, the sheer volume of plays submitted to certain companies and the specific requirements of others make a blanket marketing campaign likely to be neither practical nor successful. An in-depth examination is needed on how to give your submission a head start.

Submitting your play

If the subject matter, form or the references in the play are specific enough, start by submitting your play to a theatre company which is likely to be predisposed towards those aspects of your play. For instance, if your play is about disability, you will want to be aware that the *raison d'etre* of the Graeae Theatre Company is to explore this theme. Likewise, if you have written a play for children you should know about the Polka Theatre for Children in Wimbledon. There is a danger of compartmentalising both writers and companies but, if your play has a distinct selling point, do the research and work to that strength.

Similarly, if your play details the life or history of a specific locale or region, send a copy of your script to the repertory theatre for that area – they may well have an interest in plays with a local appeal.

If a character in your play has a specific and discernible quality for which you think a particular actor may be uniquely suitable, it may be worth contacting them

Types of theatre companies

- **Metropolitan new writing theatre companies:** Largely London-based theatres which specialise in new writing, such as Hampstead Theatre, Royal Court, Bush Theatre, Soho Theatre, etc.
- **Regional repertory theatre companies:** Theatres based in towns and cities across the country which may do new plays as part of their repertoire.
- **Commercial producing managements:** Unsubsidised profit-making theatre producers who may occasionally be interested in new plays to take on tour or to present in the West End.
- **Small and/or middle-scale touring companies:** Companies – mostly touring – which may exist to explore or promote specific themes or are geared towards specific kinds of audiences.
- **Independent theatre practitioners:** For example, actors who may be looking for interesting plays in which to appear.
- **Independent theatre producers:** For example, young directors or producers who are looking for plays to produce at the onset of their career.
- **Drama schools and amateur dramatics companies.**

through their agent. Of course, there is no point in contacting an actor merely because they are famous – they will already receive many more scripts than they could ever read. Therefore, only consider doing this if there is genuinely something specific about the play that demands their attention.

Further options

If your play does not obviously fit any such niche, there are still plenty of companies which are keen to read exciting new writing irrespective of subject matter.

Metropolitan new writing companies, the regional repertory theatres and commercial producers are all, to different degrees, in the market for new plays. Additionally, and often most successfully, there is the plethora of young directors and other practitioners who institute productions under the aegis of their own independent theatre companies. An all-inclusive list of these latter organisations would be daunting, so research their interests and be selective. Reading reviews in the national and local press and listings magazines, such as *Time Out*, will give you some idea of which are the most productive and successful companies and practitioners.

Choosing which company to approach can be difficult as past productions and achievements rarely give precise indications of the way a company wants to move forward. Likewise, the notion of a successful 'commercial' company or play is not straightforward. For example, recent new plays with youthful, urban and often violent content have proved big commercial hits despite appearing anathema to the cliché of a well-made West End play.

Amateur companies/drama schools

Two other avenues to consider are amateur theatres and drama schools. Certain amateur theatre companies, such as the Questors Theatre in Ealing, have premiered plays by both new and established writers. The Leisure Department of your local council should be able to give information on groups which exist in your area.

One good reason for approaching such a company is that they are often the only organisations (apart from the RSC and RNT) which can afford to mount large cast plays. It is a reality of modern theatre that, if you write a play requiring a cast of more than 10, it will prove financially problematic for many companies.

Similar considerations are at work regarding drama schools, with the added incentive that the people involved – directors and actors – may form an attachment to the play and want to work on it professionally elsewhere. The publication *Contacts* lists and gives contact details of the drama schools which are recognised by and accredited to the Conference of Drama Schools.

How to approach a company

Although some details may be obvious, they are worth noting and of course much depends on who you are approaching. At the very least, only ever submit a script which is legible, typed and bound, and always include a stamped addressed envelope large enough for its return. Find out the name and position of the best person to receive and assess your script. Do this not only a matter of courtesy but also because it will help if you need to follow up anything at a later date.

Do your best to ensure that you are happy with the script as it stands. Mistakes are inevitable but it is unprofessional to send rewrites before the original draft has even been read. Obviously, always keep a copy of your play.

Some theatres employ a literary manager or dramaturg whose job is specifically to facilitate the passage of plays through the administrative and artistic channels. In such cases, submissions should be simple and, under their management, the theatre should always be willing and ready to read plays by writers previously unknown to them (although some may not be interested in musicals, revues or translations and adaptations).

Useful addresses

Arts Council of England
14 Great Peter Street,
London SW1P 3NQ
Contact The Drama Director
Publishes a brochure, *Schemes for Writers & Theatre Companies*, which gives details of various forms of assistance available to playwrights and to theatres wishing to commission new plays. The Council awards Bursaries (e.g. the John Whiting Award) and helps writers who are being commissioned or encouraged by a theatre company. A number of Resident Dramatists' Attachment Awards are available. See also page 461.

Writernet
(formerly New Playwrights Trust)
Interchange Studios, Dalby Street,
London NW5 3NQ
A useful organisation which provides members with the fruits of its extensive knowledge of the industry through publications, forums and databases.

The Spotlight
7 Leicester Place, London WC2H 7BP
tel 020-7437 7631
Publishes a book, *Contacts*, which contains all the addresses for professional organisations and theatre companies listed in the article. The 2000-01 edition is available from October.

However, in the majority of cases there will be no one person whose main function is to deal with writers and their plays. Therefore, you will need to be particularly rigorous in finding out the theatre's policy (remember that due to the pressure of work, dealing with writers may not be the highest of priorities).

Some companies may only accept submission of scripts through agents or with some sort of recommendation. Others may want a brief description of the play so they can decide whether it is worth their time looking at it. They may want this either sent by post, or they may prefer a brief telephone conversation.

What to expect

Since working practices vary from organisation to organisation, the response you can expect and how long before you get it will also vary. After submitting your script, do not expect any response for two to three months. If you have heard nothing from the company after six months, make a gentle inquiry. Obviously, badgering the company for a response is unlikely to work to your advantage.

The company is likely to give one or more of the following responses:

- a straightforward rejection of the play;
- an explanation for the rejection of the play;
- the offer of a 'getting to know you' meeting;
- a more formal dramaturgical meeting to discuss possible textual changes or clarifications;
- a reading or workshop on the play;
- advice on where else to send the play;
- an offer of a more formal recommendation for the play to colleagues working elsewhere;
- an offer of a production.

Agents

When you enter into any kind of contractual relationship with a theatre company you should find an agent. An agent can help you on all the legal aspects of selling a play and ensure that your rights are protected. He or she will also help to promote you and your work and in guiding your career. As the relationship between you and your agent is crucial to your long-term development as a writer, meet as many agents as possible to seek out someone with whom you feel at ease and have an affinity. See *Literary agents for television, film, radio and theatre* on page 383.

New writing support agencies

Aside from theatre companies and practitioners, there is a burgeoning industry of organisations which exist to help writers develop their craft, their contacts and their appreciation of the industry. One cross-over organisation is the National Theatre Studio, which is part of the Royal National Theatre but exists more as a service to theatre artists and the industry at large rather than directly for the scheduling of the company's three theatres. The national organisation Writernet exists as an information and research organisation.

Attached and supported by most of the Regional Arts Boards are regional forums, such as Stage Coach for the Midlands and North West Playwrights for that region. It is worth making contact with these organisations, especially if you are based outside one of the metropolitan areas as they can act on your behalf. Some are very good at the national promotion of the work of their local writers, while others are more active in putting writers and directors in contact with each other. Contact your local Regional Arts Board (see page 492) or repertory theatre for more information.

Bursaries and prizes

There are various schemes run by theatre companies, arts boards, television companies and independent organisations to financially assist writers. These fall into two categories: bursaries and prizes. Bursaries relate to the writer rather than their work, and can sometimes include an attachment to a theatre or arts organisation. Some writers can apply for themselves (e.g. The Arts Council's Writers Bursaries), while for other awards a theatre company applies on the writer's behalf. Prizes usually (though not always) relate to the judging of a play. Because the prize for such a scheme may be either a production or sufficient money to encourage one to happen, it is worth familiarising yourself with the various schemes and their deadlines. This is best done either through membership of Writernet or by being in contact with the regional forums, mentioned above. Also, watch out for announcements in the Press, especially the *Observer*, the *Author*, *Amateur Stage* and the *Stage*. A list of magazines dealing with the theatre is on page 131; see also *Prizes and awards* on page 512.

Ben Jancovich is Literary Manager of Hampstead Theatre. Previously Literary Assistant at the Royal Shakespeare Company, he has directed plays in the London fringe and has worked as a freelance theatre critic with *City Limits*.

Theatre producers

This list is divided into London theatres (below), provincial theatres (page 339) and touring companies (page 344). See also Marketing a stage play on page 333.

London

Bush Theatre

Shepherd's Bush Green, London W12 8QD
tel 020-7602 3703 *fax* 020-7602 7614
e-mail thebush@dircon.co.uk
Literary Manager Tim Fountain

Welcomes unsolicited full-length stage scripts (plus one small and one large sae). Commissions writers, including those at an early stage in their career. Produces 9 premieres a year.

Michael Codron Plays Ltd

Aldwych Theatre Offices, Aldwych, London WC2B 4DF
tel 020-7240 8291 *fax* 020-7240 8467

Hampstead Theatre

Swiss Cottage Centre, Avenue Road, London NW3 3EX
tel 020-7722 9224 *fax* 020-7722 3860
Contact Ben Jancovich

New plays and the occasional modern classic. After initial assessment, promising scripts are then read by the literary manager and/or artistic director. It can therefore take 2-3 months to reach a decision.

Bill Kenwright Ltd

BKL House, 106 Harrow Road,
London W2 1RR
tel 020-7446 6200 *fax* 020-7446 6222
e-mail info@kenwright.com
Managing Director Bill Kenwright, *General Manager* John Dalston

Commercial producing management presenting revivals and new works for the West End and for touring theatres.

King's Head Theatre

115 Upper Street, London N1 1QN
tel 020-7226 8561 *fax* 020-7226 8507
Contact The Administrator

Pub theatre producing revivals and some new works. No unsolicited submissions.

Lyric Theatre Hammersmith

King Street, London W6 0QL
tel 020-8741 0824 *fax* 020-8741 5965
e-mail enquiries@lyric.co.uk
web site http://www.lyric.co.uk
Directors Sue Storr, Simon Mellor

A producing theatre as well as a receiving venue for work by new writers, translators, performers and composers. Unsolicited scripts for in-house productions not accepted.

Man in the Moon Theatre

392 King's Road, London SW3 5UZ
tel 020-7351 5701 *fax* 020-7351 1873
Programming Director Nick Elsen

65-seat theatre. Part of each season is reserved for new writing which links with the season theme. Phone theatre for details. Plays scheduled in seasons of 3-4 months for in-house productions.

Moral Support

Tabard Theatre, 2 Bath Road,
London W4 1LW
tel 020-8994 5985 *fax* 020-8747 8256
web site http://www.moralsupport.org.uk
Contact Zoe Klinger

The company brings together writers, musicians and other freelance practitioners to create new work with the emphasis on producing new writing and performance styles, to be performed in a variety of locations. Its performance technique has been described as 'an utterly original theatrical language'. Available for commissions of new plays, performance and dance. Founded 1993.

The Old Red Lion Theatre

418 St John Street, London EC1V 4NJ
tel 020-7833 3053 *fax* 020-7833 3053
Artistic Director Ken McClymont

Interested in contemporary pieces, especially from unproduced writers. No funding: incoming production company pays to rent the theatre. Sae essential with enquiries. Founded 1977.

Orange Tree Theatre

1 Clarence Street, Richmond, Surrey TW9 2SA
tel 020-8940 0141 *fax* 020-8332 0369

Producing venue. The theatre does not currently have a literary manager and no longer has a studio theatre. New works presented generally come from agents or through writers' groups.

Polka Theatre for Children

240 The Broadway, London SW19 1SB
tel 020-8542 4258 *fax* 020-8542 7723
e-mail polkatheatre@dial.pipex.com
web site http://www.polkatheatre.com
Artistic Director Vicky Ireland

Exclusively for children, the Main Theatre seats 300 and The Adventure Theatre seats 80. Programmed for 18 months to 2 years in advance. Theatre of new writing, with targeted commissions. Founded 1967.

The Questors Theatre

Mattock Lane, London W5 5BQ
tel 020-8567 0011 *fax* 020-8567 8736
e-mail alice@questors.org.uk
web site http://www.questors.org.uk
Theatre Manager Paul Maurel

Considers unsolicited scripts if sent with sae.

Really Useful Theatres

Manor House, 21 Soho Square,
London W1V 5FD
tel 020-7494 5200 *fax* 020-7434 1217
e-mail info@stoll-moss.com
web site http://www.stoll.moss.com
Production Director Nica Burns

Owns 13 West End theatres: Adelphi, Apollo, Cambridge, Duchess, Garrick, Gielgud, Her Majesty's, London Palladium, Lyric Shaftesbury Avenue, New London, Palace, Queens and Theatre Royal Drury Lane. Now commissions new plays from both established writers and new talent. Founded 1978.

Royal Court Theatre

(English Stage Company Ltd)
Sloane Square, London SW1W 8AS

tel 020-7565 5050 *fax* 020-7565 5002
Literary Manager Graham Whybrow
New plays.

Royal National Theatre

South Bank, London SE1 9PX
tel 020-7452 3323 *fax* 020-7452 3350
Literary Manager Jack Bradley
Limited opportunity for the production of unsolicited material, but submissions welcome. No synopses or treatments. Send to Jack Bradley, Literary Manager, together with an sae with postage covering the return of the script.

Royal Shakespeare Company

Barbican Theatre, Barbican, London EC2Y 8BQ
tel 020-7628 3351 *fax* 020-7382 2320
Artistic Director Adrian Noble, *Literary Manager* Simon Reade, *Literary Assistant* Esther Richardson
The RSC is a classical theatre company with a repertory ensemble, based in Stratford-upon-Avon, bringing its repertoire to the Barbican Theatre for 6 months of the year, and with residencies in Newcastle and Plymouth. It also tours both nationally and internationally.

As well as Shakespeare, English classics and foreign classics in translation, ambitious new plays counterpoint the RSC's repertory, especially those which celebrate language. The Literary Department is proactive rather than reactive, and seeks out the plays and playwrights it wishes to commission. It will read translations of classic foreign works submitted, or of contemporary works where the original writer and/or translator is known. It is unable to read unsolicited works from less established writers, and can only return scripts if an sae is enclosed with the submission.

Soho Theatre Company

21 Dean Street, London W1V 6NE
tel 020-7287 5060 *fax* 020-7287 5061
e-mail writer@sohotheatre.com
web site http://www.sohotheatre.com
Artistic Director Abigail Morris, *Literary Manager* Paul Sirett
Always on the look out for new plays and playwrights and welcome unsolicited scripts. These are read by a professional panel who write a detailed critical report. Also offer various levels of workshop facilities, including rehearsed reading and platform performances, for promising playwrights, and in-depth script development with the Artistic Director and Literary Manager. See also the Verity Bargate Award on page 515.

The Steam Industry

Finborough Theatre, 118 Finborough Road, London SW10 9ED
tel 020-7244 7439 *fax* 020-7835 1853
Contact Gill Foreman
Produces 1-2 seasons each year featuring new plays alongside well-known classics. Writers whose work is produced have developed a relationship with the company over a period of time. Does not accept unsolicited scripts and only occasionally attends rehearsed readings. Writers who submit a brief CV and a synopsis (max. 2 pages) may be invited to one of the company's new writers workshops. Founded 1994.

Tabard Theatre

2 Bath Road, London W4 1LW
tel 020-8995 6035
Artistic Directors Hamish Gray, Ben Brown
Aims to promote new work of contemporary relevance with particular emphasis on new writing and experimental performance styles. It hosts workshops, readings, evening performances, and has its own in-house theatre company.

Theatre Royal, Stratford East

Gerry Raffles Square, London E15 1BN
tel 020-8534 7374 *fax* 020-8534 8381
Artistic Director Philip Hedley
Associate Director Mr Kerry Michael
Middle-scale producing theatre. Specialises in new writing: currently developing contemporary British musicals. Welcomes new plays that are unproduced, full in length, and which relate to its diverse multicultural, Black and Asian audience.

The Tricycle Theatre Company

Tricycle Theatre, 269 Kilburn High Road, London NW6 7JR
tel 020-7372 6611 *fax* 020-7328 0795
Contact Nicolas Kent
Metropolitan new writing theatre company. Script-reading service but fee charged for unsolicited scripts.

Triumph Proscenium Productions Ltd

Suite 4, Waldorf Chambers, 11 Aldwych, London WC2B 4DA

tel 020-7343 8800 *fax* 020-7343 8801
e-mail dcwtpp@aol.com

Unicorn Theatre for Children

St Mark's Studios, Chillingworth Road, London N7 8QJ
tel 020-7700 0702 *fax* 020-7700 3870
Administrative Director Christopher Moxon, *Artistic Director* Tony Graham, *Associate Director* Emily Gray

Six productions a year for children aged 4-12 and their families – new writing and adaptations.

Warehouse Theatre

Dingwall Road, Croydon CR0 2NF
tel 020-8681 1257 *fax* 020-8688 6699
e-mail warehous@dircon.co.uk
web site http://www.warehousetheatre.co.uk
Artistic Director Ted Craig

South London's new writing theatre. Seats 100-120. Produces 3-5 in-house plays a year and co-produces with companies which share the commitment to new work. It continues to build upon a tradition of discovering and nurturing new writers, with activities including a monthly writers' workshop and the annual International Playwriting Festival (see page 524). Unsolicited scripts are welcome but it is more advisable to submit plays via the Playwriting Festival. Also hosts youth theatre workshops and Saturday morning children's theatre.

Michael White

48 Dean Street, London W1V 5HL
tel 020-7734 7707 *fax* 020-7734 7727
Contact Mac MacKenzie

Provincial

Abbey Theatre

Lower Abbey Street, Dublin 1, Republic of Ireland
tel (01) 8872200 *fax* (01) 8729177
Artistic Director Ben Barnes, *General Manager* Martin Fahy, *Managing Director* Richard Wakeley

Mainly produces plays written by Irish authors or on Irish subjects. Foreign classics are however regularly produced.

Actual Theatre

25 Hamilton Drive, Glasgow G12 8DN
tel/fax 0141-339 0654
Artistic Director Susan C. Triesman

Produces 'difficult and taboo subjects' and experimental theatre. Welcomes scripts from new writers. Founded 1980.

Yvonne Arnaud Theatre Management Ltd

Millbrook, Guildford, Surrey GU1 3UX
tel (01483) 440077 *fax* (01483) 564071
e-mail yat@yvonne-arnaud.co.uk
web site http://www.yvonne-arnaud.co.uk
Contact James Barber

Receives and produces Number One touring and pre-West End product.

The Belgrade Theatre

Belgrade Square, Coventry CV1 1GS
tel 024-7625 6431 *fax* 024-7655 0680
e-mail admin@belgrade.co.uk
web site http://www.belgrade.co.uk
Contact Denise Atcheson

Produces new plays developed in conjunction with Theatre Absolute, through the Writing House.

Birmingham Repertory Theatre Ltd

Broad Street, Birmingham B1 2EP
tel 0121-236 6661 *fax* 0121-236 6177
e-mail info@birmingham-rep.co.uk
web site http://www.birmingham-rep.co.uk
Artistic Director Bill Alexander, *Artistic Director* Tony Clark, *Literary Manager* Ben Payne

Aims to provide a platform for the best work from new writers from both within and beyond the West Midlands region. The development, commissioning and production of new writing takes place across the full range of the theatre's programme including: the Main House (capacity 830); the Door (capacity 190 max.), a space dedicated to new work; and its biannual Community tours. Unsolicited submissions are welcome principally from the point of view of beginning a relationship with a writer. Priority in such development work is given to writers from the region.

Bristol Old Vic

Theatre Royal, King Street, Bristol BS1 4ED
tel 0117-949 3993 *fax* 0117-949 3996
web site http://www.bristol-old-vic.co.uk
Artistic Director Andy Hay, *General Manager* Sarah Smith

Programme includes classical and new plays. Committed to commissioning and producing new writing in the Theatre Royal (650 seats) and New Vic Studio (150 seats). Plays must have enough popular appeal to attract an audience of significant size. Will read and report on unsolicited scripts for a fee of £25 per script.

Also seeks emerging talent to the Basement, a profit share venue (50 seats) committed to producing one-act plays by unproven writers. Will read plays free of charge but no report can be provided. New Vic Studio often receives productions of new plays from visiting companies.

The Byre Theatre of St Andrews Ltd

Abbey Street, St Andrews KY16 9LA
tel (01334) 476288 *fax* (01334) 475370
Artistic Director Ken Alexander

Currently involved in a major rebuilding programme. On reopening (scheduled for late autumn 2000), the theatre will operate a blend of in-house productions and touring productions. The Byre Theatre Company meanwhile maintains a policy of producing a wide variety of new and established work, theatre-in-education projects, youth theatre and community work in Fife. The company also offers support for new writing through the Byre Writers, a well-established and successful playwrights group.

Chester Gateway Theatre Trust Ltd

Hamilton Place, Chester CH1 2BH
tel (01244) 344238 *fax* (01244) 317277
web site http://www.gateway-theatre.org
Artistic Director Deborah Shaw, *Administrative Director* Shea Connolly

Regional producing theatre presenting a wide range of plays, from classics to new writing and re-discoveries.

Chichester Festival Theatre Productions Company Ltd

Chichester Festival Theatre, Oaklands Park, Chichester, West Sussex PO19 4AP
tel (01243) 784437 *fax* (01243) 787288
e-mail admin@cft.org.uk
web site http://www.cft.org.uk
Theatre Director Andrew Welch

Festival Season May-Oct in Festival and Minerva Theatres; rest of year seasons of touring plays, opera, ballet, dance, jazz, orchestral concerts and Minerva Movies.

Clwyd Theatr Cymru

Mold, Flintshire CH7 1YA
tel (01352) 756331 *fax* (01352) 758323
e-mail drama@celtic.co.uk
web site http://www.clwyd-theatr-cymru.co.uk
Director Terry Hands, *Literary Manager* William James

Produces a season of plays each year performed in repertoire by a resident company, along with tours throughout Wales (in English and Welsh). Plays are a mix of classics, revivals, contemporary drama and new writing. Considers plays by Welsh writers or with Welsh themes.

Colchester Mercury Theatre Ltd

Balkerne Gate, Colchester, Essex CO1 1PT
tel (01206) 577006 *fax* (01206) 769607
e-mail mercury.theatre@virgin.net
Contact (Playwrights' Group) Adrian Stokes

Regional repertory theatre presenting works to a wide audience. Produces some new work, mainly commissioned. Runs local Playwrights' Group for adults with a serious commitment to writing plays.

The Coliseum Theatre

Fairbottom Street, Oldham OL1 3SW
tel 0161-624 1731 *fax* 0161-624 5318
Chief Executive Kenneth Alan Taylor

Special interest in northern plays. Contact by letter initially.

Contact Theatre Company

Oxford Road, Manchester M15 6JA
tel 0161-274 3434 *fax* 0161-274 0640
Artistic Director John E. McGrath

Interested in working with and for young people aged 13-30. Send sae for writers' guidelines.

Derby Playhouse Ltd

Theatre Walk, Eagle Centre, Derby DE1 2NF
tel (01332) 363271 *fax* (01332) 294412
e-mail admin@derbyplayhouse.demon.co.uk
web site http://www.derbyplayhouse.demon.co.uk
Artistic Director Mark Clements

Regional repertory company. Unsolicited scripts: send a letter with synopsis, a resumé of your writing experience and any 10 pages of your script. A review of this material will determine whether a complete copy of the script is required.

Druid Theatre Company

Druid Lane Theatre, Chapel Lane, Galway, Republic of Ireland
tel (091) 568617/568660 *fax* (091) 563109
e-mail druidth@indigo.ie
Managing Director Ciarán Walsh, *Artistic Director* Garry Hynes

Producing company presenting a wide range of national and international plays. Emphasis on new Irish writing.

The Dukes Playhouse

Moor Lane, Lancaster LA1 1QE
tel (01524) 67461 *fax* (01524) 846817
Artistic Director Ian Hastings

Dundee Repertory Theatre

Tay Square, Dundee DD1 1PB
tel (01382) 227684
Artistic Director Hamish Glen

Regional repertory theatre company. Its policy is to concentrate resources on commissions for contemporary Scottish writers.

Everyman Theatre

Regent Street, Cheltenham, Glos. GL50 1HQ
tel (01242) 512515 *fax* (01242) 224305
e-mail admin@everymantheatre.org.uk
web site http://www.everymantheatre.org.uk
Chief Executive Philip Bernays, *Artistic Director* Sue Colverd

Regional presenting theatre promoting a wide range of plays. Small-scale experimental, youth and educational work encouraged in The Other Place studio theatre. Contact the Artistic Director before submitting material.

Everyman and Playhouse Theatres

Liverpool and Merseyside Theatres Trust Ltd, 13 Hope Street, Liverpool L1 9BH
tel 0151-708 0338 *fax* 0151-709 0398
e-mail info@everyman.org.uk
web site http://everyman.merseyworld.com/
Executive Director Jo Beddoe, *Administrative Director* Chris Ricketts

Produces and presents theatre.

Focus Theatre Company (Scotland)

c/o The Ramshorn Theatre, 98 Ingram Street, Glasgow G1 1ES
tel 0141-552 3489 *fax* 0141-553 2036
e-mail ramshorn.theatre@strath.ac.uk
Artistic Director Susan C. Triesman

Produces women's plays and feminist work. Also holds workshops. Welcomes scripts from new writers. Founded 1982.

Grand Theatre

Singleton Street, Swansea SA1 3QJ
tel (01792) 475242 *fax* (01792) 475379
e-mail swansea.grand.theatre@business.ntl.com
web site http://www.swansea.gov.uk/grandtheatre
General Manager Gary Iles

Regional receiving theatre.

Haymarket Theatre Company

The Haymarket Theatre, Wote Street, Basingstoke, Hants RG21 7NW
tel (01256) 323073 *fax* (01256) 357130
e-mail info@haymarket.org.uk
web site http://www.haymarket.org.uk

Produces up to 8 shows a year plus up to 4 visiting shows. Interested in co-production with other theatres or producers.

Leicester Haymarket Theatre

Belgrave Gate, Leicester LE1 3YQ
tel 0116-253 0021 *fax* 0116-251 3310
e-mail enquiry@haymarkettheatre.demon.co.uk
web site http://www.leicester-haymarket-theatre.co.uk

Regional repertory theatre company.

Library Theatre Company

St Peter's Square, Manchester M2 5PD
tel 0161-234 1913 *fax* 0161-228 6481
Contact Artistic Director

Contemporary drama, classics, plays for children. Aims to produce drama which illuminates the contemporary world; scripts from new writers considered.

LLt/productionline

Unity Theatre, 1 Hope Place, Liverpool L1 9BG
tel 0151-709 4332 *fax* 0151-709 7182
e-mail lltpro@dircon.co.uk
Contact Paul Goetzee

Regional new writing development company. As part of a 3-year project, promising scripts will be developed to production standard for presentation in the Liverpool theatres, and links created with other media and with other new writing theatres and organisations. Stages one full production, 20 readings, and 9 3-day workshops a year. Send sae for return of script. Founded 1983.

New Vic Theatre

Etruria Road, Newcastle under Lyme ST5 0JG
tel (01782) 717954 *fax* (01782) 712885
e-mail VicTheatre@aol.com
Artistic Director Gwenda Hughes, *General Manager* Ludo Keston

Europe's first purpose built theatre in the round, presenting classics, adaptations, contemporary plays, new plays.

Northcott Theatre

Stocker Road, Exeter, Devon EX4 4QB
tel (01392) 223999
Artistic Director Ben Crocker

Regional producing theatre company.

Northern Stage (Theatrical Productions) Ltd

Newcastle Playhouse, Barras Bridge, Newcastle upon Tyne NE1 1RH
tel 0191-232 3366 *fax* 0191-261 8093
e-mail info@northernstage.com
Artistic Director Alan Lyddiard

Major company producing and presenting international work.

Nottingham Playhouse

Nottingham Theatre Trust Ltd, Wellington Circus, Nottingham NG1 5AF
tel 0115-947 4361 *fax* 0115-947 5759
e-mail sales@nottinghamplayhouse.co.uk/playhouse
web site http://www.nottinghamplayhouse.co.uk/playhouse
Executive Director Venu Dhupa, *Artistic Director* Giles Croft

Works closely with communities of Nottingham and Nottinghamshire. Takes 6 months to read unsolicited MSS.

Nuffield Theatre

University Road, Southampton SO17 1TR
tel 023-8031 5500 *fax* 023-8031 5511
Script Executive tba

Repertory theatre producing straight plays and musicals, and some small-scale fringe work. Interested in new plays.

Octagon Theatre

Howell Croft South, Bolton BL1 1SB
tel (01204) 529407 *fax* (01204) 380110
Executive Director Simon Stallworthy, *Administrator* Christine Cunningham

Fully flexible professional theatre. Year round programme of own productions and visiting companies. No script advisory service.

The Palace Theatre Watford Ltd

Clarendon Road, Watford, Herts. WD1 1JZ
tel (01923) 235455 *fax* (01923) 819664
Contact Lawrence Till

Regional repertory theatre. Produces 8 plays each year, both classic and contemporary drama. Welcomes synopses of new plays before submitting scripts.

Peacock Theatre

The Abbey Theatre, Lower Abbey Street, Dublin 1, Republic of Ireland
tel (01) 8872200 *fax* (01) 8729177
Artistic Director Ben Barnes, *General Manager* Martin Fahy, *Managing Director* Richard Wakeley

Experimental theatre associated with the Abbey Theatre; mostly new writing.

Perth Theatre Ltd

185 High Street, Perth PH1 5UW
tel (01738) 472700 *fax* (01738) 624576
e-mail theatre@perth.org.uk
web site http://www.perth.org.uk/perth/theatre.htm
Artistic Director Michael Winter, *General Manager* Paul Hackett

Combination of 3- and 4-weekly repertoire of plays and musicals, incoming tours, studio productions and local out-touring.

Plymouth Theatre Royal

Theatre Royal, Royal Parade, Plymouth PL1 2TR
tel (01752) 668282 *fax* (01752) 671179
Chief Executive Adrian Vinken, *Artistic Director* Simon Stokes

Major regional theatre company which encourages new writing. All scripts are read and considered for production.

Queen's Theatre Hornchurch

(Havering Theatre Trust Ltd)
Billet Lane, Hornchurch, Essex RM11 1QT
tel (01708) 456118 *fax* (01708) 452348
e-mail info@queens-theatre.co.uk
Artistic Director Bob Carlton

500-seat producing theatre serving outer East London with permanent company of actors/musicians producing popular comedy, drama and musicals. Scripts from new writers welcome, especially as co-productions with commercial producer or additional funding.

The Ramshorn Theatre/Strathclyde Theatre Group

98 Ingram Street, Glasgow G1 1ES
tel 0141-552 3489 *fax* 0141-553 2036
e-mail ramshorn.theatre@strath.ac.uk
Contact Susan C. Triesman (Director of Drama, University of Strathclyde)

Develops new writing (including experimental) through Ramshorn New Playwrights Initiative. Founded 1992.

Royal Exchange Theatre Company Ltd

St Ann's Square, Manchester M2 7DH
tel 0161-833 9333 *fax* 0161-832 0881
web site http://www.royalexchange.co.uk
Executive Director Patricia Weller

Varied programme of major classics, new plays, musicals, contemporary British and European drama; also explores the creative work of diverse cultures.

Royal Lyceum Theatre Company

Royal Lyceum Theatre, Grindlay Street, Edinburgh EH3 9AX
tel 0131-248 4848 *fax* 0131-228 3955
e-mail royallyceumtheatre@cableinet.co.uk
web sites http://www.infoser.com/infotheatre/lyceum *and* http://www.infoser.com/infotheatre/vtour
Artistic Director Kenny Ireland, *Associate Literary Director* Tom McGrath

Edinburgh's busiest repertory company, producing an all-year-round programme of classic, contemporary and new drama. Interested in work of Scottish writers.

Salisbury Playhouse

Malthouse Lane, Salisbury, Wilts. SP2 7RA
tel (01722) 320117 *fax* (01722) 421991
e-mail directors@salisburyplayhouse.com
Artistic Director Joanna Read

Regional repertory theatre producing a broad programme of classical and modern plays.

Scarborough Theatre Trust Ltd

Stephen Joseph Theatre, Westborough, Scarborough, North Yorkshire YO11 1JW
tel (01723) 370540 *fax* (01723) 360506
e-mail response@sjt.onyxnet.co.uk
web site http://www.webart.co.uk/clients/sjt/
Literary Manager Laura Harvey

Regional repertory theatre company which produces about 10 plays a year, around half of which are premieres. The theatre has an excellent reputation for comedy. Plays should have a strong narrative and a desire to entertain, though nothing too lightweight will be considered. Please enclose a sae with all submissions.

Sheffield Theatres

(Crucible, Crucible Studio & Lyceum), 55 Norfolk Street, Sheffield S1 1DA
tel 0114-249 5999 *fax* 0114-249 6003
Chief Executive Grahame Morris

Large-scale producing house with distinctive thrust stage; smallish studio; Victorian proscenium arch theatre used mainly for touring productions.

Sherman Theatre

Senghennydd Road, Cardiff CF24 4YE
tel 029-2064 6901 *fax* 029-2064 6902
General Manager Margaret Jones

Plays mainly for 15-25 age range. Founded 1974.

Show of Strength Theatre Company Ltd

Hebron House, Sion Road, Bedminster, Bristol BS3 3BD
tel 0117-902 1356
Artistic Director Sheila Hannon

Small-scale company committed to producing new and unperformed work. Theatre season: Oct-Jan. Send sae for return of MSS. Founded 1986.

Sionnach Theatre Company

The New Theatre, Temple Bar, 43 East Essex Street, Dublin 2, Republic of Ireland
tel (1) 6703361 *fax* (1) 6711943
e-mail sionnach@indigo.ie
Artistic Director Anthony Fox

Innovative theatre producing plays by Irish writers whose work deals with issues pertaining to young people in contemporary Irish society. Welcomes scripts from new writers. Founded 1997.

Swan Theatre

The Moors, Worcester WR1 3EF
tel (01905) 726969 *fax* (01905) 723738
Artistic Director Jenny Stephens

A building-based producing theatre company with a mixed programme, including some new plays. A writing group meets at the theatre. Unsolicited scripts are discouraged.

Theatre Royal

Windsor, Berks. SL4 1PS
tel (01753) 863444 *fax* (01753) 831673
Executive Producer Bill Kenwright, *Executive Director* Mark Piper

Regional producing theatre presenting a wide range of productions from classics to new plays.

Traverse Theatre

10 Cambridge Street, Edinburgh EH1 2ED
tel 0131-228 3223 *fax* 0131-229 8443
Literary Director John Tiffany, *Literary Assistant* Hannah Rye, *Literary Associate (international scripts)* Katherine Mendelsohn
e-mail john@traverse.co.uk, hannah@traverse.co.uk, katherine@traverse.co.uk
web site http://www.traverse.co.uk

As Scotland's new writing theatre, the Traverse will read unsolicited scripts, but prefers a phone call, letter or e-mail in the first instance. Please include a sae for return of script.

The West Yorkshire Playhouse

Playhouse Square, Quarry Hill, Leeds LS2 7UP
tel 0113-213 7800 *fax* 0113-213 7250
e-mail mail@wyp.org.uk
Artistic Director Jude Kelly

Twin auditoria complex – with a policy of encouraging new writing; community theatre.

The Wolsey Theatre

Civic Drive, Ipswich, Suffolk IP1 2AS
tel (01473) 218911 *fax* (01473) 212946
Administrative Director Lorna Anderson, *Artistic Director* Andrew Manley

Producing theatre plus occasional touring/community weeks. Youth theatre and writers' workshop. New writing and coproductions always condsidered.

York Citizens' Theatre Trust Ltd

Theatre Royal, St Leonard's Place,
York YO1 7HD
tel (01904) 658162 *fax* (01904) 611534
Executive Director Elizabeth Jones, *Artistic Director* Damian Cruden

Repertory productions, tours.

Touring companies

Actors Touring Company

Alford House, Aveline Street, London SE11 5DQ
tel 020-7735 8311 *fax* 020-7735 1031
e-mail atc@cwcom.net
Executive Producer Gavin Barlow

Small to medium-scale company producing new theatre from old stories, myths and legends.

Compass Theatre Company

Carver Street Institute, 24 Rockingham Lane,
Sheffield S1 4FW
tel 0114-275 5328 *fax* 0114-278 6931
Artistic Director Neil Sissons, *General Manager* Craig Dronfield

Touring classical theatre nationwide. Does not produce new plays.

Graeae Theatre Company

Interchange Studios, Dalby Street,
London NW5 3NQ
tel 020-7267 1959 *fax* 020-7267 2703
Contact Jenny Sealey

Small-scale company. Welcomes scripts from disabled writers. Founded 1980.

The Hiss & Boo Company

1 Nyes Hill, Wineham Lane, Bolney,
West Sussex RH17 5SD
tel (01444) 881707 *fax* (01444) 882057
e-mail ian@hissboo.co.uk

Not much scope for new plays, but will consider comedy thrillers/chillers and plays/musicals for children. Send synopsis first. Plays/synopses will be returned only if accompanied by an sae.

Hull Truck Theatre Co. Ltd

Hull Truck Theatre, Spring Street,
Hull HU2 8RW
tel (01482) 224800 *fax* (01482) 581182
e-mail admin@hulltruck.co.uk
web site http://www.hulltruck.co.uk
General Manager Joanne Gower

World-renowned small-cast touring company presenting popular and accessible theatre. Produces some new work, mainly commissioned.

The London Bubble

(Bubble Theatre Company)
3-5 Elephant Lane, London SE16 4JD
tel 020-7237 4434 *fax* 020-7231 2366
e-mail londonbubble@gn.apc.org

M6 Theatre Company

Hamer C.P. School, Albert Royds Street,
Rochdale, Lancs. OL16 2SU
tel (01706) 355898 *fax* (01706) 711700
e-mail info@m6theatre.freeserve.co.uk
Contact Jane Milne

Theatre-in-education company providing high quality theatre for children, young people and community audiences.

Made in Wales

Chapter, Market Road, Canton, Cardiff CF5 1QE
tel 029-2034 4737 *fax* 029-2034 4738
e-mail madein.wales@virgin.net
Artistic Director Jeff Teare

Three productions per year of new plays relevant to Wales; scripts from new writers always welcome.

New Perspectives Theatre Company

The Old Library, Leeming Street, Mansfield,
Notts. NG18 1NG
tel (01623) 635225 *fax* (01623) 635240
e-mail newperspectives@cwcom.net
Artistic Director Gavin Stride

Has a policy of employing writers for new work. Regret unsolicited scripts returned, unless writers are local to the East Midlands region.

New Victoria Theatre

The Peacocks, Woking, Surrey GU21 1GQ
tel (01483) 747422 *fax* (01483) 740477
Contact Robert Cogo-Fawcett, Beaufort Cottage,
Grosvenor, Bath BA1 6PZ
tel (01225) 311248 *fax* (01225) 317207

Large-scale touring house. Interested to co-produce or produce.

Nitro

(formerly Black Theatre Co-operative Ltd)
6 Brewery Road, London N7 9NH
tel 020-7609 1331 *fax* 020-7609 1221
e-mail black.theatreco-op@virgin.net
web site http://www.nitro.co.uk
Artistic Director Felix Cross, *General Manager* Olivia Jacobs

Interested in Black plays, especially those that relate to the experiences of Black people both in Britain and outside Britain.

NTC Touring Theatre Company

(formerly Northumberland Theatre Company)
The Playhouse, Bondgate Without, Alnwick,
Northumberland NE66 1PQ

tel (01665) 602586 *fax* (01665) 605837
e-mail info@ntc.connectfree.co.uk
Artistic Director Gillian Hambleton

Performs a wide cross-section of work: new plays, extant scripts, classic and modern. Particularly interested in non-naturalism, physical theatre and plays with direct relevance to rural audiences.

Oxford Stage Company

131 High Street, Oxford OX1 4DH
tel (01865) 723238 *fax* (01865) 790625
e-mail info@oxfordstage.co.uk
web site http://www.oxfordstage.co.uk
Contact Executive Producer

A middle-scale touring company presenting 4 productions per year: Shakespeare, modern classics, and new work. Founded 1989.

Paines Plough

4th Floor, 43 Aldwych, London WC2B 4DA
tel 020-7240 4533 *fax* 020-7240 4534
e-mail paines.plough@dial.pipex.com
Artistic Director Vicky Featherstone, *Literary Manager* Jessica Dromgoole

Tours new plays by British writers to a national audience and is increasingly developing an international profile. The company believes that the playwright's voice should be at the centre of contemporary theatre and works with new and experienced writers. A programme of workshops and readings develops new work and approx. 4 playwrights a year are commissioned by the company. A new programme seeks to develop the company's relationship with writers outside London. For script-reading service send 2 saes, one for acknowledgement, and one for return of script with reader's report.

Proteus Theatre Company

Fairfields Arts Centre, Council Road, Basingstoke, Hants RG21 3DH
tel (01256) 354541 *fax* (01256) 356186
e-mail proteus@dircon.co.uk
Artistic Director Mark Helyar, *Associate Director* Deborah Wilding, *General Manager* Jason Knight

Small-scale touring company particularly committed to new writing and new work, education and community collaborations. Produces 3 touring shows per year plus several urban and rural community projects. Founded 1981.

Quicksilver National Touring Theatre

4 Enfield Road, London N1 5AZ
tel 020-7241 2942 *fax* 020-7254 3119
e-mail qsilver@easynet.co.uk
web site http://www.quicksilvertheatre.org
Artistic Director Guy Holland

A professional touring theatre company which brings live theatre to theatres and schools all over the country. Delivers good stories, original music, kaleidoscopic design and humorous, poignant writing to entertain and make children and adults think. Three new plays a year for 3-5 year-olds, 7-11 year-olds and 6+ years and families. Founded 1977.

Red Ladder Theatre Company

3 St Peters Buildings, York Street, Leeds LS9 8AJ
tel 0113-245 5311 *fax* 0113-245 5351
e-mail red-ladder@geo2.poptel.org.uk
Artistic Director Wendy Harris

Theatre performances for young people (14-25) in youth clubs and small-scale theatre venues. Commissions at least two new plays each year. Training/residentials for youth workers/young people.

Red Shift Theatre Company

TRG2 Trowbray House, 108 Weston Street, London SE1 3QB
tel 020-7378 9787 *fax* 020-7378 9789
e-mail rstc@dircon.co.uk
web site http://www.rstc.dircon.co.uk
Artistic Director Jonathan Holloway

Productions include adaptations, classics, new plays. No commissions planned before 2002.

Shared Experience Theatre

The Soho Laundry, 9 Dufours Place, London W1V 1FE
tel 020-7434 9248 *fax* 020-7287 8763
e-mail admin@setheatre.co.uk
Joint Artistic Directors Nancy Meckler, Polly Teale

Middle-scale touring company presenting 2 productions per year: adaptations or translations of classic texts, and some new writing. Tours nationally and interntionally. Founded 1975.

Snap People's Theatre Trust

45-47 South Street, Bishop's Stortford, Herts. CM23 3AG
tel (01279) 461607 *fax* (01279) 506694
Contact A. Graham

Produces classic adaptations, children's theatre and new writing. Welcomes scripts from new writers. Founded 1979.

Solent Peoples Theatre

The Heathfield Centre, Valentine Avenue, Sholing, Southampton SO19 0EQ
tel 023-8044 3943 *fax* 023-8044 0752
minicom 023-8043 4177
Administrative Director Caroline Routh

Produces 3 plays a year, one of which is always a family show and another is generally a new commission. All productions endeavour to be relevant to the communities in which the theatre works. Currently looking to develop cross art form work – in particular video and computer imaging – and also to create work which can tour to non-typical performance spaces. Welcomes plays from new writers.

Also runs a year-round programme of participatory work targeting marginalised groups such as the homeless, the disabled and mental health service users.

The Sphinx Theatre Co. Ltd

25 Short Street, London SE1 8LJ
tel 020-7401 9993/4 *fax* 020-7401 9995
Artistic Director Sue Parrish

Women writers only.

Stage One Theatre Company

34 Jasmine Grove, London SE20 8JW
tel 020-8778 5213 *fax* 020-8778 1756
e-mail admin@stageone.demon.co.uk
web site http://www.stageone.demon.co.uk
Scripts Buddy Dalton, c/o 12 The Porticos, 53-59 Belsize Avenue, London NW3 4BN

Scripts from new writers considered.

Talawa Theatre Company

3rd Floor, 23-25 Great Sutton Street, London EC1V 0DN
tel 020-7251 6644 *fax* 020-7251 5969
e-mail hq@talawa.com
Artistic Director Yvonne Brewster

Scripts from new writers considered. Particularly interested in scripts from black writers and plays portraying a black experience.

Theatre Centre

Units 7 & 8, Toynbee Workshops, 3 Gunthorpe Street, London E1 7RQ
tel 020-7377 0379 *fax* 020-7377 1376
e-mail theacen@aol.com
web site http://www.theatre-centre.co.uk
General Manager Jackie Alexis

New writing company producing and touring (nationally). Professional theatre for young people – schools, arts centres, venues.

Theatre Workshop Company

34 Hamilton Place, Edinburgh EH3 5AX
tel 0131-225 7942 *fax* 0131-220 0112
Contact Robert Rae

Plays include new writing/community/children's/disabled. Scripts from new writers considered.

Publishers of plays

Playwrights are reminded that it is unusual for a publisher of trade editions of plays to publish plays which have not had at least reasonably successful, usually professional, productions on stage first. *See listings beginning on page 151 for addresses.*

Marion Boyars Publishers
Brown, Son & Ferguson
Chapman Publishing
Cló Iar-Chonnachta Teo
Cressrelles Publishing Co.
diehard
Dublar Scripts
Everyman's Library
Faber & Faber
Samuel French
The Gallery Press (Ire.)
Gee & Son (Denbigh)
Nick Hern Books
Kenyon-Deane
Kevin Mayhew
Methuen Publishing
J. Garnet Miller
New Playwrights' Network
New Theatre Publications
The Playwrights Publishing Company
SCP Publishers
Seren
Josef Weinberger Plays

Literary agents

The role of the literary agent

The primary task of a literary agent is to look after a writer's commercial interests and to exploit fully the rights in the material he or she handles. This can mean anything from placing work with a British publisher to the sale of US, translation, dramatic, film, television, audio, electronic or other rights.

Agents are the link between the author and the publisher/purchaser. They can also supply editorial guidance, advise on career strategy, and – in the increasingly fluid and unpredictable world of modern publishing – provide the author with a degree of continuity.

What agents cannot be expected to do is comment at length on unsuitable work or sell the unsaleable. Nor can they guarantee that the writer's life is without disappointments.

Approaching an agent

Try to define your needs and choose an agent who seems most likely to meet them. Work from an up-to-date edition of this *Yearbook* and either ring (but check the entry first as some smaller agencies prefer initial contact by letter, perhaps accompanied by a synopsis and the first few pages or chapters), or write a preliminary letter (with a sae) to the agent(s) of your choice to ascertain whether the agent is taking on new clients. Describe as succinctly as possible the nature of your work, your future plans, and give any biographical information that might be relevant to your writing.

Enquire about the agent's terms. Some of this information will be given in the listings that follow, but make sure you understand how the agency operates. Does it use associates for the sale of subsidiary rights, and how does this affect commission? Does it have a letter of agreement for its clients which details its terms of business?

When submitting your work, make sure the typescript is well presented (see *Preparing and submitting a typescript*, page 248) and enclose the right-sized stamped addressed envelope for its return. Bear in mind that it is not good practice to send work to more than one agent at the same time.

Code of practice

The Association of Authors' Agents (see page 463) is the trade association of British agents. Members, designated with an asterisk in the following list, meet regularly and are committed to a code of practice. They do not charge authors a reading fee. Agents that do charge a reading fee usually refund the fee (which covers a report on the typescript) on acceptance of the material by a publisher. This fee is not to be confused with commission, which is the agreed percentage charged by the agent to the author and deducted by the agent from publishers' advances, royalties earned and any other monies paid to the author.

The listings

All the agents listed on the following pages have been sent a *Writers' & Artists' Yearbook* questionnaire designed to provide pertinent information. Each one is asked regularly to update this information. The list is not exhaustive. If any literary agents who are not included would like to be considered for inclusion, please contact the publishers.

Literary agents UK and Ireland

**Full member of the Association of Authors' Agents*

A & B Personal Management Ltd

4th Floor, Plaza Suite, 114 Jermyn Street, London SW1Y 6HJ
tel 020-7839 4433 *fax* 020-7930 5738
Directors R.W. Ellis, R. Ellis

Full-length MSS. Scripts for TV, theatre, cinema; also novels, fiction and non-fiction (home 12.5%, overseas 15%), performance rights (12.5%). Synopsis required initially from writers submitting work for first time. No reading fee for synopsis, plays or screenplays, but fee charged for full-length MSS. Return postage required. Founded 1982.

The Susie Adams Rights Agency

8 Sullivan Road, London SE11 4UH
tel 020-7582 6765 *fax* 020-7582 7279
e-mail susieara@aol.com
Agent Susie Adams

Subsidiary rights agent: foreign language and co-editions worldwide, UK serial, book club, merchandise and other sub rights. Founded 1998.

The Agency (London) Ltd*

24 Pottery Lane, London W11 4LZ
tel 020-7727 1346 *fax* 020-7727 9037
e-mail info@theagency.co.uk
Executives Stephen Durbridge, Leah Schmidt, Sebastian Born, Julia Kreitman, Bethan Evans, Wendy Gresser, Hilary Delamere, Katie Haines

Represents writers for theatre, film, TV, radio and children's book writers and illustrators. Also film and TV rights in novels and non-fiction. Adult novels represented only for existing clients. Commission: 10% unless sub-agents employed overseas; works in conjunction with agents in USA and overseas. No unsolicited MSS. Founded 1995.

Gillon Aitken Associates Ltd*

(and Hughes Massie Ltd)
29 Fernshaw Road, London SW10 0TG
tel 020-7351 7561 *fax* 020-7376 3594
e-mail reception@aitkenassoc.demon.co.uk
Directors Gillon Aitken, Clare Alexander, Antony Harwood, Sally Riley

Full-length MSS (home 10%, USA 15%, translations 20%). Preliminary letter and return postage essential.

Authors include John Banville, Josephine Cox, Sebastian Faulks, Niall Ferguson, Helen Fielding, Germaine Greer, Alan Hollinghurst, Susan Howatch, A.L. Kennedy, Douglas Kennedy, Candia McWilliam, Pauline Melville, V.S. Naipaul, Caryl Phillips, Colin Thubron, A.N. Wilson.

Michael Alcock Management

7 Kensington Church Court, London W8 4SP
tel 020-7938 4332 *fax* 020-7938 4677
e-mail michaelalcock@compuserve.com
Director Michael Alcock

Full length MSS (home 15%, overseas 20%, performance rights 15%). General fiction and (mainly) non-fiction. Specialises in health and personal development; biography, history, current affairs, lifestyle and media. No reading fee. No unsolicited MSS: send letter, CV including previous writing and media experience, and synopsis (for fiction, first 2 chapters) with sae.

Authors include Michael Brunson, James Burke, Tom Dixon, Philip Dunn, Kevin Gould, Mark Griffiths, Kathryn Marsden, Lynne Robinson, Barnaby Rogerson, Ruby & Millie.

Jacintha Alexander Associates – see Lucas Alexander Whitley*

Darley Anderson Literary, TV and Film Agency*

Estelle House, 11 Eustace Road, London SW6 1JB
tel 020-7385 6652 *fax* 020-7386 5571
e-mail darley.anderson@virgin.net
Proprietor Darley Anderson, *Associates* Elizabeth Wright (love stories and 'tear jerkers'/women's

fiction), Kerith Biggs (crime/foreign rights), Petra Sluka (non-fiction), Carrie Goodman (children's books/TV)

Full-length MSS. Popular commercial fiction and non-fiction, and children's fiction. Special fiction interests: all types of thrillers and crime (American/hard boiled/cosy/historical); young male fiction and women's fiction including contemporary, 20th century romantic sagas, love stories, 'tear jerkers', women in jeopardy and erotica; thrillers, horror; comedy (TV and books); and all types of American and Irish novels.

Special non-fiction interests: investigative books, revelatory history and science, TV tie-ins, celebrity autobiographies, true life women in jeopardy, diet, beauty, health, cookery, gardening, popular psychology, self improvement, inspirational, popular religion and supernatural (home 15%, US 20%, translation 22.5%, film/TV/radio 20%). No poetry, plays or academic books. Can arrange PR and author publicity and specialist financial advice; editorial guidance on selected MSS. Preliminary letter, synopsis and first 3 chapters. Return postage/sae must accompany submission to receive a reply. No reading fee. Overseas associates: APA Talent & Literary Agency (LA/Hollywood) and leading foreign agents worldwide.

Authors include Anne Baker, Catherine Barry, Gyles Brandreth, Paul Carson, Lee Child, Martina Cole, John Connolly, Joseph Corvo, Joan Jonker, Frank Lean, Carole Matthews, Lesley Pearse, Allan Pease, Adrian Plass, Ben Richards, Mary Ryan, Fred Secombe, Rebecca Shaw, Peter Sheridan, Linda Taylor.

Anubis Literary Agency

79 Charles Gardner Road, Leamington Spa, Warks. CV31 3BG
tel (01926) 832644 *fax* (01926) 311607
Partners Steve Calcutt and Maggie Heavey

Full-length MSS. Mainstream adult and literary fiction (home 15%, overseas 20%). No reading fee. Will suggest revision. Send preliminary letter with synopsis. No phone calls. Founded 1994.

Artellus Ltd

30 Dorset House, Gloucester Place, London NW1 5AD
tel 020-7935 6972 *fax* 020-7487 5957
Director Leslie Gardner, *Chairman* Gabriele Pantucci

Full-length and short MSS (home 10%, overseas 12.5-20%). Crime, science fiction, historical, contemporary and literary fiction; non-fiction: science, art history, current affairs, biography, general history. Works directly in USA and with agencies in Europe, Japan and Russia. Will suggest revision. No reading fee. Founded 1986.

Associated Publicity Holdings Ltd

7 Kensington Church Court, London W8 4SP
tel 020-7937 5277 *fax* 020-7937 2833
e-mail Jonathan.Harris@aph-agent.demon.co.uk
Managing Director Jonathan G. Harris

Full-length MSS. Fiction and non-fiction, particularly sport, history, archaeology, biographies, thrillers and crime novels (home 15%, overseas 20%), performance, film and TV rights (15%). Send outline, 2 sample chapters and sae. Works with foreign agencies. No reading fee. Founded 1987.

Author Literary Agents

53 Talbot Road, London N6 4QX
tel/fax 020-8341 0442 *mobile* (07989) 318245
e-mail agile@authors.co.uk
web site http://www.authors.co.uk
Contact John Havergal

New writers and creatives welcome. Most fiction and non-fiction genres and media considered, especially content which targets strongly sensed, well-researched and clearly defined commercial readerships and audiences. Send e-mail or sae for submission guidelines. Commission: publishing, film, TV and radio 15% UK, 25% Europe, US and Asia; marketing, advertising, design and merchandising 33-34%; creatives working in illustration, digital, mixed and other media 25% publishing, 33-34% marketing. Founded 1997.

Don Baker Associates

25 Eley Drive, Rottingdean, East Sussex BN2 7FH
tel/fax (01273) 386842
Directors Donald Baker, Katy Quayle

Full-length MSS. Fiction, film, TV and theatre scripts (home 12.5%, overseas 15%). No reading fee. Send sae. No unsolicited MSS. Founded 1996.

Yvonne Baker Associates

8 Temple Fortune Lane, London NW11 7UD
tel 020-8455 8687 *fax* 020-8458 3143

Television, film, theatre, radio (10%). Particularly interested in contemporary drama and TV comedy drama series. No books, short stories, articles, poetry. No reading fee but preliminary letter essential with full information and sae. Founded 1987.

Blake Friedmann Literary, TV & Film Agency Ltd*

122 Arlington Road, London NW1 7HP
tel 020-7284 0408 *fax* 020-7284 0442
e-mail firstname@blakefriedmann.co.uk
Directors Carole Blake, Julian Friedmann, Barbara Jones, Conrad Williams, Beverley Jones

Full-length MSS. Fiction: thrillers, women's novels and literary fiction; non-fiction: investigative books, biography, travel; no poetry or plays (home 15%, overseas 20%). Specialises in film and TV rights; place journalism and short stories for existing clients only. Represented worldwide in 26 markets. Preliminary letter, synopsis and first 2 chapters preferred. No reading fee.

Authors include Gilbert Adair, Ted Allbeury, Jane Asher, Elizabeth Chadwick, Teresa Crane, Stephanie Dowrick, Barbara Erskine, Ann Granger, Maeve Haran, John Harvey, Ken Hom, Glenn Meade, Lawrence Norfolk, Joseph O'Connor, Sheila O'Flanagan, Michael Ridpath, Tim Sebastian. Founded 1977.

David Bolt Associates

12 Heath Drive, Send, Surrey GU23 7EP
tel/fax (01483) 721118

Specialises in biography, fiction, theology. Full-length MSS (home 10%, overseas 19%; all other rights including film, video and TV 10%). No unsolicited short stories or play scripts. Will sometimes suggest revision. Works in association with overseas agencies worldwide. Preliminary letter essential. Reading fee terms on application.

Authors include Chinua Achebe, David Bret, John Cannon, Keith Cory-Jones, Nicci Mackay, Joseph Rhymer, Colin Wilson.

The Book Bureau Literary Agency

1st Floor, 4 Great Strand Street, Dublin 1, Republic of Ireland
tel (01) 6670528 and 8735023 *fax* (01) 8735078
web site http://www.script2screen.net
Managing Director Geraldine Nichol

Full-length MSS (home 10%, USA 15%, translation 20%). Fiction only – thrillers, women's novels, Irish novels, literary fiction. No horror, science fiction, children's or poetry. Strong editorial support before submission to publishers. No reading fee. Preliminary letter with sample material plus return postage essential. Works with agents overseas. Founded 1998.

BookBlast Ltd

21 Chesterton Road, London W10 5LY
tel 020-8968 3089 *fax* 020-8932 4087
Director G. de Chamberet

Full-length MSS (home 10%, overseas 20%), TV and radio (15%), film (20%). Fiction and non-fiction; traditional and underground literature. No unsolicited material; no submissions on disk, by fax or by e-mail. Preliminary letter, synopsis, 3-4 sample chapters and biographical information. Return postage essential. No reading fee. Founded 1997.

Authors include Jamika Ajalon, Garth Cartwright, Aamer Hussein, S.I. Martin, Christov Rühn, Onyekachi Wambu.

Alan Brodie Representation Ltd

(incorporating Michael Imison Playwrights)
211 Piccadilly, London W1V 9LD
tel 020-7917 2871 *fax* 020-7917 2872
e-mail alanbrodie@aol.com
Directors Alan Brodie, Sarah McNair
Consultant Michael Imison

Specialises in stage plays, radio, TV, film (home 10%, overseas 15%); no fiction or general MSS. Represented in all major countries. No unsolicited scripts; recommendation from known professional required.

Rosemary Bromley Literary Agency

Avington, Winchester, Hants SO21 1DB
tel/fax (01962) 779656

Specialises in biography, travel, leisure, cookery, health (home 10%, overseas from 15%.) No poetry. No unsolicited MSS. Send full details of work on offer with return postage. No fax or telephone enquiries. For children's books see **Juvenilia**.

Felicity Bryan*

2A North Parade, Banbury Road, Oxford OX2 6LX
tel (01865) 513816 *fax* (01865) 310055

Fiction and general non-fiction; no light romance, science fiction, short stories, plays or children's (home 10%, overseas

20%). Translation rights handled by Andrew Nurnberg Associates; works in conjunction with US agents. Return postage essential.

Peter Bryant (Writers)

94 Adelaide Avenue, London SE4 1YR
tel 020-8691 9085 *fax* 020-8692 9107

Special interests: animation, children's fiction and TV comedy; also handles drama scripts for theatre, radio and TV (home/USA 10%). Overseas associate: Hartmann and Stauffacher, Germany. No reading fee for the above categories, but sae essential for all submissions.

Authors include Isabelle Amyes, Joe Boyle, Andrew Brenner, Jimmy Hibbert, Penny Lloyd, Allan Plenderleith, Ruth Silvestre, Peter Symonds, George Tarry. Founded 1980.

Campbell Thomson & McLaughlin Ltd*

1 King's Mews, London WC1N 2JA
tel 020-7242 0958 *fax* 020-7242 2408
Directors John McLaughlin, Charlotte Bruton

Full-length book MSS (home 10%, overseas up to 20% including commission to foreign agent). No poetry, plays or TV/film scripts, short stories or children's books. USA agents represented: Raines & Raines, The Fox Chase Agency, Inc. Representatives in most European countries. Preliminary letter with sae essential. No unsolicited synopses or MSS. No reading fee.

Casarotto Ramsay & Associates Ltd

(formerly Margaret Ramsay Ltd and Casarotto Company Ltd)
National House, 60-66 Wardour Street, London W1V 4ND
tel 020-7287 4450 *fax* 020-7287 9128
e-mail agents@casarotto.uk.com
Directors Jenne Casarotto, Giorgio Casarotto, Tom Erhardt, Tracey Hyde, Sara Pritchard

MSS – theatre, films, TV, sound broadcasting only (10%). Works in conjunction with agents in USA and other foreign countries. Preliminary letter essential. No reading fee.

Authors include Paul Abbott, Alan Ayckbourn, J.G. Ballard, Peter Barnes, Edward Bond, Caryl Churchill, Pam Gems, Christopher Hampton, David Hare, Nick Hornby, Amy Jenkins, Neil Jordan, Frank McGuiness, Phyllis Nagy, Mark Ravenhill, Willy Russell, Martin Sherman, Shawn Slovo, Fay Weldon, Timberlake Wertenbaker, David Wood. Founded 1992.

Celia Catchpole

56 Gilpin Avenue, London SW14 8QY
tel 020-8255 7200 *fax* 020-8288 0653

Specialises as agent for children's writers and illustrators (home 10% writers, 15% illustrators; overseas 20%). No unsolicited MSS. Founded 1996.

Chapman & Vincent

The Mount, Sun Hill, Royston, Herts. SG8 9AT
tel (01763) 245005 *fax* (01763) 243033
Directors Jennifer Chapman, Gilly Vincent

Original non-fiction and (occasionally) quality fiction (home 15%; overseas 20%). No children's, genre fiction or poetry. No reading fee. Clients come mainly from personal recommendation. No phone calls; no submissions by fax. Send synopsis and 2 sample chapters with sae. Associates in Boston, Stockholm and Zurich.

Authors include George Carter, Leslie Geddes-Brown, Sara George, Rowley Leigh, John Miller, Dorit Peleg. Founded 1995.

Mic Cheetham Literary Agency

11-12 Dover Street, London W1X 3PH
tel 020-7495 2002 *fax* 020-7495 5777
Director Mic Cheetham

General and literary fiction, science fiction, some non-fiction (home 10%, overseas 20%); film, TV and radio rights (10-15%); will suggest revision. Works with The Marsh Agency for foreign rights. No unsolicited MSS. Founded 1994.

Judith Chilcote Agency*

8 Wentworth Mansions, Keats Grove, London NW3 2RL
tel 020-7794 3717 *fax* 020-7794 7431
e-mail judybks@aol.com
Director Judith Chilcote

Fiction, non-fiction – sports, self-help and health, cookery, autobiography and biography, cinema, current affairs, TV tie-ins (home 15%, overseas 20-25%). No short stories, science fiction, children's, poetry. Works in conjunction with overseas agents and New York affiliate. No reading fee but preliminary letter with 3 chapters only, CV and sae essential.

Authors include Jane Alexander, Alison Bowyer, Paul Kilduff, Douglas Thompson. Founded 1990.

Teresa Chris Literary Agency
43 Musard Road, London W6 8NR
tel 020-7386 0633
Director Teresa Chris

All fiction, especially crime, women's commercial, general and literary fiction; all non-fiction, especially health, cooking, arts and crafts. No science fiction, horror, fantasy, short stories, poetry, academic books (home 10%, USA 15%, rest 20%). Own US office: Thompson & Chris Literary Agency. No reading fee. No unsolicited MSS. Send introductory letter describing work, sample chapter and sae. Founded 1988.

Christy & Moore Ltd – see Sheil Land Associates Ltd*

Mary Clemmey Literary Agency*
6 Dunollie Road, London NW5 2XP
tel/fax 020-7267 1290 *fax* 020-7482 7360

High quality fiction and non-fiction with an international market (home 10%, overseas 20%), performance rights (15%). No children's books, science fiction or fantasy. TV, film, radio and theatre scripts from existing clients only. Works in conjunction with US agent. No reading fee. No unsolicited MSS. Approach by letter (including sae). Founded 1992.

Jonathan Clowes Ltd*
10 Iron Bridge House, Bridge Approach, London NW1 8BD
tel 020-7722 7674 *fax* 020-7722 7677
Directors Jonathan Clowes, Ann Evans

Full-length MSS fiction and non-fiction; no academic or text books (home 15%, overseas 20%). TV, film, theatre and radio. Works in association with agents abroad. Founded 1960.

Elspeth Cochrane Personal Management
11-13 Orlando Road, London SW4 0LE
tel 020-7622 0314 *fax* 020-7622 5815
Contact Elspeth Cochrane

Send synopsis with covering letter and sae in first instance (home and overseas 12.5%), performance rights (12.5%). No reading fee.

Authors include Nick Hennegan, Royce Ryton, Robert Tanitch. Founded 1960.

Rosica Colin Ltd
1 Clareville Grove Mews, London SW7 5AH
tel 020-7370 1080 *fax* 020-7244 6441
Directors Sylvie Marston, Joanna Marston

All full-length MSS (excluding sci-fi and poetry); also theatre, film and sound broadcasting (home 10%, overseas 10-20%). No reading fee, but may take 3-4 months to consider full MSS. Send synopsis only in first instance, with letter outlining writing credits and whether MS has been previously submitted, plus return postage.

Authors include Richard Aldington, Simone de Beauvoir (in UK), Samuel Beckett (publication rights), Steven Berkoff, Alan Brownjohn, Sandy Brownjohn, Donald Campbell, Nick Dear, Neil Donnelly, J.T. Edson, Bernard Farrell, Rainer Werner Fassbinder (in UK), Jean Genet, Mary Halpin, Franz Xaver Kroetz, Don McCamphill, Heiner Müller (in UK), Graham Reid, Botho Strauss (in UK), Anthony Vivis, Wim Wenders (in UK). Founded 1949.

Jane Conway-Gordon*
(in association with Andrew Mann Ltd)
1 Old Compton Street, London W1V 5PH
tel 020-7494 0148 *fax* 020-7287 9264

Full length MSS, performance rights (home 10%, overseas 20%). Represented in all foreign countries. No reading fee but preliminary letter and return postage essential. Founded 1982.

Coombs Moylett Literary Agency
3 Askew Road, London W12 9AA
tel 020-8740 0454 *fax* 020-8354 3065
e-mail lisamoylett@dial.pipex.com
Proprietor Lisa Moylett

Specialises in crime, thrillers, contemporary women's fiction and literary fiction (home 10%; overseas 15%). Send first 3 chapters and synopsis. Will help with revision as appropriate. Return postage essential.

Rupert Crew Ltd*
1A King's Mews, London WC1N 2JA
tel 020-7242 8586 *fax* 020-7831 7914
e-mail rupertcrew@compuserve.com
Directors Kathleen A. Crew, Doreen Montgomery, Caroline Montgomery

International representation, handling volume and subsidiary rights in fiction and non-fiction properties (home 15%, elsewhere 20%); no plays, poetry, journalism or short stories. No reading fee, but preliminary letter and return postage essential. Also acts independently as publishers' consultants. Founded 1927 by F. Rupert Crew.

Curtis Brown Group Ltd*

Haymarket House, 28-29 Haymarket, London SW1Y 4SP
tel 020-7396 6600 *fax* 020-7396 0110
e-mail cb@curtisbrown.co.uk
Chairman Paul Scherer, *Group Managing Director* Jonathan Lloyd, *Financial Director* Mark Collingbourne, *Australia: Joint Managing Directors* Tim Curnow, Fiona Inglis
Books London Jonathan Lloyd, Anna Davis, Jonny Geller, Hannah Griffiths, Ali Gunn, Camilla Hornby, Anthea Morton-Saner, Peter Robinson, Vivienne Schuster, Michael Shaw, Elizabeth Stevens
Books Edinburgh 37 Queensferry Street, Edinburgh EH2 4QS
tel 0131-225 1286/1288 *fax* 0131-225 1290
e-mail cb@curtisbrown.co.uk
Contact Giles Gordon, Jane Bradish-Ellames, *Foreign Rights* Diana Mackay, Carol Jackson, Kate Cooper, *Film/TV/Theatre* Nick Marston (Managing Director, Media Division), Ben Hall, Peter Murphy, Philip Patterson, *Actors* Sue Latimer (Managing Director, Talent Division), Amanda Scott, *Presenters* Sue Freathy, Julian Beynon

Agents for the negotiation in all markets of novels, general non-fiction, children's books (home 10%, overseas 20%) and associated rights (including multimedia), as well as film, theatre, TV and radio scripts. Outline for non-fiction and short synopsis for fiction with 2 or 3 sample chapters and autobiographical note. No reading fee. Return postage essential. Also represents directors, designers, presenters and actors. Return postage essential. Founded 1899.

Judy Daish Associates Ltd

2 St Charles Place, London W10 6EG
tel 020-8964 8811 *fax* 020-8964 8966
Agents Judy Daish, Sara Stroud, Deborah Harwood, Lee Newman

Theatre, film, TV, radio (rates by negotiation). No unsolicited MSS. Founded 1978.

Caroline Davidson Literary Agency

5 Queen Anne's Gardens, London W4 1TU
tel 020-8995 5768 *fax* 020-8994 2770

Handles literary novels and non-fiction of all kinds, including highly illustrated books and reference works (12.5%). Will sometimes help to structure a book, advise on revisions and edit if necessary; if the work involved is extensive, an additional development fee may be charged, by mutual agreement. Send preliminary letter with detailed book proposal/synopsis and/or first 50 pages of novel, CV and large sae. Return postage essential. No reading fee.

Authors include Susan Aldridge, Robert Baldock, Nigel Barlow, Elizabeth Bradley, Lisa Chaney, Stuart Clark, Andrew Dalby, Emma Donoghue, Robert Feather, Anissa Helou, Paul Hillyard, Tom Jaine, Huon Mallalieu, Simon Nolan, Diane Purkiss, Roland Vernon. Founded 1988.

Merric Davidson Literary Agency

12 Priors Heath, Goudhurst, Kent TN17 2RE
tel/fax (01580) 212041
Contact Merric Davidson, Wendy Suffield

Specialising in contemporary adult fiction (home 10%, overseas 20%). No unsolicited MSS. Preliminary letter with synopsis, author information and sae. No initial reading fee, may suggest revision, subsequent editorial advice by arrangement.

Authors include Valerie Blumenthal, Alys Clare, Francesca Clementis, Murray Davies, Harold Elletson, Alison Habens, Frankie Park, Mark Pepper, Simon Scarrow, Luke Sutherland. Founded 1990.

Felix De Wolfe

Garden Offices, 51 Maida Vale, London W9 1SD
tel 020-7289 5770 *fax* 020-7289 5731

Theatre, films, TV, sound broadcasting, fiction (home 10-12.5%, overseas 20%). Works in conjunction with many foreign agencies.

Dorian Literary Agency (DLA)

Upper Thornehill, 27 Church Road, St Marychurch, Torquay, Devon TQ1 4QY
tel/fax (01803) 312095
Proprietor Mrs D. Lumley

Full-length MSS. Specialises in women's fiction, science fiction, fantasy and horror, crime, thrillers and mainstream (home 10%, USA 15%, translations 20-25%), performance rights (10%). No poetry, children's or short stories. Works in conjunction with agencies in most countries; negotiates direct with USA. No reading fee. Enquiries or submissions by fax or e-mail are not acceptable. Contact by letter only with first chapter and synopsis; return postage essential.

Authors include Brian Lumley, Dee Williams, Amy Myers, Stephen Jones. Founded 1986.

Anne Drexl

8 Roland Gardens, London SW7 3PH
tel 020-7244 9645

Special interest in commercial women's fiction and reference books. Also illustrated books for young readers, activity titles, and juvenile fiction (home 12.5%, overseas 20-25%). Works in conjunction with foreign agencies. No reading fee, but no unsolicited MSS; return postage and preliminary letter essential. Founded 1988.

Toby Eady Associates Ltd

3rd Floor, 9 Orme Court, London W2 4RL
tel 020-7792 0092 *fax* 020-7792 0879
e-mail toby@tobyeady.demon.co.uk
Directors Toby Eady, Jessica Woollard

Fiction and non-fiction (home 10-15%, overseas 20%). Approach by personal recommendation. Send letter and sae. No film scripts or poetry. Special interests: China, Middle East, Africa, India. Works with overseas associates.

Authors include Jung Chang, Fadia Faqir, Ma Jian, David Landau, Kenan Makiya, Nuha Al Radi, Lin Ping, Amir Taheri, Xinran Xue, John Carey, Bernard Cornwell, Julia Blackburn, Mark Burnell, Kuki Gallmann, Francesca Marciano, Shyama Perera, Fiammetta Rocco, Ann Wroe. Founded 1968.

Eddison Pearson Ltd

3rd Floor, 22 Upper Grosvenor Street, London W1X 9PB
tel 020-7629 2414 *fax* 020-7629 7181
e-mail box1@eddisonpearson.com
Contact Clare Pearson

Literary fiction and non-fiction, contemporary fiction, children's books, poetry for the literary market (home 10%, overseas 15%). No unsolicited MSS. Enquire in writing with sae. E-mail enquiries welcome but no e-mail submissions please. No reading fee. May suggest revision where appropriate.

Authors include G.H Fleming, Abdullah Hussein, Valerie Bloom.

Edwards Fuglewicz*

49 Great Ormond Street, London WC1N 3HZ
tel 020-7405 6725 *fax* 020-7405 6726
Partners Ros Edwards and Helenka Fuglewicz

Literary and commercial fiction; non-fiction: biography, current affairs, business books, music and film (home 10%, USA/translation 20%). No scripts. Unsolicited MSS welcome. In first instance send covering letter, synopsis and up to 3 sample chapters plus sae for return of MSS. Submissions on disk or by e-mail are not acceptable. No reading fee. Founded 1996.

Faith Evans Associates*

27 Park Avenue North, London N8 7RU
tel 020-8340 9920 *fax* 020-8340 9410

Small agency (home 15%, overseas 20%). New clients by personal recommendation only. Sub-agents in most countries. No phone calls, scripts or unsolicited MSS.

Authors include Melissa Benn, Shyam Bhatia, Eleanor Bron, Caroline Conran, Helen Falconer, Midge Gillies, Ed Glinert, Saeed Jaffrey, Helena Kennedy, Seumas Milne, Tom Paulin, Christine Purkis, Sheila Rowbotham, Lorna Sage, Hwee Hwee Tan, Marion Urch, Harriet Walter, Andrea Weiss, Elizabeth Wilson. Founded 1987.

John Farquharson Ltd* – see Curtis Brown Group Ltd*

Janet Fillingham Associates

52 Lowther Road, London SW13 9NU
tel 020-8748 5594 *fax* 020-8748 7374
e-mail jfillassoc@aol.com
Director Janet Fillingham

MSS for film, TV, radio and theatre (10%). No unsolicited MSS before introductory letter, which should detail achievements rather than aspirations.

Authors include Graham Alborough, Marty Cruickshank, Steve Griffiths, Chris Green, Charles McKeown, Tina Pepler, Rob Rohrer, Guy Slater, Brendan Somers, James Stevenson. Founded 1992.

Film Rights Ltd

Southbank Commercial Centre, 140 Battersea Park Road, London SW11 4NB
tel 020-7720 2000 *fax* 020-7720 6000
e-mail information@filmrights.ltd.uk
web site http://www.filmrights.ltd.uk
Directors Brendan Davis, Joan Potts

Theatre, films, TV and sound broadcasting (home 10%, overseas 15%). Represented in USA and abroad. Founded 1932.

Laurence Fitch Ltd

(incorporating The London Play Company 1922)
Southbank Commercial Centre, 140 Battersea Park Road, London SW11 4NB
tel 020-7720 2000
Directors F.H.L. Fitch, Joan Potts, Brendan Davis

Theatre, films, TV and sound broadcasting (home 10%, overseas 15%). Also works with several agencies in USA and in Europe.

Authors include The Estate of the Late Dodie Smith, Ray Coony, John Chapman, Carlo Ardito, John Graham, Edward Taylor, Dawn Lowe-Watson, Peter Coke, Glyn Robbins.

Jill Foster Ltd

9 Barb Mews, Brook Green, London W6 7PA
tel 020-7602 1263 *fax* 020-7602 9336

Theatre, films, TV, and sound broadcasting (12.5%). Particularly interested in film and TV comedy and drama. No novels or short stories. No reading fee. Preliminary letter essential. Founded 1978.

Fox & Howard Literary Agency

4 Bramerton Street, London SW3 5JX
tel 020-7352 8691 *fax* 020-7352 8691
Partners Chelsey Fox, Charlotte Howard

Full-length MSS. General non-fiction: biography, history and popular culture, reference, business, gardening, mind, body and spirit, self-help and health (home 10-15%, overseas 20%); will suggest revision where appropriate. No poetry, plays, short stories, children's, science fiction, fantasy or horror. No reading fee, but preliminary letter and synopsis with sae essential.

Authors include Sarah Bartlett, Tony Clayton Lea, Maryon Stewart, Jane Struthers. Founded 1992.

Fraser & Dunlop Ltd, Fraser & Dunlop Scripts Ltd – see PFD*

French's

9 Elgin Mews South, London W9 1JZ
tel 020-7266 3321 *fax* 020-7286 6716
Director Mark Taylor

All MSS; specialises in novels and screenplays (home/overseas 10%); theatre, films, TV, radio (10%). Reading service available, details on application. Sae must be enclosed with all MSS.

Futerman, Rose & Associates*

(formerly Vernon Futerman Associates)
17 Deanhill Road, London SW14 7DQ
tel 020-8286 4860 *fax* 020-8286 4861
e-mail grose17@aol.com
web site http://www.caso.clara.net
Contacts Vernon Futerman (academic/politics/current affairs), Alexandra Groom (music/art), Guy Rose (fiction/show business/TV & film scripts), Christopher Oxford (theatre scripts)

Fiction and non-fiction, including biography, show business, music, art, politics; also scripts for film, TV and theatre. Literature (home 12.5%, overseas 17.5%); drama, screenplays (home 15%, overseas 20%). No unsolicited MSS. Send preliminary letter with a brief resumé, detailed synopsis and sae. Overseas associates: USA, Canada, Australia, South Africa, France, Germany, Austria, Switzerland.

Clients include Sally Becker, Lorraine Chase, Alexandra Connor, Diana Douglas Darrid, Aubrey Dillon-Malone, Sir Martin Ewans, Hon. Kingsley Fielding, Susan George, Angus Graham-Campbell, Nigel St John Groom, Russell Warren Howe, Peter King, Sue Lenier, Angela Meredith, Joseph Miller, Valerie Grosvenor Myer, Judy Upton, Simon Woodham, Prof Wu Ningkun. Founded 1984.

Jüri Gabriel

35 Camberwell Grove, London SE5 8JA
tel/fax 020-7703 6186

Quality fiction and non-fiction (current specialisations: medical, practical art, popular academic); radio, TV and film, but mainly selling these rights in existing works by existing clients. Full-length MSS (home 10%, overseas 20%), performance rights (10%); will suggest revision where appropriate. No short stories, articles, verse or books for children. No reading fee; return postage essential. Jüri Gabriel is the chairman of Dedalus (publishers).

Authors include Nigel Cawthorne, Diana Constance, Stephen Dunn, Miriam Dunne, Pat Gray, James Hawes, Robert Irwin, Mike Jay, 'David Madsen', David Miller, Prof Cedric Mims, John Outram, Stefan Szymanski, Dr Terence White, Dr Robert Youngson.

Eric Glass Ltd

28 Berkeley Square, London W1X 6HD
tel 020-7629 7162 *fax* 020-7499 6780

Director Janet Glass

Full-length MSS only; also theatre, films, TV, and sound broadcasting. No unsolicited MSS. Founded 1932.

David Godwin Associates

55 Monmouth Street, London WC2H 9DG
tel 020-7240 9992 *fax* 020-7395 6110
e-mail davidgodwinassociates@compuserve.com
Directors David Godwin, Heather Godwin

Literary fiction and general non-fiction (home 10%, overseas 20%). No reading fee; send sae for return of MSS. Founded 1995.

Annette Green Authors' Agent

6 Montem Street, London N4 3BE
tel 020-7281 0009 *fax* 020-7686 5884
e-mail agreen@literaryagency.freeserve.co.uk
Proprietor Annette Green

Full-length MSS (home 15%, overseas 20%). Literary and general fiction and non-fiction, upmarket popular culture, celebrity biography/autobiography. No dramatic scripts, poetry or children's. No reading fee. Preliminary letter, synopsis, sample chapter and sae essential.

Authors include Nick Barlay, Bill Broady, Anna Burns, Max Kinnings, Maria McCann, Ian Marchant, Rev. Victor Stock. Founded 1998.

Christine Green Authors' Agent*

40 Doughty Street, London WC1N 2LF
tel 020-7831 4956 *fax* 020-7405 3935

Fiction and general non-fiction. Full-length MSS (home 10%, overseas 20%). Works in conjunction with agencies in Europe and Scandinavia. No reading fee, but preliminary letter and return postage essential. Founded 1984.

Louise Greenberg*

The End House, Church Crescent, London N3 1BG
tel 020-8349 1179 *tel/fax* 020-8343 4559
e-mail louisegreenberg@msn.com

Full-length MSS (home10%, overseas 15%). Fiction and non-fiction. Will suggest revision. No reading fee. Return postage essential. Founded 1997.

Greene & Heaton Ltd*

37 Goldhawk Road, London W12 8QQ
tel 020-8749 0315 *fax* 020-8749 0318
Directors Carol Heaton, Judith Murray, Charles Elliott, Antony Topping

Full-length MSS, fiction and non-fiction (home 10%, overseas 20%). No plays, TV or film scripts, science fiction, fantasy, or children's books. Works in conjunction with agencies in most countries. No reading fee. No reply or return of MSS without sae and/or correct postage. Founded 1962.

Gregory & Radice Authors' Agents*

3 Barb Mews, London W6 7PA
tel 020-7610 4676 *fax* 020-7610 4686
Contact Jane Gregory (rights), Lisanne Radice (editorial)

Full-length fiction and non-fiction (home 15%, newspapers 20%, US and translation 20%, radio/film/TV 15%). Specialises in literary and commercial fiction, crime, thrillers, politics. Particularly successful in selling foreign rights. No original plays, film or TV scripts, science fiction, fantasy, poetry, academic or children's books. Represented throughout Europe, Asia and USA. Send preliminary letter, synopsis and first 3 chapters plus return postage. No reading fee. Editorial advice given to authors represented. No submissions by fax or e-mail. Founded 1987.

David Grossman Literary Agency Ltd

118B Holland Park Avenue, London W11 4UA
tel 020-7221 2770 *fax* 020-7221 1445

Full-length MSS (home 10-15%, overseas 20% including foreign agent's commission), performance rights (15%). Works in conjunction with agents in New York, Los Angeles, Europe, Japan. No reading fee, but preliminary letter required. Founded 1976.

The Rod Hall Agency Ltd

7 Goodge Place, London W1P 1FL
tel 020-7637 0706 *fax* 020-7637 0807
e-mail rod.hall@dial.pipex.com
Directors Rod Hall, Clare Barker

Specialises in writers for stage, screen and radio but also deals in TV and film rights in novels and non-fiction (home 10%, overseas 15%). No reading fee.

Clients include Simon Beaufoy, Jeremy Brock, Dario Fo, Lee Hall, Susan Hill, Arthur Hopcraft, Liz Lochhead, Martin McDonagh, Andrea Newman, Simon Nye. Founded 1997.

Richard Hatton Ltd

29 Roehampton Gate, London SW15 5JR
tel 020-8876 6699 *fax* 020-8876 8278
Director Richard Hatton

Stage plays; TV, cinema and radio scripts (15%). No reading fee. Preliminary letter with outline and sae only. No unsolicited MSS. Founded 1954.

A.M. Heath & Co. Ltd*

79 St Martin's Lane, London WC2N 4AA
tel 020-7836 4271 *fax* 020-7497 2561
Directors William Hamilton, Sara Fisher, Sarah Molloy, Victoria Hobbs

Full-length MSS. Literary and commercial fiction and non-fiction, children's (home 10-15%, USA 20%, translation 20%), performance rights (15%). No screenplays, poetry or short stories except for established clients. No reading fee. Agents in USA and all European countries and Japan.

Clients include Joan Aiken, Bella Bathurst, Anita Brookner, Helen Cresswell, Patricia Duncker, Geoff Dyer, Katie Fforde, Graham Hancock, Tobias Hill, Hilary Mantel, Tim Pears, Ricardo Pinto, Susan Price, Adam Thorpe, Barbara Trapido. Founded 1919.

David Higham Associates Ltd*

(incorporating Murray Pollinger)
5-8 Lower John Street, Golden Square, London W1R 4HA
tel 020-7437 7888 *fax* 020-7437 1072
Directors Anthony Goff, Bruce Hunter, Jacqueline Korn, Elizabeth Cree, Ania Corless, Caroline Walsh

Agents for the negotiation of all rights in fiction, general non-fiction, children's fiction and picture books, plays, film and TV scripts (home 10%, USA/translation 20%). USA associate agency: Harold Ober Associates Inc. Represented in all foreign markets. Preliminary letter and return postage essential. No reading fee. Founded 1935.

Vanessa Holt Ltd*

59 Crescent Road, Leigh-on-Sea, Essex SS9 2PF
tel (01702) 473787 *fax* (01702) 471890

General adult fiction and non-fiction (home 15%, overseas 20%, TV/film/radio 15%). Works in conjunction with foreign agencies in all markets. No reading fee, but preliminary letter and sae essential. Founded 1989.

Valerie Hoskins Associates

20 Charlotte Street, London W1P 1HJ
tel 020-7637 4490 *fax* 020-7637 4493
e-mail ValerieHoskinsAss@compuserve.com
Proprietor Valerie Hoskins, *Agent* Rebecca Watson

Film, TV and radio only (12.5% home and maximum 20% overseas). No reading fee, but sae essential. Works in conjunction with overseas agents. No unsolicited MSS; preliminary letter essential.

Tanja Howarth Literary Agency*

19 New Row, London WC2N 4LA
tel 020-7240 5553 *fax* 020-7379 0969
e-mail tanja.howarth@virgin.net

Full-length MSS. General fiction and non-fiction, thrillers, contemporary and historical women's novels and sagas (home 15%, USA/translation 20%). Represented in the USA by various agents. Please submit preliminary letter, synopsis and 3 sample chapters with return postage. No reading fee. Founded 1970.

ICM Ltd

Oxford House, 76 Oxford Street, London W1N 0AX
tel 020-7636 6565 *fax* 020-7323 0101
e-mail admin@icmlondon.co.uk
Directors Duncan Heath, Susan Rodgers, Sally Long-Innes, Paul Lyon-Maris, *Literary Agents* Susan Rodgers, Jessica Sykes, Catherine King, Greg Hunt, Alan Radcliffe, Hugo Young, Michael McCoy, Duncan Heath, Paul Lyon-Maris

Specialises in scripts for film, theatre, TV, radio (home 10%, overseas 10%). Part of International Creative Management Inc., Los Angeles and New York. No reading fee.

IMG Literary UK

The Pier House, Strand on the Green, London W4 3NN
tel 020-8233 5000 *fax* 020-8233 5001
Chairman Mark H. McCormack, *Agents* Sarah Wooldridge (London), Mark Reiter (New York), Fumiko Matsuki (Japan)

Celebrity books, sports-related books, commercial fiction, non-fiction and how-to business books (home/US 20%, elsewhere 25%). No theatre, children's, academic or poetry.

Intercontinental Literary Agency*

33 Bedford Street, London WC2E 9ED
tel 020-7379 6611 *fax* 020-7379 6790
e-mail ila@ila-agency.co.uk
jbuckman@pfd.co.uk
Contacts Anthony Guest Gornall, Nicki Kennedy, Jessica Buckman, Mary Esdaile

Represents translation rights for PFD, London, Harold Matson Company Inc., New York, The Turnbull Agency (John Irving) Inc., and Lucas Alexander Whitley Ltd. Founded 1965.

International Copyright Bureau Ltd

22A Aubrey House, Maida Avenue, London W2 1TQ
tel 020-7724 8034 *fax* 020-7724 7662
Director Joy Westendarp

Now mainly representing authors' estates and not taking on new clients.

International Scripts

1 Norland Square, London W11 4PX
tel 020-7229 0736 *fax* 020-7792 3287
Directors H.P. Tanner, J. Lawson

Specialises in full-length contemporary and women's fiction, biographies, business and general non-fiction (home 15%, overseas 20%), performance rights (15-20%); no poetry or short stories. Works with overseas agents. Preliminary letter and sae required. Return postage required plus a £30 editorial contribution may be requested for reading MSS.

Authors include Zita Adamson, Simon Clark, Charla Devereux, Paul Devereux, Ed Gorman, Peter Haining, Julie Harris, Robert A. Heinlein, Anna Jacobs, Michael Jefferson-Brown, Richard Laymon, Rowena Cory Lindquist, Nick Oldham, Mary Ryan, John and Anne Spencer, Jerry Sykes. Founded 1979.

John Johnson (Authors' Agent) Ltd*

Clerkenwell House, 45-47 Clerkenwell Green, London EC1R 0HT
tel 020-7251 0125 *fax* 020-7251 2172
e-mail johnjohnson@btinternet.com
Contacts Andrew Hewson, Margaret Hewson, Elizabeth Fairbairn

Full-length MSS (home 10%, USA 15-20%, translation 20%). General fiction and non-fiction. No science fiction, technical or academic material. Scripts from existing clients only. No unsolicited MSS; send preliminary letter and sae. No reading fee. Founded 1956.

Jane Judd Literary Agency*

18 Belitha Villas, London N1 1PD
tel 020-7607 0273 *fax* 020-7607 0623

Full-length MSS only (home 10%, overseas 20%). Works with agents in USA and most foreign countries. No reading fee, but preliminary letter with synopsis and sae essential. Founded 1986.

Juvenilia

Avington, Winchester, Hants SO21 1DB
tel/fax (01962) 779656
Proprietor Mrs Rosemary Bromley

Full-length MSS for the children's market, fiction and non-fiction (home 10%, overseas from 15%), illustration (10%), performance rights (10%). Short stories only if specifically for picture books, radio or TV. No unsolicited MSS; preliminary letter with sae and full details essential. Postage for acknowledgement and return of material imperative. No fax or telephone enquiries. Founded 1973.

Michelle Kass Associates*

36-38 Glasshouse Street, London W1R 5RH
tel 020-7439 1624 *fax* 020-7734 3394
Proprietor Michelle Kass, *Associate* Tishna Molla

Full-length MSS. Literary fiction and drama scripts for film (home 10%, overseas 15-20%). Will suggest revision where appropriate. Works with agents overseas. No reading fee. Absolutely no unsolicited MSS without a preliminary phone call. Also agent for film directors. Founded 1991.

Frances Kelly Agency*

111 Clifton Road, Kingston-upon-Thames, Surrey KT2 6PL
tel 020-8549 7830 *fax* 020-8547 0051

Full-length MSS. Non-fiction: general and academic, reference and professional books, all subjects (home 10%, overseas 20%), TV, radio (10%). No reading fee, but no unsolicited MSS; preliminary letter with synopsis, CV and return postage essential. Founded 1978.

Peter Knight Agency

20 Crescent Grove, London SW4 7AH
tel 020-7622 1467 *fax* 020-7622 1522
e-mail pknight@easynet.co.uk
Director Peter Knight, *Associates* Ann King-Hall, Gaby Martin, Andrew Knight

Motor sports, cartoon books, business, history, and factual and biographical material. No poetry, science fiction or cookery. Overseas associates: United Media (USA), Auspac Media (Australia). No unsolicited MSS. Send letter accompanied by CV and sae with synopsis of proposed work. Founded 1985.

Labour & Management Ltd – Tricia Sumner Literary Agency

Milton House, Milton Street, Waltham Abbey, Essex EN9 1EZ
tel/fax (01992) 711511
e-mail triciasumner@email.msn.com
Director Tricia Sumner

Writers for film, theatre, TV, radio. Also full-length MSS, fiction and non-fiction (home 12.5%, overseas 20%). Special interests (not exclusively): multicultural, gay, feminist, anti-establishment. No reading fee. Send preliminary letter, synopsis, sample chapters and sae for return.

Clients include Marion Baraitser, John Gordon, Sophia Kingshill, Roland Moore, Catherine Muschamp, Olusola Oyeleye, Shiraz Randeria, Richard Stone. Founded 1995.

Cat Ledger Literary Agency*

33 Percy Street, London W1P 9FG
tel 020-7436 5030 *fax* 020-7631 4273

General non-fiction and fiction but no short stories, film/TV scripts, poetry or plays (home 10%, overseas 20%). No reading fee but preliminary letter, synopsis and sae essential. Represented in all foreign countries.

Lemon Unna & Durbridge Ltd – see The Agency (London) Ltd*

Lenz-Mulligan Rights & Co-editions

15 Sandbourne Avenue, London SW19 3EW
tel 020-8543 7846 *fax* 020-8543 8909
e-mail glenz-mulligan@dial.pipex.com
Proprietor Gundhild Lenz-Mulligan

Specialises in the sale of translation rights in children's books (fiction, picture books, novelty and activity titles) and illustrated non-fiction (home 10%, overseas 15%). Represents foreign and UK authors, publishers and packagers in the UK, US, German, Dutch and Scandinavian markets. Preliminarly letter with synopsis and/or sample text, CV and sae required. Founded 1998.

Barbara Levy Literary Agency*

64 Greenhill, Hampstead High Street, London NW3 5TZ
tel 020-7435 9046 *fax* 020-7431 2063
Director Barbara Levy, *Associate* John Selby (solicitor)

Full-length MSS only; also film and TV rights (home 10%, overseas by arrangement). No reading fee, but informative preliminary letter and return postage essential. Founded 1986.

Limelight Management*

33 Newman Street, London W1P 3PD
tel 020-7637 2529 *fax* 020-7637 2538
e-mail limelight.management@virgin.net
web site http://www.limelightmanagement.com
Directors Fiona Lindsay, Linda Shanks

Full-length and short MSS. Food, wine, health, crafts, gardening, interior design (home 15%, overseas 20%), TV and radio rights (10-20%); will suggest revision where appropriate. No reading fee. Founded 1991.

Litopia® Corporation

186 Bickenhall Mansions, London W1H 3DE
tel 020-7224 1748 *fax* 020-7224 1802
e-mail info@litopia.com
web site http://www.litopia.com
Directors Peter Cox, Andrew Gillman

Specialises in works with international potential. See web site for submission guidelines. Commission by negotiation. No reading fee. Will suggest revision. Founded 1993.

The Christopher Little Literary Agency*

10 Eel Brook Studios, 125 Moore Park Road, London SW6 4PS
tel 020-7736 4455 *fax* 020-7736 4490
e-mails christopher@clittle.demon.co.uk
pwalsh@clittle.demon.co.uk
Contacts Christopher Little, Patrick Walsh (fiction, non-fiction); *Office Manager* Emma Schlesinger

Commercial and literary full-length fiction and non-fiction (home 15%; US, translation, motion picture 20%, Canada 20%). Special interests: crime, thrillers, popular science and narrative and investigative non-fiction. No poetry, plays, science fiction, fantasy, textbooks, illustrated children's books. Film scripts for established clients only. No reading fee. Send letter giving a summary of present and future intentions together with track record, if any, plus synopsis and/or first 2 chapters and sae in first instance.

Authors include Marcus Berkmann, Harriet Castor, Michael Cordy, Mike Dash, John Emsley, Steve Erikson, Penny Faith, Caron Freeborn, Janet Gleeson, John Gordon-Davis, Brian Hall, Jamie Holland, Tom Holland, Vivien Kelly, Charles Kennedy-Scott, Alastair MacNeill, Hector McDonald, Robert Mawson, Darren O'Shaughnessy, Marcus Palliser, Ruriko Pilgrim, A.J. Quinnell, Rebbecca Ray, Patrick Redmond, Candace Robb, J.K. Rowling, Laura Roychowdhury, Simon

Singh, Alan Smith, Frank Tallis, Laura Thompson, John Watson, James Whitaker, Tiger Woods. Founded 1979.

London Independent Books

26 Chalcot Crescent, London NW1 8YD
tel 020-7706 0486 *fax* 020-7724 3122
Proprietor Carolyn Whitaker

Specialises in commercial, fantasy and teenage fiction, show business, travel. Full-length MSS (home 15%, overseas 20%), films, TV and sound broadcasting (15%). Will suggest revision of promising MSS. No reading fee.

Authors include Bruce Crowther, Nigel Frith, Keith Gray, Andre Launay, Glenn Mitchell, Connie Monk, Emma Sinclair, Chris Wooding. Founded 1971.

Andrew Lownie Literary Agency*

17 Sutherland Street, London SW1V 4JU
tel 020-7828 1274 *fax* 020-7828 7608
e-mail lownie@globalnet.co.uk
web site http://www.andrew.lownie.co.uk
Director Andrew Lownie

Full-length MSS. Biography, history, reference, current affairs, and packaging journalists and celebrities for the book market (worldwide 15%). No reading fee; will suggest a revision.

Authors include Juliet Barker, Guy Bellamy, the Joyce Cary Estate, Tom Devine, Timothy Good, Lawrence James, Norma Major, Sir John Mills, Nick Pope, Richard Ridgley, Alan Whicker; *The Oxford Classical Dictionary*, *The Cambridge Guide to Literature in English*. Founded 1988.

Lucas Alexander Whitley*

14 Vernon Street, London W14 0RJ
tel 020-7471 7900 *fax* 020-7471 7910
e-mail law@lawagency.co.uk
Contacts Mark Lucas, Julian Alexander, Araminta Whitley, Roger Houghton, Peta Nightingale, Lucinda Cook, Celia Hayley

Full length MSS. Fiction and general non-fiction (home 15%, overseas 20%). No poetry, plays, science fiction, fantasy, textbooks or children's books. Film or TV scripts for established clients only. Works with agents and publishers worldwide. Preliminary letter, synopsis and 2 chapters with sae required. No reading fee. Founded 1996.

Jennifer Luithlen Agency

88 Holmfield Road, Leicester LE2 1SB
tel 0116-273 8863 *fax* 0116-273 5697
Agent Jennifer Luithlen

Not looking for new clients. Children's books; adult fiction: crime, historical, saga (home 10%, overseas 20%), performance rights (15%). Founded 1986.

Lutyens & Rubinstein*

231 Westbourne Park Road, London W11 1EB
tel 020-7792 4855 *fax* 020-7792 4833
Directors Sarah Lutyens, Felicity Rubinstein
Submissions Susannah Godman

Fiction and non-fiction, commercial and literary (home 10%, overseas 20%). Send outline/two sample chapters and sae. No reading fee. Founded 1993.

Duncan McAra

28 Beresford Gardens, Edinburgh EH5 3ES
tel/fax 0131-552 1558

Literary fiction; non-fiction: art, architecture, archaeology, biography, military, Scottish, travel (home 10%, overseas 20%). Preliminary letter with sae essential. No reading fee. Founded 1988.

McLean & Slora Literary Agents

20A Eildon Street, Edinburgh EH3 5JU
tel/fax 0131-624 4029
Partners Barbara McLean and Annie Slora

Full-length MSS. Literary fiction, biography, Scottish interest (home 15%, overseas 20%). No reading fee; will suggest a revision and undertake for a fee.

Authors include Tom Bryan, John Herdman, Ruari McLean.

Eunice McMullen Children's Literary Agent Ltd

38 Clewer Hill Road, Windsor, Berks. SL4 4BW
tel (01753) 830348 *fax* (01753) 833459
Director Eunice McMullen

All types of children's books, particularly picture books (home 10%, overseas 15%). No unsolicited scripts.

Authors include Wayne Anderson, Reg Cartwright, Richard Fowler, Charles Fuge, Susie Jenkin-Pearce, Moira Maclean, Graham Oakley, Sue Porter, Angela McAllister, Carol Thompson, David Wood. Founded 1992.

Andrew Mann Ltd*

(in association with Jane Conway-Gordon)
1 Old Compton Street, London W1V 5PH
tel 020-7734 4751 *fax* 020-7287 9264
Directors Anne Dewe, Tina Betts

Full-length MSS. Scripts for TV, cinema, radio and theatre (home 15%, USA and

Europe 20%). Associated with agents worldwide. No reading fee, but no unsolicited MSS without preliminary enquiry and sae. Founded 1974.

Manuscript ReSearch

PO Box 33, Bicester, Oxon OX6 7PP
tel (01869) 323447 *fax* (01869) 324096
Proprietor T.G. Jenkins

Now concentrating on film/TV and radio scripts. No reading fee, but sae for script return essential. Founded 1988.

Marjacq Scripts

34 Devonshire Place, London W1N 1PE
tel 020-7935 9499 *fax* 020-7935 9115
e-mail enquiries@marjacq.com
web site http://www.marjacq.com
Contact Mark Hayward

Full-length MSS (home10%, overseas 20%). Crime, thrillers, science fiction, women's commercial fiction. Will suggest revision.

Authors include James Follett, Elizabeth Lord, Mike Ripley, R.D. Wingfield. Founded 1974.

The Marsh Agency*

11-12 Dover Street, London W1X 3PH
tel 020-7399 2800 *fax* 020-7399 2801
e-mail enquiries@marsh-agency.co.uk
web site http://www.marsh-agency.co.uk
Partners Paul Marsh, Susanna Nicklin

Specialises in international rights. Founded 1994.

Judy Martin

The Basement, 94 Goldhurst Terrace, London NW6 3HS
tel 020-7372 8422 *fax* 020-7372 8423

Fiction, non-fiction, biography and popular culture (home 15%, overseas 20%). No plays, poetry, cookery, gardening or children's stories. Translation rights handled by The Marsh Agency. No reading fee, but sae required for all unsolicited MSS, together with details of publishing history. Founded 1990.

Martinez Literary Agency

60 Oakwood Avenue, London N14 6QL
tel 020-8886 5829
Contacts Françoise Budd, Mary Martinez

Fiction, children's books, arts and crafts, interior design, alternative health and complementary medicine, cookery, autobiographies, popular music, sport and memorabilia (home 15%; US, overseas and translation 20%; performance rights 20%). Not accepting any new writers. Founded 1988.

Blanche Marvin

21A St John's Wood High Street, London NW8 7NG
tel/fax 020-7722 2313

Full-length MSS (home 12.5%, 12.5% overseas), performance rights. No reading fee but return postage essential.

Authors include Christopher Bond.

MBA Literary Agents Ltd*

62 Grafton Way, London W1P 5LD
tel 020-7387 2076 *fax* 020-7387 2042
e-mail agent@mbalit.co.uk
Contact Diana Tyler, John Richard Parker, Meg Davis, Laura Longrigg

Handles fiction and non-fiction, and TV, film, radio and theatre scripts (home 15%, overseas 20%; theatre, TV, radio 10%; films 10-20%). No poetry. No unsolicited material. Works in conjunction with agents in most countries. UK representative for **Writers House LLC**, the Donald Maass Agency and the **Susan Schulman Literary & Dramatic Agents Inc.**

Clients include Campbell Armstrong, A.L. Barker, Estate of Harry Bowling, Jeffrey Caine, Glenn Chandler, Andrew Cowan, Patricia Finney, Maggie Furey, Sue Gee, the estate of B.S. Johnson, Paul J. McAuley, Anne McCaffrey, Susan Oudot, Sir Roger Penrose, Anne Perry, Gervase Phinn, Iain Sinclair, Mark Wallington, Douglas Watkinson, Paul Wilson, Valerie Windsor. Founded 1971.

Midland Exposure

4 Victoria Court, Oadby, Leicester LE2 4AF
tel 0116-271 8332 *fax* 0116-281 2188
e-mail partners@midlandexposure.co.uk
web site http://www.midlandexposure.co.uk
Partners Cari Crook and Lesley Gleeson

Women's magazine fiction only (home initially 25%, overseas 20%). Phone for current reading fee rates. Will suggest revision. Founded 1996.

William Morris Agency (UK) Ltd*

1 Stratton Street, London W1X 6HB
tel 020-7355 8500 *fax* 020-7355 8600
e-mail eif@wma.com
Contacts Stephanie Cabot, Eugenie Furniss (books), Holly Pye (TV/film)

Worldwide theatrical and literary agency with offices in New York, Beverly Hills and Nashville, and associates in Sydney. Handles film, TV and radio scripts; fiction and general non-fiction (film/TV/UK books 10%, US books and translation 20%). No unsolicited material; MSS only when preceded by letter. No reading fee. Founded 1898.

Judith Murdoch Literary Agency*

19 Chalcot Square, London NW1 8YA
tel 020-7722 4197

Full-length fiction only (home 15%, overseas 20%). No thrillers, science fiction/fantasy, poetry, short stories or children's. Approach by letter, *not* telephone, sending the first 2 chapters and synopsis. Return postage/sae essential. Editorial advice given; no reading fee. Translation rights handled by The Marsh Agency. Founded 1993.

Negotiate Ltd

99 Caiyside, Edinburgh EH10 7HR
tel 0131-445 7571 *fax* 0131-445 7572
e-mail gavin@neg1.demon.co.uk
web site http://www.negotiate.co.uk
Contact Gavin Kennedy

Specialises in the negotiation of author's contracts and subsidiary rights. Established authors only or new authors with draft contract from a publisher. Preliminary letter or fax please. Founded 1986.

New Authors Showcase

Rivendell, Kingsgate, Torquay TQ2 8QA
tel/fax (01803) 326617
e-mail james@newauthors.org.uk
web site http://www.newauthors.org.uk
Contact Barrie E. James

Internet site for new writers and poets to display their work to publishers. No unsolicited MSS. Send preliminary letter with sae. Founded 1997.

Maggie Noach Literary Agency*

22 Dorville Crescent, London W6 0HJ
tel 020-8748 2926 *fax* 020-8748 8057
e-mail m-noach@dircon.co.uk

General fiction and non-fiction, especially biography, travel, history and current events; non-illustrated children's books. Full-length MSS (home 15%, US/translation 20%). No scientific, academic or specialist non-fiction; no poetry, plays, short stories or books for the very young. Very few new clients taken on as it is considered vital to give individual attention to each author's work. Unsolicited MSS not welcome. Approach by letter (not by telephone), giving a brief description of the book and enclosing a few sample pages. Return postage essential. No reading fee. Founded 1982.

Andrew Nurnberg Associates Ltd*

Clerkenwell House, 45-47 Clerkenwell Green, London EC1R 0HT
tel 020-7417 8800 *fax* 020-7417 8812
e-mail all@nurnberg.co.uk

Specialises in the sale of translation rights of English and American authors into European languages.

Alexandra Nye, Writers & Agents

44 Braemar Avenue, Dunblane, Perthshire FK15 9EB
tel (01786) 825114
Director Alexandra Nye

Literary fiction, Scottish history, biographies; no poetry or plays (home 10%, overseas 20%, translation 15%). Unsolicited MSS with sae welcome with sae for return, but preliminary letter with synopsis preferred. Reading fee for supply of detailed report on MSS. Founded 1991.

David O'Leary Literary Agency

10 Lansdowne Court, Lansdowne Rise, London W11 2NR
tel 020-7229 1623 *fax* 020-7727 9624
e-mail d.o'leary@virgin.net

Popular and literary fiction and non-fiction: special interests Russia, Ireland, history, science (home 10%, overseas 20%), performance rights (15%). Will suggest revision; no reading fee. Write or call before submitting MSS; please enclose sae.

Authors include Alexander Cordell, David Crackanthorpe, Jim Lusby, Gretta Mulrooney, Ken Russell. Founded 1988.

Deborah Owen Ltd*

78 Narrow Street, Limehouse, London E14 8BP
tel 020-7987 5119/5441 *fax* 020-7538 4004
Contact Deborah Owen, Dawn Fozard

Full-length MSS (home 10%, overseas 15%). All types of literary material except plays, scripts, children's books, short stories or poetry. No unsolicited MSS. No new authors at present.

Authors include Charlie Ross, Ellis Peters, Amos Oz, Delia Smith. Founded 1971.

Mark Paterson & Associates*

10 Brook Street, Wivenhoe, Colchester, Essex CO7 9DS
tel (01206) 825433 *fax* (01206) 822990

e-mail info@markpaterson.co.uk
Book-length MSS; general but with special experience in psychoanalysis, psychotherapy, history and education (20% worldwide including sub-agents' commission). No fiction, articles or short stories except for existing clients. Preliminary letter with synopsis, sample material and return postage essential.

Authors include Sigmund Freud, Anna Freud, Hugh Brogan, Donald Winnicott, Peter Moss, Sir Arthur Evans, Dorothy Richardson, Hugh Schonfield, Georg Groddeck, Patrick Casement, John Seely. Founded 1955.

John Pawsey

60 High Street, Tarring, Worthing, West Sussex BN14 7NR
tel (01903) 205167 *fax* (01903) 205167
Full-length popular fiction and non-fiction MSS (home 10-15%, overseas 19%). No unsolicited material, poetry, short stories, journalism or original film and stage scripts. Preliminary letter and return postage with all correspondence essential. Works in association with agencies in the USA, Europe and the Far East. Will suggest revision if MS sufficiently promising. No reading fee.

Authors include Jonathan Agnew, Dr David Lewis, Peter Hobday, Jon Silverman. Founded 1981.

Maggie Pearlstine Associates Ltd*

31 Ashley Gardens, Ambrosden Avenue, London SW1P 1QE
tel 020-7828 4212 *fax* 020-7834 5546
e-mail post@pearlstine.co.uk
General non-fiction and fiction. Special interests: history, current affairs, biography, health (home 10-12.5%; overseas, journalism and media 20%). Translation rights handled by Gillon Aitken Associates Ltd. No children's, poetry, horror, science fiction, short stories or scripts. Seldom takes on new authors. Prospective clients should write an explanatory letter and enclose a sae and the first chapter only. No submissions accepted by fax, e-mail or from abroad. No reading fee.

Authors include Debbie Beckerman, John Biffen, Matthew Baylis, Kate Bingham, Menzies Campbell, James Cox, Kim Flecher, Dr Frank Furedi, Uri Geller, Roy Hattersley, Rachel Holmes, Prof Lisa Jardine, Charles Kennedy, Mark Leonard, Prof Nicholas Lowe, Alex Parsons, Claire Macdonald, Sara Morrison, Dr Raj Persaud, Prof Lesley Regan, Hugo Rifkind, Jackie Rowley, Henrietta Spencer-Churchill, Alan Stewart, Jack Straw, Prof Robert Winston, Shaun Woodward. Founded 1989.

The Peters Fraser and Dunlop Group Ltd – see PFD

PFD*

(incorporating A.D. Peters & Co. Ltd, Fraser & Dunlop Scripts Ltd, Fraser & Dunlop Ltd, June Hall Literary Agency Ltd, Watergate Film Services Ltd)
Drury House, 34-43 Russell Street, London WC2B 5HA
tel 020-7344 1000 *fax* 020-7836 9539
e-mail postmaster@pfd.co.uk
web site http://www.pfd.co.uk
Joint Chairmen Anthony Jones, *Managing Director* Anthony Baring, *Books* Caroline Dawnay, Michael Sissons, Pat Kavanagh, Charles Walker, Rosemary Canter, Rosemary Scoular, Robert Kirby, Simon Trewin, Annabel Hardman, James Gill, *Serial* Pat Kavanagh, Carol Macarthur, *Film/TV* Tim Corrie, Anthony Jones, Norman North, Charles Walker, Vanessa Jones, St John Donald, Natasha Galloway, Louisa Thompson, Jago Irwin, *Actors* Maureen Vincent, Ginette Chalmers, Dallas Smith, Lindy King, Ruth Cooper, Ruth Young, Lucy Brazier, Chris Harris, *Theatre* Kenneth Ewing, St John Donald, Nicki Stoddart, Rosie Cobbe, *Children's* Rosemary Canter, *New Media* Rosemary Scoular, *Translation Rights* Intercontinental Literary Agency, *US Illustrators' Representation* Harriet Kasak
Handles the full range of books including fiction, children's and non-fiction as well as scripts for film, theatre, radio and TV, actors and multimedia projects (home 10%; US and translation 20%). Has 75 years of international experience in all media. Send a full outline for non-fiction and short synopsis for fiction with 2 or 3 sample chapters and autobiographical note. Material submitted on an exclusive basis preferred; in any event it should be disclosed if material is being submitted to other agencies or publishers. Return postage essential. No reading fee. No guaranteed response to submissions by e-mail.

Laurence Pollinger Ltd*

18 Maddox Street, London W1R 0EU
tel 020-7629 9761 *fax* 020-7629 9765
e-mail laurence.pollinger@compuserve.com
Directors Gerald J. Pollinger, Lesley Hadcroft,

Secretary Leigh Pollinger, *Dramatic Associate* Micheline Steinberg

All material except original film stories, poetry and freelance journalistic articles. Commission: 15%, translation (20%). No reading fee.

Murray Pollinger – see David Higham Associates Ltd*

Shelley Power Literary Agency Ltd*

Le Montaud, 24220 Berbiguières, France
tel 53 29 62 52 *fax* 53 29 62 54
e-mail puissant@easynet.fr

General fiction and non-fiction. Full-length MSS (home 10%, USA and translations 19%). No children's books, poetry or plays. Works in conjunction with agents abroad. No reading fee, but preliminary letter with return postage as from UK or France essential. No submissions by e-mail. Also based in the UK. Founded 1976.

Elizabeth Puttick Literary Agency

46 Brookfield Mansions, Highgate West Hill, London N6 6AT
tel 020-8340 6383 *fax* 020-8340 6384
e-mail liz@puttick.com
web site http://www.puttick.com
Director Elizabeth Puttick

Full-length MSS (home 15%, overseas 20%). General non-fiction with special interest in self-help, MindBodySpirit, health, childcare, cookery, leisure, business, narrative and investigative non-fiction, popular science, biography, history, politics, women's issues, social issues, illustrated books. No poetry, drama, children's books. No reading fee. Send preliminary letter with synopsis; return postage essential.

Authors include William Bloom, Anne Baring, Nitya Lacroix. Founded 1995.

PVA Management Ltd

Hallow Park, Worcester WR2 6PG
tel (01905) 640663 *fax* (01905) 641842
e-mail pva@pva.co.uk
Managing Director Paul Vaughan

Full-length MSS. Non-fiction only (home 15%, overseas 20%, performance rights 15%). Please send synopsis and sample chapters together with return postage.

Radala & Associates

17 Avenue Mansions, Finchley Road, London NW3 7AX
tel 020-7794 4495 *fax* 020-7431 7636
Director Richard Gollner, *Associates* Neil Hornick, Anna Swan, Andy Marino

Full-length MSS (home 10%, overseas 15%). Fiction and non-fiction. Books, TV, sound broadcasting. Submit synopsis in first instance; evaluation of MSS charged (fee based on length and complexity); outlines, proposals, etc at no charge. Founded 1970.

Margaret Ramsay Ltd – now Casarotto Ramsay & Associates Ltd

Rogers, Coleridge & White Ltd*

20 Powis Mews, London W11 1JN
tel 020-7221 3717 *fax* 020-7229 9084
Directors Deborah Rogers, Gill Coleridge, Patricia White (USA), David Miller, Laurence Laluyaux, *Consultant* Ann Warnford-Davis, *USA Associate* International Creative Management, Inc.

Full-length book MSS, including children's books (home 10%, USA 15%, translations 20%). No unsolicited MSS please, and no submissions by fax or e-mail. Founded 1967.

Elizabeth Roy Literary Agency

White Cottage, Greatford, Nr Stamford, Lincs. PE9 4PR
tel/fax (01778) 560672

Children's fiction and non-fiction – writers and illustrators (home 10-15%, overseas 20%). Will suggest revision. Preliminary letter, synopsis and sample chapters essential with names of publishers and agents previously contacted. Return postage essential. No reading fee. Founded 1990.

Hilary Rubinstein Books

32 Ladbroke Grove, London W11 3BQ
tel 020-7792 4282 *fax* 020-7221 5291
Director Hilary Rubinstein

Full-length MSS. Fiction and non-fiction (home 10%, overseas 20%); will suggest revision where appropriate. No plays, scripts, children's books or poetry. No reading fee, but no unsolicited MSS without preliminary letter or call.

Authors include Eric Lomax, Donna Williams, Lucy Irvine. Founded 1992.

Uli Rushby-Smith

72 Plimsoll Road, London N4 2EE
tel/fax 020-7354 2718
Director Uli Rushby-Smith

Fiction and non-fiction, literary and commercial (home 10%, USA/foreign 20%). Work in conjunction with foreign sub-agents in some countries. UK representatives of **Curtis Brown Ltd**, New York (children's books) and Penguin Canada, Penguin South Africa, Columbia University Press (USA), Alice Toledo Agency (Netherlands). Send outline, sample chapters and sae; no reading fee. Founded 1993.

Rosemary Sandberg Ltd

6 Bayley Street, London WC1B 3HB
tel 020-7304 4110 *fax* 020-7304 4109
Directors Rosemary Sandberg, Ed Victor, Graham Greene CBE

Children's – writers and illustrators, general fiction and non-fiction (home 10-15%, overseas 20%). Absolutely no unsolicited MSS: client list is full. Founded 1991.

Tessa Sayle Agency*

11 Jubilee Place, London SW3 3TE
tel 020-7823 3883 *fax* 020-7823 3363
Publishing Rachel Calder, *Film, TV* Jane Villiers, Matthew Bates

Full-length MSS (home 10%, overseas 20-25%), film, TV (home 10%, overseas 15-20%). No science fiction, fantasy, children's books, plays or poetry. No reading fee, but preliminary letter and return postage essential. USA Associates: Darhansoff & Verrill and **Elaine Markson Literary Agency**. Represented in all foreign countries by the **Marsh Agency**.

The Sharland Organisation Ltd

The Manor House, Manor Street, Raunds, Northants. NN9 6JW
tel (01933) 626600 *fax* (01933) 624860
e-mail tsoshar@aol.com
Directors Mike Sharland, Alice Sharland

Specialises in film, TV, stage and radio rights throughout the world (home 15%, overseas 20%); also negotiates multimedia, interactive TV deals and computer game contracts. Works in conjunction with overseas agents. Preliminary letter and return postage is essential. Founded 1988.

Sheil Land Associates Ltd*

(incorporating Richard Scott Simon Ltd 1971 and Christy & Moore Ltd 1912)
43 Doughty Street, London WC1N 2LF
tel 0207-405 9351 *fax* 0207-831 2127
e-mail info@sheilland.co.uk
Agents UK and US Sonia Land, Luigi Bonomi, Sam Boyce, Vivien Green, John Rush (film/drama/TV), *Foreign and US* Amelia Cummins, Paul Rainbow

Full-length general, commercial and literary fiction and non-fiction, including: social politics, military history, gardening, thrillers, crime, romance, fantasy, drama, biography, travel, cookery, humour, UK and foreign estates (home 10-15%, USA/translations 20%). Also theatre, film, radio and TV scripts. Welcomes approaches from new clients either to start or to develop their careers. Preliminary letter with sae essential. No reading fee. Overseas associates: Georges Borchardt, Inc. (Richard Scott Simon). UK representatives for Farrar, Straus & Giroux, Inc. US film and TV representation: CAA, APA and others.

Clients include Peter Ackroyd, John Blashford-Snell, Simon van der Borgh, Melvyn Bragg, Stephanie Calman, Catherine Cookson Estate, Lynda Chater, Seamus Deane, Alan Drury, John Fowles, Alan Garner, Susan Hill, Richard Holmes, HRH The Prince of Wales, John Humphrys, Bernard Kops, Charlotte Lamb, Richard Mabey, Colin McDowell, Van Morrison, Patrick O'Brian Estate, Esther Rantzen, Pam Rhodes, Martin Riley, Colin Shindler, Tom Sharpe, Brian Sibley, Alan Titchmarsh, Rose Tremain, Sally Ward, John Wilsher, Paul Wilson. Founded 1962.

Caroline Sheldon Literary Agency*

London office 71 Hillgate Place, London W8 7SS
tel 020-7727 9102
mailing address Thorley Manor Farm, Thorley, Yarmouth, Isle of Wight PO41 0SJ
tel (01983) 760205
Proprietor Caroline Sheldon

Full-length MSS. General fiction, women's fiction, and children's books (home 10%, overseas 20%). No reading fee. Synopsis and first 3 chapters with large sae in case of return required initially. Founded 1985.

Jeffrey Simmons

10 Lowndes Square, London SW1X 9HA
tel 020-7235 8852 *fax* 020-7235 9733

Specialises in fiction (no sci-fi, horror or fantasy), biography, autobiography, show business, personality books, law, crime, politics, world affairs. Full-length MSS (home from 10%, overseas from 15%). Will suggest revision. No reading fee, but preliminary letter essential.

Richard Scott Simon Ltd – see Sheil Land Associates Ltd*

Simpson Fox Associates*

52 Shaftesbury Avenue, London W1V 7DE
tel 020-7434 9167 *fax* 020-7494 2887
Directors David Watson, Angela Fox, John Simpson, Anita Land, Georgina Capel, Robert Fox

General fiction and non-fiction, scripts (worldwide 15%). No reading fee. Write to Georgina Capel with synopsis, sample chapter and sae.

Authors include Julie Burchill, Lucy Moore, Henry Porter, Andrew Roberts.

Sinclair-Stevenson

3 South Terrace, London SW7 2TB
tel/fax 020-7581 2550
Directors Christopher Sinclair-Stevenson, Deborah Sinclair-Stevenson

Full-length MSS (worldwide 10%). General – no children's books. No reading fee; will suggest a revision. Founded 1995.

Robert Smith Literary Agency*

12 Bridge Wharf, 156 Caledonian Road, London N1 9UU
tel 020-7278 2444 *fax* 020-7833 5680
Partners Robert Smith and Anne Smith

Non-fiction: autobiography and biography, health and nutrition, mind, body and spirit, cookery, lifestyle, popular culture, music, TV and film tie-ins, true crime, investigative journalism, illustrated books (home 15%, overseas 20%). No unsolicited MSS. Will suggest revision.

Authors include Peter Gerrard, Neil and Christine Hamilton, James Haspiel, Christine Keeler, Norman Parker, Mike Reid, Christopher Warwick. Founded 1997.

Abner Stein*

10 Roland Gardens, London SW7 3PH
tel 020-7373 0456 *fax* 020-7370 6316

Full-length and short MSS (home 10%, overseas 20%). No reading fee, but no unsolicited MSS; preliminary letter and return postage required.

Micheline Steinberg Playwrights' Agent

409 Triumph House, 187-191 Regent Street, London W1R 7WF
tel 020-7287 4383 *fax* 020-7287 4384
e-mail SteinPlays@aol.com

Full-length MSS – theatre, films, TV, radio (home 10%, overseas 15%). Dramatic Associate for Laurence Pollinger Ltd; works in conjunction with agents in USA and other countries. No reading fee, but preliminary letter essential and return postage with MSS. Founded 1987.

Rochelle Stevens & Co.

2 Terretts Place, Upper Street, London N1 1QZ
tel 020-7359 3900 *fax* 020-7354 5729
Proprietor Rochelle Stevens, *Associate* Frances Grannum

Drama scripts for film, TV, theatre and radio (10%); will suggest revision where appropriate. No reading fee, but preliminary letter and return postage essential. Founded 1984.

Shirley Stewart Literary Agency

36 Brand Street, London SE10 8SR
tel 020-8853 1381 *fax* 020-8305 2175
Director Shirley Stewart

Specialises in literary fiction and general non-fiction (home 10%, overseas 20%). No poetry, plays, film scripts or children's books. No reading fee. Send preliminary letter, synopsis and first 3 chapters plus return postage. Founded 1993.

The Susijn Agency

820 Harrow Road, London NW10 5JU
tel 020-8968 7435 *fax* 020-8354 0415
e-mail LSusijn@aol.com
Director Laura Susijn

Specialises in world rights in English and non-English language literature: literary fiction and general non-fiction (home 10-15%, overseas 15-20%, theatre/film/TV/radio 15%). Send synopsis and 2 sample chapters. No reading fee.

Authors include Peter Ackroyd, Robin Baker, Adam Zameenzad, Anita Nair, Karl Shaw, Stephen Thompson, Joydeep Roy-Bhattacharya, Alex Wheatle. Founded 1998.

J.M. Thurley Management

30 Cambridge Road, Teddington, Middlesex TW11 8DR
tel 020-8977 3176 *fax* 020-8943 2678
e-mail JMThurley@aol.com
Contact Jon Thurley

Specialises in commercial and literary full-length fiction and commercial work for film and TV. No plays, poetry, short stories, articles or fantasy. No reading fee but preliminary letter and sae essential.

Editorial/creative advice provided to clients (home 15%, overseas 20%). Links with leading US and European agents. Founded 1976.

Lavinia Trevor*

The Glasshouse, 49A Goldhawk Road, London W12 8QP
tel 020-8749 8481 *fax* 020-8749 7377

Fiction and non-fiction, including popular science, for the general trade market. No reading fee. Brief autobiographical letter and approx. first 50 pages required plus sae. Founded 1993.

Jane Turnbull*

13 Wendell Road, London W12 9RS
tel 020-8743 9580 *fax* 020-8749 6079

Fiction and non-fiction (home 10%, USA 15%, translation 20%), performance rights (15%). No science fiction, romantic fiction, children's or short stories. Works in conjunction with **Gillon Aitken Associates Ltd** for sale of translation rights. No reading fee. Preliminary letter and sae essential; no unsolicited MSS. Founded 1986.

United Authors Ltd

11-15 Betterton Street, London WC2H 9BP
tel 020-7470 8886 *fax* 020-7470 8887
e-mail utdauthors@clara.net

Fiction, non-fiction, children's, biography, travel. Full-length MSS (home 10%, overseas 15%), short MSS (12%/20%), film and radio (15%/20%), TV (15%/15%). Will suggest revision.

Authors include Charlotte Bingham, John Bingham (estate), Sydney Gilliatt (estate), Peter Willet, C.S. Youd. Founded 1998.

Harvey Unna & Stephen Durbridge Ltd – see The Agency (London) Ltd*

Ed Victor Ltd*

6 Bayley Street, Bedford Square, London WC1B 3HB
tel 020-7304 4100 *fax* 020-7304 4111
Executive Chairman Ed Victor, *Joint Managing Directors* Sophie Hicks, Margaret Phillips, *Directors* Carol Ryan, Graham C. Greene CBE, Leon Morgan, Hitesh Shah

Full-length MSS, fiction and non-fiction, but no short stories, film/TV scripts, poetry or plays (home 15%, USA 15%, translation 20%), performance rights (15%). Represented in all foreign markets. No unsolicited MSS.

Authors include Douglas Adams, Sir Ranulph Fiennes, Frederick Forsyth, Josephine Hart, Jack Higgins, Erica Jong, Kathy Lette, Dame Iris Murdoch, Nigel Nicolson, Lisa St Aubin de Terán, Erich Segal, and the estates of Irving Wallace, Raymond Chandler, Sir Stephen Spender. Founded 1976.

Watson, Little Ltd*

Capo Di Monte, Windmill Hill, London NW3 6RJ
tel 020-7431 0770 *fax* 020-7431 7225
Directors Sheila Watson, Amanda Little, Sugra Zaman

Full-length MSS. Special interests: business books, popular science, psychology, all leisure activities, popular culture, history, fiction; no short stories or play scripts (home 15%, serial 15%, translation 19%, US 24%; electronic rights 20%; all other rights including film, video and TV 10%). Works in association with US agencies and many foreign agencies. Preliminary letter please.

A.P. Watt Ltd*

20 John Street, London WC1N 2DR
tel 020-7405 6774 *fax* 020-7831 2154 (books) 020-7430 1952 (drama)
e-mail apw@apwatt.co.uk
Directors Caradoc King, Linda Shaughnessy, Derek Johns, Jo Frank, Sam North

Full-length MSS; dramatic works for all media (home 10%, US and foreign 20% including commission to foreign agent). No poetry. No reading fee. No unsolicited MSS. Founded 1875.

WCA Licensing

3 Calais Street, London SE5 9LP
tel 020-7564 5898 *fax* 020-7564 3501
e-mail ecollins@wca.co.uk
Partners Elaine Collins and Arabella Woods

Specialises in non-fiction: cookery, lifestyle, gardening, etc, TV tie-ins (home 15%, overseas 20%). No reading fee; will suggest a revision. Founded 1993.

Josef Weinberger Plays Ltd

(formerly Warner/Chappell Plays Ltd)
12-14 Mortimer Street, London W1N 7RD
tel 020-7580 2827 *fax* 020-7436 9616

Specialises in stage plays. Works in conjunction with overseas agents. No unsolicited MSS; preliminary letter essential. Founded 1938.

Dinah Wiener Ltd*

12 Cornwall Grove, London W4 2LB
tel 020-8994 6011 *fax* 020-8994 6044

Full-length MSS only, fiction and general non-fiction (home 15%, overseas 20%), film and TV in association (15%). No plays, scripts, poetry, short stories or children's books. No reading fee, but preliminary letter and return postage essential.

Jonathan Williams Literary Agency

Ferrybank House, 6 Park Road, Dun Laoghaire, Co. Dublin, Republic of Ireland
tel/fax (01) 2803482
Director Jonathan Williams

General fiction and non-fiction, preferably by Irish authors (home 10%). Will suggest revision; usually no reading fee. Return postage appreciated (no British stamps – please use International Reply Coupons). Founded 1981.

Elisabeth Wilson

24 Thornhill Square, London N1 1BQ
fax 020-7609 6045

Rights agent and consultant. Founded 1979.

The Wylie Agency (UK) Ltd

4-8 Rodney Street, London N1 9JH
tel 020-7843 2150 *fax* 020-7843 2151
Directors Andrew Wylie (president), Georgia Garrett, Benita Edzard

Literary fiction and non-fiction (home 10%, overseas 20%, USA 15%). No unsolicited MSS; send preliminary letter with 2 sample chapters and sae in first instance. Founded 1996.

Literary agents for children's books

The following literary agents will consider work suitable for children's books, from both authors and illustrators. See also Writing and the children's book market on page 252 and Art agents and commercial art studios on page 390.

The Agency (London) Ltd
Darley Anderson Literary, TV and Film Agency*
Peter Bryant (Writers)
Celia Catchpole
Curtis Brown Group Ltd
Darley Anderson Literary, TV and Film Agency
Anne Drexl
Eddison Pearson Ltd
A.M. Heath & Co. Ltd
David Higham Associates Ltd
Juvenilia
Lenz-Mulligan Rights & Co-editions
Christopher Little Literary Agency
Jennifer Luithlen Agency
McLean & Slora Literary Agents
Eunice McMullen Children's Literary Agent Ltd
Andrew Mann Ltd
Martinez Literary Agency
Jay Morris & Co. Authors' Agents
Maggie Noach Literary Agency
PFD (Rosemary Canter)
Laurence Pollinger Limited
Rogers, Coleridge & White Ltd
Elizabeth Roy Literary Agency
Rosemary Sandberg Ltd
Caroline Sheldon Literary Agency
United Authors Ltd
Ed Victor Ltd (Sophie Hicks)
A.P. Watt Ltd

Literary agents overseas

Before submitting material, writers are advised to send a preliminary letter with an sae (or an International Reply Coupon) and to ascertain terms. Listings for overseas literary agents other than in the USA start on page 378.

**Member of the Association of Authors' Representatives*

USA

American Play Company Inc.

19 West 44th Street, Suite 1204, New York, NY 10036
tel 212-921-0545 *fax* 212-869-4032
President Sheldon Abend

AMG/Renaissance

9465 Wilshire Boulevard, Beverly Hills, CA 90212
tel 310-860-8000 *fax* 310-860-8100
e-mail alan.nevins@amg-la.com
Partners Alan Nevins, Joel Gotler, Irv Schwarz, *Agents* Judi Farkas, Michael Prevett

Full-length MSS. Fiction and non-fiction, plays (home 15%, overseas 20%), film and TV rights (home 10%, overseas 20%), performance rights. No unsolicited MSS; query first, submit outline. No reading fee. Founded 1934.

The Axelrod Agency*

54 Church Street, Lenox, MA 01240
tel 413-637-2000 *fax* 413-637-4725
President Steven Axelrod

Full-length MSS. Fiction and non-fiction, software (home 10%, overseas 20%), film and TV rights (10%); will suggest revision where appropriate. Works with overseas agents. No reading fee. Founded 1983.

The Balkin Agency Inc.*

PO Box 222, Amherst, MA 01004
tel 413-548-9835 *fax* 413-548-9836
e-mail balkin@crocker.com
Director Richard Balkin
European and British Representative Chandler Crawford Agency USA

Full-length MSS – adult non-fiction only (home 15%, overseas 20%). Query first. May suggest revision. No reading fee.

Virginia Barber Literary Agency Inc. – see The Writers Shop

Berman, Boals & Flynn Inc.*

208 West 30th Street, Suite 401, New York, NY 10001
tel 212-868-1068 *fax* 212-868-1052
Agents Judy Boals, Jim Flynn

Dramatic writing only (and only by recommendation).

Georges Borchardt Inc.*

136 East 57th Street, New York, NY 10022
tel 212-753-5785 *fax* 212-838-6518
Directors Georges Borchardt, Anne Borchardt

Full-length and short MSS (home/British/performance 15%, translations 20%). Agents in most foreign countries. No unsolicited MSS. No reading fee. Founded 1967.

Brandt & Brandt Literary Agents Inc.*

1501 Broadway, New York, NY 10036
tel 212-840-5760 *fax* 212-840-5776
British Representative A.M. Heath & Co. Ltd

Full-length and short MSS (home 15%, overseas 20%), performance rights (10%). No reading fee.

The Helen Brann Agency Inc.*

94 Curtis Road, Bridgewater, CT 06752
tel 860-354-9580 *fax* 860-355-2572

Maria Carvainis Agency Inc.*

235 West End Avenue, New York, NY 10023
tel 212-580-1559 *fax* 212-877-3486
President Maria Carvainis

Fiction: all categories (except science fiction), especially general fiction/literary and mainstream; mystery, thrillers and suspense; fantasy; young adult and children's; historical, Regency and category romance. Non-fiction: political and film biographies; medicine and women's issues; business, finance, psychology and popular science (home 15%, overseas 20%). Maria Carvainis views the author's editorial needs and career development as integral components of the literary agent's role, in addition to the negotiation of intricate contracts. Works in conjunction with foreign, TV and movie agents. No reading fee. Query first; no unsolicited MSS.

Faith Childs Literary Agency Inc.*

915 Broadway, Suite 1009, New York, NY 10010
tel 212-995-9600 *fax* 212-995-9709
Director Faith Hampton Childs, *Associate* Lori A. Pope

Literary fiction; non-fiction (home 15%, overseas 20%). Works in conjunction with overseas agents. Will suggest revision. No reading fee. Founded 1990.

Frances Collin Literary Agent

PO Box 33, Wayne, PA 19087-0033
tel 610-254-0555

Full-length MSS (specialisations of interest to UK writers: mysteries, women's fiction, history, biography, science fiction, fantasy) (home 15%, overseas 20%), performance rights (20%). No screenplays. Works in conjunction with agents worldwide. No reading fee. No unsolicited MSS please. Letter queries must include sufficient international postage response coupons. Founded 1948; successor to Marie Rodell-Frances Collin Literary Agency.

Don Congdon Associates Inc.*

156 Fifth Avenue, Suite 625, New York, NY 10010
tel 212-645-1229 *fax* 212-727-2688
e-mail doncongdon@aol.com
Agents Don Congdon, Michael Congdon, Susan Ramer

Full-length and short MSS. General fiction and non-fiction (home 10%, overseas 19%), performance rights (10%); will sometimes suggest revision. Works with co-agents overseas. No reading fee, but no unsolicited MSS – query first. Founded 1983.

Richard Curtis Associates Inc.*

171 East 74th Street, Floor 2, New York, NY 10021
tel 212-772-7363 *fax* 212-772-7393
web site http://curtisagency.com
President Richard Curtis, *Associate* Amy Victoria Meo

All types of commercial fiction; also non-fiction (home 15%P overseas 20%), multimedia, film, TV rights (15%). Works in conjunction with overseas agents. Will suggest revision. No reading fee. Send sase with all queries. Founded 1970.

E-Rights division
web site http://www.e-rights.com

Assists authors adapt work to electronic publishing formats.

Curtis Brown Ltd*

10 Astor Place, New York, NY 10003
tel 212-473-5400
Ceo Timothy Knowlton
Contact Query Department
1750 Montgomery Street, San Francisco, CA 94111
tel 415-954-8566
President Peter Ginsberg

Fiction and non-fiction, juvenile, film and TV rights. No unsolicited MSS; query first with sase. No reading fee; no handling fees.

Joan Daves Agency

21 West 26th Street, New York, NY 10010
tel 212-685-2663 *fax* 212-685-1781
Director Jennifer Lyons, *Assistant* Heather Currier

Sample chapter or detailed outline of non-fiction projects (home 15%, overseas 20%). No reading fee. No unpublished writers. Subsidiary of **Writers House LLC.** Founded in 1952 by Joan Daves.

Elaine Davie Literary Agency

620 Park Avenue, Rochester, NY 14607
tel 716-442-0830
President Elaine Davie

Full-length MSS. Specialises in books by and for women, especially genre romance (home 15%, overseas 20%); will sometimes suggest revision. Works with overseas agents. No reading fee, but preliminary letter with sase essential. Query or first 100 pages/synopsis. Founded 1986.

Sandra Dijkstra Literary Agency*

PMB 515, 1155 Camino Del Mar, Del Mar, CA 92104-2605
tel 858-755-3115 *fax* 858-792-1494
President Sandra Dijkstra

Non-fiction: narrative, history, business, psychology, science, memoir/biography, how-to; adult fiction, especially literary/contemporary, women's, crime; selected children's projects (home 15%, overseas 20%). Works in conjunction with foreign agents. Will suggest revision. No reading fee. Send first 50 pages and sase for response/return. No queries by fax or e-mail. Response period 4-6 weeks; do not call to enquire. Founded 1981.

Donadio & Ashworth Inc.*

121 West 27th Street, Suite 704, New York, NY 10001
tel 212-691-8077 *fax* 212-633-2837

Literary fiction and non-fiction.

Jane Dystel Literary Management*

One Union Square West, New York, NY 10003
tel 212-627-9100 *fax* 212-627-9313
web site http://www.dystel.com
President Jane D. Dystel, *Vice-President* Miriam Goderich, Todd Keithley, Jo Fagan, Stacey Glick, Kyung Cho

General fiction and non-fiction: literary and commercial fiction; narrative non-fiction; self-help; cookbooks; parenting; children's books; science fiction/fantasy. Full-length and short MSS (home 15%, overseas 10%); film, TV and radio (15%). No reading fee. Founded 1991.

Peter Elek Associates

5111 Boulevard East, West New York, NJ 07093
tel 212-431-9368/9371 *fax* 212-966-5768
e-mail info@theliteraryagency.com
web site http://www.theliteraryagency.com
Directors Peter Elek, Helene W. Elek
Submissions Lauren Mactas

Full-length fiction/non-fiction. Illustrated adult non-fiction: style, culture, popular history, popular science, current affairs; juvenile picture books (home 15%, overseas 20%), performance rights (20%); will sometimes suggest revision. Works with overseas agents. No reading fee. Experienced in licensing for multimedia, on-line and off-line. Founded 1979.

Ann Elmo Agency Inc.*

60 East 42nd Street, New York, NY 10165
tel 212-661-2880 *fax* 212-661-2883
Director Lettie Lee

Full-length fiction and non-fiction MSS (home 15%, overseas 20%), theatre (15%). Works with foreign agencies. No reading fee. Send query letter only with sase or IRC.

Frieda Fishbein Associates

PO Box 723, Bedford, NY 10506
tel 914-234-7232 *fax* 914-234-4196
e-mail fishbein@juno.com
Contacts Heidi Carlson, Douglas Michael

TV, plays, books, screenplays, film and TV rights. No unsolicited MSS; query first. Reading fee for new writers, or published writers in a new genre.

ForthWrite Literary Agency

23852 W. Pacific Coast Hwy, Suite 701, Malibu, CA 90265
tel 310-456-5698 *fax* 310-456-6589
e-mail literaryag@aol.com
Owner Wendy Keller

Only non-fiction: business, self-help popular psychology, how-to. Subjects include: animals, art, horticulture/gardening, archaeology, European history (especially English), biography, health (especially homeopathy and alternative medicines), parenting, coffee table (illustrated) books, crafts (bobbin lace, handicrafts, etc), nature, psychology. Send IRC with query. Response in 8 weeks. Founded 1988.

The Fox Chase Agency Inc.*

Walnut Hill Plaza, Suite 140, 150 South Warner Road, King of Prussia, PA 19406
tel 610-341-9840 *fax* 610-341-9842

Jeanne Fredericks Literary Agency Inc.*

221 Benedict Hill Road, New Canaan, CT 06840
tel/fax 203-972-3011
e-mail jfredrks@optonline.net

Quality non-fiction, especially health, science, women's issues, gardening, antiques and decorative arts, biography, cookbooks, popular reference, business, natural history (home 15%, overseas 20%). No reading fee. Query first, enclosing sase. Member of Authors Guild. Founded 1997.

Robert A. Freedman Dramatic Agency Inc.*

(Formerly Harold Freedman Brandt & Brandt Dramatic Dept. Inc.)
1501 Broadway, Suite 2310, New York, NY 10036
tel 212-840-5760

Plays, motion picture and TV scripts. Send letter of enquiry first, with sase.

Samuel French Inc.*

45 West 25th Street, New York, NY 10010
tel 212-206-8990 *fax* 212-206-1429
President Charles R. Van Nostrand

Play publishers; authors' representatives.

Sarah Jane Freyman Literary Agency

(formerly Stepping Stone Literary Agency)
59 West 71st Street, Suite 9B, New York, NY 10023
tel 212-362-9277 *fax* 212-501-8240
President Sarah Jane Freymann, *Associate* Katharine Sands

Fiction and non-fiction, especially commercial and mainstream non-fiction (home/ overseas 15%). Works in conjunction with Abner Stein and Marsh & Sheil in London. No reading fee. Founded 1974.

Jay Garon-Brooke Associates Inc.* – see Pinder, Lane & Garon-Brooke Associates Ltd

Gelfman Schneider Literary Agents Inc.*

250 West 57th Street, Suite 2515, New York, NY 10107
tel 212-245-1993 *fax* 212-245-8678
Directors Jane Gelfman, Deborah Schneider

General adult fiction and non-fiction (home 15%, overseas 20%). Works in conjunction with Curtis Brown, London. Will suggest revision. No reading fee but please send sase for return of material.

Goodman Associates, Literary Agents*

500 West End Avenue, New York, NY 10024
tel 212-873-4806
Partners Arnold P. Goodman, Elise Simon Goodman

Adult book length fiction and non-fiction (home 15%, overseas 20%). No reading fee. Founded 1976.

Sanford J. Greenburger Associates Inc.*

55 Fifth Avenue, New York, NY 10003
tel 212-206-5600 *fax* 212-463-8718
Contacts Heide Lange, Faith Hamlin, Beth Vesel, Theresa Park, Elyse Cheney, Daniel Mandel

Fiction and non-fiction, film and TV rights. No unsolicited MSS; query first. No reading fee.

The Joy Harris Literary Agency Inc.*

156 Fifth Avenue, Suite 617, New York, NY 10010-7002
tel 212-924-6269 *fax* 212-924-6609
e-mail jhlitagent@aol.com
President Joy Harris

John Hawkins & Associates Inc.*

(formerly Paul R. Reynolds Inc.)
71 West 23rd Street, Suite 1600, New York, NY 10010
tel 212-807-7040 *fax* 212-807-9555
President John Hawkins, *Vice-President* William Reiss, *Foreign Rights* Moses Cardona, *Permissions* Holly Cohen, *Other Agents* Elinor B. Sidel, Warren Frazier, Anne Hawkins

Fiction, non-fiction, juvenile. Founded 1893.

The Jeff Herman Agency LLC*

332 Bleecker Street, Suite 631, New York, NY 10014
tel 212-941-0540 *fax* 212-941 0540
e-mail jeff@jeffherman.com
web site http://www.jeffherman.com

Business, reference, popular psychology, computers, health and beauty, spirituality, general non-fiction (home/overseas 15%); will suggest revision where appropriate. Works with overseas agents. No reading fee. Founded 1986.

Frederick Hill Associates

1842 Union Street, San Francisco, CA 94123
tel 415-921-2910 *fax* 415-921-2802
Branch office 505 North Robertson Blvd, Los Angeles, CA 90048
tel 310-860-9605 *fax* 310-860-9672

Full-length fiction and non-fiction (home 15%, overseas 20%). Will suggest revision. Works in conjunction with agents in Scandinavia, France, Germany, Holland, Japan, Spain. No reading fee. Founded 1979.

IMG Literary – see Mark Reiter IMG Literary

International Creative Management Inc.*

40 West 57th Street, New York, NY 10019
tel 212-556-5600 *fax* 212-556-5665

No unsolicited MSS, please; send query letters.

JCA Literary Agency Inc.*

27 West 20th Street, Suite 1103, New York, NY 10011
tel 212-807-0888

Contacts Jeff Gerecke, Tony Outhwaite
Adult fiction and non-fiction. No unsolicited MSS; query first.

Ben F. Kamsler Ltd
5501 Noble Avenue, Sherman Oaks, CA 91411
tel 818-785-4167 *fax* 818-988-8304
Directors Ben Kamsler, Irene Kamsler
Full-length novel MSS, plays, TV specials, screenplays (home 10%, overseas 20%), performance rights (10%). Will suggest revision on promising MSS. No reading fee, but preliminary letter with sase essential. Founded 1990.

Barbara S. Kouts, Literary Agent*
PO Box 560, Bellport, NY 11713
tel 631-286-1278 *fax* 631-286-1538
Full-length MSS. Fiction and non-fiction, children's and adult (home 10%, overseas 20%); will suggest revision. Works with overseas agents. No reading fee. Query first. Founded 1980.

The Lazear Agency Inc.
800 Washington Avenue North, Suite 660, Minneapolis, MN 55401
tel 612-332-8640 *fax* 612-332-4648
Contacts Jonathon Lazear, Wendy Lazear, Christi Cardenas, Tanya Cromey
Fiction: full-length MSS; non-fiction: proposals. Adult fiction and non-fiction; film and TV rights; foreign language rights; audio, video and electronic rights (home 15%, overseas 20%). No reading fee. No unsolicited MSS; 2-3 page query first with sase for response. No faxed queries. Founded 1984.

Lescher & Lescher Ltd*
47 East 19th Street, New York, NY 10003
tel 212-529-1790 *fax* 212-529-2716
Directors Robert Lescher, Susan Lescher
Full-length and short MSS (home 15%, overseas 25%). No unsolicited MSS; query first with sase. No reading fee. Founded 1966.

Ellen Levine Literary Agency Inc.*
Suite 1801, 15 East 26th Street, New York, NY 10010
tel 212-899-0620 *fax* 212-725-4501
Contacts Elizabeth Kaplan, Diana Finch, Louise Quayle, *UK Representative* A.M. Heath
Full-length MSS: biography, contemporary affairs, women's issues, history, science, literary and commercial fiction (home 15%, overseas 20%); in conjunction with co-agents, theatre, films, TV (15%). Will suggest revision. Works in conjunction with agents in Europe, Japan, Israel, Brazil, Argentina, Australia, Far East. No reading fee; preliminary letter and sase and US postage essential. Founded 1980.

Margret McBride Literary Agency*
7744 Fay Avenue, Suite 201, La Jolla, CA 92037
tel 858-454-1550 *fax* 858-454-2156
President Margret McBride
Business, mainstream fiction and non-fiction; no poetry or children's books (home 15%, overseas 25%). No reading fee. Submit query letter with sase to Margret McBride. Founded 1981.

Gerard McCauley Agency Inc.*
PO Box 844, Katonah, NY 10536
tel 914-232-5700
Specialises in history, biography, public affairs for the general reader.

Anita D. McClellan Associates*
50 Stearns Street, Cambridge, MA 02138
tel 617-576-6950
Director Anita D. McClellan
General fiction and non-fiction. Full-length MSS (home 15%, overseas 20%). Will suggest revision for agency clients. No unsolicited MSS. Send preliminary letter and sase bearing US postage or IRC.

McIntosh & Otis Inc.*
353 Lexington Avenue, New York, NY 10016
tel 212-687-7400 *fax* 212-687-6894
Adult Eugene H. Winick, Samuel L. Pinkus, Barbara Kennedy, *Adult, Subsidiary Rights* Whitney Calam, Sean Ferrell, *Juvenile* Dorothy Markinko, Tracey Adams, *Film and TV* Evva Joan Pryor
Adult and juvenile literary fiction and non-fiction, film and TV rights. No unsolicited MSS; query first with outline, sample chapters and sase. No reading fee. Founded 1928.

Carol Mann Agency*
55 Fifth Avenue, New York, NY 10003
tel 212-206-5635 *fax* 212-675-4809
Associates Carol Mann, Gareth Esersky, James Fitzgerald
Psychology, popular history, biography, pop culture, general non-fiction; fiction (home 15%, overseas 20%). Works in conjunction with foreign agents. No reading fee. Founded 1977.

Elaine Markson Literary Agency*

44 Greenwich Avenue, New York, NY 10011
tel 212-243-8480 *fax* 212-691-9014
Directors Elaine Markson, Geri Thoma, Sally Wofford-Girand, Elizabeth Sheinkman

Literary and mainstream commercial fiction (no genre); biography, sociology, history, popular culture, feminism (home 15%, overseas 20%), performance rights (10%); will suggest revision. Works with overseas agents. No reading fee. No unsolicited MSS; please send query letter. Founded 1973.

Mildred Marmur Associates Ltd*

2005 Palmer Avenue, Suite 127, Larchmont, NY 10538-2469
tel 914-834-1170 *fax* 914-834-2840
e-mail marmur@westnet.com, lebowitz@westnet.com
President Mildred Marmur, *Associate* Jane Lebowitz

Serious non-fiction, literary fiction, juveniles, cookbooks. Full-length and short MSS (home licences 15%, overseas licences 20%), performance rights (15%). Works with co-agents in all major countries. No reading fee. Queries must include sase or International Reply Coupons. Founded 1987.

The Evan Marshall Agency*

6 Tristam Place, Pine Brook, NJ 07058-9445
tel 973-882-1122 *fax* 973-882-3099
e-mail evanmarshall@thenovelist.com
web site http://www.thenovelist.com
President Evan Marshall

General fiction (home 15%, overseas 20%). Works in conjunction with overseas agents. Will suggest revision; no reading fee. Founded 1987.

The Marton Agency Inc.*

1 Union Square, Suite 612, New York, NY 10003-3303
tel 212-255-1908 *fax* 212-691-9061
e-mail martonagcy@aol.com
Owner Tonda Marton

Stage plays only.

Harold Matson Company Inc.*

276 Fifth Avenue, New York, NY 10001
tel 212-679-4490 *fax* 212-545-1224

Full-length MSS (home 15%, UK 19%, translation 19%). No unsolicited MSS. No reading fee. Founded 1937.

Scott Meredith Literary Agency LP

845 Third Avenue, New York, NY 10022
tel 212-751-4545 *fax* 212-755-2972
web site http://www.writingtosell.com
President Arthur Klebanoff, *Vice-President* Lisa J. Edwards, *Director, Subsidiary Rights* Barry N. Malzberg
London office A.M. Heath & Co. Ltd

Full-length and short MSS. General fiction and non-fiction, books and magazines, juveniles, plays, TV scripts, motion picture rights and properties (home 10%, overseas 20%), performance rights (10%). Will read unsolicited MSS, queries, outlines. Single fee charged for readings, criticism and assistance in revision. Founded 1946.

Helen Merrill Ltd*

295 Lafayette Street, Suite 915, New York, NY 10012

No unsolicited MSS. No books. No phone calls or faxes.

William Morris Agency Inc.*

1325 Avenue of the Americas, New York, NY 10019
tel 212-586-5100

Multimedia Product Development Inc.*

410 South Michigan Avenue, Suite 724, Chicago, IL 60605
tel 312-922-3063 *fax* 312-922-1905
Contact Jane Jordan Browne

General fiction and non-fiction (home 15%, overseas 20%), performance rights (15%). Works in conjunction with foreign agents. Will suggest revision; no reading fee. Founded 1971.

Jean V. Naggar Literary Agency*

216 East 75th Street, Suite 1E, New York, NY 10021
tel 212-794-1082
President Jean V. Naggar, *Agents* Frances Kuffel, Alice Tasman, Jennifer Weltz (rights)

Mainstream commercial and literary fiction (no formula fiction); non-fiction: psychology, science, biography (home 15%, overseas 20%), performance rights (15%). Works in conjunction with foreign agents. No reading fee. Founded 1978.

Ruth Nathan Agency

53 East 34th Street, Suite 207, New York, NY 10016
tel/fax 212-481-1185
Director Ruth Nathan

Fine art, decorative arts, show biz, biographies pertaining to those areas; fiction (Middle Ages). Home (15%), overseas (10-15%). No reading fee. Founded 1981.

New England Publishing Associates Inc.*

PO Box 5, Chester, CT 06412
tel 860-345-READ *fax* 860-345-3660
e-mail nepa@nepa.com
Directors Elizabeth Frost-Knappman, Edward W. Knappman, Ron Formica, Kris Schiavi

Serious non-fiction for the adult market (home 15%, overseas varies), performance rights (varies). Works in conjunction with foreign publishers. No reading fee; will suggest revision – if undertaken; 15% fee for placing MSS. London representative: Scott Ferris. Dramatic rights: **AMG/ Renaissance**, Beverly Hills. Founded 1982.

Harold Ober Associates Inc.*

425 Madison Avenue, New York, NY 10017
tel 212-759-8600 *fax* 212-759-9428
Directors Phyllis Westberg, Emma Sweeney, Wendy Schmalz, Knox Burger

Full-length MSS (home 15%, British 20%, overseas 20%), performance rights (15%). Will suggest revision. No reading fee. Founded 1929.

Fifi Oscard Agency Inc.*

24 West 40th Street, New York, NY 10018
tel 212-764-1100 *fax* 212-840-5019
President Fifi Oscard, *Agents* Ivy Fischer Stone, Carolyn French (plays)

Full-length MSS (home 15%, overseas 20%), theatrical performance rights (10%). Will suggest revision. Works in conjunction with many foreign agencies. No reading fee, but no unsolicited submissions.

James Peter Associates Inc.*

151 Sunset Lane, PO Box 772, Tenafly, NJ 07670
tel 201-568-0760 *fax* 201-568-2959
e-mail bertholtje@compuserve.com
Contact Bert Holtje

Non-fiction, especially history, politics, popular culture, health, psychology, reference, biography (home 15%, overseas 20%). Foreign rights handled by: Bobbe Siegel, 41 West 83rd Street, New York, NY 10024. Will suggest revision. No reading fee. Founded 1981.

The Pimlico Agency Inc.

Box 20447, Cherokee Station, New York, NY 10021
tel 212-628-9729 *fax* 212-535-7861
Contacts Christopher Shepard, Catherine Brooks, *Directors* Kay McCauley, Kirby McCauley

Adult non-fiction and fiction. No unsolicited MSS.

Pinder, Lane & Garon-Brooke Associates Ltd*

159 West 53rd Street, Suite 14, New York, NY 10019
tel 212-489-0880 *fax* 212-586-9346
London Representative Abner Stein

Specialises in fiction and non-fiction: biographies and lifestyle. Writer must be referred by an editor or a client. Will not read unsolicited MSS

PMA Literary and Film Management Inc.

Old Chelsea Station, PO Box 1817, New York, NY 10011
tel 212-929-1222 *fax* 212-206-0238
e-mail pmalitfilm@aol.com
web site http://www.pmalitfilm.com
President Peter Miller

Full-length MSS. Specialises in commercial fiction (especially thrillers), true crime, non-fiction (all types), and all books with global publishing and film/TV potential (home 15%, overseas 25%), films, TV (10-20%). Works in conjunction with agents worldwide. Preliminary enquiry with career goals, synopsis and resumé essential. Founded 1976.

Raines & Raines*

71 Park Avenue, New York, NY 10016
tel 212-684-5160 *fax* 212-685-6593
Directors Theron Raines, Joan Raines, Keith Korman

Full-length MSS (home 15%, overseas 20%). Works in conjunction with overseas agents. No unsolicited MSS. Founded 1961.

Renaissance – A Literary Talent Agency – see AMG Renaissance

Helen Rees Literary Agency*

123 N. Washington Street, Boston, MA 02114
tel 617-723 5232 *fax* 617-723 5211
Contact Joan Mazmanian, *Associate* Barbara Rifkind

Business books, self-help, biography, autobiography, political, literary fiction (home 15%). Works with foreign agent. No reading fee. Submit query letter with sase. Founded 1982.

Mark Reiter IMG Literary*

825 Seventh Avenue, 9th Floor, New York, NY 10019
tel 212-489-5400 *fax* 212-246 1118

Fiction (no science fiction) and non-fiction. Send query letter with sase.

Rosenstone/Wender*

3 East 48th Street, New York,
NY 10017
tel 212-832-8330 *fax* 212-759-4524
Contacts Phyllis Wender, Susan Perlman Cohen, Sonia Pabley

Fiction, non-fiction, film and TV rights. No unsolicited MSS; query first. No reading fee.

Russell & Volkening Inc.*

50 West 29th Street, Suite 7E, New York,
NY 10001
tel 212-684-6050 *fax* 212-889-3026
Contacts Jennie Dunham, Timothy Seldes, Joseph Regal

General fiction and non-fiction, film and TV rights. No screenplays. No unsolicited MSS; query first with letter and sase. No reading fee.

Susan Schulman Literary & Dramatic Agents Inc.*

454 West 44th Street, New York, NY 10036
tel 212-713-1633 *fax* 212-581-8830
e-mail schulman@aol.com

Agents for negotiation in all markets (with co-agents) of fiction, general non-fiction, children's books, academic and professional works, and associated subsidiary rights including plays, film and TV (home 15%, UK 7.5%, overseas 20%). Return postage required.

The Shukat Company Ltd*

340 West 55th Street, Suite 1A, New York,
NY 10019
tel 212-582-7614 *fax* 212-315-3752
e-mail staff@shukat.com
President Scott Shukat, *Contact* Patricia McLaughlin, Maribel Rivas

Theatre, films, TV, radio (15%). No reading fee. No unsolicited material accepted.

The Spieler Agency

154 West 57th Street, Room 135, New York,
NY 10019
tel 212-757-4439 *fax* 212-333-2019
Directors F. Joseph Spieler, Lisa M. Ross, John F. Thornton

Full- and short-length MSS. History, politics, ecology, business, consumer reference, some fiction (home 15%, overseas 20%). No reading fee. Query first with sample and sase. Founded 1982.

Philip G. Spitzer Literary Agency*

50 Talmage Farm Lane, East Hampton,
NY 11937
tel 516-329-3650 *fax* 516-329-3651

General fiction and non-fiction; specialises in mystery/suspense, sports, politics, biography, social issues.

Sterling Lord Literistic Inc.

65 Bleecker Street, New York, NY 10012
tel 212-780-6050 *fax* 212-780-6095
Directors Peter Matson, Sterling Lord, Philippa Brophy, Jody Hotchkiss

Full-length and short MSS (home 15%, overseas 20%), performance rights (15%). Will suggest revision. No reading fee.

Gloria Stern Agency*

12535 Chandler Boulevard, Suite 3,
North Hollywood, CA 91607-1934
tel 818-508-6296 *fax* 818-508-6296
Director Gloria Stern

Fiction and films, electronics and multimedia (home 10%, overseas 15%). Reading fee; consultation fee for revisions; some author expenses for placing MSS. Founded 1984.

Roslyn Targ Literary Agency Inc.*

105 West 13th Street, New York, NY 10011
tel 212-206-9390 *fax* 212-989-6233
e-mail roslyntarg@aol.com

Non-fiction: query with outline, publication history and CV. Fiction: query with synopsis or outline, and CV and publication history. All submissions require sase. No phone queries. Affiliates in most foreign countries. No reading fee.

Ralph M. Vicinanza Ltd*

111 8th Avenue, Suite 1501, New York,
NY 10011
tel 212-924-7090
Contact Ralph Vicinanza, Christopher Lotts, Christopher Schelling

Fiction: literary, women's, 'multicultural', popular (especially science fiction, fantasy, thrillers), children's. Non-fiction: history, business, science, biography, popular culture. Foreign rights specialists. No unsolicited MSS.

Austin Wahl Agency Inc.

1820 North 76th Court, Elmwood Park,
IL 60707-3631
tel 708-456-2301 *fax* 708-456-2031
President Thomas Wahl

Full-length and short MSS (home 15%, overseas 20%), theatre, films, TV (10%). No reading fee; professional writers only. Founded 1935.

Wallace Literary Agency Inc.

177 East 70th Street, New York, NY 10021
tel 212-570-9090 *fax* 212-772-8979
Director Lois Wallace

Full-length MSS. No cookery, humour, how-to; film, TV, theatre for agency clients. Will suggest revision. No unsolicited MSS; no faxed queries. Will only answer queries with return postage. Founded 1988.

T.C. Wallace Ltd*

Suite 1001, 425 Madison Avenue, New York, NY 10017
tel 212-759-8600 *fax* 212-759-9428
e-mail twallace@rngfint.com
Managing Director Tom Wallace

Full-length MSS. Non-fiction: history, biography, travel, memoirs. Fiction: thrillers, mystery novels, literary fiction (home 15%, overseas 20%. No unsolicited MSS. No reading fee. Will suggest a revision. Founded 1998.

Watkins/Loomis Agency Inc.

133 East 35th Street, New York, NY 10016
tel 212-532-0080 *fax* 212-889-0506
President Gloria Loomis, *Associate* Nicole Aragi, *Contact* Katherine Fausset

Fiction and non-fiction. No unsolicited MSS; query first with sase. No reading fee. Representatives: **Abner Stein** (UK), Marsh Agency (foreign).

Sandra Watt and Associates

8033 Sunset Boulevard, Suite 4053, Hollywood, CA 90046
tel 213-653-2339
Owner Sandra Watt

Lead women's fiction, suspense, mysteries, New Age, cyber-punk; psychological self-help, gardening, single-volume reference works; screenplays (home 15%, overseas 25%), films (10%). Works in conjunction with foreign agents. Will suggest revision; no reading fee; $100 marketing fee for unpublished authors. Founded 1978.

Wecksler-Incomco

170 West End Avenue, New York, NY 10023
tel 212-787-2239 *fax* 212-496-7035
President Sally Wecksler, *Associate* Joann Amparan

Illustrated books, non-fiction, some literary fiction, children's books (home 15%, overseas 20%); will suggest revision where appropriate. No reading fee. Founded 1971.

Rhoda Weyr Agency*

151 Bergen Street, Brooklyn, NY 11217
tel 718-522-0480 *fax* 718-522-0410

General non-fiction and fiction, particularly science, history, biography (home 15%, overseas 20%), performance rights (15%). Letter with proposal; sase required. Co-agents in all foreign markets. Founded 1983.

Writers House LLC*

21 West 26th Street, New York, NY 10010
tel 212-685-2400 *fax* 212-685-1781
President Albert Zuckerman, *Executive Vice-President* Amy Berkower

Fiction and non-fiction, including all rights; film and TV rights. No screenplays or software. Query first; no reading fee. Founded 1974.

The Writers Shop*

(formerly Virginia Barber Literary Agency)
101 Fifth Avenue, New York, NY 10003
tel 212-255-6515 *fax* 212-691-9418
Co-Presidents Virginia Barber, Jennifer Rudolph Walsh, *Contacts* Jay Mandel, Kristin Lewandowski, Sarah Almodovar

General fiction and non-fiction (home 15%, overseas 20%), performance rights (15%); will suggest revision. Has co-agents in all major countries; Abner Stein handles UK rights. No reading fee. Founded 1974.

The Wylie Agency Inc.

250 West 57th Street, New York, NY 10107
tel 212-246-0069 *fax* 212-586-8953
e-mail mail@wylieagency.com
Directors Andrew Wylie (president), Sarah Chalfant

Literary fiction/non-fiction. No unsolicited MSS accepted. London office: **The Wylie Agency UK Ltd**.

Mary Yost Associates Inc.*

59 East 54th Street, Suite 72, New York, NY 10022
tel 212-980-4988

Full-length and short MSS (home and overseas 10%). Works with individual agents in all foreign countries. Will suggest revision. No reading fee. Founded 1958.

Overseas literary agents – other

Most of the agents listed here work in association with an agent in London. Before submitting a typescript, writers are advised to send a preliminary letter and to ascertain terms.

Argentina

International Editors Co.

Avenida Cabildo 1156, 1426 Buenos Aires
tel 54-11-4788-2992 *fax* 54-11-4786-0888

The Nancy H. Smith Literary Agency

(formerly The Lawrence Smith Agency)
Ayacucho 1867, 2B, Buenos Aires 1112
tel/fax (54 11) 4804 5508
e-mail meg@interlink.com.ar
Contact Margaret Murray
London office 30 Acton Lane, London W4 5ED
tel 020-8995 4769 *fax* 020-8747 4012
e-mail distobart@cs.com
Contact Diana Stobart

Founded 1938.

Australia

Curtis Brown (Australia) Pty Ltd

27 Union Street, Paddington, Sydney, NSW 2021
tel (02) 9331 5301/9361 6161 *fax* (02) 9360 3935
e-mail info@curtisbrown.com.au

Literary Resources

26 Robert Street, Willoughby, NSW 2068
fax (02) 9967 2102
e-mail dougnanc@ozemail.com.au
Principal Doug Nancarrow

Full-length and short MSS, adult fiction (home 10%, overseas 20%), performance rights (10%); will suggest revision. Works with overseas agents. Reading fee. Founded 1992.

Brazil

Agencia Literária Balcells Mello e Souza Riff/BMSR

Rua Visconde de Pirajá, 414 s1 1108 Ipanema, 22410-002 Rio de Janeiro, RJ
tel (55-21) 287-6299 *fax* (55-21) 267-6393
e-mail lucia@bmsr.com.br
Contact Lucia de Mello e Souza Riff

Karin Schindler and Suely Pedro dos Santos Rights Representatives

Caixa Postal 19051, 04505-970 São Paulo, SP
tel 55-11-241-9177 *fax* 55-11-241-9077
e-mail sysantos@internetcom.com.br

Canada

Acacia House Publishing Services Ltd

51 Acacia Road, Toronto, Ontario M4S 2K6
tel/fax 416-484-8356
Managing Director Mrs Frances A. Hanna

Literary fiction/non-fiction, quality commercial fiction, most non-fiction, except business books (15% English worldwide, 30% translation), performance rights (15-30%). No science fiction, horror or occult. Works with overseas agents. Reading fee payable in advance if a detailed evaluation is requested. Founded 1985.

Authors' Marketing Services Ltd

55 Kennedy Avenue, Toronto M65 2X6
tel 416-763 8797 *fax* 416-763-1504
e-mail 102047.111@compuserve.com
Director Larry Hoffman

Adult fiction, biography and autobiography (home 15%, overseas 20%). Reading fee charged for unpublished writers; will suggest a revision. Founded 1978.

Anne McDermid & Associates

92 Willcocks Street, Toronto, Ontario M5S 1C8
tel 416-324 8845 *fax* 416-324 8870
e-mail amcdermid@sympatico.ca
Director Anne McDermid

Literary fiction and non-fiction, and quality commercial fiction; no children's literature (home 15%, US 15%, overseas 20%). No reading fee. Founded 1996.

Eastern Europe

Artisjus

Mészáros u. 15-17, 1016 Budapest, Hungary
postal address H-1538 Budapest, Pf. 593, Hungary
tel (36) 1 488 2600 *fax* (36) 1 212 1544
e-mail pgyertyánfy@artisjus.com
AHSPAR tel/fax (36) 1 488 2706

Agency for theatre and literature of the Artisjus Hungarian Society for the Protection of Authors' Rights.

Aura-Pont, Theatrical and Literary Agency Ltd

Radlická 99, Prague 5, Czech Republic
tel/fax (420) 2 53 99 09, 53 63 51
e-mail aurapont@login.cz
web site http://www.aura-pont.cz
Director Zuzana Jezková

Handles authors' rights in books, theatre, film, TV, radio, software – both Czech and foreign (home 10%, overseas 15%). Founded 1990.

DILIA, Theatrical and Literary Agency

Krátkého 1, 190 03 Prague 9, Czech Republic

tel (420) 2 82 68 41-8 *fax* (420) 2 82 40 09
e-mail info@dilia.cz
web site http://www.dilia.cz
Theatrical and Literary Agency.

Lex Copyright
Szemere utca 21, 1054 Budapest, Hungary
tel (36) 1 332 9340 *fax* (36) 1 331 6181
e-mail lexcopy.bp@mail.datanet.hu
Director Dr Gyorgy Tibor Szanto
Specialises in representing American and British authors in Hungary. Founded 1991.

Lita
Partizánska 21, 815 30 Bratislava, Slovakia
tel/fax (421) 7 313645
Slovak Literary Agency.

Andrew Nurnberg Associates Prague, s.r.o
Seifertova 81, 130 00 Prague 3, Czech Republic
tel (420) 2 22 78 20 41 *fax* (420) 2 22 78 23 08
e-mail nurnprg@mbox.vol.cz
Contact Petra Tobisková

Prava i Prevodi
Koste Jovanovica 18, 11000 Belgrade, Yugoslavia
tel (381) 11 460 290 *fax* (381) 11 472 146
e-mails ana@pip.co.yu office@pip.co.yu
Director Ana Milenkovic
Specialises in representing American and British authors in former Eastern Europe (15 languages). Founded 1983.

France

Bureau Littéraire International Marguerite Scialtiel
14 rue Chanoinesse, 75004 Paris
tel (1) 43 54 71 16
Contact Geneviéve Ulmann

Agence Hoffman
77 Boulevard Saint-Michel, 75005 Paris
tel (1) 43 26 56 94 *fax* (1) 43 26 34 07
e-mail hoffman@starnet.fr

Agence Michelle Lapautre
6 rue Jean Carriès, 75007 Paris
tel (1) 47 34 82 41 *fax* (1) 47 34 00 90
e-mail lapautre@club-internet.fr

La Nouvelle Agence
7 rue Corneille, 75006 Paris
tel (1) 43 25 85 60 *fax* (1) 43 25 47 98
e-mail lnaparis@aol.com
Contact Mary Kling

Germany (see also Switzerland)

Agence Hoffman
Bechsteinstrasse 2, 80804 Munich
tel 089-308 48 07 *fax* 089-308 21 08

Michael Meller Literary Agency
PO Box 400323, 80703 Munich
tel (089) 366371 *fax* (089) 366372
e-mail meller@ibu.de
Full-length MSS. Fiction and non-fiction, screenplays for films and TV (home 15%, overseas 20%). Own US office. No reading fee. Founded 1988.

Thomas Schlück GmbH
Literary Agency, Hinter der Worth 12, 30827 Garbsen
tel 05131-497560 *fax* 05131-497589
e-mail mail@schlueckagent.de

India

Ajanta Books International
1 U.B. Jawahar Nagar, Bungalow Road, Delhi 110007
tel 7415016, 2926182, 7258630
fax 91-11-7415016
e-mail ajantabi@ndf.vsnl.net.in
Proprietor S. Balwant
Full-length MSS in social sciences and humanities (commission varies according to market – Indian books in Indian and foreign languages, foreign books into Indian languages). Will suggest revision; charges made if agency undertakes revision; reading fee. Founded 1975.

Israel

I. Pikarski Ltd Literary Agency
200 Hayarkon Street, PO Box 4006, Tel Aviv 61040
tel 03-5270159/5231880 *fax* 03-5270160
e-mail gabpikar@inter.net.il
Director Ilana Pikarski
General trade publishing and merchandising rights. Founded 1977.

Italy

Eulama SRL
Via Guido de Ruggiero 28, 00142 Rome
tel (06) 540 73 09 *fax* (06) 540 87 72
Directors Harald Kahnemann, Karin von Prellwitz, Norbert von Prellwitz, Pina Ocello von Prellwitz

Quality fiction and non-fiction; Latin American literature; represents publishers, authors and agencies in Europe and the world. Founded 1962.

Grandi Associati SRL

Via Caradosso 12, 20123 Milan
tel (02) 469 55 41/481 89 62
fax (02) 481 95108
e-mail agenzia@grandieassociati.it
Directors Laura Grandi, Stefano Tettamanti

Provides publicity and foreign rights consultation for publishers and authors as well as sub-agent services; will suggest revision where appropriate. Reading fee. Founded 1988.

ILA – International Literary Agency – USA

I-18010 Terzorio-IM
tel (0184) 48 40 48 *fax* (0184) 48 72 92
e-mail libri.gg@dmw.it

Publishers' and authors' agent, interested only in series of best-selling and mass market books by proven, published authors with a track record. Also interested in published books on antiques and collectibles. Founded 1969.

Agenzia Letteraria Internazionale SRL

Via Fratelli Gabba 3, 20121 Milan
tel (02) 86 54 45/86 46 34 18/86 15 72
fax (02) 87 62 22
e-mail alidmb@tin.it

New Blitz Literary & TV Agency

Via di Panico 67, 00186 Rome, Italy
tel/fax (06) 686 4859
e-mail bono@uniroma3.it
Literary Department Giovanni A.S. Congiu

Japan

The English Agency (Japan) Ltd

Sakuragi Building 4F, 6-7-3 Minami Aoyama, Minato-ku, Tokyo 107-0062
tel 03-3406 5385 *fax* 03-3406 5387
Managing Director William Miller

Handles work by English-language writers living in Japan; arranges Japanese translations for internationally established publishers, agents and authors; arranges Japanese localisations for CD-Rom. Standard commission: 10%. Own representatives in New York and London. No reading fee. Founded 1979.

Orion Literary Agency

1-7-12-4F Kanda-Jimbocho, Chiyoda-ku, Tokyo 101
tel 03-3295-1405 *fax* 03-3295-4366

Netherlands

Auteursbureau Greta Baars-Jelgersma

Clingelbeeck, Utrechtseweg 131-6, NL-6812, AA Arnhem
tel (026) 446 24 31 *fax* (026) 446 21 97

Literature; illustrated co-productions, including children's, art, handicraft, hobby and nature (home/overseas 20%). Works with overseas agents. Occasionally charges a reading fee. Founded 1951.

Internationaal Literatuur Bureau B.V.

Postbus 10014, 1201 DA, Hilversum
tel (035) 621 35 00 *fax* (035) 621 57 71
e-mail mkohn@wxs.nl
Contact Menno Kohn

New Zealand

Glenys Bean Writers' Agent

PO Box 60509, Titirangi, Auckland
tel (09) 812 8486 *fax* (09) 812 8188
e-mail g.bean@clear.net.nz

Adult and children's fiction, educational, non-fiction, film, TV, radio (10%-20%). Send preliminary letter, synopsis and sase. Represented by **Sanford Greenburger Associates Ltd** (USA). Translation/foreign rights: Paul Marsh Agency. Founded 1989.

Richards Literary Agency

48C Aberdeen Road, Castor Bay, Auckland 9
postal address PO Box 31240, Milford, Auckland 9
tel (09) 410-5681 *fax* (09) 410-6389
Partners Ray Richards, Nicki Richards Wallace

Full-length MSS, fiction, non-fiction, adult, juvenile, educational, academic books; films, TV, radio (home 10%, overseas 10-20%). Preliminary letter, synopsis with sase required. No reading fee. Founded 1977.

Nigeria

Joe-Tolalu & Associates (Nigeria) Ltd

Apt. 4, Tomoloju Estate, 4-6 Yaya Abatam Street, Ogba, PO Box 7031, Ikeja, Lagos

tel/fax 01-4922681
Directors Joseph Omosade Awolalu, Tosin Awolalu, Foluke Awolalu

Full-length MSS: fiction and non-fiction; Christian literature; short MSS: picture books only (home 10-15%, overseas 15-20%; translation 15%, performance/film/TV 10%); will suggest revision. Works with overseas agents. Preliminary letter essential; no reading fee. Founded 1983.

Portugal

Ilidio da Fonseca Matos

Avenida Gomes Pereira, 105-3°-B, 1500-326 Lisbon
tel (21) 716 2988 *fax* (21) 715 4445

Russia

Prava I Perevody

(Permissions & Rights Ltd, Moscow)
Bolshaya Bronnaya Street 6A, Moscow 103670
tel (095) 203 5280 *fax* (095) 203 0229
e-mail prava@aha.ru
Director Konstantin Palchikov

Specialises in representing US and British authors in Russia, Latvia, Lithuania, Estonia and Ukraine. Founded 1993.

Scandinavia, inc. Finland, Iceland

Bookman Literary Agency

Bastager 3, DK-2950 Vedbaek, Denmark
tel (45) 45 89 25 20 *fax* (45) 45 89 25 01
e-mail ihl@bookman.dk

Handles rights in Denmark, Sweden, Norway, Finland and Iceland for foreign authors.

Gösta Dahl & Son, AB

Aladdinsvägan 14, S-167 61 Bromma, Sweden
tel 08 25 62 35 *fax* 08 25 11 18

Leonhardt & Høier Literary Agency aps

Studiestraede 35, DK-1455 Copenhagen K, Denmark
tel 33 13 25 23 *fax* 33 13 49 92
e-mail anneli.lh@adr.dk

Lennart Sane Agency AB

Holländareplan 9, S-374 34 Karlshamm, Sweden
tel 0454 123 56 *fax* 0454 149 20
Directors Lennart Sane, Elisabeth Sane, Ulf Töregård

Fiction, non-fiction, children's books. Founded 1969.

Gustaf von Sydow

Lorensbergsvägen 76, S 136 69 Haninge, Sweden
tel/fax 08 776 10 54
Directors Gustaf von Sydow, Elizabeth von Sydow

Handles TV, film, celebrity and news features in Sweden, Norway, Denmark and Finland. Literary agent working in Sweden, Norway, Denmark and Finland. Founded 1988.

Sane Töregård Agency

Holländareplan 9, S-374 34 Karlshamn, Sweden
tel (46) 454 12356 *fax* (46) 454 14920
e-mail toregard@algonet.se
Directors Lennart Sane, Elisabeth Sane, Ulf Töregård

Represents authors, agents and publishers in Scandinavia and Holland for rights in fiction, non-fiction and children's books. Founded 1995.

South Africa

Frances Bond Literary Services

32B Stanley Teale Road, Westville North 3630, KwaZulu-Natal
postal address PO Box 223, Westville 3630
tel (031) 2624532 *fax* (031) 2622620
e-mail fbond@mweb.co.za
Managing Editor Frances Bond, *Chief Editor* Eileen Molver

Full length MSS. Fiction and non-fiction; juvenile and children's literature. Consultancy service on contracts and copyright. Preliminary phone call or letter and sase required. Representation in UK by MS Literary Services. Founded 1985.

International Press Agency (Pty) Ltd

PO Box 67, Howard Place 7450
tel (021) 5311926 *fax* (021) 5318789
e-mail inpra@iafrica.com
Manager Terry Temple
UK office Ursula A. Barnett, 17 Fairmount Road, London SW2 2BJ
tel/fax 020-8674 9283

Literary Dynamics

PO Box 51037, Musgrave 4062
tel/fax (031) 2016919
e-mail literary@saol.com
web site http://enterest.co.za/literarydynamics
Managing Editor Isabel Cooke

Full-length MSS, fiction and non-fiction, screenplays. Reading fee for in-depth evaluation. Public speaking consultant, company profiles, project reports, editorial services. Founded 1985.

Sandton Literary Agency

PO Box 785799, Sandton 2146
tel (011) 4428624
Directors J. Victoria Canning, M. Sutherland

Full-length MSS and screenplays; lecture agents. Professional editing. Write or phone first. Works in conjunction with Renaissance-Swan Film Agency Inc., Los Angeles, USA. Founded 1982.

Spain

ACER Literary Agency

Amor de Dios 1, 28014 Madrid
tel 1-369-2061 *fax* 1-369-2052
Directors Elizabeth Atkins, Laure Merle d'Aubigné

Represents UK, US, French and German publishers for Spanish and Portuguese translation rights; represents Spanish- and Portuguese-language authors (home/overseas 10%); will suggest revision where appropriate. £20 reading fee. Founded 1959.

Agencia Literaria Carmen Balcells S.A.

Diagonal 580, 08021 Barcelona
tel 93-200-89-33, 93-200-85-65
e-mail ag-balcells@mx2.redcstb.es
Contact Miss Carmen Balcells *fax* 414 23 76
Miss Gloria Gutiérrez *fax* 200 70 41

Mercedes Casanovas Literary Agency

Iradier 24, 08017 Barcelona
tel 93-212-47-91 *fax* 93-417-90-37

Literature, non-fiction, children's books (home 10%, overseas 20%). Works with overseas agents. No reading fee. Founded 1980.

International Editors Co., S.A.

Rambla Cataluña 63, 3º-1ª, 08007 Barcelona
tel 93-215-88-12 *fax* 93-487-35-83
e-mail ieco@abafcrum.es

RDC Agencia Literaria SL

Plaza de las Salesas 9, 1ºB-28004 Madrid
tel 91-308-55-85 *fax* 91-308-56-00
Director Raquel de la Concha

Representing foreign fiction, non-fiction, children's books and Spanish authors. No reading fee.

Lennart Sane Agency AB

Paseo de Mejico 65, Las Cumbres-Elviria, E-29600 Marbella (Malaga)
tel 95-283-41-80 *fax* 95-283-31-96

Fiction, non-fiction, children's books, film and TV scripts. Founded 1965.

Julio F. Yañez

Agencia Literaria S.L., Via Augusta 139, 6º-2ª, 08021 Barcelona
tel 93-200-71-07, 93-200-54-43 *fax* 93-209-48-65
e-mail yanezag@arcaip.net

Switzerland

Paul & Peter Fritz AG Literary Agency

Jupiterstrasse 1, CH-8032 Zürich
postal address Postfach 1773, CH-8032 Zürich
tel (01) 388 41 40 *fax* (01) 388 41 30
e-mail info@fritzagency.com

Represents authors, agents and publishers in German-language areas.

Liepman AG

Maienburgweg 23, CH-8044 Zürich
tel (01) 261 76 60 *fax* (01) 261 01 24
Contacts Eva Koralnik, Ruth Weibel

Represents authors, agents and publishers from all over the world for German translation rights, and selected international authors for world rights.

Mohrbooks AG, Literary Agency

Klosbachstrasse 110, CH-8032 Zürich
tel (01) 251 16 10 *fax* (01) 262 52 13
Contact Sabine Ibach

Niedieck Linder AG

Zollikerstrasse 87, Postbox, CH-8034 Zürich
tel (01) 381 65 92 *fax* (01) 381 65 13

Represents German-language authors and Italian-language authors on the German market.

West Indies

CMS Literary Services

PO Box 993, Road Town, Tortola, British Virgin Islands
tel 284-495-9202 *fax* 284-495-9043
e-mail maczero@caribsurf.com
Directors Allan McNaught, Ndigo Naka

Children's and adult fiction; Caribbean literature and poetry (10%). Will suggest revision; no reading fee. Willing to work with other agencies in publishing Caribbean writers. Founded 1994.

Literary agents for television, film, radio and theatre

Listings for these and other literary agents start on page 348.
**US literary agents*

A & B Personal Management Ltd
American Play Company Inc.*
AMG/Renaissance*
Yvonne Baker Associates
Berman, Boals & Flynn Inc.*
Blake Friedmann Literary, TV & Film Agency Ltd
Alan Brodie Representation Ltd
Peter Bryant (Writers)
Casarotto Ramsay & Associates Ltd
Jonathan Clowes Ltd
Elspeth Cochrane Personal Management
Rosica Colin Ltd
Jane Conway-Gordon
Richard Curtis Associates Inc.*
Curtis Brown Group Ltd
Curtis Brown Ltd*
Judy Daish Associates Ltd
Felix De Wolfe
Ann Elmo Agency Inc.*
Film Rights Ltd
Frieda Fishbein Associates*
Laurence Fitch Ltd
Jill Foster Ltd
Robert A. Freedman Dramatic Agency Inc.*
Samuel French Inc.*
French's
Futerman, Rose & Associates
Jüri Gabriel
Eric Glass Ltd
Richard Hatton Ltd
David Higham Associates Ltd
Valerie Hoskins Associates
ICM Ltd
Juvenilia
Ben F. Kamsler Ltd*
Michelle Kass Associates
The Lazear Agency Inc.*
Ellen Levine Literary Agency Inc.*
Barbara Levy Literary Agency
Limelight Management
Andrew Mann Ltd
Manuscript ReSearch
Martinez Literary Agency
The Marton Agency Inc.*
Blanche Marvin
MBA Literary Agents Ltd
Scott Meredith Literary Agency LP*
Helen Merrill Ltd*
William Morris Agency Inc.*
William Morris Agency (UK) Ltd
Multimedia Product Development Inc.*
Fifi Oscard Agency Inc.*
PFD
PMA Literary and Film Management Inc.*
PVA Management Ltd
Radala & Associates
Rosenstone/Wender*
Tessa Sayle Agency
Susan Schulman Literary & Dramatic Agents Inc.*
The Sharland Organisation Ltd
Sheil Land Associates Ltd
The Shukat Company Ltd*
Simpson Fox Associates
Micheline Steinberg Playwrights' Agent
Sterling Lord Literistic Inc.*
Gloria Stern Agency*
Rochelle Stevens & Co.
J.M. Thurley Management
Austin Wahl Agency Inc.*
Watkins/Loomis Agency Inc.*
A.P. Watt Ltd
Sandra Watt and Associates*
Joesef Weinberger Plays Ltd

Merchandising agents

BBC Licensing, BBC Worldwide Ltd
Woodlands, 80 Wood Lane, London W12 0TT
tel 020-8576 2404 *fax* 020-8576 2228
Representing BBC TV and Radio and a selection of copyright owners. Properties: *Animal Hospital, Antiques Roadshow, The Archers, BBC News & Current Affairs, BBC Sport, Big Knights, Blue Peter, Doctor Who, EastEnders, Emlyn the Gremlyn, Fawlty Towers, Fireman Sam, Gardeners' World, Girl Talk, Grandstand, Keeping Up Appearances, Live & Kicking, Match of the Day, Masterchef, Mr Blobby, One Foot in the Grave, Only Fools & Horses, Pingu, A Question of Sport, Radio 1, Radio 2, Radio 3, Radio 4, Radio 5 Live, Red Dwarf, Robot Wars, Rotten Ralph, Star Hill Ponies, Stressed Eric, Teletubbies, Top Gear, Top*

of the Pops, Tweenies, Walking with Dinosaurs, Wallace & Gromit.

Copyright Promotions Ltd

12th Floor, Metropolis House, 22 Percy Street, London W1P 0DN
tel 020-7580 7431 *fax* 020-7631 1147
e-mail clairea@copyrightpromotions.co.uk
Managing Director Claire Atherton

Properties: *Dennis the Menace, Gnasher, Desperate Dan, Korky the Cat, Minnie the Minx, the Bash Street Kids, Beril the Peril, Bannanaman, The Beano, The Dandy, The Three Bears; Max Steel, Charlie's Angels, Stuart Little, Dawsons Creek, Vip, Party of Five, Starship Troopers: the series, Big Guy and Rusty the Boy, Robot, Godzilla, Men in Black, Extreme Ghostbusters; Pink Panther, Stargate SG1, Fame LA, Robocop; Star Trek* (movies and TV), *Sabrina Live Action, Sabrina Animation, Frasier, Cheers, The Italian Job, Audrey Hepburn; Austin Powers, The Mask, Lost in Space; Rupert Bear; Mr Men and Little Miss Timbuctoo; Dream Street; Sonic the Hedgehog; Ricky Martin; Westlife, Boyzone;* England and Wales Cricket Board, Rugby Football, Union, EURO 2000, *Star Wars, Indiana Jones, M&Ms®, NSPCC Happy Kids,* Tonino Lamborghini, *Practical Parenting, Amateur Gardening, Ideal Home.* Founded 1974.

The Copyrights Company (UK) Ltd

Manor Barn, Milton, Nr Banbury, Oxon OX15 4HH
tel (01295) 721188 *fax* (01295) 720145
London office 1 Ivory House, Plantation Wharf, Gartons Way, London SW11 3TN
tel 020-7924 3292 *fax* 020-7924 3208
Directors Nicholas Durbridge (Managing), Linda Pooley, Mark Robinson, Julie Nellthorp, Kären Addison, Elizabeth Lamont

Properties include *Beatrix Potter, Paddington Bear, Brambly Hedge, Postman Pat, Flower Fairies, The Wombles,* and other book-related properties for merchandise licensing.

Hawk Books

309 Canalot Studios, 222 Kensal Road, London W10 5BN
tel 020-8969 8091 *fax* 020-8968 9012
Director Patrick Hawkey

Properties: *Billy Bunter, Dopey Dinosaur.*

Link Licensing Ltd

7 Baron's Gate, 33-35 Rothschild Road, London W4 5HT
tel 020-8996 4800 *fax* 020-8747 9452
e-mail info@linklicensing.co.uk
web site http://www.linklicensing.com
Directors Claire Derry, David Hamilton

Properties: *Animorphs, Asterix, Barbie, Camberwick Green, First Snow of Winter, The Forgotten Toys, Goosebumps,* Lord's, *The Magic Roundabout,* The Natural History Museum, *Noah's Island, Teddy-bears, J17,* Fisher Price. Founded 1986.

Patrick, Sinfield (PSL)

95 White Lion Street, London N1 9PF
tel 020-7837 5440 *fax* 020-7837 5334
e-mail licensing@psluk.com
Directors Christopher Patrick, John Sinfield

Properties: *Snoopy and The Peanuts, Dilbert, Fido Dido; Rugrats, Clarissa Explains It All; The Mask of Zorro, Zorro* (the animated TV series); *Garfield; Lettuce the Rabbit, Felicity Wishes; The Wanna-Bs; Face Offs; Beavis and Butt-Head; Crayola; Arthur; Lavender Castle; Felix the Cat.* Founded 1980.

Michael Woodward Creations Ltd

Parlington Hall, Aberford, West Yorkshire LS25 3EG
tel 0113-281 3913 *fax* 0113-281 3911
e-mail art@mwc.uk.com
Contacts Michael Woodward, Janet Woodward (Project Director, Rambling Ted), Rebecca Cunningham (Licensing Director)

International licensing company with own US office and associated office in Australia. Artist management, licensing of design and character merchandise worldwide. Current properties include: *Rambling Ted, Robots in Big Boots, Teddy Tum Tum,* Debbie Cook, Christine Jopling, James Hearne. New artists and concepts considered. Send sase with synopsis/illustrations; scripts only not accepted. Founded 1979.

Art and illustration

Freelancing for beginners

Full-time posts for illustrators are not only highly specialised but, sadly, very rare. Because the needs of those who commission illustration tend to change on a regular basis, most artists have little choice but to offer their skills to a variety of clients in order to make a living. ***Fig Taylor*** *describes the opportunities open to the freelance illustrator.*

As a freelance illustrator you will be entering a hugely competitive arena and a professional attitude towards targeting, presenting, promoting and delivering your work will be vital to your success. Equally crucial is a realistic understanding of how the illustration industry works and of your place within the scheme of things. Without adequate research into your chosen field of interest it is all too easy to approach inappropriate clients – a frustrating and disheartening experience for both parties, to say nothing of its being both expensive and time-consuming.

Who commissions illustration?

Magazines and newspapers

Whatever your eventual career goals, your first stop for research should be your largest local newsagent. Most illustrators receive their first commissions from editorial clients who, whilst offering comparatively modest fees, are actively keen to try out fresh talent. Briefs are by and large fairly loose, though deadlines can be short, particularly in the case of daily and weekly publications. However, fast turnover also ensures a swift appearance in print – positive proof of your professional status to clients in other, more lucrative, spheres. Given then that it is possible to use the editorial field as a springboard, it is essential to appreciate its breadth when seeking to identify your own individual market. Between them, magazines and newspapers accommodate an infinite variety of illustrative styles and techniques. Don't limit your horizons by approaching only the most obvious titles and/or those you would read yourself. Consider also trade and professional journals, free publications and those available on subscription from membership organisations or charities. Remember, the more potential clients you uncover, the brighter your future will be.

Greetings cards

Many decorative, humorous and fine art-biased illustrators are interested in providing designs for greetings cards and giftwrap, where there is a definite market for their skills. As with editorial, fees are unlikely to be high but many small card companies are keen to use new or lesser known artists. You may be expected to produce samples of artwork on a speculative basis prior to receiving a definite commission – therefore it makes sense to target those companies who are likely to be most responsive (see *Winning the greeting card game*, page 395).

In addition to card shops and the gift departments of larger stores (many of whom employ commissioning buyers for their own ranges), you may find trade fairs such as London's bi-annual Top Drawer and Birmingham's International Spring and Autumn Shows yield the best results for your research. Geared primarily towards buyers, trade fairs offer you the opportunity to check out the forthcoming ranges of numerous card, stationery and giftware manufacturers as well as enabling you to make contacts.

Be warned, however, that most exhibitors will be far too busy selling to go through your work there and then. It is best to make a separate appointment to do this after the fair has ended. For further details, contact Top Drawer organisers, Clarion Events Ltd, or Trade Promotion Services Ltd, which organise the International Shows (see page 388).

Book publishing

With the exception of adult illustrated non-fiction, where the emphasis is on decorative, specialist and technical illustration, the majority of pro-illustration publishers are interested in full-colour figurative work for use on paperback and hardback book covers. Strong, realistic work which shows the figure in a narrative context is invaluable to those who commission massmarket fiction, which includes such genres as historical and contemporary romance, thrillers, family sagas, horror, science fiction and fantasy. On the whole, publishing deadlines are civilised and massmarket covers well paid. Illustrators whose work is more stylised or experimental would be better advised to approach those smaller imprints and independent publishing houses which deal with more literary, upmarket fiction. Although fees are significantly lower and commissions less frequent, briefs are less restrictive and a wider range of styles can be accommodated.

Children's publishers use a diversity of styles, covering the gamut from baby books, activity and early-learning through to full-colour picture books, older children's novels with black and white spot illustrations and teenage fiction and non-fiction. Author/illustrators are particularly welcomed by picture book publishers – though, whatever your style, you must be able to draw children well and to sustain a character throughout a narrative. See *Illustrating for children's books* on page 256.

Design

It is unnecessary for you to have design training in order to approach a design group for illustration work. However, it is advisable that you be in print. Both designers and their clients – who are largely uncreative and will ultimately be footing the bill – will be impressed and reassured by relevant, published work. Although fees are higher than those in editorial and publishing, this third-party involvement generally means a more restrictive brief. Deadlines may vary while styles favoured range from conceptual through to realistic, decorative, humorous and technical.

For research purposes, look at *Design Week* or the monthly *Creative Review* (both published by Centaur Communications), or the monthly *Graphics International* (published by Market Link Publishing). Design groups have different biases and specialities – for instance, some might concentrate on packaging while others may deal exclusively with corporate and financial literature.

The Creative Handbook (published by Variety Media Publications), available at some reference libraries, carries many listings. Individual contact names are also available at a price from File FX, which specialises in providing creative suppliers with up-to-date information on commissioning clients in all spheres.

Advertising

As with design, you should ideally be quite well established before seeking commissions in advertising. Fees can be high, deadlines short and clients extremely demanding. Illustration has been enjoying something of a renaissance with agencies of late, particularly in areas relating to lifestyle such as food, travel and alcohol. A fairly wide range of styles are used and commissions might be incorporated into direct mail or press advertising, hoardings or animated for television – fees will vary depending on whether a campaign is locally or nationally based.

Most agencies employ an art buyer to

look at portfolios. A good one will know what each creative team is working on at any given time and may refer you to specific art directors. Agency listings and client details may be found in *ALF* (Account List File, published by the BRAD Group, a subsidiary of EMAP Media), available at reference libraries. File FX can supply individual contact names. Magazines such as *Creative Review* and Haymarket's weekly, *Campaign*, also carry agency news.

Portfolio presentation

Obviously, the more outlets you can find for your talents the better. However, do not be tempted to develop a myriad of styles in an attempt to please every client you see. Firstly it's unlikely that you will and secondly, in the UK market, you'll stand a better chance of being remembered for one strong, consistent style. You'll also get far more commissions that way. Thus, when assembling your professional portfolio, try to exclude samples which are, in your own eyes, weak, irrelevant, uncharacteristic or simply unenjoyable to do – it is worth noting that even published work counts for little if the content is substandard. For maximum impact, aim to focus solely on your strengths. Should you be one of those rare, multi-talented individuals who find it hard to limit themselves stylistically, try splitting conflicting media or subject matter into separate portfolios geared towards different types of clients.

Having no formal illustrative training need not be a handicap providing your portfolio accurately reflects the needs of potential clients. With this is mind, some find it useful to assemble 'mock-ups' using existing magazine layouts. By responding to the copy, working in proportion to original images and replacing them with your own illustrations, both you and the client will be able to see how your work will look in context. Eventually, as you become more established, you'll be able to augment these with published pieces.

Ideally, your folder should be of the zip-up, ringbound variety and never any bigger than A2 as clients usually have very little desk space. Complexity of style and diversity of subject matter will be key elements in deciding how many pieces to include but all should be neatly, consistently mounted on lightweight paper or card and placed inside protective plastic leaves. Professional photographs of originals are acceptable to clients, as are good quality lasercopies or bubblejet prints. However, tacky, out-of-focus snapshots are not. Also avoid including too many sketchbooks and academic studies – particularly life drawings, which are anathema to clients. It will be taken for granted that you know how to draw from observation.

Interviews and beyond

Making appointments can be hard work but clients take a dim view of spontaneous visits from passing illustrators. Having identified the most relevant person to see (either from a written source or by asking the company directly), clients are best approached by letter or telephone call. Most magazines and publishing houses are happy to see freelances, though portfolio 'drop-offs' are becoming increasingly common within the industry. Some clients will automatically take photocopies of your work for their files. However, it is always advisable to have some form of self-promotional material to leave behind, such as a disk, CD, full-colour postcard or advertising tearsheet. In the case of larger companies, it is also worth asking your contact if others might be interested in your work. An introduction by word of mouth has a distinct advantage over cold-calling.

Cleanliness, punctuality and enthusiasm are more important to clients than the kind of clothes you wear – as is a professional attitude towards taking and fulfilling a brief. A thorough understanding of what a job entails is paramount from the outset. You will need to know all your client's requirements regarding roughs; format, size and flexibility of artwork; preferred medium and whether the image is

Useful addresses

Artists and Illustrators
Quarto Magazines Ltd, The Fitzpatrick Building, 188-194 York Way, London N7 9QR
tel 020-78500 *fax* 020-7700 4985
Runs an annual *Student Showcase* exhibition open to illustrators and fine artists.

Basement Publishing
6 Mulgrave Chambers, 26-28 Mulgrave Road, Sutton, Surrey SM2 6LE
tel 020-8642 4412 *fax* 020-8661 0152
e-mail gary.clement@basement.co.uk
Publishes *Student Design Yearbook*.

BRAD Group
33-39 Bowling Green Lane, London EC1R 0DA
tel 020-7505 8000
web site http://www.brad.co.uk
Publishes *ALF* (Account List File).

Centaur Communications
49-50 Poland Street, London W1V 4AX
tel 020-7439 4222
e-mail patrickb@centaur.co.uk
web site http://www.creativereview.co.uk
Publishes *Design Week*, *Creative Review*.

Clarion Events Ltd
Earls Court Exhibition Centre, Warwick Road, London SW5 9AT
tel 020-7370 8210
web site http://www.eco.co.uk
Organises Top Drawer.

Elfande Ltd
Surrey House, 31 Church Street, Leatherhead, Surrey KT22 8EF
tel (01372) 220300 *fax* (01372) 220340
e-mail mail@contact-uk.com
web site http://www.contact-uk.com
Publishes *Contact Illustrators*.

File FX
Unit 14, 83-93 Shepperton Road, London N1 3DF
tel 020-7226 6646
e-mail name@filefx.demon.co.uk
Specialises in providing creative suppliers with up-to-date information on commissioning clients in all spheres.

Association of Illustrators
81 Leonard Street, London EC2A 4QS
tel 020-7613 4328 *fax* 020-7613 4417
web site http://www.aoi.co.uk
Publishes *Survive – the Illustrators Guide to a Professional Career* and *Rights – the Illustrators Guide to Professional Practice*.

Market Link Publishing
The Mill, Bearwalden Business Park, Wendens Ambo, Saffron Walden, Essex CB11 4JX
tel (01799) 544200
e-mail chris@graphics-intl.demon.co.uk
Publishes *Graphics International*.

Razor Publications
Waterside House, Falmouth Road, Penryn, Cornwall TR10 8BE
tel (01326) 376211 *fax* (01326) 376753
e-mail info@exhibita.co.uk
web site http://www.exhibita.co.uk
Publishes *Exhibit A*.

Redstart
23 Craven Terrace, London W2 3QH
tel 020-7402 6473 *fax* 020-7221 8732
e-mail support@redstart.co.uk
web site http://www.redstart.net
Operatates an on-line directory of illustrators, designers and photographers.

RotoVision SA
Sheridan House, 112-116A Western Road, Hove, East Sussex BN3 1DD
tel (01273) 727268 *fax* (01273) 727269
e-mail mail@rotovision.com
web site http://www.creative-index.com
Publishes *The Creative Index* and *Images*.

Trade Promotion Services Ltd
Exhibition House, 6 Warren Lane, London SE18 6BW
tel 020-8855 9201
e-mail sfb@tps.emap.co.uk
web site http://www.gift-gardenmart.com
Organises the International Gift Fairs.

Variety Media Publications
6 Bell Yard, London WC2A 2JR
tel 020-7520 5233 *fax* 020-7520 5237
Publishes *The Creative Handbook*.

WARP Interactive
1-5 Beehive Place, London SW9 7QR
tel 020-7978 9868 *fax* (07070) 601 835
e-mail info@warp-i.com
web site http://www.aoi.co.uk
The promotion web site of the AOI.

to be executed in colour or black and white. You will also need to know when the deadline is. Never, under any circumstances, agree to undertake a commission unless you are certain you can deliver on time and always work within your limitations. Talent is nothing without reliability.

Self-promotion

There are many ways an illustrator can ensure their work stays uppermost in the industry's consciousness, some involving more expense than others. For those with their own computer/scanner set-up, artwork can be digitised, stored on a suitable application such as KPT Quickshow, which offers a simple slideshow format, or a more sophisticated application such as Iview or Extensis Portfolio. From there, your images can be e-mailed to clients or copied onto a zip disk or CD. (Floppy disks can be used for this purpose but capacity is limited and they are rapidly becoming obsolete.) Should you opt for CD but lack a compatible writer, a reputable image bureau will be happy to do the necessary.

Annuals, such as *Contact Illustrators* (see box) enjoy a high profile, thanks to the extensive free distribution to commissioners. However, this kind of advertising is not cheap and in the case of RotoVision's *Images* (the book which accompanies the Association of Illustrators' annual showcase of the best of British illustration) only those selected to exhibit are permitted to buy pages for their winning entries. A more affordable alternative for illustration graduates is Basement Publishing's *Student Design Yearbook*. Entries are unlimited, inexpensive to submit and, like *Images*, are judged by a panel of professionals.

The *Artists and Illustrators* magazine runs an annual *Student Showcase* exhibition. In addition to seeing their work in print, winners receive a year's subscription to the magazine. *Exhibit A* magazine (published by Razor Publications), offers free publicity to a variety of artists, providing the work is of a suitably high standard and meets the magazine's strict submission policy.

As more and more commissioners turn towards the Internet for inspiration, web sites are becoming a viable and affordable method of self-promotion for illustrators. The Association of Illustrators' web site, *AOI Online*, created by WARP Interactive, is open to all but offers reduced rates for AOI members. Artists can publish anything from a single image to their entire portfolio. Pricing is per image with substantial reductions for those publishing more than five pieces. The site also carries regularly updated information about the illustration industry plus an extensive archive of material previously published in AOI magazines. Redstart, a company of web site designers, operates a directory of illustrators, designers and photographers. Inclusion – in the form of four images plus biographical and contact details – is free to those with Internet access. For those lacking the requisite technology, Redstart will scan and upload images onto the web for a modest fee. Individual web sites, incorporating a dozen images, are also competitively priced.

Be organised!

Once your career is off the ground it is imperative to keep organised records of all your commissions. Contracts can be verbal as well as written, though details – financial and otherwise – should always be confirmed in writing and duplicated for your files. Likewise, file away corresponding client faxes, letters and order forms. *Survive – the Illustrators Guide to a Professional Career* and *Rights – the Illustrators Guide to Professional Practice* (both published by the Association of Illustrators) offer artists a wealth of practical, legal and ethical information. Subjects covered include contracts, licences, royalties, copyright and ownership of artwork.

Money

Try not to undertake a commission before agreeing on a fee, although this may not always prove practicable in the case of rush jobs. Most publishing and editorial fees are fixed and, unfortunately, there are no hard and fast rules for negotiation where design and advertising are concerned. As a pointer, however, take into consideration the type of client involved and the distribution of the final printed product – obviously a national 48-sheet poster advertising a well-known supermarket chain is likely to pay better than a local press advertisement for a poodle parlour! Some illustrators find it helpful to work out a daily rate incorporating various overheads such as the cost of computer equipment, rent, heating, materials, travel and telephone charges – while others prefer to negotiate on a flat fee basis. Some clients will actually tell you if they have a specific figure in mind, though you may have to put them on the spot. Certainly, as you become more established, you'll be able to use comparable jobs as benchmarks when negotiating a fee.

Basic book-keeping – making a simple, legible record of all your financial transactions, both incoming and outgoing – will be vital to your sanity once the tax inspector starts to loom. It will also make your accountant's job easier, thereby saving you money. If your annual turnover is less than £15,000, it is unnecessary to provide the Inland Revenue with detailed accounts of your earnings. Information regarding your turnover, allowable expenses and net profit may simply be entered on your tax return. Although an accountant is not integral to this process, many find it advantageous to employ one. The tax system is complicated and dealing with the Inland Revenue can be stressful, intimidating and time-consuming – not least since the recent introduction of 'self-assessment'. Accountants offer invaluable advice on tax allowances, National Insurance and tax assessments as well as dealing expertly with the Revenue on your behalf – thereby enabling you to attend to the business of illustrating. See *Income tax* on page 659, *Social security contributions* on page 669 and *Social security benefits* on page 677.

Fig Taylor began her career as an illustrators' agent in 1983. For 15 years she has been resident 'portfolio surgeon' at the Association of Illustrators and also operates as a private consultant to non-AOI member artists. In addition, she lectures extensively in Business Awareness to BA and HND illustration students.

Art agents and commercial art studios

Before submitting work, artists are advised to make preliminary enquiries and to ascertain terms of work. Commission varies but averages 25-30%. The Association of Illustrators (see page 480) provides a valuable service for illustrators, agents and clients.

**Member of the Society of Artists Agents*
†Member of the Association of Illustrators

Advocate

Gloucester House, 4 Stroud Crescent, London SW15 3EJ
tel (07000) 238622 *fax* 020-8788 0388
Director Edward Burns

Represents 45 artists working in all mediums and styles. Will consider artwork for design-led products, for advertising, books, etc. Operates as a co-operative. Founded 1988.

Allied Artists Ltd

5 Fauconberg Road, London W4 3JZ
tel 020-8995 5500 *fax* 020-8995 8844
e-mail info@alliedartists.ltd.uk
web site http://www.alliedartists.ltd.uk
Contacts Gary Mills (director), Mary Burtenshaw

Represents over 40 artists specialising in highly finished realistic figure illustrations, stylised juvenile illustrations for children's books, and cartoons for magazines, books, plates, prints, cards and advertising. Extensive library of stock illustrations.

Arena*†

144 Royal College Street, London NW1 0TA
tel 020-7267 9661 *fax* 020-7284 0486
Contacts Tamlyn Francis, Valerie Paine, Alison Eldred

Represents 45 artists working mostly for book covers, children's books and design groups. Average commission 30%. Founded 1970.

The Art Market*

27 Old Gloucester Street, London WC1N 3AF
tel 020-7209 1123 *fax* 020-7209 1129
e-mail the.artmarket@btinternet.com
web site http://www.artmkt.co.uk
Director Philip Reed

Represents 20 artists creating illustrations for publishing, design and advertising. Founded 1989.

Art Solutions

4 Granville Road, Sevenoaks, Kent TN13 1ER
tel/fax (01732) 458917
e-mail buky@centrenet.co.uk
Director Anne Buky

Varied and versatile artwork suitable for reproduction on greetings cards, giftwrap, stationery, ceramics, gifts; children's and adult's publishing. No cartoons. Send sae with samples please. Commission: 30%. Founded 1992.

Associated Freelance Artists Ltd

124 Elm Park Mansions, Park Walk, London SW10 0AR
tel 020-7352 6890 *fax* 020-7352 8125
e-mail pekes.afa@virgin.uk
Directors Eva Morris, Doug FitzMaurice

Freelance illustrators mainly in children's educational fields; and lots of greetings cards.

Aviation Artists, The Guild of

Unit 410, Bondway Business Centre, 71 Bondway, London SW8 1SQ
tel/fax 020-7735 0634
President Michael Turner PGAVA, *Secretary* Ian Burnstock

Professional body of 350 artists specialising in aviation art in all mediums. The Guild sells, commissions and exhibits members' work. Commission: 25%. Founded 1971.

Sarah Brown Agency†

10 The Avenue, London W13 8PH
tel 020-8998 0390 *fax* 020-8843 1175
e-mail sbagency@globalnet.com.uk
Contact Brian Fennelly

Illustrations for publishing and advertising. Sae essential for unsolicited material. Commission: 25% UK, 33.3% USA. Founded 1977.

Central Illustration Agency*†

36 Wellington Street, London WC2E 7BD
tel 020-7240 8925/836 1106 *fax* 020-7836 1177
e-mail c.illustration.a@dial.pipex.com
web site http://www.centralillustration.com
Director Brian Grimwood

Illustrations for design, publishing and advertising. Commission: 30%. Founded 1983.

David Lewis Illustration Agency†

Worlds End Studios, 134 Lots Road, London SW10 0RJ
tel 020-7351 3401 *fax* 020-7351 5044
mobile (07931) 824674
Director David Lewis, *Associate Directors* Rob Davies, Robin Broadway

Considers all types of illustration for a variety of applications but mostly suitable for book publishers, design groups, recording companies and corporate institutions. Also offers a comprehensive selection of images suitable for subsidiary rights purposes. Please send return postage with samples. Commission: 30%. Founded 1974.

Début Art*†

30 Tottenham Street, London W1 9PN
tel 020-7636 1064 *fax* 020-7580 7017
e-mail debutart@coningsbygallery.demon.co.uk
web site http://www.debutart.com
Directors Andrew Coningsby, Jane Harris, Benjamin Cox

Represents 60 artists working in mixed media, digital, photographic 3D and 2D collage and montage. Commission: 25%. Founded 1985.

Barry Everitt Associates†

23 Mill Road, Stock, Essex CM4 9LJ
tel (01277) 840639 *fax* (01277) 841223
Director Barry M. Everitt

Design and art resource specialising in licensing reproduction rights for greetings cards, fine art prints, calendars, giftware, etc. Always pleased to see the work of new and established artists and illustrators. Colour copies or photographs required initially with sae for return.

Jacqui Figgis*†

Unit 4, Eel Brook Studios, 125 Moore Park Road, London SW6 4PS
tel 020-7610 9933 *fax* 020-7610 9944
Director Jacqui Figgis

Illustrations for advertising, design, publishing and editorial. Commission: 33%. Founded 1986.

Folio Illustrators' & Designers' Agents*†

10 Gate Street, Lincoln's Inn Fields, London WC2A 3HP
tel 020-7242 9562 *fax* 020-7242 1816

All areas of illustration. Please send sae with samples. Founded 1976.

Graham-Cameron Illustration†

The Studio, 23 Holt Road, Sheringham, Norfolk NR26 8NB
tel (01263) 821333 *fax* (01263) 821334
Partners Mike Graham-Cameron, Helen Graham-Cameron

Represents 37 artists. Undertakes all forms of illustration for publishing and communications. Specialist in educational and children's books. Founded 1988.

John Hodgson Agency*†

38 Westminster Palace Gardens, Artillery Row, London SW1P 1RR
tel 020-7580 3773 *fax* 020-7222 4468

Publishing (children's picture books) and advertising. Sae with samples please. Commission: 25%. Founded 1965.

Illustrators Co Ltd*†

3 Richborne Terrace, London SW8 1AR
tel 020-7793 7000 *fax* 020-7735 2565
e-mail artists@illustrators.co.uk
web site http://www.illustrators.co.uk

Illustrations in a variety of styles for advertising, design groups and publishing. Founded 1976.

Image by Design

PO Box 2554, Trowbridge, Wilts. BA14 6YF
tel (01225) 783534 *fax* (01225) 783536
e-mail imagebydesign@compuserve.com
Contact Burniece M. Brown

Artwork for prints, greetings cards, calendars, posters, stationery, jigsaw puzzles, tableware, ceramics. Commission: negotiable. Founded 1987.

The Inkshed*

98 Columbia Road, London E2 7QB
tel 020-7613 2323 *fax* 020-7613 2726
e-mail inkshed@globalnet.co.uk
Directors Tim Woolgar, Jacqueline Hollister, *Contact* David Male

Represents 30 artists who work across the board – advertising, design, publishing, editorial. Commission: 25%. Founded 1985.

Kathy Jakeman Illustration†

Richmond Business Centre, 23-24 George Street, Richmond, Surrey TW9 1HY
tel 020-8875 9525 *fax* (07071) 225 115
e-mail kathy@kji.co.uk
web site http://www.kji.co.uk

Illustration for publishing – especially children's; also design, editorial and advertising. Please send sae with samples. Commission: 25%.

Libba Jones Associates

The Coach House, Victoria Mill, Bakewell, Derbyshire DE45 1DA
tel (01629) 815186 *fax* (01629) 813426
e-mail ljassociates@easynet.co.uk
web site http://www.libbajonesassociates.com
Contacts Libba Jones, Ieuan Jones

High quality artwork and design for china, greetings cards and giftwrap, jigsaw puzzles, calendars, prints, posters, stationery, book illustration, fabric design. Submission of samples required for consideration. Founded 1983.

Lavapepper Ltd

40 Weir Road, London SW12 0NA
tel (07050) 192354 *fax* (07050) 286 044
e-mail its@lavapepper.com
web site http://www.lavapepper.com
Directors Izabella Knights, James Muchmore

Seeks strong, idiosyncratic styles, including computer-generated images and collage. Please send sae with samples. Commission 25-35%. Founded 1998.

John Martin & Artists Ltd

18 Maddox Street, London W1R 0EU
tel 020-7734 9000 *fax* 020-7226 6069

Represents 40 illustrators, mainly producing artwork for children's fiction/non-fiction and educational books. Please include return postage with submissions. Founded 1956.

Meiklejohn Illustration*†

5 Risborough Street, London SE1 0HF
tel 020-7593 0500 *fax* 020-7593 0501
e-mail mjn@mjgrafix.demon.co.uk
web site http://www.theartbook.com
Contacts Paul Meiklejohn, Malcolm Sanders

All types of illustration.

N.E. Middleton

Richmond Business Centre, 23-24 George Street, Richmond, Surrey TW9 1HY
tel 020-8875 9525 *fax* (07071) 225 115

Designs for greetings cards, stationery, prints, calendars and china. Sae with samples, please.

Maggie Mundy Illustrators' Agency†

14 Ravenscourt Park Mansions, Dalling Road, London W6 0HG
tel 020-8748 2029 *fax* 020-8748 0353
e-mail maggiemundy@compuserve.com

Represents 20 artists in varying styles of illustration for children's books. Return postage must be included with submissions.

MWC Group

Parlington Hall, Aberford, West Yorkshire LS25 3EG
tel 0113-281 3913 *fax* 0113-281 3911
e-mail art@mwc.uk.com
web site http://www.mwc.uk.com
Managing Director Michael Woodward, *Licensing Directors* Janet Woodward, Rebecca Cunningham

International concept and character licensing agency with US office and representation in the Far East, Australia and Europe. Licensing concepts, artwork and children's TV concepts for gifts, stationery, toys, etc. Properties include *Rambling Ted*, *Kit 'n' Kin*, *Diezel Power Pigs*. Freelance contributions welcome but ideas must be well developed. Samples with sae. Founded 1979.

Elizabeth Oakes

9 The Beeches, Newcastle-under-Lyme, Staffs. ST5 8RX
tel 020-8393 1503 *fax* 020-8393 9555
Directors Jayne E. Follows, Hayden U. Woodhams

Design consultancy (including colour and trend forecasting) to the international textile, stationery, table and giftware trades. Represents 50 designers/artists. Portfolio management and the opportunity to undertake design briefs may be provided for freelance designers with expertise in these markets (particularly surface pattern). Send small range of samples, CV and return postage. Commission: negotiable. Established 1996.

The Organisation*†

The Basement, 69 Caledonian Road, London N1 9BT
tel 020-7833 8268 *fax* 020-7833 8269
e-mail organise@easynet.co.uk
Contact Lorraine Owen

Various styles of illustration supplied for book work in adult, children's and educational markets. Also for print, advertising, packaging and editorial. Average commission: 30%. Sae essential for unsolicited samples. Founded 1986.

Oxford Designers & Illustrators

Aristotle Lane, Oxford OX2 6TR
tel (01865) 512331 *fax* (01865) 512408
e-mail richard@oxford-illustrators.co.uk
web site http://www.oxford-illustrators.co.uk
ISDN (01865) 310876

Studio of 25 full-time illustrators working for publishers, business and industry. All types of artwork including science, technical, airbrush, graphic, medical, biological, botanical, natural history, figure, cartoon, maps, diagrams, and charts. Artwork supplied as PMT, bromide, film, or on a Syquest, Zip optical disk or ISDN, Mac or PC, with both b&w and colour proofs. Not an agency. Founded 1968.

Pennant Inc.*†

16 Littleton Street, London SW18 3SY
tel 020-8947 4002 *fax* 020-8946 7667
e-mail matthew@pennantinc.co.uk
web site http://www.pennantinc.co.uk
Director Matthew Doyle

Illustrations for publishing, design and advertising. Samples must be accompanied by an sae. Commission: 30%. Founded 1992.

Pink Barge

13 Wyndham Place, London W1H 1AS
tel 020-7486 1053 *fax* 020-7262 1130
Director Maggee Barge

Represents 20 artists working in advertising, publishing and corporate art. Commission: 25%. Founded 1982.

Linda Rogers Associates†

PO Box 330, 163 Half Moon Lane, London SE24 9WB
tel 020-7501 9106 *fax* 020-7501 9175
e-mail lr@lrassoc.force9.co.uk
web site http://www.lrassoc.force9.co.uk
Partners Linda Rogers and Peter Sims

Represents 65 illustrators and author/illustrators in all fields of illustration. Specialises in children's books, educational, information books; adult leisure books and magazines. Reply only with sae. Commission: 25%. Founded 1973.

SGA

(formerly Simon Girling & Associates)
Mountbatten Lodge, 2-6 The Green, Hadleigh, Suffolk IP7 6AE
tel (01473) 824083 *fax* (01473) 827846
e-mail info@sgadesignart.com
web site http://www.sgadesignart.com

Representing over 50 illustrators, accepting commissions for book publishing (children's and adult), encyclopedias, magazines, dust jackets, as well as a portfolio of licensed characters. See web site for portfolio. Commission: 30%. Founded 1985.

Specs Art†

93 London Road, Cheltenham, Glos. GL52 6HL
tel (01242) 515951 *fax* (01242) 518862
e-mail roland@specsart.com
web site http://www.specsart.com
Partners Roland Berry and Stephanie Prosser

High quality illustration work for advertisers, publishers and all other forms of visual communication. Specialises in licensed character illustration.

Summer Lane Pictures Ltd

Grays Court, 1 Nursery Road, Edgbaston, Birmingham B15 3JX
tel 0121-683 7705 *fax* 0121-683 7703
e-mail images@summer-lane-pics.freeserve.co.uk
Managing Director Malcolm McGivan

Design-led agency licensing artists' work to manufacturers and publishers in the gift industry; in-house reproduction facilities available. Freelance artists and surface pattern designers are invited to send samples; sae essential. Founded 1993.

Temple Rogers Artists' Agency

120 Crofton Road, Orpington, Kent BR6 8HZ
tel (01689) 826249 *fax* (01689) 896312
Contact Patrick Kelleher

Illustrations for children's educational books and magazine illustrations. Commission: by arrangement.

Vicki Thomas Associates

195 Tollgate Road, London E6 5JY
tel 020-7511 5767 *fax* 020-7473 5177
Consultant Vicki Thomas

Considers the work of illustrators and designers working in greetings and gift industries, and promotes such work to gift, toy, publishing and related industries. Written application and b&w photocopies required. Commission: 30%. Founded 1985.

Thorogood Illustration Ltd*

5 Dryden Street, London WC2E 9NW
tel 020-7829 8468/9 *fax* 020-7497 1300
e-mail draw@thorogood.net
web site http://www.thorogood.net
Directors Doreen Thorogood, Stephen Thorogood

Represents 30 artists for advertising, design, publishing and animation work. Please send return postage with samples. Commission: 30%. Founded 1977.

Wildlife Art Ltd†

Studio 16 Muspole Workshops, 25-27 Muspole Street, Norwich, Norfolk NR3 1DJ
tel (01603) 617868 *fax* (01603) 219017
e-mail info@wildlife-art.co.uk

Illustrations of all things natural, including gardening and food. Clients range from children's/adults' books to design and advertising agencies. Sae must be included with work submitted for consideration. Commission: 30%. Founded 1992.

Michael Woodward Fine Art

Parlington Hall, Aberford, West Yorkshire LS25 3EG
tel 0113-281 3913 *fax* 0113-281 3911
e-mail art@mwc.com
web site http://www.woodward-fineart.co.uk
Managing Director Michael Woodward

Artist management company representing: Anthony Christian, Terry Durham, Jude Roberts, David Greenwood. Own publishing division. Artists should send transparencies or laser copies of work with biography, plus sae. Division of MWC Group. Founded 1996.

Winning the greeting card game

*The UK population spends £1 billion a year on greeting cards yet finding a route into this fiercely competitive industry is not always easy. **Jacqueline Brown** steers artists through the greeting card maze.*

The UK greeting card industry leads the world on two counts – design and innovation and per capita send. On average people in the UK send 44 cards a year, 85% of which are bought by women.

But just how do you, as an artist, go about satisfying this voracious appetite of the card-sending public? There are two main options: either to become a greeting card publisher yourself or to supply existing greeting card publishers with your artwork and be paid a fee for doing so.

The idea of setting up your own greeting card publishing company may sound exciting, but this decision should not be taken lightly. Going down this route will involve taking on all the set up and running costs of a publishing company as well as the production, selling and administrative responsibilities. This often leaves little time for you to do what you do best – creating the artwork.

There are estimated to be around 800 greeting card publishers in the UK, ranging in size from one-person operations to multinational corporations, roughly 200 of which are regarded as 'serious' publishers (see page 398). Not all of them accept freelance artwork, but a great many do. Remember, whatever the size of the company, all publishers rely on good designs.

Finding the right publishers

While some publishers concentrate on producing a certain type of greeting card (e.g. humorous, fine art or juvenile), the majority publish a variety of greeting card ranges. Unfortunately, this makes it more difficult for you as an artist to target the most appropriate potential publishers for your work. There are various ways in which you can research the market, quickly improve your publisher knowledge and, therefore, reduce the amount of wasted correspondence:

- **Go shopping.** Browse the displays in card shops, newsagents and other high street shops, department stores and gift shops. This will not only give you an insight into what is already available but also which publishers may be interested in your work. Most publishers include their contact details on the backs of the cards.
- **Trade fairs.** There are a number of trade exhibitions held during the year at which

Some greeting card language

Own brand/bespoke publishers. These design specific to a retailer's needs.
Spring Seasons. The industry term to describe greeting cards for Valentine's Day, Mother's Day, Easter and Father's Day. Publishers generally launch these ranges all together in June/July.
Greeting card types. Traditional; cute or whimsical; contemporary/quirky art; juvenile; handmade or hand-finished; fine art; photographic, humorous.
Finishes and treatments. Artists will not be expected to know the production techniques and finishes, but a working knowledge is often an advantage. Some of the most commonly used finishes and treatments include: embossing (raised portion of a design), die-cutting (where the card is cut into a shape or includes an aperture), foiling (metallic film) and flitter (a glitter-like substance).

publishers exhibit their greeting card ranges to retailers and overseas distributors. By visiting these exhibitions, you will gain a broad overview of the design trends in the industry, as well as the current ranges of individual publishers. Some publishers are willing to meet artists and look through their portfolios on the stand but others are not. If you believe your work could be relevant for them, ask for a contact name and follow it up afterwards. Have a supply of business cards handy, perhaps illustrated with some of your work, to leave with publishers.

Types of publishers

There are two broad categories of publisher – wholesale and direct-to-retail – each employing a different method of distribution to reach the retailer.

Wholesale publishers distribute their products to the retailer via greeting card wholesalers or cash-and-carry outlets. They work on volume sales and have a rapid turnover of designs, many being used with a variety of different captions. For example, the same floral design may be used for cards for mothers, grandmothers, aunts and sisters. It is therefore usual for the artist to leave a blank space on the design to accommodate the caption. Until recently, wholesale publishers were generally only interested in traditional, cute and juvenile designs, but they now publish across the board, including contemporary, humorous ranges.

Direct-to-retail (DTR) publishers supply retailers via sales agents or reps. Most greeting cards sold through specialist card shops and gift shops are supplied by DTR publishers, which range from multinational corporations down to small, trendy niche publishing companies. These publishers market series of ranges based on distinctive design themes or characters. Categories of DTR cards include contemporary art/fun, fine art, humour, children's, photographic and traditional.

Approaching a publisher

Unfortunately, there is no standard way of approaching and submitting work to a card publisher. The first step is to establish that the publisher you wish to approach accepts work from freelance artists; then find out their requirements for submission and to whom it should be addressed.

It is always better to send several examples of your work to show the breadth of your artistic skills. Some publishers prefer to see finished designs while others are happy with well-presented sketches. *Never* send originals: instead send photocopies, laser copies or photographs, and include at least one design in colour. Never be tempted to sell similar designs to two publishers – a bad reputation will follow you around.

Some publishers will be looking to purchase individual designs for specific sending occasions while others will be more intent on looking for designs which could be developed to make up a range. Bear in mind that publishers work a long way in advance, e.g. Christmas ranges are launched to the retailers in January. Development of a range may take up to six months prior to launching.

Also remember that cards in retail outlets are rarely displayed in their entirety. Therefore, when designing a card make sure that some of the 'action' appears in the top half.

When interest is shown

Some publishers respond to submissions from artists immediately while others prefer to deal with them on a monthly basis. A publisher's response may be in the form of a request for more submissions of a specific design style or of a specific character. This speculative development work is usually carried out free of charge. Always meet your deadline (news travels fast in the industry).

A publisher interested in buying your artwork will probably then issue you with a contract. This may cover aspects such as the terms of payment; rights of usage of the design (e.g. is it just for greeting cards or will it include giftwrap and/or stationery?); territory of usage (most publishers want worldwide rights); and ownership of copyright or license period.

There is no set industry standard rate of pay for greeting card artists. Publishers

Further information

The Greeting Card Association
United House, North Road, London N7 9DP
tel 020-7619 0396
The UK trade association for greeting card publishers. As a result of a survey of its 110 members, it has produced 2 information leaflets, one on design and one on writing, each of which contains a list of members accepting freelance work. Write with a sae to Sharon Little.

Trade fairs

Autumn Fair Birmingham at the NEC
Contact TPS *tel* 020-8301 8600
Takes place 3-6 Sept 2000, 2-5 Sept 2001

Top Drawer at Earls Court
Contact Clarion Events *tel* 020-7370 8210
web site http://www.topdrawer.co.uk
Takes place 10-12 Sept 2000 and 13-15 May 2001

Spring Fair Birmingham at the NEC
Contact TPS *tel* 020-8301 8600
web site http://www.springfair.com
Takes place 4-8 Feb 2001

Home and Gift in Harrogate
Contact Clarion Events *tel* 020-7370 8359
web site http://www.homeandgift.co.uk
Takes place 15-18 July 2001

Trade magazines

Progressive Greetings Worldwide
Max Publishing, United House, North Road, London N7 9DP
tel 020-7700 6740 *fax* 020-7609 4222
12 p.a. (£40 p.a.)
The official magazine of the Greeting Card Association. Provides an insight to the industry, including an up-to-date list of publishers. Also includes special supplements such as *Focus on Art Cards* (annual) and *Focus on Humorous Cards.*

Progressive Greetings hosts the Henries, the greeting card industry awards. The September edition includes details of the finalists in the different categories and the November issue features the winners.

Greetings Today
(formerly Greetings Magazine)
Lema Publishing, Unit No. 1, Queen Mary's Avenue, Watford, Herts. WD1 7JR
tel (01923) 250909 *fax* (01923) 250995
Publisher Malcolm Naish, *Editor* Vicky Hancocks
Monthly £35 p.a. (other rates on application)
Articles, features and news related to the greetings card industry. Includes Artists Directory for aspiring artists wishing to attract the eye of publishers.

pay artists either on a per design or per range basis in one of the following ways:

- **Flat fee.** A one-off payment is made to the artist for ownership of a design for an unlimited period. The industry standard is around £200-£250 for a single design, and payment on a sliding scale for more than one design.
- **Licensing fee.** The publisher is granted the right to use a piece of artwork for a specified number of years, after which the full rights revert to the artist. Payment to the artist is approximately £150 upwards per design.
- **Licensing fee plus royalty.** As above plus a royalty payment on each card sold. Artists would generally receive a minimum of £100 for the licensing fee plus 3% of the trade price of each card sold.
- **Advance royalty deal.** A goodwill advance on royalties is paid to the artist. In the case of a range, the artist would receive a goodwill advance of say £500-£1000 plus 5% additional royalty payment once the threshold is reached.
- **Royalty only.** The artist receives regular royalty payments, generally paid quarterly, based on the number of cards sold. Artists should expect a sales report and royalty statement.

The fees stated above should only be regarded as a rough guideline. Fees and advances are generally paid on completion of artwork. Publishers which have worldwide rights pay royalties for sales overseas to artists, although these will be on a *pro rata* basis to the export trade price.

Jacqueline Brown is editor of *Progressive Greetings Worldwide* and general secretary of the Greeting Card Association.

Card and stationery publishers which accept illustrations and verses

Before submitting work, artists are advised to write giving details of the work they have to offer, and asking for requirements.

**Member of the Greeting Card Association*

The Andrew Brownsword Collection – see Hallmark Cards UK – Bath*

Card Connection Ltd*
Park House, South Street, Farnham, Surrey GU9 7QQ
tel (01252) 892300 *fax* (01252) 892339
e-mail ho@cardconnection.co.uk
Managing Director Adrian Atkinson, *Product Manager* Louise Pallister
Cute, humour, traditional, floral, contemporary, sport. Submit artwork, colour copies or 5 x 4in transparencies of originals. No verses. Founded 1992.

Carlton Cards Ltd*
Mill Street East, Dewsbury, West Yorkshire WF12 9AW
tel (01924) 465200
Marketing Director Keith Auty
Creative Director for Alternative Ranges Ged Backland
All types of artwork, any size; submit as colour roughs, colour copies or transparencies. Especially interested in humorous artwork and ideas.

Caspari Ltd*
9 Shire Hill, Saffron Walden, Essex CB11 3AP
tel (01799) 513010 *fax* (01799) 513101
Managing Director Keith Entwisle
Traditional fine art/classic images; 5 x 4in transparencies. No verses. Founded 1990.

C.C.A. Art & Design Ltd*
Eastway, Fulwood, Preston PR2 9WS
tel (01772) 662967 *fax* (01772) 662987
Contact Design Department
Designers and manufacturers of greetings cards. Original design ideas considered, including humour.

C.C.A. Stationery Ltd
Eastway, Fulwood, Preston PR2 9WS
tel (01772) 662800 *fax* (01772) 662900
Contact Design Department
Designers and manufacturers of personalised wedding stationery and Christmas cards. Pleased to consider original artwork, preferably of relevant subject matter.

The Classic Card Company Ltd – see Hallmark Cards UK – Bath*

J. Arthur Dixon*
Forest Side, Newport, Isle of Wight PO30 5QW
tel (01983) 523381 *fax* (01983) 529719
Managing Director Andy McGarrick, *Head of Design* Carlton Knight
All subjects considered – artwork and photographs (transparencies 35mm or larger). Verses considered. Acquired by **Second Nature Ltd**. Founded 1930.

Gallery Five Ltd*
121 King Street, London W6 9JG
tel 020-8741 8394 *fax* 020-8741 4444
Contact Françoise Yates, Art Manager
Send samples which give an idea of style; or phone for an appointment on the day. Appointment further ahead can be arranged for artists living outside London. No verses. Founded 1960.

Gibson Greetings International Ltd*
Gibson House, Hortonwood 30, Telford, Shropshire TF1 4ET
tel (01952) 608333 *fax* (01952) 608363
Marketing Director Jan Taylor
All everyday and seasonal illustrations: cute, humorous, juvenile, traditional and contemporary designs, as well as surface pattern. Greeting card traditional and humorous verse. Founded 1991.

The Gordon Fraser Gallery* – see Hallmark Cards UK – Bath*

Graphic Humour Ltd

4 Britannia House, Point Pleasant, Wallsend, Tyne & Wear NE28 6HA
tel 0191-295 4200 *fax* 0191-295 3916
e-mail enquiries@graphic-humour.demon.co.uk
web site http://www.graphic-humour.demon.co.uk

Risqué and everyday artwork ideas for greetings cards; short, humorous copy. Founded 1984.

Greetings Cards By Noel Tatt Ltd

t/a Noel Tatt Group, Appledown House, Barton Business Park, Appledown Way, New Dover Road, Canterbury, Kent CT1 3TE
tel (01227) 455540 *fax* (01227) 458976
Directors Jarle Tatt, Diane Tatt, Richard Parsons, Ian Hylands

Greetings cards, giftwrap and découpage. No verses. Founded 1988.

Hallmark Cards UK*

Henley office Hallmark House, Station Road, Henley-on-Thames, Oxon RG9 1LQ
tel (01494) 578383 *fax* (01494) 578817
Product and Marketing Director Jane Edwards, *Creative Manager* Frances Billington

Traditional imagery reviewed for everyday, Christmas and spring seasons, for greetings cards and other associated products. Submit colour copies, transparencies or preferably original artwork. Please ensure all artwork is named and enclose a sae.

Bath office James Street West, Bath BA1 2BS
tel (01225) 444486 *fax* (01225) 444096
Creative Manager, Cute Roger Hutchings, *Creative Manager, Art* Nick Adsett, *Creative Manager, Humour* Jill Ramsay

Cute, art and humour imagery reviewed for everyday, Christmas and spring seasons, for greetings cards and other associated products. Submit colour copies, transparencies or preferably original artwork to the appropriate Creative Manager listed. Please ensure all artwork is named and enclose a sae. Humorous editorial ideas also considered, including short jokes and punchlines. Brand names: Forever Friends, Country Companions, Harbottle & Co., Peanuts, Looney Tunes, Victoria Plum, Hallmark Gallery, Gordon Fraser Gallery, Rosina Wachtmeister, Keepsakes, Paul Greenwood.

Hambledon Studios Ltd

Metcalf Drive, Altham Industrial Estate, Altham, Accrington, Lancs. BB5 5SS
tel (01282) 687300 *fax* (01282) 687404
e-mail hambledon@aol.com
Studio Manager W. Hudson, *Art Managers* D. Jaundrell, K. Ellis, J. Ashton, *Trainee Art Manager* L. Thompson, *Marketing Manager* C. Holmes

Designs suitable for reproduction as greetings cards. Brands: Arnold Barton, Donny Mac, Reflections, New Image.

Hammond Gower Publications

14 Tideway Yard, Mortlake High Street, London SW14 8SN
tel 020-8878 5210 *fax* 020-8876 1487
Director Nicci Gower

Greetings cards: children's, contemporary, occasions, blank cards. All types of artwork considered: paintings, silk, line drawing, embroidery, etc. Founded 1985.

Hanson White

9th Floor, Wettern House, 56 Dingwall Road, Croydon, Surrey CR0 0XH
tel 020-8260 1200 *fax* 020-8260 1212
e-mail sarah.litchfield@hansonwhite.co.uk
Product Development Manager Sarah Litchfield

Artwork for greetings cards, giftwrap and related stationery items: humorous, contemporary, design-led. Humorous copy lines, including rude jokes, poems and punchlines; occasionally accept non-humorous verses. Founded 1958.

Images & Editions*

Bourne Road, Essendine, Nr Stamford, Lincs. PE9 4UW
tel (01780) 757118 *fax* (01780) 754629
Directors Lesley Forrow, Maurice Miller

Greetings card artwork: cute, floral, animals. Founded 1984.

Jarrold Publishing

Whitefriars, Norwich NR3 1TR
tel (01603) 763300 *fax* (01603) 662748
e-mail publishing@jarrold.com
web site http://www.jarrold-publishing.co.uk
Managing Director Caroline Jarrold

Decorative colour artwork – floral, kitchen, animals. Humour. Calendars only; no cards. Please send sae with all submissions. Imprint: Papermill. Founded 1770.

Jodds

PO Box 353, Bicester, Oxon OX6 0GS
tel (01869) 278550 *fax* (01869) 278551
e-mail design@jodds.demon.co.uk
Partners M. Payne and J.S. Payne

Bright contemporary art style greetings cards which include humour; must give out a warm feel. Submit colour photocopies with sae. No verses. Founded 1988.

Jooles

PO Box 804, Arundel, West Sussex BN18 0BR
tel (01903) 734545 *fax* (01903) 734546
Contact Art Department

Write with sae for submission of artwork. Artwork for greetings cards: humorous, traditional, cute.

Leeds Postcards

4 Granby Road, Leeds LS6 3AS
tel/fax 0113-278 7540
e-mail leedspostcards@geo2.poptel.org.uk
web site http://www.poptel.org.uk/leedspostcards
Contact Christine Buckley Hankinson

Publisher and distributor of postcards worldwide. Artwork that challenges and amuses. See web site or request catalogue with sae for suitability. Send copies of artwork initially with sae. Very little published. Founded 1979.

Ling Publishing Ltd*

The Old Brewery, Newtown, Bradford on Avon, Wilts. BA15 1NF
tel (01225) 863991 *fax* (01225) 863992
Creative Director Kirsten Boyd

Artwork for greetings cards; no verses.

M.G. Media

Bolton Enterprise Centre, Washington Street, Bolton, Lancs., BL3 5EY
tel (01204) 524262 *fax* (01204) 535995
e-mail mgmedia@aol.com
Proprietor Marcia J. Galley

Produces a bi-monthly newsletter aimed at writers and artists who wish to place their work with greeting card publishers. Publishes the artwork and editorial needs of top publishers both in England and overseas. Subscription: £25 (6 issues). Not an agency. Founded 1995.

Medici

Grafton House, Hyde Estate Road, London NW9 6JZ
tel 020-8205 2500 *fax* 020-8205 2552
Contact The Art Department

Requirements: full colour or black and white paintings/sketches/etchings/designs suitable for reproduction as greetings cards. Send preliminary letter with brief details of work and colour copies.

The Paper House Group plc

Shepherd Road, Gloucester, Glos. GL2 6EL
tel (01452) 423451 *fax* (01452) 410312
Creative Director Chris Wilcox

Publishers of greetings cards depicting old masters, the Impressionists, contemporary artists and humorous themed cartoon illustration.

Paper Studios

4 Britannia House, Point Pleasant, Wallsend, Tyne and Wear NE28 6HA
tel 0191-295 4200 *fax* 0191-295 3916
e-mail paperstudios@graphic-humour.demon.co.uk
Directors Alan Picton, Mike Rowell

Traditional, floral and cute designs for greetings cards for all occasions – artwork and 35mm transparencies. Verses considered. Founded 1999.

Paperlink Ltd*

356 Kennington Road, London SE11 4LD
tel 020-7582 8244 *fax* 020-7587 5212
Directors Louise Tighe, Jo Townsend, Tim Porte, Tim Purcell

Publishers of ranges of humorous and contemporary art greetings cards, giftwrap, calendars, notelets, mugs, prints. Produce products under licence for charities. Founded 1986.

Pepperpot

Godalming Business Centre, Woolsack Way, Godalming, Surrey GU7 1XW
tel (01483) 426277 *fax* (01483) 426947
e-mail kdg@quad-pub.co.uk
Publishing Controller Kate Gorman, *Design Manager* Deborah Granger

Gift stationery, photo albums, gift cards. Colour illustrations; cute/traditional/floral. Submit original artwork or 5 x 4in transparencies. No verses. Division of Quadrillion Publishing Ltd.

Pineapple Park Ltd*

58 Wilbury Way, Hitchin, Herts. SG4 0TP
tel (01462) 442021 *fax* (01462) 440418
e-mail info@pineapplepark.co.uk
Directors Peter M. Cockerline, Sarah M. Parker

Illustrations and photographs for publication as greetings cards. Contemporary, cute, humour: submit artwork or laser copies with sae. Transparencies of animals, babies, children and floral.

Pomegranate Editorial Europe

Submissions from Europe only 3 Wilsdon Way, Lyne Meads, Kidlington, Oxford OX5 1TN
tel (01865) 460661 *fax* (01865) 378005
e-mail andy.swapp@lineone.net

web site http://www.pomegranate.com
Project Editor (Europe) Andy Swapp
Submissions from outside Europe Pomegranate Communications Inc., 210 Classic Court, Rohnert Park, California 94928, USA
tel 800-227-1428 *fax* 787-586-5522
e-mail info@pomegranate.com

Extensive range of calendars as well as posters, notecards, postcards, books of postcards, occasion, holiday and general greeting cards; bookmarks, gift enclosures and magnets; mouse mats and screen savers; address books, games and learning decks (marketed under the trademark Knowledge Cards). Founded 1993.

Powell Publishing

57 Coombe Valley Road, Dover, Kent CT17 0EX
tel (01304) 213999 *fax* (01304) 240151
Directors B.W. Powell (chairman), T.J. Paulett (managing)

Greetings card publishers. Interested in Christmas designs for the charity card market. Division of Powell Print Ltd.

Nigel Quiney Publications Ltd*

Cloudesley House, Shire Hill, Saffron Walden, Essex CB11 3FB
tel (01799) 520200 *fax* (01799) 520100
Contact Ms J. Arkinstall

Everyday and seasonal greetings cards (sizes: 7 x 5in, 9 x 6in and 12 x 9in) and giftwrap. Submit original artwork, 5 x 4in transparencies of originals or colour photocopies.

Rainbow Cards Ltd*

Albrighton Business Park, Newport Road, Albrighton, Wolverhampton, West Midlands WV7 3ET
tel (01902) 374347
Directors M. Whitehouse, J. Whitehouse, I. Mackintosh

Artwork for humorous greetings cards. Founded 1977.

The Really Good Card Company Ltd*

Osney Mead, Oxford OX2 0ES
tel (01865) 246888 *fax* (01865) 246999
Director David Hicks

Fun and humorous cards and stationery. Please do not send originals; send photocopies or snapshots with sae. No verses. Founded 1987.

Felix Rosenstiel's Widow & Son Ltd

Fine Art Publishers, 33-35 Markham Street, London SW3 3NR
tel 020-7352 3551 *fax* 020-7351 5300
e-mail sales@felixr.com

Invites offers of original oil paintings and strong watercolours of a professional standard for reproduction as picture prints for the picture framing trade. Any type of subject considered; send photographs of work.

Royle Publications Ltd – see The Paper House Group plc

Santoro Graphics Ltd

342-344 London Road, Cricket Green, Mitcham, Surrey CR4 3ND
tel 020-8640 9777 *fax* 020-8640 2888
Directors Lucio Santoro, Meera Santoro (art)

Publishers of innovative and award-winning designs for greetings cards, giftwrap and gift stationery. Bold contemporary images with an international appeal. Subjects covered: quirky and humorous, whimsical, 'Fifties, 'Seventies, futuristic! Submit photographs or colour photocopies. Founded 1985.

Scandecor Ltd

3 The Ermine Centre, Hurricane Close, Huntingdon, Cambs. PE18 6XX
tel (01480) 456395 *fax* (01480) 456269
Managing Director Derek Shirley

Drawings all sizes. Founded 1967.

Second Nature Ltd*

10 Malton Road, London W10 5UP
tel 020-8960 0212 *fax* 020-8960 8700
e-mail rods@secondnature.co.uk
web site http://www.secondnature.co.uk
Publishing Director Rod Schragger

Contemporary artwork for greetings cards; jokes for humorous range; short modern sentiment; verses. Founded 1981.

W.N. Sharpe Ltd – see Hallmark Cards UK*

Solomon & Whitehead Ltd

Lynn Lane, Shenstone, Staffs. WS14 0DX
tel (01543) 480696 *fax* (01543) 481619
e-mail sales@fineartgroup.co.uk

Fine art prints, limited editions and originals, framed and unframed.

Soul

Osney Mead, Oxford OX2 0ES
tel (01865) 434444 *fax* (01865) 454444
Director David Hicks

Publishers of contemporary, fine and quirky art. Send photocopies or snapshots (no originals) with sae. No verses.

Trumpet Limôn

Osney Mead, Oxford OX2 0ES
tel (01865) 240140 *fax* (01865) 454444

Publishers of limited edition prints. Send photocopies, snapshots or samples of published work (no originals) with sae.

Twin Oaks Publishing

Cloudesley House, Shire Hill, Saffron Walden, Essex CB11 3FB
tel (01799) 520200 *fax* (01799) 520100
e-mail firstname-surname@twinoaks.co.uk
Product & Marketing Director Jo Arkinstall

Contemporary, cute and photographic. Do not send original artwork. Brands: Objects of Desire, The Cat's Pyjamas, Just Bears, Teddies of Desire. Founded 1996.

Valentines – see Hallmark Cards UK*

Webb Ivory (Burton) Ltd

Queen Street, Burton-on-Trent, Staffs. DE14 3LP
tel (01283) 566311

High quality Christmas cards and paper products.

A serious look at marketing cartoons

There are many freelance opportunities for comic artists and illustrators. ***John Byrne*** *explores potential markets and offers guidance for success.*

Although in the business of being funny, cartoonists can sometimes be a morose bunch, bemoaning the passing of the original *Punch* and complaining that the market for general cartoons is growing smaller. Yet many of the most lucrative merchandising properties in recent years, from *Garfield* to *Judge Dredd*, started life as cartoons. Freelance cartooning has its share of ups and downs, but there are still many opportunities for comic artists and for illustrators and writers, too. Many cartoonists are certainly accomplished artists, but today funny ideas and sharp captions are just as important as the visuals. Writers with comic flair may consider collaborating with an artist or even trying their own simple drawings.

Research and presentation

See page 405 for *Newspapers and magazines which accept cartoons*.

Study the publication you are planning to submit to. What cartoon subjects feature most frequently, especially for joke or 'gag' cartoons (see 'Markets', below): married couples? children? animals? Are all the cartoons domestic or office based, or is there a mixture? Are the characters drawn in semi-realistic or more distorted styles? Are the jokes mainly in the captions or is the humour visual?

Be aware of changing fashions in humour. Thanks to Gary Larson's *The Far Side* the pun, formerly derided as a low form of wit, is currently very much in vogue. Consider technical details: Are the cartoons colour or black and white? What shape are they? It is pointless sending portrait-shaped cartoons to publications that only use landscape ones.

While many magazines still typeset cartoon captions, some also accept hand-drawn captions or balloons. Avoid spelling mistakes for which cartoonists are notorious and which often result in rejection of otherwise saleable drawings. This can also happen if a clever cartoon becomes illegible when reduced to printed size. Editors often squeeze cartoons into very small spaces – be sure your drawings are simple and bold enough to survive reduction.

It is useful to have a knowledge of copyright and libel. See *British copyright law* on page 633 and *Libel* on page 651.

Useful organisations

For specialist advice, and to meet other members of what can be a solitary profession, make contact with:

Cartoon Art Trust
7 Brunswick Centre, London WC1N 1AF
tel 020-7278 7172

The Cartoonists' Guild and The Cartoonists' Club of Great Britain
46 Strawberry Vale, Twickenham TW1 4SE
tel 020-8892 3621

Comics Creators Guild
48 Siddons Road, London SE23 2JQ
tel/fax 020-8699 4012

Submitting cartoons

A preliminary letter saves wasted effort and can yield useful information. Busy editors find unsolicited phone calls very unamusing – but one call you will need to make is to check exactly who to address your letter to: full-time cartoon editors are rare and the person who chooses cartoons can be anyone from the art director to the person in charge of the puzzle page. Sending a number of cartoons together increases the chance of at least one being accepted, but quality is better than quantity. A few good jokes will get a better response when the editor doesn't have to extract them from a mountain of 'fillers'.

Rejections

While current fashions in cartoons encompass a wide range of styles, both visual and in terms of being funny, humour is still very subjective. Rejections are a fact of life for even the most successful cartoonists, but one editor's rejected cartoon may be snapped up by another publication.

One way to lessen the sting is to have several submissions on the go at once. A strong pre-paid envelope will ensure that work comes back in one piece, ready for its next expedition. (Put your name and address on the back of each cartoon in case it gets detached from the main bundle.) If you are sending lots of cartoons back and forth to different publications it is wise to create a filing system. Otherwise you'll inevitably receive the dreaded response 'You've sent this one before ... and it wasn't funny the first time'.

Markets

General gag cartoons

The demise of the *Cartoonist*, *Squib* and other brave attempts to launch cartoon magazines in the wake of *Punch* may have suggested that the traditional gag cartoon is an endangered species. However, *Punch* has been resurrected (although with a different flavour), magazines like *Private Eye* and the *Spectator* still publish joke or gag cartoons alongside more topical items, and new cartoon magazines continue to appear.

Topical cartoons

Topical cartoons are a good market for the quick-witted artist. Remember that the cartoon must still be topical on the day it is published. This is (relatively) easy if the cartoon is for a newspaper coming out the next day, but a topical cartoon can become very outdated in the time it takes a weekly or fortnightly magazine to publish. Faxing roughs to the editor can save time. If accepted, you may need to produce finished artwork to very tight deadlines.

Try to get your cartoons back after publication – people featured in topical cartoons sometimes ask to buy the original artwork.

Specialist and trade publications

This is an under-exploited market for cartoonists who are able to tailor jokes to particular subjects – but remember you are dealing with an expert audience. A stereotypical cartoon chef may suffice for general cartoons, but you'd better get the terminology and different uniforms right for *Bakery World* or *Catering*.

Try creating your own markets. Think about jobs you've had, past or present, or your particular sports, hobbies and interests. No matter how obscure, there may be a related publication just waiting to be brightened up by your combination of cartoon skills and specialist knowledge.

Regular comic strips and syndication

For regular comic strips or cartoon features, editors need to see that you can produce not only funny material but that you can maintain a consistent output. Submit a good supply of roughs along with examples of finished cartoons to show that you can sustain the idea. The same applies when approaching a syndicate with your strip and feature ideas (see *Syndicates, news and press agencies* on page 143). Cartoons may be in syndication for a long time, and in different countries, so very topical humour and local references are best avoided. If cartoons are syndicated in other languages humour based on verbal puns may not translate very well.

Other

Card and stationery publishers which accept illustrations and verses on page 398 and *Merchandising agents* on page 383 should suggest other markets for cartoons. Cartoons are often used to illustrate books for both adults and children (listings of *Book publishers UK and Ireland* start on page 151 and *Book packagers* start on page 214). Some of the *Art agents and commercial art studios* listed on page 390 represent cartoonists.

Cartoon sites on the Internet are some of the most frequently visited and cartoonists selling their wares through this new medium have reported very good responses.

Finally ...

The life of a full-time funny person can be precarious, but properly researching and tailoring work to specific markets and adopting an organised approach to submissions should greatly reduce your rejection collection.

John Byrne combines his own writing and drawing career with internationally acclaimed training workshops on cartooning and comedy writing.

Further reading

Byrne, John, *Drawing Cartoons that Sell*, HarperCollins, 1997
Byrne, John, *Learn to Draw Cartoons*, HarperCollins, 2nd edn, 1999
Byrne, John, *Writing Comedy*, A & C Black, 1999
Hall, Robin, *The Cartoonist's Workbook*, A & C Black, 1995
Whitaker, Steve, *The Encyclopaedia of Cartooning Techniques*, Headline, reprinted 1996

Newspapers and magazines which accept cartoons

Listed below are newspapers and magazines which take cartoons – either occasionally, or on a regular basis. Approach in writing in first instance (see listings starting on pages 3, 11 and 21 for addresses) to ascertain the editor's requirements.

Newspapers and colour supplements

Aberdeen Evening Express
Advertiser (Adelaide, Aus.)
Christchurch Star (NZ)
Daily Dispatch (S.A.)
The Daily News (New Plymouth, NZ)
The Daily Telegraph (Napier, NZ)
Daily Sport
Evening Gazette
Evening Herald
The Evening Post (Wellington, NZ)
Evening Press
Grimsby Evening Telegraph
The Guardian Weekend
Hartlepool Mail
Herald Sun (Melbourne, Aus.)
The Independent Magazine
Independent on Sunday
Lancashire Evening Post
Liverpool Echo
Mail on Sunday
The Mirror
Morning Star
The Press (Christchurch, NZ)
The Scotsman
South Wales Echo
Southern Cross (S.A.)
The Southland Times (Invercargill, NZ)
The Star (Sheffield)
The Sun
The Sun (Glasgow)
The Sunday Business Post
Sunday Independent (Ire.)
Sunday Mail
The Sunday Mail (Brisbane, Aus.)
Sunday Mercury
The Sunday Times
The Sunday Times Scotland
The Sunday Tribune
Sunderland Echo
Telegraph Magazine
The Times
The Western Mail
Yorkshire Evening Post
Yorkshire Post

Consumer and special interest magazines

Aeroplane Monthly
The Aquarist and Pondkeeper
Aquila
Back Street Heroes
Bella
Best
The Big Issue Australia
Bike
Bird Watching
Boards
Bowls International
British Chess Magazine
The Bulletin with Newsweek (Aus.)
Bunty
Canadian Yachting (Can.)
Car (NZ)
Catholic Gazette
Catholic Pictorial
Caxton Magazines (S.A.)
Chapman
Christian Herald
Church of England Newspaper
Classic Cars
Classic CD
Computer Weekly
Computing
Countryman (Aus.)
The Cricketer International
Cycling Weekly
Dance Australia
The Dandy
Darts World
Dirt Bike Rider
Dogs Today
Dolly (Aus.)
East Lothian Life
Electronics Australia with ETI (Aus.)
The Erotic Review
Everyday Practical Electronics
Football Picture Story Library
Fortean Times
Garden News
Gay Times
Golf Monthly
Golf World
GQ
Guiding
H & P
Health and Efficiency – H&E Magazine
Home and Country
Home Words
Index on Censorship
Ireland of the Welcomes
Ireland's Own
Jewish Telegraph
Kids Alive!
Life and Work
Making Music
Maxim
Modern Woman Nationwide
Motor Caravan Magazine
Musical Opinion
My Weekly Puzzle Time
New Electronics
New Internationalist
New Musical Express
New Scientist
New Statesman
The New Welsh Review
New World
The Oldie
Opera Now
Organic Gardening
Overland (Aus.)
Park Home & Holiday Caravan
Picture Postcard Monthly

Planet
Poetry Review
Pony Magazine
Practical Photography
Pride
Private Eye
Punch
Real Money
Red Pepper
Reform
Rugby World
Runner's World
Running Fitness
Scottish Home and Country
Scouting
She
Shoot
Sight and Sound
Ski and Board
Smallholder
The Spectator
The Squash Player
Suffolk Norfolk Life
The Tablet
that's life!
Tribune
Trout and Salmon
The Universe
The Vegan
Viz
War Cry
Waterways World
The Weekly News
Weight Watchers Magazine
West Lothian Life
What's on TV
The Word (Ire.)
World Soccer
Yachting Monthly
Yachting World
Young People Now
Young Writer
Yours

Business and professional magazines

Accountancy
Air International
Army Quarterly & Defence Journal
Art Business Today
The Author
BMA News Review
British Printer
Broadcast
Building Design
BusinessMatters
Child Education
Control & Instrumentation
Drapers Record
Education Journal
Electrical Review
Electrical Times
Electronics Times
Estates Gazette
Hospital Doctor
Hotel and Catering Review
HouseBuilder
Irish Medical Times
Journalist
Local Government Chronicle
The Log
Mobile and Cellular Magazine
MoneyMarketing
Nursing Times
PCS, The Magazine
Pilot
Police Review
Post Magazine & Insurance Week
Printing World
Therapy Weekly
The Times Educational Supplement
Truck & Driver

Photography and picture research

The freelance photographer

Many photographers make the mistake of thinking that technical perfection and creativity alone will take them to the top, but even the most well-known photographers continually have to sell themselves to maintain a strong foothold in this highly competitive profession. ***Bruce Coleman*** *and* ***Ian Thraves*** *discuss possibilities for the freelance photographer.*

Becoming a successful freelance photographer is as much about marketing as photographic talent. Having an outstanding portfolio is one thing, but to receive regular commissions takes a good business head and sound market knowledge. Although working as a professional photographer can be tough, it is undoubtedly one of the most interesting and rewarding ways of earning a living.

Entering professional photography

A good starting point is to embark on one of the many college courses available, which range from GCSE to degree level, and higher. These form a good foundation, though most teach only the technical aspects of photography and very few cover the basics of running a business. But a good college course will provide students with the opportunity to become familiar with photographic equipment and develop skills without the restrictions and pressures found in the workplace.

In certain fields, such as commercial photography, it is possible to learn the trade as an assistant to an established photographer. A photographer's assistant will undertake many varied tasks, including preparing camera equipment and lighting, building sets, obtaining props and organising locations, as well as general mundane chores. It usually takes only a year or two for an assistant to become a fully competent photographer, having during that time learnt many technical aspects of a particular field of photography and the fundamentals of running a successful business. There is, however, the danger of a long-standing assistant becoming a clone of the photographer worked for, and it is for this reason that some assistants prefer to gain experience with other photographers rather than working for just one for a long period of time. The Association of Photographers can help place an assistant.

However, in other fields of photography, such as photojournalism or wildlife photography, an assistant is not generally required, and photographers in these fields have to learn for themselves as they work.

Identifying your market

From the outset, identify which markets are most suitable for the kind of subjects you photograph. Study each market carefully and only offer images which suit the client's in-house requirements.

Usually photographers who specialise in a particular field do better than those who generalise. By concentrating on one or two subject areas they become expert at what they do. Those who make a name for themselves are invariably specialists, and it is far easier for the images of, for example, an exceptional fashion photographer or an award-winning wildlife photographer to be remembered than the work of someone who covers a broad range of subjects.

In addition, photographers who produce work with individual style (e.g. by experimenting with camera angles or manipulating film to create unusual effects) are far more likely to make an impact. Alternative images which attract attention and can help sell a product are always sought after. This is especially true of advertising photography, but applies also to other markets such as book and magazine publishers, who are always seeking eye-catching images to use on front covers.

Promoting yourself

Effective self-promotion tells the market who you are and what service you offer. A first step should be to create an outstanding portfolio of images, tailored to appeal to the targeted market. Photographers targeting a few different markets should create an individual portfolio for each rather than presenting a single general one, including only a few relevant images. A portfolio containing between 10 and 20 images is enough for a potential client to judge a photographer's abilities.

Images should be presented in a format which the client is used to handling. Transparencies (perhaps duplicated to a larger size for easier viewing and general impact) are usually suitable for the editorial markets, but often more general companies prefer to view high-quality prints. Images can also be presented on CD-Rom and, unlike a traditional portfolio, can be left with potential clients to keep and refer to. Any published material (often referred to as 'tear sheets') should also be added to a portfolio. Tear sheets are often presented mounted and laminated in plastic.

Business cards and letterheads should be designed to reflect style and professionalism. Consider using a good graphic designer to design a logo for use on cards, letterheads and any other promotional literature. Many photographers produce postcard-size business cards and include an image as well as their name and logo.

Other than word of mouth, advertising is probably the best way of making your services known to potential clients. For a local market, a business directory such as *Yellow Pages* is a good start. Specialist directories in which photographers can advertise include *The Creative Handbook* and *Contact Photographers* (see page 410).

Cold calling by telephone is probably the most cost-effective and productive way of making contacts, and these should be followed up by an appointment for a personal visit (if possible) in order to show a portfolio of images. This helps to ensure you will not be forgotten.

Many photographers now use the Internet as an alternative medium to promote themselves. A cleverly designed web site is a stylish and cost-effective way to expose a photographer's portfolio to a global market, as well as being a convenient way for a potential client to view a photographer's work. A personal web site address can be added to business stationery and to other forms of advertising together with the usual address and telephone number information.

Creating a web site is usually much cheaper than advertising using conventional published print media. However, the design of a web site should be carefully composed and is probably best left to a professional web site designer. Although many images and details about your business can be placed on a web site, one limiting factor is the time it can take to download the images due to the size of the files. Unless this is a relatively quick process the viewer may lose patience and cancel access to the site.

A well-organised exhibition of images is a very effective way of bringing your work to the attention of current and potential new clients. Throw a preview party with refreshments for friends, colleagues and specially invited guests from the industry. A show which is well reviewed by critics who write for newspapers and magazines can generate additional interest. Many photographic organisations have regular exhibitions. An excellent example is the Photographers Gallery in London, where work selected by the gallery board is exhibited free.

As a photographer's career develops, the budget for self-promotion should increase. Many established photographers will go as far as producing full-colour mailers, posters, and even calendars, which all contain examples of their work.

Digital photography

Digital photography and image-enhancement and manipulation using computer technology are now widely used in the photographic industry. Since the cost of digital cameras (which do not require film) and other hardware can be considerably cheaper than using large quantities of film, many studio photographers are now using this technology for large photographic shoots, such as product photography for catalogue companies. Image-enhancement and manipulation using a computer program such as Adobe Photoshop provides photographers with an on-screen darkroom where the possibilities for creating imaginative images are endless. As well as being useful for retouching purposes and creating photo compositions, it provides the photographer with an opportunity to create more unusual images. It is therefore especially useful for targeting the advertising market, where fantasy images are more important than reality.

Using a stock library

As well as undertaking commissions, photographers have the option of selling their images through a photographic stock library or agency. There are many stock libraries in the UK, some specialising in specific subject areas, such as wildlife photography, and others covering general subjects (see *Picture agencies and libraries*, page 412).

Stock libraries are fiercely competitive, all fighting for a share of the market, and it is therefore best to aim to place images with an established name, although com-

Professional organisations

It may be worthwhile joining one of the reputable photographic organisations. For an annual fee, these offer services to photographers such as legal support, and also organise events where photographers can meet and share information.

Association of Photographers
Co-Secretary Gwen Thomas,
81 Leonard Street, London EC2A 4QS
tel 020-7739 6669 *fax* 020-7739 8707
web site http://www.aophoto.co.uk
Protects and promotes the interests of fashion advertising and editorial photographers. Produces (amongst many other things) a prestigious annual photographic awards book, and can also help its members find anything from a model agency to an assistant. Annual subscription: £72-£355.

BAPLA (British Association of Picture Libraries and Agencies)
See page 464.

British Institution of Professional Photography
Amwell End, Ware, Herts. SG12 9HN
tel (01920) 464011
web site http://www.bipp.com
See page 489.

Master Photographers Association
Hallmark House, 1 Chancery Lane, Darlington, Co. Durham DL1 5QP
tel (01325) 356555 *fax* (01325) 357813
e-mail generalenquiries@mpauk.com
web site http://www.mpa@mpauk.com
Promotes and protects professional photographers. Members qualify for awards of Licentiate, Associate and Fellowship. Annual subscription: £99.

The Royal Photographic Society
The Octagon, Milsom Street, Bath BA1 1DN
tel (01225) 462841 *fax* (01225) 448688
e-mail rps@rps.org
web site http://www.rps.org
Open membership organisation which promotes the art and science of photography and electronic imagery; publishes *The Photographic Journal* (monthly) and the *Imaging Science Journal* (quarterly).

petition amongst photographers will be strong. Each stock library has different specific requirements and established markets, so contact them first before making a submission. Some libraries will ask to see a few hundred images from a photographer in order to judge for consistency of quality and saleability. Stock libraries selling images through catalogues or over the Internet will often consider an initial submission of just a few images, knowing that it is possible to accumulate significant fees from a small number of outstanding individual images marketed this way.

Images placed with a library remain the property of the photographer and libraries do not normally sell images outright to clients, but lease them for a specific use for a fee, from which commission is deducted. This means that a single image can accumulate many sales over a period of time. The commission rate is usually about 50% of every sale generated by the library. This may sound high, but it should be borne in mind that the library takes on all overheads, marketing costs and other responsibilities involved in the smooth running of a business, allowing the photographer the freedom to spend more time taking pictures.

Photographers should realise, however, that stock photography is a long-term investment and it can take some time for sales to build up to a significant income. Clearly, photographers who supply the right images for the market, and are prolific, are those who do well, and there are a good number of photographers who make their entire living as full-time stock photographers, never having to undertake commissioned work.

Useful information

Bureau of Freelance Photographers
Focus House, 497 Green Lanes,
London N13 4BP
tel 020-8882 3315 *fax* 020-8886 5174
Chief Executive John Tracy
Helps the freelance photographer by providing information on markets and a free advisory service. Publishes *Market Newsletter* (monthly). Annual membership: £40.

Directories

Variety Media Publications
6 Bell Yard, London WC2A 2JR
tel 020-7520 5233
Publishes *The Creative Handbook.*

Elfande Ltd
Surrey House, 31 Church Street, Leatherhead, Surrey KT22 8EF
tel (01372) 220300 *fax* (01372) 220340
Publishes *Contact Photographers.*

Royalty-free CD companies

In recent years, a number of companies have started marketing royalty-free images on CD-Rom. These companies obtain images by purchasing them from photographers for a flat fee. Once a CD has been purchased by a client (usually at very low cost) they, in effect, own the images on the CD and are therefore able to reproduce them as many times as they wish, paying no further fees. Some royalty-free companies, however, do pay to photographers royalties related to CD sales in addition to a flat fee for the images. A typical CD usually contains approximately one hundred high-resolution reproduction-quality images in a variety of subject areas, including most specialist subjects.

Although photographers may be tempted to sell images to these companies in order to gain an instant fee, they should be aware that placing images with a traditional stock library can be far more fruitful financially in the long term, since a good image can accumulate very high fees over a period of time and go on selling for many years to come. Furthermore, the photographer always retains the rights to his or her own images.

Running your own library

Photographers choosing to market their own images or start up their own library have the advantage of retaining a full fee for every picture sale they make. But it is unlikely that an individual photographer could ever match the rates of an established library, or make the same volume of sales per image. However, the Internet has opened a new marketing avenue for photographers, who now have the opportunity to sell their images worldwide. Previously, only an established stock library would have been able to do this. Before embarking on establishing a home library, photographers should be aware that the business of marketing images is essentially a desk job which involves a considerable amount of paperwork, and time, which could be spent taking pictures.

When setting up a picture library, your first consideration should be whether to build up a library of your own images, or to take on other contributing photographers. Many photographers running their own libraries submit additional images to bigger libraries to increase the odds of making a good income. Often, a photographer's personal library is made up of work rejected by the larger libraries, which are usually only interested in images that will regularly sell and generate a high turnover. However, occasional sales can generate a significant amount of income for the individual. Furthermore, a photographer with a library of specialised subjects stands a good chance of gaining recognition with niche markets, which can be very lucrative if the competition for those particular subjects is low.

If you take on contributing photographers, the responsibility for another's work becomes yours, so it is important to draw up a contract with terms of business for both your contributing photographers and your clients. Loss or damage of images is the most important consideration when sending pictures to clients (most libraries will charge clients a fee of between £400-£600 per image for loss or damage of originals). It is often worth checking that a company wishing to receive transparencies does have adequate insurance to cover these fees, which can amount to a considerable figure if a large quantity of images is lost or damaged. On no account should images be sent to companies which refuse to take responsibility for loss or damage, nor to private individuals, unless they are working on a freelance basis for an established company. It should also be clearly stated in your terms that all pictures in the client's possession become the client's responsibility until they are returned and inspected for damage by the library.

Reproduction fees should also be established on a strict basis, bearing in mind that you owe it to your contributing photographers to command fees which are as high as possible when selling the rights to their images. It is also essential that you control how pictures will be used and the amount of exposure they will receive. The fees should be established according to the type of client using the image and how the image itself will be reproduced. Important factors to consider are where the image will appear, to what size it will be reproduced, the size of the print run, and the territorial rights required by the client. Many libraries also apply holding fees in cases where clients hold on to pictures for periods of time longer than a month.

Bruce Coleman is Managing Director of the Bruce Coleman Collection and past President of the British Association of Picture Libraries. **Ian Thraves** is a freelance photographer and former picture editor at the Bruce Coleman Collection.

Picture agencies and libraries

As well as supplying images to picture editors, picture researchers and others who use pictures, picture agencies and libraries provide a service to the freelance photographer as one way of selling their work. Most of the picture agencies and libraries listed in this section take work from other photographers.

If you want to introduce your work to a library or agency, send tear sheets, colour photocopies, disks or CDs that do not need to be returned. Never send unsolicited transparencies. Picture agencies and libraries are approached by photographers daily so do your homework to find the best agency to work for you, and consider which work they would most be interested in marketing. Remember that libraries are only interested in images that will sell. If you are approached by an agency, ask to see their terms and conditions. Members of BAPLA have signed a code of conduct that promotes fair dealing with photographers and customers.

To find agencies and libraries which cover specific subjects, start by referring to the *Picture agencies and libraries by subject area* on page 444, or see the listing for BAPLA (http://www.bapla.org.uk) on page 464.

See also ...

- *Card and stationery publishers which accept photographs* on page 451
- *Syndicates, news and press agencies* on page 143
- *The freelance photographer* on page 407
- *Picture research* on page 452
- *National newspapers UK and Ireland* on page 3
- *Magazines by subject area* on page 121
- *Children's book publishers and packagers* on page 259.

**Member of the British Association of Picture Libraries and Agencies (BAPLA)*

A.A. & A. Ancient Art & Architecture Collection*

Suite 7, 2nd Floor, 410-420 Rayners Lane, Pinner, Middlesex HA5 5DY
tel 020-8429 3131 *fax* 020-8429 4646
e-mail library@aaacollection.co.uk
web site http://www.aaacollection.com

Specialises in the history of civilisations of the Middle East, Mediterranean countries, Europe, Asia, Americas, from ancient times to recent past, their arts, architecture, beliefs and peoples.

A-Z Botanical Collection Ltd*

192 Goswell Road, London EC1V 7DT
tel 020-7253 0991 *fax* 020-72553 0992
e-mail a-z@image-data.com
web site http://www.a-z.picture-library.com
Library Manager James Wakefield

Colour transparencies of plant life worldwide, including named gardens, habitats, gardening, still life, romantic seasonal shots, fungi, pests and diseases, etc (6 x 6cm, 35mm, 5 x 4in).

Abode Interiors Photographic Library*

Albion Court, 1 Pierce Street, Macclesfield, Cheshire SK11 6ER
tel (01625) 500070 *fax* (01625) 500910
web site http://www.sldirect.co.uk/abode/
Contact Mary Jarvis or Judi Goodwin

Colour photo library specialising in English and Scottish house interiors of all styles, types and periods. High quality material only; terms by agreement. Please phone before sending material. Founded 1993.

Academic File News Photos

Eastern Art Publishing Group, PO Box 13666, 27 Wallorton Gardens, London SW14 8WF

tel 020-8392 1122 *fax* 020-8392 1422
e-mail afis@eapgroup.com
web site http://www.eapgroup.com
Director Sajid Rizvi

Daily news coverage in UK and general library of arts, cultures, people and places, with special reference to the Middle East, North Africa and Asia. New photographers welcomed to cover UK and abroad. Sample pictures accepted over e-mail. Founded 1985.

Ace Photo Agency*

Satellite House, 2 Salisbury Road, London SW19 4EZ
tel 020-8944 9944 *fax* 020-8944 9940
e-mail info@acestock.com
web site http://www.acestock.com

General library: people, industry, business, travel, commerce, skies, sport, music and natural history. Worldwide syndication. Sae for enquiries. Very selective editing policy. Terms: 50%. Founded 1980.

Action Plus*

54-58 Tanner Street, London SE1 3PH
tel 020-7403 1558 *fax* 020-7403 1526
e-mail info@actionplus.co.uk

Specialist sports and action picture library. Comprehensive collection of creative images, including all aspects of 130 professional and amateur sports worldwide. Covers all age groups, all ethnic groups and all levels of ability. 35mm colour stock and on-line digital archive accessible by ISDN or modem. Terms: 50%. Founded 1986.

Lesley and Roy Adkins Picture Library

Longstone Lodge, Aller, Langport, Somerset TA10 0QT
tel (01458) 250075 *fax* (01458) 250858

Colour library covering archaeology and heritage; prehistoric, Roman, Greek, Egyptian and medieval sites and monuments; landscape, countryside, architecture, towns, villages and religious monuments. Founded 1989.

Aerofilms*

Aerofilms Ltd, Gate Studios, Station Road, Borehamwood, Herts. WD6 1EJ
tel 020-8207 0666 *fax* 020-8207 5433
e-mail library@aerofilms.com

Comprehensive library – over 1.5 million photos going back to 1919 – of vertical and oblique aerial photographs of UK; large areas with complete cover. Founded 1919.

Air Photo Supply

42 Sunningvale Avenue, Biggin Hill, Kent TN16 3BX
tel (01959) 574872

Aircraft and associated subjects, South-east England, colour and monochrome. No other photographers' material required. Founded 1963.

AKG London*

(The Arts and History Picture Library)
5 Melbray Mews, 158 Hurlingham Road, London SW6 3NS
tel 020-7610 6103 *fax* 020-7610 6125
e-mail enquiries@akg-london.co.uk
web site http://www.akg-london.co.uk

Principal subjects covered: art, archaeology and history. Exclusive UK and US representative for the Archiv für Kunst und Geschichte (AKG) with full access to the 10 million images held by AKG Berlin. Also exclusively represents the Erich Lessing Culture and Fine Art Archives in the UK. Founded 1994.

Bryan and Cherry Alexander Photography*

Higher Cottage, Manston, Sturminster Newton, Dorset DT10 1EZ
tel (01258) 473006 *fax* (01258) 473333
e-mail alexander@arcticphoto.co.uk
web site http://www.arcticphoto.co.uk

Polar regions with emphasis on indigenous peoples of the North. Landscape and wildlife: Alaska to Siberia and Antarctica. Founded 1973.

Rev. J. Catling Allen

St Giles House, Little Torrington, Devon EX38 8PS
tel (01805) 622497

Library of colour transparencies (35mm) and b&w photos of Bible Lands, including archaeological sites and the religions of Christianity, Islam and Judaism. Medieval abbeys and priories, cathedrals and churches in Britain. Also historic, rural and scenic Britain. (Not an agent or buyer.)

Allied Artists Ltd

31 Harcourt Street, London W1H 1DT
tel 020-7724 8809 *fax* 020-7262 8526
e-mail info@alliedartists.ltd.uk
web site http://www.alliedartists.ltd.uk
Contacts Gary Mills (director), Mary Burtenshaw

Agency for illustrators specialising in a wide range of styles for magazines, books, children's books and advertising. Large colour library. Founded 1983.

Allsport UK

3 Greenlea Park, Prince George's Road, London SW19 2JD
tel 020-8685 1010 *fax* 020-8648 5240
web site http://www.allsport.com

International sport and leisure. Founded 1968.

American History Picture Library

3 Barton Buildings, Bath BA1 2JR
tel (01225) 334213 *fax* (01225) 480554

Photographs, engravings, colour transparencies covering the exploration and social, political and military history of North America from 15th to 20th century: conquistadors, civil war, railroads, the Great Depression, advertisements, Prohibition and gangsters, moon landings and space.

AMIS

(Atlas Mountains Information Services)
26 Kirkcaldy Road, Burntisland, Fife KY3 9HQ
tel (01592) 873546
Proprietor Hamish Brown

Picture library on Moroccan sites, topography, mountains, travel. Illustration service. Commissions undertaken. No pictures purchased.

Ancient Egypt Picture Library*

6 Branden Drive, Knutsford, Cheshire WA16 8EJ
e-mail BobEgyptPL@aol.com
tel/fax (01565) 633106
Proprietor Bob Partridge

Images of Egypt, including most of the ancient sites and views of modern Egypt. All photographs (over 15,000 colour transparencies) taken by an Egyptologist, who can also provide full historical/ archaeological information. Founded 1996.

Andalucía Slide Library

Apto 499, Estepona, Málaga 29680, Spain
tel/fax (34) 952-793647
e-mail library@andalucia.com
web site http://www.andalucia.com
Contact Chris Chaplow

Colour transparencies (35mm and medium format) covering all aspects of Andalucía and Spain, principally its geography and culture. Digitised images available by ISDN or modem. Commissions undertaken. Founded 1991.

Andes Press Agency*

26 Padbury Court, London E2 7EH
tel 020-7613 5417 *fax* 020-7739 3159
e-mail photos@andespress.demon.co.uk
Director Carlos Reyes

Social, political and economic aspects of Latin America, Africa, Asia, Middle East, Europe and Britain; specialises in Latin America and contemporary world religions. Founded 1983.

Heather Angel/Natural Visions*

Highways, 6 Vicarage Hill, Farnham, Surrey GU9 8HJ
tel (01252) 716700 *fax* (01252) 727464
e-mail hangel@naturalvisions.co.uk
web site http://www.naturalvisions.co.uk

Colour transparencies (35mm and 2¼in square) with worldwide coverage of natural history and biological subjects including animals, plants, natural habitats (deserts, polar regions, rainforests, wetlands, etc), landscapes, gardens, close-ups and underwater images; also man's impact on the environment – pollution, acid rain, urban wildlife, etc. Large China file including pandas in all seasons. See web site for subject range. Pictures cannot be supplied *gratis* for personal use.

Animal Photography*

4 Marylebone Mews, New Cavendish Street, London W1M 7LF
tel 020-7935 0503 *fax* 020-7487 3038
e-mail thompson@animal-photography.co.uk

Horses, dogs, cats, small pets, East Africa, Galapagos. Other photographers' work not represented. Founded 1955.

Aquarius Library*

PO Box 5, Hastings, East Sussex TN34 1HR
tel (01424) 721196 *fax* (01424) 717704
e-mail aquarius.lib@clara.net
Contact David Corkill

Showbusiness specialist library with over one million colour and b&w images: film stills, classic portraiture, candids, archive material to present. New material added every week. Archival situation stills for advertising and magazine illustration use. Also television, vintage pop, opera, ballet and stage. Worldwide representation and direct sales. Collections considered, either outright purchase or 50%-50% marketing. Division of SPM London Ltd.

Aquila Wildlife Images
PO Box 1, Studley, Warks. B80 7JG
tel (01527) 852357 *fax* (01527) 857507
e-mail interbirdnet @birder.co.uk
Specialists in ornithological subjects, but covering all aspects of natural history, also pets and landscapes, in both colour and b&w.

Arcaid Architectural Photography and Picture Library*
The Factory, 2 Acre Road, Kingston, Surrey KT2 6EF
tel 020-8546 4352 *fax* 020-8541 5230
e-mail arcaid@arcaid.co.uk
web site http://www.arcaid.co.uk
'The built environment' – international collection: architecture, interior design, lifestyle interiors, gardens, travel, museums, historic and contemporary. Terms: 50%.

Archivio Veneziano – see Venice Picture Library*

Arctic Camera
66 Ashburnham Grove, London SE10 8UJ
tel/fax 020-8692 7651
e-mail Derek.Fordham@btinternet.com
Contact Derek Fordham
Colour transparencies of all aspects of Arctic life and environment. Founded 1978.

Ardea Wildlife & Pets*
35 Brodrick Road, London SW17 7DX
tel 020-8672 2067 *fax* 020-8672 8787
e-mail ardea@ardea.co.uk
Contact Sophie Napier
Specialist worldwide natural history photographic library of animals, birds, plants, fish, insects, reptiles, worldwide scenics and domestic pets.

The Associated Press Ltd
News Photo Department, The Associated Press House, 12 Norwich Street, London EC4A 1BP
tel 020-7427 4260/4266, 020-7353 1515 ext 4264 (library manager) *fax* 020-7353 0836
web site http://www.photoarchive.ap.org
News, features, sports.

Australia Pictures
28 Sheen Common Drive, Richmond, London TW10 5BN
tel/fax 020-8898 0150 *fax* 020-8876 3637
Contact John Miles
Comprehensive library covering Australia, Aboriginals and their art, indigenous peoples, underwater, Tibet, Peru, Bolivia, Iran, Irian Jaya, Pakistan, Yemen. Founded 1988.

Aviation Picture Library* (Austin J. Brown)
116 The Avenue, St Stephen's, London W13 8 JX
tel 020-8566 7712 *fax* 020-8566 7714
cellphone (0860) 670073
e-mail avpix@avnet.co.uk
web site http://www.aviationpictures.com
Worldwide aviation photographic library, including dynamic views of aircraft. Aerial and travel library including Europe, Caribbean, USA, and East and West Africa. Material taken since 1960. Specialising in air-to-air and air-to-ground commissions. Chief photographers for *Flyer* magazine. Founded 1970.

B. & B. Photographs
Prospect House, Clifford Chambers, Stratford upon Avon, Warks. CV37 8HX
tel (01789) 298106 *fax* (01789) 292450
e-mail bucz1@btinternet.com
35mm/medium format colour library of horticulture (especially pests and diseases) and biogeography (worldwide), natural history (especially Britain) and biological education. Other photographers' work not represented. Founded 1974.

Bandphoto Agency
(division of UPPA Ltd)
29-31 Saffron Hill, London EC1N 8SW
tel 020-7421 6000 *fax* 020-7421 6006
International news and feature picture service for British and overseas publishers.

Barnaby's Picture Library*
19 Rathbone Street, London W1P 1AF
tel 020-7636 6128/9 *fax* 020-7637 4317
e-mail barnabyspicturelibrary@ukbusinesss.com
web site http://www.ukbusiness.com/barnabyspicturelibrary/
General library of 4 million photos, colour and b&w, illustrating yesterday, today and tomorrow. Plus 500,000 engravings from 1500 to 1900.

Barnardo's Photographic Archive*
Tanners Lane, Barkingside, Ilford, Essex IG6 1QG
tel 020-8550 8822 *fax* 020-8550 0429
Extensive collection of b&w and colour images dating from 1874 to the present day covering social history with the

emphasis on children and child care. Also 300 films dating from 1905. Founded 1874.

BBC Natural History Unit Picture Library*

BBC Broadcasting House, Whiteladies Road, Bristol BS8 2LR
tel 0117-9746720 *fax* 0117-9238166
e-mail nhu.picture.library@bbc.co.uk
web site http://www.bbcwild.com

Holds photographs relating to the Unit's film-making activities and represents the work of top wildlife photographers from around the world. Also has a unique collection of archive photographs relating to the history of film-making in the Unit. Founded 1995.

Dr Alan Beaumont

52 Squires Walk, Lowestoft, Suffolk NR32 4LA
tel (01502) 560126

Worldwide collection of monochrome prints and colour transparencies (35mm and 6 x 7cm) of natural history, countryside, windmills and aircraft. Brochure and subject lists available. No other photographers required.

Bee Photographs – see Heritage & Natural History Photography

Stephen Benson Slide Bureau

45 Sugden Road, London SW11 5EB
tel 020-7223 8635

World: agriculture, archaeology, architecture, commerce, everyday life, culture, environment, geography, science, tourism. Speciality: South America, the Caribbean, Australasia, Nepal, Turkey, Israel and Egypt. Assignments undertaken.

Bird Images

28 Carousel Walk, Sherburn in Elmet, North Yorkshire LS25 6LP
tel/fax (01977) 684666
Principal P. Doherty

Specialist in the birds of Britain and Europe, including video footage from Europe and North America. Expert captioning service available. Founded 1989.

John Birdsall Photography*

75 Raleigh Street, Nottingham NG7 4DL
tel 0115-978 2645 *fax* 0115-978 5546
e-mail photos@johnbirdsall.co.uk
web site http://www.johnbirdsall.co.uk
Contact Clare Marsh

Contemporary social documentary library covering children, youth, old age, health, disability, education, housing, work; also Nottingham and surrounding area; Spain, India – commissions and stock pictures. Founded 1980.

The Anthony Blake Photo Library*

54 Hill Rise, Richmond, Surrey TW10 6UB
tel 020-8940 7583 *fax* 020-8948 1224
e-mail info@abpl.co.uk
web site http://www.abpl.co.uk

Food and wine images from around the world, including raw ingredients, finished dishes, shops, restaurants, markets, agriculture and viticulture. Commissions undertaken. Contributors welcome. Brochure available.

John Blake Picture Library

204 Northfield Avenue, London W13 9SJ
tel 020-8840 4141 *fax* 020-8566 2568
Manager Alan Denny

General topography of England, Europe and the rest of the world. Landscapes, architecture, churches, gardens, countryside, towns and villages. Horse trials covered including Badminton and Gatcombe Park. Terms: 50%. Founded 1975.

Sarah Boait Photography and Picture Library

tel/fax (01458) 832600
e-mail sarahboait@compuserve.com

Covers the British Isles, especially the West Country and ancient sites; also world travel, world religions. No contributors' work accepted.

Bodleian Library*

Oxford OX1 3BG
tel (01865) 277214/277153 *fax* (01865) 277187
e-mail western.manuscripts@bodley.ox.ac.uk
web site http://www.bodley.ox.ac.uk/

Library of 32,000 35mm colour transparencies in slides or filmstrips for immediate sale (not hire). There is an iconographical index to the images, which are mostly from medieval manuscripts. Large format transparencies more suitable for reproduction are available to order, as are copies, photographs and microfilm of any other items from the Bodleian's vast collections.

BookArt & Architecture Picture Library

1 Woodcock Lodge, Epping Green, Hertford SG13 8ND

tel (01707) 875253 *fax* (01707) 875286
e-mail sharpd@globalnet.co.uk
Modern and historic buildings, landscapes, works of named architects in Great Britain, Europe, Scandinavia, North America, India, Southeast Asia, Japan, North and East Africa; modern sculpture. Listed under style, place and personality. Founded 1991.

Boxing Picture Library

3 Barton Buildings, Bath BA1 2JR
tel (01225) 334213 *fax* (01225) 480554
Prints, engravings and photos of famous boxers, boxing personalities and famous fights from 18th century to recent years.

Bridgeman Art Library*

17-19 Garway Road, London W2 4PH
tel 020-7727 4065 *fax* 020-7792 8509
e-mail info@bridgeman.co.uk
web site http://www.bridgeman.co.uk
Source of fine art images for publication. Acts as an agent for over 1000 museums, galleries and private collections throughout the world. Every subject, era and style represented in an archive of images from cave paintings to pop art and beyond, including many historical events and personalities. Also offers research service and acts as copyright agent to a growing number of contemporary artists. Images may be viewed and ordered on-line. CD-Rom and printed catalogues available. Founded 1971.

Britain on View*

43 Drury Lane, London WC2B 5RT
tel 020-7836 6608 *fax* 020-7836 6553
e-mail jcrabb@bta.org.uk
web site http://www.britainonview.com
Photo library of the British Tourist Authority. British culture, society, events, landscapes, towns and villages, tourist attractions.

British Library Picture Library*

96 Euston Road, London NW1 2DB
tel 020-7412 7614 *fax* 020-7412 7771
e-mail bl-repro@bl.uk
web site http://www.bl.uk
Illustrative and historical material from manuscripts, printed books, oriental and Indian items, maps, music and stamps. In addition to the stock collection, images from 15 million books can be sourced. Founded 1996.

David Broadbent/Peak District Pictures

12 Thomas Street, Glossop, Derbyshire SK13 8QN
tel/fax (01457) 862997
e-mail dbphoto@btinternet.com
web site http://www.firebomb.com/broadbent
The Peak District fully covered, landscape, natural history, birds a speciality; sports. Commissions undertaken. New material welcome. Terms: 50%. Founded 1989.

David Broadbent/Birds
Highly stylised and pictorial library of British birds, bird reserves and important wildlife landscapes.

Hamish Brown, Scottish Photographic

26 Kirkcaldy Road, Burntisland, Fife KY3 9HQ
tel (01592) 873546
Picture library on Scottish sites, topography, mountains, travel. Book illustrations. Commissions undertaken. No pictures purchased.

Butterflies

27 Lucastes Lane, Haywards Heath, West Sussex RH16 1LE
tel (01444) 454254
Proprietors Dr J. Tampion, Mrs M.D. Tampion
Worldwide: butterflies, silkmoths, hawkmoths, adults, larvae, pupae, their foodplants, poisonous plants, wild, garden, greenhouse and tropical plants, botanical and gardening science, ecology, environment. Articles and line illustrations also available; commissions undertaken. No new photographers required. Founded 1990.

Camera Press Ltd*

21 Queen Elizabeth Street, London SE1 2PD
tel 020-7378 1300 *fax* 020-7278 5126
B&w prints and colour transparencies including up-to-date coverage of British royalty, portraits of world statesmen, politicians, entertainers, reportage, humour, nature, pop, features. Terms: 50%. Founded 1947.

Camerapix – see C.P.L. (Camerapix Picture Library)

La Casa Photos

PO Box One, Newtown, Mid Wales SY16 2WP
tel (01686) 621421 *fax* (01686) 621421
e-mail info@org.uk
web site http://www.art71.com
Director Mike Slater

Specialises in photo-art images. Promotes the art of photography and work of other artists in creating innovative exhibitions. Principal area is abstract images of colour and shape and themed exhibitions. Welcomes proposals from other artists. Founded 1998.

J. Allan Cash Photolibrary (J. Allan Cash Ltd)*

204 Northfield Avenue, London W13 9SJ
tel 020-8840 4141 *fax* 020-8566 2568
Manager Alan Denny

Worldwide photographic library: travel, landscape, natural history, sport, industry, agriculture. Details available for photographers interested in contributing.

Cephas Picture Library*

Hurst House, 157 Walton Road, East Molesey, Surrey KT8 0DX
tel 020-8979 8647 or 07000 CEPHAS
fax 020-8224 8095
e-mail mickrock@cephas.co.uk
web site http://www.cephas.co.uk

Comprehensive library of food and drink photos: wine and vineyards, spirits, beer and cider, food and drink worldwide. Free catalogue available; specialist knowledge.

City Syndication Ltd* – see Monitor Syndication

COI Photo Library – see Stockwave*

Michael Cole Camerawork*

The Coach House, 27 The Avenue, Beckenham, Kent BR3 2DP
tel/fax 020-8658 6120
web site http://www.tennisphotos.com

Probably the largest and most comprehensive tennis library in the world comprising over half a million colour and b&w images. Includes over 50 years of the Wimbledon Championships. All grand slam and major events covered. Founded 1945.

Bruce Coleman Inc.

117 East 24th Street, New York, NY 10010-2919, USA
tel 212-979-6252 *fax* 212-979-5468
e-mail norman@bciusa.com
web site http://www.bciusq.com
President Norman Owen Tomalin

Specialises exclusively in traditional colour transparencies and digital stock. All formats from 35mm acceptable. All subjects required.

Bruce Coleman Collection*

16 Chiltern Business Village, Arundel Road, Uxbridge, Middlesex UB8 2SN
tel (01895) 257094 *fax* (01895) 272357
e-mail alison@brucecoleman.co.uk
web site http://www.brucecoleman.co.uk

Colour transparencies on natural history, ecology, environment, geography, archaeology, anthropology, agriculture, science, scenics and travel.

Collections*

13 Woodberry Crescent, London N10 1PJ
tel 020-8883 0083 *fax* 020-8883 9215

The British Isles only: places, people, buildings, industry, leisure; specialist collections on customs, castles, bridges, London, plus an extensive collection on Ireland. Founded 1990.

Colorific Photo Library*

The Innovation Centre, 225 Marsh Wall, London E14 9FX
tel 020-7515 3000 *fax* 020-7538 3555
e-mail davidl@visualgroup.com

Handles the work of international celebrity and features photographers. Most subjects currently on file, upwards of 250,000 images. Represents the following agencies: Black Star (New York), Contact Press Images (New York/Paris), Visages (Los Angeles), Shooting Star (Los Angeles), Matrix (New York), Icone (Paris), Regards (Paris), ANA Press (Paris). Also represents *Sports Illustrated*.

Concannon Golf History Library

11 Cheyney Gardens, Westcliff, Bournemouth BH4 8AS
tel (01202) 766145
e-mail c.golflib.@newsfactory.net
Contact Dale Concannon

Golfing images 1750-1950: famous players, courses, Ryder Cup, open championships, golf course architecture, memorabilia, US golf and artwork. Specialist advice available. Commissions undertaken. Founded 1997.

Dee Conway Ballet & Dance Picture Library

110 Sussex Way, London N7 6RR
tel/fax 020-7272 7845
e-mail library@ddance.demon.co.uk
Proprietor Dee Conway

Classical ballet, modern dance, flamenco, tango, rock, jive, mime; dance from India, Africa, Russia, China, Japan,

Thailand; informal class pictures of dance, music and drama. Colour and b&w images. Founded 1995.

Sylvia Cordaiy Photo Library
45 Rotherstone, Devizes, Wilts. SN10 2DD
tel (01380) 728327 *fax* (01380) 728328
e-mail sylviacordaiy@compuserve.com
web site http://www.sylvia-cordaiy.com
Worldwide travel and architecture, global environmental topics, wildlife and domestic animals, veterinary, comprehensive UK files, Paul Kaye b&w archive. Terms: 50%. Founded 1990.

Country Collections Photolibrary
Unit 9, Ditton Priors Trading Estate, Bridgnorth, Shropshire WV16 6SS
tel (01746) 712533, 861330
Contact Robert Foster
Specialises in Celtic culture from stone circles to the present day. Also an expanding collection of rivers and streamside vegetation. Colour transparencies. Founded 1985.

C.P.L. (Camerapix Picture Library)
8 Ruston Mews, London W11 1RB
tel 020-7221 0077 *fax* 020-7792 8105
e-mail camerapixuk@btinternet.com
and PO Box 45048 Nairobi, Kenya
tel 448923 *fax* 448926
e-mail info@camerapix.com
Kenya, Tanzania, Pakistan, Jordan, Namibia, Nepal, Maldives, Mauritius, Seychelles, Zimbabwe; portraits, agriculture, industry, tribal cultures, landscapes; wildlife including rare species; extensive collection on Aldabra Island; Islamic portfolio: Mecca, Medina, Muslim pilgrimage. News material available and special assignments arranged. Further material available from collection held in Nairobi.

Crafts Council Picture Library*
44A Pentonville Road, London N1 9BY
tel 020-7806 2504 *fax* 020-7837 6891
e-mail photostore@craftscouncil.org.uk
Comprehensive source of visual material for contemporary British crafts. Spanning the last 30 years, subject areas cover: jewellery, ceramics, furniture, glass, woodwork, paperwork, bookbinding, domestic objects, decorative forms, lettering, textiles, fashion accessories, basketry, musical instruments and public art. Images can be accessed through Photostore, the Council's interactive database, open during working hours (no appointment necessary). Images are available on a range of formats including digital files. Founded 1973.

Peter Cumberlidge Photo Library
Sunways, Slapton, Kingsbridge, Devon TQ7 2PR
tel (01548) 580461 *fax* (01548) 580588
e-mail cumberlidge@shines.swis.net
Contact Jane Cumberlidge
Nautical, travel and coastal colour transparencies 35mm and 6 x 6cm. Specialities: boats, harbours, marinas, inland waterways. Travel and holiday subjects in Northern Europe, the Mediterranean, and New England, USA. No other photographers' material required. Founded 1982.

Lupe Cunha
Photo-Arte Gallery, 19 Ashfield Parade, London N14 5EH
tel (07071) 225351 *fax* 020-8882 6303
e-mail lupe.cunha@btinternet.com
Specialist library on all aspects of childhood from pregnancy to school age, also women's interest and health/medical with focus on the patient and nursing care. Commissioned photography undertaken. Also represents collection on Brazil for Brazil Photo Agency. Terms: 50%. Founded 1987.

Sue Cunningham Photographic*
56 Chatham Road, Kingston-upon-Thames, Surrey KT1 3AA
tel 020-8541 3024 *fax* 020-8541 5388
e-mail pictures@scphotographic.com
web site http://www.scphotographic.com
International coverage on many subjects: Latin America, Africa and Eastern Europe. Also Western Europe, London (including aerial).

Das Photo
Chalet le Pin, Domaine de Bellevue 181, 6940 Septon, Belgium
tel/fax (32) 86-322426
e-mail dasphotogb@aol.com
Old School House, Llanfilo, Brecon, Powys LD3 0RH
tel (01874) 711953
Arab countries, Americas, Europe, Caribbean, Southeast Asia, Amazon, world festivals, archaeology, people, biblical, education, schools, modern languages. Founded 1975.

Barry Davies
Dyffryn, Bolahaul Road, Cwmffrwd, Carmarthen, Carmarthenshire SA31 2LW
tel/fax (01267) 233625
Natural history, landscape, Egypt, children, outdoor activities and general subjects. Formats 35mm, 6 x 6cm, 6 x 7cm, 6 x 17cm, 5 x 4in. Other photographers' work not accepted. Founded 1983.

Dennis Davis Photography
9 Great Burrow Rise, Northam, Bideford, Devon EX39 1TB
tel (01237) 475165
Gardens, wild and garden flowers, domestic livestock including rare breeds and poultry, agricultural landscapes, architecture – interiors and exteriors, landscape, coastal, rural life. Commissions welcomed. No other photographers required. Founded 1984.

James Davis Travel Photography
65 Brighton Road, Shoreham, West Sussex BN43 6RE
tel (01273) 452252 *fax* (01273) 440116
Proprietor Paul Seheult
Stock transparency library specialising in worldwide travel photos.

Peter Dazeley*
The Studios, 5 Heathmans Road, London SW6 4TJ
tel 020-7736 3171 *fax* 020-7371 8876
e-mail dazeleyp@aol.com
Extensive golf library dating from 1970. Colour and b&w coverage of major tournaments, with over 250,000 images of players, courses worldwide, action shots, portraits, trophies, including miscellaneous images: clubs, balls and teaching shots.

George A. Dey
'Drumcairn', Aberdeen Road, Laurencekirk, Kincardineshire AB30 1AJ
tel (01561 37) 8845
Scottish Highland landscapes, Highland Games, forestry, seabirds, castles of Northeast Scotland, gardens, spring, autumn, winter scenes, veteran cars, North Holland, New Zealand (North Island). Mostly 35mm, some 6 x 6cm. Founded 1986.

Douglas Dickins Photo Library
2 Wessex Gardens, London NW11 9RT
tel 020-8455 6221
Worldwide collection of colour transparencies (mostly 6 x 6cm, some 35mm) and b&w prints (10 x 8in originals), specialising in Asia, particularly India and Indonesia; also USA, Canada, France, Austria and Switzerland, Japan, China, Burma. Founded 1946.

C.M. Dixon*
The Orchard, Marley Lane, Kingston, Canterbury, Kent CT4 6JH
tel (01227) 830075 *fax* (01227) 831135
Europe, Ethiopia, Iceland, Jordan, Sri Lanka, Tunisia, Turkey, former USSR. Main subjects include agriculture, ancient art, archaeology, architecture, clouds, geography, geology, history, horses, industry, meteorology, mosaics, mountains, mythology, occupations, people.

Earth Images Picture Library
PO Box 43, Keynsham, Bristol BS18 2TH
tel/fax 0117-986 1144/(01275) 839643
Director Richard Arthur
Earth from Space (satellite remote sensing); earth science and art-in-science imagery – from cosmic to sub-atomic. Founded 1989.

Ecoscene*
The Oasts, Headley Lane, Passfield, Liphook, Hants GU30 7RX
tel (01428) 751056 *fax* (01428) 751057
e-mail sally@ecoscene.com
web site http://www.ecoscene.com
Contact Sally Morgan
Specialists in environment and ecology. Subjects include agriculture, conservation, energy, industry, pollution, habitats and habitat loss, sustainability, wildlife; worldwide coverage. Terms: 55% to photographer. Founded 1987.

Edinburgh Photographic Library*
Mercat International, 14 Garscube Terrace, Edinburgh EH12 6BQ
tel 0131-337 7615 *fax* 0131-337 0303
e-mail epl@mercat.co.uk
web site http://www.mercat.co.uk
Proprietor James Young
15,000 colour transparency images of Scotland – castles, scenic, mountains, festivals, pipe bands. Founded 1986.

English Heritage Photo Library*
23 Savile Row, London W1X 1AB
tel 020-7973 3338/3339 *fax* 020-7973 3027
Wide range of high quality colour transparencies, ranging from ancient monuments to artefacts, legendary castles to stone circles, elegant interiors to industrial architecture and post-war listed buildings.

Environmental Investigation Agency
69-85 Old Street, London EC1V 9HX
tel 020-7490 7040 *fax* 020-7490 0436
e-mail communications@eia-international.org
web site http://www.eia-international.org
Communications Officer Matthew Snead
Specialists in images of the illegal trade in endangered species, ozone-depleting substances and illegal logging; also animals in their natural environment. Founded 1984.

Greg Evans International Photo Library*
6 Station Parade, Sunningdale, Ascot, Berks. SL5 0EP
tel 020-7636 8238 *fax* 020-7637 1439
e-mail greg@gregevans.net
web site http://www.gregevans.net
Comprehensive, general colour library with over 300,000 transparencies. Subjects include: abstract, aircraft, arts, animals, beaches, business, children, computers, couples, families, food/restaurant, women, industry, skies, sports (action and leisure), UK scenics, worldwide travel. Visitors welcome; combined commissions undertaken; first search fee. Photographers' submissions welcome. Free brochure/CD-Rom. Founded 1979.

Mary Evans Picture Library*
59 Tranquil Vale, London SE3 0BS
tel 020-8318 0034 *fax* 020-8852 7211
e-mail lib@mepl.co.uk
web site http://www.mepl.co.uk
Millions of historical illustrations documenting social, political, cultural, technical, geographical and biographical themes from ancient times to the mid 20th century. Photographs, original prints, and ephemera backed by a large international book and magazine collection. Special collections include Sigmund Freud, the Fawcett Library (women's rights), the Meledin Collection (20th-century Russian history) and individual photographers active from the 1930s to the 1970s. Colour brochure available. Compilers of the *Picture Researcher's Handbook*, published every 3 years by Pira International.

Eyeline Photography
259 London Road, Cheltenham, Glos. GL52 6YG
tel (01242) 513567
e-mail colin.jarman@btinternet.com
Watersports, particularly sailing; windvanes; sheepdog trials. Founded 1979.

Famous Pictures & Features Agency*
13 Harwood Road, London SW6 4QP
tel 020-7731 9333 *fax* 020-7731 9330
e-mail info@famous.uk.com
web site http://www.famous.uk.com
Colour pictures and features library covering music, film and TV personalities. Terms: 50%. Founded 1990.

Feature-Pix Colour Library – see World Pictures*

Financial Times Pictures*
Number One, Southwark Bridge, London SE1 9HL
tel 020-7873 3671 *fax* 020-7873 4606
e-mail photosynd@ft.com
Colour and b&w library serving the *Financial Times*. Specialises in world business, industry and commerce; world politicians and statespeople; cities and countries; plus many other subjects. Also *FT* maps and graphics. All material available in colour and b&w, print and electronic formats. Library updated daily.

Fine Art Photographic Library*
Rawlings House, 2A Milner Street, London SW3 2PU
tel 020-7589 3127 *fax* 020-7584 1944
e-mail info@fineartphotolibrary.com
Holds over 25,000 transparencies of paintings by British and European artists, from Old Masters to contemporary. Free brochure. CD-Rom available. Founded 1980.

FirePix International*
68 Arkles Lane, Anfield, Liverpool L4 2SP
tel/fax 0151-260 0111
e-mail info@firepix.com
web site http://www.firepix.com
Contact Tony Myers ARPS, GIFireE
Holds 17,000 images of fire and firefighters at work in the UK, USA, Japan and China. Established by photographer Tony Myers after 28 years in service with the British Fire Service. Many images are stored digitally; CD-Rom available. Founded 1993.

Fogden Wildlife Photographs*
Basement, 10 Bellevue, Bristol BS8 1DA
tel 0117-923 8849 *fax* 0117-923 8543
e-mail susan.fogden@virgin.net
Library Manager Susan Fogden

Wide coverage of natural history, including camouflage, warning coloration, mimicry, breeding strategies, feeding, animal/plant relationships, environmental studies, especially in rainforests and deserts. Founded 1980.

Ron and Christine Foord

155B City Way, Rochester, Kent ME1 2BE
tel/fax (01634) 847348

Colour picture library of over 1000 species of wild flowers. Also British insects, garden flowers, pests and diseases, lichen, mosses and cacti.

Footprints Colour Picture Library

Goldfin Cottage, Maidlands Farm, Broad Oak, Rye, East Sussex TN31 6BJ
tel (01424) 883076 *fax* (01424) 883078
Proprietor Paula Leaver

Specialises in underwater and above water coverage of holiday destinations in the tropics; also food and flowers by Debbie Patterson. Founded 1991.

Forest Life Picture Library

Forestry Commission, 231 Corstorphine Road, Edinburgh EH12 7AT
Picture Researcher Neill Campbell
tel 0131-314 6411
e-mail n.campbell@forestry.gov.uk
Business Manager Douglas Green
tel 0131-314 6200 *fax* 0131-314 6285
e-mail d.green@forestry.gov.uk

Tree species, forest and woodland views and management, landscapes, wildlife, flora and fauna, conservation, sport and leisure. Founded 1983.

Werner Forman Archive*

36 Camden Square, London NW1 9XA
tel 020-7267 1034 *fax* 020-7267 6026
e-mail wfa@btinternet.com
web site http://www.btinternet.com/~wfa

Art, architecture, archaeology, history and peoples of ancient, oriental and primitive cultures. Founded 1975.

Format Photographers*

19 Arlington Way, London EC1R 1UY
tel 020-7833 0292 *fax* 020-7833 0381
e-mail format@formatphotogs.demon.co.uk
Contact Maggie Murray

A library and agency representing the work of 20 women documentary photographers. The images, mainly from the last 20 years, are constantly updated and offer a unique perspective of the world. Subjects covered: social and political life in Britain and abroad, health, education, women's issues, work, the elderly and the very young, disability, gay and lesbian, Black and Asian culture, the environment, housing and homelessness, transport and leisure. Countries from Albania to Zambia. Colour and b&w. Commissions undertaken. Founded 1983.

Fortean Picture Library*

Henblas, Mwrog Street, Ruthin LL15 1LG
tel (01824) 707278 *fax* (01824) 705324
e-mail janet.bord@forteanpix.demon.co.uk
web site http://www.forteanpix.demon.co.uk

Colour and b&w pictures covering strange phenomena: UFOs, Loch Ness Monster, ghosts, Bigfoot, witchcraft, etc; also antiquities (especially in Britain – prehistoric and Roman sites, castles, churches).

Fotoccompli – The Picture Library

166 Boldmere Road, Sutton Coldfield B73 5UD
tel 0121-240 8950

Comprehensive library, ranging from abstracts to zoology, serving all of Britain, especially the Birmingham and West Midlands areas. Terms: 50%. Minimum retention period: 3 years. Founded 1989.

Fotomas Index*

12 Pickhurst Rise, West Wickham, Kent BR4 0AL
tel/fax 020-8776 2772 *fax* 020-8776 2236

Specialises in supplying pre-20th century (mostly pre-Victorian) illustrative material to publishing and academic worlds, and for TV and advertising. Complete production back-up for interior décor, exhibitions and locations.

Freelance Focus

7 King Edward Terrace, Brough, East Yorkshire HU15 1EE
tel/fax (01482) 666036
Contact Gary Hicks

UK/international network of photographers. Over 2 million stock pictures available, covering all subjects, worldwide, at competitive rates. Assignments undertaken for all types of clients. Subject list available on request. Also publishes directory of photographers and photo libraries/agencies. Founded 1988.

Frontline Photo Press Agency

18 Wall Street, Norwood, SA 5067
postal address PO Box 162, Kent Town, SA 5071, Australia
tel (08) 8333 2691 *fax* (08) 8364 0604

e-mail info@frontline.net.au
web site http://www.frontline.net.au
Photo Editor Carlo Irlitti

Stock photo agency, picture library and photographic press agency with 400,000 images. Covers sport, people, personalities, travel, scenics, environmental, agricultural, industrial, natural history, concepts, science, medicine, social documentary and press images. Seeking worldwide stock contributors. Assignments undertaken. Prefers high resolution image files on CD-Rom. Write, fax or e-mail for submission guidelines, photo requirements and other details. Terms: 60% to photographer (stock); assignment rates negotiable. Founded 1988.

Frost Historical Newspaper Collection

8 Monks Avenue, New Barnet, Herts. EN5 1DB
tel/fax 020-8440 3159

Headline stories from 60,000 British and overseas newspapers reporting major events since 1850.

Brian Gadsby Picture Library

17 route des Pyrénées, 65700 Labatut-Riviere, Hautes Pyrénées, France
tel (33) 5 62 96 38 44
e-mail GadsbyJB@aol.com

Colour transparencies (6 x 4.5cm, 35mm) and b&w prints. Wide range of subjects but emphasis on travel and the environment: UK, Europe (particularly France), Ecuador and Galapagos Islands, Patagonia, Sri Lanka. Natural history: mainly birds and plant life (wild and garden). Large wildfowl file. Catalogue on request by picture researchers. No other photographers' material required.

Andrew N. Gagg's Photo Flora*

Town House Two, Fordbank Court, Henwick Road, Worcester WR2 5PF
tel (01905) 748515
e-mail gagg@cwcom.net
web site http://www.gagg.mcmail.com/photoflora.htm
Contact Andrew N. Gagg

Comprehensive collection of British and European wild plants. Travel: Egypt, India, Tibet, China, Nepal, Thailand, Mexico. Founded 1982.

Galaxy Picture Library*

1 Milverton Drive, Ickenham, Uxbridge, Middlesex UB10 8PP
tel (01895) 637463 *fax* (01895) 623277
e-mail galaxypix@compuserve.com
web site http://ourworld.compuserve.com/homepages/galaxypix
Contact Robin Scagell

Astronomy: specialities include the night sky, amateur astronomy, astronomers and observatories. Founded 1992.

Garden Matters Photographic Library*

Marlham, Henley's Down, Battle, East Sussex TN33 9BN
tel (01424) 830566 *fax* (01424) 830224
e-mail gardens@ftech.co.uk
web site http://web.ftech.net/~gardens
Contact Dr John Feltwell

Plants 8000 Over 8000 scientifically named species and cultivars of garden flowers, wild plants, trees (over 1000 species), grasses, crops, herbs, spices, houseplants, carnivorous plants, climbers (especially Clematis), roses and pests.

General gardening How-to, gardening techniques, garden design and embellishments, cottage gardens, USA designer-gardens, 200 garden portfolios from 16 states in the USA, 100 portfolios from 12 European countries. Several photographers now represented. Founded 1993.

Colin Garratt – see Railways – Milepost 92½*

Genesis Space Photo Library*

Greenbanks, Robins Hill, Raleigh, Bideford, Devon EX39 3PA
tel (01237) 471960 *fax* (01237) 472060
e-mail tim@spaceport.co.uk
web site http://www.spaceport. co.uk
Contact Tim Furniss

Specialises in rockets, spacecraft, spacemen, Earth, Moon, planets. Founded 1990.

Geo Aerial Photography*

4 Christian Fields, London SW16 3JZ
tel/fax 020-8764 6292, 0115-981 9418
e-mail geo-aerial@geo-group.demon.co.uk
web site http://www.geo-group.demon.co.uk
Director J.F.J. Douglas

Air-to-air and air-to-ground colour library: natural and cultural/man-made landscapes and individual features. Subjects from UK, Scandinavia, Middle East, Asia and Africa. Commissions undertaken. Terms: 50%. Founded 1992.

GeoScience Features*

(incorporates K.S.F. and RIDA photolibraries)
6 Orchard Drive, Wye, Kent TN25 5AU
tel (01233) 812707 *fax* (01233) 812707
e-mail gsf@geoscience.demon.co.uk
web site http://www.geoscience.demon.co.uk
Director Dr Basil Booth

Colour library (35mm to 5 x 4in). Animals, biology, birds, botany, chemistry, earth science, ecology, environment, geology, geography, habitats, landscapes, macro/micro, peoples, plants, travel, sky, weather, wildlife and zoology; Americas, Africa, Australasia, Europe, India, Southeast Asia. Over one third million colour images available as film or high resolution digital images. CD-Rom available to order.

Geoslides*

4 Christian Fields, London SW16 3JZ
tel/fax 020-8764 6292 or 0115-981 9418
e-mail geoslides@geo-group.demon.co.uk
web site http://www.geo-group.demon.co.uk
Library Director John Douglas

Broadly based and substantial collections from Africa, Asia, Antarctic, Arctic and sub-Arctic areas, Australia (Blackwood Collection). Worldwide commissions undertaken. Terms: 50% on UK sales. Founded 1968.

Mark Gerson Photography

3 Regal Lane, Regents Park Road, London NW1 7TH
tel 020-7286 5894 *fax* 020-7267 9246

Portrait photographs of personalities, mainly literary, in colour and b&w from 1950 to the present. No other photographers' material required.

John Glover Photography

Fairfield, Hale House Lane, Churt, Farnham, Surrey GU10 2NQ
tel (01428) 717196 *mobile* (0973) 307078
fax (01428) 717129
e-mail john@glovphot.demon.co.uk
web site http://www.glovphot.demon.co.uk

Gardens and gardening, from overall views of gardens to plant portraits with Latin names; UK landscapes including ancient sites, Stonehenge, etc. Founded 1979.

Martin and Dorothy Grace

40 Clipstone Avenue, Mapperley, Nottingham NG3 5JZ
tel 0115-920 8248 *fax* 0115-962 6802
e-mail graces@lineone.net

General British natural history, specialising in native trees, shrubs, flowers, ferns, habitats and ecology. Founded 1984.

Tim Graham Picture Library

31 Ferncroft Avenue, London NW3 7PG
tel 020-7435 7693 *fax* 020-7431 4312

Royal family in this country and on tours; background pictures on royal homes, staff, hobbies, sports, cars, etc; English and foreign country scenes; international Heads of State, VIPs and celebrities. Founded 1978.

Angela Hampton – Family Life Picture Library

Holly Tree House, The Street, Walberton, Arundel, West Sussex BN18 0PH
tel/fax (01243) 555952
Proprietor Angela Hampton

Contemporary lifestyle images including pregnancy, childbirth, babies and children, parenting, behaviour, education, medical, holidays, pets, families, couples, teenagers, women's health, men's health, retirement. Also domestic and farm animals. Over 50,000 colour transparencies. Founded 1991.

Harper Horticultural Slide Library*

219 Robanna Drive, Seaford, VA 23696, USA
tel 757-898-6453 *fax* 757-890-9378
e-mail pamharper@mindspring.com

160,000 35mm slides of plants, gardens and native habitats.

Heritage & Natural History Photography

37 Plainwood Close, Summersdale, Chichester, West Sussex PO19 4YB
tel (01243) 533822 *fax* (01243) 533822
Contact Dr John B. Free

Archaeology, history, agriculture: Arabia, China, India, Iran, Ireland, Japan, Kenya, Mediterranean countries, Mexico, Nepal, North America, Oman, Russia, Thailand, UK. Bees and bee keeping, insects and small invertebrates, tropical crops and flowers.

Pat Hodgson Library & Picture Research Agency

Jasmine Cottage, Spring Grove Road, Richmond, Surrey TW10 6EH
tel 020-8940 5986

Small collection of b&w historical engravings, book illustrations, ephemera, etc;

some colour and modern photos. Subjects include history, Victoriana, ancient civilisations, occult, travel. Text written and research undertaken on any subject.

Holt Studios International Ltd*

The Courtyard, 24 High Street, Hungerford, Berks. RG17 0NF
tel (01488) 683523 *fax* (01488) 683511
e-mail library@holt-studios.co.uk
web site http://www.holt-studios.co.uk

80,000 pictures on worldwide agriculture, horticulture, crops and associated pests (and their predators), diseases and deficiencies, farming people and practices, livestock, machinery, landscapes, diverse environments, natural flora and fauna. Founded 1981.

Horizon International

Photographers' enquiries Horizon International Images Ltd, Horizon House, Route de Picaterre, Alderney, Guernsey GY9 3UP
tel (01481) 822587 *fax* (01481) 823880
e-mail mail@hrzn.com
Picture research and sales enquiries The Studio, 1A Rutland Road, Twickenham TW2 5ER
tel 020-8898 2255 *fax* 020-8755 1630
web site http://www.hrzn.com

Specialist stock library for advertising covering leisure and lifestyle, business and industry, science and medicine, environment and nature, world travel. Founded 1978.

David Hosking FRPS

Pages Green House, Wetheringsett, Stowmarket, Suffolk IP14 5QA
tel (01728) 861113 *fax* (01728) 860222
e-mail pictures@flpa-images.co.uk
web site http://www.flpa-images.co.uk

Natural history subjects, especially birds covering whole world. Also Dr D.P. Wilson's unique marine photo collection.

Houses & Interiors Photographic Features Agency*

192 Goswell Road, London EC1V 7DT
tel 020-7253 0991 *fax* 020-7253 0992
web site http://www.a-z.picture-library.com
Contact Justine Moss

Stylish house interiors and exteriors, people in their homes and gardens, home dossiers, renovations, architectural details, interior design, gardens and houseplants. Also step-by-step photographic sequences of DIY subjects, fresh and dried flower arrangements and gardening techniques. Food. Colour only. Commissions undertaken. Terms: 50%, negotiable. Founded 1985.

Hulton Getty Picture Collection*

Unique House, 21-31 Woodfield Road, London W9 2BA
tel 020-7266 2662 *fax* 020-7266 3154
web site http://www.hultongetty.com

Over 15 million b&w and colour images. Specialises in social history, royalty, transport, war, fashion, sport, entertainment, people, places and early photography. Collections include *Picture Post*, *Express*, *Evening Standard*, Keystone, Fox and Topical Press. Publisher of CD-Roms for creative image access.

Hutchison Picture Library*

118B Holland Park Avenue, London W11 4UA
tel 020-7229 2743 *fax* 020-7792 0259
e-mail library@hutchisonpic.demon.co.uk

General colour library; worldwide subjects: agriculture, the environment, festivals, human relationships, industry, landscape, peoples, religion, towns, travel. Founded 1976.

The Illustrated London News Picture Library*

20 Upper Ground, London SE1 9PF
tel 020-7805 5585 *fax* 020-7805 5905
e-mail iln.pictures@seacontainers.com

Engravings, photos, illustrations in b&w and colour from 1842 to present day, especially 19th and 20th century social history, wars, portraits, royalty.

The Image Bank*

17 Conway Street, London W1P 6EE
tel 020-7312 0300 *fax* 020-7391 9111
web site http://www.imagebank.co.uk

Image Bank Dublin

11 Upper Mount Street, Dublin 2
tel (01) 676 0872 *fax* (01) 676 0873

Image Bank Manchester

4 Jordan Street, Manchester M15 4PY
tel 0161-236 9226 *fax* 0161-236 8723

Image Bank Scotland

57 Melville Street, Edinburgh EH3 7HL
tel 0131-225 1770 *fax* 0131-225 1660

Still and moving imagery for the advertising, publishing and corporate sector. On-line searching available.

Image Diggers

618B Finchley Road, London NW11 7RR
tel/fax 020-8455 4564
e-mail zip@phancap.demon.co.uk
Contact Neil Hornick

Stills archive covering performing arts, popular culture, human interest, natural history, architecture, nautical, children and people, strange phenomena, etc. Also audio and video for research purposes, and ephemera including magazines, books, comic books, sheet music, postcards. Founded 1980.

Imagefinder Pte Ltd

228A South Bridge Road, Singapore 058777
tel (65) 324 3747 *fax* (65) 324 3748
e-mail imagef@mbox4.singnet.com.sg
Director Rashidah Hamid

General photo library with strong focus on Asian-related material. Founded 1998.

Images Colour Library Ltd*

Leeds Office Manager Jess Diebel
15-17 High Court Lane, The Calls, Leeds LS2 7EU
tel 0113-243 3389 *fax* 0113-242 5605
London Office Manager Julie Chamberlain
Ramillies House, 1-2 Ramillies Street, London W1V 1DF
tel 020-7734 7344 *fax* 020-7287 3933

General, contemporary stock library including people, business, UK and world travel, industry and sport. Founded 1983.

Images of Africa Photobank*

11 The Windings, Lichfield, Staffs. WS13 7EX
tel (01543) 262898 *fax* (01543) 417154
e-mail info@imagesofafrica.co.uk
web site http://www.imagesofafrica.co.uk
Contact Jacquie Shipton, Library Manager
Proprietor David Keith Jones, FRPS

135,000 images covering 14 African countries: Botswana, Egypt, Ethiopia, Kenya, Malawi, Namibia, Rwanda, South Africa, Swaziland, Tanzania, Uganda, Zaire, Zambia and Zimbabwe. Specialities: wildlife, people, landscapes, tourism, hotels and lodges, National Parks and Reserves. Colour brochure available. Terms: 50%. Founded 1983.

Imperial War Museum*

Photograph Archive, Austral Street, London SE11 4SL
tel 020-7416 5333/8 *fax* 020-7416 5355
e-mail photos@iwm.org.uk

National archive of over 5 million photos, dealing with war in the 20th century involving the armed forces of Britain and the Commonwealth countries. Open by appointment Mon-Fri. Prints made to order. Founded 1917.

International Press Agency (Pty) Ltd

PO Box 67, Howard Place 7450, South Africa
tel (021) 531 1926 *fax* (021) 531 8789
e-mail inpra@iafrica.com

Press photos for South African market. Founded 1934.

Isle of Wight Photo Library

The Old Rectory, Calbourne, Isle of Wight PO30 4JE
tel (01983) 531247 *fax* (01983) 531253

Specialist library of colour transparencies of the Isle of Wight: landscapes, seascapes, architecture, gardens, flora and boats. In association with **S. & O. Mathews**. Founded 1995.

Isle of Wight Pictures

60 York Street, Cowes, Isle of Wight PO31 7BS
tel/fax (01983) 290366 *mobile* (0468) 877914
web site http://www.isleofwight.uk.com/iowpictures
Proprietor Patrick Eden

Covers all aspects of the Isle of Wight, including Cowes Week, sailing events, nautical aspects. Commissions undertaken. Founded 1985.

Japan Archive

9 Victoria Drive, Horsforth, Leeds LS18 4PN
tel 0113-258 3244 *fax* 0113-216 3441
e-mail stephen.turnbull@virgin.net
web site http://freespace.virgin.net/stephen.turnbull/japanarchive.htm
Contact S.R. Turnbull

Japan: modern, daily life, architecture, religion, history, personalities, gardens, natural world. Founded 1993.

Jazz Index*

26 Fosse Way, London W13 0BZ
tel 020-8998 1232 *fax* 020-8998 2880
e-mail christianhim@jazzindex.co.uk
web site http://www. jazzindex.co.uk

Photo library of jazz, blues and contemporary musicians. Also photos of instruments, clubs, crowds at concerts. Photos sold on behalf of photographers. Terms: 50%. Founded 1979.

Joe Filmbase Photo Agency/Library

1 Town Mead Business Centre, William Morris Way, London SW6 2SZ
tel/fax 020-7371 9902
e-mail joefilmbase@btconnect.com
web site http://www.joefilmbase.com

General library: fashion, catwalk, people, ideas, art photos, business, traders, travel, dance, concerts, cars, boats, lifestyle, nature, worldwide. Transparencies only: 35mm, 6 x 7cm etc. Founded 1991.

J.S. Library International

101A Brondesbury Park, London NW2 5JL
tel 020-8451 2668 *fax* 020-8459 0223/8517
e-mail jjohnpbshelley@msn.com

The J.S. Royal collection, Art collection, Hollywood collection, Celebrity service, particularly authors. Travel, fauna and flora and general pictures. New photographers and material required. Assignments worldwide undertaken. Founded 1979.

Just Europe

50 Basingfield Road, Thames Ditton, Surrey KT7 0PD
tel/fax 020-8398 2468

Specialises in Europe – major cities, towns, people and customs. Assignments undertaken; background information available; advice/research service. Founded 1989.

Kilmartin House Trust

Kilmartin House, Kilmartin, Argyll PA31 8RQ
tel (01546) 510278 *fax* (01546) 510330
e-mail museum@khouse.demon.co.uk
web site http://www.kht.org.uk
Contact D.J. Adams McGilp

Ancient monuments, archaeological sites; artefacts and excavations. Aerial photographs of Mid Argyll. Colour prints and transparencies. Founded 1994.

Lakeland Life Picture Library

Langsett, Lyndene Drive, Grange-over-Sands, Cumbria LA11 6QP
tel (015395) 33565 (answerphone)

English Lake District: industries, crafts, sports, shows, customs, architecture, people. Also provides colour and b&w, illustrated articles. Not an agency. Catalogue available on request. Founded 1979.

Frank Lane Picture Agency Ltd*

Pages Green House, Wetheringsett, Stowmarket, Suffolk IP14 5QA
tel (01728) 860789 *fax* (01728) 860222
e-mail pictures@flpa-images.co.uk
web site http://www.flpa-images.co.uk

Natural history, ecology, environment, farming, geography, trees and weather.

Michael Leach

Brookside, Kinnerley, Oswestry SY10 8DB
tel/fax (01691) 682639
e-mail mike.leach@lineone.net

General worldwide wildlife and natural history subjects, with particular emphasis on mammals and urban wildlife. Comprehensive collection of owls from all over the world. No other photographers required.

Lebrecht Collection*

58B Carlton Hill, London NW8 0ES
tel 020-7625 5341 and 020-7372 8233
fax 020-7625 5341
e-mail pictures@lebrecht.co.uk
web site http://www.lebrecht.co.uk
Director Elbie Lebrecht

Colour and b&w images of classical music from antiquity to the 21st century: composers, musicians, opera singers, musical scores, concert halls and opera houses, instruments, world music. Founded 1992.

Dave Lewis Nostalgia Collection

20 The Avenue, Starbeck, Harrogate, North Yorkshire HG1 4QD
tel/fax (01423) 888642
e-mail davelewis@beckstar.freeserve.co.uk
web site http://www.harrogate.com/davel

A collection of advertising, packaging, points of sale and magazine reference from 1800-1970s. Founded 1995.

Link Picture Library*

33 Greyhound Road, London W6 8NH
tel 020-7381 2261/2433 *fax* 020-7385 6244
e-mail lib@linkpics.demon.co.uk
web site http://www.linkphotographers.com
Proprietor Orde Eliason

Specialist archives on Central and Southern Africa, India, Southeast Asia and Israel. Commissions accepted. Terms: 50%. Founded 1982.

Elizabeth Linley Collection

The Elizabeth Linley Studio, 29 Dewlands, Godstone, Surrey RH9 8BS
tel (01883) 742702 *fax* (01883) 742451
Contact Audrey I.B. Thomas

Prints, b&w photos and colour transparencies of 18th- and 19th-century artists, portraits, illustrations, theatre, society events, architecture.

London Metropolitan Archives

(formerly Greater London Record Office)
40 Northampton Road, London EC1R 0HB
tel 020-7332 3820 *fax* 020-7833 9136
minicom 020-7278 8703
e-mail lma@corpoflondon.gov.uk

Over 350,000 photographic prints and 1,500,000 negatives of London and the London area from *c.*1860 to 1986. Especially strong on local authority projects, including schools, public housing and open spaces.

Lonely Planet Images

192C Burwood Road, Hawthorn, Melbourne, Victoria 3122, Australia
tel (03) 9819 1877 *fax* (03) 9819 6459
web site http://www.lonelyplanetimages.com
Manager Louise Poultney

Online library with 38,000 colour travel images, including those used in the *Lonely Planet* guidebooks. Founded 1998.

The Billie Love Historical Collection

Reflections, 3 Winton Street, Ryde, Isle of Wight PO33 2BX
tel (01983) 812572 *fax* (01983) 811164
Proprietor Billie Love

Photos (late 19th century-1930s), engravings, coloured lithographs, covering subjects from earliest times, people, places and events up to the Second World War; also more recent material. Founded 1969.

Ludvigsen Library Ltd

73 Collier Street, London N1 9BE
tel 020-7837 1700 *fax* 020-7837 1776
e-mail library@ludvigsen.com
Photographic resources Paul Parker

Specialist automotive and motor racing photo library. Includes much rare and unpublished material from John Dugdale, Edward Eves, Max le Grand, Peter Keen, Karl Ludvigsen, Rodolfo Mailander, Ove Nielsen, Stanley Rosenthall and others. Founded 1984.

The MacQuitty International Collection*

7 Elm Lodge, River Gardens, Stevenage Road, London SW6 6NZ
tel/fax 020-7385 5606
e-mail miranda.macquitty@btinternet.com

300,000 photos covering aspects of life in 70 countries: archaeology, art, buildings, flora and fauna, gardens, museums, people and occupations, scenery, religions, methods of transport, surgery, acupuncture, funeral customs, fishing, farming, dancing, music, crafts, sports, weddings, carnivals, food, drink, jewellery and oriental subjects. Period: 1920 to present day.

Mander & Mitchenson Theatre Collection*

The Mansion, Beckenham Place Park, Beckenham, Kent BR3 2BP
tel 020-8658 7725 *fax* 020-8663 0313
e-mail richard@mander-and-mitchenson.co.uk

Prints, drawings, photos, programmes, etc, theatre, opera, ballet, music hall, and other allied subjects including composers, playwrights, etc. All periods.

Mansell/Time Inc.

c/o Katz Pictures, Zetland House, 5-25 Scrutton Street, London EC2A 4LP
tel 020-7377 5888 *fax* 020-7377 5558

General historical material up to the 1920s, 1930s.

John Massey Stewart

20 Hillway, London N6 6QA
tel 020-8341 3544 *fax* 020-8341 5292

Large collection Russia/USSR, including topography, people, culture, Siberia, plus Russian and Soviet history, 3000 pre-revolutionary PCs, etc. Also Britain, Europe (including Bulgaria, Poland, Slovenia and Turkey), Alaska, USA, Israel, Sinai desert, etc.

S. & O. Mathews*

The Old Rectory, Calbourne, Isle of Wight PO30 4JE
tel (01983) 531247 *fax* (01983) 531253

Gardens, flowers and landscapes.

Chris Mattison

138 Dalewood Road, Sheffield S8 0EF
tel/fax 0114-236 4433
e-mail chris.mattison@btinternet.com
web site http://www.btinternet.com/~Chris.Mattison

Colour library specialising in reptiles and amphibians; other natural history subjects; habitats and landscapes in Africa, Southeast Asia, South America, USA, Mexico, Mediterranean. Captions or detailed copy supplied if required. No other photographers' material required.

Bill Meadows Picture Library

11 Tollhouse Drive, Oldbury Road, St Johns, Worcester WR2 6AD
tel/fax (01905) 429254
Proprietor Bill Meadows

Aspects of Great Britain: general scenic including towns and villages; buildings and monuments; agricultural, industrial and building sites; urban scenes and services; misuse of the environment, vandalism, etc; recreational, 'people at play'; natural history subjects. 20,000 b&w photographs and 50,000 (6 x 6cm and 35mm) colour transparencies. Founded 1968.

Medimage

32 Brooklyn Road, Coventry CV1 4JT
tel/fax (01203) 668562

e-mail chambersking@clara.co.uk
Contact Anthony King
Specialist library of medium format transparencies of subjects in Mediterranean countries: agriculture, architecture, crafts, festivals, flora, industry, landscapes, markets, portraits, recreation, seascapes, sport and transport. Commissions undertaken. Other photographers' work not accepted. Founded 1992.

Merseyside Photo Library

Suite 1, Egerton House, Tower Road, Birkenhead, Wirral CH41 1FN
tel 0151-650 6975 *fax* 0151-650 6976
e-mail ron@merseywide.demon.co.uk
Operated by Ron Jones Associates
Library specialising in images of Liverpool and Merseyside but includes other destinations. Founded 1989.

Microscopix

Middle Travelly, Beguildy, Nr Knighton, Powys LD7 1UW
tel (01547) 510242 *fax* (01547) 510317
e-mail mik@micropix.demon.co.uk
web site http://www.micropix.demon.co.uk/sem
Scientific photo library specialising in scanning electron micrographs and photomicrographs for technical and aesthetic purposes. Commissioned work, both biological and non-biological, undertaken offering a wide variety of applicable microscopical techniques. Founded 1986.

Military History Picture Library

3 Barton Buildings, Bath BA1 2JR
tel (01225) 334213 *fax* (01225) 480554
Prints, engravings, photos, colour transparencies covering all aspects of warfare and uniforms from ancient times to the present.

Monitor Syndication

(incorporates the City Syndication Ltd)
5-23 Old Street, London EC1V 9HF
tel 020-7253 7071 *fax* 020-7250 0966
tel/fax (01279) 792139 (archive)
e-mail monitor@ftech.co.uk
Contact Stewart White
Specialists in portrait photos of leading national and international personalities from politics, trade unions, entertainment, sport, royalty, business and law, and well-known buildings in London. Plus editorial archive library dating back to the early days of photography. Founded 1960.

Motorcycles Unlimited

48 Lemsford Road, St Albans, Herts. AL1 3PR
tel (01727) 869001 *fax* (01727) 869014
e-mail rolandbrown@motobike.demon.co.uk
Owner Roland Brown
Motorbikes of all kinds, from latest roadsters to classics, racers to tourers. Detailed information available on all machines pictured. Founded 1993.

Motoring Picture Library, Beaulieu*

National Motor Museum, Beaulieu, Hants SO42 7ZN
tel (01590) 614656 *fax* (01590) 612655
e-mail nmmt@compuserve.com
All aspects of motoring, cars, commercial vehicles, motor cycles, personalities, etc. Illustrations of period scenes and motor sport. Also large library of 5 x 4in and smaller colour transparencies of veteran, vintage and modern cars, commercial vehicles and motorcycles. Over 800,000 images in total.

Mountain Dynamics

Heathcourt, Morven Way, Monaltrie, Ballater AB35 5SF
tel (013397) 55081 *fax* (013397) 55526
e-mail gpa@globalnet.co.uk
Proprietor Graham P. Adams
Scottish and European mountains – from ground to summits – in panoramic (6 x 17cm), 5 x 4in and medium format. Commissions undertaken. Terms: 50%. Founded 1990.

Mountain Visions and Faces

25 The Mallards, Langstone, Havant, Hants PO9 1SS
tel 023-9247 8441
e-mail ozroz@talk21.com
Contact Graham Elson and Roslyn Elson
Colour transparencies of mountaineering, skiing, and tourism in Europe, Africa, Himalayas, Arctic, Far East, South America and Australia. Does not act as agent for other photographers. Founded 1984.

The Mustograph Agency

19 Rathbone Street, London W1P 1AF
tel 020-7636 6128/9 *fax* 020-7637 4317
Britain only: b&w general subjects of countryside life, work, history and scenery.

National Maritime Museum Picture Library*

National Maritime Museum, Park Row, Greenwich, London SE10 9NF
web site http://www.nmm.ac.uk/

Contact David Taylor *tel* 020-8312 6631, Eleanor Heron *tel* 020-8312 6704

Maritime, transport, time and space and historic photographs.

National Museums & Galleries of Northern Ireland, Ulster Folk & Transport Museum*

153 Bangor Road, Cultra, Holywood, Co. Down BT18 0EU, Northern Ireland
tel 028-9042 8428 *fax* 028-9042 8728
Head of Dept of Photography T.K. Anderson

Photographs from 1850s to the present day, including the work of W.A. Green, Rose Shaw and R.J. Welsh while he was under contract to Harland and Wolff Ltd. Subjects include Belfast shipbuilding (80,000 photographs, including 70 original negatives of the *Titanic*), road and rail transport, folk life, agriculture and the linen industry. B&w and colour (35mm, medium and large format). Founded 1962.

National Portrait Gallery Picture Library*

St Martin's Place, London WC2H 0HE
tel 020-7312 2473/4/5/6 *fax* 020-7312 2464
e-mail picturelibrary@npg.org.uk
web site http://www.npg.org.uk
Contact Tom Morgan

Specialists in portraits of the makers of British history: paintings, drawings, sculptures, engravings and photographs. Definitive captioning data. The most comprehensive collection of its kind in the world. 10,000 images can be viewed on web site. Founded 1856.

Natural History Photographic Agency – see NHPA*

Natural Image

31 Shaftesbury Road, Poole, Dorset BH15 2LT
tel (01202) 675916 *fax* (01202) 242944
e-mail bob.gibbons@which.net
Contact Dr Bob Gibbons

Colour library covering natural history, habitats, countryside and gardening (UK and worldwide); special emphasis on conservation. Commissions undertaken. Terms: 50%. Founded 1982.

The Nature and Landscape File

24 Southleigh Crescent, Leeds LS11 5TW
tel/fax 0113-2715535 *mobile* (0802) 540537
web site http://www.photosource.co.uk/photosource/Nature&Landscape.htm
Proprietor Dr Mark Lucock

Natural history subjects and landscapes from around the world, especially the UK, southern Europe, North America. Specialises in photomacrographic images. Examples and subject list on web site. 30,000 large- and small-format colour transparencies. Founded 1997.

Peter Newark Pictures

3 Barton Buildings, Bath BA1 2JR
tel (01225) 334213 *fax* (01225) 480554

One million pictures: engravings, prints, paintings and photographs on all aspects of world history from ancient times to the present.

New Blitz Literary & TV Agency

Via di Panico 67, 00186 Rome, Italy
tel/fax (06) 686 4859
e-mail bono@uniroma3.it
Contact Giovanni A.S. Congiu

News and general library.

NHPA*

(Natural History Photographic Agency)
57 High Street, Ardingly, West Sussex RH17 6TB
tel (01444) 892514 *fax* (01444) 892168
e-mail nhpa@nhpa.co.uk
web site http://www.nhpa.co.uk

Represents more than 120 of the world's leading natural history photographers covering a wide range of wildlife, marine life, domestic animals and pets, plants, landscapes and environmental subjects. Specialisations include the unique high-speed photography of Stephen Dalton, comprehensive coverage on North America and Africa, and the ANT collection of Australasian material (for which NHPA is UK agent). Recent acquisitions include Japanese wildlife, giant pandas, extensive Indian and Australian files, plus new coverage on UK landscapes and agriculture. Pictures are generally supplied to commercial companies only and are sent to freelance writers and artists by agreement with the publisher or commissioning company.

Northern Picture Library – see Stockwave*

Operation Raleigh – see Raleigh International Picture Library

Christine Osborne Pictures/MEP*

53A Crimsworth Road, London SW8 4RJ
tel/fax 020-7720 6951

e-mail co@middleeastpictures.com
web site http://www.middleeastpictures.com
Specialises in the developing world, notably Africa, Indian subcontinent, Southeast Asia and Middle East/Arab states (covers 30 Muslim countries). Major files on Eastern cultures – religions (worship, rites of passage and festivals), geography, agriculture and food production, architecture – rural and urban environments, family life, education and social services, traditional crafts, plus more than 50 travel destinations. Pictures updated by a small team of contributors. Commissions undertaken. In-depth caption information provided. Member of the British Guild of Travel Writers. French spoken. Founded 1984.

Oxford Scientific Films Ltd, Photo Library*

(incorporating the Survival Anglia Photo Library)
Lower Road, Long Hanborough, Oxon OX8 8LL
tel (01993) 881881 *fax* (01993) 882808
e-mail photo.library@osf.uk.com
web site http://www.osf.uk.com
300,000 colour transparencies of wildlife, underwater, natural science, plants, gardens, landscapes, habitats, agriculture, fossils, dinosaur illustrations, domestic animals, tribal people, weather, space and environmental images supplied by over 300 photographers worldwide. UK agents for *Animals Animals*, New York; *Okapia*, Frankfurt; *Dinodia*, India.

PA News Photo Library*

292 Vauxhall Bridge Road, London SW1V 1AE
tel 020-7963 7032/34/35 *fax* 020-7963 7066
e-mail photo-sales@pa.press.net
web site http://www.paphotos.com
Over 6 million photos dating from the turn of the century, covering news, sport, royalty and showbiz. Library updated daily. Searches undertaken, or customers are welcome to visit.

PAL (Performing Arts Library)*

1st Floor, Production House, 25 Hackney Road, London E2 7NX
tel 020-7749 4850 *fax* 020-7749 4858
e-mail peformingartspics@pobox.com
web site http://www.performingartslibrary.co.uk
Continually updated specialist image collection covering classical music, opera, theatre, musicals, instruments, festivals, venues, circus, ballet and contemporary dance. Almost one million images from late 19th century onwards.

Panos Pictures*

1 Chapel Court, Borough High Street, London SE1 1HH
tel 020-7234 0010 *fax* 020-7357 0094
e-mail panospics@corporate.nethead.co.uk
Third World and Eastern European documentary photos focusing on social, political and economic issues with a special emphasis on environment and development. Files on agriculture, conflict, education, energy, environment, family life, festivals, food, health, industry, landscape, people, politics, pollution, refugees, religions, rural life, transport, urban life, water, weather. Terms: 50%. Founded 1986.

Papilio Natural History & Travel Library

44 Palestine Grove, London SW19 2QN
tel 020-8687 2202 *mobile* (0973) 310072
fax 020-8640 2011
e-mail justine@papilio.demon.co.uk
web site http://www.papilio.demon.co.uk
Contacts Robert Pickett, Justine Bowler
Worldwide coverage of natural history and environment subjects including travel section; commissions undertaken. Over 100,000 images held. Colour catalogue available. Founded 1988.

Ann and Bury Peerless*

22 King's Avenue, Minnis Bay, Birchington-on-Sea, Kent CT7 9QL
tel (01843) 841428 *fax* (01843) 848321
Art, craft (including textiles), archaeology, architecture, dance, iconography, miniature paintings, manuscripts, museum artefacts, social, cultural, agricultural, industrial, historical, political, educational, geographical subjects and travel in India, Pakistan, Bangladesh, Afghanistan, Burma, Cambodia, China, Egypt, Indonesia (Borobudur, Java), Iran, Israel, Kenya, Libya, Malta, Malaysia, Morocco, Nepal, Russia (Moscow, St Petersburg, Samarkand and Bukhara, Uzbekistan), Sri Lanka, Spain, Sudan, Taiwan, Thailand, Tunisia, Uganda, Vietnam, Zambia and Zimbabwe. Specialist material on historical and world religions: Hinduism, Buddhism, Jainism, Judaism, Christianity, Confucianism, Islam, Sikhism, Taoism, Zoroastrianism (Parsees of India).

Chandra S. Perera Cinetra

437 Pethiyagoda, Kelaniya-11600, Sri Lanka
tel (94) 1-911885 *fax* (94) 1-541414/332867

B&w and colour library including news, wildlife, religious, social, political, sports, adventure, environmental, forestry, nature and tourism. Photographic and journalistic features on any subject. Founded 1958.

Cinetra Worldwide Createch (Pvt) Ltd
126/3rd Floor, 10B, YMBA Building, Fort, Colombo 1, Sri Lanka
tel/fax (94) 1-323910
Managing Director Chandra S. Perera

Photo Link

126 Quarry Lane, Northfield, Birmingham B31 2QD
tel 0121-475 8712 *fax* 0121-604 0480
e-mail vines_photolink@compuserve.com
Contact Mike Vines

Colour and b&w aviation library, covering subjects from 1909 to the present day. Specialises in air-to-air photography. Assignments undertaken. Over 10,000 aviation images from around the world are added every year. Can also research, advise and write aviation stories and press releases. Founded 1990.

Photo Resources

The Orchard, Marley Lane, Kingston, Canterbury, Kent CT4 6JH
tel (01227) 830075 *fax* (01227) 831135

Ancient civilisations, art, archaeology, world religions, myth, and museum objects covering the period from 30,000 BC to AD 1900. European birds, butterflies, trees.

Photofusion*

17A Electric Lane, London SW9 8LA
tel 020-7738 5774 *fax* 020-7738 5509
e-mail library@photofusion.org
web site http://www.photofusion.org

Covers all aspects of UK contemporary life with an emphasis on social issues. Catalogue available. Photographers available for commission.

The Photographers' Library*

81A Endell Street, London WC2H 9AJ
tel 020-7836 5591 *fax* 020-7379 4650

Requires transparency material on business, lifestyles, worldwide travel, industry, agriculture, sport, scenic. Colour only. Terms: 50%. Founded 1978.

The Photolibrary Wales*

2 Bro-nant, Church Road, Pentyrch, Cardiff CF15 8QG
tel 029-2089 0311 *fax* 029-2089 2650
e-mail info@photo-lib-wales.co.uk
web site http://www.photo-lib-wales.co.uk
Director Steve Benbow

Comprehensive collection of contemporary images of Wales. Subjects include landscape, lifestyle, current affairs, sport, industry, people. Over 100 photographers represented. Digital files and transmission available. Colour transparencies and b&w prints. Commission: 50%. Founded 1998.

Pictor International Ltd

Lymehouse Studios, 30-31 Lyme Street, London NW1 0EE
tel 020-7482 0478 *fax* 020-7267 5759
e-mail postmaster@pictor.demon.co.uk
web site http://www.pictor.co.uk

Offices and agents in over 20 countries. All subjects. Terms: 50%.

The Picture Company

11C Turnford Villas, High Road, Turnford, Broxbourne, Herts. EN10 6BE
tel/fax (01992) 443066 *Mobile* (07850) 971491
Contact Chris Bonass

Colour transparencies (2¼ x 2¼in and 35mm) of people and places worldwide. Taken by award-winning film and TV cameraman and largely unseen and unpublished. Also aviation pictures old and new, including air-to-air photography and a unique archive on 16mm film and broadcast videotape. Used by BBC, C4, etc. Assignments undertaken. Founded 1993.

Picture Research Service

Rich Research, One Bradby, 77 Carlton Hill, London NW8 9XE
tel/fax 020-7624 7755
Contact Diane Rich

Visuals found for all sectors of the media and publishing. Artwork and photography commissioned. Rights and permissions negotiated.

Picturepoint Ltd – see Topham Picturepoint*

Picturesmiths Ltd*

Manor Farm Cottage, Main Road, Curbridge, Witney, Oxon OX8 7NT
tel (01993) 771907 *fax* (01993) 706383
e-mail picturesmiths@mcmail.com
web site http://www.picturesmiths.mcmail.com
Managing Director Roger M. Smith

Plant photography, from portraits, close-ups and macrophotography to plant associations, colour themes and garden scenes.

Also prehistoric archaeology, medieval castles, butterflies, military aircraft, fire-fighting, Falkland Islands wildlife. Colour transparencies. Founded 1997.

Sylvia Pitcher Photo Library

75 Bristol Road, London E7 8HG
tel/fax 020-8552 8308

Musicians: blues, jazz, old-time country and bluegrass, cajun and zydeco plus related ephemera. Views and details of the USA: countryside, 'small-town America', shacks, railroads, rural Americana. Archival: early 20th century – mainly cottonfields, riverboats and various cities in the USA. 1960s-1970s: girls (both white and black) and couples. Founded 1968.

Pixfeatures

5 Latimer Road, Barnet, Herts. EN5 5NU
tel 020-8449 9946 *fax* 020-8441 2725
Contact Peter Wickman

Pictures and features covering big news events, royalty, showbiz and travel (all countries). National newspapers' extensive collection of people in the news to 1970. *Stern* magazine features (before 1985). Documentary and historical photos. Special collections: Dukes of Windsor and Kent, Kennedys, Beatles, Keeler/Levy, trainrobbers. Terms: 50%.

Planet Earth Pictures*

The Innovation Centre, 225 Marsh Wall, London E14 9FX
tel 020-7293 2999 *fax* 020-7293 2998
e-mail planetearth@visualgroup.com

All aspects of natural history and the natural environment, farming, fishing, pollution and conservation. Founded 1969.

POPPERFOTO (Paul Popper Ltd)*

The Old Mill, Overstone Farm, Overstone, Northampton NN6 0AB
tel (01604) 670670 *fax* (01604) 670635
e-mail popperfoto@msn.com
web site http://www.popperfoto.com

Over 14 million images, covering 150 years of photographic history. Unrivalled archival material, world-famous sports library and extensive stock photography. Credit line includes Reuters, Bob Thomas Sports Photography, UPI, AFP and EPA, Acme, INP, Planet, Paul Popper, Exclusive News Agency, Victory Archive, Odhams Periodicals Library, *Illustrated*, Harris Picture Agency, and H.G. Ponting which holds the Scott 1910-12 Antarctic expedition material.

Colour from 1940, b&w from 1870 to present. Major subjects covered worldwide include: events, personalities, wars, royalty, sport, politics, transport, crime, history and social conditions. POPPERFOTO policy is to make material available, same day, to clients throughout the world. Mac-desk accessible. Researchers welcome by appointment. Free catalogue available.

Premaphotos Wildlife

Amberstone, 1 Kirland Road, Bodmin, Cornwall PL30 5JQ
tel (01208) 78258 *fax* (01208) 72302
e-mail pics@premaphotos.co.uk
web site http://www.premaphotos.co.uk
Contact Dr Rod Preston-Mafham

Library of 35mm transparencies; wide range of natural history subjects from around the world, including camouflage, mimicry, warning coloration, parental care, courtship, mating, flowers, fruits, fungi, habitats (particularly rainforests and deserts), and many more. Specialists in invertebrate behaviour and cacti. Captions and copy can be provided. Founded 1978.

Press Association Photos – see PA News Photo Library*

Press Features Syndicate

9 Paradise Close, Eastbourne, East Sussex BN20 8BT
tel (01323) 728760

For full details see page 147.

Public Record Office Image Library*

Public Record Office, Ruskin Avenue, Kew, Surrey TW9 4DU
tel 020-8392 5225 *fax* 020-8392 5266
e-mail image-library@pro.gov.uk
web site http://www.pro.gov.uk/imagelibrary

Unique collection of millions of historical documents on a wide range of formats from 1066 to 1960s. Special collections include: Victorian and Edwardian advertisements and photographs, Second World War propaganda, military history, maps, decorative and technical designs and medieval illuminations. Founded 1995.

Punch Cartoon Library*

100 Brompton Road, London SW3 1ER
tel 020-7225 6711/6710 *fax* 020-7225 6712
e-mail edit@punch.co.uk

Comprehensive collection of cartoons and illustrations, indexed under subject categories: humour, historical events, politics, fashion, sport, personalities, etc.

Railways – Milepost 92½*

Milepost 92½, Newton Harcourt, Leics. LE8 9FH
tel 0116-259 6068 *fax* 0116-259 3001
e-mail contacts@milepost92-half.co.uk
web site http://www.milepost92-half.co.uk

Comprehensive library representing all aspects of modern railway operations and scenic pictures from the UK and abroad. Includes Colin Garratt's collection of world steam trains as well as archive b&w photos. Welcomes contributing photographers and also archives, and markets picture collections on behalf of individuals. Founded 1969.

Raleigh International Picture Library

Raleigh House, 27 Parson's Green Lane, London SW6 4HS
tel 020-7371 8585 *fax* 020-7371 5116
e-mail sophie@raleigh.org.uk
web site http://raleigh.org.uk
Contact Sophie Annesley

Source of stock colour images from locations around the world: the 100,000-plus images are updated 10 times a year. Open to researchers by appointment Mon-Fri, 9.30 a.m.-4.00 p.m.

Redferns Music Picture Library*

7 Bramley Road, London W10 6SZ
tel 020-7792 9914 *fax* 020-7792 0921
e-mail info@redferns.com
web site http://www.redferns.com
Contact Dede Millar

All styles of music, from 1920s jazz to current Top 10, plus instruments, crowds, festivals and atmospherics. Brochure available. Commission 50%. Founded 1963.

Retna Pictures Ltd*

53-56 Great Sutton Street, London EC1V 0DE
tel 020-7608 4800 *fax* 020-7608 4805

Library of colour transparencies and b&w prints of rock and pop performers, show business personalities, celebrities, actors and actresses. Also extensive lifestyle and stock library. Founded 1984.

Retrograph Nostalgia Archive Ltd

164 Kensington Park Road, London W11 2ER
tel 020-7727 9378 *fax* 020-7229 3395
e-mail MBreese999@aol.com

Worldwide advertising, packaging, posters, postcards, decorative and fine art illustrations from 1880-1970. Special collections include Victoriana illustrations and scraps (1860-1901), fashion and beauty (1880-1975), RetroTravel Archive: travel and tourism, RetroGourmet Archive: food and drink (1890-1950). Research service and Image Consultancy services; Retro-Montages: Victoriana montage design service. Free colour leaflets. Founded 1984.

Ritmeyer Archaeological Design

50 Tewit Well Road, Harrogate, North Yorkshire HG2 8JJ
tel (01423) 530143 *fax* (01423) 504921
e-mail ritmeyer@dial.pipex.com
web site http://ds.dial.pipex.com/ritmeyer/
Contact Leen and Kathleen Ritmeyer

Colour transparencies of the archaeology of the Holy Land with the emphasis on Jerusalem and the Temple Mount. Architectural reconstruction drawings of ancient sites, such as temples, synagogues, mosques and churches. Special collection of scenes of Jewish temple ritual illustrated on to-scale model of the first century temple in Jerusalem. Drawing commissions undertaken. Founded 1983.

robertharding.com*

58-59 Great Marlborough Street, London W1V 1DD
tel 020-7478 4000 *fax* 020-7631 1070
e-mail info@robertharding.com
web site http://www.robertharding.com

Picture library with extensive range of subjects, in particular travel, geography, culture and the natural world; also lifestyle, business and industry, sport, wildlife, botany, architecture, science and medicine. Full e-commerce web site with over 40,000 searchable images.

Ann Ronan at Image Select

2nd Floor, Heron House, 109 Wembley Hill Road, Wembley, Middlesex HA9 8DA
tel 020-8900 2898 *fax* 020-8900 9969

Woodcuts, engravings, etc, social and political history plus history of science and technology, including military and space, literature and music.

Roundhouse Ornithology Collection

Mathry Hill House, Mathry, Pembrokeshire SA62 5HB
tel/fax (01348) 837008
Contact John Stewart-Smith

Colour library specialising in birds of

UK, Europe, Middle East (especially), North Africa, Far East and South America. Founded 1991.

Royalpics – see Stockwave*

Royal Geographical Society Picture Library*
1 Kensington Gore, London SW7 2AR
tel 020-7591 3060 *fax* 020-7591 3061
e-mail pictures@rgs.org
web site http://www.rgs.org/picturelibrary
Contact Picture Library Manager

Worldwide coverage of geography, travel, exploration, expeditions and cultural environment from 1870s to the present. Founded 1830.

The Royal Photographic Society*
The Octagon, Milsom Street, Bath BA1 1DN
tel (01225) 462841 *fax* (01225) 448688
e-mail sam@collection.rps.org
Contact Sam Johnson

History of photography from 1827 to the present day. Founded 1853.

The Royal Society for Asian Affairs
2 Belgrave Square, London SW1X 8PJ
tel 020-7235 5122 *fax* 020-7259 6771
e-mail info@rsaa.org.uk
web site http://www.rsaa.org.uk

Archive library of original 19th and 20th century b&w photos, glass slides, etc, of Asia. Publishes *Asian Affairs* (3 p.a.).

Royal Society of Chemistry Library and Information Centre*
Burlington House, Piccadilly, London W1V 0BN
tel 020-7437 8656 *fax* 020-7287 9798
e-mail library@rsc.org
web site http://www.rsc.org

Covers all aspects of chemistry information. Images collection dating from 1538 includes prints and photographs of famous chemists, *Vanity Fair* cartoons, scenes, lantern slides of similar subjects and colour photomicrographs of crystal structures. Founded 1841.

RSPCA Photolibrary*
RSPCA Trading Ltd, Causeway, Horsham, West Sussex RH12 1HG
tel (01403) 223150 *fax* (01403) 241048
e-mail photolibrary@rspca.org.uk
Manager Andrew Forsyth

A comprehensive collection of natural history pictures representing the work of over 350 photographers, including the Wild Images collection. Its files include wild, domestic and farm animals, birds, marine life, veterinary work, animal welfare and environmental issues and a record of the work of the RSPCA. Founded 1993.

Dawn Runnals Photographic Library
5 St Marys Terrace, Kenwyn Road, Truro, Cornwall TR1 3SW
tel (01872) 279353

General library: land and seascapes, flora and fauna, sport, animals, people, buildings, boats, harbours, miscellaneous section; details of other subjects on application. Other photographers' work not accepted. Sae appreciated with enquiries. Founded 1985.

Russia and Eastern Images*
Sonning, Cheapside Lane, Denham, Uxbridge, Middlesex UB9 5AE
tel (01895) 833508 *fax* (01895) 831957
e-mail easteuropix@btinternet.com
Library Manager Mark Wadlow

Architecture, cities, landscapes, people and travel images covering Russia and the former Soviet Union. Excellent background knowledge available and Russian language spoken. Founded 1988.

Salamander Picture Library
8 Blenheim Court, Brewery Road, London N7 9NT
tel 020-7700 7799 *fax* 020-7700 3918
e-mail pictures@salamander-books.demon.co.uk
Picture Manager Terry Forshaw

General collection including American history, collectables, cookery, crafts, military, natural history, space and transport. Founded 1996.

Peter Sanders Photography*
24 Meades Lane, Chesham, Bucks. HP5 1ND
tel/fax (01494) 773674
e-mail petersanders.photography@btinternet.com

Specialises in Islamic world, but now expanding into other world religions, beliefs, cultures, architecture and industry. Founded 1987.

Steffi Schubert, Wildlife Conservation Collection Photographic Library
Bramble Cottage, Foxhill, St Cross, South Elmham, Harleston, Norfolk IP20 0NX
tel/fax (01986) 782279

All aspects of British wildlife and fauna. Founded 1990.

Science Photo Library*
327-329 Harrow Road, London W9 3RB
tel 020-7432 1100 *fax* 020-7286 8668

e-mail info@sciencephoto.com
web site http://www.sciencephoto.com
Contact Luci Gosling, Sales Manager

Specialises in pictures of science, medicine, technology, earth, space and nature. Over 120,000 images created by photographers, illustrators, scientists and medical specialists. Free colour catalogue. Visit web site to view images. Founded 1979.

Science & Society Picture Library*

Science Museum, Exhibition Road, London SW7 2DD
tel 020-7942 4400 *fax* 020-7942 4401
e-mail piclib@nmsi.ac.uk
web site http://www.nmsi.ac.uk/piclib/

Subjects include: science and technology, medicine, industry, transport, social documentary and the media. Extensive collection; images drawn from the Science Museum in London, the National Railway Museum in York and the National Museum of Photography, Film and Television in Bradford. Free brochure available on request. Founded 1993.

Scotland in Focus Picture Library

Ladhope Vale House, Ladhope Vale, Galashiels, Selkirkshire TD1 1BT
tel (01896) 755124 *fax* (01896) 752370
e-mail library@scotfocus.sol.co.uk
web site http://www.scotfocus.com

Specialist library offering thousands of stock images to illustrate every aspect of Scottish life and work.

Scottish Wildlife Library

Environmental and natural history.

All Scottish material required on 35mm and upwards, medium format preferred. Photographers must enclose return postage. Terms: 50%. Founded 1988.

SCR Photo Library

Society for Co-operation in Russian and Soviet Studies, 320 Brixton Road, London SW9 6AB
tel 020-7274 2282 *fax* 020-7274 3230

Russian and Soviet life and history. Comprehensive coverage of cultural subjects: art, theatre, folk art, costume, music; agriculture and industry, architecture, armed forces, education, history, places, politics, science, sport. Also material on contemporary life in Russia, the CIS and the Baltic states; posters and theatre props, artistic reference, advice. Research by appointment only. Founded 1924.

Seaco Picture Library*

Sea Containers House, 20 Upper Ground, London SE1 9PF
tel 020-7805 5831/5834 *fax* 020-7805 5807

Stills and video footage of: container shipping; fast ferries and ports; produce and fruit farming; Orient-Express. Hotels and resorts in Botswana, South Africa, Portugal, USA, Brazil, Peru, Italy and Australia. Founded 1995.

Sealand Aerial Photography Ltd*

Unit 2, Breadbares Barns, Clay Lane, Chichester, West Sussex PO18 8DJ
tel (01243) 576688 *fax* (01243) 575528

Aerial photo coverage of any subject that can be photographed from the air in the UK. Most stock on 2¼in format colour negative/transparency. Subjects constantly updated from new flying. Founded 1976.

S & G Press Agency Ltd

63 Gee Street, London EC1V 3RS
tel 020-7336 0632 *fax* 020-7253 8419

Press photos and vast photo library. Send photos, but negatives preferred.

Mick Sharp Photography

Eithinog, Waun, Penisarwaun, Caernarfon, Gwynedd LL55 3PW
tel/fax (01286) 872425

Archaeology, ancient monuments, buildings, churches, countryside, environment, history, landscape, past cultures and topography. Emphasis on British Isles, but material also from other countries. Access to other specialist collections on related subjects. B&w prints from 5 x 4in negatives, and 35mm and 6 x 4.5cm colour transparencies. Founded 1981.

Shout Picture Library

Rowan House, Aston-le-Walls, Northants. NN11 6UF
tel (01295) 660374 *fax* (01295) 660518
e-mail john@shout-pictures.demon.co.uk
web site http://www.shout-pictures.demon.co.uk
Contact John Callan

Specialises in the emergency services: fires, road traffic accidents, surgery, various police and hospital units. Commissions accepted. Founded 1994.

Brian and Sal Shuel – see Collections*

Sites, Sights and Cities

1 Manchester Court, Moreton-in-Marsh, Glos. GL56 0BY

tel/fax (01608) 652829
e-mail devereuxp@aol.com
Director Paul Devereux

Ancient monuments, mainly in Britain, Egypt, Greece and USA; city features in UK, Europe and USA; general nature shots. Founded 1990.

Skishoot – Offshoot*

Hall Place, Upper Woodcott, Whitchurch, Hants RG28 7PY
tel (01635) 255527 *fax* (01635) 255528
e-mail skishoot@surfersparadise.net
web site http://www.skishoot.net
Librarians Jane Blount, Fiona Foote

Library specialising in all aspects of skiing and snowboarding. Also France, all year round. Assignments undertaken. Terms: 50%. Founded 1986.

Skyscan Photolibrary*

Oak House, Toddington, Cheltenham, Glos. GL54 5BY
tel (01242) 621357 *fax* (01242) 621343
e-mail info@skyscan.co.uk
web site http://www.skyscan.co.uk

Based on the unique Skyscan Balloon views of Britain, the library has expanded to include collections from across the aviation spectrum. Ballooning, paragliding and other aerial sports; aircraft both military and civil, air-to-air, RAF life; aviation; international air-to-ground images, etc. Terms: 50%. Founded 1984.

The Slide File*

79 Merrion Square South, Dublin 2, Republic of Ireland
tel (01) 6766850 *fax* (01) 6624476
e-mail admin@slidefile.ie
web site http://www.slidefile.ie

Over 130,000 images, evenly divided between Irish and general material. Diverse subject range: cottages, castles, golf courses, Celtic archaeological sites, landscapes. Special interest in Irish gardens, traditional and contemporary cultural activities. All 32 counties covered. Founded 1978.

The Harry Smith Collection Horticultural Photographic Library*

Mayfield Studio, South Hanningfield Road, Wickford, Essex SS11 7PF
tel (01268) 710044 *fax* (01268) 710122
e-mail hsmithhortphoto@compuserve.com
web site http://www.harrysmithcollection.co.uk
Partners Françoise Davis and Barbara Elkington

All aspects of horticulture, including large and small gardens, specialist sections on all subjects including trees, fruit, vegetables, herbs, cacti, orchids, grasses, cultivated and wild flowers from all over the world, pests and diseases, action shots. Founded 1974.

Patrick Smith Associates

c/o Arioma, PO Box 53, Aberystwyth SY24 5WG
tel (01970) 871296 *fax* (01970) 871733

South London 1950-1977, mid-Wales, aviation; also The Patrick Smith Collection of London photos, now in The Museum of London. Founded 1964.

Snookerimages (Eric Whitehead Photography)*

PO Box 33, Kendal, Cumbria LA9 4SU
tel (015394) 48894 *fax* (015394) 48294
mobile (0468) 808249
e-mail eric@snookerimages.co.uk
web site http://www.snookerimages.co.uk
Contact Eric Whitehead

Specialist picture library covering the sport of snooker. Over 20,000 images of all the professional players dating from 1984 to the present day: players away from the table in locations throughout the world as well as action images.

Society for Anglo-Chinese Understanding

Sally & Richard Greenhill Photo Library, 357 Liverpool Road, London N1 1NL
tel 020-7607 8549 *fax* 020-7607 7151

Colour and b&w prints of China, late 1960s-1989. Founded 1965.

Society for Co-operation in Russian and Soviet Studies – see SCR Photo Library

Spectrum Colour Library

41-42 Berners Street, London W1P 3AA
tel 020-7637 1587 *fax* 020-7637 3681

Extensive general library of high-quality transparencies, for worldwide marketing, including electronically. Photographer's information pack available. Purchases photos and collections of photos.

Sporting Pictures (UK) Ltd*

7A Lambs Conduit Passage, London WC1R 4RG
tel 020-7405 4500 *fax* 020-7831 7991
e-mail photos@sportingpictures.demon.co.uk
web site http://www.sporting-pictures.com
Director Crispin J. Thruston, *Librarian* Simon Anning

Specialises in sports, sporting events, sportspersons, amateur sport.

Peter Stiles Picture Library
49 Palmerston Avenue, Goring by Sea, West Sussex BN12 4RN
tel/fax (01903) 503147 *mobile* (0976) 351369
e-mail enquiries@peterstiles.com
web site http://www.peterstiles.com

A stock picture library specialising in horticultural/gardening subjects. Also pictorial views of UK and the Channel Islands, tropical marine fish and invertebrates. Sequences and illustrated features for gardening press. Commissions undertaken. Visit web site to view images.

The Still Moving Picture Company*
67A Logie Green Road, Edinburgh EH7 4HF
tel 0131-557 9697 *fax* 0131-557 9699
e-mail stillmovingpictures@compuserve.com
web site http://www.stillmovingpictures.com

250,000 pictures of Scotland and all things Scottish; sport (Allsport agent for Scotland). Founded 1991.

STILL Pictures Whole Earth*
199 Shooters Hill Road, London SE3 8UL
tel 020-8858 8307 *fax* 020-8858 2049
e-mail info@stillpictures.com
web site http://www.stillpictures.com
Proprietor Mark Edwards

Specialises in people and the environment; the Third World; nature; wildlife and habitats. Includes industry, agriculture, indigenous peoples and cultures, nature and endangered species. Terms: 50%. Founded 1970.

Stockwave
Headquarters Aylesbury office
tel (01296) 747878 *fax* (01296) 748648
e-mail enquiries@stockwave.com
web site http://www.stockwave.com

Collections encompassing Britain, Europe and the world. British events (including social calendar), social/political news, government, politicians, industrial, tourism, science and technology, defence, lifestyle, Royal family, film and stage personalities.

COI Photo Library

Includes many important and previously unseen images of Britain's government, political events, interior views of the Houses of Parliament and 10 Downing Street, etc, British Royal archives, Festival of Britain, industrial and manufacturing archives, agriculture, education, defence.

Northern Picture Library

Northern England scenery; cities of Northern England and Scotland; architecture and industrial scenes of Northern England past and present.

Royalpics
web site http://www.royalpics.com

Dedicated site for Royal pictures from Stockwave, COI Archives and other major photo libraries.

Tony Stone Images*
101 Bayham Street, London NW1 0AG
tel 020-7544 3333 *fax* 020-7544 3334
e-mail info@tonystone.com
web site http://www.tonystone.com
Contact Creative Dept

International photo library. Subjects required: travel, people, natural history, commerce, industry, technology, sport, concepts etc. Terms: variable.

Survival Anglia Photo Library – see **Oxford Scientific Films Ltd***

Sutcliffe Gallery
1 Flowergate, Whitby, North Yorkshire YO21 3BA
tel (01947) 602239 *fax* (01947) 820287
e-mail photographs@sutcliffe-gallery.fsnet.co.uk
web site http://www.sutcliffe-gallery.fsnet.co.uk

Collection of 19th century photography, all by Frank M. Sutcliffe Hon. FRPS (1853-1941), especially inshore fishing boats and fishing community; also farming interests. Period covered 1872 to 1910.

Swift Imagery
Media House, 76 Queen Street, Newton Abbot TQ12 2ER
tel (01626) 208011/2 *fax* (01626) 208014 *and* Media House, Hexworthy, Yelverton PL20 6SD
tel/fax (01364) 631405
e-mail imagery@theswiftgroup.co.uk
web site http://www.theswiftgroup.co.uk
Picture Editor Richard Bennett

Travel, documentary, lifestyle plus general stock, colour transparencies and b&w prints. Over 120 contributing photographers/photojournalists. Commission: 50%. Founded 1980.

Syndication International*
One Canada Square, Canary Wharf, London E14 5AP
tel 020-7293 3700 *fax* 020-7293 2712
e-mail desk@mirpix.com

web site http://www.mirpix.com
Specialises in current affairs, personalities, royalty, sport, cinema and travel. Agents for Mirror Group Newspapers.

Charles Tait Photo Library

Kelton, St Ola, Orkney KW15 1TR
tel (01856) 873738 *fax* (01856) 875313
e-mail charles.tait@zetnet.co.uk
web site http://www.charles-tait.co.uk
Colour photo library specialising in Scottish islands: Orkney, Shetland and Western Isles, including outliers; also mainland Scotland and France. Archaeology, landscapes, seascapes, craft and industry, transport, events, people and wildlife. 10,000 images in formats ranging from 35mm to 70mm and 5 x 4in, all with detailed captions and bar coded. Publisher of postcards, calendars, guidebooks. See web site. Founded 1978.

The Tank Museum Photo Library & Archive

The Tank Museum, Bovington, Dorset BH20 6JG
tel (01929) 405070 *fax* (01929) 405360
e-mail library@tankmuseum.co.uk
web site http://www.tankmuseum.co.uk
International collection, from 1900 to present, of armoured fighting vehicles and military transport, including tanks, armoured cars, personnel carriers, self-propelled artillery carriers, missile launchers, cars, lorries and tractors. Founded *c.*1946.

Telegraph Colour Library*

The Innovation Centre, 225 Marsh Wall, London E14 9FX
tel 020-7293 2929 *fax* 020-7538 3309
Stock photography agency covering a wide subject range: business, sport, people, industry, animals, medical, nature, space, travel and graphics. Sameday service for all UK clients. Free catalogues available upon request.

Theatre Museum

National Museum of the Performing Arts, 1E Tavistock Street, London WC2E 7PA
tel 020-7943 4700 *fax* 020-7943 4777
web site http://www.theatremuseum.org
In addition to extensive public displays on live entertainment and education programme, the Museum has an unrivalled collection of programmes, playbills, prints, photos, videos, texts and press cuttings relating to performers and productions from the 17th century onwards. Available by appointment (book 3 weeks in advance), free of charge through the Study Room. Open Wed-Fri 10.30am-4.30pm. Reprographic services available.

3rd Millennium Music Ltd

22 Avon, Hockley, Tamworth, Staffs. B77 5QA
tel/fax (01827) 286086
e-mail Neil3MMLtd@aol.com
web site http://members.aol.com/Neil3MMLtd/NWCC.htm
Contact Neil Williams (Managing Director)
Specialises in classical music ephemera, including portraits of composers, musicians, conductors, opera singers, ballet stars, impresarios, and music-related literary figures. Old and sometimes rare photographs, postcards, antique prints, cigarette cards, stamps, concert programmes, Victorian newspapers, etc. Also modern photographs of composer references such as museums, statues, memorials etc.

Other subjects: music in art, musical instruments, manuscripts, concert halls, opera houses and other music venues. Founded 1996.

Tibet Pictures*

38 Camac Road, Twickenham TW2 6NU
tel/fax 020-8898 0150 *tel* 020-8876 3637
Contact Jonathan Miller
Specialises in the people, architecture, history, religion and politics of Tibet. Also Yemen. Colour and b&w. Founded 1992.

Topham Picturepoint*

PO Box 33, Edenbridge, Kent TN8 5PB
tel (01342) 850313 *fax* (01342) 850244
e-mail admin@topfoto.co.uk
web site http://www.topfoto.co.uk
Contact Bernice Fairchild
Eight million contemporary and historical images, including the United Nations Environment Programme (UNEP) library. Delivery on-line if requested. New photographers – sample submission of 50 transparencies; 5-year contract, 50% commission.

B.M. Totterdell Photography*

Constable Cottage, Burlings Lane, Knockholt, Kent TN14 7PE
tel/fax (01959) 532001
Specialist volleyball library, covering all aspects of the sport. Founded 1989.

Transworld/Scope

26 St Cross Street, London EC1N 8UH
tel 020-7405 2997 *fax* 020-7831 4549
Contact Valerie Dobson

Colour: situations/beauty pictures.

Travel Images

Harpers Barn, Summerhill, Goudhurst, Kent TN17 1JU
tel (01580) 211132
Sales and Marketing Manager Frances Main Wilson

Comprehensive travel library, covering over 90 countries. Founded 1990.

Travel Ink Photo & Feature Library*

The Old Coach House, 14 High Street, Goring-on-Thames, Nr Reading, Berks. RG8 9AR
tel (01491) 873011 *fax* (01491) 875558
e-mail info@travel-ink.co.uk
web site http://www.travel-ink.co.uk

Travel, tourism and lifestyles covering around 150 countries – including the UK. Specialist sections include Hong Kong (including construction of the Tsing Ma Bridge), North Wales and Greece. Founded 1988.

Travel Photo International

9 Halsall Green, Wirral CH63 9NA
tel/fax 0151-334 2300

Touristic interest including scenery, towns, monuments, historic buildings, archaeological sites, local people. Specialises in travel brochures and books. Terms: 50%.

TRH Pictures

Bradley's Close, 74-77 White Lion Street, London N1 9PF
tel 020-7520 7647 *fax* 020-7520 7606
e-mail trh@trhpictures.co.uk
web site http://www.trhpictures.co.uk
Director Ted Nevill

Specialises in colour transparencies and b&w photos of the history of civil and military aviation, modern warfare from the American Civil War, transport on land and sea, and the exploration of space. Commission: 50%. Founded 1983.

Tropix Photo Library*

156 Meols Parade, Meols, Wirral CH47 6AN
tel/fax 0151-632 1698
e-mail tropixphoto@talk21.com
web site http://www.merseyworld.com/tropix/

All human and environmental aspects of tropics, sub-tropics and non-tropical developing countries. Positive, progressive and model-released images especially welcome. Preliminary enquiry in writing essential, preferably by e-mail. Visit web site for full submission guidelines. Terms: 50%. Founded 1973.

True North Picture Source

5 Brunswick Street, Hebden Bridge, West Yorkshire HX7 6AJ
tel/fax (01422) 845532
e-mail john@trunorth.demon.co.uk
web site http://www.trunorth.demon.co.uk
Proprietor John Morrison

The life and landscape of the North of England. No other photographers' work required. 30,000 transparencies (35mm and medium format). Commissions undertaken. Founded 1992.

Ulster Folk & Transport Museum – see National Museums & Galleries of Northern Ireland, Ulster Folk & Transport Museum*

Ulster Photographic Agency

22 Casaeldona Park, Belfast BT6 9RB
tel (01232) 795738

Motoring and motorsport. Terms: 50% or outright purchase. Founded 1985.

Universal Pictorial Press & Agency Ltd (UPPA)*

29-31 Saffron Hill, London EC1N 8SW
tel 020-7421 6000 *fax* 020-7421 6006
e-mail postmaster@uppa.demon.co.uk

Photo library containing notable Royal, political, company, academic, legal, diplomatic, church, military, pop, arts, entertainment and sports personalities and well-known views and buildings. Commercial, industrial, corporate and public relations photo assignments undertaken. Founded 1929.

Colin Varndell Natural History Photography

The Happy Return, Whitecross, Netherbury, Bridport, Dorset DT6 5NH
tel (01308) 488341
Proprietor Colin Varndell

UK wildlife and landscape with particular emphasis on birds, mammals, butterflies, wild flowers and habitats. 110,000 colour transparencies. Founded 1980.

Venice Picture Library*

(formerly Archivio Veneziano)
Rawlings House, 2A Milner Street, London SW3 2PU

tel 020-7589 3127 *fax* 020-7584 1944
e-mail info@fineartphotolibrary.com
Contact Michelle Wood

Specialises in Venice, covering most aspects of the city, islands and lagoon, especially architecture and the environment. Commissions undertaken; visitors welcome by appointment. Founded 1990.

John Vickers Theatre Collection

27 Shorrolds Road, London SW6 7TR
tel 020-7385 5774

Archives of British theatre and portraits of actors, writers and musicians by John Vickers from 1938-1974.

Vidocq Photo Library

162 Burwell Meadow, Witney, Oxon OX8 7GD
tel/fax (01993) 778518
e-mail vidocq@which.net

Specialist in photographs for language and educational text books. Detailed coverage of France. Assignments undertaken. Founded 1983.

Visions in Golf

Noblethorpe Hall, Silkstone, Barnsley, South Yorkshire S75 4NG
tel (01226) 791001 *fax* (01226) 791601
e-mail mark@visionsingolf.freeserve.co.uk
Proprietor Mark Newcombe

Every aspect of worldwide golf, including an archive dating back to the late 19th century and world-famous golf courses. Over 150,000 colour transparencies and 5000 b&w images. Commission: 50%. Founded 1984.

The Charles Walker Collection

c/o Images Colour Library Ltd, Ramillies House, 1-2 Ramillies Street, London W1V 1DF
tel 020-7734 7344 *fax* 020-7287 3933
Contact Richard Heys

World's largest archive of colour pictures relating to the occult, magical, esoteric, mystical and mythological traditions. Founded 1983.

John Walmsley Photography*

April Cottage, Warners Lane, Albury Heath, Guildford, Surrey GU5 9DE
tel/fax (01483) 203846
e-mail john@johnwalmsleyphotos.co.uk
web site http://www.johnwalmsleyphotos.co.uk
Proprietor John Walmsley

Colour transparencies of education, careers, portraits of ordinary people, alternative medicine. Commissions undertaken. Founded 1987.

Christopher Ware Photography

65 Trinity Street, Barry, South Glamorgan CF62 7EX
tel/fax (01446) 732816
web site http://www.soundandvision-wales.com
Proprietor Christopher Ware

Colour and b&w photos of industry and transport of the southeast Wales area; also civil and military aircraft. Commissions undertaken. Founded 1970.

Simon Warner

Whitestone Farm, Stanbury, Keighley, West Yorkshire BD22 0JW
tel/fax (01535) 644644
e-mail photos@imagenet.prestel.co.uk

Landscape photographer with own stock pictures of northern England, North Wales and Northwest Scotland.

Waterways Photo Library*

39 Manor Court Road, London W7 3EJ
tel 020-8840 1659 *fax* 020-8567 0605
e-mail watphot39@aol.com
Contact Derek Pratt

British inland waterways; canals, rivers; bridges, aqueducts, locks and all waterside architectural features; watersports; waterway holidays, boats, fishing; town and countryside scenes. No other photographers' work required. Founded 1976.

Welfare History Picture Library

Heatherbank Museum of Social Work, Caledonian University, City Campus, Cowcaddens Road, Glasgow G4 0BA
tel 0141-331 3000 *fax* 0141-331 8637
e-mail a.ramage@gcal.ac.uk
web site http://www.lib.gcal.ac.uk/heatherbank/

Social history and social work, especially child welfare, poorhouses, prisons, hospitals, slum clearance, women's movement, social reformers and their work. Catalogue on request and on web site. Founded 1975.

Wellcome Trust Medical Photographic Library*

210 Euston Road, London NW1 2BE
tel 020-7611 8348 fax 020-7611 8577
e-mail photolib@wellcome.ac.uk
web site http://www.wellcome.ac.uk
Library Manager Catherine Draycott

Medical and social history; contemporary clinical and general medicine. Over 170,000 images. Founded 1936; renamed 1992.

Richard Welsby Photography

37 Grieveship Brae, Stromness,
Orkney Islands KW16 3BG
tel/fax (01856) 850910
e-mail richard.welsby@orkney.com
web site http://www.orknet.com.uk/welsby/index.htm
Contact Richard Welsby

Specialist library of the Orkney Islands: business and industry, scenics, geology, archaeology and historic; wide coverage of flowers, plants and other natural history subjects; aerials. Founded 1984.

Westcountry Pictures

10 Headon Gardens, Countess Wear, Exeter,
Devon EX2 6LE
tel (01392) 426640 *fax* (01392) 209080
e-mail petercooper@eclipse.co.uk
web site http://www.westcountrypictures.co.uk
Contact Peter Cooper

All aspects of Devon and Cornwall – culture, places, industry and leisure. Founded 1989.

Western Americana Picture Library

3 Barton Buildings, Bath BA1 2JR
tel (01225) 334213 *fax* (01225) 480554

Prints, engravings, photos and colour transparencies on the American West, cowboys, gunfighters, Indians, including pictures by Frederic Remington and Charles Russell, etc.

Roy J. Westlake ARPS

West Country Photo Library, 31 Redwood Drive,
Plympton, Plymouth PL7 2FS
tel/fax (01752) 336444

Landscapes, seascapes, architecture, leisure activities, etc. Also camping, caravanning and inland waterways subjects in Britain, including rivers and canals. Some world travel. Other photographers' work not accepted.

Eric Whitehead Photography – see Snookerimages*

Derek G. Widdicombe

Worldwide Photographic Library, 'Oldfield',
High Street, Clayton West,
Huddersfield HD8 9NS
tel/fax (01484) 862638 *mobile* (0839) 764024

Landscapes, seascapes, architecture, human interest of Britain and abroad. Moods and seasons, buildings and natural features. Holds copyright of Noel Habgood FRPS Collection.

Wilderness Photographic Library*

Mill Barn, Broad Raine, Sedbergh,
Cumbria LA10 5ED
tel (015396) 20196 *fax* (015396) 21293
Director John Noble FRGS

Specialist library in mountain and wilderness regions, especially polar. Associated aspects of people, places, natural history, geographical features, exploration and mountaineering, adventure sports, travel.

Wildlife Matters Photographic Library*

Marlham, Henley's Down, Battle,
East Sussex TN33 9BN
tel (01424) 830566 *fax* (01424) 830224
e-mail gardens@ftech.co.uk, jfeltwell@aol.com
web site http://web.ftech.net/~gardens
Contact Dr John Feltwell

Ecology, conservation and environment; habitats and pollution; agriculture and horticulture; general natural history, entomology; Mediterranean wildlife; rainforests (Amazon, Central America, Costa Rica and Indonesia); aerial pics of countryside UK, Europe, USA. Founded 1980.

David Williams Picture Library*

50 Burlington Avenue, Glasgow G12 0LH
tel 0141-339 7823 *fax* 0141-337 3031

Specialises in colour transparencies of Scotland and Iceland (2¼in and 35mm). Subjects include landscapes, towns, villages, buildings, antiquities, geology and physical geography. Smaller collections include many European countries (Faroe Islands, France, Spain, Czech Republic, Hungary, Portugal, Canary Islands), and Western USA. Commissions undertaken. Catalogue available. Founded 1989.

S. & I. Williams, Power Pix International Picture Library

Castle Lodge, Wenvoe, Cardiff CF5 6AD
tel/fax (029) 2059 5163

Worldwide travel, people and views, girl and 'mood-pix', sub-aqua, aircraft, flora, fauna, agriculture, children. Agents worldwide. Founded 1968.

Windrush Photos*

99 Noah's Ark, Kemsing, Sevenoaks,
Kent TN15 6PD
tel (01732) 763486 *fax* (01732) 763285
Owner David Tipling

Worldwide wildlife and landscapes; birds a speciality. Captioning and text services; ornithological consultancy. Photographic and features commissions undertaken. Terms: 50%. Founded 1991.

Tim Woodcock

45 Lyewater, Crewkerne, Somerset TA18 8BB
tel (01460) 74488 *fax* (01460) 74988
e-mail timwoodc@aol.com

British and Eire landscape, seascape, architecture and heritage; children, parenthood, adults and education; gardens and containers; mountain biking. Location commissions undertaken. Terms: 50%. Founded 1983.

Woodmansterne Publications Ltd*

1 The Boulevard, Blackmoor Lane, Watford, Herts. WD1 8YW
tel (01923) 228236 *fax* (01923) 245788
e-mail pictures@woodmansterne.co.uk

Britain, Europe, Holy Land; architecture, cathedral and stately home interiors; general art subjects; museum collections; volcanoes, transport, Space; opera and ballet; major state occasions; British heritage, contemporary artists.

World Pictures*

(formerly Feature-Pix Colour Library)
85A Great Portland Street, London W1N 5RA
tel 020-7437 2121/436 0440 *fax* 020-7439 1307
e-mail worldpictures@btinternet.com
Directors Joan Brenes, David Brenes

Over 600,000 medium and large format colour transparencies aimed at travel and travel-related markets. Extensive coverage of cities, countries and specific resort areas, together with material of an emotive nature, i.e. children, couples and families on holiday, all types of winter and summer sporting activities, motoring abroad, etc. Terms: 50%; major contributing photographers 60%.

Murray Wren Picture Library

3 Hallgate, London SE3 9SG
tel 020-8852 7556
e-mail murraywren@aol.com

Outdoor nudes; nudist holiday resorts and activities in Europe and elsewhere; historic and erotic art of the nude through the ages. Media enquiries only; no new photographers required.

The Allan Wright Photo Library

t/a Cauldron Press Ltd, The Stables, Parton, Castle Douglas, Kirkcudbrightshire DG7 3NB
tel (016444) 70260 *fax* (016444) 70202
e-mail allan@lyricalscotland.com
web site http://www.lyricalscotland.com

North Sea oil, offshore life 'on the rigs', Dumfries and Galloway, Argyll and Scottish highlands, scenic and environmental. Founded 1986.

Yemen Pictures

38 Camac Road, Twickenham TW2 6NU
tel/fax 020-8898 0150 or 020-8876 3637
Contact John Miles

Specialist colour library of Yemen, covering all aspects of culture, people, architecture, dance, qat and music. Also Africa, Australia, Middle East and Asia. Founded 1995.

York Archaeological Trust Picture Library

Cromwell House, 13 Ogleforth, York YO1 7FG
tel (01904) 663000 *fax* (01904) 663024
e-mail postmaster@yorkarch.demon.co.uk
web site http://www.yorkarch.demon.co.uk
Picture Librarian H. Dawson

York archaeology covering Romans, Dark Ages, Vikings and Middle Ages; traditional crafts; scenes of York and Yorkshire. Founded 1987.

Zoological Society of London*

Regent's Park, London NW1 4RY
tel 020-7449 6293 *fax* 020-7586 5743
e-mail library@zsl.org
Librarian Ann Sylph

Archive collection of photographs, paintings and prints, from the 16th century onwards, covering almost all vertebrate animals, many now extinct or rare, plus invertebrates. Founded 1826.

Picture agencies and libraries by subject area

This index gives the major subject area(s) only of each entry in the main listing which begins on page 412, and should be used with discrimination.

Aerial photography

Aerofilms
Aviation Picture Library
Sue Cunningham Photographic (London)
Geo Aerial Photography
Sealand Aerial Photography
Skyscan Photolibrary

Africa

Academic File News Photos
AMIS (Morocco)
Ancient Egypt Picture Library
Andes Press Agency
Animal Photography
Sue Cunningham Photographic
C.M. Dixon (Ethiopia, Tunisia)
Geoslides
Images of Africa Photobank
Link Picture Library (Central and Southern Africa)
Tibet Pictures (Yemen)
Yemen Pictures

Agriculture and farming

Stephen Benson Slide Bureau
The Anthony Blake Photo Library
Dennis Davis Photography
Ecoscene
Heritage & Natural History Photography
Frank Lane Picture Agency
Holt Studios International
Planet Earth Pictures
Seaco Picture Library
Sutcliffe Gallery

Aircraft and aviation

Air Photo Supply
Aviation Picture Library
Dr Alan Beaumont
Photo Link
The Picture Company
Skyscan Photolibrary
Patrick Smith Associates
TRH Pictures

Archaeology, antiquities, ancient monuments and heritage

A.A. & A. Ancient Art & Architecture Collection
Lesley and Roy Adkins Picture Library
AKG London
Rev. J. Catling Allen
Ancient Egypt Picture Library
Stephen Benson Slide Bureau
Sarah Boait Photography and Picture Library
Country Collections Photolibrary (Celtic)
C.M. Dixon
English Heritage Photo Library
Werner Forman Archive
Fortean Picture Library
John Glover Photography
Heritage & Natural History Photography
Kilmartin House Trust
Photo Resources
Ritmeyer Archaeological Design (Holy Land)
Mick Sharp Photography
Sites, Sights and Cities
Travel Photo International
Woodmansterne Publications
York Archaeological Trust Picture Library

Architecture, houses and interiors

A.A. & A. Ancient Art and Architecture Collection
Abode Interiors Photographic Library
Arcaid Architectural Photography and Picture Library
Stephen Benson Slide Bureau
John Blake Picture Library
BookArt & Architecture Picture Library
Rev. J. Catling Allen
Sylvia Cordaiy Photo Library
Dennis Davis Photography
English Heritage Photo Library
Werner Forman Archive
Houses & Interiors Photographic Features Agency
Mick Sharp Photography
The Venice Picture Library
Woodmansterne Publications

Art, sculpture and crafts

AKG London
Allied Artists
Bodleian Library
BookArt & Architecture Picture Library
Bridgeman Art Library
La Casa Photos
Crafts Council Picture Library
Fine Art Photographic Library
Werner Forman Archive
National Portrait Gallery Picture Library
Ann and Bury Peerless
Photo Resources
Retrograph Nostalgia Archive
The Venice Picture Library

Asia

Academic File News Photos
Andes Press Agency
Australia Pictures (Tibet, Pakistan)
Das Photo
Douglas Dickins Photo Library
C.M. Dixon (Sri Lanka, Turkey)
Andrew N. Gagg's Photo Flora
Geoslides
Imagefinder Pte Ltd
Japan Archive
Link Picture Library
Ann and Bury Peerless
The Royal Society for Asian Affairs
Society for Anglo-Chinese Understanding
Tibet Pictures
Travel Ink Photo & Feature Library (Hong Kong)
Yemen Pictures

Australia and New Zealand

Australia Pictures
George A. Dey
Frontline Photo Press Agency
Geoslides
Yemen Pictures

Britain (see also Ireland, Scotland, Wales)

Air Photo Supply (southeast)
Rev. J. Catling Allen
John Birdsall Photography (Nottingham)
John Blake Picture Library
Sarah Boait Photography and Picture Library
Britain on View
David Broadbent/Peak District Pictures
COI Photo Library
Collections
English Heritage Photo Library
Isle of Wight Photo Library
Isle of Wight Pictures
Lakeland Life Picture Library (Lake District)
Bill Meadows Picture Library
Merseyside Photo Library
The Mustograph Agency
Photofusion
Skyscan Photolibrary
Britain on View
True North Picture Source (North England)
Simon Warner (North England)
Westcountry Pictures (Devon, Cornwall)
Roy J. Westlake
Derek G. Widdicombe
Tim Woodcock
Woodmansterne Publications
York Archaeological Trust Picture Library

Business, industry and commerce

Ace Photo Agency
Financial Times Pictures
Horizon International
The Photographers' Library
Christopher Ware Photography

Camping and caravanning

Roy J. Westlake

Children and people (see also Social issues)

Barnardo's Photographic Archive
Lupe Cunha
Das Photo
Barry Davies
Format Photographers
Angela Hampton – Family Life Picture Library

Cities and towns (see also London)

Lesley and Roy Adkins Picture Library
Financial Times Pictures
Bill Meadows Picture Library
Sites, Sights and Cities
Skyscan Photolibrary

Civilisations, cultures and way of life

A.A. & A. Ancient Art and Architecture Collection
Bryan and Cherry Alexander Photography
Andalucía Slide Library (Spain)
Australia Pictures
Bruce Coleman Collection
Dee Conway Ballet & Dance Picture Library
Country Collections Photolibrary (Celtic)
Werner Forman Archive
Angela Hampton – Family Life Picture Library
Christine Osborne Pictures/MEP
Photo Resources
Royal Geographical Society Picture Library
Peter Sanders Photography
The Slide File (Irish, Celtic)
STILL Pictures Whole Earth
Tibet Pictures (Tibet, Yemen)

Countryside and rural life (see also Landscapes)

Andalucía Slide Library (Spain)
Dr Alan Beaumont
Forest Life Picture Library
National Museums and Galleries of Northern Ireland, Ulster Folk and Transport Museum
Wildlife Matters Photographic Library

Developing countries

Geoslides
Christine Osborne Pictures/MEP
Panos Pictures
STILL Pictures Whole Earth
Tropix Photo Library

Environment, conservation, ecology and habitats

Heather Angel/Natural Visions
Arctic Camera
Butterflies
Bruce Coleman Collection
Sylvia Cordaiy Photo Library
Ecoscene
Environmental Investigation Agency
Fogden Wildlife Photographs
Forest Life Picture Library
Brian Gadsby Picture Library
GeoScience Features
Martin and Dorothy Grace
Harper Horticultural Slide Library
Holt Studios International
Horizon International
Frank Lane Picture Agency
Chris Mattison
Natural Image
NHPA
Oxford Scientific Films Ltd, Photo Library

Panos Pictures
Papilio Natural History & Travel Library
Planet Earth Pictures
Premaphotos Wildlife
STILL Pictures Whole Earth
Tropix Photo Library
Colin Varndell Natural History Photography
Wildlife Matters Photographic Library

Europe and Eastern Europe (excluding UK/Ireland)

Andalucía Slide Library (Spain)
Andes Press Agency
John Birdsall Photography (Spain)
Sue Cunningham Photographic
Das Photo
C.M. Dixon
Just Europe
John Massey Stewart
Medimage (Mediterranean)
Panos Pictures (Eastern Europe)
Russia and Eastern Images
Skishoot – Offshoot (France)
Charles Tait Photo Library (France, Venice)
Venice Picture Library
Vidocq Photo Library (France)
David Williams Picture Library (Iceland)

Fashion and lifestyle

Joe Filmbase Photo Agency/ Library

Food and drink

The Anthony Blake Photo Library
Cephas Picture Library
Footprints Colour Picture Library
Retrograph Nostalgia Archive

Gardens, gardening and horticulture (see also Plant life)

A-Z Botanical Collection
Arcaid Architectural Photography and Picture Library
Butterflies
Dennis Davis Photography
Forest Life Picture Library
Garden Matters Photographic Library
John Glover Photography
Harper Horticultural Slide Library
Houses & Interiors Photographic Features Agency
S. & O. Mathews
Natural Image
The Harry Smith Collection Horticultural Photographic Library
Peter Stiles Picture Library
Tim Woodcock

General and stock libraries

Ace Photo Agency
Barnaby's Picture Library
Stephen Benson Slide Bureau
J. Allan Cash Photolibrary
Bruce Coleman Inc.
Bruce Coleman Collection
Colorific Photo Library
C.P.L. (Camerapix Picture Library)
Barry Davies
C.M. Dixon
Greg Evans International Photo Library
Fotoccompli – The Picture Library
Freelance Focus
Frontline Photo Press Agency
GeoScience Features
Geoslides
Horizon International
Hulton Getty Picture Collection
Hutchison Picture Library
The Image Bank
Image Diggers
Imagefinder
Images Colour Library
Joe Filmbase Photo Agency/ Library
The MacQuitty International Collection
News Blitz International
Chandra S. Perera Cinetra
Photofusion
The Photographers' Library
Pictor International
POPPERFOTO (Paul Popper)
Raleigh International Picture Library
Retna Pictures
robertharding.com
Dawn Runnals Photographic Library
Salamander Picture Library
S & G Press Agency
Spectrum Colour Library
Tony Stone Images
Telegraph Colour Library
Topham Picturepoint
Universal Pictorial Press & Agency (UPPA)
S. & I. Williams, Power Pix International Picture Library
Woodmansterne Publications

Geography, biogeography and topography

Arctic Camera
B. & B. Photographs
John Blake Picture Library
Geoslides
GeoScience Features
Royal Geographical Society Picture Library
Mick Sharp Photography
John Massey Stewart

Glamour, moods and nudes

Transworld/Scope
S. & I. Williams, Power Pix International Picture Library
Murray Wren Picture Library

Health and medicine

Lupe Cunha
Angela Hampton – Family Life Picture Library
Science Photo Library
Science & Society Picture Library
Shout Picture Library
John Walmsley Photography
Wellcome Trust Medical Photographic Library

High-tech, high-speed, macro/micro, special effects and step-by-step

Earth Images Picture Library (high-tech)
GeoScience Features (macro/ micro)
Houses & Interiors Photographic Features Agency (step-by-step)
The Image Bank (high-tech, special effects)

The Nature and Landscape File
Microscopix (electron micrographs, photomicrographs)
NHPA (high-speed)
Oxford Scientific Films, Photo Library (special effects)

History

AKG London
American History Picture Library
Bodleian Library
British Library Picture Library
Mary Evans Picture Library
Frost Historical Newspaper Collection
Heritage & Natural History Photography
Pat Hodgson Library
Dave Lewis Nostalgia Collection
Elizabeth Linley Collection
London Metropolitan Archives
The Billie Love Historical Collection
Mansell/Time
National Museums and Galleries of Northern Ireland, Ulster Folk and Transport Museum
Peter Newark Pictures
Sylvia Pitcher Photo Library (USA)
Pixfeatures
Public Record Office Image Library
Retrograph Nostalgia Archive
Ann Ronan at Image Select
The Royal Photographic Society
Royal Society for Asian Affairs
Royal Society of Chemistry Library
Salamander Picture Library (USA)
SCR Photo Library
The Tank Museum Photo Library & Archive (military)
Topham Picturepoint

Illustrations, prints, engravings, lithographs and cartoons

Allied Artists
American History Picture Library
Barnaby's Picture Library
Bodleian Library
British Library Picture Library
Mary Evans Picture Library
Fotomas Index
Pat Hodgson Library & Picture Research Agency
The Illustrated London News Picture Library
Elizabeth Linley Collection
The Billie Love Historical Collection
Mansell/Time
National Portrait Gallery Picture Library
Peter Newark Pictures
Public Record Office Image Library
Punch Cartoon Library
Retrograph Nostalgia Archive
Ann Ronan at Image Select
Royal Society of Chemistry Library
Western Americana Picture Library
Zoological Society of London

Ireland

Collections
Heritage & Natural History Photography
National Museums and Galleries of Northern Ireland, Ulster Folk and Transport Museum
The Slide File

Landscapes and scenics

Lesley and Roy Adkins Picture Library
Andalucía Slide Library (Spain)
Ardea Wildlife & Pets
BookArt & Architecture Picture Library
Barry Davies
George A. Dey (Scottish)
John Glover Photography
Isle of Wight Photo Library
Isle of Wight Pictures
S. & O. Mathews
Bill Meadows Picture Library
Medimage (Mediterranean)
The Nature and Landscape File
The Photolibrary Wales
Railways – Milepost 9½
Peter Stiles Picture Library
Charles Tait Photo Library
Simon Warner
Richard Welsby Photography (Orkney Islands)
Roy J. Westlake
Derek G. Widdicombe
Windrush Photos
The Allan Wright Photo Library (Scotland)

Latin America

Andes Press Agency
Sue Cunningham Photographic
Das Photo

London

The Illustrated London News Picture Library
London Metropolitan Archives
Monitor Syndication
Patrick Smith Associates

Middle East

Academic File News Photos
Ancient Egypt Picture Library
Australia Pictures (Iran, Yemen)
Stephen Benson Slide Bureau
Das Photo
Barry Davies (Egypt)
Link Picture Library (Israel)
Christine Osborne Pictures/MEP
Ann and Bury Peerless
Yemen Pictures

Military and armed forces

Air Photo Supply
Imperial War Museum
Military History Picture Library
Public Record Office Image Library
Salamander Books Picture Archive
The Tank Museum Photo Library & Archive

Mountains

AMIS
Hamish Brown, Scottish Photographic
Mountain Dynamics
Mountain Visions and Faces
Royal Geographical Society Picture Library
Wilderness Photographic Library

Natural history (see also Environment, Plant life)

A-Z Botanical Collection
Heather Angel/Natural Visions
Animal Photography
Aquila Wildlife Images
Ardea Wildlife & Pets

B. & B. Photographs
BBC Natural History Unit Picture Library
Dr Alan Beaumont
Bird Images
David Broadbent/Peak District Pictures
David Broadbent/Birds
Butterflies
Bruce Coleman Collection
Sylvia Cordaiy Photo Library
Barry Davies
Ecoscene
Environmental Investigation Agency
Fogden Wildlife Photographs
Ron and Christine Foord
Footprints Colour Picture Library
Forest Life Picture Library
Brian Gadsby Picture Library
GeoScience Features
Martin and Dorothy Grace
Heritage & Natural History Photography
David Hosking
Image Diggers
Frank Lane Picture Agency
Michael Leach
Chris Mattison (reptiles, amphibians)
Natural Image
The Nature and Landscape File
NHPA
Oxford Scientific Films, Photo Library
Papilio Natural History & Travel Library
Photo Resources
Planet Earth Pictures
Premaphotos Wildlife
robertharding.com
Roundhouse Ornithology Collection
RSPCA Photolibrary
Steffi Schubert, Wildlife Conservation Collection Photographic Library
Scottish Wildlife Library
Peter Stiles Picture Library
STILL Pictures Whole Earth
Colin Varndell Natural History Photography
Richard Welsby Photography (Orkney Islands)
Wildlife Matters Photographic Agency
Windrush Photos
Zoological Society of London

Nautical and maritime

Peter Cumberlidge Photo Library
National Maritime Museum Picture Library
National Museums and Galleries of Northern Ireland, Ulster Folk and Transport Museum
Seaco Picture Library

News, features and photo features

Academic File News Photos
The Associated Press
Bandphoto Agency
Financial Times Pictures
Frontline Photo Press Agency
Frost Historical Newspaper Collection
International Press Agency
News Blitz International
PA News Photo Library
Chandra S. Perera Cinetra
Pixfeatures
Press Features Syndicate
S & G Press Agency
Swift Imagery
Syndication International
Topham Picturepoint

North America

American History Picture Library
Douglas Dickins Photo Library
Sylvia Pitcher Photo Library
Western Americana Picture Library

Nostalgia, ephemera and advertising

Fotomas Index
Dave Lewis Nostalgia Collection
Retrograph Nostalgia Archive

Performing arts
(theatre, dance, music)

Aquarius Library
Camera Press
Dee Conway Ballet & Dance Picture Library
Famous Pictures & Features Agency
Image Diggers
Jazz Index
Lebrecht Collection
Link Picture Library (music)
Mander & Mitchenson Theatre Collection
PA News Photo Library
PAL (Performing Arts Library)
Sylvia Pitcher
Redferns Music Picture Library
Retna Pictures
Theatre Museum
3rd Millennium Music
John Vickers Theatre Collection

Personalities and portraits (see also Royalty)

Aquarius Library
Camera Press
Famous Pictures & Features Agency
Financial Times Pictures
Mark Gerson Photography
Tim Graham Picture Library
Pat Hodgson Library (historical)
J.S. Library International
Mander & Mitchenson Theatre Collection
Monitor Syndication
National Portrait Gallery Picture Library
PAL (Performing Arts Library)
Pixfeatures
POPPERFOTO (Paul Popper)
Punch Cartoon Library
Retna Pictures
The Royal Photographic Society
Royal Society of Chemistry Library
Syndication International
Topham Picturepoint
Universal Pictorial Press & Agency (UPPA)
John Vickers Theatre Collection

Plant life (see also Gardens)

A-Z Botanical Collection
Heather Angel/Natural Visions
Ardea Wildlife & Pets
B. & B. Photographs
Butterflies
Ron and Christine Foord
Footprints Colour Picture Library
Andrew N. Gagg's Photo Flora
Garden Matters Photographic Library
John Glover Photography
Martin and Dorothy Grace
Harper Horiticultural Slide Library
Heritage & Natural History Photography
NHPA
Picturesmiths
Premaphotos Wildlife
The Harry Smith Collection Horticultural Photographic Library
Richard Welsby Photography (Orkney Islands)

Polar and Arctic

Bryan and Cherry Alexander Photography
Arctic Camera
Geoslides
POPPERFOTO (Paul Popper)
Royal Geographical Society Picture Library
Wilderness Photographic Library

Religions and religious monuments

Lesley and Roy Adkins Picture Library
Rev. J. Catling Allen
Andes Press Agency
Sarah Boait Photography and Picture Library
Ann and Bury Peerless
Photo Resources
Ritmeyer Archaeological Design (Holy Land)
Peter Sanders Photography

Royalty

Camera Press
Tim Graham Picture Library
J.S. Library International
Monitor Syndication
Pixfeatures
Syndication International

Russia

C.M. Dixon
John Massey Stewart
Russia & Eastern Images
SCR Photo Library

Science, technology and meteorology

Ace Photo Agency
Bruce Coleman Collection
Earth Images Picture Library
GeoScience Features
Horizon International
Frank Lane Picture Agency
Microscopix
Oxford Scientific Films Ltd, Photo Library
Ann Ronan at Image Select
Royal Society of Chemistry Library
Science Photo Library
Science & Society Picture Library

Scotland

Edinburgh Photographic Library
Hamish Brown, Scottish Photographic
George A. Dey
Kilmartin House Trust
Scotland in Focus Picture Library
The Still Moving Picture Company
Charles Tait Photo Library
Simon Warner
Richard Westby Photography (Orkney Islands)
David Williams Picture Library
The Allan Wright Photo Library

Social issues and social history

Barnardo's Photographic Archive
John Birdsall Photography
COI Photo Library
Mary Evans Picture Library
FirePix
Format Photographers
Hulton Getty Picture Collection
The Illustrated London News Picture Library
Imperial War Museum
Elizabeth Linley Collection
London Metropolitan Archives
Photofusion
RSPCA Photolibrary
Ann Ronan at Image Select
Science & Society Picture Library
Shout Picture Library
Stockwave
Swift Imagery (lifestyle)
John Walmsley Photography (education/careers)
Welfare History Picture Library
Wellcome Trust Medical Photographic Library

South America

Animal Photography (Galapagos)
Australia Pictures (Bolivia, Peru)
Stephen Benson Slide Bureau
Lupe Cunha (Brazil)
Das Photo
David Hosking (Falklands)

Space and astronomy

Earth Images Picture Library
Galaxy Picture Library
Genesis Space Photo Library
National Maritime Museum Picture Library
Oxford Scientific Films Ltd, Photo Library
Science Photo Library
TRH Pictures

Sport and leisure

Action Plus
Allsport UK
The Associated Press
John Blake Photo Library (equestrian)
Boxing Picture Library
David Broadbent
Michael Cole Camerawork (tennis)
Concannon Golf History Library
Sylvia Cordaiy Photo Library (ocean racing)
Peter Dazeley (golf)

George A. Dey (Highland Games)
Eyeline Photography (watersports, sheepdog trials)
Frontline Photo Press Agency
Isle of Wight Pictures (sailing)
Ludvigsen Library (motor racing)
Mountain Visions and Faces (mountaineering, skiing)
PA News Photo Library
POPPERFOTO (Paul Popper)
Skishoot – Offshoot
Skyscan Photo Library (aerial)
Snookerimages
Sporting Pictures
The Still Moving Picture Company
Syndication International
B.M. Totterdell Photography (volleyball)
Ulster Photography Agency (motorsport)
Universal Pictorial Press & Agency (UPPA)
Visions in Golf
Waterways Photo Library (watersports)
Tim Woodcock (mountain biking)
World Pictures

Strange phenomena, occult and mystical

Fortean Picture Library
Image Diggers
Sites, Sights and Cities
The Charles Walker Collection

Transport (cars and motoring, railways)

Das Photo (motorbikes)
George A. Dey (veteran cars)
Ludvigsen Library
Motorcycles Unlimited
Motoring Picture Library, Beaulieu
National Museums and Galleries of Northern Ireland, Ulster Folk and Transport Museum
Railways – Milepost 9½
Science & Society Picture Library
Seaco Picture Library
TRH Pictures
Ulster Photographic Agency
Christopher Ware Photography

Travel and tourism

Ace Photo Agency
Arcaid Architectural Photography and Picture Library
Aviation Picture Library
Sarah Boait Photography and Picture Library
Britain on View
J. Allan Cash Photolibrary
Sylvia Cordaiy Picture Library
Peter Cumberlidge Photo Library
James Davis Travel Photography
Douglas Dickins Photo Library
C.M. Dixon
Ecoscene
Greg Evans International Photo Library
Footprints Colour Picture Library
Format Photographers
Brian Gadsby Picture Library
Andrew N. Gagg's Photo Flora
The Hutchinson Library
The Illustrated London News Picture Library
Lonely Planet Images
J.S. Library International
Just Europe
Mountain Visions and Faces
Papilio Natural History & Travel Library
The Photographers' Library
The Picture Company
Raleigh International Picture Library
robertharding.com
Royal Geographical Society Picture Library
Seaco Picture Library
Spectrum Colour Library
Swift Imagery
Charles Tait Photo Library
Telegraph Colour Library
Travel Images
Travel Ink Photo & Feature Library
Travel Photo International
Wilderness Photographic Library
World Pictures

Wales

The Photolibrary Wales
Patrick Smith Associates
Travel Ink Photo & Feature Library
Christopher Ware Photography
Simon Warner

Waterways

Country Collections Photolibrary (rivers/streams)
Peter Cumberlidge Photo Library
Waterways Photo Library
Roy J. Westlake

Card and stationery publishers which accept photographs

Before submitting work, photographers are advised to ascertain requirements, including terms and conditions. Only top quality material should be submitted; inferior work is never accepted. Postage for return of material should be enclosed.

**Member of the Greeting Card Association*

Britannia Products Ltd

Dawson Lane, Dudley Hill, Bradford, West Yorkshire BD4 6HW
tel (01274) 784200 *fax* (01274) 651218
Managing Director Steve McNally

Designs and manufactures greetings cards, giftwrap and calendars. Submit transparencies (5 x 4in). Brands: Fine Art Graphics, Paws for Thought, The Comedy Club, Just Kiddin', Academy, Mother Earth, Animates, Fleurs, Truffles. Division of Hallmark Cards (Holdings) Ltd. Founded 1980.

Caspari Ltd*

9 Shire Hill, Saffron Walden, Essex CB11 3AP
tel (01799) 513010 *fax* (01799) 513101
Managing Director Keith Entwisle

Traditional fine art/classic images; 5 x 4in transparencies. No verses. Founded 1990.

Chapter and Verse

Granta House, 96 High Street, Linton, Cambs. CB1 6JT
tel (01223) 891951 *fax* (01223) 894137

Buildings, animals, flowers, scenic, or domestic subjects in series, suitable for greetings cards and postcards. All sizes of transparency. No verses. Founded 1981.

Hambledon Studios Ltd

Metcalf Drive, Altham Industrial Estate, Altham, Accrington, Lancs. BB5 5SS
tel (01282) 687300 *fax* (01282) 687404
Art Managers D. Jaundrell, J. Ashton, D. Fuller, N. Harrison, K. Ellis

Photos for reproduction as greetings cards. *Brands* Arnold Barton, Donny Mac, Reflections, New Image.

Images & Editions*

Bourne Road, Essendine, Nr Stamford, Lincs. PE9 4UW
tel (01780) 757118 *fax* (01780) 754629
Directors Lesley Forrow, Maurice Miller

Greetings cards, giftwrap, gift products and social stationery: flowers, gardens and landscape, animals, especially cats and dogs. Any format accepted; transparencies preferred. Founded 1984.

Jarrold Publishing

Whitefriars, Norwich NR3 1TR
tel (01603) 763300 *fax* (01603) 662748
Managing Director Caroline Jarrold
Photographic Librarian Vivienne Buckingham
tel (01603) 227325

Transparencies for calendars only; no cards. UK scenic, animals, floral. No constraint on format. Verses not required. All submissions to be accompanied by an sae, but prefer telephone enquiry in first instance. Imprints: Jarrold, Papermill. Founded 1770.

Papermill – calendar range of Jarrold Publishing

Pomegranate Editorial Europe

Submissions from Europe only 3 Wilsdon Way, Lyne Meads, Kidlington, Oxford OX5 1TN
tel (01865) 460661 *fax* (01865) 378005
e-mail andy.swapp@lineone.net
web site http://www.pomegranate.com
Project Editor (Europe) Andy Swapp
Submissions from outside Europe Pomegranate Communications Inc., 210 Classic Court, Rohnert Park, California 94928, USA
tel 800-227-1428 *fax* 787-586-5522
e-mail info@pomegranate.com

Extensive range of calendars as well as posters, notecards, postcards, books of postcards, occasion, holiday and general greeting cards; bookmarks, gift enclosures and magnets; mouse mats and screen savers; address books, games and learning decks (marketed under the trademark Knowledge Cards). Founded 1993.

J. Salmon Ltd

100 London Road, Sevenoaks, Kent TN13 1BB
tel (01732) 452381 *fax* (01732) 450951

Picture postcards, calendars and local view booklets.

Santoro Graphics Ltd

342-344 London Road, Cricket Green, Mitcham, Surrey CR4 3ND
tel 020-8640 9777 *fax* 020-8640 2888
web site http://www.santorographics.com
Directors L. Santoro, M. Santoro

Publishers of innovative and award-winning designs for greetings cards, giftwrap and gift stationery. Bold contemporary images with an international appeal. Subjects covered: black and white, colour floral, quirky and humorous, whimsical, 'Fifties, 'Seventies, futuristic! All formats accepted in both b&w and colour; transparencies ideally 5 x 4in but will accept 35mm. Founded 1985.

Scandecor Ltd

3 The Ermine Centre, Hurricane Close, Huntingdon, Cambs. PE18 6XX
tel (01480) 456395 *fax* (01480) 456269
Managing Director Derek Shirley

Transparencies all sizes. Founded 1967.

Twin Oaks Publishing

Cloudesley House, Shire Hill, Saffron Walden, Essex CB11 3FB
tel (01799) 520200 *fax* (01799) 520100
Product and Marketing Director Jo Arkinstall

Send transparencies or prints. Brands: Objects of Desire, The Cat's Pyjamas, Just Bears, Teddies of Desire. Founded 1996.

Picture research

A multitude of pictures are reproduced in the media and their images consumed by the viewer as part of daily life. The role of the picture researcher is to obtain these pictures and to be conversant with the legal implications concerning their reproduction. ***Jennie Karrach*** *explains.*

Picture research is the art of obtaining pictures – photos and illustrations – suitable for reproduction, which suit the project's brief, budget and deadline. It also includes the clearance of permissions, copyright, the negotiation of rights and fees, and the eventual return of pictures to their owners at the end of the project.

Picture researchers are responsible for supplying a vast range of clients: in the book and magazine industry – both publishers and packagers – advertising agencies, film, television and video companies, newspapers and exhibition organisers. Although the skills involved in picture research are relevant in all these contexts, the type of pictures required varies enormously. Consequently, researchers tend to specialise in the type of work they undertake, and they may well have a specialist knowledge of one particular area, such as science and technology.

Picture researchers are employed either as staff members or on a freelance basis, paid by the hour or day, or for the duration of a project, as appropriate. An employee working full time on a long-running project may have time to carry out extensive research, but freelance work is often constrained by the client's budget and schedule. It is here that experience counts. Knowing where to find material quickly to suit the brief saves time and therefore money.

The researcher's fees are often included in the total budget, so that although the final deadline for delivery of pictures to the client may be a month away, the total allowed for picture research amounts to three days' work. It may be that this is unrealistic, and that the job will require five days. These details all need to be clarified at the outset and some sort of agreement listing the picture brief, deadlines, budget and invoicing particulars needs to be drawn up. It is important to put everything in writing so that in the event of dispute both parties can refer back to the agreement. Pictures are often worth large amounts of money, and in the event of loss it will become difficult to agree who will pay compensation unless this has been pre-arranged. It can also prove difficult to collect payment for work completed, so it may be advisable to agree upon regular payments and an advance to cover expenses such as travel, postage and telephone, etc.

The brief

It is important to clarify the brief so that both parties, the picture researcher and the editor/design team, are agreed upon the image required. It may be that the picture requested needs no further description – a work of art, by a well-known artist, e.g. *The Mona Lisa* by Leonardo da Vinci, to be used in colour. Or it may be that the picture is to depict an historical event which occurred long before the advent of photography. What is required? A photo of a contemporary manuscript which describes the incident, or perhaps a contemporary illumination exists. Or does the client have in mind an illustration executed by a more recent artist, perhaps a nineteenth-century engraving? Or a photograph of the remains of an historic site? It may be that the client has no one image in mind, but rather needs to evoke a specific mood, or provoke a reaction. This is often the case in advertising campaigns. Pictures are highly subjective, and what is evocative to some will appear bleak to others. A good picture researcher is able to capture the image conjured up in a picture meeting, responding to the ideas of an art director or editor.

It may be that the picture required must be a specific shape – portrait (upright) or landscape (horizontal), or it may need to have an area lacking in detail, such as sky, into which text can fit. Or a dark area suitable for text reversal. If there are too many design constraints it may be cost effective to commission a photographer, rather than to search for a non-existent 'existing' photo.

The budget, rights and deadline

Once the brief has been agreed, the budget, rights and deadline must be confirmed. These are interdependent. Picture fees increase according to the size and use made of the image; for instance, a picture used at quarter-page size in a school textbook will cost less than one used quarter-page size in a glossy, adult non-fiction book. Fees vary according to the media: books, magazines, television, video, CD-Rom, etc. The print run/circulation of a book/magazine also affects the price charged for use. Fees are calculated also according to the rights requested. The larger the territory, the larger the fee, although the percentage increase between the various categories will vary from agency to agency. The territories sold are usually:

- UK only
- UK and first foreign edition
- English language, world rights, excluding US
- English language, world rights, including US
- world rights, all languages.

It may well be that, as the European Union attempts to remove trade barriers, the rights available will change.

Other fees will need to be budgeted for. Many commercial picture agencies charge 'research' or 'service' fees. These may be linked to the amount of material they are loaning or there may be a fixed charge levied. In both cases the source should advise of this at the initial enquiry stage. Some will only charge if a personal visit is not possible and pictures are despatched by a member of their staff. The levying of these fees can erode the total picture budget quickly. It is not unusual to receive a service fee of £30, which may be acceptable if this is the only source used, and the pictures obtained are accepted by the client. However, on projects where a selection of pictures to cover a wider range of topics is required, many sources will have to be approached. It is worth discussing service fees at the outset. It is not unknown for agencies to waive or reduce them if it increases the likelihood of a sale. Some only charge the service fee if all pictures are returned and none selected for use. Other sources do not loan out material but instead sell copy transparencies or prints. This is usually the case with museums which can supply a transparency of a particular object or manuscript, but are unable to respond to a vague request for a selection of pictures for possible use. Museums often charge a monthly hire fee as well as the final reproduction fee.

Most commercial picture libraries or agencies operate on a loan system. Pictures are selected and loaned for an agreed period, usually a month. After this time material not required should be returned and some indication given as to the fate of the pictures still held. Is a subsequent picture selection to be made, or are those retained going to be used? If material is kept longer than the agreed loan period, then holding fees may be charged. These should only be levied if a reminder sent fails to elicit news of the pictures or return. (Freelance picture researchers need to make sure that such reminders are forwarded to them either by the source or sent on by the client.) Holding fees are charged per picture, per week over the deadline, and are usually waived if a reasonable extension to the free loan period is requested.

Useful directories

Picture Sources UK
by Rosemary Eakins, Macdonald, 1985
Now out of print but may be available through a library.

Picture Researcher's Handbook
by Hilary and Mary Evans, 7th edn, Pira, £50.00 (plus £3.00 p&p)
Available from bookshops and:
The Mary Evans Picture Library
59 Tranquil Vale, London SE3 0BS
tel 020-8318 0034 *fax* 020-8297 9819

BAPLA Directory
BAPLA, 18 Vine Hill, London EC1R 5DZ
tel 020-7713 1780 *fax* 020-7713 1211
£10
Lists all the current members of the British Association of Picture Libraries and Agencies (BAPLA), at present totalling over 380.

Picture sources

Sources are many and various. They include government departments, institutions, companies, libraries, commercial picture libraries and agencies, individual collectors, and individual photographers. Some of these sources supply pictures without charge, but that is not to say that they are necessarily easy to obtain, or that no copyright pertains. Many sources are not primarily concerned with the supply of pictures and give it low priority. Access to the collection may be limited to research students and those who hold a reader's card. Enquiries may have to be made in writing, and the idea of urgency is an alien one. Or lack of resources may prevent an efficient service.

There is no one source book which lists all picture sources and if one existed it would run to many volumes and be in need of constant updating. Commercial libraries and agencies maintain a high profile, advertising by mail shots to prospective clients. The larger ones produce glossy catalogues, usually free, which include a selection of their images, enough to give a flavour of the type of stock held.

New technology is affecting picture storage and use. Some large agencies produce CD-Roms which clients can purchase for future reference. These discs allow rapid viewing of thousands of images. On-line facilities at news agencies allow quick transmission of pictures to clients and use of the World Wide Web via the Internet enables subscribers to browse and download high resolution images for use. There are serious implications for copyright control resulting from electronic storage, e.g. unauthorised use or manipulation of photographs. Several systems are available which 'fingerprint' or 'watermark' the image so that pirate use is minimised.

General stock libraries

'General stock libraries' hold pictures which fall into broad categories, namely: travel, architecture, food, business, science/medicine, people, sport, nature, animals, transport, etc. They would almost certainly hold pictures of famous foreign landmarks, e.g. the Eiffel Tower, photographed from the ground, the air, by night, by day, with lovers ... It is much more difficult to find pictures of less glamorous sites. Street furniture, cars and pedestrians date quickly, and some agencies, keen to keep pictures saleable for as long as possible, will attempt to keep such features to a minimum. The result is strange; London, peopled only by bobbies and red buses, Venice reduced to St Mark's Square and gondoliers on the Grand Canal, Los Angeles depicted by traffic on freeways. This problem extends to the 'people' pictures, which tend to be stereotypes posed by models. It is not impossible to find pictures of 'real' people going about everyday activities, but it can be time-consuming. Directories cannot hope to express the nuances of photographic collections, and it is only over time, after visits to many sources, that an overview of the range available will emerge. Specialist picture libraries are usually one-subject libraries, and cover the whole range of picture needs. The level of captioning is usually higher in specialist sources as the photographer has expert knowledge. It can be the case that a good quality photograph badly captioned is rendered useless. A photo filed in the 'elderly people' category of a general stock agency showed a woman standing in a slight depression in the desert somewhere. The woman was actually a famous anthropologist, but her name meant nothing to the library so she had been miscaptioned and then wrongly filed. It may be that for certain purposes any train, boat, car, etc will be acceptable, but if the picture required is of a specific model then it is frustrating to find insubstantial captions and undated pictures.

Use of photos

Permission

Once pictures have been found which fit the brief, the next stage is clearance for use. Permission must be sought from the copyright holder for use of particular photos in set contexts. The supply of photos does not automatically guarantee permission to reproduce. It may be that the agency or picture source is not the copyright holder, and permission has to be sought elsewhere. This is often the case with photos of works of art still in copyright. The artist, or the artist's estate, may be represented by a copyright protection society such as DACS (Design and Artists Copyright Society – see page 474), which will approach the estate or artist on behalf of a picture researcher and, if permission is granted, often subject to conditions, issue a licence. Conditions could include the right to approve colour proofs. The production department or designer of the project would therefore need to be informed to allow time in the schedule. DACS has reciprocal representation agreements with similar copyright protection societies in some 26 countries. This simplifies a copyright enquiry considerably but sufficient time should be allowed for clearance. It may take a day or several weeks. If the copyright holder and the supplier of the photograph are not one and the same, then a fee may be due to both parties.

Context

It may be that the context in which the photo is to appear is a sensitive one, perhaps an article about child abuse, divorce, AIDS, or that the caption is to make some derogatory statement about the subject. If this is the case it is important to be honest

Useful organisations

BAPLA (British Association of Picture Libraries and Agencies)
18 Vine Hill, London EC1R 5DZ
tel 020-7713 1780 *fax* 020-7713 1211
e-mail enquiries@bapla.org.uk
web site http://www.bapla.org.uk
Chief Administrator Linda Royles
See page 464.

DACS (Design and Artists Copyright Society)
13 Northburgh Street,
London EC1V 0JP
tel 020-7336 8811 *fax* 020-7336 8822
e-mail info@dacs.co.uk
See page 474.

The Association of Photographers
81 Leonard Street, London EC2A 4QS
tel 020-7739 6669 *fax* 020-7739 8707
e-mail aop@dircon.co.uk
web site http://www.aophoto.co.uk
Includes fashion and advertising photographers amongst its members.

The Picture Research Association
(formerly SPREd)
2 Culver Drive, Oxted, Surrey RH8 9HP
tel (01883) 730123 *fax* (01883) 730144
e-mail pra@lippmann.co.uk
Chair Charlotte Lippman
A professional body for picture researchers, managers, picture editors and all those involved in the research, management and supply of visual material to all forms of the media.

The Association's main aims are to promote the interests and specific skills of its members internationally; to bring together those involved in the research and publication of visual material; to provide a forum for the exchange of information and to provide guidance to its members. It offers a free advisory service for members, meetings, a quarterly magazine, a monthly newsletter and Freelance Register. Founded in 1977 as the Society of Picture Researchers & Editors (SPREd).

about the context with the supplier of the photo. If the article is educational and positive in its approach, then the photo will play a different role from one appearing in an exposé of shameful goings on. It is prudent to enquire whether the photographer has obtained 'model release' from the subject in the photo. In return for a sum of money the model grants the photographer the right to sell the photos taken. This is standard procedure at photo sessions, where a particular shot has been commissioned by a client, or a personality has granted a shoot. The release may have certain riders attached as to use, precisely to avoid certain contexts.

An agency may grant permission to use the photo in a sensitive area, but insist on a declaration appearing with it or with the photo credits 'all photos posed by models'. Or it may be that the agency or photographer do not have model release for the photo. At present in the UK, if a person is photographed in public they cannot prevent that photo being published. Hence the breed of paparazzi photographers. There is as yet no law protecting against the invasion of privacy. (The situation is different in the USA.) As a result many British photo libraries hold photos of members of the public, taken 'in the public domain' for which they hold no model release. Most agencies reproduce the following or similar statement in their Terms & Conditions: 'although the agency takes all reasonable care, the agency shall not be liable for any loss or damage suffered by the client or by any third party arising from any defect in the picture or its caption, or in any way from its reproduction.' The onus is put onto the picture user. It is fair to say that if the context of the photo is an innocent one, most members of the public are pleased to be in the spotlight, and require no more than a complimentary copy of the book, magazine, or whatever.

Captions

It is important for picture researchers to make caption writers aware that litigation may result from derogatory or inappropriate captions. Staff researchers should attempt to prevent pictures which were obtained for one project, e.g. a book on health care, being transferred to another, such as a booklet on safe sex. Freelance researchers would be well advised to include a paragraph in the agreement mentioned above which would disclaim responsibility for use by the client of pictures supplied in any use other than that stated in the brief, and any subsequent copyright infringement by the client. It is not unknown for clients to withhold information or mislead picture researchers as to the length of the print run, or the production of foreign language editions.

Picture researchers do not generally write captions themselves but may be asked to provide information for captions. This can be very time-consuming if the pictures do not already have a reasonable amount of caption information attached, supplied by the source or photographer.

Picture research courses

The Publishing Training Centre at Book House
45 East Hill, London SW18 2QZ
tel 020-8874 2718/4608 *fax* 020-8870 8985
e-mail publishing.training@bookhouse.co.uk
web site http://www.train4publishing.co.uk
Offers a 2-day course in picture research, designed for people working in book publishing. Its objectives are to give a professional approach to the search for and use of suitable sources; to make picture researchers aware of all the implications of their task: suitability for reproduction, legal and financial aspects, and efficient administration. Held in June and in December.

The London School of Publishing and PR
David Game House, 69 Notting Hill Gate, London W11 3JS
tel 020-7221 3399 *fax* 020-7243 1730
e-mail lsp@easynet.co.uk
Course Director John Dalton
Offers a 10-week course in picture research 3 times a year. Each course takes place between 6.30-8.30pm, one evening per week. On successful completion a certificate in picture research is awarded. NUJ approved.

Credits and copyright

Once pictures have been selected, captioned, and sized for the project in hand, the credit or acknowledgement list will need to be drawn up. This usually includes a courtesy line thanking the various picture sources for permission to reproduce photographs. Sources are either listed alphabetically, with page numbers as to where their pictures appear, or the name of the source appears next to the picture.

Copyright

Under the provisions of the Copyright, Designs and Patents Act 1988, photographers have 'moral rights' which include the right to be identified as the author of a photograph (see *British copyright law*, page 633). Newspapers, magazines, encyclopedias, and other works of reference, are exempt from crediting contributors but most will include credits as a matter of course. Under the terms of the 1988 Act photography is copyright for the same duration and in the same way as other works of art. This was for 50 years after the death of the photographer until 1 January 1996, when 'the Term Directive' was implemented. The Term Directive harmonised copyright laws throughout the European Union and it extends the term of copyright in the UK to 70 years after the death of the photographer. Commissioned work, where previously the copyright belonged to the commissioner, is now the property of the photographer. This means that photos can only be kept for a limited period after a photo session, and rights must be agreed in the same way as for stock library images. All photos, used and unused, must be returned to the photographer. Staff photographers as employees do not own copyright on their photos.

A short booklet produced by the British Photographers Liaison Committee (BPLC), *The ABC Guide to UK Photographic*

Copyright, summarises the changes in copyright relevant to photographers brought about by the 1988 Act. The new edition is available from the Association of Photographers.

Last stages

When the pictures are ready to go off to the printer, a final check should be made to see that they have not been damaged by any of the people who have handled them – editors, designers, etc. If the printer returns photos damaged it will be easier to refute claims that pictures were already scratched if everything is checked as a matter of course. If prints or transparencies are damaged, a fee to compensate the agency or photographer is due. This will vary in amount according to whether the picture was an original or a duplicate. Some photographs are irreplaceable. The amount due for loss is stated in the Terms & Conditions listed on the reverse of most delivery notes. This may be in the region of £400 for an original. Sometimes pictures are not damaged irreparably but are returned by the printer with torn mounts, or still sticky from origination. It is best to return such pictures to the printer for cleaning, in case any damage occurs during a DIY cleaning session. Pictures should then be returned to their owners and one or two copies of the book or proofs supplied as evidence of use, as stated in the Terms & Conditions of the source.

Getting into picture research

This can be difficult as employers are loath to employ people without experience, and some picture sources are nervous about loaning pictures. A job with a picture library would give an insight into that particular source and might lead into a job as a picture researcher. Jobs in picture libraries, and picture research work, are advertised in the Creative, Media and Sales section of the *Guardian* on Saturdays and Mondays and in the *Independent* on Mondays. Sometimes such ads appear in the *Bookseller*, the weekly publishing journal, and *Campaign*, the weekly advertising magazine. These may all be available to read at your local library. Salaries tend to be low initially as one learns the skills involved. The idea of working freelance may appeal but it is difficult to obtain enough freelance work without the contacts amassed over a period of time.

Many picture researchers build up experience working for an employer full time, and then go freelance. This is not without risks. Getting enough work, being paid for work completed, sorting out tax and National Insurance to be paid, motivation, and loneliness are some of the problems which may arise.

Jennie Karrach is a freelance picture researcher and former chair of SPREd, who has worked with major national and international clients.

Societies, prizes and festivals

Societies, associations and clubs

The societies, associations and clubs listed here will be of interest to both writers and artists. They include appreciation societies devoted to specific authors, professional bodies and national institutions. Some also offer prizes and awards (see page 512).

Academi (Welsh Academy)
3rd Floor, Mount Stuart House, Mount Stuart Square, Cardiff CF10 5FQ
tel 029-2047 2266 *fax* 029-2049 2930
e-mail post@academi.org
web site http://www.academi.org
North Wales Office Ty Newydd, Llanystumdwy, Cricieth, Gwynedd LL52 0LW
tel (01766) 522817
e-mail academi.gog@dial.pipex.com
Chief Executive Peter Finch

Academi is shorthand for Yr Academi Gymreig, the national society of Welsh writers which exists to promote the literature of Wales. It runs courses, competitions (including the Cardiff International Poetry Competition), conferences, tours by authors, festivals and represents the interests of Welsh writers and Welsh writing both inside Wales and beyond. Its publications include *Taliesin* (quarterly), a literary journal in the Welsh language; *A470* (bi-monthly), a literature information magazine; *The Oxford Companion to the Literature of Wales, The Welsh Academy English-Welsh Dictionary*, and a variety of translated works.

In 1998 Academi won the franchise from the Arts Council of Wales to establish a Welsh National Literature Promotion Agency. The new, much enlarged Academi now administers a range of schemes including Writers on Tour, Writers Residencies, Writing Squads for young people, has field workers based in North and West Wales, and co-ordinates a number of literature development projects. It promotes an annual literary festival and runs a dedicated programme of literary activity. In addition, the Academi is in receipt of a lottery grant to publish the first *Encyclopaedia of Wales*. Associate membership: £15 p.a., £7.50 (unwaged). Founded 1959.

Acrylic Painters' Association, National (NAPA)
134 Rake Lane, Wallasey, Wirral, Merseyside CH45 1JW
tel 0151-639 2980 *fax* 0151-639 2980
web sites http://www.artarena force9.co.uk/napa
http://www.watercolor-online.com/napa
President Alwyn Crawshaw, *Vice-President* vacant, *Director/Founder* Kenneth J. Hodgson

Promotes interest in, and encourages excellence and innovation in, the work of painters in acrylic. Holds an annual open exhibition and regional shows: awards are made. Worldwide membership. Publishes a newsletter known as the International Napa Newspages. American Division established 1995. Membership: £20 p.a. (full), £15 p.a. (associate). Founded 1985.

Agricultural Journalists, Guild of
President Prof John Nix, *Chairman* Daphne MacCarthy, *Hon. General Secretary* Don Gomery, Charmwood, 47 Court Meadow, Rotherfield, East Sussex TN6 3LQ
tel (01892) 853187 *fax* (01892) 853551
e-mail don.gomery@farmline.com
web site http://www.gaj.org.uk

Established to promote a high standard among journalists who specialise in agricultural matters and to assist them to increase their sources of information and technical knowledge.

American Correspondents, Association of
President William Glauber
Secretary Sandra Marshall, Associated Press, 12 Norwich Street, London EC4A 1BP
tel 020-7353 1515 ext 4202 *fax* 020-7936 2229

American Publishers, Association of Inc.
71 Fifth Avenue, New York, NY 10003, USA
tel 212-255-0200 *fax* 212-255-7007
President and Ceo Patricia S. Schroeder
Founded 1970.

American Society of Composers, Authors and Publishers
One Lincoln Plaza, New York, NY 10023
tel 212-621-6000 *fax* 212-874 8480
President and Chairman Marilyn Bergman

American Society of Indexers (ASI)
11250 Roger Bacon Drive, Suite 8, Reston, VA 22090, USA
tel 703-437-4377 *fax* 703-435-4390
e-mail info@asindexing.org
web site http://www.asindexing.org
Aims to increase awareness of the value of high-quality indexes and indexing; offer members access to educational resources that enable them to strengthen their indexing performance; keep members up to date on indexing technology; defend and safeguard the professional interests of indexers.

Art and Design, National Society for Education in
The Gatehouse, Corsham Court, Corsham, Wilts. SN13 0BZ
tel (01249) 714825 *fax* (01249) 716138
web site http://www.nsead.org
General Secretary Dr John Steers NDD, ATC, DAE, PhD
The leading national authority concerned with art, craft and design across all phases of education in the UK. Offers the benefits of membership of a professional association, a learned society and a trade union. Has representatives on National and Regional Committees concerned with Art and Design Education. Publishes *Journal of Art and Design Education* (3 p.a.), (Blackwells). Founded 1888.

Art Club, New English
17 Carlton House Terrace, London SW1Y 5BD
tel 020-7930 6844 *fax* 020-7839 7830
Hon. Secretary Ken Howard RA
For all those interested in the art of painting, and the promotion of fine arts. Open Annual Exhibition at the Mall Galleries, The Mall, London SW1.

Art Historians, Association of (AAH)
70 Cowcross Street, London EC1M 6EJ
tel 020-7490 3211 *fax* 020-7490 3277
e-mail admin@aah.org.uk
web site http://www.aah.org.uk
Administrator Andrew Falconer
Formed to promote the study of art history and ensure wider public recognition of the field. Publishes *Art History* journal, *The Art Book* magazine, *Bulletin* newsletter. Annual conference and bookfair in March/April. Various options for personal membership, depending upon the choice of publications; special rates for students/unwaged; corporate membership available. Founded 1974.

Artists, Federation of British
17 Carlton House Terrace, London SW1Y 5BD
tel 020-7930 6844 *fax* 020-7839 7830
Administers 9 major National Art Societies at The Mall Galleries, The Mall, London SW1.

Artists, The International Guild of
Briargate, 2 The Brambles, Ilkley, West Yorkshire LS29 9DH
tel (01943) 609075
Director Leslie Simpson FRSA
Organises 4 seasonal exhibitions per year for 3 national societies: Society of Miniaturists, British Society of Painters in Oils, Pastels & Acrylics and British Watercolour Society. Promotes these 3 societies in countries outside the British Isles.

Artists Agents, Society of
21 Croftdown Road, London NW5 1EL
tel/fax 020-7424 0121
e-mail smptilly@compuserve.com
web site http://www.illustratorsagents.co.uk
Contact Sabine Tilly
Formed to promote professionalism in the illustration industry and to forge closer links between clients and artists through an agreed set of guidelines. The Society believes in an ethical approach through proper terms and conditions, thereby protecting the interests of the artists and clients. Founded 1992.

Artists Association of Ireland
43 Temple Bar, Dublin 2, Republic of Ireland
tel (01) 8740529 *fax* (01) 6771585
e-mail artists.ireland@indigo.ie
web site http://www.artistsireland.com
Executive Director Stella Coffey
Information and advice resource for professional visual artists in Ireland. Publishes *Art Bulletin* (6 p.a.), available on subscription. Annual membership: £35. Founded 1981.

Artists, Royal Birmingham Society of

Dakota House, St Paul's Square,
Birmingham B3 1SA
tel 0121-643 3768 *fax* 0121-644 5298 (until 6 Dec)

Society has its own galleries and rooms in the city centre. Members (RBSA) and Associates (ARBSA) are elected annually. Holds 3 Open Exhibitions: Oil & Sculpture (February), Watercolour & Crafts (May), Pastel & Drawing (December) – send sae for schedules, available 6 weeks prior to Exhibition. A further Open £1000 First Prize Exhibition is held (June/July) for works in any media. Other substantial money prizes can be won with no preference given to Members and Associates. Also an Exhibition of Printmakers (April), an Autumn Exhibition open to Members and Associates, and 2 Friends Exhibitions (February and August). Friends of the RBSA pay an annual subscription of £14, which entitles them to attend various functions and to submit work for the Annual Exhibitions.

Artists, Royal Society of British

17 Carlton House Terrace, London SW1Y 5BD
tel 020-7930 6844 *fax* 020-7839 7830
President Cav. Romeo di Girolamo, *Keeper* Alfred Daniels

Incorporated by Royal Charter for the purpose of encouraging the study and practice of the arts of painting, sculpture and architectural designs. Annual Open Exhibition at the Mall Galleries, The Mall, London SW1.

Arts Boards – see Regional Arts Boards

Arts Club

40 Dover Street, London W1X 3RB
tel 020-7499 8581 *fax* 020-7409 0913
Membership Secretary Ursula Keeling

For all those connected with or interested in the arts, literature and science. Founded 1863.

The Arts Council/An Chomhairle Ealaíon

Literature Officer, 70 Merrion Square, Dublin 2, Republic of Ireland
tel (01) 6611840 *fax* (01) 6761302
web site http://www.artscouncil.ie
Literature Officer Sinéad MacAodha, *Visual Arts Officer* Oliver Dowling

The national development agency for the arts in Ireland. Founded 1951.

Arts Council of England

14 Great Peter Street, London SW1P 3NQ
tel 020-7333 0100 *fax* 020-7973 6590
web site http://www.artscouncil.org.uk
Chairman Gerry Robinson, *Chief Executive* Peter Hewitt, *Executive Director of Arts* Kim Evans, *Director of Literature* Gary McKeone, *Director of Visual Arts* Marjorie Allthorpe-Guyton

To develop and improve the knowledge, understanding and practice of the arts, and to increase their accessibility to the public throughout England. The Council distributes public money from government and the lottery to artists and arts organisations, both directly and through the 10 Regional Arts Boards. The arts with which the Council is mainly concerned are dance, drama, literature, music and opera, collaborative arts, the visual arts, including new media, photography, architecture, crafts, and artists' film and video.

Within literature, 15 annual writers' awards are given competitively (see also page 513). Subsidies are provided to literary organisations and magazines, and schemes include support for translation, writers' residencies in prisons, tours by authors and the promotion of literature in libraries and education.

The Visual Arts Department is committed to the long-term improvement of visual artists' and makers' economic standing and working conditions in England. It now has responsibility for crafts and funds the Crafts Council. In collaboration with the Regional Arts Boards, which provide grants for the benefit of individual practitioners, it supports a number of national artists' agencies and promotes artists' professional development initiatives.

Arts Council of Northern Ireland

MacNeice House, 77 Malone Road,
Belfast BT9 6AQ
tel 028-9038 5200 *fax* 028-90661715
Chief Executive Brian Ferran, *Literature Officer* Ciaran Carson, *Visual Arts Officer* Paula Campbell

Promotes and encourages the arts throughout Northern Ireland. Artists in drama, dance, music and jazz, literature, the visual arts, traditional arts and community arts, can apply for support for specific schemes and projects. The value of the grant will be set according to the aims of the application. Applicants must have contributed regularly to the artistic activities of the community, with residency of at least one year in Northern Ireland.

Arts Council of Wales
9 Museum Place, Cardiff CF10 3NX
tel 029-2037 6500 *fax* 029-2022 1447
e-mail information@ccc-acw.org.uk
web site http://www.ccc-acw.org.uk
Chairman Sybil Crouch, *Chief Executive* Joanna Weston, *Senior Literature Officer* Tony Bianchi, *Senior Officer: Dance and Drama* Anna Holmes, *Senior Visual Arts and Crafts Officer* John Hambley
National organisation with specific responsibility for the funding and development of the arts in Wales. ACW receives grants from central and local government; also distributes the National Lottery funds in Wales. From these resources, ACW makes grants to support arts activity and facilities. Some of the funds are allocated in the form of annual revenue grants to full-time arts organisations; also operates schemes which provide financial and other forms of support for individual activities or projects. Undertakes this work in both the English and Welsh languages.

North Wales Regional Office
36 Princes Drive, Colwyn Bay LL29 8LA
tel (01492) 533440 *fax* (01492) 533677

West Wales Regional Office
6 Gardd Llydaw, Jackson Lane, Carmarthen SA31 1QD
tel (01267) 234248 *fax* (01267) 233084

Asian Affairs, The Royal Society for
2 Belgrave Square, London SW1X 8PJ
tel 020-7235 5122 *fax* 020-7259 6771
e-mail info@rsaa.org.uk
web site http://www.rsaa.org.uk
President The Lord Denman CBE, MC, TD, *Chairman of Council* Sir Donald Hawley KCMG, MBE, *Secretary* David Easton MA, FRSA, FRGS
For the study of all Asia past and present; fortnightly lectures, etc; library. Publishes *Asian Affairs* (3 p.a.), free to members. Subscription: £55 London, £45 more than 60 miles from London and overseas, Junior Members (to 25) £10. Founded 1901.

Aslib (The Association for Information Management)
Staple Hall, Stone House Court, London EC3A 7PB
tel 020-7903 0000 *fax* 020-7903 0011
e-mail aslib@aslib.com
web site http://www.aslib.com
Ceo Roger Bowes
Actively promotes best practice in the management of information resources. It represents its members and lobbies on all aspects of the management of and legislation concerning information at local, national and international levels. Aslib provides consultancy and information services, professional development training, conferences, specialist recruitment, and publishes primary and secondary journals, conference proceedings, Directories and monographs. Founded 1924.

The Jane Austen Society
Secretary Mrs Susan McCartan, Carton House, Redwood Lane, Medstead, Alton, Hants GU34 5PE
tel/fax (01420) 562469
e-mail janeaustensoc@freeuk.com
web site http://www.janeaustensociety.org.uk
Founded in 1940 to promote interest in, and enjoyment of, Jane Austen's novels and letters. Twelve branches in UK. Membership: UK £10, life £150; overseas £12, life £180.

Australia Council
PO Box 788, Strawberry Hills, NSW 2012, Australia
located at 372 Elizabeth Street, Surry Hills, NSW 2010
tel (02) 9215 9000 *fax* (02) 9215 9111
e-mail mail@ozco.gov.au
web site http://www.ozco.gov.au
Chairperson Dr Margaret Seares
Provides a broad range of support for the arts in Australia, embracing music, theatre, literature, visual arts, crafts, Aboriginal arts, community and new media arts. It has 8 major Funds: Literature, Visual Arts/Craft, Music, Theatre, Dance, New Media, Community Cultural Development, Major Organisations, as well as the Aboriginal and Torres Strait Islander Arts Board.

The Literature Fund's chief objective is to support the writing of all forms of creative literature – novels, short stories, poetry, plays and literary non-fiction. It also assists with the publication of literary magazines, has a book publishing subsidies programme, and initiates and supports projects of many kinds designed to promote Australian literature both within Australia and abroad.

Australian Library and Information Association

PO Box E441, Kingston, ACT 2604, Australia
tel (02) 6285 1877 *fax* (02) 6282 2249
e-mail enquiry@alia.org.au
web site http://www.alia.org.au/
Executive Director Jennefer Nicholson

Aims to promote and improve the services of libraries and other information agencies; to improve the standard of library and information personnel and foster their professional interests; to represent the interests of members to governments, other organisations and the community; and to encourage people to contribute to the improvement of library and information services by supporting the association.

Australian Publishers Association (APA)

89 Jones Street, Ultimo, NSW 2007, Australia
tel (02) 9281 9788 *fax* (02) 9281 1073
e-mail apa@magna.com.au
web site http://www.publishers.asn.au

The Australian Society of Authors

PO Box 1566, Strawberry Hills, NSW 2012, Australia
located at 98 Pitt Street, Redfern, NSW 2016, Australia
tel (02) 9318 0877 *fax* (02) 9318 0530
e-mail asa@asauthors.org
web site http://www.asauthors.org
Executive Director José Borginho

Authors, The Society of

84 Drayton Gardens, London SW10 9SB
tel 020-7373 6642
e-mail authorsoc@writers.org.uk
web site http://www.writers.org.uk/society
Chairman Deborah Moggach, *General Secretary* Mark Le Fanu

Founded in 1884 by Sir Walter Besant with the object of representing, assisting and protecting authors. A limited company and independent trade union, the Society's scope has been continuously extended; specialist associations have been created for translators, broadcasters, educational, medical and children's writers and illustrators (details are elsewhere in this *Yearbook*). Members are entitled to legal as well as general advice in connection with their work, their contracts, their choice of a publisher, problems with publishers, broadcasting organisations, etc. Annual subscription: £75 (£70 by direct debit) with reductions available to authors under 35 or over 65. Full particulars of membership from the Society's offices (see also page 507).

Authors' Agents, The Association of

President Jonathan Lloyd, *Vice President* Julian Alexander, *Treasurer* Barbara Levy
Secretary Meg Davis, 62 Grafton Way, London W1P 5LD
tel 020-7387 2076 *fax* 020-7387 2042

Maintains a code of professional practice to which all members commit themselves; holds regular meetings to discuss matters of common professional interest; and provides a vehicle for representing the view of authors' agents in discussion of matters of common interest with other professional bodies. Founded 1974.

Authors' Club (at the Arts Club)

40 Dover Street, London W1X 3RB
tel 020-7499 8581 *fax* 020-7409 0913
Secretary Ann de La Grange

Founded by Sir Walter Besant, the Authors' Club welcomes as members writers, publishers, critics, journalists, academics and anyone involved with literature. Administers the Authors' Club Best First Novel Award and the Sir Banister Fletcher Award. Membership: apply to Secretary. Founded 1891.

Authors' Licensing and Collecting Society Ltd (ALCS)

Marlborough Court, 14-18 Holborn, London EC1N 2LE
tel 020-7395 0600 *fax* 020-7395 0660
e-mail alcs@alcs.co.uk
web site http://www.alcs.co.uk
Chief Executive Dafydd Wyn Phillips

ALCS is the British rights management society for all writers. It is a non-profit, non-union organisation owned by writers. Its principal business is to distribute fees for secondary use to writers whose work has been photocopied, broadcast or recorded. Since its foundation ALCS has paid writers over £60 million in fees, most of which they would not have been able to collect independently.

The monies collected by ALCS are often difficult, time-consuming and sometimes legally impossible for individuals or their agents to claim. However, authors can receive their fees quickly and cost-effectively by mandating ALCS to administer on their behalf those rights which they cannot exercise as an individual, or which are best handled on a collective basis. Through its network of international contacts, and reciprocal agreements with foreign collecting societies, the ALCS is able to maximise the amount of revenue authors receive.

The main aims of ALCS are:

- to ensure hard-to-collect revenues due to authors are efficiently collected and speedily distributed;
- to protect and promote authors rights;
- to campaign for the establishment of collective rights schemes by statute and voluntary agreement;
- to identify and develop new sources of income for writers; and
- to foster an awareness of intellectual property issues among the UK writing community and beyond.

It is financed primarily by a commission levied on distributions. Further income is derived from rights and media services, licensing activities and membership fees.

ALCS is internationally recognised as a leading authority on copyright matters and authors' collective interests. It maintains a watching brief on all matters affecting copyright both in the UK and abroad, making representations to UK government authorities and the European Union.

ALCS members are writers of all kinds and their heirs. Subscription: £7.50 (inc. VAT) UK residents; £7.50 EEA and EFTA country residents; £10 other overseas residents. Members of the Society of Authors and/or the Writers' Guild of Great Britain receive free membership. Rightsholders who do not fulfil the membership criteria may also receive payments from ALCS, but are subject to a higher rate of commission. Registration forms and further information may be obtained from the Membership Secretary or the ALCS web site. Founded 1977.

Authors' Representatives Inc., Association of

PO Box 237201, Ansonia Station, New York, NY 10023, USA
tel 212-252-3695
web site http://www.aar-online.org

Founded 1991.

Aviation Artists, The Guild of

(incorporating the Society of Aviation Artists)
The Bondway Business Centre, 71 Bondway, Vauxhall Cross, London SW8 1SQ
tel/fax 020-7735 0634
President Michael Turner PGAvA, *Secretary* Ian Burnstock

Formed in 1971 to promote aviation art through the organisation of exhibitions and meetings. Holds annual open exhibition in July in London; £1000 for 'Aviation Painting of the Year'. quarterly members' journal. Associates £40, Members £55 (by invitation), non-exhibiting artists and friends £20.

AXIS

Visual Arts Information Service, Leeds Metropolitan University, 8 Queen Square, Leeds LS2 8AJ
tel 0113-245 7946 *fax* 0113-245 7950
Axis Information Service 0930-170130 (UK only 50p/min)
e-mail axis@lmu.ac.uk
web site http://www.axisartists.org.uk

Provides information on contemporary artists and makers living/working in Britain to national and international clients. The Axis database features 11,000+ images by over 3000 artists (professionals and recent graduates). The database can be accessed in 4 different ways: on CD-Rom, on-line, at Axispoint host organisations throughout the UK, and on the Axis Information Service line. Printouts of artist CVs, artwork images, and contact details are available to potential buyers, commissioners, exhibitors and collaborators. Axis receives funding from the Arts Councils of England, Scotland and Wales, and 7 Regional Arts Boards. Founded 1991.

BAPLA (British Association of Picture Libraries and Agencies)

18 Vine Hill, London EC1R 5DZ
tel 020-7713 1780 *fax* 020-7713 1211
e-mail enquiries@bapla.org.uk
web site http://www.bapla.org.uk
Chief Executive Linda Royles

Represents the interests of the British picture library industry. Works on UK and worldwide levels on issues such as copyright, industry statistics and technology. It offers researchers free telephone referrals from its database, and through its web site, from over 380 members.

Publishes a *Directory*, the definitive guide to UK picture libraries, and *Light Box* (quarterly) magazine. Founded 1975.

BASCA (British Academy of Songwriters, Composers and Authors) – **see British Academy of Composers and Songwriters**

The Beckford Society
Secretary Sidney Blackmore, 15 Healey Street, London NW1 8SR
tel 020-7267 7750 *fax* (01985) 213239
e-mail sidney.blackmore@btinternet.com

Aims to promote an interest in the life and works of William Beckford of Fonthill (1760-1844) and his circle. Encourages Beckford studies and scholarship through exhibitions, lectures and publications, including *The Beckford Journal* (annual) and occasional newsletters. Annual subscription: £10 minimum. Founded 1995.

Thomas Lovell Beddoes Society
11 Laund Nook, Belper, Derbyshire DE56 1GY
tel (01773) 828066
e-mail tlbeddoes@tlbeddoes.force9.co.uk
web site http://www.nortexinfo.net/mcdaniel/tlb.htm

Aims to promote an interest in the life and works of Thomas Lovell Beddoes (1803-1849). The Society promotes and undertakes Beddoes studies, and disseminates and publishes useful research. Founded 1994.

Beer Writers, British Guild of
Secretary Barry Bremner
tel (01462) 685844 *fax* (01462) 685783
e-mail bsb@tccnet.co.uk

Aims to improve standards in beer writing and at the same time extend public knowledge of beers and brewing. The Gold and Silver Tankard Awards are given annually to writers and broadcasters judged to have made the most valuable contribution to this end. Publishes a directory of members with details of their publications and their particular areas of interest, which is circulated to the media. Subscription: £40.00 p.a. Founded 1988.

The E.F. Benson Society
The Old Coach House, High Street, Rye, East Sussex TN31 7JF
tel (01797) 223114
Secretary Allan Downend

To promote interest in the author E.F. Benson and the Benson family. Arranges annual literary evening, annual outing to Rye (July), talks on the Bensons and exhibitions. Archive includes the Austin Seckersen Collection, transcriptions of the Benson diaries and letters. Publishes postcards, anthologies of Benson's works, a Benson biography and an annual journal, *The Dodo*. Also sells out-of-print Bensons to members. Annual subscription: £7.50 single, £8.50 2 people at same address, £12.50 overseas. Founded 1984.

E.F. Benson: The Tilling Society
5 Friars Bank, Guestling, Hastings TN35 4EJ
Secretaries Cynthia and Tony Reavell

To bring together enthusiasts, wherever they may live, for E.F. Benson and his Mapp & Lucia novels; annual gathering in Rye. Publishes 2 lengthy newsletters p.a. Annual subscription: £8, overseas £10; full starters membership (including all back newsletters) £28, overseas £32. Founded 1982.

Bibliographical Society
c/o Wellcome Library, 183 Euston Road, London NW1 2BE
tel 020-7611 7244 *fax* 020-7611 8703
e-mail jm93@dial.pipex.com
President D. McKitterick, *Hon. Secretary* D. Pearson

Acquisition and dissemination of information upon subjects connected with historical bibliography. Founded 1892.

The Blackpool Art Society
The Studio, Wilkinson Avenue, Blackpool FY3 9HB
President Don Ruther ARPS
Hon. Secretary Denise Fergyson, 1 Thirlmere Avenue, Carleton, Poulton-le-Fylde, Lancs. FY6 7NF
tel (01253) 884645

Summer and autumn exhibition (members' work only). Studio meetings, practicals, lectures, etc, out-of-door sketching, workshops. Founded 1884.

Book Trust
Book House, 45 East Hill, London SW18 2QZ
tel 020-8516 2977 *fax* 020-8516 2978
Chair Jane Carr, *Director* Chris Meade

Book Trust exists to open up the world of books and reading to people of all ages and cultures. Its services include the Book Information Service, a unique, specialist information and research service for all queries on books and reading (business callers are charged via a premium rate telephone service and should phone 0906-516 1193; calls are charged at £1.50 per minute). Book Trust administers a number of literary prizes, including the Booker Prize and produces a wide range of books, pamphlets and leaflets designed to make books more easily accessible to the public. Founded 1925 as the National Book Council.

Young Book Trust
The arm of Book Trust concerned with children's literature, YBT provides practical help and advice on all aspects of children's books and reading. An on-site collection of children's literature contains the vast majority of titles published in the UK during the last 2 years. Subscribers receive copies of all Young Book Trust publications, information, posters, etc, plus author information, Book Week material and book lists. YBT produces a termly children's book magazine, ideal for schools, libraries, booksellers and publishers. Annual YBT subscription: £36.50 plus VAT. Book Trust also coordinates the national Bookstart (books for babies) programme.

Books Across the Sea
The English-Speaking Union of the Commonwealth, Dartmouth House, 37 Charles Street, London W1X 8AB
tel 020-7493 3328 *fax* 020-7495 6108
e-mail esu@esu.org
web site http://www.esu.org
The English Speaking Union of the United States, 16 East 69th Street, New York, NY 10021, USA
tel 212-879-6800 *fax* 212-772-2886
World voluntary organisation devoted to the promotion of international understanding and friendship. Exchanges books with its corresponding BAS Committees in New York, Russia and Australia. The books are selected to reflect the life and culture of each country and the best of its recent publishing and writing. New selections are announced by bulletin, *The Ambassador Booklist.*

The Booksellers Association of the United Kingdom and Ireland Ltd
272 Vauxhall Bridge Road, London SW1V 1BA
tel 020-7834 5477 *fax* 020-7834 8812
e-mail mail@booksellers.org.uk
Chief Executive T.E. Godfray
Founded 1895.

The George Borrow Society
Hon. Secretary Dr James H. Reading, The Gables, 112 Irchester Road, Rushden, Northants. NN10 9XQ
tel/fax (01933) 312965
Promotes knowledge of the life and works of George Borrow (1803-81), traveller and author. Publishes *Bulletin* (bi-annual). Annual membership: £10. Founded 1991.

Botanical Artists, The Society of
Founder President Suzanne Lucas FLS, PRMS, FPSBA, *Hon. Treasurer* Pamela Davis, *Executive Vice President* Margaret Stevens
Executive Secretary Mrs Pam Henderson, 1 Knapp Cottages, Wyke, Gillingham, Dorset SP8 4NQ
tel (01747) 825718, 020-7222 2723 (during exhibitions)
e-mail hendersons@dial.pipex.com
web site http://www.soc-botanical-artists.org
Aims to encourage the art of botanical painting. Membership through selection. Annual Open Exhibition held in May at the Westminster Gallery, Westminster Central Hall, Storey's Gate, London SW1H 9NH; hand in end March. Information and entrance forms available from the Executive Secretary from January, on receipt of sae. Membership: £90; lay members £20. Founded 1985.

British Academy
10 Carlton House Terrace, London SW1Y 5AH
tel 020-7969 5200 *fax* 020-7969 5300
e-mail secretary@britac.ac.uk
web site http://www.britac.ac.uk
President Sir Tony Wrigley, *Vice-Presidents* Prof H.C.G. Matthew, Prof R.J.P. Kain *Treasurer* Mr J.S. Flemming, *Foreign Secretary* Prof C.N.J. Mann, *Publications Secretary* Prof F.G.B. Millar, *Secretary* P.W.H. Brown CBE
The national Academy for the humanities and social sciences: an independent and self-governing fellowship of scholars, elected for distinction and achievement in one or more branches of the academic disciplines that make up the humanities and social sciences. Its primary purpose is to promote research and scholarship in those areas: through research grants and other awards, the sponsorship of a number of research projects and of research institutes overseas; the award of prizes and medals; and the publication both of sponsored lectures and seminar papers and of fundamental texts and research aids prepared under

the direction of Academy committees. It also acts as a forum for the discussion of issues of interest and concern to scholars in the humanities and the social sciences, and it provides advice to the Government and other public bodies. Founded 1901.

British Academy of Composers and Songwriters

(incorporating the Association of Professional Composers, The British Academy of Songwriters, Composers and Authors, and The Composers' Guild of Great Britain)
British Music House, 25-27 Berners Street, London W1P 3DB
tel 020-7636 2929 *fax* 020-7636 2212
e-mail info@britishacademy.com
web site http://www.britishacademy.com
Contact Chris Green (Chief Executive)

The Academy represents the interests of composers and songwriters across all genres, providing advice on professional and artistic matters. It administers a number of major awards and events, including the prestigious Ivor Novello Awards, and publishes *The Works* magazine (quarterly), which is available to non-members on subscription.

British Academy of Film and Television Arts (BAFTA)

Executive Director John Morrell, 195 Piccadilly, London W1V 0LN
tel 020-7734 0022 *fax* 020-7437 0473
e-mail jmorrell@bafta.org
web site http://www.bafta.org

The pre-eminent organisation in the UK for film, TV and interactive entertainment, recognising and promoting the achievement and endeavour of industry practitioners. BAFTA Awards are awarded annually by members to their peers in recognition of their skills and expertise. The Academy's premises provide club facilities with a 200-seat cinema and 40-seat preview theatre. Provides a full and varied programme of industry-related events, masterclasses, seminars and panel discussions, which are open to both members and non-members. Membership: £165 p.a., £80 (age under 30), £75 (overseas). Founded 1947.

British American Arts Association (BAAA) – see Centre for Creative Communities

The British Council

10 Spring Gardens, London SW1A 2BN
tel 020-7930 8466 *fax* 020-7839 6347
web site http://www.britcoun.org/
Chair Baroness Helena Kennedy, *Director-General* David Green, *Director of Literature* Alastair Niven, *Director, Arts Group* Paul Smith

The British Council promotes Britain abroad, by providing access to British ideas, talent and experience in education and training, books and the English language, information, the arts, the sciences and technology. The Council is an authority on teaching English as a second or foreign language and gives advice and information on curriculum, methodology, materials and testing. It also promotes British literature overseas through writers' tours, academic visits, seminars and exhibitions. The Council works in 110 countries where it runs over 225 libraries and resource centres and 135 teaching centres.

The Council's lending and reference libraries throughout the world stock material appropriate to the Council's priorities in individual countries. Where appropriate the libraries act as showcases for the latest British publications. They vary in size from small reference collections and information centres to comprehensive libraries equipped with reference works, CD-Rom, on-line facilities and a selection of British periodicals. Bibliographies of British books on special subjects are prepared on request.

The Council organises book and electronic publishing exhibitions for showing overseas, ranging from small specialist displays to larger exhibitions at major international book fairs such as Frankfurt.

The Council publishes *New Writing*, an annual anthology; a series of literary bibliographies, including *The Novel in Britain since 1970*; *Contemporary Writers*, a series of over 30 pamphlets on modern British writers; and exhibitions on literary topics such as translation. A catalogue is available on request.

The Visual Arts Department, part of the Council's Arts Division, develops and enlarges overseas knowledge and appreciation of British achievement in the fields of painting, sculpture, printmaking, design, photography, the crafts and architecture, working closely with the

Council's overseas offices and with professional colleagues in Britain and abroad.

The Council helps manage book aid projects for developing countries. In 2000/2001 the Council also supported over 3000 events in the visual arts, film and TV, drama, literature, dance and music, ranging from the classical to the contemporary.

Further information about the work of the British Council is available from the Press and Public Relations Department at the headquarters in London or from British Council offices and libraries overseas.

British Film Institute (BFI)

21 Stephen Street, London W1P 2LN
tel 020-7255 1444 *fax* 020-7436 0439
24-hour BFI Events Line 0870-240 4050
web site http://www.bfi.org.uk
Chair Joan Bakewell CBE, *Director* Jon Teckman

Offers opportunities to experience, enjoy and discover more about the world of film and TV. Its 3 main departments are:

• BFI Education comprises the BFI National Library, BFI Publishing, *Sight and Sound* magazine and BFI Education Projects, which encourages a life-long learning about the moving image;
• BFI Exhibition runs the National Film Theatre on London's South Bank and the annual London Film Festival, and supports local cinemas and festivals UK-wide;
• BFI Collections preserves the UK's moving image heritage and promotes access to it through a variety of means, including film, video and DVD releases and touring exhibitions. The BFI also runs the BFI London IMAX® Cinema at Waterloo, featuring the UK's largest screen. Founded 1933.

British Interactive Multimedia Association (BIMA)

5-6 Clipstone Street, London W1P 7EB
tel 020-7436 8250 *fax* 020-7436 8251
e-mail enquiries@bima.co.uk
web site http://www.bima.co.uk
Office Administrator Janice Cable

BIMA was established to promote a wider understanding of the benefits of interactive multimedia to industry, government and education and to provide a regular forum for the exchange of views amongst members. Membership is open to any organisation or individual with an interest in multimedia. Publishes regular newsletters. Membership: commercial £650; institutional £300; individual £150. Founded 1984.

Broadcasting Entertainment Cinematograph and Theatre Union (BECTU), Writers Section

111 Wardour Street, London W1V 4AY
tel 020-7437 8506 *fax* 020-7437 8268
e-mail mgoodman@bectu.org.uk
web site http://www.bectu.org.uk
Assistant General Secretary Marilyn Goodman, *General Secretary* R. Bolton

To defend the interests of writers in film, TV and radio. By virtue of its industrial strength, the Union is able to help its writer members to secure favourable terms and conditions. In cases of disputes with employers, the Union can intervene in order to ensure an equitable settlement. Its production agreement with PACT lays down minimum terms for writers working in the documentary area. Founded 1946.

Broadcasting Group

84 Drayton Gardens,
London SW10 9SB
tel 020-7373 6642

Specialist group within the Society of Authors (see page 507) for radio and TV writers and others involved in broadcasting.

The Brontë Society

Membership Secretary, The Brontë Parsonage Museum, Haworth, Keighley,
West Yorkshire BD22 8DR
tel (01535) 642323 *fax* (01535) 647131
e-mail bronte@bronte.prestel.co.uk
web site http://www.bronte.org.uk

Examination, preservation, illustration of the memoirs and literary remains of the Brontë family; exhibitions of MSS and other subjects. Publishes *The Transactions of the Brontë Society* (bi-annual) and *The Brontë Gazette* (bi-annual). Its Museum is open throughout the year.

The Browning Society

Secretary Ralph Ensz, 163 Wembley Hill Road, Wembley Park, Middlesex HA9 8EL
tel 020-8904 8401
web site http://www.ucl.ac.uk/~uclesle

Aims to widen the appreciation and understanding of the lives and poetry of Robert Browning and Elizabeth Barrett Browning, and other Victorian writers and poets. Membership: £15. Founded 1881; refounded 1969.

The John Buchan Society

Membership Secretary Russell Paterson, Limpsfield, 16 Ranfurly Road, Bridge of Weir, Renfrewshire PA11 3EL
tel (01505) 613116

Promotes a wider understanding and appreciation of the life and works of John Buchan. Encourages publication of a complete annotated edition of Buchan's works, and supports the John Buchan Centre and Museum at Broughton, Borders. Holds regular meetings and social gatherings; produces a Newsletter and a Journal. Annual subscription: £10 full/overseas; other rates on application. Founded 1979.

Byron Society (International)

Byron House, 6 Gertrude Street, London SW10 0JN
tel 020-7352 5112 *fax* 020-7352 1226
Hon. Director Mrs Elma Dangerfield OBE

To promote research into the life and works of Lord Byron by seminars, discussions, lectures and readings. Publishes *The Byron Journal* (annual, £5 plus postage). Annual subscription: £20. Founded 1971.

Randolph Caldecott Society

Secretary Kenn Oultram, Clatterwick House, Little Leigh, Northwich, Cheshire CW8 4RJ
tel (01606) 891303 (office), 781731 (evening)

To encourage an interest in the life and works of Randolph Caldecott, the Victorian artist, illustrator and sculptor. Meetings held in Chester and London. Annual subscription: £7-£10. Founded 1983.

Canada, Writers Guild of

123 Edward Street, Suite 1225, Toronto, Ontario M5G 1EZ, Canada
tel 416-979-7907 *toll free* 1-800-567-9974
fax 416-979-9273
e-mail info@writersguildofcanada.com
web site http://www.writersguildofcanada.com
Executive Director Maureen Parker

To further the professional, creative and economic rights and interests of writers in film, TV, radio and multimedia and all recorded media; to promote full freedom of expression and communication, and to oppose censorship unequivocally. Annual membership: $150, plus 2% of fees earned in the Guild's jurisdiction.

Canada, The Writers' Union of

24 Ryerson Avenue, Toronto, Ontario M5T 2P3, Canada
tel 416-703-8982 *fax* 416-703-0826
e-mail twuc@the-wire.com
web site http://www.swifty.com/twuc

Canadian Authors Association

PO Box 419, Campbellford, Ontario K0L 1L0, Canada
tel 705-653-0323 *fax* 705-653-0593
e-mail canauth@redden.on.ca
web site http://www.CanAuthors.org/national.html
President Gillian Foss, *Administrator* Alec McEachern

Canadian Magazine Publishers Association

130 Spadina Avenue, Suite 202, Toronto, Ontario M5V 2L4, Canada
tel 416-504-0274 *fax* 416-504-0437
e-mail cmpainfo@cmpa.ca
web site http://www.cmpa.ca
Executive Director Mark Jamison

Founded 1973.

Canadian Poets, League of

54 Wolseley Street, 3rd Floor, Toronto, Ontario M5T 1A5, Canada
tel 416-504-1657 *fax* 416-504 0096
e-mail league@ican.net
web site http://www.poets.ca
Executive Director Edita Petrauskaite

To promote the interests of poets and to advance Canadian poetry in Canada and abroad. Administers 3 annual awards; runs an annual poetry competition, a Canadian chapbook manuscript competition, and a youth poetry competition; publishes a newsletter and *Poetry Markets for Canadians, Who's Who in The League of Canadian Poets, Poets in the Classroom* (teaching guide), *Vintage* (contest anthology). Promotes and sells members' poetry books. Founded 1966.

Canadian Publishers, Association of

110 Eglinton Avenue West, Suite 401, Toronto, Ontario M4R 1A3, Canada
tel 416-487-6116 *fax* 416-487-8815
e-mail info@canbook.org
web site http://www.publishers.ca
Executive Director Monique Smith

Founded 1976; formerly Independent Publishers Association, 1971.

Canadian Publishers' Council

250 Merton Street, Suite 203, Toronto, Ontario M4S 1B1, Canada
tel 416-322-7011 *fax* 416-322-6999
e-mail pubadmin@pubcouncil.ca
web site http://www.pubcouncil.ca
Executive Director Jacqueline Hushion

Career Development Group
(formerly Association of Assistant Librarians)
c/o The Library Association, 7 Ridgmount Street, London WC1E 7AE
President Anne Partridge BSc, MSc
Hon. Secretary Joanna Ball BA, MA, ALA

Publishes bibliographical aids, the journal *Impact*, works on librarianship; and runs educational courses. Founded 1895.

Careers Writers' Association
Membership Secretary Barbara Buffton, 71 Wimborne Road, Colehill, Wimborne, Dorset BH21 2RP
tel/fax (01202) 880320
e-mail Barbara.Buffton@wsmail.co.uk

Society for established writers on the inter-related topics of education, training and careers. Holds occasional meetings on subjects of interest to members, and circulates details of members to information providers. Annual membership: £20. Founded 1979.

(Daresbury) Lewis Carroll Society
Secretary Kenn Oultram, Clatterwick House, Little Leigh, Northwich, Cheshire CW8 4RJ
tel (01606) 891303 (office), 781731 (evening)

To encourage an interest in the life and works of Lewis Carroll, author of *Alice's Adventures*. Meetings at Carroll's birth village (Daresbury, Cheshire). Elects an annual 'Alice'. Annual subscription: £5. Founded 1970.

The Lewis Carroll Society
Secretary Alan White, 69 Cromwell Road, Hertford, Herts. SG13 7DP
e-mail alanwhite@tesco.net
web site http://aznet.co.uk/lcs

To promote interest in the life and works of Lewis Carroll (Revd Charles Lutwidge Dodgson) and to encourage research. Activities include regular meetings, exhibitions, and a publishing programme that includes the first annotated, unexpurgated edition of his diaries in 9 volumes, the Society's journal *The Carrollian* (2 p.a.), a newsletter, *Bandersnatch* (quarterly) and the *Lewis Carroll Review* (occasional). Annual subscription: £13 (UK), £15 (Europe), £17 (elsewhere); special rates for institutions. Founded 1969.

Cartoonists Club of Great Britain
Secretary Terry Christien, 46 Strawberry Vale, Twickenham TW1 4SE
tel 020-8892 3621 *fax* 020-8891 5946
e-mail terry@cartoonology.com

Aims to encourage social contact between members and endeavours to promote the professional standing and prestige of cartoonists. Fee on joining: full, provisional, or associate £40; thereafter annual fee £25.

Centerprise Literature Development Project
Centerprise Trust, 136-138 Kingsland High Street, London E8 2NS
tel 020-7254 9632 ext. 211, 214
fax 020-7923 1951
e-mail cldd@cnpr.demon.co.uk
New Writing Eva Lewin, *Black Literature* Catherine Johnson

An advice and resource centre for writers of fiction and poetry, servicing Central, East and North London. Runs courses and workshops in creative writing, organises poetry and book readings, discussions and debates on literary and relevant issues, writers' surgeries, and telephone information on resources for writers in London. Publishes *Calabash* newsletter for Writers of Black and Asian origin. Funded by London Arts Board. See also page 575. Founded 1995.

Centre for Creative Communities (CCC)
118 Commercial Street, London E1 6NF
tel 020-7247 5385 *fax* 020-7247 5256
e-mail info@creativecommunities.org.uk
Director Jennifer Williams

A non-profit-making organisation working in the field of arts, education and community development. Conducts research, organises conferences, produces a quarterly newsletter and is part of an international network of arts and education organisations. As well as a specialised arts, education and community development library, it has a more general library holding information on opportunities for artists and performers both in the UK and abroad. CCC is not a grant-giving organisation.

The Raymond Chandler Society
UK contact Simon Beckett, 6 Barkers Road, Nether Edge, Sheffield S7 1SE
tel/fax 0114-255 6302
e-mail william.adamson@zsp.uni-ulm.de

Promotes the works of Raymond Chandler (1888-1959) and his influence and reception within a historical and contemporary context, as well as the genre of the crime novel in general. Publishes the *Chandler Yearbook*, a scholarly publication containing reviews and articles on crime writing in both English and German. Based in Germany with an international membership. Organises the Chandler symposium, usually held in Germany in July. Membership: £15 p.a. (£7 concessions). Founded 1991.

The Chesterton Society

Hon. Secretary Robert Hughes KHS,
11 Lawrence Leys, Bloxham, Nr Banbury,
Oxon OX15 4NU
tel (01295) 720869

To promote interest in the life and work of G.K. Chesterton and those associated with him or influenced by his writings. Two lectures a year. Publishes the *Chesterton Quarterly Review* (4 p.a.). Subscription: £12.50 p.a. Founded 1974.

Children's Book Circle

c/o Susan Barry, The Watts Publishing Group Ltd,
96 Leonard Street, London EC2A 4XD
tel 020-7739 2929 *fax* 020-7739 2318
e-mail susan.barry@wattspub.co.uk
Membership Secretary Jonathan Douglas
tel 020-7255 0636

Provides a discussion forum for anybody involved with children's books. Monthly meetings are addressed by a panel of invited speakers and topics focus on current and controversial issues. Holds the annual Patrick Hardy lecture and administers the Eleanor Farjeon Award. Annual membership: £15 if working inside M25; outside £12. Founded 1962.

Children's Books History Society

Secretary Mrs Pat Garrett, 25 Field Way,
Hoddesdon, Herts. EN11 0QN
tel/fax (01992) 464885
e-mail cbhs@abcgarrett.demon.co.uk

Aims 'to promote an appreciation of children's books, and to study their history, bibliography and literary content'. Holds approx. 6 meetings and produces 3 substantial *Newsletters* and an occasional paper per year. The Harvey Darton Award is given biennially for a book that extends knowledge of British children's literature of the past. Subscription: £10 p.a.; overseas rates on application. Founded 1969.

Children's Writers and Illustrators Group

84 Drayton Gardens, London SW10 9SB
tel 020-7373 6642

Subsidiary group for writers and illustrators of children's books, who are members of the Society of Authors (see page 507).

Christian Literature, United Society for

Albany House, 67 Sydenham Road, Guildford,
Surrey GU1 3RY
tel (01483) 888580 *fax* (01483) 888581
e-mail feedtheminds@gn.apc.org
Chairman John Clark, *General Secretary* Dr Alwyn Marriage

To aid Christian literature principally in the world's poorest countries. Founded 1799.

Christian Writers, Association of

Administrator W.G. Crawford, 73 Lodge Hill
Road, Farnham, Surrey GU10 3RB
tel (01252) 715746

Aims to see the quality of writing in every area of the media, either overtly Christian or shaped by a Christian perspective, reaching the widest range of people across the UK and beyond. To inspire and equip people to use their talents and skills with integrity to devise, write and market excellent material which comes from a Christian world view. Membership: £17 p.a. (direct debit £15). Founded 1971.

Agatha Christie Society

PO Box 1896, Radio City Station, New York,
NY 10101-1896, USA
e-mail agathaus@aol.com
Director Kate Stine

To promote communication between the fans of Agatha Christie and the various media who bring her works to the public. Publishes newsletters (4 p.a.). Annual subscription: £12.50 (UK), £15 (Europe), $24 (USA), £15 (rest of world). Founded 1993.

Civil Service Authors, Society of

Secretary Mrs J.M. Hykin, 4 Top Street,
Wing, Nr Oakham, Rutland LE15 8SE

Aims to encourage authorship by present and past members of the Civil Service (and some other public service bodies). Holds annual competitions for poetry, short stories, autobiography, etc, open to members only, and annual 'Writer of the Year' award. Publishes *The Civil Service Author* magazine, free to members; subscription £15 p.a. Poetry Workshop offers newsletter, weekend, anthology; subscription additional £3.

The John Clare Society

The Stables, 1A West Street, Helpston, Peterborough PE6 7DU
tel (01733) 252678
web site http://vzone.virgin.net/linda.curry/jclaresociety.htm

Promotes a wider appreciation of the life and works of the poet John Clare. Annual subscription: £9.50 (UK individual); other rates (including overseas) on application. Founded 1981.

Classical Association

Secretary (Council) Dr M. Schofield, St John's College, Cambridge CB2 1TP
Publicity Officer Dr J. March, PO Box 38, Alresford, Hants SO24 0ZQ
Administrator Clare Roberts, Senate House, Malet Street, London WC1E 7HU
tel 020-7862 8706 *fax* 020-7802 8729
e-mail croberts@sas.ac.uk
web site http://www.sas.ac.uk/icls/classass

To promote and sustain interest in classical studies, to maintain their rightful position in universities and schools, and to give scholars and teachers opportunities for meeting and discussing their problems.

Clé: The Irish Book Publishers' Association

43-44 Temple Bar, Dublin 2, Republic of Ireland
tel (01) 6707 393 *fax* (01) 6707 642
e-mail cle@iol.ie
President John Murphy, *Executive Director* Orla Martin

The William Cobbett Society

Chairman Molly Townsend, Johnsons Farm, Sheet, Petersfield, Hants GU32 2BY
tel (01730) 262060

To make the life and work of William Cobbett better known. Annual subscription: £8. Founded 1976.

The Wilkie Collins Society

Membership Secretary Paul Lewis, 47 Hereford Road, London W3 9JW
e-mail paul@paullewis.co.uk
Chairman Andrew Gasson

To promote interest in the life and works of Wilkie Collins. Publishes a newsletter, an occasional scholarly journal and reprints of Collins's lesser known works. Annual subscription: £9.50 (EU), £15 (international). Founded 1981.

Comedy Writers Association UK (CWAUK)

44 Cherry Avenue, Swanley, Kent BR8 7DU
tel/fax (01322) 410742
e-mail marknich@freelancewriter.co.uk
web site http://www.cwauk.co.uk
Contact Mark Nicholson

For people who take comedy writing seriously; aims to encourage and promote comedy writing as a profession. Holds annual weekend and one-day seminars, with invited industry speakers. Associate membership is open to aspiring comedy writers and full membership to existing ones. Members receive a monthly newsletter. Membership: £40 p.a. Founded 1981.

Comhairle nan Leabhraichean/ The Gaelic Books Council

22 Mansfield Street, Glasgow G11 5QP
tel 0141-337 6211 *fax* 0141-353 0515
Chairman Boyd Robertson

Stimulates Scottish Gaelic publishing by awarding publication grants for new books, commissioning authors and providing editorial services and general assistance to writers and readers. Has its own bookshop of all Gaelic and Gaelic-related books in print and runs a book club. Founded 1968.

Comics Creators Guild

(formerly Society for Strip Illustration)
48 Siddons Road, London SE23 2JQ
tel/fax 020-8699 4012
web site http://www.comicscreators.org.uk

Open to all those concerned with, or interested in, professional comics creation. Holds monthly meetings and publishes a newsletter (monthly), a Directory of Members' Work, Submission Guidelines for the major comics publishers, sample scripts for artists, a 'Guide to Contracts' and 'Getting Started in Comics', a beginners' guide to working in the industry, and *Comics Forum* (quarterly), a magazine of art and criticism.

Commonwealth Institute

Kensington High Street, London W8 6NQ
tel 020-7603 4535 *fax* 020-7602 7374
e-mail info@commonwealth.org.uk
web site http://www.commonwealth.org.uk/
Chief Executive David French

Promotes Commonwealth education and culture in the UK. The Resource Centre offers services to teachers and school groups, and includes a specialist Literature Library. Open to the public Mon-Sat 10am-4pm. Founded 1893.

Communicators in Business, The British Association of
42 Borough High Street, London SE1 1XW
tel 020-7378 7139 *fax* 020-7378 7140
e-mail bacb@globalnet.co.uk
web site http://www.bacb.org.uk
Aims to be the market leader for those involved in corporate media management and practice by providing professional, authoritative, dynamic, supportive and innovative services. Founded 1949.

Composers, The Association of Professional – **see British Academy of Composers and Songwriters**

The Composers' Guild of Great Britain – **see British Academy of Composers and Songwriters**

The Joseph Conrad Society (UK)
Chairman Keith Carabine, *President* Philip Conrad, *Secretary* Hugh Epstein
The Conradian, Dept. of English, St Mary's University College, Twickenham, Middlesex TW1 4SX
Editor Allan Simmons
Maintains close and friendly links with the Conrad family. Activities include an annual international conference; publication of *The Conradian* and a series of pamphlets; and maintenance of a study centre at the Polish Cultural Centre, 238-246 King Street, London W6 0RF. Administers the Juliet McLauchlan Prize: £100 annual award for the winner of an essay competition. Founded 1973.

Copyright Clearance Center Inc.
222 Rosewood Drive, Danvers, MA 01923, USA
tel 978-750-8400 *fax* 978-750-4470
web site http://www.copyright.com

Copyright Council, The British
Copyright House, 29-33 Berners Street, London W1P 4AA
tel (01986) 788 122 *fax* (01986) 788 847
e-mail copyright@bcc2.demon.co.uk
President Denis de Freitas OBE, *Vice-Presidents* Geoffrey Adams, Maureen Duffy, *Chairman* Prof Gerald Dworkin, *Vice Chairmen* Rachel Duffield, David Lester, Kate Pool, *Secretary* Janet Ibbotson, *Treasurer* Lord Brain
Aims to defend and foster the true principles of creators' copyright and their acceptance throughout the world, to bring together bodies representing all who are interested in the protection of such copyright, and to keep watch on any legal or other changes which may require an amendment of the law.

The Copyright Licensing Agency Ltd (CLA)
90 Tottenham Court Road, London W1P 0LP
tel 020-7631 5555 *fax* 020-7631 5500
e-mail cla@cla.co.uk
web site http://www.cla.co.uk
Chief Executive Peter Shepherd
The CLA administers collectively photocopying and other copying rights that it is uneconomic for writers and publishers to administer for themselves. The Agency issues collective and transactional licences, and the fees it collects, after the deduction of its operating costs, are distributed at regular intervals to authors and publishers via their respective societies. See also page 624. Founded 1982.

Crime Writers' Association
PO Box 6939 Brimingham B14 7LT
Secretary Judith Cutler
For professional writers of crime novels, short stories, plays for stage, TV and radio, or of other serious works on crime. Associate membership open to publishers, journalists, booksellers specialising in crime literature. Publishes *Red Herrings* (monthly), available to members only. Founded 1953.

The Critics' Circle
President George Perry, *Hon. General Secretary* Charles Hedges
Contact Catherine Cooper, Administrator, c/o 69 Marylebone Lane, London W1M 5GB
tel 020-7224 1410 (office hours)
Aims to promote the art of criticism, to uphold its integrity in practice, to foster and safeguard the professional interests of its members, to provide opportunities for social intercourse among them, and to support the advancement of the arts. Membership is by invitation of the Council. Such invitations are issued only to persons engaged professionally, regularly and substantially in the writing or broadcasting of criticism of drama, music, films, dance and the visual arts. Founded 1913.

Cultural Desk, International
3 Bruntsfield Crescent, Edinburgh EH10 4HD
tel 0131-446 3001 *fax* 0131-446 3048
e-mail info@icd.org.uk

Development Manager Hilde Bollen, *Information Officer* Kerry Jardine

Aims to assist Scottish artists and arts organisations to take up international opportunities by providing timely and targeted information and advice. The Desk provides information and advice on funding sources, European cultural policy development, international cultural networks, basic data on international opportunities, and contact and partner finding as a starting point for international collaborations. Publishes *Communication* (bimonthly) and *InFocus*, a new series of specialised guides with an international focus. Founded 1994.

Cyngor Llyfrau Cymru – see Welsh Books Council

Deaf Broadcasting Council

70 Blacketts Wood Drive, Chorleywood, Rickmansworth, Herts. WD3 5QQ
tel/fax (01923) 283127 (text phone only)
e-mail dmyers@cix.co.uk
web site http://www.waterlow.com.dbc
Secretary Ruth Myers

Design and Artists Copyright Society Ltd (DACS)

Parchment House, 13 Northburgh Street, London EC1V 0JP
tel 020-7336 8811 *fax* 020-7336 8822
e-mail info@dacs.co.uk
Chief Executive Rachel Duffield, *Administrator* Janet Tod

DACS is an independent, non-profit-making membership society open to all visual artists and photographers. Its primary functions are:

- to provide access to works of visual art and photography by developing both individual and blanket licensing schemes;
- to protect and administer the rights of visual artists in the UK;
- to ensure that visual artists receive payments for use of reproduction of their work by others and to collect and distribute royalties to individual creators;
- to provide advice and support on legal matters arising from any infringement of visual artists' copyright;
- to campaign and lobby for a fair working environment for visual artists at national and international levels. DACS is currently involved in lobbying for the introduction in the UK of Artist's Resale Rights, which would ensure that artists receive a percentage of the selling price each time a work is sold, after the original sale. This would bring the UK into line with other European countries.

DACS issues licences on behalf of its members for the reproduction of artistic works as authorised by the artist concerned or by the artist's estate. It acts as exclusive licensee on behalf of its national members, and it also acts as agent for artists and estates who are members of sister societies abroad.

As a collecting society, DACS helps to secure revenue for artists for rights which are difficult to administer as an individual. In 1999 DACS had available £300,000 for distribution to visual artists – the first such distribution in the UK for artists and photographers. Further distributions will follow annually. Registration is free. For information or to register, contact Distribution at the above address.

Life membership: £25 (inc. VAT). Founded 1983.

Designers, The Chartered Society of

First Floor, 32-38 Saffron Hill, London EC1N 8FH
tel 020-7831 9777 *fax* 020-7831 6277
e-mail csd@csd.org.uk
web site http://www.designweb.co.uk/csd
Director Brian Lymbery

Works to promote and regulate standards of competence, professional conduct and integrity, including representation on government and official bodies, design education and competitions. The services to members include general information, publications, guidance on copyright and other professional issues, access to professional indemnity insurance and a credit-checking/debt collection service. Activities in the regions are included in an extensive annual programme of events and training courses. The Society publishes a Code of Conduct, and has developed a Business and Design Programme to strengthen the links between designers and clients in business and industry.

Designers in Ireland, Institute of

8 Merrion Square, Dublin 2, Republic of Ireland
tel/fax (01) 4962806

Irish design profession's representative

body, covering every field of design. Details from the honorary secretary. Annual membership: IR£130 (full), IR£45 (licentiate). Founded 1972.

Dickens Fellowship
The Dickens House, 48 Doughty Street, London WC1N 2LF
tel 020-7405 2127 *fax* 020-7831 5175
Hon. Secretary Dr Tony Williams
Based in house occupied by Dickens 1837-9; publishes *The Dickensian* (3 p.a.). Membership rates and particulars on application. Founded 1902.

Directory & Database Publishers Association
Secretary Rosemary Pettit, PO Box 23034, London W6 0RJ
tel 020-8846 9707
Maintains a code of professional practice; aims to raise the standard and professional status of UK directory and database publishing and to protect (and promote) the legal, statutory and common interests of directory publishers; provides for the exchange of technical, commercial and management information between members. Annual subscription: £120-£1200. Founded 1970.

'Sean Dorman' Manuscript Society
Cherry Trees, Crosemere Road, Cockshutt, Ellesmere, Shropshire SY12 0JP
tel (01939) 270293
Director Mary Driver
Provides mutual help among writers and aspiring writers in the UK. By means of circulating MSS parcels, members receive constructive criticism of their own work and read and comment on the work of others. Each 'Circulator' has up to 9 participants and members' contributions may be in any medium: short stories, chapters of a novel, poetry, magazine articles etc. Send sae for full details and application form. Founded 1957.

The Arthur Conan Doyle Society
Organisers Christopher and Barbara Roden, PO Box 1360, Ashcroft, B.C., Canada V0K 1A0
tel 250-453-2045 *fax* 250-453-2075
e-mail ashtree@ash-tree.bc.ca
web site http://www.ash-tree.bc.ca/acdsocy.html
Promotes the study of the life and works of Sir Arthur Conan Doyle. Publishes *ACD* journal (bi-annual) and occasional reprints of Conan Doyle material. Occasional conventions. Subscription: £16 p.a. (airmail extra). Founded 1989.

Early English Text Society
Christ Church, Oxford OX1 1DP
Hon. Director Prof John Burrow
Executive Secretary R.F.S. Hamer
To bring unprinted early English literature within the reach of students in sound texts. Annual subscription: £15. Founded 1864.

The Eckhart Society
Summa, 22 Tippings Lane, Woodley, Reading, Berks. RG5 4RX
tel/fax 0118-9690118
e-mail ashleyyoung@aysumma.demon.co.uk
web site http://www.op.org/eckhart
Secretary Ashley Young
Aims to promote the understanding and appreciation of Eckhart's writings and their importance for Christian thought and practice; to facilitate scholarly research into Eckhart's life and works; and to promote the study of Eckhart's teaching as a contribution to inter-religious dialogue. Offers an annual Essay Prize (£250). Membership: £15 p.a.; £8 p.a. OAPs/students. Founded 1987.

Edinburgh Bibliographical Society
c/o National Library of Scotland, George IV Bridge, Edinburgh EH1 1EW
tel 0131-226-4531
Secretary R. Ovenden, *Treasurer* P. Freshwater
Encourages bibliographical activity through organising talks for members, particularly on bibliographical topics relating to Scotland, and visits to libraries. Also publishes *Transactions* (bi-annual, free to members) and other occasional publications. Membership: £10 p.a. (£15 p.a. institutions; £5 full-time students). Founded 1890.

Editors, Society of
Director Bob Satchwell, The University Centre, Granta Place, Mill Lane, Cambridge CB2 1RU
tel (01223) 304080 *fax* (01223) 304090
e-mail society@ukeditors.com
Formed from the merger of the Guild of Editors and the Association of British Editors, the Society has more than 450 members in national, regional and local newspapers, broadcasting, new media, journalism education and media law, campaigning for media freedom. Publishes *Briefing* (monthly). Annual subscription: £200 (full). Founded 1999.

Educational Writers Group

84 Drayton Gardens, London SW10 9SB
tel 020-7373 6642

Specialist group within the membership of the Society of Authors (see page 507).

The George Eliot Fellowship

President Jonathan G. Ouvry
Secretary Mrs K.M. Adams, 71 Stepping Stones Road, Coventry CV5 8JT
tel 024-7659 2231

Promotes an interest in the life and work of George Eliot (1819-80) and helps to extend her influence; arranges meetings; produces an annual journal and a quarterly newsletter. Awards the annual George Eliot Fellowship Prize (£250) for an essay on Eliot's life or work, which must be previously unpublished and not exceed 2500 words. Annual subscription: £10. Founded 1930.

English Association

University of Leicester, University Road, Leicester LE1 7RH
tel 0116-252 3982 *fax* 0116-252 2301
e-mail engassoc@le.ac.uk
web site http://www.le.ac.uk/engassoc/
Chairman Martin Blocksidge, *Chief Executive* Helen Lucas

Aims to further knowledge, understanding and enjoyment of English literature and the English language, by working towards a fuller recognition of English as an essential element in education and in the community at large; by encouraging the study of English literature and language by means of conferences, lectures and publications; by fostering the discussion of methods of teaching English of all kinds; and by the establishment of local groups for the exchange of views and to work to further the status of English literature and language in the community.

English Regional Arts Boards – see Regional Arts Boards

English Speaking Board (International) Ltd

26A Princes Street, Southport PR8 1EQ
tel (01704) 501730 *fax* (01704) 539637
e-mail admin@esbuk.demon.co.uk
web site http://www.esbuk.demon.co.uk
President Christabel Burniston MBE, *Chairman* Richard Ellis

Aims to foster all activities concerned with oral communication. The Board conducts examinations and training courses for teachers and students in schools and colleges where stress is on individual oral expression; also for those engaged in technical or industrial concerns, and for those using English as an acquired language. Members receive *Speaking English* (Mar/Sept); articles are invited on any special aspect of spoken English. Members can purchase other ESB publications at reduced rates. Conference and AGM in the spring. Membership: individuals, £22 p.a., corporate £40 p.a.

The English-Speaking Union

Dartmouth House, 37 Charles Street, London W1X 8AB
tel 020-7493 3328 *fax* 020-7495 6108
e-mail esu@esu.org
web site http://www.esu.org
Director-General Mrs Valerie Mitchell

Aims to promote international understanding and human achievement through the widening use of the English language throughout the world. The ESU is an educational charity which sponsors scholarships and exchanges, educational programmes promoting the effective use of English, and a wide range of international and cultural events. Members contribute to its work across the world. Administers the Marsh Biography Award. Annual membership: various categories. See also Books Across the Sea. Founded 1918.

European Broadcasting Union

Ancienne Route 17A, CH-1218 Grand Saconnex (Geneva), Switzerland
tel (22) 7172111 *fax* (22) 7174000
e-mail ebu@ebu.ch
web site http://www.ebu.ch
Secretary-General Dr Jean-Bernard Münch

Supports and promotes co-operation between its members and broadcasting organisations worldwide; represents the interests of its members in programme, legal, technical and other fields. Founded 1950.

European Publishers, Federation of

204 avenue de Tervuren, 1150 Brussels, Belgium
tel (2) 770 11 10 *fax* (2) 771 20 71
e-mail fep.alemann@brutele.be
President Ulrico C. Hoepli, *Director* Mechthild von Alemann

Represents the interests of European publishers on EU affairs; informs members on the development of EU policies which could affect the publishing industry. Founded 1967.

Fabian Society
11 Dartmouth Street, London SW1H 9BN
tel 020-7227 4900 *fax* 020-7976 7153
e-mail info@fabian-society.org.uk
web site http://www.fabian-society.org.uk
General Secretary Michael Jacobs
Current affairs, political thought, economics, education, environment, foreign affairs, social policy. Also controls NCLC Publishing Society Ltd. Founded 1884.

Fantasy Society, The British
201 Reddish Road, South Reddish,
Stockport SK5 7HR
tel 0161-476 5368 (after 6pm)
e-mail faliol@yahoo.com
web site http://www.herebedragons.co.uk/bfs
President Ramsey Campbell, *Secretary* Robert Parkinson
For devotees of fantasy, horror and related fields, in literature, art and the cinema. Publications include *British Fantasy Newsletter* (bi-monthly) featuring news and reviews and several annual booklets, including: *Dark Horizons*; *Masters of Fantasy* on individual authors. There is a small-press library and an annual convention and fantasy awards sponsored by the Society. Annual membership: £20. Founded 1971.

Federation Against Copyright Theft Ltd (FACT)
7 Victory Business Centre, Worton Road,
Isleworth, Middlesex TW7 6DB
tel 020-8568 6646 *fax* 020-8560 6364
Contact Director General
FACT aims to protect the interests of its members and others against infringement in the UK of copyright in cinematograph films, TV programmes and all forms of audio-visual recording. Founded 1982.

Financial Journalists' Group
Secretary Suzanne Moore, c/o Association of British Insurers, 51 Gresham Street,
London EC2V 7HQ
tel 020-7216 7411 *fax* 020-7367 8606
e-mail suzanne.moore@abi.org.uk
Aims to give journalists working in the area of, or with an interest in, finance and financial services, a forum to learn more about some of the issues involved, and meet colleagues with similar interests. No membership fee. Founded 1997.

The Fine Art Trade Guild
16-18 Empress Place,
London SW6 1TT
tel 020-7381 6616 *fax* 020-7381 2596
e-mail information@fineart.co.uk
web site http://www.fineart.co.uk
Managing Director Rosie Sumner
Promotes the sale of fine art prints and picture framing in the UK and overseas markets; establishes and raises standards amongst members and communicates these to the buying public. The Guild publishes *The Directory* and *Art Business Today*, the trade's longest established magazine and various specialist books. Founded 1910.

FOCAL (Federation of Commercial AudioVisual Libraries International Ltd)
Pentax House, South Hill Avenue, South Harrow,
Middlesex HA2 0DU
tel/fax 020-8423 5853 *fax* 020-8933 4826
e-mail info@focalint.org
web site http://www.focalint.org
Commerical Manager Anne Johnson
Founded 1985.

The Folklore Society
University College, Gower Street,
London WC1E 6BT
tel 020-7387 5894
Hon. Secretary Dr Jacqueline Simpson
Collection, recording and study of folklore. Founded 1878.

Food Writers, Guild of
Administrator Christina Thomas,
48 Crabtree Lane, London SW6 6LW
tel 020-7610 1180 *fax* 020-7610 0299
e-mail gfw@gfw.co.uk
Aims to bring together professional food writers including journalists, broadcasters and authors, to print and issue an annual list of members, to extend the range of members' knowledge and experience by arranging discussions, tastings and visits, and to encourage the development of new writers by every means including competitions and awards. Membership: £70 p.a. Founded 1984.

Foreign Press Association in London
Registered Office 11 Carlton House Terrace,
London SW1Y 5AJ
tel 020-7930 0445 *fax* 020-7925 0469
President Tomohiko Taniguchi, *Secretaries* Davina Crole and Catherine Flury
Aims to promote the professional interests of its members. Full Membership open to

overseas professional journalists residing in the UK; Associate Membership available for British press and freelance journalists. Entrance fee: £147.50; annual subscription: £124. Founded 1888.

Free Painters & Sculptors
Loggia Gallery and Sculpture Garden,
15 Buckingham Gate, London SW1E 6LB
tel 020-7828 5963
Exhibits progressive work of all artistic allegiances and provides opportunities for FPS members to meet and discuss their work in either one-person or group shows.Gallery hours: Mon-Fri 6-8pm, Sat 11am-5pm Sun 1-5pm.

Freelance Editors and Proofreaders, Society of (SFEP)
Office Mermaid House, 1 Mermaid Court,
London SE1 1HR
tel 020-7403 5141
e-mail admin@sfep.demon.co.uk
web site http://www.sfep.org.uk
Aims to promote high editorial standards and achieve recognition of its members' professional status, through local and national meetings, an annual conference, a monthly newsletter and a programme of reasonably priced workshops/training sessions. These sessions help newcomers to acquire basic skills, enable experienced editors to update their skills or broaden their competence, and also cover aspects of professional practice or business for the self-employed. An annual Directory of members' services is available to publishers. The Society supports moves towards recognised standards of training and accreditation for editors and proofreaders. It has close links with the Publishing Training Centre and the Society of Indexers, is represented on the BSI Technical Committee dealing with copy preparation and proof correction (BS 5261), and works to foster good relations with all relevant bodies and organisations in the UK and worldwide. Founded 1988.

Freelance Photographers, Bureau of
Focus House, 497 Green Lanes, London N13 4BP
tel 020-8882 3315 *fax* 020-8886 5174
Chief Executive John Tracy
To help the freelance photographer by providing information on markets, and free advisory service. Publishes *Market Newsletter* (monthly). Annual membership: £40. Founded 1965.

French Publishers' Association
(Syndicat National de l'Edition)
115 Blvd St Germain, 75006 Paris, France
tel (1) 44 41 40 50 *fax* (1) 44 41 40 77

The Gaelic Books Council – see Comhairle nan Leabhraichean

Garden Writers Guild
Secretary Angela Clarke, c/o Institute of
Horticulture, 14-15 Belgrave Square,
London SW1X 8PS
tel/fax 020-7245 6943
e-mail gwg@horticulture.org.uk
web site http://www.gardenwriters.co.uk
Aims to raise the standards of gardening communicators. Administers annual awards to encourage excellence in garden writing, trade and consumer press journalism, TV and radio broadcasting, as well as garden photography. Membership: £30 p.a. Founded 1991.

The Gaskell Society
Far Yew Tree House, Over Tabley, Knutsford,
Cheshire WA16 0HN
tel (01565) 634668
e-mail JoanLeach@aol.com
web site http://www.gaskellsociety.cwc.net
Hon. Secretary Mrs Joan Leach
Promotes and encourages the study and appreciation of the work and life of Elizabeth Cleghorn Gaskell. Holds regular meetings in Knutsford, London and Manchester, visits and residential conferences; produces an annual Journal and bi-annual Newsletters. Annual subscription: £8, corporate and overseas £12. Founded 1985.

Gay Authors Workshop
Kathryn Byrd, BM Box 5700, London WC1N 3XX
tel 020-8520 5223
To encourage writers who are lesbian, gay or bisexual. Quarterly newsletter. Membership: £7; unwaged £3. Founded 1978.

General Practitioners Writers Association
President Dr Robin Hull, West Carnliath,
Strathtay, Pitlochry, Perthshire PH9 0PG
tel (01887) 840380
Aims to improve the writing by, for, from or about general medical practice. Publishes *The GP Writer* (2 p.a.); register of members' writing interests is sent to medical editors and publishers. Founded 1985.

German Publishers' and Booksellers' Association

(Börsenverein des Deutschen Buchhandels e.V.)
Postfach 100442, 60004 Frankfurt am Main, Germany
tel (069) 13060 *fax* (069) 1306201
e-mail info@boev.de
web site http://www.boersenverein.de
General Manager Dr Hans-Karl von Kupsch

Graphic Fine Art, Society of

15 Willow Way, Hatfield, Herts AL10 9QD
President Michael Taylor

A fine art society holding an annual open exhibition. Membership by election, requires work of high quality with an emphasis on good drawing, whether by pen, pencil (with our without wash), watercolour, pastel or any of the forms of print making. Founded 1919.

Graphical, Paper & Media Union

Keys House, 63-67 Bromham Road, Bedford MK40 2AG
tel (01234) 351521 *fax* (01234) 270580
e-mail general@gpmu.org.uk
web site http://www.gpmu.org.uk
General Secretary Tony Dubbins

The Greeting Card Association

United House, North Road, London N7 9DP
tel/fax 020-7619 0396
Administrator Sharon Little

Official magazine: *Progressive Greetings Worldwide* (12 p.a.). See page 397.

Guernsey Arts Council

St James Concert and Assembly Hall, St Peter Port, Guernsey, CI
tel (01481) 721902
Secretary Elizabeth Eales *tel* (01481) 63189

Haiku Society, The British

Secretary Alan J. Summers, PO Box 1974, Bristol BS88 3BB
tel (07979) 656775

Aims to pioneer the appreciation and writing of haiku, senryu, renku and tanka in the UK and the rest of Europe, and to establish links with haiku societies throughout the world. Membership: £15 UK/Europe, £11 concession/unwaged. Publishes the journal *Blithe Spirit*, and a newsletter, *The Brief*, and holds national events. Founded 1990.

Hakluyt Society

c/o The Map Library, The British Library, 96 Euston Road, London NW1 2DB
tel (01986) 788359 *fax* (01986) 788181
e-mail office@hakluyt.com
web site http://www.hakluyt.com
President Sarah Tyacke CB, *Hon. Secretary* Dr Andrew Cook

Publication of original narratives of voyages, travels, naval expeditions, and other geographical records. Founded 1846.

The Thomas Hardy Society Ltd

PO Box 1438, Dorchester, Dorset DT1 1YH
tel/fax (01305) 251501

Publishes *The Thomas Hardy Journal* (3 p.a.). Biennial conference in Dorchester, 1998. Annual subscription: £12 (£15 overseas). Founded 1967.

Harleian Society

College of Arms, Queen Victoria Street, London EC4V 4BT
tel 020-7236 7728 *fax* 020-7248 6448
Chairman J. Brooke-Little CVO, MA, FSA, *Hon. Secretary* T.H.S. Duke, Chester Herald of Arms

Instituted for transcribing, printing and publishing the heraldic visitations of Counties, Parish Registers and any manuscripts relating to genealogy, family history and heraldry. Founded 1869.

Health Writers, Guild of

Administrator Jatinder Dua, 1 Broadmead Close, Hampton, Middlesex TW12 3RT
tel/fax 020-8941 2977
e-mail admin@healthwriters.com

Brings together professional journalists dedicated to providing accurate, broad-based information about health and related subjects to the public. Publishes a directory of members. Membership: £40 plus VAT p.a. Founded 1995.

Heraldic Arts, Society of

46 Reigate Road, Reigate, Surrey RH2 0QN
tel (01737) 242945
Secretary John Ferguson ARCA, SHA, DFACH, FRSA

Aims to serve the interests of heraldic artists, craftsmen, designers and writers, to provide a 'shop window' for their work, to obtain commissions on their behalf and to act as a forum for the exchange of information and ideas. Also offers an information service to the public. Candidates for admission as craft members should be artists or craftsmen whose work comprises a substantial element of heraldry and is of a sufficiently high standard to satisfy the requirements of the society's advisory council.Annual membership: £12 (associate); £17 (craft). Founded 1987.

Historical Novel Society
Secretary Richard Lee, Marine Cottage, The Strand, Starcross, Devon EX6 8NY
tel (01626) 891962 *fax* (01392) 438714
e-mail histnovel@aol.com
web site http://www.historical-novel-society.freeserve.co.uk

Promotes the historical novel via short story competitions, a society magazine *Solander* (2 p.a.) and reviews (*Historical Novels Review*, quarterly). Members include eminent novelists: Wilbur Smith, Bernard Cornwell, Joanna Trollope, Beryl Bainbridge, *et al.* Annual membership: £15. Founded 1997.

The Sherlock Holmes Society of London
President A.D. Howlett MA, LLB, *Chairman* Peter L. Horrocks LLB
General enquiries Heather Owen, 64 Graham Road, London SW19 3SS
tel/fax 020-8540 7657
e-mail abcc@msn.com
web site http://www.sherlock-holmes.org.uk
Membership R.J. Ellis, 13 Crofton Avenue, Orpington, Kent BA6 8DU
tel/fax (01689) 811314

Aims to bring together those who have a common interest as readers and students of the literature of Sherlock Holmes, and to encourage the pursuit of knowledge of the public and private lives of Sherlock Holmes and Dr Watson. Annual subscription: £14 (UK/Europe), £18 (Far East), US$30.50 (USA), including *The Sherlock Holmes Journal* (2 p.a.). Founded 1951.

Hopkins Society
Secretary 41 North Drive, Rhyl, Denbighshire LL18 4SW

To promote and celebrate the work of the poet, Gerard Manley Hopkins, to inform members about the latest publications about Hopkins and to support educational projects concerning his work. Annual lecture held in North Wales in the spring; publishes a newsletter (2 p.a.) Annual subscription: £7 (£10 outside Europe). Founded 1990.

Housman Society
80 New Road, Bromsgrove, Worcs. B60 2LA
tel (01527) 874136 *fax* (01527) 837274
e-mail jimpage@btinternet.com
web site http://www.knowledge.co.uk/housman/
Chairman Jim Page

Aims to foster interest in and promote knowledge of A.E. Housman and his family. Sponsors a lecture at the Hay Festival and the biennial National Poetry Competition. Membership: £10 p.a. Founded 1973.

Hesketh Hubbard Art Society
17 Carlton House Terrace, London SW1Y 5BD
tel 020-7930 6844 *fax* 020-7839 7830
President Simon Whittle

Weekly life drawing classes open to all.

Illustrators, The Association of
81 Leonard Street, London EC2A 4QS
tel 020-7613 4328 *fax* 020-7613 4417
web site http://www.aoi.co.uk
Contact Samantha Taylor

To support illustrators, promote illustration and encourage professional standards in the industry. Publishes monthly magazine; presents an annual programme of events; annual competition, Images – the Best of British Illustration: call for entries March/April. Founded 1973.

Indexers, Society of
Administrator Wendy Burrow, Globe Centre, Penistone Road, Sheffield S6 3AE
tel 0114-281 3060
e-mail admin@socind.demon.co.uk

Aims to improve the standard of indexing, and to raise the status of indexers and to safeguard their interests. Maintains a Register of Indexers; acts as an advisory body on the qualifications and remuneration of indexers; publishes or communicates books, papers and notes on the subject of indexing; publishes and runs an open-learning indexing course, 'Training in Indexing'. The Society's journal, *The Indexer*, is sent free to members. Annual subscription: £50 UK/Europe (£65 overseas), corporate £75 (£100 overseas).

Indian Publishers, The Federation of
18/1-C Institutional Area, Aruna Asaf Ali Marg (near JNU), New Delhi 110067, India
tel 6964847, 6852263 *fax* 91-11-6864054
e-mail india.ifb@aworld.net.in

The Irish Book Publishers' Association – see Clé

The Irish Copyright Licensing Agency
19 Parnell Square, Dublin 1, Republic of Ireland
tel (01) 8729202 *fax* (01) 8722035
Executive Director Orla O'Sullivan

Licences schools and other users of copyright material to photocopy extracts of such material, and distributes the monies collected to the authors and publishers whose works have been copied. Founded 1992.

Irish Playwrights and Screenwriters Guild

(formerly the Society of Irish Playwrights)
Irish Writers' Centre, 19 Parnell Square, Dublin 1, Republic of Ireland
tel (01) 8721302 *fax* (01) 8726282
e-mail moffatts@intigo.ie
Secretary Sean Moffatt

Represents writers' interests in theatre, radio and screenwriting. Founded 1969.

Irish Translators' Association

Irish Writers' Centre, 19 Parnell Square, Dublin 1, Republic of Ireland
tel (01) 8721302 *fax* (01) 8726282
e-mail translation@tinet.ie
web site http://homepage.tinet.ie/~translation
Secretary Miriam Lee

Promotes translation in Ireland, the translation of Irish authors abroad and the practical training of translators, and promotes the interests of translators. Catalogues the works of translators in areas of Irish interest; secures the awarding of prizes and bursaries for translators; and maintains a detailed register of translators. Annual membership: IR£20 (member), IR£40 (professional member). Founded 1986.

Irish Writers' Union/Comhar na Scríbhneoirí

Irish Writers' Centre, 19 Parnell Square, Dublin 1, Republic of Ireland
tel (01) 8721302 *fax* (01) 8726282
e-mail iwc@iol.ie
Chairman Sam MacAughtry

The Union aims to advance the cause of writing as a profession, to achieve better remuneration and more favourable conditions for writers and to provide a means for the expression of the collective opinion of writers on matters affecting their profession. Founded 1986.

The Richard Jefferies Society

Hon. Secretary Phyllis Treitel, Eidsvoll, Bedwells Heath, Boars Hill, Oxford OX1 5JE
tel (01865) 735678

Worldwide membership. Promotes interest in the life, works and associations of the naturalist and novelist, Richard Jefferies; helps to preserve buildings and memorials, and co-operates in the development of a Museum in his birthplace. Arranges regular meetings in Swindon, and occasionally elsewhere; organises outings and displays; publishes a Journal and Newsletter in spring and an Annual Report in September. Annual subscription: £7. Founded 1950.

The Johnson Society

Johnson Birthplace Museum, Breadmarket Street, Lichfield, Staffs. WS13 6LG
tel (01543) 264972
Hon. General Secretary Norma Hooper

To encourage the study of the life and works of Dr Samuel Johnson; to preserve the memorials, associations, books, manuscripts, letters of Dr Johnson and his contemporaries; preservation of his birthplace.

Johnson Society of London

President The Viscountess Eccles
Secretary Mrs Zandra O'Donnell MA, 255 Baring Road, London SE12 0BQ
tel 020-8851 0173

To study the life and works of Dr Johnson, and to perpetuate his memory in the city of his adoption. Founded 1928.

Journalists, The Chartered Institute of

General Secretary Christopher Underwood FCIJ, FRSA
2 Dock Offices, Surrey Quays Road, London SE16 2XU
tel 020-7252 1187 *fax* 020-7232 2302
e-mail memberservices@ioj.co.uk

The senior organisation of the profession, founded in 1884 and incorporated by Royal Charter in 1890. The Chartered Institute maintains an employment register and has accumulated funds for the assistance of members. A Freelance Division links editors and publishers with freelances and a Directory is published of freelance writers, with their specialisations. There are special sections for broadcasters, motoring correspondents, public relations practitioners and overseas members. Occasional contributors to the media may qualify for election as Affiliates. Annual subscription: maximum £160, trainees £80; affiliate £110.

Journalists, National Council for the Training of

Latton Bush Centre, Southern Way, Harlow, Essex CM18 7BL
tel (01279) 430009 *fax* (01279) 438008
e-mail nctjtraining@aol.com
web site http://www.nctj.com
Chief Executive Rob Selwood

A registered charity which aims to advance the education and training of trainee journalists, including press photographers. Founded 1952.

The Sheila Kaye-Smith Society
Secretary Grace Chatfield, 5 Leeds Close, Ore Village, Hastings, East Sussex TN35 5BX
tel (01424) 437413 *fax* (01424) 883268
Aims to stimulate and widen interest in the work of the Sussex writer and novelist, Sheila Kaye-Smith (1887-1956). Produces *The Gleam* (annual) and occasional papers, and organises talks. Annual membership: £6 single, £9 joint. Founded 1987.

Keats-Shelley Memorial Association
Hon. Secretary Mr D.R. Leigh-Hunt, 1 Satchwell Walk, Leamington Spa, Warks. CV32 4QE
tel (01926) 427400 *fax* (01926) 335133
Patron HM Queen Elizabeth the Queen Mother, *Chairman* Hon. Mrs H. Cullen
Owns and supports house in Rome where John Keats died as a museum open to the public, and celebrates the poets Keats, Shelley and Leigh Hunt. Occasional meetings; poetry competitions; annual *Review,* 2 literary awards, and progress reports. Subscription to 'Friends of the Keats-Shelley Memorial', minimum £10 p.a. Founded 1903.

Kent and Sussex Poetry Society
President Laurence Lerner, *Chairman* Clive Eastwood
Hon. Secretary Joyce Mandel Walter, 23 Arundel Road, Tunbridge Wells, Kent TN1 1TB
e-mail walter.scape@which.net
Based in Tunbridge Wells, the society was formed in 1946 to create a greater interest in Poetry. Well-known poets address the Society, a Folio of members' work is produced and a full programme of recitals, discussions, competitions and readings is provided. See page 525 for details of Open Poetry Competition. Annual subscription: full members £10, country members/concessions £5.

The Kipling Society
Hon. Secretary J.W. Michael Smith, 2 Brownleaf Road, Brighton, East Sussex BN2 6LB
tel (01273) 303719
e-mail kipling@fastmedia.demon.co.uk
web site http://www.kipling.org.uk
Aims to honour and extend the influence of Rudyard Kipling (1865-1936), to assist in the study of his writings, to hold discussion meetings, to publish a quarterly journal, and to maintain a Kipling Library in London and a Kipling Room in The Grange, Rottingdean, near Brighton. Membership details on application.

The Lancashire Authors' Association
General Secretary Eric Holt, 5 Quakerfields, Westhoughton, Bolton BL5 2BJ
tel (01942) 791390
'For writers and lovers of Lancashire literature and history.' Publishes *The Record* (quarterly). Annual subscription: £9. Founded 1909.

The T.E. Lawrence Society
PO Box 728, Oxford OX2 6YP
web site http://www.telawrence.org
Promotes the memory of T.E. Lawrence and furthers knowledge by research into his life; publishes *Journal* (bi-annual) and *Newsletter* (quarterly). Annual subscription: £15, overseas £20. Founded 1985.

Learned and Professional Society Publishers, The Association of
Secretary-General Sally Morris, South House, The Street, Clapham, Worthing, West Sussex BN13 3UU
tel (01903) 871 686 *fax* (01903) 871457
e-mail sec-gen@alpsp.org.uk
web site http://www.alpsp.org
Aims to promote and develop the publishing activities of learned and professional organisations. Membership is open to professional and learned societies and allied organisations. Founded 1972.

Librarians, Association of Assistant – see Career Development Group

The Library Association
7 Ridgmount Street, London WC1E 7AE
tel 020-7255 0500 *fax* 020-7255 0501
textphone 020-7255 0505
e-mail info@la-hq.org.uk
web site http://www.la-hq.org.uk
Chief Executive Bob McKee PhD, MIIN, FSc, FRSA, ALA
For over a century, the Library Association has promoted and defended the interests of the Library and Information Service profession, those working within it and the people who use the services. The journal *The Library Association Record* (monthly), is distributed free to all members. Subscription: varies according to income. Founded 1877.

Limners, The Society of
Founder/President Elizabeth Davys Wood MBE, PSLm, 2 Glentrammon Close, Green Street Green, Orpington, Kent BR6 6DL
tel (01689) 851158

Aims to promote an interest in miniature painting (in any medium), calligraphy and heraldry and encourage their development to a high standard. New members are elected after the submission of 4 works of acceptable standard and guidelines are provided for new artists. Members receive up to 4 newsletters a year and 2 annual exhibitions are arranged. Annual membership: £25; Friends (£12). Friends membership is open to non-exhibitors and includes newsletters and invitations to exhibitions and seminar. Founded 1986.

Linguists, Institute of
Saxon House, 48 Southwark Street, London SE1 1UN
tel 020-7940 3100 *fax* 020-7940 3101
e-mail info@iol.org.uk
web site http://www.iol.org.uk

To provide language qualifications; to encourage Government and industry to develop the use of modern languages and encourage recognition of the status of professional linguists in all occupations; to promote the exchange and dissemination of information on matters of concern to linguists.

Literacy Trust, National
Swire House, 59 Buckingham Gate, London SW1E 6AJ
tel 020-7828 2435 *fax* 020-7931 9986
e-mail contact@literacytrust.org.uk
web site http://www.literacytrust.org.uk
Director Neil McClelland, *PA* Jacky Taylor

A registered charity that aims to make an independent, strategic contribution to the creation of a society in which all can enjoy the appropriate skills, confidence and pleasures of literacy to support their educational, economic, social and cultural goals. Maintains an extensive web site with literacy issues, research news and a searchable database detailing literacy practice nationwide; promotes and facilitates literacy partnerships; organises an annual conference, courses and training events; publishes quarterly magazine *Literacy Today* (£16 p.a.). Organised and implemented the National Year of Reading 1998-9 and is coordinating the National Reading Campaign. Runs Reading is Fundamental, UK which provides books free to children. Founded 1993.

Literary Societies, Alliance of
Secretary Rosemary Culley, 22 Belmont Grove, Havant, Hants PO9 3PU
tel 023-9247 5855 *fax* (0870) 056 0330
e-mail rosemary@sndc.demon.co.uk
web site http://www.sndc.demon.co.uk
Open Book, Greta, Sandford Avenue, Church Stretton, Shropshire SY6 7AB
tel (01694) 722821
Editor Thelma Thompson

Aims to enable close cooperation between societies so that the ideas for expansion to membership and the preservation of our literary heritage can flourish. It is currently producing a handbook of information for each member society.

Literature, Royal Society of
Somerset House, Strand, London WC2R 0RN
tel 020-7845 4676 *fax* 020-7845 4679
e-mail RSLit@aol.com
Chairman of Council Michael Holroyd CBE, FRSL, FRHistS, *Secretary* Maggie Fergusson

For the advancement of literature by the holding of lectures, discussions, readings, and by publications. Administers the Royal Society of Literature Award under the W.H. Heinemann Bequest, the V.S. Pritchett Memorial Prize and the Winifred Holtby Memorial Prize. Annual subscription: £30. Founded 1820.

Little Theatre Guild of Great Britain
Public Relations Officer Marjorie Havard, 20 Abbey Road, Grimsby DN32 0HW
tel (01472) 343424

Aims to promote closer co-operation amongst the little theatres constituting its membership; to act as co-ordinating and representative body on behalf of the little theatres; to maintain and advance the highest standards in the art of theatre; and to assist in encouraging the establishment of other little theatres. Yearbook available to non-members £5.

Marine Artists, Royal Society of
17 Carlton House Terrace, London SW1Y 5BD
tel 020-7930 6844 *fax* 020-7839 7830
President Bert Wright

To promote and encourage marine painting. Open Annual Exhibition at the Mall Galleries, London.

The Marlowe Society
Secretary Roger Hards, Venusmead, Congresbury, Bristol BS49 5EZ
tel (01934) 834780
To extend appreciation and widen recognition of Christopher Marlowe (1564-93) as the foremost poet and dramatist preceding Shakespeare, whose development he influenced. Holds meetings and cultural visits, and issues a bi-annual magazine. Annual subscription: £12, concessions £7, overseas £15/$26. Founded 1955.

The John Masefield Society
Chairman Peter J.R. Carter, The Frith, Ledbury, Herefordshire HR8 1LW
tel (01531) 633800 *fax* (01531) 631647
e-mail petercarter@btinternet.com
web site http://www.ucl.ac.uk/~uczzpwe/jms1.htm
To stimulate interest in and public awareness and enjoyment of the life and works of the poet John Masefield. Holds an annual lecture and other, less formal, readings and gatherings; publishes an annual journal and frequent newsletters. Annual membership: £5, overseas £10, family/institutions £8. Founded 1992.

Mechanical-Copyright Protection Society Ltd (MCPS)
Copyright House, 29-33 Berners Street, London W1P 4AA
tel 020-7580 5544 *fax* 020-7306 4455
and Elgar House, 41 Streatham High Road, London SW16 1ER
tel 020-8664 4400 *fax* 020-8769 8792
e-mail info@mcps.co.uk
web site http://www.mcps.co.uk
Chief Executive John Hutchinson

The Media Society
Secretary Peter Dannheisser, 56 Roseneath Road, London SW11 6AQ
tel/fax 0171-223 5631
To promote and encourage collective and independent research into the standards, performance, organisation and economics of the media and hold regular discussions, debates, etc. on subjects of topical or special interest and concern to print and broadcast journalists and others working in or with the media. Annual subscription: £25. Founded 1973.

Medical Journalists Association
Hon. Secretary Sue Lowell, 101 Cambridge Gardens, London W10 6JE
tel 020-8968 1614 *fax* 020-8968 7910
e-mail sue4382@aol.com
Chairman John Illman
Aims to improve the quality and practice of health and medical journalism. Administers major awards for health and medical journalism and broadcasting. Publishes The *MJA Directory* and *MJA News* newsletter. Annual membership: £30. Founded 1966.

Medical Writers Group
84 Drayton Gardens, London SW10 9SB
tel 020-7373 6642
Specialist group within the membership of the Society of Authors (see page 507) giving contractual and legal advice. Also organises talks, day seminars covering many aspects of medical writing, and administers the medical prizes sponsored by the Royal Society of Medicine.

Miniature Painters, Sculptors and Gravers, The Royal Society of
Executive Secretary Mrs Pam Henderson, 1 Knapp Cottages, Wyke, Gillingham, Dorset SP8 4NQ
tel (01747) 825718; 020-7222 2723 (during exhibitions)
e-mail hendersons@dial.pipex.com
web site http://www.royal-miniature-society.org.uk
President Suzanne Lucas FLS, PRMS, FPSBA, *Treasurer* Alastair MacDonald, *Hon. Secretary* Pauline Gyles
Membership is by selection and standard of work over a period of years (ARMS associate, RMS full member). Annual Open Exhibition in November at the Westminster Gallery in London. Hand in Sept/Oct; schedules available in July (send sae). Applications and enquiries to the Executive Secretary. Founded 1895.

Miniaturists, British Society of
Director Margaret Simpson, Briargate, 2 The Brambles, Ilkley, West Yorkshire LS29 9DH
tel (01943) 609075
'The world's oldest miniature society.' Holds 2 open exhibitions p.a. Membership by selection. Founded 1895.

Miniaturists, The Hilliard Society of
The Executive Officer Pauline Warner, 11 Portway, Wells, Somerset BA5 2BA
tel (01749) 674472 *fax* (01749) 672918
web site http://ourworld.compuserve.com/homepages/bulldancer/miniatur.htm
President Cdr. G.W.G. Hunt, RMS, HS, MASF, RN
International society with approx. 300

members. Founded to increase knowledge and promote the art of miniature painting. Annual Exhibition held in May/June at Wells; seminars; Young People's Awards (11-19 years). Encourages Patron membership to keep collectors in touch with artists. Informative Newsletter includes technical section and news from miniature societies around the world. Membership: from £25. Founded 1982.

William Morris Society
Kelmscott House, 26 Upper Mall,
London W6 9TA
tel/fax 020-8741 3735
e-mail wmsoc@compuserve.com
Secretary Peter Faulkner
To spread knowledge of the life, work and ideas of William Morris; publishes *Newsletter* (quarterly) and *Journal* (2 p.a.). Library and collections open to the public Thu and Sat, 2-5pm. Founded 1955.

Motoring Artists, The Guild of
Administrator David Purvis, 71 Brook Court, Watling Street, Radlett, Herts. WD7 7JA
tel (01923) 853803
web site http://www.guildofmotoringartists.co.uk
To promote, publicise and develop motoring fine art; to build a recognised group of artists interested in motoring art, holding events and exchanging ideas and support; to hold motoring art exhibitions. Annual membership: £27.50, associate £22.50, friend £18. Founded 1986.

Motoring Writers, The Guild of
Contact General Secretary, 30 The Cravens, Smallfield, Surrey RH6 9QS
tel (01342) 843294 *fax* (01342) 844093
To raise the standard of motoring journalism. For writers, broadcasters, photographers on matters of motoring, but who are not connected with the motor industry.

Music Publishers Association Ltd
3rd Floor, Strandgate, 18-20 York Buildings, London WC2N 6JU
tel 020-7839 7779 *fax* 020-7839 7776
e-mail mpa@musicpublishers.co.uk
Chief Executive Sarah Faulder
The only trade organisation representing the UK music publishing industry: promotes its members' interests in copyright, trade and related matters. A number of sub-committees and groups deal with particular interests. Details of subscriptions available on request. Founded 1881.

Musical Association, The Royal
Secretary Bruce Phillips, 20 Third Acre Rise, Oxford OX2 9DA
tel/fax (01865) 862524
e-mail phillips@patrol.i-way.co.uk
web site http://www.soton.ac.uk/~stilwell/rma.html

Musicians, Incorporated Society of
10 Stratford Place,
London W1N 9AE
tel 020-7629 4413 *fax* 020-7408 1538
e-mail membership@ism.org
web site http://www.ism.org
President 2000-01: Sarah Walker CBE, *Chief Executive* Neil Hoyle
Professional body for musicians. Aims to promote the art of music; protect the interests and raise the standards of the musical profession; provide services, support and advice for its members. Publishes *Music Journal* (12 p.a.); Yearbook and 3 Registers of Specialists annually. Annual subscription: £93.

National Campaign for the Arts (NCA)
Pegasus House, 37-43 Sackville Street,
London W1X 2DL
tel 020-7333 0375 *fax* 020-7287 9959
Director Victoria Todd, *Deputy Director* Anna Leatherdale
Aims to be a strong advocate for all art forms on the national stage; to fight government funding cuts; to seek recognition for the value of the arts in a civilised society; to represent the diverse views and wishes of its members. Membership: £21.50; unwaged £15; special rates for organisations. Founded 1985.

The National Small Press Centre
BM BOZO, London WC1N 3XX
Director John Nicholson, *Press Officer* Cecilia Boggis, *Treasurer* Andy Hopton
Provides a focus for small presses and independent self-publishers and actively promotes them by collecting and disseminating information in the form of exhibitions, talks, courses, workshops, conferences and fairs. Publishes *News from the Centre* (bi-monthly) and *Small Press Listings* (quarterly) – joint subscription: £12 p.a.; *Handbook* £12 plus £1.50 p&p.

Small Press Fairs are held annually in the Royal Festival Hall, London. The Centre is twinned with the Mainz Mini-Press Archive in Mainz, Germany and the New York Small Press Center. Founded 1992.

National Union of Journalists
Head Office Acorn House, 314-320 Gray's Inn Road, London WC1X 8DP
tel 020-7278 7916 *fax* 020-7837 8143
e-mail nuj@mcr1.poptel.org.uk
Trade union for working journalists with 28,000 members and 147 branches throughout the UK and the Republic of Ireland, and in Paris, Brussels, Geneva and the Netherlands. It covers the newspaper press, news agencies and broadcasting, the major part of periodical and book publishing, and a number of public relations departments and consultancies, information services and Prestel-Viewdata services. Administers disputes, unemployment, benevolent and provident benefits. Official publications: *The Journalist*, *Freelance Directory*, *Freelance Fees Guide* and policy pamphlets.

National Viewers' and Listeners' Association
Director John C. Beyer, 3 Willow House, Kennington Road, Ashford, Kent TN24 0NR
tel (01233) 633936 *fax* (01233) 633836
e-mail info@nvala.org
web site http://www.nvala.org
Aims to encourage viewers and listeners to react effectively to programme content; to initiate and stimulate public discussion and parliamentary debate concerning the effects of broadcasting, and other mass media, on the individual, the family and society; to secure – then uphold – effective legislation to control obscenity and pornography in the media. Membership: £10 p.a. Founded 1965.

The Edith Nesbit Society
73 Brookehowse Road, London SE6 3TH
tel 020-8698 8907
Aims to promote an interest in the life and works of Edith Nesbit (1858-1924) by means of talks, a regular newsletter and and other publications, and visits to relevant places. Annual membership: £5; organisations/overseas £10. Founded 1996.

New Science Fiction Alliance (NSFA)
Chris Reed, BBR, PO Box 625, Sheffield S1 3GY
web site http://www.bbr-online.com/catalogue
Publicity Officer Chris Reed
The NSFA is committed to supporting the work of new writers and artists by promoting independent and small press publications worldwide. It was founded by a group of independent publishers to give writers the opportunity to explore the small press and find the right market for their material. It offers a mail order service for magazines. Founded 1989.

New Writing North
7-8 Trinity Chare, Quayside, Newcastle upon Tyne NE1 3DF
tel 0191-232 9991 *fax* 0191-230 1883
e-mails clarie.malcolm@virgin.net, john.mcgagh@virgin.net
web site http://www.newwritingnorth.com
Director Claire Malcolm, *Administrator* John McGagh
The literature development agency for the Northern Arts region. Organises events, readings and courses for writers; produces writing guides and a regular magazine with literary news, events and opportunities. Administers The Northern Playwriting Panel (aiding new drama) and the Northern Writers' Awards, which include tailored development packages for writers (mentoring and financial help). Has strong links with the post of Northern Literary Fellow. Founded 1996.

Book Publishers Association of New Zealand Inc.
PO Box 36477, Northcote, Auckland, New Zealand
tel (09) 480-2711 *fax* (09) 480-1130
e-mail bpanz@copyright.co.nz
President Daphne Brasell, *Secretary* Kathy Sheat

Copyright Council of New Zealand Inc.
PO Box 36477, Northcote, Auckland, New Zealand
tel (09) 480-2711 *fax* (09) 480-1130
Chairman Terence O'Neill-Joyce, *Secretary* Kathy Sheat

Newspaper Press Fund
Dickens House, 35 Wathen Road, Dorking, Surrey RH4 1JY
tel (01306) 887511 *fax* (01306) 888212
web site http://www.foundation.reuters.com/npf
Secretary D.J. Ilott
For the relief of hardship amongst member journalists, their widows and dependants. Financial assistance and retirement housing are provided. Limited help is available for non-member journalists and their dependants. For further information see web site.

The Newspaper Publishers Association Ltd
34 Southwark Bridge Road, London SE1 9EU
tel 020-7207 2200 *fax* 020-7928 2067

Newspaper Society

Bloomsbury House, 74-77 Great Russell Street, London WC1B 3DA
tel 020-7636 7014 *fax* 020-7631 5119
AdDoc DX35701 Bloomsbury
e-mail ns@newspapersoc.org.uk
Director David Newell

Oil Painters, Royal Institute of

17 Carlton House Terrace, London SW1Y 5BD
tel 020-7930 6844 *fax* 020-7839 7830
President Dr Richard Baines

Promotes and encourages the art of painting in oils. Open Annual Exhibition at the Mall Galleries, London.

Oils, Pastels and Acrylics, British Society of Painters in

Briargate, 2 The Brambles, Ilkley, West Yorkshire LS29 9DH
tel (01943) 609075
Director Margaret Simpson

Promotes interest and encourages high quality in the work of painters in these media. Holds 2 open exhibitions p.a. Membership by selection. Founded 1988.

Outdoor Writers' Guild

Secretary Terry Marsh, PO Box 520, Bamber Bridge, Preston, Lancs. PR5 8LF
tel/fax (01772) 696732
web site http://www.owg.org.uk

Aims to promote and maintain a high professional standard among writers and photographers who specialise in outdoor activities; represents members' interests to representative bodies in the outdoor leisure industry; circulates members with news of media opportunities; provides a forum for members to meet colleagues and others in the outdoor leisure industry. Presents annual literary and photographic awards. Annual membership: £45 plus £10 joining fee. Founded 1980.

Wilfred Owen Association

17 Belmont, Shrewsbury SY1 1TE
tel/fax (01743) 235904

To commemorate the life and work of Wilfred Owen, and to encourage and enhance appreciation of his work through visits, public events and a newsletter. Annual subscription: £4 (£6 overseas), groups/institutions £10, senior citizens/students/unemployed £2. Founded 1989.

PACT (Producers Alliance for Cinema and Television)

45 Mortimer Street, London W1N 7TD
tel 020-7331 6030 *fax* 020-7331 6700
e-mail enquiries@pact.co.uk
web site http://www.pact.co.uk
Chief Executive Shaun Williams, *Membership Officer* David Alan Mills

Pact Scotland
249 West George Street, Glasgow G2 4QE
tel 0141-302 1720 *fax* 0141-302 1721
e-mail margaret@pactscot.co.uk
web site http://www.pactscot.co.uk
Manager Margaret Scott

The main trade association for feature film and independent TV production companies. Represents the interests of over 1000 production companies throughout the UK: promotes and protects the commercial interests of its members; lobbies government and regulators on their behalf; negotiates terms of trade with broadcasters; provides a range of membership services including advice on business affairs, industrial relations and legal advice; operates a copyright registration service for members' proposals and treatments for films and TV programmes. Its representative office in Glasgow serves the interests of its Scottish members.

Painter-Printmakers, Royal Society of

Bankside Gallery, 48 Hopton Street, London SE1 9JH
tel 020-7928 7521
e-mail re&rws@bankside-gallery.demon.co.uk
President Prof David L. Carpanini Hon. RWS, RBA, RWA, NEAC

Membership (RE) open to British and overseas artists. An election of Associates is held annually, and applications for the necesssary forms and particulars should be addressed to the Secretary. The Society organises workshops and lectures on original printmaking; holds one members' exhibition per year. Friends of the RE open to all those interested in artists' original printmaking. Founded 1880.

Painters, Sculptors and Printmakers, National Society of

President Denis Baxter PNS, UA, FRSA
Hon. Secretary Gwen Spencer, 122 Copse Hill, London SW20 0NL
tel 020-8946 7878
web site http://www.wwid.co.uk/nationalsociety

An annual exhibition in London representing all aspects of art for artists of every creed and outlook. Newsletter (2 p.a.) for members. Founded 1930

The Pastel Society
17 Carlton House Terrace,
London SW1Y 5BD
tel 020-7930 6844 *fax* 020-7839 7830
President Thomas Coates

Pastel and drawings in pencil or chalk. Annual Exhibition open to all artists working in dry media held at the Mall Galleries, London. Members elected from approved candidates' list. Founded 1899.

The Mervyn Peake Society
Hon. President Sebastian Peake, *Chairman* Brian Sibley
Secretary Frank Surry, 2 Mount Park Road, London W5 2RP

Devoted to recording the life and works of Mervyn Peake; publishes a journal and newsletter. Annual subscription: £12 (UK and Europe), £5 (students), £16 (all other countries). Founded 1975.

PEN, International
International President Homero Aridjis
International Secretary Terry Carlbom,
9-10 Charterhouse Buildings, Goswell Road,
London EC1M 7AT
tel 020-7253 4308 *fax* 020-7253 5711

English PEN Centre
President Rachel Billington
Executive Director Diana Reich, 152-6 Kentish Town Road, London NW1 9QB
tel 020-7267 9444
e-mail enquiries@pen.org.uk

Scottish PEN Centre
President Robin Lloyd-Jones
Secretary Simon Berry, Greenleaf Editorial, 15A Lynedoch Street, Glasgow G3 6EF
tel/fax 0141-564 1958
e-mail greenenter@aol.com

Irish PEN Centre
President John B. Keane
Secretary Arthur Flynn, 26 Rosslyn, Killarney Road, Bray, Co. Wicklow, Republic of Ireland
tel (353) 1 282 8053

A world association of writers. PEN was founded in 1921 by C.A. Dawson Scott under the presidency of John Galsworthy, to promote friendship and understanding between writers and to defend freedom of expression within and between all nations. The initials PEN stand for Poets, Playwrights, Editors, Essayists, Novelists – but membership is open to all writers of standing (including translators), whether men or women, without distinction of creed or race, who subscribe to these fundamental principles. PEN takes no part in state or party politics. The International PEN Writers in Prison Committee works on behalf of writers imprisoned for exercising their right to freedom of expression, a right implicit in the PEN Charter to which all members subscribe. The International PEN Translations and Linguistic Rights Committee strives to promote the translations of works by writers in the lesser-known languages and to defend those languages. The Writers for Peace Committee exists to find ways in which writers can work for peaceful co-existence in the world. The Women Writers' Committee works to promote women's writing and publishing in developing countries. International Congresses are held most years. The 67th Congress was held in Moscow in 2000 and the 68th will be held in Manilla in 2001.

Membership of any one Centre implies membership of all Centres; at present 130 autonomous Centres exist throughout the world. Membership of the English Centre is £30 p.a. for country and overseas members, £35 for London members. Associate membership is available for writers not yet eligible for full membership and for persons connected with literature. The English Centre has a programme of literary lectures, discussion, dinners and parties. A yearly Writers' Day is open to the public as are some literary lectures.

Please apply to the Scottish and Irish Centres for information about their membership fees and activities.

Performing Right Society Ltd (PRS)
Copyright House, 29-33 Berners Street,
London W1P 4AA
tel 020-7580 5544 *fax* 020-7306 4455
and Elgar House, 41 Streatham High Road,
London SW16 1ER
tel 020-8664 4400 *fax* 020-8769 8792
e-mail info@prs.co.uk
web site http://www.prs.co.uk
Chief Executive John Hutchinson

Periodical Publishers Association
Queens House, 28 Kingsway, London WC2B 6JR
tel 020-7404 4166 *fax* 020-7404 4167
e-mail info1@ppa.co.uk
web site http://www.ppa.co.uk
Chief Executive Ian Locks

The Personal Managers' Association Ltd
Liaison Secretary Angela Adler, 1 Summer Road, East Molesey, Surrey KT8 9LX
tel/fax 020-8398 9796
e-mail aadler@pma-office.fsbusiness.co.uk
Association of theatrical agents in the theatre, film and entertainment world generally.

Photographers, The Association of
Co-Secretary Gwen Thomas, 81 Leonard Street, London EC2A 4QS
tel 020-7739 6669 *fax* 020-7739 8707
e-mail general@dophoto.co.uk
web site http://www.aophoto.co.uk
To protect and promote the interests of fashion advertising and editorial photographers. Annual subscription: £72-£355, depending on turnover. Founded 1969.

Photographers Association, Master
Hallmark House, 1 Chancery Lane, Darlington, Co. Durham DL1 5QP
tel (01325) 356555 *fax* (01325) 357813
e-mail generalenquiries@mpauk.com
web site http://www.mpa@mpauk.com
To promote and protect professional photographers. Members qualify for awards of Licentiate, Associate and Fellowship. Annual subscription: £105.

Photographic Society, The Royal
The Octagon, Milsom Street, Bath BA1 1DN
tel (01225) 462841 *fax* (01225) 448688
e-mail rps@rps.org
web site http://www.rps.org
Open membership organisation which promotes the art and science of photography and electronic imagery; publishes *The RPS Journal* (monthly) and *Imaging Science Journal* (quarterly). Founded 1853.

Photography, British Institute of Professional
Fox Talbot House, Amwell End, Ware, Herts. SG12 9HN
tel (01920) 464011
To represent all who practise photography as a profession in any field; to improve the quality of photography; establish recognised examination qualifications and a high standard of conduct; to safeguard the interests of the public and the profession. Admission can be obtained either via examinations, or by submission of work and other information to the appropriate examining board. Fellows, Associates and Licentiates are entitled to the designation Incorporated Photographer or Incorporated Photographic Technician. Organises numerous meetings and conferences in various parts of the country throughout the year; publishes *The Photographer* journal (monthly), and an annual Register of Members and *Guide to Buyers of Photography*, plus various pamphlets and leaflets on professional photography. Founded 1901, incorporated 1921.

Picture Libraries and Agencies, British Association of – see BAPLA

The Picture Research Association
(formerly SPREd)
2 Culver Drive, Oxted, Surrey RH8 9HP
tel (01883) 730123 *fax* (01883) 730144
e-mail pra@lippmann.co.uk
Chair Charlotte Lippman
Professional organisation of picture researchers and picture editors. See page 456.

Player-Playwrights
Secretary Peter Thompson, 9 Hillfield Park, London N10 3QT
tel 020-8883 0371
Meets on Monday evenings at St Augustine's Church Hall, Queen's Gate, London SW1. The society reads, performs and discusses plays and scripts submitted by members, with a view to assisting the writers in improving and marketing their work. Newcomers and new acting members are always welcome. Membership fees: £10 in the first year and £6 thereafter (and £1 per attendance). Founded 1948.

Playwrights Trust, New – see Writernet

Poetry Book Society
Book House, 45 East Hill, London SW18 2QZ
tel 020-8870 8403 *fax* 020-8877 1615
e-mail info@poetrybooks.co.uk
web site http://www.poetrybooks.co.uk
Chairman Maura Dooley, *Director* Clare Brown
Foremost in getting books of new poetry to readers through quarterly selections, special offers, and 300-strong backlist which it sells at favourable rates to members.

Publishes *Bulletin* (quarterly) and holds quarterly readings at the Royal Festival Hall. Runs the annual T.S. Eliot Prize for the best collection of new poetry. Operates as a charitable Book Club with annual membership (£10, £32, £125) open to all. Education resources for secondary schools and Children's Poetry Bookshelf for primary schools and libraries.

The Poetry Society
22 Betterton Street, London WC2H 9BU
tel 020-7420 9880 *fax* 020-7240 4818
e-mail poetrysoc@dial.pipex.com
web site http://www.poetrysoc.com
Subscriptions Subscriptions and Membership Dept, Freepost LON5410, London SW6 5YY
tel 020-7384 3261 *fax* 020-7736 9239
Chairman Judith Palmer, *Director* Christina Patterson

National membership body, open to all, to help poets and poetry thrive in Britain today. Publishes *Poetry Review* (quarterly) and *Poetry News* (quarterly), has an information and imagination service, runs promotions and educational projects, helps to co-ordinate National Poetry Day and the annual National Poetry Competition in association with British Telecommunications plc (see page 530). Provides a unique critical service, Poetry Prescription, where poetry of up to 100 lines is appraised by a chosen poet. Runs the Poetry Café at its premises in Covent Garden, which is also a venue for regular and one-off events, and is also available for hire for small readings and seminars (contact Jess York *tel* 020-7420 9887). Founded 1909.

The John Polidori Literary Society
Contact The Secretary, PO Box 6078, Nottingham NG16 4HX
Founder/President Franklin Charles Bishop

Promotes and encourages the appreciation of the life and works of Anglo-Italian John William Polidori MD (1795-1821) – novelist, poet, tragedian, philosopher, diarist, essayist, reviewer, traveller and one of the youngest ever students to obtain a medical degree at the age of 19. He introduced into English literature the icon of the vampire portrayed as an aristocratic, handsome seducer both cynical and amoral with his seminal work *The Vampyre – A Tale* (1819). The Society has a programme of republishing many of Polidori's literary works, including a recently found cache of previously unknown letters. The Society houses a collection of rare letters and memorabilia connected with Polidori. Subscription: £30 p.a. Founded 1990.

Portrait Painters, Royal Society of
17 Carlton House Terrace, London SW1Y 5BD
tel 020-7930 6844 *fax* 020-7839 7830
President Daphne Todd

Annual Exhibition at the Mall Galleries, London, of members' work and that of selected non-members. Three high-profile artists' awards are made: the Ondaatje Prize for Portraiture (£10,000), the Carroll Foundation Young Portrait Painters Award (£3000), and the Prince of Wales Award for Portrait Drawing (£2000). Also commissions consultancy service. Founded 1891.

Beatrix Potter Society
The Administrator, The Beatrix Potter Society Office, Resources for Business, South Park Road, Macclesfield, Cheshire SK11 6SH
tel (01625) 267880 *fax* (01625) 267879
e-mail bps@resources.demon.co.uk
Chairman Judy Taylor

Promotes the study and appreciation of the life and works of Beatrix Potter as author, artist, diarist, farmer and conservationist. Annual subscription: UK £10, overseas US$25/Can$30/Aus$30. Founded 1980.

The Powys Society
Hon. Secretary Chris Gostick, Old School House, George Green Road, George Green, Wexham, Bucks. SL3 6BJ
tel (01753) 578632
e-mail gostick@altavista.net
web site http://www.iaehv.nl/users/tklijn/pws/powys.htm

Aims to promote the greater public recognition and enjoyment of the writings, thought and contribution to the arts of the Powys family, particularly John Cowper (1872-1963), Theodore (1875-1953) and Llewelyn (1884-1939) Powys, and the many other family members and their close friends. Publishes an annual scholarly journal (*The Powys Journal*) and 3 newsletters per year, and holds an annual weekend conference in August, as well as other activities. Founded 1967.

Press Agencies, National Association of
The Administrator, 41 Lansdowne Crescent, Leamington Spa, Warks. CV32 4PR

tel (01926) 424181 *fax* (01926) 424760
Trade association representing the interests of the leading national news and photographic agencies. Annual subscription: £250. Founded 1983.

The Press Complaints Commission
Chairman The Rt Hon Lord Wakeham
Director Guy Black, 1 Salisbury Square, London EC4Y 8JB
tel 020-7353 1248 *Helpline tel* 020-7353 3732
fax 020-7353 8355
e-mail pcc@pcc.org.uk
web site http://www.pcc.org.uk
Independent body founded to oversee self-regulation of the Press. Deals with complaints by the public about the contents and conduct of British newspapers and magazines and advises editors on journalistic ethics. Complaints must be about the failure of newspapers or magazines to follow the letter or spirit of a Code of Practice, drafted by newspaper and magazine editors, adopted by the industry and supervised by the Commission. Founded 1991.

The J.B. Priestley Society
Secretary Rod Slater, 54 Framingham Road, Sale, Greater Manchester M33 3RJ
tel 0161-962 1477 (evening) *fax* 0161-905 3103
web site priestleysociety@slatersweb.demon.co.uk
Aims to widen the knowledge, understanding and appreciation of the published works of J.B. Priestley (1894-1984) and to promote the study of his life and career. Holds lectures and discussions and shows films. Publishes a newsletter. Organises walks to areas with Priestley connections, Annual Priestley Night and other social events. Annual membership: £10 single, £15 family, £3 concessionary. Founded 1997.

Printmakers Council
Clerkenwell Workshops, 31 Clerkenwell Close, London EC1R 0AT
tel/fax 020-7250 1927
President Stanley Jones, *Chair* Sheila Sloss
Artist-led group which aims 'to promote the use of both traditional and innovative printmaking techniques by:
• holding exhibitions of prints;
• providing information on prints and printmaking to both its membership and the public;
• encouraging co-operation and exchanges between members, other associations and interested individuals.'
Annual membership: £50; students £25. Founded 1965.

Private Libraries Association
Ravelston, South View Road, Pinner, Middlesex HA5 3YD
web site http://www.praxis.co.uk/ppuk/pla.htm
President B.C. Bloomfield, *Hon. Editors* David Chambers and Paul W. Nash, *Hon. Secretary* Frank Broomhead
International society of book collectors and private libraries. Publications include *The Private Library* (quarterly), annual *Private Press Books*, and other books on book collecting. Annual subscription: £25. Founded 1956.

The Publishers Association
1 Kingsway, London WC2B 6XF
tel 020-7565 7474 *fax* 020-7836 4543
e-mail mail@publishers.org.uk
web site http://www.publishers.org.uk
Chief Executive Ronnie Williams OBE, *Director of International and Trade Divisions (BDC)* Ian Taylor, *Director of Educational and Academic and Professional Publishing* John Davies
Founded 1896.

Publishers Association, International
3 avenue de Miremont, CH-1206 Geneva, Switzerland
tel (022) 346-30-18 *fax* (022) 347-57-17
President Alain Gründ, *Secretary-General* Mr Benoît Müller
Founded 1896.

Publishers Guild, Independent
PO Box 93, Royston, Herts. SG8 5GH
tel (01763) 247014 *fax* (01763) 246293
Full membership is open to new and established publishers and book packagers; supplier membership is available to specialists in fields allied to publishing (but not printers and binders). The Guild offers a forum for the exchange of ideas and information and represents the interests of its members. Annual membership: £75 (plus VAT). Founded 1962.

Publishers Licensing Society Ltd (PLS)
5 Dryden Street, London WC2E 9NW
tel 020-7829 8486 *fax* 020-7829 8488
Chairman Neil McRae, *Chief Executive* Jens Bammel
PLS has mandates from over 1600 publishers. These non-exclusive licences allow

PLS to include those publishers' works as part of the repertoire offered to licensees by CLA. The licences permit photocopying and some digitisation of parts of copyright works. The money collected from these licences is shared between publishers and authors and PLS has responsibility for distributing the publishers' share to the mandating companies. PLS represents the interests of a wide range of publishers from the multinationals to the single-title publisher. Founded 1981.

Publishers Publicity Circle

Secretary/Treasurer Heather White, 65 Airedale Avenue, London W4 2NN
e-mail ppc-@lineone.net
tel/fax 020-8994 1881

Enables all book publicists to meet and share information regularly. Monthly meetings provide a forum for press journalists, TV and radio researchers and producers to meet publicists collectively. Awards are presented for the best PR campaigns. Monthly newsletter includes recruitment advertising. Founded 1955.

Puzzle Writers, International Association of

Secretary Dr Jeremy Sims, 42 Brigstocke Terrace, Ryde, Isle of Wight PO33 2PD
e-mail drsims@cyber-hospital.org.uk
tel (01983) 811688

Aims to bring puzzle writers and games designers worldwide, both amateur and professional, closer together and to provide support and information. Promotes the art of puzzle writing and games design to publishers, games manufacturers and the general public. Membership: £25 p.a. Members must have e-mail commissions invited from publishers and Internet developers. Founded 1996.

The Radclyffe International Philosophical Association

BM-RIPhA, Old Gloucester Street, London WC1N 3XX
e-mail riphassoc@aol.com
President William Mann FRIPhA, *Secretary General* John Khasseyan FRIPhA

Aims to dignify those achievements which might otherwise escape formal recognition; to promote the interests and talent of its members; to encourage their good fellowship; and to form a medium for the exchange of ideas between members. Annual subscription: £30 (Fellows, Members and Associates). Published authors and artists usually enter at Fellowship level. Founded 1955.

The Radio Academy

5 Market Place, London W1N 7AH
e-mail info@radioacademy.org
web site http://www.radioacademy.org
Director John Bradford

The professional association for those engaged in the UK radio industry with over 1800 individual members and 30 corporate patrons. Organises conferences, seminars, debates, the annual UK Radio Festival and social events for members; publishes *Off Air* (monthly) newsletter and an annual *Yearbook*. Provides administrative support for the student Radio Association and the Radio Studies Network and organises a series of regional training events for those interested in getting into radio.

Railway Artists, Guild of

Chief Executive Officer F.P. Hodges Hon. GRA, 45 Dickins Road, Warwick CV34 5NS
tel (01926) 499246

Aims to forge a link between artists depicting railway subjects and to give members a corporate identity; also stages railway art exhibitions and members' meetings. Founded 1979.

Regional Arts Boards (RABs)

web site http://www.arts.org.uk

The 10 English RABs are each limited companies with charitable status. They are partners with the Arts Council of England (ACE), now merged with the Crafts Council, the British Film Institute (BFI) and the local authorities in developing, sustaining and promoting the arts in England. They work as arts development agencies (in the broadest sense), identifying needs and formulating strategies for arts provision in conjunction with their key partners, with government departments (e.g. in relation to EU Structural Funds, social inclusion and SRB), the private sector (including regional media and broadcasters) and Higher Education.

Financial support The RABs provide financial support for professional theatre companies, dance and mime companies, music ensembles, literature, film, art and new media centres, galleries, community projects, arts education and training, and a wide range of local arts bodies which promote arts events. The greater part of RAB funding is allocated to the professional sector, largely because of the greater expenses of professional arts companies and because amateur activities are more generally seen as the responsibility of local rather than regional authorities. Nevertheless, some assistance is provided to support high quality amateur work. Changes in Lottery distribution rules and greater decentralisation are also expanding the possibilities for supporting participation. Each RAB establishes its own priorities from year to year, in line with a strategy agreed with the Arts Council and, from 2000-01, with the Film Council. Generally, RABs are concerned to develop ventures in areas where provision is poor.

The Lottery The RABs act as agents for the ACE in the assessment of applications for awards. RABs are also able to help potential applicants with advice and discussion of their Lottery bids before applications are formally made. As a result of the 1998 Lottery Act, RABs are now delegated Lottery distributors of the ACE. Owing to the scale of existing committed projects, Lottery capital funding will be more difficult to access than hitherto. RABs will be handling the decisions on all capital bids up to £100,000 and supporting development work at regional level through the Regional Arts Lottery Programme (the successor to Arts for Everyone).

Wales and Scotland do not have regional boards but work directly through the Arts Council of Wales and the Scottish Arts Council.

English Regional Arts Boards
5 City Road, Winchester, Hants SO23 8SD
tel (01962) 851063 *fax* (01962) 842033
e-mail info@erab.org.uk
Chief Executive Christopher Gordon, *Assistant* Carolyn Nixson
The representative body for the 10 Regional Arts Boards in England. Its secretariat provides project management, services and information for the members and acts on their behalf in appropriate circumstances.

Eastern Arts Board
Cherry Hinton Hall, Cherry Hinton Road, Cambridge CB1 4DW
tel (01223) 215355 *fax* (01223) 248075
e-mail info@eab.eastern-arts.co.uk
Chief Executive Andrea Stark, *Literature Officer* Emma Drew, *Visual Arts Officer* Niki Braithwaite
Bedfordshire, Cambridgeshire, Essex, Hertfordshire, Norfolk and Suffolk; unitary authorities of Luton, Peterborough, Southend-on-Sea, Thurrock. Founded 1971.

East Midlands Arts Board
Mountfields House, Epinal Way, Loughborough, Leics. LE11 0QE
tel (01509) 218292 *fax* (01509) 262214
e-mail info@em-arts.co.uk
Chief Executive John Buston, *Literature Officer* Sue Stewart, *Visual Arts Officer* Alison Lloyd
Derbyshire (excluding High Peak District), Leicestershire, Northamptonshire and Nottinghamshire; unitary authorities of Derby, Leicester, Nottingham and Rutland. Founded 1969.

London Arts Board
Elme House, 133 Long Acre, London WC2E 9AF
Helpline 020-7670 2410
tel 020-7240 1313 *fax* 020-7670 2400
e-mail chrissie.cochrane@lonab.co.uk
Head of Literature Nick McDowell, *Principal Visual Arts and Crafts Officer* Holly Tebbutt
The area of the 32 London Boroughs and the City of London. Founded 1991.

North West Arts Board
Manchester House, 22 Bridge Street, Manchester M3 3AB
tel 0161-834 6644 *fax* 0161-834 6969
e-mail info@nwarts.co.uk
Chief Executive Sue Harrison, *Director Visual Arts and Media* Howard Rifkin, *Literature Officer* Bronwen Williams
Cheshire, Lancashire, High Peak District of Derbyshire; unitary authorities of Blackburn with Darwen, Blackpool, Halton, Warrington; metropolitan districts of Bolton, Bury, Knowsley, Liverpool, Manchester, Oldham, Rochdale, St Helens, Salford, Sefton, Stockport, Tameside, Trafford, Wigan, Wirral. Founded 1966.

Northern Arts
9-10 Osborne Terrace, Newcastle upon Tyne NE2 1NZ
tel 0191-281 6334 *fax* 0191-281 3276
e-mail nab@norab.demon.co.uk

Chief Executive Andrew Dixon, *Head of Published and Broadcast Arts* Mark Robinson, *Head of Visual Arts* James Bustard

Cumbria, Durham, Northumberland, metropolitan districts of Newcastle, Gateshead, Sunderland, North Tyneside and South Tyneside; unitary authorities of Darlington, Hartlepool, Middlesbrough, Redcar and Cleveland, and Stockton. Founded 1961.

South East Arts Board
Union House, Eridge Road, Tunbridge Wells, Kent TN4 8HF
tel (01892) 507200 *fax* (01892) 549383
e-mail info@seab.co.uk
Chief Executive Felicity Harvest, *Literature Officer* Suzanne Joinson, *Visual Arts Officer* Jim Shea

Kent, Surrey, East Sussex and West Sussex; unitary authorities of Brighton and Hove, Medway. Information and publications list available. Founded 1973.

South West Arts
Bradninch Place, Gandy Street, Exeter, Devon EX4 3LS
tel (01392) 218188 *fax* (01392) 413554
e-mail info@swa.co.uk
Chief Executive Nick Capaldi, *Visual Arts and Crafts Officer* Judith Robinson, *Director, Media and Published Arts* David Drake

Cornwall, Devon, Dorset (except Districts of Bournemouth, Christchurch and Poole), Gloucestershire, Somerset; unitary authorities of Bristol, Bath and North-East Somerset, South Gloucestershire, North Somerset, Plymouth, Torbay. Founded 1956.

Southern Arts Board
13 St Clement Street, Winchester, Hants SO23 9DQ
tel (01962) 855099 *fax* (01962) 861186
e-mail info@southernarts.co.uk
Chief Executive Robert Hutchison, *Literature Officer* Keiren Phelan, *Visual Arts Officer* Philip Smith

Berkshire, Hampshire, Oxfordshire, Wiltshire; unitary authorities of Bournemouth, Bracknell Forest, Isle of Wight, Milton Keynes, Poole, Portsmouth, Reading, Slough, Southampton, Swindon, West Berkshire, Windsor and Maidenhead, Wokingham; district council of Christchurch. Founded 1968.

West Midlands Arts Board
82 Granville Street, Birmingham B1 2LH
tel 0121-631 3121 *fax* 0121-643 7239
e-mail info@west-midlands-arts.co.uk
Chief Executive Sally Luton, *Director, Visual Arts, Crafts and Media* Caroline Foxhall

Worcester, Shropshire, Staffordshire, Warwickshire; unitary authorities of Herefordshire, Stoke on Trent, Telford and Wrekin; metropolitan districts of Birmingham, Coventry, Dudley, Sandwell, Solihull, Walsall, Wolverhampton. Founded 1971.

Yorkshire Arts
21 Bond Street, Dewsbury, West Yorkshire WF13 1AX
tel (01924) 455555 *fax* (01924) 466522
e-mail info@yarts.co.uk
Chief Executive Roger Lancaster, *Visual Arts and Crafts Officer* Jennifer Hallam, *Literature Officer* Steve Dearden

North Yorkshire; unitary authorities of East Riding, Kingston upon Hull, North Lincolnshire, York; metropolitan districts of Barnsley, Bradford, Calderdale, Doncaster, Kirklees, Leeds, Rotherham, Sheffield, Wakefield. Funds schemes and projects for the promotion of contemporary literature and writing activities. Provides grants for festivals, events, courses, residencies, publishing. Offers advice and information on various aspects of literature. Preliminary enquiry advised. Founded 1991.

Ridley Art Society
50 Crowborough Road, London SW17 9QQ
tel 020-8682 1212
e-mail ridley@artboy.demon.co.uk
President Ken Howard RA, *Chairman* dickon

Represents a wide variety of attitudes towards the making of art. In recent years has sought to encourage young artists. At least one central London exhibition annually. Founded 1889.

The Romantic Novelists' Association
Chairman Norma Curtis, 13 Makepeace Avenue, London N6 6EL
tel/fax 020-8341 6175
Hon. Secretary Annie Murray, 99 Connaught Road, Reading RG30 2UE
tel/fax 0118-958 7802
web site http://www.rna-uk.org

To raise the prestige of Romantic Authorship. Open to romantic and historical novelists. See also page 532.

Royal Academy of Arts
Piccadilly, London W1V 0DS
tel 020-7300 8000 *fax* 020-7300 8001

web site http://www.royalacademy.org.uk
President Prof Phillip King, *Keeper* Brendan Neiland RA, *Secretary* David Gordon
Academicians (RA) are elected from the most distinguished artists in the UK. Major loan exhibitions throughout the year with the Annual Summer Exhibition, June to August. Also runs art schools for 60 post-graduate students in painting and sculpture.

The Royal Literary Fund
3 Johnson's Court, off Fleet Street, London EC4A 3EA
tel 020-7353 7150 *fax* 020-7353 1350
e-mail egunnrlf@globalnet.co.uk
President His Honour Sir Stephen Tumim, *General Secretary* Eileen Gunn
Founded in 1790, the Fund is the oldest and largest charity serving literature, set up to help writers and their families who face hardship. It does not offer grants to writers who can earn their living in other ways, nor does it provide financial support for writing projects. But it sustains authors who have for one reason or another fallen on hard times – illness, family misfortune, or sheer loss of writing form. Applicants must have published work of approved literary merit, which may include important contributions to periodicals. The literary claim of every new applicant must be accepted by the General Committee before the question of need can be considered.

The Royal Society
6 Carlton House Terrace, London SW1Y 5AG
tel 020-7839 5561 *fax* 020-7930 2170
e-mail press@royalsoc.ac.uk
web site http://www.royalsoc.ac.uk
President Sir Aaron Klug OM, FRS, *Treasurer* Sir Eric Ash CBE, FRS, *Biological Secretary* Prof P.P.G. Bateson FRS, *Physical Secretary* Prof J.S. Rowlinson F.Eng, FRS, *Foreign Secretary* Prof B. Heap CBE, FRS, *Executive Secretary* Mr S. Cox CVO

Royal Society for the encouragement of Arts, Manufactures and Commerce (RSA)
8 John Adam Street, London WC2N 6EZ
tel 020-7930 5115 *fax* 020-7839 5805
e-mail general@rsa-uk.demon.co.uk, editor@rsajournal.co.uk
web site http://www.rsa.org.uk
Chairman of Council Sir Stuart Hampson, *Director* Penny Egan, *Commercial Director* Chris Bond, *Programme Director* Geoffrey Botting, *Communication Director* Paul Crake, *Director of Finance* Bernard Kelly, *Editor, RSA Journal* Celia Joicey, *Press Officer* Barbara Ormston
With over 20,000 Fellows, the RSA sustains a forum for people from all walks of life to come together to address issues, shape new ideas and stimulate action. It works through projects, award schemes and its lecture programme, the proceedings of which are recorded in *RSA Journal*. Founded 1754.

The Ruskin Society
Hon. Secretary Dr C.J. Gamble, 49 Hallam Street, London W1N 5LN
Aims to encourage a wider understanding of John Ruskin (1819-1900) and his contemporaries. Organises lectures and events which seek to explain to the public the nature of Ruskin's theories and to place these in a modern context. Affiliated to the Ruskin Foundation. Membership: £10. Founded 1997.

The Ruskin Society of London
Chairman and General Secretary Miss O.E. Forbes-Madden
Membership Secretary Mrs A. Hardy, 351 Woodstock Road, Oxford OX2 7NX
tel (01865) 310987/515962 *fax* (01865) 240448
Promotes literary and biographical interest in John Ruskin and his contemporaries. The Society publishes an annual *Ruskin Gazette* free to members. Members are also affiliated to other literary societies. Annual subscription: £10. Founded 1985.

SAA (Society of Amateur Artists)
PO Box 50, Newark, Notts. NG23 5GY
tel (01949) 844050 *fax* (01949) 844051
e-mail inspiration@saa.co.uk
web site www.saa.co.uk
Founded to inform, encourage and inspire everyone, whatever their ability, who wants to paint, and to promote friendship and companionship amongst fellow artists. Holds meetings and events at local level, organises painting holidays, workshops, local and international exhibitions and competitions, publishes newsletter *Paint* (quarterly). Membership: £17.50-£39.50; exhibition insurance included. Affiliated art club membership starts at £25 for third party public liability insurance. Overseas membership: £27.50. Founded 1992.

The Malcolm Saville Society
Secretary Mark O'Hanlon, 10 Bilford Road, Worcester WR3 8QA
e-mail mystery@witchend.demon.co.uk

web site http://www.witchend.demon.co.uk
Aims to remember and promote interest in the work of Malcolm Saville (1901-82), children's author. Regular social activities, book search, library, contact directory and magazine (3 p.a.). Membership: £7.50 p.a. (UK and EU), £12 p.a. (outside EU). Founded 1994.

The Dorothy L. Sayers Society
Chairman Christopher J. Dean, Rose Cottage, Malthouse Lane, Hurstpierpoint, West Sussex BN6 9JY
tel (01273) 833444 *fax* (01273) 835988
web site http://www.sayers.org.uk/
Secretaries Lenelle Davis, Jasmine Simeone
To promote and encourage the study of the works of Dorothy L. Sayers; to collect relics and reminiscences about her and make them available to students and biographers; to hold an annual seminar and other meetings; to publish proceedings, pamphlets and a bi-monthly bulletin. Annual subscription: £14. Founded 1976.

Scattered Authors Society
Secretary Anne Cassidy, 150 Wanstead Lane, Ilford, Essex IG1 3SG
e-mail anne.cassidy@cwcom.net
Aims to provide a forum for informal discussion, contact and support for professional writers in children's fiction. Founded 1998.

Science Fiction Association Ltd, The British
President Arthur C. Clarke
Membership Secretary Paul Billinger, 1 Long Row Close, Everdon, Daventry, Northants. NN11 3BE
e-mail bsfa@enterprise.net
For authors, publishers, booksellers and readers of science fiction, fantasy and allied genres. Publishes *Matrix*, an informal magazine of news and information; *Focus*, an amateur writers' magazine; *Vector*, a critical magazine and The Orbiter Service, a network of postal writers workshops. Founded 1958.

Science Writers, Association of British
c/o British Association for the Advancement of Science, 23 Savile Row, London W1X 2NB
tel 020-7439 1205 *fax* 020-7973 3051
e-mail absw@absw-demon.co.uk
Chairman Peter Wrobel, *Administrator* Barbara Drillsma
Association of science writers, editors, and radio, film and TV producers concerned with the presentation and communication of science, technology and medicine. Aims to improve the standard of science writing and to assist its members in their work.

Scottish Academy, Royal
The Mound, Edinburgh EH2 2EL
tel 0131-225 6671 *fax* 0131-225 2349
President Ian McKenzie Smith OBE, PRSA, *Secretary* Bill Scott RSA, *Treasurer* Isi Metzstein RSA
Academicians (RSA) and Associates (ARSA) and non-members may exhibit in the Annual Exhibition of Painting, Sculpture and Architecture, held approximately mid April to July; Festival Exhibition August/October. Other artists' societies' annual exhibitions, normally between October and January. Royal Scottish Academy Student Competition held in March. Founded 1826.

Scottish Arts
24 Rutland Square, Edinburgh EH1 2BW
tel 0131-229 8157 *fax* 0131-229 8887
Hon. Secretary Colin J.M. Sutherland
tel 0131-229 8157
Art, literature, music. Annual subscription: £275 (full); reductions available.

Scottish Arts Council
12 Manor Place, Edinburgh EH3 7DD
tel 0131-226 6051
Chairman Magnus Linklater, *Director* Tessa Jackson, *Literature Director* Jenny Brown, *Visual Arts Director* tba
Principal channel for government funding of the arts in Scotland, the Scottish Arts Council is funded by the Scottish Office. It aims to develop and improve the knowledge, understanding and practice of the arts, and to increase their accessibility throughout Scotland. It offers about 1300 grants a year to artists and arts organisations concerned with the visual arts, drama, dance and mime, literature, music, festivals, and traditional, ethnic and community arts. It is also the distributor of National Lottery funds to the arts in Scotland.

Scottish Book Marketing Group
Scottish Book Centre, 137 Dundee Street, Edinburgh EH11 1BG
tel 0131-228 6866 *fax* 0131-228 3220
e-mail allan@scottishbooks.org
Co-ordinator Allan Shanks
Co-operative venture set up by the Scottish Publishers Association and the

Booksellers Association (Scottish Branch) which aims to promote Scottish books through member booksellers. Founded 1986.

Scottish Book Trust
The Scottish Book Centre, 137 Dundee Street, Edinburgh EH11 1BG
tel 0131-229 3663 *fax* 0131-228 4293
e-mail scottish.book.trust@dial.pipex.com
With a particular responsibility towards Scottish writing, the Trust exists to promote literature and reading, and aims to reach (and create) a wider reading public than has existed before. It also organises exhibitions, readings and storytellings, operates an extensive children's reference library available to everyone and administers literary prizes, including the Scottish Writer of the Year and the Fidler Award. The Trust also publishes posters, literary guides and Directories and advises other relevant art organisations.

In addition, the Trust administers the Writers in Scotland scheme which supports writers' visits throughout Scotland. Readiscovery Touring, the Trust's touring arm, runs the Readiscovery Book Bus and publishes the literary *Touring Co-ordination Newsletter* (quarterly). Founded 1960.

Scottish Daily Newspaper Society
48 Palmerston Place, Edinburgh EH12 5DE
tel 0131-220 4353 *fax* 0131-220 4344
e-mail info@sdns.org.uk
Director J.B. Raeburn FCIS

Scottish Literary Studies, Association for (ASLS)
c/o Dept of Scottish History, 9 University Gardens, University of Glasgow G12 8QH
tel 0141-330 5309
e-mail cmc@arts.gla.ac.uk
Hon. President Dorothy McMillan, *Hon. Secretary* Jim Alison, *Hon. Treasurer* Dr Elaine Petrie, *Publishing Manager* Duncan Jones
Promotes the study, teaching and writing of Scottish literature and furthers the study of the languages of Scotland. Publishes annually an edited text of Scottish literature, an anthology of new Scottish writing, a series of academic journals and a Newsletter (2 p.a.). Also publishes *Scotnotes* – comprehensive study guides to major Scottish writers – literary texts and commentary cassettes designed to assist the classroom teacher, and a series of occasional papers. Organises 3 conferences a year. Annual membership: individuals/schools £33, UK students £19, corporate £61. Founded 1970.

Scottish Newspaper Publishers Association
48 Palmerston Place, Edinburgh EH12 5DE
tel 0131-220 4353 *fax* 0131-220 4344
e-mail info@snpa.org.uk
web site http://www.snpa.org.uk
President S. McPherson
Director J.B. Raeburn FCIS

Scottish Publishers Association
Scottish Book Centre, 137 Dundee Street, Edinburgh EH11 1BG
tel 0131-228 6866 *fax* 0131-228 3220
e-mail enquiries@scottishbooks.org
web site http://www.scottishbooks.org
Director Lorraine Fannin, *Administrator* Davinder Bedi, *Marketing Manager* Alison Rae, *Scottish Book Marketing Group/Training* Allan Shanks
Founded 1973.

Scottish Screen
249 West George Street, Glasgow G2 4QE
tel 0141-302 1700 *fax* 0141-302 1711
e-mail info@scottishscreen.com
web site http://www.scottishscreen.com
Information Officer Isabella Edgar
Responsible to the Scottish parliament for developing all aspects of screen industry and culture in Scotland through script and company development, short film production, distribution of National Lottery production finance, training, education, exhibition funding, the Film Commission locations support, and the Scottish Film and Television Archive. Founded 1997.

Screenwriters' Workshop
(formerly London Screenwriters' Workshop)
Suffolk House, 1-8 Whitfield Place, London W1P 5SF
tel 020-7387 5511
web site http://www.lsw.org.uk
Contact Alan Denman, Paul Gallagher
Forum for contact, information and tuition, the SW helps new and established writers work successfully in the film and TV industry, and organises a continuous programme of activities, events, courses and seminars, all of which are reduced to members and open to non-members at reasonable rates. The SW is the largest screenwriting group in

Europe and supports Euroscript, a Media II-funded organisation developing scripts for film and TV throughout the EU. Annual subscription: £30. Founded 1983.

Scribes and Illuminators, Society of (SSI)
Hon. Secretary 6 Queen Square, London WC1N 3AR
e-mail scribe@calligraphy.org
web site http://www.calligraphy.org

Aims to advance the crafts of writing and illumination. International membership of professional calligraphers and those with a committed interest. Holds regular exhibitions, provides opportunities for discussion, demonstration and sharing of research. Membership: £27 Lay Members, £22 Friends. Founded 1921.

SCRIBO
Contact K. & P. Sylvester, Flat 1, 31 Hamilton Road, Bournemouth BH1 4EQ

A postal forum for novelists (published and unpublished), SCRIBO aims to give friendly, informed encouragement and help, to discuss all matters of interest to novelists and to offer criticism via MSS folios: crime/thrillers, fantasy/sci-fi, mainstream, aga-saga/popular women's fiction, 2 literary folios (mostly graduates writing serious fiction). Porn is not accepted. Joining fee: £5 (send sae). Founded 1971.

The Shaw Society
Secretary Barbara Smoker, 51 Farmfield Road, Downham, Bromley, Kent BR1 4NF
tel 020-8697 3619
e-mail anthnyellis@aol.com

Improvement and diffusion of knowledge of the life and works of Bernard Shaw and his circle. Meetings in London; annual festival at Ayot St Lawrence in July; publishes *The Shavian*. Annual membership: £12/$20.

Society of Authors – see Authors, The Society of, and page 507

Society of Young Publishers
Contact The Secretary, c/o The Bookseller, 12 Dyott Street, London WC1A 1DF
e-mail thesyp@thesyp.demon.co.uk
web site http://www.thesyp.demon.co.uk

Organises monthly speaker meetings at which senior figures talk on topics of key importance to the industry today. Membership is open to anyone employed in publishing or hoping to be soon, with associate membership available to those over the age of 35. Also organises social and other events and runs a job database which matches candidates with potential employers. London meetings are held at the Publishers Association, usually on the last Wednesday of the month at 6.30pm. Also a branch in Oxford. Founded 1949.

Songwriters & Composers, The Guild of International
Sovereign House, 12 Trewartha Road, Praa Sands, Penzance, Cornwall TR20 9ST
tel (01736) 762826 *fax* (01736) 763328
e-mail songmag@aol.com
web site http://www.songwriters-guild.co.uk
Secretary Carole Ann Jones

Gives advice to members on contractual and copyright matters; assists with protection of members rights; assists with analysis of members' works; international collaboration register free to members; outlines requirements to record companies, publishers, artists. Publishes *Songwriting & Composing* (quarterly). Annual subscription: £38 (UK), £50 (EU/overseas).

Songwriters, Composers and Authors, British Academy of – see British Academy of Composers and Songwriters

South Africa, Publishers' Association of (PASA)
PO Box 22640, Fish Hoek 7974, South Africa
tel (021) 782-7677 *fax* (021) 782-7679
e-mail pasa@publishsa.co.za
web site http://www.publishsa.co.za/

South African Writers' Circle
Secretary Mr Pat Lister, PO Box 10558, Marine Parade, Durban 4056, South Africa
tel (031) 205-1769
e-mail sawc@xoommail.com

Aims to help and encourage all writers, new and experienced, in the art of writing. Publishes a monthly *Newsletter*, and runs competitions with prizes for the winners. Annual subscription: R80 (local), R90 (overseas). Founded 1960.

South & Mid Wales Association of Writers (SAMWAW)
Secretary Julian Rosser, c/o IMC Consulting Group, Denham House, Lambourne Crescent, Cardiff CF4 5ZW
tel 029-2076 1170 *fax* 029-2076 1304

Aims to encourage the art of writing in all its forms, for both beginners and established writers. Offers a range of courses (see page 577). Membership is drawn from all over the UK as well as overseas. Publishes a newsletter and runs competitions, including the Mathew Prichard Award for Short Story Writing (see page 533). Membership: £7 p.a. single, £12 joint. Founded 1965.

Southwest Scriptwriters
Secretary John Colborn *tel* 0117-902 0788
e-mail southwest_scriptwriters@hotmail.com
web site http://www.southwest-scriptwriters.co.uk
Workshops members' drama scripts for stage, screen, radio and TV with the aim of improving their chances of professional production, meeting at the Bristol Old Vic. Also hosts regular talks by professional dramatists. Presents short annual seasons of script-in-hand performances of members' work at the New Vic Studio. Bi-monthly newsletter. Membership: £5 p.a. Founded 1994.

Spanish Publishers' Association, Federation of
(Federación de Gremios de Editores de España)
Cea Bermúdez, 44-2° Dcha. 28003 Madrid, Spain
tel (91) 534 51 95 *fax* (91) 535 26 25
e-mail fgee@fujitsu.es
President Josef Lluis, *Secretary* Ana Moltó Blasco

Spoken Word Publishing Association (SWPA)
Secretary Lynne Powell, 2 Richmond Road, Basingstoke, Hants. RG21 5NX
tel (01256) 358343
web site http://www.swpa.org.uk
The UK trade association for the spoken word industry, SWPA is an umbrella organisation which brings together all those involved – publishers, performers, producers, distributors, retailers, manufacturers. It aims to increase the profile of the spoken word in the media, the retail trade and among the general public, and to provide a forum for discussion. Membership: £50-£600 p.a. Founded 1994.

Sports Writers' Association of Great Britain (SWA)
Secretary Trevor Bond, 244 Perry Street, Billericay, Essex CM12 0QP
tel (01277) 651708 *fax* (01277) 622890
Represents sports journalists across the country and is Britain's voice in international sporting affairs. Offers advice to members covering major events, acts as a consultant to organisers of major sporting events on media requirements. Member of the BOA Press Advisory Committee. Membership: £23.50 p.a. Founded 1948.

SPREd (Society of Picture Researchers and Editors) – see The Picture Research Association

Stationers and Newspaper Makers, Worshipful Company of
Stationers' Hall, London EC4M 7DD
tel 020-7248 2934 *fax* 020-7489 1975
Master Richard T.H. Harrison, *Clerk* Brig. Denzil Sharp, AFC
One of the Livery Companies of the City of London. Connected with the printing, publishing, bookselling, newspaper and allied trades. Founded 1557.

The Robert Louis Stevenson Club
Secretary Margaret Bean, c/o 37 Lauder Road, Edinburgh EH9 1UE
tel 0131-667 6256 *fax* 0131-662 0353
e-mail mbeanconferences@compuserve.com
Aims to foster interest in Stevenson's life (1850-94) and works through various events and its newsletter. Membership: £15 p.a., £100 life. Founded 1920.

Strip Illustration, Society for – now Comics Creators Guild

Sussex Authors, The Society of
Secretary Michael Legat, Bookends, Lewes Road, Horsted Keynes, Haywards Heath, West Sussex RH17 7DP
tel/fax (01825) 790755
e-mail michael@bookends.claranet.com
Aims to encourage social contact between members, and to promote interest in literature and authors. Membership open to writers living in Sussex who have had at least one book commercially published or who have worked extensively in journalism, radio, TV or the theatre. Annual subscription: £10. Founded 1969.

Sussex Playwrights' Club
Hon. Secretary, Sussex Playwrights' Club, 2 Princes Avenue, Hove, East Sussex BN3 4GD

Swedish Publishers' Association
(Svenska Förläggareföreningen)
Drottninggaten 97, 2 tr., 113 60 Stockholm, Sweden
tel 08-736 19 40 *fax* 08-736 19 44

e-mail svf@forlagskansli.se
web site http://www.forlagskansli.se
Director Kristina Ahlinder

Founded 1843.

Television Society, Royal

Holborn Hall, 100 Gray's Inn Road,
London WC1X 8AL
tel 020-7430 1000 *fax* 020-7430 0924
e-mail membership@rts.org.uk
web site http://www.rts.org.uk
Executive Director Michael Bunce, *Membership Services Manager* Deborah Halls

The Tennyson Society

Secretary Kathleen Jefferson, Brayford House, Lucy Tower Street, Lincoln LN1 1XN
tel (01522) 552851 *fax* (01522) 552858
e-mail lincs.lib@dial.pipex.com
web site http://www.tennysonsociety.org.uk

Promotes the study and understanding of the life and work of the poet Alfred, Lord Tennyson and supports the Tennyson Research Centre in Lincoln; holds lectures, visits and seminars; publishes the *Tennyson Research Bulletin* (annual), Monographs and Occasional Papers; tapes/recordings available. Annual membership: £8, family £10, institutions £15. Founded 1960.

Theatre Exchange, International

Registered office Drama Association of Wales, Cardiff
Secretariat 20 Abbey Road, Grimsby DN32 0HW
tel (01472) 343424

To encourage, foster and promote exchanges of theatre; student, educational, adult, puppet theatre activities at international level. To organise international seminars, workshops, courses and conferences, and to collect and collate information of all types for national and international dissemination.

Theatre Research, The Society for

c/o The Theatre Museum, 1E Tavistock Street, London WC2E 7PA
Hon. Secretaries Eileen Cottis and Frances Dann
e-mail e.cottis@btinternet.com
web site http://www.blot.co.uk/str

Publishes annual volumes and journal (3 p.a.), *Theatre Notebook*, holds lectures and makes annual research grants (current total sum approx. £4000). Starting in 1998, the Society's 50th anniversary, it awards an annual prize of £400 for the best book published in English on the historical or current practice of the British theatre.

Theatre Writers' Union – incorporated into The Writers' Guild of Great Britain

Angela Thirkell Society

Chairman Mrs I.J. Cox, 32 Murvagh Close, Cheltenham, Glos. GL53 7QY
tel (01242) 251604
Secretary Mrs P. Aldred, 54 Belmont Park, London SE13 5BN
tel 020-8244 9339
web site http://www.angelathirkell.org

Aims 'to honour the memory of Angela Thirkell (1890-1960) as a writer, and to make her works available to new generations'. Publishes an *Annual Journal*, and encourages Thirkell studies. Annual membership: £7. Founded 1980.

The Edward Thomas Fellowship

Butler's Cottage, Halswell House, Goathurst, Nr Bridgwater, Somerset TA5 2DH
tel (01278) 662856
Hon. Secretary Richard N. Emeny

To perpetuate the memory of Edward Thomas, poet and writer, foster an interest in his life and work, to assist in the preservation of places associated with him and to arrange events which extend fellowship amongst his admirers. Annual subscription: £7. Founded 1980.

The Tolkien Society

Secretary Sally Kennett, 210 Prestbury Road, Cheltenham, Glos. GL52 3ER
Membership Secretary Trevor Reynolds, 65 Wentworth Crescent, Ash Vale, Surrey GU12 5LF
e-mail trevor@caerlas.demon.co.uk
web site http://www.tolkiensociety.org

Translation & Interpreting, The Institute of (ITI)

Contact The Secretary, 377 City Road, London EC1V 1ND
tel 020-7713 7600 *fax* 020-7713 7650
e-mail info@iti.org.uk
web site http://www.iti.org.uk

The ITI is a professional association of translators and interpreters which aims to promote the highest standards in translating and interpreting. It has a strong corporate membership and runs professional development courses and conferences, sometimes in conjunction with its language, regional and subject networks. Membership is open to those with a genuine and proven involvement in translation and interpreting of all kinds, but particularly technical and commercial translation. As a full and active member of the International Federation of Translators, it maintains good contacts with translators and interpreters worldwide. ITI's directory of members (on-line and in CD-Rom and paper format) and its bi-monthly bulletin are available from the Secretariat.

The Translators Association
84 Drayton Gardens, London SW10 9SB
tel 020-7373 6642
e-mail authorsoc@writers.org.uk
Specialist unit within the membership of the Society of Authors (see page 507), exclusively concerned with the interests and special problems of translators into English whose work is published or performed commercially in Great Britain and English-speaking countries overseas. Members are entitled to general and legal advice on all questions connected with their work, including remuneration and contractual arrangements with publishers, editors, broadcasting organisations. Publishes a *Quick Guide* to literary translation (£2 to non-members). Administers a range of translation prizes. Annual subscription: £70 by direct debit, £75 by cheque – includes membership of the Society of Authors. Founded 1958.

Travel Writers, The British Guild of
Hon. Secretary Adele Evans, Springfield, Hangersley Hill, Ringwood, Hants BH24 3JN
tel/fax (01425) 470946
e-mail adeleevans@compuserve.com
Arranges meetings, discussions and visits for its 190 members (who are all professional travel journalists) to promote and encourage the public's interest in travel. Publishes a monthly newsletter (for members only) and an annual *Yearbook*, which contains details of members and lists travel industry PRs and contacts.

The Trollope Society
9A North Street, London SW4 0HN
tel 020-7720 6789
e-mail <trolsoc@barset.fsnet.co.uk
Chairman John Letts, *Secretary* Phyllis Eden
Aims to produce the first ever complete edition of the novels of Anthony Trollope (46 vols now available). Membership: £24 p.a., £240 (life). Founded 1987.

The Turner Society
BCM Box Turner, London WC1N 3XX
Chairman Evelyn Joll
To foster a wider appreciation of all facets of Turner's work; to encourage exhibitions of his paintings, drawings and engravings. Publishes *Turner Society News* (3 p.a.). Annual subscription: £10; other rates on application. Founded 1975.

Typographic Designers, Society of
President John Harrison FSTD, *Chair* David Quay FSTD/Freda Sack FSTD
Hon. Secretary Helen Cornish, Chapelfield Cottage, Randwick, Stroud, Glos. GL6 6HS
tel (01453) 759311 *fax* (01453) 767466
Advises and acts on matters of professional and educational practice, provides a better understanding of the typographic craft and the rapidly changing technology in the graphic industries by lectures, discussions and through the journal *Typographic*. Students of typography and graphic design are encouraged to gain Membership of the Society by entering the annual student assessment project. Founded 1928.

Vampire Research Society
International Secretary Dennis Crawford, PO Box 542, London N6 6BG
The Society's sole purpose is to study and investigate vampirological phenomena, and publishes its research findings in books and academic reports. Holds the largest archive of vampire-related material in the world, to which membership allows access. Publishes a newsletter. Not affiliated to any other vampire interest group and remains aloof from the wider subculture. Membership: by invitation. Founded 1970.

Ver Poets
Organiser/Editor May Badman, Haycroft, 61-63 Chiswell Green Lane, St Albans, Herts. AL2 3AL
tel (01727) 867005
Encourages the writing and study of poetry as a part of our culture. Help and advice, assessment and comment on work are available on request. Holds meetings (fortnightly) in St Albans; organises workshops and competitions for members, and produces anthologies of members' work. The annual Open Competition is also open to non-

members. Annual membership: £12-£50 UK, £15 ($30) overseas. Founded 1966.

Visiting Arts

11 Portland Place, London W1N 4EJ
tel 020-7389 3019 *fax* 020-7389 3016
e-mail office@visitingarts.demon.co.uk
web site http://www.britcoun.org/visitingarts/
Director Terry Sandell OBE

The national agency for promoting the flow of international arts into the UK and developing related cultural links abroad to help build cultural awareness and positive cultural relations. Activities include providing advice, information, training, consultancy and publications, as well as special projects and project development. Visiting Arts is a joint venture of the Arts Councils of England, Scotland, Wales and Northern Ireland, the Crafts Council, the Foreign Commonwealth Office and the British Council. It has a project development award scheme, open to British-based promoters and venues promoting quality foreign work that has a clear country-specific dimension, which can demonstrate its contribution to the development of cultural awareness and cultural relations and which will produce some kind of continuing impact, influence or follow-up. Founded 1977.

Visual Communication Association, International (IVCA)

Bolsover House, 5-6 Clipstone Street, London W1P 8LD
tel 020-7580 0962 *fax* 020-7436 2606
e-mail info@ivca.org
web site http://www.ivca.org
Membership Secretary Nick Gardiner

For those who use or supply visual communication. Aims to promote the industry and provide a collective voice; provides a range of services, publications and events to help existing and potential users to make the most of what video, film, multimedia and live events can offer their business. Annual membership: from £165. Founded 1987.

Voice of the Listener & Viewer (VLV)

101 King's Drive, Gravesend, Kent DA12 5BQ
tel (01474) 352835
Chairman Jocelyn Hay, *Administrative Secretary* Linda Forbes

Independent association representing the citizen and consumer interest in broadcasting and the interests of listeners and viewers on all broadcasting issues. Concerned to maintain the principle of public service plus independence, quality and diversity in British broadcasting. Has over 2000 individual members, 20 charities as corporate members and more than 50 colleges in academic membership. Holds frequent public conferences. Publishes a quarterly newsletter and briefings on broadcasting developments. Founded 1983.

Wales, Arts Council of – see Arts Council of Wales

The Walmsley Society

Secretary Fred Lane, April Cottage, 1 Brand Road, Hampden Park, Eastbourne, East Sussex BN22 9PX
Membership Secretary Mrs Elizabeth Buckley, 21 The Crescent, Hipperholm, Halifax, West Yorkshire HX3 8NQ

Aims to promote and encourage an appreciation of the literary and artistic heritage left to us by Leo and J. Ulric Walmsley. Founded 1985.

Water Colours, Royal Institute of Painters in

17 Carlton House Terrace, London SW1Y 5BD
tel 020-7930 6844 *fax* 020-7839 7830
President Ronald Maddox Hon. RWS

The Institute promotes the appreciation of watercolour painting in its traditional and contemporary forms, primarily by means of an annual exhibition at the Mall Galleries, London SW1 of members' and non-members' work and also by members' exhibitions at selected venues in Britain and abroad. Members elected from approved candidates' list. Founded 1831.

Watercolour Society, British

Director Margaret Simpson, Briargate, 2 The Brambles, Ilkley, West Yorkshire LS29 9DH
tel (01943) 609075

Promotes the best in traditional watercolour painting. Holds 2 open exhibitions p.a. Membership by selection. Founded 1830.

Watercolour Society, Royal

Bankside Gallery, 48 Hopton Street, London SE1 9JH
tel 020-7928 7521
e-mail re&rws@bankside-gallery.demon.co.uk

President John Doyle MBE

Membership (RWS) open to British and overseas artists. An election of Associates is held annually, and applications for the necessary forms and particulars should be addressed to the Secretary. The Society gives lectures on watercolour paintings; organises residential/non-residential courses; holds open exhibition in summer. Exhibitions: spring and autumn. Friends of the RWS open to all those interested in watercolour painting. Founded 1804.

Mary Webb Society

Secretary Sue Higginbotham, 8 The Knowe, Willaston, Neston, Cheshire CH64 1TA
tel 0151-327 5843
web site http://www.wlv.qc.uk/~me1927/mwebb.html/

For devotees of the literature and works of Mary Webb and of the beautiful Shropshire countryside of her novels. Publishes an annual journal, organises summer schools and other events in various locations related to Webb's life and works. Archives, lectures; tours arranged for individuals and groups. Founded 1972.

The H.G. Wells Society

Hon. General Secretary J.R. Hammond, 49 Beckingthorpe Drive, Bottesford, Nottingham NG13 0DN
web site http://www.rdg.ac.uk/~lhsjamse/wells/wells.htm

Promotes an active interest in and an appreciation of the life, work and thought of H.G. Wells. Publishes *The Wellsian* (annual) and *The Newsletter* (bi-annual). Annual subscription £16, corporate £20. Founded 1960.

Welsh Academy – see Academi

Welsh Books Council/Cygngor Llyfrau Cymru

Castell Brychan, Aberystwyth, Ceredigion SY23 2JB
tel (01970) 624151 *fax* (01970) 625385
e-mail castellbrychan@cllc.org.uk
web site http://www.cllc.org.uk
Director Gwerfyl Pierce Jones

Founded in 1961 to promote Welsh-language and English-language books of Welsh interest. Editorial, design, marketing, distribution and children's books promotion services provided for publishers.

Welsh Union of Writers

Secretary Jean Henderson, 13 Tyn-y-Coed Road, Pentyrch, Cardiff CF15 9NP
tel 029-2089 0428
e-mail wuw@btinternet.com
web site http://info.cf.ac.uk/ccin/wuw/wuwhome.html

Independent union open to persons born or working in Wales with at least one publication in a quality outlet, fiction, non-fiction or poetry. Lobbies for writing in Wales; represents members in disputes; annual conference; occasional events and publications. Annual subscription: £15 plus £5 joining fee. Associate membership for others with a committed interest in writing: £5 plus £5 joining fee. Particularly welcomes applications from younger writers. Founded 1982.

The West Country Writers' Association

President Christopher Fry FRSL, DLitt, *Chair* Dr John Harcup
Hon. Secretary Anne Double, Malvern View, Garway Hill, Hereford HR2 8EZ
tel (01981) 580495

To foster love of literature in the West Country and to give authors an opportunity of meeting to exchange news and views. Holds Annual Weekend Congress and Regional Meetings. Newsletter (2 p.a.). Membership open to published authors. Annual subscription: £10.

West of England Academy, Royal

Queens Road, Clifton, Bristol BS8 1PX
tel 0117-973 5129 *fax* 0117-923 7874
web site http://www.rwa.org.uk
President Derek Balmer, *Academy Secretary* Rachel Fear

Aims to further the interests of practising painters and sculptors. Holds art exhibitions and is a meeting place for artists and their work. Founded 1844.

The Oscar Wilde Society

9 Ingram House, Park Road, Hampton Wick, Kingston upon Thames KT1 4BA
tel 020-8977 5671
Secretary Rosemary McGlashon

Wildlife Artists, Society of

17 Carlton House Terrace, London SW1Y 5BD
tel 020-7930 6844 *fax* 020-7839 7830
President Bruce Pearson

To promote and encourage the art of wildlife painting and sculpture. Open Annual Exhibition at the Mall Galleries, The Mall, London SW1.

Charles Williams Society
Secretary Richard Sturch, 3 The Rise, Islip, Kidlington, Oxon OX5 2TG
To promote interest in the life and work of Charles Walter Stansby Williams (1886-1945) and to make his writings more easily available. Founded 1975.

The Henry Williamson Society
Chairman Will Harris
General Secretary/Membership Secretary Mrs Margaret Murphy, 16 Doran Drive, Redhill, Surrey RH1 6AX
tel (01737) 763228
web site http://www.hwsoc.org.uk
Aims to encourage a wider readership and greater understanding of the literary heritage left by Henry Williamson. Two meetings annually; also weekend activities. Publishes an annual journal. Annual subscription: £12; family, student and overseas rates available. Founded 1980.

Circle of Wine Writers
Secretary Stephen Skelton, 21 Golden Square, Tenterden, Kent TN30 6RN
tel (01580) 765242 *fax* (01580) 765224
e-mail spskelton@btinternet.co
An association for those engaged in communicating about wines and spirits. Produces *Circle Update* newsletter (5 p.a.), organises tasting sessions as well as a programme of meetings and talks. Membership is by election (£45 p.a.). Founded 1960.

The P.G. Wodehouse Society (UK)
Details Tony Ring, 34 Longfield, Great Missenden, Bucks. HP16 0EG
tel (01494) 864848 *fax* (01494) 863048
e-mail tring@sauce34.freeserve.co.uk
web site http://www.eclipse.co.uk/wodehouse
Aims to promote enjoyment of P.G. Wodehouse (1881-1975). Publishes *Wooster Sauce* (quarterly) and *By The Way* papers (3 p.a.) which cover diverse subjects of Wodehousean interest. Holds events, entertainments and meetings throughout Britain. Membership: £15. Founded 1997.

Women Artists, The Society of
Executive Secretary 1 Knapp Cottages, Wyke, Gillingham, Dorset SP8 4NQ
tel (01747) 825718 *fax* (01747) 826835
e-mail hendersons@dial.pipex.com
web site http://www.mcis.net.uk/swa
President Elizabeth Meek RMS, HS
Founded in 1855 when women were not considered as serious contributors to art and could not compete for professional honours, the Society continues to promote art by women. Receiving day end January for annual open exhibition held just before Easter at Westminster Gallery, Westminster Central Hall, Storey's Gate, London SW1H 9NH. Election to membership by invitation, based on work submitted to the exhibition.

Women in Publishing
c/o The Publishers Association, 1 Kingsway, London WC2B 6XF
web site http://www.cyberiacafe.net/wip/
Promotes the status of women within publishing; encourages networking and mutual support among women; provides a forum for the discussion of ideas, trends and subjects to women in the trade; offers practical training for career and personal development; supports and publicises women's achievements and successes. Each year WiP presents 2 awards: the Pandora Award is given in recognition of significant personal contributions to women in publishing, and the New Venture Award is presented to a recent venture which reflects the interests and concerns of women in the 21st century. Annual subscription: £20. Founded 1977.

Women Writers and Journalists, Society of
Secretary Jean Hawkes, 110 Whitehall Road, London E4 6DW
tel 020-8529 0886
e-mail swwriters@aol.com
For women writers: lectures, monthly lunchtime meetings; free literary advice for members. *The Woman Writer* (4 p.a.). Annual subscription: town £30, country £25, overseas £20; joining fee £10. Founded 1894.

Women Writers Network
Membership Secretary Cathy Smith, 23 Prospect Road, London NW2 2JU
tel 020-7794 5861
London-based network serving both salaried and independent women writers from all disciplines, and providing a forum for the exchange of information, support and networking opportunities. Holds monthly meetings, workshops and publishes a newsletter and members' Directory. Send A5 or A4 sae for informa-

tion. Annual membership: £35. Meetings only: £5 at door. Founded 1985.

Virginia Woolf Society of Great Britain

Details Paul Evans, Advertising Officer, 13 Berriedale Drive, Sompting, Lancing, Sussex BN15 0LE
tel/fax (01903) 764655
e-mail paul@evansp38.fsnet.co.uk
web site http://orlando.jp.org/vwsgb/

Acts as a forum for British admirers of Virginia Woolf (1882-1941) to meet, correspond and share their enjoyment of her work. Publishes the *Virginia Woolf Bulletin*. Membership £12 p.a. (£15 overseas). Founded 1998.

Worker Writers and Community Publishers, The Federation of

67 The Boulevard, Tunstall, Stoke-on-Tent ST6 6BD
tel/fax (01782) 822327
e-mail fwwcp@cwcom.net
web site http://www.fwwcp.mcmail.com

A network of writers groups and community publishers which promotes working-class writing and publishing. Annual membership: funded groups £40; unfunded £20. Founded 1976.

Writernet

(formerly New Playwrights Trust)
Interchange Studios, Dalby Street, London NW5 3NQ
tel 020-7284 2818 *fax* 020-7482 5292
e-mail npt@easynet.co.uk
Executive Director Jonathan Meth

Research and development organisation for writers and aspiring writers for all forms of live and recorded performance, and those interested in developing and producing new work. Services include script-reading; information guides; writer/company Link Service; 6-weekly *Newsletter*. Subscription: rates on application.

Writers' Circles

Contact Jill Dick, Oldacre, Horderns Park Road, Chapel-en-le-Frith, High Peak SK23 9SY
tel (01298) 812305
e-mail jillie@cix.co.uk
web site http://www.cix.co.uk/~oldacre

The *Directory of Writers' Circles*, containing addresses of over 600 writers' circles, guilds, workshops, literary clubs, societies and organisations, is published regularly. Copies of the 8th edition (£5 post free) are available from the compiler/editor, Jill Dick, to whom cheques should be made payable.

Writers' Groups, National Association of

The Arts Centre, Biddick Lane, Washington, Tyne and Wear NE38 8AB
tel 0191-416 9751 *fax* 0191-431 1263
Secretary Brian Lister

Aims 'to advance the education of the general public throughout the UK, including the Channel Islands, by promoting the study and art of writing in all its aspects.' Membership: £20 p.a. plus £5 registration per group; Associate individuals £10 p.a. Founded 1995.

Writers Guild of America, East Inc. (WGAE)

Executive Director Mona Mangan, 555 West 57 Street, Suite 1230, New York, NY 10019, USA
tel 212-767-7800

Represents writers in screen and TV for collective bargaining. It provides member services including pension and health, as well as educational and professional activities. Annual membership: 1.5% of covered earnings. Founded 1954.

Writers Guild of America, West Inc. (WGA)

Executive Director John McLean, 7000 West 3rd Street, Los Angeles, CA 90048, USA
tel 323-951-4000 *fax* 323-782-4800
web site http://www.wga.org

Union representing and servicing 9000 writers in film, broadcast, cable and multimedia industries for purposes of collective bargaining, contract administration and other services, and functions to protect and advance the economic, professional and creative interests of writers. Monthly publication, *Written By*, available by subscription. Membership: initiation $2500, quarterly $25, annually 1.5% of income. Founded 1933.

The Writers' Guild of Great Britain

430 Edgware Road, London W2 1EH
tel 020-7723 8074 *fax* 020-7706 2413
e-mail postie@wggb.demon.co.uk
web site http://www.writers.org.uk/guild
Acting General Secretary Jacob Ecclestone

Founded in 1959 as the Screenwriters' Guild, now a trade union affiliated to the TUC, representing writers' interests in film, radio, TV, theatre and publishing.

Its scope extends into all areas of freelance writing and copyright protection and, where necessary, discusses at Government level policies on legislative matters affecting writers. The Guild's basic function is to negotiate minimum terms in those areas in which its members work. The Guild, by constitution non-political, employs a permanent secretariat and staff and is administered by an Executive Council of 26 members. There are also Regional/Branch Committees representing Scotland, Wales, and all the English regions. See also page 509.

Writers in Oxford
41 Kingston Road, Oxford OX2 6RH
tel (01865) 513844 *fax* (01865) 510017
Membership Secretary Antony Sanderson, 47 Southdale Road, Oxford OX2 7SE
e-mail antony.sanderson@conted.ox.ac.uk

To promote valuable discussion and social meetings among all kinds of professional writers in and around Oxfordshire. Activities include: topical lunches and dinners, where subjects important to the writer are discussed; showcase evenings; parties. Quarterly newsletter, *The Oxford Writer*. Annual subscription: £15. Founded 1992.

Yachting Journalists' Association
3 Friars Lane, Maldon, Essex CM9 6AG
tel (01621) 855943 *fax* (01621) 852212
e-mail petercookyja@compuserve.com
Secretary Peter Cook

Aims to further the interests of yachting, sail and power, and yachting journalism. Members vote annually for the Yachtsman of the Year, headline title of the British Nautical Awards. Membership: £30 p.a. Founded 1969.

The Yorkshire Dialect Society
Hon. Secretary Michael Park, 51 Stepney Avenue, Scarborough YO12 5BW

Aims to encourage interest in: dialect speech, the writing of dialect verse, prose and drama; the publication and circulation of dialect literature; the study of the origins and the history of dialect and kindred subjects. Organises meetings; publishes *Transactions* (annual) and *The Summer Bulletin* free to members; list of other publications on request. Annual subscription: £7. Founded 1897.

Young Book Trust – see Book Trust

Francis Brett Young Society
Secretary Mrs J. Hadley, 92 Gower Road, Halesowen, West Midlands B62 9BT
tel 0121-422 8969

To provide opportunities for members to meet, correspond, and to share the enjoyment of the author's works. Journal published 2 p.a. Annual subscription: £7 (individual), life membership £70 (other rates on application). Founded 1979.

The Society of Authors

The Society of Authors is an independent trade union, representing writers' interests in all aspects of the writing profession, including publishing, broadcasting, television and films, theatre and translation.

Founded over 100 years ago by Walter Besant, the Society now has more than 6500 members. It has a professional staff, responsible to a Management Committee of 12 authors, and a Council (an advisory body meeting twice a year) consisting of 60 eminent writers. There are specialist groups within the Society to serve the particular needs of broadcasters, literary translators, educational writers, medical writers and children's writers and illustrators. There are also regional groups representing Scotland, the North of England and the Isle of Man.

> 'When we begin working, we are so poor and so busy that we have neither the time nor the means to defend ourselves against the commercial organisations which exploit us. When we become famous, we become famous suddenly, passing at one bound from the state in which we are, as I have said, too poor to fight our own battles, to a state in which our time is so valuable that it is not worth our while wasting any of it on lawsuits and bad debts. We all, eminent and obscure alike, need the Authors' Society. We all owe it a share of our time, our means, our influence'
>
> – *Bernard Shaw*

What the Society does for members

Through its permanent staff (including a solicitor), the Society is able to give its members a comprehensive personal and professional service covering the business aspects of authorship, including:

- providing information about agents, publishers, and others concerned with the book trade, journalism, broadcasting and the performing arts;
- advising on negotiations, including the individual vetting of contracts, clause by clause, and assessing their terms both financial and otherwise;
- taking up complaints on behalf of members on any issue concerned with the business of authorship;
- pursuing legal actions for breach of contract, copyright infringement, and the non-payment of royalties and fees, when the risk and cost preclude individual action by a member and issues of general concern to the profession are at stake;
- holding conferences, seminars, meetings and social occasions;
- producing a comprehensive range of publications, free of charge to members, including the Society's quarterly journal, *The Author*. *Quick Guides* cover many aspects of the profession such as: copyright, publishing contracts, libel, income tax, VAT, authors' agents, permissions, indexing, and the protection of titles. The Society also publishes occasional papers on subjects such as film agreements, packaged books, revised editions, multimedia, and vanity publishing.

Further membership benefits

Members have access to:

- the Retirement Benefit Scheme;
- a group Medical Insurance Scheme with BUPA;
- the Pension Fund (which offers discretionary pensions to a number of members);
- the Contingency Fund (which provides

financial relief for authors or their dependents in sudden financial difficulties);
- automatic free membership of the Authors' Licensing and Collecting Society (ALCS);
- books at special rates;
- membership of the Royal Over-Seas League at a discount;
- use of the Society's photocopier at special rates.

The Society frequently secures improved conditions and better returns for members. It is common for members to report that, through the help and facilities offered, they have saved more, and sometimes substantially more, than their annual subscriptions (which are an allowable expense against income tax).

What the Society does for authors

The Society lobbies Members of Parliament, Ministers and Government Departments on all issues of concern to writers. Recent issues have included the operation and funding of Public Lending Right, the threat of VAT on books, copyright legislation and European Community initiatives. Concessions have also been obtained under various Finance Acts.

The Society litigates in matters of importance to authors. For example, the Society backed Andrew Boyle when he won his appeal against the Inland Revenue's attempt to tax the Whitbread Award.

The Society campaigns for better terms for writers. With the Writers' Guild, it has negotiated 'minimum terms agreements' with many leading publishers. The translators' section of the Society has also drawn up a minimum terms agreement for translators which has been adopted by Faber & Faber, and has been used on an individual basis by a number of other publishers.

The Society is recognised by the BBC for the purpose of negotiating rates for writers' contributions to radio drama, as well as for the broadcasting of published material. It was instrumental in setting up the Authors' Licensing and Collecting Society (ALCS), which collects and distributes fees from reprography and other methods whereby copyright material is exploited without direct payment to the originators.

The Society keeps in close touch with the Arts Councils, the Association of Authors' Agents, the British Council, the Broadcasting Entertainment Cinematograph and Theatre Union, the Institute of Translation and Interpreting, the Secretary of State for National Heritage, the National Union of Journalists, the Publishers Association and the Writers' Guild of Great Britain.

The Society is a member of the European Writers Congress, the British

Membership

The Society of Authors
84 Drayton Gardens, London SW10 9SB
tel 020-7373 6642

Membership at the discretion of the Committee of Management is open to authors who have had a full-length work published, broadcast or performed commercially in the UK or have an established reputation in another medium. It is also open to authors who have had a full-length work accepted for publication, but not yet published; and those authors who have had occasional items broadcast or performed, or translations, articles, illustrations or short stories published.

The owner or administrator of a deceased author's copyrights can become a member on behalf of the author's estate.

The annual subscription (which is tax deductible under Schedule D) is £75 (£70 by direct debit after the first year), and there are special joint membership terms for husband and wife. Authors under 35, who are not yet earning a significant income from their writing, may apply for membership at a lower subscription of £55. Authors over 65 may apply to pay at the reduced rate after their first year of membership.

Contact the Society for a free booklet and copy of *The Author*.

Copyright Council, the National Book Committee and the International Confederation of Societies of Authors and Composers (CISAC).

Awards

The Society of Authors administers:
- two travel awards: the Somerset Maugham Awards and the Travelling Scholarships;
- four prizes for novels: the Betty Trask Awards, the Encore Award, the McKitterick Prize and the Sagittarius Prize;
- two poetry awards: the Eric Gregory Awards and the Cholmondeley Awards;
- the Tom-Gallon Award for short story writers;
- the Authors' Foundation and Kathleen Blundell Trust, which are endowed with wide powers to support work in progress;
- the Margaret Rhondda Award for women journalists;
- awards for translations from French, German, Italian, Dutch, Portuguese, Spanish, Swedish and Japanese into English;
- the Francis Head Bequest for assisting authors who, through physical mishap, are temporarily unable to maintain themselves or their families.

The Writers' Guild of Great Britain

The Writers' Guild of Great Britain is the writers' trade union and is affiliated to the TUC.

The Writers' Guild of Great Britain is the writers' trade union, affiliated to the TUC, and represents writers' interests in film, radio, television, theatre and publishing. Formed in 1959 as the Screenwriters' Guild, the union gradually extended into all areas of freelance writing activity and copyright protection. In 1974, when book authors and stage dramatists became eligible for membership substantial numbers joined. In June 1997 the Theatre Writers' Union membership unified with that of the Writers' Guild to create a larger, more powerful writers' union. Each branch of writing is represented on the Executive Council of the Guild.

Apart from necessary dealings with Government and policies on legislative matters affecting writers, the Guild is, by constitution, non-political, has no involvement with any political party, and pays no political levy.

The Guild employs a permanent secretary and staff and is administered by an Executive Council of 31 members. The Guild has a national and regional/branch structure with committees representing Scotland, Wales, London and the South East, the North West, the North East, the Midlands and the South West of England.

The Guild comprises practising professional writers in all media, united in common concern for one another and regulating the conditions under which they work.

The Writers' Guild and agreements

The Guild's basic function is to negotiate minimum terms in those areas in which its members work. Those agreements form the basis of the individual contracts signed by members. Further details are given below. The Guild also gives individual advice to its members on contracts and other matters which the writer encounters in his or her professional life.

Television

The Guild has national agreements with the BBC and the ITV companies which regulate minimum fees and going rates, copyright licence, credit terms and conditions for television plays, series and serials, dramatisations and adaptations. One of the most important achievements in recent years has been the establishment of pension rights for Guild members. The BBC pay an additional 7.5% of the going rate on the understanding that the Guild member pays 5% of his or her fee. ITV companies now pay an additional 8% and the writer 5%. The Guild Pension Fund at present amounts to well over £3 million.

The advent of digital and cable television channels and the creation of the BBC's commercial arm has seen the Guild in constant negotiation. The Guild now has agreements for all of the BBC's digital channels and for its joint venture channels. In addition, the Guild has concluded an agreement with the BBC for use of programme clips on the Internet.

In 1997, the Guild negotiated substantial revised terms and conditions for writers who are commissioned by the ITV companies. The new agreement includes a provision for the non-arms length sale of material to digital and cable channels, thus ensuring that writers receive market prices for the use of their material on these new channels.

Film

On 11 March 1985, an important agreement was signed with the two producer organisations: the British Film and Television Producers' Association and the Independent Programme Producers Association (now known as PACT, the Producers' Alliance for Cinema and Television). For the first time, there exists an industrial agreement which covers both independent television productions and independent film productions. Pension fund contributions have been negotiated for Guild members in the same way as for the BBC and ITV. The Agreement was comprehensively renegotiated and concluded in February 1992. The areas of participation have been improved and the money paid up front is considerably more than it was in the past.

The Guild is involved in constant negotiations in this important field. At the time of writing, negotiations were well under way for a new PACT agreement. The Guild is also involved in ensuring that its members receive proper screenwriting credits and is often involved in credit arbitrations where disputes arise.

Radio

The Guild has fought for and obtained a standard agreement for Radio Drama with the BBC, establishing a fee structure which is annually reviewed. The current agreement includes a Code of Practice which is important for establishing good working conditions for the writer working for the BBC. In December 1985 the BBC agreed to extend the pension scheme already established for television writers to include radio writers. In 1994 a comprehensive revision of the Agreement was undertaken. The Guild negotiated special agreements for the new daily serial on Radio 4 for the new World Service soap *West Way*, the BBC Radio Wales soap *Station Road*, and for the on-line streaming of BBC Radio services.

Books

The Guild fought long, hard and successfully for the loans-based Public Lending Right to reimburse authors for books lent in libraries. This is now law and the Guild is constantly in touch with the Registrar of the scheme, which is administered from offices in Darlington.

The Guild, together with the Society of Authors, has drawn up a draft Minimum Terms Book Agreement which has been widely circulated amongst publishers. In 1984, the unions achieved a significant breakthrough by signing agreements with two major publishers; negotiations were also opened with other publishers. The publishing agreements will, it is hoped, improve the relationship between the writer and publisher and help to clarify what writers might reasonably expect from the exploitation of copyright in works written by him or her.

Agreements have now been signed with BBC Publications, Bloomsbury, Chapmans, André Deutsch, Faber & Faber, HarperCollins, Hodder Headline, Random House, Penguin Books, Transworld Publishers and Viking. Negotiations are currently taking place with Macmillan.

Theatre

In 1979, the Guild, together with the Theatre Writers' Union, negotiated the first ever industrial agreement for theatre writers. The Theatre National Committee Agreement covered the Royal Shakespeare Company, the National Theatre Company and the English Stage Company.

In June 1986, a new agreement was signed with the Theatrical Management Association, which covers some 95 provincial theatres. In 1993, this agreement was comprehensively revised and included a provision for a year-on-year increase in fees in line with the Retail Price Index.

After many years of negotiation, an agreement was concluded in 1991 between the Guild and the Independent Theatre Council, which represents some 200 of the smaller and fringe theatres as well as educational, touring companies.

Copies of all the above agreements are available; there is a charge to non-members.

Membership

The Writers' Guild of Great Britain
(incorporating the Theatre Writers' Union)
430 Edgware Road, London W2 1EH
tel 020-7723 8074 *fax* 020-7706 2413
e-mail postie@wggb.demon.co.uk
web site http://www.writers.org.uk/guild

Membership of the Guild is open to all persons entitled to claim a single piece of written work of any length for which payment has been received under written contract in terms not less favourable than those existing in current minimum terms agreements negotiated by the Guild.

Candidate membership (£50) is open to all those who are taking their first steps into writing but who have not yet received a contract.

The minimum subscription is currently £100 plus 1% of that part of an author's income earned from professional writing sources in the previous calendar year with a cap of £930.

All Full members are automatically members of the Authors Licensing and Collecting Society (ALCS). The Guild is a corporate member of the ALCS and maintains its links through representation on its board.

Members receive the *Writers' Newsletter*, which carries articles, letters and reports written by members.

Members are entitled to various other benefits, such as free entry to the British Library reading rooms, and reduced entry to the National Film Theatre.

Other activities

The Guild is in constant touch with Government and national institutions wherever and whenever the interests of writers are in question or are being discussed. The Guild has been holding cross-party Parliamentary lobbies every 18 months since 1989 with Equity and the Musicians Union to ensure that the various art forms they represent are properly cared for.

Working with the Federation of Entertainment Unions, the Guild makes its views known to Government bodies on a broader basis. It keeps in touch with the Arts Council of Great Britain, the Independent Television Commission and other national bodies.

The Guild has close working relationships with Equity and the Musicians Union. All three unions have agreed to work closely together where they share a common interest. Representatives of the three governing bodies meet regularly.

Internationally, the Guild plays a leading role in the International Affiliation of Writers' Guilds, which includes the American Guilds East and West, the Canadian Guilds (French and English), and the Australian and New Zealand Guilds. When it is possible to make common cause, the Guilds act accordingly.

The Guild takes a leading role in the European Writers' Congress, which is becoming increasingly important and successful. An initiative from the Guild saw the setting up of a Copyright Committee to protect writers' interests within the EU in particular and throughout Europe in general. The Guild is becoming more and more involved with matters at European level where the harmonisation of copyright law and the regulation of a converged audiovisual/telecommunications are of immediate interest.

Membership activities

The Guild in its day-to-day work takes up problems on behalf of individual members, gives advice on contracts, and helps with any problems which affect the lives of its members as professional writers. It now has a legal hotline so that members can quickly and easily seek legal advice.

Regular Craft Meetings are held by all the Guild's specialist committees. This gives Guild members the opportunity of meeting those who control, work within, or affect the sphere of writing within which they work.

In conclusion

The writer is an isolated individual in a world in which individual voices are not always heard. The Guild brings together those writers in order to make common cause in respect of the many vitally important matters which are susceptible to influence only from the position of the collective strength which the Guild enjoys. The writer properly cherishes his or her individuality; it will not be lost within a union run by other writers.

Prizes and awards

This list provides details of many British prizes, competitions and awards for writers and artists, including grants, bursaries and fellowships, as well as details of major international prizes. *See page 540 for a quick reference to its contents.*

Academi 2001 Cardiff International Poetry Competition

Details/entry form Academi 2001 Cardiff International Poetry Competition, PO Box 438, Cardiff CF10 5YA

Eight prizes totalling £5000 are awarded for unpublished poetry written in English (prizes: 1st £3000; 2nd £700; 3rd £300; plus 5 prizes of £200). Closing date: 30 June 2001.

J.R. Ackerley Prize for Autobiography

Information PEN, 152-6 Kentish Town Road, London NW1 9QB
tel 020-7267 9444 *fax* 020-7267 9304

An annual prize given for an outstanding work of literary autobiography written in English and published during the previous year by an author of British nationality or an author who has been a long-term resident in the UK. No submissions please – books are nominated by the judges only. First awarded in 1982.

Further information

In the UK, details of awards for novels, short stories and works of non-fiction, as they are offered, will be found in such journals as *The Author*.

Book Trust

Book House, 45 East Hill, London SW18 2QZ
tel 020-8516 2977

Publishes a list of prizes, *Guide to Literary Prizes 2000* (£6.99) and a free leaflet on grants and awards.

The Alexander Prize

Literary Director, Royal Historical Society, University College London, Gower Street, London WC1E 6BT

tel/fax 020-7387 7532
e-mail royalhistsoc@ucl.ac.uk
web site http://www.rhs.ac.uk

An annual award of £250 or a silver medal for a paper based on original historical research. Candidates must either be under the age of 35 or be registered for a higher degree now or within the last 3 years. Closing date: 1 November each year.

The Hans Christian Andersen Medals

Details International Board on Books for Young People, Nonnenweg 12, Postfach, CH-4003 Basel, Switzerland
tel (61) 272 29 17 *fax* (61) 272 27 57
e-mail ibby@eye.ch
web site http://www.ibby.org

The Medals are awarded every 2 years to a living author and an illustrator who by the outstanding value of their work are judged to have made a lasting contribution to literature for children and young people.

Artists' Residencies in Tuscany

Enquiries B.D. Gomperts, 31 Addison Avenue, London W11 4QS
e-mail rmka101@ucl.ac.uk

Established in memory of Juliet Gomperts who was killed when studying at the National College of Art in Lahore, Pakistan. Three annual bursaries (value up to £2000) provide board, lodging and studio facilities for up to 4 weeks at the Verrocchio Arts Centre in Italy. Open to artists aged 18-40 (UK and Ireland only). Closing date: end of January. Send sae for details. Founded 1990.

The Arts Council/An Chomhairle Ealaíon, Ireland

Details The Arts Council/An Chomhairle Ealaíon, 70 Merrion Square, Dublin 2, Republic of Ireland
tel (01) 618 0200 *fax* (01) 676 1302, 661 0349
e-mail info@artscouncil.ie
web site http://www.artscouncil.ie

Awards in Literature are available to those of Irish birth or resident in Ireland or Northern Ireland.

Bursaries in Literature

Offered to creative writers of drama, poetry, fiction and non-fiction (E5100-10,200). Applications assessed once a year.

Travel awards

Applications assessed 3 times a year (maximum value of E2000).

Triennial Awards

Macaulay Fellowship (IR£3500). Next awarded in Literature in 2002.

The Marten Toonder Award (E9000). Next awarded in Literature in 2001.

Denis Devlin Award (IR£3000). Award made for the finest book of poetry in the English language in the 3 years preceding the award. Next award: 2001.

An Duais don bhFilíocht i nGaeilge (IR£3000). Award made for the finest book of poetry in the Irish language in the 3 years preceding the award. Next award: 2001.

Arts Council of England

Details Arts Council of England, 14 Great Peter Street, London SW1P 3NQ
tel 020-7333 0100

The Arts Council of England is undergoing a substantial change of role and function which aims to serve the arts, artists and audiences more effectively. One of the imperatives guiding this change is the belief that arts activity should be funded as close to its source as possible. This will result in the devolution of Development Fund money to Regional Arts Boards and, where appropriate, the delegation of Arts Council-funded organisations to Regional Arts Boards. Contact the Literature Dept for details of schemes and funding available for the financial year 2000-1.

The Arts Council of England Children's Award

Details Theatre Writing Dept, Arts Council of England, 14 Great Peter Street, London SW1P 3NQ
tel 020-7973 6431
e-mail info.drama@artscouncil.org.uk

An award of £6000 will be made for a playwright who writes for children up to the age of 12. Plays must have been produced professionally between 1 July 2000 and 30 June 2001 and must be at least 45 minutes long. It may be a first, second or third production of a play written within the last 10 years. Closing date: 6 July 2001.

The Arts Council of Wales Awards to Writers

Literature Department, The Arts Council of Wales, Museum Place, Cardiff CF10 3NX
tel 029-2037 6500 *fax* 029-2022 1447
e-mail information@ccc-acw.org.uk
web site http://www.ccc-acw.org.uk

Book of the Year Award
A £3000 prize is awarded to winners, in Welsh and English, and £1000 to 4 other short-listed authors for works of exceptional merit by Welsh authors (by birth or residence) published during the previous calendar year in the categories of poetry, fiction and creative non-fiction.
Bursaries
Bursaries totalling about £75,000 are awarded annually to authors writing in both Welsh and English. Write for further details of the Arts Council of Wales' policies.

Arvon Foundation International Poetry Competition

Details Arvon Foundation Poetry Competition, 11 Westbourne Crescent, London W2 3DB
tel 020-7262 2788
e-mail london@arvonfoundation.org

A biennial competition for previously unpublished poems written in English. First prize £5000, plus at least £5000 in other cash prizes. Founded in 1980.

Authors' Club Awards

Details Ann de La Grange, Secretary, Authors' Club, 40 Dover Street, London W1X 3RB
tel 020-7499 8581 *fax* 020-7409 0913

Best First Novel Award
An award of £750 is presented at a dinner held in the Club, to the author of the most promising first novel published in the UK during each year. Entries (one from each publisher's imprint) are accepted during October and November and must be full-length novels – short stories are not eligible. Instituted by Lawrence Meynell in 1954.
Sir Banister Fletcher Award for Authors' Club
The late Sir Banister Fletcher, a former President of both the Authors' Club and the Royal Institute of British Architects instituted an annual prize 'for the book on architecture or the arts most deserving'. The award is made on the recommendation of the Professional Literature Committee of RIBA, to whom nominations for eligible titles (i.e. those written by British authors or those resident in the UK and published under a British imprint) should be submitted by the end of May of the year after publication. The prize of £750 is awarded by the Authors' Club during September. First awarded in 1954.

The Authors' Foundation

The Society of Authors, 84 Drayton Gardens, London SW10 9SB

Grants are available to novelists, poets and writers of non-fiction who are published authors working on their next book. The aim is to provide funding (in addition to a proper advance) for research, travel or other necessary expenditure. Closing dates: 30 April and 31 October. Send sae for an information sheet. Founded in 1984 to mark the centenary of the Society of Authors.

The Aventis Prizes for Science Books

Details COPUS, c/o The Royal Society, 6 Carlton House Terrace, London SW1Y 5AG
tel 020-7839 5561 *fax* 020-7451 2693
e-mail anna.link@royalsoc.ac.uk
web site http://www.royalsoc.ac.uk/

These prizes, established in 1988 by COPUS and the Science Museum and sponsored by Aventis, are awarded annually for the best popular science books for the non-specialist reader. Eligible books must be written in English and published in the UK in the year preceding the prize. The Aventis Prize (£10,000) is for a book with a general readership; the Junior Prize (£10,000), is for a book written specifically for young people (under 14); remaining shortlisted authors will receive £1000 – total prize fund is £30,000. Publishers may enter any number of books for each prize. Entries may cover any aspect of science and technology, including biography and history, but books published as educational textbooks or for professional or specialist audiences are not eligible. A prize-winning author will be ineligible for another Aventis Prize for 2 years.

BA/Whitaker Author of the Year

Details The Booksellers Association of Great Britain and Ireland, 272 Vauxhall Bridge Road, London SW1V 1BA
tel 020-7834 5477 *fax* 020-7834 8812

This annual award of £1000 is judged by members of the Booksellers Association of Great Britain and Ireland (3200 bookshops) in a postal ballot. Any living, British or Irish published writer is eligible and the award is given to the author judged to have had the most impact in the year. Founded in 1993.

Verity Bargate Award
Details The Literary Officer, Verity Bargate Award, Soho Theatre Company, 21 Dean Street, London W1V 6NE
e-mail writer@sohotheatre.com
web site http://www.sohotheatre.com

A bi-annual award, set up in honour of the company's co-founder, is made to the writer of a new and previously unperformed full-length play. The prize (£1500) represents an option to produce the play by Soho Theatre Company. Next award: 2002.

The Samuel Beckett Award
Details Editorial Department, Faber and Faber, 3 Queen Square, London WC1N 3AU

This award is open to residents of the UK and the Republic of Ireland for new dramatic writing, professionally performed. The provisions of the award are currently under review. Founded in 1983.

The David Berry Prize
Council of the Royal Historical Society, University College London, Gower Street, London WC1E 6BT
tel/fax 020-7387 7532
e-mail royalhistsoc@ucl.ac.uk
web site http://www.rhs.ac.uk

Candidates may select any subject dealing with Scottish history. Value of prize: £250. Closing date: 31 October each year.

BG Wildlife Photographer of the Year
Details BG Wildlife Photographer of the Year, The Natural History Museum, Cromwell Road, London SW7 5BD
tel 020-7942 5015 *fax* 020-7942 5084
e-mail wildphoto@nhm.ac.uk
web site http://www.nhm.ac.uk/WildPhoto

An annual award given to the photographer whose individual image is judged to be the most striking and memorable. The winner receives a bronze trophy and £2000. Open to anyone aged 18 and over. Closing date for entries: April/May 2001. Sponsored by BG plc. Founded 1983.

BG Young Wildlife Photographer of the Year
Details BG Young Wildlife Photographer of the Year, The Natural History Museum, Cromwell Road, London SW7 5BD
tel 020-7942 5015 *fax* 020-7942 5084
e-mail wildphoto@nhm.ac.uk
web site http://www.nhm.ac.uk/WildPhoto

An annual competition open to photographers aged 17 or under for pictures showing wild animals or plants, or wild landscapes. The award will be given to the photographer whose image is judged to be the most striking and memorable. The winner receives a bronze trophy of an ibis and £500, plus a day out with photographer Heather Angel. Sponsored by BG plc. Closing date for entries: April/May May 2001. Founded 1984.

The Bisto Book of the Year Awards
Details The Coordinator, The Bisto Book of the Year Awards, Children's Books Ireland, 19 Parnell Square, Dublin 1, Republic of Ireland
tel/fax (01) 872 5854
e-mail childrensbooksire@eircom.net

Annual awards open to authors and/or illustrators who were born in Ireland, or who were living in Ireland at the time of a book's publication.

The Bisto Book of the Year Award
An award of £1500 and a bronze trophy is presented to the overall winner (text and/or illustration).

Bisto Merit Awards
Awards of £500 each are awarded to 3 authors or illustrators.

Bisto Eilís Dillon Award
An award of £500 and a glass trophy is presented to an author for a first children's book (text only).
Closing date: 31 January 2001 for work published during 1 January-31 December 2000. Submission forms are available from September. Founded in 1990.

The James Tait Black Memorial Prizes
Submissions Department of English Literature, David Hume Tower, George Square, Edinburgh EH8 9JX
tel 0131-650 3619 *fax* 0131-650 6898
web site http://www.ed.ac.uk/englit/jtbinf.htm

Two prizes of £3000 are awarded annually: one for the best biography or work of that nature, the other for the best novel, published during the calendar year. The adjudicator is the Professor of English Literature in the University of Edinburgh. Eligible novels and biographies are those written in English, originating with a British publisher, and usually first published in Britain in the year of the award. Both prizes may go to the same author, but neither to the same author a second time. Publishers should submit a copy of any appropriate biography, or work of fiction, as early as possible with a note of the date of publication, marked 'James Tait Black Prize'. Closing date for submissions: 30 September. Founded in memory of a partner in the publishing house of A & C Black, these prizes were instituted in 1918.

The Kathleen Blundell Trust

Kathleen Blundell Trust, The Society of Authors, 84 Drayton Gardens, London SW10 9SB

Awards are given to published writers under the age of 40 to assist them with their next book. Applications should be in the form of a letter giving reasons for the application, and must be accompanied by a copy of the author's latest book. The author's work must 'contribute to the greater understanding of existing social and economic organisation', but fiction is not excluded. Closing dates: 30 April and 31 October. Send sae for an information sheet.

The Boardman Tasker Prize

Details Mrs Dorothy Boardman, 14 Pine Lodge, Dairyground Road, Bramhall, Stockport, Cheshire SK7 2HS

This annual prize of £2000 is given for a work of fiction, non-fiction or poetry, the central theme of which is concerned with the mountain environment. Authors of any nationality are eligible but the work must be published or distributed in the UK. Entries from publishers only. Founded in 1983.

The Booker Prize

Book Trust, Book House, 45 East Hill, London SW18 2QZ
tel 020-8516 2973/2972 *fax* 020-8516 2978
e-mail sandra@booktrust.org.uk
Contact Sandra Vince, Tarryn McKay

This annual prize for fiction of £26,000, including £1000 to each of 6 shortlisted authors, is awarded to the best novel published each year. It is open to novels written in English by citizens of the British Commonwealth and Republic of Ireland and published for the first time in the UK by a British publisher, although previous publication of a book outside the UK does not disqualify it. Entries only from UK publishers who may each submit not more than 2 novels with scheduled publication dates between 1 October of the previous year and 30 September of the current year, but the judges may also ask for other eligible novels to be submitted to them. In addition, publishers may submit one eligible title by authors who have been shortlisted or won the Booker Prize previously. Sponsored by Booker plc.

BP Natural World Book Prize

(in partnership with The Wildlife Trusts)
Details/entry form Book Trust, Book House, 45 East Hill, London SW18 2QZ
tel 020-8516 2973/2972 *fax* 020-8516 2978
e-mail sandra@booktrust.org.uk
Contacts Sandra Vince,Tarryn McKay

Awards of £5000 to the winner and £1000 to the runner up for an adult book which most imaginatively promotes the conservation of the natural environment and all its animals and plants. Books must have been published in the UK between 1 October of the previous year and 31 October of the year of the award. An amalgamation of the BP Conservation Book Prize and the Natural World Book of the Year Award.

BP Portrait Award

Details National Portrait Gallery, St Martin's Place, London WC2H 0HE
tel 020-7306 0055 *fax* 020-7306 0056
web site http://www.npg.org.uk

An annual award to encourage young artists (EC citizens aged 18-41) to focus upon and develop the theme of portraiture within their work. 1st prize: £10,000 plus at the judges' discretion a commission worth £3000 to be agreed between the NPG and the artist; 2nd prize £5000; 3rd prize: £3000; commendation: up to 5 entrants may be awarded £1000 each. Closing date: April. A selection of entrants' work is exhibited at the National Portrait Gallery between June and October. Founded 1978.

Alfred Bradley Bursary Award

Details BBC Radio Drama Department, BBC North, New Broadcasting House, Oxford Road, Manchester M60 1SJ
tel 0161-244 4260

This biennial bursary of £6000 (over 2 years, plus a full commission for a radio play) is awarded to a writer resident or born in the North of England who has had a small amount of work published or produced. The scheme also allows for a group of finalists to receive small bursaries and participate in workshops. Founded in 1992.

The Bridport Prize

Details Competition Secretary, Arts Centre, South Street, Bridport, Dorset DT6 3NR
tel (01308) 427183 *fax* (01308) 459166
e-mail arts@bridport.co.uk
web site http://www.wdi.co.uk/arts

Annual prizes are awarded for poetry and short stories – 1st £2500, 2nd £1000, 3rd £500 in both categories. Entries should be in English, original work, typed or clearly written, and never published, read on radio/television/stage or entered for any other current competition. Closing date: 30 June each year. Winning stories are read by leading London literary agent, without obligation, and an anthology of winning entries is published each autumn. Send sae for entry form.

British Academy of Film and Television Arts (BAFTA) Awards

Executive Director John Morrell, 195 Piccadilly, London W1V 0LN
tel 020-7734 0022 *fax* 020-7437 0473
e-mail jmorrell@bafta.org
web site http://www.bafta.org

The pre-eminent organisation in the UK for film and TV, recognising and promoting the achievement and endeavour of industry practitioners. BAFTA Awards are awarded annually by members to their peers in recognition of their skills and expertise. Founded 1947.

British Academy Medals and Prizes

The British Academy, 10 Carlton House Terrace, London SW1Y 5AH
tel 020-7969 5200 *fax* 020-7969 5300
e-mail secretary@britac.ac.uk

A number of medals and prizes are awarded for outstanding work in various fields of the humanities on the recommendation of specialist committees: Burkitt Medal for Biblical Studies; Derek Allen Prize (made annually in turn in musicology, numismatics and Celtic studies); Sir Israel Gollancz Prize (in English studies); Grahame Clark Medal for Prehistory; Kenyon Medal for Classical Studies; Rose Mary Crawshay Prize (for English literature); Serena Medal for Italian Studies.

The British Academy Research Awards

Details/application form The British Academy, 10 Carlton House Terrace, London SW1Y 5AH
tel 020-7969 5200 *fax* 020-7969 5300
e-mail secretary@britac.ac.uk
web site http://www.britac.ac.uk

These awards are made quarterly to scholars conducting advanced academic research in the humanities and social sciences, and normally resident in the UK. Applications are accepted for travel and maintenance expenses in connection with an approved programme of research, and costs of preparation of research for publication. There are also awards for attendance at scholarly conferences overseas; and for postdoctoral fellowships, research readerships and research professorships.

British Book Awards

Details Merric Davidson, 12 Priors Heath, Goudhurst, Cranbrook, Kent TN17 2RE
tel/fax (01580) 212041

Presented annually, major categories include: Author of the Year, Publisher of the Year, Bookseller of the Year, Children's Book of the Year. Founded 1989.

British Fantasy Awards

Details Robert Parkinson, Secretary, The British Fantasy Society, 201 Reddish Road, South Reddish, Stockport SK5 7HR
e-mail faliol@yahoo.com

Members of the British Fantasy Society vote annually for the best novel, short fiction, artist, small press and anthology of the preceding year. A further award, the Committee Award, is decided separately. The awards take the form of a statuette. Closing date for nominations: end August each year. Founded in 1972.

The Raymond Chandler Society's 'Marlowe' Award for Best International Crime Novel

Heidenheimer Str. 106, 89075 Ulm, Germany
UK contact tel/fax 0114-255 6302
e-mail william.adamson@zsp.uni-ulm.de

Annual award for the best English language crime novel. Also awards for best German language crime novel and best German language short story. Send submissions direct to the Society. Founded 1991.

Children's Book Award

Details Marianne Adey, The Old Malt House, Aldbourne, Marlborough, Wilts. SN8 2DW
tel (01672) 540629 *fax* (01672) 541280

This award is given annually to authors of works of fiction for children published in the UK. Children participate in the judging of the award. 'Pick of the Year' booklist is published in conjunction with the award. Founded in 1980 by the Federation of Children's Book Groups.

The Children's Laureate

Details The Administrator, 18 Grosvenor Road, Portswood, Southampton SO17 1RT

A biennial award of £10,000 to honour a writer or illustrator of children's books for a lifetime's achievement which highlights the importance of children's book creators in making readers of the future. Founded 1998.

Cholmondeley Awards

Administered by The Society of Authors, 84 Drayton Gardens, London SW10 9SB

These honorary awards are to recognise the achievement and distinction of individual poets. Submissions are not accepted. Total value of awards about £8000. Established by the then Dowager Marchioness of Cholmondeley in 1965.

Arthur C. Clarke Award

Details Paul Kincaid, 60 Bournemouth Road, Folkestone, Kent CT19 5AZ
e-mail clarke@appomattox.demon.co.uk

An annual award of £1000 plus engraved bookend is given for the best science fiction novel with first UK publication during the previous calendar year. Titles are submitted by publishers. Founded 1985.

The David Cohen British Literature Prize

Details The Literature Department, Arts Council of England, 14 Great Peter Street, London SW1P 3NQ
tel 020-7333 0100

This prize of £30,000 is awarded every 2 years to a living writer, novelist, short story writer, poet, essayist or dramatist in recognition of a lifetime's substantial body of achievement. Work must be written primarily in English and the writer must be a British citizen. In addition, the Arts Council will make available an extra £10,000 to enable the winner to encourage reading or writing among younger people. No application needed; the choice of the winner is made by a distinguished jury on the basis of its collective reading.

Commonwealth Writers Prize

Details/entry form Book Trust, Book House, 45 East Hill, London SW18 2QZ
tel 020-8516 2973/2972 *fax* 020-8516 2978
e-mail sandra@booktrust.org.uk
Contact Sandra Vince, Tarryn McKay

This annual award is for the best work of fiction in English by a citizen of the Commonwealth published in the year prior to the award. A prize of £10,000 is awarded for best entry and a prize of £3000 for best first published book, selected from 8 regional winners who each receive prizes of £1000. Sponsored by the Commonwealth Foundation.

The Duff Cooper Prize

Details Artemis Cooper, 54 St Maur Road, London SW6 4DP
tel 020-7736 3729 *fax* 020-7731 7638

An annual prize for a literary work in the field of biography, history, politics or poetry published in English or French and submitted by a recognised publisher during the previous 12 months. The prize of £3000 comes from a Trust Fund established by the friends and admirers of Duff Cooper, 1st Viscount Norwich (1890-1954) after his death.

The Rose Mary Crawshay Prizes

The British Academy, 10 Carlton House Terrace, London SW1Y 5AH
tel 020-7969 5200 *fax* 020-7969 5300
e-mail secretary@britac.ac.uk

One or more prizes are awarded each year to women of any nationality who, in the judgement of the Council of the British Academy, have written or published within the 3 calendar years immediately preceding the date of the award an historical or critical work of sufficient value on any subject connected with English literature, preference being given to a work regarding Byron, Shelley or Keats. Founded in 1888.

CWA Awards

Crime Writers' Association, PO Box 6939, Brimingham B14 7LT
web site http://www.twbooks.co.uk/cwa/cwa.html

CWA Cartier Diamond Dagger

This award is for an outstanding contribution to the genre. Nominations are not required. Sponsored by Cartier in conjunction with the CWA. First awarded 1986.

CWA John Creasey Memorial Dagger
An award given annually for the best crime novel by an author who has not previously published a full-length work of fiction. Nominations by publishers only. Sponsored by Chivers Press. Founded in 1973 following the death of John Creasey, to commemorate his foundation of the CWA.

CWA Macallan Gold Dagger and Silver Dagger
Annual awards for crime novels published in the UK. Nominations by publishers only. Sponsored by The Macallan in conjunction with the CWA. Founded in 1955.

CWA Macallan Gold Dagger for Non-Fiction
An annual award for a non-fiction crime book to an author published in the UK. Chosen by 4 judges of different professions. Nominations by publishers only. Sponsored by The Macallan in conjunction with the CWA. Founded in 1977.

CWA Macallan Short Story Dagger
An award for the best published short story of the year, to be submitted by publishers. Panels of judges vary from year to year. The winner receives a cheque and a Dagger lapel pin. Sponsored by The Macallan. Instituted in 1993.

David Thomas Charitable Trust Awards

David Thomas Self-Publishing Awards
Details/entry form Self-Publishing Awards, David Thomas Charitable Trust, PO Box 6055, Nairn IV12 4YB
tel (01667) 453351

These awards are given annually to anyone resident in the UK who has self-published a book during the calendar year preceding the award. The awards are in 5 categories – fiction, non-fiction, poetry, educational, children – with a prize of £250 in each category. Closing date: 15 January each year. (In addition, the Trust sponsors other writing competitions; details available from Lorna Edwardson.) Established in 1993.

David Thomas Charitable Trust Open Poetry Competition
Details/entry form Lorna Edwardson, David Thomas Charitable Trust, PO Box 6055, Nairn IV12 4YB
tel (01667) 453351

This annual award is open to anyone aged over 16 and writing in the English language. Poems can be up to 30 lines. Usually divided into 4 categories, changing each year; send for subject details. The total prize money is £1200 and the overall winner holds the Silver Cup for one year. Established in 1994.

David Thomas Charitable Trust Annual Ghost Story Competition
Details/entry form Lorna Edwardson (as above)

Open to anyone aged over 16, this competition is for a ghost story in 1600-1800 words. First prize is £1000 plus publication in *Writing Magazine*; 2 runners up of £100. The winner holds the Ghost Story Silver Cup for one year. Closing date: 15 February each year.

David Thomas Charitable Trust Annual Love Story Competition
Details/entry form Lorna Edwardson (as above)

Open to anyone aged over 16, this competition is for a love story in 1600-1800 words. First prize is £1000 plus publication in *Writing Magazine*; 2 runners up of £100. The winner holds the Love Story Silver Cup for one year. Closing date: 15 January each year.

The Rhys Davies Trust
Details Mr Meic Stephens, The Secretary, The Rhys Davies Trust, 10 Heol Don, Whitchurch, Cardiff CF14 2AU
tel 029-2062 3359 *fax* 029-2052 9202
e-mail meic@heoldon.fsnet.co.uk

The Trust aims to foster Welsh writing in English and offers financial assistance to English-language literary projects in Wales, directly or in association with other bodies.

The Dundee Book Prize
Details Anne Rendall, Dundee City Council, Economic Development Dept, 3 City Square, Dundee DD3 1BE
tel (01382) 434275 *fax* (01382) 434096

A biennial prize (£6000 and the chance of publication by Polygon) awarded for an unpublished novel. Next award: 2002. Founded 1996.

The T.S. Eliot Prize
Applications Poetry Book Society, Book House, 45 East Hill, London SW18 2QZ
tel 020-8870 8403
e-mail info@poetrybooks.co.uk
web site http://www.poetrybooks.co.uk

An annual prize of £5000 is awarded to the best collection of new poetry published in the UK or the Republic of Ireland during the year. Submissions are invited from publishers in the autumn. Founded in 1993.

Encore Award

Details Awards Secretary, The Society of Authors, 84 Drayton Gardens, London SW10 9SB
tel 020-7373 6642

This annual award of £7500 is for the best second novel of the year. The work submitted must be:

- a novel by one author who has had one (and only one) novel published previously, and
- in the English language, first published in the UK.

Closing date: 30 November.

European Jewish Publication Society Grants

Details Dr Colin Shindler, Editorial Director, European Jewish Publication Society, PO Box 19948, London N3 3ZJ
tel 020-8346 1668 *fax* 020-8346 1776
e-mail cs@ejps.org.uk
web site http://www.ejps.org.uk

Awards of up to £3000 are given to publishers to assist in the publication of books of Jewish interest, including fiction, non-fiction and poetry. Translations from other languages are considered eligible. Founded 1995.

Christopher Ewart-Biggs Memorial Prize

Details The Secretary, Memorial Prize, Flat 3, 149 Hamilton Terrace, London NW8 9QS
fax 020-7328 0699

This prize of £5000 is awarded once every 2 years to the writer, of any nationality, whose work is judged to contribute most to:

- peace and understanding in Ireland;
- to closer ties between the peoples of Britain and Ireland;
- or to co-operation between the partners of the European Union.

Eligible works must be published during the 2 years to 31 December 2000.

The Geoffrey Faber Memorial Prize

An annual prize of £1000 is awarded in alternate years for a volume of verse and for a volume of prose fiction, first published originally in the UK during the 2 years preceding the year in which the award is given which is, in the opinion of the judges, of the greatest literary merit. Eligible writers must be not more than 40 years old at the date of publication of the book and a citizen of the UK and Colonies, of any other Commonwealth state or of the Republic of Ireland. The 3 judges are reviewers of poetry or fiction who are nominated each year by the literary editors of newspapers and magazines which regularly publish such reviews. Faber and Faber invite nominations from reviewers and literary editors. No submissions for the prize are to be made. Established in 1963 by Faber and Faber Ltd, as a memorial to the founder and first Chairman of the firm.

Fallen Leaves Short Story Competition

Details Cork Campus Radio, Level 3, Áras na Mac Léinn, University College Cork, Cork City, Republic of Ireland
tel (021) 902170 *fax* (021) 903108
e-mail radio@ucc.ie
Contact Sinéad O'Donnell, Station Manager

Fallen Leaves is a short story radio series devised to provide new and innovative Irish short story writers with an opportunity to write for radio. Stories should be 1800-2000 words long and unpublished. Fee: £4 for the first story and £2 for each subseqent story. Founded 1996.

The Eleanor Farjeon Award

An annual prize of (minimum) £750 may be given to a librarian, teacher, author, artist, publisher, reviewer, TV producer or any other person working with or for children through books. Sponsored by Scholastic Ltd. Instituted in 1965 by the Children's Book Circle for distinguished services to children's books and named after the much-loved children's writer.

The Fidler Award

Administered by Scottish Book Trust, The Scottish Book Centre, 137 Dundee Street, Edinburgh EH11 1BG
tel 0131-229 3663

An annual award for an unpublished novel for children aged 8-12 years, to encourage authors new to writing for this age group. Entries should be from writers who have not previously had books for children published. The winner will receive £1000 and the work will be published by Hodder Children's Books, the sponsors of the award. Send sae for details and conditions of entry.

The Fish Short Story Competition

Durrus, Bantry, Co. Cork, Republic of Ireland
tel (353) 2761246
e-mail fishpublishing@eircom.ie
web site http://www.sleeping-giant.ie/fishpublishing
Contact Clem Cairns

An annual award which aims to discover, encourage and publish exciting new literary talent. Stories up to 5000 words long which have not been previously published are eligible. First prize: £1000; the best 16 stories are published in an anthology. Entry fee: £8 for the first entry, £5 for subsequent entries. Critiques available. Closing date: 30 November. Founded 1994.

E.M. Forster Award

The distinguished English author, E.M. Forster, bequeathed the American publication rights and royalties of his posthumous novel *Maurice* to Christopher Isherwood, who transferred them to the American Academy of Arts and Letters (633 West 155th Street, New York, NY 10032, USA), for the establishment of an E.M. Forster Award, currently $15,000, to be given annually to a British or Irish writer for a stay in the USA. Applications for this award are not accepted.

Forward Poetry Prizes

Details Forward Poetry Prize Administrator, Colman Getty PR, Carrington House, 126-130 Regent Street, London W1R 5FE
tel 020-7439 1783 *fax* 020-7439 1784

Three prizes are awarded annually:

- The Forward Prize for best collection of poetry published between 1 October and 30 September (£10,000);
- The Waterstones Prize for best first collection of poetry published between 1 October and 30 September (£5000); and
- The Tolman Cunard Prize for best individual poem, published but not as part of a collection between 1 May 2000 and 30 April 2001 (£1000).

All poems entered are also considered for inclusion in the *Forward Book of Poetry*, an annual anthology. Entries must be submitted by book publishers and editors of newspapers, periodicals and magazines in the UK and Eire. Entries from poets will not be accepted. Established 1992.

Miles Franklin Literary Award

Details Arts Management Pty Ltd, Station House, Rawson Place, 790 George Street, Sydney, NSW 2000, Australia
tel (02) 9212 5066 *fax* (02) 9211 7762
e-mail claudia@artsmanagement.com.au

This annual award of $28,000 is for a novel or play first published in the preceding year, which presents Australian life in any of its phases. More than one entry may be submitted by each author, and collaborations between 2 or more authors are eligible. Biographies, collections of short stories or children's books are not eligible. Closing date: approx. 15 December. Founded in 1957.

Freedom Award

Details The Hon. Secretary, London Press Club, St Bride Institute, 14 Bride Lane, Fleet Street, London EC4Y 8EQ
tel/fax 020-7353 7086
e-mail lpressclub@aol.com

An annual award of a crystal globe for the individual and/or organisation doing most to promote the freedom of the press. Founded 1998.

The Lionel Gelber Prize

Details Prize Manager, The Lionel Gelber Prize, c/o Meisner Publicity, 112 Braemore Gardens, Toronto, Ontario M6G 2C8, Canada
tel 416-656-3722 *fax* 416-658-5205
e-mail meisner@interlog.com

This international prize of $50,000 is awarded annually in Canada to the author of the year's most outstanding work of non-fiction in the field of international relations. Submissions must be published in English or in English translation between 1 September and 31 August of the following year. Submissions deadline: 31 May, i.e. 3 months before the end of the period in question. Books must be submitted by the publisher. Established in 1989.

The Gilchrist-Fisher Award

Contact Matthew Sturgis, 33 Warren Street, London W1P 5DL

Biennial prize (approx. £3500) awarded to a young artist (aged under 30) for landscape painting. Award exhibition for finalists held at Rebecca Hossack Gallery, London W1. Founded 1987.

Gladstone History Book Prize
Submissions Executive Secretary, Royal Historical Society, University College London, Gower Street, London WC1E 6BT
e-mail royalhistsoc@ucl.ac.uk

An annual award (value £1000) for a history book. The book must:
• be on any historical subject which is not primarily related to British history;
• be its author's first solely written history book;
• have been published in English during the calendar year of 2000 by a scholar normally resident in the UK;
• be an original and scholarly work of historical research.

Three non-returnable copies of an eligible book should be submitted before 31 December.

Glaxo Wellcome ABSW Science Writers Awards
Details Claire Jowett, Glaxo Wellcome plc, Glaxo Wellcome House, Berkeley Avenue, Greenford, Middlesex UB6 0NN
tel 020-8966 8000 *fax* 020-8966 8827

Awards are given to the writers who, in the opinion of the judges, have done most to enhance the quality of science journalism. Entries will be accepted from specialist writers, newspaper reporters and freelances. There are 7 categories, each worth £2500. Organised in conjunction in the Association of British Science Writers. Closing date: 31 January. Founded 1966.

Glenfiddich Food & Drink Awards
Details The Glenfiddich Awards, 4 Bedford Square, London WC1B 3RA
tel 020-7255 1100 *fax* 020-7631 0602

Awards are given annually to recognise excellence in writing, publishing and broadcasting relating to the subjects of food and drink. £800 is given to each of 12 categories, together with a case of Glenfiddich single malt Scotch whisky and an award. The overall winner receives The Glenfiddich Trophy and an additional £3000. Founded in 1970.

E.C. Gregory Trust Fund
Details Awards Secretary, The Society of Authors, 84 Drayton Gardens, London SW10 9SB

A number of substantial awards are made annually for the encouragement of young poets who can show that they are likely to benefit from an opportunity to give more time to writing. An eligible candidate must:
• be a British subject by birth but not a national of Eire or any of the British dominions or colonies and be ordinarily resident in the UK or Northern Ireland;
• be under the age of 30 on 31 March in the year of the Award (i.e. the year following submission);
• submit for consideration a published or unpublished work of belles-lettres, poetry or drama poems (not more than 30 poems). Closing date: 31 October.

The Guardian Children's Fiction Prize
tel 020-7239 9694
e-mail books@guardian.co.uk

The *Guardian's* annual prize of £1500 is for a work of children's fiction (for children over 8; no picture books) published by a British or Commonwealth writer. The winning book is chosen by the Children's Book Editor together with a team of 3 or 4 other authors of children's books.

The Guardian First Book Award
Contact Claire Armitstead
tel 020-7239 9694 *fax* 020-7713 4366
e-mail books@guardian.co.uk
Submissions Literary Editor, The Guardian, 119 Farringdon Road, London EC1R 3ER

Open to first-time authors published in English in the UK across all genres of writing, the award will recognise and reward new writing by honouring an author's first book. The winner will receive £10,000 plus an advertising package within the *Guardian* and the *Observer.* In addition, an endowment of £1000 worth of books will be made by the *Guardian* to a UK school of the author's choice. Publishers may submit up to 3 titles per imprint with publication dates between January and December 2000. Closing date: late July.

The Paul Hamlyn Foundation Awards to Artists
Details The Administrator, 18 Queen Anne's Gate, London SW1H 9AA
tel 020-7227 3500 *fax* 020-7222 0601
e-mail phf@globalnet.co.uk

Five awards of £30,000 spread over 3 years will be made to visual artists in 2001 to support the creative process. Strength of talent, promise and need, as well as achievement, are all assessed. Nominations will be made by a nationwide panel of 20 artists and others. Founded 1993.

The Hawthornden Prize

Details The Administrator, 42A Hays Mews, Berkeley Square, London W1X 7RU

This prize is awarded annually to the author of what, in the opinion of the Committee, is the best work of imaginative literature published during the preceding calendar year by a British author. Books do not have to be specially submitted.

Hawthornden Writers' Fellowships

Details The Administrator, Hawthornden Castle International Retreat for Writers, Hawthornden Castle, Lasswade, Midlothian EH18 1EG
tel 0131-440 2180

Applications are invited from novelists, poets, dramatists and other creative writers whose work has already been published. Four-week fellowships are offered to those working on a current project.

The Martin Healy Short Story Award

Details The Martin Healy Short Story Award, Model Arts Centre, The Mall, Sligo, Republic of Ireland
tel (71) 41405 *fax* (71) 43694
e-mail modelart@iol.ie

A competition for short stories of 3000 words or less open to Irish writers or writers resident in Ireland. Prizes £1000 (1st), £200 (2nd), £100 (3rd). Entry fees: £5 for first entry, £3 for subsequent entries. Closing date: mid July each year. Founded 1997.

The Felicia Hemans Prize for Lyrical Poetry

Submissions The Registrar, The University of Liverpool, PO Box 147, Liverpool L69 3BX
tel 0151-794 2458 *fax* 0151-794 3765
e-mail wilderc@liv.ac.uk

This annual prize of books or money, open to past and present members and students of the University of Liverpool only, is awarded for a lyrical poem, the subject of which may be chosen by the competitor. Only one poem, either published or unpublished, may be submitted. The prize shall not be awarded more than once to the same competitor. Poems, endorsed 'Hemans Prize', must be sent on or before 1 May.

Heywood Hill Literary Prize

Administration Heywood Hill Booksellers, 10 Curzon Street, London W1Y 7FJ

An award of £12,000 is given annually to a person chosen for their lifetime's contribution to the enjoyment of books. No applications. Established in 1995.

William Hill Sports Book of the Year Award

Details Graham Sharpe, William Hill Organisation, Greenside House, 50 Station Road, London N22 4TP
tel 020-8918 3731

This award is given annually in November for a book with a sporting theme (record books and listings excluded). The title must be in the English language, and published for the first time in the UK during the relevant calendar year. Total value of prize is £12,000, including £10,000 in cash. An award for the best cover design has total value of £1000. Founded in 1989.

The Calvin and Rose G. Hoffman Memorial Prize for Distinguished Publication on Christopher Marlowe

Applications The Headmaster, The King's School, Canterbury, Kent CT1 2ES
tel (01227) 595501 *fax* (01227) 595595

This annual prize of between £5000 and £6000 is awarded to the best unpublished work that examines the life and works of Christopher Marlowe and the relationship between the works of Marlowe and Shakespeare. Closing date: 1 September.

The Winifred Holtby Memorial Prize

Submissions The Royal Society of Literature, Somerset House, Strand, London WC2R 0RN
tel 020-7845 4676 *fax* 020-7845 4679

This prize (value £1000) is awarded for the best regional novel of the year written in the English language. The writer must be of British or Irish nationality, or a citizen of the Commonwealth. Translations, unless made by the author of the work, are not eligible for consideration. If in any year it is considered that no regional novel is of sufficient merit the prize may be awarded to an author, qualified as aforesaid, of a literary work of non-fiction or poetry, concerning a regional subject. Novels published during the current year should be submitted by 15 December. Contact the Secretary for details.

L. Ron Hubbard's Writers and Illustrators of the Future Contests

Administrator Andrea Grant-Webb, PO Box 218, East Grinstead, West Sussex RH19 4GH

Aims to encourage new and aspiring writers and illustrators of science fiction, fantasy and horror. In addition to the quarterly prizes there is an annual prize of £2500 for each contest. All 24 winners are invited to the annual L. Ron Hubbard Achievement Awards, which include a series of writers' and illustrators' workshops, and their work is published in an anthology. Write for an entry form.

Writers of the Future Contest
Entrants should submit a short story of up to 10,000 words or a novelette of less than 17,000 words. Prizes of £640 (1st), £480 (2nd) and £320 (3rd) are awarded each quarter. Founded 1984.

Illustrators of the Future Contest
Entrants should submit three black and white illustrations on different themes. Three prizes of £320 are awarded each quarter. Founded 1988.

Hunting Art Prizes

Details Parker Harris & Co., PO Box 279, Esher, Surrey KT10 8YZ
tel (01372) 462190 *fax* (01372) 460032

An annual national art competition open to all artists resident in the UK. Total prize monies: £20,500. Entry fee is £10 (£4 students) per work and artists may submit up to 3 works. Closing date: end November 2000. Winning entries will be exhibited at the Royal College of Art February 2001. Established 1980.

Images – The Best of British Illustration

Details Association of Illustrators, 81 Leonard Street, London EC2A 4QS
tel 020-7613 4328 *fax* 020-7613 4417
e-mail info@a-o-illustrators.demon.co.uk
web site http://www.aoi.co.uk
Contact Samantha Taylor

Illustrators are invited to submit work for possible inclusion in the *Images Annual*, a jury-selected showcase of the best of contemporary British illustration. Selected work forms the Images exhibition, which tours the UK. UK illustrators or illustrators working for UK clients are all eligible. Entry forms available mid April. Closing date: beginning of June each year. Founded 1976.

The Richard Imison Memorial Award

Details/entry form The Secretary, The Broadcasting Committee, The Society of Authors, 84 Drayton Gardens, London SW10 9SB
tel 020-7373 6642

This annual prize of £1500 is awarded to any new writer of radio drama first transmitted within the UK during the period 1 January-31 December 2000 by a writer new to radio. Founded in 1993.

International IMPAC Dublin Literary Award

Details The International IMPAC Dublin Literary Award Office, Dublin City Public Libraries, Administrative Headquarters, Cumberland House, Fenian Street, Dublin 2, Republic of Ireland
tel (01) 6619000 *fax* (01) 6761628
e-mail dubaward@iol.ie
web site http://www.impacdublinaward.ie/

An annual award of IR£100,000 is presented to the author of a work of fiction, written and published in the English language or written in a language other than English and published in English translation, which in the opinion of the judges is of high literary merit and constitutes a lasting contribution to world literature. Nominations accepted from library systems of major cities from all over the world, regardless of national origin of the author or the place of publication. Founded in 1995.

International Playwriting Festival

Details/entry form Festival Administrator, Warehouse Theatre, Dingwall Road, Croydon CR0 2NF
tel 020-8681 1257 *fax* 020-8688 6699
e-mail warehouse@dircon.co.uk
web site http://www.uk-line.co.uk/warehouse_theatre

An annual competition for full-length unperformed plays, judged by a panel of theatre professionals. Selected plays are given rehearsed readings during the festival week in November. Entries are welcome from all parts of the world. For further details and entry forms send an sae. Deadline for entries: usually by the end of June. Founded 1985.

Irish Times Literary Prizes

Details Gerard Cavanagh (Administrator), Paul Anderson (Co-ordinator)
tel (3531) 679 2022 *fax* (3531) 670 9383
e-mail gcavanagh@irish-times.ie

These 5 biennial prizes are awarded from nominations submitted by literary editors, critics, writers and academics. The 2001 Irish Literature Prizes are £5000 each for 4 categories and are open only to Irish authors:

- fiction (a novel, novella or a collection of short stories);
- non-fiction (history, biography, autobiography, criticism, politics, sociological interest, travel, current affairs and belles-lettres);
- poetry (a collection of works, a long poem or sequence of poems or revised/updated edition of previously published selection or collection of a poet's work);
- Irish language (works of fiction, non-fiction or poetry written in the Irish language).

A separate International Fiction Prize of £7500 is also awarded (novels, novellas, short stories), open to authors of any nationality for work in the English language.

Work must be first published between 31 July 1999 and 1 August 2001, and apart from the Irish language prize, all entries must have been originally published in English.

Japan Festival Awards

Details The Japan Festival Fund, Swire House, 59 Buckingham Gate, London SW1E 6AJ
tel 020-7630 5552 *fax* 020-7931 8453

Prizes are awarded annually for recent outstanding achievements in furthering the understanding of Japanese culture in the UK. A literary prize (£1000) is given to this end for a new work of fiction or non-fiction. Closing date: 31 March each year. Founded 1993.

Jewish Quarterly Literary Prizes

Details The Administrator, Jewish Quarterly, PO Box 2078, London W1A 1JR
tel 020-7629 5004 *fax* 020-7629 5110

Prizes are awarded annually for a work of fiction (£4000) and non-fiction (£4000) which best stimulate an interest in and awareness of themes of Jewish concern among a wider reading public. Founded in 1977.

The Samuel Johnson Prize for Non-Fiction

Details Booksellers Association, Minster House, 272 Vauxhall Bridge Road, London SW1V 1BA
tel 020-7834 5477 *fax* 020-7834 8812
e-mail sharon.down@booksellers.org.uk

A prize of £30,000 will be awarded to the winning writer of a non-fiction book in the areas of current affairs, history, politics, science, sport, travel, biography, autobiography and the arts. Each short-listed author will receive £2500. Books must be published in English in the UK between 1 May 2000 and 30 April 2001, and authors must be alive when the books are submitted. Books must not be written by more than 2 authors. Both hardback and paperback originals are eligible. Founded 1998.

The Petra Kenney Poetry Competition

Details Morgan Kenney, 1B The Crescent, Filey, North Yorkshire YO14 9HZ

This annual competition is for unpublished poems on any theme and in any style, and is open to everyone. Poems should be no more than 80 lines. Prizes: £1000 (1st), £500 (2nd), £250 (3rd); all the winning entries will be published in Writers' Forum magazine. Entry fee: £3 per poem. Closing date: 1 December each year. Founded 1995.

Kent and Sussex Poetry Society Open Poetry Competition

Submissions The Organiser, 13 Ruscombe Close, Southborough, Tunbridge Wells, Kent TN4 0SG

This competition is open to all unpublished poems, no longer than 40 lines in length. Prizes: 1st £500, 2nd £200, 3rd £100, 4th 4 at £50. Closing date: 31 January. Entries should include an entry fee of £3 per poem, the author's name and address and a list of poems submitted. Founded in 1985.

The John Kobal Photographic Portrait Award

The John Kobal Foundation, PO Box 3838, London WC1X 0NP
tel/fax 020-7278 8482

Portrait photography is defined here as 'photography concerned with portraying people with the emphasis on their identity as individuals' and the award is open to anyone over the age of 18. Total prize monies: £5500. Deadline for entries: 5 June. Established 1992.

Kraszna-Krausz Awards

Details Andrea Livingstone, Administrator, Kraszna-Krausz Foundation, 122 Fawnbrake Avenue, London SE24 0BZ

tel/fax 020-7738 6701
e-mail k-k@dial.pipex.com
web site http://www.editor.net/k-k

Awards totalling over £10,000 are made each year, alternating annually between the best books on:

- still photography: art, culture and history; craft, technology and scientific (2000);
- moving image (film, TV and video): culture and history; business, techniques and technology (2001).

The prize in each category will be awarded to the best book published in the preceding 2 years. Closing date: 1 July. The Foundation is also open to applications for grants (UK only) concerned with the literature of photography and the moving image. Instituted in 1985.

LAB/LBC London Radio Playwrights' Festival

Details London Radio Playwrights' Festival, IRDP, PO Box 518, Manningtree, Essex CO11 1XD

Organised by Independent Radio Drama Productions and LBC Radio, the festival falls into 2 parts: a workshop programme and a script competition. It is hoped that writers attending the workshops will enter the competition but this is not a condition. Two commissions are offered, one for an established writer and the other for a writer who has previously completed one play for radio. Three other plays will be chosen by open competition. Entrants must live, work or study in London. Send sae for details. Founded 1987.

The Lady Short Story Competition

The Lady, 39-40 Bedford Street, London WC2E 9ER

This competition is open to anyone possessing a coupon from the first October issue of the *Lady*. First prize is £1000. Subjects for short stories change each year. Further information in the relevant issue – please do not contact the magazine office directly in connection with the competition. Founded in 1993.

The Laing Art Competition

Details Mrs J. Donlevy, John Laing plc (Art Competition), Maxted House, 13 Maxted Road, Hemel Hempstead, Herts HP2 7DX
tel (01442) 286752

An annual national open art competition (seascapes and landscapes) open to all artists resident in the UK and held at regional venues. 1st prize: £5000; 5 highly commended prizes: £1000; regional 1st prizes: £1000. Winning entries will be exhibited in the spring regionally and at the Mall Galleries, London. Founded 1972.

Langhe Ceretto Prize for Food and Wine Culture, The International

Details Segreteria del Premio, Biblioteca Civica 'G. Ferrero', Via Paruzza 1, 12051 Alba, Italy
tel (0) 173 290092 *fax* (0) 173 362075

The Langhe Ceretto Prize is awarded for the work judged best at dealing with a topic relating to a historic, scientific, dietological, gastronomic or sociological aspect of food and wine (It.L 15,000,000). Publishers should send 13 copies to the Prize Secretariat, usually by mid March each year. Founded 1991.

Leverhulme Research Fellowships and Grants

The Leverhulme Trust, 1 Pemberton Row, London EC4A 3BG
tel 020-7822 6964 *fax* 020-7822 5084
e-mail jcater@leverhulme.org.uk
web site http://www.leverhulme.org.uk

The Leverhulme Trustees offer annually approx. 120 Fellowships and Grants to individuals in aid of original research – not for study of any sort. These awards are not available as replacement for past support from other sources. Applications will be considered in all subject areas. The maximum total of a Fellowship or Grant is £16,920. Completed application forms must be received by mid November 2000. Founded 1933.

The Library Association Carnegie and Kate Greenaway Awards

e-mail info@la-hq.org.uk
web site http://www.la-hq.org.uk/

Recommendations for the following 2 awards are invited from members of the Library Association, who are asked to submit a preliminary list of not more than 2 titles for each award, accompanied by a 50-word appraisal justifying the recommendation of each book. The awards are selected by the Youth Libraries Group of the Library Association.

Carnegie Medal

Awarded annually for an outstanding book for children (fiction or non-fiction) written in English and first published in the UK during the preceding year or co-published elsewhere within a 3-month time lapse.

Kate Greenaway Medal

Awarded annually for an outstanding illustrated book for children first published in the UK during the preceding year or co-published elsewhere within a 3-month time lapse. Books intended for older as well as younger children are included, and reproduction will be taken into account. The Colin Mears Award (£5000) is awarded annually to the winner of the Kate Greenaway Medal.

The Library Association Reference Awards

e-mail info@la-hq.org.uk
web site http://www.la-hq.org.uk/

The Besterman Medal

Awarded annually for an outstanding bibliography or guide to the literature first published in the UK during the preceding year either in print or in electronic form. Recommendations are invited from members of the Library Association, who are asked to submit a preliminary list of not more than 3 titles; submissions from publishers are also welcome.

The McColvin Medal

Awarded annually for an outstanding reference work either in print or in electronic form first published in the UK during the preceding year. Works eligible for consideration are encyclopedias, general and special; dictionaries, general and special; biographical dictionaries; annuals, yearbooks and directories; handbooks and compendia of data; atlases. Recommendations for the award are invited from members of the Library Association, who are asked to submit a preliminary list of not more than 3 titles, and submissions from publishers are welcome.

The Walford Award

Awarded annually to an individual who has made a sustained and continued contribution to the science and art of British bibliography over a period of years. The bibliographer's work can encompass effort in the history, classification and description of printed, written, audiovisual and machine-readable materials. Recommendations may be made for the work of a living person or persons, or for an organisation. The award can be made to a British bibliographer or to a person or organisation working in the UK.

The Wheatley Medal

Awarded annually for an outstanding index published during the preceding 3 years. Printed indexes to any type of publication may be submitted for consideration, providing that the whole work, including the index, or the index alone has originated in the UK. Recommendations for the award are invited from members of the Library Association and the Society of Indexers, publishers and others. The final selection is made by a committee consisting of representatives of the Library Association Cataloguing and Indexing Group and the Society of Indexers.

The Lichfield Prize

Details Tourist Information Centre, Donegal House, Bore Street, Lichfield, Staffs. WS13 6NE
tel (01543) 308215 *fax* (01543) 308211
e-mail prize@lichfield-tourist.co.uk

Lichfield District Council's biennial prize of £5000 and the chance of publication by Hodder & Stoughton, is for the best novel based recognisably on the geographical area of Lichfield District, Staffordshire. Quote 'WA' on all correspondence. Next closing date: 30 April 2001. Instituted in 1988.

The London New Writing Competition

Entry form London Arts Board, Elme House, 133 Long Acre, London WC2E 9AF
tel 020-7240 1313 *fax* 020-7670 2400
e-mail nick.mcdowell@lonab.co.uk

Open to adults resident in Greater London, this biennial competition offers awards of £200 each (plus publication in an anthology) for the best creative pieces about London. Next closing date: May 2001. Founded in 1992.

London Writers Competition

Details Arts Office, Room 224A, Wandsworth Town Hall, High Street, London SW18 2PU
tel 020-8871 8711
e-mail ants@wandsworth.gov.uk
web site http://www.wandsworth.gov.uk

Open to writers who live, work or study in the Greater London Area. Awards are made annually in 3 classes (Poetry, Short Story and Play) and prizes total £1000 in each class. Entries must be previously unpublished work. Judging is under the chairmanship of Martyn Goff.

The Sir William Lyons Award

Details General Secretary, 30 The Cravens, Smallfield, Surrey RH6 9QS
tel (01342) 843294 *fax* (01342) 844093

This annual award (trophy, £1000 and 2 years' probationary membership of The Guild of Motoring Writers) was set up to encourage young people in automotive journalism, including broadcasting, and to foster interest in motoring and the motor industry through these media. Open to any person of British nationality resident in the UK under the age of 23, it consists of writing 2 essays and an interview with the Award Committee.

The Macallan/Scotland on Sunday Short Story Competition

Details The Administrator, The Macallan/ Scotland on Sunday Short Story Competition, 20 North Bridge, Edinburgh EH1 1YT

These annual prizes (1st £6000; 2nd £600; 4 runners up £100 each; publication of winning entries in *Scotland on Sunday*) are awarded for the best short story of less than 3000 words written by a person born in Scotland, now living in Scotland or by a Scot living abroad. The best 20 stories will be published in a special collection. Instituted 1990.

The McKitterick Prize

Details Awards Secretary, The Society of Authors, 84 Drayton Gardens, London SW10 9SB

This annual award of £4000 is open to first published novels and unpublished typescripts by authors over the age of 40. Closing date: 20 December. Endowed by the late Tom McKitterick.

The Enid McLeod Literary Prize

Details Executive Secretary, Franco-British Society, Room 623, Linen Hall, 162-168 Regent Street, London W1R 5TB
tel/fax 020-7734 0815

This annual prize of £250 is given for a full-length work of literature which contributes most to Franco-British understanding. It must be first published in the UK and written in English by a citizen of the UK, British Commonwealth, the Republic of Ireland, Pakistan, Bangladesh or South Africa.

Bryan MacMahon Short Story Award

Writers' Week, PO Box 147, Listowel, Co. Kerry, Republic of Ireland
tel (353) 6821074 *fax* (353) 6822893
e-mail writersweek@eircom.net

An annual award for the best short story (up to 3000 words) on any subject. Prize: £1500. Entry fee: £5. Closing date: March. Founded 1971.

The Macmillan Prize for a Children's Picture Book

Applications Marketing Dept, Macmillan Children's Books, 25 Eccleston Place, London SW1W 9NF

Three prizes are awarded annually for unpublished children's book illustrations by art students in higher education establishments in the UK. Prizes: £1000 (1st), £500 (2nd) and £250 (3rd).

Macmillan Silver Pen Award for Fiction

Details PEN, 152-6 Kentish Town Road, London NW1 9QB
tel 020-7267 9444 *fax* 020-7267 9304

This award of £500 is given annually for an outstanding collection of short stories written in English and published during the previous year by an author of British nationality or an author who has been a long-term resident in the UK. No submissions please – books are nominated by members of the PEN Executive Committee. Sponsored by Macmillan since 1986. Founded in 1969.

The Mail on Sunday/John Llewellyn Rhys Prize

Entry form The Mail on Sunday/John Llewellyn Rhys Prize, c/o Book Trust, Book House, 45 East Hill, London SW18 2QZ
tel 020-8516 2973/2972 *fax* 020-8516 2978
e-mail sandra@booktrust.org.uk
Contact Sandra Vince, Tarryn McKay

This annual prize of £5000 (plus £500 to each shortlisted author) is offered to the author of the most promising literary work of any kind published for the first time during the current year. The author must be a citizen of this country or the Commonwealth, and not have passed his or her 35th birthday by the date of the publication of the work submitted. Publishers only may submit books. Inaugurated in memory of the writer John Llewellyn Rhys.

Marsh Award for Children's Literature in Translation

Administered by National Centre for Research into Children's Literature, Digby Stuart College, University of Surrey, Roehampton, Roehampton Lane, London SW15 5PU
tel 020-8392 3008
Contact Dr Gillian Lathey

This biennial award of £750 is given to a British translator of a book for children (aged 4-16) from a foreign language into English and published in the UK by a British publisher. Electronic books, and encyclopedias and other reference books, are not eligible. Next award: January 2001. Founded in 1995.

Marsh Biography Award

Administered by The English-Speaking Union, Dartmouth House, 37 Charles Street, London W1X 8AB
tel 020-7529 1550 *fax* 020-7495 6108
e-mail lucy_passmore@esu.org

This major national biography prize of £3500 plus a trophy is presented every 2 years. Entries must be serious biographies written by British authors and published in the UK. Next award: October 2001. Founded 1985-86.

The Kurt Maschler Award

Details Book Trust, Book House, 45 East Hill, London SW18 2QZ
tel 020-8516 2973/2972 *fax* 020-8516 2978
e-mail sandra@booktrust.org.uk
Contact Sandra Vince, Tarryn McKay

This annual prize of £1000 is awarded to a British author/artist or an author/artist who has been resident in Britain for more than 10 years for a children's book in which text and illustrations are of excellence and enhance and balance each other. Founded in 1982.

The Somerset Maugham Awards

Details Awards Secretary, The Society of Authors, 84 Drayton Gardens, London SW10 9SB

These annual awards, totalling about £12,000, are for young writers. Mr Maugham urged that originality and promise should be the touchstones: he did not wish the judges to 'play for safety' in their choice. A candidate must be a British subject by birth and ordinarily resident in the UK or Northern Ireland, must be under 35 and must submit a published literary work in the English language, of which the candidate is the sole author. Poetry, fiction, non-fiction, belles-lettres or philosophy, but not dramatic works, are eligible. Four, non-returnable copies of one published work should be submitted, and must be accompanied by a statement of the author's date and place of birth, and other published works. Closing date: 20 December.

MCA Book Prize

Details Andrea Livingstone, Administrator, MCA Book Prize, 122 Fawnbrake Avenue, London SE24 0BZ
tel/fax 020-7738 6701

An annual main prize of £5000, and a Young Writers Award (under 40 years old) of up to £2000, are given to books which contribute stimulating, original and progressive ideas on management issues. Authors must be British subjects domiciled in the UK. Next closing date: end February 2000. Founded in 1993.

Meyer-Whitworth Award

Details Theatre Writing Section, Drama Department, Arts Council of England, 14 Great Peter Street, London SW1P 3NQ
tel 020-7973 6431
e-mail info.drama@artscouncil.org.uk

Set up to help further the careers of UK contemporary playwrights who are not yet established, this award of up to £8000 is given annually for an English-language play which shows writing of individual quality and the promise of a developing new talent. Candidates will have had no more than 2 of their plays professionally produced. Nominated plays must have been produced professionally in the UK for the first time between 1 August and 31 July; closing date: last Friday in August.

Millfield Arts Projects

Atkinson Gallery, Millfield, Butleigh Road, Street, Somerset BA16 0YD
tel (01458) 442291 *fax* (01458) 447276
Director of Art Len Green

'The mandate of the Millfield Arts Project programme is to search for, promote and support, primarily but not exclusively, young aspiring artists at local, regional, national and international levels.' In a professional art context MAP offers:

- Sculpture Commission. Artists work on campus for 8 weeks (£7500). Deadline for entries: mid January.
- Summer Show. An open exhibition.

Application forms available: March.

- Six Gallery exhibitions selected by the Director of Art. Interested artists should send slides and CV to the Director of Art.
- Sculpture Summer Show. Campus sculpture exhibition in July/Aug/Sept.

Mind Book of the Year/Allen Lane Award

Details Anny Brackx, Corporate Promotion Department, Granta House, 15-19 Broadway, London E15 4BQ
tel 020-8519 2122 *fax* 020-8522 1725

This £1000 award is given to the author of any book (fiction or non-fiction) published in the UK in the current year which outstandingly furthers public understanding of the prevention, causes, treatment or experience of mental health problems. Entries by 31 December. Administered by Mind, the National Association for Mental Health. Inaugurated in memory of Sir Allen Lane in 1981.

The Oscar Moore Screenwriting Prize

Details The Oscar Moore Foundation, 33-39 Bowling Green Lane, London EC1R 0DA
tel 020-7505 8080 *fax* 020-7505 8087
e-mail clarissa.caleo-green@media.emap.com
web site http://www.screendaily.com

The Foundation works to build for a Europe-wide culture of screenwriting excellence and to this end makes this annual award (£10,000) to finance the second draft of a promising screenplay. A different genre is chosen for each year.

John Moores Liverpool Exhibition

Walker Art Gallery, William Brown Street, Liverpool L3 8EL
tel 0151-478 4199 *fax* 0151-478 4190
Contact Stephen Guy

Biennial painting exhibition open to any artist living or working in the UK. Cash prize of £25,000 plus acquisition (by gift) of prize-winning painting by the Walker Art Gallery. Exhibition September 2001-January 2002. Founded 1957.

Shiva Naipaul Memorial Prize

Details The Spectator, 56 Doughty Street, London WC1N 2LL

This annual prize of £3000 is given to an English language writer of any nationality under the age of 35 for an essay of not more than 4000 words giving the most acute and profound observation of a culture alien to the writer. Founded 1985.

The National Art Library Illustration Awards

Enquiries The National Art Library, Victoria and Albert Museum, South Kensington, London SW7 2RL
tel 020-7938 8313
web site http://www.nal/vam.ac.uk
Contact Dr Leo De Freitas *tel/fax* (01295) 256110

These annual awards are given to practising book and magazine illustrators, for work first published in Great Britain in the 12 months preceding the judging of the awards. Book covers, illustrations of a purely technical nature and photographs together with works produced as limited editions are excluded. Cover illustrations to magazines are eligible. Sponsored by The Enid Linder Foundation.

National Poetry Competition

Contact Competition Organiser, The Poetry Society, 22 Betterton Street, London WC2H 9BU
tel 020-7420 9880 *fax* 020-7240 4818
e-mail poetrysoc@dial.pipex.com
web site http://www.poetrysoc.com

One of Britain's major annual open poetry competitions. Poems on any theme, up to 40 lines. Prizes: 1st £5000, 2nd £1000, 3rd £500, plus 10 commendations of £50. There will be an additional 6 prizes for 1999-2001, courtesy of British Telecommunications plc. Entries are appraised by a chosen poet. For rules and entry form send an sae. Entries also accepted via the web site. Closing date: 31 October each year.

The Néstle Smarties Book Prize

Details Book Trust, Book House, 45 East Hill, London SW18 2QZ
tel 020-8516 2973/2972 *fax* 020-8516 2978
e-mail sandra@booktrust.org.uk
Contact Sandra Vince, Tarryn McKay

A prize (Gold Award) of £2500 is awarded to each of the 3 age category winners (0-5, 6-8 and 9-11 years). Runners-up (Silver Award) receive £1500 each, and third prize (Bronze Award) winners receive £500 each. Eligible books must be published in the UK in the 12 months ending 30 September of the year of presentation and be a work of fiction or poetry for children written in English by a citizen or resident of the UK. Closing date for entries: 31 July of the year of presentation. Sponsored by Nestlé Smarties. Established in 1985.

New London Writers Awards
Details Nick McDowell, Head of Literature, London Arts Board, Elme House, 133 Long Acre, London WC2E 9AF
tel 020-7240 1313 *fax* 020-7670 2400
e-mail nick.mcdowell@lonab.co.uk
Five bursaries of £4000 each are offered to London writers who have published a first book of fiction or poetry, and who need to 'buy time' to complete a second work. (Fiction is taken to mean novels, short stories and other less easily defined creative work.) Writers can be of any nationality but must be resident in Greater London. Closing date: 12 January 2001. Founded 1993-4.

New Millennial Science Essay Competition
Details The Wellcome Trust, 210 Euston Road, London NW1 2BE
tel 020-7611 7221 *fax* 020-7611 8269
e-mail comm+ed@wellcome.ac.uk
web site http://www.wellcome.ac.uk/ScienceEssay
Postgraduate students (in science, engineering or technology) currently writing up their theses are invited to write an entertaining essay of no more than 700 words on their research. The aim is to make the research topic interesting and accessible to a wider non-specialist audience. Applicants must be registered at an internationally recognised institution. The competition is open from mid February to mid May each year and winners are announced at the BA Festival of Science. A collaboration between the Wellcome Trust and *New Scientist* magazine. Prizes: £1500 and publication in *New Scientist* (1st), £750 (2nd), two 3rd prizes of £375 each. All winners, including the next 10 best essays, receive a one-year subscription to *New Scientist*. Founded 1993.

The New Writer Poetry Prizes
Details The New Writer Poetry Prizes, PO Box 60, Cranbrook, Kent TN17 2ZR
tel (01580) 212626 *fax* (01580) 212041
e-mail thenewwriter@hotmail.com
web site http://homestead.dejanews.com/tnw/index.html
Poets may submit either one or a collection of 6-10 previously unpublished poems. Up to 25 prizes (total prize money £2500) will be presented as well as publication for the prize-winning poets in an anthology, plus the chance for a further 10 shortlisted poets to have their work published in the *New Writer* magazine. Entry fees: £3 per poem; £10 for a collection of 6-10 poems. Closing date: 20 November 2000. Founded 1997.

The Nobel Prize in Literature
Awarding authority Swedish Academy, Box 2118, S-10313 Stockholm, Sweden
tel (08) 10-65-24 *fax* (08) 24-42-25
e-mail sekretariat@svenskaakademien.se
web site http://www.svenskaakademien.se
This is one of the awards stipulated in the will of the late Alfred Nobel, the Swedish scientist who invented dynamite. No direct application for a prize will be taken into consideration. For authors writing in English it was bestowed upon Rudyard Kipling in 1907, W.B. Yeats in 1923, George Bernard Shaw in 1925, Sinclair Lewis in 1930, John Galsworthy in 1932, Eugene O'Neill in 1936, Pearl Buck in 1938, T.S. Eliot in 1948, William Faulkner in 1949, Bertrand Russell in 1950, Sir Winston Churchill in 1953, Ernest Hemingway in 1954, John Steinbeck in 1962, Samuel Beckett in 1969, Patrick White in 1973, Saul Bellow in 1976, William Golding in 1983, Wole Soyinka in 1986, Joseph Brodsky in 1987, Nadine Gordimer in 1991, Derek Walcott in 1992, Toni Morrison in 1993 and Seamus Heaney in 1995.

Northern Writers' Awards
Administered by New Writing North, 7-8 Trinity Chare, Quayside, Newcastle upon Tyne NE1 3DF
tel 0191-232 9991 *fax* 0191-230 1883
e-mail subtext.nwn@virgin.net
web site http://www.newwritingnorth.com
Contact John McGagh
Awards (from £1500 to £8000) are aimed at developing writers at 3 different stages in their careers. A panel of professional writers shortlists and makes minor awards once a year. Deadline for all applications: 31 January.

The Observer Hodge Award/Exhibition
The Observer Hodge Award, The Observer, 119 Farringdon Road, London EC1R 3ER
tel 020-7278 2332 *fax* 020-7713 4368
e-mail anna.sinfield@guardian.co.uk
Contact Anna Sinfield
Set up in memory of photographer David Hodge who died aged 30, this annual

award is given to student and professional photographers under 30. First prize: £3000 plus a photographic assignment for the *Observer*; best student prize: £1500. Deadline: varies. Founded 1986.

P.J. O'Connor Awards

P.J. O'Connor Awards, RTE Radio Drama, Donnybrook, Dublin 4, Republic of Ireland
tel (01) 2083111 *fax* (01) 2082045
Producer in Charge Michael Campion

An annual competition for a 30-minute original radio play, open to unproduced writers born in or living in Ireland. Prizes: £2000 (1st), £1500 (2nd), £750 (3rd). Closing date: November 2000.

Orange Prize for Fiction

Orange Prize for Fiction, Book Trust, Book House, 45 East Hill, London SW18 2QZ
tel 020-8516 2973/2972 *fax* 020-8516 2978
e-mail sandra@booktrust.org.uk
Contact Sandra Vince, Tarryn McKay

This award of £30,000 is for a full-length novel written in English by a woman of any nationality and first published in the UK between 1 April and the following 31 March.

George Orwell Memorial Prize

Details Specialist Conferences Ltd, The Orwell Prize, 21 The Lodge, Kensington Park Gardens, London W11 3HA
tel 020-7727 9732 *fax* 020-7221 5187

Two prizes of £1000 each are awarded in March each year – one for the best political book, and one for best political journalism – of the previous year, giving equal merit to content and good style accessible to the general public. Founded in 1993.

Catherine Pakenham Memorial Award

Entry form Charlotte Ibarra, Public Relations Dept, The Sunday Telegraph, 1 Canada Square, Canary Wharf, London E14 5DT
tel 020-7538 6257 *fax* 020-7513 2512

This award is open to young women journalists aged 18-25 who have at least one piece of published work. Entrants are asked to submit a non-fiction 750-2000-word article by early March 2000. The winner will receive £1000 and the chance to write for a *Telegraph* publication. Three runners-up each receive £200. Entry forms are available after 1 September. Founded in 1970 in memory of Catherine Pakenham, who died in a car crash whilst working for the *Telegraph Magazine*.

The Parker Romantic Novel of the Year Award

Details Anthea Kenyon, The Old Bakehouse, 36 Eastgate, Hallaton, Market Harborough, Leics. LE16 8UB
tel (01858) 555602
web site http://www.rna-uk.org

This annual award for the best romantic novel of the year is open to both members and non-members of the Romantic Novelists' Association, provided non-members are domiciled in the UK. Novels must be published between the previous 1 December and 30 November of the year of entry. Three copies of the novel are required. Entry forms and details are available from July onwards.

New Writers' Award

Details Margaret James, 21 Copse Way, Finchampstead, Berks. RG40 4EJ
tel (01189) 733942
e-mail margaret@jamesk.freeserve.co.uk

For writers previously unpublished in the romantic novel field and who are probationary members of the Association. MSS can be submitted until the end of September under the New Writers' Scheme. All receive a critique. Any MSS which have passed through the Scheme and which are subsequently accepted for publication become eligible for the Award.

Peterloo Poets Open Poetry Competition

Details Peterloo Poets, 2 Kelly Gardens, Calstock, Cornwall PL18 9SA

This annual competition offers a first prize of £3000 and 5 other prizes totalling £2100. Closing date: 2 March 2000. Founded in 1986.

Poetry Life Open Poetry Competition

Details 1 Blue Ball Corner, Water Lane, Winchester, Hants SO23 0ER
e-mail adrian.abishop@virgin.net
web site http://freespace.virgin.net/poetry.life/

Competitions are held 3 times a year with a first prize of £500. Any style is acceptable with an 80-line limit on each poem. Poems must be previously unpublished (in book form) and must not have won a prize in another competition. All winning poems are published in *Poetry Life* magazine and on its web site. Send sae for further details. Founded 1994.

The Portico Prize

Details Miss Emma Marigliano, Librarian, Portico Library, 57 Mosley Street, Manchester M2 3HY
tel 0161-236 6785 *fax* 0161-236 6803

This biennial prize of £3000 is awarded for a published work of fiction or non-fiction, of general interest and literary merit set wholly or mainly in the North-West of England (Lancashire, Manchester, Liverpool, High Peak of Derbyshire, Cheshire and Cumbria). Next award: 2002. Founded in 1985.

Dennis Potter Play of the Year Award

Details Jeremy Howe,
BBC Broadcasting House,
Whiteladies Road, Bristol BS8 2LR

Information about this award is obtainable from the above office after October 2000. Founded in 1994.

The Mathew Prichard Award for Short Story Writing

Details The Competition Secretary, The Mathew Prichard Award, 2 Rhododendron Close, Cyncoed, Cardiff CF2 7HS

Total prize money of £2000 is awarded annually in this open competition for original short stories in English of not more than 2500 words. Adjudication is organised in May each year by the South and Mid Wales Association of Writers.

Real Writers Short Story Competition

PO Box 170, Chesterfield, Derbyshire S40 1FE
tel/fax (01246) 238492
e-mail realwrtrs@aol.com
web site http://www.turtledesign.com/realwriters/

An annual open competition for stories of up to 5000 words. There is no theme. First prize: £1000. Send sae for entry form. Closing date: 30 September. Founded 1994.

Trevor Reese Memorial Prize

Details Events and Publicity Officer, Institute of Commonwealth Studies, 28 Russell Square, London WC1B 5DS
tel 020-7862 8825 *fax* 020-7862 8820
e-mail skearins@sas.ac.uk
web site http://www.sas.ac.uk/commonwealthstudies/

This prize of £1000 is awarded biennially, usually for a scholarly work by a single author in the field of Imperial and Commonwealth history. The next award (for a book published in 1998 or 1999) will be given in 2001.

The Margaret Rhondda Award

Details Awards Secretary, The Society of Authors, 84 Drayton Gardens, London SW10 9SB

This award is given every 3 years to a woman writer as a grant-in-aid towards the expenses of a research project in journalism, in recognition of the service which women journalists give to the public through journalism. Closing date for next award: 20 December 2001. First awarded in July 1968 on the tenth anniversary of Lady Rhondda's death.

The Rio Tinto David Watt Memorial Prize

Details/entry form The Administrator, The Rio Tinto David Watt Memorial Prize, Rio Tinto plc, 6 St James's Square, London SW1Y 4LD

This £5000 prize is awarded for outstanding written contributions towards the greater understanding of international and political issues. Those eligible for the prize are writers actively engaged in writing for newspapers and journals in the English language. Entries should comprise a published article in English of not more than 3000 words. Closing date for entries and nominations: end March. Funded and administered by Rio Tinto plc. Founded in 1988.

The Rooney Prize for Irish Literature

Details J.A. Sherwin, Strathin, Templecarrig, Delgany, Co. Wicklow, Republic of Ireland
tel (01) 287 4769 *fax* (01) 287 2595
e-mail jsherwin@iol.ie

This prize is to encourage young Irish writing talent. IR£5000 is awarded annually to a different individual, who must be Irish, published in either Irish or English and under 40 years of age. The prize is non-competitive and there is no application procedure or entry form. Founded in 1976.

The Royal Society of Literature Award under the W.H. Heinemann Bequest

Details/Submissions The Secretary, Royal Society of Literature, Somerset House, Strand, London WC2R 0RN
tel 020-7845 4676 *fax* 020-7845 4679
e-mail RSLit@aol.com

Works of any kind of literature may be submitted by publishers under this award of £5000, which aims to encourage genuine contributions to literature. Books must be written in the English language and have been published in the previous year. Translations are not eligible for consideration, nor are single poems, nor collections of pieces by more than one author, nor may individuals put forward their own work. Final entry date: 15 December.

The Royal Society of Medicine Prizes
Details The Secretary, MWG, The Society of Authors, 84 Drayton Gardens, London SW10 9SB
Closing date for submissions of medical basic books; advanced authored books; advanced multi-contributor books; medical history: 30 June. The Medical Writers Group of the Society of Authors administers the prizes sponsored by the Royal Society of Medicine.

RSPCA Young Photographer Awards
Details Publications Department, RSPCA, Causeway, Horsham, West Sussex RH12 1HG
tel (01403) 223145 *fax* (01403) 241048
e-mail publications@rspca.org.uk
Annual awards are made for animal photographs taken by young people in 2 age categories: under 12 and 12-18. Prizes: overall winner (£250 cash, £300 camera, and £250 books), age group winners (£100 cash, £180 camera, £100 books). Four runners-up in each age group receive £150 camera. Sponsored by Olympus and Hodder Wayland. Closing date for entries: September 2001. Founded 1994.

Runciman Award
Details The Administrator, The Anglo-Hellenic League, 16-18 Paddington Street, London W1M 4AS
tel 020-7486 9410
An annual prize of not less than £2000 for a work wholly or mainly about some aspect of Greece or the Hellenic scene, which has been published in its first English edition in the UK during the previous year and listed in Whitaker's Books in Print. The Award may be given for a work of fiction, drama or non-fiction; concerned academically or non-academically with the history of any period; biography or autobiography, the arts, archaeology; a guidebook or a translation from the Greek of any period. Established 1985.

Sainsbury's Baby Book Award
Book Trust, Book House, 45 East Hill, London SW18 2QZ
tel 020-8516 2973 *fax* 020-8516 2978
e-mail sandra@booktrust.org.uk
web site http://www.booktrust.org.uk
An annual award of £2000 for the author and/or illustrator of the best book for babies under one year of age. Closing date: 1 June 2001.

Alastair Salvesen Art Scholarship
The Royal Scottish Academy, The Mound, Edinburgh EH2 2EL
tel 0131-225 6671 *fax* 0131-225 2349
The Scholarship consists of 2 parts:
• A 3-6 months travel scholarship of up to £10,000 depending on the plan submitted; and
• An exhibition in Nov/Dec organised by the Royal Scottish Academy.
Applicants must be painters aged 25-35 who have been trained at one of the 4 Scottish colleges of art; are currently living and working in Scotland; have worked for a minimum of 3 years outside a college or student environment; and have during 2000 had work accepted for an exhibition in the Annual Exhibition organised by certain Scottish institutes or, in a recognised gallery, have held a one-artist exhibition or participated in a group exhibition. Founded 1989.

Scoop of the Year Award
Details The Hon. Secretary, London Press Club, St Bride Institute, 14 Bride Lane, Fleet Street, London EC4Y 8EQ
tel/fax 020-7353 7086
e-mail lpressclub@aol.com
Chosen by a panel of senior editors, this annual award of a bronze statuette is given for the reporting scoop of the year, appearing in either a newspaper or electronic media. Founded in 1990.

The Scottish Arts Council

Writers' Bursaries
Contact Jenny Brown, Literature Director, The Scottish Arts Council, 12 Manor Place, Edinburgh EH3 7DD
tel 0131-226 6051
e-mail jenny.brown.sac@arts.fb.org
A limited number of bursaries – of between £1000 and £10,000 each – are offered to enable professional writers, including writers for children, to devote more time to writing. Priority is given to writers of fiction and verse, but writers of literary non-fiction are also considered.

Application normally open only to writers who have been living and working in Scotland for at least 2 years. Applications may be discussed with Jenny Brown.

Book Awards
Details Gavin Wallace, Literature Officer, The Scottish Arts Council, 12 Manor Place, Edinburgh EH3 7DD
tel 0131-226 6051
e-mail gavin.wallace.sac@arts.fb.org

Four awards of £1000 each are made in both spring and autumn. Preference is given to literary fiction and verse, but literary non-fiction is also considered. Authors should be Scottish or resident in Scotland, but books of Scottish interest by other authors are eligible for consideration. Books by Scottish writers for children are eligible for 3 new annual awards. Publishers should apply for further information.

The Scottish Book of the Year and Scottish First Book

Details The Saltire Society, 9 Fountain Close, 22 High Street, Edinburgh EH1 1TF
tel 0131-556 1836 *fax* 0131-557 1675
e-mail saltire@saltire.org.uk
web site http://www.saltire-socity.demon.co.uk

These 2 annual awards (£5000 and £1500) are open to any author of Scottish descent or living in Scotland, or for a book by anyone which deals with the work or life of a Scot or with a Scottish problem, event or situation. Nominations are made by literary editors of Scottish newspapers and periodicals. Supported by the Post Office. Established in 1982 and 1988 respectively.

The Scottish Writer of the Year Award

Details Scottish Book Trust, Scottish Book Centre, 137 Dundee Street, Edinburgh EH11 1BG
tel 0131-229 3663 *fax* 0131-228 4293

An annual prize of £1000 is awarded to each of 5 shortlisted writers, plus a further £9000 to the winner. Submissions include novels, volumes of short stories, poetry, biography, autobiography, journalism, science fiction and children's books as well as theatre, cinema, radio and television scripts. Open to writers who were born or have been resident in Scotland, who have Scottish parents, or who take Scotland as their inspiration. Closing date: 31 July for work first made public during the previous 12 months.

The Seebohm Trophy – Age Concern Book of the Year

Application form Age Concern England, Astral House, 1268 London Road, London SW16 4ER
tel 020-8765 7456
e-mail marshav@ace.org.uk

An annual award is made to the author and publisher of a non-fiction title (published in the previous calendar year) which, in the opinion of the judges, is most successful in promoting the wellbeing and understanding of older people. The author receives £1000, the publisher the silver Seebohm Trophy. Nominations must be received before the end of April each year. Founded in 1995 in memory of Frederic, Lord Seebohm, President of Age Concern, 1971-89.

The Signal Poetry for Children Award

Details The Thimble Press, Lockwood, Station Road, South Woodchester, Stroud, Glos. GL5 5EQ

A prize of £100 is given annually for an outstanding book of poetry published for children in Britain and the Commonwealth during the previous year, whether single poem or anthology and regardless of country of original publication. Articles about the winning book are published in *Signal* each May. Not open to unpublished work.

The André Simon Memorial Fund Book Awards

Details Tessa Hayward, 5 Sion Hill Place, Bath BA1 5SJ
tel (01225) 336305 *fax* (01225) 421862

Two awards (£2000 each) are given annually, one each for the best new book on food and on drink, plus one Special Commendation of £1000 in either category. Closing date: November each year. Founded in 1978.

Singer & Friedlander/Sunday Times Watercolour Competition

Details Parker Harris Partnership, PO Box 279, Esher, Surrey KT10 8YZ
tel (01372) 462190 *fax* (01372) 460032
e-mail sf@parkerharris.co.uk

An annual competition 'to promote the continuance of the British tradition of fine watercolour painting'. Total prize money: £25,000. Open to artists born or resident in the UK. Closing date: mid June 2001. Winning entries will be exhibited in London, Manchester, Leeds and Birmingham. Launched 1987.

WHSmith Book Prize

Details WHSmith PLC, Nations House, 103 Wigmore Street, London W1H 0WH
tel 020-7409 3222 *fax* 020-7629 3600

A new prize to celebrate all forms of excellence in book publishing with a range of categories. Contact WHSmith for fuller details.

The Jill Smythies Award

The Linnean Society of London, Burlington House, Piccadilly, London W1V 0LQ
tel 020-7434 4479 *fax* 020-7287 9364
e-mail john@linnean.demon.co.uk
web site http://www.linnean.org.uk

Established in honour of Jill Smythies whose career as a botanical artist was cut short by an accident to her right hand. The rubic states that 'the Award, to be made by Council usually annually consisting of a silver medal and a purse (currently £1000) ... is for published illustrations, such as drawings and paintings, in aid of plant identification, with the emphasis on botanical accuracy and the accurate portrayal of diagnostic characteristics. Illustrations of cultivars of garden origin are not eligible.' Closing date for nominations: 30 September. Founded 1988.

Sony Radio Awards

Details Sony Radio Awards Secretariat, Zafer Associates, 47-48 Chagford Street, London NW1 6EB
tel 020-7723 0106 *fax* 020-7724 6163
e-mail secretariat@radioawards.org

'The Sony Radio Awards celebrate excellence in broadcast work. They reward creative achievement through imagination, originality, wit and integrity. The Awards offer an opportunity to enter work in a range of categories which reflect today's local, regional and national radio. The Awards are for everyone regardless of resources – for stations big and small, for a team or for one person with a microphone.' Send for further information. Founded 1981.

Stand Magazine Awards

Details Stand Magazine, Haltwhistle House, George Street, Newcastle upon Tyne NE4 7JL
tel/fax 0191-273 3280 *fax* 0191-273 0555

Stand Magazine Short Story Competition

Biennial competition is for an original, untranslated short story in English (up to 8000 words) not previously published, broadcast or under consideration elsewhere. Prizes to the value of £2500. Entry fee: £4/$8 per story. Closing date: 31 May 2001. Send a UK sae or 2 IRCs for an entry form. Founded 1980.

Stand Poetry Competition

Biennial competition for original poems, in English and untranslated, and previously unpublished. Prizes to the value of £2500. Entrants may submit as many poems as they wish. Entry fee: £4.50/ $8.50 for the first, and £3/$7 for each subsequent poem. Closing date: May 2002. Send a UK sae or 2 IRCs for entry form.

The Stern Silver Pen Award for Non-Fiction

Details PEN, 152-6 Kentish Town Road, London NW1 9QB
tel 020-7267 9444 *fax* 020-7267 9304

This award of £1000 is given annually for an outstanding work of non-fiction written in English and published during the previous year by an author of British nationality or an author who has been a long-term resident in the UK. No submissions please – books are nominated by members of the PEN Executive Committee. Sponsored by the Stern family since 1996. Founded in 1969.

Tabla Poetry Competition

Tabla, Dept of English, University of Bristol, 3-5 Woodland Road, Bristol BS8 1TB
fax 0117-928 8860
e-mail stephen.james@bris.ac.uk
web site http://www.bris.ac.uk/tabla

An annual competition for poems of any length and on any subject. Selected entries are published alongside work by established authors in the annual *Tabla Book of New Verse*. Prizes: £500 (1st), £200 (2nd), £100 (3 runners up). Closing date: 30 September.

TAPS (Television Arts Performance Showcase)

Teddington Studios, Broom Road, Teddington TW11 9NT
tel 020-8977 3252 *fax* 020-8614 2337
e-mail taps@tvarts.demon.co.uk

Writers with less than 2 hours on network TV may submit their script to TAPS at any time throughout the year, and selected scripts are showcased. There are 3 award categories of showcased writers: shorts, comedy and full-length scripts. In addition, there is an overall Writer of the Year award. Awards are between £500 and £1500. Awards date: October/November.

Reginald Taylor and Lord Fletcher Essay Competition

Submissions Hon. Editor, Dr Martin Henig, British Archaeological Association, Institute of Archaeology, 36 Beaumont Street, Oxford OX1 2PG

A prize of a medal and £300 is awarded biennially for the best unpublished essay of high scholarly standard, not exceeding 7500 words, which shows original research on a subject of archaeological, art-historical or antiquarian interest within the period from the Roman era to AD 1830. The successful competitor will be invited to read the essay before the Association and the essay may be published in the Association's *Journal*. Competitors should notify the Hon. Editor in advance of the intended subject of their work. Next award: November 2002. The essay should be submitted not later than 1 June 2002, enclosing an sae. Founded in memory of E. Reginald Taylor FSA and Lord Fletcher FSA.

Society for Theatre Research Book Prize

Details The Society for Theatre Research, c/o The Theatre Museum, 1E Tavistock Street, London WC2E 7PA
e-mail e.cottis@btinternet.com
web site http://www.blot.co.uk/str

An annual award (£400) is given to the author whose book, in the opinion of the judges, is the best original research into any aspect of the history and technique of the British theatre. Books must have been published in English in the preceding calendar year. Founded 1997.

The Thomas Cook Daily Telegraph Travel Book Award

Details Travel Book Award, Thomas Cook Publishing, PO Box 227, Thorpe Wood, Peterborough PE3 6PU
tel (01733) 503566 *fax* (01733) 503596
e-mail joan.lee@thomascook.com

This annual award is given to encourage the art of travel writing. Travel narrative books (150pp minimum) written in English and published between 1 January and 31 December of the preceding year are eligible. Established in 1980.

The Times Educational Supplement Book Awards

Details TES Book Awards, The Times Educational Supplement, Admiral House, 66-68 East Smithfield, London E1 9XY
tel 020-7782 3000 *fax* 020-7782 3200
e-mail friday@tes.co.uk

The Times Educational Supplement Information Book Awards

There are 2 annual awards for the best information books for children. The Junior Award is for books for children to the age of 11, and the Senior Award is for books for 11-16 year-olds.

The Times Educational Supplement Schoolbook Awards

There are 2 annual awards for the best primary and secondary school textbooks. The subject varies each year.

Tir Na N-og Awards

Details Welsh Books Council, Castell Brychan, Aberystwyth, Ceredigion SY23 2JB
tel (01970) 624151 *fax* (01970) 625385
e-mail menai.williams@cllc.org.uk
web site http://www.cllc.org.uk

There are 3 annual awards to children's authors and illustrators: best original Welsh fiction, including short stories and picture books; best original Welsh non-fiction book of the year; best English book with an authentic Welsh background. Total prize value is £3000. Founded 1976.

The Tom-Gallon Trust

Submissions Awards Secretary, The Society of Authors, 84 Drayton Gardens, SW10 9SB

A biennial award is made to fiction writers of limited means who have had at least one short story accepted for publication. An award of £1000 was made in 1999. Authors should send: a list of their already published fiction, giving the name of the publisher or periodical in each case and the approximate date of publication; one published or unpublished short story; a brief statement of their financial position and their date of birth; an undertaking that they intend to devote a substantial amount of time to the writing of fiction as soon as they are financially able to do so; an sae for the return of the work submitted. Next closing date: 20 September 2002.

The Translators Association Awards

Details Dorothy Wright, The Translators Association, 84 Drayton Gardens, London SW10 9SB

The Translators Association of the Society of Authors administers a number of prizes for translations into English. They include prizes for translations of Dutch and Flemish, French, German, Italian, Japanese, Portuguese, Spanish and Swedish works.

The Betty Trask Awards

Details Awards Secretary, The Society of Authors, 84 Drayton Gardens, London SW10 9SB

These awards are for the benefit of young authors under the age of 35 and are given on the strength of a first novel (published or unpublished) of a romantic or traditional nature. It is expected that prizes totalling at least £25,000 will be presented each year. The winners are required to use the money for a period or periods of foreign travel. Closing date: 31 January. Made possible through a generous bequest from Miss Betty Trask.

The Travelling Scholarships

These are honorary awards administered by the Society of Authors. Submissions are not accepted.

The Trewithen Poetry Prize

Details The Competition Secretary, Chy-an-Dour, Trewithen Moor, Stithians, Truro, Cornwall TR3 7DU

An annual prize to promote poetry with a rural theme. Poems can reflect contemporary rural living, environmental concerns, or any other aspect of nature or rural life in any country. Total prize money: £800. In addition, prize-winners will have their poems published in the *Trewithen Chapbook*, a biennial limited edition publication. Entry fee: £3. Send sae for entry form. Closing date: 31 October each year.

T.E. Utley Memorial Fund Award

Details Virginia Utley, 111 Sugden Road, London SW11 5ED
tel 020-7228 1665

One prize of £2500 and one of £1500 are awarded annually for an essay on a given subject.

'Charles Veillon' European Essay Prize

Details The Secretary, Charles Veillon Foundation, CH 1017 Lausanne, Switzerland
tel (021) 706 9029

A prize of 30,000 Swiss francs is awarded annually to a European writer or essayist for essays offering a critical look at modern society's way of life and ideology. Founded in 1975.

Ver Poets Open Competition

Organiser May Badman, Ver Poets, 61-63 Chiswell Green Lane, St Albans, Herts. AL2 3AL
tel (01727) 867005

A competition open to all for poems of up to 30 lines of any genre or subject matter, which must be unpublished work in English. Prizes: £500 (1st), £300 (2nd), £100 (2 x 3rd). Entry fee: £2.50 per poem with 2 copies of each poem (each year a gift to charity is made). Closing date 30 April each year.

Edgar Wallace Award

Details The Hon. Secretary, London Press Club, St Bride Institute, 14 Bride Lane, Fleet Street, London EC4Y 8EQ
tel/fax 020-7353 7086
e-mail lpressclub@aol.com

Chosen by a panel of senior editors, this annual award of a silver inkstand is given for outstanding writing or reporting by a journalist. Founded in 1990.

Wellcome Trust Prize

Details The Wellcome Trust, 210 Euston Road, London NW1 2BE
tel 020-7611 7221 *fax* 020-7611 8269
e-mail comm+ed@wellcome.ac.uk
web site http://www.wellcome.ac.uk

A bi-annual prize of £25,000 (paid quarterly over one year) gives the opportunity for a professional life scientist to take a break from their normal routine to write a popular book about their work which will educate, captivate and inspire the non-specialist lay reader. The winning work will be published by either HarperCollins or Weidenfeld & Nicolson. Applicants must be resident in the UK and have not previously published a popular science book. Founded 1997.

Whitbread Book Awards

Details Denise Bayat, The Booksellers Association, Minster House, 272 Vauxhall Bridge Road, London SW1V 1BA
tel 020-7834 5477 *fax* 020-7834 8812
e-mail denise.bayat@booksellers.org.uk
web site http://www.whitbread.co.uk

The awards celebrate well-written, enjoyable British books of the previous year. Judged in 2 stages and offering a total of £39,000 prize money, the awards are open to 5 categories: Novel, First Novel, Biography/Autobiography, Poetry and Children's Book of the Year. The winner in each category receives a Whitbread Award of £3500. These 5 nominations are then judged for the Whitbread Book of the Year, the overall winner receiving an additional £21,000. Writers must have lived in Great Britain or Ireland for 3 or more years. Submissions only from publishers. Closing date: end of June. Sponsored by Whitbread plc. Founded 1965.

The Whitfield Prize

Submissions Executive Secretary, Royal Historical Society, University College London, Gower Street, London WC1E 6BT
tel/fax 0171-387 7532
e-mail royalhistsoc@ucl.ac.uk
web site http://www.rhs.ac.uk

The Prize (value £1000) is announced in July each year for the best work on a subject within a field of British history. It must be its author's first solely written history book, an original and scholarly work of historical research and have been published in the UK in the preceding calendar year. Three non-returnable copies of an eligible book should be submitted before 31 December to the Executive Secretary.

John Whiting Award

Details Writing Theatre Dept, Arts Council of England, 14 Great Peter Street, London SW1P 3NQ
tel 0171-973 6431
e-mail info.drama@artscouncil.org.uk

This prize of £6000 is given annually. Eligible to apply are any writers who have received during the previous 2 calendar years an award through the Arts Council new theatre writing schemes, or who have had a commission or premier production by a theatre company in receipt of an annual subsidy. Founded 1965.

David T.K. Wong Fellowship

Details David T.K. Wong Fellowship, School of English & American Studies, University of East Anglia, Norwich NR4 7TJ
tel (01603) 592810 *fax* (01603) 507728

Founded by David Wong, retired senior civil servant, journalist and businessman, the annual Fellowship (worth £25,000) at the University of East Anglia will give writers of exceptional talent the chance to produce a work of fiction in English which deals seriously with some aspect of life in the Far East. Write for further details. Closing date: 31 October each year. Founded 1997.

Write A Story for Children Competition

Entry forms The Academy of Children's Writers, PO Box 95, Huntingdon, Cambs. PE17 5RL
tel (01487) 832752

Three prizes are awarded annually (1st £1000, 2nd £200, 3rd £100) for a short story for children, maximum 1000 words, by an unpublished writer of children's fiction. Send sae for details. Founded in 1984.

Writers' Forum Short Story Competition

Details Writers' International Ltd, 1st Floor, Briggs House, 26 Commercial Road, Ashley Cross, Poole BH14 0JR
tel (01202) 716043 *fax* (01202) 740995
e-mail writintl@globalnet.co.uk
web site http://www.users.globalnet.co.uk/~writintl

An annual competition open to unpublished short stories of up to 2000 words. Prizes are £300 (1st), £100 (2nd), £50 (3rd); all the winning entries will be published in *Writers' Forum* magazine. Entry fee: £4. Next closing date to be advised. Founded 1991.

Yorkshire Post Book of the Year

Submissions Margaret Brown, Yorkshire Post Literary Awards, Yorkshire Post Newspapers Ltd, PO Box 168, Wellington Street, Leeds LS1 1RF

A prize of £1200 annually for the Best Book, either fiction or non-fiction. Submissions are accepted only from publishers, and authors should be British or resident in the UK. Next closing date: 31 December.

Young Writers' Season

Details Young Writers' Season, Royal Court Young Writers' Programme, Sloane Square, London SW1W 8AS
tel 020-7565 5034 *fax* 020-7565 5001

Anyone aged 25 or under can submit a play on any subject. A selection of plays is professionally presented by the Royal Court Theatre with the writers fully involved in rehearsal and production. Pre-Festival Development Workshops are run by professional theatre practitioners and designed to help everyone attending to write a play.

Prizes and awards by subject area

This list provides a quick reference to the main listings of prizes, competitions and awards which starts on page 512.

Biography

J.R. Ackerley Prize
James Tait Black Memorial Prize
The Duff Cooper Prize
Marsh Biography Award
The Royal Society of Literature Award under the W.H. Heinemann Bequest
The Runciman Award
The Scottish Writer of the Year Award
Whitbread Book Awards

Children

Hans Christian Andersen Medal
The Arts Council of England Children's Award
The Bisto Book of the Year Award
Children's Book Award
The Children's Laureate
The Eleanor Farjeon Award
The Fidler Award
The Guardian Children's Fiction Prize
The Independent/Scholastic Story of the Year Competition
The Library Association Carnegie and Kate Greenaway Awards
The Macmillan Prize for a Children's Picture Book
Kurt Maschler Award
The Néstle Smarties Book Prize
Sainsbury Baby Book Award
The Signal Poetry for Children Award
The Times Educational Supplement Book Awards
Tir Na N-og Awards
Write a Story for Children Competition

Drama – theatre, TV and radio

The Arts Council of England Children's Award
British Academy of Film and Television Arts Awards
The David Cohen British Literature Prize
Verity Bargate Award
Samuel Beckett Award
Miles Franklin Literary Award
The Richard Imison Memorial Award
LAB/LBC London Radio Playwrights' Festival
Meyer-Whitworth Award
P.J. O'Connor Awards
Dennis Potter Play of the Year Award
Sony Radio Awards
TAPS (Television Arts Performance Project)
John Whiting Award
Young Writers' Season

Essays

The David Cohen British Literature Prize
Shiva Naipaul Award
New Millennial Science Essay Competition
Reginald Taylor and Lord Fletcher Essay Competition
T.E. Utley Memorial Fund Award
Charles Veillon European Essay Prize

Fiction

Authors' Club Best First Novel Award
James Tait Black Memorial Prize
The Booker Prize
The Raymond Chandler Society's 'Marlowe' Award for Best International Crime Novel
Arthur C. Clarke Award
The David Cohen British Literature Prize
Commonwealth Writers Prize
CWA Awards
The Dundee Book Prize
Encore Award
Christopher Ewart-Biggs Memorial Prize
The Geoffrey Faber Memorial Prize
Miles Franklin Literary Award
Mind Book of the Year/Allen Lane Award
The Guardian First Book Award
The Hawthornden Prize
The Winifred Holtby Memorial Prize
International IMPAC Dublin Literary Award
Irish Times Literary Prizes
Japan Festival Awards
Jewish Quarterly Literary Prizes
The Lichfield Prize
The McKitterick Prize (published/unpublished)
The Enid McLeod Literary Prize
Macmillan Silver Pen Award for Fiction
The Mail on Sunday-John Llewellyn Rhys Prize
The Somerset Maugham Awards
Mind Book of the Year/Allen Lane Award
New London Writers Awards
Orange Prize for Fiction
The Parker Romantic Novel of the Year Award
The Portico Prize
The Runciman Award
Scottish Arts Council Book Awards
WHSmith Book Prize
The Scottish Writer of the Year Award
The Betty Trask Awards
Whitbread Book Awards

David T.K. Wong Fellowship
Yorkshire Post Book of the Year

Fine art – see Visual art

Grants, bursaries and fellowships

Arts Council of England
The Arts Council of Ireland
Arts Council of Wales
Authors' Foundation
Kathleen Blundell Trust
Alfred Bradley Bursary
British Academy Research Awards
The Rhys Davies Trust
European Jewish Publication Society Grants
E.M. Forster Award
E.C. Gregory Trust Fund
Hawthornden Writers' Fellowships
Leverhulme Research Fellowships and Grants
New London Writers Awards
Northern Writers' Awards
The Margaret Rhondda Award
Scottish Arts Council
The Travelling Scholarships
Wellcome Trust Prize
David T.K. Wong Fellowship

Illustration

Hans Christian Andersen Medal
Bisto Book of the Year Award
British Fantasy Awards
The Eleanor Farjeon Award
L. Ron Hubbard's Illustrators of the Future Contest
Images – The Best of Illustration
The Macmillan Prize for a Children's Picture Book
Kurt Maschler Award
The National Art Library Illustration Awards
Sainsbury Baby Book Award
The Jill Smythies Award
Tir Na N-og Awards

Journalism

Freedom Award
Glaxo Wellcome ABSW Science Writers Awards
George Orwell Memorial Prize
Catherine Pakenham Memorial Award
Margaret Rhondda Award
Scoop of the Year Award
The Scottish Writer of the Year Award
Edgar Wallace Award

Non-fiction

Alexander Prize (History)
Authors' Club Sir Banister Fletcher Award (Architecture)
The Aventis Prizes for Science Books
David Berry Prize (History)
BP Natural World Book Prize
British Academy Medals and Prizes
The Duff Cooper Prize
The Rose Mary Crawshay Prizes
CWA Awards
Christopher Ewart-Biggs Memorial Prize
Gladstone History Book Prize
Glenfiddich Food & Drink Awards
The Calvin and Rose G. Hoffman Memorial Prize
IrishTimes Literary Prizes
Jewish Quarterly Literary Prizes
Kraszna-Krausz Awards
The International Langhe Ceretto Prize for Food and Wine Culture
Japan Festival Awards
The Samuel Johnson Prize for Non-Fiction
The Library Association Reference Awards
The Mail on Sunday-John Llewellyn Rhys Prize
The Somerset Maugham Awards
MCA Book Prize (Management)
Enid McLeod Prize
Mind Book of the Year/Allen Lane Award
The Portico Prize
Trevor Reese Memorial Prize
The Royal Society of Literature Award under the W.H. Heinemann Bequest
The Royal Society of Medicine Prizes
The Rio Tinto David Watt Memorial Prize
Runciman Award
Scottish Arts Council Book Awards
The André Simon Memorial Fund Book Awards (Food and Drink)
WHSmith Book Prize
The Society for Theatre Research Book Prize
The Stern Silver Pen Award for Non-Fiction
The Thomas Cook Daily Telegraph Travel Book Award (Travel writing)
The Times Educational Supplement Book Awards
The Whitfield Prize (History)
Yorkshire Post Book of the Year

Photography – see Visual art

Poetry

Academi 2001 Cardiff International Poetry Competition
Arvon Foundation
The David Cohen British Literature Prize
Denis Devlin Memorial Award
Arts Council of Ireland
Arts Council of Wales
The Bridport Prize
Cholmondeley Award
DT Charitable Trust Open Poetry Competition
The T.S. Eliot Prize
Geoffrey Faber Memorial Prize
Forward Poetry Prizes
The Felicia Hemans Prize for Lyrical Poetry
Irish Times Literary Prizes
Kent & Sussex Poetry Society Open Poetry Competition
London Writers Competition
The Somerset Maugham Awards
National Poetry Competition
The Néstle Smarties Book Prize
New London Writers Awards
The New Writer Poetry Prizes
Peterloo Poets Open Poetry Competition
Poetry Life Open Poetry CompetitionThe Royal Society of Literature Award under the W.H. Heinemann Bequest
The Runciman Award
Scottish Arts Council Book Awards
The Signal Poetry for Children Award
The Scottish Writer of the Year Award
Stand Poetry Competition
Tabla Poetry Competition

The Trewithen Poetry Prize
Ver Poets Open Competition
Whitbread Book Awards

Short stories

The Bridport Prize
The David Cohen British Literature Prize
CWA/The Macallan Short Story Dagger
DT Charitable Trust Annual Ghost Story Competition
DT Charitable Trust Annual Love Story Competition
The Fish Short Story Competition
The Martin Healy Short Story Award
L. Ron Hubbard's Writers of the Future Contest
The Lady Short Story Competition
London Writers Competition
Macallan/Scotland on Sunday Short Story Competition
Bryan MacMahon Short Story Award
Macmillan Silver Pen Award for Fiction
The Matthew Prichard Award for Short Story Writing
Real Writers Short Story Competition
The Scottish Writer of the Year Award
Stand Magazine Short Story Competition
The Tom-Gallon Trust Award
Write A Story for Children Competition
Writers' Forum Short Story Competition

Translation

European Translation Prize
Marsh Award for Children's Literature in Translation
The Translators Association Awards

Specialist

BA/Whitaker Author of the Year Award
European Literary Prize (Literature)
The Boardman Tasker Prize (Mountain Literature)
British Academy Medals and Prizes
British Book Awards
British Fantasy Awards
DT Charitable Trust Awards – Self-Publishing Award
The Lionel Gelber Prize (International Relations)
Heywood Hill Literary Prize
William Hill Sports Book of the Year Award
The Library Association Wheatley Medal (Indexing)
The London New Writing Competition
The Enid McLeod Literary Prize
The Somerset Maugham Awards
The Nobel Prize in Literature
The Portico Prize
The Rooney Prize for Irish Literature
The Runciman Award (Greece)
Scottish Arts Council Book Awards
Scottish Book of the Year and Scottish First Book
The Seebohm Trophy – Age Concern Book of the Year
Times Educational Supplement Book Awards

Visual art

Artists' Residencies in Tuscany
BG Young Wildlife Photographer of the Year
BG Wildlife Photographer of the Year
BP Portrait Award
The Gilchrist-Fisher Award
The Paul Hamlyn Foundation Awards to Artists
Hunting Art Prizes
Images – The Best of British Illustration
The John Kobal Photographic Portrait Award
Laing Art Prize
Millfield Arts Projects
John Moores Liverpool Exhibition
The Observer Hodge Award/Exhibition
RSPCA Young Photographer Awards
Alastair Salvesen Art Scholarship
Singer & Friedlander/Sunday Times Watercolour Competition

Literature festivals

There are hundreds of arts festivals held in the UK each year – too many to mention in this Yearbook and many of which are not applicable specifically to writers. We give here a selection of literature festivals and general arts festivals which include literature events. Space constraints and the nature of an annual publication together determine that only brief details are given; contact festival organisers for a full programme of events. The British Council will supply a list of forthcoming literature festivals on receipt of a large sae.

Aldeburgh Poetry Festival

Aldeburgh Poetry Trust, Goldings, Goldings Lane, Leiston, Suffolk IP16 4EB
tel (01728) 830631 *fax* (01728) 832029
Festival Director Naomi Jaffa
Takes place First weekend in Nov

An annual international festival of contemporary poetry. The weekend includes readings, workshops, a public masterclass, a lecture and a children's event. Twenty different poets as well as fringe events. Preceded by an extended residency for one of the invited poets. Festival prize for the year's best first collection.

Aspects Festival

North Down Heritage Centre, The Castle, Bangor, Co. Down BT20 4BT
tel (01247) 271200 *fax* (01247) 271370
Festival Director Kenneth Irvine
Contact Paula Clamp (Arts Officer)
Takes place 26 Sept-1 Oct 2000

An annual celebration of contemporary Irish writing with novelists, poets, playwrights and non-fiction writers. Includes readings, discussions, workshops and a children's day.

Ballymena Arts Festival

Ballymena Borough Council, Ardeevin, 80 Galgorm Road, Ballymena, Co. Antrim BT42 1AB
tel (01266) 660300 *fax* (01266) 660400
Takes place Oct

Bath Literature Festival

Bath Festivals Trust, 5-6 Broad Street, Bath BA1 5LJ
tel (01225) 462231 *fax* (01225) 445551
e-mail info@bathlitfest.org.uk
web site http://www.bathlitfest.org.uk
Director Rachel Cottam
Takes place 3-11 March 2001

An annual 9-day festival with leading guest writers. Includes readings, debates, discussions and workshops, and children's activities. Education & Community Programme includes author visits to schools and a children's writing competition. Each year has a chosen theme. Also a major on-line festival, with on-line debates, critical commentary, games and collaborative writing projects.

Belfast Festival at Queen's

Festival House, 25 College Gardens, Belfast BT9 6BS
tel 028-9066 7687 *fax* 028-9066 3733
e-mail festival@gub.ac.uk
web site http://www.gub.ac.uk/festival
Assistant Director Rosie Turner
Takes place 26 Oct-11 Nov 2000

The largest annual arts event in Ireland. Includes literature events. Programme available mid-September.

Birmingham Readers & Writers Festival

Festival Office, Central Library, Chamberlain Square, Birmingham B3 3HQ
tel 0121-303 4244 *fax* 0121-233 9702
e-mail readers.writers@dial.pipex.com
Festival Director Helen Cross
Takes place Oct/Nov

Book Now!

Leisure Service Department, London Borough of Richmond upon Thames, Langholm Lodge, 146 Petersham Road, Richmond, Surrey TW10 6UX
tel 020-8332 0534 *fax* 020-8891 7787
e-mail n.cutting@richmond.gov.uk
Principal Arts Officer Nigel Cutting
Takes place Throughout Nov

An annual literature festival covering a broad range of subjects. Leading British and overseas guest writers and poets hold discussions, talks, debates and workshops and give readings. There are also exhibitions, storytelling sessions and a schools programme.

Brighton Festival

12A Pavilion Buildings, Castle Square, Brighton BN1 1EE
tel (01273) 700747 *fax* (01273) 707505
e-mail info@brighton-festival.org.uk
web site http://www.brighton-festival.org.uk
Takes place May

An annual general arts festival with a large literature programme. Leading guest writers cover a broad range of subjects in a diverse programme of events. Programme published end of February.

Cambridge Conference of Contemporary Poetry

c/o Dr Ian Patterson, Queens' College, Cambridge CB3 9ET
tel (01223) 335523
e-mail ikp1000@cam.ac.uk
Takes place April

An annual weekend of poetry readings, discussion and performance of international poetry in the modernist tradition.

Canterbury Festival

Festival Office, Christ Church Gate, The Precincts, Canterbury, Kent CT1 2EE
tel (01227) 472820 *fax* (01227) 781830
e-mail info@canterburyfestival.co.uk
Takes place 14-28 Oct 2000

An annual general arts festival with a literature programme. Programme published in July.

Chaucer Festival

Chaucer Heritage Trust, Chaucer Centre, 22 St Peter's Street, Canterbury, Kent CT1 2BQ
tel/fax 020-7229 0635 *fax* (01227) 761416
Director Martin Starkie, *Manager and Events Organiser* Zoran Tesic *tel* (01227) 470379
Takes place Spring, Summer and Autumn

An annual festival which includes commemoration services, theatre productions, exhibitions, readings, recitals, Chaucer site visits, medieval fairs, costumed cavalcades, educational programmes for schools. Takes place in London, Canterbury and the County of Kent in the Spring (Easter Chaucer Pilgrimage), Summer (June-July), and Autumn (Oct).

Cheltenham Festival of Literature

Town Hall, Imperial Square, Cheltenham, Glos. GL50 1QA
tel (01242) 521621 *fax* (01242) 256457
tel (01242) 237377 (brochures)
web site http://www.cheltenhamfestivals.co.uk
Festival Director Sarah Smyth
Takes place 13-22 Oct 2000

This annual festival is the largest of its kind in Europe. Events include talks and lectures, poetry readings, novelists in conversation, exhibitions, discussions, workshops and a large bookshop. *Book It!* is a festival for children within the main festival with an extensive programme of events and a multimedia room. Brochures are available in August.

Chester Literature Festival

8 Abbey Square, Chester CH1 2HU
tel (01244) 319985 *tel/fax* (01244) 341200
Festival Administrator Freda Hadwen
Takes place 7-22 Oct 2000

An annual festival with events including international and national writers, events by local literary groups, events for children, a Literary Lunch, workshops and competitions.

Chichester Festivities

Canon Gate House, South Street, Chichester, West Sussex PO19 1PU
tel (01243) 785718 *fax* (01243) 528356
Takes place June/July

City of London Festival

Bishopsgate Hall, 230 Bishopsgate, London EC2M 4HW
tel 020-7377 0540 *fax* 020-7377 1972
e-mail admin@colf.org
web site http://www.colf.org
Takes place 26 June-19 July 2001

An annual multi-arts festival with a programme of literary events. Programme published in April.

City Voice

Word Arena, Library Headquarters, 32 York Road, Leeds LS9 7SJ
tel 0113-214 3341 *fax* 0113-214 3339
e-mail sean.burn@leeds.gov.uk
web site http://www.leeds.gov.uk/wordarena
Manager, Word Arena Sean Burn
Takes place First 2 weeks of June

An annual celebration of the voices of the city – provides a platform for Leeds writers alongside established names. World Arena also supports new writing, reading, and the region's literary activities.

Durham Literature Festival: Word 4 Word

c/o Durham City Arts Ltd, Byland Lodge, Hawthorn Terrace, Durham DH1 4TD
tel/fax 0191-301 8821
Takes place Oct/Nov 2001

Edinburgh International Book Festival

Scottish Book Centre, 137 Dundee Street, Fountainbridge, Edinburgh EH11 1BG
tel 0131-228 5444 *fax* 0131-228 4333
e-mail admin@edbookfest.co.uk
web site http://www.edbookfest.co.uk
Director tba
Takes place 11-27 Aug 2001

Now regarded as Europe's largest book event for the public. In addition to the displays of books, over 350 writers contribute to the programme of events. Programme details available in June. Runs concurrently with Edinburgh International Festival.

Edinburgh International Festival

The Hub, Edinburgh's Festival Centre, Castlehill, Royal Mile, Edinburgh EH1 2NE
tel 0131-473 2001 *fax* 0131-473 2002
e-mail eif@eif.co.uk
web site http://www.eif.co.uk
Takes place 13 Aug-2 Sept 2000, 12 Aug-1 Sept 2001

An annual international arts festival including world class theatre, dance, opera and music. Programme published late March.

Eisteddfod Genedlaethol Frenhinol Cymru

(Royal National Eisteddfod of Wales)
40 Parc Ty Glas, Llanishen, Cardiff CF14 5WU
tel 029-2076 3777 *fax* 029-2076 3737
web site http://eisteddfod.org.uk
Marketing Officer Betsan Williams
Takes place 4-11 Aug 2001

An annual festival promoting the Welsh language and the culture of Wales. Over 200 competitions in all artistic fields are held each year. A contemporary art exhibition is one of the highlights with over 4000 submissions each year. The 2001 festival will be held in Denbigh. Eisteddfod dates back to 1176; founded as annual arts festival 1880.

Exeter Festival

Festival Office, Civic Centre, Exeter EX1 1JJ
tel (01392) 265200 *fax* (01392) 265265
web site http://www.exeter.gov.uk
Festival Manager Lesley Maynard
Takes place July

An annual general arts festival which includes a programme of literary activities. Programme of events available in April.

Federation of Worker Writers and Community Publishers Festival of Writing

PO Box 540, Burslem, Stoke-on-Trent ST6 6DR
tel/fax (01782) 822327
web site http://www.fwwcp.mcmail.com
Takes place April

Female Eye National Festival of Women's Writing

Female Eye, Watersmead, Norwood Green Hill, Halifax, West Yorkshire HX3 8QX
tel/fax (01274) 670181
Takes place June

Festival at the Edge

c/o 3 Highpoint, Little Wenlock, Telford, Shrops. TF6 5BT
tel (01952) 504929
Contact Jackie Douglas
Takes place Second full weekend of July

Guildford Book Festival

c/o Arts Office, University of Surrey, Guildford GU2 5XH
tel (01483) 879167
e-mail s.wallach@surrey.ac.uk
web site http://www.surreyweb.org.uk/
Festival Organiser Glenis Pycraft
Takes place 22 Oct-4 Nov 2000

An annual festival on a chosen theme, with a programme of over 40 events at 12 different venues. Includes readings, literary lunches and dinners, discussions, performance poetry, writing competitions, a writer in residence, the annual University of Surrey Poetry Lecture and children's events.

Harrogate International Festival

1 Victoria Avenue, Harrogate, North Yorkshire HG1 1EQ
tel (01423) 562303 *fax* (01423) 521264
e-mail info@harrogate-festival.org.uk
web site http://www.harrogate-festival.org.uk
Takes place July/Aug

An annual international multi-arts festival. Programme available in May.

Hastings Poetry Festival

c/o The Snoring Cat, 136 Harold Road, Hastings, East Sussex TN35 5NN
tel (01424) 428855 *fax* (01424) 428855
Organiser and Editor of First Time Josephine Austin
Takes place 4-5 Nov 2000

Started in 1968, this national festival is

now held in the Marina Pavilion, St Leonards-on-Sea. Includes the prize-giving of the *Hastings National Poetry Competition.* Poems are invited for consideration for the bi-annual *First Time* poetry magazine. Please include sae.

Huddersfield Poetry Festival

The Word Hoard Ltd, Kirklees Media Centre, 7 Northumberland Street, Huddersfield HD1 1RL
tel (01484) 452070 *fax* (01484) 455049
e-mail hoard@zoo.co.uk
web site http://www.wordhoard.co.uk
Takes place Spring (April) and Autumn (Oct)

Both seasons of this annual festival include multi-art form performances, participatory projects, and workshops.

Ilkley Literature Festival

The Manor House, Ilkley LS29 9DT
tel (01943) 601210 *fax* (01943) 817079
e-mail ilf@pop3.poptel.org.uk
web site http://www.openingline.co.uk/ilf
Festival Director Dominic Gregory
Takes place Autumn

The north of England's oldest and largest literature festival organises a full programme of writing and reading workshops, performances, readings, lectures and debates.

International Playwriting Festival

Warehouse Theatre, Dingwall Road, Croydon CR0 2NF
tel 020-8681 1257 *fax* 020-8688 6699
e-mail warehouse@dircon.co.uk
web site http://www.warehousetheatre.co.uk
Festival Administrator Carolyn Braby
Takes place Nov

An annual competition for full-length unperformed plays (see page 524). The weekend festival includes readings of selected plays and work from the leading Italian festival, the Premio Candoni Arta Terme.

King's Lynn Festival

27 King Street, King's Lynn, Norfolk PE30 1ET
tel (01553) 767557 *fax* (01553) 767688
web site http://www.kl-festival.freeserve.co.uk
Administrator Joanne Rutterford
Takes place 19-28 July 2001

An annual general arts festival with literature events featuring leading guest writers.

King's Lynn Festivals

19 Tuesday Market Place, King's Lynn, Norfolk PE30 1JW
tel (01553) 691661 *fax* (01553) 691779
Chairman Tony Ellis

Fiction Festival
Takes place 9-11 March 2001

An annual festival which brings 8 published novelists to King's Lynn for the weekend for readings and discussions.

Poetry Festival
Takes place 28-30 Sept 2001

An annual festival which brings 8 published poets to King's Lynn for the weekend for readings and discussions. The King's Lynn Poetry Prize (value £1000) is awarded at the festival.

Lancaster LitFest

Sun Street Studios, 23-29 Sun Street, Lancaster LA1 1EW
tel (01524) 62166
e-mail info@lancslitfest.demon.co.uk
web site http://www.folly.co.uk/litfest
Contact Andrew Darby
Takes place End of Oct

Annual festival featuring readings, performances and workshops by contemporary writers for adults, young people and children; includes performance of several new commissioned works each year. The LitFest also acts as a year-round literature development agency, organising readings and workshops, and offering advice and information to writers and readers in Lancashire.

Ledbury Poetry Festival

Town Council Offices, Church Street, Ledbury HR8 1DH
tel (01531) 631456
e-mail prog@poetry-festival.com
web site http://www.poetry-festival.com
Festival Manager Alan Lloyd
Takes place 30 June-8 July 2001

An annual festival featuring top poets from around the world, together with a poet-in-residence programme, competitions (send sae for entry form), workshops and exhibitions. Full programme available in May.

Leicester Literature Festival

Leicester City Council, 12th Floor, New Walk Centre, Welford Place, Leicester LE1 6ZG
Contact Bob Parsons
Takes place Oct

Lincolnshire Literature Festival

Education and Cultural Services Directorate, Lincolnshire County Council, County Offices, Lincoln LN1 1YL
tel (01522) 552831 *fax* (01522) 552811
e-mail david.lambert@lincolnshire.gov.uk

County Arts Development Officer David Lambert
Takes place Throughout the year

A monthly series of literary events throughout Lincoln. Occasional festivals throughout the county.

Lit Up!

Beaford Arts, The Plough Arts Centre, 9-11 Fore Street, Torrington, Devon EX38 8HQ
tel (01805) 622552 *fax* (01805) 622113
Contact Richard Wolfenden-Brown
Takes place Throughout the year

An occasional literature programme including workshops, readings, performances and exhibitions, as part of a larger programme of arts work, including community and educational workshops, projects and residencies.

The London Festival of Literature: The Word

245 St John Street, London EC1V 4NB
tel 020-7837 2555 *fax* 020-7278 0480
e-mail admin@theword.org.uk
Festival Director Peter Florence, *Development Manager* Michelle Birch
Takes place 22 Sept-1 Oct 2000

A carnival celebration of The Word from the first steps of literacy to the greatest poets of the age. It will give the people of London access to the best contemporary writing in every media in a programme of events, performances and conversations featuring the world's largest gathering of writers, musicians and artists.

Manchester Poetry Festival

2nd Floor, Enterprise House, 15 Whitworth Street West, Manchester M1 5WG
tel 0161-907 0031 *fax* 0161-907 0032
e-mail mpf@dial.pipex.com
web site http://www.53degrees.co.uk
Festival Director Richard Michael

An annual festival catering for all tastes, including readings, children's events, slams, workshops and many live events.

Norfolk and Norwich Festival

42-58 St George's Street, Norwich NR3 1AB
tel (01603) 614921 *fax* (01603) 632303
e-mail info@nnfest.demon.co.uk
web site http://www.eab.org.uk/festivals
Festival Director Marcus Davey
Takes place Oct

North East Lincolnshire Annual Literature Festival

Arts Development Unit, North East Lincolnshire Council, Knoll Street, Cleethorpes DN35 8LN
tel (01472) 323007
Festival Programmer Lynne Conlan
Takes place Feb/March

Reflecting the heritage and culture of the area, this annual festival aims to make literature accessible to all ages and abilities through a varied and unusual programme. Write or telephone for details.

Off the Shelf Literature Festival

c/o Sheffield Libraries and Information Services, Central Library, Surrey Street, Sheffield S1 1XZ
tel 0114-273 4716 *fax* 0114-273 5009
Contacts Maria de Souza, Su Walker
Takes place 14-28 Oct 2000

The festival comprises a wide range of events for adults and children, including author visits, writing workshops, storytelling, competitions, theatre performances and exhibitions. Programme available in September.

Poetry International

Literature Department, Royal Festival Hall, London SE1 8XX
tel 020-7921 0906 *fax* 020-7928 2049
e-mail literature&talks@rfh.org.uk
web site http://www.sbc.org.uk
Takes place 6-14 Oct 2000 (biennial)

The biggest poetry festival in the British Isles, bringing together a wide range of poets from around the world. Includes readings, workshops, discussions and events for children. The Literature Section also runs a year-round programme of readings, talks and discussions.

Royal Court Young Writers' Festival

The Royal Court Young Writers' Programme, Sloane Square, London SW1W 8AS
tel 020-7565 5000
Contact Aoife Mannix
Takes place Biennially

A national festival which anyone up to the age of 25 can enter. Promising plays which arise from the workshops are then developed and performed at the Royal Court's Theatre Upstairs (see page 539).

Rye Festival

Lamb House, West Street, Rye, East Sussex TN31 7ES
tel (01797) 224982 *fax* (01797) 224226
Literary Events Manager Mrs Hilary Brooke
Takes place First 2 weeks of Sept (15days); Winter Series held last weekend Jan and first weekend Feb (4 days)

An annual festival of 15 literary events featuring novelists, biographers, and political and scientific writers, with book signings and discussions. Runs concurrently with the Rye festival of music and visual arts.

Salisbury Festival

75 New Street, Salisbury, Wilts. SP1 2PH
tel (01722) 323883 *fax* (01722) 410552
Director Helen Marriage
Takes place May/June

An annual general multi-arts festival with a literature programme of events. Programme published in April.

Stratford-upon-Avon Poetry Festival

Shakespeare Centre, Henley Street, Stratford-upon-Avon CV37 6QW
tel (01789) 204016 *fax* (01789) 296083
e-mail info@shakespeare.org.uk
web site http://www.shakespeare.org.uk
Director Roger Pringle
Takes place Usually Sunday evenings throughout July and Aug

An annual festival which aims to present poetry of many different ages and to provide opportunities for readings by contemporary poets. Sponsored by the Shakespeare Birthplace Trust. Founded 1954.

The Sunday Times Hay Festival

Festival Office, Hay-on-Wye HR3 5BX
tel (01497) 821217 *fax* (01497) 821066
e-mail admin@litfest.co.uk
web site http://www.LitFest.co.uk
Takes place May/June

This annual festival aims to celebrate the best in writing and performance from around the world, to commission new work, and to promote and encourage young writers of excellence and potential. Over 200 events in 10 days with leading guest writers. Programme published April.

Dylan Thomas – The Celebration 2000

The Dylan Thomas Centre, Somerset Place, Swansea SA1 1RR
tel (01792) 463980 *fax* (01792) 463993
Events Manager David Woolley
Takes place 29 Oct-9 Nov 2000, 29 Oct-9 Nov 2001

An annual festival celebrating the life and work of Swansea's most famous son. Performances, lectures, debates, poetry, music and film.

Warwick & Leamington Festival

Warwick Arts Society, Northgate, Warwick CV34 4JL
tel (01926) 410747 *fax* (01926) 407606
Festival Director Richard Phillips
Takes place First half of July

A music festival which includes some literature and poetry events: readings, performances and workshops.

Ways With Words Literature Festival

Droridge Farm, Dartington, Totnes, Devon TQ9 6JQ
tel (01803) 867311 *fax* (01803) 863688
e-mail wwwords@globalnet.co.uk
web site http://www.wayswithwords.co.uk
Contact Kay Dunbar
Takes place 10 days in middle of July each year

200 speakers give readings, talks, interviews, discussions, seminars, workshops with leading guest writers. Literary weekends in York, Southwold and Bury St Edmunds; writing courses also organised.

Wells Festival of Literature

Tower House, St Andrew Street, Wells, Somerset BA5 2UN
tel (01749) 673385
web site http://www.somersite.co.uk/wellsfest.htm
Takes place Late Oct

This annual festival features leading guest writers and poets; includes writing workshops and competitions. The main venue is the historic Bishop's Palace, Wells.

The Internet

Writers and the Internet

*Although the Internet is no longer in its infancy, many people still want to know what all the hype adds up to. Do writers really need it? **Jane Dorner** explains why authors should join the on-line community.*

You can write a novel, short story, poem or textbook without being wired up to the superhighways transmitting digital material all over the world. You can also write without resort to a telephone. However, people who do not have telephones these days are considered to be out of touch, and that is increasingly true of the Internet.

Contact with co-authors, publishers and readers has never been easier. Dialling up information on the Internet is quicker and cheaper than going to a library. If you already have the computer equipment for word processing, you can save time and costs by taking the further step of connecting to the Internet, which provides four basic services: e-mail, news, the World Wide Web and Chat.

So where do you start?

Equipment

You need a present-generation computer: a PC or Apple Mac not more than five years old. If it did not come fitted with a modem, you will have to buy one. An external modem is easier to fit, though an internal card modem might be cheaper. It is a false economy to get anything less than the fastest in the shop, but a dedicated ISDN or ADSL line is probably overkill.

You also need an Internet service provider, or access provider (known as an ISP), which is the company that connects you to the networks. There are many free providers to choose from, all grounded in product advertising. They are all similar; the choice is how you want to define your personality. Do you like the ring of yourname@tesco.net, or @classicfm or @virgin or @arsenal? These companies receive revenue either by getting a percentage of the cost of the call, by charging 50p to £1 a minute for support, or by irritating you with advertising banners on the entry page. As they are not primarily service providers, their level of service is variable. They are not offering quality service; they are offering a 'free' service – for which you are effectively paying. Paying a rental fee (around £10 a month) will guarantee reliability and added-value services. But if you do not intend to rely on e-mail for delivery of copy, then a free ISP may be all you need.

Telephone companies are now agreeing fixed monthly charges for Internet telephone connections. Cable networks are offering Surf Unlimited at £10 a month and BT's SurfTime has a range of options tailored to different levels of usage. For those who prefer a pay-as-you-go scheme, Internet calls are charged at local rates – e-mails to California, or Russia or Chile only cost 1p a minute during the evening or at weekends and 2p a minute during the day. Some ISPs are even offering free connections on 0800 numbers. For further information about getting on-line see *Research and the Internet* on page 553.

E-mail

E-mail offers the most obvious benefits. It is infinitely cheaper than either post or telephone and the fastest way of delivering copy.

The mailing program is a notepad unit for creating, sending and filing messages – it usually holds finished messages in a queue waiting to be transmitted when you next dial in to your server. Incoming post is dumped into the mailbox for viewing when you come off-line – this is so that you do not waste telephone time reading or writing e-mail. Remember that when you press the button marked 'Send', your 'mail' may go into the outbox until you next dial in when it will be transmitted. It's like putting it in a postbox, except that you decide on collection times yourself.

You can have several different mailboxes on one computer and each one is password-protected so no one else can read your mail if you do not want them to.

Sending messages and attachments

The joy of e-mail is that it is instant, unobtrusive – and cheap. You can contact one, two or 50 people with a single phone connection. Quite often the reply is waiting for you when you next log on – this is most useful for connections abroad. The etiquette (known as netiquette) is that you reply briefly and quickly. You do not waste time in letter-writing niceties, but plunge straight in to the matter in hand. Many people return the original message with the reply to maintain speed and continuity. There is also a level of flippancy in e-mail that has become acceptable discourse, enabling helpful informality. Many people consider this a culturally interesting development and useful in our communication-intensive age.

An e-mail is more like a memo than a letter, but the medium can also transmit longer documents. Anything that goes into several pages, or relies to some extent on layout (even if it is just italicisation), is best sent as an 'attachment'. Most mailer programs display an icon of a paper clip or clothespeg which, when selected, will attach a file to the message. Anything electronic can be attached in this way, e.g. a word-processed file, a desktop published file, digital pictures – even music. It takes much longer to send (and receive) attachments than a plain text e-mail, but it still works out cheaper than paper, envelopes and postage stamps. And it is immediate. For example, a 120,000-word typed book would be about 1 Mb in size (compared to this article which is 35K) and it could take 5p of telephone time to send it. Generally speaking, it will arrive at the destination mailbox within a quarter of an hour, but it might take longer, depending on the service provider's traffic and capacity.

(When selecting a service provider, make sure the off-line mailer is up to date and can cope with attachment files. If not, consider using Outlook, Eudora or Netscape.)

E-mail is essential for some writing genres and a significant time saver for others. For example, journalists increasingly rely on e-mail to file copy – especially if they are communicating from abroad. Newspaper and magazine editors also prefer to receive copy by e-mail because they can then bring it directly into their own word processor to work on rather than have it retyped or wait for the disk to be delivered. Whole books and book proposals should only be submitted by e-mail to publishers and literary agents by arrangement as they usually prefer to receive a printout. In fact, many of them get irritated when they receive unsolicited manuscripts by e-mail.

Technology is unforgiving: an e-mail address must be keyed in correctly. The '@' sign in the address joins the unique identifier (which may be your name) with the service provider's address and the dots in the address separate the different parts of it. It can be useful to know what the suffixes in e-mail addresses stand for as they give clues about who your correspondent is: 'co.uk' is a UK company; 'ac.uk' signifies 'academic'; 'com' means commercial. E-mail addresses are usually written in lower case.

Disadvantages

Disadvantages of having e-mail are slight. It is rare to catch a virus from an e-mail because viruses usually occur in program files. But if you have an e-mail program that automatically opens an attachment file then be very wary and don't open anything from an unknown source unless you have an up-to-date virus checker.

Another worry is junk mail. This is

unlikely to be acute unless you advertise. Some people send more trivial communications than are strictly necessary, but you can deal with them briefly and the corollary is that friends and relatives abroad are delightfully accessible.

News

There are thousands of newsgroups on Usenet, a network linked to the Internet. Every special interest, hobby or professional grouping is represented here – food and drink buffs, violin makers, model aeroplane hobbyists, meteorologists, fast car freaks, depressives, diabetics, pagans, cinema lovers – everything. This is a cause for concern for some people because the laws of freedom of speech mean that these groups are uncensored. The individual, however, can get filtering software (e.g. Net Nanny) that can exclude undesirables, so if there are children in the house access can be restricted. The research opportunities offered by newsgroups are outlined on page 555.

Newsgroups offer some new opportunities for writers in the form of e-zines (electronic magazines) and webzines. I haven't yet come across any of these that pay contributors, but times may change.

The World Wide Web (WWW)

The World Wide Web, WWW, or the 'web' for short, is the nerve centre of the Internet. It is a giant network of interconnected information which is available through computers. Access is via a program known as a browser (e.g. Netscape, Internet Explorer and Opera). It works by embedding links into documents using a code called HTML (HyperText Mark-up Language) which is being replaced by XML (Extensible Mark-up Language). The user doesn't see any of this coding but moves through 'pages' of information by clicking the mouse on a hotspot link, or hyperlink – usually an underlined phrase appearing on-screen in blue. (A 'page' can be of variable length; generally half to three printed A4 pages.)

Hyperlinks are coded instructions to a computer to fetch a document from another address. When the mouse is clicked on a hyperlink, the browser sends a message across the Internet requesting information from another program (known as a server) running on a computer somewhere else in the world. The server sends back a message containing the information.

Web addresses for writers

An address on the web is called a Uniform Resource Locator (URL) and starts with the prefix 'http://'. For further information on this, and on the opportunities for using the web for research, see page 554.

On the Internet there are web sites that explore experimental writing forms such as interactive novels or electro-poetry. Other sites offer software tools for writers, and others give (or sell) writing advice. Be prepared to use your own judgement when looking at these.

You must be sure in your own mind what you are looking for and why you have come to a particular site. Otherwise, the chances are that you will sink into unfocused channel hopping. Once there, you can tell a lot by the look and feel of the web site. Poor spelling and grammar abounds: it's usually the sign of a poorly thought-out site (though even the best have typos here and there).

The URL itself gives clues – it's like reading any other address. Is it Belgravia or Brixton? It's unadventurous to be prejudiced and your presumptions can be wrong, but it is worth looking for:

- a statement of the aims and objectives of the site;
- author and publisher details and e-mail link to back up authenticity;
- details of origin of any data or information;
- mention of any quality checks or referencing of information;
- creation dates – age may or may not matter;
- last updated dates – shows how active a site is;
- clearly marked archival information;
- good design and awareness of readability – though many excellent academic

sites do not fit these criteria;
• a good search box – vital on an information-rich site.

In judging the content of a web site, ask yourself:

• Does the resource appear to be honest and genuine?
• Is the resource available in another format, e.g. a book or CD-Rom?
• Do any of the materials infringe copyright?
• Is the information well researched?
• Is any bias made clear and of an acceptable level?
• Is it the result of a personal hobby horse?
• Is the information durable in nature?
• Is there adequate maintenance of the information content?

Internet addresses change just as any other addresses do. Quite often, a site that began life as a subdirectory on an enthusiast's personal web space registers its own domain name and moves to another server. Many now have redirection URLs to link old addresses to a new one, but it isn't always possible (e.g. if the original enthusiast no longer has the same space). So if you use any of the web site addresses in the *Writers' & Artists' Yearbook*, do not assume they have disappeared if the address given turns out to be wrong. Type the name into a search engine and try again.

For useful web site addresses see *Web sites for writers* on page 561.

A web site of your own

The web is also a personal publishing or self-advertising medium. Most service providers give 5-15 Mb of web space with an e-mail account so that users can create web sites of their own. This enables you to have a sophisticated brochure or pamphlet about yourself, available all the time, never out-of-print and as up-to-date as you make it. Links can be made to point to details of all your publications or your work-in-progress. For further information, see *Setting up a web site* on page 557.

Chat

Internet Relay Chat (IRC) is a way of talking – via your keyboard – in real time with people all over the world. Sound and video chat is just a step away. It is an eerie experience. The computer, logged on to the Internet, transmits your typed words directly on to someone else's screen. This is synchronous communication that is not quite like spoken or written language yet uses conventions from both. It is a written form that is transmitted, received and responded to within a time frame that was formerly thought relevant to only spoken communication.

This is the world of 'muds' and 'moos' – silly words that describe a conferencing system that can be a lifeline for writers working in remote areas or for genre writers sharing a specialised interest.

Writing groups arrange to 'meet' on-line at a specified time and a good place to learn about this is at the TrAce Online Writing Community (http://trace.ntu.ac.uk/). It has a Sunday evening chat hour which welcomes people from anywhere in the world who can 'talk', on the screen, about their experiences or aspects of writing. Simply log in and follow the community joining instructions. Relationships are often begun in such chat rooms that are creatively continued by e-mail afterwards – it can simply be an extension of the time-honoured tradition of writers meeting in a literary pub.

The Internet and the future

So is the Internet all hype? I don't think so. It is a remarkable medium of exchange that is both inspirational and useful. The impact on creative work will be significant in the 21st century.

Jane Dorner is the author of 15 books and represents authors' interests on the Boards of ALCS and CLA. She is author of *The Internet: A Writer's Guide* (A & C Black), which has listings of almost 1000 web sites for writers (see page 561).

Research and the Internet

The Internet is an almost infinite library that is constantly being updated. Users can often find the facts they seek in a few minutes, without leaving their desk, and at relatively low cost. ***David Couchman*** *introduces the Internet as a research tool for writers.*

Recently, I was trying to locate a vaguely remembered quotation from a 19th-century American poet. My wife wanted to find out about Chronic Fatigue Syndrome; and my daughter needed to discover large prime numbers for her maths homework. A few years ago we would have gone to the library. It might not have had the information we were seeking, and whatever it did have would probably have been out of date. Today we use the Internet.

The Internet is a worldwide network of computers. It began in the USA as a military communication system designed to keep going in the event of a nuclear war. It expanded significantly as universities and commercial organisations joined, and today it continues to grow explosively.

Getting on-line

There are more and more opportunities to explore the Internet through library, 'Cyber-Café' and university or college sites. These allow you to dip your toe in the water, but if you decide to go further you will need your own Internet access. This requires:

- A computer – if you have a PC which can use Microsoft Windows, or an Apple 'Mac', you are already well on the way.
- A modem – this device makes it possible for one computer to communicate with another over an ordinary telephone line.
- An 'Internet access provider' – this enables a computer to be connected to the Internet, just as a telephone company connects telephone users to the worldwide phone network.
- Special computer programs – these will be supplied by the access provider.

Once the modem has been linked up, the programs installed, and a connection established to an access provider, the computer is 'on-line'.

Choosing an access provider

Today it is not necessary to pay for access to the Internet. There has been a huge increase over the past two years in the number of free services. These range from British Telecom's BTClick to Tesco's TescoNet to Netscape Online, with new providers throwing their hats into the ring every week. The largest and best established free access provider is Freeserve, which attracted half a million subscribers in its first two months of operation, and its CD-Rom can be obtained from many large electrical and computer stores. Other free access providers' CD-Roms can be found at supermarket checkouts, on magazine covers, as well as from numerous other sources.

Although you do not pay to use a free Internet service, you will be charged for your telephone calls for the time you are on-line – usually to a local-rate number. In addition, if you need to call the helpline of a free service to solve a problem, this is usually an expensive premium rate call – so you may find it helpful to have a tame computer guru to hand, especially while you are starting your explorations of the web. The CD-Rom usually gives instructions on how to install it, an almost completely automatic process which is generally problem free.

The longer established free-paying service providers, e.g. Compuserve, give more than just access to the Internet, providing information and discussion groups (see below) within their service, and may be easier to use than 'raw' Internet access. However, they charge a monthly or annual fee for this service.

The service provider situation continues to change rapidly, so it is worth investigating what is available. Quality of service is important: How quickly can you get a connection? How fast does the data you need reach you? (Remember that the whole time you spend on-line is being charged to your telephone bill. It may only be a local call but charges mount up.) Some access providers offer a much better service than others do. It can be helpful to consult friends and colleagues who are already using the Internet, to find out what they think of their access providers. Internet magazines carry advertisements for access providers and up-to-date comparative reviews – essential reading in a sphere that is changing so rapidly. If the service of your access provider proves unsatisfactory, it is easy to change to another.

Early in 2000 it was rumoured in the press that BT would start offering unmetered local calls 'within a year'. If that happens, it will effectively make Internet access completely free at the point of use.

Research using the World Wide Web

The most important part of the Internet for research is the 'World Wide Web', often abbreviated to WWW, or just 'the web'. The web is a vast collection of linked pages of information about every imaginable subject. In order to read these pages a special computer program called a 'web browser' is required, the two most widely used of which are Netscape Navigator and Microsoft Internet Explorer. A browser program will be provided (free) on the installation CD-Rom from the access provider, and installed automatically on to your computer.

Each page of information on the web has its own unique address – usually beginning http://www. To access a page, have the web browser program running and type in the address. The browser will fetch the appropriate page from the computer where it is stored and display it on the screen. That computer could be anywhere in the world – you may not even know where it is – but it does not matter. Distance is not an issue as your computer is connected by phone to your access provider, and the cost is usually that of a local phone call.

A web page displayed on the screen incorporates 'hyperlinks' to other pages. A hyperlink may be a key word in the text (usually underlined), a small graphic, or part of a larger graphic. It is a 'link' because it points the computer towards the address of another web page. Hyperlinks are a powerful cross-referencing system: by clicking the mouse on a hyperlink the web browser automatically fetches the new page to which the link points. (The on-screen help files in 'Windows' are similar to a hyperlink.) Some useful web site addresses are listed in the box opposite.

Finding information

How do you know where to find the key facts you need among all the millions of pages of information? If the Internet is like a vast library, beautifully cross-referenced, it is unfortunately also the worst indexed library in the world. To help with the task there are a number of 'search engines', which are themselves sites on the Internet.

One of the most widely used search engines is the Altavista web site. By typing

Some major search engines

Altavista
http://www.altavista.digital.co.uk

Lycos
http://www.uk.lycos.de/

Mamma.com
http://www.mamma.com

Yahoo UK
http://www.yahoo.co.uk/

in a key word or phrase Altavista gives you a list of all the sites it can find which contain that word or phrase. The list will contain hyperlinks to these sites, so you can simply click the mouse on the links to access them. For example, when we were trying to find out more about Chronic Fatigue Syndrome, we typed this name into the Altavista search engine. One of the first sites it found was the CFS home page of the American Centers for Disease Control and Prevention – a goldmine of information (http://www.cdc.gov/ncidod/diseases/cfs/).

Some of the other major search engines are listed in the box on page 554. Each search engine uses a different approach. For example, while Altavista searches for key words, 'Yahoo' is based on a directory or 'tree' structure, organised into major search areas including Arts and Humanities, Business and Economy, Education, Health, News and Media, and Society and Culture.

Newsgroups

In addition to the World Wide Web, there are other sources of information on the Internet. Most important among these are the discussion groups or newsgroups which go under the collective name of 'Usenet'. Discussion groups are just that – groups where anyone can send a message and everyone else in the group receives it. There are more than 20,000 such groups covering every interest under the sun – including some specifically for writers, for example:

alt.publish.books
alt.writing
misc.writing
rec.arts.prose

The Deja News web site is dedicated to helping find newsgroup postings on particular subjects (http://www.deja.com/). The quality of newsgroups is variable; however a question to an appropriate group can often elicit information that cannot be found elsewhere. Your access provider can give you a list of the discussion groups that it carries.

Join only a few carefully chosen groups that cover your key interests. If you join too

Useful web addresses

In addition to the addresses given below, many of the listings in this *Yearbook* include a web site address.

Amazon Bookshop UK
http://www.amazon.co.uk/

Associated Press
http://wire.ap.org/

BAISE
http://portico.bl.uk/
The British Library's automated information service.

The CIA
http://www.odci.gov/

CNN
http://www.cnn.com/

Government departments (UK)
http://www.open.gov.uk/

Internet Movie Database
http://www.imdb.com/

The Library of Congress
http://www.loc.gov/

NASA
http://www.nasa.gov/

New WWW sites
http://www.whatsnew.com/

New York Times
http://www.nytimes.com/

Reuters
http://www.reuters.com/

The Royal Family
http://www.royal.gov.uk/

W.H. Smith Online
http://www.bookshop.co.uk/

The White House
http://www.whitehouse.gov/

Writers and their Copyright Holders (WATCH)
http://www.lib.utexas.edu/hre/watch.html

The Writers' Site
http://www.writers.org.uk/
http://www.writers.org.uk/society/
http://www.writers.org.uk/guild/
Contains both the Society of Authors and the Writers Guild of Great Britain.

many you will be inundated by the number of messages and will soon reach the point where you do not read any of them.

Sending a message to a group is called 'posting'. When you first join a group it is a good idea to 'lurk' for a while – to read the messages posted by existing members before you start to post your own. This helps you to get a feel for the 'style' of the group and thus avoid blunders.

As in any sphere, beginners often ask the same questions over and over again. The Internet has evolved its own particular solution to this problem – the FAQ, an information 'sheet' containing the answers to Frequently Asked Questions. The FAQ may be posted to the group on a regular basis. FAQs on particular subjects are often made available on the World Wide Web too and can be a goldmine of useful information, so are well worth reading.

Subscription services

Discussion groups are free. So is the World Wide Web – mostly. However, more and more commercial services are being launched that provide quality information not available elsewhere, but at a cost. For example, the Electronic Share Information site (http://www.esi.co.uk/) provides several grades of share price information. The lowest grades are free, but if you need the most current prices you have to pay to access them. These services are usually too expensive for an individual subscriber, but they may be worth investigating if you need a specific kind of information. Open web sites of commercial organisations often give information about related subscription services (e.g. the Reuters' site).

Where next?

An article as brief as this can only begin to introduce the power of the Internet as a research tool. So where do you go to find out more? The Internet is changing so fast that books current today could be completely out of date in a few months' time. However, a few suggestions for further reading are given below. The Internet itself is the most useful tool to find out more. For example, Charlie Harris has written an essential guide for writers wanting to use the Internet for research (http://www.purefiction.com/pages/res1. htm).

No turning back

Today I can usually research the information I need without leaving my desk and my findings are more comprehensive and more up to date than ever before. I cannot imagine going back to a pre-Internet world any more than I can imagine throwing away my word processor and taking up a quill.

David Couchman is a project manager at Focus Radio, where he previously worked as a scriptwriter and producer. He is a former lecturer in computing and has set up a public web site as a research tool for businessmen and academics working in part of the former Soviet Union. He uses the Internet regularly for his own research.

Further reading

Kennedy, Angus J., *The Rough Guide to the Internet 2000*, Rough Guides/Penguin 1999. A 'must have' guide: it includes excellent coverage of how to get started and different aspects of using the Internet, as well as a directory of over a thousand web sites.

Wentk, Richard, *The Which? Guide to the Internet*, Which? Books, 1997. An excellent introduction, and reasonably non-technical.

Setting up a web site

*Computer users who have e-mail almost certainly have web space available to them. **Jane Dorner** explains the points for writers to consider when setting up a personal web site and how to best make it work for them.*

This article assumes that readers are familiar with web sites and have read *Writers and the Internet* on page 549. To set up your own web site the main investment you need to make is in time, perhaps more than you initially think. The process may have its frustrating moments, but it is ultimately creative.

A writer's personal web site

A web site can be an astonishing self-publicity medium for writers. It can be especially useful if you self-publish, but equally worthwhile for showing the world a portfolio of your accomplishments. Many writers are polymaths and the web shows up such diversity to advantage.

A personal web site can be set up to demonstrate your writing style(s) and areas of interest with examples of work so that commissioning editors can see if they are choosing the right writer for the job. You can include an outline of your skills and achievements, and list your publications – or you could even offer a personal syndication service for stories and articles (if first or resale rights are yours).

You need to let people know that your web site exists – there is no point having a wonderful site if no one visits it – for which old-fashioned marketing techniques are necessary. Posting your site on the web and registering hopefully with a few (or even a hundred) search engines is no substitute for careful targeting, although it is helpful once initial contact has been made. Refer potential clients to your web site, and make sure it attracts them sufficiently to explore it.

Choosing the designer

In order to create the web site yourself, you will need to have:

- a capacity for logical thinking;
- secure language expertise;
- some technical understanding;
- good visual sense;
- patience; and
- familiarity with applicable law.

If you don't have (or can't acquire) these skills then it is worth thinking about asking someone else to build the site for you. Expect to pay for at least one day of a professional designer's time (between £150 and £350) to create a modest suite of individually tailored pages with some attention to what you want and need. Bear in mind that the less you pay, the more likely it is that your material is simply being poured into a standard template.

Planning a web site

Whether you get involved with the technological side or not, you will still have to plan and write the copy yourself. Here you have the advantage over most other people. Writing for the web is a new art form that uses writerly skills: it is genuinely creative; requires writers, not programmers; and needs editors with an understanding of traditional editorial values.

Writing the text for a web site is like any other writing project. The more effort that goes into the planning stage, the better the result. You need to identify who you are targeting and be clear about the purpose of the web site. For instance, is it your calling card; a PR brochure; a sales outlet;

an information resource; a literary club or part of a network; or a medium of self-expression? The web site needs to be planned and created accordingly. For example, if you just want a simple calling card, then a single screen – called a splash page – might suffice. It would have your name, perhaps a photograph of you, a few lines about your specialist writing skills and interests, possibly some titles you have had published, and your contact details. You can then be found by anyone who visits your web site; your personal front cover is on the world bookshelf.

The simplest way of achieving a splash page is to visit the Authors Direct web site (see page 560) and find on the busy front page their offer to 'link to any author's site and even provide authors with a free web page if they don't yet have a site'. All you have to do is give your name, address and list of books by e-mail and they do the rest.

Writing for screen reading

If you write for radio, you will have an advantage over other writers. Writing for the web is a bit like writing for broadcasting: the style has to compensate for the loss of the visual impact of words. It's a common mistake to cut and paste from documents created for print because the text will not read as well on a web site.

The average adult spends eight hours a week reading as opposed to 27 hours watching television. And that's reading from paper – reading from a screen has so far proved less efficient than paper.

When writing the introductory text for a web site, aim for the reluctant reader with a less than three-minute attention span and use easy words and short sentences. As readers delve deeper into a site, their acceptance of more discursive reading matter increases. Once they are committed to the subject material, you can write in your normal style and assume they will print out the text and read from paper. Take writing for radio or television as the paradigm and then make it even simpler. Here are a few pointers:

- **Use the tadpole or pyramid structure**. Hit your reader with the main points at the top of the page (people are reluctant to scroll). Use interior pages to unfold details.
- **Be concise**. The overall length of a radio or television piece is about a third of a print article; a web page should be even shorter. Cut every word that doesn't contribute. A good web page length is under 500 words – it is better to divide anything longer than that into sub-topics.
- **Write short paragraphs**. Paragraph breaks refresh the eye: between two and five sentences is enough.
- **Write simple sentences**. Ideas are easier to digest in a simple subject-verb-object progression. Make subclauses into separate sentences. Use one idea per sentence and make them under the 17-word print average.
- **Use the present or present perfect tense**. The web is here and now. Keep passives away.
- **Be consistent**. Use the same font, type size, alignment and background colour throughout your site. Or use different colour bands to denote different 'areas' (novels, poetry, teaching and so on). Remember that capital letters on-screen look like SHOUTING.
- **Consider navigation**. If a visitor makes Choice A here, what are the ramifications for Choice B there? Web writing is not static, but writing dynamically is something that most writers have not learned. It is, perhaps, something we will all have to discover as we progress into the web publishing age.
- **Links**. Don't link every prompt phrase that leads somewhere else. If you want readers to stay with you to absorb your point, put the link outside the main text area. Don't link just because you can.
- **Influence design**. Use white or pale cream backgrounds and black type (studies show that sharp contrasts aid readability). Use (or ask your web designer to use) invisible tables so that the line length is limited to about 10 words in standard browsers – this is an optimum reading line length. If you do not set a limit, the chances are that at high screen resolutions readers might get a line length of 25 words on the default reading

typeface. This leads to what is known as 'regression pauses' while the reader struggles to make sense of the text.

• **Use graphics sparingly**. Bullet points or graphic elements help pick out key words, but animations can be irritating. Studies show that the message is lost when television images fail to reinforce spoken words. The same is true of the web.

• **Define the main areas of your site**. Consider synonyms for your top level labels (the four to six main areas of your site). How often have you got lost in a web site simply because the way in which your mind works isn't the same as the mindset of the person who created it? Try to second guess what visitors to your site will want to see when they come to each page then find a single word that most unambiguously describes it. (This is what writers should be good at. An input from the writing community can only have a beneficial effect on the 'grammar' of web sites generally. After all, writers have always understood that the point of grammar is not to be regimental, or proprietorial, but to diminish the chances of being misunderstood.)

Going on-line

Once you have the planning and writing of your web site organised, you need a little basic technical understanding to get it on-line. Your service provider will have a starter kit of instructions – although whether they make sense is another matter. You may well have to turn to other sources for instruction.

The Internet is chock-a-block with instructional material. The best I've found is 1st Site Free (see page 560), which outlines and expands on seven easy steps – plan, design, code, upload, test, promote and maintain. It is nice and clear, offers good advice and gives links to all the various free useful tools on offer that will help someone with no previous experience to produce a first web site. Bill Green of Texas assures me he will continue to maintain his site.

An alternative is to use software that 'talks you through' setting up a small site with what are called 'wizards'. TescoNet and Webb Net are two of the many free providers which offer a wizard-operated template that will produce some linked pages on the basis of answers to standard questions. Few writers will find these adequate for their needs, but you might want to try one of them, perhaps with a pen name, just to see what happens.

Other wizards come in software programs such as FrontPage (part of Microsoft Office Premium) and its free look-a-like Site Aid. Both resemble word processors and keep the coding hidden from view. Hard core web designers will sneer at these programs, because programmers like to control the way the code works themselves. What they do not realise is that writers want to concentrate on the words, not the coding, and as long as it functions, the refinements of the underlying structure are of less importance.

Once the pages are ready, the next step is to transmit them to the service provider's machines. The mechanics of this are frequently opaque even when you are offered a handy button that says 'Publish'. The chances are that your service provider will not have the extensions that make the 'Publish' button work and you will have to acquire a (free) File Transfer Protocol program – ftp for short. If you are technophobe, this may seem frightening at first. However, it is really very simple and once you have successfully transferred (or uploaded) the pages from your computer to the web space on the remote server, you will wonder what the problem was. For this transfer process you will need to know the host name, your user ID and your password, information available from your provider.

HTML

If you want to learn HTML (HyperText Markup Language) – the code that tags elements such as text, links and graphics so that browser software will know how to display a document – then you need only a plain text program, like Notepad,

Useful URLs

Amazon Bookshop Associates Scheme
http://www.amazon.co.uk/associates
For linking to sales of your own (or recommended) books.

Alert Box
http://www.useit.com/alertbox
Web usability and readability analysis. Opinionated but pertinent.

Authors Direct
http://www.authors-direct.com
An easy way to create a splash page.

The CGI Resource Index
http://www.cgi-resources.com
Scripts that you can buy (some are free), e.g. automatic forms and page counters.

1st Site Free
http://www.1stsitefree.com/
Create a web site in 7 easy steps. A good starting point; links to useful tools.

FTP Explorer
http://www.ftpx.com
File transfer software for PCs.

The HTML Writers Guild
http://www.hwg.org
Free membership and access to resources.

Namezero
http://www.namezero.com/
Free domain names (.com, .net, .org).

Netfinder
http://www.ozemail.com.au/~pli/netfinder
File transfer software for Macs.

Site Aid
http://www.siteaid.com
Freeware HTML editor. Looks similar to Microsoft's FrontPage.

TescoNet
http://www.tesco.net
Free web space with wizard to help you set it up.

UK2.Net
http://uk2.net
Inexpensive domain registration and web forwarding.

Validator
http://validator.w3.org/
Free on-line validation of HTML code.

Webb Net
http://www.webb.net/webb
Free web space with wizard.

Yale Style Manual
http://info.med.yale.edu/caim/manual
Excellent guide to aspects of web writing.

and an HTML primer (there are plenty online as well as in printed form). Find some web site pages which you like and look at their source code to see how they have been constructed (click the subsidiary button of the mouse, usually the right button, and select View Source). If the originators have used JavaScript or Cascading Style Sheets, this may well be more code than you want to know about so look at simple pages first.

Going a step further

You may wish to have a web address or URL that is short or memorable so that it is easier for people to find your web site. You can choose this domain name yourself, and is now relatively cheap and can even be free (see box).

It is probably best to leave e-commerce (having a secure site that can handle credit card sales) till later. In the meantime, however, a simple way to boost your income is to become an Amazon Associate. If your book titles are linked to Amazon, you'll make 15% on a direct sale made from your site.

Jane Dorner is the author of 15 books and represents authors' interests on the Boards of ALCS and CLA. She is author of *The Internet: A Writer's Guide* (A & C Black), which has listings of almost 1000 web sites for writers. A selection of these follows.

Web sites for writers

The Internet: A Writer's Guide *by Jane Dorner (http://www.internetwriter.co.uk password 'qixotica') is published by A & C Black and has the full listing of nearly 1000 resources for writers from which the sites below have been selected.*

New to the Internet

Acronym Expander
http://www.ucc.ie/info/net/acronyms/index.html
Web abbreviations and acronyms.

BBC Web Wise
http://www.bbc.co.uk/education/webwise/
How to get started on the Internet.

FAQ
http://www.faqs.org
Frequently Asked Questions on just about anything to do with the Internet.

New to the Web
http://home.netscape.com/netcenter/newnet
A basic tutorial with a good glossary.

Searching

All-One-Search
http://www.allonesearch.com
500 search engines, databases, indexes, and directories in a single site; plus price comparisons on books. Impressively comprehensive and worth looking at if only to find the engine that specialises in something esoteric.

Askjeeves
http://www.askjeeves.co.uk
Selected sites picked by real editors and searches across AltaVista, Excite, Infoseek, Webcrawler and Yahoo!; a good starting point.

Subject-based gateways
http://www.lub.lu.se/desire/sbigs.html
Clearing houses to quality-assessed Internet resources.

Fact finding on-line

Bartlett's Familiar Quotations
http://www.bartleby.com

Bibliomania
http://www.bibliomania.com
Excellent full text with a good word or phrase retrieval; includes the wonderful *Brewer's Dictionary of Phrase & Fable* (which no author can do without).

British Library
http://portico.bl.uk
Free search for material held in the major Reference and Document Supply collections of the British Library.

Glasgow University Library
http://www.gla.ac.uk/Library/E-Journals
Catalogues, national biographies, indexes to periodical contents, and a list of all on-line services provided by the European national libraries at Glasgow University Library.

CIA World Factbook
http://www.cia.gov/cia/publications/factbook
Statistical data about countries and other useful data.

Encyclopaedia Britannica
http://www.britannica.com
Full text and searching, with a huge resource of free information, grammar and reference links.

Press Association News Centre (UK)
http://www.pa.press.net
Latest stories from the UK's top news and information web sites; useful free daily round-up of news, sport and information by e-mail.

Roget's Thesaurus
http://humanities.uchicago.edu/forms_unrest/ROGET.html
1911 version (out of copyright, and inevitably out of currency too).

WISDOM: Knowledge & Literature Search
http://thinkers.net
Links to writing and literature sites under the headings Creativity, Literature, Authors, Thoughts, Publishing, Words, Languages.

Interactivity

Eastgate
http://www.eastgate.com
New hypertext technologies; publication of serious hypertext, fiction and non-fiction: serious, interactive writing.

Fiction Writer's Connection
http://www.fictionwriters.com
Provides help with novel writing and information on finding agents/editors and getting published; useful mailing list.

Hypertext Kitchen
http://www.HypertextKitchen.com

Inklings
http://www.inkspot.com/inklings
Newsletter for writers on the Web.

Interactive Fiction Now Magazine
http://www.if-now.demon.co.uk

InterNovel Home Page
http://www.internovel.com/~novel
Experimental site; exercises in composition, creative writing and screenplay adaptation.

Response Source
http://sourcewire.com/frames/pr
UK journalists can request business information in a single step from over 300 organisations.

SmarterWork
http://www.smarterwork.com
On-line workplace, connecting writers and editors to clients for clearly defined, short-term projects.

TrAce Online Writing Community
http://trace.ntu.ac.uk/
Arts Council-funded experimental fiction and poetry site; has chat areas.

Miscellany

Eponym
http://www.eponym.org/
Aimed at new parents and handy if you are looking for a suitable name for a character; names from just about everywhere in the world at different times in history.

Famous Birthdays
http://www.famousbirthdays.com
Month-by-month and day-by-day listing of birth dates, historical and in the media.

Famous Firsts
http://www.corsinet.com/trivia/1-triv.html
People-who-did-something-first arranged in ascending date order.

Dying Words
http://www.corsinet.com/braincandy/dying.html
For the historical novelist.

Literary Calendar: An Almanac of Literary Information
http://litcal.yasuda-u.ac.jp/LitCalendar.shtml
Significant literary events: births, deaths, publications.

Perpetual Virtual Calendars
http://www.mnsinc.com/utopia/Calendar/Virtual_Calendars.html
A historical or science fiction novelist's dream: verify any date or day of the week in the 20th and 21st centuries.

Research-it
http://www.itools.com/research-it
Little battery of dictionaries and acronym converters.

Rhyming dictionary
http://www.link.cs.cmu.edu/dougb/rhyme-doc.html

Time Zone Converter
http://www.timezoneconverter.com
What time it is or will be anywhere in the world.

Who is or Was
http://www.biography.com
Good for checking people's dates; incorporates the *Cambridge Dictionary of American Biography.*

World Wide Words
http://www.quinion.com/words/
Verbal cornucopia for anyone interested in words; circulates a newsletter.

Texts on-line

Classics
http://the-tech.mit.edu/Classics/titles.d.html
Links to the full text of 400 Greek and Roman classics in translation.

The English Server
http://english-server.hss.cmu.edu
Large collection of interesting resources.

Electronic Text Center
http://etext.lib.virginia.edu/english.html
Collection of on-line English language texts; links to other texts on-line by subject or by author.

Etext Archives
http://www.etext.org
Archives of religious, political, legal and fanzine text.

Literature Online
http://lion.chadwyck.co.uk
Poetry, literature and reference databases aimed

at libraries. High charge, but you can try it free; also some free access to poetry and to a writer-in-residence.

Oxford Text Archive

http://www.hcu.ox.ac.uk/ota/
Distributes more than 2500 resources in over 25 different languages for study purposes only.

Project Gutenberg

http://www.gutenberg.net
The official sites (many mirrors all over the world); vast library of e-texts, mostly public domain; all in plain text format.

Shakespeare Resources

http://www.shakespeare.com
Links to many other sites.

ePublishing

Sites to submit work to or buy from. In all cases, authors should study the standard contracts in detail and make sure all rights have reverted to them. Be wary, too, of vanity publishers.

Association of Electronic Publishers

http://members.tripod.com/~BestBooksCom/AEP/aepmembers.html
Links to publishers' author guidelines.

Back-in-print

http://www.backinprint.com
One of a growing number of on-demand printing services for out-of-print titles. Member of US Guild of Writers only, but UK societies are looking at reciprocal arrangements; authors get 55%.

Book-on-Disk

http://www.book-on-disc.com/
Creates e-books in downloadable or disk format; pays royalties and appears to have been vetted by the American Guild of Writers; authors retain copyright. Not a vanity press.

eBooks.com

http://www.ebooks.com
Internet Digital Bookstore; authors should check rights deals with their publishers.

Fiction Works

http://www.fictionworks.com
About e-books and audio book opportunities.

iUniverse

http://www.iuniverse.com
A service for redeploying out-of-print books; possibly vetted by the Authors' Guild of America, but check the author contract carefully.

Overdrive Systems

http://www.overdrive.com/news
How to publish with Microsoft Reader and other e-publishing solutions which authors may need to know about.

Questia

http://www.questia.com
Company in Dallas which is looking for authors' out-of-print non-fiction. Be sure you own the rights to scan before negotiations begin.

Scribes' World

http://www.scribesworld.com
For readers and writers; authors can ask for their books to be reviewed.

Small Press Center

http://www.smallpress.org
Non-profit institution for independent publishers, based in New York; useful articles and information for small publishers.

Storyteller UK

http://www.storyteller.org.uk
A showcase where established writers may experiment and the unpublished and frustrated may take their first steps.

Storywise

http://www.storywise.co.uk
Non-profit making Library of Books from UK writers of fiction who have not managed, or don't wish to have, their work published in the traditional format; no money changes hands.

e-books and e-readers

eBookNet

http://www.ebooknet.com
An e-book community packed with information about e-publishers; find out about the latest hand-held devices from here.

eBookCity

http://www.ebookcity.com
Overcrowded portal for people looking for entry points to e-Net resources.

Microsoft Reader

http://www.microsoft.com/reader/authors
The page about the Reader (e-books designed to be read on pocket PCs) aimed at authors; keep your eye on this one.

Open eBook initiative

http://www.openebook.org
Format specifications, sponsored by the National Institute of Standards and Technology.

Xlibris reading machine

http://www.fxpal.xerox.com/PersonalMobile/xlibris
Experimental site to see how technology affects reading.

Writing tools

Screenwriting

Dramatica
http://www.dramatica.com/
Screenplay software; not free – compare it with ScreenForge below.

Final Draft
http://www.finaldraft.com/
Apparently the bees knees of scripting software – expensive (about £150), high functionality and cross-platform compatibility.

Hollywood Screenwriter
http://www.writerspage.com/hsbase.htm
Apparently very like FinalDraft but a third of the price.

ScreenForge
http://www.execpc.com/~jesser/
Almostfree Hollywood scriptwriting format bolt-on for Word.

Scrnplay.dot
http://www.erols.com/lehket/Dale/scrnplay.html
Free template for Word 6/7 for screenplay writers; both this and ScreenForge are worth looking at.

Writers' Guild of America
http://www.wga.org./tools/ScriptSoftware/
Guide to writing software; sensible advice.

Storyware

Alice
http://www.cs.virginia.edu/~alice
Software program for storyboard modelling; quite technical but interesting.

Brutus Story Generator
http://www.rpi.edu/dept/ppcs/BRUTUS/brutus.html#Sample

Storycraft Writer's Software
http://www.storycraft-soft.com
Fiction-writing program that claims to turn ideas into complete novels, screenplays, plays or short stories.

Creativity Unleashed
http://www.cul.co.uk/
Software to stimulate creative thinking, originally intended for business.

Creativity Web
http://www.ozemail.com.au/~caveman/Creative/
Resources for creativity and innovation; emphasis on lateral thinking.

StoryBoard Quick
http://www.powerproduction.com/
Storyboard software for films, animation, games and other uses.

Writers' Software
http://www.starcomp.net/
Includes some dedicated items such as plot assistants.

Web Store for Writers and Creative Pros
http://www.masterfreelancer.com/
Plots Unlimited, Writer's Software Companion and other software aids.

Writer's Toolbox
http://www.geocities.com/Athens/6346
Software resources for writers with slightly annoying advertising.

Word-processing aids

Bibliographic software
http://www.isinet.com/products/refman.html
Advanced tools such as Reference Manager, ProCite and EndNote (free trials).

Mind Mapping
http://www.mindman.co.uk/
Software to help individuals organise, generate and learn ideas and information; free trial available.

Tricks and Trinkets
http://www.tricksandtrinkets.com/pk/
To make word processing easier, e.g. autotext for often-used phrases.

WordTips
http://www.VitalNews.com/wordtips/
How to get the best out of Microsoft Word; useful tips, many a real boon for writers.

Setting up a web site – see page 560

***The Internet: A Writer's Guide* by Jane Dorner** (A & C Black) (http://www.internetwriter.co.uk *password* qixotica) has the full listing of nearly 1000 resources for writers. The following genre areas have substantial listings: academic writing; business writing; children's writing; crime writing and mystery; fantasy; fiction; health writers; historical research; horror; interactive fiction and experimental forms; journalism; literature festivals; literature resources; mystery; poetry; prizes; residencies; romance; science fiction, fantasy and horror; specialist subjects; screen, TV and playwriting; translation; travel writing; STM writers; technical writing; women's and gender issues; writing courses and many other themes.

Resources for writers

Books, research and reference

Almost every writing project will involve the use of books or research at some stage. Some references are quickly found; other projects require numerous books or information files on a specific topic, visits to specialist libraries and to other relevant places or people. ***Margaret Payne*** *ALA gives an introduction to printed sources.*

Although research can be an interest or pleasure in itself, it can also be time-consuming, cutting into writing or earning time. Even checking a single fact can take hours or days if you ask the wrong question or check the wrong source first. No article or book can hope to solve all problems – sometimes there are no answers, or the lack of information is itself the answer – but a few guidelines as to routines and sources may save much time and money.

Many reference books are now on CD-Rom and the Internet is increasingly being used for research (see *Research and the Internet*, page 553), but this article is an introduction to printed sources. For a more detailed approach, Ann Hoffmann's *Research for Writers* (A & C Black, 6th edn 1999, £11.99) includes guides to original and unpublished material, and covers methods, sources, specific organisations and specialist libraries.

Suggestions for a core collection of reference books to own are given under 'A writer's reference bookshelf' on page 568. The final choice of title often depends on personal preference and interests, space, the frequency with which it needs to be consulted, its cost and the proximity of your nearest public reference library. Anyone living in or near a large city has an advantage over the country dweller, with a choice of major reference libraries; a variety of specialist sources such as headquarters of various societies, companies and organisations; academic and other specialist libraries and the government. Often a question can be answered much nearer home, but you may find the further back in time you go, or the more detailed your research, the further afield you need to travel.

Checking a fact

What do you really want to know?

Clarifying your question in advance can save much work for you or your researcher. If you want to check someone's date of birth and know the person is alive or very recently dead and in *Who's Who*, then ask for that book, or phrase your telephone request so that the librarian goes straight to that source. Do not start with general questions such as 'Where are the biographies?' In a branch library you may be shown sections of individual lives; on the telephone you are adding unnecessarily to your telephone bill, as well as wasting time. If the person is dead, did he or she die recently enough to have a newspaper obituary – it often mentions the date of birth – or long enough ago to be in a volume of *Who Was Who* or the *Dictionary of National Biography*? Never assume that information that you know is necessarily common knowledge; it needs to be specified.

Go straight to the index

Most reference books are arranged in alphabetical order but, if not, they should have an index. Some indexes may seem inadequate, but have you used the right key word? A good index should refer you from the one not used. For example, some will use carpentry and ignore woodwork as an entry. Others will ignore both and go straight to the object to be made or repaired. If there is no index, turn first to the contents page, as in some books the index is at the front rather than the back.

Is it important to be up to date?

Most books have the date of publication on the back of the title page. Is the answer given in the book one which may be surpassed or superseded? Despite some instant publishing, when dealing with statistics most books have a built-in obsolescence. There is a cut-off date when the text goes to the printer and the updating must wait for the next edition. Some current events are too recent to be found in books at all, although well documented at the time in newspapers and magazines (see box).

If in doubt, re-check your answer

If the answer is of importance, try not to depend on one source. Mistakes can occur in print or in transcribing. Sometimes it is necessary to check another source for verification or to obtain another point of view. In all cases you should …

Note your source

Even if you think you will remember, always note where you find your information, preferably next to the answer, or in a card file or book where it can be easily found. Note the title, author, publisher and date of publication as well as the page number. Nothing is more annoying than having to undertake the same search twice.

Researching a subject

Reference has already been made to Ann Hoffmann's book for detail, but Kipling's six honest serving men can still be the basis for any subject: What? Why? When? How? Where? Who? cover aspects of most enquiries. The starting point depends on the writer's personal knowledge of the subject. Where it is unfamiliar always start from the general and go on to the particular. An article in an encyclopedia can fill in the background and often recommend bibliographies or other references. If an article in a multi-volume encyclope-

Sources of information

Reference libraries. Use the largest one in your vicinity for encylopedias, specialised reference books, annuals and for back numbers of newspapers and periodicals. Ask for *Walford's Guide to Reference Material*: three volumes list the standard reference works of subjects, most of which should be available for consultation.

Lending libraries. Find the class number of the books you want, and see what is available.

Special libraries. *The Aslib Directory of Information Sources in the United Kingdom* should be available in your reference library. It gives details of special libraries of industries, organisations and societies.

Catalogues, bibliographies and subject guides. Most library catalogues are now on-line, with author, title or key word access. There is a series of subject catalogues to the British Library up to 1975 and the *British National Bibliography* updates this (see 'Compiling a bibliography' on page 567).

Newspapers and bibliographies. There is a monthly index to *The Times*, cumulated annually, which often provides the date of an event. The index also includes the *The Times Supplements*. For periodical articles, begin with the *British Humanities Index*, and, if necessary, check also the specialist indexes and abstracting journals such as *Current Technology Index*. Your public library can often locate runs of periodicals and magazines, and the interloan service can obtain specific periodical articles if you have the details. *Profile*, an on-line index to quality newspapers (most of whom now have their own on-line access), is the most up to date available, but retrospective only to 1985. *Clover* is a printed index to the same broadsheet press.

The Internet. See page 553.

dia is too detailed or too complex, try *The World Book* which can be found in the children's library. Because *The World Book* has to appeal to a wider readership, the text and illustrations are clearer. Avoid a detailed book on the subject until you need it; it may tell you more than you want to know.

Compiling a bibliography

Checking what books are already available may reveal both the range of titles already in print and the potential market for your work. If yours is to be the tenth book on the subject published in the last two years, saturation point may be near. On the other hand, if you know the books and believe you can do better, or have evolved a different approach, you can mention this in a covering letter to a potential publisher. A quick way to evaluate what is available is by checking the shelves of a public library or bookshop, but it should be remembered that in a library, many of the best books will be on loan. This practice also makes one aware of publishers' interests.

A more comprehensive and systematic list of recent books can be compiled by consulting the *British National Bibliography*, a cumulating list based on the copyright books in the British Library, with advance notice (up to three months) of new books through the Cataloguing in Publication scheme. The arrangement is by the Dewey Decimal Classification used in all public libraries. Other subject lists are less satisfactory to consult. The British Library has a series of subject indexes up to 1975, and many British books are included in the American *Cumulative Book Index* (1928 on). *Whitaker's Books in Print* is predominantly an author-title list, but does index some books under the key word of a subtitle; as its name implies, out-of-print books are excluded.

A bibliography on any subject may be obtained by using one of the computer data banks based on the British Library, the Library of Congress or commercial firms and the Internet.

Obtaining books

Books in print

In 1999, 110,155 different books were published in the United Kingdom alone, joining the many thousands of other titles still in print from previous years. The number of books available means that the chances of finding a copy of what you want on your bookseller's shelf, when you want it, may be slim. But if it is in print it can be ordered for you, although delivery times vary with each publisher. Most large bookshops and libraries now have the online, microfiche or CD-Rom editions of *Whitaker's Books in Print* giving details of author, publisher, price, number of pages and ISBN. Supplying the ISBN number is often useful for speeding the order.

Out of print books

Out of print books present more difficulty. Generally the older the book, the more difficult it may be to obtain. Such books are no longer available from the publishers, who retain only a file copy, all other stocks having been sold. Therefore unless you are lucky enough to find an unsold copy on a bookseller's shelves, it must be sought in the second-hand market or through a library loan. There are many specialist second-hand and antiquarian booksellers, and a number of directories listing them and their interests. The most well known are *Sheppard's Book Dealers in the British Isles*, now published by R. Joseph. Copies of these should be in your local reference library. Many advertise in *Book and Magazine Collector*, a monthly magazine, which has extensive 'wants' and 'for sale' columns.

Public libraries

Public libraries should be able to obtain books for you, whether or not they are in print, either from their own stock, from other libraries in the system or through the interloan scheme. This operates through the British Lending Library, but all requests must go through your library as you cannot apply direct. Your local library tickets may sometimes be used in other libraries, but different issuing systems have discouraged this in recent years. Most library systems now have a databased catalogue of all branch stock.

A writer's reference bookshelf

The increasing use of personal computers and the Internet is extending the sources of information from print to multimedia. Many reference books are available on CD-Rom and much knowledge can be accessed through web sites. But as yet few libraries in the UK have the funds, expertise or space to make such sources available, and in the meantime there is a growing division between individuals who prefer or only have access to print and those who are computer literate and can afford and have the time to explore what knowledge is available electronically, as well as what is not.

However good and accessible a public library may be, there are some books required for constant or instant consultation, which should be within easy reach of your work area. The choice of title may vary, but the following list is offered as suggestions for a core collection.

Dictionaries

With the use of word processor packages, a dictionary is no longer quite so essential for spelling checks, although still needed to clarify definitions and meanings. A book is often easier to consult, and portable. The complete *Oxford English Dictionary* is not, although now available on-line, neither the full nor the compact edition with its magnifying glass, nor the two volume *Shorter Oxford Dictionary* is easy to handle for quick reference, so a one volume dictionary is more practical. The number of new words and meanings coming into vogue suggests a replacement every five years or so, or supplementing your choice by a good paperback edition. If you use an old copy, you will be surprised by the improved format and readability of the new editions, now with continuous revision.

For a visual, encyclopedic approach, the *DK Illustrated Oxford Dictionary* has 4500 illustrations and 187,000 entries (Dorling Kindersley, 1998, £30.00). The most popular one volume dictionaries are the *Concise Oxford Dictionary* (£16.99 – 80,000 definitions), *Chambers' English Dictionary* (£35.00 – 150,000 entries, appeals to Scrabble and crossword addicts), *The Collins English Dictionary* (HarperCollins, £29.99 – 140,000 entries). A recommended paperback dictionary is the *Oxford Paperback Dictionary and Thesaurus* (£10.99 – 50,000 entries). If you write for the American market, it is advisable also to have an American dictionary to check variant spellings and meanings. The equivalent of the Oxford family of dictionaries is Webster's, the most popular one volume edition being Webster's *New World Dictionary* (Random House, £17.95).

Roget's Thesaurus

When the exact word or meaning eludes you, a thesaurus may help clear a mental block. There are many versions of Roget available, both in hardback and paperback, including a revision by E.M. Kirkpatrick (Penguin, 1998, £14.99). *The Bloomsbury Thesaurus* (Bloomsbury, 1993, £15.99) is a new compilation which includes 1000 knowledge categories and 1500 quotations.

Grammar and English usage

A wide choice is available but *New Fowler's Modern English Usage* remains a standard work (3rd edn 1998, revised R.W. Burchfield, Oxford UP, £17.99). Many prefer Sir Ernest Gowers' *Complete Plain Words* (4th edn 1994, rev. Sidney Greenbaum and Jane Whitcut, Penguin, £7.99). More recent works are *The Oxford Guide to English Usage* (Oxford UP, 2nd edn 1994, £4.99), and Michael Legat's *The Nuts and Bolts of Writing* (Hale, 1989, £9.95 and £5.99).

Encyclopedias and annuals

Multi-volume encyclopedias are both expensive and space consuming. They are best left for consultation at the nearest reference library, where the most up-to-date versions should be available, unless your need justifies ownership or you prefer the CD-Rom version. Of the single volumes, *Pears Cyclopaedia* contains a surprising amount of general information and a new edition is issued annually (Penguin Books, 1999-2000, £16.99). For those concerned with current affairs, the complete edition of *Whitaker's Almanack* has valuable statistics and information on government and countries, as well as many miscellaneous facts not found elsewhere. For annual replacement if constantly used.

Atlases, gazetteers and road maps

These also need replacing with updated editions from time to time. An old edition can be misleading with recent changes of place names and metrication. The *The Times Atlas of the World* is the definitive work, but it is expensive and bulky for quick reference. The *The Times Concise Atlas of the World* (HarperCollins, 8th edn 1998, £60.00) has the most comprehensive gazetteer-index. It is a little more manageable but still requires special shelving.

With the building of the M25 and other motorways, many existing road atlases of Britain may be out of date and need replacing. There are many paperback editions at 3 miles to 1 inch (1:190,080) for less than £5.00, but most detailed is *A-Z Great Britain Road Atlas* (Geographers A-Z, 1999, £7.95; 1:250,000) with 31,000 place names and 56 town maps. For London and environs *Greater London Street Atlas* (Nicholson, rev. edn 1999, £26.99 and £14.99) is a detailed 3.17 miles to 1 inch, 1:20,000 street map for the whole M25 area.

Literary companions and dictionaries

There are many to choose from, and frequency of consultation will determine whether all or some of the following are desirable. *Brewer's Dictionary of Phrase and Fable* (Cassell, 15th edn 1995, £25.00 and £17.99) and its companion volume *Brewer's Twentieth Century Dictionary of Phrase and Fable* (Cassell, 1996, £25.00 and £16.99) avoid many distractions by settling queries, as does *The Oxford Companion to English Literature* (new edn edited by Margaret Drabble, Oxford UP, 2000, £25.00). This new edition complements rather than replaces Sir Paul Harvey's earlier editions. Either can be used for checking an author's work, but the definitive and exhaustive lists are to be found in the *New Cambridge Bibliography of English Literature*. The four volumes and the index volume can be found in major reference libraries.

Books of quotations

Once divorced from their text and unattributed, quotations are not easy to trace. This should be a warning to any writer or researcher to note author, title and page number to any item copied. Tracing quotations often needs resort to more than one collection, but the most popular anthologies are *The Oxford Dictionary of Quotations* (Oxford UP, 4th edn 1996, £25.00) and the *Bloomsbury Dictionary of Quotations* (Bloomsbury, 3rd edn 1997, paperback, £16.99) and *The New Penguin Dictionary of Quotations* (Penguin, 1993, £7.99). Most large reference libraries stock many titles.

Biographical dictionaries

Pears Cyclopaedia contains a brief but useful section, but for a fuller working tool the standard works are *Chambers' Biographical Dictionary* (Chambers, 6th edn 1997, £40.00 – 15,000 entries) or the American-biased Webster's *New Biographical Dictionary* (Merriam-Webster Inc., 1996, £17.95 – 150,000 entries). Frequency of consultation will determine whether you need a personal copy of *Who's Who* or the *Concise Dictionary of National Biography*, which are available in most libraries.

Dates, anniversaries and names

Dent's Everyman's Dictionary of Dates (Weidenfeld, 8th edn 1995, £20.00) and *The Independent Book of Anniversaries* (Headline, 1993, o.p.) are useful. For historical facts *The Companion to British History* by Charles Arnold-Baker (Longcross Press, 1997, £48.00) is a comprehensive dictionary of events and people. Leslie Dunkling's *Guinness Book of Names* (Guinness, 7th edn 1995, £11.99) is an encyclopedic source on its subject from first names to places and pubs, with a comprehensive index.

Working directories for writers

A current copy of *Writers' & Artists' Yearbook* is essential, as recent moves and mergers have made so many publishers' details out of date. It is useful for very much more information besides that found in the first section. Browse through, or use the index, in spare moments to familiarise yourself with its contents for future reference.

Cassell's Directory of Publishing complements all the above, but gives more information about publishing personnel not found elsewhere.

Margaret Payne ALA has worked in public and academic libraries in the UK and Canada and also as a librarian in a book trade library, in which subject she retains a special interest.

PCs for writers

A computer won't make anyone a better writer, but it can give practical help in getting their words into print. ***Richard Williams*** *explains how to use a computer to best advantage, both for word processing and desktop publishing.*

There is a natural tendency to assume that a word processor is just a hi-tech typewriter, but to get the best from it you need to rethink the way you work. Let the words flow without worrying about spelling or punctuation – these can be easily put right when you revise. If your word processing program automatically corrects your spelling while you write, turn off this feature and check the whole document afterwards.

Once your first draft is complete, put it aside for a while so that you come back to revise it with a fresh eye. For this task word processing comes into its own – you can move or delete chunks of text and add whole paragraphs or even sections, all without the slog of any retyping.

But just because it is so easy to change things, you can fall into the bad habit of tinkering endlessly with a draft. Instead, try to work steadily through it, making corrections as you go, then, as with the first draft, put it aside for a while.

Getting the most from your program

Using your computer as a word processor gives you access to many other useful features besides spell checking. Auto correct can put right common mistakes like transposition or incorrect capitalisation, while an automatic word count is invaluable.

Search and replace makes revision easier. For instance, if you decide that a character's name doesn't work, the computer can change it to a new one everywhere, just with a click of the mouse button. Similarly, by substituting single for double spaces, it can quickly get rid of unwanted spaces that crept in during revision.

An outliner facility can help to organise a mass of facts into a coherent article or book. Once you have set up a structure, text can be added to it anywhere and in any order. Radical reorganisation is just a matter of dragging headings around the skeleton.

The computer can also give you fast access to tools such as a dictionary and thesaurus. If stuck for a word, or unsure of its meaning, you can get the computer to search a CD-Rom version for you, then copy the chosen word directly into the word processor text.

For research or fact checking, you can turn to one of the CD-Rom versions of encyclopedias or to a 'bookshelf' CD-Rom which combines dictionaries with other reference works. For instance, the Writers Shelf CD-Rom (Oxford University Press, £19.99) includes the *Pocket Oxford Dictionary*, plus the *Oxford Mini Dictionary of Quotations*, the *Oxford Dictionary for Writers and Editors*, the *Oxford Guide to English Usage* and a compact encyclopedia. The Internet provides another huge resource for writers; see *Writers and the Internet* on page 549.

Saving and backing up your work

Modern word processing programs save work automatically every few minutes, but for peace of mind make sure you save, as a minimum, whenever you leave the machine, or make major changes. Don't rely solely on the computer's hard disk to save your work – you may regret it if you do. Disks can crash or corrupt, and computers (particularly portables) can be stolen.

To guard against this, back up your work separately on a removable disk. For plain text, a floppy disk will probably be sufficient, but if you need room for illustrations one of the new super-floppies, such as the Zip or Superdisk, is best.

Store your disks away from the computer if possible and back up each draft separately (not only to increase security, but to allow the luxury of second thoughts about a change). For even greater security, print out a copy of each draft before switching off the machine.

Preparing the final version

When submitting a typescript, produce the final double-spaced version by altering the line spacing for the whole document just before printing, instead of setting double spacing from the start. This not only makes drafts easier to read, but saves paper too.

Try to break yourself of ingrained habits like using two dashes for a hyphen, putting two spaces after a full stop or blank lines between paragraphs, and using underlining or capitals for emphasis (use bold for a few words and italics for longer passages). All these are unnecessary for the typescript and will have to be changed when a file is used for typesetting.

Now that most books and magazines are computer typeset, many publishers prefer to use an author's word processor file to save the cost of inputting text. Remember, when you prepare such a file, that the final layout will be done in a desktop publishing program and resist the temptation to pre-empt this. However attractive it may look, fancy formatting will have to be stripped out by the typesetter. Instead, use a single typeface and confine formatting to necessities like headings, bulleted lists, and tables.

Unfamiliar file formats are another potential problem for the typesetter. All modern systems should allow you to create files in formats other than their own, so ask which would be the best – this is likely to be plain text (otherwise known as ASCII) or, if you want to preserve basic formatting, Rich Text Format.

Any graphics files should be kept separate, so that these can be modified if necessary and placed in the correct position in the final layout. As well as the computer files, provide a printout of the typescript that can be marked up for typesetting. See also *Preparing and submitting a typescript* on page 248.

At this point most writers will prefer to let the professionals take over, but if you want to retain complete control over your work's appearance you can use desktop publishing software to produce your own printed version. The rest of this article is intended to guide you along this path (though if you intend to do without a publisher completely and publicise and market your book yourself, see *Doing it on your own* on page 262).

Layout and design

The key to successful desktop publishing (DTP) is thorough planning. Before you start writing you should know what type of book you want to produce, but now you need to think about the detailed layout.

Fiction is relatively easy to deal with, as people normally read a book from beginning to end, and such a book needs only a simple page layout to guide the reader. Non-fiction readers require more help. They won't necessarily read a book straight through, and even if they do, they may later need to find a particular piece of information in a hurry.

There are various ways to help the reader navigate a book. An informative contents page and the use of section headings to indicate the topics covered not only allows a browser to decide whether the book is worth buying, but helps a reader to find relevant information. If there is a significant number of illustrations or tables, a separate listing makes these easier to find.

Within a chapter, section headings, perhaps repeated in a header at the top of a page, help the reader to find the relevant part. Any serious book needs an index to pinpoint particular facts or references, and more detailed or esoteric information may be best relegated to an appendix.

Page format

Apart from these structural considerations, the format of pages and treatment of illustrations need to be considered. Pages should have sufficient variety to be attractive, but the various elements should form an integrated whole. Ruling lines and white space can play a useful part here, providing these are used with discretion.

If possible, use the master page feature of your DTP program to create the basic page format. You can set up a grid on this as a guide to the size and placing of illustrations – keeping these to a few standard sizes and positions helps to unify the book's appearance.

Don't try too hard to be original – book design has conventions which have evolved over centuries, and readers are accustomed to these. If in doubt, look at books of the same type, and copy from those which you think work best (though you can also learn from other peoples' mistakes).

The printing and binding method you choose may determine the page format – new machines, more akin to laser printers, can be more economical for short runs but the choice of page size may be limited. Discuss your ideas with potential printers to ensure that the number and size of pages you choose can be produced as efficiently (and therefore cheaply) as possible on their machines. Often a small adjustment can make a big difference.

Typography

As well as the basic format of the book, you also need to decide on the typography. Remember that the primary aim of the book is to communicate and resist the temptation to use too many, or too colourful typefaces.

Many successful book designs, like this one, use a single serif typeface, gaining the necessary variety with different sizes and weights for text and headings. A serif face is generally preferred for text as being more readable, but it can be combined with a sans-serif face for headings. Apart from special cases, two typefaces should be the limit.

The right line length and spacing is as important to readability as the right typeface. Seventy characters is about the maximum line length for readable text. Lines much shorter than 40 characters will still be readable, but excessive hyphenation may be a problem, particularly with justified text. For text spacing the accepted rule is that space between letters should be less than space between words, which in turn should be less than space between lines. Within this guideline, the precise amount of spacing is a matter of personal taste, but you should aim for an even texture, with no obvious variation over the page.

Default spacing settings for DTP programs tend to allow too wide a range of spacing, so I prefer to turn off letter spacing completely, reduce the maximum word spacing substantially, and the average slightly. The important thing is to try different combinations until you find one that satisfies you. Again, if unsure, look at books of the same type for guidance.

Headings and subheadings

These should not be overdone – three different levels should be sufficient. Make sure that each level is distinguished from the others by type size and positioning (for example, by throwing major headings into the margin with a ruling line below).

Spacing for headings is also critical. There should be more space above a heading than below, so that it clearly relates to the following text, and the total space occupied by headings (including the type itself) should be a multiple of the space occupied by a line of body text. This ensures that all the lines on a page automatically align with those on the facing page. Space above and below other elements, such as tables or graphics, should also be set to preserve this alignment.

Finalising the layout

At some stage you need to decide on the treatment of pages that come before or after the main text – contents, lists of illustrations, foreword, index and appendices. Although not essential, it is preferable to do this before finalising the design of the main text, so that you have a complete idea of the book's final appearance.

Once you have decided on the format and typography, lay out some sample pages. For fiction a double page spread for the main text, plus another showing the treatment of the chapter start and finish, should be sufficient. Sample pages for more complex books should show all the possible variations of headings and treatment of illustrations, plus contents pages, foreword, index and appendices. It is worth spending some time to get these samples right – if in doubt put them to one side for a few days and remember that if something doesn't look right, then it probably isn't.

If you can, also get your printer to check the samples for potential problems – a good printer will be happy to do this, knowing that snags found at this stage will prevent trouble later. When you feel happy with the result, produce a whole sample chapter as a final check, before proceeding to the final layout.

Final stages

Checking proofs is a tedious task but a crucial one – mistakes overlooked at this stage are expensive to correct later. Manual checking is essential, since a spell check program can find wrongly spelt words, but not wrong, missing or unnecessary words.

The compilation of an index is best left until the book is in its final form. DTP programs can help in the purely mechanical task of referencing pages, but someone still has to decide which words and cross references to include, and a professional indexer is best qualified for this task.

If you have not already done so, discuss with your printer the precise form in which your work is to be handed over (including illustrations and fonts). PostScript files will probably be preferred, though files in the DTP program's native format may also be acceptable. Apart from short-run direct printing, where a single large file is preferred, separate files for each chapter are best, as this makes recovery from problems easier. Increasingly, files are used to produce film or even printing plates directly, thus saving the cost of intermediate stages, but making it even more vital that mistakes are found and corrected beforehand. Make sure you send the printer a proof copy of the output with the files, and include your telephone number in case problems do occur.

Richard Williams is the author of several books on desktop publishing and other computer applications and works as a consultant.

Creative writing courses

The information included in this section has been provided by the institutions running the courses. Every effort has been made to include only those courses which offer a high standard. However, anyone who wishes to participate in a course should first satisfy themselves as to its content and quality. For day and evening courses consult your local Adult Education Centre. See also Editorial, literary and production services on page 578.

Alston Hall Residential College for Adult Education

Alston Lane, Longridge, Preston PR3 3BP
tel (01722) 784661 *fax* (01722) 785835
e-mail info@alstonhall.u-net.com
web site http://www.alstonhall.u-net.com

Creative Writing (monthly). Day courses for writers to use the focus and discipline of a group to enable them to tap into their own material. Writing exercises are used to produce prose, poetry and performance pieces. Run by a practising writer; open to both new and experienced writers.

Annual Writers' Conference

Chinook, Southdown Road, Winchester, Hants SO21 2BY
tel (01962) 712307
e-mail Writerconf@aol.com
web site http://www.gmp.co.uk/writers/conference
Conference Director Barbara Large MBE
Venue King Alfred's College, Winchester

Ten-day residential conference (29 June-6 July) for aspiring and published writers. Includes workshops, seminars, lectures, one-to-one appointments, and mini courses run by published authors, poets, playwrights and producers, literary agents and publishers. Also 15 writing competitions with critiques on each submitted work and a 2-day bookfair.

The Arvon Foundation

Lumb Bank, Heptonstall, Hebden Bridge, West Yorkshire HX7 6DF
tel/fax (01422) 843714
e-mail l-bank@arvonfoundation.org
web site http://www.arvonfoundation.org
Contact Ann Anderton

The Arvon Foundation, Moniack Mhor,Teavarran, Kiltarlity, Beauly, Inverness-shire IV4 7HT
tel (01463) 741675 *fax* (01463) 741733
e-mail m-mhor@arvonfoundation.org
Contact Chris Aldridge

The Arvon Foundation, Totleigh Barton, Sheepwash, Beaworthy, Devon EX21 5NS
tel (01409) 231338 *fax* (01409) 231144
e-mail t-barton@arvonfoundation.org
Contact Julia Wheadon

A broad range of courses for both the beginner and the experienced writer offering the opportunity to work in groups and individually with 2 professional writers. The Arvon Foundation is a registered charity which receives funding from the Arts Council and other public bodies and from the private sector.

Belstead House Education & Conference Centre

Belstead, Ipswich, Suffolk IP8 3NA
tel (01473) 686321 *fax* (01473) 686664
e-mail belsteadhouse@talk21.com

Writing and marketing science fiction and fantasy (September). Story ideas, setting and character. Looks at tradition, and how to market to the media.

Memoir writing (November). Techniques for researching, recording and presenting material in interesting and original ways.

Myths, dreams and impossibilities (March). Techniques for accessing the subconscious and using it as a resource in creative writing.

Writing for radio (August). Pinpointing the unique demands of radio. How to grab your audience and techniques for creating a punchy script.

Burton Manor College

Burton, Neston, Cheshire CH64 5SJ
tel 0151-336 5172 *fax* 0151-336 6586
e-mail enquiry@burtonmanor.com
Principal Keith Chandler

Midweek, weekend and day courses, residential and non-residential. Contact the college for courses running in 2001.

Irish Writing (September). How varied styles and techniques are used to deal with recurrent themes, issues and concerns are considered through close reading of a broad range of examples.

Creative writing (October). An opportunity to make poetry or prose out of what you see around you.

Writing for radio (November). Explores the unique demands of radio drama and the step-by-step techniques that create a punchy script.

Unleash your writing power (January). How to write faster and more easily by tapping into your latent talents for creative expression.

Travel writing (February).

Comedy writing (March).

Easter writing (April)

Write a successful novel (August). Covers all the essential elements a successful novel needs.

Centerprise Black Literature and New Writing Development Projects

136 Kingsland High Street, London E8 2NS
tel 020-7254 9632 ext. 211, 214 *fax* 020-7923 1951

A resource service for writers and readers in London. Courses for new and experienced writers, including a 1-year writing course and an advanced critical fiction workshop. Specialist groups for Asian, Black, male and female writers. See also page 470.

Dingle Writing Courses Ltd

Ballintlea, Ventry, Co. Kerry, Republic of Ireland
tel/fax 66 91 59052
e-mail dinglewc@iol.ie
web site http://www.iol.ie/~dinglewc
Directors Abigail Joffe and Nicholas McLachlan

Various weekend and 5-day courses for both beginners and experienced writers.

The Earnley Concourse

Earnley Trust Ltd, Earnley, Chichester, West Sussex PO20 7JL
tel (01243) 670392 *fax* (01243) 670832
e-mail info@earnley.co.uk
web site http://www.earnley.co.uk

A private educational trust, registered as a charity.

You can write for publication (January). Aims to bring out the talent in students of writing articles, short stories and poems suitable for publication.

Writing a novel (May). Explains how ideas for novels are found and then structured into plots, how to create realistic characters, how to write successful dialogue and how to build up suspense. Includes sections on writing fiction from fact and on how to present finished work.

You can write for publication (June). Aims to bring out the talent in participants of writing articles, short stories and poems suitable for publication.

International Summer Courses Centre for Continuing Education (University of Edinburgh)

University of Edinburgh, 11 Buccleuch Place, Edinburgh EH8 9LW
tel 0131-650 4400 *fax* 0131-667 6097
e-mail ccesummer@ed.ac.uk
web site http://www.cce.ed.ac.uk

Creative writing (July). Consists of 3 week-long units.

Introductory unit. Covers the basic techniques of writing short stories, poetry and plays.

Short story unit. Follows a logical process of short story writing from inspiration to the finished product. Concentrates on techniques, planning, structure, characterisation, etc. Also looks at marketing of the finished work.

Playwriting unit. Analyses what a play is and how it is constructed, explores how dialogue works and how a character is created. Students work with professional actors on the scenes they write and the course culminates in a rehearsed reading performance of their work.

Gowland Farm Craft Workshop

Gowland Farm, Gowland Lane, Cloughton, Scarborough YO13 0DU
tel (01723) 870924
Contact Mrs M.A. Martin

Creative writing and poetry (spring and autumn). Residential courses for beginners and practised writers.

The Indian King Arts Centre

Fore Street, Camelford, Cornwall PL32 9PG
tel (01840) 212111
e-mail info@indianking.co.uk
web site http://www.indianking.co.uk

Residential writing and painting courses. Tutors include John Greening, Philip Gross, Karen Hayes, Ian Parks, David Rudkin, Ray Atkins, June Lisle, Robin Paris. Contact the Centre for course details.

Short stories for magazines; Writing retreat; Self-hypnosis for creativity; Genre writing (September); **Painting, music, poetry and landscape** (October); **Setting it free; Getting started** (April); **From reality to fiction; Writing retreat** (May); **Poetry workshop; Earthwords; Women writers 2000** (June); **Writing retreat; Writing for radio; Getting started** (July); **Teaching the language to sing; Return of teaching the language to sing; Dealing with the novel** (August).

Summer Academy, Keynes College

The University, Canterbury, Kent CT2 7NP
tel (01227) 470404/823473 *fax* (01227) 784338
e-mail summeracademy@ukc.ac.uk
web site http://www.ukc.ac.uk/sa/index.html
Contact Andrea McDonnell
Venues Norwich, Durham

Creative writing – the sea and waterways (21-28 July) and **Creative writing – people and histories** (4-11 August). Designed to stimulate the imagination and to provide the opportunity to write. Workshops and discussion groups with the focus on writing short stories and poetry. Includes 2 field trips to gain inspiration.

Knuston Hall

Irchester, Wellingborough, Northants. NN29 7EU
tel (01933) 312104 *fax* (01933) 357596
e-mail enquiries@knustonhall.org.uk
web site http://www.knustonhall.org.uk
Contact Daphne Brittin

Writing and illustrating: picture books for children (September). Starting with a blank sheet, participants will write and illustrate (or decorate) a picture book for children. For beginners and more experienced individuals.
Creative writing (April). Designed for both the beginner and the more experienced writer.

Lancaster University

Dept of Continuing Education, Lonsdale College, Lancaster University LA1 4YN
tel (01524) 592623 *fax* (01524) 592448
e-mail Conted@lancaster.ac.uk

Summer Studies at Lancaster University (July). Two courses are held:
Performance writing (mornings). Explores the process of creating character through a combination of reading improvisation, analysis, writing and rehearsal. Also how to perform dramatic material.
Creative writing (afternoons). Designed to support the nervous beginner and rejuvenate the jaded writer. Aims to develop and explore the individual voice of the writer and relate it to wide-ranging ways of working with words.

Missenden Abbey

Great Missenden, Bucks HP16 0BN
tel (01494) 862904 *fax* (01494) 890087
e-mail enquiries@missendenabbey.ac.uk
web site http://www.aredu.org.uk/missendenabbey

Writing for pleasure and profit: freelance journalism (September). Strong practical emphasis with lively exercises rather than lecture format. No experience necessary.
Writing for self-discovery (November). Aims to show different ways of using creative writing to explore oneself and to help participants develop a personal approach in writing prose and poetry.
A voyage into writing (March). An opportunity to unleash creativity in a safe and supportive environment. Group work and one-to-one guidance. For new and experienced writers.
Travel to success (May). Travel-writing markets, planning and writing. No experience necessary.
Writers' toolkit (June). Through exercises, each session will focus on different aspects of writing including plot, dialogue, description and characterisation.

Learn at Leisure (University of Nottingham)

School of Continuing Education, University of Nottingham, Jubilee Campus, Wollaton Road, Nottingham NG8 1BB
tel 0115-951 6526 *fax* 0115-951 6556

Writing is fun (July). Aims to give

confidence to those who are unsure of their creativity, to awaken the imagination of those who have let it fall asleep and to strengthen the resolve of those who are wavering in their writing endeavours. Also examines techniques and rules that transform pieces of writing that please only the author into pieces that others want to read. Uses a combination of workshops, exercises, talks, discussions and readings. Part of the Nottingham University Summer School.

The Old Rectory Adult Education College

Fittleworth, Pulborough, West Sussex RH20 1HU
tel/fax (01798) 865306
e-mail oldrectory@mistral.co.uk
web site http://www.oldrectory.mistral.co.uk

Write a short, short story (November). Covers how to write saleable material for the short story market (e.g. *Bella*, *Best*, *Chat* and *Take a Break*). Looks at different styles.

Writing fantasy and historical fiction (February).

How to be a travel writer (March). Aims to equip students with the skills needed to record travel experiences. Includes practical assignments and individual advice from the tutor.

Write your autobiography (May). Examines fiction and drama from an autobiographical point of view to help with autobiographical writing.

South and Mid Wales Association of Writers

c/o IMC Consulting Group, Denham House, Lambourne Crescent, Cardiff CF4 5ZW
tel 029-2076 1170 *fax* 029-2076 1304
Contact Julian Rosser

South and Mid Wales Association of Writers Weekend Course (May). Includes study groups on writing feature articles, stories, novels and children's books, and how to get published. Open to members of the Association and the general public.

Southern Writers' Conference

Stable House, Home Farm, Coldharbour Lane, Dorking, Surrey RH4 3JG
Contact Lucia White
Venue The Earnley Concourse, Chichester

Southern Writers' Conference (June). Includes a full programme of talks and discussions covering practically every aspect of writing, with some distinguished guest speakers from the literary world. Takes place annually.

Ty Newydd

Ty Newydd, National Creative Writing Centre of Wales, Llanystumdwy, Cricieth, Gwynedd LL52 0LW
tel (01766) 522811 *fax* (01766) 523095
e-mail tynewydd@dial.pipex.com

Residential 4½-day courses for writers at all levels of experience: poetry, fiction, media, songwriting, etc.

Urchfont Manor College

Urchfont, Devizes, Wilts. SN10 4RG
tel (01380) 840495 *fax* (01380) 840005

Creative writing (October).

Writing for pleasure (March).

Wedgwood Memorial College

Station Road, Barlaston, Stoke-on-Trent ST12 9DG
tel (01782) 372105/373427 *fax* (01782) 372393

Contact college for details.

Writers' Summer School, Swanwick

Contact The Secretary, PO Box 5532, Heanor DE75 7YF
web site http://www.wss.org.uk
Venue The Hayes, Swanwick, Derbyshire

One-week summer school held in August. Informal talks and discussion groups, forums, panels, quizzes and competitions. For beginners and published authors.

Editorial, literary and production services

The following specialists offer a wide variety of services to writers (both new and established), to publishers, journalists and others. Services include advice on manuscripts, editing and book production, indexing, translation, research and writing. For an index of the services offered here, see page 592.

'A Feature Factory' Editorial Services

(incorporating Academic Projects)
4 St Andrews Court, 53 Yarmouth Road, Norwich NR7 0EW
tel/fax (01603) 435229 *mobile* (0777) 3045679
Editors Dr Dennis Chaplin, Alexandra Ross

Produces company magazines, brochures, company histories, press releases/features (including sameday turnaround), advertisement features, ghostwriting, autobiographies, research briefs for press/broadcasting, backgrounders, writing and research tuition, DTP. Extra researchers often needed for projects – send CV, work samples and sae.

Abbey Writing Services

Twitchen Cottage, Holcombe Rogus, Wellington, Somerset TA21 0PT
tel/fax (01823) 672762
e-mail john.mcilwain@virgin.net
Director John McIlwain

Comprehensive non-fiction writing, project management and editorial service. Educational consultants. Lexicography. Founded 1989.

Academic File

(in association with The Centre for Near East Afro-Asia Research – NEAR)
27 Wallorton Gardens, PO Box 13666, London SW14 8WF
tel 020-8392 1122 *fax* 020-8392 1422
web site http://www.eapgroup.com
Director Sajid Rizvi

Research, advisory and consultancy services related to politics, economics and societies of the Near and Middle East, Asia and North Africa and related issues in Europe. Risk analysis, editorial assessment, editing, contract publishing, design and production. Founded 1985.

Advice and Criticism Service

1 Beechwood Court, Syderstone, Norfolk PE31 8TR
tel (01485) 578594 *fax* (01485) 578138
e-mail hilary@hilaryjohnson.demon.co.uk
web site http://www.hilaryjohnson.demon.co.uk
Contact Hilary Johnson

Authors' consultant: detailed and constructive assessment of typescripts/practical advice regarding publication. Former organiser of Romantic Novelists' Association's New Writers' Scheme, adjudicator of literary awards and publishers' reader. Specialities: crime/thrillers/popular women's fiction. Advice also available on science fiction/fantasy, children's books and non-fiction.

Alpha Word Power

3 Bluecoat Buildings, Claypath, Durham DH1 1RF
tel 0191-384 7219 *fax* 0191-384 3767
e-mail p.g.h@btinternet.com
web site http://www.btinternet.com/~p.g.h/awp.htm

Publishing services: camera-ready copy, word processing, text from and/or to disk, desk editing, proofreading, liaison with printers/binders/graphic design; full secretarial services including audio-typing; business services. Specialises in versatility and speed of turnaround. Founded 1985.

Amolibros

5 Saxon Close, Watchet, Somerset TA23 0BN
tel/fax (01984) 633713
e-mail amolibros@aol.com
web site http://www.author.co.uk/amolibros
Managing Consultant Jane Tatam

A self-publishing consultancy/packager.

Also offers copy-editing, proofreading, typesetting, advice on marketing and sales. Established 1992.

Anchor Editorial Services

Anchor House, 5 High Street, Dulverton, Somerset TA22 9HB
tel/fax (01398) 324350
Editorial Director Leigh-Anne Perryman, *Photographic Director* Martyn Collins

A complete editorial, research and photographic service for company brochures and magazines; guidebooks, publicity leaflets and tourism projects; press releases and newsletters. Established 1998.

Angel Books

6 Lancaster Road, Harrogate, North Yorkshire HG2 0EZ
tel (01423) 566804
e-mail angelbooks@classicfm.net
Contact Angela Sibson BA AFBPsS

Professional author (20 titles) and tutor in creative writing offers comprehensive, sympathetic assessment of ficiton MSS. Revision suggested with a view to getting into print. Special interests: psychological suspense, crime, thrillers, women's, teenage. Established 1994.

Arioma Editorial Services

PO Box 53, Aberystwyth, Ceredigion SY24 5WG
tel (01970) 871296 *fax* (01970) 871733
Proprietor Moira W. Smith

Research, co-writing, ghost-writing, DTP, complete book production service. Specialities: military, naval, aviation history and autobiography.

Arkst Publishing

1 Lindsey House, Lloyds's Place, London SE3 0QF
tel 020-8297 9997 *fax* 020-8318 4359
e-mail jim@arkst.demon.co.uk
Director James H. Willis MA, FRCP (Edin.)

Advice on rewrites. Independent appraisal of MSS – fiction and non-fiction. Founded 1995.

Authors' Advisory Service

Halfway House, 24A Lyndale Avenue, Childs Hill, London NW2 2QA
tel 020-7794 3285

All typescripts professionally evaluated in depth and edited by long-established publishers' reader specialising in constructive advice to new writers and with wide experience of current literary requirements. Lecture service on the craft and technique of writing for publication. Founded 1972.

Authors' Aid

11 Orchard Street, Fearnhead, Warrington WA2 0PL
tel (01925) 838431
e-mail chris.sawyer@btinternet.com
web site http://www.authorsaid.co.uk
Partners Mrs C.A. Sawyer and Miss D.E. Ramage

Provides an honest critical appraisal of MSS and offers advice and guidance on such topics as style, presentation, characterisation, plot and marketability. A personalised service by an established writer with the aim of getting the work published. Other services: word processing, editing, reappraisal. Established 1991.

Authors Appraisal Service

12 Hadleigh Gardens, Boyatt Wood, Eastleigh, Hants SO5 4NP
Literary consultant J. Evans

Professional writer offers critical appraisal of MSS – fiction only. Specialises in romantic and historical fiction. Competitive rates. Preliminary letter essential and sae for reply. Founded 1988.

Authors' Research Services

32 Oak Village, London NW5 4QN
tel 020-7284 4316
e-mail rmwindserv@aol.com
Contact Richard Wright

Offers comprehensive research service to writers, academics and business people worldwide, including fact checking, bibliographical references and document supply. Specialises in English history, social sciences, business. Founded 1966.

Authors OnLine Ltd

Adams Yard, Maidenhead Street, Hertford SG14 1DR
tel (01992) 503151 *fax* 020-7681 2847
e-mail theeditor@authorsonline.co.uk
web site http://www.authorsonline.co.uk
Contact Richard Fitt (editor), Derek Reece (technical), Gary Lee (marketing)

Publishes MSS (including short stories and poetry) on the AuthorsOnLine web site. Authors retain control of editorial content and copyright, leaving them free to pursue hard copy contracts. Works closely with publishers and literary agents. New and established authors welcome. Fee for book-length MS: £25 plus £10 p.a. Founded 1997.

Richard A. Beck

49 Curzon Avenue, Stanmore, Middlesex HA7 2AL
tel 020-8933 9787 *fax* 020-8904 5182

Editing, proofreading, indexing, research, writing and rewriting. Reduced rates for new authors, senior citizens, the unemployed, etc. Founded 1991.

Beswick Writing Services

19 Haig Road, Stretford M32 0DS
tel 0161-865 1259
Contact Francis Beswick

Editing, research, information books. Special interests: religious, philosophical and educational. Expertise in correspondence courses and Open Learning materials. Founded 1988.

Black Ace Book Production

PO Box 6557, Forfar DD8 2YS
tel (01307) 465096 *fax* (01307) 465494
Directors Hunter Steele, Boo Wood

Book production and text processing, including text capture (or scanning), editing, proofing to camera-ready/film, printing and binding, jacket artwork and design. Delivery of finished books; can sometimes help with distribution. Founded 1990.

Blair Services

Blair Cottage, Aultgrishan, Melvaig, Gairloch, Wester Ross IV21 2DZ
tel/fax (01445) 771228
e-mail blairservices@aultgrisham.fsnet.co.uk
Director Ian Mertling-Blake MA, DPhil

Editing and revision: fiction and non-fiction (such as prospectus for schools and other educational purposes). Also specialist academic revision for books/articles on archaeology and associated subjects. Founded 1992.

The Book Guild Ltd

Temple House, 25 High Street, Lewes, East Sussex BN7 2LU
tel (01273) 472534 *fax* (01273) 476472
e-mail info@bookguild.co.uk
web site http://www.bookguild.co.uk
Directors G.M. Nissen CBE (chairman), Carol Biss (managing), Anthony Nissen, Jane Nissen, David Ross, Paul White (financial), Janet Wrench (production)

Offers a range of publishing options:

• Comprehensive package for authors incorporating editorial, design, production, marketing, publicity and distribution.

• Editorial and production only for authors requiring private editions.

• A complete service for companies and organisations requiring books for internal or promotional purposes – from brief to finished book. Founded 1982.

Book Production Consultants plc

25-27 High Street, Chesterton, Cambridge CB4 1ND
tel (01223) 352790 *fax* (01223) 460718
e-mail [name]@tlebpccam.co.uk
web site http://www.bpccam.co.uk
Directors A.P. Littlechild, C.S. Walsh

Complete publishing service: writing, editing, designing, illustrating, translating, indexing, photography; production management of printing and binding; specialised sales and distribution; advertising sales. For books, journals, manuals, reports, magazines, catalogues, electronic media. Founded 1973.

Book-in-Hand Ltd

20 Shepherds Hill, London N6 5AH
tel/fax 020-8341 7650
Contact Ann Kritzinger

Production of cost-effective short-run books for small and self-publishers, from typescript (or disk) to bound copies (hardbacks or paperbacks, sewn or unsewn). Enquiries with sae, or by fax, please.

Bookwatch Ltd

15-up, East Street, Lewin's Yard, Chesham, Bucks. HP5 1HQ
tel (01494) 792269 *fax* (01494) 784850
e-mail 100615.1643@compuserve.com
Directors Peter Harland, Jennifer Harland

Bestseller lists, book reviews, features.

David Bradley Science Writer

18 Pelham Way, Cottenham, Cambridge CB4 8TQ
tel/fax (01954) 202218
e-mail bradley@enterprise.net
web site http://homepages.enterprise.net/bradley/
Partners David Bradley BSc (Hons) CChem MRSC and Patricia Bradley BSc (Hons), GIPD, Dip RSA

General and specialist articles and scripts on science, technology and medicine. Editing and rewriting of articles, newsletters, scripts, brochures and technical MSS. Member of ABSW and recipient of several writing awards. Most word processing and picture formats handled; HTML aware. Established 1989.

Brittan Design Partnership

7 The Old Fire Station Annex, Fairfield Road, Market Harborough, Leics. LE16 9QJ
tel (01858) 466950 *fax* (01858) 434632
e-mail b.d.p@virgin.net
web site http://www.freespace.virgin.net/b.d.p
Partners Derek W. Brittan MCSD, Nick J. Brittan

Complete editorial design and publishing service; in-house typesetting; high end computer graphics and pre-press; film production. Founded 1978.

Brooke Projects

21 Barnfield, Urmston, Manchester M41 9EW
tel 0161-746 8140 *fax* 0161-746 8132
e-mail urmston@brooke.u-net.com

Research, editing and contract writing. Specialises in business, management, tourism, history, biography and social science.

Mrs D. Buckmaster

51 Chatsworth Road, Torquay, Devon TQ1 3BJ
tel/fax (01803) 294663

General editing of non-fiction, with particular attention to clarity of expression and meaning, grammar, punctuation and flow. Experience editing architecture, photography, financial, religious, natural health and human potential MSS. Founded 1966.

John Button – Editorial Services

Tower House, 6 Burnham Court, Martello Bay, Clacton on Sea, Essex CO15 1RE
tel (01255) 470404

Copy-editing and proofreading, specialising in government committee of enquiry reports, legal, financial, taxation, business education and corporate identity publications; Legal Reference Library series. Founded 1991.

Causeway Resources

8 The Causeway, Teddington, Middlesex TW11 0HE
tel/fax 020-8977 8797
Director Keith Skinner

Genealogical, biographical and historical research, specialising in police history and true crime research. Founded 1989.

Vanessa Charles

38 Ham Common, Richmond, Surrey TW10 7JG
tel/fax 0181-940 9225
e-mail 101361,1176@compuserve.com

Design and book production services. Founded 1975.

Karyn Claridge Book Production

244 Bromham Road, Biddenham, Bedford MK40 4AA
tel (01234) 347909

Complete book production management service offered from MS to bound copies; graphic services available; sourcing service for interactive book projects. Founded 1989.

Johnathon Clifford

27 Mill Road, Fareham, Hants PO16 0TH
tel/fax (01329) 822218
web site http://www.ourworld.compuserve.com/homepages/jonathonclifford

Offers a free, unbiased advice service for anyone looking for a publisher or who has experienced difficulties with a publishing house. Has extensive knowledge of vanity publishing and acted as adviser to the Advertising Standards Authority regarding the wording of the 'Advice Note Vanity Publishing July 1997'. See web site for his report on the government White Paper against rogue traders and its effectiveness where authors are concerned. Established 1994.

Combrógos

Mr Meic Stephens, 10 Heol Don, Whitchurch, Cardiff CF14 2AU
e-mail meic@heoldon.fsnet.co.uk
tel 029-2062 3359 *fax* 029-2052 9202

Specialises in books (including fiction and poetry) about Wales or by Welsh authors, providing a full editorial service and undertaking arts and media research. Founded 1990.

Cornerstones

PO Box 22534, London W8 4GP
tel 020-7727 2478 *fax* 020-7727 6983
mobile (07971) 457358
Proprietor Helen Corner

Specialist team of readers (authors, editors and literary reviewers) provides general literary guidance and constructive assessment of MSS. Clients range from best sellers to unpublished authors. Strong contacts with agents and publishers. Established 1998.

Ingrid Cranfield

16 Myddelton Gardens, London N21 2PA
tel/fax 020-8360 2433
e-mail ingrid_cranfield@hotmail.com

Advisory and editorial services for authors, publishers and media, including critical assessment, rewriting, proofreading, copy-editing, indexing, research, interviews, transcripts. Special interests: geography, travel, exploration, adventure (own archives), language, education, youth training, art and architecture (notably Japanese). Translations from

German and French. Not an employer or agency. Founded 1972.

Clarissa Cridland

4 Rock Terrace, Coleford, Bath, Somerset BA3 5NF
tel (01373) 812705 *fax* (01373) 813517
e-mail cridland@rockterrace.demon.co.uk

Full service on all aspects of author and publisher contracts, including but not limited to reading, typing and negotiating contracts. Not an agent. Does not undertake typing of MSS. Established 1994.

David A. Cross

75 Croslands Park, Barrow-in-Furness,
Cumbria LA13 9LB
tel (01229) 822694

Research and information service; editing texts, specialising in art history, English literature, biography and genealogy; creative writing tutorials; lectures on artists and writers of the Lake District.

D & N Publishing

Membury Business Park, Lambourn Woodlands,
Hungerford, Berks. RG17 7TJ
tel (01488) 71210 *fax* (01488) 71220
e-mail DandNPub@aol.com
Partners David and Namrita Price-Goodfellow

Complete project management including commissioning, editing, picture research, illustration and design, page layout, proofreading, indexing, printing and repro. All stages managed in-house and produced on Apple Macs running Quark, FreeHand and Photoshop. Founded 1991.

David Wineman, Solicitors

Craven House, 121 Kingsway, London WC2B 6NX
tel 020-7400 7800 *fax* 020-7400 7890
e-mail law@davidwineman.co.uk
web site http://www.davidwineman.co.uk
Partners Irving David, Vivian Wineman, Neil Aspess, Malcolm Brahams, Stuart Killen
Contact Irving David

A broadly based media law firm. Offers legal advice to authors, illustrators, photographers, composers, songwriters and their agents on all forms of publishing agreement, including negotiation and review of commercial terms, where required, with book and music publishers, film, TV and theatrical production companies, packagers and merchandisers. Founded 1981.

Meg Davies

31 Egerton Road, Ashton, Preston, Lancs. PR2 1AJ
tel (01772) 725120 *fax* (01772) 723853
e-mail megindex@aol.com

Indexing at general and post-graduate level in the arts and humanities. Also proofreading and copy-editing. Registered Indexer with Society of Indexers since 1971.

Editorial Solutions

537 Antrim Road, Belfast BT15 3BU
tel 028-9077 2300 *fax* 028-9078 1356
e-mail inbox@editorialsolutions.com
web site http://www.editorialsolutions.com
Partners Sheelagh Hughes, Michael Johnston

Offers a comprehensive editorial and publications service, including news and feature writing, copywriting, editing and copy-editing, proofreading, publication design, page layout and complete publication management, and on-line publications. Qualified journalists. Specialisms: business, public sector, education, religious communications, multimedia.

Editorial/Visual Research

21 Leamington Road Villas, London W11 1HS
tel 020-7727 4920 *mobile* (07973) 820020
Contact Angela Murphy

Comprehensive research service including historical, literary, film and picture research for writers, publishers, film and TV companies. Services also include copy-writing, editing, and travel and feature writing. Founded 1973.

Dr Martin Edwards

Flat 1, St Donats, De La Warr Parade,
Bexhill-on-Sea, East Sussex TN40 1NR
tel/fax (01424) 210737

Specialist editorial and research service in the medico-scientific field: copy-editing, co-editorial/-authorship, proofreading, abstracting and conference productions. Special interest in the improvement of foreign texts. Founded 1985.

Lewis Esson Publishing

45 Brewster Gardens, London W10 6AQ
tel 020-7854 0668 *fax* 020-8968 1623
e-mail lewisesson@supanet.com

Project management of illustrated books in areas of food, art and interior design; editing and writing of food books; copywriting, especially in the area of food packaging and FMCGs. Founded 1989.

etr (Edward Twentyman Resources)

4 Little Green, Cheveley, Newmarket CB8 9RG
tel/fax (01638) 731332
e-mail freelance@etr.co.uk
web site http://www.etr.co.uk
Proprietor Edward Twentyman

Employment agency specialising solely in freelance people experienced in publishing. Founded 1992.

Finers Stephens Innocent

179 Great Portland Street, London W1N 6LS
tel 020-7323 4000 *fax* 020-7344 5600
e-mail nsolomon@fsilaw.co.uk
web site http://www.finersstephensinnocent.co.uk
Contact Nicola Solomon, Partner

Services include: drafting and negotiating agency and publishing agreements; advice on copyright and moral rights, libel reading, defamation advice and insurance; breaches or termination of contract; errors in printing and failure or refusal to publish or delay in publishing; debt collection for payment of royalties, commission or fees, including suing or insolvency proceedings where necessary; injunctions; preparation of wills, administering artistic and literary estates; permissions, rights, copyright infringement and negligent misstatement; electronic rights and international sales. Solicitors to the Society of Authors and the Association of Illustrators.

First Edition Translations Ltd

6 Wellington Court, Wellington Street,
Cambridge CB1 1HZ
tel (01223) 356733 *fax* (01223) 321488
e-mail info@firstedit.co.uk
web site http://www.firstedit.co.uk
Directors Sheila Waller, Jeremy Waller

Translation, interpreting, voice recording, editing, proofreading, Americanisation, DTP; books, manuals, reports, journals and promotional material. Founded 1981.

FJN Associates

Little Theobald, Sandy Cross, Heathfield,
East Sussex TN21 8BT
tel (01435) 866653 *fax* (01435) 868998
e-mail fred@nixonf.freeserve.co.uk
Partners Frederick J. Nixon, Brenda Mellen Nixon

Comprehensive DTP and editorial service including magazine and newsletter design and production; advice to authors, editing and preparation of manuscripts for submission to publishers/editors; proofreading. Founded 1990.

Christine Foley Secretarial Services

Glyndedwydd, Login, Whitland,
Carmarthenshire SA34 0TN
tel/fax (01994) 448414
Partners Christine Foley, Michael Foley

Word processing service: preparation of MSS from handwritten/typed notes and audio-transcription. Complete secretarial support. Founded 1991.

Brian J. Ford

Rothay House, 6 Mayfield Road, Eastrea,
Cambs. PE7 2AY
tel/fax (01733) 350888
e-mail bjford@sciences.demon.co.uk
web site http://www.sciences.demon.co.uk

Scientist and adviser on scientific matters; author, producer/director scientific films and programmes in addition to editor/contributor to many leading books and journals. Has hosted many leading BBC TV and radio programmes, and overseas documentaries.

the Freelance Editorial Service

45 Bridge Street, Musselburgh,
Midlothian EH21 6AA
tel 0131-663 1238
Contact Bill Houston BSc, DipLib, MPhil

Editing, proofreading, indexing, abstracting, translations, bibliographies; particularly scientific and medical. Founded 1975.

Freelance Market News

Sevendale House, 7 Dale Street,
Manchester M1 1JB
tel 0161-228 2362 *fax* 0161-228 3533
e-mail fmn@writersbureau.com
web site http://www.writersbureau.com
Contact Angela Cox, Editor

A monthly market newsletter (£29 p.a.). A good rate of pay made for news of editorial requirements. Information on UK and overseas publications with editorial content, submission requirements and contact details. Founded 1968.

Freelance Services, Joan Shannon

41A Newal Road, Ballymoney,
Co. Antrim BT53 6HB
tel 028-2766 2953 *fax* 028-2766 5019

Writing, editorial and desktop design service. Natural light photography. Postcard publisher. Founded 1991.

Frost Historical Newspaper Collection

8 Monks Avenue, New Barnet,
Herts. EN5 1DB
tel/fax 020-8440 3159

Headline stories from 60,000 British and overseas newspapers reporting major events since 1850.

Shelagh Furness

Hallgarth Farmhouse, The Hallgarth, Durham, Co. Durham DH1 3BJ
tel 0191-384 3840

Research and information service, specialising in environmental, scientific and geographical topics, also North East England; word processing service. Founded 1992.

Geo Group & Associates

4 Christian Fields, London SW16 3JZ
tel/fax 020-8764 6292 *fax* 0115-981 9418
e-mail geo.group@geo-group.demon.co.uk

Publishing services. From copy-editing and proofreading to complete package. Research and publishing consultancy. Publishing imprint: Nyala Publishing. Two photo libraries (including aerial); photography commissioned. Special rates to author-publishers. Established 1968.

C.N. Gilmore

27 Salisbury Street, Bedford MK41 7RE
tel (01234) 346142
e-mail Intel_Thug@compuserve.com

Sub-editing, slush-pile reading, reviewing. Will also collaborate. Undertakes work in all scholarly and academic fields as well as fiction and practical writing. Specialises in editing translated works. Founded 1987.

Graham-Cameron Publishing

The Studio, 23 Holt Road, Sheringham, Norfolk NR26 8NB
tel (01263) 821333 *fax* (01263) 821334
Partners Helen Graham-Cameron, Mike Graham-Cameron

Complete editorial, including writing, editing, illustration and production services. Absolutely no unsolicited MSS. Founded 1984.

Guildford Reading Services

17 Burwood Gardens, Ash Vale, Aldershot, Hants GU12 5HN
tel (01252) 317950
Director B.V. Varney

Proofreading, press revision, copy preparation, sub-editing. Founded 1978.

John Hall

20 Drury Avenue, Horsforth, Leeds LS18 4BR
tel 0113-258 4902

Writing, editing, proofreading. Specialises in crime fiction but all subjects covered. Established 1990.

Bernard Hawton

6 Merdon Court, Merdon Avenue, Chandler's Ford, Hants SO53 1FP
tel 023-8026 7400

Proofreading, copy-editing.

Heath Associates

Garden Flat, 15 South Hill Park Gardens, London NW3 2TD
tel/fax 020-7435 4059
e-mail 74101.624@compuserve.com
Proprietor Richard Williams

Consultancy on desktop publishing, word processing and graphics programs for IBM PC; design and illustration specialising in academic and technical works; writing and editing for computing and related topics. Founded 1988.

Antony Hemans

Maranatha, 1 Nettles Terrace, Guildford, Surrey GU1 4PA
tel (01483) 574511

Biographical and historical research, specialising in industrial archaeology – railways, canals and shipping, air, military and naval operations – genealogy and family history. Founded 1981.

Mark P. Hempshell

9 Heath Drive, Boston Spa, West Yorkshire LS23 6PB
tel/fax (01937) 845585
e-mail markhempshell@compuserve.com

Freelance writer specialising in careers/employment, business, live and work abroad, and how-to books and articles. Also research and all kinds of advertising copywriting, especially direct mail. Established 1986.

Rosemary Horstmann

122 Mayfield Court, 27 West Savile Terrace, Edinburgh EH9 3DR
tel 0131-667 1377

Broadcasting scripts evaluated; general consultancy on editorial and marketing matters.

E.J. Hunter

6 Dorset Road, London N22 7SL
tel 020-8889 0370

Editing, copy-editing, proofreading; appraisal of MSS. Special interests: novels, short stories, drama, children's stories; primary education, complementary medicine, New Age.

Hurst Village Publishing

Henry and Elizabeth Farrar, High Chimneys, Davis Street, Hurst, Reading RG10 0TH
tel 0118-9345211 *fax* 0118-9342073
e-mail hf@hurstvp.demon.co.uk

Offers design, photography, typesetting using the latest desktop publishing programs, photographic equipment and high resolution colour and laser printers. Founded 1989.

Indexers, Society of

Globe Centre, Penistone Road, Sheffield S6 3AE
tel 0114-281 3060 *fax* 0114-281 3061
e-mail admin@socind.demon.co.uk
web site http://www.socind.demon.co.uk

See pages 480 and 595 for further details.

Indexing Specialists

202 Church Road, Hove, East Sussex BN3 2DJ
tel (01273) 738299 *fax* (01273) 323309
e-mail richardr@indexing.co.uk
web site http://www.indexing.co.uk
Director Richard Raper BSc, DTA

Indexes for all types: books, journals and reference publications on professional, scientific and general subjects; copy-editing, proofreading services; consultancy on indexing and electronic indexing. Founded 1965.

The Information Bureau

(formerly Daily Telegraph Information Bureau)
51 The Business Centre, 103 Lavender Hill, London SW11 5QL
tel 020-7924 4414 *fax* 020-7924 4456
e-mail infobureau@dial.pipex.com
Contact Jane Hall

Offers an on-demand research service on a variety of subjects including current affairs, business, marketing, history, the arts, media and politics. Resources include range of cuttings amassed by the bureau since 1948.

Library Research Agency

Burberry, Devon Road, Salcombe, Devon TQ8 8HJ
tel (01548) 842769 *fax* (01548) 842293
Directors D.J. Langford MA, B. Langford

Research and information service for writers, journalists, artists, businessmen from libraries, archives, museums, record offices and newspapers in UK, USA and Europe. Sources may be in English, French, German, Russian, Serbo-Croat, Bulgarian, and translations made if required. Founded 1974.

The Literary Consultancy (TLC)

PO Box 12939, London N8 9WA
tel/fax 020-8372 3922
e-mail swifttlc@dircon.co.uk
web site http://www.literaryconsultancy.co.uk
Director Rebecca Swift

Offers a detailed assessment of fiction, non-fiction and autobiography from a team of professional editors and writers. Fees based on length. Quick turnaround. Personal links with agents and publishers. Established 1996.

Dr Kenneth Lysons

Lathom, Scotchbarn Lane, Whiston, Nr Prescot, Merseyside L35 7JB
tel 0151-426 5513
Contact Dr Kenneth Lysons MA, MEd, DPA, DMS, FCIS, FInstPS, FBIM

Company and institutional histories, support material for organisational management and supervisory training, house journals, research and reports service. Full secretarial support. Founded 1986.

Duncan McAra

28 Beresford Gardens, Edinburgh EH5 3ES
tel/fax 0131-552 1558
e-mail duncanmcara@hotmail.com

Consultancy on all aspects of general trade publishing; editing; proof correction. Main subjects include art, architecture, archaeology, biography, military, Scottish and travel. See also page 360. Founded 1988.

McText

Denmill, Tough, By Alford, Aberdeenshire AB33 8EP
tel/fax (019755) 62582
e-mail mctext@highland-pony.com
web site http://www.highland-pony.com/mctext.htm
Partners K. and Duncan McArdle

Proofreading, editing, copy-editing, web site authoring. Specialist interests: archaeology, equestrian. Founded 1986.

Manuscript Appraisals

Lanetrees, Simpson Cross, Haverfordwest, Pembs. SA62 6AE
tel/fax (01437) 710534
Proprietor Norman Price
Consultants Ray Price, Mary Hunt

Independent appraisal of authors' MSS (fiction and non-fiction, but no poetry) with full editorial guidance and advice. In-house editing, copy-editing, rewriting and proofreading if required. Overseas enquiries welcome. Interested in the work of new writers. Founded 1984.

Marlinoak

22 Eve's Croft, Birmingham B32 3QL
tel/fax 0121-475 6139
Proprietor Hazel J. Billing JP, BA, DipEd

Preparation of scripts, plays, books, MSS service, proofreading, research; also audio-transcription, word processing and full secretarial facilities. Founded 1984.

Susan Moore Editorial Services

65 Albion Road, London N16 9PP
tel/fax 020-7923 2480

Troubleshooting service for publishers, packagers and agents: co-authorship with specialists, ghostwriting, rewriting, translation fine tuning, re-drafting. Founded 1994.

Murder Files

81 Churchfields Drive, Bovey Tracey, Devon TQ13 9QU
tel (01626) 833487 *fax* (01626) 835797
e-mail enquiry@murderfiles.com
web sites http://www.murderfiles.com
Director Paul Williams

Crime writer and researcher specialising in UK murders. Holds information on thousands of well-known and less well-known murders dating from 1400 to the present day. Copies of press cuttings on murder cases available from 1920 to date. Details of executions, particularly at the Tyburn and Newgate. Information on British Hangmen. Service available to general enquirers, writers, TV, radio, video, etc. Founded 1994.

Elizabeth Murray

3 Gower Mews Mansions, Gower Mews, London WC1E 6HR
tel/fax 020-7636 3761

Literary, biographical, historical, crime, military, cinema, genealogy research for authors, journalists, radio and TV from UK, European and USA sources. Founded 1975.

My Word!

138 Railway Terrace, Rugby, Warks. CV21 3HN
tel (01788) 571294 *fax* (01788) 550957
e-mail enquiries@myword.co.uk
web site http://www.myword.co.uk
Partners Roddie Grant, Janet Grant

Complete graphic design and DTP service; word processing service either to hard copy or disk; web site design and database development. Brochures, leaflets, magazines, books, theses, CVs, etc. Founded 1994.

Paul Nash

Munday House, Aberdalgie, Perth PH2 0QB
tel/fax (01738) 621584
e-mail paulnash@zetnet.co.uk

Indexer specialising in sciences, technology, environmental science. Registered with the Society of Indexers. Winner of Library Association Wheatley Medal (1992) for outstanding index. Founded 1979.

Peter Nickol

50 St Leonards Road, Exeter EX2 4LS
tel/fax (01392) 255512
e-mail pnickol@ninoakes.freeserve.co.uk

Editing and page layout; typesetting and music engraving; copyright licensing; project management including mixed media coordination, CD recording and production. Specialises in music and music education. Established 1987.

Nidaba Publishing Services

19 Khartoum Road, London SW17 0JA
tel 020-8767 8470
Contact Ali Glenny PhD Eng. Lit.

Copy-editing, text keying (Word, Quark, etc), proofreading. Experienced with many major publishing houses. Established 1997.

Paul H. Niekirk

40 Rectory Avenue, High Wycombe, Bucks. HP13 6HW
tel (01494) 527200

Text editing for works of reference and professional and management publications, particularly texts on law; freelance writing. Founded 1976.

Northern Writers Advisory Services

77 Marford Crescent, Sale, Cheshire M33 4DN
tel 0161-969 1573
e-mail grovesjill@aol.com
Proprietor Jill Groves

Offers copy-editing and typesetting to small publishers, societies and authors. Local history only. Founded 1986.

Oriental Languages Bureau

Lakshmi Building, Sir P. Mehta Road, Fort, Bombay 400001, India
tel 2661258/2665640 *fax* 2664598
Proprietor Rajan K. Shah

Undertakes translations, phototypesetting-

DTP, artwork and printing in all Indian languages and a few foreign languages.

Ormrod Research Services

Weeping Birch, Burwash, East Sussex TN19 7HG
tel (01435) 882541
and 4 Croftleigh Gardens, Solihull B91 1TG
tel 0121-711 7200

Comprehensive research service: literary, historical, academic, biographical, commercial. Critical reading with report (novels, theses, non-fiction), editing, indexing, proofreading, ghosting. Founded 1982.

Oxford Designers & Illustrators

(formerly Oxford Illustrators and Oxprint Design)
Aristotle House, Aristotle Lane,
Oxford OX2 6TR
tel (01865) 512331 *fax* (01865) 512408
e-mail [name]@odi-illustration.co.uk
web site http://www.oxford-illustrators.co.uk
Directors Peter Lawrence, Richard Corfield, Andrew King

Over 30 years' experience in the design, typesetting and illustration of educational and general books. In-house artists for all subjects including scientific and technical, medical, natural history, cartoons, maps and diagrams. Full project management and repro service. Not an agency.

Pages Editorial & Publishing Services

Ballencrieff Cottage, Ballencrieff Toll, Bathgate, West Lothian EH48 4LD
tel (01506) 632728 *fax* (01506) 635444
e-mail suse@pages.clara.net
Director Susan Coon

Editorial and production service of magazines/newspapers for companies or for commercial distribution; promotional literature; publishing service for authors wishing to self-publish. Founded 1995.

Geoffrey D. Palmer

47 Burton Fields Road, Stamford Bridge, York YO41 1JJ
tel/fax (01759) 372874
e-mail gdp@lineone.net
web site http://www.website.lineone.net/~gdp/index.htm

Editorial and production services, including STM and general copy-editing, on-screen editing, artwork editing, proofreading and indexing. Pre-press project management. Founded 1987.

Roger Palmer Ltd

Antonia House, 262 Holloway Road,
London N7 6NB
tel 020-7609 4828 *fax* 020-2697 8877
e-mail contracts@rogerpalmerltd.co.uk
Directors Roger Palmer, Stephen Aucutt *Senior Senior Consultants* Angela Elkins, Gareth Shannon

Drafts, advises on and negotiates all media contracts for publishers, packagers, agents, authors and others; operates complete outsourced contracts department functions for publishers; undertakes contractual audits and devises contracts and permissions systems; provides advice on copyright and related issues; provides training and seminars. Special terms for members of the Society of Authors and the Writers' Guild of Great Britain. Founded 1993.

Phoenix 2

Lantern House, Lodge Drove, Woodfalls, Salisbury, Wilts SP5 2NH
tel (01725) 512200 *fax* (01725) 511819
e-mail walker@phoenix2.prestel.co.uk
Partners Bryan Walker, Amanda Walker

Writing, editing, sub-editing, typesetting and design of magazines, newsletters, journals, brochures and promotional literature. Specialist areas are business, tourism, social affairs and education. Founded 1994.

Christopher Pick

41 Chestnut Road, London SE27 9EZ
tel 020-8761 2585 *fax* 020-8761 6388
e-mail cpick@netcomuk.co.uk

Publications consultancy, project management, writing and editing for companies and public-sector and voluntary-sector institutions, and publishers: e.g. annual reports, brochures and booklets, information materials and training manuals, multimedia, strategy documents, research reports, company histories. Special expertise in presenting information clearly and concisely for non-specialist readers.

Picture Research Agency

Jasmine Cottage, Spring Grove Road, Richmond, Surrey TW10 6EH
tel 020-8940 5986
Contact Pat Hodgson

Illustrations found for books, films and TV. Written research also undertaken particularly on historical subjects, including photographic and film history. Small picture library.

Picture Research Service – see Rich Research

Reginald Piggott

Decoy Lodge, Decoy Road, Potter Heigham, Norfolk NR29 5LX
tel (01692) 670384

Cartographer to the University Presses and academic publishers in Britain and overseas. Maps and diagrams for academic and educational books. Founded 1962.

Keith Povey Editorial Services

Stoneleigh House, South Brentor, Tavistock, Devon PL19 0NW
tel (01822) 810190 *fax* (01822) 810191
e-mail Povedservs@aol.com

Copy-editing, indexing, proofreading, publisher/author liaison. Partnership with:

T & A Typesetting Services
189 Drake Street, Rochdale, Lancs. OL11 1EF
tel (01706) 861662 *fax* (01706) 861673
e-mail a.edmondson@zen.co.uk

Specialist book-typesetting to final output of any kind, graphic design.

David Price

4 Harbidges Lane, Long Buckby, Northampton NN6 7QL
tel/fax (01327) 844119
e-mail dprice@appleonline.net

Copy-editing, proofreading, research, writing, rewriting. Special interests: fine art (particularly modern art), operetta and musicals, modern European history (including the former Soviet Union), alternative health. Founded 1995.

Victoria Ramsay

Abbots Rest, Chilbolton, Stockbridge, Hants SO20 6BE
tel (01264) 860251 *fax* (01264) 860026
e-mail victoredit@supanet.com

Freelance editing, copy-editing and proofreading; non-fiction research and writing of promotional literature and pamphlets. Any non-scientific subject undertaken. Special interests: education, cookery, travel, Africa and Caribbean and works in translation. Established 1981.

Reading and Righting (Robert Lambolle Services)

618B Finchley Road, London NW11 7RR
tel/fax 020-8455 4564
e-mail zip@phancap.demon.co.uk

MSS/script analysis and evaluation service: fiction, non-fiction, stage plays and screenplays; editorial services; one-to-one tutorials, creative writing courses, lectures and research. Send sae for leaflet. Founded 1987.

Repertoire

21 Hindsleys Place, London SE23 2NF
tel 020-8244 5816
Contact John Parker

Offers writing service: anything from a letter to ghosting a novel. Detailed advice and rewriting of scripts, plays, fiction, etc. Personal tuition available. Fees: £5 per 1000 words or £20 for general appraisal of a novel. Established 1991.

S. Ribeiro Literary Services

42 West Heath Court, North End Road, London NW11 7RG
tel 020-8458 9082
Contact S. Ribeiro BA

Copywriting, book reviews, rewriting, MSS appraisal and analysis with sensitive editing and proofreading. Author's disk (all systems) can be edited to publication standard. Offers guidance in submission to publishers and agents, and in self-publishing. New writers welcome. Special interests and experience: fiction, general non-fiction and memoirs. Telephone or send sae for further information. Founded 1986.

Rich Research

One Bradby, 77 Carlton Hill, London NW8 9XE
tel/fax 020-7624 7755
Contact Diane Rich

Picture research service. Visuals found for all sectors of the media and publishing. Artwork and photography commissioned. Rights and permissions negotiated. Founded 1978.

Anton Rippon Press Services

Breedon House, 3 The Parker Centre, Derby DE21 4SZ
tel (01332) 384235 *fax* (01332) 292755/521548
cellphone 0402-693864
e-mail anton@breedonbooks.co.uk

General feature and sports writing for newspapers and magazines. Ghost writing (preliminary letter essential). Radio and film documentary treatments and scripts. Complete book production service. Part of the Breedon Publishing Group.

Sandhurst Editorial Consultants

36 Albion Road, Sandhurst, Berks. GU47 9BP
tel (01252) 877645 *fax* (01252) 890508
e-mail mail@sand-con.demon.co.uk
web site http://www.sand-con.demon.co.uk

Partners Lionel Browne, Janet Browne

Specialists in technical, professional and reference work. Project management, editorial development, writing, rewriting, copy-editing, proofreading, and general editorial consultancy. Founded 1991.

Sandton Literary Agency

PO Box 785799, Sandton 2146, South Africa
tel (011) 442-8624
Directors J. Victoria Canning, M. Sutherland

Evaluating, editing and/or indexing book MSS. Preparing reports, company histories, house journals, etc. Critical but constructive advice to writers. Lecture agents. Please write or phone first. Founded 1982.

SciText

18 Barton Close, Landrake, Saltash, Cornwall PL12 5BA
tel/fax (01752) 851451
e-mail bg@scitext.fsnet.co.uk
Contact Dr Brian Gee

Proofreading and editing in science, chemical and electrical engineering and the history of science and technology; IBM compatible PC. Founded 1988.

Scriptmate

20 Shepherd's Hill, London N6 5AH
tel/fax 020-8341 7650
Contact Ann Kritzinger

An editing service in conjunction with **Book-in-Hand Ltd** for selected work in fiction and non-fiction. Enquiries with sae, or by fax, please. Founded 1985.

Mrs Ellen Seager

3 Hereford Court, Hereford Road, Harrogate, North Yorkshire HG1 2PX
tel (01423) 509770

Critical assessment of fiction and non-fiction work with helpful direction, tuition and advice; creative writing tutor; ghost writing; publishing and market information.

SeaStar Publishing

76 Buccleuch Street, Kettering NN16 9EF
tel (01536) 412844
e-mail Terry-Scott@msn.com
Proprietor Terry E. Scott

Compilation; desktop publishing services, Internet research.

Serpentine Editorial

50 Quaker's Hall Lane, Sevenoaks, Kent TN13 3TU
tel/fax (01732) 457360
e-mail molly@perham.freeserve.co.uk
Partners Molly Perham, Julian Rowe

Publishing service for children's books: editing, writing and rewiting, planning and management of complete projects to CRC; DTP on PC or Apple Mac. All subjects, but science a speciality. Founded 1991.

SFEP (Society of Freelance Editors and Proofreaders) – see page 478

Gill Shepherd

87 Elm Park Mansions, Park Walk, London SW10 0AP
tel 020-7352 1770
e-mail rgbshepherd@msn.com

Research, fact checking, rewriting for authors. Specialises in history, politics, biography and genealogy. Established 1985.

I.R. Sinclair

Saltire, Livermere Road, Gt Barton, Bury St Edmunds, Suffolk IP31 2RZ
tel (01284) 788312
e-mail ian_sinclair@lineone.net
web site http://www.webspace.lineone.net/~ian_sinclair

Technical writing (electronics and computing). Typesetting to CRC or Postscript files on CD-Rom, particularly mathematical setting. Founded 1984.

Small Print

The Old School House, 74 High Street, Swavesey, Cambridge CB4 5QU
tel (01954) 231713 *fax* (01954) 232777
e-mail info@smallprt.demon.co.uk
Proprietor Naomi Laredo

Editorial, design, project management, and audio production services, specialising in ELT and foreign language courses for secondary schools and home study; also phrase books, travel guides, general humanities. Translation from/to and editing in many European and Asian languages. Photography and picture research. Founded 1986.

Special Edition Pre-press Services

Partners Romilly Hambling, 17 Almorah Road, London N1 3ER
tel/fax 020-7226 5339 and
Corinne Orde, 2 Caledonian Wharf, London E14 3EW
tel/fax 020-7987 9600

Integrated Mac-based editing and page make-up for publishers of general and STM titles. Linguistics and music a speciality. Design and project management undertaken. Established 1993.

Mrs Gene M. Spencer

63 Castle Street, Melbourne, Derbyshire DE73 1DY
tel (01332) 862133

Editing, copy-editing and proofreading; feature writing; theatrical profiles; book reviews; freelance writing. Founded 1970.

SPREd (Society of Picture Researchers and Editors) – now The Picture Research Association – see page 456

Strand Editorial Services

16 Mitchley View, South Croydon,
Surrey CR2 9HQ
tel/fax 020-8657 1247
Joint Principals Derek and Irene Bradley

Provide a comprehensive service to publishers, editorial departments, and public relations and advertising agencies. Proofreading and copy-editing a speciality. Founded 1974.

Hans Tasiemka Archives

80 Temple Fortune Lane, London NW11 7TU
tel 020-8455 2485 *fax* 020-8455 0231
Proprietor Mrs Edda Tasiemka

Comprehensive newspaper cuttings library from 1850s to the present day on all subjects for writers, publishers, picture researchers, film and TV companies. Founded 1950.

Lyn M. Taylor

(Eve-Line Editorial Proofs)
Mill of Auldallan, Balintore, By Kirriemuir,
Angus DD8 5JS
tel (01575) 560 380 *fax* (01575) 560 780
e-mail LynTaylor@compuserve.com

General comprehensive editorial service for publishers: copy-editing and proofreading in all subjects. Specialises in scientific and medical books, journals and reports. Hard copy or on-screen. For authors: editorial treatment of accepted or unsolicited MSS undertaken.

Tecmedia Ltd

Bruce House, 258 Bromham Road, Biddenham,
Beds. MK40 4AA
tel (01234) 325223 *fax* (01234) 353524
e-mail jojobaxter@compuserve.com
Managing Director J.D. Baxter

Specialists in the design, development and production of training and information packages, newsletters and promotional material. Founded 1972.

Teral Research Services

111 The Avenue, Bournemouth,
Dorset BH9 2UX
tel (01202) 519220
Contact Alan C. Wood
and 45 Forest View Road, Bournemouth BH9 3BH
tel/fax (01202) 516834
Contact Terry C. Treadwell

Research and consultancy on military aviation, army, navy, defence, space, weapons (new and antique), police, intelligence, medals, uniforms and armour. Founded 1980.

3 & 5 Promotion

Crag House, Witherslack, Grange-over-Sands,
Cumbria LA11 6RW
tel (015395) 52286 *fax* (015395) 52013
web site http://www.rdooley.demon.co.uk
e-mail musicbks @rdooley.demon.co.uk
Proprietor Rosemary Dooley

Collaborative publishers' exhibitions: music books. Founded 1985.

Felicity Trotman

Downside, Chicklade, Salisbury,
Wilts. SP3 5SU
tel/fax (01747) 820503
e-mail F.Trotman@btinternet.com

Editing, copy-editing, proofreading, writing, rewriting for publishers only. Specialises in children's books, fiction and non-fiction, all ages. Established 1982.

John Vickers

27 Shorrolds Road, London SW6 7TR
tel 020-7385 5774

Archives of British Theatre photographs by John Vickers, from 1938-1974.

Valerie Vogel Picture Research

141 Chestnut Street, Montclair, NJ 07042, USA
tel 973-746-8560 *fax* 973-746-8471
e-mail vvpics@adsight.com

Freelance picture researcher/photo editor. Diverse experience in wide range of subjects for books, magazines, advertising, corporate and film. Uses traditional and online sources. Established 1980.

Gordon R. Wainwright

22 Hawes Court, Sunderland SR6 8NU
tel/fax 0191-548 9342
e-mail gordon@gordonwainwright.co.uk
web site http://www.gordonwainwright.co.uk

Criticism, advice and revision for authors; information detective; grant writer; authors' publishing consultant. Established 1961.

Caroline White

78 Howard Road, London E17 4SQ
tel/fax 020-8521 5791
e-mail cwhite@bmjgroup.com

Research and writing of features for newspapers, magazines and radio, specialising in health and social issues. Corporate literature and reports. Press and public relations. Written and spoken Italian, Spanish and French. Founded 1985.

Derek Wilde

59 Victoria Road, Woodbridge, Suffolk IP12 1EL
tel/fax (01394) 384557
e-mail jill001@aol.com

Copy-editing, proofreading, indexing, research. Particular expertise in directories and reference books. Special interests: higher education, performing arts, travel and transport. Languages: French and Latin plus some knowledge of German and Italian. Established 1991.

David L. Williams

7 Buckbury Heights, Newport,
Isle of Wight PO30 2LX
tel (01983) 528729 *fax* (01983) 822116

Picture and text research. Specialises in transport, particularly maritime and aviation; military and naval, particularly the World Wars. Also indexing and proofreading. Established 1982.

David Winpenny

33 St Marygate, Ripon, North Yorkshire HG4 1LX
tel (01765) 608320 *fax* (01765) 607641
e-mail david@dwpr.freeserve.co.uk
web site http://www.dwpr.freeserve.co.uk

Writer and editor, including research and writing of features, news stories, brochures, speeches, advertising copy. Special interest in architectural history, the arts, music, landscape, heritage, business and the North. Founded 1991.

Rita Winter Editorial Services

'Kilrubie', Eddleston, Peeblesshire EH45 8QP
tel/fax (01721) 730353
e-mail rita@ednet.co.uk

On-screen editing, copy-editing and proofreading (English and Dutch). Academic and general material, books, dictionaries, company literature. Special interests: art, art history, exhibition catalogues.

Witan Publishing Services

Cherry Tree House, 8 Nelson Crescent,
Cotes Heath, via Stafford ST21 6ST
tel (01782) 791673
Director Jeff Kent

Editing, proofreading, typesetting, publishing advice, design and artwork, printing, marketing, publicity, repping, distribution advice. Established 1980.

The Word Service

Bob Gallagher, 143 Sirdar Road,
London N22 6QS
tel 020-8888 6962

Radio drama script analysis, evaluation and polishing; copy-editing and proofreading; research, specialising in Irish history, literary lives and the history of psychiatry. Founded 1994.

Wordwise

37 Elmthorpe Road, Wolvercote,
Oxford OX2 8PA
tel (01865) 510098 *fax* (01865) 310556
e-mail wordwise@mendes.demon.co.uk
Director Valerie Mendes

Provides a range of publishing services, including creative writing, particularly for children. Founded 1990.

WordWise

66 Russell Road, Lee-on-the-Solent,
Hants. PO13 9HP
tel 023-9235 9960 *fax* 023-9255 4842
e-mail martyn@wordwise.co.uk
web site http://www.wordwise.co.uk
Contact Martyn Yeo

The following services are offered to publishers only: copy-editing, proofreading, indexing, on-screen editing, HTML and SGML mark-up, data entry, database publishing, typesetting, project management. Member of SFEP. Established 1984.

Richard M. Wright

32 Oak Village,
London NW5 4QN
tel 020-7284 4316
e-mail rmwindserv@aol.com

Indexing, copy-editing, specialising in politics, history, business, social sciences. Founded 1977.

Write on...

62 Kiln Lane, Oxford OX3 8EY
tel (01865) 761169 *fax* (01865) 744336
e-mail writeon1989@aol.com
Contact Yvonne Newman

Non-fiction book planning workshops and consultations, including family history and biography. Founded 1989.

The Writers Advice Centre for Children's Books

Palace Wharf, Rainville Road, London W6 9HN
tel/fax 020-8874 7347
e-mail enquiries@writersadvice.co.uk
web site http://www.writersadvice.co.uk
Director Louise Jordan

Editorial and marketing advice to children's writers; courses, including home study, newsletter; mail order books; agency service.Founded 1994.

The Writers' Exchange

14 Old School Mews, Bacup, Lancs. OL13 0QN
tel (01706) 877480
e-mail writers'exchange@j-m-wright.freeserve.co.uk
web site http://www.world-wide-words.co.uk
Secretary Mike Wright

Copywriting, ghostwriting, DTP, design/print and editorial services, including appraisal service for amateur writers preparing to submit material to literary agents/publishers. Offers 'constructive, objective evaluation service, particularly for those who cannot get past the standard rejection slip barrier, or who have had work rejected by publishers and need an impartial view of why it did not sell'; fee £10 per 1000 words. Novels, short stories, film, TV, radio and stage plays. Send sae for details. Founded 1977.

Hans Zell, Publishing Consultant

11 Richmond Road, PO Box 56, Oxford OX1 2SJ
tel (01865) 511428 *fax* (01865) 311534
e-mail hzell@dial.pipex.com
web site http://www.hanszell.co.uk

Consultancies, project evaluations, market assessments, feasibility studies, research and surveys, funding proposals, freelance editorial work, commissioning, journals management, Internet training. Specialises in services to publishers and the book community in Third World countries and provides specific expertise in these areas. Also mailing list services. Founded 1987.

Editorial, literary and production services by specialisation

Addresses for editorial, literary and production services start on page 578.

Complete editorial, literary and book production services

'A Feature Factory' Editorial Services
Academic File
Anchor Editorial Services
The Book Guild
Book Production Consultants
Brittan Design Partnership
Karyn Claridge Book Production
D & N Publishing
Editorial Solutions
Geo Group & Associates
Graham-Cameron Publishing
Oxford Designers & Illustrators
Pages Editorial & Publishing Services
Keith Povey Editorial Services
Anton Rippon Press Services

Advisory and consultancy services, critical assessments, reports

Academic File
Advice and Criticism Service
Amolibros
Angel Books
Arkst Publishing
Authors' Aid
Authors Advisory Service
Authors' Appraisal Service
Bookwatch
Jonathon Clifford
Cornerstones
Ingrid Cranfield
Clarissa Cridland
FJN Associates
Brian J. Ford
Geo Group & Associates
C.N. Gilmore
Heath Associates
Rosemary Horstmann
E.J. Hunter
Indexing Specialists
The Literary Consultancy (TLC)
Duncan McAra
Manuscript Appraisals
Ormrod Research Services
Christopher Pick
Reading and Righting
S. Ribeiro Literary Services
Sandhurst Editorial Consultants
Sandton Literary Agency
Mrs Ellen Seager
Teral Research Services
Felicity Trotman
Gordon R. Wainwright
Witan Publishing Services
The Word Service
Wordwise
Write on ...
The Writers Advice Centre for Children's Books
The Writers' Exchange
Hans Zell, Publishing Consultant

Editing, copy-editing, proofreading

Abbey Writing Services
Alpha Word Power
Amolibros
Arkst Publishing
Authors' Aid
Richard A. Beck
Beswick Writing Services
Black Ace Book Production
Blair Services
The Book Guild
David Bradley Science Writer
Brooke Projects
Mrs D. Buckmaster
John Button – Editorial Services
Combrógos
Ingrid Cranfield
David A. Cross
Meg Davies
Editorial Solutions
Editorial/Visual Research
Dr Martin Edwards
Lewis Esson Publishing
First Edition Translations
FJN Associates
the Freelance Editorial Service
Freelance Services, Joan Shannon
C.N. Gilmore
Guildford Reading Services
John Hall
Bernard Hawton
Heath Associates
E.J. Hunter
Indexing Specialists
Duncan McAra
McText
Manuscript Appraisals
Marlinoak
My Word!
Peter Nickol
Nidaba Publishing Services
Paul H. Niekirk
Northern Writers Advisory Services
Ormrod Research Services
Geoffrey D. Palmer
Phoenix 2
Christopher Pick
Keith Povey Editorial Services
David Price
Victoria Ramsay
Reading and Righting
S. Ribeiro Literary Services
Sandhurst Editorial Consultants
Sandton Literary Agency
SciText
Scriptmate
Serpentine Editorial
Small Print
Mrs Gene M. Spencer
Strand Editorial Services
Lyn M. Taylor
Felicity Trotman
Derek Wilde
David L. Williams
David Winpenny
Rita Winter Editorial Services
Witan Publishing Services
The Word Service
WordWise
Richard M. Wright
The Writers' Exchange
Hans Zell, Publishing Consultant

Design, typing, word processing, DTP, book production

'A Feature Factory' Editorial Services
Alpha Word Power
Arioma Editorial Services
Authors' Aid
Black Ace Book Production
The Book Guild
Book-in-Hand
Vanessa Charles
Editorial Solutions
First Edition Translations
FJN Associates
Christine Foley Secretarial Services
Freelance Services, Joan Shannon
Shelagh Furness
Heath Associates
Hurst Village Publishing
Marlinoak
My Word!
Peter Nickol
Nidaba Publishing Services
Northern Writers Advisory Services
Oriental Languages Bureau
Phoenix 2
SeaStar Publishing
Serpentine Editorial
I.R. Sinclair
Small Print
Special Edition Pre-press Services
Tecmedia
Witan Publishing Services
WordWise
The Writers' Exchange

Research and/or writing, rewriting, picture research

'A Feature Factory' Editorial Services
Abbey Writing Services
Academic File
Arioma Editorial Services
Authors' Research Services
Richard A. Beck
Beswick Writing Services
Blair Services
Bookwatch
David Bradley Science Writer
Brooke Projects
Causeway Resources
Combrógos
Ingrid Cranfield
David A. Cross
Editorial Solutions
Editorial/Visual Research
Dr Martin Edwards
Lewis Esson Publishing
Freelance Services, Joan Shannon
Shelagh Furness
Geo Group & Associates
John Hall
Heath Associates
Antony Hemans
Mark Hempshell
The Information Bureau
Library Research Agency
Dr Kenneth Lysons
Manuscript Appraisals
Marlinoak
Susan Moore Editorial Services
Murder Files
Elizabeth Murray
Paul H. Niekirk
Ormrod Research Services
Phoenix 2
Christopher Pick
Picture Research Agency
David Price
Victoria Ramsay
Repertoire
S. Ribeiro Literary Services
Rich Research
Anton Rippon Press Services
Sandhurst Editorial Consultants
Sandton Literary Agency
Mrs Ellen Seager
SeaStar Publishing
Serpentine Editorial
Gill Shepherd
I.R. Sinclair
Small Print
Mrs Gene M. Spencer
Teral Research Services
Felicity Trotman

Valerie Vogel Picture Research
Gordon R. Wainwright
Caroline White
David L. Williams
David Winpenny
The Word Service
Wordwise
WordWise
The Writers' Exchange
Hans Zell, Publishing Consultant

Indexing

Richard A. Beck
Ingrid Cranfield
Meg Davies
the Freelance Editorial Service
Society of Indexers
Indexing Specialists
Paul Nash
Ormrod Research Services
Geoffrey D. Palmer
Keith Povey Editorial Services
Sandton Literary Agency
David L. Williams
WordWise
Richard M. Wright

Translations

Ingrid Cranfield
First Edition Translations
the Freelance Editorial Service
Oriental Languages Bureau
Small Print

Specialist services

Archives

Frost Historical Newspaper Collection
The Information Bureau
Murder Files
Hans Tasiemka Archives
John Vickers

Cartography

Reginald Piggott

Cassettes, visual aids

Small Print

Contracts and copyright services

Clarissa Cridland
Peter Nickol
Roger Palmer

Freelance agency

etr

Interpreting

First Edition Translations

Legal services

David Wineman, Solicitors
Finers Stephens Innocent

Media and publicity services

Bookwatch
Freelance Market News
3 & 5 Promotion

Multimedia/web site/Internet/database services

AuthorsOnLine
Editorial Solutions
McText
My Word!
Peter Nichol
WordWise
Hans Zell, Publishing Consultant

Indexing

A good index is a joy to the user of a non-fiction book; a bad index will downgrade an otherwise good book. The function of indexes, together with the skills needed to compile them, are examined here.

An index is a detailed key to the contents of a document, in contrast to a contents list, which gives only the titles of the parts into which the document is divided (chapters, for example). Precisely, an index is 'A systematic arrangement of entries designed to enable users to locate information in a document'. The document may be a book, a series of books, an issue of a periodical, a run of several volumes of a periodical, an audiotape, a map, a film, a picture, a computer disk, an object, or any other information source in print or non-print form.

The objective of an index is to guide enquirers to information on given subjects in a document by providing the terms of their choice (single words, phrases, abbreviations, acronyms, dates, names, and so on) in an appropriately organised list which refers them to specific locations using page, column, section, frame, figure, table, paragraph, line or other appropriate numbers.

An index differs from a catalogue, which is a record of the documents held in a particular collection, such as a library; though a catalogue may require an index, for example to guide searchers from subject words to class numbers.

A document may have separate indexes for different classes of heading, so that personal names are distinguished from subjects, for example, or a single index in which all classes of heading are interfiled.

The Society of Indexers

The Society of Indexers is a non-profit organisation founded in 1957 and is the only autonomous professional body for indexers in the UK. It is affiliated with the American Society of Indexers, the Australian Society of Indexers, the Indexing and Abstracting Society of Canada, and the Association of South African Indexers and Bibliographers, and has close ties with the Library Association and the Society of Freelance Editors and Proofreaders.

The main objectives of the Society are to promote all types of indexing standards and techniques and the role of indexers in the organisation of knowledge; to provide, promote and recognise facilities for both the initial and the further training of indexers; to establish criteria for assessing indexing standards; and to conduct research and publish guidance, ideas and information about indexing. It seeks to establish good relationships between indexers, librarians, publishers and authors both to advance good indexing and to improve the role and wellbeing of indexers.

Services to indexers

The Society publishes a learned journal *The Indexer*, a newsletter and *Occasional Papers in Indexing*. Meetings are held regularly on a wide range of subjects while local and special interest groups provide the chance for members to meet to discuss common interests. A weekend conference is held every year. All levels of training are supported by regular workshops held at venues throughout the country.

Professional competence is recognised in two stages by the Society. Accredited Indexers who have completed the open-learning course qualification (see below) have shown theoretical competence in indexing while Registered Indexers have proved their experience and competence in practical indexing through an assessment procedure and admission to the Register of Indexers. The services of Registered Indexers are actively promoted by the Society while all trained and experienced members have the opportunity of an annual entry in *Indexers Available*, a directory published by the Society and distributed without charge to over 1000 publishers to help them find an indexer.

The Society sets annually a minimum recommended indexing rate (£14.50 per hour in 2000) and provides advice on the business side of indexing to its members.

Services to publishers and authors

Anyone who commissions indexes needs to be certain of engaging a professional indexer working to the highest standards and able to meet deadlines.

Indexers Available lists only members of the Society and gives basic contact details, subject specialisms and indexing experience. Those accepted for listing need to fall into the following categories:

- Registered Indexers who have had their competence in practical indexing recognised by the Society;
- Accredited Indexers who have passed the Society's tests of technical competence; and
- others who have successfully completed other recognised training courses.

Advice on the selection of indexers is available from the Registrar, who may also be able to suggest names of professionals able to undertake related tasks such as thesaurus construction, terminology control or database indexing. The Registrar will also advise on relations with indexers.

The Society co-operates with the Library Association in the award of the Wheatley Medal for an outstanding index.

Training in indexing

The Society's course is based on the principle of open learning with Units, tutorial support and formal tests all available separately so that individuals can learn in their own way and at their own pace. The Units cover five core subjects and contain practical exercises and self-administered tests. Members of the Society receive a substantial discount on the cost although anyone can purchase the Units. Only members of the Society can apply for the formal tests or for tutorial support.

Further information

Society of Indexers, Globe Centre,
Penistone Road, Sheffield S6 3AE
tel 0114-281 3060 *fax* 0114-281 3061
e-mail admin@socind.demon.co.uk
web site http://www.socind.demon.co.uk
Administrator Wendy Burrow

Write to the Secretary for further information. Enquiries from publishers and authors seeking to commission an indexer should be made to the Registrar.

Further reading

British Standards Institution, *British Standard recommendations for examining documents, determining their subjects and selecting indexing terms*, BSI, 1984 (BS6529:1984)

Information and documentation – guidelines for the content, organization and presentation of indexes (ISO 999:1996)

Correcting proofs

The following notes and table are extracted from BS 5261: Part 2: 1976 (1995) and are reproduced by permission of the British Standards Institution. Copies of the complete Standard are available from the British Standards Institution, 2 Park Street, London W1A 2BS.

The marks to be used for marking up copy for composition and for the correction of printers' proofs shall be as shown in table 1.

The marks in table 1 are classified in three groups as follows.

(a) Group A: general.
(b) Group B: deletion, insertion and substitution.
(c) Group C: positioning and spacing.

Each item in table 1 is given a simple alpha-numeric serial number denoting the classification group to which it belongs and its position within the group.

The marks have been drawn keeping the shapes as simple as possible and using sizes which relate to normal practice. The shapes of the marks should be followed exactly by all who make use of them.

For each marking-up or proof correction instruction a distinct mark is to be made:

(a) in the text: to indicate the exact place to which the instruction refers;
(b) in the margin: to signify or amplify the meaning of the instruction.

It should be noted that some instructions have a combined textual and marginal mark.

Where a number of instructions occur in one line, the marginal marks are to be divided between the left and right margins where possible, the order being from left to right in both margins.

Specification details, comments and instructions may be written on the copy or proof to complement the textual and marginal marks. Such written matter is to be clearly distinguishable from the copy and from any corrections made to the proof. Normally this is done by encircling the matter and/or by the appropriate use of colour (see below).

Proof corrections shall be made in coloured ink thus:

(a) printer's literal errors marked by the printer for correction: green;
(b) printer's literal errors marked by the customer and his agents for correction: red;
(c) alterations and instructions made by the customer and his agents: black or dark blue.

Table 1. Classified list of marks

NOTE. The letters M and P in the notes column indicate marks for marking-up copy and for correcting proofs respectively.

Group A General

Number	Instruction	Textual mark	Marginal mark	Notes
A1	Correction is concluded	None	/	P Make after each correction
A2	Leave unchanged	------ under characters to remain	(✓)	M P
A3	Remove extraneous marks	Encircle marks to be removed	X	P e.g. film or paper edges visible between lines on bromide or diazo proofs
A3.1	Push down risen spacing material	Encircle blemish	⊥	P
A4	Refer to appropriate authority anything of doubtful accuracy	Encircle word(s) affected	(?)	P

Group B Deletion, insertion and substitution

Number	Instruction	Textual mark	Marginal mark	Notes
B1	Insert in text the matter indicated in the margin	⅄	New matter followed by ⅄	M P Indentical to B2
B2	Insert additional matter identified by a letter in a diamond	⅄	⅄ Followed by for example ◇A	M P The relevant section of the copy should be supplied with the corresponding letter marked on it in a diamond e.g. ◇A
B3	Delete	/ through character(s) or ├──┤ through words to be deleted	∂	M P
B4	Delete and close up	/ through character or ├──┤ through characters e.g. charaacter charaacter	∂	M P

Table 1 *(continued)*

Number	Instruction	Textual mark	Marginal mark	Notes
B5	Substitute character or substitute part of one or more word(s)	/ through character or ├──┤ through word(s)	New character or new word(s)	M P
B6	Wrong fount. Replace by character(s) of correct fount	Encircle character(s) to be changed	⊗	P
B6.1	Change damaged character(s)	Encircle character(s) to be changed	×	P This mark is identical to A3
B7	Set in or change to italic	─── under character(s) to be set or changed	⊔⊔	M P Where space does not permit textual marks encircle the affected area instead
B8	Set in or change to capital letters	≡ under character(s) to be set or changed	≡	
B9	Set in or change to small capital letters	═ under character(s) to be set or changed	═	
B9.1	Set in or change to capital letters for initial letters and small capital letters for the rest of the words	≡ under initial letters and ═ under rest of the word(s)	≡	
B10	Set in or change to bold type	∿∿∿ under character(s) to be set or changed	∿	
B11	Set in or change to bold italic type	∿∿∿ (with line above) under character(s) to be set or changed	⊔⊔ over ∿	
B12	Change capital letters to lower case letters	Encircle character(s) to be changed	≢	P For use when B5 is inappropriate

Table 1 *(continued)*

Number	Instruction	Textual mark	Marginal mark	Notes
B12.1	Change small capital letters to lower case letters	Encircle character(s) to be changed		P For use when B5 is inappropriate
B13	Change italic to upright type	Encircle character(s) to be changed		P
B14	Invert type	Encircle character to be inverted		P
B15	Substitute or insert character in 'superior' position	/ through character or where required	under character e.g. 2	P
B16	Substitute or insert character in 'inferior' position	/ through character or where required	over character e.g. 2	P
B17	Substitute ligature e.g. ﬃ for separate letters	through characters affected	e.g. ﬃ	P
B17.1	Substitute separate letters for ligature		Write out separate letters	P
B18	Substitute or insert full stop or decimal point	/ through character or where required		M P
B18.1	Substitute or insert colon	/ through character or where required		M P
B18.2	Substitute or insert semi-colon	/ through character or where required	;	M P

Table 1 *(continued)*

Number	Instruction	Textual mark	Marginal mark	Notes
B18.3	Substitute or insert comma	/ through character or ⋏ where required	,	M P
B18.4	Substitute or insert apostrophe	/ through character or ⋏ where required	’	M P
B18.5	Substitute or insert single quotation marks	/ through character or ⋏ where required	‘ and/or ’	M P
B18.6	Substitute or insert double quotation marks	/ through character or ⋏ where required	“ and/or ”	M P
B19	Substitute or insert ellipsis	/ through character or ⋏ where required	• • •	M P
B20	Substitute or insert leader dots	/ through character or ⋏ where required	(• • •)	M P Give the measure of the leader when necessary
B21	Substitute or insert hyphen	/ through character or ⋏ where required	|–|	M P
B22	Substitute or insert rule	/ through character ⋏ where required	|—|	M P Give the size of the rule in the marginal mark e.g. |1 em| |4 mm|

Table 1 *(continued)*

Number	Instruction	Textual mark	Marginal mark	Notes
B23	Substitute or insert oblique	/ through character or ⅄ where required	ⓘ/	M P
Group C	**Positioning and spacing**			
C1	Start new paragraph			M P
C2	Run on (no new paragraph)			M P
C3	Transpose characters or words	between characters or words, numbered when necessary		M P
C4	Transpose a number of characters or words	3 2 1 | | |	123	M P To be used when the sequence cannot be clearly indicated by the use of C3. The vertical strokes are made through the characters or words to be transposed and numbered in the correct sequence
C5	Transpose lines			M P
C6	Transpose a number of lines	——— 3 ——— 2 ——— 1		P To be used when the sequence cannot be clearly indicated by C5. Rules extend from the margin into the text with each line to be transposed numbered in the correct sequence
C7	Centre	[enclosing matter to be centred]	[ ]	M P
C8	Indent			P Give the amount of the indent in the marginal mark

Table 1 *(continued)*

Number	Instruction	Textual mark	Marginal mark	Notes
C9	Cancel indent	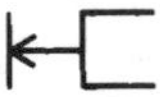		P
C10	Set line justified to specified measure	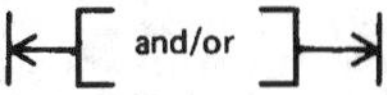 and/or		P Give the exact dimensions when necessary
C11	Set column justified to specified measure			M P Give the exact dimensions when necessary
C12	Move matter specified distance to the right	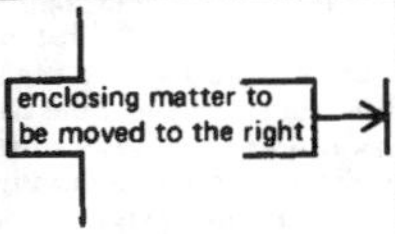 enclosing matter to be moved to the right		P Give the exact dimensions when necessary
C13	Move matter specified distance to the left	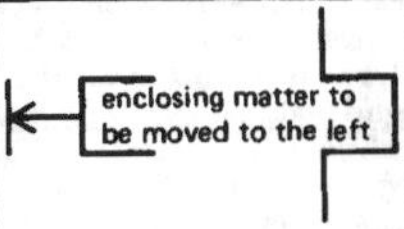 enclosing matter to be moved to the left		P Give the exact dimensions when necessary
C14	Take over character(s), word(s) or line to next line, column or page			P The textual mark surrounds the matter to be taken over and extends into the margin
C15	Take back character(s), word(s), or line to previous line, column or page			P The textual mark surrounds the matter to be taken back and extends into the margin
C16	Raise matter	 over matter to be raised under matter to be raised		P Give the exact dimensions when necessary. (Use C28 for insertion of space between lines or paragraphs in text)
C17	Lower matter	over matter to be lowered  under matter to be lowered		P Give the exact dimensions when necessary. (Use C29 for reduction of space between lines or paragraphs in text)
C18	Move matter to position indicated	Enclose matter to be moved and indicate new position		P Give the exact dimensions when necessary

Marked galley proof of text

At the sign of the red pale

The Life and Work of William Caxton, by H W Larken

[An Extract]

Few people, even in the field of printing, have any clear conception of what William Caxton did or, indeed, of what he was. Much of this lack of knowledge is due to the absence of information that can be counted as factual and the consequent tendency to vague generalsation.

Though it is well known that Caxton was born in the county of Kent, there is no information as to the precise place. In his prologue to the *History of Troy*, William Caxton wrote for in France I was never and was born and learned my English in Kent in the Weald where I doubt not is spoken as broad and rudeEnglish as in any place of England.[1] During the fifteenth century there were a great number of Flemish cloth weavers in Kent; most of them had come to Engld at the instigation of Edward III with the object of teaching their craft to the English. So successful was this venture thar the English cloth tradeflourished and the agents who sold the cloth (the mercers) became very wealthy people. There have bi There have been many speculations concerning the origin of the Caxton family and much research has been carried out. It is assumed often that Caxton's family must have bee connected with the wool trade in order to have secured his apprenticeship to an influential merchant.

W. Blyth Crotch (Prologues and Epilogues of William Caxton) suggests that the origin of the name Caxton (of which there are several variations in spelling) may be traced to Cambridgeshire but notes that many writers have suggested that Caxton was connected with a family at Hadlow or alternatively a family in Canterbury.

Of the Canterbury connection a William Caxton became freeman of the City in 1431 and William Pratt, a mercer who was the printer's friend, was born there. H. R. Plomer suggests that Pratt and Caxton might possibly have been schoolboys together, perhaps at the school St. Alphege. In this parish there lived a John Caxton who used as his mark three cakes over a barrel (or tun) and who is mentioned in an inscription on a monument in the church of St. Alphege.

In 1941, Alan Keen (an authority on manuscripts) secured some documents concerning Caxton; these are now in the BRITISH MUSEUM. Discovered in the library of Earl Winterton at Shillinglee Park by Richard Holworthy, the documents cover the period 1420 to 1467. One of Winterton's ancestors purchased the manor of West Wratting from a family named Caxton, the property being situated in the Weald of Kent.

There is also record of a property mentioning Philip Caxton and his wife Dennis who had two sones, Philip (born in 1413) and William

Particularly interesting in these documents is one recording that Philip Caxton junior sold the manor of Little Wratting to John Christemasse of London in 1436 the deed having been witnessed by two aldermen, one of whom was Robert Large, the printer's employer. Further, in 1439 the other son, William Caxton, con Wratting to John Christemasse, and an indenture of 1457 concerning this property mentions one William Caxton veyed his rights in the manor Bluntes Hall at Little alias Causton. It is an interesting coincidence to note that the lord of the manor of Little Wratting was the father of Margaret, Duchess of Burgundy.

In 1420, a Thomas Caxton of Tenterden witnessed the will of a fellow townsman; he owned property in Kent and appears to have been a person of some importance.

[1] See 'William Caxton'.

(A) *attached to Christchurch Monastery in the parish of*

Revised galley proof of text incorporating corrections

AT THE SIGN OF THE RED PALE

The Life and Work of William Caxton, *by H W Larken*

An Extract

FEW PEOPLE, even in the field of printing, have any clear conception of what William Caxton did or, indeed, of what he was. Much of this lack of knowledge is due to the absence of information that can be counted as factual and the consequent tendency to vague generalisation.

Though it is well known that Caxton was born in the county of Kent, there is no information as to the precise place. In his prologue to the *History of Troy*, William Caxton wrote '. . . for in France I was never and was born and learned my English in Kent in the Weald where I doubt not is spoken as broad and rude English as in any place of England.'

During the fifteenth century there were a great number of Flemish cloth weavers in Kent; most of them had come to England at the instigation of Edward III with the object of teaching their craft to the English. So successful was this venture that the English cloth trade flourished and the agents who sold the cloth (the mercers) became very wealthy people.

There have been many speculations concerning the origin of the Caxton family and much research has been carried out. It is often assumed that Caxton's family must have been connected with the wool trade in order to have secured his apprenticeship to an influential merchant.

W. Blyth Crotch (*Prologues and Epilogues of William Caxton*) suggests that the origin of the name Caxton (of which there are several variations in spelling) may be traced to Cambridgeshire but notes that many writers have suggested that Caxton was connected with a family at Hadlow or alternatively a family in Canterbury.

Of the Canterbury connection: a William Caxton became freeman of the City in 1431 and William Pratt, a mercer who was the printer's friend, was born there. H. R. Plomer[1] suggests that Pratt and Caxton might possibly have been schoolboys together, perhaps at the school attached to Christchurch Monastery in the parish of St. Alphege. In this parish there lived a John Caxton who used as his mark three cakes over a barrel (or tun) and who is mentioned in an inscription on a monument in the church of St. Alphege.

In 1941, Alan Keen (an authority on manuscripts) secured some documents concerning Caxton; these are now in the British Museum. Discovered in the library of Earl Winterton at Shillinglee Park by Richard Holworthy, the documents cover the period 1420 to 1467. One of Winterton's ancestors purchased the manor of West Wratting from a family named Caxton, the property being situated in the Weald of Kent. There is also record of a property mentioning Philip Caxton and his wife Dennis who had two sons, Philip (born in 1413) and William.

Particularly interesting in these documents is one recording that Philip Caxton junior sold the manor of Little Wratting to John Christemasse of London in 1436—the deed having been witnessed by two aldermen, one of whom was Robert Large, the printer's employer. Further, in 1439, the other son, William Caxton, conveyed his rights in the manor Bluntes Hall at Little Wratting to John Christemasse, and an indenture of 1457 concerning this property mentions one William Caxton alias Causton. It is an interesting coincidence to note that the lord of the manor of Little Wratting was the father of Margaret, Duchess of Burgundy.

In 1420, a Thomas Caxton of Tenterden witnessed the will of a fellow townsman; he owned property in Kent and appears to have been a person of some importance.

[1] See 'William Caxton'.

Table 1 ***(continued)***

Number	Instruction	Textual mark	Marginal mark	Notes
C19	Correct vertical alignment	‖	‖	P
C20	Correct horizontal alignment	Single line above and below misaligned matter e.g. misaligned	═	P The marginal mark is placed level with the head and foot of the relevant line
C21	Close up. Delete space between characters or words	linking ⁀‿ characters	⁀‿	M P
C22	Insert space between characters	| between characters affected	Y	M P Give the size of the space to be inserted when necessary
C23	Insert space between words	Y between words affected	Y	M P Give the size of the space to be inserted when necessary
C24	Reduce space between characters	| between characters affected	↑	M P Give the amount by which the space is to be reduced when necessary
C25	Reduce space between words	↑ between words affected	↑	M P Give amount by which the space is to be reduced when necessary
C26	Make space appear equal between characters or words	| between characters or words affected	X	M P
C27	Close up to normal interline spacing	(each side of column linking lines)		M P The textual marks extend into the margin

Table 1 *(continued)*

Number	Instruction	Textual mark	Marginal mark	Notes
C28	Insert space between lines or paragraphs		or	M P The marginal mark extends between the lines of text. Give the size of the space to be inserted when necessary
C29	Reduce space between lines or paragraphs		or	M P The marginal mark extends between the lines of text. Give the amount by which the space is to be reduced when necessary

Government offices and public services

Enquiries to any of the following bodies should be sent to the Public Relations Officer, accompanied by a sae. The names and addresses of many other public bodies can be found in Whitaker's Almanack.

Advertising Standards Authority
2 Torrington Place, London WC1E 7HW
tel 020-7580 5555 *fax* 020-7631 3051
web site http://www.asa.org.uk

Agriculture, Fisheries and Food, Ministry of
3-8 Whitehall Place, London SW1A 2HH
Helpline (0645) 335577
tel 020-7270 8000 *fax* 020-7270 8419
web site http://www.maff.gov.uk

Apsley House, The Wellington Museum
149 Piccadilly, Hyde Park Corner,
London W1V 9FA
tel 020-7499 5676 *fax* 020-7493 6576
web site http://www.vam.ac.uk/apsley/welcome.html
Open Tues-Sun, 11.00am-17.00pm.

Architecture and the Built Environment, Commission for
7 St James's Square, London SW1Y 4JU
tel 020-7839 6537 *fax* 020-7839 8475
e-mail enquiries@cabe.org.uk
web site http://www.cabe.org.uk

Arts Council of England
14 Great Peter Street, London SW1P 3NQ
tel 020-7333 0100
Library/enquiry line 020-7973 6517
fax 020-7973 6590
e-mail enquiries@artscouncil.org.uk
web site http://www.artscouncil.org.uk
For full details, see page 461.

Arts Council of Northern Ireland
MacNeice House, 77 Malone Road,
Belfast BT9 6AQ
tel 028-9038 5200 *fax* 028-9066 1715

Arts Council of Wales
9 Museum Place, Cardiff CF10 3NX
tel 029-2037 6500 *fax* 029-2022 1447
e-mail information@ccc-acw.org.uk
web site http://www.ccc-acw.org.uk
North Wales Regional Office
36 Prince's Drive, Colwyn Bay LL29 8LA
tel (01492) 533440 *fax* (01492) 533677
West Wales Regional Office
6 Gardd Llydaw, Jackson's Lane,
Carmarthen SA31 1QD
tel (01267) 234248 *fax* (01267) 233084

Australian High Commission
Australia House, Strand, London WC2B 4LA
tel 020-7379 4334 *fax* 020-7240 5333
web site http://www.australia.org.uk

Austrian Embassy
18 Belgrave Mews West, London SW1X 8HU
tel 020-7235 3731 *fax* 020-7344 0292
e-mail embassy@austria.org.uk

Bahamas High Commission
Bahamas House, 10 Chesterfield Street, London W1X 8AH
tel 020-7408 4488 *fax* 020-7499 9937
e-mail bahamas.hicom.lon@cableinet.co.uk

Bangladesh High Commission
28 Queen's Gate, London SW7 5JA
tel 020-7584 0081-4 *fax* 020-7225 2130
e-mail bdesh-Lon@dial.pipex.com

The Bank of England
Threadneedle Street, London EC2R 8AH
tel 020-7601 4444 *fax* 020-7601 4771
web site http://www.bankofengland.co.uk

Barbados High Commission
1 Great Russell Street, London WC1B 3JY
tel 020-7631 4975 *fax* 020-7323 6872
e-mail barcomuk@dial.pipex.com

Belgian Embassy
103 Eaton Square, London SW1W 9AB
tel 020-7470 3700 *fax* 020-7259 6213
e-mail info@belgium-embassy.co.uk
web site http://www.belgium-embassy.co.uk

Benefits Agency, Pensions and Overseas Benefits Directorate (POD) – see Social Security, Department of

Bodleian Library
Oxford OX1 3BG
tel (01865) 277000 *fax* (01865) 277182
e-mail enquiries@bodley.ox.ac.uk
web site http://www.bodley.ox.ac.uk

Bosnia-Herzegovina, Embassy of
320 Regent Street, London W1R 5AB
tel 020-7255 3758 *fax* 020-7255 3760

Botswana High Commission
6 Stratford Place, London W1N 9AE
tel 020-7499 0031

British Broadcasting Corporation
Broadcasting House, London W1A 1AA
tel 020-7580 4468
web site http://www.bbc.co.uk

British Coal – see The Coal Authority

The British Council
10 Spring Gardens, London SW1A 2BN
tel 020-7930 8466 *fax* 020-7839 6347

British Film Commission
10 Little Portland Street, London W1N 5DF
tel 020-7224 5000 *fax* 020-7224 1013
e-mail info@bfc.co.uk
web site http://www.bfc.co.uk

British Film Institute
21 Stephen Street, London W1P 2LN
tel 020-7255 1444 *fax* 020-7436 0439
web site http://www.bfi.org.uk

The British Library
96 Euston Road, London NW1 2DB
tel 020-7412 7111 *fax* 020-7412 7168

British Library Document Supply Centre
Boston Spa, Wetherby, West Yorkshire LS23 7BQ
tel (01937) 546060 *fax* (01937) 546333
e-mail dsc-customer-services@bl.uk
web site http://www.bl.uk

Offers remote supply of photocopies and loans either direct to registered customers or through a national network of local and academic libraries. Free access to material (preferably with advance notice), including recordings from the National Sound Archive, in the Reading Room. Many catalogues are available on the web site, which also offers a document ordering link for registered and non-registered customers.

British Library Newspaper Library
Colindale Avenue, London NW9 5HE
tel 020-7412 7353 *fax* 020-7412 7379
e-mail newspaper@bl.uk
web site http://www.bl.uk/collections/newspaper/

British Museum
Great Russell Street, London WC1B 3DG
tel 020-7636 1555 *fax* 020-7323 8118
e-mail info@british-museum.ac.uk
web site http://www.british-museum.ac.uk

British Railways Board
Whittles House, 14 Pentonville Road, London N1 9HF
tel 020-7904 5000 *fax* 020-7904 5040
e-mail ji79@dial.pipex.com
web site http://www.brb.gov.uk

British Standards Institution
Technical Information Group, 389 Chiswick High Road, London W4 4AL
tel 020-8996 7111 *fax* 020-8996 7048
e-mail info@bsi.org.uk
web site http://www.bsi.org.uk/

British Tourist Authority
Thames Tower, Black's Road, London W6 9EL
tel 020-8846 9000 *fax* 020-8563 0302
web sites http://www.visitbritain.com
www.britishtouristauthority.org

Broadcasting Standards Commission
7 The Sanctuary, London SW1P 3JS
tel 020-7233 0544 *fax* 020-7222 3172
web site http://www.bsc.org.uk

Bulgaria, Embassy of the Republic of
186-188 Queen's Gate, London SW7 5HL
tel 020-7584 9400/9433, 020-7581 3144 (5 lines)
fax 020-7584 4948
e-mail bgembasy@globalnet.co.uk

The Cabinet Office
70 Whitehall, London SW1A 2AS
tel 020-7270 0070
Horse Guards Road, London SW1P 3AL
tel 020-7270 6430

Cadw: Welsh Historic Monuments
Crown Building, Cathays Park,
Cardiff CF10 3NQ
tel 029-2050 0200 *fax* 029-2082 6375
e-mail cadw@wales.gsi.gov.uk
web site http://www.cadw.wales.gov.uk

Canadian High Commission
Cultural Affairs Section, Canada House,
Trafalgar Square, London SW1Y 5BJ
tel 020-7258 6412 *fax* 020-7258 6434
Contact Literature Officer

The Caribbean Council for Europe
Nelson House, 8-9 Northumberland Street,
London WC2N 5RA
tel 020-7976 1493 *fax* 020-7976 1541
e-mail caribbean@compuserve.com

Central Office of Information
Hercules Road, London SE1 7DU
tel 020-7928 2345

In the UK conducts press, TV, radio and poster advertising; produces booklets, leaflets, films, radio and TV material, exhibitions and other visual material on behalf of other government organisations.

Central Statistical Office – now part of National Statistics, Office for

Centre for Information on Language Teaching and Research (CILT)
20 Bedfordbury, London WC2N 4LB
tel 020-7379 5101 *fax* 020-7379 5082
e-mail library@cilt.org.uk
web site http://www.cilt.org.uk

Supports the work of all professionals concerned with modern language teaching and learning throughout the UK, across every sector and stage of education. Offers a full conference programme, plus INSET for teachers, a complete range of publications and the CILT Resources Library with extensive IT and AV facilities. CILT also provides a comprehensive information service and knowledge of research and developmental activity.

Charity Commission
Head Office Harmsworth House, 13-15 Bouverie Street, London EC4Y 8DP
tel (0870) 3330123 *fax* 020-7674 2300
2nd Floor, 20 King's Parade, Queen's Dock,
Liverpool L3 4DQ
tel (0870) 3330123 *fax* 0151-703 1555
Woodfield House, Tangier, Taunton,
Somerset TA1 4B1
tel (0870) 3330123 *fax* (01823) 345003

The Coal Authority
200 Lichfield Lane, Mansfield, Notts. NG18 4RG
tel (01623) 427162 *fax* (01623) 622072
web site http://www.coal.gov.uk

College of Arms (or Heralds' College)
Queen Victoria Street, London EC4V 4BT
tel 020-7248 2762 *fax* 020-7248 6448
e-mail enquiries@college-of-arms.gov.uk
web site http://www.college-of-arms.gov.uk

Committee on Standards in Public Life
Horse Guards Road, London SW1P 3AL
tel 020-7270 5875 *fax* 020-7270 5874

Commonwealth Institute
Commonwealth Resource Centre, Kensington
High Street, London W8 6NQ
tel 020-7603 4535 *fax* 020-7602 7374
e-mail info@commonwealth.org.uk
web site http://www.commonwealth.org.uk
For full details, see page 472.

Competition Commission
(formerly Monopolies and Mergers Commission)
New Court, 48 Carey Street, London WC2A 2JT
tel 020-7271 0243 *fax* 020-7271 0367
e-mail info@competition-commission.org.uk
web site http://www.competition-commission.org.uk

Contributions Agency, International Services (InS) – see Inland Revenue, Board of

Copyright Directorate – see under Patent Office

Copyright Tribunal
Room 1/8, Harmsworth House,
13-15 Bouverie Street, London EC4Y 8DP
tel 020-7596 6510 *fax* 020-7596 6526
textphone (0645) 222250
e-mail copyright.tribunal@patent.gov.uk
web site http://www.patent.gov.uk

Countryside Agency
John Dower House, Crescent Place, Cheltenham, Glos. GL50 3RA
tel (01242) 521381 *fax* (01242) 584270
web site http://www.countryside.gov.uk

Court of the Lord Lyon
HM New Register House, Edinburgh EH1 3YT
tel 0131-556 7255 *fax* 0131-557 2148

Crafts Council
44A Pentonville Road, London N1 9BY
tel 020-7278 7700 *fax* 020-7837 6891
e-mail reference@craftscouncil.org.uk
web site http://www.craftscouncil.org.uk
Exhibition gallery, picture library, reference library, reference service, shop, education workshop, café.

Croatia, Embassy of the Republic of
21 Conway Street, London W1P 5HL
tel 020-7387 1790 *fax* 020-7387 3289

Culture, Media and Sport, Department for
2-4 Cockspur Street, London SW1Y 5DH
tel 020-7211 6000
Responsible for government policy relating to the arts, broadcasting, the press, museums and galleries, libraries, sport and recreation, historic buildings and ancient monuments, tourism and the music industry. It funds the Arts Councils and other arts bodies, is responsible for policy on the National Lottery and the Millenium, and sponsors the Millennium Commission. Established in July 1977 from the former Department of National Heritage.

Cyprus High Commission
93 Park Street, London W1Y 4ET
tel 020-7499 8272 *fax* 020-7491 0691
e-mail presscounsellor@chclondon.com
web site http://www.pio.gov.cy

Czech Republic, Embassy of the
26 Kensington Palace Gardens, London W8 4QY
tel 020-7243 1115 *fax* 020-7727 9654
e-mail london@embassy.mzv.cz

Royal Danish Embassy
55 Sloane Street, London SW1X 9SR
tel 020-7333 0200 *fax* 020-7333 0270
e-mail dkembassy@compuserve.com
web site http://www.denmark.org.uk

Data Protection Commissioner, Office of the
Wycliffe House, Water Lane, Wilmslow, Cheshire SK9 5AF
tel (01625) 545745(enquiries) (01625) 545700 (switchboard) *fax* (01625) 524510
e-mail mail@dataprotection.gov.uk
web site http://www.dataprotection.gov.uk

Defence, Ministry of
Main Building, Whitehall, London SW1A 2HB
tel 020-7218 9000
web site http://www.mod.uk/

Design Council
34 Bow Street, London WC2E 7DL
tel 020-7420 5200 *fax* 020-7420 5300
web site http://www.design-council.org.uk

DFID: Department for International Development
94 Victoria Street, London SW1E 5JL
tel 020-7917 7000
web site http://www.dfid.gov.uk
Abercrombie House, Eaglesham Road, East Kilbride, Glasgow G75 8EA
tel (01355) 844000
Public Enquiry Point tel (0845) 3004100 (local rate)
tel (01355) 843132 (for enquiries from overseas)
e-mail enquiry@dfid.gov.uk

DTI: Department of Trade and Industry
1 Victoria Street,
London SW1H 0ET
tel 020-7215 5000 (general enquiries)
fax 020-7222 0612
minicom/textphone 020-7215 6740
web site http://www.dti.gov.uk

Economic and Social Research Council
Polaris House, North Star Avenue, Swindon, Wilts. SN2 1UJ
tel (01793) 413000 *fax* (01793) 413130
web site www.esrc.ac.uk

Education and Employment, Department for
Sanctuary Buildings, Great Smith Street, London SW1P 3BT
tel (0870) 0012345 (switchboard) 020-7925 5555 (public enquiries)

Electricity & Gas Regulation Northern Ireland, Office of (OFREG)
Brookmount Buildings, 42 Fountain Street, Belfast BT1 5EE
tel 028-9031 1575 *fax* 028-9031 1740
e-mail ofreg@nics.gov.uk
web site http://ofreg.nics.gov.uk/

Electricity Regulation, Office of (OFFER) – see Gas and Electricity Markets, Office of (OFGEM)

Engineering and Physical Sciences Research Council
Polaris House, North Star Avenue, Swindon, Wilts. SN2 1ET

tel (01793) 444000 *fax* (01793) 444010
e-mail infoline@epsrc.ac.uk
web site http://www.epsrc.ac.uk

English Heritage
23 Savile Row, London W1X 1AB
tel 020-7973 3000 *fax* 020-7973 3001
web site http://www.english-heritage.org.uk

English Regional Arts Boards
5 City Road, Winchester, Hants SO23 8SD
tel (01962) 851063 *fax* (01962) 842033
e-mail info@erab.org.uk
web site http://www.arts.co.uk
Representative body for the 10 Regional Arts Boards in England; see page 492.

English Tourism Council
Thames Tower, Black's Road, London W6 9EL
tel 020-8563 3000 *fax* 020-8563 0302
web site http://www.englishtourism.co.uk

The Environment Agency
Head Office Rio House, Waterside Drive, Aztec West, Almondsbury, Bristol BS12 4UD
tel (01454) 624400 *fax* (01454) 624409
Carries out work formerly undertaken by the National Rivers Authority, HM Inspectorate of Pollution, the waste regulation authorities and some technical units of the Dept of the Environment.

Environment, Transport and the Regions, Department of
Eland House, Bressenden Place,
London SW1E 5DU
tel 020-7890 3000
76 Marsham Street, London SW1P 4DR
tel 020-7271 4800

Equal Opportunities Commission
Overseas House, Quay Street, Manchester M3 3HN
tel 0161-833 9244 *fax* 0161-835 1657
e-mail info@eoc.org.uk
web site http://www.eoc.org.uk/

The European Commission
8 Storey's Gate, London SW1P 3AT
tel 020-7973 1992 *fax* 020-7973 1900
e-mail press@cec.org.uk
web site http://www.cec.org.uk

European Parliament
UK Office 2 Queen Anne's Gate,
London SW1H 9AA
tel 020-7227 4300 *fax* 020-7227 4302
library fax 020-7227 4301
web site http://www.europarl.org.uk

Fair Trading, Office of
Fleetbank House, 2-6 Salisbury Square,
London EC4Y 8SX
tel 020-7211 8000 *fax* 020-7211 8800
e-mail enquiries@oft.gov.uk
web site http://www.oft.gov.uk

Film Classification, British Board of
3 Soho Square, London W1V 6HD
tel 020-7439 7961 *fax* 020-7287 0141
e-mail webmaster@bbfc.co.uk
web site http://www.bbfc.co.uk
Director Robin Duval

Finland, Embassy of
38 Chesham Place, London SW1W 8HW
tel 020-7838 6200 *fax* 020-7235 3860 (general)
020-7259 5602 (press and information)
web site http://www.finemb.org.uk

Foreign and Commonwealth Office
King Charles Street, London SW1A 2AH
tel 020-7270 3000
web site http://www.fco.gov.uk

Forestry Commission
231 Corstorphine Road, Edinburgh EH12 7AT
tel 0131-334 0303 *fax* 0131-334 4473
e-mail info@forestry.gov.uk
web site http://www.forestry.gov.uk

French Embassy
58 Knightsbridge, London SW1X 7JT
tel 020-7201 1000
web site http://www.ambafrance.org.uk
Cultural Department 23 Cromwell Road,
London SW7 2EL
tel 020-7838 2055

Gambia High Commission
57 Kensington Court, London W8 5DG
tel 020-7937 6316/7/8 *fax* 020-7937 9095

Gas and Electricity Markets, Office of (OFGEM)
(combined functions of the former OFGAS and OFFER)
OFGEM Head Office 130 Wilton Road,
London SW1V 1LQ
tel 020-7838 0898
OFGEM Scotland Regents Court,
70 West Regent Street, Glasgow G2 2QZ
tel 0141-331 2673
Freephone helpline 0800-887777 (for customer queries about gas and electricity competition)
web site http://www.ofgem.gov.uk
The regulator of the gas and electricity markets. It aims to bring choice and value to all electricity and gas customers by promoting competition and regulating monopolies.

German Embassy
23 Belgrave Square, London SW1X 8PZ
tel 020-7824 1300 *fax* 020-7824 1435
e-mail mail@german-embassy.org.uk
web site http://www.german-embassy.org.uk

Ghana High Commission
13 Belgrave Square, London SW1X 8PN
tel 020-7235 4142-5 *fax* 020-7245 9552

Government Offices for the Regions
1st Floor, Eland House, Bressenden Place, London SW1E 5DU
tel 020-7944 5157 *fax* 020-7944 5019
Combination of the former regional offices of the Depts of the Environment, Trade and Industry, Education and Employment, and Transport. Established April 1994.

Greece, Embassy of
Press and Information Office, 1A Holland Park, London W11 3TP
tel 020-7727 3071 *fax* 020-7727 8960

Guyana High Commission
3 Palace Court, Bayswater Road, London W2 4LP
tel 020-7229 7684 *fax* 020-7727 9809

Hayward Gallery
Belvedere Road, London SE1 8XZ
tel 020-7960 5226 *fax* 020-7401 2664
web site http://www.hayward-gallery.org.uk

Health, Department of
Richmond House, 79 Whitehall, London SW1A 2NS
tel 020-7210 3000
web site http://www.open.gov.uk/doh.dhhome.htm

Health and Safety Executive
Rose Court, 2 Southwark Bridge, London SE1 9HS
tel (0541) 545500 *fax* 0114-289 2333
web site http://www.open.gov.uk/hse/hsehome.htm

Historic Scotland
Longmore House, Salisbury Place, Edinburgh EH9 1SH
tel 0131-668 8600 *fax* 0131-668 8699
web site http://www.historic-scotland.gov.uk

HMSO Books – see The Stationery Office

Home Office
Queen Anne's Gate, London SW1H 9AT
tel 020-7273 3757
Director, Communication B. Butler

Housing Corporation
149 Tottenham Court Road, London W1P 0BN
tel 020-7393 2000 *fax* 020-7393 2111
web site http://www.housingcorp.gov.uk

Hungary, Embassy of the Republic of
35 Eaton Place, London SW1X 8BY
tel 020-7235 5218 *fax* 020-7823 1348

Independent Television Commission
33 Foley Street, London W1P 7LB
tel 020-7255 3000 *fax* 020-7306 7800

High Commission of India, Press & Information Wing
India House, Aldwych, London WC2B 4NA
tel 020-7836 8484 ext 147, 286, 327
fax 020-7836 2632
e-mail 106167.1470@compuserve.com

Inland Revenue, Board of
Somerset House, London WC2R 1LB
Library tel 020-7438 6648 *fax* 020-7438 7562
InS at IR, Contributions Office, Longbenton, Newcastle Upon Tyne NE98 1ZZ
tel (0645) 154 811 *fax* (0645) 157 800
e-mail w.clark@new040.dss.gov.uk
web site http://www.dss.gov.uk
Contact Inland Revenue, International Services (InS) for queries about working abroad and paying National Insurance contributions.

International Services (InS) – see Inland Revenue, Board of

Ireland, Embassy of
17 Grosvenor Place, London SW1X 7HR
tel 020-7235 2171 *fax* 020-7245 6961

Israel, Embassy of
2 Palace Green, London W8 4QB
tel 020-7957 9500 *fax* 020-7957 9555
e-mail info@israel-embassy.org.uk
web site http://www.israel-embassy.org.uk

Italian Embassy
14 Three Kings Yard, Davies Street, London W1Y 2EH
tel 020-7312 2200 *fax* 020-7312 2230
e-mail press@embitaly.org.uk
web site http://www.embitaly.org.uk

Jamaican High Commission
1-2 Prince Consort Road, London SW7 2BZ
tel 020-7823 9911 *fax* 020-7589 5154
e-mail jis@jhcuk.com

Japan, Embassy of
101-104 Piccadilly, London W1V 9FN
tel 020-7465 6500 *fax* 020-7491 9347 (information) 020-7491 9348 (other departments)
e-mail jicc@jicc.demon.co.uk
web site http://www.embjapan.org.uk

Kenya High Commission
45 Portland Place, London W1N 4AS
tel 020-7636 2371 *fax* 020-7323 6717
e-mail kcomm45@aol.com

HM Land Registry
Lincoln's Inn Fields, London WC2A 3PH
tel 020-7917 8888 *fax* 020-7955 0110
web site http://www.land.reggov.uk/
Head of Information Mrs M. Bennett

Law Commission
Conquest House, 37-38 John Street,
Theobalds Road, London WC1N 2BQ
tel 020-7453 1220 *fax* 020-7453 1297
e-mail secretary.lawcomm@gtnet.gov.uk
web site http://www.lawcom.gov.uk
Covers England and Wales.

The Legal Deposit Office
The British Library, Boston Spa, Wetherby,
West Yorkshire LS23 7BY
tel (01937) 546267/546268 *fax* (01937) 546176

Legal Services Commission
(formerly Legal Aid Board)
85 Gray's Inn Road, London WC1X 8AA
tel 020-7813 1000

Legal Services Ombudsman, Office of the
22 Oxford Court, Oxford Street,
Manchester M2 3WQ
tel 0161-236 9532 *fax* 0161-236 2651
Lo call 0845-6010794 (charged at local rate)
e-mail enquiries.olso@gtnet.gov.uk

Lesotho, High Commission of the Kingdom of
7 Chesham Place, London SW1 8HN
tel 020-7235 5686 *fax* 020-7235 5023
e-mail lesotholondonhighcom@compuserve.com

London Museum – see Museum of London

London Records Office, Corporation of
Guildhall, London EC2P 2EJ
tel 020-7332 1251 *fax* 020-7710 8682
e-mail clro@ms.corpoflondon.gov.uk
web site http://www.cityoflondon.gov.uk

London Transport
55 Broadway, London SW1H 0BD
tel 020-7222 5600 (administration)
020-7222 1234 (travel information)

Luxembourg, Embassy of
27 Wilton Crescent, London SW1X 8SD
tel 020-7235 6961 *fax* 020-7235 9734

Malawi High Commission
33 Grosvenor Street, London W1X 0DE
tel 020-7491 4172/7 *fax* 020-7491 9916

Malaysian High Commission
45 Belgrave Square, London SW1X 8QT
tel 020-7235 8033 *fax* 020-7235 5161

Malta High Commission
Malta House, 36-38 Piccadilly, London W1V 0PQ
tel 020-7292 4800 *fax* 020-7734 1831

Mauritius, High Commission for the Republic of
32-33 Elvaston Place, London SW7 5NW
tel 020-7581 0294/5 *fax* 020-7823 8437

Medical Research Council
20 Park Crescent, London W1N 4AL
tel 020-7636 5422 *fax* 020-7436 6179
e-mail firstname.surname@headoffice.mrc.ac.uk
web site http://www.mrc.ac.uk

Millennium Commission
Portland House, Stag Place, London SW1E 5EZ
tel 020-7880 2001 *fax* 020-7880 2000
Information line 020-7880 2030
web site http://www.millennium.gov.uk

Monopolies and Mergers Commission – now Competition Commission

Museum of London
London Wall, London EC2Y 5HN
tel 020-7600 3699 *fax* 020-7600 1058
e-mail info@museumoflondon.org
web site http://www.museumoflondon.org
Tells the story of London from prehistoric times to the present day.

National Audit Office
157-197 Buckingham Palace Road,
London SW1W 9SP
tel 020-7798 7000 *fax* 020-7828 3774
e-mail nao@gtnet.gov.uk
22 Melville Street, Edinburgh EH3 7NS
tel 0131-244 2736 *fax* 0131-244 2721
Audit House, 23-24 Park Place,
Cardiff CF1 3BA
tel 029-2037 8661 *fax* 029-2038 8415
Provides independent information, advice and assurance to Parliament and the public about all aspects of the financial operations of government departments and many other bodies receiving public funds.

National Consumer Council
20 Grosvenor Gardens, London SW1W 0DH
tel 020-7730 3469 *fax* 020-7730 0191
e-mail info@ncc.org.uk
web site http://www.ncc.org.uk

National Gallery
Trafalgar Square, London WC2N 5DN
tel 020-7747 2885 (general information)
Press Office fax 020-7930 4764
Information fax 020-7747 2423
e-mail information@ng-london.org.uk
web site http://www.nationalgallery.org.uk

National Lottery Commission
2 Monck Street, London SW1P 2BQ
tel 020-7227 2000 *fax* 020-7227 2005
web site http://www.natlotcomm.gov.uk

National Maritime Museum
Greenwich, London SE10 9NF
tel 020-8858 4422 *fax* 020-8312 6632

e-mail research@nmm.ac.uk
web sites http://www.nmm.ac.uk
http://www.port.nmm.ac.uk (gateway site for maritime information)
http://www.rog.nmm.ac.uk (for astronomy information)
Information also for the Queen's House and the Royal Observatory of Greenwich. Extensive reference library (Mon-Fri).

The National Monuments Record
National Monuments Record Centre,
Kemble Drive, Swindon, Wilts. SN2 2GZ
tel (01793) 414600 *fax* (01793) 414606
e-mail info@rchme.gov.uk
web site http://www.english-heritage.org.uk
The public archive of English Heritage.

National Savings
Commerical Directorate, Charles House,
375 Kensington High Street, London W14 8SD
tel 020-7605 9300 *fax* 020-7605 9432/9481
web site http://www.nationalsavings.co.uk

National Statistics, Office for
1 Drummond Gate, London SW1V 2QQ
tel 020-7533 5725 (economic statistics); 020-7533 5702 (social statistics) *fax* 020-7533 5719

Natural Environment Research Council
Polaris House, North Star Avenue, Swindon,
Wilts. SN2 1EU
tel (01793) 411500 *fax* (01793) 411501
e-mail requests@nerc.ac.uk
web site http://www.nerc.ac.uk

The Natural History Museum
Cromwell Road, London SW7 5BD
tel 020-7942 5000

Royal Netherlands Embassy
38 Hyde Park Gate, London SW7 5DP
tel 020-7590 3200
Press and Cultural Affairs fax 020-7581 0053
e-mail cultural@netherlands-embassy.org.uk
web site http://www.netherlands-embassy.org.uk

New Zealand High Commission
New Zealand House, Haymarket,
London SW1Y 4TQ
tel 020-7930 8422 *fax* 020-7839 4580
web site http://www.newzealandhc.org.uk

Nigeria High Commission
Nigeria House, 9 Northumberland Avenue,
PO Box 29041, London WC2N 5QJ
tel 020-7839 1244 *fax* 020-7839 8746

Northern Ireland Assembly
Parliament Buildings, Belfast BT4 3XX
tel 028-9052 1333

Northern Ireland Office
11 Millbank, London SW1P 4PN
tel 020-7210 3000
Castle Buildings, Belfast BT4 3ST
tel 028-9052 0700
web site http://www.nio.gov.uk/index.htm

Northern Ireland Tourist Board
59 North Street, Belfast, Northern Ireland BT1 1NB
tel 028-9023 1221 *fax* 028-9024 0960
e-mail info@nitb.com
web site http://www.ni-tourism.com

Royal Norwegian Embassy
25 Belgrave Square, London SW1X 8QD
tel 020-7591 5500 *fax* 020-7245 6993
e-mail embassy@embassy.norway.org.uk
web site http://www.norway.org.uk/

Royal Observatory of Greenwich – see National Maritime Museum

Oftel – see Telecommunications, Office of

OFWAT – see Water Services, Office of

Ordnance Survey
Romsey Road, Maybush, Southampton SO16 4GU
tel 023-8079 2000 *fax* 023-8079 2615
Press Officer tel (02380) 792635
Help Line (08456) 050505
e-mail custinfo@ordsvy.gov.uk
web site http://www.ordsvy.gov.uk/

Particle Physics and Astronomy Research Council (PPARC)
Polaris House, North Star Avenue, Swindon,
Wilts. SN2 1SZ
tel (01793) 442000 *fax* (01793) 442002
e-mail pr_pus@pparc.ac.uk
web site http://www.pparc.ac.uk

Patent Office
General enquiries (designs, patents, trade marks)
Central Enquiry Unit, Room 1L02, Concept House,
Cardiff Road, Newport, South Wales NP9 1RH
tel (0645) 500505 *text phone* (0645) 222250
e-mail enquiries@patent.gov.uk
web site http://www.patent.gov.uk
Copyright enquiries Copyright Directorate,
The Patent Office, Room 1/10, Harmsworth House,
13-15 Bouverie Street, London EC4Y 8DP
tel 020-7596 6566 *fax* 020-7596 6526
textphone (0645) 222250
e-mail copyright@patent.gov.uk
web site http://www.patent.gov.uk

Pensions Ombudsman, The
11 Belgrave Road, London SW1V 1RB
tel 020-7834 9144 *fax* 020-7821 0065

Pensions and Overseas Benefits Directorate (POD) – see Social Security, Department of

PLR Office
Richard House, Sorbonne Close,
Stockton-on-Tees TS17 6DA
tel (01642) 604699 *fax* (01642) 615641
e-mail enquiries@plr.uk.com
web site http://www.plr.uk.com

Poland, Embassy of the Republic of
47 Portland Place, London W1N 4JH
tel 020-7580 4324 *fax* 020-7323 4018
e-mail pol-emb@dircon.co.uk
web site http://www.poland-embassy.org.uk/
Polish Cultural Institute
34 Portland Place, London W1N 4HQ
tel 020-7636 6032 *fax* 020-7637 2190
e-mail PCI-LOND@pcidiv.demon.co.uk

Police Complaints Authority
10 Great George Street, London SW1P 3AE
tel 020-7273 6450 *fax* 020-7273 6401
web site http://www.pca.gov.uk

Population Census and Surveys, Office of – now Office for National Statistics

Portuguese Embassy
11 Belgrave Square, London SW1X 8PP
tel 020-7235 5331 *fax* 020-7245 1287 and 020-7235 0739
e-mail Portembassy-London@dialin.net

Post Office Headquarters
5th Floor, 148 Old Street, London EC1V 9HQ
tel 020-7490 2888

Privy Council Office
2 Carlton Gardens, London SW1Y 5AA
tel 020-7210 1033 *fax* 020-7210 1071

Public Record Office
Ruskin Avenue, Kew, Richmond, Surrey TW9 4DU
tel 020-8392 5200 *fax* 020-8878 8905
web site http://www.pro.gov.uk

Records of Government Departments and central courts of law.

Public Service, Office of (OPS) – merged with the Cabinet Office

Public Trust Office
Stewart House, 24 Kingsway,
London WC2B 6JX
tel 020-7664 7000 *fax* 020-7664 7705

Qualifications and Curriculum Authority (QCA)
29 Bolton Street, london W1Y 7PD
tel 020-7509 5555 *fax* 020-7509 6666
e-mail info@qca.org.uk
web site http://www.qca.org.uk/
Chairman Sir William Stubbs, *Deputy Chairman* Sir Dominic Cadbury, *Chief Executive* Dr Nicholas Tate

Racial Equality, Commission for
Elliot House, 10-12 Allington Street,
London SW1E 5EH
tel 020-7828 7022 *fax* 020-7630 7605

The Radio Authority
Holbrook House, 14 Great Queen Street,
London WC2B 5DG
tel 020-7430 2724 *fax* 020-7405 7062
e-mail info@radioauthority.org.uk
web site http://www.radioauthority.org.uk

Regional Arts Boards – see English Regional Arts Boards

Romania, Embassy of
4 Palace Green, London W8 4QD
tel 020-7937 9666 *fax* 020-7937 8069
e-mail romania@roemb.demon.uk.co

Royal Commission on the Ancient and Historical Monuments of Scotland
(with National Monuments Record of Scotland)
John Sinclair House, 16 Bernard Terrace,
Edinburgh EH8 9NX
tel 0131-662 1456 *fax* 0131-662 1477/1499
e-mail postmaster@rcahms.gov.uk
web site http://www.rcahms.gov.uk

Royal Commission on the Ancient and Historical Monuments of Wales
(with National Monuments Record of Wales)
Crown Building, Plas Crug,
Aberystwyth,
Ceredigion SY23 1NJ
tel (01970) 621200 *fax* (01970) 627701
e-mail nmr.wales@rcahmw.org.uk
web site http://www.rcahmw.org.uk

Royal Commission on Historical Manuscripts
Quality House, Quality Court, Chancery Lane,
London WC2A 1HP
tel 020-7242 1198 *fax* 020-7831 3550
e-mail nra@hmc.gov.uk
web site http://www.hmc.gov.uk

Royal Commission on the Historical Monuments of England – merged with English Heritage

Royal Fine Art Commission for Scotland
Bakehouse Close, 146 Canongate,
Edinburgh EH8 8DD
tel 0131-556 6699 *fax* 0131-556 6633
e-mail rfacscot@gtnet.co.uk

Royal Mint
Llantrisant, Pontyclun CF72 8YT
tel (01443) 222111
e-mail ldoster@rmint.demon.co.uk
web site http://www.royalmint.com

Royal National Theatre Board
South Bank, London SE1 9PX
tel 020-7452 3333 *fax* 020-7452 3344
web site http://www.nt-online.org
Chairman Christopher Hogg

Russian Federation, Embassy of the
6-7 Kensington Palace Gardens, London W8 4QP
tel 020-7229 3628, 020-7229 6412
fax 020-7727 8625

Science and Technology, Office of
Department of Trade and Industry, Albany House, Petty France, London SW1H 9ST
tel 020-7271 2000

Science Museum
Exhibition Road, London SW7 2DD
tel 020-7942 4000
Information Desk tel 020-7942 4454/4455
Press Office tel 020-7942 4352/4357
fax 020-7942 4351
web site http://www.sciencemuseum.org.uk

Scotland, The National Archives of
HM General Register House,
Edinburgh EH1 3YY
tel 0131-535 1314 *fax* 0131-535 1360
e-mail research@nas.gov.uk

Scotland, National Galleries of
National Gallery of Scotland
The Mound, Edinburgh EH2 2EL
Scottish National Portrait Gallery
1 Queen Street, Edinburgh EH2 1JD
Scottish National Gallery of Modern Art
Belford Road, Edinburgh EH4 3DR
The Dean Gallery
Belford Road, Edinburgh EH4 3DS
tel 0131-624 6200, 0131-624 6332 (press office)
fax 0131-343 3250 (press office)

Scotland, National Library of
George IV Bridge, Edinburgh EH1 1EW
tel 0131-226 4531 *fax* 0131-622 4803
e-mail enquiries@nls.uk
web site http://www.nls.uk

Scottish Arts Council
12 Manor Place, Edinburgh EH3 7DD
tel 0131-226 6051 *fax* 0131-225 9833
Help Desk tel 0131-240 2443/2444
e-mail administrator.SAC@artsfb.org.uk
web site http://www.sac.org.uk

The Scottish Executive Information Directorate
St Andrew's House, Edinburgh EH1 1DG
tel 0131-556 8400
web site http://www.scotland.gov.uk

Scottish Law Commission
140 Causewayside, Edinburgh EH9 1PR
tel 0131-668 2131 *fax* 0131-662 4900

Scottish Legal Aid Board
44 Drumsheugh Gardens, Edinburgh EH3 7SW
tel 0131-226 7061 *fax* 0131-220 4878

Scottish Natural Heritage
12 Hope Terrace, Edinburgh EH9 2AS
tel 0131-447 4784 *Press Office fax* 0131-446 2279
web site http://www.snh.org.uk

The Scottish Office
Dover House, Whitehall, London SW1A 2AU
tel 020-7270 3000

The Scottish Parliament
Edinburgh EH99 1SP
tel 0131-348 5000 (public information service)
(0845) 278 1999 (general enquiries)
fax 0131-348 5601
e-mail sp.info@scottish.parliament.uk
web site www.scottish parliament.uk

Scottish Tourist Board
Thistle House, Beechwood Park North,
Inverness IV2 3ED
tel (01463) 716996 *fax* (01463) 717299

The Security Service (MI5)
PO Box 3255, London SW1P 1AE

Serpentine Gallery
Kensington Gardens, London W2 3XA
tel 020-7402 6075 *fax* 020-7402 4103
Public information 020-7298 1515

Seychelles High Commission
2nd Floor, Eros House, 111 Baker Street,
London W1M 1FE
tel 020-7224 1660 *fax* 020-7487 5756

Shadow Strategic Rail Authority
25 Victoria Street, London SW1H 0EU
tel 020-7654 6000 *fax* 020-7654 6010
web site http://www.sra.gov.uk

Sierra Leone High Commission
33 Portland Place, London W1N 3AG
tel 020-7636 6483-5 *fax* 020-7323 3159

Singapore High Commission
9 Wilton Crescent, London SW1X 8SP
tel 020-7235 8315 *fax* 020-7245 6583
e-mail schlondon@singcomm.demon.co.uk
web site http://www.gov.sg

Slovak Republic, Embassy of the
25 Kensington Palace Gardens,
London W8 4QY
tel 020-7243 0803 *fax* 020-7727 5824
e-mail mail@slovakembassy.co.uk
web site http://www.slovakembassy.co.uk

Slovenia, Embassy of
Suite One, Cavendish Court,
11-15 Wigmore Street, London W1H 9LA
tel 020-7495 7775 *fax* 020-7495 7776

e-mail slovene-embassy.london@virgin.net
web site http://www.embassy-slovenia.org.uk

Social Security, Department of
Richmond House, 79 Whitehall,
London SW1A 2NS
tel 020-7238 0800
POD at DSS, Benefits Agency, Tyneview Park, Whitley Road, Newcastle Upon Tyne NE98 1BA
tel 0191-218 7777 *fax* 0191-218 7293
e-mail pod-customer-care-ba@ms04.dss.qsi.gov.uk
web site http://www.podcustcareba

Contact Benefits Agency, Pensions and Overseas Benefits Directorate (POD) for queries about benefits being paid abroad.

South Africa, Republic of
South African High Commission,
South Africa House, Trafalgar Square,
London WC2N 5DP
tel 020-7451 7299 *fax* 020-7451 7283/7284
e-mail general@southafricahouse.com
web site http://www.southafricahouse.com

Spanish Embassy
39 Chesham Place, London SW1X 8SB
tel 020-7235 5555 *fax* 020-7259 5392

Sport England
16 Upper Woburn Place, London WC1H 0QP
tel 020-7273 1500 *fax* 020-7383 5740
e-mail info@english.sports.gov.uk
web site http://www.english.sports.gov.uk

Sri Lanka, High Commission of the Democratic Socialist Republic of
13 Hyde Park Gardens, London W2 2LU
tel 020-7262 1841 *fax* 020-7262 7970

Standards in Education, Office for (OFSTED)
Alexandra House, 33 Kingsway, London WC2B 6SE
tel 020-7421 6800 *fax* 020-7421 6707

The Stationery Office
St Crispins, Duke Street, Norwich NR3 1PD
tel 020-7873 0011 (publication enquiries)

Swaziland High Commission
20 Buckingham Gate, London SW1E 6LB
tel 020-7630 6611 *fax* 020-7630 6564

Sweden, Embassy of
11 Montagu Place, London W1H 2AL
tel 020-7917 6400 *fax* 020-7917 6477
e-mail embassy@swednet.org.uk
web site http://www.swedish-embassy.org.uk

Swiss Embassy Cultural Section
16-18 Montagu Place, London W1H 2BQ
tel 020-7616 6000 *fax* 020-7724 7001
e-mail vertretung@lon.rep.admin.ch
web site http://www.swissembassy.org.uk

Tanzania High Commission
43 Hertford Street, London W1Y 8DB
tel 020-7499 8951 *fax* 020-7491 9321
e-mail balozi@tanzarep.demon.co.uk
web site http://www.tanzania-online.gov.uk

Tate
Tate Britain, Millbank, London SW1P 4RG
tel 020-7887 8008
e-mail information@tate.org.uk
web site http://www.tate.org.uk
Tate Modern, Bankside, London SE1 9TG
tel 020-7887 8008
Tate Liverpool, Albert Dock,
Liverpool L3 4BB
tel 0151-702 7400
Tate St Ives, Porthmeor Beach, St Ives,
Cornwall TR26 1TG
tel (01736) 796226

Telecommunications, Office of
50 Ludgate Hill, London EC4M 7JJ
tel 020-7634 8700 *fax* 020-7634 8946
e-mail infocent.oftel@gtnet.gov.uk
web site http://www.oftel.gov.uk

Theatre Museum
National Museum of the Performing Arts,
1E Tavistock Street, London WC2E 7PA
tel 020-7943 4700 *fax* 020-7943 4777
web site http://theatremuseum.org

See page 439 for reprographic services.

Transport, Department of – see Environment, Transport and the Regions, Department of

HM Treasury
Parliament Street, London SW1P 3AG
tel 020-7270 5000
Press Office tel 020-7270 5238 *fax* 020-7270 5244
Public Enquiry Unit tel 020-7270 4558
web site http://www.hm-treasury.gov.uk

Trinidad and Tobago High Commission
42 Belgrave Square, London SW1X 8NT
tel 020-7245 9351 *fax* 020-7823 1065
e-mail trintogov@tthc.demon.co.uk

Trinity House, Corporation of
Tower Hill, London EC3N 4DH
tel 020-7481 6900 *fax* 020-7480 7662
web site http://www.trinityhouse.co.uk

Turkish Embassy
43 Belgrave Square, London SW1X 8PA
tel 020-7393 0202 *fax* 020-7393 0066
e-mail info@turkishembassy.co.uk

Uganda High Commission
Uganda House, 58-59 Trafalgar Square,
London WC2N 5DX
tel 020-7839 5783 *fax* 020-7839 8925

United States Embassy
24 Grosvenor Square, London W1A 1AE
tel 020-7499 9000
web site http://www.usembassy.org.uk

Victoria and Albert Museum
South Kensington, London SW7 2RL
tel 020-7942 2000 *fax* 020-7942 2266
web site http://www.vam.ac.uk

Visiting Arts
11 Portland Place, London W1N 4EJ
tel 020-7389 3019 *fax* 020-7389 3016
e-mail office@visitingarts.demon.co.uk
web site http://www.britcoun.org/visitingarts/
Director T. Sandell OBE

Vocational Qualifications, National Council for (NCVQ) – see Qualifications and Curriculum Authority (QCA)

Wales Office
Office of the Secretary of State for Wales, Gwydyr House, Whitehall, London SW1A 2ER
tel 020-7270 3000 *fax* 020-7270 0568
web site http://www.ossw.wales.gov.uk

Wales, National Assembly for
Public Information and Education Service, Cardiff Bay, Cardiff CF99 1NA
tel 029-2089 8200
e-mail Assembly.Info@wales.gsi.gov.uk
web site http://www.wales.gov.uk

Wales, The National Library of
Aberystwyth, Ceredigion SY23 3BU
e-mail holi@llgc.org.uk
web site http://www.llgc.org.uk

Wales Tourist Board
Brunel House, 2 Fitzalan Road, Cardiff CF24 0UY
tel 029-2047 5214 *fax* 029-2048 2436
e-mail info@tourism.wales.gov.uk
web site http://www.visitwales.com

Water Services, Office of (OFWAT)
Centre City Tower, 7 Hill Street, Birmingham B5 4UA
tel 0121-625 1300 *fax* 0121-625 1400
web site http://www.open.gov.uk/ofwat

Women's National Commission
Cabinet Office, 4th Floor, Horse Guards Road, London SW1P 3AL
tel 020-7238 0386 *fax* 020-7238 0387
web site http://www.thewnc.org.uk

Yugoslavia, Embassy of the Federal Republic of
5-7 Lexham Gardens, London W8 5JJ
tel 020-7370 6105 *fax* 020-7370 3838
e-mail mark@yuembassylondon.demon.co.uk

Zambia High Commission
2 Palace Gate, London W8 5NG
tel 020-7589 6655 *fax* 020-7581 1353

Zimbabwe, High Commission of the Republic of
Zimbabwe House, 429 Strand, London WC2R 0QE
tel 020-7836 7755 *fax* 020-7379 1167

Publishing practice

Publishing agreements

Publisher's agreements are not a standard form. Before signing one, the author must check it carefully, taking nothing for granted. ***Michael Legat*** *navigates the reader through this complex document.*

Any author, presented with so complex a document as a publisher's agreement, should read it carefully before signing, making sure that every clause is understood, and not taking anything for granted. Bear in mind that there is no such thing as a standard form. A given publisher's 'standard' contract may not only differ substantially from those of other publishers, but will often vary from author to author and from book to book. Don't be fooled into believing that it is a standard form because it appears to have been printed – each agreement can be individually produced on a word processor to give exactly that effect.

A fair and reasonable agreement

You should be able to rely on your agent, if you have one, to check the agreement for you, or – if you are a member – you can get it vetted by the Society of Authors or the Writers' Guild of Great Britain. But if you are on your own, you must either go to one of the solicitors who specialise in publishing business (probably expensive) or Do It Yourself. In the latter case it will help to compare the contract you have been offered, clause by clause, with a typical Minimum Terms Agreement such as those printed in my own books, *An Author's Guide to Publishing* and *Understanding Publishers' Contracts.*

Minimum Terms Agreement

The Minimum Terms Agreement (MTA), developed jointly by the Society of Authors and the Writers' Guild, is signed by a publisher on the one hand and the Society and the Guild on the other. It is not an agreement between a publisher and an individual author. It commits the publisher to offering his or her authors terms which are at least as good as those in the MTA. The intention is that only members of the Society and Guild should be eligible for this special treatment, but in practice publishers who sign the agreement tend to offer its terms to all their authors. There is no standard MTA, and most signatory publishers have insisted on certain variations in the agreement; nevertheless, the more important basic principles have always been accepted. It must be pointed out that the MTA does not usually apply to:

- books in which illustrations take up 40% or more of the space;
- specialist works on the visual arts in which illustrations fill 25% or more of the space;
- books involving three or more participants in royalties; or
- technical books, manuals and reference books.

Since its origins in 1980, comparatively few publishers have signed a Minimum Terms Agreement, although the signatories include several major publishing houses. Some publishers have refused, claiming to treat their authors quite well enough already, while others say that each author and each book is so different that standard terms cannot be laid down. Nonetheless, the MTA has been a resounding success. Almost all non-signatory publishers have adopted some or all of its provisions, and even in the case of the excluded books mentioned above, the terms have tended to improve. All authors can now argue, from a position of some strength, that their own agreements should meet the MTA's standards.

The provisions of the MTA

The MTA is a royalty agreement (usually the most satisfactory form for an author), and it lays down the minimum acceptable royalties on sales, and the levels at which the rate should rise. These royalties are expressed as percentages of the book's retail price but can easily be adjusted to apply to royalties based on price received, a system to which a number of publishers are changing, increasing the percentages so that the author's earnings are not adversely affected. The MTA also covers the size of the advance (calculated in accordance with the expected initial print quantity and retail price), and recommended splits between publisher and author of moneys from the sale of subsidiary rights (including US and translation rights).

However, the MTA is not by any means concerned solely with money, but with fairness to the author in all clauses of a publishing agreement, special attention being paid to provisions designed to make the author/publisher relationship more of a partnership than it has often been in the past. While recognising the publisher's right to take final decisions on such matters as print quantity, publication date, retail price, jacket or cover design, wording of the blurb, promotion and publicity, and remaindering, the MTA insists that the author has a right to consultation (which should not be an empty formality but should mean that serious consideration is given to his or her views), in all such cases. Also the author's approval must be sought for the sale of any subsidiary rights.

Some essential clauses

Any publisher's agreement you sign should contain, in addition to acceptable financial terms, clauses covering:

- **Rights licensed.** A clear definition of which rights you are licensing to the publisher. The publisher will normally require volume rights but the agreement must specify whether such rights will apply in all languages (or perhaps only in English) and throughout the world (or only in an agreed list of territories). The duration of the publisher's licence should be spelt out; commonly this is for the period of copyright (currently the author's lifetime plus 70 years), although some publishers now accept a shorter term. A list of those subsidiary rights of which control is granted to the publisher must be included (make sure that the splits of moneys earned from these rights are in accordance with, or approximate reasonably to, those in the MTA, especially in the currently growing area of merchandising). Because the development of non-traditional forms of publishing, such as the Internet, continues to be so rapid, it may be advisable for the author not to grant the publisher control of electronic and multimedia rights, or of any additional rights as yet unknown resulting from advances in technology, or at least to require the split of income from such sources to be negotiated as and when their sale occurs.
- **Publication date.** Commitment by the publisher to publication of the book by a specific date (usually within a year or 18 months from the delivery of the typescript). Avoid signing an agreement which is vague on this point, saying, for instance, only that the book will be published 'within a reasonable period'.
- **Copyright.** Confirmation that in all copies of the book the publisher will print a copyright notice in the author's name and a statement that the author has asserted his or her 'Right of Paternity' (the right to be identified as the author in future exploitation of the material in any form), and that a similar commitment will be required from any subsidiary licensee.
- **Fees and permissions.** Clarification, if the book is to include a professionally prepared index or material the copyright of which does not belong to the author,

of whether the author or the publisher will be responsible for the fees (or if costs are to be shared, in what proportions) and the clearance of permissions.

- **Acceptable accounting procedures.** Most publishers divide the year into two six-month periods, accounting to the author, and paying any sums due, three months after the end of each period. Look askance at any less frequent accounting or longer delay after the royalty period. The publisher should also agree to pay the author the due share of any subsidiary moneys promptly on receipt, provided that the advance on the book has been earned.
- **Termination.** A clear definition of the various conditions under which the agreement shall be terminated, with reversion of rights to the author.

Clauses to question

You can question anything in a publisher's agreement before you sign it. Provided that you do so politely and are not just being difficult, the publisher should be prepared to answer every query, to explain, and where possible to meet your objections. Most publishing contracts are not designed to exploit the author unfairly, but you should watch out for:

- **Rights assigned elsewhere.** It is unwise to accept a clause which allows the publisher to assign the rights in your book to another firm or person without your approval.
- **Non-publication.** The contract for a commissioned book often includes wording which alludes to the publisher's acceptance of the work, implying that there is no obligation to publish it if he or she deems it unacceptable. It may be understandable that the publisher wants an escape route in case the author turns in an inferior work, but he or she should be obliged to justify the rejection, and to give the author an opportunity to revise the work to bring it up to standard. If, having accepted the book, the publisher then wishes to cancel the contract prior to publication, the author can usually expect to receive financial compensation, which should be non-returnable even if the book is subsequently placed with another publisher. However, this point is not normally covered in a publishing agreement.
- **Sole publisher.** Some agreements prohibit the author from writing similar material for any other publisher. This may clearly affect the author's earning ability.
- **Editing consultation.** Don't agree to the publisher's right to edit your work without any requirement for him or her to obtain your approval of any changes made.
- **Royalty rate.** While it is normal practice for an agreement to allow the publisher to pay a lower royalty on books which are sold at high trade discounts, such sales are more frequently made nowadays than in the past, and you should therefore make sure the royalty rate on high discount sales is not unfairly low.
- **Future books.** The Society of Authors and the Writers' Guild are both generally opposed to clauses giving the publisher the right to publish the author's next work, feeling that this privilege should be earned by the publisher's handling of the earlier book. If you accept an option clause, at least make sure that it leaves all terms for a future book to be agreed.

Joint and multiple authorship

In the case of joint authorship (a work so written that the individual contributions of the authors cannot be readily separated), the first written agreement should be between the authors themselves, setting out the proportions in which any moneys earned by the book will be split, specifying how the authors' responsibilities are to be shared, and especially laying down the procedure to be adopted should the authors ever find themselves in dispute. The terms of any publishing agreement which they sign (each author having an identical copy) should reflect their joint understanding. The total earnings should not be less than would be paid were the book by a single author, and the authors should have normal rights of consultation.

In the case of multiple authorship (when the work of each contributor can be clearly separated), each author is likely to have an individual contract, and may not be aware of what terms are offered to the others involved. Because of the possibility of disagreement between the authors, the publisher will probably offer little in the way of consultation. All the individual author can do is to ensure that the agreement appears to be fair in relation to the amount of work contributed, and that the author's responsibilities indicated by the contract refer only to his or her work.

Outright sale

As a general rule no author should agree to surrender his or her copyright to the publisher, although this may be unavoidable in the case of a book with many contributors, such as an encyclopedia. Even then, give up your copyright with great reluctance and only after an adequate explanation from the publisher of why you should (and probably a substantial financial inducement, including, if possible, provision for the payment of a further fee each time the book is reprinted). The agreement itself will probably be no more than a brief and unequivocal letter.

Subsidies and vanity publishing

Few commercial publishers will be interested in publishing your book on a subsidy basis (i.e. with a contribution from you towards costs), unless perhaps it is of a serious, highly specialised nature, such as an academic monograph, when a publisher who is well established within that particular field will certainly behave with probity and offer a fair contract. Vanity publishers, on the other hand, will accept your book with enthusiasm, ask for 'a small contribution to production costs' (which turns out to be a very substantial sum, not a penny of which you are likely to see again), and will fail to achieve any sales for your book apart from the copies which you yourself buy. If you want to put your own money into the publication of your book, try self-publishing (see page 262) – you will be far better off than going to a vanity house. How do you tell which are the vanity publishers? That's easy – they're the ones who put advertisements in the papers saying things like, 'Authors Wanted!'. Regular publishers don't need to do that.

Michael Legat became a full-time writer after a long and successful publishing career. He is the author of a number of highly regarded books on publishing and writing.

Further reading

Clark, Charles (ed.), *Publishing Agreements: A Book of Precedents*, Butterworths, 5th edn, 1997

Flint, Michael F., *A User's Guide to Copyright*, Butterworths, 5th edn, 2000

Legat, Michael, *An Authors' Guide to Publishing*, Robert Hale, 3rd edn revised, 1998

Legat, Michael, *Understanding Publishers' Contracts*, Robert Hale, 1992

Unwin, Sir Stanley, *The Truth About Publishing*, Unwin Hyman, 8th edn, 1976, o.p. (An edition is available from the US publishers Lyons & Burford)

Frequently asked questions about ISBNs

The Standard Book Numbering Agency receives a large number of enquiries about the ISBN system. The most frequently asked questions are answered here.

What is an ISBN?
An International Standard Book Number.

What is the purpose of an ISBN?
An ISBN is a product number, used by publishers, booksellers and libraries for ordering, listing and stock control purposes. The number enables them to identify a particular publisher and allows the publisher to identify a specific edition of a specific title in a specific format within their output.

What is the format of an ISBN?
It is always a 10-digit number divided into four parts, which can be of varying length, and separated by spaces or hyphens:
• Group Identifier – Identifies a national, geographic or language grouping of publishers. It tells you where in the world the publisher is based (not the language of the book).
• Publisher Prefix – Identifies a specific publisher or imprint.
• Title Number – Identifies a specific edition of a specific title in a specific format.
• Check Digit – This is always and only the final digit which mathematically validates the rest of the number.

Do all books need to have an ISBN?
There is no legal requirement for an ISBN and it conveys no form of legal or copyright protection. It is a product number.

What can be gained from using an ISBN?
If you wish to sell your publication through major bookselling chains, or Internet booksellers, they will require you to have an ISBN to assist their internal processing and ordering systems.

The ISBN also provides access to Bibliographic Databases such as Whitaker BookBank, which are organised using ISBNs as references. These databases are used by the book trade and libraries to provide information for customers. The ISBN therefore provides access to additional marketing tools which could help sales of your product.

Where can we get an ISBN?
ISBNs are assigned to publishers in the country where the publisher's main office is based. This is irrespective of the language of the publication or the intended market for the book.

The Standard Book Numbering Agency Ltd is the ISBN Agency for the UK and Republic of Ireland. Publishers should contact the Agency for an application pack. Publishers based elsewhere will not be able to get numbers from the UK Agency but should contact them for details of the relevant Agency.

Who is eligible for ISBNs?
Any publisher who is publishing a qualifying product (i.e. making a work available to the public) for general sale or distribution to the market is eligible.

What is a publisher?
It is sometimes difficult to decide who the publisher is and who their agent may be, but the publisher is generally the person or body who takes the financial risk in making a product available. For example, if a product went on sale and sold no copies at all, the publisher is usually the person or body who loses money. If you get paid anyway, you are likely to be a designer, printer, author or consultant of some kind.

How long does it take to get an ISBN?
In the UK the Standard service time is 10 working days. There is also a Fast Track service, which is a three-working day processing period.

How much does it cost to get an ISBN?
In the UK there is a one-off, flat rate registration fee which is payable by all new publishers. The fees are £50.00 plus VAT for the Standard service and £75.00 plus VAT for the Fast Track service.

What if we only want one ISBN?
ISBNs are only available in blocks. The smallest block is 10 numbers. It is not possible to obtain a single ISBN.

Which products do not qualify for ISBNs?
Calendars; diaries; greetings cards, videos for entertainment; documentaries on video/CD-Rom; computer games; computer application programs; items which are available to a restricted group of people, e.g. a history of a golf club which is only for sale to members, or an educational course book only available to those registered as students on the course.

What is an ISSN?
An International Standard Serial Number is the numbering system for journals, magazines, periodicals, newspapers and newsletters. It is administered by the British Library (*tel* (01937) 546959).

Contact details

Standard Book Numbering Agency Ltd
12 Dyott Street, London WC1A 1DF
tel (0906) 8132 100 – 24-hour application line (60p/min)
tel 020-7420 6008 – general queries Mon-Fri 9am-2pm *fax* 020-7836 4342
e-mail isbn@whitaker.co.uk

The Copyright Licensing Agency Ltd

The Copyright Licensing Agency (CLA) is the UK's reproduction rights organisation which looks after the interests of rightsholders for the photocopying of extracts from books, journals and periodicals.

Formed in 1982, CLA is a non-profit making company limited by guarantee. The Agency is owned by its members, the Authors' Licensing and Collecting Society (ALCS) and the Publishers Licensing Society (PLS) to promote and enforce the intellectual property rights of British authors and their publishers, both at home and abroad.

In turn, members of ALCS are the Society of Authors and the Writers' Guild of Great Britain as well as a number of individual authors. Members of PLS are the Publishers Association, the Periodical Publishers Association and the Association of Learned and Professional Society Publishers.

The role of CLA

- CLA licenses the photocopying of extracts from books, journals and periodicals;
- collects fees from licensed users for such copying;
- forwards to rightsholders the copying fees collected;
- encourages and promotes copyright awareness;
- institutes legal proceedings for copyright compliance if necessary.

Balancing mechanism

CLA has been described as the intermediary between various competing needs. Through the collective administration of licensing schemes, CLA is committed to providing its users with the easiest means of obtaining authorisation for photocopying. At the same time it is able to exercise sensible control over copying limits and to obtain fair recompense for that copying for authors and publishers alike.

Licensing

CLA licenses major users of copyright text, which fall into three main groups:
• Education (schools, further and higher education, charities and churches);
• Government (central, local, public bodies); and
• Business (business, industry, professions).
In each sector, CLA offers flexibility by negotiating a licence tailored to the need of each particular user group. Depending on the particular requirements, there are both blanket and transactional services.

A CLA licence allows, subject to certain terms and conditions, photocopying from most books, periodicals and journals published in the UK. The limitations of copying under a CLA licence are clearly stated in notices provided to all licensees for display alongside their photocopiers, together with reminder stickers for the top of each machine. At the present time, certain categories of works remain excluded (e.g. music, maps and newspapers).

International agreements

Many countries have established counterpart organisations to CLA, and the number of such agencies continues to grow. Nearly all these agencies, including CLA, are members of the International Federation of Reproduction Rights Organisations (IFRRO).

Through reciprocal arrangements with these organisations, a CLA licence also allows copying from an expanding list of publications in other countries. These currently are: Australia, Canada (including Quebec), Denmark, Finland, France, Germany, Greece, Iceland, Ireland, The Netherlands, New Zealand, Norway, South Africa, Spain, Sweden, Switzerland and the USA.

Distribution

The fees collected from licensees are forwarded to authors and publishers, via ALCS and PLS respectively, on the basis of statistical surveys, transactional usage and records of copying activity. Since 1982, CLA has distributed over £70 million (US$112 million). For the year ending 31st March 1998, £16.2 million was returned to rightsholders, a 14% increase on the previous year.

The digital era

In 1998, CLA was given the go-ahead by rightsholders to develop licences for the electrocopying and digitisation of existing print material, in response to the increasing influence of digital technology in everyday life. This exciting and historic development has now been made CLA's highest priority. Rightsholders will be given the opportunity to opt in to CLA's licensing schemes on a non-exclusive, sector-by-sector basis. Licensees will be able to scan, store and electronically send extracts from copyright works. The first licences will be offered to the higher education community and the pharmaceuticals industry, followed by further education, press cuttings agencies and other business sectors.

Copyright awareness

As a champion of collective licensing and a believer in voluntary agreement rather than coercion, CLA is continually raising copyright awareness through a programme of marketing and public relations activities. It has a comprehensive web site, and CLA's newsletter, *Clarion*, is mailed regularly to all licensees and to those individuals and groups concerned with copyright. At the same time, CLA takes an active role speaking and lobbying on behalf of copyright and digital rights management issues, particularly through its membership of IFRRO. Recently, this has included monitoring the progress of the European Commission's Directive on Copyright through the European Parliament.

Compliance

As a last resort, under the Copyright, Designs and Patents Act 1988, CLA has the authority to take legal action as and when appropriate, and will not hesitate to seek the maximum penalties possible. For example, Fournier Pharmaceuticals Ltd, in an out-of-court settlement, accepted that copyright had been infringed in an internal 'awareness bulletin' through the unauthorised copying of articles from trade journals. Likewise, one of the UK's leading engineering firms, Dar Al Handasah Consultants (UK), settled for £50,000 in damages and costs, following High Court action for extensive copyright infringement over a long period of time.

Further information

The Copyright Licensing Agency Ltd
90 Tottenham Court Road, London W1P 0LP
tel 020-7631 5555 *fax* 020-7631 5500
e-mail cla@cla.co.uk
web site http://www.cla.co.uk
CBC House, 24 Canning Street,
Edinburgh EH3 8E9
tel 0131-272 2711 *fax* 0131-272 2811

Public Lending Right

Under the PLR system, payment is made from public funds to authors (writers, translators, illustrators and some editors/compilers) whose books are lent out from public libraries. Payment is made once a year, in February, and the amount authors receive is proportionate to the number of times (established from a sample) that their books were borrowed during the previous year (July to June).

The legislation

PLR was created, and its principles established, by the Public Lending Right Act 1979 (HMSO, 30p). The Act required the rules for the administration of PLR to be laid down by a scheme. That was done in the Public Lending Right Scheme 1982 (HMSO, £2.95), which includes details of transfer (assignment), transmission after death, renunciation, trusteeship, bankruptcy, etc. Amending orders made in 1983, 1984, 1988, 1989 and 1990 were consolidated in December 1990 (S.I. 2360, £3.90). Some further amendments affecting author eligibility came into effect in December 1991 (S.I. 2618, £1.00) and July 1997 (S.I. 1576, £1.10).

How the system works

From the applications he receives, the Registrar of PLR compiles a register of authors and books which is held on computer. A representative sample of book issues is recorded, consisting of all loans from selected public libraries. This is then multiplied in proportion to total library lending to produce, for each book, an estimate of its total annual loans throughout the country. Each year the computer compares the register with the estimated loans to discover how many loans are credited to each registered book for the calculation of PLR payments. The computer does this using code numbers – in most cases the ISBN printed in the book.

Most borrowed authors in UK public libraries

Based on PLR sample loans July 1998-June 1999. Includes all writers, both registered and unregistered, but not illustrators where the book has a separate writer. Writing names are used; pseudonyms have not been combined.

Most borrowed authors

1. Catherine Cookson
2. Danielle Steel
3. Dick Francis
4. Josephine Cox
5. Jack Higgins
6. Ruth Rendell
7. Agatha Christie
8. Emma Blair
9. Audrey Howard
10. Terry Pratchett
11. Barbara Taylor Bradford
12. Harry Bowling
13. Patricia Cornwell
14. Maeve Binchy
15. Virginia Andrews
16. Mary Higgins Clark
17. John Grisham
18. Bernard Cornwell
19. Dean R. Koontz
20. Mary Jane Staples

Most borrowed children's authors

1. R.L. Stine
2. Janet & Allan Ahlberg
3. Roald Dahl
4. Enid Blyton
5. Ann M. Martin
6. Dick King-Smith
7. Lucy Daniels
8. John Cunliffe
9. Mick Inkpen
10. Eric Hill
11. Roderick Hunt
12. Shirley Hughes
13. Nick Butterworth
14. Martin Waddell
15. Goscinny
16. Jacqueline Wilson
17. Tony Bradman
18. Jill Murphy
19. David McKee
20. Colin & Jacqui Hawkins

Parliament allocates a sum each year (£5,150,000 for 2000-01) for PLR. This Fund pays the administrative costs of PLR and reimburses local authorities for recording loans in the sample libraries. The remaining money is then divided by the total registered loan figure in order to work out how much can be paid for each estimated loan of a registered book.

Limits on payments

Bottom limit. If all the registered interests in an author's books score so few loans that they would earn less than £5 in a year, no payment is due.

Top limit. If the books of one registered author score so high that the author's PLR earnings for the year would exceed £6000, then only £6000 is paid. No author can earn more than £6000 in PLR in any one year.

Money that is not paid out because of these limits belongs to the Fund and increases the amounts paid that year to other authors.

The sample

The basic sample represents only public libraries (no academic, school, private or commercial libraries are included) and only loans made over the counter (not consultations of books on library premises). It follows that only those books which are loaned from public libraries can earn PLR and make an application worthwhile.

The sample consists of the entire loans records for a year from libraries in 30 public library authorities spread through England, Scotland, Wales and Northern Ireland. Sample loans represent 10% of the national total. Several computerised sampling points in an authority contribute loans data ('multi-site' sampling). This change has been introduced gradually, and began in July 1991. The aim has been to increase the sample without any significant increase in costs. In order to counteract sampling error, libraries in the sample change every two to three years. Loans are totalled every 12 months for the period 1 July to 30 June.

An author's entitlement to PLR depends, under the 1979 Act, on the loans accrued by his or her books in the sample. This figure is multiplied to produce first regional and then finally national estimated loans.

Summary of the 17th year's results

Registration: authors When registration closed for the 17th year (30 June 1999) the number of shares in books registered was 304,769 for 30,674 authors. This included 739 German authors.

Eligible loans Of the 480.4 million estimated loans from UK libraries, 215 million belong to books on the PLR register. The loans credited to registered books – 44.8% of all library borrowings – qualify for payment. The remaining 55.2% of loans relate to books that are ineligible for various reasons, to books written by dead or foreign authors, and to books that have simply not been applied for.

Money and payments PLR's administrative costs are deducted from the fund allocated to the Registrar annually by Parliament. Operating the Scheme this year cost £845,000*, representing some 16.7% of the PLR fund. The Rate per Loan for 1999-2000 increased to 2.18 pence and was calculated to distribute all the £4,206,000 available. The total of PLR distribution and costs is therefore the full £5,051,000 which the Government provided in 1999-2000.

The numbers of authors in various payment categories are as follows:

**138	payments at	5000-6000
241	payments between	2500-4999.99
578	payments between	1000-2499.99
747	payments between	500-999.99
3,455	payments between	100-499.99
12,248	payments between	5-99.99
17,407	TOTAL	

There were also 13,267 registered authors whose books earned them nil payment. As a result of the £6000 maximum payment rule some £470,949 became available for redistribution to other authors.

* includes the extra cost of replacing PLR's computer system.

** includes 100 authors where the maximum threshold applied.

ISBNs

PLR depends on the use of code numbers to identify books lent and to correlate loans with entries on the register so that payment can be made. The system uses the International Standard Book Number (ISBN), which is required for all new registrations. Different editions (e.g., 1st, 2nd, hardcover, paperback, large print) of the same book have different ISBNs.

Authorship

In the PLR system the author of a book is the writer, illustrator, translator, compiler, editor or reviser. Authors must be named on the book's title page, or be able to prove authorship by some other means (e.g. receipt of royalties). The ownership of copyright has no bearing on PLR eligibility.

Co-authorship/illustrators

In the PLR system the authors of a book are those writers, translators, editors, compilers and illustrators as defined above. Authors must apply for registration before their books can earn PLR. There is no restriction on the number of authors who can register shares in any one book as long as they satisfy the eligibility criteria.

Writers and/or illustrators

At least one must be eligible and they must jointly agree what share of PLR each will take. This agreement is necessary even if one or two are ineligible or do not wish to register for PLR. Share sizes should be based on contribution. The eligible authors will receive the share(s) specified in the application. PLR can be any whole percentage. Detailed advice is available from the PLR office.

Translators

Translators may apply, without reference to other authors, for a 30% fixed share (to be divided equally between joint translators).

Editors and compilers

An editor or compiler may apply, either with others or without reference to them, to register a 20% share. Unless in receipt of royalties an editor must have written at least 10% of the book's contents or more than 10 pages of text in addition to normal editorial work. The share of joint editors/compilers is 20% in total to be divided equally. An application from an editor or compiler to register a greater percentage share must be accompanied by supporting documentary evidence of actual contribution.

Dead or missing co-authors

Where it is impossible to agree shares with a co-author because that person is dead or untraceable, then the surviving co-author or co-authors may submit an application without the dead or missing co-author but must name the co-author and provide supporting evidence as to why that co-author has not agreed shares. The living co-author(s) will then be able to register a share in the book which will be 20% for the illustrator (or illustrators) and the residual percentage for the writer (or writers). If this percentage is to be divided between more than one writer or illustrator, then this will be in equal shares unless some other apportionment is requested and agreed by the Registrar.

The PLR Office keeps a file of missing authors (mostly illustrators) to help locate co-authors. Help is also available from publishers, the writers' organisations, and the Association of Illustrators.

Life and death

Authors can only be registered for PLR during their lifetime. However, for authors so registered, books can later be registered if first published within one year before their death or 10 years afterwards. New versions of titles registered by the author can be registered posthumously.

Residential qualifications

Eligibility for PLR is restricted to authors who are resident in the United Kingdom or Germany. However, the government is expected to extend eligibility to authors resident in all European Community countries with effect from 1 July 2000. A resident in these countries (for PLR purposes) has his or her only or principal home there. The United Kingdom does not include the Channel Islands or the Isle of Man.

Further information

Public Lending Right
PLR Office, Richard House, Sorbonne Close, Stockton-on-Tees TS17 6DA
tel (01642) 604699 *fax* (01642) 615641
web sites http://www.plr.uk.com
http://www.plrinternational.com
Contact The Registrar

Application forms, information, publications and a copy of its *Annual Report* are all obtainable from the PLR Office. Further information on eligibility for PLR, loans statistics and forthcoming developments may be found on PLR's web site.

PLR Advisory Committee

Advises the Secretary of State for Culture, Media and Sport and the Registrar on the operation of the PLR scheme.

Eligible books

In the PLR system each separate edition of a book is registered and treated as a separate book. A book is eligible for PLR registration provided that:

- it has an eligible author (or co-author);
- it is printed and bound (paperbacks counting as bound);
- copies of it have been put on sale (i.e. it is not a free handout and it has already been published);
- it is not a newspaper, magazine, journal or periodical;
- the authorship is personal (i.e. not a company or association) and the book is not crown copyright;
- it is not wholly or mainly a musical score;
- it has an ISBN.

Notification and payment

Every registered author receives from the Registrar an annual statement of estimated loans for each book and the PLR due.

Sampling arrangements

Libraries

To help minimise the unfairnesses that arise inevitably from a sampling system, the Scheme specifies the eight regions within which authorities and sampling points have to be designated and includes libraries of varying size. Part of the sample drops out by rotation each year to allow fresh libraries to be included. The following library authorities have been designated for the year beginning 1 July 2000 (all are multi-site authorities):

- Wales: Flintshire, Gwynedd, Cardiff;
- Scotland: West Lothian, Glasgow, Highland;
- Northern Ireland: North-Eastern Education & Library Board (NEELB), Belfast;
- London: Barking and Dagenham, Bromley, Ealing, Southwark;
- Metropolitan Boroughs: Birmingham, Stockport, Sheffield, Bradford, Wakefield;
- Counties SE: Hertfordshire, Northamptonshire, Suffolk, Surrey, Essex;
- Counties SW: Cornwall, Somerset, Southampton, Warwickshire;
- Counties N: Cheshire, Durham, Hull, Stockton.

Participating local authorities are reimbursed on an actual cost basis for additional expenditure incurred in providing loans data to the PLR Office. The extra PLR work mostly consists of modifications to computer programs to accumulate loans data in the local authority computer and to transmit the data to the PLR Office at Stockton-on-Tees.

Reciprocal arrangements

In 1981-2 reciprocal arrangements with West Germany were sought by British writers to help ensure that they did not lose the German PLR payments they had enjoyed since 1974 under international copyright law. The German Scheme, although loan based, is very different in most other respects and operates under German copyright law. Reciprocity was brought into effect in January 1985. Authors can apply for German PLR through the Authors' Licensing and Collecting Society. (Further information on PLR schemes internationally and recent developments within the EC towards wider recognition of PLR is available from the PLR office or on the international web site.)

Copyright and libel

Copyright questions

Copyright is a vital part of any writer's assets, and should never be assigned or sold without due consideration and the advice of a competent authority, such as the Society of Authors, the Writers' Guild of Great Britain, or the National Union of Journalists. ***Michael Legat*** *answers some of the most commonly asked questions about copyright.*

Is there a period of time after which the copyright expires?
Copyright in the European Union lasts for the lifetime of the author and for a further 70 years from the end of the year of death, or, if the work is first published posthumously, for 70 years from the end of the year of publication. In most other countries of the world copyright exists similarly for the lifetime and for either 50 years or 70 years after death or posthumous publication.

If I want to include an extract from a book, poem or article, do I have to seek copyright? How much may be used without permission? What happens if I apply for copyright permission but do not get a reply?
It is essential to seek permission to quote from another author's work, unless that author has been dead for 70 years or more, or 70 years or more has passed from the date of publication of a work published posthumously. Only if you are quoting for purposes of criticism or review are you allowed to do so without obtaining permission, and even then the Copyright, Designs and Patents Act of 1988 restricts you to 400 words of prose in a single extract from a copyright work, or a series of extracts of up to 300 words each, totalling no more than 800 words, or up to 40 lines of poetry, which must not be more than 25% of the poem. However, a quotation of no more than, say, half a dozen words may usually be used without permission since it will probably not extend beyond a brief and familiar reference, as, for example, Rider Haggard's well-known phrase, 'she who must be obeyed'. If in doubt, always check. If you do not get a reply when you ask for permission to quote, insert a notice in your work saying that you have tried without success to contact the copyright owner, and would be pleased to hear from him or her so that the matter could be cleared up – and keep a copy of all the relevant correspondence, in order to back up your claim of having tried to get in touch.

If a newspaper pays for an article and I then want to sell the story to a magazine, am I free under the copyright law to do so?
Yes, provided that you have not granted copyright to the newspaper. When selling your work to newspapers or magazines you should make it clear, in writing, that you are selling only First or Second Serial Rights, not your copyright.

If I agree to have an article published for no payment do I retain any rights over how it appears?
Whether or not you are paid for the work has no bearing on the legal situation. However, the Moral Rights which apply to books, plays, television and radio scripts, do not cover you against a failure to acknowledge you as the author of an article, nor against the mutilation of your text, when it is published in a newspaper or magazine.

I want to publish a photograph that was taken in 1950. I am not sure how to

contact the photographer or even if he is still alive. Am I allowed to go ahead and publish it?
The Copyright, Designs and Patents Act of 1988 works retrospectively, so a photograph taken in 1950 is bound to be in copyright until at least 2020, and the copyright will be owned by the photographer, even though, when it was taken, the copyright would have belonged to the person who commissioned it, according to the laws then in place. You should therefore make every effort to contact the photographer, keeping copies of any relevant correspondence, and in case of failure take the same course of action as described above in relation to a textual extract the copyright owner of which you have been unable to trace.

I recently read an article on the same subject as one I have written. It contained many identical facts. Did this writer breach my copyright? What if I send ideas for an article to a magazine editor and those ideas are used despite the fact that I was not commissioned? May I sue the magazine?
Facts are normally in the public domain and may be used by anyone. However, if your article contains a fact which you have discovered and no one else has published, there could be an infringement of copyright if the author who uses it fails to attribute it to you. There is no copyright in ideas, so you cannot sue a writer or a journal for using ideas that you have put forward; in any case you would find it very difficult to prove that the idea belonged to you and to no one else. There is also no copyright in titles.

Does being paid a kill fee affect my copyright in a given piece?
No, provided that you have not sold the magazine or newspaper your copyright.

Do I need to copyright a piece of writing physically – whether an essay or a novel – or is it copyrighted automatically? Does it have to carry the © symbol?
Anything that you write is your copyright, assuming that it is not copied from the work of someone else, as soon as you have written it on paper or recorded it on the disk of a computer or on tape, or broadcast it. It is not essential for the work to carry the © symbol, although its inclusion may act as a warning and help to stop another writer from plagiarising it.

Am I legally required to inform an interviewee that our conversation is being recorded?
The interviewee owns the copyright of any words that he or she speaks as soon as they are recorded on your tape. Unless you have received permission to use those words in direct quotation, you could be liable to an action for infringement of copyright. You should therefore certainly inform the interviewee that the conversation is being recorded and seek permission to quote what is said directly.

More and more newspapers and magazines have versions both in print and on the Internet. How can I ensure that my work is not published on the Internet without my permission?
Make sure that any clause granting electronic rights to anyone in any agreement that you sign in respect of your work specifies not only the proportion of any fees received which you will get, but that your agreement must be sought before the rights are sold. Copyright extends to electronic rights, and therefore to publication on the Internet, in just the same way as to other uses of the material.

I commissioned a designer to design a business card for me, and I paid her well. Does the design belong to me or to her?
The design right in the design belongs to you as the person who commissioned the work. This is in contrast to the position regarding photographs, where the copyright belongs to the photographer, even if the photograph was commissioned. The design right expires 15 years after the end of the year in which the design was made.

Michael Legat became a full-time writer after a long and successful publishing career. He is the author of a number of highly regarded books on publishing and writing.

British copyright law

Copyright is a creature of statute. There have been a series of Copyright Acts over the years, gradually extending the scope of this area of the law so as to offer protection to the widening range of media used by writers and artists of all types. In an article of this length, it is not possible to deal fully with all the complexities of this technical area of the law. Rather, ***Amanda L. Michaels****, barrister, sets out the basic principles of copyright protection, and identifies topics which may be of particular interest to readers of this Yearbook.*

Since 1 August 1989, the law relating to copyright in the United Kingdom has been governed by the Copyright, Designs & Patents Act 1988 ('the Act'), which replaced the Copyright Act 1956. The Act largely restated the existing law (mere changes of expression did not denote a substantive change: see section 172) but certain parts of the Act were innovative, in particular in the creation of a new 'design right' offering protection (generally speaking in lieu of copyright) for many industrial or commercial designs, and in the wider protection of an author or artist's moral rights.

Changes to the law since 1989

On 1 January 1996, further important changes were made to UK copyright law, upon the implementation of EC Directive 93/98 ('the Term Directive') by the Duration of Copyright and Rights in Performances Regulations 1995 (SI 1995 No 3297). The Term Directive harmonised copyright laws throughout the European Union as to the period of copyright protection offered to various types of copyright work, with a view to avoiding distortions within the internal market. Rather than take away vested rights in any one state, the term was harmonised 'upwards' to meet the longest protection already offered in Germany. The end result is that the term of copyright in the UK and in some other countries has been extended from the 'life of the author plus 50 years' to life plus 70 years. Numerous works may, as a result, benefit from a 'revived' term of copyright protection in the UK and this may well make the task of deciding whether a work is still protected by copyright fraught with difficulty (see below). The Regulations also deal with what is to happen to a variety of existing rights (e.g. publishing contracts) in works offered an extended term of protection.

Further amendments continue to be made to the Act, for instance in the Copyright and Rights in Databases Regulations 1997, implementing EC Council Directive No 96/9/EC, which came into force on 1 January 1998.

Continuing relevance of old law

Copyright is a long-term right, and an important element of the Act is the provision made for 'existing works', and the other transitional provisions contained in Schedule 1 of the Act. Whilst generally speaking works in copyright on 1 August 1989 when the Act came into force will have obtained the protection offered to more modern works under the Act, certain categories of work did not fare so well, and, in particular, artistic works protected under the Act only by design right (see below) which were given a 10-year 'grace period' of copyright protection by Schedule 1, will now have lost that protection. When looking at a work made before 1 August 1989, therefore, it may well be necessary to look not simply at the Act, and its Schedule 1, but also at earlier copyright Acts, and where foreign works are concerned, it will also be necessary to look at subordinate legislation for all relevant periods.

Users of this *Yearbook* particularly need to note that publishing and similar agreements and licences drafted for use before 1989 may well need revision to protect all necessary rights, and especially moral rights (see below).

Copyright protection of works

Copyright has always protected the form in which the artist/author has set out his or her inspiration, not the underlying idea. Plots, artistic ideas, systems and themes cannot be protected as such by copyright. Whilst an idea remains no more than that, it can be protected only by the law relating to confidential information (contrast the cases of *Green* v. *Broadcasting Corp. of New Zealand* [1989] RPC 700: no copyright in 'format' of *Opportunity Knocks*, and *Fraser* v. *Thames TV Ltd* [1984] QB 44: plot of a projected television series protected by law of confidence). The law of copyright prevents the copying of the material form in which the idea has been presented, or of a substantial part of it, measured in terms of quality, not quantity.

The Act therefore starts out, in section 1, by setting out a number of different categories of works which can be the subject of copyright protection. These are:

- original literary, dramatic, musical or artistic works,
- sound recordings, films, broadcasts or cable programmes, and
- typographical arrangements of published editions.

These works are further defined in sections 3 to 8 (see box for examples).

The definitions of literary and musical works do not, however, contradict the basic rule that copyright protects the form (or the 'expression of the idea') and not the idea; works are not protected before being reduced into tangible form. Section 3(2) specifically provides that no copyright shall subsist in a literary, musical or artistic work until it has been recorded in writing or otherwise.

Definitions under the Act

Literary work is defined as: 'any work, other than a dramatic or musical work, which is written, spoken or sung, and accordingly includes: (a) a table or compilation other than a database, (b) a computer program, (c) preparatory design material for a computer program and (d) a database.'

A musical work means: 'a work consisting of music, exclusive of any words or action intended to be sung, spoken or performed with the music.'

An artistic work means: '(a) a graphic work, photograph, sculpture or collage, irrespective of artistic quality, (b) a work of architecture being a building or model for a building, or (c) a work of artistic craftsmanship.'

On the other hand, all that is required to achieve copyright protection is to record the original work in any appropriate medium. Once that has been done, copyright will subsist in the work (assuming that the qualifying features set out below are present) without any formality of registration or otherwise. As long as the work is recorded in some tangible form there is, for instance, no need for it to be published in any way for the protection to attach to it. (Please note, however, that although this lack of formality applies here and in most European countries, the law of the United States does differ). The common idea that one must register a work at Stationers Hall, or send it to oneself or to, say, a bank, in a sealed envelope so as to obtain copyright protection is incorrect. All that this precaution may do is provide some proof in an infringement action (whether as claimant or defendant) of the date of creation and form of one's work.

Originality

In order to gain copyright protection, literary, dramatic, artistic and musical works must be original. Sound recordings or films which are mere copies of pre-existing sound recordings and films, broadcasts which infringe rights in another broadcast or cable programmes which consist of immediate retransmissions of broadcasts are not protected by copyright.

The test of originality may not be quite that expected by the layperson. Just as the law protects the form, rather than the idea, originality relates to the 'expression of the thought', rather than to the thought itself. A work need not be original in the sense of showing innovative or cultural merit, it needs only to have been the product of skill and labour on the part of the author. This can be seen from various sections in the Act, for instance in the definition of certain artistic works, and in the fact that it offers copyright protection to works such as compilations (like football pools coupons or directories) and tables (including mathematical tables).

There may be considerable difficulty, at times, in deciding whether a work is of sufficient originality, or has original features, where there have been a series of similar designs or amendments of existing works. See *L.A. Gear Inc.* v. *Hi-Tec Sports plc* [1992] FSR 121 and *Biotrading* v. *Biohit* [1998] FSR 109. A new edition of an existing work, or an adaptation of one, may obtain a new copyright depending upon the scope of the changes to the work; this will not affect the earlier copyright protection. See *Cala Homes (South) Ltd* v. *Alfred McAlpine Homes East Ltd* [1995] FSR 818. What is clear, though, is that merely making a 'slavish copy' of a drawing will not create an original work: see *Interlego AG* v. *Tyco Industries* [1989] AC 217.

On the other hand, 'works' comprising the titles of books or periodicals, or advertising slogans, which may have required a good deal of original thought, generally are not accorded copyright protection, because they are too short to be deemed literary works. See, too, the limited protection given to drawings of a functional or engineering type in the sections on infringement and design right below.

Qualification

The Act is limited in its effects to the UK (and to colonies to which it may be extended by Order in Council). It is aimed primarily at protecting the works of British citizens, or works which were first published here. However, in line with the requirements of various international conventions to which the UK is a party, copyright protection in the UK is also accorded to the works of nationals of many foreign states which are also party to these conventions, as well as to works first published in those states, on a reciprocal basis.

The position is somewhat different where copyright in works of nationals of other member states of the European Union are concerned, as there is a principle of equal treatment which applies to copyright protection, so that protection must be offered to such works here: see *Phil Collins* v. *Imtrat Handelsgesellschaft mbH* (Case C92/92) [1993] 2 CMLR 773.

The importance of these rules mainly arises when one is trying to find out whether a pre-existing foreign work is protected by copyright here, for instance, if one wishes to make a film based upon a foreign novel.

Ownership

The general rule is that a work will initially be owned by its author, the author being the creator of the work, or in the case of a film or sound recording, the person who makes the arrangements necessary for it to be made. The Term Directive provided that the 'principal director' of a film shall be deemed to be its author or one of its authors.

One important exception to the general rule is that the copyright in a work made by an employee in the course of his or her employment will belong to their employer, subject to any agreement to the contrary. However, this rule applies only to true employees, not to freelance designers, journalists, etc, and not even to nominally self-employed company directors. This obviously may lead to problems if the question of copyright ownership is not agreed (see box on page 637).

Where a work is produced by several people who collaborate in such a way that each one's contribution is not distinct from that of the other(s), then they will be the joint authors of the work. Where two people collaborate to write a song, one producing the lyrics and the other the music, there will be two separate copyright works, the copyright of which will be owned by each of the authors separately. But where two people write a play, each rewriting what the other produces, there will be a joint work.

The importance of knowing whether the work is joint or not arises:

- in working out the duration of the copyright, and
- from the fact that joint works can only be exploited with the agreement of all the joint authors, so that all of them have to join in any licence, although each of them can sue for infringement without joining the other(s) in the proceedings.

Duration of copyright

As a result of the amendments brought into effect on 1 January 1996, copyright in literary, dramatic, musical or artistic works expires at the end of the period of 70 years from the end of the calendar year in which the author dies (new section 12(1)). Where there are joint authors (see 'Ownership', above), then the 70 years runs from the year of the death of the last of them to die. If the author is unknown, there will be 70 years protection from the date the work was first made or (where applicable) first made available to the public by being performed, etc.

The extended 70-year term also applies to films, and runs from the end of the calendar year in which the death occurs of the last to die of the principal director, the author of the screenplay, the author of the dialogue or the composer of any music especially created for the film (new section 13B). This could obviously be a nightmare to establish, and there are certain presumptions in section 66A which may help someone wishing to use material from an old film.

However, sound recordings are still protected by copyright for only 50 years from the year of making or release (new section 13A); similarly, broadcasts and cable programmes still get only 50 years protection. Computer-generated works keep a 50-year term of protection.

The new longer term obviously applies without difficulty to works created after 1 January 1996. Nor is the extension of term especially hard to apply to works which were in copyright here on 31 December 1995, as the term will simply be extended for a further 20 years. The owner of that extended copyright will be the person who owned it on 31 December 1995, unless that person had only a limited term of ownership, in which case the extra 20 years will be added on to the reversionary term (see paragraph 18 of the Regulations).

Where copyright had expired here, but the author died between 50 and 70 years ago, the position is more complicated. The Term Directive provided that if a work was protected by copyright anywhere in the European Union on 1 July 1995, then copyright protection should revive for it in any other state in which it had expired, until the end of the same 70-year period (this was given effect by paragraph 16(d) of the 1995 Regulations). This is not, unfortunately, simply a question of looking at the date of the author's death, since protection may not have been offered to a particular work even by Germany, the state offering the 70-year period of protection prior to the Directive, for other reasons, e.g. lack of originality according to German law. It might therefore be necessary to look at the position in the other states offering a longer term of protection, namely France and Spain.

Ownership of the revived term of copyright will belong to the person who was the owner of the copyright when the initial term expired, save that if that person died (or a company, etc, ceased to exist) before 1 January 1996, then the revived term will vest in the author or his or her personal representatives, and in the case of a film, in the principal director or his personal representatives (paragraph 19 of the Regulations).

The increased term offered to works of other EU nationals as a result of the Term Directive is not offered automatically to the nationals of other states, but will only apply where an equally long term is offered in their state of origin (new subsections 12(6), 13A(4) and 13B(7)).

Where acts are carried out in relation to such revived copyright works, pursuant to things done whilst they were in the public domain prior to such revival, certain protection from infringement is available (see paragraph 23 of the Regulations). A licence as of right may also be available, on giving notice to the copyright owner and paying a royalty (see paragraph 24).

Finally, where one is dealing with a work made before the Act came into force, one needs to look at the law in force when it was made, as well as at the transitional provisions of the 1956 Act (for pre-1957 works) and/or of the Act (for pre-1989 works).

Dealing with copyright works

Ownership of the copyright in a work confers upon the owner the exclusive right to deal with the work in a number of ways, and essentially stops all unauthorised exploitation of the work. Ownership of the copyright is capable of being separated from ownership of the material form in which the work is embodied, and whether the purchase of the latter includes the former will depend upon the terms of any agreement or the circumstances. Buying a copy of a book does not transfer the ownership of the copyright in the underlying work, but purchasing an original manuscript or a unique piece of sculpture might do so, depending upon the circumstances and/or any express agreement between the parties.

Copyright works can be exploited by their owners in two ways:

- Assignment: rights in the work may be sold, with the owner retaining no interest in it (except, possibly, for payment by way of royalties or some reversionary rights in certain agreed circumstances); or
- Licensing: the owner may grant a licence to another to exploit the right, whilst retaining overall ownership.

Agreements dealing with copyright should make it clear whether an assignment or a licence is being granted, and should clearly define the scope of any assignment or licence. There may be significant advantages in granting a licence rather than an assignment, for where the assignee sells the rights to a third party, or perhaps the rights are sold by the liquidator or trustee in bankruptcy of an insolvent assignee, it may prove impossible to require the purchaser to pay royalties or abide by other contractual obligations on the part of the original assignee (see e.g. *Barker* v. *Stickney* [1919] 1 KB 121). If the agreement is unclear, the Court is likely to find that the grantee took the minimum rights necessary for his intended use of the work (see *Ray* v. *Classic FM plc* [1998] F.S.R. 622). The question of moral rights (see below) will also have to be considered by parties negotiating an assignment or licence.

Both assignments and licences can, and frequently do, split up the various rights contained within the copyright. So, for instance, a licence might be granted to one

Assignments

In an assignment, rights in the work are sold, with the owner retaining no interest in it (except, possibly, for payment by way of royalties).

An assignment must be in writing, signed by or on behalf of the assignor, but no other formality is required. One can make an assignment of future copyright (under section 91). Where the author of a projected work agrees in writing that he will assign the rights in a future work to another, the copyright vests in the assignee immediately upon the creation of the work, without further formalities.

These rules do not affect the common law as to beneficial interests in copyright. One possibility may be that a court will, in the right circumstances, find or infer an agreement to assign the copyright in a work, e.g. where a sole trader had title to the copyright used in his business incorporated his business and allowed the company to exploit the software as if it were its own, an agreement to assign was inferred (see *Lakeview Computers plc* v. *Steadman* 26/1/99). Alternatively, if the court finds that a work was commissioned to be made, but the copyright has not automatically vested in the 'commissioner', despite a common intention that he should own the copyright, the court may order the author to assign the copyright to the commissioner. 'Commission' in this context means only to order a particular piece of work to be done: see *Apple Corps Ltd* v. *Cooper* [1993] FSR 286 (on the 1956 Act). If no sufficient agreement is found of this sort, then the arrangement is likely to be found to have conferred a licence, whether exclusive or not, upon the 'commissioner'.

Licensing

A licence is granted to another to exploit the right whilst retaining overall ownership.

Licences do not need to take any form in particular, and may indeed be granted orally. However, an exclusive licence (i.e. one which excludes even the copyright owner himself from exploiting the work in the manner authorised by the licence) must be in writing, if the licensee is to enjoy rights in respect of infringements concurrent with those of the copyright owner.

person to publish a novel in hardback and to another to publish in softback, a third person might be granted the film, television and video rights, and yet a fourth the right to translate the novel into other languages.

Assignments and licences may also confer rights according to territory, dividing the USA from the EU or different EU countries one from the other. Two comments must be made about this. Firstly, any such agreement would be dealing with a bundle of different national copyrights, as each country's law extends only to its own borders; each country's law on copyright protection, on licensing and on infringement may differ and will continue to do so even after the implementation of the Term Directive. Secondly, when seeking to divide rights between different territories of the EU there is a danger that one will infringe the competition rules of the EU. Professional advice should be taken to ensure that there is no breach of these rules, which would render the parties liable to a fine, as well as making the agreement void in whole or in part.

Licences can also, of course, be of varying lengths. There is no need for a licence to be granted for the whole term of copyright; indeed this would be unusual, if not foolish. Well-drafted licences will provide for termination on breach, including the failure of the licensee to exploit the work properly, and on the bankruptcy or winding up of the licensee.

Copyright may be assigned by will, and where a bequest is given of an original document, etc embodying an unpublished copyright work, the bequest will carry the copyright.

Any licence affecting a copyright work which subsisted on 31 December 1995 and was then for the full term of the copyright, shall continue to have effect during any extended term of copyright, subject to any agreement to the contrary (paragraph 21 of the Regulations).

Infringement

Copyright is infringed by doing any of a number of specified acts in relation to the copyright work, without the authority of the owner. In all forms of infringement, it suffices if a substantial part of the original is used, and the question is one to be judged according to quality not quantity (see e.g. *Ravenscroft* v. *Herbert* [1980] RPC 193). The form of infringement common to all forms of copyright works is that of copying. This means reproducing the work in any material form. It is important to note that primary infringement, such as copying, can be done innocently of any intention to infringe.

Infringement may occur where an existing work provides the inspiration for a later one, if copying results, e.g. by including edited extracts from a history book in a novel (*Ravenscroft* v. *Herbert*, see above) or using a photograph as the inspiration for a painting (*Baumann* v. *Fussell* [1978] RPC 485). Infringement will not necessarily be prevented merely by the application of significant new skill and labour by the infringer, nor by a change of medium. On the other hand, if the work gives particular expression to a fairly commonplace idea or to an old tale, copyright may subsist in that particular expression of the familiar notion, (see e.g. *Christoffer* v. *Poseidon Film Distributors Limited* [unreported, 6/10/99] in which it was held that a script for an animated film of a story from Homer's *Odyssey* was an original literary work). Copyright protection will be limited to the original features of the work, or those features created or chosen by the author's input of skill and labour. See *Biotrading* above.

In the case of a two-dimensional artistic work, reproduction can mean making a copy in three dimensions, and vice versa, although there is an important limitation on this general rule in section 51 of the Act, which provides that in the case of a 'design document or model' (defined as a record of a design of any aspect of the shape or configuration, internal or external, of the whole or part of an article, other than surface decoration) for something which is not itself an artistic work, it is no infringement to make an article to that design. This means that whilst it would be an infringement of copyright to make an article from a design drawing for, say, a sculpture, it will not be an infringement of copyright to make a handbag from a copy of the design drawing for it, or from a handbag which one has purchased. In order to protect such designs one will have to rely upon design right or upon a registered design (for both see below).

Copying a film, broadcast or cable programme can include making a copy of the whole or a substantial part of any image from it (see section 17(4)). This means that copying one frame of the film will be an infringement, as it was under the previous law (see *Spelling Goldberg Productions* v. *BPC* [1981] RPC 283). It is not an infringement of copyright in a film (though there could be an infringement of the copyright in underlying works) to reshoot the film. See *Norowzian* v. *Arks* [2000] FSR 363.

Copying is generally proved by showing substantial similarities between the original and the alleged copy, plus an opportunity to copy. Surprisingly often, minor errors in the original are reproduced by an infringer.

Copying need not be direct, so that, for instance, where the copyright is in a fabric design, copying the material, without ever having seen the original drawing, will still be an infringement, as will 'reverse engineering' of industrial designs e.g. to make unlicensed spare parts (subject to any defence of implied licence: see *British Leyland Motor Corp* v. *Armstrong Patents Co Ltd* [1984] FSR 591; also see *Mars* v. *Teknowledge* [2000] FSR 138).

Issuing copies of a work to the public when they have not previously been put into circulation in the UK is also an infringement of all types of work.

Other acts which may amount to an infringement depend upon the nature of the work. It will be an infringement of the copyright in a literary, dramatic or musical work to perform it in public, whether by live performance or by playing recordings. Similarly, it is an infringement of the copyright in a sound recording, film, broadcast or cable programme to play or show it in public. Many copyright works will also be infringed by the rental or lending of copies of the work.

One rather different form of infringement is to make an adaptation of a literary, dramatic or musical work. An adaptation includes, in the case of a literary work, a translation, in the case of a non-dramatic work, making a dramatic work of it, and in the case of a dramatic work, making a non-dramatic work of it. A transcription or arrangement of a musical work is an adaptation of it. There are also a number of 'secondary' infringements – see box.

'Secondary' infringements

Secondary infringements consist not of making infringing copies, but of dealing with them in some way. It is an infringement to import an infringing copy into the UK, and to possess in the course of business, or to sell, hire, offer for sale or hire, or distribute in the course of trade an infringing copy. However, none of these acts will be an infringement unless the alleged infringer knew or had reason to believe that the articles were infringing copies. What is sufficient knowledge will depend upon the facts of each case (see *LA Gear Inc.* v. *Hi-Tec Sports plc* [1992] FSR 121 and *ZYX Records* v. *King* [1997] 2 All ER 132). Merely putting someone on notice of a dispute as to ownership of copyright may not suffice to give him or her reason to believe in infringement for this purpose: *Hutchison Personal Communications* v. *Hook Advertising* [1995] FSR 365.

Other secondary infringements consist of permitting a place to be used for a public performance in which copyright is infringed and supplying apparatus to be used for infringing public performance, again, in each case, with safeguards for innocent acts.

Exceptions to infringement

The Act provides a large number of exceptions to the rules on infringement, many of which are innovatory. They are far too numerous to be dealt with here in full, but they include:

- fair dealing with literary, dramatic, musical or artistic works for the purpose of research or private study;
- fair dealing for the purpose of criticism or review or reporting current events, as to which there have been a number of important decisions recently (see e.g. *Pro Sieben Media* v. *Carlton UK TV Limited* [1999] FSR 610; *Hyde Park Residence Limited* v. *Yelland* [unreported, 10/2/2000]);
- incidental inclusion of a work in an artistic work, sound recording, film, broadcast or cable programme;
- various educational exceptions (see sections 32-36);
- various exceptions for libraries (see sections 37-44); various exceptions for public administration (see sections 45-50);
- backing-up, or converting a computer program or accessing a licensed database (see sections 50A-D);
- dealing with a work where the author cannot be identified and the work seems likely to be out of copyright;
- public recitation, if accompanied by a sufficient acknowledgement;
- recording broadcasts or cable programmes at home for viewing at a more convenient time.

Remedies for infringements

The copyright owner has all the remedies offered to other owners of property. Usually the owner will want two things: firstly, to prevent the repetition or continuation of the infringement, and, secondly, compensation.

In almost all cases an injunction will be sought at trial, stopping the continuation of the infringement. The Courts have useful powers to grant an injunction preventing an alleged infringement at an early stage, indeed, even before any infringement takes place, if a real threat of damaging infringement can be shown. Such an interim injunction can be applied for on three days notice (or without notice in appropriate cases), with a view to stopping damaging infringement without having to await the outcome of a full trial. An injunction will not be granted unless the claimant has a reasonably good case and can show that he would suffer 'unquantifiable' damage if the defendant's activities continued pending trial. Certainly, it is always worth considering the matter as soon as an infringement comes to notice, for delay in bringing an interlocutory application may be fatal to its success. The terms of the injunction granted may cover any type of infringement of the work, or may be more narrowly tailored to the acts already carried out by the defendant (see *Microsoft Corporation* v. *Plato Technology Limited* [1999] FSR 834).

Financial compensation may be sought in one of two forms. Firstly, damages may be granted for infringement. These will usually be calculated upon evidence of the loss caused to the claimant, sometimes based upon loss of business, at others upon the basis of what would have been a proper licence fee had the defendant sought a licence for the acts complained of. Additional damages may be awarded in rare cases for flagrant infringements.

Damages will not be awarded for infringement where the infringer did not know, and had no reason to believe, that copyright subsisted in the work. This exception is of limited use to a defendant, though, in the usual situation where he had no actual knowledge of the copyright, but the work was of such a nature that he should have known that copyright would subsist in it.

The alternative to a claim for damages is a claim for an account of profits, that is, the profits made by the infringer by virtue of his illicit exploitation of the copyright. Where an account of profits is sought, no award of flagrant damages can be made. See *Redrow Homes Ltd* v. *Betts Brothers plc* [1998] FSR 345.

A copyright owner may also apply for delivery up of infringing copies of his or her work (sections 99 and 113-15).

Finally, there are various criminal offences relating to the making, importation, possession, sale, hire, distribution, etc of infringing copies (see sections 107-110).

Design right

Many industrial designs are excluded from copyright protection, by reason of the provisions of section 51 of the Act, described above. Alternatively, the term of their copyright protection is limited to 25 years from first industrial exploitation, by section 52 of the Act. However, they may instead be protected by the new 'design right' created by sections 213-64 of the Act. Like copyright, design right does not depend upon registration, but upon the creation of a suitable design by a qualified person.

The protection of the new right is given to original designs consisting of the shape or configuration (internal or external) of the whole or part of an article and not being merely 'surface decoration'. A design is not to be considered original if it was commonplace in the design field in question at the time of its creation. In *Ocular Sciences Ltd* v. *Aspect Vision Care Ltd* [1997] RPC 289 and *Farmers Build* v. *Carier Bulk Materials* [1999] RPC 461, 'commonplace' was defined as meaning a design of a type which would excite no 'peculiar attention' amongst those in the trade, or one which amounts to a run-of-the-mill combination of well-known features. Designs are not protected if they consist of a method or principle of construction, or are dictated by the shape, etc of an article to which the new article is to be connected or of which it is to form part, the so-called 'must-fit' and 'must-match' exclusions. In *Ocular Sciences*, these exclusions had a devastating effect upon numerous design rights claimed for contact lens designs.

Design right will be granted to designs made by qualifying persons (in this part of the Act meaning UK and EU citizens or residents or others to whom the right may be extended) or commissioned by a qualifying person, or first marketed in the UK, another EU state or any other country to which the provision may be extended by Order in Council.

Design right lasts only 15 years from the end of the year in which it was first recorded or an article made to the design, or (if shorter) 10 years from the end of the year in which articles made according to the design were first sold or hired out. During the last five years of the term of protection, a licence to use the design can be obtained 'as of right' but against payment of a proper licence fee.

The designer will be the owner of the right, unless he or she made it in pursuance of a commission, in which case the commissioner will be the first owner of the right. The same rule applies as in copyright, that an employee's designs made in the course of his or her employment will belong to the employer.

The right given to the owner of a design right is the exclusive right to reproduce the design for commercial purposes. The rules as to assignments and licensing and as to infringement, both primary and secondary, are substantially similar to those described above in relation to copyright, as are the remedies available.

Design right coexists with the scheme of *registered* designs of the Registered Designs Act 1949 (as amended by the Act), which provides a monopoly right renewable for up to 25 years in respect of designs which have been accepted on to a register. Registered designs must contain features which appeal to and are judged by the eye, which is not a requirement for design right protection.

Moral rights

The Act also provides for the protection of certain so-called 'moral rights', commonly known as the rights of 'paternity' and 'integrity'.

The right of 'paternity' is for the author of a copyright literary, dramatic, musical or artistic work, and the director of a copyright film, to be identified as the author/director in a number of different situations, largely whenever the work is published, performed or otherwise commercially exploited (section 77).

However, the right does not arise unless it has been 'asserted' by appropriate words in an assignment, or otherwise by an instrument in writing (section 78), or in the case of an artistic work by ensuring that the artist's name appears on the frame, etc. Writers should therefore aim to ensure that all copies of their works carry a clear assertion of their rights under this provision (see end). There are exceptions to the right, in particular where the first ownership of the copyright vested in the author's or director's employer.

The right of 'integrity' is not to have one's work subjected to 'derogatory treatment'. This is defined as meaning an addition to, deletion from, alteration or adaptation of a work (save for a translation of a literary or dramatic work or an arrangement of a musical work involving no more than a change of key or register) which amounts to distortion or mutilation of the work or is otherwise prejudicial to the honour or reputation of the author/director.

Again, infringement of the right takes place when the maltreated work is published commercially or performed or exhibited in public. There are various exceptions set out in section 81 of the Act, in particular where the publication is in a newspaper, etc, and the work was made for inclusion in it or made available with the author's consent.

Where the copyright in the work vested first in the author's or director's employer, he or she has no right to 'integrity' unless identified at the time of the relevant act or on published copies of the work.

These rights subsist for as long as the copyright in the work subsists.

A third moral right conferred by the Act is not to have a literary, dramatic, musical or artistic work falsely attributed to one as author, or to have a film falsely attributed to one as director, again where the work in question is published, etc. This right subsists until 20 years after a person's death.

None of these rights can be assigned during the person's lifetime, but all of them either pass on the person's death as directed by his or her will or fall into his residuary estate.

A fourth but rather different moral right is conferred by section 85. It gives a person who has commissioned the taking of photographs for private purposes a right to prevent copies of the work being issued to the public, etc.

The remedies for breach of these moral rights again include damages and an injunction, although section 103(2) specifically foresees the granting of an injunction qualified by a right to the defendant to do the acts complained of, if subject to a suitable disclaimer.

Moral rights are exercisable in relation to works in which the copyright has revived subject to any waiver or assertion of the right made before 1 January 1996 (see details as to who may exercise rights in paragraph 22 of the Regulations).

NOTICE

I, AMANDA LOUISE MICHAELS, hereby assert and give notice of my right under section 77 of the Copyright, Designs and Patents Act 1988 to be identified as the author of the foregoing article.

AMANDA MICHAELS

Amanda L. Michaels is a barrister in private practice in London, and specialises in copyright, designs, trade marks, and similar intellectual property and 'media' work. She is author of *A Practical Guide to Trade Mark Law* (Sweet & Maxwell, 2nd edn 1996).

Further reading

Garnett, Rayner James and Davies, *Copinger and Skone James on Copyright*, Sweet & Maxwell, 14th edn, 1999

Laddie, Prescott and Vitoria, *The Modern Law of Copyright*, Butterworths, 2nd edn, 1995

Flint, *A User's Guide to Copyright*, Butterworths, 4th edn, 1997

Bainbridge, David, *Intellectual Property*, Pearson Education, 4th edn, 1999

Copyright Acts

Copyright, Designs and Patents Act 1998

The Duration of Copyright and Rights in Performances Regulations 1995 (SI 1995 No 3297)

see also Numerous Orders in Council

US copyright law

When authors and other artists take their work overseas, the complex subject of copyright can become even more daunting. ***Gavin McFarlane****, barrister, introduces US copyright law and points out the differences, and similarities, of British copyright law.*

International copyright

International copyright conventions

There is no general principle of international copyright which provides a uniform code for the protection of right owners throughout the world. There are, however, two major international copyright conventions which lay down certain minimum standards for member states, in particular requiring member states to accord to right owners of other member states the same protection which is granted to their own nationals. One is the higher standard Berne Convention of 1886, the most recent revision of which was signed in Paris in 1971. The other is the Universal Copyright Convention signed in 1952 with lower minimum standards, and sponsored by Unesco. This also was most recently revised in Paris in 1971, jointly with the Berne Convention. To this latter Convention the United States has belonged since 1955. On 16 November 1988, the Government of the United States deposited its instrument of accession to the Paris Revision of the Berne Convention. The Convention entered into force as regards the United States on 1 March 1989. Together with certain new statutory provisions made in consequence of accession to Berne, this advances substantially the process of overhaul and modernisation of US copyright law which was begun in the 1970s.

Effect on British copyright owners

The copyright statute of the United States having been brought into line with the requirements of the Berne compliance with the formalities required by American law has been largely removed. The Berne Convention Implementation Act of 1988 makes statutory amendments to the way foreign works are now treated in US law. These are now inserted in the US codified law as Title 17 – The Copyright Act. 'Foreign works' are works having a country of origin other than the United States. The formalities which were for so long a considerable handicap for foreign copyright owners in the American system have now become optional, though not removed altogether. The new system provides incentives to encourage foreign right owners to continue to comply with formalities on a voluntary basis, in particular notice, renewal and registration.

US copyright law – summary

Introduction of new law

After many years of debate, the new Copyright Statute of the United States was passed on 19 October 1976. The greater part of its relevant provisions came into force on 1 January 1978. It has extended the range of copyright protection, and further eased the requirements whereby British authors can obtain copyright protection in America. New Public Law 100-568 of 31 October 1988 has made further amendments to the Copyright Statute which were necessary to enable ratification of the Berne Convention to take place. The Universal Copyright

Convention is now for all practical purposes moribund. The problems which derived from the old system of common law copyright no longer exist.

The rights of a copyright owner

(1) To reproduce the copyrighted work in copies or phonorecords.
(2) To prepare derivative works based upon the copyrighted work.
(3) To distribute copies or phonorecords of the copyrighted work to the public by sale or other transfer of ownership, or by rental, lease or lending.
(4) In the case of literary, musical, dramatic and choreographic works, pantomimes, and motion pictures and other audiovisual works, but not sound recordings, to perform the copyrighted work publicly. However, in 1995 Congress granted a limited performance right to sound recordings in digital format in an interactive medium.
(5) In the case of literary, musical, dramatic, and choreographic works, pantomimes, and pictorial, graphic, or sculptural works, including the individual images of a motion picture or other audiovisual work, to display the copyrighted work publicly.
(6) By the Record Rental Amendment Act 1984, s.109 of the Copyright Statute is amended. Now, unless authorised by the owners of copyright in the sound recording and the musical works thereon, the owner of a phonorecord may not, for direct or indirect commercial advantage, rent, lease or lend the phonorecord. A compulsory licence under s.115(c) includes the right of a maker of a phonorecord of non-dramatic musical work to distribute or authorise the distribution of the phonorecord by rental, lease, or lending, and an additional royalty is payable in respect of that. This modifies the 'first sale doctrine', which otherwise permits someone buying a copyright work to hire or sell a lawfully purchased copy to third parties without compensating the copyright owners, and without his or her consent.
(7) A further exception to the 'first sale doctrine' and s.109 of the Copyright Act is made by the Computer Software Rental Amendments Act. A similar restriction has been placed on the unauthorised rental, lease or lending of software, subject to certain limited exceptions. Both the phonorecord and software exceptions to the first sale doctrine terminated, and were extended by Congress on 1 October 1997.
(8) The Semiconductor Chip Protection Act 1984 adds to the Copyright Statute a new chapter on the protection of semiconductor chip products.
(9) The Visual Artists Rights Act 1990 has added moral rights to the various economic rights listed above. These moral rights are the right of integrity, and the right of attribution or paternity. A new category of 'work of visual art' is defined broadly as paintings, drawings, prints and sculptures, with an upper limit of 200 copies. Works generally exploited in mass market copies such as books, newspapers, motion pictures and electronic information services are specifically excluded from these moral rights provisions. Where they apply, they do so only in respect of works created on or after 1 June 1991, and to certain works previously created where title has not already been transferred by the author.

Manufacturing requirements

With effect from 1 July 1986, these ceased to have effect. Prior to 1 July 1986, the importation into or public distribution in the United States of a work consisting preponderantly of non-dramatic literary material that was in the English language and protected under American law was prohibited unless the portions consisting of such material had been manufactured in the United States or Canada. This provision did not apply where, on the date when importation was sought or public distribution in the United States was made, the author of any substantial part of such material was not a national of the United States or, if a national, had been domiciled outside the United States for a continuous period of at least one year immediately preceding that date.

Works protected in American law

Works of authorship include the following categories:

- Literary works. Note: Computer programs are classified as literary works for the purposes of United States copyright. In *Whelan Associates Inc.* v. *Jaslow Dental Laboratory Inc.* (1987) FSR1, it was held that the copyright of a computer program could be infringed even in the absence of copying of the literal code if the structure was part of the expression of the idea behind a program rather than the idea itself.
- Musical works, including any accompanying words.
- Dramatic works, including any accompanying music.
- Pantomimes and choreographic works.
- Pictorial, graphic and sculptural works.
- Motion pictures and other audiovisual works. Note: copyright in certain motion pictures has been extended by the North American Free Trade Agreement Information Act 1993.
- Sound recordings, but copyright in sound recordings is not to include a right of public performance.
- Architectural works: the design of a building as embodied in any tangible medium of expression, including a building, architectural plans or drawings. The Architectural Works Copyright Protections Act applies this protection to works created on or after 1 December 1990.

Since 1 July 1986, there is no manufacturing requirement in respect of works of British authors. With American ratification of the Berne Convention, the formalities previously required in relation to copyright notice, deposit and registration have been greatly modified.

Formalities

Notice of copyright. Whenever a work protected by the American Copyright Statute is published in the United States or elsewhere by authority of the copyright owner, a notice of copyright should be placed on all publicly distributed copies. This should consist of:

- either the symbol © or the word 'Copyright' or the abbreviation 'Copr.' plus
- the year of first publication of the work, plus
- the name of the copyright owner.

Since the Berne Amendments, both US and works of foreign origin which were first published in the US after 1 March 1989 without having notice of copyright placed on them will no longer be unprotected. In general, authors are advised to place copyright notices on their works, as this is a considerable deterrent to plagiarism. Damages may well be lower in a case where no notice of copyright was placed on the work.

Deposit. The owner of copyright or the exclusive right of publication in a work published with notice of copyright in the United States must within three months of such publication deposit in the Copyright Office for the use or disposition of the Library of Congress two complete copies of the best edition of the work (or two records, if the work is a sound recording). Failure to comply with the deposit requirements does not result in the loss of copyright, but a court could assess fines and issue an injunction.

Registration. Registration for copyright in the United States is optional. However, any owner of copyright in a work first published outside the United States may register a work by making application to the Copyright Office with the appropriate fee, and by depositing one complete copy of the work. This requirement of deposit may be satisfied by using copies deposited for the Library of Congress. Whilst registration is still a requirement for works of US origin and from non-Berne countries as a precondition to filing an infringement action, it is no longer necessary for foreign works from Berne countries. But as a matter of practice there are procedural advantages in any litigation where there has been registration. The United States has interpreted the Berne Convention as allowing formalities which are not in themselves conditions for obtaining copyright protection, but which lead to improved protection. The law allows statutory damages and attorneys' fees only if the work was registered prior to the infringement.

Restoration of copyright

Works by non-US authors which lost copyright protection in the United States because of failure to comply with any of these formalities may have had protection automatically restored in certain circumstances. Works claiming restoration must still be in copyright in their country of origin. If a work succeeds in having copyright restored, it will last for the remainder of the period to which it would originally have been entitled in the United States.

Duration of copyright

Copyright in a work created on or after 1 January 1978 endures for a term of the life of the author, and a period of 50 years after the author's death. The further amendments made by Public Law 100-568 of 31 October 1988 have enabled the government to ratify the higher standard Berne Convention. Copyright in a work created before 1 January 1978, but not published or copyrighted before then, subsists from 1 January 1978, and lasts for the life of the author and a post-mortem period of 50 years.

Any copyright, the first term of which under the previous law was still subsisting on 1 January 1978, shall endure for 28 years from the date when it was originally secured, and the copyright proprietor or his or her representative may apply for a further term of 47 years within one year prior to the expiry of the original term. Until 1992, application for renewal and extension was required. Failure to do so produced disastrous results with some material of great merit passing into the public domain in error. By Public Law 102-307 enacted on 26 June 1992, there is no longer necessity to make a renewal registration in order to obtain the longer period of protection. Now renewal copyright vests automatically in the person entitled to renewal at the end of the 28th year of the original term of copyright.

The duration of any copyright, the renewal term of which was subsisting at any time between 31 December 1976 and 31 December 1977, or for which renewal registration was made between those dates, is extended to endure for a term of 75 years from the date copyright was originally secured.

All terms of copyright provided for by the sections referred to above run to the end of the calendar year in which they would otherwise expire.

Public performance

Under the previous American law the provisions relating to performance in public were less generous to right owners than those existing in United Kingdom copyright law. In particular, performance of a musical work was formerly only an infringement if it was 'for profit'. Moreover, the considerable American coin-operated record-playing machine industry (juke boxes) had obtained an exemption from being regarded as instruments of profit, and accordingly their owners did not have to pay royalties for the use of copyright musical works.

Now by the new law one of the exclusive rights of the copyright owner is, in the case of literary, musical, dramatic and choreographic works, pantomimes, and motion pictures and other audiovisual works, to perform the work publicly, without any requirement of such performance being 'for profit'. By Section 114 however, the exclusive rights of the owner of copyright in a sound recording are specifically stated not to include any right of public performance, although this provision was modified in 1995.

The position of coin-operated record players (juke boxes) is governed by the new Section 116A, inserted by Public Law 100-568 of 31 October 1988. It covers the position of negotiated licences. Limitations are placed on the exclusive right if licences are not negotiated.

Mechanical right

Where sound recordings of a non-dramatic musical work have been distributed to the public in the United States with the authority of the copyright owner, any other person may, by following the provisions of the law, obtain a compulsory licence to make and distribute sound recordings of the work. This right is known in the United Kingdom as 'the mechanical right'. Notice must be served on the copyright owner, who is entitled to a royalty in respect of each of his or her works recorded of either two and three fourths cents or one half of one cent per minute of playing time or fraction thereof, whichever amount is the larger. These rates are adjusted periodically by the Copyright Arbitration Royalty Panels (CARP). Failure to serve or file the required notice forecloses the possibility of a compulsory licence and, in the absence of a negotiated licence, renders the making and distribution of such records actionable as acts of infringement.

Transfer of copyright

Under the previous American law copyright was regarded as indivisible, which meant that on the transfer of copyright, where it was intended that only film rights or some other such limited right be transferred, the entire copyright nevertheless had to be passed. This led to a cumbersome procedure whereby the author would assign the whole copyright to his or her publisher, who would return to the author by means of an exclusive licence those rights which it was not meant to transfer.

Now it is provided by Section 201(d) of the Copyright Statute that (1) the ownership of a copyright may be transferred in whole or in part by any means of conveyance or by operation of law, and may be bequeathed by will or pass as personal property by the applicable laws of intestate succession and (2) any of the exclusive rights comprised in a copyright (including any subdivision of any of the rights set out in 'The rights of a copyright owner' above) may be transferred as provided in (1) above and owned separately. The owner of any particular exclusive right is entitled, to the extent of that right, to all the protection and remedies accorded to the copyright owner by that Statute. This removes the difficulties which existed under the previous law, and brings the position much closer to that existing in the copyright law of the United Kingdom. All transfers and assignments of copyright must be recorded in the US Copyright Office to have full legal effect.

Copyright Arbitration Royalty Panels

In 1993, the Copyright Royalty Tribunal which had been established by the Copyright Act was eliminated by Congress. In its place a new administrative mechanism was established in the Copyright Office with the purpose of making adjustments of reasonable copyright royalty rates in respect of the exercise of certain rights, mainly affecting the musical interests. The newly formed Copyright Arbitration Royalty Panels are constituted on an ad hoc basis and perform in the United States a function similar to the Copyright Tribunal in the United Kingdom.

The new American law spells out the economic objectives which the CARP is to apply in calculating the relevant rates. These are:

- to maximise the availability of creative works to the public;
- to afford the copyright owner a fair return for his or her creative work and the copyright user a fair income under existing economic conditions;
- to reflect the relative roles of the copyright owner and the copyright user in the product made available to the public with respect to relative creative contribution, technological contribution, capital investment, cost, risk, and contribution to the opening of new markets for creative expression and media for their communication.
- to minimise any disruptive impact on the structure of the industries involved and on generally prevailing industry practices.

Every final determination of the CARP shall be published in the Federal Register. It shall state in detail the criteria that the CARP determined to be applicable to the particular proceeding, the various facts that it found relevant to its determination in that proceeding, and the specific reasons for its determination. Any final decision of the CARP in a proceeding may be appealed to the United States Court of Appeals by an aggrieved party, within 30 days after its publication in the Federal Register.

Fair use

One of the most controversial factors which held up the revision of the American copyright law for at least a decade was the extent to which a balance should be struck between the desire of copyright owners to benefit from their works by extending copyright protection as far as possible, and the pressure from users of copyright to obtain access to copyright material as cheaply as possible – if not completely freely.

The new law provides by Section 107 that the fair use of a copyright work, including such use by reproduction of excerpts, for purposes such as criticism, comment, news reporting, teaching (including multiple copies for classroom use), scholarship or research is not an infringement of copyright. In determining whether the use made of a work in any particular case is a fair use, the factors to be considered include:

- the purpose and character of the use, including whether such use is of a commercial nature or is for non-profit educational purposes;
- the nature of the copyrighted work;
- the amount and substantiality of the portion used in relation to the copyrighted work as a whole; and
- the effect of the use upon the potential market for or value of the copyrighted work.

It is not an infringement of copyright for a library or archive, or any of its employees acting within the scope of their employment, to reproduce or distribute no more than one copy of a work, if:

- the reproduction or distribution is made without any purpose of direct or indirect commercial advantage;
- the collections of the library or archive are either open to the public or available not only to researchers affiliated with the library or archive or with the institution of which it is a part, but also to other persons doing research in a specialised field; and
- the reproduction or distribution of the work includes a notice of copyright.

It is not generally an infringement of copyright if a performance or display of a work is given by instructors or pupils in the course of face-to-face teaching activities of a non-profit educational institution, in a classroom or similar place devoted to instruction.

Nor is it an infringement of copyright to give a performance of a non-dramatic literary or musical work or a dramatico-musical work of a religious nature in the course of services at a place of worship or other religious assembly.

It is also not an infringement of copyright to give a performance of a non-dramatic literary or musical work other than in a transmission to the public, without any purpose of direct or indirect commercial advantage and without payment of any fee for the performance to any of the performing artists, promoters or organisers if either:

- there is no direct or indirect admission charge; or
- the proceeds, after deducting the reasonable costs of producing the performance, are used exclusively for educational, religious or charitable purposes and not for private financial gain.

In this case the copyright owner has the right to serve notice of objection to the performance in a prescribed form.

Note the important decision of the Supreme Court in *Sony Corporation of America* v. *Universal City Studios* (No. 81-1687, 52 USLW 4090). This decided that the sale of video recorders to the public for the purpose of recording a copyrighted programme from a broadcast signal for private use for time-switching purposes alone (not for archiving or 'librarying') does not amount to contributory infringement of the rights in films which are copied as a result of television broadcasts of them.

Remedies for copyright owners

Infringement of copyright

Copyright is infringed by anyone who violates any of the exclusive rights referred to in 'The rights of a copyright owner' above, or who imports copies or records into the United States in violation of the law. The owner of copyright is entitled to institute an action for infringement so long as that infringement is committed while he or she is the owner of the right infringed. Previously, no action for infringement of copyright could be instituted until registration of the copyright claim had been made, but this requirement has been modified now that the United States has ratified the Berne Convention. Under the new provision, US authors must register, or attempt to register, but non-US Berne authors are exempt from this requirement.

Injunctions

Any court having civil jurisdiction under the copyright law may grant interim and final injunctions on such terms as it may deem reasonable to prevent or restrain infringement of copyright. Such injunction may be served anywhere in the United States on the person named. An injunction is operative throughout the whole of the United States, and can be enforced by proceedings in contempt or otherwise by any American court which has jurisdiction over the infringer.

Impounding and disposition

At any time while a copyright action under American law is pending, the court may order the impounding on such terms as it considers reasonable of all copies or records claimed to have been made or used in violation of the copyright owner's exclusive rights; it may also order the impounding of all VCRs, tape recorders, plates, moulds, matrices, masters, tapes, film negatives or other articles by means of which infringing copies or records may be reproduced. A court may order as part of a final judgement or decree the destruction or other disposition of all copies or records found to have been made or used in violation of the copyright owner's exclusive rights. It also has the power to order the destruction of all articles by means of which infringing copies or records were reproduced.

Damages and profits

An infringer of copyright is generally liable either for the copyright owner's actual damage and any additional profits made by the infringer, or for statutory damages.

- The copyright owner is entitled to recover the actual damages suffered by him or her as a result of the infringement, and in addition any profits of the infringer which are attributed to the infringement and are not taken into account in computing the actual damages. In establishing the infringer's profits, the copyright owner is only required to present proof of the infringer's gross revenue, and it is for the infringer to prove his or her deductible expenses and the elements of profit attributable to factors other than the copyright work.
- Except where the copyright owner has persuaded the court that the infringement was committed wilfully, the copyright owner may elect, at any time before final judgement is given, to recover, instead of actual damages and profits, an award of statutory damages for all infringements involved in the action in respect of any one work, which may be between $750 and $30,000 according to what the court considers justified.
- However, where the copyright owner satisfies the court that the infringement was committed wilfully, the court has the discretion to increase the award of statutory damages to not more than $150,000. Where the infringer succeeds in proving that he or she was not aware and had no reason to believe that his or her acts constituted an infringement of copyright, the court has the discretion to reduce the award of statutory damages to not less than $200.

Costs: time limits

In any civil proceedings under American copyright law, the court has the discretion to allow the recovery of full costs by or against any party except the Government of the United States. It may also award a reasonable sum in respect of an attorney's fee.

No civil or criminal proceedings in respect of copyright law shall be permitted unless begun within three years after the claim or cause of action arose.

Counterfeiting

By the Piracy and Counterfeiting Amendment Act 1982, pirates and counterfeiters of sound recordings and of motion pictures now face maximum penalties of up to five years imprisonment or fines of up to $250,000.

Criminal proceedings in respect of copyright

- Anyone who infringes a copyright wilfully and for purposes of commercial advantage and private financial gain shall be fined not more than $10,000 or imprisoned for not more than 3 years, or both. However, if the infringement relates to copyright in a sound recording or a film, the infringer is liable to a fine of not more than $250,000 or imprisonment for not more than 5 years or both on a first offence, which can be increased to a fine of up to $250,000 or imprisonment for not more than 10 years or both for a subsequent offence.
- Following a conviction for criminal infringement a court may in addition to these penalties order the forfeiture and destruction of all infringing copies and records, together with implements and equipment used in their manufacture.
- It is also an offence knowingly and with fraudulent intent to place on any article a notice of copyright or words of the same purport, or to import or distribute such copies. A fine is provided for this offence of not more than $2500. The fraudulent removal of a copyright notice also attracts the same maximum fine, as does the false representation of a material particular on an application for copyright representation.

Colouring films

The United States Copyright Office has decided that adding colour to a black and white film may qualify for copyright protection whenever it amounts to more than a trivial change.

Satellite home viewers

The position of satellite home viewers is controlled by the Satellite Home Viewer Act of 1988. (Title II of Public Law 100-667 of 16 November 1988.)

The Copyright Remedy Clarification Act has created s.511 of the Copyright Act, in order to rectify a situation which had developed in case law. By this, the component States of the Union, their agencies and employees are placed in the same position as private individuals and entities in relation to their liability for copyright infringement.

Digital Millennium Copyright Act

The US Congress in 1998 passed new legislation to make clear that the copyright law applies to all works transmitted, or simply made available to, users over the Internet.

This measure is unique in that for the first time it gives its copyright owner the right to control access to the digital work, which is so crucial to security on the Internet. To allow the United States to ratify two new WIPO (World Intellectual Property Organisation) treaties – the WIPO Copyright Treaty and the WIPO Performance and Phonograms Treaty, negotiated in 1996 – the Digital Millennium Copyright Act (DMCA) makes two changes in US law. First, it outlaws, with substantial criminal and civil penalties, any tampering with copyright management information – the invisible digital coding embedded on sound recordings, software, motion pictures, and databases that identify the owner of the work and stipulate the price and conditions of use. This encoding will help promote e-commerce and curtail Internet piracy.

Second, the DMCA prohibits anyone from disabling anti-copying circuitry in a machine or signal. It also bans the manufacture, sale, and importation of electronic devices that would permit the disabling of that circuitry. Here, too, the DMCA specifies stiff civil and criminal penalties for acts of circumvention and for the manufacture or sale of the devices.

With the DMCA passed, the United States quickly joined the two new WIPO treaties in the hope that its action would serve as an example to other countries.

General observations

The copyright law of the United States was improved as a result of the statute passed by Congress on 19 October 1976. (Title 17, United States Code.) Apart from lifting the general standards of protection for copyright owners to a higher level than that which previously existed, it has on the whole shifted the balance of copyright protection in favour of the copyright owner and away from the copyright user in many of the areas where controversy existed. But most important for British and other non-American authors and publishers, it has gone a long way towards bringing American copyright law up to the same standards of international protection for non-national copyright proprietors which have long been offered by the United Kingdom and the other major countries, both in Europe and elsewhere in the English-speaking world. The ratification by the United States of the Berne Convention with effect from 1 March 1989 was an action which at that time put American copyright law on par with the protection offered by other major countries.

Gavin McFarlane LLM, PhD is a barrister at Dechert. He specialises in international trade law, and is particularly interested in the involvement of the World Trade Organisation in intellectual property matters. He is a visiting professor at London Guildhall University.

Libel

Any writer should be aware of the law of libel. ***Antony Whitaker*** *gives an outline of the main principles, concentrating on points which are most frequently misunderstood. But this article is no more than that, and specific legal advice should be taken when practical problems arise.*

The law discussed is the law of England and Wales. Scotland has its own, albeit somewhat similar, rules. A summary of the main differences between the two systems appears in the box on page 652.

The Defamation Act 1996, designed mainly to streamline and simplify libel litigation, was brought into force in stages, and became fully effective in February 2000.

Libel: liability to pay damages

English law draws a distinction between defamation published in permanent form and that which is not. The former is libel, the latter slander. 'Permanent form' includes writing, printing, drawings and photographs and radio and television broadcasts. It follows that it is the law of libel rather than slander which most concerns writers and artists professionally, and the slightly differing rules applicable to slander will not be mentioned in this article.

Publication of a libel can result in a civil action for damages, an injunction to prevent repetition and/or in certain cases a criminal prosecution against those responsible, who include the author (or artist or photographer), the publishers and the editor, if any, of the publication in which the libel appeared. 'Innocent disseminators', such as printers, distributors,

The main differences between English and Scottish law

Much of the terminology of the Scots law of defamation differs from that of English law, and in certain minor respects the law itself is different. North of the border, libel and slander are virtually indistinguishable, both as to the nature of the wrongs and their consequences; and Scots law does not recognise the offence of criminal libel. Where individual English litigants enjoy absolute privilege for what they say in court, their Scottish counterparts have only qualified privilege. 'Exemplary', or 'punitive', damages are not awarded by the Scottish courts. Until recently, libel cases in Scotland were for the most part heard by judges sitting alone, but there is now a marked trend towards trial by jury, which has been accompanied by a significant increase in the levels of damages awarded.

broadcasters, Internet service providers and retailers, who can show they took reasonable care and had no reason to believe what they were handling contained a libel, are protected under the 1996 Act. Prosecutions are rare. Certain special rules apply to them and these will be explained below after a discussion of the question of civil liability, which in practice arises much more frequently.

Libel claims do not qualify for legal aid, although the closely analagous remedy of malicious falsehood does. Most libel cases are usually heard by a judge and jury, and it is the jury which decides the amount of any award, which is tax-free. It is not necessary for the plaintiff to prove that he or she has actually suffered any loss, because the law presumes damage. While the main purpose of a libel claim is to compensate the plaintiff for the injury to his or her reputation, a jury may give additional sums either as 'aggravated' damages, if it appears a defendant has behaved malevolently or spitefully, or as 'exemplary', or 'punitive', damages where a defendant hopes the economic advantages of publication will outweigh any sum awarded. Damages can also be 'nominal' if the libel complained of is trivial. It is generally very difficult to forecast the amounts juries are likely to award, though awards against newspapers disclose a tendency towards considerable generosity. The Court of Appeal has power to reduce excessive awards of damages.

In an action for damages for libel, it is for the plaintiff to establish that the matter he or she complains of:

- has been published by the defendant,
- refers to the plaintiff,
- is defamatory.

If this is done, the plaintiff establishes a *prima facie* case. However, the defendant will escape liability if he or she can show he has a good defence. There are five defences to a libel action. They are:

- Justification
- Fair Comment
- Privilege
- Offer of Amends: ss. 2-4 of the Defamation Act, 1996
- Apology, etc, under the Libel Acts, 1843 and 1845.

A libel claim can also become barred under the Limitation Acts, as explained below. These matters must now be examined in detail.

The plaintiff's case

The meaning of 'published'

'Published' in the legal sense means communicated to a person other than the plaintiff. Thus the legal sense is wider than the lay sense but includes it. It follows that the content of a book is published in the legal sense when the manuscript is first sent to the publishing firm just as much as it is when the book is later placed on sale to the public. Subject to the 'innocent dissemination' defence referred to above, both types of publication are sufficient for the purpose of establishing liability for libel, but the law differentiates between them, since the scope of publication can properly be taken into account by the jury in considering the actual amount of damages to award. Material placed on the Internet is unquestionably 'published' there, and the extent of publication can be judged by the number of visits made to the relevant web site.

Establishing identity

The plaintiff must also establish that the matter complained of refers to him or her. It is of course by no means necessary to mention a person's name before it is clear that he or she is referred to. Nicknames by which he or she is known or corruptions of his name are just two ways in which his or her identity can be indicated. There are more subtle methods. The sole question is whether the plaintiff is indicated to those who read the matter complained of. In some cases he or she will not be unless it is read in the light of facts known to the reader from other sources, but this is sufficient for the plaintiff's purpose. The test is purely objective and does not depend at all on whether the writer intended to refer to the plaintiff.

It is because it is impossible to establish reference to any individual that generalisations, broadly speaking, are not successfully actionable. To say boldly 'All lawyers are crooks' does not give any single lawyer a cause of action, because the statement does not point a finger at any individual. However, if anyone is named in conjunction with a generalisation, then it may lose its general character and become particular from the context. Again, if one says 'One of the X Committee has been convicted of murder' and the X Committee consists of, say, four persons, it cannot be said that the statement is not actionable because no individual is indicated and it could be referring to any of the committee. This is precisely why it is actionable at the suit of each of them as suspicion has been cast on all.

Determining what is defamatory

It is for the plaintiff to show that the matter complained of is defamatory. What is defamatory is decided by the jury except in the extreme cases where the judge rules that the words cannot bear a defamatory meaning. Various tests have been laid down for determining this. It is sufficient that any one test is satisfied. The basic tests are:

- Does the matter complained of tend to lower the plaintiff in the estimation of society?
- Does it tend to bring him or her into hatred, ridicule, contempt, dislike or disesteem with society?
- Does it tend to make him shunned or avoided or cut off from society? The mere fact that what is published is inaccurate is not enough to involve liability; it is the adverse impact on the plaintiff's reputation that matters. For example, merely to overstate a person's income is not defamatory; but it will be if the context implies he has not fully declared it to the tax authorities.

'Society' means right-thinking members of society generally. It is by reference to such people that the above tests must be applied. A libel action against a newspaper which had stated that the police had taken a statement from the plaintiff failed, notwithstanding that the plaintiff gave evidence that his apparent assistance to the police (which he denied) had brought him into grave disrepute with the underworld. It was not by their wrongheaded standards that the matter fell to be judged.

Further, it is not necessary to imply that the plaintiff is at fault in some way in order to defame him. To say of a woman that she has been raped or of someone that he is insane imputes to them no degree of blame, but nonetheless both statements are defamatory. Lawyers disagree over whether the claim that an individual is 'ugly' is, or could be, defamatory.

Sometimes a defamatory meaning is conveyed by words which on the face of them have no such meaning. 'But Brutus is an honourable man' is an example. If a jury finds that words are meant ironically they will consider this ironical sense when determining whether the words are defamatory. In deciding, therefore, whether or not the words are defamatory, the jury seeks to discover what, without straining the words or putting a perverse construction on them, they will be understood to mean. In some cases this may differ substantially from their literal meaning.

Matter may also be defamatory by innuendo. Strictly so called, an innuendo is a meaning that words acquire by virtue of facts known to the reader but not stated in the passage complained of. Words, quite innocent on the face of them, may acquire a defamatory meaning when read in the light of these facts. For example, where a newspaper published a photograph of a man and a woman, with the caption that they had just announced their engagement, it was held to be defamatory of the man's wife since those who knew that she had cohabited with him were led to the belief that she had done so only as his mistress. The newspaper was unaware that the man was already married, but some of its readers were not. In general, however, imputations of unchastity against members of either sex would today be regarded as far less defamatory than they were in 1929 when this case was decided.

Defences to a libel action

Justification

English law does not protect the reputation that a person either does not or should not possess. Stating the truth therefore does not incur liability, and the plea of justification – namely, that what is complained of is true in substance and in fact – is a complete answer to an action for damages. However, this defence is by no means to be undertaken lightly. For instance, to prove one instance of using bad language will be insufficient to justify the allegation that a person is 'foulmouthed'. It would be necessary to prove several instances, and the defendant is obliged in most cases to particularise in his pleadings giving details, dates and places. However, the requirement that the truth of every allegation must be proved is not absolute, and is qualified by the 'multiple charge – no worse off' defence. This applies where two or more distinct charges are levelled against a plaintiff, and some of what is said turns out to be inaccurate. If his or her reputation in the light of what is shown to be true is made no worse by the unprovable defamatory allegations – for example, mistaken accusations that a convicted pickpocket and car thief is also a shoplifter – the publisher will be safe. This is the extent of the law's recognition that some individuals are so disreputable as to be beyond redemption by awards of damages regardless of what is said about them. Subject to this, however, it is for the defendant to prove that what he or she has published is true, not for the plaintiff to disprove it, though if he can do so, so much the better for him.

One point requires special mention. It is insufficient for the defendant to prove that he or she has accurately repeated what a third person has written or said or that such statements have gone uncontradicted when made on occasions in the past. If X writes 'Y told me that Z is a liar', it is no defence to an action against X merely to prove that Y did say that. X has given currency to a defamatory statement concerning Z and has so made it his own. His only defence is to prove that Z is a liar by establishing a number of instances of Z's untruthfulness. Nor does it help a defence of justification to prove that the defendant genuinely believed what he or she published to be true. This may, however, form part of a qualified privilege defence (see below), and might well be a complete answer in an action, other than a libel action, based on a false but non-defamatory statement. For such statements do not incur liability in the absence of fraud or malice which, in this context, means a dishonest or otherwise improper motive. Bona fide belief, however, may be relevant to the assessment of damages, even in a libel action.

Special care should be taken in relation to references to a person's convictions, however accurately described. Since the Rehabilitation of Offenders Act, 1974, a person's convictions may become 'spent' and thereafter it may involve liability to refer to them. Reference to the Act and orders thereunder must be made in order to determine the position in any particular case.

Fair comment

It is a defence to prove that what is complained of is fair comment made in good faith and without malice on a matter of public interest.

'Fair' in this context means 'honest'.

'Fair comment' means therefore the expression of the writer's genuinely held opinion. It does not necessarily mean opinion with which the jury agree. Comment may therefore be quite extreme and still be 'fair' in the legal sense. However, if it is utterly perverse the jury may be led to think that no one could have genuinely held such views. In such a case the defence would fail, for the comment could not be honest. 'Malice' here includes the popular sense of personal spite, but covers any dishonest or improper motive.

The defence only applies when what is complained of is comment as distinct from a statement of fact. The line between comment and fact is notoriously difficult to draw in some cases. Comment means a statement of opinion. The facts on which comment is made must be stated together with the comment or be sufficiently indicated with it. This is merely another way of saying that it must be clear that the defamatory statement is one of opinion and not of fact, for which the only defence would be the onerous one of justification. The exact extent to which the facts commented on must be stated or referred to is a difficult question, but some help may be derived in answering it by considering the purpose of the rule, which is to enable the reader to exercise his own judgement and to agree or disagree with the comment. It is quite plain that it is not necessary to state every single detail of the facts. In one case it was sufficient merely to mention the name of one of the Press lords in an article about a newspaper though not one owned by him. He was so well known that to mention his name indicated the substratum of fact commented upon, namely his control of his group of newspapers. No universal rule can be laid down, except that, in general, the fuller the facts set out or referred to with the comment, the better. All these facts must be proved to be true subject, however, to the flexibility of the 'proportionate truth' rule. This means that the defence remains available even if, for example, only three out of five factual claims can be proved true, provided that these three are by themselves sufficient to sustain, and are proportionate to, the fairness of the comment. The impact of the two unproven claims would probably fall to be assessed in accordance with the 'multiple charge – no worse off' rule in justification, set out above.

The defence only applies where the matters commented on are of public interest, i.e. of legitimate concern to the public or a substantial section of it. Thus the conduct of national and local government, international affairs, the administration of justice, etc, are all matters of public interest, whereas other people's private affairs may very well not be, although they undoubtedly interest the public, or provoke curiosity.

In addition, matters of which criticism has been expressly or impliedly invited, such as publicly performed plays and published books, are a legitimate subject of comment. Criticism need not be confined merely to their artistic merit but equally may deal with the attitudes to life and the opinions therein expressed.

It is sometimes said that a man's moral character is never a proper subject of comment for the purpose of this defence. This is certainly true where it is a private individual who is concerned, and some authorities say it is the same in the case of a public figure even though his or her character may be relevant to his or her public life. Again, it may in some cases be exceeding the bounds of fair comment to impute a dishonourable motive to a person, as is frequently done by way of inference from facts. In general, the imputation is a dangerous and potentially expensive practice.

Privilege

Privilege in the law of libel is either 'absolute' or 'qualified', and denotes the two levels of protection from liability afforded, in the public interest, to defamatory statements made on certain occasions. Absolute privilege – where the individual defamed has no remedy whatever – has applied to Parliamentary papers published by the direction of either House, or full republications thereof, since early in the nineteenth century. Following the implementation of section 14 of the 1996 Defamation Act, this privilege also applies to fair, accurate and contemporaneous reports of public judicial proceedings in the United Kingdom, the European Courts of Justice and Human Rights, and any international criminal tribunal established by the Security Council.

Qualified privilege confers protection provided publication is made only for the reason that the privilege is given and not for some wrongful or indirect motive. In October 1999 the House of Lords extended the defence to protect publications where a defamatory mistake on a matter of public concern has been made by a writer who can show he did his best to uncover the truth. The precise limits of this defence are not clear, and will only become so as other cases are decided in the future.

The defence also applies, under section 15 of the Act, to fair and accurate reports of public proceedings before a legislature, a court, a government inquiry and an international organisation or conference anywhere in the world, and of certain documents, or extracts from such documents, issued by those bodies. While there is no requirement to correct or publish explanations concerning these reports, such an obligation does arise under section 15 in respect of a separate category of reports of notices issued by various bodies within the European Community and of proceedings of certain bodies or organisations within the United Kingdom. Apart from the Act, such privilege also attaches to extracts from Parliamentary papers and fair and accurate reports of Parliamentary proceedings.

This list of privileged occasions is by no means exhaustive, and the second category may now be expanded by an order of the Lord Chancellor. The privilege defence is extended to the media generally, rather than being restricted, as it was hitherto, simply to newspapers.

Offers of Amends under the 1996 Act

Sections 2, 3 and 4 of the 1996 Act offer a flexible method of nipping in the bud potential libel actions by those who have been unintentionally defamed. The range of libel meanings for which this defence caters is much wider than that previously available. It envisages the payment of damages as well as costs, together with the offer of a correction and apology, and the damages figure will be fixed by a judge if the parties cannot agree. He or she will do this bearing in mind the generosity of the correction and apology, and the extent of its publication. While recourse to this defence excludes reliance on the defences of justification, privilege and fair comment, it offers a considerable incentive to settle complaints and will save substantially on costs.

Apology under 1843 and 1845 Acts

This defence is rarely utilised, since if any condition of it is not fulfilled, the plaintiff must succeed and the only question is the actual amount of damages. It only applies to actions in respect of libels in newspapers and periodicals. The defendant pleads that the libel was inserted without actual malice and without gross negligence and that before the action commenced or as soon afterwards as possible he inserted a full apology in the same newspaper, etc, or had offered to publish it in a newspaper, etc, of the plaintiff's choice, where the original newspaper is published at intervals greater than a week. Further a sum must be paid into court with this defence to compensate the plaintiff.

'Fast-track disposal' procedure

In its recognition of the generally cumbersome nature of libel litigation, the 1996 Act provides a simplified mechanism for dealing with less serious complaints. Sections 8, 9 and 10 enable a judge alone to dismiss unrealistic claims at the outset; and he will also be able to dispose 'summarily' of relatively minor, but well-founded, claims, on the basis of an award of up to £10,000, a declaration that the publication was libellous, an order for an apology and an order forbidding repetition.

Apologies in general

Quite apart from the provisions concerning statutory apologies mentioned above, a swift and well publicised apology will always go some way towards assuaging injured feelings and help reduce an award of damages.

Limitation and death

As from September 1996, the new Act has reduced from three years to one the period within which a libel action must generally be started if it is not to become 'statute-barred' through lapse of time. But successive and subsequent publications, such as the issue of later editions of the same book, or the sale of surplus copies of an old newspaper, can give rise to fresh claims.

Civil claims for libel cannot be brought on behalf of the dead. If an individual living plaintiff or defendant in a libel case dies before the jury gives their verdict, the action 'abates', i.e. comes to an end, so far as their involvement is concerned, and no rights arising out of it survive either for or against their personal representatives.

Insurance

For an author, the importance of at least an awareness of this branch of law lies first, in the fact that most book contracts contain a clause enabling the publisher to look to him should any libel claims result; and second, in the increasingly large awards of damages. It is therefore advisable to check what libel insurance a publisher carries, and whether it also covers the author who, if he or she is to have the benefit of it, should always alert the publisher to any potential risk. One company which offers libel insurance for authors is Royal Sun Alliance, Professional and Financial Risks, 1st Floor, Leadenhall Court, Leadenhall Street, London EC3V 1PP (*tel* 020-7283 9000). Premiums start at £1000, and can be substantially higher if the book is tendentious or likely to be controversial. The company generally insists on the author obtaining, and paying for, a legal opinion first. Indemnity limits vary between £50,000 and £1 million, and the author is required to bear at least the first £5000 of any loss. It is worth remembering that 'losses' include legal costs as well as damages, which they can often exceed. Libel insurance can also be obtained through a Lloyds broker.

Criminal liability in libel

Whereas the object of a civil action is to obtain compensation for the wrong done or to prevent repetition, the object of criminal proceedings is to punish the wrongdoer by fine or imprisonment or both. There are four main types of writing which may provoke a prosecution:
- defamatory libel;
- obscene publications;
- sedition and incitement to racial hatred;
- blasphemous libel.

Defamatory libel

The publication of defamatory matter is in certain circumstances a crime as well as a civil wrong. But whereas the principal object of civil proceedings will normally be to obtain compensation, the principal object of a criminal prosecution will be to secure punishment of the accused, for example by way of a fine. Prosecutions are not frequent, but there have been signs of late of a revival of interest. There are important differences between the rules applicable to criminal libel and its civil counterpart. For example, a criminal libel may be 'published' even though only communicated to the person defamed and may be found to have occurred even where the person defamed is dead, or where only a group of persons but no particular individual has been maligned. During election campaigns, it is an 'illegal practice' to publish false statements about the personal character or conduct of a candidate irrespective of whether they are also defamatory.

Obscene publications

It is an offence to publish obscene matter. By the Obscene Publications Act, 1959, matter is obscene if its effect is such as to tend to deprave and corrupt persons who are likely, having regard to all relevant circumstances, to read, see or hear it. 'To deprave and corrupt' is to be distinguished from 'to shock and disgust'. It is a defence to a prosecution to prove that publication of the matter in question is justified as being for the public good, on the ground that it is in the interests of science, literature, art or learning, or of other objects of general concern. Expert evidence may be given as to its literary, artistic, scientific or other merits. Playwrights, directors and producers should note that the Theatres Act, 1968, though designed to afford similar protection to stage productions, does not necessarily prevent prosecutions for indecency under other statutes.

Sedition and incitement to racial hatred

Writings which tend to destroy the peace of the realm may be prosecuted as being seditious or as amounting to incitement to racial hatred. Seditious writings include those which advocate reform by unconstitutional or violent means or incite contempt or hatred for the monarch or Parliament. These institutions may be criticised stringently, but not in a manner which is likely to lead to insurrection or civil commotion or indeed any physical force. Prosecutions are a rarity, but it should be remembered that writers of matter contemptuous of the House of Commons, though not prosecuted for seditious libel are, from time to time, punished by that House for breach of its privileges, although, if a full apology is made, it is often an end of the matter. The Public Order Act 1986 makes it an offence, irrespective of the author's or publisher's intention, to publish, or put on plays containing, threatening, abusive or insulting matter if hatred is likely to be stirred up against any racial group in Great Britain.

Blasphemous libel

Blasphemous libel consists in the vilification of the Christian religion or its ceremonies. Other religions are not protected. The offence lies essentially in the impact of what is said concerning, for instance, God, Christ, the Bible, the Book of Common Prayer, etc; it is irrelevant that the publisher does not intend to shock or arouse resentment. While temperate and sober writings on religious topics however anti-Christian in sentiment will not involve liability, if the discussion is 'so scurrilous and offensive as to pass the limit of decent controversy and to outrage any Christian feeling', it will.

Antony Whitaker, a barrister, is Legal Consultant to Times Newspapers Ltd and to City solicitors Theodore Goddard & Co.

Finance for writers and artists

Income tax

Despite attempts by successive Governments to simplify our taxation system, the subject has become increasingly complicated. ***Peter Vaines****, a chartered accountant and barrister, gives a broad outline of taxation from the point of view of writers and other creative professionals. At the time of writing the proposals in the March 2000 Budget have just been announced and these are broadly reflected in this article.*

How income is taxed

Generally

Authors are usually treated for tax purposes as carrying on a profession and are taxed in a similar fashion to other professionals, i.e. as self-employed persons assessable under Schedule D. This article is directed to self-employed persons only, because if a writer is employed he or she will be subject to the rules of Schedule E where different considerations apply – substantially to his or her disadvantage.

Attempts are often made by employed persons to shake off the status of 'employee' and to attain 'freelance' status so as to qualify for the advantages of Schedule D, such attempts meeting with varying degrees of success. The problems involved in making this transition are considerable and space does not permit a detailed explanation to be made here – individual advice is necessary if difficulties are to be avoided.

Particular attention has been paid by the Inland Revenue to journalists and to those engaged in the entertainment industry with a view to reclassifying them as employees so that PAYE is deducted from their earnings. This blanket treatment has been extended to other areas and, although it is obviously open to challenge by individual taxpayers, it is always difficult to persuade the Inland Revenue to change its views.

There is no reason why employed people cannot carry on a freelance business in their spare time. Indeed, aspiring authors, painters, musicians, etc, often derive so little income from their craft that the financial security of an employment, perhaps in a different sphere of activity, is necessary. The existence of the employment is irrelevant to the taxation of the freelance earnings although it is most important not to confuse the income or expenditure of the employment with the income or expenditure of the self-employed activity. The Inland Revenue is aware of the advantages which can be derived by an individual having 'freelance' income from an organisation of which he or she is also an employee, and where such circumstances are contrived, it can be extremely difficult to convince an Inspector of Taxes that a genuine freelance activity is being carried on. Where the individual operates through a company or partnership providing services personally to a particular client, and would be regarded as an employee if the services were supplied directly by the individual, additional problems arise on which professional advice is essential.

For those starting in business or commencing work on a freelance basis the Inland Revenue produces a very useful booklet, *Starting in Business (IR28)*, which is available from any tax office.

Income

For income to be taxable it need not be substantial, nor even the author's only source of income; earnings from casual writing are also taxable but this can be an advantage, because occasional writers do not often make a profit from their writing. The expenses incurred in connection with writing may well exceed any income receivable and the resultant loss may then be used to reclaim tax paid on other income. There may be deducted from the income certain allowable expenses and capital allowances which are set out in more detail below. The possibility of a loss being used as a basis for a tax repayment is fully appreciated by the Inland Revenue, which sometimes attempts to treat casual writing as a hobby so that any losses incurred cannot be used to reclaim tax; of course by the same token any income receivable would not be chargeable to tax. This treatment may sound attractive but it should be resisted vigorously because the Inland Revenue does not hesitate to change its mind when profits begin to arise. In the case of exceptional or non-recurring writing, such as the autobiography of a sports personality or the memoirs of a politician, it could be better to be treated as pursuing a hobby and not as a professional author. Sales of copyright cannot be charged to income tax unless the recipient is a professional author. However, the proceeds of sale of copyright may be charged to capital gains tax, even by an individual who is not a professional author.

Royalties

Where the recipient is a professional author, a series of cases has laid down a clear principle that sales of copyright are taxable as income and not as capital receipts. Similarly, lump sums on account of, or in advance of royalties are also taxable as income in the year of receipt, subject to a claim for spreading relief (see below).

Copyright royalties are generally paid without deduction of income tax. However, if royalties are paid to a person who normally lives abroad, tax will be deducted by the payer or his agent at the time the payment is made unless arrangements are made with the Inland Revenue for payments to be made gross.

Arts Council category A awards

- Direct or indirect musical, design or choreographic commissions and direct or indirect commission of sculpture and paintings for public sites.
- The Royalty Supplement Guarantee Scheme.
- The contract writers' scheme.
- Jazz bursaries.
- Translators' grants.
- Photographic awards and bursaries.
- Film and video awards and bursaries.
- Performance Art Awards.
- Art Publishing Grants.
- Grants to assist with a specific project or projects (such as the writing of a book) or to meet specific professional expenses such as a contribution towards copying expenses made to a composer or to an artist's studio expenses.

Arts Council grants

Persons in receipt of grants from the Arts Council or similar bodies will be concerned whether or not such grants are liable to income tax. The Inland Revenue has issued a Statement of Practice after detailed discussions with the Arts Council regarding the tax treatment of such awards. Grants and other receipts of a similar nature have now been divided into two categories (see boxes) – those which are to be treated by the Inland Revenue as chargeable to tax and those which are not. Category A awards are considered to be taxable; awards made under category B are not chargeable to tax.

This Statement of Practice has no legal force and is used merely to ease the administration of the tax system. It is open to anyone in receipt of a grant or award to disregard the agreed statement and challenge the Inland Revenue view on the merits of their particular case. However, it must be recognised that the Inland Revenue does not issue such statements lightly and any challenge to their

Arts Council category B awards

- Bursaries to trainee directors.
- In-service bursaries for theatre directors.
- Bursaries for associate directors.
- Bursaries to people attending full-time courses in arts administration (the practical training course).
- In-service bursaries to theatre designers and bursaries to trainees on the theatre designers' scheme.
- In-service bursaries for administrators.
- Bursaries for actors and actresses.
- Bursaries for technicians and stage managers.
- Bursaries made to students attending the City University Arts Administration courses.
- Awards, known as the Buying Time Awards, made not to assist with a specific project or professional expenses but to maintain the recipient to enable him or her to take time off to develop his personal talents. These at present include the awards and bursaries known as the Theatre Writing Bursaries, awards and bursaries to composers, awards and bursaries to painters, sculptures and print makers, literature awards and bursaries.

view would almost certainly involve a lengthy and expensive action through the Courts.

The tax position of persons in receipt of literary prizes will generally follow a decision by the Special Commissioners in connection with the Whitbread Literary Award. In that case it was decided that the prize was not part of the author's professional income and accordingly not chargeable to tax. The precise details are not available because decisions of the Special Commissioners were not, at that time, reported unless an appeal was made to the High Court; the Inland Revenue chose not to appeal against this decision. Details of the many literary awards which are given each year start on page 512, and this decision is of considerable significance to the winners of each of these prizes. It would be unwise to assume that all such awards will be free of tax as the precise facts which were present in the case of the Whitbread award may not be repeated in another case; however it is clear that an author winning a prize has some very powerful arguments in his or her favour, should the Inland Revenue seek to charge tax on the award.

Allowable expenses

To qualify as an allowable business expense, expenditure has to be laid out wholly and exclusively for business purposes. Strictly there must be no 'duality of purpose', which means that expenditure cannot be apportioned to reflect the private and business usage, e.g. food, clothing, telephone, travelling expenses, etc. However, the Inland Revenue does not usually interpret this principle strictly and is prepared to allow all reasonable expenses (including apportioned sums) where the amounts can be commercially justified.

It should be noted carefully that the expenditure does not have to be 'necessary', it merely has to be incurred 'wholly and exclusively' for business purposes. Naturally, however, expenditure of an outrageous and wholly unnecessary character might well give rise to a presumption that it was not really for business purposes. As with all things, some expenses are unquestionably allowable and some expenses are equally unquestionably not allowable – it is the grey area in between which gives rise to all the difficulties and the outcome invariably depends on negotiation with the Inland Revenue.

Great care should be taken when claiming a deduction for items where there is a 'duality of purpose' and negotiations should be conducted with more than usual care and courtesy – if provoked the Inspector of Taxes may well choose to allow nothing. An appeal is always possible although unlikely to succeed as a string of cases in the Courts has clearly demonstrated. An example is the case of *Caillebotte* v. *Quinn* where the taxpayer (who normally had lunch at home) sought to claim the excess cost of meals incurred because he was working a long way from his home. The taxpayer's arguments failed because he did not eat only in

Allowable expenses

(a) Cost of all materials used up in the course of preparation of the work.
(b) Cost of typewriting and secretarial assistance, etc; if this or other help is obtained from one's spouse then it is entirely proper for a deduction to be claimed for the amounts paid for the work. The amounts claimed must actually be paid to the spouse and should be at the market rate although some uplift can be made for unsocial hours, etc. Payments to a wife (or husband) are of course taxable in her (or his) hands and should therefore be most carefully considered. The wife's earnings may also be liable for National Insurance contributions and it is important to take care because otherwise you may find that these contributions may outweigh the tax savings. The impact of the National Minimum Wage should also be considered.
(c) All expenditure on normal business items such as postage, stationery, telephone, e-mail, fax and answering machines, agent's fees, accountancy charges, photography, subscriptions, periodicals, magazines, etc, may be claimed. The cost of daily papers should not be overlooked if these form part of research material. Visits to theatres, cinemas, etc, for research purposes may also be permissible (but not the cost relating to guests). Unfortunately, expenditure on all types of business entertaining is specifically denied tax relief.
(d) If work is conducted at home, a deduction for 'use of home' is usually allowed providing the amount claimed is reasonable. If the claim is based on an appropriate proportion of the total costs of rent, light and heat, cleaning and maintenance, insurance, etc (but not the Council Tax), care should be taken to ensure that no single room is used 'exclusively' for business purposes, because this may result in the Capital Gains Tax exemption on the house as the only or main residence being partially forfeited. However, it would be a strange household where one room was in fact used exclusively for business purposes and for no other purpose whatsoever (e.g. storing personal bank statements and other private papers); the usual formula is to claim a deduction on the basis that most or all of the rooms in the house are used at one time or another for business purposes, thereby avoiding any suggestion that any part was used exclusively for business purposes.
(e) The appropriate business proportion of motor running expenses may also be claimed although what is the appropriate proportion will naturally depend on the particular circumstances of each case; it should be mentioned that the well-known scale benefits, whereby one is taxed according to the size and cost of the car, do not apply to self-employed persons.
(f) It has been long established that the cost of travelling from home to work (whether employed or self-employed) is not an allowable expense. However, if home is one's place of work then no expenditure under this heading is likely to be incurred and difficulties are unlikely to arise.
(g) Travelling and hotel expenses incurred for business purposes will normally be allowed but if any part could be construed as disguised holiday or pleasure expenditure, considerable thought would need to be given to the commercial reasons for the journey in order to justify the claim. The principle of 'duality of purpose' will always be a difficult hurdle in this connection – although not insurmountable.
(h) If a separate business bank account is maintained, any overdraft interest thereon will be an allowable expense. This is the only circumstance in which overdraft interest is allowed for tax purposes and care should be taken to avoid overdrafts in all other circumstances.
(i) Where capital allowances (see page 663) are claimed for a personal computer, fax, modem, television, video, CD or tape player, etc, used for business purposes the costs of maintenance and repair of the equipment may also be claimed.

order to work, one of the reasons for his eating was in order to sustain his life; a duality of purpose therefore existed and no tax relief was due.

Other cases have shown that expenditure on clothing can also be disallowed if it is the kind of clothing which is in everyday use, because clothing is worn not only to assist the pursuit of one's profession but also to accord with public decency. This duality of purpose may be sufficient to deny relief – even where the particular type of clothing is of a kind not otherwise worn by the taxpayer. In the case of *Mallalieu* v. *Drummond* a lady barrister failed to obtain a tax deduction for items of sombre clothing purchased specifically for wearing in Court. The House of Lords decided that a duality of purpose existed because clothing represented part of her needs as a human being.

Despite the above, Inspectors of Taxes are not usually inflexible and the expenses listed in the box on page 622 are among those generally allowed. Clearly many other allowable items may be claimed in addition to those listed. Wherever there is any reasonable business motive for some expenditure it should be claimed as a deduction although it is necessary to preserve all records relating to the expense. It is sensible to avoid an excess of imagination as this would naturally cause the Inspector of Taxes to doubt the genuineness of other expenses claimed.

The question is often raised whether the whole amount of an expense may be deducted or whether the VAT content must be excluded. Where VAT is reclaimed from the Customs and Excise (on the quarterly returns made by a registered person), the VAT element of the expense cannot be treated as an allowable deduction. Where the VAT is not reclaimed, the whole expense (inclusive of VAT) is allowable for income tax purposes.

Capital allowances

Allowances

Where expenditure of a capital nature is incurred, it cannot be deducted from income as an expense – a separate and sometimes more valuable capital allowance being available instead. Capital allowances are given for many different types of expenditure, but authors and similar professional people are likely to claim only for 'plant and machinery'; this is a very wide expression which may include motor cars, personal computers, fax and photocopying machines, modems, televisions, CD, video and cassette players used for business purposes, books – and even a horse! Plant and machinery generally qualify for a 40% allowance in the year of purchase and 25% of the reducing balance in subsequent years. Expenditure on information technology for the purposes of the business now benefits from a special 100% allowance in the year of purchase. Where the useful life of an asset is expected to be short, it is possible to claim special treatment as a 'short life asset' enabling the allowances to be accelerated.

The reason these allowances can be more valuable than allowable expenses is that they may be wholly or partly disclaimed in any year that full benefit cannot be obtained – ordinary business expenses cannot be similarly disclaimed. Where, for example, the income of an author does not exceed his personal allowances, he would not be liable to tax and a claim for capital allowances would be wasted. If the capital allowances were to be disclaimed their benefit would be carried forward for use in subsequent years. Careful planning with claims for capital allowances is therefore essential if maximum benefit is to be obtained.

As an alternative to capital allowances, claims can be made on the 'renewals' basis whereby all renewals are treated as allowable deductions in the year; no allowance is obtained for the initial purchase, but the cost of replacement (excluding any improvement element) is allowed in full. This basis is no longer widely used, as it is considerably less advantageous than claiming capital allowances as described above.

Leasing is a popular method of acquiring fixed assets, and where cash is not available to enable an outright purchase to be made, assets may be leased over a period of time. Whilst leasing may have financial benefits in certain circumstances, in normal cases there is likely to be no tax advantage in leasing an asset where the alternative of outright purchase is available. Indeed, leasing can be a positive disadvantage in the case of motor cars with a new retail price of more than £12,000. If such a car is leased, only a proportion of the leasing charges will be tax deductible.

Books

The question of whether the cost of books is eligible for tax relief has long been a source of difficulty. The annual cost of replacing books used for the purposes of one's professional activities (e.g. the annual cost of a new *Writers' & Artists' Yearbook*) has always been an allowable expense; the difficulty arose because the initial cost of reference books, etc (e.g. when commencing one's profession) was treated as capital expenditure but no allowances were due as the books were not considered to be 'plant'. However, the matter was clarified by the case of *Munby* v. *Furlong* in which the Court of Appeal decided that the initial cost of law books purchased by a barrister was expenditure on 'plant' and eligible for capital allowances. This is clearly a most important decision, particularly relevant to any person who uses expensive books in the course of exercising his or her profession.

Pension contributions

Personal pensions

Where a self-employed person pays annual premiums under an approved personal pension policy, tax relief may now be obtained each year for the following amounts:

Age at 6/4/2000	Maximum %
35 and under	17.5% (max) £16,065
36 – 45	20% (max) £18,360
46 – 50	25% (max) £22,950
51 – 55	30% (max) £27,540
56 – 60	35% (max) £32,130
61 and over	40% (max) £36,720

These figures do not apply to existing retirement annuity policies; these remain subject to the old limits which are unchanged.

These arrangements can be extremely advantageous in providing for a pension as premiums are usually paid when the income is high (and the tax relief is also high) and the pension (taxed as earned income when received) usually arises when the income is low and little tax is payable. The reduction in the rates of income tax to a maximum of 40% makes this decision a little more difficult because the tax advantages could go into reverse. When the pension is paid it could, if rates rise again, be taxed at a higher rate than the rate of tax relief at the moment. One would be deferring income in order to pay more tax on it later. However, this involves a large element of guesswork, and many people will be content simply with the long-term pension benefits.

Class 4 NI contributions

Allied to pensions is the payment of Class 4 National Insurance contributions, although no pension or other benefit is obtained by the contributions; the Class 4 contributions are designed solely to extract additional amounts from self-employed persons and are payable in addition to the normal Class 2 (self-employed) contributions. The rates are changed each year and for 2000/01 self-employed persons will be obliged to contribute 7% of their profits between the range £4385-£27,820 per annum, a maximum liability of £1640 for 2000/01. This amount is collected in conjunction with the Schedule D income tax liability.

Spreading relief

Relief for copyright payments

Special provisions enable authors and similar persons who have been engaged on a literary, dramatic, musical or artistic work for a period of more than 12 months, to spread certain amounts received over two or three years depending on the time spent in preparing the work. If the author was engaged on the work for a period exceeding 12 months, the receipt may be spread backwards over two years; if the author was engaged on the work for more than 24 months, the receipt may be spread backwards over three years. (Analogous provisions apply to sums received for the sale of a painting, sculpture or other work of art.) The relief applies to:

- lump sums received on the assignment of copyright, in whole or in part;
- sums received on the grant of any interest in the copyright by licence;
- non-returnable advances on account of royalties;

- any receipts of or on account of royalties or any periodical sums received within two years of first publication.

A claim for spreading relief has to be made within eight years from 5 April following the date of first publication.

Relief: copyright sold after 10 years

Where copyright is assigned (or a licence in it is granted) more than 10 years after the first publication of the work, then the amounts received can qualify for a different spreading relief. The assignment (or licence) must be for a period of more than two years and the receipt will be spread forward over the number of years for which the assignment (or licence) is granted – but with a maximum of six years. The relief is terminated by death, but there are provisions enabling the deceased author's personal representatives to re-spread the amounts if it is to the beneficiaries' advantage.

The above rules are arbitrary and cumbersome, only providing a limited measure of relief in special circumstances. The provisions can sometimes be helpful to repair matters when consideration of the tax position has been neglected, but invariably a better solution is found if the likely tax implications are considered fully in advance.

Collection of tax

Self-assessment

The year ended 5 April 1997, i.e. the tax year 1996/7, brought with it two profound changes to the method of taxing individuals, particularly those carrying out a self-employed activity such as writing. The old system of sending in a tax return showing all your income and the Inland Revenue raising an assessment to collect the tax has gone. So has the idea that you pay tax on your profits for the preceding year. Now, when you send in your tax return you have to work out your own tax liability and send a cheque; this is called 'self-assessment'. If you get it wrong, or if you are late with your tax return or the payment of tax, interest and penalties will be charged.

Under this new system, the Inland Revenue will rarely issue assessments; they are no longer necessary because the idea is that you assess yourself. A new colour-coded tax return has been designed to help individuals meet their new tax obligations. This is a daunting task but the term 'self-assessment' is not intended to imply that individuals have to do it themselves; they can (and often will) engage professional help. The term is only intended to convey that it is the taxpayer, and not the Inland Revenue, who is responsible for getting the tax liability right and for it to be paid on time.

The deadline for sending in the tax return is 31 January following the end of the tax year; so for the tax year 1999/2000, the tax return has to be submitted to the Inland Revenue by 31 January 2001. If for some reason you are unwilling or unable to calculate the tax payable, you can ask the Inland Revenue to do it for you, in which case it is necessary to send in your tax return by 30 September.

Income tax on self-employed earnings remains payable in two instalments but the payment dates have been moved to 31 January and 31 July each year. Because the accurate figures may not necessarily be known, these payments in January and July will therefore be only payments on account based on the previous year's liability. The final balancing figure will be paid the following 31 January together with the first instalment of the liability for the following year.

When the Inland Revenue receives the self-assessment tax return, it is checked to see if there is anything obviously wrong; if there is, a letter will be sent to you immediately. Otherwise, the Inland Revenue has 12 months from the filing date of 31 January in which to make further enquiries; if it doesn't, it will have no further opportunity to do so and your tax liabilities are final – unless there is something seriously wrong such as the omission of income or capital gains. In that event, the Inland Revenue will raise an assessment later to collect any extra tax together with appropriate penalties. It is essential for the operation of the new system that all records relevant to your tax returns are retained for at least 12 months in case they are needed by the Inland Revenue. For the self-employed, the record-keeping requirement is much more onerous because the records need to be kept for nearly six years. One important change in the rules is that if you claim a tax deduction for an expense, it will be necessary to have a receipt or other document proving that the expenditure has been made. Because the existence of the underlying records is so important to the operation of self-assessment, the Inland Revenue treats them very seriously and there is a penalty of £3000 for any failure to keep adequate records.

Interest

Interest is chargeable on overdue tax at a variable rate, which at the time of writing is 8.5% per annum. It does not rank for any tax relief, which can make the Inland Revenue an expensive source of credit.

However, the Inland Revenue can also be obliged to pay interest (known as repayment supplement) tax-free where repayments are delayed. The rules relating to repayment supplement are less beneficial and even more complicated than the rules for interest payable but they do exist and can be very welcome if a large repayment has been delayed for a long time. Unfortunately, the rate of repayment supplement is only 4%, much lower than the rate of interest on unpaid tax.

Value added tax

The activities of writers, painters, composers, etc, are all 'taxable supplies' within the scope of VAT and chargeable at the standard rate. (Zero rating which applies to publishers, booksellers, etc on the supply of books does not extend to the work performed by writers.) Accordingly, authors are obliged to register for VAT if their income for the past 12 months exceeds £52,000 or if their income for the coming month will exceed that figure.

Delay in registering can be a most serious matter because if registration is not effected at the proper time, the Customs and Excise can (and invariably do) claim VAT from all the income received since the date on which registration should have been made. As no VAT would have been included in the amounts received during this period the amount claimed by the Customs and Excise must inevitably come straight from the pocket of the author.

The author may be entitled to seek reimbursement of the VAT from those whom he or she ought to have charged VAT but this is obviously a matter of some difficulty and may indeed damage his commercial relationships. Apart from these disadvantages there is also a penalty for late registration. The rules are extremely harsh and are imposed automatically even in cases of innocent error. It is therefore extremely important to monitor the income very carefully because if in any period of 12 months the income exceeds the £52,000 limit, the Customs and Excise must be notified within 30 days of the end of the period. Failure to do so will give rise to an automatic penalty. It should be emphasised that this is a penalty for failing to submit a form and has nothing to do with any real or potential loss of tax. Furthermore, whether the failure was innocent or deliberate will not matter. Only the existence of a 'reasonable excuse' will be a defence to the penalty. However, a reasonable excuse does not include ignorance, error, a lack of funds or reliance on any third party.

However, it is possible to regard VAT registration as a privilege and not a penalty, because only VAT registered persons can reclaim VAT paid on their expenses such as stationery, telephone, professional fees, etc, even typewriters and other plant and machinery (excluding cars). However, many find that the administrative inconvenience – the cost of maintaining the necessary records and completing the necessary forms – more than outweighs the benefits to be gained from registration and prefer to stay outside the scope of VAT for as long as possible.

Overseas matters

The general observation may be made that self-employed persons resident and domiciled in the United Kingdom are not well treated with regard to their overseas work, being taxable on their worldwide income. It is important to emphasise that if fees are earned abroad, no tax saving can be achieved merely by keeping the money outside the country. Although exchange control regulations no longer exist to require repatriation of foreign earnings, such income remains taxable in the UK and must be disclosed to the Inland Revenue; the same applies to interest or other income arising on any investment of these earnings overseas. Accordingly, whenever foreign earnings are likely to become substantial, prompt and effective action is required to limit the impact of UK and foreign taxation. In the case of non-resident authors it is important that arrangements concerning writing for publication in the UK, e.g. in newspapers, are undertaken with great care. A case concerning the wife of one of the great train robbers who provided detailed information for a series of articles in a Sunday newspaper is most instructive. Although she was acknowledged to be resident in Canada for all the relevant years, the income from the articles was treated as arising in this country and fully chargeable to UK tax.

The United Kingdom has double taxation agreements with many other countries and these agreements are designed to ensure that income arising in a foreign country is taxed either in that country or in the UK. Where a withholding tax is deducted from payments received from another country (or where tax is paid in full in the absence of a double taxation agreement), the amount of foreign tax paid can usually be set off against the related UK tax liability. Many successful authors can be found living in Eire because of the complete exemption from tax which attaches to works of cultural or artistic merit by persons who are resident there. However, such a step should only be contemplated having careful regard to all the other domestic and commercial considerations and specialist advice is essential if the exemption is to be obtained and kept; a careless breach of the conditions could cause the exemption to be withdrawn with catastrophic consequences.

Companies

When an author becomes successful the prospect of paying tax at the higher rate may drive him or her to take hasty action such as the formation of companies, etc, which may not always be to his advantage. Indeed some authors seeing the exodus into tax exile of their more successful colleagues even form companies in low tax areas in the naive expectation of saving large amounts of tax. The Inland Revenue is fully aware of the opportunities and have extensive powers to charge tax and combat avoidance. Accordingly, such action is just as likely to increase tax liabilities and generate other costs and should never be contemplated without expert advice; some very expensive mistakes are often made in this area which are not always able to be remedied.

To conduct one's business through the medium of a company can be a most effective method of mitigating tax liabilities, and providing it is done at the right time and under the right circumstances very substantial advantages can be derived. However, if done without due care and attention the intended advantages will simply evaporate. At the very least it is essential to ensure that the company's business is genuine and conducted properly with regard to the realities of the situation. If the author continues his or her activities unchanged, simply paying all the receipts from his work into a company's bank account, he cannot expect to persuade the Inland Revenue that it is the company and not himself who is entitled to, and should be assessed to tax on, that income.

It must be strongly emphasised that many pitfalls exist which can easily eliminate all the tax benefits expected to arise by the formation of the company. For example, company directors are employees of the company and will be liable to pay much higher National Insurance contributions; the company must also pay the employer's proportion of the contribution and a total liability of over 20% of gross salary may arise. This compares most unfavourably with the position of a self-employed person. Moreover, on the commencement of the company's business the individual's profession will cease and the possibility of revisions being made by the Inland Revenue to earlier tax liabilities means that the timing of a change has to be considered very carefully.

The tax return

No mention has been made above of personal reliefs and allowances; this is because these allowances and the rates of tax are subject to constant change and are always set out in detail in the explanatory notes which accompany the Tax Return. The annual Tax Return is an important document and should be completed promptly with extreme care, particularly since the introduction of self-assessment. If filling in the Return is a source of difficulty or anxiety, comfort may be found in the Consumer Association's publication *Money Which? – Tax Saving Guide*; this is published in March of each year and includes much which is likely to be of interest and assistance.

Peter Vaines FCA, ATII, barrister, of Haarmann Hemmelrath writes and speaks widely on tax and related matters. He is Managing Editor of *Personal Tax Planning Review*, on the Editorial Board of *Taxation*, and tax columnist for *New Law Journal.*

Social security contributions

In general, every individual who works in Great Britain either as an employee or as a self-employed person is liable to pay social security contributions. The law governing this subject is complicated and **Peter Arrowsmith** *FCA gives here a summary of the position. This article should be regarded as a general guide only.*

All contributions are payable in respect of years ending on 5 April. The classes of contributions are:

Class 1 These are payable by employees (primary contributions) and their employers (secondary contributions) and are based on earnings.
Class 1A Use of company car, and fuel, for private purposes.
Class 1B In respect of PAYE Settlement Agreements entered into by employers.
Class 2 These are weekly flat rate contributions, payable by the self-employed.
Class 3 These are weekly flat rate contributions, payable on a voluntary basis in order to provide, or make up entitlement to, certain social security benefits.
Class 4 These are payable by the self-employed in respect of their trading or professional income and are based on earnings.

Employed or self-employed?

The question as to whether a person is employed under a contract *of* service and is thereby an employee liable to Class 1 contributions, or performs services (either solely or in partnership) under a contract *for* service and is thereby self-employed liable to Class 2 and Class 4 contributions, often has to be decided in practice. One of the best guides can be found in the case of *Market Investigations Ltd* v. *Minister of Social Security* (1969 2 WLR 1) when Cooke J. remarked:

'... the fundamental test to be applied is this: "Is the person who has engaged himself to perform these services performing them as a person in business on his own account?" If the answer to that question is "yes", then the contract is a contract for services. If the answer is "no", then the contract is a contract of service. No exhaustive list has been compiled and perhaps no exhaustive list can be compiled of the considerations which are relevant in determining that question, nor can strict rules be laid down as to the relative weight which the various considerations should carry in particular cases. The most that can be said is that control will no doubt always have to be considered, although it can no longer be regarded as the sole determining factor; and that factors which may be of importance are such matters as:
• whether the man performing the services provides his own equipment,
• whether he hires his own helpers,
• what degree of financial risk he takes,
• what degree of responsibility for investment and management he has, and
• whether and how far he has an opportunity of profiting from sound management in the performance of his task.'

The above case was also considered as recently as November 1993 by the Court of Appeal in the case of *Hall* v. *Lorimer*. In this case a vision mixer with around 20 clients and undertaking around 120-150 separate engagements per annum was held to be self-employed. This follows the, perhaps surprising, contention of the Inland Revenue that the taxpayer was an employee.

Further guidance

There have been three cases dealing with musicians, in relatively recent times, which provide further guidance on the question as to whether an individual is employed or self-employed.

- ***Midland Sinfonia Concert Society Ltd* v. *Secretary of State for Social Services* (1981 ICR 454).** A musician, employed to play in an orchestra by separate invitation at irregular intervals and remunerated solely in respect of each occasion upon which he does play, is employed under a contract for services. He is therefore self-employed, not an employed earner, for the purposes of the Social Security Contributions and Benefits Act 1992, and the orchestra which engages him is not liable to pay National Insurance contributions in respect of his earnings.
- ***Addison* v. *London Philharmonic Orchestra Ltd* (1981 ICR 261).** This was an appeal to determine whether certain individuals were employees for the purposes of section 11(1) of the Employment Protection (Consolidation) Act 1978.

The Employment Appeal Tribunal upheld the decision of an industrial tribunal that an associate player and three additional or extra players of the London Philharmonic Orchestra were not employees under a contract of service, but were essentially freelance musicians carrying on their own business. The facts found by the industrial tribunal showed that, when playing for the orchestra, each appellant remained essentially a freelance musician, pursuing his or her own profession as an instrumentalist, with an individual reputation, and carrying on his or her own business, and they contributed their own skills and interpretative powers to the orchestra's performances as independent contractors.

- ***Winfield* v. *London Philharmonic Orchestra Ltd* (1979 ICR 726).** This case dealt with the question as to whether an individual was an employee within the meaning of section 30 of the Trade Union and Labour Relations Act 1974. The following remarks by the appeal tribunal are of interest in relation to the status of musicians:

'... making music is an art, and the co-operation required for a performance of Berlioz's *Requiem* is dissimilar to that required between the manufacturer of concrete and the truck driver who takes the concrete where it is needed ... It took the view, as we think it was entitled on the material before it to do, that the company was simply machinery through which the members of the orchestra managed and controlled the orchestra's operation ... In deciding whether you are in the presence of a contract of service or not, you look at the whole of the picture. This picture looks to us, as it looked to the industrial tribunal, like a co-operative of distinguished musicians running themselves with self and mutual discipline, and in no sense like a boss and his musician employees.'

Other recent cases have concerned a professional dancer and holiday camp entertainers (all of whom were regarded as employees). In two recent cases income from part-time lecturing was held to be from an employment.

Accordingly, if a person is regarded as an employee under the above rules, he or she will be liable to pay contributions even if his employment is casual, part time or temporary. Furthermore, if a person is an employee and also carries on a trade or profession either solely or in partnership, there will be a liability to more than one class of contributions (subject to certain maxima – see below).

Exceptions

There are certain exceptions to the above rules, those most relevant to artists and writers being:

- The employment of a wife by her husband, or vice versa, is disregarded for social security purposes unless it is for the purposes of a trade or profession (e.g. the employment of his wife by an author would not be disregarded and would result in a liability for contributions if her salary reached the minimum levels).
- The employment of certain relatives in a private dwelling house in which both employee and employer reside is disre-

garded for social security purposes provided the employment is not for the purposes of a trade or business carried on at those premises by the employer. This would cover the employment of a relative (as defined) as a housekeeper in a private residence.

• In general, lecturers, teachers and instructors engaged by an educational establishment to teach on at least four days in three consecutive months are regarded as employees, although this rule does not apply to fees received by persons giving public lectures.

Freelance film workers

As regards the status of workers in the film and allied industries, the Inland Revenue made the following announcement on 30 March 1983:

'The Inland Revenue has recently carried out a review of the employment status of workers engaged on "freelance" terms within the industry. Following this review there has been an extensive series of discussions with representative bodies in the industry, including Independent Programme Producers Association, British Film and Television Producers Association, Advertising Film and Video Tape Producers Association, National Association of Theatrical and Kine Employees, and Association of Cinematograph, Television and Allied Technicians.

'As a result of that review and the subsequent discussions, the Inland Revenue considers that a number of workers engaged on "freelance" terms within the industry are engaged as employees under contracts of service, either written or oral, and should be assessed under Schedule E. Many workers in the industry already pay employee's National Insurance contributions.

'The Inland Revenue, however, accepts that a number of "freelance" workers in certain types of work within the industry are likely to be engaged under contracts for services, as people in self-employment, and should therefore be assessed under Schedule D. Any individual who does not agree with the Revenue's determination of his position has the normal right of appeal to the independent Income Tax Commissioners.'

There is a list of grades in the film industry in respect of which PAYE need not be deducted and who are regarded as self-employed for tax purposes.

Further information can be obtained from the March 1992 edition of the Inland Revenue guidance notes on the application of PAYE to casual and freelance staff in the film industry. In view of the Inland Revenue announcement that the same status will apply for PAYE and NIC purposes, no liability for employee's and employer's contributions should arise in the case of any of the grades mentioned above. However, in the film and TV industry this general rule has not always been followed in practice. In December 1992, after a long review, the DSS agreed that individuals working behind the camera and who have jobs on the Inland Revenue Schedule D list are self-employed for social security purposes. The National Insurance Contributions Office will accept claims for repayment of Class 1 contributions where persons were correctly to have been treated as self-employed. It was announced on 23 June 1995 that a provision had been included in the Pensions Bill to enable a self-employed person who had erroneously been charged Class 1 contributions to forego a refund of the employee's contributions and retain the right to earnings-related state pension entitlement and, if applicable, personal pension rebates. The provision does not prevent the 'employer' reclaiming the employer's portion of contributions. The individual's benefit position will be preserved provided that it is only the employer's contributions that are refunded. Individuals or employers wishing to seek refunds should write to the National Insurance Contributions Office Refunds Group.

There are special rules for, *inter alia*, personnel appearing before the camera, short engagements, payments to limited companies and payments to overseas personalities.

Artistes, performers/non-performers

From 6 April 1990 to 5 April 1996 artistes and performers (excluding established performers with 'reserved Schedule D status' and guest artistes engaged by opera companies) working under standard Equity contracts were treated as employees for income tax purposes so far as earnings from such employments were concerned. This brought the income tax treatment into line with that of social security, as it had been the view of the DSS for many years that the vast majority of performers are employees for social security contribution purposes because of the general conditions under which they usually work.

However, from 6 April 1994 it is understood that the Inland Revenue accepts that the earnings of many artistes should be assessed under Schedule D Case I. This does not, of itself, affect the social security position but the DSS had always acknowledged that there is some scope for self-employment for performers (especially 'act as known' engagements), and specific claims to self-employment are looked into in detail. Accordingly 'act as known' engagements will normally be treated as self-employment for both social security and income tax purposes.

The NICO does, however, permit subsistence allowances to be paid without liability to contributions, and special rules apply to travelling expenses.

The industry also uses standard agreements for the engagement of non-performers. The Inland Revenue has looked at some of these and concluded that some are normally contracts for services (self-employed) and others contracts of service (employed). However, new regulations which took effect on 17 July 1998 require most actors, musicians or similar performers to be treated as employees for social security purposes, whether or not this status applies under general law. It also applies whether or not the individual is supplied through an agency.

Personal service companies

From 6 April 2000, those who have control of their own 'one-man service companies' will be subject to special rules. If the work that the owner of the company does for the company's customers would – but for the one-man company – fall to be considered as an employment of that individual (i.e. rather than self-employment), a deemed salary may arise. If it does, then some or all of the income of the company will be treated as salary liable to PAYE and National Insurance contributions. This will be the case whether or not such salary is actually paid by the company.

The calculations required by the Inland Revenue are complicated and have to be done very quickly at the end of each tax year (even if the company's year-end is different). It is essential that affected businesses seek detailed professional advice about these new rules which may, in certain circumstances, also apply to partnerships.

Class 1 contributions

As mentioned above, these are related to earnings, the amount payable depending upon whether the employer has applied for his employees to be 'contracted-out' of the State earnings-related pension scheme; such application can be made where the employer's own pension scheme provides a requisite level of benefits for his or her employees and their dependants or, in the case of a money purchase scheme (COMPS) certain minimum safeguards are covered.

Contributions are only payable by employees once earnings exceed the lower earnings limit and are then due on the balance of earnings up to the upper earnings limit ('primary contributions'). Contributions are payable by employers ('secondary contributions') once earnings exceed the earnings threshold but without any upper limit. Contributions are normally collected via the PAYE tax deduction machinery, and there are penalties for late submission of returns and for errors therein. From 19 April 1993, interest will be charged automatically on unpaid PAYE and social security contributions.

Employees liable to pay

Contributions are payable by any employee who is aged 16 years and over (even though he or she may still be at school) and who is paid an amount equal to, or exceeding, the lower earnings limit (see below). Nationality is irrelevant for contribution purposes and, subject to special rules covering employees not normally resident in Great Britain, Northern Ireland or the Isle of Man, or resident in EEA countries or those with which there are reciprocal agreements, contributions must be paid whether the employee concerned is a British subject or not provided he is gainfully employed in Great Britain.

Employees exempt from liability to pay

Persons over pensionable age (65 for men; 60 – until 2010 – for women) are exempt from liability to pay primary contributions, even if they have not retired. However, the fact that an employee may be exempt from liability does not relieve an employer from liability to pay secondary contributions in respect of that employee.

Rate of employees' contributions

From 6 April 2000, the rate of employees' contributions on earnings from the employees earnings threshold to the upper earnings limit is 10% (8.4% for contracted-out employments).

Certain married women who made appropriate elections before 12 May 1977 may be entitled to pay a reduced rate of 3.85%. However, they will have no entitlement to benefits in respect of these contributions.

Employers' contributions

All employers are liable to pay contributions on the gross earnings of employees. As mentioned above, an employer's liability is not reduced as a result of employees being exempted from contributions, or being liable to pay only the reduced rate (3.85%) of contributions.

For earnings paid on or after 6 April 2000 employers are liable at a rate of 12.2% on earnings paid above the employers earnings threshold (without any upper earnings limit), 9.2% where the employment is contracted out (salary related) or 11.6% (money purchase). In addition, special rebates apply in respect of earnings falling between the lower earnings limit and the earnings thresholds. This provides, effectively, a negative rate of contribution in that small band of earnings. It should be noted that the contracted-out rates of 9.2% and 11.6% apply only up to the upper earnings limit. Thereafter, the not contracted-out rate of 12.2% is applicable.

The employer is responsible for the payment of both employees' and employer's contributions, but is entitled to deduct the employees' contributions from the earnings on which they are calculated. Effectively, therefore, the

Rates of Class 1 contributions and earnings limits from 6 April 2000

Earnings per week	*Rates payable on earnings in each band*			
	Not contracted-out		*Contracted-out*	
	Employee	*Employer*	*Employee*	*Employer*
£	%	%	%	%
Below 67.00	—	—	—	—
67.00 – 75.99	—	—	— (*)	— (*)
76.00 – 83.99	10	—	8.4	— (*)
84.00 – 535.00	10	12.2	8.4	9.2 or 11.6
Over £535.00	—	12.2	—	9.2 or 11.6

* Special rebates deductible in respect of these bands of earnings.

employee suffers a deduction in respect of his or her social security contributions in arriving at his weekly or monthly wage or salary. Special rules apply to company directors and persons employed through agencies.

Items included in, or excluded from, earnings

Contributions are calculated on the basis of a person's gross earnings from his or her employment. This will normally be the figure shown on the tax deduction working sheet, except where the employee pays superannuation contributions and, from 6 April 1987, charitable gifts – these must be added back for the purposes of calculating Class 1 liability. Profit-related pay exempt from income tax was not exempt from social security contributions.

Earnings include salary, wages, overtime pay, commissions, bonuses, holiday pay, payments made while the employee is sick or absent from work, payments to cover travel between home and office, and payments under the statutory sick pay and statutory maternity pay schemes.

However, certain payments, some of which may be regarded as taxable income for income tax purposes, are ignored for social security purposes. These include:

- certain gratuities paid other than by the employer,
- redundancy payments and some payments in lieu of notice,
- certain payments in kind,
- reimbursement of specific expenses incurred in the carrying out of the employment,
- benefits given on an individual basis for personal reasons (e.g. wedding and birthday presents),
- compensation for loss of office.

IR Booklet CWG 2 (April 2000 edition) gives a list of items to include in or exclude from earnings for Class 1 contribution purposes.

Maximum contributions

There is a limit to the total liability for social security contributions payable by a person who is employed in more than one employment, or is also self-employed or a partner.

Where only not contracted-out Class 1 contributions, or not contracted-out Class 1 and Class 2 contributions, are payable, the maximum contribution is limited to 53 primary Class 1 contributions at the maximum weekly not contracted-out standard rate. For 2000/01 the maximum will thus be £2432.70.

However, where contracted-out Class 1 contributions are payable, the maximum primary Class 1 contributions payable for 1999/2000 where all employments are contracted out are £2043.68.

Where Class 4 contributions are payable in addition to Class 1 and/or Class 2 contributions, the Class 4 contributions are restricted so that they shall not exceed the excess of £1746.45 (i.e. 53 Class 2 contributions plus maximum Class 4 contributions) over the aggregate of the Class 1 and Class 2 contributions.

Miscellaneous rules

There are detailed rules covering a person with two or more employments; where a person receives a bonus or commission in addition to a regular wage or salary; and where a person is in receipt of holiday pay. From 6 April 1991 employers' social security contributions arise under Class 1A in respect of the private use of a company car, and of fuel provided for private use therein. The rate is currently 12.2%. From 6 April 2000, this charge is extended to cover most benefits in kind. From 6 April 1999, Class 1B contributions are payable by employers using PAYE Settlement Agreements in respect of small and/or irregular expense payments and benefits, etc. This rate is also currently 12.2%.

Class 2 contributions

Class 2 contributions are payable at the weekly rate of £2.00 as from 6 April 2000. Exemptions from Class 2 liability are:

- A man over 65 or a woman over 60.
- A person who has not attained the age of 16.

• A married woman or, in certain cases, a widow who elected prior to 12 May 1977 not to pay Class 2 contributions.
• Persons with small earnings (see below).
• Persons not ordinarily self-employed (see below).

Small earnings

Application for a certificate of exception from Class 2 contributions may be made by any person who can show that his or her net self-employed earnings per his profit and loss account (as opposed to taxable profits):
• for the year of application are expected to be less than a specified limit (£3825 in the 2000/01 tax year); or
• for the year preceding the application were less than the limit specified for that year (£3770 for 1999/2000) and there has been no material change of circumstances.

Certificates of exception must be renewed in accordance with the instructions stated thereon. At the Inland Revenue's discretion the certificate may commence up to 13 weeks before the date on which the application is made. Despite a certificate of exception being in force, a person who is self-employed is still entitled to pay Class 2 contributions if they wish, in order to maintain entitlement to social security benefits.

Persons not ordinarily self-employed

Part-time self-employed activities (including as a writer or artist) are disregarded for contribution purposes if the person concerned is not ordinarily employed in such activities and has a full-time job as an employee. There is no definition of 'ordinarily employed' for this purpose but the DSS formerly regarded a person who has a regular job and whose earnings from spare-time occupation are not expected to be more than £800 per annum as falling within this category. Persons qualifying for this relief do not require certificates of exception. It should be noted that many activities covered by this relief would probably also be eligible for relief under the small earnings rule (see above).

Method of payment

From April 1993, Class 2 contributions may be paid by monthly direct debit in arrears or, alternatively, by cheque, bank giro, etc following receipt of a quarterly (in arrears) bill.

Overpaid contributions

If, following the payment of Class 2 contributions, it is found that the earnings are below the exception limit (e.g. the relevant accounts are prepared late), the Class 2 contributions that have been overpaid can be reclaimed for tax years 1988/89 onwards, provided a claim is made between 6 April and 31 December immediately following the end of the tax year.

Class 3 contributions

Class 3 contributions are payable voluntarily, at the weekly rate of £6.55 per week from 6 April 2000, by persons aged 16 or over with a view to enabling them to qualify for a limited range of benefits if their contribution record is not otherwise sufficient. In general, Class 3 contributions can be paid by employees, the self-employed and the non employed.

Broadly speaking, no more than 52 Class 3 contributions are payable for any one tax year, and contributions are not payable after the end of the tax year in which the individual concerned reaches the age of 64 (59 for women).

Class 3 contributions may be paid in the same manner as Class 2 (see above) or by annual cheque in arrears.

Class 4 contributions

In addition to Class 2 contributions, self-employed persons are liable to pay Class 4 contributions. These are calculated at the rate of 7% on the amount of profits or gains chargeable to income tax under Schedule D Case I or II which exceed £4385 per annum but which do not exceed £27,820 per annum for 2000/01. Thus the maximum Class 4 contribution is 7% of £23,435 – i.e. £1640.45 for 2000/01.

The income tax profits on which Class 4 contributions are calculated is after deducting capital allowances and losses, but before deducting personal tax allowances or retirement annuity or personal pension plan premiums.

Class 4 contributions produce no additional benefits, but were introduced to ensure that self-employed persons as a whole pay a fair share of the cost of pensions and other social security benefits without the self-employed who make only small profits having to pay excessively high flat rate contributions.

From 6 April 1996 no income tax relief is available for Class 4 contributions. Previously, half the liability attracted income tax relief.

Payment of contributions

In general, contributions are now self-assessed and paid to the Inland Revenue together with the income tax under Schedule D Case I or II, and accordingly the contributions are due and payable at the same time as the income tax liability on the relevant profits. Under self-assessment, interim payments of Class 4 contributions are payable at the same time as interim payments of tax.

Class 4 exemptions

The following persons are exempt from Class 4 contributions:

- Men over 65 and women over 60 at the commencement of the year of assessment (i.e. on 6 April).
- An individual not resident in the United Kingdom for income tax purposes in the year of assessment.
- Persons whose earnings are not 'immediately derived' from carrying on a trade, profession or vocation (e.g., sleeping partners and, possibly, limited partners).
- A child under 16 on 6 April of the year of assessment.
- Persons not ordinarily self-employed (see above as for Class 2 contributions).

Further information

Further information can be obtained from the many booklets published by the Inland Revenue, available from local National Insurance Contributions Office sites.

National Insurance Contributions Office, International Services
Newcastle upon Tyne NE98 1ZZ
tel (08459) 154811 (local call rates apply)
Address for enquiries for individuals resident abroad.

Married persons and partnerships

Under independent taxation of husband and wife from 1990/91 onwards, each spouse is responsible for his or her Class 4 liability.

In partnerships, each partner's liability is calculated separately. If a partner also carries on another trade or profession, the profits of all such businesses are aggregated for the purposes of calculating his or her Class 4 liability.

When an assessment has become final and conclusive for the purposes of income tax, it is also final and conclusive for the purposes of calculating Class 4 liability.

Transfer to Inland Revenue

The administrative functions of the former Contributions Agency transferred to the Inland Revenue from 1 April 1999. Responsibility for NIC policy matters was also transferred from DSS Ministers to the Inland Revenue and Treasury Ministers on the same date.

Peter Arrowsmith FCA is a sole practitioner specialising in National Insurance matters. He is chairman of the Employers Issues Committee of the Institute of Chartered Accountants in England and Wales and Consulting Editor to *Tolley's National Insurance Contributions 2000/01*.

Social security benefits

*There are many leaflets produced by the Department of Social Security. However, due to the nature of the subject social security benefits can be quite difficult to understand. In this article, **K.D. Bartlett** FCA has summarised some of the more usual benefits that are available under the Social Security Acts.*

This article deliberately does not cover every aspect of the legislation but the references given should enable the relevant information to be easily traced. These references are to the leaflets issued by the Department of Social Security.

It is usual for only one periodical benefit to be payable at any one time. If the contribution conditions are satisfied for more than one benefit it is the larger benefit that is payable. Benefit rates shown below were those payable from the week commencing 6 April 2000.

Employed persons (Category A or D contributors) are covered for all benefits. Certain married women and widows (Category B and E contributors) who elected to pay at the reduced rate receive only attendance allowance, guardian's allowance and industrial injuries benefits. Other benefits may be available dependent on their husbands' contributions.

Self-employed persons (Class 2 and Class 4 contributors) are covered for all benefits except earnings-related supplements, unemployment benefit, widow's and invalidity pensions, widowed mother's allowance and industrial injury benefits.

Family benefits

Child benefits

Leaflet CH 1

Child benefit is payable for all children who are either under 16 or under 19 and receiving full-time education at a recognised educational establishment. The rate is £15.00 for the first or eldest child and £10.00 a week for each subsequent child. It is payable to the person who is responsible for the child but excludes foster parents or people exempt from UK tax. Furthermore, one-parent families receive £17.55 per week for the eldest child.

Maternity benefits

Help with maternity expenses is given to selected people from the social fund. To be eligible the claimant must be receiving income support or family credit. £100 is paid for each new or adopted baby, reduced by the amount of any savings over £500 held by the claimant or his or her family (£1000 for those aged 60 or over). A payment can be obtained from the social fund for an adopted baby provided the child is not more than 12 months old when the application is made. The claimant has three months to make the claim from when adoption has taken place.

Maternity pay

Leaflet NI 17A

Statutory maternity pay (SMP) was introduced for female employees who leave employment because of pregnancy. SMP is applicable to those who have worked for 26 weeks by the 15th week before the expected date of confinement. This 15th week is known as the qualifying week (QW). The other qualifying conditions are that the woman must:

- be pregnant at the 11th week before the expected week of confinement, or

already have been confined;
- have stopped working for her employer wholly or partly because of pregnancy or confinement;
- have average earnings of not less than the lower earnings limit for the payment of National Insurance contributions which is in force during her QW;
- provide her employer with evidence of her expected week of confinement;
- provide her employer with notice of her maternity absence.

Rates of SMP

There is a higher and a lower rate. The higher rate of SMP is 90% of an employee's weekly earnings and is paid for the first six weeks for which there is entitlement to SMP. To be eligible for the higher rate, a woman must meet all the qualifying conditions and have been employed by the employer for a continuous period of at least two years (at between 8 and 16 hours a week). Her service must continue into the QW.

The lower rate of SMP is a set rate reviewed each year. The rate for the tax year beginning 6 April 2000 is £60.20 per week. It is paid for 18 weeks to those not entitled to the higher amount and for up to 12 weeks to those who receive the higher rate for the first six weeks.

SMP is taxable and also subject to National Insurance contributions. The gross amount of SMP and the employer's portion of National Insurance payable on the SMP can be recovered from the State by deducting the amounts from the amount normally due for PAYE and National Insurance deductions payable to the Collector of Taxes.

Guardian's allowance

Leaflet NI 14

This is paid at the rate of £7.30 a week. For each subsequent child the rate of benefit is £11.35 a week to people who have taken orphans into their own family. Usually both of the child's parents must be dead and at least one of them must have satisfied a residence condition.

The allowance can only be paid to the person who is entitled to child benefit for the child (or to that person's spouse). It is not necessary to be the legal guardian. The claim should be made within three months of the date of entitlement.

Disability living allowance

Disability living allowance (DLA) was introduced on 6 April 1992 and replaces attendance allowance for disabled people before they reach the age of 65. It has also replaced mobility allowance.

Those who are disabled after reaching 65 may be able to claim attendance allowance. The attendance allowance board decide whether, and for how long, a person is eligible for this allowance. Attendance allowance is not taxable.

The care component is divided into three rates whereas the mobility allowance has two rates. The rate of benefit from 6 April 2000 is as follows:

	Per week
Care component	
Higher rate (day and night, or terminally ill)	£53.55
Middle rate (day or night)	£35.80
Lower rate (if need some help during day, or over 16 and need help preparing a meal)	£14.20
Mobility component	
Higher rate (unable or virtually unable to walk)	£37.40
Lower rate (can walk but needs help when outside)	£14.20

Benefits for the ill or unemployed

Statutory sick pay (SSP)

Leaflets NI 27, NI 16, NI 244

In the majority of cases the employer now has the responsibility of paying sick pay to its employees. The payment is dependent on satisfying various conditions in respect of periods of incapacity, periods of entitlement, qualifying days and rules on notification of absence. The rules are quite complicated and reference should be made to the relevant booklets for further clarification but the key points are:

- Payment is made by the employer.
- There is a possibility of two rates of payment dependent on the employee's gross average earnings.
- The employee must not be capable of work and must do no work on the day concerned.
- SSP is not usually payable for the first three working days.
- The maximum entitlement is 28 weeks in any period of incapacity.
- Notification must be made by the employer but this procedure must be within statutory guidelines.
- Payment can be withheld if notification of sickness is not given in due time.

From 6 April 1996 most employers will no longer be able to reclaim any SSP back. Small employers may, in certain circumstances, receive compensation called the New Relief Scheme which will help all employers faced with exceptionally high levels of sickness absence.

Incapacity benefit

Leaflet DS 700

Incapacity benefit replaced sickness benefit and invalidity benefit. The contribution conditions haven't changed but a new medical test has been brought in which includes a comprehensive questionnaire. The rates from 13 April 2000 are:

Long-term incapacity benefit	£67.50
Short-term incapacity benefit	£50.90
Increase of long-term incapacity benefit for age:	
Higher rate	£14.20
Lower rate	£7.10

Invalid care allowance

Leaflet NI 212

This is a taxable benefit paid to people of working age who cannot take a job because they have to stay at home to look after a severely disabled person. The basic allowance is £40.40 per week. An extra £9.90 is paid for the first dependent child and £11.35 for each subsequent child.

Disabled person's tax credit

This is a benefit for people under pensionable age who cannot work because of physical or mental ill health and do not have sufficient National Insurance contributions to qualify for sickness or invalidity benefit. The basic allowance is £40.36 a week. There are increases of £23.95 a week for adult dependants and £11.35 for each child.

Jobseekers' allowance

Jobseekers' allowance (JSA) is a new social security benefit that came in force on 7 October 1996. It has taken the place of unemployment benefit and income support for unemployed people. JSA differs from unemployment benefit in that there are no additional amounts payable for dependants. The rates are:

Rates of JSA	Post-April 2000
Single under 18	£31.45
18-24	£41.35
25 or over	£52.20

Claimants will be able to claim JSA if they have paid National Insurance contributions equal to 25 times the lower earnings level in one of the last two complete tax years before the claim; and either paid or have been credited in respect of each of the last two complete tax years before the year of the claim 50 times the lower earnings limit for that tax year.

JSA is not normally paid for the first three waiting days. Exceptions are made for those under 18 who are considered to be in severe hardship or if a person has received income support, incapacity benefit or invalid care allowance in the 12 weeks prior to the claim for JSA. Contributory-related JSA is only payable for a maximum of 182 days.

People ineligible for contributory-related JSA may be able to claim income-related JSA. If a claimant satisfies the entitlement conditions he or she is entitled to income-related JSA indefinitely.

Eligibility conditions

In order to be eligible for JSA a potential claimant must not have capital exceeding £8000. If he or she has capital of £3000 or more, £1 is deducted for every £250 above the £3000. The claimant is not allowed to work more than 24 hours a week and his or her partner is only allowed to work 16 hours a week.

Claimants must usually be available to take up employment immediately unless they can show that they are doing part-time work and need to give notice. Once that notice has ended the claimant must take up work immediately afterwards.

Claims should be made at the nearest office of the Department for Education and Employment (DfEE) – in most cases this will be a job centre. Benefit is normally paid fortnightly in arrears via giro cheque either at a post office or via a bank account. JSA is a taxable benefit.

Seeking work

A claimant must agree to a 'jobseekers' agreement' based on the job search plan which will be discussed at the 'new jobseeker' interview. The jobseeker will attend thereafter for a job search review. If the conditions for JSA are still being met, benefit will be paid. If it seems that the jobseeker has made himself unemployed and refuses a job without good cause, payment of JSA can be stopped for up to 26 weeks. People unemployed for at least 13 weeks will not be subject to sanctions if they start a full-time job and then leave it within a period of five to eight weeks.

Pensions and widow's benefits

Leaflets NP 23, NP 35, NP 31

The state pension is divided into two parts – the basic pension, presently £67.50 per week for a single person or £107.90 per week for a married couple, and the State Earnings Related Pension Scheme (SERPS), which will after it matures on the present basis pay a pension of 25% of revalued earnings between the lower and upper earnings limits.

The cost of SERPS has been a major political consideration for some time. In order to reduce the long-term cost of the scheme, benefits will be reduced for those retiring or widowed after the year 2000. The benefits will be reduced as follows:

- The pension will be based on lifetime average earnings rather than the best 20 years as at present.
- The pension will be calculated on the basis of 20% of earnings between the lower and upper earnings limit rather than 25%. This will be phased in over 10 years from the tax year 2000/2001.
- Presently all of a member's state earnings-related benefit is inherited by a surviving spouse. For deaths occurring after April 2000 this will be reduced to 50%.

Women paying standard rate contributions into the scheme are eligible for the same amount of pension as men but five years earlier, from age 60. If a woman stays at home to bring up her children or to look after a person receiving attendance allowance she can have her basic pension rights protected without paying contributions.

The widow's pension and widowed mother's allowance also consists of a basic pension and an additional earnings-related pension. The full amount of the additional pension applies only if the husband has contributed to the new scheme for at least 20 years.

Widow's benefits

From 11 April 1988 there are three main widow's benefits:

- widow's payment, which has replaced the widow's allowance
- widowed mother's allowance
- widow's pension.

Widow's payment

This is an allowance, currently a lump sum payment of £1000 payable to widows who were bereaved on or after 11 April 1988. It is payable immediately on the death of the husband. Entitlement to this benefit is based on the late husband's contribution record but no payment will be made if the widow is living with another man as husband and wife at the date of death. The late husband must have actually paid contributions on earnings of at least 25 times the weekly or lower earnings limit for a given tax year in any tax year ending before his death (or ending before he reached pensionable age if he was over 65 when he died). The equivalent number of Class 2 or voluntary Class 3 contributions will be sufficient.

When claiming, the widow should complete the form on the back of the death certificate and send it to the local social security office. On receipt of this information the DSS will send the claimant a more detailed form (BD8) which, once completed, has to go back to the social security office. It is important to claim the benefit within 12 months of the husband's death.

Widowed mother's allowance

Leaflet NP 45

If a widow is left with children to look after, she is entitled to a widowed mother's allowance provided that her late husband had paid sufficient national insurance contributions. These contributions are:

- 25 Class 1, 2 or 3 contributions before age 65 and before 6 April 1975; or
- contributions in any one tax year after 6 April 1975 on earnings of at least 25 times the weekly lower earnings limit for that year.

It is important that the widow is looking after either her own child or her husband's child and that the child is under 16 or, if between the age of 16 and 19, is continuing in full-time education.

The allowance stops immediately if the widow remarries and will be suspended if she lives with a man as his wife. From April 1999 the amounts payable are:

Basic allowance	£67.50
Increase for each child	£11.35

Where a husband's contributions only satisfied the first test above, the basic allowance may be payable at a reduced rate. This reduction does not alter the rate of an increase for a child.

Widow's pension

Leaflet NP 45

A widow who is over the age of 45 when her husband dies may be eligible for a widow's pension unless she is eligible for the widowed mother's allowance. In this situation the widow's pension becomes payable when the widowed mother's allowance ends, provided she is still under the age of 65. However, where a woman had been receiving the widowed mother's allowance, she becomes entitled to a widow's pension if she is between the ages of 45 and 65 when the allowance ends, no matter what her age may have been when her husband died. Before 11 April 1988 a widow aged 40 or over could qualify for a widow's pension.

Qualification conditions

- The contributions conditions must be satisfied and these conditions are the same as those for the widowed mother's allowance above.
- The widow must not be receiving the widowed mother's allowance.
- When her husband died she was aged between 45 and 65 or she was entitled to widowed mother's allowance and is aged between 45 and 65 when her widowed mother's allowance finished.

Cessation of widow's pension

- Entitlement finishes if the widowed mother's allowance stops because she has remarried.
- Widow's pension must not be claimed when the payment of the widowed mother's allowance has been suspended because the widow is in pension or is living with a man as his wife.

From 11 April 1988 both the basic and additional pension are paid at a reduced rate if the widow was aged under 55:

- when her husband died, if she did not subsequently become entitled to widowed mother's allowance; or
- when her widowed mother's allowance ceased to be paid. The relevant rates from 6 April 1999 are as follows:

Age related	£	%
Basic	67.50	100
Age 54 (49)	62.78	93
53 (48)	58.05	86
52 (47)	53.33	79
51 (46)	48.60	72
50 (45)	43.88	65
49 (44)	39.15	58
48 (43)	34.43	51
47 (42)	29.70	44
46 (41)	24.98	37
45 (40)	20.25	30

(The ages given in parentheses apply to women for whom widow's pension was payable before 11 April 1988.)

Funeral expenses

The death grant was abolished from 6 April 1987. It has been replaced by a payment from the social fund where the claimant is in receipt of income support, family credit or housing benefit. The full cost of a reasonable funeral is paid, reduced by any savings of over £500 held by the claimant or his or her family (£1000 for couples over 60).

Working Families' Tax Credit (WFTC)

WFTC replaced Family Credit on 5 October 1999. It entitles families who have at least one partner who works 16 hours or more a week who have at least one child in full-time education up to and including A level or equivalent to claim. Both self-employed and employed people are covered.

WFTC is now administered and paid by the Inland Revenue. An application form can be obtained by phoning the helpline on (0845) 609 5000.

WFTC is paid for a fixed period of 26 weeks but the claimant can keep re-applying every 26 weeks. It usually runs for the 26-week period even if the circumstances change. There is an exception to this when the last remaining child leaves full-time education when the family's WFTC is terminated from the pay week following the change. The rates of WFTC effective from April 2000 are:

£53.15	Basic (adult) tax credit (one payable per family)
£11.25	30-hour tax credit (payable if the claimant or partner is working 30 hours or more a week – one payable per family)

Childcare tax credit

One credit is paid in respect of each child – the amount depends on their age when the WFTC is awarded:

£21.25	From birth to September following 16th birthday
£26.35	From September following 16th birthday to age 18
£70.00	Maximum childcare tax credit (one child only)
£105.00	Maximum childcare tax credit (2 or more children)
£91.45	Applicable amount (i.e. threshold)
55%	Taper
70%	Childcare taper

For each family there is a maximum level of WFTC. If the family's net income exceeds £91.45 per week, 55 pence of every excess £1 is deducted from the maximum WFTC. Net income is earnings (gross pay less tax, National Insurance contributions and half of any occupational or personal pension contributions) and most other forms of income.

Childcare tax credit will be worth up to 70% of eligible childcare costs. The maximum limit for eligible childcare costs will be £100 per week for one child and £150 per week for two or more children. This means that for a family with one child currently paying eligible childcare costs of £100, £70 per week childcare will be included in their WFTC award. Eligible childcare means childcare provided by registered childminders, nurseries and out-of-hours clubs on school premises, run by the school or local authority; and childcare schemes run on crown property. From April 2000 the range of eligible childcare providers will be extended to include 'approved providers'.

Approved providers are those which have applied to and met the quality standards of new accredited organisations appointed for the purpose by the Department for Education and Employment (DfEE). Each approved provider will be allocated a unique reference number that must be quoted when a WFTC application is made.

Capital of between £3000 and £8000 will affect the level of income to be taken into account. A weekly income of £1 is assumed for each £250, or part of £250, of capital above £3000.

Disabled Persons' Tax Credit (DPTC)

This is a new tax credit to help people with an illness or disability who are in work depending on their circumstances. It replaces Disability Working Allowance (DWA), and is administered by the Inland Revenue. It is similar to Working Families' Tax Credit (WFTC), and from April 2000 will be paid through the wage packet. It is intended for people with an illness or disability, who:

- work at least 16 hours a week
- are resident in the United Kingdom, and entitled to work here
- have savings of £16,000 or less
- have one of a number of qualifying benefits.

There are four parts to DPTC:

- basic tax credit – £54.30; or £83.55 for a couple
- 30-hour credit – £11.05
- tax credit for each child –
  Age 0-11 – £19.85
  Age 11-16 – £20.90
  Age 16-18 – £25.95
  disabled child's credit of £21.90
- childcare tax credit – up to 70% of eligible costs up to maximum costs of £100 for one child and £150 for two or more children.

DPTC payment is calculated by adding the credits together. If net income of the family is above £90 per week, this is reduced by 55 pence for each £1 above £90. For single people the threshold is £70. A DPTC award will normally last for 26 weeks.

Further information

This article does not set out to cover every aspect of the Social Security Acts legislation. Further information can be obtained from the local office of the Department of Social Security or from Accountants Digest No. 370 published by the Institute of Chartered Accountants in England and Wales. Readers resident abroad who have queries should write to the Department's Overseas Branch, Newcastle upon Tyne NE98 1BA.

How to apply

From April 2000 applications are made to the Inland Revenue, which assess and calculate how much DPTC a claimant will receive. For employees payment will be made in the pay packet, and for the self-employed payment will be made directly.

Those who are directly receiving DWA will continue for the full 26-week period. Depending on individual circumstances, a person can then apply for DPTC. An application form for DPTC is automatically sent before an existing DWA award runs out. You cannot receive both DWA and DPTC.

Grants from local authorities

Housing benefit

People will be able to claim benefit are those who:

- are on a low income, or
- are in receipt of income support
- share the house with certain other persons who are receiving income support.

The maximum benefit entitlement for a liable person claiming will be 100% of the liability.

K.D. Bartlett FCA qualified as a Chartered Accountant in 1969 and became a partner in a predecessor firm of Horwath Clark Whitehill in 1972.

Index

Order form

Writing Handbooks

—	Freelance Copywriting	£9.99
—	Freelance Writing for Newspapers	£9.99
—	Writing about Food	£8.99
—	Writing for Children	£8.99
—	Writing Comedy	£9.99
—	Writing Crime Fiction	£7.99
—	Writing Dialogue for Scripts	£8.99
—	Writing Historical Fiction	£8.99
—	Writing Horror Fiction	£8.99
—	Writing for a Living	£8.99
—	Writing for Magazines	£9.99
—	Writing a Play	£8.99
—	Writing Popular Fiction	£9.99
—	Writing for Radio	£8.99
—	Writing Romantic Fiction	£8.99
—	Writing for Television	£10.99
—	Writing a Thriller	£9.99
—	Writing about Travel	£7.99

Other books for writers

—	The Internet: A Writer's Guide	£9.99
—	The Journalist's Handbook	£10.99
—	Novel Writing	£9.99
—	Research for Writers	£11.99
—	Rewriting	£10.99
—	Sports Writing	£9.99
—	Word Power	£10.99

These books are available from bookshops or direct from the publisher using this form. Postage and packing is free in the UK. Please add 20% of the total cost for overseas delivery. Airmail prices available on application. Tick the titles you want and fill in the form below. Prices and availability are subject to change without notice. Please send this form (or photocopy) to:

A & C Black (Publishers) Ltd, Dept YB2001, PO Box 19, Huntingdon, Cambs PE19 8SF

***tel* (01480) 212666 *fax* (01480) 405014 *e-mail* sales@acblackdist.co.uk**

Card number ______________________________

Mastercard/Visa/Switch (delete as appropriate)

Amount ______________________ Expiry date ______________

Signed ______________________

Name (please print) ______________________________

Address ______________________________

____

______________________ Postcode ______________